A Companion to Philosophy in the Middle Ages

Blackwell Companions to Philosophy

This outstanding student reference series offers a comprehensive and authoritative survey of philosophy as a whole. Written by today's leading philosophers, each volume provides lucid and engaging coverage of the key figures, terms, topics, and problems of the field. Taken together, the volumes provide the ideal basis for course use, representing an unparalleled work of reference for students and specialists alike.

Already published in the series:

1. The Blackwell Companion to Philosophy, Second Edition
   Edited by Nicholas Bunnin and Eric Tsui-James

2. A Companion to Ethics
   Edited by Peter Singer

3. A Companion to Aesthetics
   Edited by David Cooper

4. A Companion to Epistemology
   Edited by Jonathan Dancy and Ernest Sosa

5. A Companion to Contemporary Political Philosophy
   Edited by Robert E. Goodin and Philip Pettit

6. A Companion to Philosophy of Mind
   Edited by Samuel Guttenplan

7. A Companion to Metaphysics
   Edited by Jaegwon Kim and Ernest Sosa

8. A Companion to Philosophy of Law and Legal Theory
   Edited by Dennis Patterson

9. A Companion to Philosophy of Religion
   Edited by Philip L. Quinn and Charles Taliaferro

10. A Companion to the Philosophy of Language
    Edited by Bob Hale and Crispin Wright

11. A Companion to World Philosophies
    Edited by Eliot Deutsch and Ron Bontekoe

12. A Companion to Continental Philosophy
    Edited by Simon Critchley and William Schroeder

13. A Companion to Feminist Philosophy
    Edited by Alison M. Jaggar and Iris Marion Young

14. A Companion to Cognitive Science
    Edited by William Bechtel and George Graham

15. A Companion to Bioethics
    Edited by Helga Kuhse and Peter Singer

16. A Companion to the Philosophers
    Edited by Robert L. Arrington

17. A Companion to Business Ethics
    Edited by Robert E. Frederick

18. A Companion to the Philosophy of Science
    Edited by W. H. Newton-Smith

19. A Companion to Environmental Philosophy
    Edited by Dale Jamieson

20. A Companion to Analytic Philosophy
    Edited by A. P. Martinich and David Sosa

21. A Companion to Genethics
    Edited by Justine Burley and John Harris

22. A Companion to Philosophical Logic
    Edited by Dale Jacquette

23. A Companion to Early Modern Philosophy
    Edited by Steven Nadler

24. A Companion to Philosophy in the Middle Ages
    Edited by Jorge J. E. Gracia and Timothy B. Noone

25. A Companion to African-American Philosophy
    Edited by Tommy L. Lott and John P. Pittman

26. A Companion to Applied Ethics
    Edited by R. G. Frey and Christopher Heath Wellman

27. A Companion to the Philosophy of Education
    Edited by Randall Curren

28. A Companion to African Philosophy
    Edited by Kwasi Wiredu

29. A Companion to Heidegger
    Edited by Hubert L. Dreyfus and Mark A. Wrathall

30. A Companion to Rationalism
    Edited by Alan Nelson

31. A Companion to Ancient Philosophy
    Edited by Mary Louise Gill and Pierre Pellegrin

32. A Companion to Pragmatism
    Edited by John R. Shook and Joseph Margolis

33. A Companion to Nietzsche
    Edited by Keith Ansell Pearson

34. A Companion to Socrates
    Edited by Sara Ahbel-Rappe and Rachanar Kamtekar

35. A Companion to Phenomenology and Existentialism
    Edited by Hubert L Dreyfus and Mark A. Wrathall

Blackwell Companions to Philosophy

A Companion to Philosophy in the Middle Ages

Edited by

JORGE J. E. GRACIA

and

TIMOTHY B. NOONE

© 2003, 2006 by Blackwell Publishing Ltd

BLACKWELL PUBLISHING
350 Main Street, Malden, MA 02148-5020, USA
9600 Garsington Road, Oxford OX4 2DQ, UK
550 Swanston Street, Carlton, Victoria 3053, Australia

The right of Jorge J. E. Gracia and Timothy B. Noone to be identified as the Author of the Editorial Material in this Work has been asserted in accordance with the UK Copyright, Designs, and Patents Act 1988.

First published 2003
First published in paperback 2006 by Blackwell Publishing Ltd

1   2006

Library of Congress Cataloging-in-Publication Data

A companion to philosophy in the middle ages / edited by Jorge J. E. Gracia and Timothy B. Noone.
    p. cm. — (Blackwell companions to philosophy; 24)
    Includes bibliographical references and index.
    ISBN 0-631-21672-3 (alk. paper) — ISBN 0-631-21673-1 (pbk: alk. paper)
    1. Philosophy, Medieval. I. Gracia, Jorge J. E.   II. Noone, Timothy B.   III. Series.

  B721 .C54 2002
  189—dc21

                                                              2002066421

ISBN-13: 978-0-631-21672-8 (alk. paper) — ISBN-13: 978-0-631-21673-5 (pbk: alk. paper)

A catalogue record for this title is available from the British Library.

Set in 10/12 pt Ehrhardt
by SNP Best-set Typesetter Ltd, Hong Kong
Printed and bound in the United Kingdom
by TJ International, Padstow, Cornwall

The publisher's policy is to use permanent paper from mills that operate a sustainable forestry policy, and which has been manufactured from pulp processed using acid-free and elementary chlorine-free practices. Furthermore, the publisher ensures that the text paper and cover board used have met acceptable environmental accreditation standards.

For further information on
Blackwell Publishing, visit our website:
www.blackwellpublishing.com

Contents

Contributors

Jan A. Aertsen Thomas Institute, University of Cologne

Robert Andrews University of Stockholm

B. Carlos Bazán University of Ottawa

Francisco Bertelloni University of Buenos Aires

Mauricio Beuchot National University of Mexico

Deborah L. Black University of Toronto

Alexander Broadie University of Glasgow

Stephen F. Brown Boston College

David B. Burrell University of Notre Dame

Peter J. Casarella The Catholic University of America

Richard Cross Oriel College, Oxford University

Christopher M. Cullen Fordham University

Brian Davies Fordham University

Silvia Donati University of Padua

Sandro D'Onofrio University of San Ignacio

Mechthild Dreyer University of Mainz

Thérèse-Anne Druart The Catholic University of America

Stephen D. Dumont University of Notre Dame

Louis Dupré Yale University

Kent Emery, Jr. University of Notre Dame

Girard J. Etzkorn Fairfield Glade, TN

Russell L. Friedman University of Copenhagen

Kimberly Georgedes Franciscan University, Steubenville

Michael Gorman The Catholic University of America

Mark D. Gossiaux St. John's University, New York

Jorge J. E. Gracia State University at Buffalo

Edward Grant Indiana University

Jeremiah Hackett South Carolina University

D. W. Hadley University of Dallas

Idris Samawi Hamid Colorado State University

Mark G. Henninger University of Detroit

Maarten J. F. M. Hoenen Catholic University, Nijmegen

Jasper Hopkins University of Minnesota

R. Edward Houser University of St. Thomas, Houston

Nancy Hudson Yale University

Alfred L. Ivry New York University

Jean Jolivet University of Paris

Elizabeth Karger Centre d'Études des Religions du Livre, CNRS

Peter King Ohio State University

Gyula Klima Fordham University

C. H. Kneepkens University of Groningen

John D. Kronen University of St. Thomas, St. Paul

Stephen E. Lahey Le Moyne College

Roberto Lambertini University of Macerata

Richard A. Lee, Jr. Pennsylvania State University

Neil Lewis Georgetown University

David C. Lindberg University of Wisconsin, Madison

Charles H. Lohr University of Freiburg

R. James Long Fairfield University

John Longeway University of Wisconsin, Parkside

Scott MacDonald Cornell University

John Magee University of Toronto

John Marenbon Cambridge University

Brian Patrick McGuire Roskilde University, Denmark

Bruce Milem State University of New York at New Paltz

M. Michèle Mulchahey Fordham University

Lauge Olaf Nielsen University of Copenhagen

Timothy B. Noone The Catholic University of America

Robert Pasnau University of Colorado

Eric D. Perl University of Dallas

Alan Perreiah University of Kentucky

Sarah Pessin University of Chicago

François-Xavier Putallaz University of Fribourg

José Luis Rivera The Catholic University of America

Philipp W. Rosemann University of Dallas

Tamar Rudavsky Ohio State University

Jonathan J. Sanford Fordham University

Christopher Schabel University of Cyprus

Mary Catherine Sommers University of St. Thomas, Houston

Gérard Sondag University Blaise-Pascal, Clermont-Ferrand

Andreas Speer University of Würzburg

James B. South Marquette University

Carlos Steel Leuven University

Edith Dudley Sylla North Carolina State University, Raleigh

Richard C. Taylor Marquette University

Roland J. Teske Marquette University

Andrew G. Traver Southeastern Louisiana University

Cecilia Trifogli Oxford University

Winthrop Wetherbee Cornell University

Kevin White The Catholic University of America

Robert Wielockx Pontifical University of the Holy Cross, Rome

Gordon A. Wilson University of North Carolina, Asheville

John F. Wippel The Catholic University of America

Rega Wood Stanford University

Jack Zupko Emory University

Preface

The Middle Ages is not only the longest period of philosophical development in the West, but also one of the richest and more complex. Its roots go back to ancient philosophy and we are still living with some of its consequences today. Indeed, a very large part of our philosophical vocabulary, whether in English, Spanish, or any other western European language, was developed in the Middle Ages, and most of the philosophical problems about which we still worry were first formulated in the version in which we know them in this period. The historical importance of the Middle Ages and its influence in the subsequent history of western thought is difficult to overestimate.

In spite of this, however, the study of the philosophy of the Middle Ages was, until relatively recently, rare outside Roman Catholic contexts. Secular universities, and even Christian colleges from denominations other than Roman Catholicism, rarely offered courses in medieval philosophy, and their faculty seldom did research in the field. The medieval period was mentioned in two kinds of courses: in history of philosophy sequences, the Middle Ages was usually appended to the ancient period, as an afterthought, and was generally given little emphasis; in courses in the philosophy of religion, where arguments for the existence of God were examined, mention was usually made of Anselm's so-called ontological argument and Aquinas's "five ways."

This dismal situation has been changing gradually, although it is still true that most of the leading philosophy departments in the English-speaking world do not yet have specialists in the Middle Ages. Some do, however, and this has not gone unnoticed in other, less prestigious, places. Medieval philosophy is gradually becoming respectable. First-rank presses are publishing books on medieval philosophy, and even bringing out anthologies of texts to be used in the classroom. Unfortunately, there is still much that needs to be done. For one thing, we do not yet have a book that contains the main facts about, and presents the main views on, the key figures of the period. And, indeed, this is the gap we aim to fill in part with this *Companion*. The idea behind it is to have, in one volume, most of the background information one needs to approach medieval texts.

With this in mind, we have divided the volume into two parts, which are preceded by a brief introduction. The introduction is intended to give a general impression of the philosophical thought of the age, whereas the first part of the volume itself provides the historical background without which medieval philosophy would be difficult to understand. The seven articles comprising the latter deal with the ancient and Patristic background of the period, the ninth and tenth centuries, the School of Chartres, religious orders, scholasticism, and the condemnations of philosophical and theological views by ecclesiastical authorities in 1270 and 1277. The second part is composed of articles of varying length dealing with the main authors of the age and is arranged alphabetically. There are several reasons for this arrangement. First, in this way the volume complements, rather than competes with, already available books, for most of the recent histories and companions to medieval philosophy have been organized topically or periodically. Second, it avoids the problem of gaps and narrow perspectives. Topical organization tends to be contentious, perspectival, and controversial, whereas organization by authors is more comprehensive. Third, the use of the volume by a larger audience is enhanced, for anyone who wishes to do something on Aquinas, for example, might consult it regardless of the specificity of his or her interests. A topically arranged volume tends to be used only by those interested in the topics the volume covers. Fourth, there is a matter of depth; essays devoted to particular authors can go deeper than surveys of many authors around a topic; they can get at the heart of the thought of the authors. Finally, the present organization makes possible overall, original interpretations, something that would be more difficult under different arrangements.

The approach and content of each article has been ultimately up to the contributors. The editors have welcomed a variety of historiographical approaches so as to illustrate the current state of scholarship on medieval philosophy. All the same, we have encouraged contributors to consider a problems approach in which the articles on historical figures in particular are presented in the context of the philosophical and theological issues they were trying to address.

Since we are constrained by strict limitations of space, we have had to make choices. First, it was necessary to leave some authors out; and second, we had to choose the space devoted to each author. This was based on our view of the relative historical and philosophical importance of the authors in question. Four towering figures received around 10,000 words each (Augustine, Thomas Aquinas, John Duns Scotus, and William of Ockham) and four others received around 8,000 words (Anselm, Averroes, Avicenna, and Maimonides). The remaining authors were allotted articles of 5,000, 3,000, or 500 words each. Obviously, many authors who got only 500, 3,000, or even 5,000 words deserve more. Indeed, even those to whom we devoted larger articles deserve much more. But to give them more space would have been impossible within the parameters imposed on the project: one physically manageable volume that could be sold at a reasonable price. We intend this volume to be of service to faculty, students, libraries, and persons among the general public with an interest in medieval philosophy. A larger volume, or a multi-volume set, would have done better justice to the authors discussed here, but it would also have had to exclude some of these prospective audiences.

We particularly regret having to leave out some authors either because of the size of the volume or because those who had agreed to compose entries for them were unable to deliver the articles in time for inclusion. Hopefully, the damage to the volume and the inconvenience to readers will not be too great.

We have made a special effort to be cosmopolitan and inclusive insofar as the contributors are concerned. Often, works of this sort are narrowly parochial in that they include contributors exclusively selected from the Anglo-American and British worlds, and sometimes even from particular scholarly traditions. On the contrary, we have tried to be broad both with respect to scholars working in languages other than English, in different countries, and within diverse scholarly traditions. This, we hope, will make the volume representative of contemporary scholarship in medieval philosophy overall, and more attractive to a larger community of scholars and students.

A few comments about conventions. Single quotation marks have been used only within double quotation marks or to indicate a linguistic term or expression that is being mentioned rather than used. The names of Islamic and Jewish authors included in the volume have been given in their common Latin form, although the Arabic or Hebrew forms have been recorded. Thus, we have chosen 'Avicenna' instead of 'Ibn Sīnā', 'Alfarabi' for 'al-Fārābī', and so on. The bibliographies of articles on authors have been divided into primary sources and secondary sources. Under 'Primary sources' generally only works by the author are included, although there are a couple of exceptions. The choice of works has been entirely up to the authors of the articles, but we have encouraged them to include mainly recently printed or reprinted works, although in some cases in which only incunabula or even unedited works exist, some incunabula and manuscripts have been listed. The bibliographies on secondary sources are specific to the authors and thus usually omit general works on the period or on particular topics. Such works are listed in a separate topical bibliography at the end of the volume.

Putting together a volume of this sort requires the effort of many persons. In particular, we are grateful to the authors of the articles who not only delivered them in time for inclusion, but adapted themselves to the parameters we had specified and often were willing to revise in accordance with our suggestions. We are also grateful to Stan Grove for doing the index, to Laura Arcilla for the translations of Mauricio Beuchot's articles, to Thérèse-Anne Druart for helping us with spelling and bilbliographic matters concerning Arabic materials, and to our respective universities for their support in the form of academic leaves and secretarial assistance. To Mary Dortch we are particularly indebted for her expert copy-editing and great patience. Gracia's introductory essay, "Philosophy in the Middle Ages," was first published in *The Blackwell Companion to Philosophy*, edited by Nicholas Bunnin and Eric Tsui-James. We appreciate their permission to reprint it here. Finally, we are most appreciative of the efforts by Steve Smith, of Blackwell Publishing, who not only came up with the idea for the volume and asked us to undertake it, but also gave us a free hand when it came to its organization and character. Without his support, the publication of the volume would have been impossible.

Jorge J. E. Gracia
Timothy B. Noone

Chronological List

Augustine (b. 354; d. 430)
Pseudo-Dionysius (fl. ca. 500)
John Philoponus (b. ca. 490; d. ca. 570)
Boethius (b. ca. 480; d. 524/5)
Isidore of Seville (b. ca. 560; d. 636)
Maximus Confessor (b. 580; d. 662)
Albumasar (b. 787; d. 886)
Alkindi (d. ca. 870)
John Scotus Eriugena (b. ca. 800; d. ca. 877)
Isaac Israeli (b. ca. 855; d. ca. 955)
Alrazi (b. ca. 865; d. ca. 925)
Alfarabi (b. ca. 870; d. ca. 950)
Saadiah (b. 882; d. 942)
Alhacen (b. 965; d. ca. 1040)
Avicenna (b. 980; d. 1037)
Peter Damian (b. 1007; d. 1072)
Avencebrol (b. 1021/2; d. 1057/8)
William of Champeaux (fl. ca. 1100)
Anselm of Canterbury (b. 1033; d. 1109)
Algazali (b. 1058; d. 1111)
Avempace (d. 1139)
Peter Abelard (b. 1079; d. 1142)
Adelard of Bath (b. ca. 1080; d. ca. 1152)
Gilbert of Poitiers (b. 1085/90; d. 1154)
Bernard of Clairvaux (b. 1090; d. 1153)
Peter the Venerable (b. ca. 1092; d. 1156)
Peter Lombard (b. 1095/1100; d. 1160)
Hugh of St. Victor (b. 1097/1101; d. 1141)
Hildegard of Bingen (b. 1098; d. 1179)
Peter Helias (b. ca. 1100; d. after 1166)
Richard of St. Victor (d. 1173)
John of Salisbury (b. 1115/20; d. 1180)
Dominicus Gundissalinus (fl. 1150–90)
Averroes (b. ca. 1126; d. 1198)

Alan of Lille (d. 1203)
Moses Maimonides (b. 1138; d. 1204)
William of Auxerre (b. ca. 1140; d. 1231)
Philip the Chancellor (b. 1165/85; d. 1236)
Robert Grosseteste (b. ca. 1168; d. 1253)
Alexander of Hales (b. ca. 1185; d. 1245)
William of Auvergne (b. 1180/90; d. 1249)
Jean de la Rochelle (b. 1190/1200; d. 1245)
Albertus Magnus (b. ca. 1200; d. 1280)
William of Sherwood (b. 1200/5; d. 1266/71)
Richard Fishacre (b. ca. 1205; d. 1248)
Richard Rufus of Cornwall (fl. 1231–56)
William Arnaud (fl. ca. 1250)
Pierre de Maricourt (fl. ca. 1267)
Peter of Spain (fl. ca. 1267)
Roger Bacon (b. 1214/20; d. ca. 1292)
Robert Kilwardby (b. ca. 1215; d. 1279)
Bonaventure (b. 1217; d. 1274)
Henry of Ghent (d. 1293)
Ulrich of Strassburg (b. ca. 1220; d. 1277)
Thomas Aquinas (b. 1224/6; d. 1274)
John Pecham (b. ca. 1230; d. 1292)
Boethius of Dacia (fl. 1270–80)
William of Ware (fl. 1290s)
James of Metz (fl. ca. 1300)
Thomas of Erfurt (fl. ca. 1300)
Martin of Dacia (d. 1304)
Peter of Auvergne (d. 1304)
John of Paris (d. 1306)
Ramon Lull (b. 1232/3; d. 1316)
Roger Marston (b. ca. 1235; d. ca. 1303)
Arnaldus of Villanova (b. 1238/40; d. 1311)
Siger of Brabant (b. ca. 1240; d. after 1282)
Matthew of Aquasparta (b. ca. 1240; d. 1302)
Giles of Rome (b. 1243/7; d. 1316)
Peter Olivi (b. ca. 1248; d. 1298)
Richard of Middleton (b. ca. 1249; d. 1302)
Godfrey of Fontaines (b. before 1250; d. 1306/9)
Dietrich of Freiburg (b. ca. 1250; d. ca. 1310)
Thomas of Sutton (b. ca. 1250; d. ca. 1315)
Hervaeus Natalis (b. 1250/60; d. 1323)
James of Viterbo (b. ca. 1255; d. 1307/8)
Simon of Faversham (b. ca. 1260; d. 1306)
Vital du Four (b. ca. 1260; d. 1327)
Meister Eckhart (b. ca. 1260; d. 1328)
Dante Alighieri (b. 1265; d. 1321)
John Duns Scotus (b. ca. 1266; d. 1308)
Thomas Wilton (fl. ca. 1312)

Gonsalvo of Spain (d. ca. 1313)
Henry of Harclay (b. ca. 1270; d. 1317)
Radulphus Brito (b. ca. 1270; d. 1320)
Durand of St. Pourçain (b. 1270/5; d. 1334)
Walter Burley (b. 1274/5; d. in or after 1344)
William of Alnwick (b. ca. 1275; d. 1333)
Peter Auriol (b. ca. 1280; d. 1322)
William Crathorn (fl. 1330s)
Michael of Massa (d. 1337)
Guido Terrena (d. 1342)
Marsilius of Padua (b. 1280; d. 1343)
Richard of Campsall (b. ca. 1280; d. ca. 1350)
Walter Chatton (b. ca. 1285; d. 1343)
John of Reading (b. ca. 1285; d. 1346)
William of Ockham (b. ca. 1285; d. 1347)
John of Jandun (b. 1285/9; d. 1328)
Francis of Meyronnes (b. 1288; d. 1328)
Gersonides (b. 1288; d. 1344)
Richard Swineshead (fl. 1340–55)
Francis of Marchia (b. ca. 1290; d. after 1344)
John Baconthorpe (b. ca. 1290; d. 1345/8)
John of Mirecourt (fl. ca. 1345)
Robert Holcot (b. ca. 1290; d. 1349)
Thomas Bradwardine (b. ca. 1290; d. 1349)
John Buridan (b. ca. 1295; d. 1361)
Peter Ceffons (fl. 1348–9)
Richard Brinkley (fl. 1350–73)
Nicholas of Autrecourt (b. ca. 1300; d. after 1350)
Robert of Halifax (b. ca. 1300; d. after 1350)
Landulph Caracciolo (d. 1351)
Gregory of Rimini (b. ca. 1300; d. 1358)
Richard Fitzralph (b. ca. 1300; d. 1360)
Berthold of Moosburg (b. ca. 1300; d. after 1361)
Adam of Wodeham (d. 1358)
Richard Kilvington (b. 1302/5; d. 1361)
John Dumbleton (b. ca. 1310; d. ca. 1349)
Ralph Strode (fl. 1360–87)
William Heytesbury (b. before 1313; d. 1372/3)
Albert of Saxony (b. ca. 1316; d. 1390)
Nicole Oresme (b. ca. 1320; d. 1382)
John Wyclif (b. ca. 1320; d. 1384)
Marsilius of Inghen (b. ca. 1340; d. 1396)
Peter of Candia (b. ca. 1340; d. 1410)
Hasdai Crescas (b. ca. 1340; d. 1410/11)
Pierre d'Ailly (b. ca. 1350; d. 1420)
John Gerson (b. 1363; d. 1429)
Paul of Venice (b. 1369; d. 1429)
Jerome of Prague (b. 1370/1; d. 1416)

John Capreolus (b. ca. 1380; d. 1444)
Paul of Pergula (d. 1455)
Gaetano of Thiene (b. 1387; d. 1465)
Heymeric of Camp (b. 1395; d. 1460)
Nicholas of Cusa (b. 1401; d. 1464)
Denys the Carthusian (b. 1402; d. 1472)
Peter de Rivo (b. ca. 1420; d. 1500)
Gabriel Biel (b. before 1425; d. 1495)

Philosophy in the Middle Ages: An Introduction

JORGE J. E. GRACIA

The concern to integrate revealed doctrine and secular learning distinguishes medieval thought from ancient, Renaissance, and modern philosophy and determines to a great extent the philosophical problems the medievals addressed and the solutions they proposed for those problems. This Introduction examines the way the medievals approached this main theme and illustrates how it affected their choice of philosophical problems and how they dealt with them. In particular, it pays attention to seven problems well discussed throughout the age: the relation of faith and reason, the existence of God, the significance of names used to speak about God, the object of theology and metaphysics, the way we know, universals, and individuation.

The use of the expression 'medieval philosophy' to refer to philosophy in the Middle Ages is paradoxical because it is hard to find anyone during the period who considered himself a philosopher, whose concerns were purely philosophical, or who composed purely philosophical works. Medieval authors from the Latin West thought of themselves rather as theologians, were primarily interested in theological issues, and very seldom composed purely philosophical works. For them, the philosophers were the ancients, Plato and Aristotle, and some of the Islamic authors, like Avicenna of Baghdad (Ibn Sīnā, b. 980; d. 1037) and Averroes of Cordoba (Ibn Rushd, b. ca. 1126; d. 1198). There are relatively few works produced in the period that can be classified strictly speaking as philosophical. Most of the philosophy that we find is contained in books of theology and used to elucidate theological doctrine. Whence the well-known phrase, popularized by Thomas Aquinas (b. ca. 1225; d. 1274) in reference to philosophy, *ancilla theologiae*, servant of theology. The expression 'medieval philosophy', moreover, has a disparaging connotation derived from the term 'Middle Ages', used first by Renaissance humanists to refer to what they thought was a barbaric and dark period of western history found between the two civilized and enlightened ages of classical antiquity and the Renaissance. In spite of the lack of philosophers, the absence of purely philosophical works, and the prejudices of Renaissance humanists, the Middle Ages is not only the longest period of philosophical development in the West, but also one of the richest. Indeed, in intensity, sophistication, and achievement, the philosophical flowering in the thirteenth century could be rightly said to rival the golden age of Greek philosophy in the fourth century BC.

The temporal and territorial boundaries of the Middle Ages are a subject of controversy among scholars. No matter which dates are picked, however, it is clear that both Augustine (b. 354; d. 430) and John of St. Thomas (b. 1589; d. 1644) were engaged in the same intellectual program and therefore belong together. Before Augustine, the intellectual life of the

West was dominated by pagan philosophy, and Descartes (b. 1596; d. 1650), generally regarded as the first modern philosopher, was contemporaneous with John. Territorially, we need to include not only Europe, but also the Middle East, where important Greek Orthodox, Jewish, and Islamic authors flourished.

A period that extends for more than a millennium is by no means uniform and easily breaks down into smaller units. The first of these might be called Patristic, and began in earnest with Augustine, although its roots went back to the second century BC. It extended to the seventh century, and closed with the death of Isidore of Seville (b. ca. 560; d. 636), author of the *Etymologies*, the first of many medieval encyclopedias. Between this time and the Carolingian renaissance nothing of philosophical importance took place. Thanks to the efforts of Charlemagne (b. 742; d. 814) to establish schools, regularize writing, and gather in his court all the great minds of the times in order to encourage learning and to replicate the magnificence of Rome, there was some important intellectual activity at the end of the eighth and the beginning of the ninth centuries, which culminated in the work of John Eriugena (b. ca. 800; d. ca. 877).

This period was followed by a dark age which ended with another, more lasting, revival of learning in the eleventh and twelfth centuries. The twelfth-century renaissance, as it is often called, produced some of the greatest of all medieval thinkers: Anselm (b. 1033; d. 1109), Gilbert of Poitiers (b. 1085/90; d. 1154), Peter Abelard (b. 1079; d. 1142), and the School of Chartres. The period from 1150 to about 1225 is of paramount importance. At this time many of the works of the ancients became available to the medievals for the first time, thanks to the conquest of territory by Christians in Spain, and western scholars engaged in a feverish attempt to assimilate them. Some of these works had been translated from Greek into Syriac in the Middle East, and later were translated into Arabic. From Arabic, they were translated into Latin with the help of Spanish Jews. Other works were rendered into Latin directly from Greek originals by scholars working in Sicily and southern Italy. Prior to 1150, the medievals had a rather meager group of technical philosophical works from Aristotle and his commentators, known as the *logica vetus*. But in a few years not only the whole *Organon*, but most other works of Aristotle, with commentaries by Islamic authors, and many scientific works from antiquity became available.

The renaissance of the twelfth century and the ferment created by the newly available texts gave rise to what is usually known as scholasticism. This is a method of teaching and learning used in various disciplines, particularly philosophy and theology. The origin of the term is to be found in medieval schools, where a lecturer, particularly one who taught the liberal arts (*trivium* and *quadrivium*) was called *scholasticus*. The aim of the method was to yield knowledge concordant with both human reason and the Christian faith, a *concordia discordantium* of opinions which the medievals regarded as authoritative. The method was practiced in the medieval university and used Aristotelian logic as a tool. As a result, the literary genres used by scholastics reflect university activities and settings. The commentary is, generally speaking, the product of classroom lectures on texts; the *quaestio* is the product of university disputations; and the *summae* were the textbooks of the age.

Among the first scholastics of note were Roger Bacon (b. 1214/20; d. ca. 1492) and Albert the Great (b. ca. 1200; d. 1280), but they were followed by a host of towering figures: Bonaventure (b. ca. 1217; d. 1274), Thomas Aquinas, John Duns Scotus (b. 1266; d. 1308), and William of Ockham (b. ca. 1285; d. 1347). In the middle of the fourteenth century, however, scholasticism suffered a nearly irreversible setback through the Black Death (ca. 1347–51), which decimated the universities of Europe. It took more than a hundred years to recover and still longer to generate a second period of greatness under the leadership of Spanish scholastics of the sixteenth century, such as Francisco Suárez (b. 1548; d. 1617) and Francisco de Vitoria (b. ca. 1483; d. 1546).

The distinguishing mark of Latin philosophy in the Middle Ages is to be found in its double aim: the understanding of Christian faith and its defense against those who attacked it. The effort at understanding produced theological works; the effort at defense produced apologetic works. This does not mean, however, that the medievals were not interested in purely philosophical problems. They were, but most often the reason for their interest was that the solutions to these problems had important implications for Christian doctrine; indeed, the solutions adopted were often governed by the doctrinal principles they wished to defend. In this sense, philosophy was generally subordinated to theology and apologetics.

This attitude separates the philosophy of the Middle Ages from both ancient and Renaissance philosophy. The medieval approach to philosophy contrasts with that of the ancient philosophy because both in classical Greece and in Rome, philosophy enjoyed a largely independent status and a predominant position. Philosophy was a pursuit unsubordinated to any other intellectual activity, whose main goal was the understanding of the world and man's place in it. On the other hand, the medieval attitude is quite distinct also from that of the Renaissance, because the humanists looked upon the classical past as a model of their activity and, therefore, restored man to the center of attention and channeled their efforts to the recovery and emulation of classical learning, particularly in the philosophy of Plato. In contrast, philosophy in the Middle Ages was subordinated to theology, and the center of intellectual attention was God and his revelation rather than human beings; human beings were studied only as creatures of God made in his image and likeness. The model adopted by the medievals was not to be found in the lives and theories of ancient philosophers, but instead in the lives of saints and their prayers.

The character of philosophy in the Middle Ages is evident in the philosophical problems medievals chose to address, the way they interpreted philosophical problems they found in ancient texts, and the solutions they gave to most of them. Three of the most important concerns the medievals inherited from the ancients were the problem of how we know, the problem of God's existence, and the problem of universals. Four questions they raised as a result of their theological concerns and commitments were the problem of the relation between faith and reason, the problem of individuation, the problem concerned with the language used to talk about God, and the relation between theology and metaphysics.

Faith and reason

No other issue concerned the medievals more than the relation of faith to reason, for the success of the program adopted in the age to a large extent depended in turn on the success in working out this relationship. For ancient philosophers, this had not been a concern, for most of them were not religious so there was no need to reconcile reason to faith, or truths derived from the study of the world independently of faith to a body of revealed truths known by faith. Under this rubric, several and different, if interrelated, issues are contained. The problem is first explicitly formulated in the second century of the Christian era, when some early Fathers of the Church questioned the merit of using secular learning by those to whom the truth has been revealed by God. Two sides are easily identifiable. Some rejected the value of secular learning altogether; this position is often called fideism because of its exclusive preference for faith. Others found a place for secular learning in the understanding of faith. Tertullian (b. ca. 160; d. 220) argued that there is no place for the learning of infidels in Christianity, and he coined a phrase that has made history: "I believe because it is absurd" (*Credo quia ineptum*). Among those who saw some merit in the use of secular learning and tried to bring it together with revealed truth was Justin Martyr (d. ca. 165).

Augustine followed in the footsteps of Justin Martyr and provided the parameters for future discussions of this issue. For him, all truth is one, regardless of the source, so the Christian can and should make use of secular learning. However, it is only in the Christian faith that one can truly understand the world and the place of human beings in it. Christian doctrine completes, illuminates, and transforms secular learning, providing answers to the most important questions and to those for which non-Christians have no answers. Moreover, it supplies us with an infallible criterion of truth. Anything found in secular learning that contradicts Christian doctrine is false and must be rejected; anything concordant with it may be used as long as it is done in the context of faith.

The controversy between the approach of those denying the value of secular learning and those advocating its use surfaced again in the eleventh and twelfth centuries. This time the focus was upon the use of logic, known then as dialectic, in the understanding of Scriptures. Among the anti-dialecticians was Peter Damian (b. 1007; d. 1072), who went so far as to reject not just logic, but even grammar because, as he put it, the Devil became the first grammarian when he declined the word *Deus* in the plural. His irrationalism was so strong, and his faith in God's power so great, that he argued that God could bring it about that the past never happened. The most outspoken dialectician was Abelard, known as the Peripatetic from Pallet because of his use of and predilection for Aristotelian logic. In a controversial book, entitled *Sic et non* (*Yes and No*), Abelard showed that Christian authorities contradict each other, and therefore an understanding of Christian faith requires the use of logic. A more moderate position was adopted by Anselm. Inspired by Augustine, he argued for a measured use of logic, in which understanding begins with faith but is achieved when the doctrines revealed in Scriptures are articulated in logical form. His view is encapsulated in two famous formulas: *Credo ut intelligam* (I believe in order that I may understand) and *Fides quaerens intellectum* (Faith seeking understanding).

The relation between faith and reason was also of concern to Islamic and Jewish thinkers during this period. One of the most controversial views on the topic was proposed by Averroes. Adopting a strict Aristotelian model of knowledge as demonstration, he argued that the understanding of Scriptures can never reach the level of knowledge, for knowledge is based on demonstrative reasoning, and reasoning founded on premises that are not self-evident can never be considered demonstrative. Theology does not yield knowledge properly speaking, and therefore must be subordinated to philosophy, which does. Averroes' position, as well as the position of those who preferred reason over faith, is usually referred to as rationalism.

In the thirteenth century, both Bonaventure and Aquinas responded to Averroes. Bonaventure rejected the universality of the Aristotelian model of knowledge, though he admitted its competence within its own sphere. Since all things in the created order are, for Bonaventure, signs of the Uncreated Wisdom, each sphere of reality must be seen in its connection to that Wisdom. As a result, although in any one science knowledge can be acquired without appeal to revelation, each science and its subject needs to be traced back (*reducere*) to the Uncreated Wisdom for a proper appreciation of its role within human life and thought. Hence Bonaventure privileges Augustinian wisdom over and against

Aristotelian science, rejecting the latter as the highest canon of judgment regarding human knowledge.

In contrast to Bonaventure, Aquinas did not reject the Aristotelian model used by Averroes, but rather argued that not all knowledge is of the same sort. Some knowledge has premisses which are self-evident principles – as is the case with metaphysics – but some have premisses which have been demonstrated in other branches of knowledge – as with optics, which takes its principles from geometry. Theology is based on faith, but it can be considered knowledge because it rests on God's own knowledge, which is the highest one there can be. Aquinas, moreover, made room for both theology and philosophy in the body of all knowledge by arguing that some truths can be known only through faith (e.g., Christ is God), some can be known only through reason (e.g., all material substances are composed of matter and form), and some can be known through either faith or reason (e.g., God exists).

In spite of the efforts of Bonaventure, Aquinas, and others, the influence of Averroes continued to be felt well into the sixteenth century and prompted repeated condemnations from various quarters. The most famous of these occurred in 1277, and included even some views which Aquinas himself had held. The popularity of Averroes was more strongly felt in the faculty of arts rather than theology. Among those in the thirteenth century accused of following Averroes too closely was Siger of Brabant (b. ca. 1240; d. after 1282). He was charged with holding a doctrine of double truth, according to which there is a truth of faith and a truth of reason, and the truths can and often do contradict each other. Clearly, this was unacceptable to most medievals, for it undermined the overall program of the age, that is, the integration of revelation and secular learning into a consistent body of doctrine.

God's existence

Proving that God exists was important for the medievals because God's existence is the angular stone on which the Christian faith rests. It was important in order both to lay down the foundation of all Christian theology and to establish a base for apologetic efforts directed toward Muslims and Jews.

The ancients had already provided some arguments for the existence of God, but it was the medievals who formulated these in elegant and parsimonious ways. These arguments break down into two types: arguments based on the analysis of concepts and arguments based on experience. Of the first, the most famous are the arguments of Anselm in the *Proslogion* and John Duns Scotus in *On the First Principle*. Both have come to be known as versions of the so-called ontological argument, a term first used by Kant to designate them. Of the second type, the most famous are the five ways presented in Aquinas's *Summa theologiae*, which comprise both cosmological and teleological arguments.

Anselm's argument derives God's existence from the conception of God as that than which a greater cannot be thought. God exists, for if he did not, than which a greater cannot be thought would not be that than which a greater cannot be thought. Anselm assumes, in line with his Augustinian-Platonic framework, that something that exists is greater than something that does not, that the notion of a being that than which a greater cannot be thought is intelligible, and that logical necessity has a bearing on existence. He has been criticized for all three assumptions. But to this day there are strong supporters of the soundness of the argument.

Each of Aquinas's five ways begins by taking note of a fact given in experience, such as that some things change. From this they go on to point out, through various steps, that these facts cannot be explained without recourse to a being who is ultimately responsible for them, and this being is God. The first way argues from the fact that there is change in the world to a first cause of the change. The second argues from the efficient causality we experience in the world to a first efficient cause. The third distinguishes between necessary and contingent beings, as well as between beings that are necessary in themselves and those that are necessary through another, ultimately concluding that there must be one necessary being whose necessary existence is not derived from any other being. The fourth argues from the gradation found in things to a being who is both the maximum and the cause of those things. And the fifth argues that all things, intelligent or not, act for an end, and there must be an intelligent being who directs them towards their end.

The names of God

Showing that we can know God was as important to the medievals as proving that he exists. Indeed, because the latter implies knowing something about God, one might say that the task of showing that we can know God logically precedes the task of proving he exists.

Several philosophers from antiquity had talked about God. Texts abound in Plato, Aristotle, and the Stoics that speak about a single divinity. In all these cases, however, God seems to have been conceived as part of the world. Knowing God, then, was not essentially different from knowing anything else, even if perhaps more difficult, for the terms we use to talk about the world are in principle applicable to God as well. The Christian conception of God, however, changed this. If God is wholly other than creation and transcends it, then it is questionable that the terms we use to speak about the world can also be applied to him.

The background of this controversy is found in both Augustine's writings and an anonymous treatise, probably written by a fifth-century Syrian monk (known as Pseudo-Dionysius) who posed as Dionysius the Areopagite, entitled *On the Divine Names*. Controversy over the ways to understand divine names heats up in the twelfth and thirteenth centuries with Moses Maimonides (Moshe ben Maimon, b. 1138; d. 1204), Aquinas, and Scotus. The issue concerns the application and understanding of terms that express perfections, such as 'good' and 'just'; no one held that terms expressing imperfections, such as 'bad' and 'unjust', are applicable to God. If terms of the first sort do not signify anything about God, then it appears that when we use them we do not understand anything in particular about God; and if they do, then it appears that we understand something about God but that he is not fundamentally different from the world. The first makes God unknowable and the Scriptures unintelligible; the second makes God part of the world and therefore not divine. Both are unacceptable to an orthodox Muslim, Jew, or Christian.

Almost every thinker in the Middle Ages tried to find a solution to this dilemma. Maimonides argued that there are two kinds of terms applicable to God. First, terms that stand for attributes do not signify anything about God himself, but rather are to be understood negatively, as denying something of God. To say that God is good is to say that he is not evil, and to say that he is just is to say that he is not unjust. Second, terms that stand for actions do convey information, but the information they convey is not about God himself but about what God has done for others.

At the other extreme, Scotus argued that, in order for the language we predicate of God to be effective in producing understanding, there must be at least one term that is used univocally (i.e., with the same meaning) of God and creatures, and proposed 'being' as such a term. The univocity of this term grounds our knowledge of God and makes possible to speak intelligibly about him. Aquinas adopts a middle position, between Maimonides and Scotus, with the doctrine of analogy. The terms we predicate of God are not used equivocally (i.e., with different meanings) or univocally, but analogically. 'God is good' does not mean that he is good like we are, or that he is not bad in the sense we are; it means that he is good in proportion to his nature and thus better than we are, in a superlative degree, as the Pseudo-Dionysius had already stated.

Theology and metaphysics

Because God is at the center of our understanding, there must be a discipline devoted to his study. But which is this discipline? On the one hand, it is clear that the Scriptures are the source where we can find revealed knowledge of God. But, on the other hand, the world also contains information about God because, as creator, he has left his imprint upon it. Indeed, thirteenth-century theologians found texts of Aristotle in the *Metaphysics* that spoke of a science concerned with God. This gave rise to a heated controversy over whether God is studied in theology or in metaphysics.

In the Islamic world already we find differing views with respect to this issue. Avicenna rejected the view that God is studied in metaphysics because no science proves the existence of what it studies and metaphysics proves the existence of God. On the contrary, Averroes argued that God is studied in metaphysics, because his existence is not proven in this science but in physics. On the Latin side, Aquinas distinguished between sacred doctrine, that is theology based on Scriptures, and what we now call natural theology, that is theology based on the study of the world. Moreover, he contrasted both of these disciplines with metaphysics. On the one hand, both sacred doctrine and natural theology study God: the first studies God as revealed in the Scriptures and the second studies God as revealed in creation. On the other hand, metaphysics does not study God primarily, but rather studies being *qua* being, that is, being insofar as it is neither this kind of (e.g., human, divine), nor this individual (e.g., Socrates, God) being. Metaphysics studies God only secondarily, as the first cause of being. Scotus agrees with Aquinas to the extent that he too believes that the proper object of study of theology is God, whereas that of metaphysics is being *qua* being.

This apparent agreement between two towering figures did not help to settle the matter, however, for the very understanding of being *qua* being was at issue. Aquinas and his followers argued that being *qua* being is to be understood as the last act (*esse*) and perfection of an essence in an individual entity, and distinct in reality from the essence. But both Scotus and Ockham rejected this conception of being. Indeed, Ockham even rejected the notion that any science has a single object of study. According to him, sciences are merely collections of mental propositions and because these propositions have different subjects, one cannot say that any science has only one subject or object.

How we know

The problem of how we know beings other than God was introduced into the Middle Ages by Augustine's dialogue *On the Teacher*. The ostensive problem raised in this work is the purpose of the use of words, but the real underlying concern is the old Platonic issue of whether we can be taught. Plato's answer to this question had been negative: We cannot be taught because the objects of knowledge are immaterial Ideas, and the only way to know these is through a direct encounter with them in a previous life, when we were not fettered to the body. Our only hope for acquiring knowledge in this life is to be reminded through language of the Ideas we once knew. Augustine followed closely on Plato's footsteps but because, as a Christian, he could not accept the pre-existence of the soul, he modified the Platonic scheme. Christ becomes the Teacher who places Ideas in our memory and it is there that we encounter them by being reminded of them through words. Augustine's view became known as the Doctrine of Illumination, because he used the Platonic metaphor of light to describe how Christ makes us see Ideas: Christ is like the Sun, which illumines our minds with knowledge of intelligible realities.

This doctrine turned into one of the most important battlegrounds between Augustinians and Aristotelians in the later Middle Ages. Almost everyone accepted Augustine's metaphor, but that is where the agreement ended. Bonaventure and Henry of Ghent (b. ca. 1217; d. 1293) among others tried to answer some of the questions raised by the doctrine and to resolve some of its ambiguities, but Aquinas and Scotus opposed these interpretations. Aquinas argued that the light about which Augustine was speaking is none other than the natural light of reason, so that illumination is a natural, rather than a supernatural, process. Scotus, although a Franciscan, opposed Bonaventure and Henry, in this. He argued that Henry's interpretation of Augustine leads to skepticism, and that knowledge is possible without illumination understood in a supernatural way.

Universals

Both Aristotle and Plato had made clear that knowledge properly speaking is of the universal, and the authority of Augustine had added further support for this view. Knowledge, in a strict sense, is not about this or that cat, but about cat, not about this man or that man, but about man in general. The medievals generally accepted this, but at the same time most of them held that not just substances in the Aristotelian sense (e.g., this cat, this man), but also the features of substances (e.g., a cat's black fur color, a man's rationality) were individual. This posed a host of epistemological and metaphysical problems, one of which is known as the problem of universals.

In the early part of the age, the problem was framed in terms of three questions Porphyry the Phoenician (b. ca. 232; d. 304) had asked in the *Isagoge* concerning genera and species, and which the medievals found in Boethius' translation of that work: (1) Are things like animal and man something in the mind only or also something outside the mind? (2) If they are something outside the mind, are they material or immaterial? And (3) are they something separate and different from individual, sensible things, or something in them and like them? Boethius himself gave rather ambiguous answers to these questions, which left much for others to do. Roughly he held that animal and man are both something in the mind and something outside the mind. They are understood in one way in the mind and exist in another way in things outside the mind; in the mind they are understood as universal, whereas outside the mind they are individual and sensible. Moreover, explicitly adopting an Aristotelian stance, which he justified because he was commenting on a work dealing with Aristotle, he rejected the view that genera and species exist separately from individual things outside the mind.

Challenged by Boethius' answers, subsequent authors developed many positions in the early Middle Ages. They ranged from the extreme realism of Eriugena, according to whom genera and species are Platonic Ideas, to the extreme nominalism of Roscelin (b. ca. 1050; d. 1120), who held they are mere individual utterances. The most sophisticated view was offered by Abelard, who argued that universals are words that are created to be predicated of several things. Although these words do not cause an understanding of any individual thing in particular, but rather of a conception common to many of them which the mind contrives, the cause of their imposition is to be found in the status of individual things. The status itself is not a thing, or any kind of reality, but merely what things are. The status of Socrates and Plato is man, but man is no entity other than Socrates and Plato. In spite of the sophistication of Abelard's theory, there were many questions that it left unanswered and which were taken up by subsequent authors.

In the thirteenth century, the terms of the controversy changed somewhat because of the introduction of new terminology found in the recent translations of Aristotle and the commentaries upon them by Averroes and Avicenna. Instead of speaking about genera, species, or universals, the talk changed to natures. Moreover, the question was framed in terms of their unity and being: What kind of being and unity do natures have? The classic moderate position was taken by Aquinas, who argued that natures can be considered absolutely or in relation to the mind or individual things. Absolutely, only what is included in their definitions belongs to natures. Therefore, they cannot be said to have being or unity, but neither can they be said to lack them. Because the definition of the nature "man" is "rational animal," only animality and rationality can be said to belong to man considered absolutely. And because being and unity, just like whiteness, are not present in the definition, these cannot be said to belong to man considered as man, but neither are they supposed not to belong to it. The nature "man" is as neutral with respect to being and unity, as it is with respect to whiteness. Being and unity belong to natures only when they are considered in relation to the mind or to individual things outside the mind. In relation to the mind, natures are concepts properly speaking and, therefore, are universal and have mental being. In relation to individual things, natures are individual and have individual being. Man, when understood, has both being and unity, the being proper to the mind, where it is found as a concept, and the unity proper to universals, because it can be used to think about not any man in particular but about each and every man. Man, considered in relation to individual men, has both individual being and unity, the being and unity of each man where it is found as their nature.

Both Scotus and Ockham developed views that disagreed with that of Aquinas, but in opposite directions. Scotus moved closer to realism and Ockham closer to nominalism. For Scotus, natures considered absolutely have a being and unity proper to themselves. Thus, in individuals, natures have a double unity and a double being, their own and that of individuals. Man has a being and unity proper to natures, so that in this man there is a double being and unity: the being and unity of the nature and the being and unity of the individual.

Ockham was quite dissatisfied with this view and applied to it his famous Razor, according to which explanations should not multiply entities beyond necessity. For him, there is no such a thing as a nature considered absolutely; there are only universal concepts in the mind and individual things outside the mind. The notion of a nature considered absolutely, whether that nature is conceived neutrally as Aquinas did, or as having some being and unity as Scotus did, is superfluous. The existence of universal concepts in the mind can be explained in terms of the natural capacity of the mind to form a general concept based on the particular experience of individuals.

Individuation

Those authors who attributed some status to natures in things outside the mind naturally asked themselves the question of what it is in things that makes them individual. If all the terms we predicate of individual things indicate something universal or common in them, what is individual in things? This was a particularly important question for medieval authors, and one which had been generally neglected by the ancients. Both Plato and Aristotle had talked about individuals, but their primary concern was with universals and their status. For the medievals, the order of importance was reversed, because for them God was not universal and had even become an individual person in the world. Moreover, God's creation was conceived as individual and endowed, as Augustine had pointed out, with a value higher than the ideas through which we know it.

The first author to raise questions concerning individuation was Boethius in *On the Trinity*, a treatise devoted to the explanation of how God can be both one substance and three persons. For him, individuality is the result of the bundle of accidents (i.e., of features which are not necessary to the thing) substances have, and ultimately, if they have all other accidents in common, of the place they occupy. Although this view is controversial, it enjoyed enormous popularity throughout the early Middle Ages. After Abelard's challenge in the twelfth century, however, it was generally rejected. He argued that accidents cannot individuate a substance because a substance is prior to its accidents insofar as particular accidents are not necessary for the substance.

Ockham and other conceptualists and nominalists did not think they needed to find a principle of individuation because they held that only individual things exist and universals, or natures, are nothing but concepts produced by mental processes. Realists, however, who held universals or natures are something real outside the mind, had to identify a principle of individuation. A popular view was to hold that substances are individual owing to their matter. In an Aristotelian framework, where substances are composed of matter and form, and form is common, this view makes sense prima facie. Upon further analysis, however, it appears that matter also is common and this makes it difficult for it to individuate. Aquinas's response was to propose that it is not matter by itself that individuates, but rather matter taken together with quantity, which he understood as dimensions. This was unsatisfactory to Scotus, who pointed out that quantity is as common as matter and therefore the combination of the two cannot explain individuality. Instead, he proposed a *sui generis* principle of individuation, a formality he called thisness. This is an unanalyzable and indefinable principle whose only function is to individuate. Each individual, then, has a common nature with a unity and being proper to itself, and also a principle of individuation which makes it a this. This principle and the common nature are distinguished more than concepts are, but less than real things are; they are distinguished formally.

Conclusion

The problems discussed above provide only a small sample of the many that the medievals addressed. Indeed, except for problems only subsequently raised because of advances in science and technology (e.g., artificial intelligence), the medievals seem to have touched upon most of the philosophical problems of perennial interest. Although medieval philosophy is significantly different from contemporary philosophy insofar as it is primarily concerned with the integration of revelation and secular learning, nonetheless it has much in common with it. For example, it shares with analytic philosophy an emphasis on linguistic precision, the use of technical language, an argumentative spirit, and the view that philosophical problems can be solved by drawing distinctions. And it shares with continental philosophy a concern with being and the existential issues that affect humans. Much can be found in medieval philosophy, therefore, that should be of interest to contemporary philosophers – not just as a matter of antiquarian curiosity, but also as a source of philosophical understanding.

PART I

THE HISTORICAL CONTEXT

1

The Ancient Philosophical Legacy and its Transmission to the Middle Ages

CHARLES H. LOHR

Medieval learning was characterized by an attitude which was dominant - though in varying degrees and varying circumstances – from the time of Alcuin to that of Bellarmine. For the Middle Ages it was not the individual who taught, but the Church through the clergy. Clerical science was the corporate transmission of traditional wisdom. The task of the monastic teacher was ordered to the service of God and centered on the understanding of God's word as recorded in the sacred writings and interpreted by the Fathers. The teacher's authority was guaranteed by Scripture and the Church Fathers. Within this conception, a standard method of interpretation was developed based on the presumed concordance of the fundamental authorities – the Bible and the Church Fathers, above all AUGUSTINE, Ambrose, Jerome, and Gregory the Great – and schools evolved whose function was the training of masters who should transmit traditional learning to God's people.

The master saw the arts of the *trivium* (logic, grammar, and rhetoric) and *quadrivium* (arithmetic, music, geometry, and astronomy) as united with theology in one comprehensive system of knowledge in accordance with Augustine's (unrealized) vision. But he knew little of Greek philosophy and science, and, apart from some notions transmitted by Cicero, Martianus Capella, and ISIDORE OF SEVILLE, very little of Aristotle. Although the Aristotelian logic fitted neatly into the scheme of the liberal arts, BOETHIUS' translations could have but little influence in the monastic schools of the early Middle Ages.

A first stage: the twelfth and early thirteenth centuries

From the eleventh century knowledge was no longer confined to remote monasteries. With the rise of the towns, new schools appeared and with them a new type of teacher. This teacher turned first to the legacy he had inherited through the ancient *trivium*. He found that he would require a new form of school and a new method of interpretation. The new master would not only transmit traditional learning, he would have to question its authority.

From about this time the new masters slowly pieced together the original fabric of Aristotelian logic, with the exception of the theory of proof as it is found in the *Posterior Analytics*. The Aristotelian method of the topics and the treatment of the fallacies were reconstructed from hints in the available works of Aristotle and Cicero and from the treatises of Boethius surrounding them.

ABELARD'S *Dialectica* is worlds away from the monastic idea of dialectic and it shows that the full range of Aristotelian logic, which became known in the latter half of the twelfth century, became known because this new generation had sought the works containing it and their searching was itself a form of interpretation. The masters' study of Aristotelian logic did not proceed without opposition from the representatives of the traditional conception of the cleric's task. The polemics of BERNARD OF CLAIRVAUX against Abelard represent the reaction of the older, monastic idea to the new, urban conception of the teacher's role. By the middle of the twelfth century these new masters had come to realize that there were whole areas of knowledge of which they knew only the names. The new generation's search for hitherto unknown sciences is the expression of its own new self-image.

Parallel to the effort to forge a new tool for the sciences, a *novum organum*, ran an awakening interest in the subjects of the old *quadrivium*. The function of the masters whose trade it was to teach was no longer simply that of transmitting traditional Latin wisdom. New translations of the Pseudo-Dionysius had to be absorbed. The School of Chartres confronted the Bible and the Fathers with the *Timaeus* of Plato. ALAN OF LILLE sought to work Platonic notions into Christian theology, employing the methodology of the newly translated *Liber de causis*. Through contact with travelers in Sicily and Spain and with Jewish scholars in southern France, the masters gained some knowledge of Greek and Arabic philosophy and science. Having learned the names of many new and strange sciences, they turned to the translators. The additions which these interpreters of the classical tradition made to medieval knowledge were immense: in geometry and optics Euclid, in astronomy Ptolemy, in medicine Hippocrates and Galen, and above all – for method, for system, for wholly new and undreamt-of sciences – the works of Aristotle, the Philosopher *par excellence*, together with his Muslim and Jewish commentators, ALFARABI, AVICENNA, ALGAZALI, AVERROES, and MAIMONIDES.

At this stage the reception of Aristotle was part of a vast effort to absorb the philosophical, medical, astrological, and natural science not only of ancient Greece, but also of past and contemporary Judaism and Islam. The Aristotelian encyclopedia provided the framework for all this new material. At Barcelona, in the Archives of the Crown of Aragon, there is a manuscript (Ripoll 109 fo. 134r–158v) which contains a guidebook or manual for students in the arts faculty in Paris. This text, which was apparently based on early thirteenth-century practice, was composed about 1230–40 by an unknown master of the faculty for the benefit of students who had to prepare for examinations. It reveals very clearly the role which the Aristotelian encyclopedia played in mastering the ancient legacy.

For the author of the guidebook, the arts are no longer simply the seven liberal arts of the *trivium* and *quadrivium*; they comprise rather all the philosophical and scientific disciplines newly recovered at his time. And because the author attempts to situate the plan of studies in the arts faculty within the context of a complete classification of the sciences, these arts include some disciplines as yet unknown to him.

After some reflections on the nature of philosophy, the author divides his subject into three branches: rational, natural, and practical or moral philosophy. Under rational philosophy he takes up the subjects of the *trivium*, assigning to grammar the works of Priscian and Donatus, to rhetoric Cicero's *De inventione*, and to dialectic Aristotle's *Organon* together with the *Isagoge* of Porphyry and the logical treatises of Boethius.

Natural philosophy he divides into metaphysics, mathematics, and physics. For metaphysics the standard texts are Aristotle's *Metaphysics* and the pseudo-Aristotelian *Liber de causis*. Under mathematics he takes up the subjects of the *quadrivium*, but assigns to some of its branches works which were unknown in the earlier Middle Ages. To astronomy he assigns Ptolemy's *Almagest*, to geometry Euclid's *Elements*, to arithmetic Boethius' *Institutio arithmetica*, and to music Boethius' *Institutio musica*. Physics, being at a lower degree of abstraction than metaphysics and mathematics, is described as *scientia naturalis inferior*. Here are taken up all the works then ascribed to Aristotle on natural philosophy: *Physics*, dealing with the general principles of change; *De caelo*, dealing with the eternal motion of the celestial bodies; *De generatione et corruptione*, dealing with the four sublunary elements which explain generation and corruption; *Meteora*, dealing with a great variety of natural phenomena; *De plantis*, *De animalibus*, *De anima*, *Parva naturalia*, and *De motu cordis*, dealing with the whole range of animate nature.

Most interesting is the author's treatment of moral philosophy, divided into the treatment of the life of the soul, first in its relation to God, then in its relation to others, and finally in itself. Here the author's assignment of texts to the different branches lacks the clarity we have found in the other sections. The study of the life of the soul in God he identifies with theology, but he indicates no standard text. The other divisions reflect Aristotle's classification of the practical disciplines into those concerning the individual, the family, and the state. But the author does not yet know the *Oeconomica* and the *Politics*, and so assigns Cicero's *De officiis* to the consideration of the life of the soul in the family, and the study of Roman and canon law to the consideration of the life of the soul in the state. He assigns Aristotle's *Ethics* only to the treatment of the life of the soul in itself. After the treatment of ethics the author adds the note that two other books are also read in the faculty of arts: Plato's *Timaeus* and Boethius' *De consolatione philosophiae*.

This students' guide marks a definite stage in the evolution of the medieval arts faculty, the final stage in the formation of a new type of school, a school representing the interests of the new, urban type of master and his basically unclerical conception of the scientific enterprise. Although the author attempts to assign theology a place among the practical disciplines, his concern is rather with the Aristotelian system of the sciences. This system will lead the masters of arts inevitably to Aristotle's division of the practical sciences. The author does not yet know all the works of Aristotle's practical philosophy. But he does know the names of the sciences, and no doubt his colleagues were searching the libraries of Europe for copies of the works to be translated.

The Aristotelian classification of the sciences was thus instrumental in the recovery of Aristotle's own works. It also supplied the framework for the vast amount of new scientific material, for the Greek, Arabic, and Hebrew works on mathematics, astrology, medicine, and natural science that the translators of the late twelfth and early thirteenth centuries had made available. Even more significantly, the Aristotelian system of the sciences was decisive for the formation of the medieval university.

A second stage: the late thirteenth and fourteenth centuries

On March 19, 1255, Aristotelianism was officially adopted in the University of Paris as the arts faculty proclaimed a new syllabus which imposed the study of all the known works of Aristotle. On that day a second stage in the attitude to the ancient philosophical legacy began. The arts faculty became what we might call a philosophical faculty, with a tendency to develop a teaching independent of the theological faculty. Such a development was bound to cause a growing rivalry between the two faculties. The conflict had broken out at least as early as the students' guide. It concerned at first moral philosophy. The author distinguished between the point of view of a philosopher and that of a theologian: "To which we reply that speaking philosophically we are the entire cause [of our good actions]; but speaking theologically, we are not capable of good actions, but it is necessary that God pour grace into us." In a few decades, questions concerning the eternity of the world and the immortality of the human soul were added to the questions regarding which philosophy and theology were thus expressly opposed. But far more profound than these particular differences was the distinction between theological and philosophical discourse to which our master of arts here appeals.

The prescription of the Aristotelian corpus as the basis of instruction in the arts faculty brought with it for the masters the obligation of interpreting the texts they had sought after. Their commentaries on the works of the Philosopher open a new epoch in the history of medieval exegesis. As early as our students' guide we find the author, in the text cited above, distinguishing between philosophical and theological discourse (*loquendo secundum philosophos; loquendo secundum theologos et secundum veritatem*). SIGER OF BRABANT explains his purpose even more explicitly: "We seek what the philosophers meant in this matter, their intention rather than the truth, because we proceed philosophically."

Medieval exegesis had been concerned with the Bible. Its premiss was that the exegete was already in possession of a truth revealed by God himself. The task of the exegete was not the discovery of new truths, but rather the unveiling of the truth concealed in the words of the sacred text. In accomplishing this task, he not only turned to the councils and Church Fathers as authorities to lead him, he also felt himself, as a living link in a corporate undertaking, endowed with the same authority to teach. In the twelfth century, as discrepancies among his authorities became increasingly obtrusive, his conviction that the tradition of which he was custodian was at bottom coherent guided his efforts to penetrate more deeply into the truth of God's word as a sort of *concordia discordantium*.

The point of departure of the masters of arts was radically different. Siger of Brabant and his fellow masters were the first to want to interpret philosophical texts "philosophically", that is, in the very unclerical way of abstracting from the question of the truth of the teaching. Their task was not the unveiling of a truth already possessed but hidden; it was rather the discussion of the opinion of a most distinguished colleague. For this reason Siger gave the following rule for the interpretation of Aristotle: "It should be noted by those who undertake to comment upon the books of the Philosopher that his opinion is not to be concealed, even though it be contrary to the truth." A further consequence of this "philosophical procedure" was that the interpreter need make no effort at a *concordia discordantium*. The theologian sought to unveil a truth concealed; the philosopher need not seek to conceal the errors in his sources. Since the work of Aristotle, the primary source for a member of the arts faculty, was for him neither a new dogma nor an infallible guide, he need make no clerical attempt at harmonizing science and the Bible. The interpreter, having abandoned the notion of truth possessed for the notion of truth to be sought, could approach the text of the Philosopher in a critical, questioning way.

Behind this revolution lay no doubt the *de facto* conflicts between Aristotle's teachings and the doctrines of faith. The masters of arts were confronted with an important literature opposing various interpretations of Aristotle: ALBERTUS MAGNUS, *De XV problematibus*; THOMAS AQUINAS, *De unitate intellectus contra Averroistas*; Giles of Rome, *De erroribus philosophorum*; the condemnations of 1270 and 1277. In the face of such opposition, it was difficult to maintain that Aristotle had spoken the whole truth. But this revolution in the theory of interpretation represents the beginning of the end of the clerical paradigm for the scientific enterprise. The masters of arts could recognize the deficiencies in Aristotle's teaching. But in him they found a new model not only for interpretation, but also for science.

The theologians had traditionally attempted to solve problems arising out of divergent authorities by seeking a standpoint from which all the relevant texts could be brought into harmony. But in the thirteenth century the newly translated philosophical and scientific sources rendered questionable the simple concordances which the twelfth century had made between authorities limited to the Latin ecclesiastical tradition. In this new situation, some rejected the new literature and attempted, by ecclesiastical condemnations, to prevent its being read; others, like BONAVENTURE and PETER OLIVI, saw in Aristotle the apocalyptic beast of the last days and took refuge in the historical speculations of Joachim of Fiore; still other theologians, like Albert the Great and Thomas Aquinas, showed themselves receptive to the new sources and tried in a new and very subtle way to continue the clerical enterprise of a *concordia discordantium.*

Thomas went furthest in the attempt to answer the challenge posed by the approach of the masters of arts to the new literature. As a theologian, he had to maintain the existence of truths revealed in the Bible that transcended human understanding. At the same time, the encounter with the religious teachings of Judaism and Islam had constrained Latin theologians to attempt the construction of an apologetic based on arguments acceptable to the three faiths. Because such arguments could be based only on rational demonstration, Thomas sought to justify the inclusion of philosophical questions in the subject matter of theology. Because theology is the science of revelation, he maintained that God had revealed not only strictly supernatural truths, but also some truths which are philosophically demonstrable. For example, God revealed his existence, for otherwise but few men would have attained certain knowledge of this truth. Nevertheless, Thomas argued, God's existence can be also demonstrated, and he proposed five ways of doing so. The first cause whose existence has been rationally demonstrated on the basis of the principles of the philosophers is that very being which the Christian by revelation knows as God.

The concord between philosophy and revelation that Thomas intended involved not only the demonstration of rationally accessible truths, but also the discovery of natural analogies to transcendent truths and the ordering of both natural and supernatural truths in a scientific way. Thomas's theologian had therefore to turn to nature and could employ in this effort the works of "the master of them that know" (Dante). In the Aristotelian logic, Thomas found prescriptions for the ordering of theological doctrine as a strict science. In the Aristotelian metaphysics, he found the principles for the demonstration of truths such as the existence, infinity, and omnipotence of God. In the Aristotelian natural philosophy, he found natural analogies to the hierarchical view of the world that the clerical tradition had handed down.

It was in dealing with Aristotelian astronomy that Thomas was forced to take a position with regard to a type of discourse different from that between dissenting theological authorities. The translators from Arabic and Greek had made available two mutually opposed discussions of the problem of celestial motion: Ptolemy's *Almagest* and Aristotle's *De caelo.* While the professional astronomers of the period adopted Ptolemy's theory of eccentrics and epicycles and paid little attention to Aristotle's theory of homocentric spheres, the theologians were very disturbed by the contradiction between Ptolemy's mathematical astronomy, which claimed to save the phenomena, and Aristotle's physical theory, which was presented as a deduction from first principles.

Thomas's attempt at a solution of this problem shows clearly the difference between his theological interpretation of Aristotle and what we may call the philosophical interpretation of the masters of arts. For Thomas the harmonious order found in Aristotle's physical theory was based on absolutely certain, metaphysical principles. To the argument that Ptolemy's hypotheses are supported by experience, Thomas rejoined that (whereas falsification invalidates an hypothesis) the experimental verification of an hypothesis does not necessarily

19

demonstrate it. Although Thomas thus formulated explicitly one of the most important principles in the theory of science, he employed it to render harmless the objections to his theological interpretation of Aristotle's astronomy – in the hope that some day a way might be found to make Aristotle's theory agree with experience. His appeal to the principle that verification does not demonstrate an hypothesis meant only that his conception of the concordance between philosophy and revelation need not be disturbed by the contrary data of experience.

Armed with Thomas's principle, the clerical worldview was able to maintain itself until the time of Bellarmine and disappeared only with the new astronomical discoveries of the sixteenth and seventeenth centuries. The falsification of the Aristotelian physics then implied for many the falsification of Thomas's approach. Thomas Aquinas's answer to the challenge posed by the new literature was in fact the last speculative attempt to save the clerical conception of science as the corporate transmission of traditional wisdom.

The rejection by the masters of arts of the method of concordance, their rejection of the notion of a prior truth known by faith to which philosophical truth must conform, conformed to the image they had of themselves as the successors of the Philosopher. Because their own status was not based on an appeal to authority, they could admit that Aristotle made mistakes. The authority of their teaching was guaranteed only by reason. Since they claimed no authority in the sacred sciences, they enjoyed a new liberty in their research, a liberty that brought with it the many new, un-Aristotelian developments of the fourteenth and fifteenth centuries.

The masters of arts regarded their work as philosophy, but it was meant to take up the vast legacy they had inherited from antiquity – a legacy which embraced logic and mathematics, mechanics and astronomy, ethics and political theory. The distinction between philosophical and theological (not truth, but) discourse enabled them not only to break with the clerical commentary tradition, but also to give the medieval arts faculty a new autonomy. No longer simply the gateway to theology, the arts faculty became an institution on an equal footing with the faculties of law, medicine, and theology. The "philosophical procedure" made it possible for the masters of arts to turn increasingly from the exposition to the question-form of commentary, to criticize the Philosopher, to ask the new logical and mathematical questions with which WILLIAM OF OCKHAM, JOHN BURIDAN, and the Merton school led philosophy in the early fourteenth century into new paths. It made it possible for NICOLE ORESME to fuse Mertonian mathematics with Parisian physics in the late fourteenth century, and for PAUL OF VENICE and others in Padua in the fifteenth century to bring these developments together with the Averroist attitude to form the secular Aristotelianism of the sixteenth-century Italian universities.

A third stage: the fifteenth and sixteenth centuries

A third stage in the tradition of the ancient philosophical legacy began in the late fourteenth century. This stage was often more philological than philosophical in character. New editions and vernacular translations of the Greek and Latin classics and new philosophical options – Platonism, Epicureanism, and Stoicism – began to appear. A new Aristotelianism also appeared. A third wave of editions, translations, and commentaries on the works of Aristotle began in the fifteenth century and lasted until about the middle of the seventeenth.

The Aristotelianism of the period 1500–1650 no longer played the role it had had in the university philosophy of the Middle Ages. In the sixteenth century, we must speak not of one, but of several Aristotelianisms. Within the Catholic Church, the Jesuits and the other religious orders attempted to maintain the old, clerical idea of philosophy, enlisting Aquinas's interpretation of Aristotle's *Metaphysics* in the service of Catholic theology. In Protestant Germany, Melanchthon constructed a new Aristotelianism – without the *Metaphysics* – for the new schools which should serve Luther's gospel. In France scholars concerned with constitutional reform searched for new ways to interpret legal doctrine. In Italy humanists turned to Aristotle's moral philosophy, literary critics to the teachings of the *Poetics*, university professors to works either unknown or ignored in the Middle Ages, like the *Problemata* and the *Mechanica* and to the Greek commentators on natural philosophy. The new Latin Aristotelians began to turn increasingly to the Greek tradition of Aristotle's works and came eventually to regard the Arabic contribution as alien to their own self-image as the successors of the Greeks and Romans.

New sources, new scientific interests, new classes of students, new geographical divisions led such groups of scholars to attend to the various parts of philosophy without reference to Aristotle's organization of science. Although these developments took different forms in different contexts, beneath them lay a new conception of what philosophy is, a conception that was born with the Parisian masters of the thirteenth century and could still be shared by Descartes and Galileo, by Bacon and Hobbes, a conception of philosophy no longer bound by traditional authority.

Bibliography

Aertsen, J. A., et al., eds. (1999), *Averroes and the Aristotelian Tradition*, Leiden: Brill.

d'Alverny, M.-T. (1993), *Avicenne en Occident: recueil d'articles*, Paris: Librairie Philosophique J. Vrin.

Bernardo, A. S., et al., eds. (1990), *The Classics in the Middle Ages*, Papers of the Twentieth Annual Conference of the Center for Medieval and Early Renaissance Studies, Binghamton, NY: Center for Medieval and Early Renaissance Studies.

Bianchi, L. (1990), *Il vescovo e i filosofi: la condanna parigina del 1277 e l'evoluzione del aristotelismo scolastico*, Bergamo: Lubrina.

Bianchi, L. and Randi, E. (1990), *Le verità dissonanti: Aristotele alla fine del medioevo*, Rome and Bari: Laterza.

Butterworth, C. E., et al., eds. (1994), *The Introduction of Arabic Philosophy into Europe*, Leiden and New York: Brill.

Colish, M. L. (1985), *The Stoic Tradition from Antiquity to the Early Middle Ages*, Leiden: Brill.

Flasch, K. (1989), *Aufklärung im Mittelalter? Die Verurteilung von 1277*, Mainz: Dietrich.

Grabmann, M. (1936), "Eine für Examinazwecke abgefasste Quaestionensammlung der Pariser Artistenfakultät aus der ersten Hälfte des XIII. Jahrhunderts," in *Mittelalterliches Geistesleben II* (pp. 183–199), Munich: Hubner.

Hankins, J. (1990), *Plato in the Italian Renaissance*, 2 vols., Leiden: Brill.

Hissette, R. (1977), *Enquête sur les 219 articles condamnés à Paris le 7 mars 1277*, Louvain and Paris: Publications Universitaires.

Imbach, R. (1996), *Dante, la philosophie et les laïcs: initiations à la philosophie médiévale*, Fribourg, Switzerland: Editions Universitaires; Paris: Éditions du Cerf.

Jones, H. (1989), *The Epicurean Tradition*, London: Routledge.

Kristeller, P. O. (1955), *The Classics and Renaissance Thought*, Cambridge, MA: published for Oberlin College by Harvard University Press.

Lafleur, C., et al., eds. (1997), *L'Enseignement de la philosophie au XIIIe siècle: autour du "Guide de l'étudiant" de MS Ripoll 109*, Turnhout: Brepols.

Lohr, C. H. (1967–74), "Medieval Latin Aristotle Commentaries," *Traditio* 23–30.

——(1988), *Commentateurs d'Aristote au moyen âge: bibliographie de la littérature secondaire récente*, Fribourg, Switzerland: Editions Universitaires; Paris: Éditions du Cerf.

——(1988), *Latin Aristotle Commentaries*, vol. II: *Renaissance Authors*, Florence: L. S. Olschki.

——(1995), *Latin Aristotle Commentaries*, vol. III: *Index initiorum, Index finium*, Florence: L. S. Olschki.

Niewöhner, F., et al., eds. (1994), *Averroismus im Mittelalter und in der Renaissance*, Zurich: Spur.

Osler, M. J. (1991), *Atoms, Pneuma and Tranquility: Epicurean and Stoic Themes in European Thought*, Cambridge and New York: Cambridge University Press.

Siraisi, N. G. (1987), *Avicenna in Renaissance Italy: The Canon and Medical Teaching in Italian Universities after 1500*, Princeton, NJ: Princeton University Press.

Thijssen, J. M. M. H. (1998), *Censure and Heresy at the University of Paris, 1200–1440*, Philadelphia: University of Pennsylvania Press.

Van Steenberghen, F. (1946), *Aristote en Occident: les origines de l'aristotelisme parisien*, Louvain: Éditions de l'Institut Supérieur de Philosophie.

A bibliography of secondary literature concerning the *fortuna* of the classics in the Middle Ages and Renaissance may be found on the internet:
www.ruf.uni-freiburg.de/theologie/forsch/lohr/lohr-ch0.htm

2

The Patristic Background

STEPHEN F. BROWN

On at least two occasions in the *Commentary on the Sentences of Peter Lombard* (II, d. 23, a. 2, q. 3; II, 547 and II, prol.; II, 1–2), BONAVENTURE speaks of his spiritual father, ALEXANDER OF HALES. In so doing, he follows a long biblical and church tradition of acknowledging indebtedness to the teachers of spiritual realities, fathers in the faith. Saint Paul in his First Letter to the Corinthians (4: 14–15) stated: "I am not writing this to make you ashamed, but to admonish you as my beloved children. For though you might have ten thousand guardians in Christ, you do not have many fathers. Indeed, in Christ Jesus I became your father through the gospel." Clement of Alexandria (*Stromata* (*Miscellanies*) I, c. 1; *PG* 8, 687–90) led a long list of those who acknowledged the importance of spiritual fathers when he explained: "It is a good thing, I reckon, to leave to posterity good children. This is the case with children of our bodies. But words are the progeny of the soul. Whence we call those who have instructed us, fathers." The Fathers of the Church, according to Clement, replaced the fathers of the pagan world, Homer and the other "theologians of vice" (*Logos protreptikos* (*Exhortation to the Heathen*), 4; *PG* 8, 133–4). In biblical times, the spiritual fathers were the writers of the Old and New Testaments. Later, the spiritual fathers became those Catholic writers who explained and witnessed the divine revelation found in the Scriptures.

Although Bonaventure might refer to Alexander of Hales as his immediate spiritual "father," the traditional Catholic Fathers of the Church had a longer claim to respect. They were generally known for their antiquity, orthodoxy, holiness, and church approval, though some who held heretical or unorthodox positions enjoyed the title due to their great influence on the deeper understanding of the teachings of the Church. The Christian Fathers extend from the Apostolic Fathers, like Clement of Rome who died around 100, to the last of the western Fathers, ISIDORE OF SEVILLE, who died around 636, and the last of the eastern Fathers, John of Damascus, who died around 750. The more famous traditional Fathers of the Church were those who were also named Doctors, or chief teachers, of the Church. This was a group that for medieval writers included the Latin Fathers, Ambrose, AUGUSTINE, Jerome, and Gregory the Great, and the Greek Fathers, John Chrysostom, Basil, Gregory of Nazianzus, and Athanasius. Augustine was the most influential Latin Father: he is quoted by the important medieval textbook writer, PETER LOMBARD, so often that many imagined Peter, as the Master of the *Sentences*, to be a compiler of Augustinian quotations rather than an author in his own right. THOMAS AQUINAS indicated that Chrysostom was the most respected of the Greek Fathers when it came to the understanding of the Scriptures (*In evangelium S. Ioannis lectura*, lect. II, n. 94).

The Fathers of the Church were not considered infallible. In a frank admission, Saint Augustine in the introduction of his *Retractationes*, indicated how much he feared God's words: "In a multitude of words you shall not avoid sin" (Prov. 10: 19). He feared the divine warning because he realized that many things could be collected from his "numerous disputations, which, if not false, yet may certainly seem or even be proved unnecessary" (*Retractationes*, I, c. 1; *PL* 32, 583–4). In his *Letter to Fortunatianus* (*Epistola 148*, n. 15; *PL* 33, 628–9), Augustine went beyond the correction of his own works and extended the invitation to criticism to the works of others: "Still, we are not obliged to regard the arguments of any writers, however Catholic and estimable they may be, as we do the canonical Scriptures, so that we may – with all due respect to the deference owed them as men – refute or reject anything we happen to find in their writings wherein their opinions differ from the established truth, or from what has been thought out by others or by us, with divine help. I wish other thinkers to hold the same attitude toward my writings as I hold toward theirs." Despite such solicitation for criticism by Augustine, and others, the Fathers commanded great authority as Christians who were attempting a more profound penetration of revelation. Such an effort demanded a loyal doctrinal communion with the Church, and although Tertullian and Origen might respectively have slipped into Montanism and into teaching the pre-existence of souls, they contributed strongly to the orthodox teachings of the Church by opposing errors and producing a deeper understanding of the faith.

Over the years, the Fathers gained stature as the Church searched for solid statements of fundamental Christian beliefs, for a strong defense of them, and for an ever-deepening understanding of their meanings. Athanasius had such a strong influence at the Councils of Nicea-Constantinople, that the conciliar creed was honorifically given the name "The Athanasian Creed." Generally, in their efforts to establish a unified collection of basic beliefs, councils appealed to the Fathers, as is evident from the statement of the acts of the fifth ecumenical council, the Second Council of Constantinople (553): "We further declare that we hold fast to the decrees of the four Councils, and in every way follow the holy Fathers, Athanasius, Hilary, Basil, Gregory the Theologian, Gregory of Nyssa, Ambrose, Theophilus, John Chrysostom, Cyril, Augustine, Proclus, Leo and their writings on the true faith" (Percival 1900, 14: p. 303). These same Fathers are praised in these conciliar acts for defending true belief against the heresies of Theodore of Mopsuestia and Nestorius. Patristic authority also grew from the Fathers' contributions to a deeper understanding and richer practice of the Christian faith, as is witnessed by the *Rule of Saint Benedict*. In chapter 73 of the *Rule*, Benedict urges monks to follow "the teachings of the holy Fathers, by observing which a man is led to the summit of perfection. For what page or what utterance of the divinely-inspired books of the Old and the New Testament is not a most unerring rule of human life? Or what book of the holy Catholic Fathers is not manifestly devoted to teaching us the straight road to our creator?" (McCann 1952, pp. 160–1). The influence of the Fathers is also evident in the reformed Benedictine tradition, as is visible in the way William of St. Thierry in *The Golden Epistle* (1971, pp. 6–7) describes the influence of particular Fathers on his works. Regarding his commentary on the Song of Songs, he declares: "I have extracted also from the works of Saint Ambrose whatever he has to say on the Song of Songs, no slight work and one deserving of esteem. . . . If you wish to transcribe *The Sentences on Faith*, which I drew principally from the works of Saint Augustine (they are indeed strong meat and weighty with meaning), they are more akin to the book I mentioned above, entitled *The Enigma of Faith*."

The Catholic Fathers facing grammatical and logical precision

Early scholastic writers often simply quoted the Fathers to confirm the Church's understanding of the chief truths of the Christian faith. We see this in Peter Lombard's *Sentences*, where he cites Augustine's commentary on a verse from Paul's Letter to the Romans (11: 36): "For from him, and through him, and in him are all things. To him be glory forever." Augustine in his *On the Trinity* (I, c. 6, n. 12: *PL* 42, 827) explains: "*From him*, he says, because of the Father; *through him*, because of the Son; and *in him*, because of the Holy Spirit. From the fact that he does not say *from them, through them*, or *in them*, nor *to them* be glory, but rather *to him* be glory, the Apostle insinuated that this Trinity is the one Lord God." This is the case, likewise, when Lombard cited Jerome's *Explanation of the Creed* concerning the union of the divine and human natures in the one person of the Son in Christ. However, with PETER ABELARD a different type of reading of the Fathers is more striking. In his *Sic et non* (*Yes and No*) Abelard gathers the sayings of the different Fathers on various questions and shows the discrepancies that arise when they are brought together. Even though he does not resolve all the particular discrepancies, in his preface to the work (*PL* 178, 1339–43), Peter attempts to pose principles that might help resolve the seeming incompatibilities. Some contrasting statements might be due to scribal errors, others to the false attribution of a work to a certain author, others to translations from another language to Latin, others to the changing meanings given to the same words, others because teachers often need to vary their language, adjusting it to the understanding level of different audiences. Peter tells us that Saint Augustine realized the need for audience considerations when he said: "Good teachers should give teaching such a high priority that a word which cannot be good Latin without being obscure or ambiguous, but is used in its colloquial form to avoid ambiguity and obscurity, should not be spoken in the form used by the educated, but rather that habitually used by the unlearned. . . . For what use is a golden key if it cannot open what we want? Or what harm is a wooden key if it can do so, when we seek only that that which has been closed should be open?" (*De doctrina Christiana*, IV, 9–11; *PL* 34, 100). Frequently, then, quotations from the Fathers had to be read not by the rules of exact expression but with one eye to the truth they intended to present and another to the manner of their expression. In such cases, the "wooden key" of colloquial language often opened the message of the Patristic texts. The Fathers knew what they intended to say; they just did not always say it in the form that would be applauded by the readers who wanted only the "golden keys" of perfect grammar and logic.

In the era of Peter Abelard and Peter Lombard, the grammatical writings of Donatus and Priscian, and the logical treatises of Aristotle, aimed at greater precision of expression. Those who had accustomed themselves to these golden keys found among the Fathers many authoritative texts that needed to be changed from colloquial language to their learned forms. Abelard tells us in his *Story of My Calamities* that he had a heated discussion at the Council of Soissons (1121) with Alberic of Reims. It centered on the opening passage of Augustine's *On the Trinity* (I, c. 1, n. 1; *PL* 42, 820), where Augustine warned against forming conceptions of God in corporeal terms, such as God as white or red, or in terms relating to the human soul, such as God as now forgetting or now remembering. Finally, Augustine cautions against those who consider that God is of such power as to have generated himself, since "there is nothing whatever that generates its own existence." By way of the *Summa sententiarum* (*PL* 171, 1087) this debate, which Abelard chronicles in *Christian*

Theology (1969, pp. 235–6, 297–334, and 335–44) became the subject matter of Peter Lombard's distinction IV of Book I of the *Sentences*, where he says: "Here it is asked whether it should be conceded that God begot himself." When Lombard's *Sentences* became an official theology textbook at Paris in the 1230s, and later at Oxford, the debate was on. Bonaventure said that "God begot God" has been granted as true by the masters and the Fathers. But what did they mean when they admitted this statement as true? The masters and Fathers had not worked out an explicit theory of supposition or reference. Did they want to say "The divine essence begot God," or "The Trinity begot God," or "The Father begot the Son?" There was a need to go back to the Fathers and to the later masters in the schools to decide what they wanted to say. Then one would better express what they intended in a way that was different from their actual statements.

One of the notable comments on this text of Lombard expressing the need for restating the declarations of the Fathers comes from Simon of Tournai. He is quoted by later authors (e.g., HENRY OF GHENT, *Summa quaestionum ordinariarum*, a. 54, q. 3; II, fo. 80rT) as holding that Augustine was not always precise in his statements; nor were other Fathers of the Church. According to Simon, Augustine said in his *Letter to Maximinus* concerning the Father: "He begot from himself another self." According to Lombard, Augustine was trying to say: "He begot another, namely, another, distinct in person, who is the same as he is, namely the same in substance, for even though the Father is other than the Son, he is not a distinct thing from the Son, but the same thing, with the result that what the Son is the same as what the Father himself is." In other words, when Augustine said, "He begot from himself another self," this statement is a true and proper expression on the side of the truth that it expresses, but it is not properly stated on the side of the way it is expressed. This is so because 'another' is understood as a masculine gender word and therefore indicates a personal other, whereas the term 'self' is a neuter gender term and expresses an essential self. The expression 'another self', therefore is an improper or mixed-up expression. If, on the contrary, we change the masculine gender 'him' to the neuter gender, to 'that which he himself is', and say "The Father begot that which He himself is," as Augustine does in his *Sermon on the Creed*, then from a proper viewpoint, the statement is false, because it would follow that Augustine would be saying that the Father begot the divine essence. So, statements of this kind, if you want not only to get at the truth but also express it correctly, have to be changed from the neuter to the masculine gender. In fact, in this and similar ways, all the propositions or statements of the Fathers which insinuate that the divine essence itself generates or is generated have to be recast into their proper forms to avoid misunderstanding.

Augustine and the other Fathers knew logic and grammar. In *On Christian Doctrine*, Augustine underscored the importance of these disciplines for students attempting to understand the Scriptures. Yet, in the era of Abelard, Peter Lombard, and Simon of Tournai demands for logical and grammatical precision questioned the authoritative Patristic sources and demanded that they be exact at all times. Of course, no one always speaks according to the letter of grammatical and logical laws. Rhetoric would disappear and listeners would be bored to tears! Yet, in the non-ordinary world of the classroom where you are training to be precise, it is good practice to rephrase imprecise expressions. This effort allows students to restate the sense of Patristic statements in as clear a manner as possible. Such logical and grammatical precision continued long after Abelard, Lombard, and Simon of Tournai; it can be found especially in the commentaries on distinctions IV–VI of Book I of Peter Lombard's *Sentences* or in the *Summae* penned by Saint Bonaventure, Saint Thomas Aquinas, Henry of Ghent, WILLIAM OF OCKHAM, and so many other medieval authors.

The Fathers and the challenges of Aristotelian philosophy

When Aristotle's more properly philosophic works became available and influential, further challenges beyond those concerned with the manner of expression started to arise. Saint Augustine, the most dominant western Father, had developed some deep philosophical convictions. Could his philosophical positions withstand the objections coming from the newly-arrived Aristotelian texts? One important area of consideration in the mid-thirteenth century concerned the role "illumination" played in Augustine's theory of knowledge. Saint Bonaventure, in q. 4 of his *Disputed Questions on the Knowledge of Christ* (1981, V, pp. 22–3) analyzes the source or sources of certain or sure human knowledge.

The question as Bonaventure considered it was formulated as: "Do we get certitude in this life in the light of the eternal reasons?" Thus stated, the question carries us back to Plato and to some of his Christian followers. It also is judged by Bonaventure an ambiguous question, because 'in the light of the eternal reasons' can be understood in three ways.

One way of understanding 'the light of the eternal reasons' is the Platonic way that antecedes Saint Augustine, yet lingers in the minds of certain Christians. Human beings, according to this version of 'the eternal reasons' do not know anything with certainty except in the Divine Word in whom the eternal reasons are found. In such an understanding, there would be no difference between knowledge here on earth and knowledge in heaven, or between knowledge in the Divine Word and knowledge of things in themselves. This first interpretation of 'the eternal reasons' leaves us with the claim that nothing is known with certainty except in the archetypal world.

A second way of understanding 'the light of the eternal reasons' argues that the eternal reasons in themselves are not the cause of certain or sure human knowledge, but rather that their influence on human judgment is such that we on our part, by the faculties that belong to our nature and that we develop, evaluate the objects we perceive and appreciate. Such an interpretation, according to Bonaventure, implies that Augustine was deceived, since it is not easy to explain his arguments in a way consistent with this view. "It would be very absurd," continues Bonaventure, "to say this about one who is such a great Father and who is the most authoritative Doctor among the interpreters of the sacred Scriptures" (1981, V, p. 23).

The third way of viewing 'the light of the eternal reasons', a way that threads between these two extreme positions, is that for certain knowledge, the eternal reasons, which are above our minds, are the regulative and motivating principle – but certainly not the sole principle. Along with our created reason, which does its part, the light of the eternal reasons is the regulative and motivating principle of our certain knowledge (1981, V, p. 23).

Neither Augustine nor Bonaventure claim that we are conscious of this light. It is only when we reflect on the sources of our true judgments that we realize that a measure beyond us must also be present to us in our true certain judgments. As an analogy, a Christian version of Plato's cave might aid our understanding: Imagine yourself in a cathedral on a sunny day, looking at the beautiful stained-glass windows there. You would see the glorious colors of the windows, the detailed figures of those portrayed in them, and praise their beauty. Yet imagine that you happened to visit the cathedral at night or on a dark dreary day on which the colors were not visible or at least did not stand out, and when the figures were hardly, if at all, recognizable. Even though you (the knower and judge) were in the cathedral each time and the windows (objects known) were the same, still there would be a noticeable difference in your perceptions and judgments. You would realize that the light,

27

although not visible directly, was the most important and determining factor. In effect, such a light is the chief, though not the only, cause of our being able to see and judge the objects that are perceived under its indirectly perceivable presence.

Varying interpretations of the same text

As different medieval authors developed their own philosophical or theological positions, they brought to the texts of the Fathers meanings that made explicit what was only implicitly stated. Henry of Ghent, for instance, developed a very elaborate theory of analogy and applied it to the case of "being." For Henry, the first thing the human mind knows is being. We grasp being in a way that is deceiving, since we think that the term has a common meaning applicable to and predicable of everything. The concept of being, for Henry, has however only a psychological unity. When we dig a bit deeper, we discover that this seeming unity really covers a duality. There are in reality two different concepts of being that we have mistakenly "con-fused" into one: there is negatively undetermined being and privatively undetermined being. The first is not capable of receiving determinations or limitations, since negatively undetermined being is God. The second, privatively undetermined being, is undetermined but determinable, since it is capable of being limited or determined. It is this concept of privatively undetermined being that is predicable of creatures.

Henry believes that he can make his position on the two types of undetermined being clearer by introducing Augustine's declaration in Book VIII of *On the Trinity*: "You understand this good and that good. Understand pure good (*bonum simpliciter*) and you will have understood God." Henry substitutes 'being' for 'good' and gives the Bishop of Hippo's expression this meaning: "You understand this being and that being. If you understand pure being (*ens simpliciter*), then you understand God – but only on the condition that your understanding of pure being is negatively undetermined being. If you mean privatively undetermined being, then you do not grasp God; you only grasp determinable created being" (*Summa*, a. 21, q. 2; I, fo. 125rQ).

When JOHN DUNS SCOTUS developed a different conception of being and opposed Henry of Ghent's position, then, expectedly, he had to comment on Henry's use of Augustine's text. For Scotus, we can have a univocal concept of being. It is a concept that is common: not proper to any being, but rather a concept that is predicable of all beings, including God. It is a concept that Scotus describes as a distinct concept, since it leaves outside its ambit modes, such as "infinite" and "finite," and ultimate differences. When Scotus reads Augustine's text from Book VIII of *On the Trinity*, he reads it differently from Henry: "You understand this good or this being and that good or that being. Leave out the 'this' and the 'that', and you end up with 'good' or 'being', which leaves aside the differences and is thus common. Augustine's 'You understand God' means not that you know Him as 'a particular essence' but you know Him in a first common concept that will become a proper concept of God when you add the mode 'infinite' to it" (*Ordinatio* I, d. 3, p. 1, q. 3; III, p. 118).

PETER AURIOL, a Franciscan critic of Scotus's theory of being, offered an alternative conception of being. He, in a way, follows both Henry of Ghent and Scotus, while yet disagreeing with both of them. Like Henry, Auriol will argue that our concept of being is confused. However, he gives 'confused' a different meaning: our concept of being is confused because it does not leave modes and ultimate differences distinctly outside its ambit. It includes them in an implicit way. Like Scotus's view, Auriol's conception of being allows it to be predicable of God and creatures. Auriol does not, however, argue for a concept of being that is distinct: it is a concept that excludes nothing. It arrives at proper concepts not by adding anything, since there is nothing outside "being." It arrives at proper concepts by making explicit what is only implicit in the concept of being. When Auriol meditates on the text of Augustine, surprisingly, he does not interpret it in a manner that would remove the 'this' and the 'that' from 'this good' or 'that good' to arrive at a most common concept that would be predicable of all. He focuses more directly on 'You understand God', and employs Augustine's text to argue that God is in no way a special being or a partial entity separate from all other beings. He interprets Augustine's text as affirming that "God is total subsistent being" (*Deus est totalis entitas simpliciter subsistens*). Auriol says "Take away the 'this' and the 'that', and you will have total being which is God" (*habebis totalem entitatem quae est Deus* (*Reportatio Parisiensis* I, d. 2, p. 2, q. 2, p. 244)). In brief, he does not use Augustine to affirm a most common concept predicable of all, including God, but takes the Patristic text to point to the richest being of all.

In this and in similar ways, medieval thinkers worked and reworked Patristic texts in terms of the philosophical and theological views they themselves had developed. They thereby had to draw out the implications of certain texts of the Fathers that had not explicitly treated the same issues as they themselves were addressing. At times this entailed the complete alteration of the way of reading the entire corpus of one or many Patristic authors. According to DURAND OF ST. POURÇAIN, for example, there are two main forms of technical theology. One is deductive theology, where the habit developed by theologians is one that starts with the articles of the faith as premises and using other faith-based or purely rational premises, draws further truths from them. The other type of theology is declarative theology, where the principles of theology are the articles of the faith and theologians attempt to bring some light to these principles themselves, by defining technical terms, showing the errors of heretical teachings, and finding suitable analogies and arguments that illuminate to some degree these articles that are accepted because of faith in the God who has revealed them. Peter Auriol, in the prooemium to his *Scriptum on the Sentences* attributes deductive theology to Thomas Aquinas, though he claims that Aquinas and other theologians also develop what he calls declarative theology:

> Now, it is certain that this Doctor, in his *Summa*, and generally all theologians who are teachers, formulate questions concerning the articles of the faith, and they go on to solve the questions and bring some light in regard to them and come to conclusions in regard to these articles, as when they ask: "Is there only one God?," or "Is there in God a trinity of persons?," or "Is the Incarnation possible?" (*Scriptum*, I, sect. 1, q. 1, n. 24; I, p. 139)

This is especially evident if we look at a number of Augustine's theological efforts. In the early part of the *De Trinitate*, he tells us that he has examined all the expositors who have written on the Trinity, and that they tried to make it clear that the Father, the Son, and the Holy Spirit express a divine unity of one and the same substance in indivisible equality. Furthermore, when the Bishop of Hippo argues against Faustus, he attempts to prove that Christ is born of the Virgin Mary and that the Holy Spirit spoke through the prophets. Augustine's writings, then, do not for the most part proceed from the articles of the faith to further truths, but much more they focus on the articles themselves and attempt to illuminate them. Theologians, Auriol concludes, should more properly build up habits that do not proceed from the articles of the faith as from premises, but that instead lead people to better grasp the truths of the very articles of the Creed, to nourish their faith in them, defend them, and strengthen the understanding of them against the attacks of those who misrepresent and distort their meanings.

> It is to these purposes that the book of the *Sentences*, and the questions of the Doctors, and the original treatises of the Fathers, and the commentaries on the Scriptures are all aimed. Thus the common dictum on which this Doctor [Thomas Aquinas] supports his position, namely, "The articles of the faith serve as principles [or premises] in theology" is false. (*Scriptum*, I, sect. 1, q. 1, n. 29; I, p. 140)

GREGORY OF RIMINI, a hermit of Saint Augustine, sides with the deductive theologians, but with a twist. He calls theology a *habitus creditivus* (a faith-developing habit) not a *habitus deductivus* (deductive habit). Theology, for Gregory, draws out what follows necessarily from the truths contained formally in sacred Scripture. It is a faith-developing habit. It is not simply belief, since a theologian develops a habit that is in some way distinct from the habit of faith that he shares with all believers. For he is able to make explicit what most believers hold only implicitly since they accept in general all that God has revealed.

Because Auriol supported his claims for declarative theology by so many appeals to Augustine, Gregory was forced to mount a counteroffensive that reinterpreted Auriol's Augustinian base. In effect, Gregory addresses Auriol's claim for Augustine's support by saying in substance: Let him go back and reread what he has read inattentively (*Lectura super I Sententiarum*, prol., q. 1, a. 2; I, p. 19). Yes, Gregory concedes, Auriol is correct when he goes to the beginning of Saint Augustine's *On the Trinity* and tells us that when Augustine examined all the Catholic expositors who had written on the Trinity, he saw that they tried to make it clear that the Father, the Son, and the Holy Spirit express a divine unity of one and the same substance in indivisible equality. In fact, they did; and so did Augustine. But the Bishop of Hippo did not say that they did so by going to other sciences, or other teachings, or probable propositions. He rather said that they tried to make it clear according to the Scriptures. For Gregory, all our knowledge of the faith is either expressly contained in sacred Scriptures or is deducible from what is contained there. Otherwise, he claims, the Scriptures would not suffice for our salvation and for the defense of our faith. This, however, is the position of Augustine, as Gregory reads him, for in the last chapter of Book II of *On Christian Teaching*, Augustine tells us: "Whatever a man might learn outside of Scripture, if it is harmful, it is condemned in the Sacred Writings; if it is useful, it is already found there (*Lectura*, prol., q. 1, a. 2; I, pp. 55–6).

Peter Auriol and Gregory of Rimini held strongly differing interpretations of Augustine's methods as well as those of other Fathers of the Church. So did all medieval commentators and interpreters of Patristic works. As the medieval authors developed their precisions in grammar and logic, faced the conflicting teachings of the Stoic, Platonic and Aristotelian traditions of philosophy, realized their own metaphysical theories, and elaborated their various views of theology, the Fathers of the Church, especially Saint Augustine, became unending stimuli and ever-repeated sources of depth and reflection.

Bibliography

Primary sources

Augustine (Augustinus) (1877), *Epistola 148*, in *Patrologia Latina*, vol. 32, Paris: J.-P. Migne.

——(1886), *De Trinitate*, in *Patrologia Latina*, vol. 42, Paris: J.-P. Migne.

——(1887), *De doctrina Christiana*, in *Patrologia Latina*, vol. 34, Paris: J.-P. Migne.

——(1902), *Retractationes*, in *Patrologia Latina*, vol. 33, Paris: J.-P. Migne.

Bonaventure (Bonaventura) (1882–1902), *Commentarii in quatuor libros Sententiarum* (*Opera omnia* I–IV), Quaracchi: Collegium S. Bonaventurae.

——(1891), *Quaestiones disputatae de scientia Christi*, in *Opera omnia* V, Quaracchi: Collegium S. Bonaventurae.

Clement of Alexandria (Clemens Alexandrinus) (1891), *Logos protreptikos*, in *Patrologia Graeca*, vol. 8, Paris: J.-P. Migne.

——(1891), *Stromata*, in *Patrologia Graeca*, vol. 8, Paris: J.-P. Migne.

Gregory of Rimini (Gregorius Ariminensis) (1981), *Lectura super primum Sententiarum*, vol. I, Berlin: De Gruyter.

Henry of Ghent (Henricus a Gandavo) (1520), *Summa quaestionum ordinariarum*, Paris: I. Badius.

John Duns Scotus (Ioannes Duns Scotus) (1954), *Ordinatio*, in *Opera omnia*, vol. III, Vatican City: Typis Polyglottis Vaticanis.

McCann, J. (1952), *The Rule of Saint Benedict*, Westminster, MD: Newman Press.

Percival, H. R. (1900), *The Seven Ecumenical Councils*, Nicene and Post-Nicence Fathers 14, New York: Charles Scribner's Sons.

Peter Abelard (Petrus Abaelardus) (1885), *Sic et non*, in *Patrologia Latina*, vol. 178, Paris: J.-P. Migne.

——(1959), *Historia calamitatum*, Paris: J. Vrin.

——(1969), *Theologia Christiana*, Corpus Christianorum continuatio mediaevalis 12, Turnhout: Brepols.

Peter Auriol (Petrus Aureoli) (1956), *Scriptum super primum Sententiarum*, vol. I, St. Bonaventure, NY: Franciscan Institute.

——(1995), *Reportatio Parisiensis*, I, d. 2, *Traditio* 50, pp. 199–248.

Peter Lombard (Petrus Lombardus) (1971), *Sententiae in IV libris distinctae*, Grottaferrata: Collegium S. Bonaventurae.

Thomas Aquinas (Thomas de Aquino) (1952), *In evangelium S. Ioannis lectura*, Turin and Rome: Marietti.

William of St. Thierry (1971), *The Golden Epistle*, trans. Theodore Berkeley, Spencer, MA: Cistercian Publications.

Secondary sources

Brown, S. F. (1993), "Medieval supposition theory in its theological context," *Medieval Philosophy and Theology* 3, pp. 121–57.

——, "Declarative and deductive theology in the early fourteenth century," Miscellanea mediaevalia 26 (pp. 648–55), Berlin and New York: De Gruyter.

Di Bernardino, A. and Studer, B., eds. (1996), *History of Theology: The Patristic Period*, Collegeville, MN: Liturgical Press.

Grassi, O. (1976), "La questione della teologia come scienza in Gregorio da Rimini," *Rivista di Filosofia Neoscolastica* 8, pp. 610–44.

Minnis, S. J. and Scott, A. B. (1988), *Medieval Literary Theory and Criticism, c.1100–c.1375*, Oxford: Clarendon Press.

Streuer, S. R. (1968), *Die theologische Einleitungslehre des Petrus Aureoli*, Werl in Westfalen: Dietrich-Coelde Verlag, Franziskaner Forschungen 20.

3

Philosophy in the Latin Christian West:
750–1050

PETER KING

The revival of philosophy after the Dark Ages (roughly 525–750) was a drawn-out process, lasting nearly three centuries. The only philosopher worthy of the name between BOETHIUS at the end of antiquity and the twelfth-century genius of ANSELM and PETER ABELARD was the anomalous JOHN SCOTUS ERIUGENA, whose extraordinary knowledge of Greek allowed him direct access to ancient philosophical and theological literature, presumably the inspiration for his strikingly original Neoplatonic metaphysics. Aside from Eriugena there was little philosophy to speak of. The work of summary, paraphrase, gloss, and transmission absorbed most of the intellectual energies of several generations. Yet there were signs and stirrings of interest in philosophy throughout the period, if not for its own sake then as an adjunct to religious and theological speculation.

The first important thinker in the revival of philosophy was the English monk Alcuin of York (b. 735; d. 804), whose sojourn at the court of Charlemagne near the end of the eighth century gave him wide influence on the continent. Alcuin and his many students were the heirs and imitators of the earlier mediaeval encyclopedists – Cassiodorus, Martianus Capella, ISIDORE OF SEVILLE – who tried to preserve classical learning for an uncertain future, and their efforts were equally wide-ranging and diffuse. Alcuin, in his *Dialogue on True Philosophy*, which serves as an introduction to his school texts collectively known as the *Didascalion*, identifies the "seven stages of philosophy" with the liberal arts: grammar, rhetoric, dialectic, arithmetic, geometry, music, and astronomy. But to identify philosophy with the whole of human intellectual endeavor is to miss the distinguishing feature of philosophy proper, namely reasoned argument directed at first principles. In this narrower sense, Alcuin's discussion of philosophy is largely confined to the treatise on dialectic, covering the material traditionally known as the "old logic" (*logica vetus*). Like most of the treatises in the *Didascalion*, it is written as an elementary question–answer catechism between Charlemagne and Alcuin. Here is a sample: "Charlemagne: 'How should a syllogism be constructed?' Alcuin: 'Typically from three elements so that from the first two premises the third follows as the conclusion.'" The raw materials of logic, philosophy of language, and metaphysics are presented in this simplified textbook fashion.

Alcuin wrote three works of dogmatic theology that suggest a wider acquaintance with philosophy than do his school texts. *Belief in the Holy and Undivided Trinity*, for the most part an epitome of AUGUSTINE's masterwork *The Trinity*, recounts the African Doctor's theory of relative predication in the Trinity and analyzes a miscellany of questions suggested by dogma, for instance whether Christ had full knowledge of his own divinity. While Alcuin does not contribute anything original to these discussions, they offer a summary of arguments and distinctions that suggest how philosophy might be done systematically. Likewise, his shorter works *The Nature of the Soul* and *The Virtues and Vices* respectively epitomize Augustine's *On the Nature and Origin of the Soul* and some of his sermons, in each case reproducing key lines of argument in the original works.

Alcuin was followed in the work of paraphrase and explanation by his student Rhabanus Maurus (b. 776; d. 856), whose massive *Rules for Clerics*, a compendium of Christian practice, follows Alcuin's identification of philosophy with the seven liberal arts. But he adds that Christians should have the same attitude to works of philosophy, especially those written by Platonists, as the Israelites had to their Egyptian masters: carry off only what is valuable (Exod. 12: 35–6). Rhabanus identifies dialectic with philosophy in the narrower sense, namely "the discipline of rational inquiry" (*Rules* 3.20), and he seems to mean by this any activity using logical or syllogistic reasoning. Rhabanus says nothing about any specifically philosophical topics or questions, though. Most of his writings on religious matters were low-level exegesis and edifying commentary rather than rigorous logical inquiries, and he generally avoided issues in dogmatic theology. Yet Rhabanus also composed a *Treatise on the Soul*, which alternated summary and paraphrase of Augustine with original discussion of the issues. For instance, Rhabanus argues that the soul cannot have a form, since forms are geometrical shapes and therefore only apply to corporeal items, whereas the soul is incorporeal. In addition to such claims, Rhabanus discusses the virtues as the psychologically distinctive feature of the soul.

Some of Alcuin's students showed a particular interest in logic and the philosophy of language, though no great sophistication. Fridugisus (b. 782?; d. 834), who succeeded Alcuin as abbot of St. Martin's in Tours, wrote a letter about the kind of being that nothingness and shadows have – a problem he took to be posed by the requirement that every finite noun signify something, in which case 'nothing' must signify something. The English monk Candidus (Wizo), who became head of Charlemagne's palace school when Alcuin departed for Tours, wrote some short notes investigating logical puzzles having to do with the Trinity. He compiled a record of such inquiries by members of Alcuin's circle, which range from mere excerpts of Patristic authors to apparently original investigations into questions such as the location of the soul in space, whether truth is something physical, and even an attempt to prove the existence of God; these short notes betray familiarity not only with Augustine but also with the old logic, and a commendable enterprise in applying their knowledge to theological issues.

The next generation of thinkers was dominated by John Scotus Eriugena and witnessed an increase in philosophical sophistication, harnessed more than ever to the service of theological problems. Around the middle of the ninth century several doctrinal controversies erupted. The first was precipitated by Gottschalk of Orbais (b. ca. 805; d. 866), who argued on scriptural and Patristic grounds that God predestined some for salvation and some for damnation, and furthermore that this was the view of Augustine; Eriugena was called in, by Hincmar, Archbishop of Reims, to write a rebuttal of Gottschalk's views, and he effectively ended the debate by uniting all opposed sides against his own views.

Around the same time Paschasius Radbertus revised his treatise on the Eucharist, *The Lord's Body and Blood*, raising questions about Christ's real presence: Is the body in the host the same Christ's historical body? How can this body be present in the host in many places and many times? What change occurs in the bread and wine in consecration? Radbertus argued that Christ's historical body is present in the host, though veiled by the continued appearance of bread and wine, and that this one body must therefore be present in all places and times, presumably by God's incomprehensible direct creative activity. Charles the Bald then asked Ratramnus of Corbie (died after 868) to respond to Radbertus. Ratramnus argued that Christ's presence in the host is spiritual rather than corporeal, so that there is no real change in the bread and wine – which are now called "the body and blood of Christ" in virtue of representing them. Furthermore, Christ's spiritual body and spiritual blood are not the same as his physical body and blood, maintains Ratramnus, so further recourse to God's creative activity is not necessary.

The Eucharistic debate between Ratramnus and Radbertus, whatever one may think of their views, is much more sophisticated than controversies of the preceding generation. The techniques of philosophy are deployed throughout: argumentation, drawing or rejecting distinctions, attempts to define issues on an abstract level, use of examples and counter-examples, drawing out consequences of positions – all these and more are part of their debate.

Ratramnus later wrote a treatise *On the Soul*, as part of another theological controversy, this time on the nature of the soul; he spends most of the treatise analyzing the relation between the individual soul and the kind of thing it is, the species, given that an individual really "is" its species. Ratramnus argues that genera and species are strictly speaking mental abstractions, not real items in the world, and therefore do not threaten the individuality of different souls. Although he does not develop his view in any detail, it is clear Ratramnus has the metaphysical problem of universals in mind, introduced by speculation on the nature of the soul.

By the end of the ninth century, then, philosophical issues were being explored in connection with dogmatic theology. Much of the tenth century was devoted to assimilating philosophical material for its own sake. The scholars of the tenth century were aided by the efforts of Remigius of Auxerre (b. ca. 841; d. 908) who, at the end of the ninth century, produced glosses or commentaries on the scattered remnants of classical learning: Donatus, Priscian, Boethius, and Martianus Cappella. To these were added the "old logic" and Boethius' monographs. This work, largely anonymous, had its flower at the close of the first millennium: Abbo of Fleury (b. 945?; d. 1004) wrote his own explanation of categorical and hypothetical syllogisms, the *Enodatio*; Notker Labeo (b. ca. 950; d. 1022), a monk at St. Gall, translated several logical works into Old High German and wrote a treatise in Latin on the syllogism.

A measure of how far such purely philosophical interests had spread may be seen in Gerbert (b. ca. 955; d. 1003), aka Pope Sylvester II, who wrote a treatise *On the Rational and the Use of Reason*. He begins with a problem drawn from Porphyry, who says that a *differentia* can be predicated of its cognate difference, as 'using reason' is predicated of what is rational; but how can this be, given that only some of those who are capable of using reason may actually be using it? Gerbert eventually concludes that this predication is indefinite, and hence logically equivalent to the claim that some people able to reason are actually doing so. His journey to this conclusion takes him through an original analysis of potency and act, inspired by a few sketchy remarks in Boethius; he manages to reconstruct a fair amount of Aristotle's doctrine with little help. But perhaps more impressive is that Gerbert takes up a purely philosophical question and treats it on its merits, a sign that philosophical research had come into its own.

Philosophy had, in fact, become enough of a specific intellectual activity to be seen by some as problematic. A controversy broke out in the first half of the eleventh century over the proper role of philosophy, namely whether it could illuminate doctrinal questions (the view held by the "dialecticians") or was a hindrance rather than a help (the view held by the "anti-dialecticians"). Around 1050, Berengar of Tours (b. ca. 999; d. 1088) challenged the traditional view that in the Eucharist the bread and wine are changed at all, roughly on the grounds that he could not sense any difference before and after their consecration. Lanfranc of Bec (b. ca. 1005; d. 1089) charges in his reply that Berengar has left behind authority and "taken refuge in dialectic," and, although he would prefer to refute Berengar by citing authoritative works, he too must therefore take up the cudgels of dialectic to defend the doctrine of Christ's real presence in the host. Berengar retorted that taking "refuge" in dialectic is simply to use reason, a divine gift to man, which cannot go against God but rather confutes his enemies.

The same conflict arose in a different context. PETER DAMIAN (b. 1007; d. 1072), in a letter on divine omnipotence, took up the question whether God could change the past. Some philosophers argued that God could not, on the grounds that it is logically impossible; what has happened is now fixed and unchangeable – in a word, necessary – but it is no restriction or limitation on God's power to say that he cannot do the impossible. Damian objects that God was able to make things now past turn out otherwise than they did, and, since God is outside of time and eternal, he still has the power to make that event turn out otherwise, even if it is now past to us (and hence unchangeable by us). Damian further objects that the necessity of the past is only a necessity relative to us, or, more precisely, to our discourse; dialectic only draws connections among statements, not things, and so is intrinsically limited in revealing the truth. Worse yet, the partisans of dialectic "discard the foundation of a clear faith because of the obscure darknesses of their arguments." Damian countenances only a subordinate role for philosophy. In a simile that was to become famous, Damian asserted that philosophy should be related to Scripture "like a handmaiden to her mistress."

No resolution to the conflict between the dialecticians and anti-dialecticians was reached in the first half of the eleventh century, and this set the stage for the different paths followed in the second half of the century by Anselm and Abelard. The sophisticated appropriation of ancient philosophical literature likewise prepared the ground, so that even critics of philosophy were relatively skilled in dialectic compared to their predecessors. There are more detailed and penetrating glosses on works of grammar, logic, and rhetoric drawn up in this period too, most anonymous. By the latter part of the eleventh century Anselm and Abelard could flourish in an intellectual world in which there was widespread familiarity with the best of the ancient philosophical literature available.

Bibliography

Marenbon, John (1981), *From the Circle of Alcuin to the School of Auxerre*, Cambridge: Cambridge University Press.

4

The School of Chartres

WINTHROP WETHERBEE

In the 1960s it would have been easy enough to treat the "School of Chartres" in a historically straightforward way. A scholarly tradition of long standing held that Chartres and its cathedral school had been a great center of humanistic, scientific, and philosophical study in northern Europe during the early twelfth century. A number of important figures had studied at Chartres or occupied official positions there, and their work exhibited common features which suggested a common enterprise. Such assumptions arose all the more readily in the light of the evidence provided by JOHN OF SALISBURY, whose *Metalogicon* (1159) presents a magnificent account of the work of Bernard, the first great master of twelfth-century Chartres, and identifies as kindred spirits three of John's own teachers, GILBERT OF POITIERS, William of Conches, and Thierry of Chartres. William and Gilbert evidently studied with Bernard; the writings of both William and Thierry have close affinities with those of Bernard; and both Gilbert and Thierry later held the office of chancellor of the cathedral. It is thus easy to think of them as closely associated, and they have been taken by modern scholars as the pillars of the school in its great days.

In 1970 Sir Richard Southern published an essay calling nearly all of this into question. No mere cathedral school, he claimed, could have supported such a group of scholars, and their major work is much more likely to have been done in Paris. In any case the allegedly innovative ventures in philosophy that have been credited to these masters were in fact no more than a reworking of old material. Rather than pioneers of the new science, they might better be seen as the last of the Carolingian grammarians.

Admirable in itself, Southern's zeal to expose a pernicious bit of historical myth-making led him to overstate his case. In fact there is a good deal more evidence for associating Gilbert, William, and Thierry with Chartres than with Paris. Gilbert and William were the students of Bernard, in all likelihood at Chartres, and it is at Chartres that John of Salisbury is likely to have heard both men. Thierry, whose writings owe a good deal to William (Ziomkowski 2000, pp. 166–72), is likely to have taught at Chartres for a period before succeeding Gilbert as chancellor in the 1140s, and it was to the cathedral library at Chartres that he left his great *Heptateuchon*, a compilation of texts fundamental to instruction in the seven liberal arts. On the other hand, while Gilbert certainly taught at Paris, the evidence that Thierry did so is minimal, and for William there is none at all.

Thus while the evidence provided by the *Metalogicon* remains debatable, it seems reasonable and useful to consider Gilbert, William, and Thierry together as having been significantly influenced by methods and ideas which flourished at Chartres, and as having in all likelihood made substantial contributions, as teachers and scholars, to the work of the school. And whatever value we assign their writings, they embody the thought, if not of the school of Chartres itself, then of the school of Bernard of Chartres. On this basis I will refer to them in what follows as the "Chartrians."

History

Almost no information has survived about education at Chartres during the first millennium of the common era. By the time of Fulbert (b. ca. 970; d. 1028), the first master of whom we have specific knowledge, the cathedral school provided a curriculum broadly grounded in the liberal arts. Fulbert, who was a deacon of Chartres cathedral by 1004, and apparently also *scholasticus* or *magister* of the cathedral school, had himself studied under the leading scholar of the previous generation, Gerbert of Reims, and must have brought with him to Chartres much of Gerbert's sophisticated approach to the teaching of dialectic, rhetoric, and literature. There is also evidence of activity in other fields. The historian Richer had come to Chartres in 991 to study medicine with one Heribrandus, and Fulbert himself clearly possessed medical knowledge. Two of his own students are said to have been well versed in music (Behrends 1976, pp. xxviii–xxxiii).

Fulbert and Chartres are warmly recalled by students who became the teachers and scholars of the next generation, but there is no real basis for speculation about the continuity of study at Chartres between Fulbert's time and the twelfth century.

Bernard of Chartres

The "School of Chartres" of modern scholarly legend originates with Bernard (d. ca. 1130), who appears in cathedral documents in 1108, was chancellor of the cathedral by 1124, and at his death left twenty-four books to the cathedral library. Not only was Bernard the teacher of William of Conches and Gilbert of Poitiers, but he is the hero of John of Salisbury's *Metalogicon* (1159), which contrasts the debased education of John's day with that provided by Bernard, "the most abundant fountain of learning of modern times in Gaul" (*Met.* 1.24).

As the student of William and Gilbert, John had good authority for what he tells us of the great teacher's habits of quotation, his famous comparison of modern scholars to dwarfs perched on the shoulders of the giants of the classical past, and his pre-Socratic habit of couching everything from pedagogical maxims to complex metaphysical principles in gnomic hexameters. But John's "old man of Chartres" is also a mythic figure, a personification of humanism. We see the ideals he represents in John's account of how one should present the texts of the *auctores* for study, a passage which surely owes as much to Martianus Capella as to twelfth-century praxis (*Met.* 1.24):

> [The ancient authors,] when they had taken up the raw material of history, argument, fable, or whatever, would refine it . . . with such abundant learning, such graceful style and adornment, that the finished work would somehow appear an image of all the arts. All the hosts of Grammar and Poetry pour forth, and take over the whole surface of the matter which is being expounded. Across this field, as it may be called, Logic, bearing the devices of dialectic, casts the golden darts of her reasoning. Rhetoric, clad in the *topoi* of persuasion and the bright trappings of eloquence, shines with the brilliance of silver. *Mathematica* is borne along in the four-wheeled chariot of her *quadrivium*, and following in the path of these others, intermingles her manifold

variety of devices and charms. Physics, having delved into the secrets of nature, brings forth
from her abundant supply the complex splendor of her own ornamentation.

The classic text is "an image of all the arts," and the teacher assumes the role of the ancient
expositor of Homer or Vergil, authorized to draw back the veil of poetic language and
imagery, and reveal the hidden treasure of philosophical and religious knowledge. Such a
teacher must himself be possessed of encyclopedic learning and a clear vision of the scope
and coherence of philosophy and the liberal arts. In such terms Bernard, William, Thierry,
and Gilbert were remembered by their disciples, and it is this encyclopedic ideal that their
writings aim to realize.

To cast Bernard as a *grammaticus* and mentor of genius is a fundamental strategy of
the *Metalogicon*, but when John calls him "the most perfect among the Platonists of our
time" (*Met.* 4.35), we should hear a veiled criticism; *perfectissimus* here probably means
"thoroughgoing," or "extreme." John was suspicious of any attempt to reconcile a Platonic
doctrine of Ideas with Aristotle's rejection of universals (*Met.* 2.17, 20), and that such an
undertaking was central to Bernard's thought is confirmed by his recently identified commentary on the *Timaeus*, that unique mixture of myth and science which, with the *opuscula
theologica* of BOETHIUS, provided the framework for the work of the Chartrians. Recognizing the need for some intermediary between Plato's eternal Ideas and the material world,
Bernard posited a secondary rank of "natural" forms (*formae nativae*) capable of union with
matter. By emphasizing the active, causal role of these forms in the production of creatures,
Bernard provided the dynamic principle lacking in the *Timaeus* itself, capable of bridging
the gap between the physical and metaphysical worlds. Both Calcidius and Boethius posit
such intermediaries, but Calcidius seeks merely to distinguish among levels of existence
within a largely static system, and Boethius to emphasize the radically transcendent character of the true Ideas. Bernard's contribution is to have focused on the Aristotelian element
in Calcidius' version of Plato, and assigned his "native forms" a function in the creative
process. From them the soul derives sense and intellect, and the Aristotelian conception of
the soul as *endelichia* or *forma corporis* defines their relationship to the created world in
general (Dutton 1991, pp. 70–96).

Bernard's glosses exhibit two distinguishing traits of the Chartrian scholars. The first is
their focus on natural causality within the framework defined by the *Timaeus*. By adapting
newly available knowledge in physics, astronomy, and human physiology to Plato's cosmology they furthered the development of a scientific approach to the natural world (Speer
1997).

A second hallmark is their willingness to engage the *Timaeus* and other ancient texts
directly and on their own terms. Biblical allusions in Bernard's *Glosae* note correspondences
of Platonic with Christian ideas at the level of primary meaning, and when he reads the text
allegorically, it is to demonstrate its inherent coherence, rather than transpose its meaning
into Christian terms. Allegory in Plato's text – what Bernard and his followers call a "veil"
or "covering," *involucrum* or *integumentum* – is a conscious recourse, a way of preserving
philosophical truth from ignorant misuse, and a fundamental property of philosophical
language (Jeauneau 1973, pp. 127–92). The meanings veiled by Plato's mathematical
formulae and mythic figures are profound, but remain products of human knowledge and
imagination. These principles are set forth in the glosses of William of Conches, and the
same assumptions inform the writings of Thierry.

John of Salisbury has less to say about the other masters traditionally linked to Chartres,
but places them firmly in the tradition of Bernard. Gilbert of Poitiers (b. ca. 1085/90; d.

1154), William of Conches (b. ca. 1085; d. 1154) and Thierry of Chartres (d. after 1156) are named, with PETER ABELARD (b. 1079; d. 1142), as "true lovers of learning" who had withstood the corruption of education in their day (*Met.* 1.5). William was "the most accomplished grammarian since Bernard," and Thierry "the most assiduous investigator of the arts," while Gilbert, by far the most important for the later history of philosophy, is recalled mainly as having labored to refine Bernard's theory of "native forms" and so further his project of reconciling Plato and Aristotle (*Met.* 2.17).

William of Conches and Thierry of Chartres

The most striking and controversial feature of the work of William and Thierry is their treatment of the World Soul, which in the *Timaeus* informs the created universe with an ordering intelligence. A natural principle for Bernard, in William's glosses this *anima mundi* becomes at once the "natural vitality" informing created life, and a "divine and benign concord" which he identifies with the Holy Spirit (Gregory 1955, pp. 135–8). The same associations appear in Thierry's *Tractatus de sex dierum operibus* (*Treatise on the Work of the Six Days*), which explains the biblical creation "according to physical law" (*secundum physicam*). Thierry describes the virtually autonomous elements, each informed by its seminal *virtus*, acting together to sustain temporal life (Häring 1971, p. 562), but then considers the primal state in which they were informed by that power which Moses calls "the spirit of the Lord"; this same spirit, in the Hermetic *Asclepius*, mediates between God and matter; for Vergil it is the "inner spirit" which imparts life to the universe; it is Plato's World Soul and the Holy Spirit of Christian belief (Häring 1971, pp. 566–7).

A commentator on the *Timaeus* familiar with William's teaching dwells on the implications of the World Soul (Gregory 1958, pp. 126–8):

> The World Soul is that eternal love in the Creator through which he created all things and governs his creation harmoniously . . . It is this love that theologians who adhere to the tenets of the Christian religion call the Holy Spirit – transferring the terms, as a certain thinker has observed, from the human sphere to the divine. For, says this thinker, just as we can tell by a man's breathing whether he is filled with joy or tormented by sorrow, so by observing this love one comes to a perception of the divine mind. Those who assign to this spirit the epithet 'holy' do well, for he is the holiest of men who enables all others to become good through participation in his holiness.
>
> Others define the World Soul thus: it is a natural vigor instilled in creatures . . . This natural vigor is called the Holy Spirit by some teachers, and this view is in no respect at odds with that given above. Though the words are different, the sense is wholly the same . . .
>
> Some have said that Plato saw the world as a great living being, whose soul, they said, is a vital heat emanating from the sun which is diffused through the whole universe and gives rise to all growth. Some declare that God established the universe as a kind of fundamental principle of all substantial existence, bodily and spiritual. For they say that all other bodies are derived from the world's body. Likewise they posit the World Soul as a sort of fountain of souls, imagining it as a great spirit diffused through the entire universe. They are not so bold as to declare that this "spirit" is the Holy Spirit: they approach this truth but will not see it clearly, and in their wilful ignorance fall back on Plato and Vergil, who speak about the World Soul in the manner of philosophers.

Like similar passages in William, these reflections may seem to recall the *testimonia philosophorum*, foreshadowings of Christian theology in pagan authors, which Patristic authors compiled to attest the prevalent truth of Christianity. But more is implied by the reliance on the metaphor of "breath" or "spirit" as an interpretive tool, the persistent emphasis on the physical operation of the power described, and the assumption that twelfth-century hermeneutics can bring to full realization the spiritual intuitions of pagans who spoke "in the manner of philosophers." Far from simply reformulating a traditional theme of Christian apologetic, this passage aims to show how the natural order is informed with divine purpose by translating Platonic myth into scientific terms.

Fundamental for William is the conviction that to study the natural world as an autonomous system is in no way to question God's authority. Repeatedly he extrapolates from naturalistic accounts of the "facts" of physical nature to the power that produced them, declaring that far from derogating God's power, such arguments enhance it, since the natural process expresses the divine will. In the same spirit Thierry, glossing Genesis in terms of natural process, passes from the formative work of the elements to the divine *spiritus* that informs them. Elsewhere he speaks of matter, form, and spirit as a secondary trinity, "perpetual powers" whose attributes are in effect *integumenta* of the divine Persons (Häring 1971, pp. 80–1).

Chartres had long possessed exceptional resources in medicine and mathematics, and was among the first centers to obtain the work of translators such as Constantinus Africanus, ADELARD OF BATH, and later Herman of Carinthia (Dronke 1969, pp. 124–6). The work of William and Thierry differs from that of Bernard largely because their approach to texts is conditioned by a fuller appreciation of what might be learned from study of the natural world (Burnett 1988, pp. 153–4). But while both are responsive to the new science, their responses take very different forms.

William was in close touch with the work of the translators. Between the first redaction of his glosses (ca. 1120) on Boethius, based only on traditional sources, and the version of his mature thought embodied in the *Dragmaticon* (1147–9), he read widely in medicine and astronomy, and we see him reassessing his views in the light of new information. He discourses at length on the importance of observation to philosophical understanding, and on the properties and interrelations of the elements. Even the *Timaeus* loses some of its authority as his scientific knowledge grows. The absence from the *Dragmaticon* of the controversial identification of the Holy Spirit with the World Soul may be due, not just to Cistercian criticisms of his earlier work, but to a preference for medical explanations of the development of organic life (Gregory 1955, pp. 148–54).

Thierry, on the other hand, makes little specific use of new resources. His commitment to the new science remains theoretical, though strikingly original. Glossing Boethius' *De Trinitate*, he expands on Boethius' definition of "natural" speculation (*De Trin.* 2.5–10), and explains "physics" as concerned with "the forms and states of material things" (*formas et status rerum in materia*) (Häring 1971, p. 161). In his *Tractatus*, he describes the order of nature in terms of the *causae seminales* of the four elements (ibid., p. 562), while at the same time grounding his description of the interaction of the elements in simple observations of the natural effects of heat and moisture (Häring 1971, p. 559; Speer 1997, pp. 140–1). This impulse to synthesize Stoic-Platonic physics with empirical data resembles William's approach, though what appears empirical in Thierry may itself be drawn wholly from traditional sources – the results of Galen's *via experimenti* raised to authoritative status, but with little of William's concern to base his work on the best available authorities.

Much of Thierry, indeed, seems like an exercise in sheer imagination. Creation is the "unfolding" of a plan first "enfolded" (*complicata*) in the simplicity of God. This orderly unfolding or "necessary continuity" brings to bear on matter "the truths of forms and images, which we call 'ideas'," mediating between form as it exists in the Divine Mind (the "form of forms") and the image of the ideal embodied in created things (Dronke 1988, pp. 368–70; Häring 1971, pp. 272–3). The mediating movement, Thierry notes, is called by many names: natural law, nature, world soul, natural justice, *eimarmene*, fate or the fates, divine intelligence – a litany which, like his discussion of the "spirit" of cosmic life, cited above, invokes the array of texts whose intuitions he seeks to reconcile with Christian theology. The process, moreover, closely parallels the creativity of the human mind, itself a formative principle (*forma artificialium specierum*) which projects images onto the material world (Häring 1971, p. 410). Similarly the work of the elements, in which fire, "the artist and efficient cause" transforms subject earth, while air and water mediate and synthesize its effects, imitates the "artist" Spirit of Genesis 1: 2 (ibid., pp. 562, 566).

It is in such analogies and allusions that the real continuity of Thierry's vision of the order of things resides, rather than in any attempt to directly explain physical causality. His essays in physics and mathematics often seem "metaphors projected by the soul in its effort at understanding," rather than attempts to give objective definition to natural law (Dronke 1988, p. 371). The intuition of continuity draws him repeatedly into an essentially poetic mode of thinking in which the interplay of the elements and the acts of the human mind are at once effects of all-informing Spirit and images, *integumenta* for its workings, interpretative gestures which are confirmed repeatedly by the marshalling of the authority of ancient poetry, philosophy, and mythography.

The imaginative element in Thierry's speculations, the ingenuity that finds new suggestions in traditional materials, is engaging, but also reveals a fundamental limitation which his work shares with that of Bernard and William. A major thrust of Professor Southern's attack on the School of Chartres centers on its limited resources, informational and methodological. In spite of the Chartrians' concern to read and think in new ways, he declares, "all their thoughts were old thoughts" (Southern 1970, p. 83), and we should see them (as to some extent they saw themselves), not as philosophers but as *grammatici* in the tradition of the late Carolingian emulators of Macrobius and Martianus Capella.

There is a good deal of truth in this assertion; the tools with which the Chartrian scholars worked were largely those of literary criticism. To bridge the gap between their newly particularized understanding of the physical world and their less certain sense of the metaphysical implications of its laws and patterns, Bernard and his followers employed a kind of "grammatical Platonism" (Jolivet 1966), exploiting the verbal arts through mythography, etymology, and other traditional ways of extracting an inner and potentially transcendent meaning from their *auctores*. Their phenomenal world was a tissue of figures and images, and the philosophy of nature involved and embodied "a transcendent form of rhetoric" (Cadden 1995). Their "discovery of nature" was first and last a rediscovery of *texts* about nature. To decode the natural world was to decipher the *integumenta* of the *Timaeus*.

But Southern is too quick to dismiss an intellectual program which, if its ambitions exceeded the means available for its realization, was nonetheless grounded in a sense of intellectual possibility that has no precedent in the Middle Ages, and did much to prepare the ground for the reception of Aristotelian physics and cosmology. For all their resemblance to their Carolingian forebears, these scholars were doing something new. Such as their learning was, it made them famous in their time, and they engaged their chosen texts with a directness and a degree of objectivity that are themselves a remarkable achievement at this period. Much in their philosophical program is anticipated in the work of JOHN SCOTUS ERIUGENA, but they managed largely to distance themselves from the mystical Neoplatonism which makes it difficult to isolate the philosophical elements in Eriugena's thought. And as

41

Southern himself acknowledges, their attempt to establish the liberal arts as essential to the pursuit of truth contributed significantly to the founding of a "scientific" theology.

Gilbert of Poitiers

In relation to all of this, Gilbert of Poitiers occupies a place of his own. Though he did more than any of the Chartrians to establish religious speculation on a foundation of scientific knowledge, his use of the liberal arts is confined to the linguistic disciplines and mathematics, and he shows no interest in cosmology or the natural world. He is as much concerned to distinguish among the sciences on the basis of the *rationes* proper to each as to pursue the implications of their interrelationship, and he differs in this respect not only from Thierry but from Boethius, the master to whom he owes his understanding of the task of theology.

Gilbert recognizes that "noble" philosophers might come to perceive the triune God through study of the order of the universe, but condemns their proud blindness in crediting their own reason, rather than God's goodness, for their insight. Far from seeing the divine love and wisdom expressed in the harmony and regularity of nature, he denies that the natural order is based on any inherent principle. What appears universal and constant is merely usual; the only true necessity is the divine will, and the sciences which comprehend the created universe are valid only when set in the perspective of theological understanding (Nielsen 1982, pp. 129–30, 136–42). The limits Gilbert imposes in applying the terms and methods of rational or natural analysis to theological questions are the source of much of the notorious difficulty of his writing, since terms "transsumed" from natural to theological contexts must continually be qualified and refined (Marenbon 1988, pp. 330–6; Nielsen 1982, pp. 149–63). Gilbert was rightly seen by John of Salisbury as having inherited from Bernard a concern with universals, but he differs sharply from Bernard on the relation of the forms of created things to the uncreated ideas, a relationship that he considers one of mere *imitatio*, devoid of ontological significance (Elswijk 1966, pp. 198–202; Nielsen 1982, pp. 72–4). What John sees as Gilbert's attempt to reconcile Plato and Aristotle is, unlike the theorizing of Bernard (the "perfect" Platonist), a significant shift in the direction of Aristotle (*Met.* 2.17).

Yet Gilbert was famous for his learning, and while his rigorous demarcation of the sphere of theology can seem to imply a searching critique of the interpretative work of his fellow Chartrians, it does not entail a rejection of philosophy and the natural sciences themselves. Implicit in the thoroughness of his subordination of these disciplines is an acknowledgment of their importance. The *rationes* proper to theology as science can only be fully understood when seen in relation to the sciences from which its terms and methods are "transsumed"; the complete theologian would necessarily be a complete philosopher-scientist as well.

Like Thierry, Gilbert is attempting in his writings to realize the full implications of Boethius' tantalizingly brief sketch of the domains of physics, mathematics, and theology. For Gilbert this involves a constant wariness in the face of the Neoplatonist assumptions that underlie Boethius' thinking and color his prose, and a refusal to let them obscure the careful distinctions that control his own use of the terms of grammar, logic, and mathematics in theological speculation. If his assumptions set him at odds with Thierry and William, they distance him still further from the relatively unreflecting use of the resources of grammar and logic in Abelard or PETER LOMBARD (Nielsen 1982, pp. 364–70). In other respects his focus on the ontology of form and his concern to make the right use of philosophy and the sciences are, as John of Salisbury recognized, in the tradition of Bernard of Chartres.

Conclusion

By the middle of the twelfth century a new generation, some of them admiring disciples of the Chartrians, were discovering in the Islamic version of Aristotelian physics a cosmology better adapted than that of the *Timaeus* to their scientific interests. The development of theology as a science in its own right, foreshadowed in the work of Gilbert, involved its increasing separation from philosophy and the liberal arts.

The effect of such developments was to render the work of Thierry and William largely obsolete. Though their writings provided a rich source of cosmological doctrine for the encyclopedists of the thirteenth century, perhaps their most significant legacy was their influence on the work of the schools of grammar and rhetoric. The form and techniques of William's glosses provided a model for commentary on a broad range of ancient texts, and the "unveiling" of the cosmology of the *Timaeus* provided the impetus for the most significant Latin poetry of the period, the *Cosmographia* (1147) of Bernardus Silvestris, dedicated to Thierry, and the *De planctu naturae* (ca. 1170) and *Anticlaudianus* (ca. 1175) of ALAN OF LILLE, where an epistemology largely drawn from the work of Gilbert and his followers defines the relation of the natural and spiritual orders. Through these channels their influence survived the radical transformation of science and philosophy in the new Aristotelian curriculum, and can be seen in the *Romance of the Rose* and Dante's *Commedia*.

Bibliography

Behrends, Frederick, ed. (1976), *The Letters and Poems of Fulbert of Chartres*, Oxford: Oxford University Press.

Burnett, Charles (1988), "Scientific speculations," in Peter Dronke, ed., *A History of Twelfth-century Western Philosophy* (pp. 151–76), Cambridge: Cambridge University Press.

Cadden, Joan (1995), "Science and rhetoric in the Middle Ages: the natural philosophy of William of Conches," *Journal of the History of Ideas* 56, pp. 1–24.

Chenu, Marie-Dominique (1957), *La Théologie au douzième siècle*, Paris: J. Vrin.

Dronke, Peter (1969), "New approaches to the School of Chartres," *Anuario de Estudios Medievales* 6, pp. 117–40.

——(1988), "Thierry of Chartres," in Peter Dronke, ed., *A History of Twelfth-century Western Philosophy* (pp. 358–85), Cambridge: Cambridge University Press.

Dutton, Paul E., ed. (1991), *Bernard of Chartres, Glosae super Platonem*, Toronto: Pontifical Institute of Mediaeval Studies.

Elswijk, H. C. van (1966), *Gilbert Porreta: sa vie, son oeuvre, sa pensée*, Louvain: Spicilegium Sacrum Lovaniense.

Gregory, Tullio (1955), *Anima mundi: la filosofia di Guglielmo di Conches e la Scuola di Chartres*, Florence: Sansoni.

——(1958), *Platonismo medievale: studi e ricerche*, Rome: Istituto Storico Italiano per il Medioevo.

Hall, J. B., ed. (1991), *Ioannis Saresberiensis Metalogicon*, Turnhout: Brepols.

Häring, Nikolaus M., ed. (1966), *The Commentaries on Boethius by Gilbert of Poitiers*, Toronto: Pontifical Institute of Mediaeval Studies.

——ed. (1971), *Commentaries on Boethius by Thierry of Chartres and his School*, Toronto: Pontifical Institute of Medieval Studies (includes the *Tractatus de sex dierum operibus*).

——(1974), "Chartres and Paris revisited," in J. R. O'Donnell, ed., *Essays in Honor of Anton Charles Pegis* (pp. 268–329), Toronto: Pontifical Institute of Mediaeval Studies.

Jeauneau, Edouard, ed. (1965), *Guillaume de Conches, Glosae super Platonem*, Paris: J. Vrin.

——(1973), *"Lectio philosophorum": Recherches sur l'Ecole de Chartres*, Amsterdam: A. M. Hakkert.

Jolivet, Jean (1966), "Quelques cas de 'platonisme grammatical' du VIIe au XIIe siècle," in Pierre Gallais and Yves-Jean Rion, eds., *Mélanges offerts à René Crozet*, 2 vols., vol. I (pp. 93–9), Poitiers: Société d'Études Médiévales.

Marenbon, John (1988), "Gilbert of Poitiers," in Peter Dronke, ed., *A History of Twelfth-century Western Philosophy* (pp. 328–52), Cambridge: Cambridge University Press.

Nauta, Lodi, ed. (1999), *Guilelmi de Conchis Glosae super Boetium*, Turnhout: Brepols.

Nielsen, Lauge Olaf (1982), *Theology and Philosophy in the Twelfth Century*, Leiden: Brill.

Ronca, I., ed. (1997), *Guilelmi de Conchis Dragmaticon philosophiae*, Turnhout: Brepols.

Southern, Richard W. (1970), "Humanism and the School of Chartres," in R. W. Southern, *Medieval Humanism and Other Studies* (pp. 61–85), Oxford: Blackwell.

——(1995), *Scholastic Humanism and the Unification of Europe*, vol. I: *Foundations*, Oxford: Oxford University Press.

Speer, Andreas (1997), "The discovery of nature: the contribution of the Chartrians to twelfth-century attempts to found a *scientia naturalis*," *Traditio* 52, pp. 135–51.

Wetherbee, Winthrop (1972), *Platonism and Poetry in the Twelfth Century*, Princeton, NJ: Princeton University Press.

——(1988), "Philosophy, cosmology, and the twelfth-century Renaissance," in Peter Dronke, ed., *A History of Twelfth-century Western Philosophy* (pp. 21–53), Cambridge: Cambridge University Press.

Ziomkowski, Robert (2000), "Science, theology, and myth in medieval creationism: cosmogony in the twelfth century," Ph.D. dissertation, Cornell University.

5

Religious Orders

M. MICHÈLE MULCHAHEY AND
TIMOTHY B. NOONE

Medieval monasticism and learning

Monasticism in the West is associated most especially with St. Benedict of Nursia and the religious order that came to bear his name. Schools and *scriptoria*, which seem to us so much a part of the life of the medieval monastery, were, however, only dimly intimated in Benedict's original conception. His *Rule* of ca. AD 525 required monks to engage daily in the *lectio divina*, that is, ruminative reading of the Bible and other spiritual classics, and to this end suggested that each year at the beginning of Lent a book be given to each brother, who would read and re-read it over the course of the year until exchanging it for a new one. Benedict said little else about education. But the demands for literacy that monastic life made upon its adherents and the growing custom of admitting child oblates soon forced the Benedictines to organize schools in which to form their youngsters. These were intended as internal schools for the community's use only, run by monk-schoolmasters who imparted a basic literary education; the education of outsiders within the cloister was, in fact, forbidden by church law starting in the ninth century.

Nevertheless, by the time Charlemagne began his program of cultural and educational reform at the end of the eighth century, monasteries had become an obvious locus of learning for a society in which learning was rare, and the Carolingians came to depend upon the monks to train their administrators and churchmen. By the twelfth century the monks were, however, attempting to reassert the separateness of the cloister. Child-oblation was gradually eliminated, and with it the claustral schools; postulants were not admitted until they had received a basic grammar education elsewhere, and at a minimum age of between 15 and 18. But an opposite trend then became evident. Men who had been very well educated indeed at the urban cathedral schools or by peripatetic masters, increasingly sought admittance to the cloister. St. BERNARD OF CLAIRVAUX, that moving force in the Cistercian reform, made a special effort to attract men from the Paris schools, and this began to change the intellectual complexion of the monastic world.

If they could not undo the background of the men who came to them, as the twelfth century gave way to the thirteenth, the monastic orders did become ever more reluctant to allow their monks to study in the urban schools, seeing it as contrary to the spirit of monasticism and a dangerous precedent. The central objection, of course, was that monks belonged in the monasteries in which they had vowed stability, and that the distractions of the city could prove deadly. But monastic leaders of the period were also deeply convinced of the fundamental incompatibility between the monk's calling and the intellectual activities of the schools. The monk is one who has devoted his life to learning how to love God, by daily disciplining his will so that he might open his mind to the divine. Monastic literature, whether in the form of biblical commentaries or saints' lives or guides to contemplation, was intended primarily as material for meditation and incentive for good behavior; it promoted prayer. The aim of the schoolmen, quite otherwise, was to explain the ways of God to men, insofar as they were able, by submitting the data of revelation to logical analysis; they wrote to question and to advance speculation. It was the new scholastic method, and the attitude it bespoke, that monastic theologians distrusted.

The gulf that separated the schools from the monasteries was bridged to some extent in the twelfth century by the new orders of canons regular, who had a foot in both worlds, one in the cloister and one in the secular arena as priests. The house of canons at St. Victor in Paris, for example, produced men, such as Andrew and HUGH OF ST. VICTOR, who were well versed in the new learning and its uses, yet were still committed to the life of the cloister and the life of prayer. Their work, as well as the continued absorption of men who had been formed in the schools before taking the habit, meant that the new methodology was ever-more present within monastic theology. With the coming of the friars, who defined a new paradigm as regular clergy who turned the learning of the schools to a manifestly religious purpose, the walls between the two worlds very nearly came tumbling down. The Cistercians and the older Benedictines began sending small contingents of their monks to the schools as a matter of course, and even established houses for them at the universities, from which they went forth to the lectures offered by the bachelors and regent masters in theology. But despite such relaxations of the rules of enclosure and the allowances made for a few to be educated in the scholastic manner, inside the cloister walls the traditional modes of monastic study were still followed and the traditional texts of spiritual formation still read. The public reading done at table in monasteries, as witnessed by surviving manuscripts that have been marked for oral presentation, continued to show a decided preference for the spiritual classics – the *Lives of the Fathers*, the *Dialogues* of Gregory the Great, the *Collations* of St. John Cassian – while the sermons offered by abbots relied as much as ever upon the mystical interpretations of Scripture that had always lain at the heart of the *lectio divina*. If anything, the new learning had heightened the monks' awareness of the differences between their way of approaching theology and the world's way, and made them work all the harder to preserve their traditions.

As a result, by the second quarter of the thirteenth century it was clear that the intellectual initiative had passed from the monasteries to the universities. And the new leaders there soon proved to be not monks but men of the new orders of mendicant friars, most particularly the Dominicans and the Franciscans.

The Dominicans

The Dominican order, founded by St. Domingo de Guzmán (b. ca. 1170; d. 1221) around 1210, was from the start a learned and clerical order. Behind their founding lay Dominic's strategy for combating the Cathar heresy, which by the early thirteenth century had become so entrenched in the society of southern France as to be almost a counter-Church. To put men in the field who would preach doctrine, use the arts of persuasion, and offer an example of apostolic poverty that might recapture the hearts and minds of the people was the original *raison d'être* of the order of Preachers. Consequently, one of the Dominicans' earliest priorities was to provide themselves with an education that was adequate to the task. When the Dominicans came to write their first Constitutions in 1220, they produced legislation that clearly embodied their understanding of the critical importance of education to the order's mission: dispensation for reasons of study was made a standard policy of the order, and every Dominican priory was required to operate a school in which the local brothers were taught the rudiments of theology. The same commitment to learning is why Dominic had early sent his brothers out from Toulouse and directed them to the great centers of learning, at Paris, Bologna, and Oxford. There the friars not only trained their minds, but found recruits whose intellectual promise was an obvious asset to the order. The Constitutions of 1220 that made of every convent also a school already contain as well mention of the order's own *studium* at Paris, greater than any local *schola*, to which each province in the order could send three of its best and brightest. *Schola* and *studium:* these were the two institutional starting points for what was to become one of the most elaborate, well-articulated educational systems Europe had ever seen.

The *schola* was the educational bedrock of the Dominican order. Every friar no matter how high-ranking was required to attend the classes offered daily in his priory. There a lector orchestrated a course in theology that, in its modest way, mimicked the pedagogy the friars had encountered at Paris. Two cycles of lectures were presented each day, one on a book of the Bible, which served to keep students abreast of current developments in exegesis, and one on the *Sentences* of PETER LOMBARD, through which they learned a basic theological method. The ambitiousness of the *schola* course can also be seen in the requirement imposed on all Dominican lectors that they hold weekly disputations, and, if their own training were up to it, even occasionally mount public *disputationes de quolibet*. A particularly important innovation came in the form of a new officer the Dominicans introduced into claustral life, the master of students, who worked alongside the lector and functioned as tutor to the community. It was his job to monitor the progress of the individual friars in his care, and to decide, for example, who might benefit from being assigned a private cell in which to study. The master of students also organized the in-house disputations, appointed helpers such as a "brother repeater" who offered daily *repetitiones* of all lectures and weekly general repetitions that summarized the disputation and put it in context, and generally managed the practicalities of academic life and discipline in his convent.

It is through the master of students that we also have a window on the less formal but no less important side of a Dominican friar's formation: his training as a preacher and a confessor, through something called the *collatio scientifica*. This was a twice-weekly meeting to which the master of students called the brothers, there to drill them through the current literature on confession, such as Raymond of Peñafort's *Summa de casibus* in the order's early years or, later, John of Freiburg's Thomistic *Summa confessorum*; to mount mock disputations in which the brothers gained some much needed experience in marshalling their own arguments; or simply to review trouble spots in recent coursework. This twice-weekly exercise also alerts us to the chameleon-like nature of the term *collatio* for the Dominicans. It could refer to these gatherings or to the meetings the novices in a community were required to attend. It could refer to the short sermons preached on ferial days as part of the Dominican compline office. And it was given a new connotation by the first generation of Dominicans at the University of Paris, for whom master-general Jordan of Saxony had secured the right that there be evening-time sermons offered to ensure that his friars, who attended class during the morning hours when preaching traditionally took place, would not miss hearing the word of God. This last type of *collatio* has left a rich scholastic literature, as the mendicants gradually transformed the vespertine university sermon into an ever more sophisticated medium through which to present new ideas (Mulchahey 1998, pp. 130–218).

47

Within a very few years of Dominic's death, however, the Dominicans found themselves confronting the reality that an education in theology, as it was currently coming to be understood, might require a more progressive outlook, that the philosophical disciplines might indeed need to be seen as propaedeutic to the pursuit of theological science. By the time the order produced a second redaction of its Constitutions in 1228, a ban on the study of the liberal arts that had figured prominently in the original Constitutions had been formally relaxed: special permission to pursue such subjects would now be considered on an individual basis. By the 1240s the Dominicans had begun experimenting with various ways of delivering training in logic to the brothers on a wider scale. Soon the first steps were taken towards creating a network of *studia artium*, schools that would rotate amongst the convents of a region and in which only a handful of students drawn from all over the province would be enrolled. In 1259 the order published a *ratio studiorum* that included amongst its recommendations a call for every province to establish at least one *studium artium*. It was long thought that this signaled the Dominicans' alignment with the new syllabus published by the faculty of arts of the University of Paris in 1255, in which Aristotelian natural philosophy loomed so large, but the order's arts schools concentrated solely upon logic (Mulchahey 1998, pp. 220–38). A surviving syllabus from Provence dated to 1321 indicates a two-year cycle: the first term of the first year in such a *studium* was devoted to the *Analytica posteriora* and to PETER OF SPAIN's *Tractatus*, save its chapter on fallacies; the second term covered Aristotle's *Praedicamenta* and *Analytica priora*, as well as the *Liber de sex principiis*; the *De sophisticis elenchis* paired with lectures on Peter of Spain's chapter on fallacies filled the first term of the second year; while the second term turned to the *Peri hermeneias* together with Porphyry's introduction to the *Praedicamenta*, the *Isagoge*. Clearly, this was only a partial answer to Parisian arts training (Mulchahey 1998, pp. 238–52).

The advent of natural philosophy within the Dominican curriculum came in the 1260s. The emergence of the first *studia naturarum* within the Dominican order coincides convincingly with ALBERTUS MAGNUS' work on his Aristotelian paraphrases. And it has been suggested that the paraphrases were, in fact, commissioned from Albert by Dominican master-general Humbert of Romans, in an attempt to develop a series of preparatory texts for use in the new schools (Mulchahey 1998, pp. 254–63). The fully-evolved curriculum of the *studium naturarum* is most clearly delineated in the surviving records of the order's Roman Province, which describe a three-year cycle that presented the *Metaphysica* and the *De anima* combined with the *Parva naturalia* one year; Aristotle's *Physica* and the *De generatione et corruptione*, coupled with the *De caelo et mundo* and the *De meteoris* the next; and the *Liber de causis* together with the Aristotelian treatises on biological subjects, the *De plantis* and the five works on animals, in the third. This reading list does seem to take the Dominicans further along the road towards assimilation with the syllabus of the Parisian arts faculty, but it still parts company with Paris in not including moral philosophy. That subject was taught elsewhere within the Dominican educational system. And a surprising hint of the old conservatism may be seen in the fact that a command to parallel the 1259 *ratio studiorum*'s call for a logic school in every province is not found for *studia naturarum* until 1305. However, even once the latter type of *studium* existed, it remained true that only select students, those chosen as *fratres studentes*, advanced through the Dominicans' *studium* system, and that the friars of the rank and file whose training is to be equated with the *schola* would have had only limited exposure to philosophical thinking (Mulchahey 1998, pp. 252–78).

At just about the same time that the Dominicans were developing their natural philosophy course, a singular experiment was unfolding at Santa Sabina, the friars' priory

48

in Rome. In 1265, THOMAS AQUINAS, recently returned to Italy after his first Parisian regency, was asked by the Roman Province to organize a *studium* in Rome, and there develop a course in theology that would occupy a level intermediate between that of the simple convent *scholae* and that of the *studia generalia*. The result was both a new textbook, the *Summa theologiae*, and a model for another new subsystem of provincial *studia*, the *studia particularis theologiae*, which became a regular feature of the order's educational apparatus in the 1280s (Boyle 1982; Mulchahey 1998, pp. 278–306). But the order was slow to adopt Aquinas's approach to theology. Apart from the fact that Thomism had undergone a severe testing with the Condemnations of 1277, the Dominicans were wedded to teaching theology according to the curriculum in effect at the universities, and at Paris in particular, if they wished to keep their men eligible for the *magisterium*. The key textbook in the university theology faculties remained the *Sentences* of Peter Lombard, as it did in Dominican priory schools, and this as much as anything explains why the *Sentences* were drafted into service in the order's *studia theologiae* as well; the *Summa* per se was kept at arm's length from the syllabus throughout the medieval period (Mulchahey 1998, pp. 306–40).

At the top of the Dominican educational pyramid stood the order's general houses of study, the *studia generalia*. The Parisian priory, St. Jacques, housed the original Dominican *studium generale*, which was already in existence in some form by 1220. The next generation of general houses appeared in 1248, with the erection of schools at Bologna, Oxford, Cologne, and Montpellier. By the early fourteenth century every province was supposed to operate one. Each province could send two students to each *studium generale*, except to Paris where the original quota had been set at three. Thus while conventual *scholae* served the local community, and provincial *studia* served the province, the *studia generalia* were intended to encourage the communication of ideas across national or other boundaries by accepting students drawn from the order at large. Although some of the most famous Dominican *studia generalia* were found in priories located within the university environment, not all of the order's general houses were actually incorporated into the universities. Thus it is necessary to be aware of differences between the Dominican *studia generalia*, their curriculum and procedures, and those of the universities: as with the Dominican understanding of the arts and the universities' understanding, the two are not identical (Mulchahey 1994; 1998, pp. 352–78).

Theology instruction in the order's general houses of study assumed a more or less tripartite form, of which we have already seen hints in the *scholae* and whose homage to the Parisian curriculum is manifest. The principal lector in each *studium generale*, who would also be a regent master should his school operate within one of the universities, presented the central lecture cycle, the ordinary lectures *de textu* on the Bible, focusing upon the most important issues within contemporary exegesis. The men who headed up *studia generalia* were also required to lecture on one of the four books of Peter Lombard's *Sentences* each year, as a framework within which the theological implications of Scripture could be examined, if, increasingly, through a lens provided by Thomas Aquinas. Each lector also presided over regularly-scheduled *quaestiones disputatae*, weekly it was hoped, on issues that arose directly from the lectures, and, in keeping with university prescriptions, also mounted the more wide-ranging quodlibetal disputations in which the order's Thomism was put on very public display. Most Dominican *studia generalia* also had a *cursor Sententiarum* working under the lector, who was expected to cover the four books of the Lombard's work over a single academic year, in a series of simple and straightforward expositions of the text, known as "cursory" or running lectures. Although the Dominican *studia* mainly imitated the theology course at the University of Paris, there was a major

49

difference: whereas the Parisian schools and Oxford tended to have a *cursor biblicus* who worked alongside the *cursor Sententiarum* and offered cursory lectures on the Bible, Dominican *studia generalia* substituted a course in moral philosophy taught by the *studium*'s master of students, in which capacity the *cursor* served in the second year of his assignment. The cycle of lectures presented by the master of students was drawn either directly from the works of Aristotle or from Aquinas's commentaries on the *Nicomachean Ethics*. What is especially noteworthy is that, in assigning young men to train as *cursores*, the Dominican order was emphatically concerned with seeing them become skilled teachers, and that year's experience as a master of students was a critical part of their formation (Mulchahey 1998, pp. 378–96).

This alerts us to an important reality about the Dominican educational system, and that is that it was geared, primarily, towards producing lectors for the order's lower schools. Prosopographical evidence as well as the order's legislative record shows quite clearly that a student's advancement through the *studium* system was punctuated by periods of service as a teacher. Before being moved from a *studium artium* to continue his studies at a *studium naturarum*, a friar would normally spend a year or two teaching logic himself; before advancing from a *studium naturarum* to a *studium particularis theologiae*, a student could expect to work first as a lector in a philosophy school. And so on. Most of the men sent to the order's *studia generalia* were there not to pursue the *magisterium* but simply to be exposed to theology taught at its highest level for two or three years before being recalled to their home provinces to take up work as teachers in the *schola*.

Also important to note in all of this, is that the Dominican contribution to the philosophical and theological explorations of the medieval period were not all made within the context of the university, as has been implicitly accepted by most scholarship in the last century and more. *Sentences* commentaries could come from the pen of a Dominican lector in a local conventual *schola* as readily as from the pen of a Parisian bachelor; Aristotelian summaries and analyses might have had a provincial *studium* in mind; disputed questions were required of every teacher in the Dominican system, be he conventual lector or regent master. The Dominican network of schools has sometimes been called a "decentralized university." Whatever the shortcomings of that analogy in institutional terms, it does embody an important truth about the wide reach of the order of Preachers' educational enterprise in the Middle Ages.

The Franciscans

The order founded in 1210/12 by St. Francis of Assisi (b. 1182; d. 1226) was not, like the Dominican order, one dedicated to extirpating heresy or even, strictly speaking, to preaching. Preaching was only one possible means of expression for the Franciscans' mission, which was to live a life of evangelical poverty and to encourage the revival of the Gospel. Teaching an authentic imitation of Christ by their own example, as Francis had before them, was the *fratres minores'* first and greatest ministry. Thus the elaboration of a formal educational system might seem an undertaking outside of, if not opposed to, the basic intention of the Franciscan order. Yet the Franciscans did take an interest in education from early in their history, and Francis himself, despite his many misgivings, seems to have recognized its potential as an instrument for fulfilling the order's purpose (Roest 2000, pp. 2–3). Within a decade of Francis's death the order had established centers of study at Paris, Bologna, Oxford, and Montpellier, shadowing those of the Dominicans.

But, as with the Dominicans, historians have often confused the educational programs that came to be in vogue in Franciscan schools with the programs offered by the secular universities, not least because the most prominent Franciscan houses of study were located in university towns or cities. Understanding the differences between the university curricula and how teaching was organized in the Franciscan order is important here, too, if we are to place many of the friars' philosophical and theological works within their proper context.

The essential form of education within the Franciscan order was theological, and by dint of the time in which they lived, scholastic. Statutes dating back perhaps as early as 1237 mandate steps to assure training in theology for the friars, and, by implication, indicate the stages for that training, which began at the local friary. It was hoped that every friary of thirty members or so would have one or two lectors, regularly teaching books of the Bible, a standard theological work such as the *Sentences*, and occasionally holding disputations on selected topics. Throughout the Middle Ages, the Franciscans' chief educational desideratum was to have enough lectors to staff every Franciscan house or community in Europe. And to create a group of qualified teachers, the order instituted and maintained a training program at its *studia generalia*, the most prominent of which was at Paris (Roest 2000, pp. 87–97).

Every province within the order could send to Paris two friars at a time to participate in the lectorate, as the training program for lectors was called. The expenses for the two were borne by the Parisian community; an additional two friars could be enrolled at the province's own expense. Such student-friars were presumed to have mastered Latin grammar, to have studied philosophy for at least two years, and theology for at least three. At a *studium generale* such as the one the Franciscans operated at Paris, lectorate students would both hear lectures and attend disputations within the order's *studium* and also do the same at other schools within the wider university community. But lectorate students were not university students and they followed their own curriculum devised by the order, consisting chiefly of the study of the Bible and the *Sentences* (Courtenay 1999, pp. 79–83). After their lectorate, which lasted four years, friars would usually return to their home provinces to begin teaching or administrative duties. Most lectors never undertook the additional work that would lead to either the baccalaureate or a magisterial degree in theology, and often terminated their education at the age of 26 or 27 (Roest 2000, pp. 91–2).

As noted, to be qualified for the lectorate course at a *studium generale* Franciscan students needed to have completed the equivalent of a university arts course. In the order's early days, when many of its new members were recruited from the ranks of university students and graduates, there was little difficulty in finding suitably prepared candidates for the lectorate. But when the success and popularity of the order brought with it a large population of very young entrants, some no more than 12 years of age, the order had to create its own schools of grammar, arts, and philosophy to ready its members for advanced theological study. Usually such schools functioned at the local or provincial level, but occasionally schools of philosophy were to be found in a Franciscan *studium generale*. For example, training in the arts was regularly provided for younger friars at Oxford. One implication of this practice is that Franciscan masters in theology, unlike their secular counterparts, might give courses in philosophy even at the most advanced stages of their scholarly careers, as they taught in general houses of study. As a result, we have texts such as JOHN DUNS SCOTUS'S *Questions on the Metaphysics* and WILLIAM OF OCKHAM's *Expositions of the Categories*, which originated in courses conducted on these texts for younger friars.

If a student were considered worthy of further education beyond the lectorate and perhaps apt for higher ecclesiastical office, the minister general and the general chapter of

51

the order could approve his pursuit of a baccalaureate in theology. At this point, the system of education inside the order and that of the universities coincided. Since the requirements for the study of theology at the baccalaureate level and the steps necessary to obtain the mastership in theology are described in the chapter SCHOLASTICISM, they need not be repeated here. What is distinctive about the Franciscans' participation in the universities' theological programs is that, for one thing, the friar-students were often considerably older than the secular students, and they were also given credit for the study they had done within the Franciscan system. Once they were deemed to have met all the requirements, Franciscans were allowed to proceed directly to the baccalaureate. Furthermore, if they actually became masters in theology, they rarely occupied their chairs for more than a year since the number of candidates for the mastership was so large that the order felt constrained to rotate chairs of theology as rapidly as possible (Courtenay 1999, pp. 91–2).

Though Franciscan candidates were exempted from many university requirements, those exemptions were always at the pleasure of the university faculties and were a continual point of friction between the mendicant orders and the universities. The issue was twofold: not only whether the arts training offered in the Franciscan or Dominican order was really equivalent to the university course in the arts, but also whether the preliminary theological training a friar received in his order matched the same kind of training in the universities. The first issue was at stake in 1253 when Oxford University initially refused to allow Thomas of York, an English Franciscan, to incept as a master in theology because he had never taught the arts in any university. The second was, apparently, at the heart of the conflicts between the Franciscans and Oxford University at the outset of the fourteenth century. Other sources of tension centered on the universities' essential character as a guild or corporation aimed at advancing the members' common interest. When the universities went on strike, as happened in the 1250s at Paris, the Franciscans and the other mendicant orders refused to participate at the behest of their religious superiors, and this was viewed by the secular masters as divisive and self-interested behavior. Moreover, the usual practice of recruiting novices from amongst the younger students meant that the Franciscans and the other orders deprived the universities of what might otherwise have been future university teachers and guild members, often ones of remarkable abilities. The resentment this caused was evident on several occasions when the universities attempted to curtail the recruitment of younger students by the friars (Roest 2000, pp. 51–64). In general, the source of tension between the Franciscan order and the universities lay in the extent to which the order represented competition to universities while simultaneously expecting university officials to accommodate the friars' special needs. But these strains were felt mainly at the northern European universities, such as Oxford, Cambridge, and Paris; in southern universities, such as Bologna and Padua, theology was a faculty that emerged later in the universities' history and often had as its nucleus Franciscans and other mendicants drawn from the orders' *studia generalia*, causing the friars' interests and the faculty's to be practically the same.

The different levels of instruction and the various pedagogical elements found in the various programs – lectorate, baccalaureate, and mastership – yielded distinctive forms of philosophical and theological literature. For example, Franciscans authors often produced two or more commentaries on the *Sentences*, as did Scotus and PETER AURIOL, the first deriving from a preliminary reading of the *Sentences* at one *studium* and a second done at the *studium* where they eventually obtained their mastership. We also have works written by Franciscan non-masters that in secular circles would come only from those who had attained their mastership: Ockham, though never a master of theology, nonetheless produced a full set of edited quodlibetal questions from a disputation held at a non-university center, namely, the London *studium* of the Franciscans. Genres also become more flexible at the friars' hands: for example, the sort of questions usually treated only in properly theological works by non-mendicants are often raised in Franciscan philosophical commentaries; there are Franciscan commentaries on the *Metaphysics* that include extensive discussions of divine foreknowledge or the acts of intellect found in angelic natures. And, as with the Dominicans, we have an interesting Franciscan variation on the theme of the *collatio*. For the Franciscans the genre seems to have encompassed two different types of activities: evening lectures and short disputations. The former is illustrated in the *Collationes in Hexaemeron* of St. BONAVENTURE; the latter in the *Collationes* of John Duns Scotus.

Conclusion

In general, then, while it has always been recognized that the mendicant orders provided some of the most outstanding philosophical thinkers of the thirteenth and fourteenth centuries, what has not been so readily acknowledged is that the friars' contributions were not made exclusively at the medieval universities. The works of Dominican and Franciscan friars, in particular, need to be assessed primarily in reference to the institutional setting of their own orders' schools: the impetus for mendicant authors to compose works or to organize them in certain ways was often provided by the educational needs of their own orders, as was so clearly the case for Thomas Aquinas when writing his *Summa theologiae*. The friars' contribution to medieval philosophy was made within the universities, but also at times quite consciously apart from the university regulations that governed the teaching and literary activities of other university men.

Bibliography

Boyle, Leonard E. (1981), "Notes of the education of the *fratres communes* in the Dominican Order in the thirteenth century," in R. Creytens and P. Künzle, eds., *Xenia medii aevi historiam illustrantia oblata Thomae Kaeppeli, O.P.* (pp. 248–67), I, Storia e letteratura 141; repr. in *Pastoral Care, Clerical Education and Canon Law, 1200–1400*, London: Variorum Reprints.

——(1982), *The Setting of the Summa Theologiae of Thomas Aquinas*, Étienne Gilson Series 5, Toronto: Pontifical Institute of Mediaeval Studies.

——(1983), "Alia lectura fratris Thome," *Mediaeval Studies* 45, pp. 18–29.

Courtenay, William J. (1993), "The Parisian community in 1303," *Franciscan Studies* 53, pp. 155–73.

——(1994), "Programs of study and genres of scholastic theological production in the fourteenth century," in Jacqueline Hamesse, ed., *Manuels, programmes de cours et techniques d'enseignement dans les universités médiévales* (pp. 325–50), Louvain-la-Neuve: Université Catholique de Louvain.

——(1996), "Between pope and king: the Parisian letters of adhesion of 1303," *Speculum* 71/3, pp. 577–605.

——(1999), "The instructional programme of the mendicant convents at Paris in the early fourteenth century," in Peter Biller and Barrie Dobson, eds., *The Medieval Church: Universities, Heresy, and the Religious Life: Eessays in Honour of Gordon Leff* (pp. 77–92), London: Boydell Press for the Ecclesiastical History Society.

Leclercq, Jean (1982), *The Love of Learning and the Desire for God: A Study of Monastic Culture*, trans. C. Misrahi, New York: Fordham University Press.

Mulchahey, M. Michèle (1994), "The Dominican *studium* system and the universities of Europe in the thirteenth century: a relationship redefined," in Jacqueline Hamesse, ed., *Manuels, programmes de cours et techniques d'enseignement dans les universités médiévales* (pp. 277–324), Louvain-la-Neuve: Université Catholique de Louvain.

——(1998), *"First the bow is bent in study . . ." Dominican Education before 1350*, Texts and Studies 132, Toronto: Pontifical Institute of Mediaeval Studies.

Roest, Bert (2000), *A History of Franciscan Education (c. 1210–1517)*, Leiden, Boston, and Cologne: Brill.

6

Scholasticism

TIMOTHY B. NOONE

Scholars of medieval thought from the middle of the nineteenth century to the present have employed the term 'scholasticism' in various senses: some have extended the term to make it practically equivalent to 'medieval philosophy', counting BOETHIUS of the sixth century the first of the scholastics and the fifteenth-century NICHOLAS OF CUSA the last (Grabmann 1909–11); others have confined the term to the period of the High Middle Ages, allowing the twelfth-century PETER ABELARD, or sometimes the late eleventh-century ANSELM, to be the first of the scholastics and closing off the main scholastic period just prior to the Reformation, while acknowledging the continuation of scholastic thought in the Iberian peninsula in such figures as Francisco Suárez and Jean Poinsot of the sixteenth and seventeenth centuries. Which of these approaches to adopt and favor is decisive in determining the subject matter at hand. The present essay, partly on historical and partly on terminological grounds, will side with the latter usage and approach; the course of scholastic thought is closely associated with the twelfth-century schools that eventually formed the burgeoning universities at Paris and Oxford, while the English 'scholasticism', despite its occasionally pejorative connotations, consistently points to the High Middle Ages as a period of thought that has distinctive features.

What are the features characteristic of the scholastic thinkers associated with the schools of the twelfth to the seventeenth centuries? Speaking in the most general terms, we can say that there are at least three overarching traits: (1) thinkers treasured rigorous argumentation and trusted logic and dialectics to uncover, through discussion and analysis, philosophical truth (the principle of reasoned argument or *ratio*); (2) they accepted, as a fundamental guide to developing their own ideas, the ancient insight (see Aristotle, *Metaphysics*, book A) that earlier philosophers whose thought and writings were remembered and preserved had so privileged a claim on one's attention that to show the legitimacy of one's own reflections involved constant reference to and dialogue with such predecessors (the principle of authority or *auctoritas*); and (3) by and large, thinkers during this period felt obliged to raise questions about the relationship of their theories to revealed truths and to coordinate the insights of philosophy with theological teaching (the principle of the harmony of faith and reason, or *concordia*).

True, some medieval thinkers during the centuries mentioned came close to suggesting the worthlessness of certain customary authorities – PETER OLIVI, for example, displays at times a fairly dismissive attitude toward Aristotle and AVERROES, as does NICHOLAS OF AUTRECOURT in the fourteenth century – but, for the most part, the range of authoritative texts was uniformly accepted as worthy of intellectual attention, though the number of such texts was subject to growth over time with the addition of new authors. Instead of rejecting authorities, philosophers of the Middle Ages tended to propose distinctions so as to allow a set of texts and their corresponding arguments to be judged correct in one respect, though wanting in other respects. Even Olivi, for example, spends considerable time arguing for certain interpretations of key passages in Aristotle to buttress his case for a given doctrinal point (Olivi 1924, *In II Sent.* q. 57 348). We must acknowledge, moreover, that some thinkers, chiefly those identified by historians as "Latin Averroists," certainly appeared at times to modify, if not reject, the third principle since they thought it incumbent upon philosophers to state what they adjudged to be the consequences of their philosophical principles solely in terms of natural reason without any effort to alter their conclusions with reference to revealed teachings. Yet even here matters are not so clear; SIGER OF BRABANT, for example, did take his faith quite seriously and would, speaking as a Christian intellectual and not as a philosopher, point out the tension between the philosophical view and the Church's doctrine (Wippel 1998). The tendency to advance intellectually by first considering alternative viewpoints expressed in earlier literature and then surmounting them through proposing a synthetic perspective wherein the truths of the opposing views can be duly recognized is the quintessentially scholastic inclination and, to the extent that such a tendency is regularly put into practice, the scholastic method.

The institutional setting and environment of thinkers during this period determines in large part the focus of their intellectual attention as well as the precise form their works take. Scholasticism is nearly unintelligible apart from the institutions in which philosophy and theology were taught and the changing and novel influences to which thinkers during this time were subject, in the form of Latin translations becoming available of works originally composed in Greek and Arabic. Consequently, this essay will begin with a description of the institutional setting of the philosophy produced in the Middle Ages, outlining in broad strokes the passage from the schools of the twelfth century to the universities of the thirteenth as well as some of the features of the latter. Thereafter, it will turn to the new literature introduced by the translations, the changes in curriculum that the new literature required, and the academic exercises and forms of discourse developed to advance philosophical and theological thought.

Institutional setting

Origins of the universities

The origins of the universities in which so much of the teaching of philosophy occurred are to be found mainly in the cathedral and local schools of the towns where the first universities appeared: Bologna, Paris, and Oxford. At Bologna, the rise of the university is associated with the growth of a school of civil law and a school of canon law. Though theology and other faculties eventually appeared in Bologna, the university did not figure in any major way in the history of philosophy until the late thirteenth century (Verger 1973, pp. 36–41). Much more typical of most northern European universities in terms of structure and curriculum was the University of Paris.

Paris grew out of the cathedral school of the cathedral of Notre Dame, where Peter Abelard taught in the early twelfth century, the monastic school of St. Geneviève, where Abelard also briefly taught, and the school of St. Victor, which had as its successive masters the illustrious teachers HUGH OF ST. VICTOR and RICHARD OF ST. VICTOR. The predominance of Paris is not, however, attributable simply to the series of distinguished philosophers and theologians, such as Abelard, the Victorines, and PETER LOMBARD who taught in its schools throughout the twelfth century – the school of Chartres had equally eminent scholars closely associated with it – but also to its urban location and its close connection with and value to the royal court. Hence it is no accident that the University of Paris is first recognized as a legal corporation and its rights acknowledged in a decree, dating to July 1200, of the French king, Philip Augustus. Since, however, Philip's decree had the effect of defending the university scholars' rights by subjecting them unreservedly to the strictures of canon law and its enforcement by the Bishop of Paris, the university as a corporation found it increasingly advantageous to appeal to the papacy to safeguard itself against arbitrary decisions on the part of the local hierarchy to refuse degrees to worthy members. As a result of these appeals to the papacy, the popes came to have a direct and, for the most part, cordial relationship with the University of Paris and the first statutes of the University of Paris were promulgated in 1215 by Robert Courson, a papal legate, as part of an effort to settle a dispute between the Bishop of Paris and the university corporation (Pedersen 1997, pp. 130–7, 158–72).

The situation at Oxford is slightly more complicated and certainly less well documented, but the pattern is in many ways similar to that found at Paris: a local group of schools enjoying a series of well-known teachers, though much less distinguished than the ones associated with Paris; a favorable location (in Oxford's case, the town was a legal center); and, in addition, the historical accident of a conflict between the English crown and the Archbishop of Canterbury, which caused the king to order all scholars home from foreign territories, thereby temporarily increasing vastly the number of teachers and students in the town (McEvoy 1998; Pedersen, 1997, pp. 159–64; Southern 1984). As at Paris, conflicts between the university's scholars and the townspeople resulted in strife – in this case students were hanged (*suspendium clericorum*) in retribution for an accidental death – and the university went on strike for five years (1209–15). When, however, the university was reconciled to the town, the latter yielded to it on all the key points and the university's rights were enshrined in the statutes issued at the time of the settlement, 1215, by Robert Courson, the papal legate ordered to negotiate the restoration of the university.

Structure of the universities

The structure of medieval universities differed considerably from that found in modern universities, though certain similarities are nonetheless discernible. The northern European universities patterned after Paris are really teaching guilds or corporations, organizations of teachers designed to teach students academic subjects and to train the next generation of scholars. The control exercised by the teaching masters over the administrative arm of the universities shows the extent to which the guild mentality was predominant; academic administrators, such as deans and provosts, were severely limited in their terms of office and were expected to return to the faculty from which they originated after the service of their terms. Once the universities gained full autonomy and legally recognized status, they established internal regulations in conformity to the general statutes mentioned above, though they were also known to "reform" or alter those statutes when they deemed it conducive to the academic well-being of their communities, as happened in Paris in the faculty of arts in 1255. The modern reader must remember that many of the steps toward MA degrees and the sequence of steps to be followed in obtaining a higher degree were modeled on the pattern of traditional education found in the case of a master craftsman and an apprentice. The graduate of a medieval university became, at graduation, a member of the faculty of masters under whom he had studied and was obliged to a period of postgraduate teaching exceeding a year as part of his postgraduate duties. A final point to note on this score is that the degree received at a university was not simply a record of academic achievement; it was also a license to teach both within one's home university and elsewhere, the right of teaching anywhere (*ius ubique docendi*). Here we have the earmark of what made a medieval university education, as opposed to a school education, worthwhile, since only a university (a *studium generale*) could grant such a universal license (*licentia*); at the same time, we have in the *licentia* the sign of what is distinctively medieval about such an education, since the practice of the craft is what the graduate is now licensed to do.

Another striking feature of medieval universities is the extent to which they mandated sequences of courses and hierarchized their faculties in a much stricter manner than we typically find in modern universities. Though in a modern university a student must have acquired a baccalaureate prior to seeking and obtaining a master's degree, what precise subject is studied and what books are read at the undergraduate level are not generally prescribed except as required by a particular department or unit within the university. In a medieval university, by contrast, every student had to take the MA prior to being accepted for a course of studies in one of the higher faculties: theology, medicine, or law (canon or civil). Furthermore there was a single curriculum set within any given university's faculty of arts that required a certain set of books be lectured on (*legere*) and argued over (*disputare*); by the end of the BA sequence the student began to do minor amounts of teaching which steadily grew until, by the completion of the MA sequence, the student was ready to take on the role of teacher in his own right (Weisheipl 1974, pp. 207, 214–15). Though, as we shall see presently, the canon – so to speak – of required readings for the arts degrees changed over time owing to the introduction of materials recently translated as well as to the introduction of texts authored by Latin writers themselves, the set of universally required texts for the MA, and hence for any advanced study, meant that medieval academics had in their university studies a common intellectual framework rarely found in modern universities.

Finally, before turning to the wave of translations, curricula, and academic exercises associated with curricula, we should note the relative youth of most entering university students and the comparative maturity of the graduates of the faculty of theology, the faculty of which so many famous medieval philosophers were alumni. Most students entered the university when they were approximately 14 years of age, though a few were known to be as old as 17 and a few as young as 12. The BA course took three years and the MA another three, with an additional year of teaching associated with it. Hence most students entering one of the higher faculties, such as theology, were approximately 22 years of age. The length and precise course of studies stipulated by university statutes varied from university to university – at Paris the sequence of hearing lectures, giving lectures, and participating in disputes involved fourteen years of study, whereas at Oxford a similar sequence took only ten or eleven years (Courtenay 1994, pp. 331–2) – but overall the average theologian who had both taken his MA and become a full-fledged member of the theology faculty would be about 36 years of age at inception, that is, at the outset of his theological teaching career. Since, as we shall see, much of this comparatively long period of time, i.e. some twenty-two years, would have been spent either in the study of philosophical texts or in the study of theological texts that often called forth philosophical speculation, we should not wonder that the best and most original philosophical works are usually the products of members of the faculty of theology.

Translations

If we examine what philosophical texts were available to the Latin West prior to the wave of Latin translations that were done in the period between 1140 and 1300, we may be surprised at how little direct knowledge of Greek, and later on Arabic, philosophical texts medieval philosophers confined to reading Latin could have had. Latin readers generally had available to them the old logic (*ars vetus*), i.e., the *Categories*, the *Perihermenias*, the *Topics* of Cicero, and the *Topical Differences* of Boethius along with the latter's translation of Porphyry's *Isagoge* (Introduction to the *Categories*) as well as his commentaries on the *Isagoge*, *Categories*, and the *Perihermenias*; these works constituted the only direct knowledge Latin readers had of Aristotle up until the middle of the twelfth century (Ebbesen 1982, pp. 104–9). The received inheritance from the Platonic tradition prior to the wave of twelfth and thirteenth-century translations was equally meager in terms of direct access to the primary texts. Only a partial translation of Plato's *Timaeus* was available, along with an extensive commentary by Calcidius, and a section of Plato's *Republic* in a translation by Cicero, though the latter did not apparently enjoy wide circulation. Indirect access to the Platonic tradition, on the other hand, was nigh on ubiquitous. The works of the pagans usually read in schools – Cicero, Seneca, Apuleius, and Martianus Capella, to mention a few – communicated much in the way of Platonic doctrines and seemed to correlate extremely well with the Platonism present in both the Latin Fathers, such as AUGUSTINE and Ambrose, and the Greek Fathers, such as PSEUDO-DIONYSIUS and Gregory of Nyssa. Hence even an author so well steeped in Aristotelian dialectic as Abelard could still feel in the second quarter of the twelfth century that the greatest philosopher of ancient times was Plato (Gregory 1988, pp. 54–63).

The advent of the translations, many of them done in the twelfth and early thirteenth centuries, changed all of this. Sometime in the middle of the twelfth century, probably as early as 1160, the writings of the Islamic philosopher AVICENNA were translated into Latin in Toledo by a group of translators that included DOMINICUS GUNDISSALINUS. Though Avicenna's works were self-standing essays and not by any means akin to the literal commentaries on Aristotelian texts to be found in Averroes writings, they did provide an overview of many key Aristotelian metaphysical and psychological notions, laying the foundation for the later Latin effort to understand Aristotle. From about the middle of the twelfth century also, Aristotle's own works on nature, science, and ethics began to appear, either in partial or complete form. The Latins came to know by the end of the twelfth century Aristotle's *Physics*, *De caelo*, most of his *Metaphysics*, *De anima*, *Parva naturalia*, the first three books of the *Nicomachean Ethics*, and the *Posterior Analytics*; among these are the Aristotelian writings on natural philosophy (*libri naturales*) proscribed in the condemnation of Paris in 1210 and the first statutes of the University of Paris in 1215. Sometime in the 1220s, Averroes' writings also began to appear in Paris and Oxford and were used by masters of arts as well as theologians. It was Averroes more than any other of the Aristotelian commentators known to the Latin West who allowed the masters of Oxford and Paris to delve into the meaning of the Aristotelian texts and come to understand their underlying structure. Finally, by the middle of the thirteenth century, nearly all of the Aristotelian corpus (the chief lacuna being the *Politics*) was available in some form, including the whole of the *Nicomachean Ethics*, a work translated in its entirety for the first time by ROBERT GROSSETESTE.

Curriculum

Faculty of arts

reaction

Reactions to the introduction of the Aristotelian writings were initially mixed: at Paris, efforts to assimilate Aristotle led to curious interpretations on the part of early figures such as Amalric of Bené and David of Dinant and resulted in their writings being banned and the prohibition of public reading of, or lecturing upon, Aristotle's works on natural philosophy. At Oxford, the works were known and read freely since there was no prohibition on their use, though there does not ever seem to have been at Oxford the kind of enthusiasm for Aristotelianism seen in the masters of arts of Paris during the 1260s and 1270s. Yet, despite the renewal of the Parisian prohibitions of 1210 and 1215 by Pope Gregory IX in 1231, by 1255 the newly translated works were incorporated into the curriculum at the University of Paris and constituted the majority of the books for which students were responsible at their examinations and disputes. The precise stages through which the increased acceptance of Aristotle's works was achieved is not known; the documentary record for the period of 1220–35 is very sparse. But that the medieval universities made the alien texts of Aristotle the primary texts for their curricula is a remarkable fact and a testimony to the desire on the part of intellectuals of that time to assimilate and appropriate whatever was of value in the earlier pagan culture. To the extent that the ideal of assimilating the wisdom of ancient culture was the guiding principle of their activity, we might suggest that the foundational aim of the medieval universities was the same as that expressed in St. Augustine's *De doctrina christiana* and repeated in the twelfth century in the *Didascalicon* of Hugh of St. Victor: the ordering of all wisdom and knowledge to the study of theology.

The curriculum adopted by the faculty of arts at Paris in 1255 represents an enormous change in medieval higher education. From the time of Boethius until the beginning of the thirteenth century, the focus of medieval learning had always been upon the *trivium* (grammar, rhetoric, and dialectic) and *quadrivium* (geometry, astronomy, arithmetic, and music). Indeed, during a good amount of the Middle Ages, these branches of study were considered not simply propaedeutic to philosophy, but also largely constitutive of it. Prior to the statute of 1255, much of the curriculum, both in the earlier schools and the nascent universities, was devoted to the classical texts presenting the liberal arts (*artes liberales*) that comprised the *trivium* and *quadrivium*, texts such as Plato's *Timaeus* for astronomy, Augustine's *De musica* for music, and Priscian's *Institutiones grammaticae* for grammar, and of course the logical works of Aristotle for dialectic. The persistence of these traditional texts may be seen in the 1215 statutes wherein, in the process of forbidding public lecturing on Aristotle's books on natural philosophy, many of these same works are mentioned as being either recommended options or obligatory for teachers and students.

In the Parisian statute of 1255, however, all of the twelfth-century emphasis upon *quadrivium* and *trivium* was set aside and efforts were made instead to accommodate the Aristotelian writings by ceding the majority of the time for lecturing and disputing to the newly translated literature. According to the terms of the statute, practically all of the Aristotelian *corpus* was required reading and material for examination, including: the *Physics*, *De generatione et corruptione*, *De anima*, the *Parva naturalia*, *Nicomachean Ethics*, *Metaphysics*, and the pseudo-Aristotelian *Liber de causis*. Shortly thereafter, further translations made available Aristotle's *Oeconomica*, *Rhetorica*, and *Politics*, which were subsequently added to the curriculum. Nor were the only additions to the traditional list of readings coming from translated literature: in mathematics, THOMAS BRADWARDINE'S *De proportione*, or at least some treatises summarizing it, became books of study at Oxford after 1328; in optics, JOHN PECHAM's *Perspectiva communis* was similarly employed by the early fourteenth century; in logic over the course of the thirteenth, fourteenth, and fifteenth centuries, the curriculum came to include various treatises by WILLIAM OF SHERWOOD, WALTER BURLEY, WILLIAM HEYTESBURY, and PAUL OF VENICE, among others (Ashworth 1994, pp. 352–60, 357–69; Weisheipl 1964, pp. 170–3).

Faculty of theology

The Bible was the main authoritative source of theological teaching and instruction through-out the Middle Ages with the Church Fathers functioning as sources of secondary impor-tance. By the end of the twelfth century, however, theologians such as Peter of Poitiers, Peter Abelard, and Peter Lombard began to assemble the sayings (*dicta*) of the Fathers as well as supporting biblical texts into collections of definitive opinions or *sententiae*. These collec-tions of theological opinions became increasingly popular as starting points for theological argument and reflection, figuring often in the academic exercises to be described below; by 1228 at the latest, ALEXANDER OF HALES, who would eventually enter the Franciscan order and become one of its earliest and most influential theologians, introduced at Paris the prac-tice of commenting upon the collection of *sententiae* drawn up nearly a century earlier by Peter Lombard. Henceforth, Lombard's *Sentences* became the main textbook in speculative theology, serving in that role until the end of the seventeenth century.

Students in theology were expected to hear lectures on the Bible and Lombard's *Sen-tences* for a number of years. Once they became bachelors of theology, students had to deliver lectures on the Bible and on the *Sentences*. After devoting three to four years to giving these lectures, candidates then proceeded to participate in disputations for at least one year prior to being admitted into the society of the masters under whom they had studied. Once they were masters, medieval theologians were to continue to lecture on the Bible, hold regular disputed questions, and communicate their theological ideas through preaching.

Academic exercises

Medieval intellectual life was characterized by a regular form of teaching and learning known as the question (*quaestio*). The distant origins of the *quaestio* may be found in the writings of Cicero, and even before the great Roman orator, in the practices of the ancient philosophical schools (Hadot 1982, pp. 2–6). The medieval form takes its proximate source, however, from the development of academic practices in the faculty of theology during the second half of the twelfth century. As mentioned above, theologians lectured primarily on the Bible, but turned their attention increasingly to collections of Patristic theological opin-ions. In the course of lecturing, masters would often raise short questions called for by the text that they were expounding. Such short questions often were hermeneutic in scope, but steadily became more and more concerned with speculative matters. Though initially questions were reserved for the end of a class meeting, they soon became too complicated to manage within the setting of the lecture period. As a result, schools began to hold special sessions in which the master would hold a dispute on the topic broached in the original lecture (Bazán 1982, pp. 32–7; 1985, pp. 25–48).

As the universities devised their curricula, they incorporated the practice of holding dis-putes in separate sessions both in the theological faculties and elsewhere. It seems, nonethe-less, that the theological faculty provided the model for the introduction of the pedagogical

61

method into the other faculties. In the university setting, questions began to take on a more formal structure and to evolve into differing types depending upon their function within the curriculum. To start with the theology faculty's practices, masters would hold regular disputes (*quaestiones ordinariae*) as part of their teaching duties and these regular disputes took one of two basic forms. If the disputes were within the confines of the master's own classes or his "school," then they were considered private since it involved only a given master and his students. But apart from such classroom disputes there were regular public disputes involving not only a given master and his students, but also the other members of the theological faculty, masters and students. These public, regular disputes were held at least once every two weeks and all university theologians were obliged to hold them. Topics for these disputes were chosen by the masters who held them and were announced in advance. The disputes followed a distinct procedure: in the first session, known as the *disputatio*, the master's advanced students or bachelors would play the role of disputing parties, one student opposing (*opponens*) the master's view by advancing arguments against it with the other responding (*respondens*) by making counterarguments and providing a preliminary solution; in the second session, known as the *determinatio* and held at least one day later, the master would make a definitive reply or "determine" the question and answer each of the objections raised in the first session against the position taken (Bazán 1985, pp. 50–70).

Such regular disputes should be distinguished sharply from the occasional disputes known as quodlibets (*quaestiones quodlibetales*). At least within a university setting, quodlibets could only be conducted by a master, could only be held at Lent or Easter rather than throughout the academic year, were on a topic decided by the attendees and not by the master (though the master organized the questions raised according to a schematic pattern prior to replying), and were not part of the regular teaching of the master since no professor was obliged to hold them. Despite the last mentioned characteristic, quodlibets were sometimes favored by certain masters as one of the chief means for expressing their thought, as may be readily seen in the numerous quodlibets of THOMAS AQUINAS, HENRY OF GHENT, and GODFREY OF FONTAINES. Just as in a regular dispute, a quodlibetal question was held over at least two days, though the interval between the original discussion among the attendees and the reply of the master holding the quodlibet is known to have been a week or more on some occasions. Just as in a regular dispute, too, the entire faculty was required to attend a quodlibet, with members of other faculties and even interested parties from outside the university being permitted to attend as well (Wippel 1982, pp. 67–77; 1985, pp. 157–73).

Much of the structure of the disputed questions is repeated in the disputes held in the faculty of arts, though with some important differences. Like in the theology faculty, masters of arts are known to have held public and private disputations, though the former were not so frequent as in theology and do not seem to have served the same pedagogic function. Private disputations or ones held in the schools were extremely common and it is just such disputations as classroom exercises that underlie the many different types of questions, problems (*sophismata*), *insolubilia*, and other forms of literary expression so commonly found in surviving manuscripts.

Types of literature

The world of learning described in the foregoing, with its set books of study and obligatory disputations, is the proximate source of the various forms of literature characteristically termed "scholastic". There is first of all the disputed question, a literary version of the exercises described above. An example of such a disputed question might be Aquinas's *Quaestiones disputatae de anima*, a series of disputations believed to have been held in Rome at the beginning of the 1270s. In the case of Aquinas's literary version of the proceedings, we know that he reworked the material for publication; but in many cases such revision is known not to have occurred and the resulting material is a report of the proceedings or a *reportatio*. Next, we have the quodlibets, which tend to survive mainly in the form of reworked copies, though a few reports are also recognized. Both of these first two types are associated primarily with faculties of theology in medieval universities. The third type of literature, however, is characteristic of the faculty of arts: the commentary on Aristotle. But, in such cases, the term 'commentary' is used in describing two different literary forms: the literal commentary, often called a *sententia* or *scriptum*; and the question commentary. Over time, the latter form came to dominate within the literature and is believed to be related to the private disputations held by arts masters within their schools, though the transition from literal commentary to question commentary is not well documented or understood. Finally, we have a type of literature associated mainly with the faculty of theology: the *summae*. *Summae* or handbooks were not exactly manuals, but rather overarching accounts of a subject, accounts often quite sophisticated. The most famous, of course, are the *Summa theologiae* and *Summa contra gentiles* of Thomas Aquinas, but the form goes back earlier to the *summae* of figures such as Alexander of Hales and WILLIAM OF AUXERRE. *Summae* are systematic renderings of entire subjects, often groups of disputed questions, organized according to an architectonic plan of relating one group of subjects to another; as such, they need not be theological in their content, despite the prevalence of the *summa* form within theology. WILLIAM OF OCKHAM'S *Summa logicae*, for example, is an architectonic treatment of all the parts of logic, composed of units that are chapters.

This description of literary forms is by no means exhaustive – many forms, such as *sophismata*, *syncategoremata*, and *insolubilia*, are in the interest of space left out of consideration entirely – but does fairly indicate the main forms the reader is likely to encounter in the course of studying the philosophy of the Middle Ages and the ones most closely associated with the activities of Scholastic authors.

Bibliography

Ashworth, Jennifer (1994), "Les manuels de logique à l'Université d'Oxford aux XIVe et XVe siècles," in Jacqueline Hamesse, ed., *Manuels, programmes de cours et techniques d'enseignement dans les universités médiévales* (pp. 351–70), Actes du Colloque international de Louvain-la-Neuve, 9–11 septembre 1993, Louvain-la-Neuve: Institut d'Études Médiévales de l'Université Catholique de Louvain.

Bazán, B. Carlos (1982), "La *quaestio disputata*," in *Les Genres littéraires dans les sources théologiques et philosophiques médiévales: définition, critique et exploitation* (pp. 31–49), Actes du Colloque international de Louvain-la-Neuve, 25–7 mai 1981, Louvain-la-Neuve: Institut d'Études Médiévales de l'Université Catholique de Louvain.

——(1985), "Les questions disputées, principalement dans les facultés de théologie," in B. Carlos Bazán, Gérard Fransen, Danielle Jacquart, and John F. Wippel, *Les Questions disputées et les questions quodlibétiques dans les facultés de théologie, de droit et de médecine* (pp. 13–149), Typologie des sources du moyen-âge occidental, fasc. 44–5, directeur L. Genicot, Louvain-la-Neuve: Institut d'Études Médiévales de l'Université Catholique de Louvain.

Ebbesen, Sten (1982), "Ancient scholastic logic as the source of medieval scholastic logic," in Norman Kretzmann, Anthony Kenny, and Jan Pinborg, eds., *The Cambridge History of Later Medieval Philosophy* (pp. 101–27), Cambridge: Cambridge University Press.

Fletcher, J. M. (1984), "The faculty of arts," in J. I. Catto, R. Evans, and T. H. Aston, eds., *The History of the University of Oxford* (pp. 369–99), Oxford: Clarendon Press.

Gregory, Tullio (1988), "The Platonic inheritance," in Peter Dronke, ed., *A History of Twelfth-century Western Philosophy* (pp. 54–80), Cambridge: Cambridge University Press.

Hadot, Pierre (1982), "La préhistoire des genres littéraires philosophiques médiévaux dans l'antiquité," in *Les Genres littéraires dans les sources théologiques et philosophiques médiévales: définition, critique et exploitation* (pp. 1–9), Actes du Colloque international de Louvain-la-Neuve, 25–7 mai 1981, Louvain-la-Neuve: Institut d'Études Médiévales de l'Université Catholique de Louvain.

Lewry, P. O. (1984), "Grammar, logic, and rhetoric: 1220–1320," in J. I. Catto, R. Evans, and T. H. Aston, eds., *The History of the University of Oxford* (pp. 401–33), Oxford: Clarendon Press.

Grabmann, Martin (1909–11), *Die Geschichte der scholastischen Methode*, Fribourg im Breisgau: Herder.

McEvoy, James (1998), "Liberal arts, science, philosophy, theology and wisdom at Oxford, 1200–1250," in Jan A. Aertsen and Andreas Speer, eds., *Was ist Philosophie im Mittelalter?* (pp. 560–70), Akten des X. Internationalen Kongresses für mittelalterliche Philosophie der Société Internationale pour l'Étude de la Philosophie Médiévale 25. bis 30. August 1997 in Erfurt, Berlin and New York: De Gruyter.

Olivi, Peter John (1924), *Quaestiones in secundum librum Sententiarum*, ed. Bernardus Jansen, Quaracchi: Collegium S. Bonaventurae.

Pedersen, Olaf (1997), *The First Universities: Studium Generale and the Origins of University Education in Europe*, Cambridge: Cambridge University Press.

Southern, Richard W. (1984), "From schools to university," in J. I. Catto, R. Evans, and T. H. Aston, eds., *The History of the University of Oxford* (pp. 1–36), Oxford: Clarendon Press.

Verger, Jacques (1973), *Les Universités au moyen âge*, Paris: Presses Universitaires de France.

——(1992), "The first French universities and the institutionalization of learning: faculties, curricula, degrees," in John Van Engen, ed., *Learning Institutionalized: Teaching in the Medieval University*, Notre Dame, IN: University of Notre Dame Press.

Weisheipl, James A. (1964), "Curriculum of the faculty of arts at Oxford in the early fourteenth century," *Mediaeval Studies* 26, pp. 143–85.

——(1966), "Developments in the arts curriculum at Oxford in the early fourteenth century," *Mediaeval Studies* 28, pp. 151–75.

——(1974), "The Parisian faculty of arts in mid-thirteenth century: 1240–1270," *The American Benedictine Review* 25, pp. 200–17.

Wippel, John F. (1982), "The quodlibetal question as a distinctive literary genre," in *Les Genres littéraires dans les sources théologiques et philosophiques médiévales: définition, critique et exploitation* (pp. 67–84), Actes du Colloque international de Louvain-la-Neuve, 25–7 mai 1981, Louvain-la-Neuve: Institut d'Études Médiévales de l'Université Catholique de Louvain.

——(1985), "Quodlibetal questions, chiefly in theological faculties," in B. Carlos Bazán, Gérard Fransen, Danielle Jacquart, and John F. Wippel, *Les Questions disputées et les questions quodlibétiques dans les facultés de théologie, de droit et de médecine*, Typologie des sources du moyen-âge occidental, fasc. 44–5, directeur L. Genicot (pp. 151–222), Louvain-la-Neuve: Institut d'Études Médiévales de l'Université Catholique de Louvain.

——(1998), "Siger of Brabant: what it means to proceed philosophically," in Jan A. Aertsen and Andreas Speer, eds., *Was ist Philosophie im Mittelalter?* (pp. 490–6), Akten des X. Internationalen Kongresses für mittelalterliche Philosophie der Société Internationale pour l'Étude de la Philosophie Médiévale 25. bis 30. August 1997 in Erfurt, Berlin and New York: De Gruyter.

7

The Parisian Condemnations of 1270 and 1277

JOHN F. WIPPEL

On March 7, 1277, Stephen Tempier, the Bishop of Paris, issued a wide-ranging condemnation of 219 propositions, or now apparently 220 in light of recent research (Piché 1999, p. 24). He also excommunicated all who would have dared to defend or support any of these in any way whatsoever, as well as those who would have listened to them, unless they presented themselves to him or to the chancellor of the university within seven days. Even then, they would be subject to proportionate penalties. He singled out for special mention a work on courtly love by Andreas Capellanus (*De amore*) and an unnamed work on geomancy, and also condemned books, rolls, or sheets dealing with necromancy, or containing experiments in fortune-telling or the invocation of demons or incantations and like things opposed to faith and morals (*Chartularium* I, p. 543; Piché 1999, pp. 72–9).

This is the most extensive doctrinal condemnation of the Middle Ages, although by no means the only one. On December 6, 1270 the same Bishop Tempier had already condemned 13 articles. Reference to these may cast some light on the general intellectual climate at the University of Paris at the time. They center on unicity of the intellect in all human beings (1), and the related denial that an individual human being understands (2), rejection of human freedom (3), whether based on determinism by heavenly bodies (4), or by the object desired (9), eternity of the world (5), or of human beings (6), mortality of the human soul (7), a denial that it suffers from fire after death (8), rejection of God's knowledge of individuals (10), or of things other than himself (11), or of his providence (12), or of his power to endow a mortal body with the gift of immortality (13) (*Chartularium* I, pp. 486–7).

In order to understand how such positions could have gained a foothold at the university by 1270, it is important to recall that beginning already in the twelfth century, and continuing throughout the major part of the thirteenth, an intensive translation movement had been underway. This effort concentrated primarily on philosophical and scientific sources originally written in Greek or Arabic. Until this time the Latin-speaking world had been deprived of most of the greatest works of ancient Greek philosophy. Now, within a few decades, all of Aristotle had become available in Latin, along with translations both of classical Greek commentators on Aristotle and Arabic interpreters such as ALKINDI, ALFARABI, AVICENNA, and AVERROES, along with a number of pseudo-Aristotelian works (Dod 1982, pp. 45–79). Since all of these writings were of non-Christian origins, western thinkers and the Church were faced with the challenge of assimilating this mass of new material and of determining how they, as Christians, should react to it (Van Steenberghen 1991, pp. 67–107).

Consequently, not long after 1200, the accepted date for the founding of the University of Paris, varying reactions on the part of theologians and members of the arts faculty can be detected, along with considerable caution on the part of certain members of the hierarchy. In 1210 a synod conducted under Archbishop Peter of Corbeil for the Archdiocese of Sens, which included the Diocese of Paris, prohibited teaching Aristotle's books on natural philosophy at Paris whether in public or in private, along with commentaries on the same. In 1215 the papal legate, Cardinal Robert of Courçon, while reorganizing the program of studies at the recently founded University of Paris, prohibited masters in arts from "reading," i.e., lecturing, on Aristotle's books on natural philosophy along with the *Metaphysics* and *Summae* of the same (probably certain works of Avicenna and perhaps of Alfarabi). The prohibition did not apply to private study of these works, nor did it apply to the theology faculty, where one finds a gradually increasing use of the new philosophical works.

On April 13, 1231, Pope Gregory issued a letter entitled *Parens scientiarum Parisius*, often regarded as the university's Magna Carta, which maintained the official prohibition against "reading" Aristotle's books on natural philosophy, but also indicated that this would remain in effect only until they had been examined and freed from all suspicion of error. But another letter from the pope dated May 10, 1231 suggested to the masters in arts that they would incur no sanction if they violated the prohibition, for it assured them that professors at the university would not be subject to excommunication for a seven year period, a privilege which was renewed again in 1237 for another seven year period (Bianchi 1999, p. 116; *Chartularium* I, pp. 147, 160). And so in the 1240s Roger Bacon lectured as a master of arts at Paris on Aristotle's books on natural philosophy, which means that the prohibition was no longer being observed. In 1252 the statutes for the English nation within the arts faculty required candidates for the licentiate examination to follow lectures on Aristotle's *De anima*, and in 1255 the statutes for the entire faculty of arts included all the known works of Aristotle in its required curriculum. In effect the faculty of arts had now become a philosophy faculty.

As this process unfolded, masters in arts gradually became more conscious of the value of philosophy pursued as an end in itself rather than as a mere preparation for study in a higher faculty, and in the 1260s and 1270s some of them were content to teach philosophy, or what the philosophers had said, without concerning themselves about the implications for Christian religious belief. Thus SIGER OF BRABANT, along with BOETHIUS OF DACIA, a leading representative of a radical Aristotelian movement developing within the arts faculty in the 1260s and 1270s, saw it as his role to determine what the philosophers had held on the points at issue "by seeking the mind of the philosophers rather than the truth since we are proceeding philosophically" (*De anima intellectiva*, c. 7; 1972b, p. 101).

In writings prior to 1270, however, Siger maintains that the human intellect is, according to Aristotle, eternally caused by God, which he considers more probable than AUGUSTINE'S view (*Qu. in librum tertium de anima*, q. 2; 1972b, pp. 5–8). This intellect is united to the bodies of individual human beings only in an accidental way, by its power (q. 7, p. 23). It is "diversified" in individual humans only by means of different "intentions" present in the imaginations of different individuals (q. 9, p. 28). The agent and the possible intellects are simply two powers of one single and separate intellect for the entire human race (q. 15, pp. 58–9). From this doctrine, taken from Averroes, it follows that there is no individual spiritual soul in human beings, and therefore no personal immortality. In a logical treatise dating from this pre-1270 period, Siger affirms the eternity of the human species and, by implication, of the world (*Qu. utrum haec sit vera: homo est animal nullo homine existente*; 1974, pp. 57–9). And in his *Qu. in librum tertium de anima* (q. 11, pp. 32–4; 1972b), he ventures into the theological arena by denying that the separated soul can suffer from corporeal fire.

Views such as these drew considerable critical reaction from theologians. Best known are remarks by BONAVENTURE in his Conferences of 1267 (*Collationes de decem praeceptis*) and of 1268 (*Collationes de donis Spiritus Sancti*). He warns against those who assert that the world is eternal, or that there is only one intellect for all humans, or that mortal beings cannot attain to immortality, or that the will is determined by the motion of heavenly bodies (*Opera omnia* 1882–1902, V; pp. 514, 497). Another Franciscan, William of Baglione, regent master of theology in 1266–7, also expressed concern about some of these views, especially about the unicity of the human intellect (Brady 1970, pp. 35–48). And in 1270 THOMAS AQUINAS directed his *De unitate intellectus contra Averroistas* against the Averroistic doctrine of the unicity of the intellect, aiming it especially at an unnamed contemporary, Siger of Brabant.

As can be seen from the above, four of the articles condemned in 1270 were defended by Siger in his pre-1270 writings: 1, 5, 6, 8. Article 2 ("that it is false to say that this individual human being understands") also follows from Siger's defense of the unicity of the intellect. Other positions condemned by the bishop were probably circulating orally within the arts faculty.

After 1270 there is some modification and development on Siger's part. His *De anima intellectiva* of 1272/3 reveals philosophical uncertainty about the unicity of the intellect, but he professes that it is true according to Christian faith that the human intellect is multiplied in individuals (c. 7; 1972b, pp. 101, 108). And in his recently discovered *Quaestiones in librum de causis* of 1274–6, q. 27, he defends a perfectly orthodox position on this, if not on every issue (1972a, pp. 112–15). In dealing with other sensitive topics after 1270, Siger usually qualifies his discussion of positions opposed to Christian belief by stating that he is presenting these not as his own view, but only according to the mind of the Philosopher (Aristotle) or the philosophers. This same stratagem is also found in writings by other radical Aristotelians of this time.

On the other hand, various theologians and members of the hierarchy continued to be concerned about certain teachings in the arts faculty during the 1270s. Moreover, on April 1, 1272 the majority of the arts faculty approved some statutes that strictly limited their own freedom to deal with theological questions (Bianchi 1999, pp. 165–98; *Chartularium* I, pp. 499–500). And on September 2, 1276, a university-wide decree was issued that prohibited teaching in secret or in private places, with the exception of logic and grammar (*Chartularium* I, p. 539).

In his *Collationes in Hexaemeron* of 1273 Bonaventure sharply criticizes Aristotle and contemporaries who follow him and the Peripatetics into heterodox positions (*Opera omnia*, V; 1882–1902, pp. 360–1; Van Steenberghen 1991, pp. 218–22). GILES OF ROME'S *De plurificatione intellectus possibilis* (ca. 1273–7) is another sign of continuing concern about the unicity of the intellect. Still another indication is an anonymous commentary on the *De anima* (Wippel 1977, p. 185 n. 38), where its unknown author emphatically rejects the claim that an individual human being can be said to understand. And on November 23, 1276, Siger of Brabant, along with his colleagues in arts, Bernier of Nivelles and Gosvin of La Chapelle, were summoned to appear before the Inquisitor of France, Simon du Val, since they were suspected of the crime of heresy. The letter of summons indicates that they were no longer present in the kingdom of France.

On January 18, 1277, Pope John XXI (PETER OF SPAIN) sent a letter to Bishop Tempier, expressing concern over dangerous doctrines about which he had heard. He instructed the bishop to conduct an investigation to determine where and by whom these doctrines were being circulated and to report back as soon as possible. Stephen formed a commission of sixteen theologians, including HENRY OF GHENT. In the relatively short period of three or four weeks, this commission apparently surveyed a large number of suspect writings and drew from them the list of articles that the bishop condemned on March 7 on his own authority.

The lack of any general organizing principle in the original list of articles has often been noted, and the hurried nature of the commission's work may account for this. But the fact that different members may have been asked to investigate different works could also partially explain it, if their results were then loosely assembled in the final listing. Repetitions abound and at times inconsistencies are found in the sense that mutually exclusive propositions are condemned. Shortly after the condemnation, in about 1277–9, an unknown writer reorganized the articles into a version preserved in a medieval *Collectio errorum in Anglia et Parisius condemnatorum*. Early in the twentieth century P. Mandonnet imposed still a third order and numbering (1908, II, pp. 175–91) which has competed with the original enumeration followed both by the *Chartularium* and the recent critical edition by D. Piché. Here both numbers for particular articles will be cited.

Tempier's letter of introduction tells us much about his intent in issuing the condemnation. Repeated reports have come to him from serious and eminent persons animated by zeal for the faith indicating that certain members of the faculty of arts (*studentes in artibus*) have been surpassing the limits of their own faculty. They dare to consider and dispute as if open to debate certain clear and damnable errors contained in the roll or on the sheets attached to his letter. They support these errors by turning to the writings of the "gentiles," and moreover, he laments, they profess themselves unable to respond to what they find in those writings. He accuses them of trying to conceal what they are really saying by holding that these things are true according to philosophy, but not according to Catholic faith, as if there were two contrary truths, and as if the truth of Sacred Scripture were opposed to the truth of the sayings of the accursed gentiles. And so, lest such imprudent speech lead the simple into error, having taken counsel both with doctors of theology and other prudent men, Tempier strictly prohibits such things and totally condemns them, and excommunicates all who presume to teach or defend them in any way whatsoever, or even to listen to them.

In light of recent scholarship, certain points should be made. First, Tempier indicates from the beginning to the end of his introductory letter that he is concerned about doctrinal errors. Hence, although some recent scholarship has tended to develop the juridical (Thijssen 1998, pp. 40–56) or the ethical and political (de Libera 1991, pp. 188–244; Piché 1999, pp. 228–83) aspects of the condemnation, Tempier's doctrinal concerns still remain fundamental. Second, Tempier refers to those "studying in arts" as exceeding the limits of their own faculty. Does this mean that none of the errors in question was drawn from the writings of others, for instance, from theologians such as Aquinas? This will be discussed below. Third, Tempier accuses them of trying to avoid responsibility for what they are teaching by holding that these conclusions are true according to philosophy, but not according to faith. Nevertheless no such "double-truth" theory has been found in the writings of any of the arts masters. Finally, a number of articles are included that would be regarded as perfectly compatible with Catholic belief today, and were, in fact, so regarded by other theologians of Tempier's time. Hence a certain doctrinal tendentiousness, whether Augustinian or neo-Augustinian, evidently influenced the censors in these cases.

Since the articles are too numerous to be considered individually, some appreciation of their wide-ranging content may be gained by considering them under some broad categories. Several highly exalt the nature of philosophy, for instance: 40 (*Chartularium*/Piché), 1 (Mandonnet): "That there is no more excellent state than to give oneself to philosophy;" 154/2: "That the wise men of the world are the philosophers alone"; 145/6: "That there is no question that can be disputed by reason that the philosopher should not dispute and determine, because arguments are taken from things. But it belongs to philosophy according to its parts to consider all things." While the first of these seems to envision Boethius of Dacia's *De summo bono* (Boethius 1976, p. 374: 137–8), the other two both appear to be aimed at his *De aeternitate mundi*. However, art. 154/2 misrepresents his thought. While he does refer to the philosophers as those who "were and are the wise men of the world" (Boethius 1976, p. 365: 828–32), he does not say that they alone are. Art. 24/7 (as revised by Piché) states: "That all the sciences are superfluous with the exception of the philosophical disciplines and that they [the other sciences] are not necessary except because of human custom."

Certain propositions have to do with our ability to know God, and two of these would be cited by GODFREY OF FONTAINES in *Quodlibet* XII, q. 5 (Godfrey 1932, p. 101) as mutually excluding one another: 36/9: "That we can know God in this mortal life by his essence"; 215/10: "That concerning God only that he is or his existence can be known." A number have to do with God's knowledge of other things. Art. 3/13 maintains "that God does not know things other than himself." According to art. 56/14, God cannot know contingent things immediately but only by means of another particular and proximate cause. Art. 42/15 argues against God's knowledge of future contingents.

Still others would restrict God's power. According to 190/16, the "first cause is the most remote cause of all things." This is rejected as an error if it is understood by abstraction by precision, i.e., in such fashion as to exclude its being the most proximate cause. According to 147/17, "What is impossible in the absolute sense cannot be done by God or by any agent." This seemingly unobjectionable claim is rejected as an error if it is taken as referring to what is impossible by nature. The infinity of divine power is restricted to God's producing an infinitely enduring motion according to 29/26, and by 62/25, which explicitly excludes his power to produce something from nothing, i.e., to create. According to 53/20, God necessarily produces whatever proceeds from him immediately. According to 44/28 a multiplicity of effects cannot come from one first agent, thereby echoing the Neoplatonic axiom that from one only one thing can proceed immediately. According to 34/27, the first cause cannot produce more than one world. The condemnation of this article has been singled out along with 49/66 ("that God could not move the heaven in a straight line, for the reason that he would then produce a vacuum") as having played a considerable role in the development of modern science by rejecting two central tenets of Aristotelian physics (P. Duhem), but this claim has been sharply contested (Murdoch 1991).

The eternity of separate substances is asserted or at least implied by a number of articles (58/34, 28/35 (by implication), 70/38, 5/39, 80/40, 72/41, 71/44, 83/45). According to arts. 96/42 and 81/43, God cannot multiply individuals within the same species without matter, and cannot, therefore, produce several intelligences within the same species. The last two positions were defended by Thomas Aquinas, as well as by Siger of Brabant and Boethius of Dacia (Wippel 1995, pp. 243–8).

Art. 218/53 states that an intelligence or an angel or a separated soul is not in a place. But, as Godfrey of Fontaines would point out, 219/54 and 204/55 seem incompatible with one another; for in commenting on the first the censors state that separate substances are not in place by reason of their substance; but they condemn the second, which states that they are in place by operating therein. How, then, is one to account for their presence in place? (Godfrey 1932, pp. 101–2). Both articles 218 and 204 seem to be aimed at views held both by Aquinas and by certain masters in arts (Wippel 1995, pp. 248–54).

Other articles attribute a creative or else some intermediary causal efficacy to separate intelligences and thereby compromise immediate divine creative and causal agency (73/56,

30/58, 84/57). God's power to produce directly the different effects of second causes is rejected by art. 69/63, as is his capacity to produce directly different effects on earth (43/68).

Certain articles assign a soul to heavenly bodies (95/31, 94/32, both of which also defend their eternity, and 92/73). Art. 91/80 states that the Philosopher's (Aristotle) argumentation to prove that the motion of the heaven is eternal is not sophistical, and that it is surprising that profound men do not see this. A number defend the eternity of the world, for instance, 99/83, 98/84, 87/85, 4/87, 205/88, 101/91. According to art. 90/191, the natural philosopher must deny absolutely that the world began to be because he bases himself on natural causes and arguments. But the believer can deny the eternity of the world because he bases himself on supernatural causes. Evidently this criticism was aiming at Boethius of Dacia's *De aeternitate mundi*, although the censors have distorted his position by inserting the term 'absolutely' in the description of the position. Art. 107/112 defends the eternity of the elements, and 6/92 asserts a theory of cyclical recurrence of events within the universe.

According to 206/106 one attributes health, sickness, life and death to the position of the stars and the glance of fortune. Versions of this astral determinism are also implied by 142/103 and 143/104. Art. 46/108 restricts God's efficient causality to that which exists potentially in matter. According to art. 191/110 forms are not divided except by reason of matter. This is rejected as an error unless it is restricted to forms educed from the potency of matter.

A considerable number deal with the unicity of the intellect, either of the agent intellect (which in itself is not necessarily opposed to faith), or of the possible intellect, or of both (32/117, 123/118, 121/126). Art. 118/140 states that the agent intellect is not united with our possible intellect, and that the possible intellect is not united with us substantially. Substantial union of a spiritual human soul with the body is rejected by 111/121, and 13/122. Eternity of the substance of the soul and of the agent and possible intellect is defended in 109/129, as well as of the human intellect (31/130), and of the human species (137/139).

A number of the articles appear to restrict human freedom whether by asserting that the will is moved by heavenly bodies (133/153, 162/164, 132/155, 161/156), or by submitting the will to appetite (164/158, 134/159, 159/164). Others were apparently condemned because in the eyes of the censors they threatened freedom by submitting the will to the intellect or to the object as presented to the will by the intellect (208/157, 173/162, 163/163, 158/165, 130/166). Some of these articles seem to be aimed at positions defended in a non-deterministic way not only by Siger or other Radical Aristotelians, but also by Aquinas (Wippel 1995, pp. 255–61).

A fair number, approximately 10 percent, deal with moral matters. For instance, art. 144/170 states that every good possible to man consists in the intellectual virtues, whereas 151/171 holds that one who is well ordered in intellect and affections by the intellectual and moral virtues discussed in Aristotle's *Ethics* is sufficiently disposed for eternal happiness. But 176/172 restricts happiness to this life, and 15/174 states that after death one loses every good. According to 20/179 natural law forbids killing irrational animals as well as rational, though not as strongly. According to 177/200 no other virtues are possible except the acquired and the innate, thereby eliminating any place for supernatural or infused virtues. Art. 155/204 indicates that one should not be concerned about burying the dead. Art. 180/202 asserts that one should not pray. Six attack Christian sexual morality (183/205, 166/206, 172/207, 168/208, 181/209, 169/210), whereas 211/171 denies that humility is a virtue if it is taken in the sense of depreciating oneself or what one has. Art. 170/212 states that one who lacks the goods of fortune cannot act well in moral matters.

Others touch on life after death. Art. 178/213 states that death is the end of all terrifying things. This is rejected as an error if it excludes the terror of hell. Art. 25/214 denies that God can give perpetual existence to something changeable and corruptible, thereby rejecting belief in resurrection of the body, while 17/215 opposes resurrection of numerically the same body. Art. 18/216 states that a philosopher must not grant the resurrection because it cannot be investigated by reason. The last three articles were derived by the censors from Boethius' *De aeternitate mundi*, in a way to make them merit condemnation, although he did not defend them in an absolute sense, but only insofar as they follow from the principles of natural philosophy. Art. 23/217 states that it is irrational to say that God gives happiness to one but not to another. And art. 19/219 denies that the separated soul suffers in any way from fire.

Finally, a number of articles attack the Christian religion directly, for instance by asserting that the Christian "Law" impedes one from learning (175/180), or that there are fables and falsities in the Christian Law, or by rejecting the doctrine of the Trinity (1/185) or the generation of the Son from the Father in the Trinity (2/186), or the doctrine of creation even though it must be believed (184/189), or creation of something from nothing or that things began to be (185/188). Four articles are aimed at belief in the Eucharist by stating that an accident in general, or quantity in particular, cannot be made to exist without a subject (138/199, 139/198, 140/196, 141/197).

R. Hissette has attempted to find the sources targeted by Tempier for each article by concentrating on edited writings of members of the arts faculty. He restricted himself to these because of the bishop's reference to them in the Introduction. For 151 articles Hissette was able to assign a source as plausible or probable or certain. But in 99 of these cases he found that the article did not accurately reflect the thought of the master in question. In 16 such cases the censors simply misinterpreted the thought of the master concerned. In 9 instances they hardened it and pushed its meaning. But in the majority of cases (64) they stated without any qualifications positions that the original masters had presented only in a qualified sense, for instance, when speaking only as a natural philosopher or as expressing the mind of the philosophers or of Aristotle, but not as reflecting their personal positions (Hissette 1977, pp. 314–17).

Moreover, the lack of success in identifying even likely sources for the other articles has led some scholars to assign a considerable degree of creativity to Tempier and his commission. Especially with respect to the articles dealing with ethical matters and sexual morality, A. de Libera has proposed that no one in fact defended these particular articles prior to the condemnation of March 7, 1277, but that in inventing them, presumably with the intention of preventing them from appearing, the censors unwittingly prompted others to develop and defend them thereafter (de Libera 1991, pp. 202–40). At this stage of research, however, some caution is advisable. It seems premature to conclude that a written source will not be found for other articles, perhaps for many, simply because an edited source has not yet been discovered.

In some instances the prohibited positions may be found both in the writings of certain masters of arts and of certain theologians, especially Thomas Aquinas. Hissette has argued that while Aquinas may have been indirectly implicated because he happened to teach the same thing as certain arts masters, he was not directly targeted. Others, this writer included, regard this approach as too restrictive. Given the fact that Aquinas's views were well known to members of the commission, especially to Henry of Ghent, it seems unlikely that they

71

could have condemned a position they knew Aquinas had defended and yet not have intended to condemn *his* position directly (Hissette 1977, *passim*; 1997, pp. 3–31; Wippel 1995).

More remains to be written about the effects of the condemnation, but a considerable amount of information has recently been assembled (Aertsen et al. 2000, *passim*; Bianchi 1999, pp. 203–30; Mahoney 2000, pp. 902–30). It was clearly taken quite seriously by members of the theology faculty at Paris for some time to come, although much less frequent reference is made to it by members of the arts faculty. Franciscan thinkers would gladly appeal to it in order to support their attacks on certain positions of Aquinas, and Dominicans would resort to various strategies in defending him. About twenty years after the event Godfrey of Fontaines would sharply criticize it and argue that many of the articles contained therein needed to be corrected, especially those seemingly taken from Aquinas (Godfrey 1932, pp. 100–4). On February 14, 1325, the Bishop of Paris, Stephen of Bourret, would judge it necessary to suspend the condemnation insofar as it touched on or was asserted to touch on the teachings of Aquinas (who had been canonized in 1323).

The extent to which its jurisdiction extended outside the Diocese of Paris was debated for decades, with some wanting to restrict its legal force to that diocese, and others wishing to extend it beyond those regions even across the Channel to England. It is clear that its moral influence did extend very widely, not only because of the prestige of the theology faculty at Paris, but also because the Parisian articles would be incorporated into the statutes of a number of universities founded after the thirteenth century.

Bibliography

Aertsen, J., Emery, K., and Speer, A., eds. (2000), *Nach der Verurteilung von 1277. Philosophie und Theologie an der Universität von Paris im letzten Viertel des 13. Jahrhunderts. Studien und Texte*, Miscellanea mediaevalia 28, Berlin and New York: De Gruyter.

Bianchi, L. (1999), *Censure et liberté intellectuelle à l'université de Paris (XIIIe–XIVe siècles)*, Paris: Les Belles Lettres.

Boethius of Dacia (1976), *Opuscula. De aeternitate mundi, De summo bono, De somniis*, in *Opera VI. 2*, ed. N. G. Green-Pedersen, Copenhagen: Gad.

Bonaventure (1882–1902), *Opera omnia*, Quaracchi: Collegium S. Bonaventurae.

Brady, I. (1970), "Background to the condemnation of 1270: Master William of Baglione, O.F.M.," *Franciscan Studies* 30, pp. 5–48.

Chartularium Universitatis Parisiensis, vol. 1 (1889), ed. H. Denifle and É. Châtelain, Paris: Delalain.

de Libera, A. (1991), *Penser au moyen âge*, Paris: Éditions du Seuil.

Dod, B. B. (1982), "Aristoteles latinus," in N. Kretzmann, A. Kenny, and J. Pinborg, eds., *The Cambridge History of Later Medieval Philosophy* (pp. 45–79), Cambridge: Cambridge University Press.

Godfrey of Fontaines (1932), *Les Quodlibets onze-quatorze de Godefroid de Fontaines*, ed. J. Hoffmans, in *Les Philosophes belges*, vol. 5, Louvain: Éditions de l'Institut Supérieur de Philosophie.

Hissette, R. (1977), *Enquête sur les 219 articles condamnés à Paris le 7 mars 1277*, Paris and Louvain: Publications Universitaires.

——(1997), "L'implication de Thomas d'Aquin dans les censures parisiennes de 1277," *Recherches de Théologie et Philosophie Médiévales* 64, pp. 3–31.

Mahoney, E. P. (2000), "Reverberations of the condemnation of 1277 in later medieval and renaissance philosophy," in J. Aertsen, K. Emery, and A. Speer, eds., *Nach der Verurteilung von 1277*, Miscellanea mediaevalia 28 (pp. 902–30), Berlin and New York: De Gruyter.

Mandonnet, P. (1908, 1911), *Siger de Brabant et l'averroïsme latin au XIIIe siècle*, 2nd edn., 2 vols., Louvain: Institut Supérieur de Philosophie de l'Université.

Murdoch, J. (1991), "Pierre Duhem and the history of late medieval philosophy and science in the Latin west," in R. Imbach and A. Maierù, eds., *Gli studi di filosofia medievale fra otto et novecento*, Rome: Edizioni di Storia e Letteratura.

Piché, D. (1999), *La Condamnation parisienne de 1277: texte latin, traduction, introduction et commentaire*, with C. Lafleur, Paris: J. Vrin.

Siger of Brabant (1972a), *Les quaestiones super librum de causis de Siger de Brabant*, ed. A. Marlasca, Louvain: Publications Universitaires.

——(1972b), *Quaestiones in tertium de anima, De anima intellectiva, De aeternitate mundi*, ed. B. Bazán, Louvain: Publications Universitaires.

——(1974), *Écrits de logique, de morale et de physique*, ed. B. Bazán, Louvain: Publications Universitaires.

Thijssen, J. M. M. H. (1998), *Censure and Heresy at the University of Paris 1200–1400*, Philadelphia: University of Pennsylvania Press.

Van Steenberghen, F. (1991), *La Philosophie au XIIIe siècle*, 2nd edn., Louvain and Paris: Peeters.

Wippel, J. F. (1977), "The condemnations of 1270 and 1277 at Paris," *Journal of Medieval and Renaissance Studies* 7, pp. 169–201.

——(1995), "Thomas Aquinas and the condemnation of 1277," *Modern Schoolman* 72, pp. 233–72.

Further reading

Flasch, K. (1989), *Aufklärung im Mittelalter? Die Verurteilung von 1277*, Mainz: Dietrich'sche Verlagsbuchhandlung.

73

PART II

THE AUTHORS

1

Adam of Wodeham

REGA WOOD

Adam de Wodeham (d. 1358) was a philosopher theologian at Oxford University, who earlier had taught at Franciscan seminaries in London and Norwich. A theologian in the Franciscan tradition, Wodeham emphasized the contingency of salvation and the dependence of the created world on God. He was a subtle and precise thinker deeply concerned with logic and semantics.

Wodeham was proud of his debts to the Franciscan doctor, JOHN DUNS SCOTUS, and to the great Franciscan logician, WILLIAM OF OCKHAM. Wodeham respected Scotus enough to study his works carefully in the original manuscripts and to accept his views in doubtful cases. He prepared an abbreviation of Ockham's theology lectures, wrote an introduction to his lectures on logic, and defended his views against attack.

Wodeham was a brilliant interpreter of Ockham and Scotus, and his allegiance to their views was responsible in part for their continued influence. More subtle than Ockham, he nonetheless trenchantly defended Ockham's views. More preoccupied with logical questions than Scotus, Wodeham was deeply impressed by the rigor of Scotus's arguments.

WALTER CHATTON and PETER AURIOL were two other Franciscan authors who influenced Wodeham. Though he considered Chatton's 1321–3 attacks on Ockham ignorant and malicious, Wodeham was influenced by Chatton on a variety of questions – about the subject of scientific or demonstrative knowledge, for example. Auriol strongly influenced Wodeham's views on certainty.

The Norwich Lectures

Wodeham's lectures on theology, loosely based on PETER LOMBARD's *Sentences*, were his most important works. Delivered first, his *London Lectures* have not survived, but he reused parts of them when he lectured at Norwich. The *Norwich Lectures*, delivered between 1329 and 1332, are cited and published as his second lectures (*Lectura secunda*). Both these works were intended for a Franciscan audience. Among contemporary thinkers, the *Norwich Lectures* consider almost exclusively Franciscan authors. Published in 1990, these *Lectures* are now the most frequently cited of Wodeham's works.

Epistemology

Unlike his teacher, William of Ockham, Wodeham considers skepticism a serious problem. For Ockham, intuitive cognition is reliable by definition. By means of intuitive cognition we know "that a thing exists when it does." When a thing does not exist, we know by intuitive cognition that it does not exist (*OTh* V, p. 256). A problem arises from the second part of Ockham's definition, his uncontroversial claim that it is logically possible that we should have intuitive cognition of something nonexistent. Our mental states, including our acts of cognition, are accidents, which for medieval philosophers exist independently of their objective contents. So it is at least logically possible that something other than the object of an act of cognition could cause that cognition.

For Ockham, intuition produces knowledge; for Wodeham, it inclines us to belief. Hence, unlike Ockham, Wodeham holds that whether the object of intuition exists or not, it will always incline us to believe that its object exists. Initially, Ockham distinguished between naturally and supernaturally produced intuitive cognition.

Subsequently, Peter Auriol forced his contemporaries to consider the possibility of naturally produced cognition of nonexistents, inferring from a series of illusory cognitions that the objects of cognition are apparent beings, not things themselves. Ockham rejected apparent beings and all other intermediates as objects of cognition. He maintained that the objects of sense perception are things themselves. Sensation itself is never illusory, though the judgments based on sensory perception can be mistaken. Ockham held, for example, that our perception of motion when we are moving past trees may be equivalent to our sensation when trees move past a stationary object (*OTh* 4, pp. 243–50). Because there are situations in which the same sensation can be produced in more than one way, the judgments we base on sensation can be mistaken. When our judgments are wrong, our sensations do not produce intuitive cognition. For Ockham, then, 'cognizing' is a success verb, so intuitive cognition of nonexistents leads to our knowing that its objects do not exist. By contrast, for Wodeham, intuitive cognition is a mental state that always inclines to judgment of existence.

In one sense, there is little disagreement. Both philosophers believed that our sensations do sometimes incline us to judge falsely, and both refer to false beliefs rather than admitting false intuitive of false cognition, as HERVAEUS NATALIS did. But Wodeham was, and Ockham was not, deeply concerned with the question of how and when we can know that our judgments are correct.

This was new, since neither Ockham nor Auriol believed that what was at issue in their debate was skepticism or the problem of certainty. Responding to their dispute, Wodeham was among the first to recognize that skeptical consequences could be drawn from Auriol's lists of sensory illusions. Wodeham defined three degrees of certainty. The greatest degree that compels the intellect is not possible regarding contingent propositions, since the intellect is aware of the possibility of error and deception. The least degree of certainty is compatible with error; I may be in some degree certain of a mistaken proposition, as for example, when I judge that a straight stick half submerged in water is bent.

Despite his preoccupation with the possible natural and supernatural obstructions in the perceptual process and the concessions he made to them, Wodeham was a reliabilist, who believed that cognition is reliably though not infallibly caused by its object. His basic reply to the sensory illusions adduced by Auriol was that reason and experience allow us to recognize illusions and not to be systematically misled by them. Illusions will continue to incline us to make false judgments, but we can correct our judgments by reference to reason and experience (1990, *L. sec.* I: pp. 163–79).

Psychology

Wodeham denied the distinction between the sensitive and intellective souls; a single soul suffices to explain all the cognitive acts we experience. On this merely philosophical issue,

Wodeham departed from the traditional Franciscan view that there is a plurality of substantial forms in man. He opposed both Scotus (formally distinct souls) and Ockham (really distinct souls). Ockham held that sensory and intellective souls must be distinct since contraries could not coexist in the same subject. Wodeham replied that sensory inclination and intellectual appetite regarding the same external object were only virtually, not formally, contraries. According to Wodeham, the same soul apprehends sensible particulars and universals; when these acts are partially caused by external objects, they are sensations; when they abstract from singulars, they are intellections (1990, *L. sec.* I: pp. 9–33).

Wodeham's reductionism also shows itself in his discussion of fruition, the enjoyment humans experience in contemplating God in the next life. Wodeham holds that all appetitive acts are cognitive acts, since we cannot experience an object without apprehending it. But though volition cannot be separated from apprehension, cognition does not necessitate volition. Like Ockham, Wodeham holds that clear knowledge of God without enjoyment is possible at least initially. Conversely, loving God necessarily includes the implied judgment that God is lovable; this leads Wodeham to ask whether acts of volition can be described as true or false. Wodeham answers in the affirmative; amusingly, he holds that rejoicing about being a Franciscan is a correct act as well as an act of enjoyment (1990, *L. sec.* I: pp. 253–85).

Semantics and ontology

Wodeham believed that external language presupposes an internal or mental language. Sentences, both of external and of mental language, are composed of terms. Terms of mental language are concepts, and concepts are acts of cognition by which things are apprehended and which signify naturally those very same things. For example, if she has come into contact, via the senses, with at least one lion, a person will normally have the general concept of "lion." This is a concept by which she apprehends lions, and not things of any other sort, a concept which, accordingly, naturally signifies lions. Terms of external language, by contrast, are significant only by conventional association with concepts; they signify whatever the concept to which they are associated signifies.

Terms, then, signify things. Aside from God, however, there are, according to Wodeham, no "things" other than individual substances (such as lions) and individual accidents inhering in substances (such as whitenesses which, by inhering in substances, make them white). Accordingly, apart from the transcendental terms, such as 'being', which include God among the things they signify, terms of external and of mental language signify individual substances and/or accidents.

A term, however, not only signifies (*significat*), but, if it is used in a sentence, also refers (*supponit*). In this respect two kinds of terms, both of external and of mental language, can be distinguished: those which can refer to all the things they signify and those which can refer only to some of the things they signify (1990, *L. sec*, III: p. 316). The term 'lion', for example, can refer to all its significates, i.e. to all actual or possible lions. By contrast, the term 'white' can refer only to white substances, although it also signifies the whitenesses inhering in them. Reference to whitenesses is of course possible, but by the term 'whiteness', not by the term 'white'. Like the term 'lion', the term 'whiteness' is a term which can refer to all the things it signifies, i.e. to all actual or possible whitenesses.

Sentences, although they do not refer, do signify, both sentences of external and of internal, mental language. But they do not signify "things" in the proper sense. Instead of things, a sentence signifies a state of affairs or, as Wodeham says, a "being the case" or a "not being the case" (1990, *L. sec.* I: p. 193). Because a state of affairs can be signified only proposi-tionally, it can also be called a "complexly signifiable." States of affairs cannot be referred to by terms properly so-called, that is by terms prior to sentences; they can, nevertheless, be referred to, namely by nominalizations of sentences. 'That a human is an animal', for example, can refer to the state of affairs signified by the sentence 'A human is an animal' (1990, *L. sec.* I: p. 194). Because they can be referred to ("supposited for"), complexly sig-nifiables belong to the ontology (Karger 1995).

Wodeham found he needed to posit states of affairs, and thereby to enlarge a strictly nom-inalist ontology, in order to provide acts of knowledge, and more generally acts of belief, with appropriate objects. Mental sentences, which are mental accidents, cannot fulfill that function, he pointed out. Although we cannot entertain a belief without forming the mental proposition that expresses the content of that belief, the object we then assent to is not the mental proposition itself, but its content, i.e. the state of affairs it expresses (1990, *L. sec.* I: p. 192).

Like his views on certainty, Wodeham developed his views on the significate of sentences in the course of defending Ockham's position. His position can be seen as a compromise between Chatton and Ockham on the question of what is the object of scientific knowledge. Are the objects of our assent external objects in the real world (Chatton's *res*) or proposi-tions (Ockham's *complexa*)? Wodeham rejects both positions.

Though the *complexe significabile* has being, i.e. ontological status, Wodeham prefers not to emphasize that consequence of his views. Instead, he emphasizes that it is neither some-thing in the external world nor a mental object. Since it is neither a substance nor an acci-dent, it does not belong to an Aristotelian category. It is not something, but neither is it nothing. Indeed, the question 'What is it?' is ill-formed. It makes no more sense than the question 'Is a people a man or a non-man?'. When we assent to a *complexe significabile*, we are not assenting to some thing, but rather we affirm that something is the case (1990, *L. sec.* I: pp. 180–208; Nuchelmans 1980, pp. 173–85).

Wodeham's attempt not to focus the discussion on the ontological status of the *complexe significabile* was unsuccessful. Those who subsequently employed the notion attracted criti-cism in their attempt to answer the question: What is its being? This debate somewhat resembles the modern controversy about whether propositions exist. NICHOLAS OF AUTRE-COURT takes a negative stance about the being of the *complexe significabile*; he holds that it has none. What we complexly signify when we say, 'God and creatures are distinguished' is not some thing, but nothing. GREGORY OF RIMINI, by contrast, describes two senses in which the *complexe significabile* is a thing. Here Rimini was following Wodeham's later Oxford dis-cussion where he allows a sense in which the *complexe significabile* is something, that is, an object of knowledge.

JOHN BURIDAN considered it unnecessary to posit anything complexly signifiable. Where Wodeham says that the *complexe significabile* is not something and not nothing, Buridan says that it is everything or nothing. Everything, if complexly signifiables are the adverbial ref-erents of sentences or nominalizations, for everything in the world is a complexly signifi-able, since we can state propositions that refer complexly even to simple objects such as God. Nothing, if they are supposed to be part of the natural order, since *complexe significa-biles* are neither substances nor accidents. More important, we need not posit them, since we can explain everything without them. Buridan's criticisms were repeated by MARSILIUS OF INGHEN and subsequently by PIERRE D'AILLY in his attack on Gregory of Rimini.

As Jack Zupko has pointed out, the debate about the *complexe significabile* did not stop with Buridan. Following Rimini, Hugolino of Orvieto held that the object of science was the total significate of the conclusion. A *complexe significabile* is a thing in the sense that it is signifiable truly, though it is not an existing essence or entity. For ALBERT OF SAXONY, the object of science is the conclusion as a sign of the complex act of knowing. So we may conclude that Wodeham was at least successful in drawing attention to the problems involved in identifying the object of science either with the external referents of terms or with propositions.

Metaphysics

Though he opposed Ockham's view that the object of scientific knowledge could be a proposition, Wodeham agreed with Ockham that universals are mental acts (1990, *L. sec.* I: p. 21). Moreover, he denied the existence of intellective species, prior or posterior to intellective acts (1990, *L. sec.* III: pp. 4–34). Wodeham argued that universals were subjectively present to the mind as acts. Their contents were single external things themselves, indistinctly and confusedly apprehended (ibid., p. 31), or as he once puts it "infinitely many things immediately and indistinctly conceived in a single act" (ibid., p. 34). Though he considered Chatton's arguments against Ockham's *fictum* theory of intellection unconvincing, he himself denied *ficta*. He refused to posit intermediates in the perceptual process.

Nonetheless, Wodeham does not entirely deny sensible species. He accepts the medieval optical theory and hence posits species in the medium, in the air through which we see things, for example (1990, *L. sec.* III: pp. 106–8). He also believes it necessary to posit internal species in order to explain certain illusions and delusions (1990, *L. sec.* I: pp. 75, 80–1), but he holds that they are the result from dysfunctional, injured senses – our eyes, for example, when we are subjected to very bright light (1990, *L. sec.* II: p. 226). Such species are not prior in the perceptual process, but posterior to it (1990, *L. sec.* III: p. 287).

Wodeham's views on universals were stated in questions entitled, "Whether we can know God," and "Whether the concept by which we know God is a common notion." This is because we cannot know God directly, but only in common notions such as essence or entity (1990, *L. sec.* III: pp. 34–5). Wodeham affirmed that these abstract concepts could be predicated univocally of God and creatures (1990, *L. sec.* II: pp. 63–5).

Turning to proofs for God's existence, Wodeham's analyzes fourteenth-century Franciscan theories of causality. He argues that Ockham was right to reject Scotus's inference: "Since the universe of essentially ordered effects is caused, the universe must be caused." Focusing on the logic of infinity, Wodeham rejects Chatton's defense of Scotus. Chatton mistakenly infers categorematic conclusions from premises that are true only if interpreted syncategorematically (see Adams 1993; 1990, *L. sec.* II: pp. 117–21). Wodeham holds that God's existence is not known to us in this life per se, but can be shown discursively (ibid., pp. 194–5)

The Oxford Lectures

Wodeham's last lectures on Lombard's *Sentences*, presented to an Oxford audience in about 1332, were his most influential work, though they are seldom studied today. They discuss the views of Wodeham's Oxford contemporaries including WILLIAM CRATHORN, Roger Gosford, ROBERT HOLCOTT, and William Skelton. They also considered such secular authors as WALTER BURLEY, RICHARD CAMPSALL, RICHARD FITZRALPH, and RICHARD KILVINGTON.

Unfortunately the *Oxford Lectures* have never been published. In 1512 John Major chose to print Henry Totting von Oyta's abbreviation of the Oxford lectures, rather than the work itself. The Major edition is generally reliable, but a bit difficult to read, and consequently seldom cited today. An admirable exception to this unfortunate neglect of the Oxford lectures is the work of Hester Gelber, who analyzed Wodeham's trinitarian logic on the basis of this work.

Logic

A thoroughgoing terminist logician, Wodeham sometimes settles theological questions by discussing logic. For example, though God's existence is not self-evident to us in this life, when the blessed understand propositions that signify God's existence, their knowledge is per se. What is more, the blessed can demonstrate the articles of faith we believe. This is because when we formulate propositions about the existence of the divine essence, we can know the terms of those propositions only by abstractive cognition; by contrast, the blessed seeing God have intuitive cognition of the terms.

Wodeham and Chatton accept Ockham's claim that demonstrative knowledge is possible only for conclusions that can be doubted and that follow from self-evident premises. But Chatton denies that the blessed can demonstrate the articles of faith, since for them the existence of God is indubitable. Ockham defends himself, saying that meeting the requirement for dubitability requires only that someone be able to doubt a conclusion (*OTh* 2, p. 441). Chatton is unimpressed, the blessed do not entertain our conclusions, but only their own, which are indubitable. Hence, they cannot prove the propositions we believe. Wodeham shows that Chatton is mistaken, since he accepted that the blessed know that our beliefs are correct. But to do that, they must be able to entertain them as formulated in the terms available to us (1990, *L. sec.* II: pp. 9–10: Lenz 1998). Here, as elsewhere, Wodeham not only brilliantly interprets Ockham, but states his position more compellingly. As Lenz puts it, he catches the logical error made by Chatton.

Wodeham relies on theories of predication in dealing with problems of trinitarian theology, which appears to violate the Aristotelian principle of non-contradiction. Thus, if 'The Father is not the Spirit' and 'The Father is the deity', then 'The deity is not the Spirit' seems to follow. Dealing with this problem, Wodeham refused to provide special qualifications of logic for this problem; that approach is deservedly derided by non-Christians. Wodeham even rejects the solutions of Ockham and Scotus. Wodeham formulates instead a distinction between identic and inherent (denominative) predication. In denominative predication subject and predicate have the same supposition; in identic predication the predicate supposits more broadly than the subject. Thus 'The Father is the deity', but 'The deity is not the Father'. Father and Spirit are really identical – that is the same as the deity. But, as Gelber points out, Father and Son are also distinct, and here Wodeham offers a new sense of what it means to be distinct (see Gelber 1974).

Wodeham's discussion of the distinction between abstract and concrete predication was based on, but differed from, Ockham's. He aimed to avoid negation in defining concrete predication. Thus for Wodeham the verbal (*quid-nominis*) definition of the term *albus* is 'having whiteness' not 'a body having whiteness'. Not including the bearer in definitions of concrete terms avoids nonsense-sentences such as 'Plato is a body having whiteness body' which would otherwise result from successive substitutions of the definition of 'white' in the sentence 'Plato is white' (see 1990, *L. sec.* II: p. 244).

Paul Spade has pointed out that Wodeham's denial that the bearer is predicated when we speak of concrete objects resembles Anselm's distinction between *per se* and *per aliud* predication. Reference is signification only in a secondary sense. What we think of when we hear a term are not necessarily the objects to which it refers (its *supposita* or *appellata*). Abstract and concrete terms have the same *per se* signification; and in the case of substances, supposition and signification coincide. Thus 'man' and 'humanity' both signify and sup-posit for 'a substance composed of body and soul'. 'Man is a humanity' is false only in the case of Christ who has both a divine and a human nature; his person cannot, therefore, be identified with his humanity.

Ethics

Wodeham agrees with Ockham that the will is the sole locus of imputability. External acts make no contribution to the goodness or badness of an act. Unlike Ockham, Wodeham provides a detailed discussion of a series of apparent counterexamples that suggest that outcomes, and not just intentions, must be considered when evaluating the moral worth of our actions.

Tractatus de indivisibilibus, *Quaestio de divisione et compositione continui*

Between 1322 and 1331, Wodeham wrote two works on the continuum, a brief question fol-lowed by a longer treatise. The *Question*'s nine arguments against indivisibilism reappear in the first of twelve principal arguments against medieval atomists stated in the first question of the *Treatise*. On one major point, Wodeham changed his mind. In the *Question*, he held that all infinities as such were equal, the traditional view. By contrast, the fifth question of the *Treatise* is a sustained argument for the claim that one infinity can be greater than another, a rare and controversial position among medieval philosophers.

Natural philosophy

An anti-indivisibilist, Wodeham repeatedly treated the logic of infinity and infinitesimal change. Wodeham presents twelve arguments against medieval atomism or indivisibilism (1988, *T. ind.* q. 1). Wodeham held that the composition of the continuum from atoms was impossible, since indivisibles cannot touch, as Aristotle established. He holds that continua could be "infinitely divided" only in a syncategorematic sense, in which divisions are pro-gressively actualized. Understood syncategorematically, the continuum can be infinitely divided; the division of the continuum does not halt at minimal parts. The continuum cannot, however, be infinitely divided in the categorematic sense, in which the divided parts are perfectly actualized.

Despite holding that the continuum can be infinitely divided only potentially, Wodeham agrees with Ockham that the infinity of parts in a continuum exists not just potentially but actually. Acceptance of this claim led Wodeham to argue for the possibility of unequal infini-ties (1988, *T. ind.* q. 5).

Wodeham bases further arguments against indivisibilism on an analysis of the compound and divided sense. Only in a divided sense can the continuum be divided; a continuous line, for example, can be divided into line segments, but once it is divided it is no longer a continuum. Strictly speaking it is not the continuum that is divided, but its parts. Norman Kretzmann described Wodeham's position as anti-Aristotelian indivisibilism, a characterization that was successfully challenged by G. Sinkler (see Kretzmann 1984; 1988, *T. ind.* q. 4).

A conceptualist, like Ockham, Wodeham believes that limits of all kinds – points, lines, surface, temporal instants, and instants of change – have no independent ontological status; 'point' is a non-referring term. On this subject, Wodeham claims not to be interpreting Ockham, but to have stated the position himself first. "Almost all these arguments were yours before Ockham would have written anything about indivisibles," he says (1988, *T. ind.*, p. 132). This claim is difficult to interpret, but since Wodeham normally acknowledges his debts carefully, it needs to be taken seriously.

Lost works by Wodeham

Wodeham's biblical commentaries have been lost. Attributed to him are commentaries on the *Canticum canticorum* and the first book of *Ecclesiasticus*. Bale also attributed to Wodeham a set of *Determinationes* directed against Richard of Wetherset, in the secular mendicant controversy.

Conclusion

"Almost infinitely many men attended his lectures," according to Luke Wadding, an ironically inappropriate tribute to a person interested in precise uses of the term 'infinite'. Still, it shows that Wodeham's reputation was considerable. John Major believed that had it not been for Ockham's political writings, Wodeham would be considered a greater philosopher than Ockham.

Wodeham exercised great influence in the history of philosophy for almost two centuries, from the 1330s until after 1512. But since the sixteenth century, little work has been done in exploring his views. The publication of Wodeham's *Norwich Lectures* has helped to change this somewhat. Until a critical edition of his most important work, the *Oxford Lectures*, is prepared, however, we will continue to be largely ignorant of his thought. This deplorable gap not only leaves us ill-equipped to understand Wodeham's own thought, but the works of John Duns Scotus, William of Ockham, John Buridan, and the subsequent tradition of medieval philosophy.

Note

Elizabeth Karger contributed the first five paragraphs of the section on semantics.

Bibliography

Primary sources
(1512), *Super quattuor libros sententiarum: Abbreviatio Henrici Totting de Oyta*, ed. J. Major, Paris: P. le Preux.

(1966), *Quaestio de divisione et compositione continui*, in J. Murdoch, "Two questions on the Continuum," *Franciscan Studies* 26, pp. 212–88.

(*OTh*) (1967–88), *Opera theologica*, 10 vols., ed. Gedeon Gál, et al., St. Bonaventure, NY: Franciscan Institute.

(1988), *Tractatus de indivisibilibus*, ed. R. Wood, Dordrecht: Kluwer.

(1990), *Lectura secunda*, ed. R. Wood and G. Gál, St. Bonaventure, NY: Franciscan Institute.

Secondary sources

Adams, M. M. (1993), Review of Wodeham's *Lectura secunda*, *Philosophical Review* 102, pp. 588–94.

Adams, M. M. and Wood, R. (1981), "Is to will it as bad as to do it?", *Franciscan Studies* 41, pp. 5–60.

Courtenay, W. (1975), "Ockhamism among the Augustinians: the case of Adam Wodeham," *Scientia Augustiniana*, ed. C. Mayer and W. Eckermann, *Cassiciacum* 30, pp. 267–75.

——(1978), *Adam Wodeham*, Leiden: Brill.

Gál, G. (1977), "Adam Wodeham's question on the *complexe significabile*," *Franciscan Studies* 37, pp. 66–102.

Gelber, Hester Goodenough (1974), "Logic and the Trinity: a clash of values in scholastic thought, 1300–1335," Ph.D. dissertation, University of Wisconsin.

Grassi, O. (1986), *Intuizione e significato: Adam Wodeham ed il problema della conoscenza nel XIV secolo*, Milan: Editoriale Jaca.

Karger, E. (1995), "William of Ockham, Walter Chatton and Adam Wodeham on the objects of knowledge and belief," *Vivarium* 33/2, pp. 171–96.

Kretzmann, N. (1984), "Adam Wodeham's anti-Aristotelian anti-atomism," *History of Philosophy Quarterly* 4, pp. 381–98.

Lenz, M. (1998), "Himmlische Sätze: Die Beweisbarkeit von Glaubenssatzen nach Wilhelm von Ockham," *Bochumer Philosophisches Jahrbuch für Antike und Mittelalter* 3, pp. 99–120.

Little, A. G. (1892), *The Grey Friars in Oxford*, Oxford: Clarendon Press.

Maierù, A. (1984), "Logique et théologie trinitaire: Pierre d'Ailly," in Z. Kaluza and P. Vignaux, eds., *Preuve et raisons à l'Université de Paris* (pp. 253–68), Paris: J. Vrin.

McGrade, A. S. (1987), "Enjoyment after Ockham: philosophy, psychology and the love of God," in A. Hudson and M. Wilks, eds., *From Ockham to Wyclif* (pp. 63–88), Oxford: Blackwell.

Nuchelmans, G. (1980), "Adam Wodeham on the meaning of declarative sentences," *Historiographia Linguistica* 7, pp. 177–86.

Reina, M. E. (1986), "Cognizione intuitiva ed esperienza interiore in Adamo Wodeham," *Rivista di Storia della Filosofia* 41, pp. 19–49, 211–44.

Spade, P. V. (1988), "Anselm and the background to Adam Wodeham's theory of abstract and concrete terms," *Rivista di Storia della Filosofia* 2, pp. 261–71.

Tachau, K. (1988), *Vision and Certitude in the Age of Ockham*, Leiden: Brill (see pp. 275–99).

Walter Chatton (Gualterus de Chatton) (1989), *Reportatio et lectura super Sententias: collatio et prologus*, ed. J. Wey, Toronto: Pontifical Institute of Mediaeval Studies.

Wood, R. (1982), "Adam Wodeham on sensory illusions," *Traditio* 38, pp. 214–52.

——(1989), "Epistemology and omnipotence," In S. Chodorow and J. Sweeney, eds., *Popes, Teachers and Canon Law in the Middle Ages* (pp. 160–78), Ithaca: Cornell University Press.

Zupko, J. (1994), "Nominalism meets indivisibilism," *Medieval Philosophy and Theology* 3, pp. 158–85.

——(1994–7), "How it played in the rue de Fouarre: the reception of Adam Wodeham's theory of the *complexe significabile* in the arts faculty at Paris in the mid-fourteenth century," *Franciscan Studies* 54, pp. 211–25.

2

Adelard of Bath

JEREMIAH HACKETT

Adelard of Bath (b. ca. 1080; d. ca. 1152), English natural philosopher, was a metaphysician, mathematician, and translator of works in the *quadrivium*; a layman, traveler, scholar of the Norman court in England, he was associated with the diocese of Bath.

When one looks back from the 1270s, and specifically from the works of ROGER BACON, it is evident that Adelard of Bath played a major philosophical role in the development of interest in natural philosophy and mathematics. Indeed, his translations and comments on Euclid's *Elements* provided the kind of training that would enable later scholars, in particular ROBERT GROSSETESTE, to understand clearly the relationship between the notion of demonstrative proof in Aristotle's *Posterior Analytics* and the forms of geometrical proof in Euclid. Yet the work of Abelard of Bath ought to be seen as a whole.

Adelard's work in metaphysics (*On the Same and the Different/ De eodem et diverso*) is modeled on BOETHIUS' *Consolation of Philosophy*. Following Boethius' project and that of scholars at Tours and Laon, Adelard attempts a reconciliation of the philosophies of Plato and Aristotle. It should be noted that Plato is seen as the "divine philosopher." Of interest here is Adelard's "indifference" theory of universals, a topic that places him in the context of Roscelin and WILLIAM OF CHAMPEAUX. His understanding of the liberal arts in relation to philosophy arise out of a concern with Cicero, Martianus Capella, and contemporary textbooks on the arts.

Adelard's very important work in natural philosophy (*Questions on Natural Science/ Quaestiones naturales*) is written in imitation of a Platonic dialogue, owing to the influence of the *Timaeus*. The work has seventy-six questions, covering many general topics in meteorology and natural science. Its philosophical significance lies in the important role given to "Questions on the Soul" (*Quaestiones de anima*). It must be seen in the context of such works as HUGH OF ST. VICTOR's *On the Union of the Soul and Body*, Isaac of Stella's *On the Soul*, and Pseudo-Augustine's (Alcher of Clairvaux) *On the Soul and the Spirit*. Two remarkable features are: (1) a preference for reason over authority in matters of science and nature, following the ways of the Arabs, and (2) the use of the literary device of invoking "the teachings of the Arabs" when presenting very controversial topics, such as the notion that brute animals possess knowledge and have souls. *Questions on Natural Science* was widely known and used in the schools. There is evidence for familiarity with this work in the *Dragmaticon* and possibly also in the *Philosophia* of William of Conches. Its influence would last into and beyond the thirteenth century but in general the teaching on natural things would be superseded by the works of Aristotle. Adelard's practical work (*Treatise on Birds/ De avibus tractatus*) is a manual on falconry and hawking, drawing on European, Arabic, and native English sources.

After a typical twelfth-century classical education, Adelard set out on a seven-year journey to the lands of the Crusaders: Greece, Asia Minor, Sicily, Antioch, Spain, and possibly Palestine. He met the "wise men" of these lands and developed a keen interest in the study and applications of mathematics (the *quadrivium*). The result of this study was his attempt to establish a whole program on the *quadrivium*. Of primary importance here are his translations and comments on Euclid's *Elements*. These would have a major impact on natural philosophy in the later Middle Ages. There are three versions. Version I is a close translation of the whole work (including the non-Euclidian Books XIV and XV) from the Arabic text (Clagett 1963, p. 63). Version II is not a copy of Version I, but rather an account of how to do proofs; it seems to have been based on an Arabic original. Version III consists of a commentary, is attributed to Adelard, and had much influence in the thirteenth century.

Adelard also introduced western Europeans to significant texts in the applications of mathematics. These include the *Ysagoge minor* (ALBUMASAR's *Shorter Introduction to Astrology*), the book on images and horoscopes by Thebit ben Qura (*Liber prestigiorum*), a *Treatise on the Astrolabe*, a *Regulae abachi*, a treatise on arithmetic, and al-Khwarismi's *Astronomical Tables*.

Clearly, Adelard of Bath helped in a major way to lay the foundations for English natural philosophy in later centuries. He was a Platonic-Aristotelian philosopher, much influenced by Latin classical texts, and some translations from Greek such as Nemesius' *On the Nature of Man*. The effect of his teaching can be seen most immediately in Robert Grosseteste and Roger Bacon.

Bibliography

Primary sources

(1992), Adelard's Commentary: see Robert of Chester (?), *Reduction of Euclid's Elements, the so-called Adelard II Version*, 2 vols., ed. H. L. L. Busard and M. Folkerts, Basle, Boston, and Berlin: Birkhäuser.

(1998), *Conversations with his Nephew: On the Same and the Different, Questions on Natural Science, and On Birds*, ed. and trans. Charles Burnett, with Italo Ronca, Pedro Mantas España, and Baudouin van den Abeele, Cambridge: Cambridge University Press.

Translations by Adelard

(1983), *Elements*, Euclid: *The First Latin Translation of Euclid's Elements Commonly Ascribed to Adelard of Bath*, ed. H. L. L. Busard, Toronto: Pontifical Institute of Mediaeval Studies.

(1994), *Ysagoga minor*, in Abu Ma'sar (Iafar), *The Abbreviation of the Introduction to Astrology Together with the Translation of Adelard of Bath*, ed. C. Burnett, K. Yamamoto, and M. Yano, Leiden: Brill.

Secondary sources

Al-Khwarizmi, *Astronomical Tables (Ezig)* (1914), edited in *Die astronomischen Tafeln des Muhommed ibn Musa al-Khwarizmi*, in *Der Bearbeitung des Maslama ibn Ahmed al-Madjriti und der lateinische Übersetzung des Athelhard von Bath*, ed. H. Suter, A. Bjornbo, and R. Bestborn, Copenhagen: Andr. Fred. Horst & Sons, KGL, Hof-Boghandel.

Burnett, Charles (1987), *Adelard of Bath: An English Scientist and Arabist of the Early Twelfth Century*, Warburg Institute Surveys and Texts 14, London: Warburg Institute.

Clagett, Marshall (1953), "The medieval Latin translations from the Arabic of the *Elements* of Euclid," *Isis* 44, pp. 16–42.

——(1963), "Adelard of Bath," in *Dictionary of Scientific Biography*, vol. 1 (pp. 61–4), New York: Scribner.

3

Alan of Lille

JOHN MARENBON

Alan of Lille, whose earliest works were written, most probably in Paris, in the 1150s and who lived until 1203, was one of the widest-ranging writers of his time. Of particular philosophical interest are his two allegorical compositions (*De planctu Naturae* and *Anticlaudianus*) and his work in systematic theology (for biography and works, see 1965, pp. 11–183).

De planctu Naturae (*Nature's Lament*) (late 1160s?) takes Boethius' *Consolation of Philosophy* as its starting point. It too is written in a mixture of prose and verse and involves an encounter between the narrator and a personification. Alan's Natura resembles Boethius' Philosophia in being a figure who, although authoritative, has no access to Christian revelation. But, whereas Boethius' Philosophia simply leaves Christianity unmentioned, Alan's Natura carefully defines her own inferior position, as a mere vicegerent of God. In the *Anticlaudianus*, a verse epic (ca. 1182–3) influenced especially by Martianus Capella's *On the Marriage of Mercury and Philology*, Alan describes the making of a perfect man and the heavenly journey to obtain his soul from God. Here he again emphasizes the subordination of philosophical reasoning to faith, although his allegorical method allows him an openness in doctrinal suggestiveness at odds with his explicit orthodoxy.

Alan also wrote three large theological textbooks. One, *De fide catholica* (1185–1200) is specially designed to refute the views of heretics (Waldensians and Cathars), Jews, and "pagans" (Muslims). One, the *Summa quoniam homines* (?1170–80), uses careful logical argumentation and shows the marked influence of GILBERT OF POITIERS and also, unusually, of JOHN SCOTUS ERIUGENA. And one, the *Regulae caelestis iuris* ("Rules of the Heavenly Law," ?1170–80), presents its teaching as a series of 134 interrelated "rules": pithy, sometimes enigmatic statements, each followed by an explanatory and justificatory commentary. The idea of theological rules is typical of the followers of Gilbert of Poitiers, but Alan's arrangement may also show the influence of the *Liber de causis* (a reworking of part of Proclus' *Elements of Theology*), which Alan was one of the first Latin writers to read. One of the rules (no. 7) is the famous statement that "God is an intelligible sphere the centre of which is everywhere, the circumference nowhere." It is also the subject of a short and intellectually adventurous sermon (1965, pp. 295–306), which posits exemplars and images on a multiplicity of levels between God and material things.

Bibliography

Primary sources

(1953), *Summa "Quoniam homines,"* ed. P. Glorieux, *Archives d'Histoire Doctrinale et Littéraire du Moyen Âge* 20, pp. 113–364.

(1955), *Anticlaudianus*, ed. R. Bossuat, Paris: J. Vrin; English trans. 1973, by J. J. Sheridan, Toronto: Pontifical Institute of Mediaeval Studies.

(1965), *Textes inédits*, ed. M.-T. d'Alverny, Paris: J. Vrin.

(1978), *De planctu Naturae*, ed. N. M. Häring, *Studi Medievali*, 3rd ser. 19, pp. 797–879; English trans. 1980, by J. J. Sheridan, Toronto: Pontifical Institute of Mediaeval Studies.

(1981), *Regulae caelestis iuris*, ed. N. M. Häring, *Archives d'Histoire Doctrinale et Littéraire du Moyen Âge* 48, pp. 97–226.

4

Albert of Saxony

EDWARD GRANT

Albert of Saxony (b. ca. 1316; d. 1390) was born in the region of Helmstedt in Germany, eventually studying at the University of Paris where he became a master of arts in 1351 and rector in 1353. He taught in the arts faculty until 1361, while also studying theology, though he did not receive a degree in theology. By the end of 1362, Albert left Paris and went to Avignon, where he worked for Pope Urban V, who rewarded him with benefices. After convincing the pope to establish the University of Vienna, Albert helped draw up the university's statutes and was named its first rector in 1365. In 1366, Albert's academic career ended when he was named Bishop of Halberstadt, an office he held until his death on July 8, 1390.

Albert composed major treatises on logic, mathematics, and natural philosophy. He is historically important because many of his works were printed in fifteenth- and sixteenth-century editions. As a result, it was often Albert's version of a particular type of treatise that came to represent that subject area of medieval scholastic thought, to both scholastic and non-scholastic thinkers of the late sixteenth and seventeenth centuries. Although his famous contemporaries, JOHN BURIDAN and NICOLE ORESME, were more original thinkers, many of Albert's works on the same topics were printed and therefore had a much greater subsequent impact.

In logic, Albert wrote a widely used textbook in which he described the basic themes that were important to medieval logicians. He also wrote independent treatises on sophisms, on obligations, and on insolubilia, and also questions on Aristotle's *Posterior Analytics*. Printed versions of all these works appeared.

Albert's analysis of motion in his mathematical *Treatise on Proportions* was based directly on the earlier, similarly titled works of THOMAS BRADWARDINE and Nicole Oresme. Indeed, all three works were published together in a single undated Parisian edition.

The most influential of Albert's works were his questions on Aristotle's *Physics, On the Heavens*, and *On Generation and Corruption*, each of which appeared in numerous printed editions of the late fifteenth and early sixteenth century. Albert presented significant ideas drawn primarily from the questions that Buridan and Oresme wrote on the same books of Aristotle, especially about projectile motion and impetus theory. If their ideas played any role in later scholasticism, it was in no small measure due to Albert's influence. In his *Questions on On the Heavens*, Albert also devoted questions to topics that neither Buridan nor Oresme included, among which were: whether one infinite can be greater or smaller than another (bk. 1, q. 8); whether the world is a finite or infinite magnitude (bk. 1, q. 9); and whether the world is eternal (bk. 1, q. 17). In his *Questions on On the Heavens*, Albert departed from most of his medieval colleagues by organizing the questions into specific themes that reflected larger cosmic relationships.

Of uncertain attribution are unpublished questions on Aristotle's *Meteorology*, *Ethics*, *On the Senses*, and *Economics*.

Bibliography

Primary sources
(1974), *Perutilis logica* [Venice 1518, 1522], Hildesheim: Olms.
(1975), *Sophismata* [Paris 1495, 1502], Hildesheim: Olms.

Secondary sources
Grant, E. (1991), "The unusual structure and organization of Albert of Saxony's *Questions on De caelo*," in J. Biard, ed., *Itinéraires d'Albert de Saxe Paris-Vienne au XIVe siècle* (pp. 205–17), Paris: Librairie Philosophique J. Vrin.
Moody, E. (1970), "Albert of Saxony," in C. C. Gillispie, ed., *Dictionary of Scientific Biography*, vol. 1 (pp. 93–5), New York: Scribner.

5

Albertus Magnus

MECHTHILD DREYER

I

Albertus Magnus (b. ca. 1200; d. 1280) was born of a family in the lower nobility in the Swabian town of Lauingen on the Danube. The thirteenth century, in which Albert lived, was in many ways an unsettling time. It was a time of greater mobility within society caused by ongoing missionary activity, the ever-increasing amount of international commerce, wars and crusades, the cultivation of entirely new tracts of land, and the growth of medieval towns. Significant changes were felt in the areas of politics, law, business, and culture, while in the Church much was also in a state of flux. It is hardly surprising, then, that a mentality of crisis became widespread, while simultaneously widely different ways of coping with it were developed. Many people felt the need to reorient themselves within the world and its activities and thereby to forge a new identity. Two historically important answers to the crisis wrought by the rapid changes of the thirteenth century made their impact felt upon the life of Albert: the movement of the mendicant religious orders and the increasing sophistication of knowledge, which found its institutional expression in the founding of the universities.

While studying law at Padua, Albert joined the Dominican Order, either in 1223 or 1229 (Anzulewicz 1999, I, pp. 4–6). St. Dominic had founded the order a few years earlier in Toulouse and since then it had become a European-wide and centralized organization, confirmed through a series of papal bulls. Albert may well have done his novitiate in Cologne; after finishing this, he was active as a teacher in a series of Dominican *studia*. At the beginning of the 1240s, the Dominican Order sent Albert to study theology at the University of Paris, probably because of the prominence of its faculty of theology.

When Albert began his period of study at the comparatively young University of Paris, he was over 40 years old. After obtaining the doctorate, he held one of the two chairs at the theology faculty of the university belonging to the Dominican Order, functioning as a regent master and having THOMAS AQUINAS as his most important student. In 1248 Albert left Paris for Cologne, where the order had entrusted him with the task of creating a *studium generale* or order-wide school. Thomas Aquinas joined him there.

II

Closely connected with the establishment of the Cologne *studium* is the beginning of the enterprise to which Albert owes his fame as an outstanding figure in the thirteenth century, namely, his commentaries upon the works of Aristotle. To grasp fully how significant Albert's project was for the history of European thought and culture, especially for the subsequent history of western European philosophy and theology, we should acquaint ourselves briefly with the background to his project.

Shortly after its entry into the Greco-Roman cultural milieu, Christianity found itself challenged by views of the world and being that, like its own teachings, laid claim to universal truth. Indeed, the Greco-Roman philosophical outlook, although relying on natural reason, might appear to concur with Christianity or be perceived by Christian thinkers as doing so. But two different views developed with regard to pagan wisdom. One view rejected the claims of philosophy as irrelevant and thereby avoided any conflict with it; the other recognized such claims and regarded their evaluation as a legitimate, even necessary, enterprise. Augustine, for example, took this position. He felt that, since philosophy argues exclusively though reason, a natural capacity of human beings, philosophy can help a person understand better her belief, communicate better the content of her belief to those who do not yet believe, and, finally, defend better her beliefs against criticisms. Although Augustine viewed philosophy as an intellectual treasure it did not find acceptance as an equal to Christian belief until the twelfth century. We must note, nonetheless, that the Latin Christian tradition did not know most of the riches of Greco-Roman philosophy until the twelfth century. Latins had familiarity only with a few texts of Plato, some representatives of Neoplatonism, and fragments of Stoic thinkers. Only a small portion of Aristotle, doubtless the most outstanding pagan philosopher after Plato, was known to the Latin West and that consisted of some of the logic, which, from an Aristotelian viewpoint, is a discipline that has value only as propaedeutics insofar as it deals with the art of rational argumentation common to all sciences.

But this situation changed around the middle of the twelfth century. In addition to other factors, what made this possible was the increased commerce in the Mediterranean and the growing mobility of people. The writings of Arabic, Greek, and Hebrew authors became, in this fashion, accessible to the Latin-speaking areas of Europe. These writings were translated and enjoyed a wide dissemination. Connected with this reception was the arrival of numerous Aristotelian treatises and the works of the Arabic philosophers who commented upon them. At this point, the full range of the rich tradition of Greek philosophical speculation became known to the Christian thinkers of the West. The newly translated materials were quickly taken up in the literary circles of the Latin West and came to be studied along with the seven liberal arts. Since, furthermore, the knowledge of the arts was presupposed for any advanced study such as theology, medicine, or law, every future theology student became acquainted with the new philosophical literature. As had happened in the early Christian period, so too in the early thirteenth century many teachers of Christian wisdom experienced difficulty in getting their bearings in regard to pagan philosophical ideas. For one thing, Christian thought had been thoroughly stamped by Augustine and thereby imprinted with a good deal of Platonic thinking, which was in tension with the Aristotelian theories being introduced; for another, essential elements of Christian doctrine contained certain claims that were in obvious contradiction to Aristotelian philosophy.

The more intense study of the Aristotelian writings and those of his Arabic commentators became, the better understood became the differences between Christian religious teachings and the thought of Aristotle. At the University of Paris, which, as mentioned, was the most important center of theological education in the Latin West, church authorities sought to protect Christian doctrine by issuing prohibitions against privately or publicly lecturing on some Aristotelian writings and punishing any who contravened the prohibitions. Other French universities, not to mention universities outside of France, did not labor under any such restrictions. Gradually, there appeared many earnest signs of a desire on the part of the theological faculty of Paris to enter into dialogue with the Aristotelian philosophy and by 1255 a new curriculum was inaugurated by the arts faculty that required the study of the Aristotelian corpus.

This is the background for Albert's ambitious project to write commentaries upon all the works of Aristotle. When Albert was studying theology at the University of Paris, the prohibitions upon lecturing on Aristotle were still in place, though there was sufficient indication that many scholars were keenly interested in entering into dialogue with Aristotelian philosophy. Albert himself must have been among these since, upon coming to Cologne to set up the new *studium generale* for the Dominican Order, he began to teach and to write commentaries on Aristotle; indeed, from the pattern of his activity we may conclude that, for Albert, a solid theological education required a thorough acquaintance with Aristotelian philosophy.

III

Despite the prohibitions, Albert was certainly not the first Latin writer to comment upon Aristotle. But Albert is, within the Latin Middle Ages, the first theologian to take so keen an interest in him and he remains to this day the only medieval theologian to have commented on so much of the Aristotelian corpus: on nearly all of it and, in the case of some works, twice. Besides the works by, or assumed to be by, Aristotle he commented on those by other writers that he believed completed or supplemented Aristotle's works in important ways. Altogether forty volumes comprise his philosophical works (the commentary on Euclid's *Geometry* probably being by Albert; see Anzulewicz 1999, I, pp. 6–11). In addition to these, however, we know of approximately thirty theological works, including commentaries on books of the Old and New Testaments and an extensive commentary on PETER LOMBARD's *Sentences*. Some of Albert's writings are still available in autographs. An absolute chronology for the composition of his philosophical works cannot be established, though a relative chronology is available (1999, I, pp. 12–17). It was sometime in 1249 or 1250 that Albert developed his plan to comment on the Aristotelian corpus, having just completed his commentaries on the writings of PSEUDO-DIONYSIUS that he had begun during his stay in Paris.

The first work on which Albert commented was the *Nicomachean Ethics*, a work he would expound twice; the remaining commentaries followed in quick succession over the next twenty years. Albert adopted Aristotle's division of philosophical sciences; distinguishing between speculative and practical philosophy, he subdivided the former philosophy into natural philosophy, mathematics, and metaphysics. Like speculative philosophy, practical philosophy too had its own parts, namely ethics and politics. Logic was assigned the role, in Peripatetic fashion, of being a propaedeutic to philosophical study.

IV

What Albert states at the beginning of the *Physics* concerning his intention and methodology holds good, more or less, for the whole of his project (1987, I tr. 1 cap. 1; 1980a, I tr. 1 cap. 1, p. 111). Albert aims to place before the reader the contents of Aristotle's writings, so as to make accessible the entire range of philosophical disciplines and at the same time to make Aristotle's work intelligible. To accomplish this goal, Albert intends to follow the leading thought in each of Aristotle's works and to trace out the stated positions, expressing by comment and example what appears necessary for the argumentation to achieve its conclusion, though there would be no detailed literal commentary. Albert's encounter with Aristotle's thought takes, then, the form of a paraphrase: he follows the order of the Aristotelian text, laying out in an orderly fashion its contents, and reformulating its major points, while emphasizing key concepts, commenting upon their significance and supporting Aristotle's train of thought by additional arguments. The aim of supplementing Aristotle's fundamental ideas by providing additional argumentation leads Albert to write short essays called *excursus* that solve philosophical problems arising from the text or to discuss extensively particular issues found in it, resulting in a substantial dialogue between the Aristotelian text and the writings of other philosophical authors. This is especially the case in those places where Albert finds that Aristotle's treatment of an issue is incomplete. Finally, Albert hopes to fill in those pieces missing in the Aristotelian corpus by supplying treatises for subjects left out altogether, or only sketchily treated in the extant writings of Aristotle.

Both in his efforts to supplement and improve the Aristotelian corpus and in his discussions of particular issues arising in it, Albert works with the full range of knowledge available to him. He draws heavily upon the writings of the Judeo-Christian tradition but also from the newly translated Arabic, Hebrew, and Greek texts. He cites a wide range of sources, including Heraclitus, Plato, Ptolemy, Galen, Vitruvius, Cicero, BOETHIUS, AVICENNA, AVERROES, ALGAZALI, and ALFARABI. He calls our attention to the fact that he consciously chooses his positions by accounting for the positions of others: he reports the opinions of earlier thinkers, adopts the doctrines that contain something valuable in them, and leaves aside whatever teachings are unsuitable, while pointing out that the doctrines themselves are worthy of attention insofar as they provide stimulation for discussion (1968, I tr. 1 cap. 7, p. 16). Furthermore, Albert adds to the commentaries on natural philosophy whatever observations or natural phenonomena he deems relevant on the basis of his own experiments or the observations and experiments of others. Unsurprisingly, because of his use of experiment and observation, Albert figures shortly after his death in folklore as a great magician and alchemist and, as a result, books of magic came to be attributed to him. Overall, we may say that in his commentaries upon the Aristotelian writings Albert presents not simply the work of Aristotle himself, but a work updated, both scientifically and philosophically, to take account of the thought, research, and experimentation of others during the years intervening between the Stagirite and himself. Because the work of Albert is practically a summary of all philosophical and scientific thought up to the thirteenth century, he earned the sobriquet of *Doctor Universalis* or "teacher of every subject."

What exactly does Albert make of Aristotle and what philosophical importance does he attribute to him? For Albert, Aristotle is, next to Plato, the philosopher whom it is most important to know if someone aims to study and be thoroughly acquainted with philosophy. Aristotle is described by Albert as the most distinguished philosopher (*praeclarus philosophus*: 1968, I tr. 1 cap. 1, p. 2), and the outstanding scholar and chief teacher of philosophy (*archidoctor philosophiae*: 1980a, I tr. 1 cap. 1, p. 49). In spite of these praises, Albert does not adopt Aristotle's views slavishly: "If someone thinks Aristotle was a god, he has to believe that Aristotle never was mistaken, but if he considers Aristotle a man, then he must admit that Aristotle could be mistaken just as we ourselves can" (1987, VIII tr. 1 cap. 14, p. 578). Even at that, Aristotle is not an authority in all areas of intellectual inquiry: "In matters of faith and morals, a person should trust Augustine more than the philosophers, in cases where they argue for views widely varying from his. But when Augustine speaks about medicine, I would trust rather more the views of Hippocrates or Galen than Augustine's. If Augustine expresses his views in the objects of natural science, I would place my trust more in Aristotle or some other experts in natural science" (1651c, II Sent d. 13, p. 137).

V

In examining the numerous philosophical writings that Albert produced during his long life, we consistently find a high degree of interest in systematizing and structuring the philosophical materials found in them. Key to Albert's understanding of science and knowledge are their epistemological, anthropological, and ethical dimensions. In what follows, we present Albert's understanding of the meaning of science and philosophical knowledge.

Knowledge, science, and scientific knowledge are part and parcel of our experience of the world and, following the views of Aristotle, essential to the fulfillment of human beings (1960, I tr. 1 cap. 1, p. 1, 16). The capacity for knowledge through the power of understanding exists as something divine in human beings, but the actualization of that capacity is a specifically human endeavor. Albert's concern for the epistemological aspect of knowledge is seen in his analysis of the subjects of the three theoretical sciences, or speculative philosophies: natural philosophy (*scientia naturalis*), mathematics (*scientia mathematica*), and metaphysics (*sapientia, scientia divina, scientia prima*). These branches of knowledge are all theoretical insofar as their goal is exclusively knowledge as such. Yet, for Albert, there is a ranking among them. The subject of natural philosophy consists in changeable material things and thus is considered the first stage of learning for the student of philosophy. Next comes mathematics, which treats of objects endowed with quantity but no sensible matter. Both mathematics and natural philosophy lead to metaphysics, a discipline that allows human beings a comprehensive view of the world but also a vision that transcends the sensible world. Metaphysics treats what is first in the order of nature; being as being and what follows upon being as such (I tr. 1 cap. 1; cap. 2, pp. 1; 3). Insofar as the first principles of things are discovered within it, metaphysics deals with divine things inasmuch as divine things are the first principles. In knowing the causes and principles of all things, the metaphysician knows the highest objects knowable by the human mind, leaving nothing else for the mode of understanding to be known appropriate to humans, and fulfilling in this way the human desire to know; in metaphysical speculation, human knowing reaches its apex and the striving for greater knowledge finds its rest. In an Aristotelian sense – and Albert endorses this view – to the extent that human beings succeed at metaphysical speculation, they find the happiness proper to them (I tr. 1 cap. 5, pp. 7 et seq.).

The human person is drawn through the means of theoretical philosophy into a deeper understanding of the world, on the one hand, but, on the other, to a knowledge of the divine. In Albert's view, however, this is simply the natural outcome of what human persons essentially are: a bond between the world and God (*nexus Dei et mundi*), since it is precisely through their concern with theoretical knowledge that human beings achieve their self-realization (1960, I tr. 1 cap. 1, p. 1). Yet, as a student of natural science, Albert is well aware that human intellectual activity is marked not simply by the natural desire to know and the human will's striving to reach its end, but is also dependent upon psychological habits and aptitudes as well as physiological dispositions. Given these other relevant factors, Albert notes the diversity among those seeking to fulfill their inborn desire to know:

some are, indeed, able to achieve their end through the study of metaphysics; others, not having the requisite psychological dispositions to do so, may fulfill their intellectual strivings through the study of languages, or natural science, or mathematics (I tr. 1 cap. 5, pp. 7 et seq.).

Both the disciplines pertaining to theoretical philosophy and those belonging to practical philosophy are sciences for Albert. The notion of science to which Albert subscribes is taken from Aristotle's *Posterior Analytics*: a science begins with underivable primitive statements, that is, principles, and develops its conclusions through such principles (1987, I tr. 1 cap. 3; cap. 5; pp. 5, 8). To be scientific knowledge, a branch of learning must deal with unchanging, necessary, and universal statements. These properties can only be found in cases, however, in which the subjects of inquiry are unchanging, necessary, and universal. Since not all areas of investigation are capable of meeting these conditions, not all disciplines qualify as sciences. The subject of a science, moreover, is the source of the science's unity; it is in reference to its subject that a science accomplishes its task of determining the subject's properties, elements, and principles. We should emphasize that Albert distinguishes sharply between scientific knowledge in the strong sense just described and dialectical or rhetorical knowledge that yields only opinion, conjecture, and hasty generalization (I tr. 1 cap. 5, p. 8). The reason that dialectical and rhetorical investigations do not yield better results is that they do not rely upon any understanding of the essential aspects of their subjects of inquiry, but rather upon general relations that hold only for the most part or even circumstantially. Drawing out the consequences of the Aristotelian viewpoint, Albert assigns a much higher value to scientific knowledge in the strong sense than to dialectical or rhetorical knowledge; so it is not surprising to find Albert spending time at the outset of his commentaries on Aristotle's logical writings, as well as his commentaries on Aristotle's *Ethics*, *Physics*, and *Metaphysics*, showing that each of the disciplines in question has a properly scientific character. Thus, at the beginning of each of his commentaries, Albert prefaces his remarks by giving an account of the science that the text of Aristotle treats, outlining its subject, goal, unity, method, and nature as a scientific discipline (Dreyer 1998a, 405–15; 1998b, pp. 1017–23).

In terms of the method used by different sciences, Albert differentiates between the method proper to a given science and the method underlying all areas of investigation and hence common to all sciences (1651a, tr. 1 cap. 1, pp. 1–2). The common methodology is characterized by Albert as one that works every discipline and allows each branch of knowledge to arrive at the unknown by way of the known; it is logic, understood in its totality. Since Albert attributes a natural desire for knowledge to human beings, he also, following Avicenna, thinks that the common method for achieving scientific knowledge, that is logic, is given by nature. But Albert does not claim that the science of logic, that is, the science that treats professedly of the rules of inference and how to proceed from the known to the unknown, is something naturally implanted in us. Rather what is given by nature is only the potentiality or disposition which must be brought to completion and perfection through proper training in the art of logic (*ars*). Still, according to Albert, no philosophical discipline will be able to be counted among the branches of scientific knowledge if it proceeds without the knowledge of logic. For, without the latter, we possess more apparent than real knowledge since we can neither know the precise grounds for reaching a conclusion in the discipline nor are capable of defending the truth of a scientific claim against objections.

If logic is necessary to pursue philosophy successfully as a science, and the highest stage of speculative knowledge as well as the zenith of human happiness consists in metaphysical knowledge, the knowledge of logic is essential for human beings and enjoys a high degree

97

of importance (1651a, tr. 1 cap. 3, pp. 3–4). Only with the help of logic – so Albert tells us – is the full activity of metaphysical contemplation possible for human beings and thereby the highest form of happiness under earthly conditions. Logic frees us from making illusory claims, shows us the falsehood of many of our inferences, and casts light upon the object of contemplation.

VI

We know from Albert himself that his project of commenting upon the pagan philosophy of Aristotle met with resistance and hostility (1651a, VIII cap. 6, p. 500; 1978, ep. 7, p. 504). Whence the hostility towards Albert's efforts to study Aristotle arose we cannot say exactly; a possible cause for the resistance to his project may well have been the attitude that he adopted toward Aristotle as the chief exponent of the claims of natural reason. Varying from some of his contemporaries and most theologians of the time who followed the line of approach taken by St. Augustine, Albert conceded a greater role to philosophy than that of being a mere tool of theology. Indeed, he conceived of philosophy as an outlook in its own right upon the world and being, one capable of existing independent of theology. At the same time, he emphasized the extent to which philosophy and theology need each other in different respects. For example, in specifying the ultimate end of human life, if we ask whether and how human beings may attain their end or salvation, Albert formulates his reply by drawing upon the received Christian tradition: philosophical knowledge, in contrast to theological teaching, can give no definitive answer to this question. The philosopher can only show that there must be an ultimate end for human beings and it must be attainable, in some sense, in the present life. But to know that the ultimate end is only realizable in its fullness in the next life and how it is realized belongs to theology to determine, relying upon Judeo-Christian revelation. Contrary to the traditional view, however, Albert does not draw the conclusion that, since philosophy's range and perspective on human life is narrow, everything knowable by natural reason must be subject to theology. Theology and philosophy are scientific disciplines, each in its own right. They each have their own subjects, principles of demonstration, and methods. While theology's subject is the being of created things and the human person as related to his ultimate end, philosophy's subject is being and man as they present themselves to us in our present condition. Accordingly, even if philosophical knowledge cannot make any definitive claims about the attainment of the ultimate end in its fullness, it can make telling claims about what is required in the present life to realize the goal of the human good.

Philosophy and theology are, in their own ways, independent approaches to the truth, but approaches that cannot contradict one another in the final analysis. God is the source of both the realms that philosophy and theology study, since he is both the creator of human beings and their powers of natural reason and the revealer of his nature through the Incarnation. To return to the theme of the ultimate end, philosophical reflection upon the problem of attaining the ultimate end depends on theology, which upon the basis of revelation claims to know the correct way to attain the end, to elaborate for philosophy the meaning and manner of attaining the end. Yet to show that theology is a science and how it meets the conditions of discourse associated with science so as to be able to speak definitively upon the subject of the ultimate end is something that theology owes to philosophy and the methodology articulated by natural reason. Hence, in regard to its method of teaching and investigation, theology bears a reference to philosophy.

VII

If a work reflects the personality of its creator, we may be entitled to ask what picture of Albert is conveyed to the reader through his vast corpus. In regard to the work of a medieval author, this question does not often arise, generally speaking; contrary to the situation nowadays, medieval scholars tend to vanish behind the works they produce. Even the positions taken by philosophers of the Middle Ages tend to be considered important not because they belong to a certain author, but simply because they cast light upon, and made a contribution to, the solution of a given philosophical problem. Significant indeed is the fact that we often cannot identify with certainty the authors of so many texts belonging to medieval philosophy and theology, though their contributions to the treatment of certain problems in those areas remain clear enough.

Albert, however, represents something of an exception to this usual pattern. He always places himself into his reflections so that some conclusions, albeit tentative ones, may reasonably be drawn regarding his personality. Since, as stated above, Albert aims to render Aristotle's works not simply intelligible to his contemporaries but even to present them with an updated version of Aristotelian philosophical wisdom, he must exude a substantial degree of confidence – at least enough to trust his own insights while engaging in disputes with opponents. If we consider to what extent Aristotle himself was a wide-ranging scholar and the extent to which Albert successfully advanced his program of mediating Aristotle to his contemporaries, we cannot fail to see in Albert a person of exceptional learning, conversant at an unusually high level with nearly all departments of life and thought. We should immediately add to the breadth of his learning such characteristics as his openness toward the unknown, his readiness to discuss such a wide range of problems, and his desire to establish a basis of harmony between seemingly irreconcilable positions. Yet, in fairness, we must say that there are also passages in which Albert shows himself not all that well disposed towards the philosophical and theological views he treats; theses he finds unconvincing are sometimes summarily dismissed or commented upon with harsh words, while arguments that are of little interest to him are presented in a haphazard manner. At the other extreme, Albert can be quite long-winded whenever he wants to convey to the reader the breadth of his learning on a certain topic; upon such occasions especially one *excursus* piles up on top of another. His own position is of great importance to Albert and it is always advanced with considerable learning. Another characteristic of his writing and personality has already been mentioned, his keen sense of observation and its importance: in support of his own views, he often enlists his own experiences, what he has seen and lived through, or what he has discovered through his own experiments, since his numerous travels provided him with plenty of opportunities of observing things. When we consider that Albert continued his Aristotelian project even into his last years despite the opposition to it, we must also attribute to him a strong sense of determination and an ability to see the importance of opening up a new approach to philosophical thought even in the face of difficulties.

All of his abilities – his intrepidness, his commitment, his openness to novelty, along with his ability to take what is true in differing standpoints precisely as different and communicate those standpoints to others – predestined Albert to political office. From 1254 until 1257 he was provincial minister of the Teutonia province, covering an area of vast size. He was actively sought after as a peacebroker and an adjudicator of conflicts; for example, his help was enlisted to resolve a conflict between the Bishop of Cologne and the town council which had legal claims attached to it involving the Holy See. Albert's most illustrious political appointment was undoubtedly that of the bishopric of Regensburg (1260–2). This appointment was surprising for at least two reasons: first, the roles of scholar and bishop were quite far apart, especially so in Albert's time; second, many of Albert's contemporaries perceived a clear contradiction between the ideal of poverty associated with the Dominican Order and the highly powerful, and economically wealthy, position of bishop. Albert, ignoring the doubts of others, accepted the papal appointment to the bishopric, probably not least because certain lifelong freedoms would accrue to him thereby from the rule of the Dominican Order. The step of taking the bishopric displays once again a trait found also in the production of his philosophical works: the ability to remain steadfast in carrying through something against steady opposition.

VIII

To assess the philosophical and theological accomplishments of Albert, we must remember the following. At a time when his contemporaries saw some of their most cherished convictions placed into question by culturally alien ideas and opposed those ideas as being skeptical and of little worth, Albert embraced them. He recognized in the novel ideas a substantial amount of ordinary human knowledge and wisdom, emphasized its importance, and opened up its hidden treasures for the benefit of his contemporaries. He made an effort to point out that the sciences represented in the new literature dealt with the created world independently of any particular theology. Such recognition of the autonomy of the sciences opened up, for Albert, the possibility of buttressing the theological teachings of the Latin Christian West, by allowing Europeans a chance of articulating their views more clearly and precisely. In working out what was proper with respect to natural knowledge and theology, Albert showed that the claims of reason and revelation reinforced each other in different, but complementary, ways.

Bibliography

Primary sources

(1651a), *De praedicabilibus*, edn. Lugdun. I, Lyon: Rigaud.
(1651b), *Politica*, edn. Lugdun. IV, Lyon: Rigaud.
(1651c), *Super II Sententiarum*, edn. Lugdun. XV, Lyon: Rigaud.
(1960), *Metaphysica*, edn. Colon. XVI/1, Münster: Aschendorff.
(1968), *De anima*, edn. Colon. VII/1, Münster: Aschendorff.
(1978), *Super Dionysii epistulas 7*, edn. Colon. XXXVII/2, Münster: Aschendorff.
(1980a), *De causis proprietatum elementorum*, edn. Colon. V/2, Münster: Aschendorff.
(1980b), *De generatione et corruptione*, ed. Colon. V/2, Münster: Aschendorff.
(1987), *Physica*, edn. Colon. IV/1, Münster: Aschendorff.

Secondary sources

Albertus Magnus Institut, Bonn edn. (1999–), *Lectio Albertina* 1ff, Münster: Aschendorff.
Aertsen, J. A. (1996), "Albertus Magnus und die mittelalterliche Philosophie," *Allgemeine Zeitschrift für Philosophie* 21, pp. 111–28.
Anzulewicz, H. (1999), *De forma resultante in speculo des Albertus Magnus. Handschriftliche Überlieferung, literargeschichtliche und textkritische Untersuchungen, Textedition, Übersetzung und Kommentar*, 2 vols., *Beiträge zur Geschichte der Philosophie und Theologie des Mittelalters* NF 53, Münster: Aschendorff.

Craemer-Ruegenberg, I. (1980), *Albertus Magnus*, Munich: Beck.

de Libera, A. (1990), *Albert le Grand et la philosophie: à la recherche de la vérité*, Paris: J. Vrin.

Bosley, R., and Tweedale, M., eds. (1992), "Aristotle and his medieval interpreters," *Canadian Journal of Philosophy*, suppl. vol. 17.

Dreyer, M. (1998a), "Alberts Kölner Vorlesungen 'Super Ethica' und die Begründung der Ethik als Wissenschaft," in N. Trippen, et al., eds., *Dombau und Theologie im mittelalterlichen Köln. Festschrift zur 750-Jahr-Feier der Grundsteinlegung des Kölner Doms und zum 65. Geburtstag von Joachim Kardinal Meisner* (pp. 405–15), Cologne: Verlag Kölner Dom.

——(1998b), "Ethik als Wissenschaft nach Albertus Magnus," in Jan A. Aertsen and A. Speer, eds., *Was ist Philosophie im Mittelalter?* Akten des 10. Internationalen Kongresses für mittelalterliche Philosophie der S.I.E.P.M. 1997 in Erfurt, Miscellanea mediaevalia 26 (pp. 1017–23), Berlin: De Gruyter.

Hufnagel, A. and Wieland, G. (1990), "Albertus Magnus," in G. Fløistad, ed., *Contemporary Philosophy: A New Survey*, vol. 6/1: *Philosophy and Science in the Middle Ages* (pp. 231–40), Dordrecht: Kluwer.

Krieger, G. (1990), "Albertus Magnus," in G. Fløistad, ed., *Contemporary Philosophy: A New Survey*, vol. 6/1: *Philosophy and Science in the Middle Ages* (pp. 241–60), Dordrecht: Kluwer.

Meyer, G. and Zimmermann, A., eds. (1980), *Albertus Magnus: Doctor Universalis, 1280/1980*, Mainz: Matthias-Grünewald-Verlag.

Thomassen, B. (1985), *Metaphysik als Lebensform. Untersuchungen zur Grundlegung der Metaphysik im Metaphysikkommentar Alberts des Großen*, Beiträge zur Geschichte der Philosophie und Theologie des Mittelalters NF 27, Münster: Aschendorff.

Van Steenberghen, F. (1980), "Albert le Grand et l'aristotélisme," *Revue Internationale de Philosophie* 34, pp. 566–74.

Weisheipl, J. A., ed. (1980), *Albertus Magnus and the Sciences: Commemorative Essays*, Toronto: Pontifical Institute of Mediaeval Studies.

Wieland, G. (1972), *Untersuchungen zum Seinsbegriff im Metaphysikkommentar Alberts des Großen*, Beiträge zur Geschichte der Philosophie und Theologie des Mittelalters NF 7, Münster: Aschendorff.

6

Albumasar

JEREMIAH HACKETT

Albumasar, also known as Abū Ma'shar al-Balkhi Ja'Far ibn Muhammad (b. 787; d. 886) was born in Balkh, Khurasan, a region which was a veritable crossroads of world religions, having Jews, Nestorian Christians, Manicheans, Buddhists, Hindus, and Zoroastrians among its inhabitants. He died in al-Wasit, Iraq. His intellectual contemporaries were inclined to a pro-Iranian view of the cosmos and to the Shi'a sect of Islam. Albumasar was a strong advocate of Iranian intellectual superiority. Philosophically, he shared a Neoplatonic emanationist view of the world, which allowed him to hold some very eclectic philosophical positions. He seems to have been relatively free of religious persecution. His philosophical career began in Baghdad during the caliphate of al-Mamun (813–33), where he moved in the same circles as ALKINDI, who became his great opponent.

Albumasar devoted himself to the account and justification of astrology. Presupposing a Ptolemaic astronomy, he set out to give an account of the influences of the heavenly bodies on the processes of generation and corruption of species and individuals on earth. He drew together into one great synthesis many ancient traditions – Indian, Greek, and Iranian. The Greek influence consisted of the teachings of Plato, Aristotle, Ptolemy, and Theon. Yet he also drew on Syriac Neoplatonic sources and on Alkindi for a general metaphysics. Further, he saw the validity of astrology as an integral part of a theory of traditionalism in which all knowledge is the result of an original revelation and is handed down through various religious and philosophical groups. This view of knowledge affected the origins of natural science and was taken up by ROGER BACON in the *Opus maius*, remaining a standard interpretation of science until the eighteenth century.

For the generation of ALBERTUS MAGNUS, Roger Bacon, and others, Albumasar was commonly referred to as the "auctor in astronomia." That is, he had the same status in general astronomy that Aristotle had in philosophy. Further, these medieval authors perceived a close connection between Albumasar's "Great introduction to astronomy," and the works of Aristotle, specifically, the *Physics, Metaphysics, On the Heavens*, and *On Generation and Corruption*. Prior to the new translations of Aristotle's natural works, the *Kitab al-mudhal al-kabir* (The book of the great introduction to astronomy) entered the Latin world in the first quarter of the twelfth century in the *Ysagoge minor* (The abbreviation of the great introduction) of ADELARD OF BATH. The whole work was translated into Latin in 1133 by John of Seville and Limia, and by Herman of Carinthia in 1140. Albumasar's astronomy and astrology fit well into the world of the School of Chartres with its Neoplatonic understanding of a hierarchical world; it also matched the worldview of the *Chaldean Oracles* (known to Latin authors through Augustine) and the hermetic writings of late antiquity.

The defence of astrology is presented in the context of an Aristotelian cosmology. One finds a doctrine of matter and form, potency and act, and the four causes. Further, the nature of scientific questioning is taken from the *Posterior Analytics*. Albumasar clearly draws on the *On Interpretation* of Aristotle to give an account of the nature of causation. His theory would be interpreted by some Latin scholastics, such as THOMAS AQUINAS, as a kind of astral determinism which compromised contingency. Yet he was seen by both Albertus Magnus and Roger Bacon as the main authority in the field of applied astronomy.

Albumasar was also known for his work *Kitab alquiranat* (The book of conjunctions). This work provides an astrological manner for interpreting world history and was widely influential in the Middle Ages, as may be seen in Roger Bacon's *Moralis philosophia*.

Bibliography

Primary sources

(1994) *Isagoge minor: The Abbreviation of the Introduction to Astrology*, ed. C. C. Burnett, Keiji Yamamoto, and Michio Yano, Leiden: Birkhäuser.

(1995) *Kitab al-mudhal al-kabir, Liber introductorii maioris ad scientiam judiciorum astrorum*, 9 vols., ed. Richard Lemay (Arabic/Latin text, notes and introduction), Naples: Istituto Universitario Orientale.

Secondary sources

Lemay, Richard (1962), *Abu Ma'shar and Latin Aristotelianism in the Twelfth Century: The Recovery of Aristotle's Natural Philosophy through Arabic Astrology*, Beirut: American University of Beirut.

Pingree, David (1970), "Abu Ma'shar," *Dictionary of Scientific Biography*, vol. 1 (pp. 32–9), New York: Scribner.

Ulmann, Manfred (1972), *Die Natur und Geheimwissenschaften im Islam*, Leiden: Brill.

7

Alexander of Hales

CHRISTOPHER M. CULLEN

Alexander of Hales (b. ca. 1185; d. 1245) was a notable thinker, important in the history of scholasticism and the Franciscan school. Alexander's importance within the tradition of scholastic thought derives from the fact that he is among the earliest scholastics to engage Aristotle's newly translated writings, in particular, the *Metaphysics*. He steered scholasticism in a more systematic direction with his momentous decision to use the *Sentences* of PETER LOMBARD as the basic textbook for treating the whole of theology.

Alexander was also "the founder of the Franciscan school. He gave the school its body of teachings and its characteristic spirit" (Bougerol 1963, p. 15). Alexander was the first Franciscan to hold a chair at the University of Paris. It was there that he was the teacher of several Franciscans who later became noteworthy thinkers; among these the most important is BONAVENTURE. Bonaventure refers to Alexander as his "father and master" and says that he wishes to follow in his footsteps (1951, v. 1, p. 20). Other important Halesian disciples include RICHARD RUFUS OF CORNWALL and JEAN DE LA ROCHELLE. Alexander's influence within the Franciscan tradition also derives from the fact that he began a theological *summa* (summary), which is among the earliest in this genre. This *Summa theologica* exercised considerable influence, especially among Franciscans. Indeed, two ministers general of the order in the fourteenth century mandated it as a textbook. Hales also bequeathed to the Franciscan school a deep-seated allegiance to the thought of AUGUSTINE; it was, however, an Augustine read through the eyes of ANSELM. Indeed, Alexander is among those thirteenth-century thinkers who helped bring Anselm's thought to the forefront of theological development.

Alexander was likely born in Hales Owen, Shropshire, between 1180 and 1186. He was from a well-to-do country family. He went on to study the arts in Paris and became a master of arts sometime before 1210. After studying theology, he joined the theology faculty as regent master around 1220 or 1221. He was made a canon of St. Paul's in London and later, of Lichfield; by 1231 he was Archdeacon of Coventry. In 1235 Henry III of England appointed him to help pursue peace with the French king. One of the most decisive moments in his life, and in thirteenth-century history, occurred at the beginning of the academic year 1236–7 when, at the age of at least 50, he entered the Franciscan order. Since he retained his academic position, he became the first Franciscan to hold a university chair. ROGER BACON tells us that he was "a good and rich man . . . and a great teacher of theology in his time"; not surprisingly, he stirred up considerable excitement when he became a friar (1951, v. 1, pp. 24–5). In 1245 Alexander was at the Council of Lyons; and, with Bishop ROBERT GROSSETESTE, served on a commission for a canonization case. Not long before his death, he resigned his chair in favor of Jean de la Rochelle; it subsequently became the custom for a Franciscan to hold this chair. Alexander died in Paris on August 21, 1245. He is known as *Doctor Irrefragabilis* (the Irrefutable Doctor), apparently as a result of comments made by Pope Alexander IV in the bull, *De fontibus paradisi* (1255/6) in which the pope praised the Halesian *Summa*.

In 1946 the prefect of the commission charged with editing the works of Alexander, Victorin Doucet, OFM (1946, p. 407) made the momentous announcement that an early manuscript of Alexander's commentary on the Lombard's *Sentences* had been found in Assisi. This text, known as *Glossa in quatuor libros sententiarum*, was subsequently edited and published in the *Bibliotheca franciscana scholastica*. The editors of the "Prolegomena" (which provides the most comprehensive biography of Alexander available [1951, v. 1, pp. 7–75]) date the *Glossa* between 1220 and 1227. The text of the *Glossa* is divided into four books: God, creation, the Incarnation, and the sacraments. Each book contains many "distinctions," each of which usually treats several different questions. (Alexander himself is probably responsible for introducing the distinctions in Lombard's text.)

Alexander engaged in many university disputations during his career as a master of theology. Indeed, many *quaestiones* have been identified as his, both from before and after he became a friar (1948, v. 4, pp. 153–97). Although Alexander did not introduce the scholastic *disputatio*, he helped lead the way in the development of it as a highly structured affair (Doucet 1946, p. 404). Some 68 of the disputed questions that he held before he became a Franciscan have been edited and published as *Quaestiones disputatae 'antequam esset frater'* (Disputed questions before he was a brother).

For centuries Alexander was best known as the author of a theological synthesis, originally called the *Summa theologica* or *Summa fratris Alexandri*. Although he certainly started this *Summa Halesiana*, as the final form of this text is now sometimes called, it has become clear that this work was not entirely written by him (Doucet 1947). Since many parts within the first three books were written before his death in 1245, Alexander may have supervised the editing. Other Franciscans attempted to complete this work and later issued an expanded edition. William of Melitona, for example, composed much of Book IV on the sacraments. As a result of this multiple authorship, the *Glossa* and the *Quaestiones disputatae* must serve as the standard for determining Alexander's own doctrines (Principe 1967, p. 15). Nevertheless, the *Summa* borrows extensively from Alexander's earlier work. It also retains historical significance, not only because it expresses the major doctrines of the Franciscan school in the mid-thirteenth century, but also because it seems to indicate, at least to some historians, the presence of an Augustinian school prior to the rise of the Latin Averroism of the 1260s.

Alexander's methodology in the *Glossa* marks a clear change from that found in twelfth-century works. The *Glossa* is not a line-by-line biblical commentary; rather, it proceeds topically. It consistently employs a dialectical structure for addressing a topic: a question is posed, arguments on both sides are presented, a response is made, and then opposing arguments are addressed. In other words, the basic structure of the scholastic question is unambiguously present. Furthermore, Alexander pursues speculative questions in the manner characteristic of high scholasticism.

Alexander draws from many sources in his *Glossa*, including PSEUDO-DIONYSIUS and the Neoplatonic *Liber de causis*, which he attributes to Aristotle. Two points about the sources are of particular note. First, Alexander makes considerable use of philosophical ones, the chief among them being Aristotle, to whom he repeatedly refers as *"Philosophus"* ("the Philosopher"). The *Glossa* thus provides a valuable glimpse of an early attempt to engage the more complete corpus of Aristotle's writings that was then becoming available. Second,

Alexander draws heavily from twelfth-century sources, especially BERNARD OF CLAIRVAUX and RICHARD OF ST. VICTOR.

The influence of Aristotle is present at various points in Alexander's philosophical views. He quotes from nearly all the major works of Aristotle, with frequent reference to the *Metaphysics*, *Physics*, and, with slightly less frequency, the *De anima*. He makes use of the distinction between substance and accident, Aristotle's division of causes, and a modified version of the theory of hylomorphism.

Alexander is keenly aware of the difference between arguments from revelation or divine authority and arguments from reason. Reason is a valuable instrument of theology and can be employed to help pierce the great mysteries of the faith and God. Nevertheless, reason and philosophy have their limits, and the relationship between faith and reason is complex. Alexander affirms at the beginning of his work the common dictum (Isa. 7: 9) that "unless you believe, you shall not understand" (1951, 1, d. 2, v. 1, p. 27).

With regard to our knowledge of God, Alexander argues that, while human reason has no direct knowledge of the essence of God, it can know that God exists from his creation (1951, 1, 3, v. 1, p. 39). He presents a number of proofs, borrowed from various sources. Among these one finds an abbreviated version of Aristotle's argument for a first mover (ibid., p. 40) and Anselm's proof of the *Proslogion*, cc. 2–4 (ibid., p. 42).

Although Alexander thinks that there is no direct knowledge of God in this life, he argues that many of the attributes of God can be known either by negation or analogy (1951, 1, 8, v. 1, pp. 108–9). Moreover, he discusses several divine attributes, including simple, infinite, omnipotent, omniscient, and immutable.

Among Alexander's most important contributions is his discussion of divine knowledge, which is prompted by Lombard's discussion of this topic in the *Sentences*. Whereas Lombard merely mentions divine knowledge and argues that good and evil are known by God in different ways – the former with an approving knowledge, the latter from afar – Alexander supplies a detailed analysis. Augustine had posited Platonic forms as ideas in the divine mind (*De diversis quaestionibus LXXXIII*, q. 46), but Alexander sees in this move a possible foundation for metaphysical realism.

As a house is in the mind of its builder, so the creature must be in the mind of its Creator (1951, 1, 8, v. 1, p. 109). All things are made according to divine ideas, which they reflect, so divine ideas serve as exemplars for created things. The forms of all things, then, have an ultimate ground in nothing less than the divine mind.

Although Alexander argues that there must be ideas in the divine mind that serve as exemplars for created things, he explains that these ideas cannot exist as independent essences separate from God. For whatever is in God must be God. "God is the exemplar of all creatures" (1951, 1, 36, v. 1, p. 357). Indeed, the ideas can really differ only according to a mode of speaking.

Alexander is careful to avoid any sort of necessitarian view of creation, such that whatever God knows must come to exist. Although in knowing himself God knows all things, not only actual but also possible (ibid.), this fact does not mean that in willing himself God wills all things insofar as knowing does not cause the object of knowledge to be (1951, 1, 45, v. 1, p. 449). God's knowledge of a thing does not entail that the thing exists as a substance in God – that which God knows is in God as in a cause and is not other than God; but willing a thing entails causing the thing really to exist, externally to the knowing agent (ibid.).

Among the important scholastic concerns in the early thirteenth century is the distinction between God and the world. On this issue, Alexander argues at considerable length against any sort of what would now be called *pantheism* (1951, 1, 19, v. 1, p. 201). He warns against understanding the statement that creatures are in God to mean that all things are God. He returns to a similar concern later when he warns against the heresy that holds that God is the matter of all things. Although God is the efficient, formal, and final cause of all things, he cannot be the material cause of the universe; for "matter is possible, incomplete, not existing in act; therefore it is not fitting to the divine persons" (1951, 1, 19, n. 22, v. 1, p. 201).

Among the more disputed issues in the thirteenth century is the possibility of an eternal creation. Even in this early text Alexander is clear that only God is eternal by nature and thus without beginning or end. Angels, for example, are not eternal by nature, even if they pre-existed the corporeal world. The angels are only eternal by participation, and this means that they had a beginning in time (1952, 2, v. 2).

Alexander is deeply imbued with a trinitarian view of creation. Granted that faith helps us to see reflections of the Trinity in creation (1951, 1, 3, v. 1, pp. 37–74), human reason can come to see a footprint (*vestigium*) of the Trinity in creatures and in the rational soul, even if only confusedly and without certainty (ibid., v. 1, pp. 44–5; also, v. 1, p. 29).

Whereas God is simple, all creatures are composed. Alexander discusses various types of composition involved in created beings (1951, 1, 8, v. 1, p. 105). Within creatures there is a composition of *quod est* (essence) and *quo est* (existence), a distinction which he borrows from BOETHIUS (1951, 1, 26, v. 1, p. 254). Another of the compositions found within creatures is the composition of matter and form, usually referred to as hylomorphism. Alexander develops a version of this theory that becomes distinctive to the Augustinian school. Matter is a sort of quasi-nonbeing (1951, 1, 19, v. 1, p. 201). It was the first thing created; and initially, it existed without any of the forms with which it was later adorned in the days of creation. In the *Glossa*, Alexander denies that angels are composed of matter and form (1952, 2, v. 2, p. 28).

Quoting Augustine's *Commentary on Genesis*, Alexander posits *rationes seminales* (seminal reasons) within matter in order to explain change. Change does not involve the conferral of a new form by the efficient cause; rather, the efficient cause brings forth, from matter, a new form, already present in it in a seminal state. The *ratio seminalis* disposes the material cause to a change (ibid., p. 153), because it is a form in germinal state.

Among living things, there are three types of soul: vegetative, sensible, and rational (1951, 1, 3, v. 1, p. 52). The rational soul is a simple substance without distinction between its substance and its powers. The intellect, will, and memory of the rational soul reflect the Trinity. The light of the intellect makes intelligible species actually so (1954, 3, 23, v. 3, p. 266). Alexander affirms that knowledge begins in the senses (1951, 1, 3, v. 1, p. 39).

In the treatment of ethical issues in the *Glossa*, Alexander's debt to Augustine is clear. Moral goodness consists in loving rightly. Indeed, love is clinging to the highest good (1951, 1, 1, v. 1, p. 27). Alexander draws extensively on the Augustinian distinction between use and enjoyment. We use something when we seek it for some purpose beyond itself; we enjoy that which is sought for itself. In light of this, we are supposed to use the created things of the world; God alone is to be enjoyed, for union with him is our happiness. This dynamic involves conforming to the divine will (1951, 1, 48, v. 1, pp. 481–5). The moral good and the virtuous life thus involve the right ordering of the human soul: justice involves the right order to God and neighbor (1951, 1, 2, v. 1, p. 29). Alexander affirms the Augustinian notion of evil as privative (1951, 1, v. 1, 53; v. 2, p. 73). Moral evil consists in a failure to love the highest good and results in disorder.

The *Summa fratris Alexandri* contains many of the doctrines that are distinctive of the Augustinian school. Several of these doctrines are of note. First, the eternity of the world is impossible. God alone is truly eternal. It is impossible for any created thing to be eternal by nature and thus without a beginning (1928, 2, v. 2, no. 67, p. 86). Second, all creatures are composed of matter and form. Universal hylomorphism is part of the created condition, because matter is sheer potentiality for form (ibid., nos. 59–61, pp. 74–6). Third, seminal reasons are present in matter, disposing matter to all its subsequent changes. Fourth, there is an identity between the soul and its powers, though Alexander understands this to refer to the substance, not the essence of the soul (ibid., no. 349, p. 425). Fifth, divine illumination is an aid in human cognition (ibid., no. 372, p. 452). The presence of these doctrines in the *Summa* seems to indicate the existence of a distinct Augustinian school prior to the rise of the radical Aristotelianism of the Averroists. Also of interest is the *Summa*'s "elaborate system" for determining whether a war is just (1928, 3, v. 4, pp. 466–70; Barnes 1982).

Bibliography

Primary sources
(1924–48), *Summa theologica*, Quaracchi, Florence: Collegium S. Bonaventurae.
(1951–7), *Glossa in quattuor libros sententiarum*, Quaracchi, Florence: Collegium S. Bonaventurae.
(1960), *Quaestiones disputatae 'antequam esset frater'*, Quaracchi, Florence: Collegium S. Bonaventurae.

Secondary sources
Barnes, J. (1982), "The just war," in N. Kretzmann, A. Kenny, and J. Pinborg, eds., *Cambridge History of Later Medieval Philosophy* (pp. 771–84), Cambridge: Cambridge University Press.
Bougerol, J. G. (1963), *Introduction to the Works of Bonaventure*, Patterson, NJ: St. Anthony Guild Press.
Brady, I. (1967), "Alexander of Hales," in P. Edwards, ed., *Encyclopedia of Philosophy*, New York: The Macmillan Company.
Doucet, V. (1946), "A new source of the *Summa fratris Alexandri*," *Franciscan Studies* 6, pp. 403–17.
——(1947), "The history of the problem of the authenticity of the *Summa*," *Franciscan Studies* 7, pp. 26–41.
Gál, G. (1998), "Alexander of Hales," in E. Craig, ed., *The Routledge Encyclopedia of Philosophy*, vol. 1 (pp. 176–8), New York: Routledge.
Gössmann, E. (1964), *Metaphysik und Heilgeschichte: eine theologische Untersuchung der Summa Halensis*, Munich.
Principe, W. (1967), *Alexander of Hales' Theology of the Hypostatic Union*, Toronto: Pontifical Institute of Mediaeval Studies.
Wood, R. (1993), "Distinct ideas and perfect solicitude: Alexander of Hales, Richard Rufus, and Odo Rigaldus," *Franciscan Studies* 53, pp. 7–31.

8

Alfarabi

DEBORAH L. BLACK

Abū Naṣr Muḥammad ibn Muḥammad al-Fārābī (b. ca. 870; d. ca. 950) was probably of Turkish origin, born in the district of Fārāb in Transoxania. Few of the details of Alfarabi's biography and education are known with certainty, however, and many of the more colorful anecdotes associated with his name are recounted by writers who lived many centuries after Alfarabi himself, and thus their historical accuracy is suspect. But Alfarabi is known to have studied philosophy in Baghdad with the Christian scholar Yuḥanna ibn Ḥaylān (d. 910), and possibly also with Abū Bishr Mattā (d. 940), the Christian translator of Aristotle's *Poetics* and *Posterior Analytics* into Arabic. Among Alfarabi's students at Baghdad was another important Christian translator and logician, Yaḥyā ibn ʿĀdī (d. 974). In 942, Alfarabi left Baghdad for Syria, traveling to Damascus and then to Aleppo at the invitation of the Ḥamdānid ruler, Sayf al-Dawlah, who became his patron for a time. Alfarabi traveled to Egypt in 948–9, later returning to Syria, where he died in Damascus around 950 (Gutas 1999).

If the attribution of over one hundred works to Alfarabi by medieval biographers is accurate, then only a fraction of his works have survived to the present day. Of these, many have only recently become available in modern editions, and a number of works still remain unavailable in translation into western languages. These works include both commentaries on Aristotle and Plato as well as independent treatises. Many are concerned with logic and the philosophy of language, although important treatises devoted to topics in metaphysics, psychology, and political philosophy also survive.

Logic and language

Alfarabi's high reputation amongst later philosophers in both the Islamic and Jewish traditions was particularly linked to his logical and linguistic writings. For example, in the preface to his *Guide for the Perplexed*, the twelfth-century Jewish philosopher Moses Maimonides praised Alfarabi as the finest logician known to him, describing his logical treatises as "faultlessly excellent" (Maimonides 1963, 1, p. lx).

Alfarabi's surviving logical and linguistic writings can conveniently be split into two categories: commentaries on the logical works of Aristotle, that is the *Organon*, and independent treatises. The commentaries include a set of epitomes covering all the works of Aristotle's *Organon*, as well as Porphyry's *Isagoge* and the *Rhetoric* and *Poetics*, which had been grouped with Aristotle's logical writings by the Greek commentators from the School of Alexandria. While these epitomes are commentaries inasmuch as they follow the general outline of Aristotle's treatises, they are neither summaries of Aristotle nor line by line expositions of his text, but rather Alfarabi's own personal consideration of the themes and issues raised in these treatises. By contrast, Alfarabi's *Long Commentary on Aristotle's On Interpretation* is a commentary in the more standard sense of the term, offering a detailed, paragraph by paragraph explication of Aristotle's theory of propositions, including his famous discussion in chapter 9 of the truth conditions for statements about future contingents.

Alfarabi's independent treatises on logic and language contain some of his most original contributions to the history of philosophy. An important theme in many of them, such as the *Utterances Employed in Logic*, the *Book of Letters, Reminder of the Way to Happiness*, and portions of the *Catalogue of the Sciences*, is the relation between philosophical logic and the grammar of ordinary language. Alfarabi conceives of logic as a sort of universal grammar, which provides the rules for correct reasoning in all languages; grammar, by contrast, is concerned only with those rules and idioms that have been established by convention for the speakers of a particular natural language, for example, English or Arabic. Logic, then, provides the rules that govern the intellect and its intelligible concepts, whereas grammar provides the rules that govern only the outward linguistic expression of those intelligibles. Alfarabi describes the relation between logic and grammar in this way in his *Reminder of the Way to Happiness*:

> Just as the art of grammar rectifies language so that nothing is expressed except by means of what is correct according to the custom of the speakers of the language, so too the art of logic rectifies the mind so that it only apprehends intellectually what is correct in all matters. And in general the relation of the art of grammar to expressions is analogous to the relation of the art of logic to intelligibles (1985b, p. 80).

The conception of logic and grammar expressed in this passage reflects Alfarabi's need to address the peculiar circumstances of practicing philosophy in the medieval Islamic world. Entire systems of Greek philosophy had been imported into Islamic culture, and thus Arabic-speaking philosophers had to face the difficulties created by translation, including the need to invent a philosophical vocabulary in Arabic. Moreover, some Arabic grammarians and their allies amongst the *mutakallimūn* (theologians) viewed Greek logic as an affront to Arabic grammar, and they suspected that the philosophers' interest in Greek logic was simply an attempt to substitute Greek grammar for Arabic. Alfarabi's logical and linguistic writings represented one of the most systematic efforts to harmonize these competing approaches to the study of language by recognizing grammar and logic as distinct sciences, each autonomous in its own sphere, and each necessary to ensure the correctness of linguistic expression and its underlying content.

While Alfarabi upheld the respective autonomy of logic and grammar, he was also keenly aware of the philosopher's dependence upon ordinary language for the expression of his ideas. Thus a number of his linguistic writings, such as the *Utterances Employed in Logic* and the *Book of Letters*, address the relation between ordinary language and the development of a technical philosophical vocabulary. The *Book of Letters* also places these concerns in the broader context of a general account of the nature and development of human language, civilization, and philosophy. The text begins with a linguistic study of how the everyday meanings of Arabic particles provide the basis for their transformation into technical philosophical terms for the ten Aristotelian categories, and in the third and final part Alfarabi examines how the various interrogative particles can be used to raise philosophical questions framed in terms of Aristotle's four causes. In the central part of the *Book of Letters*, Alfarabi presents his larger theory of the origins of human language, explaining how the natural evolution of language culminates in the development of practical arts, philosophy and science, and political and religious institutions. In this context, two of the most central themes in Alfarabi's philosophical outlook are woven together: the logical theme of the nature of language and the political theme of the relation between philosophy and religion. Alfarabi views religion as essentially the popular expression of philosophy communicated to the non-philosophical masses by prophets, who employ the two popular logical arts of rhetoric and poetics. Logic, then, provides one of the key foundations for Alfarabi's claim that philosophy is both absolutely and temporally prior to religion, "in the same way that the user of tools precedes the tools in time" (1969a, p. 132).

The connection between Alfarabi's logic and his philosophy of religion is especially evident in his discussions of the nature of demonstration and its relation to other methods of reasoning found in his accounts of syllogistic theory. As already noted, he followed the tradition that considered Aristotle's *Rhetoric* and *Poetics* as logical treatises, which implied that they must in some way involve the application of syllogistic models to oratory and poetry. This meant that rhetoric and poetics, as well as dialectic and sophistry, had to be fitted into Alfarabi's hierarchical conception of logic, according to which the purpose of logic can only be fully realized in the demonstrative theory given in Aristotle's *Posterior Analytics*. Logic seeks primarily to produce certain and scientific knowledge through the use of demonstration, and the remaining logical arts are ancillary to this aim. Alfarabi expresses this point as follows in his *Catalogue of the Sciences*:

> The fourth [part of logic] contains the rules by which demonstrative statements are tested, the rules which pertain to those things from which philosophy is welded together, and everything by which its activity becomes most complete, most excellent, and most perfect. . . . And the fourth part is the most vigorous of them, pre-eminent in dignity and authority. Logic seeks its principal intention only in this fourth part, the remainder of its parts having been invented only for its sake (1968, pp. 87–9).

This does not mean, of course, that the non-demonstrative logical arts are of no utility in Alfarabi's view, only that they do not contribute directly to the perfection of the theoretical knowledge that is the principal aim of philosophy. Where these arts, and in particular rhetoric and poetics, are of special importance to philosophy is in the political and religious arena. Following Plato in the *Republic*, Alfarabi held the view that the true philosopher must not only seek his own perfection, but must also attempt to communicate his philosophy to others and to make it a political reality, as he asserts in his *Attainment of Happiness*: "To be a truly perfect philosopher one has to possess both the theoretical sciences and the faculty for exploiting them for the benefit of all others according to their capacity" (1969b, p. 43). It is the function of a virtuous religion to ensure this practical realization of philosophical truths, and thus Alfarabi maintains in his political writings that the ideal philosopher is also a prophet and a political leader. And in turn his principal means of communicating philosophical truths to the common people, and of persuading them to behave justly and virtuously, is through the persuasive and imaginative arts of rhetoric and poetics. In this way these arts are for Alfarabi an indispensable part of philosophy and a necessary complement to demonstrative science, just as religion is a necessary partner with philosophy in the formation of the ideal political state.

Alfarabi's theory of demonstration is found principally in two texts, the *Book of Demonstration*, which is part of the series of epitomes of the Aristotelian *Organon*, and a short independent treatise, *The Conditions of Certitude*. In these works Alfarabi identifies certain knowledge or science as the cognitive act that is the goal of demonstration. The pillar around which his analysis of certitude revolves is the distinction between two basic types of knowledge, concept-formation (*taṣawwur*) and assent (*taṣdīq*), a distinction that became standard in discussions of logic amongst all the major Islamic philosophers. Concept-formation is the apprehension of simple concepts which culminates in the mind's grasping of the essence of the conceived object. In contrast to concept-formation, which is neither true nor false, assent always implies a judgment of truth or falsehood and admits of varying degrees, the highest of which confers complete certitude about the object known. According to Alfarabi, then, demonstration is the logical method that yields perfect and complete acts of concept-formation and assent, the former through definitions and the latter through demonstrative syllogisms, the main topics of Aristotle's *Posterior Analytics*.

One of the most interesting and unusual aspects of Alfarabi's interpretation of the Aristotelian theory of demonstration is his discussion of the concept of certitude itself. Contrary to what might be expected, Alfarabi does not identify certitude with necessity, either on the part of the object known or on the part of the knower. Rather, he distinguishes between necessary and non-necessary certitude, the latter of which holds "only at a particular time." While Alfarabi continues to maintain that demonstration in its strictest sense culminates in necessary certitude, which requires an object that is "necessarily existent," the category of non-necessary certitude provides a theoretical foundation for the claim that some form of certitude can be had of contingent and variable objects as well as of necessary and immutable ones.

In addition to extending the concept of certitude to contingent objects of knowledge, Alfarabi also adds conditions pertaining to the knower to his definition of absolute certitude, so that it becomes a form of second-order knowledge. In order to claim absolute certitude, then, he argues that the knower must not merely know that a proposition is true, but she must also know *that* she knows it:

> Certitude is for us to believe, concerning the truth to which we have assented, that it is not possible at all for what we believe about this matter to be different from what we believe. In addition to this it is for us to believe, concerning our belief, that another belief is not possible – to the extent that whenever some belief about the first belief is formed, it is impossible for it to be otherwise, and so on *ad infinitum* (1987, p. 20).

Psychology and metaphysics

Alfarabi's views on the nature of mind are primarily contained in his metaphysical treatises, although one brief treatise devoted to the topic of mind, the *Letter Concerning the Intellect*, does survive. In keeping with his linguistic approach, in this treatise and in metaphysical works such as the *Book of Letters* and *On One and Unity*, Alfarabi approaches his topic by way of an analysis of the multiple meanings of which key technical terms, such as 'intellect' (*ʿaql*), 'one' (*wāḥid*), 'substance' (*jawhar*), and so on, admit both in philosophical and in popular usage. In the *Letter Concerning the Intellect* he isolates six basic meanings of 'intellect' and 'intelligent', ranging from its popular use denoting someone who is practically wise, to its use to denote the various intellectual powers of the human soul in Aristotle's *De anima*, as interpreted by the later Greek commentators. These powers, according to Alfarabi, are four in number: (1) the potential intellect, the pure capacity for thought; (2) the intellect in act, after it has realized its capacity to think; (3) the acquired intellect, the stage reached when the mind has perfected itself and become an object of thought for itself; and (4) the agent intellect of *De anima* 3.5, a separate substance and the moving cause of all human understanding (Alfarabi 1963).

The fullest picture of both Alfarabi's psychology and his metaphysics is found in his two latest works, *The Opinions of the People of the Virtuous City*, and *The Political Regime*, both of which combine metaphysical and psychological with political topics, after the model of Plato's *Republic*. These texts employ an emanational framework adapted from Neoplatonism and Ptolemaic astronomy in their explanation of the relations between God, the celestial intellects and bodies, and our sublunar world. Not all of Alfarabi's metaphysical writings present this emanational picture, however, and this has led some modern interpreters to question his commitment to the theory of emanation as well as his general interest in metaphysical issues. Despite the doubts of modern readers, however, Alfarabi was an important source on metaphysical themes to later Islamic philosophers, especially AVICENNA. Indeed Avicenna, who was not generally renowned for his modesty, credited Alfarabi's treatise, *On the Aims of Aristotle's Metaphysics*, with unlocking for him the secrets of Aristotle's text, which remained opaque to him even after he had read it over forty times! One of the principal themes of this short Alfarabian text is that many people become perplexed when reading Aristotle's *Metaphysics* because they expect it to deal extensively with theological topics, such as God and the separate intellects, when in fact these topics are confined to book Lambda (Twelve). Alfarabi holds that this is a misconception of the nature of philosophical metaphysics which results from confusing it with dialectical theology (*kalām*). While metaphysics does include the study of divine beings as one of its parts, it derives its status as first philosophy not from the fact that it studies the highest beings but from the fact that its consideration of being *qua* being provides the most comprehensive and universal explanation of reality (Alfarabi 1988).

On this account of metaphysics, then, it is quite consistent that Alfarabi, like Aristotle, should spend most of his energies on metaphysical matters pertaining to general ontology and the signification of metaphysical terms. But emanation remains an important aspect of metaphysics, since it completes the causal explanation of the principles of all beings with an account of how God, the first being, produces the world through intermediary causes – an account not found in Aristotle himself, but developed by the Neoplatonic tradition that influenced many of Aristotle's later commentators (Druart 1987a). As noted above, the mechanics of emanation are drawn from the realm of Ptolemaic cosmology, in which the world is taken to consist of a series of concentric spheres: the first heaven, the sphere of the fixed stars, and the spheres of Saturn, Jupiter, Mars, the Sun, Venus, Mercury, and the Moon. As an explanation of God's production of the world, Alfarabian emanation draws upon both Aristotelian and Neoplatonic conceptions of the nature of divine being. With Neoplatonism, Alfarabi agrees in taking God to be the first cause of the existence of all other beings, and not merely, as in Aristotle, the first cause of motion. God is one, immaterial, and eternal, and his creative act is a necessary outpouring of his goodness. In the emanational scheme, however, the most important divine attribute is one that ultimately derives from Aristotle's description of God's activity as a "thinking of thinking," since it is the divine activity of self-contemplation that links God to the world as its creator. Through God's self-contemplation, there is an emanation (*fayḍ*) from him of a second intellect. But since this second intellect is dependent upon God for its own existence, *its* peculiar act of self-contemplation, unlike God's, is not fully self-contained, but also entails the contemplation of God. This intellect's self-contemplation generates its corresponding heavenly sphere,

113

whereas its thinking of God generates a third intellect. This dyadic pattern of contemplation is repeated for the remainder of the spheres, generating a total of ten separate intellects in addition to God. The use of a dyadic model sets Alfarabi apart from most other Neoplatonic thinkers, who use triadic models to account for the emanation of a distinct soul for each celestial body. By contrast, Alfarabi does not distinguish the soul as mover of the sphere from its intellect, as he makes clear in the *Political Regime*, so there is no room in his system for a third emanation. The terminus of the emanational process is our own sublunar world, whose corresponding intellect is none other than the Agent Intellect of Aristotle's *De anima* 3.5, which as we have noted is in Alfarabi's philosophy one for all human beings, illuminating intelligibles for individual human intellects in much the same way as the sun illuminates visible objects.

Through its termination in the agent intellect, emanation allows Alfarabi to link together into a single system cosmology, metaphysics, and human psychology. This link in turn has repercussions for his political philosophy and his philosophy of mind, since it forms the foundation for his account of prophecy. We have already noted with reference to Alfarabi's *Letter Concerning the Intellect* that Alfarabi adopted the basic tenets of Aristotle's psychology of the intellect, as systematized by later Greek commentators. In other respects his psychology is also Aristotelian: the soul's principal faculties are identified as the nutritive, sensitive, imaginative, and rational powers. The appetitive powers of the soul correspond to its cognitive powers, so that the soul's powers of sensation, imagination, and reason or intellect give rise to a corresponding appetite towards the objects apprehended by that faculty. Of the soul's pre-rational powers, the imagination is of special note because of the function it plays in Alfarabi's account of prophecy. According to Alfarabi, the imagination includes amongst its operations the capacity for imitation, which allows it to represent under sensible guise objects that are not themselves sensible and material. In this way, the imagination is able to depict even intelligible concepts and abstract philosophical truths, a capacity central to the prophet's ability to communicate truths about God to the non-philosophical populace. This is not to say, however, that Alfarabi's view of the prophet makes him dependent entirely upon the imaginative faculty. Rather, he argues that prophets must first possess full intellectual understanding of the truths that they are to communicate through images, and that all prophets must also be philosophers. What distinguishes the prophet from the philosopher is that after his rational faculty has been perfected, its contents are able to overflow or emanate into his imaginative faculty, thereby enabling him to imitate for others what he himself comprehends intellectually. Here again, then, the concept of emanation is a key element in Alfarabi's explanation of the workings of the prophetic imagination.

Political philosophy

Most of the elements of Alfarabi's theoretical philosophy are essentially Aristotelian. But the absence of an Arabic translation of Aristotle's *Politics* meant that Alfarabi's chief inspirations in political philosophy were Plato's *Republic* and his *Laws*, modified to suit the social and historical circumstances of Alfarabi's own milieu, and to reflect his interest in the political aspects of religious institutions. An excellent expression of the interplay between Alfarabi's Platonic and Islamic heritage occurs in the *Attainment of Happiness*, where he argues that the concepts of philosopher, lawgiver, and *imām* are one and the same, the different labels reflecting the different religious and philosophical aspects of political leadership (1969a, p. 47). This entails, of course, that just as the true prophet is also a philosopher, the true philosopher, while not necessarily a prophet, is, as in Plato, obliged to assume political and also religious leadership or risk rendering his philosophy futile.

Alfarabi's political Platonism is especially evident in his sketch of the conditions for an ideal state and the various ways in which, through a failure to fulfill those conditions, corrupt states arise. In *The Political Regime* Alfarabi provides anthropological and ethical foundations for his political theory that reflect the variety of cultures and religions embraced by the Islamic empire in his day. Alfarabi echoes the Aristotelian dictum that human beings are by nature political animals whose perfection requires that they live together in organized societies. He recognizes international, national, and civic organizations as the most important human institutions, whereas community and family associations are subordinate to these larger associations. He also recognizes that a variety of diverse political institutions is a necessary corollary of the diversity of nations and ethnic groups into which humanity is divided, since these groups vary in their physiological attributes and develop different diets and customs as a result of their diverse geographical environments and the resources that they yield. Alfarabi does not allow, however, that these differences affect the essential humanity of different groups, nor does he accept that local variations make some groups better suited than others to the practice of philosophy or the founding of an ideal state. Rather, he argues that local differences entail religious pluralism, that is, the view that there may be a plurality of equally virtuous religions appropriate to the different nations, each one reflecting the truth through the symbols and images most familiar and significant to the peoples to whom it is addressed (1963, pp. 32–3, 41).

But if all peoples are equally equipped by nature to cultivate philosophy and thereby develop an ideal political state, why in practice does this so seldom come about? The reason is essentially the rarity of individual leaders who combine all the intellectual, moral, and spiritual qualities required of the first lawgiver of an ideal state. This first ruler must have attained theoretical perfection, since otherwise he could not direct his subjects towards such perfection. Hence the founder of any virtuous state must, in Platonic terms, be a Philosopher-King. Still, while it is necessary for such a ruler to be a philosopher, philosophy is not sufficient for his success. In the *Virtuous City*, Alfarabi lists a number of additional moral and even physical attributes that the ideal ruler must possess. Most importantly, however, this first ideal ruler must also have the prophetic gifts that will allow him to institute a religion that will ensure that all citizens share in the virtues exemplified in the state. Once founded, moreover, the maintenance of the ideal state and its virtuous religion poses a challenge. For while Alfarabi does allow that subsequent rulers need not be prophets, and in some cases a group of leaders rather than a single person may rule, the ideal state cannot survive unless both its philosophical foundations and its religious observances remain strong. Thus Alfarabi, again echoing Plato, provides an elaborate typology of the ways in which these conditions can either deteriorate or fail to arise at all.

He initially identifies three major types of corruption to which the ideal state may fall prey. The first, to which Alfarabi devotes the most attention, are ignorant cities, in which philosophy has never taken hold. In them both the leader and the citizens fail to understand their true nature and purpose, and in their ignorance substitute some other vain goal for the true end discerned by philosophy. Ignorant cities are subdivided in turn according to the various corrupt goals that they seek. Among them Alfarabi lists the following: indispensable cities, which seek mere subsistence as their goal, and appear to be envisaged as primitive agrarian societies; vile cities, which pursue the accumulation of wealth; base cities, which exist solely for the sake of pleasure and amusement; timocratic cities, which have as their goal honor and fame; despotic or tyrannical cities, in which power and domination over

115

others is the principal goal; and finally democratic cities, in which there is no single motivating end, but each citizen is left to seek whatever he or she deems best, so that the dominant pursuit is simply freedom from all external and internal constraints. All of these cities are considered corruptions by Alfarabi, with the despotic city being the most corrupt, the timocratic the least, and the democratic combining both the greatest goods and the greatest evils in a single state.

Unlike ignorant cities, Alfarabi's other two classes of corrupt cities, the immoral (or wicked) and the errant, are corrupt in the strict sense of the term, in that they possess now or once possessed some sort of knowledge of the true human end but fail to follow that knowledge. In immoral cities the entire community, ruler and citizens alike, has lapsed in its pursuit of the true good and reverted to pursuing one of the aims of ignorant cities. By contrast, in errant cities the leader himself is a lapsed philosopher and a false prophet who possesses true knowledge of the proper end that his city should follow, but because his own desires have been corrupted he deceives his citizens into pursuing unworthy goals.

Alfarabi's political writings also mention people whom he calls the "weeds" in virtuous cities, those who, either because of their lack of ability or their viciousness, inhabit the virtuous city and conform to its laws, while failing to participate personally in its goals. Although some of these people may be harmless, others carry with them the seeds for corrupting the entire city, by misinterpreting its laws either intentionally or through ignorance. In the weeds, then, we have yet another reason why the ideal state remains elusive despite its foundations in the rational and political nature that Alfarabi identifies as distinctively human.

Bibliography

Primary sources

(1963), *The Political Regime*, trans. F. M. Najjar, in Ralph Lerner and Muhsin Mahdi, eds., *Medieval Political Philosophy: A Sourcebook* (pp. 31–57), Ithaca, NY: Cornell University Press.

(1968), *Ihsā' al-ʿulūm (Catalogue of the Sciences)*, ed. Uthman Amin, Cairo: Librarie Anglo-Egyptienne.

(1969a), *Book of Letters (Kitāb al-ḥurūf): Commentary on Aristotle's Metaphysics*, ed. M. Mahdi, Beirut: Dar el-Mashreq.

(1969b), *Philosophy of Plato and Aristotle*, trans. M. Mahdi, Ithaca, NY: Cornell University Press.

(1973), "The letter concerning the intellect," trans. A. Hyman, in A. Hyman and J. J. Walsh, eds., *Philosophy in the Middle Ages: The Christian, Islamic, and Jewish Traditions* (pp. 215–21), Indianapolis: Hackett.

(1985a), *On the Perfect State: Abū Naṣr al-Fārābī's Mabādi' arā' ahl al-madīnah al-fāḍilah*, ed. and trans. Richard Walzer, Oxford: Clarendon Press.

(1985b), *Kitāb al-tanbīh ʿalā sabīl al-saʿādah (Reminder of the Way to Happiness)*, ed. Jafar Al Yasin, Beirut: Dar al-Manahel.

(1987), *Kitāb al-burhān (Demonstration)*, ed. M. Fakhry, Beirut: Dar el-Mashreq.

(1988), *On the Aims of Aristotle's Metaphysics*, trans. D. Gutas, in Dimitri Gutas, *Avicenna and the Aristotelian Tradition* (pp. 240–2), Leiden: Brill.

Secondary sources

Abed, S. B. (1991), *Aristotelian Logic and the Arabic Language in Alfarabi*, Albany, NY: State University of New York Press.

Davidson, H. A. (1992), *Alfarabi, Avicenna, and Averroes on Intellect: Their Cosmologies, Theories of the Active Intellect, and Theories of Human Intellect*, Oxford: Oxford University Press.

Druart, T.-A. (1987a), "Al-Farabi and emanationism," in John F. Wippel, ed., *Studies in Medieval Philosophy* (pp. 23–43), Washington, DC: The Catholic University of America Press.

——(1987b), "Substance in Arabic philosophy: Al-Fārābī's discussion," *Proceedings of the American Catholic Philosophical Association* 61, pp. 88–97.

Galston, Miriam (1990), *Politics and Excellence: The Political Philosophy of Alfarabi*, Princeton, NJ: Princeton University Press.

Gutas, Dimitri (1999), Fārābī: "Biography," in Ehsan Yarshater, ed., *Encyclopaedia Iranica*, vol. 9 (fasc. 2, pp. 213–16), New York: Bibliotheca Persica Press.

Mahdi, M. (1972), "Alfarabi," in L. Strauss and J. Cropsey, eds., *History of Political Philosophy*, 2nd edn. (pp. 182–202), Chicago: Rand McNally.

Maimonides, Moses (1963), *The Guide of the Perplexed*, 2 vols., trans. S. Pines, Chicago and London: University of Chicago Press.

Netton, I. R. (1989), *Al-Fārābī and his School*, London and New York: Routledge.

Parens, J. (1995), *Metaphysics as Rhetoric: Alfarabi's Summary of Plato's Laws*, Albany: State University of New York Press.

9

Algazali

THÉRÈSE-ANNE DRUART

Abū Hāmid Muhammad al-Ghazālī (b. 1058; d. 1111), not to be confused with his brother Ahmad, was a Persian born in Tus, and wrote most of his numerous works in Arabic. They cover Islamic jurisprudence, *kalām* (Islamic theology or apologetics), various religious topics, and a large *summa, The Revivification of the Religious Sciences* (*'Ihyā' 'ulūm al-dīn*). So impressive were these works that people called Algazali "The Proof of Islam." He had a distinguished teaching career in various *madrasahs* (Islamic colleges) including the prestigious Nizamiyya School in Baghdad. There, around 1095, a spiritual crisis – and maybe some political events – prompted him to give up his post in order to lead an ascetic and reclusive life in Damascus and Jerusalem and to become a Sufi. At that time he made the pilgrimage to Mecca and Medina. In 1106, he returned to teaching, first in Nishapur and finally in Tus, where he died.

In philosophical circles Algazali is well known for his staunch defense of Sunni Islamic orthodoxy and for his vigorous opposition to the *falāsifa* (the Hellenized philosophers) epitomized in his famous *The Incoherence of the Philosophers* (*Tahāfut al-falāsifa* (*TF*), known in Latin as *Destructio philosophorum*). So powerful was this attack that AVERROES (b. 1126; d. 1198) deemed necessary to rebut it point by point and at great length in his own *Incoherence of the Incoherence* (*Tahāfut at-tahāfut* (*TT*) or *Destructio destructionis*). Yet ironically, history played a trick on Algazali. As preparation for the *Incoherence*, after careful reading and study of the works of the philosophers, Algazali had written *The Aims of the Philosophers* (*Maqāsid al-falāsifa* (*MF*)), which presents a summation of mainly AVICENNA'S views. In the Middle Ages, when *MF* was translated, the passages explaining that this work presented positions the author opposed and which he intended to criticize systematically were somehow omitted from the Latin version. Besides, at that time its follow-up, *TF*, had not been translated. Therefore, Latin philosophers, such as AQUINAS, mistook Algazali for an Avicennan philosopher and innocently attributed to him views he rejected. In the early Renaissance, when *TF* and *TT* began to circulate in Latin, the error was finally spotted.

Algazali and philosophy

Too often Algazali is presented as an enemy of philosophy. In fact he is not opposed to philosophy as such, but rather to those who uncritically assent to some kind of Hellenic philosophical orthodoxy and to Aristotelian naturalist tenets in particular. For instance, Algazali penned *The Standard for Knowledge* (*Mi'yār al-'ilm*), an exposition of Avicennan

118

logic, not to refute it but rather to promote its use among theologians. His intellectual auto-biography, *Freedom and Fulfillment (Al-Munqidh min adalāl (MmD))*, unknown to the Latins and often called "Deliverance from error" in English), states that both logic and mathe-matics are religiously neutral. Rejecting them in the name of faith makes of Islam an object of ridicule (1980, pp. 74–5, nn. 43–4). *Freedom and Fulfillment* also asserts that the philoso-phers' logic is more precise and more sophisticated than that of the theologians but that philosophers, contrary to their own claims, are far from always following it rigorously, par-ticularly in metaphysics.

Interestingly, in this autobiography, Algazali chides the theologians for their unsophisti-cated ontology and the weakness of their criticisms of the philosophers. They had not studied their texts carefully enough to really understand them (1980, p. 69, n. 24, and p. 70, n. 26). Algazali, therefore, exerts his philosophical skills and unusual acumen to attack the uncriti-cal conformism of the philosophers, particularly in what concerns emanationism. He uses any argument apt to show that the philosophers fall into self-contradictions but is careful often not to endorse them. This makes it difficult to determine whether he upholds the posi-tions and arguments he uses (*TF*, third introduction, pp. 7–8, n. 22). One must, therefore, be very cautious in attributing any of the *TF*'s views or arguments to Algazali himself.

This first interpretive problem leads to a second. Already Ibn Tufayl (d. as an old man in 1185) and Averroes complained that Algazali seems to claim different things in different texts and some scholars have called Algazali's sincerity into doubt. For instance, though in *TF* Algazali presents harsh criticisms of the philosophers and their emanationism in particular, in the probably later work *The Niche of Lights (Mishkāt al-'anwār)*, overtly a Sufi work, he does not hesitate to use emanationist language. Averroes, therefore, accused Algazali of duplicity since he openly attacks emanationism but esoterically endorses it in his Sufi works. Though formally professing the Ash'arite theological orthodoxy, Algazali would in fact have concealed his agreement with the philosophers on some issues and hinted that such was the case. Some contemporary scholars, such as Herbert H. Davidson, have fol-lowed Averroes (Algazali 1998, p. xxviii). Recently R. M. Frank (1992 and 1994) has argued that Algazali is very cautious in what he says, never really contradicts himself, and, while rejecting some rather tame Avicennan theses concerning God's relation to the cosmos as its creator, he adopted important ones (1992, p. 86). Frank contends, for instance, that Algazali does give a role to intermediary or secondary causes and, therefore, departs from strict Ash'arite occasionalism, but M. E. Marmura (1994 and 1995) disputes his conclusions. More recently, Jules Janssens (2001) has shown that, while in the *MF*, the presentation of the philosophers' views is very close to Avicennan passages, in the *TF* it is much less so. He wonders then whether in the *TF* Algazali is not more concerned with Aristotelian natural-ism than with Avicenna, who had already distanced himself from it. In his *TT* and other works Averroes bitterly reproaches Avicenna for his innovations. Algazali may have thought that Avicenna was moving in the right direction, even if he did not go far enough.

Algazali and causation

One thing is clear: Algazali himself took the core of the debate between the Sunni Islamic view and that of the Neoplatonizing Aristotelians to be a key philosophical notion: cause. In his intellectual autobiography (*MmD*), a late work, while discussing the philosophers' physics, Algazali asserts that religion does not require the repudiation of this science, except for some specific points all resting on a conception of nature. For Algazali, contrary to the

Aristotelian conception, nature does not act by itself since it is subject to God and, therefore, does not have an internal principle of motion and rest. Nature is simply used by its creator; it is inert. If the philosophers had realized this, they would not have fallen into their three main false metaphysical positions:

1 Denying human bodies will be assembled on the Last Day. If such were the case, then there would be an infinite number of souls. Algazali objects that the problem of the infinity of souls arises only if one considers the world to be eternal (Marmura 1989).
2 Maintaining the eternity of the world, past and future. Since for Algazali the world is utterly contingent on God's free will it cannot be eternal, whereas the philosophers conceive only of a necessary emanation, which, therefore, must be eternal. Hence, Algazali defends a conception of modality (necessity and contingency), different from that of Avicenna who himself had already developed that of Aristotle, while radically modifying it (Kukkonen 2000);
3 Affirming that God knows universals, but not particulars. Since for Algazali creation is an act of the will and will requires knowledge of what is willed in order to evaluate alternatives, such knowledge must include that of particulars.

In the *TF* and in his autobiography, Algazali insists that his main problem with philosophers concerns metaphysical issues, all of which depend on a certain conception of causation. Avicenna deals with the four Aristotelian causes in a special treatise of his physics but also shows in his *Metaphysics*, VI, 1 and 2, that there is a metaphysical type of cause, which, contrary to a physical efficient cause, does not temporally precede its effect but rather is simultaneous with it. Such metaphysical causes are the only true causes, physical causes being only necessary, and even at times sufficient conditions, for their efficacy. For Avicenna, such metaphysical causes are linked to a necessary emanationist and, therefore, eternal causal system which does not involve the will of the agent. Yet, contrary to Aristotle who held that the prime mover had no knowledge of any being inferior to itself, Avicenna claims that the first cause, God, knows universals but not particulars. Algazali is adamant that God must know particulars and act by will.

In *TF*, discussion 17, when finally directly confronting the physical causation issue, Algazali presents two views of causation in order to refute the philosophers and their assertion that miracles are impossible. One is a strict Ash'arite occasionalism, but the other grants natures to created things as well as some causal efficacy while maintaining that the divine act remains voluntary, and that divine power is such that it can intervene in the natural order and, therefore, operate miracles. Marmura claims that Algazali upholds the Ash'arite theory (*TF*, p. xxv, and 1994, 1995), whereas Frank considers the second, which is close to Avicenna's modified reformulation of Aristotle, minus the necessary emanation, as the one Algazali truly accepts (1992, 1994). As scholarship on the discussion 17 is extensive, it seems more useful to concentrate on Algazali's conception of agency, particularly as it is presented in other passages of the *TF*, since this is the text most accessible to the majority of readers. (Studies of Algazali's views on causation in other texts can be found in Abrahamov 1988; Frank 1992, 1994; Marmura 1994, 1995; for a contrast with those of Averroes see Kogan 1985.)

Algazali's conception of the agent in the *Incoherence*

Algazali, who claims that the whole dispute with the *falāsifa* turns on a different conception of causation, highlights some aspects of contrast between the "Aristotelian" positions and the one he uses to defeat them. What is, therefore, the position he presents as an alternative to that of the followers of Aristotle? But is it really an alternative or rather simply an attack against the philosophers' reductionist approach to causation? It is clear that he argues that they do not leave much room for voluntary action and, in particular, posit a God who does not act voluntarily but rather by some kind of natural causation, grounded in necessary emanationism. For Algazali, properly speaking, something inanimate does not act. Acting requires cognition as well as will. The philosophers deny proper cognition and will to God and so reduce his causation to that of the inanimate. The prime mover, i.e., God, does not act in any sense; the eternal motion of the heavens is grounded in its own act of desiring to imitate the unmoved mover and, therefore, Aristotle and his followers have made of the heavens an animal by ensouling it.

In the *Munqidh* (*MdD*), a work posterior to the *TF*, Algazali presents the philosophical disciplines in the traditional order and, therefore, consideration of physics precedes that of metaphysics. In his brief evaluation of the natural sciences, he maintains, in opposition to Aristotle, that nature does not have an inner principle of motion or rest. Nature is inert and the Creator simply uses it as one would a tool. "The sun, moon, stars and the elements are subject to God's command: none of them does any act (*fi'l*) by itself or from itself (*bi-dhātihi 'an dhātihi*)" (1980, n. 45). This explains why in discussion 17 of the *TF* Algazali attacks the philosophers' contention that they can show the heavens are an animal. For him the celestial bodies do not act, since they have no purposive activity, and so are inert or inanimate.

The *TF* discussions proceed in reverse order, i.e., metaphysical considerations precede physical ones and, therefore, the famous discussion 17 and its analysis of the burning of a piece of cotton. Following the order Algazali adopted in the *TF* may help us better to understand his conception of voluntary action, or more exactly of action, since for him any action must be voluntary. His emphasis on voluntary action leads him often to equate an agent and a craftsman since most of the book focuses on the temporal origination of the world. The book begins with a refutation of the philosophers' arguments for the eternity of the world, the first consideration of which rests on an analysis of the will. Philosophers do not pay attention to the will and so do not properly distinguish "mechanical" or natural causation from action, which by definition must be voluntary. Nature "does" nothing; only a voluntary agent acts or does.

But what is the will, through which the world temporally originates, for Algazali? The first discussion gives us a definition: "the will is an attribute whose function is to differentiate a thing from its similar" (1980, n. 41). What does similar mean here? It means something identical in every respect to something and, therefore, indiscernible from it. Algazali's story of someone who is hungry and needs to choose between two identical dates, makes it clear. For the philosophers, the problem of the past-eternity of the world arises from the impossibility of something external to God differentiating between two indiscernible instants at which the world could originate. But, counters Algazali, if God can specify one of these indiscernible "instants," then he is able to originate a temporal event as well as time and duration, without some new external condition having occurred. The will can determine itself and specify one of the indiscernibles, even if the intellect cannot differentiate between them, because the will is not necessarily determined by the intellect, or more exactly by its object. Since two instants are undistinguishable, particularly since temporal succession has not yet begun, then the will can only determine itself. To establish this point, Algazali proceeds by analogy to the human will. The philosophers object to that analogy. Human will implies an end but God of course cannot act for an end, which would

121

be external to him. Algazali grants that God does not act for an end but otherwise accepts the validity of the analogy. The philosophers also object to the human will's own ability to specify one of two indiscernibles but rather hold that the will is differentiated by some specific feature of one of the two "indiscernibles," such as a different weight for two glasses of water. Algazali retorts that the philosophers, in order to avoid a self-determining will, simply deny the existence of true indiscernibles. He concludes that anyone reflecting on the true nature of a voluntary act must affirm the existence of an attribute able to distinguish between indiscernibles in specifying one of them, i.e., the will or one of its aspects. This, of course, implies recognition that the intellect could not distinguish the objects from one another.

Discussion 3, as Kwame Gyekye already argued in 1987, maintains that an action must be voluntary and, therefore, include will and knowledge. It offers a very systematic examination of the agent (*fā'il*) and his act. Algazali asserts that the philosophers cannot show that God is the agent and maker of the world, failing to do so in three respects: with respect to the agent's will, with respect to the act's temporal origination, and with respect to a relationship common to effect and agent, i.e., that just as the agent is one so should the effect be.

The discussion begins with a definition of the agent. An agent is "one (*man*, i.e., a person) from whom the act proceeds together with the will to act by way of choice and the knowledge of what is willed" (1997, III, n. 4). The formulation implies that not all that proceeds (*iusduru*, a verb also used to describe emanation) need be an act. For an act to be truly an act it must proceed through will and, therefore, the agent must will by way of choice and with knowledge of what is willed. The voluntariness essential to any and every act stems from the agent's will and knowledge. So the primary meaning of acting requires origination through will and knowledge. Therefore, inanimate beings strictly speaking cannot act; only animals can. If anyone says that a "thing" is acting, then he is speaking metaphorically. When the philosophers claim that God is an agent, they simply use that word in a metaphorical manner since they deny he acts by will.

Algazali justifies his claim that only people – and eventually animals – can truly act by analyzing the way we judge and speak of an event combining voluntary agency and natural causation.

> If we suppose that a temporal event depends for its occurrence on two things, one voluntary and the other not, the intellect relates the act to the voluntary. The same goes for the way we speak. For if someone throws another into the fire and [the latter] dies, one says that [the former], not the fire, is the killer. (1997, n. 13, translation with some modification)

Intellect and the normal way of speaking attribute the killing to the person who voluntarily threw another into the fire but not to the efficacy (*ta'thīr*, not act, *fi'l*) of the fire, which does not involve the will. Algazali seems to view the fire, which he calls a proximate cause, simply as a tool in the hand of the murderer. For him blurring the distinction between act, which by definition is voluntary, and natural causation makes nonsense of the intellect's judgment, the normal way of speaking, and by implication of moral and juridical responsibility, as well as of the distinction between animate and inanimate.

Algazali here does not object to the existence of two types of cause (*sabab*), natural and voluntary, but he rejects the philosophers' contention that these types of causation can both be called "acts" in the same and proper way. For him, cause (*sabab*) is more extensive than agent (*fā'il*), which should be reserved for a being originating something through will informed by knowledge. He counts among the well-known and true universal principles the affirmation that "act does not belong to what is inanimate" but rather to what is animate. The requirement that an act arise through will implies the necessity of knowing what is willed, since "will necessarily entails knowledge." He concludes that the philosophers who in fact deny will and choice to God cannot really show that he is the agent and maker of the world, since for him making implies acting in the proper sense. If God has no will, then he cannot be an agent and its pseudo-act cannot be distinguished from the efficacy of inanimate beings.

Moving then to what concerns the act as such, Algazali claims that it must be understood as a temporal origination, for not every origination is an act. Again, Algazali begins this section with a definition. An act is "the bringing forth of something from non-being to being by means of its temporary origination" (1997, n. 18). Therefore, what is pre-eternal and pre-exists, not coming from non-being to being, is not temporally originated and cannot be an act. A necessary condition for an act to be a true act is that it be temporally originated. If the blurring, if not the disappearance of the distinction between voluntary and natural causation, is indeed a problem, and such is the case, then Algazali is right to reject it. But that temporal origin is a necessary condition for an act is less obvious.

In accordance with Avicenna's famous analysis of causation in the *Metaphysics* of the *Shifa'*, the philosophers counter that non-being, which, Algazali claims, should temporally precede the coming into being, is not a condition depending on the agent. Non-being does not require any agent and, therefore, is an irrelevant condition for an act. The agent is an agent of being or existence simply, however that existence originates, be it eternally or temporally. Therefore, an eternal world can be the act of God. Algazali, who grants to the philosophers that non-being does not have an agent, retorts that act attaches to agent strictly in terms of its temporal origination and not in terms of its previous non-being or in terms of its being an existent only. Therefore, what is perpetual as such cannot be the act of an agent. That the previous non-being does not originate from the agent is no problem insofar as many things can be conditions of the act of an agent without originating from that agent, such as the agent's own essence, power, will, knowledge, and even his very existence. For Algazali, strictly speaking, no act can be eternal as such but he accepts that an act be perpetually temporally originated. The condition of temporal origination certainly holds in the case of human makers, such as a tailor, weaver, and builder, to which he refers in the next discussion about the *falāsifa*'s inability to show that God is the maker of the world. There (1997, IV, nn. 4–10) he describes a maker as an agent who chooses and who acts after not having acted, as observation shows. However, Algazali does not explain in what way such a requirement would apply to God, and his immutability in particular. The philosophers call God a maker but by sheer metaphor and, therefore, their claim that God is a maker is empty. Algazali seems to imply that the essential characteristics of a human agent or maker apply to God univocally.

The third aspect of the analysis of agency focuses on the common relation between an agent and the result of his act, as posited by the philosophers, i.e., that both an agent and its effect must be one. This stems from a Neoplatonic dictum that from the one only the one proceeds. The philosophers deem God to be one in every respect. In order to explain how plurality arises from such strict oneness, they posit intermediaries. According to them, multiplicity in act can only stem: (1) From different acting powers, just as we do through the appetitive power which differs from what we do through the irascible; (2) from different matters, as the sun whitens washed garments but darkens people's faces; (3) from different instruments or tools; (4) or from mediation, the one agent doing one sole act, and that act in its turn (the Arabic uses the same term for the act and its result) producing another, etc. Though Algazali does not say so, the first three candidates for explaining multiplicity already assume it. Anyway, in the case of God's creation of the world, the One cannot act through a multiplicity of powers since he is perfectly one, nor can he act on pre-existing matters or by means of instruments that would precede their own creation. Therefore, the only possibility left is mediation through a series of intermediaries, each of a different kind.

Algazali shows that the principle that from one only one proceeds leads to endless inconsistencies. If one follows the principle, then one can never give an account of a multiplicity of beings of the same kind or species, and if one does not strictly follow it, then one has already compromised it. The philosophers, already at the level of the first intelligence, i.e., the first intermediary, accept a certain multiplicity, at least in that intelligence's objects of thought, which gives rise to the triadic Avicennan emanation. Even in the first emanation, i.e., the first intelligence, there is a meeting point of oneness and multiplicity and a slippage in the application of the principle. Therefore, why not jettison this principle altogether and assume such meeting points to God himself? This would ensure his knowledge of a multiplicity of particulars, required for his being a true agent, acting through will.

In order to save God's perfect oneness, Aristotle had drastically limited his knowing to self-knowledge. Avicenna himself felt compelled to introduce some multiplicity in God's knowledge and had broadened it to encompass universals. Algazali concludes that the philosophers' effort to magnify God has backfired in leading them to negate everything one understands by greatness. "They have rendered his state approximating that of the dead person who has no information of what takes place in the world, differing from the dead, however, only in His self-awareness" (1997, n. 58). The God of the philosophers is "half-dead" so to speak, and, therefore, no agent or maker.

Algazali brilliantly criticizes and ridicules the Neoplatonic principle that from the one only one proceeds, but carefully refrains from offering a solution to the problem of how multiplicity arises from oneness. He rejects the axiom that it is impossible for two things to proceed from one since it is known neither through necessity nor through theoretical reflection. Hence "what is there to prevent one from saying that the First Principle is knowing, powerful, willing; that He does [or acts] as He wishes, governs what He wills, creates things that are varied as well as things that are homogeneous as He wills and in the way He wills?" (1997, n. 79) Algazali then adds: "investigating the manner of the act's proceeding from God through will is presumption and coveting of what is unattainable" (ibid.). Yet such an act presupposes God's knowledge of particulars, his ability to specify one of two indiscernibles, which constitutes or is an aspect of the will. Note that in most of his attempts to preserve a true voluntary causation for God, Algazali gives priority to the will. His dodging the issue of how multiplicity arises from the one is maddening, but he reiterates his warning that his stance is purely critical.

Besides affirming the necessity to distinguish voluntary acts from natural causation, the third discussion claims that a true agent must act through will and that the act must be temporally originated. As for the common relation between the agent and its act, it cannot be based on the axiom that from the one only the one proceeds and, therefore, mediation is no solution for explaining how multiplicity stems from oneness. Algazali may hint that some faint kind of multiplicity must be assumed in God, particularly to endow him with the knowledge required for his acting through will. This raises the delicate issue of the relation between God's essence and his attributes.

In the fourth discussion, Algazali maintains that one should logically claim either that the world is temporally originated and so must have a maker or that the world is eternal and so has no need of a maker. The philosophers' attempt to assert both that the world is eternal and has a maker that is a necessary being who is no real agent fails because the very notion of a necessary being is unintelligible. This claim reminds one of Hume's similar assertion.

Discussion 17 attacks the philosophers' claim that the heavens are an animal that obeys God through circular motion. As our soul voluntarily moves our body towards its goal, so does the heavenly animal in order to worship the Lord of the world. Such voluntary act aims at an end. As earlier Algazali acknowledged that God cannot act for an end, the analogy between God's voluntary action and that of one of his creatures fails, at least in some respect. Philosophers grant to the heavens conceived as an animal, which wills and knows, the voluntary agency of which they deprive God. Algazali claims here that it is not impossible that the heavens be an animal but that this cannot be known through rational proof. For the philosophers, a motion is either natural, compulsory, or voluntary. A process of elimination leads to the conclusion that the heavens move through will. Philosophers eliminate the possibility that God moves the heavens compulsorily by arguing that such compulsory motion entails that God treats that body differently from the way he treats all the other bodies and, therefore, has an ability to differentiate between indiscernibles. Algazali counters once again that the ability to specify one indiscernible rests in the will and, therefore, can be attributed to God who may move the heavens compulsorily. Therefore, the heavens need not be conceived as an animal.

In conclusion, Algazali criticizes the philosophers for blurring the distinction between natural and voluntary causes and for depriving God of voluntary agency and, thereby, demoting him to a level close to the inanimate. Necessary emanation, besides not explaining multiplicity, reduces God's agency to natural causation. Inanimate things cannot act but God surely does.

Bibliography

Primary sources

(*Mmd*) (1969), *Al-Munqidh min adalāl (Erreur et délivrance)*, 2nd edn., ed. and trans. F. Jabre, Beirut: Commission Libanaise pour la Traduction des Chefs-d'œuvres.

(*MdD*) (1980), *Freedom and Fulfillment: An Annotated Translation of "Al-Munqidh min al-Dalāl" and Other Relevant Works*, trans. R. J. McCarthy, Boston: Twayne.

(*TF*) (1997), *The Incoherence of the Philosophers: A Parallel English–Arabic Text*, trans. M. E. Marmura, Provo, UT: Brigham Young University Press.

(1998), *The Niche of Lights: A Parallel English–Arabic Text*, trans. D. Buchman, Provo, UT: Brigham Young University Press.

Secondary sources

Abrahamov, B. (1988), "Al-Ghazālī's theory of causality," *Studia Islamica* 67, pp. 75–98.

Frank, R. M. (1992), *Creation and the Cosmic System: Al-Ghazālī and Avicenna*, Heidelberg: Carl Winter Universitätsverlag.

——(1994), *Al-Ghazālī and the Ash'arite School*, Durham, NC: Duke University Press.

Gyekye, K. (1987), "Al-Ghazālī on action," in *Ghazālī, la raison et le miracle* (pp. 83–91), Paris: Maisonneuve & Larose.

Hourani, G. F. (1984), "A revised chronology of Ghazālī's writings," *Journal of the American Oriental Society* 104, pp. 289–302.

Janssens, J. (2001), "Al-Ghazzālī's *Tahāfut*: Is it really a rejection of Ibn Sīnā's philosophy?," *Journal of Islamic Studies* 12, pp. 1–17.

Kogan, B. S. (1985), *Averroes and the Metaphysics of Causation*, Albany, NY: State University of New York Press.

Kukkonen, T. (2000), "Possible worlds in the *Tahāfut al-Falāsifa*: Al-Ghāzalī on creation and contingency," *Journal of the History of Philosophy* 38, pp. 479–502.

Marmura, M. E. (1989), "Algazali on bodily resurrection and causality in Tahafut and the Iqtisad," *Aligarh Journal of Islamic Thought* 2, pp. 46–75.

——(1994), "Ghazali's chapter on divine power in the *Iqtisād*," *Arabic Sciences and Philosophy* 4, pp. 279–315.

——(1995), "Ghazālian causes and intermediaries" (review article of R. M. Frank (1992)), *Journal of the American Oriental Society* 115, pp. 89–100.

10

Alhacen

DAVID C. LINDBERG

Alhacen (b. 965; d. ca. 1040), Abū 'Alī al-Ḥasan ibn al-Ḥasan ibn al-Haytham, known in Christian Europe as Alhacen (erroneously, Alhazen), was born in Basra and died in Cairo. An enormously talented natural philosopher and mathematician, Alhacen is known to have written approximately 140 treatises on mathematical, astronomical, and optical topics, several of which were translated into Latin. Alhacen's western influence depended primarily on his great optical treatise, *De aspectibus* or *Perspectiva*.

Alhacen was thoroughly acquainted with the principal works representing the major Greek optical traditions. These traditions disagreed not merely about theoretical matters such as the nature of light or the directionality of vision-causing rays, but also about the criteria a theory needed to satisfy in order to be judged successful: physical or causal criteria for Aristotle and his followers, mathematical criteria for Euclid and Ptolemy, and anatomical and physiological criteria for Galen and the physicians. Refusing to cast his lot with any one set of criteria and the visual theory it spawned, Alhacen set out to merge all three into a single unit: a comprehensive theory of vision capable of satisfying all three kinds of criteria.

Delivering on this promise proved a formidable challenge. The challenge was not primarily empirical, though at every point Alhacen took empirical data seriously as measures of theoretical adequacy. His project required him to submit the theoretical claims on which the various traditions were founded to careful scrutiny and criticism. He was obliged to identify error, adjudicate rival claims, craft compromises, and construct arguments. The goal was to demonstrate the mutual compatibility of the core achievements (corrected as necessary) of Aristotelians, Euclideans, and Galenists.

Alhacen's theory of vision is undoubtedly his greatest optical achievement. Rejecting the theories of the extramissionists, Euclid and Ptolemy, who attributed vision to rays emanating from the observer's eye, Alhacen assigned the cause of vision (following Aristotle) to intromitted rays, which pass from visible object to observer's eye, where they stimulate the visual power. The rays efficacious in vision are those, he argued, that fall on the eye perpendicularly and enter without refraction, one from each point of the visible object. These, he demonstrated, form a cone of rays with the object as base and apex in the eye. At one stroke, Alhacen thereby joined the mathematical analysis of the extramissionists (associated with the visual cone) to the causal and physical concerns of Aristotle and the intromissionists. Set, in its fully-developed form, within the anatomical and physiological framework of the Galenic tradition, Alhacen's theory achieved the unification he sought. Championed by ROGER BACON, it dominated western thought until the seventeenth century.

Bibliography

Lindberg, David (1976), *Theories of Vision from Al-Kindi to Kepler*, Chicago: University of Chicago Press.

Sabra, A. I. (1972), "Ibn al-Haytham, Abu 'Ali al-Hasan ibn al-Hasan," in *Dictionary of Scientific Biography*, vol. VI (pp. 189–210), New York: Scribner.

——ed. and trans. (1989), *The Optics of Ibn al-Haytham; Books I–III, on Direct Vision*, 2 vols., London: Warburg Institute.

11

Alkindi

JEAN JOLIVET

Abū Yūsuf Ya'qūb ibn Ishāq Al-Kindi (d. ca. 870) was born at the end of the eighth century or the beginnng of the ninth century of the common era (that is, the end of the second century of the Hegirian age). This period began several decades after the coming to power of the Abassid dynasty supported by the Muslims of Persia, a dynasty much more in keeping with the culture of the Persians than the Ommayad dynasty had been. The coming to power of the Abassid dynasty was an important development, providing support for intellectual pursuits within the Islamic empire, especially for the study of medicine, astronomy, and mathematics. The Near East, moreover, which the Arabs had conquered during the beginning of the expansion of Islam, was already deeply influenced by Greek culture, following upon the conquests of Alexander the Great; centuries later, during the theological controversies of the Christian churches of the fourth century, part of the logical works of Aristotle had even been translated into Syriac, the cultural language of the area.

During the period of Alkindi's birth, a number of scientific and philosophical texts became available and were being studied in connection with the intellectual disciplines of grammar, law, and theology, which had already been established in Islam. In spite of the predominant religious currents of thought, the Abassid caliphs undertook a cultural policy useful for the furtherance of their political power: they favored the expansion of the new "foreign" disciplines, notably by encouraging translations of scientific and philosophical texts from Greek into Arabic and supporting scholars who devoted themselves to the study of such texts (Gutas 1998). Aiming at the same practical goal of upholding their political power, the caliph al-Ma'mūn and his successor al-Mu'tasim also supported, vigorously and at times brutally, the theological party of the Mu'tazilites, who were sympathetic towards philosophy in several regards. We must bear in mind this intellectual and spiritual setting in which Alkindi worked, for he was in favor under both of the caliphs mentioned; thereafter, he fell into disgrace under the second successor of al-Mu'tasim and died around the time of the birth of ALFARABI.

The enormous and complex enterprise of translations began at the outset of the ninth century and continued until the beginning of the tenth century. During this period, all the philosophical and scientific works then known and available were translated from Greek into Syriac and Arabic. Alkindi himself was part of these translation efforts; he had a translation made of Aristotle's *Metaphysics* and *On the Heavens* as well as some of Proclus' writings, while he also had "improved" the translation of the apocryphal work *The Theology of Aristotle*. His own philosophy was nourished on the reading of Greek sources, but it was far from being a mere sequel to Greek thought or a restatement of it, as some historians have suggested. But before entering into the question of the character of Alkindi's philosophy, we should note that he was a scholar of wide learning. His abundant corpus contains works on mathematics and medicine wherein he showed undeniable originality, especially in pharmacology and optics (Rashed 1997). The catalogue of his works found in the bio-bibliographical study of al-Nadim contains nearly 250 titles, most of which are now lost. Some fifty of his works treated philosophy (to which we should add the commentaries on Aristotle's *Organon* as being by himself); only fifteen or so of these works, however, have come down to us and have been published.

The manner in which Alkindi aligned himself in relation to Greek thought, and, by the same token, the manner in which he conceived of and pursued his life as a philosopher, are best expressed in his principal work, *The Book of First Philosophy*, dedicated to the caliph, al-Mu'tasim; perhaps we should say that his outlook is best expressed in the part of his work that survives (the first part, which is divided into four chapters), since, according to certain historical witnesses, it was originally much longer. The first lines present philosophy as "the highest of the human arts" and first philosophy as "the science of the First Truth which is the cause of every truth." Alkindi says elsewhere that the second is the science of the first cause. Thereafter, he gives a quite general outline of an overall theoretical system by ennumerating the four causes (matter, form, agent, and end) as well as the four "scientific questions" (Does it exist?, What is it?, What sort is it?, and Why?) and claims that to know the causes of a thing is to determine its genus, species, and difference. Accordingly, the first page of his work as well as its title place it in the framework of Aristotle's philosophy as filtered through Porphyry and, as certain details indicate, the Alexandrine commentators. The remainder of the first chapter is replete with praise for the ancient philosophers who "have smoothed out for us the pathways of truth" through the work they pursued over the centuries. Our task is "to acquire the truth from wherever it may arise, even if it comes from nations distant in place and different from our own; what the ancients expressed fully we should explain in the most direct and accessible manner, but what they have not fully expressed we should complete, following the language and the custom of the present time." There is no need to criticize philosophy – here Alkindi gives a sharp reproof of those who revile philosophy – inasmuch as philosophy contains "the science of Sovereignty and the science of Unicity" (that is to say, theology) and the science of virtue; in a word, philosophy contains all that "the true Prophets" have taught. This is clear: philosophy, the science that the ancients (the *falāsifa*, from a word transliterating the Greek term 'philosophy') developed, encompasses in its entirety the same content that the books of the prophets do. Hence, what is needed is to accept philosophy and carry it forward to its completion in the effort to recover, following the philosophical path, the truths already expounded in revelation. The last point remains implicit in the text of Alkindi under discussion, but appears clearly enough in the body of his philosophical work.

This first part of *The Book of First Philosophy* is, in a sense, a manifesto, ending with a general statement of the program that the three other parts of the work begin to put into practice. At the outset of the second of these parts, considerations of method are introduced. Alkindi first distinguishes between the knowledge of the senses and knowledge of the intellect, the latter being a knowledge acquired without deploying images, but gained rather by turning away from images. Every branch of knowledge has its own proper method, one that is entirely distinct from that employed by other branches of knowledge.

With these distinctions in place, Alkindi passes immediately to the characteristics of the eternal: the eternal is alone necessary, it does not come forth from any other cause, it does not have a genus, it neither corrupts nor changes, and it is necessarily perfect. Thereupon, having shown that no body can be infinite in act, Alkindi infers that the world is not eternal since body, movement, and time have no mutual priority and none of these continuous quantities can be infinite. The world has begun and will come to an end. Up to this passage of his text, Alkindi is generally faithful to Aristotle; at this point, he breaks with him and aligns himself with the Christian Alexandrian, JOHN PHILOPONUS, who had written a critique of Proclus on the issue of the eternity of the world. This doctrine is quite important for Alkindi, who wrote three chapters upon the same subject, where he came to the same conclusion (1950, pp. 186–93, 194–8, 201–7; 1998, pp. 136–47, 150–5, 158–65).

In chapter 3, he shows dialectically that one thing cannot be the cause of its own essence; he distinguishes between what is essential and non-essential within a thing. At that point, he displays a theoretical redirection of capital importance, turning from Aristotle to Neoplatonism by placing the concept of the One at the center of his thought. He lists the ways in which the predicate 'one' may be attributed to a subject. We could say that species, genus, and accident are each one, but such unity that is in them is associated with a multiplicity that is inherent to them. As a matter of fact, no created thing is able to be purely multiple or purely unitary; each thing shares at one and the same time in unity and plurality and the association of the two principles of unity and plurality in a thing is the effect of a cause distinct from the thing in question: that cause is the cause of the thing's existence and of its subsistence, a thing that itself is absolutely one.

The fourth chapter establishes that there is neither a great absolute nor a small absolute; that the One is not a number; and that every predication of quantity is relative and restricted to one genus. As a result of these rather lengthy demonstrations, the True One appears as eternal, absolute, lacking any plurality; hence we cannot attribute to it any of the predicates attributable to other things. It is the first cause of the unity within things and which exist because unity flows down upon them, arising from the True One. The One is the Creator, for creation consists in this gift of unity, which, within the domain of created things, remains necessarily bound up with multiplicity.

If we consider the overall scheme of this first part of *The Book of First Philosophy*, we find that Alkindi is faithful within the work to the program he defined in chapter 1. He welcomes the results arrived at by Greek philosophers; notable in this regard are the fundamental concepts of Aristotle's philosophy (the couplets substance/accident, act/potency, and cause/effect, as well as the list of the four causes), but also the concept of the One, a notion essential to the Neoplatonic outlook and one that allows Alkindi to make a transition from the physics and the metaphysics of Aristotle to a theology that can be rendered harmonious with the fundamental dogma of Islam, the dogma of the divine unity and the divine unicity. But it is also just one of the points upon which the theologians divide themselves; some allow us to say, in accord with traditional doctrine, that, though God remains one, he has attributes, such as science and power, whereas others, such as the Mu'tazilites to whom allusion was made earlier in the work, affirm that such attributes are incompatible with the divine unity. Yet, in the last few lines of the first part of the *The Book of First Philosophy* we find these words: "the True One is indeed above these attributes that ascribe to Him what belongs to the order of becoming." This is one of the points of agreement between Alkindi and the Mu'tazilites. Certain historians have thought that the philosopher, already closely connected with the caliphs, who had made of Mu'tazilism an official doctrine, professed the same views. Other historians, however, make the observation that he stands apart from them on several points, notably in physics where he follows Aristotle. He wrote a treatise, now lost, to refute "those who believe that a body is indivisible"; yet, for all the theologians, whether Mu'tazilites or not, the existence of atoms was an essential point. What we can say with certainty is that Alkindi showed an important degree of agreement, albeit only on certain points, between the theological school in question and certain themes of Greek philosophy, especially in regard to the One. It is significant that the theologian al-Aš'arī accused the Mu'tazilites of being "the brothers of philosophers," because "they thought, without daring to state as much, that God was merely an essence and nothing more."

In general, then, *The Book of First Philosophy* poses the relation of dependence and the distinction between the world and God from the viewpoint of ontology. A very short work that considers the relationship of creaturely dependence from the viewpoint of efficient causality is the *Epistle on the True, First, and Perfect Agent and on the Deficient Agent which is an Agent by Extension*. There are two modes of action, according to Alkindi: (1) to make things be simply; (2) to exercise an action upon them. The first type of action is proper to God alone; the second should be understood in two senses since we should distinguish between the True Agent which acts without anything else acting upon it, i.e., God, and the "agents by extension." The first among the latter agents receives the action of God and thereupon communicates that action to another, which, in turn, communicates the action to a third, etc.; the causal process as communicated through the agents by extension is no longer, however, truly an action. In fact, creatures do nothing but transmit among themselves what they have received and thus do not act, but rather suffer action. The *Epistle* is too short for us to discern the solutions that might be given to the problems it raises, but it does orient us in two different directions. First, it raises issues of cosmology, suggesting the kind of hierarchical universe whose structure and details Alkindi sketches out in other works. Second, it leads us into theology and Alkindi's thought regarding the following issue: if every action results immediately from the action of God, what becomes of human activity and, more particularly, human free choice? The Mu'tazilites, differing on this matter from general theological opinion, used to claim that man is the "creator of his own acts," that is to say, free; only on such a condition would man be responsible for his own actions and be rightly punished or rewarded by God (divine justice being a principal part of their doctrine). The *Epistle on the True Agent*, placed by al-Nadīm among the theological writings of Alkindi, does not appear to be headed in this direction and this would be a point upon which the philosopher might distinguish his views from those of the Mu'tazilites. But we cannot really tell since we would have to be more fully acquainted than we are with works that do not survive; we know that Alkindi wrote an *Epistle on Free Choice*, but it is lost (as an aside, we should note that he also wrote on astrology, a practice in which he engaged).

The abstract concepts of motion are discussed in the cosmological chapters. The *Epistle on the Prosternation of the First Body*, whose title arises from a verse of the Koran about "the star that bows down," shows, through a tightly reasoned chain of arguments, that the heavenly sphere is a living being endowed with reason, the agent cause of living things subject to generation and corruption, and is not itself generated but rather created by God for a determined amount of time (this last point Alkindi often discusses and it is a theme of the Mu'tazilites). The general structure of the universe is reflected in the "little world" that is man and therein lies for Alkindi one of the things that provides the greatest evidence for "true and perfect power" of God, whom he calls "the Generous." This divine name, which is also found in the Koran, calls to mind Plato's *Timaeus*, a work available in Arabic in the form of a summary derived from Galen's writings. Such convergences of Greek philosophy and Koranic sources are not unusual in Alkindi. He also says, in this chapter and elsewhere, that God created the world in the best possible manner, thus picking up a theme of

Mu'tazilite theology. We find the same theme once again in the *Epistle on the Proximate Cause of Generation and Corruption*, written prior to the *Epistle on Prosternation*, but which should follow it according to the logical order of presentation. Unfortunately, only the first chapter of the former survives. Aristotelian physics furnishes the fundamental concepts: the four causes, the four elements, and the four types of motion. After describing the properties of the four elements, Alkindi shows that generation and corruption arise partially from something besides the elements themselves. The variation of hot and cold, dry and wet depend upon the distance, which changes from one season to another, of the "heavenly substances." In this fashion bodily changes are wrought upon which the "acts of the soul" depend; thus there is a chain of causes and effects, encompassing the movements of the stars, the climate, the different physiologies of human beings, their psychological attitudes, and their moral dispositions. The sun and the planets are the causes of our being and, more generally, of the items subject to generation and corruption; the movements of the sun and the moon will continue to be the conserving causes of the various biological species until the end predestined by the Creator.

The works that we have examined belong simultaneously to metaphysics and physics in their cosmological dimension; other works also belong to these areas, namely the works that deal with the soul. In a short chapter Alkindi establishes that there exist incorporeal substances (*That there Exist Incorporeal Substances*, in 1950, pp. 265–9), which are souls and species (the latter "realist" aspect of Alkindi's philosophy warrants close examination). In several works, he treats psychology, noetic and eschatology, but he keeps close to the thought of the Greek philosophers in these works; it is their philosophical psychology that he shows himself capable of reading critically in such works as *A Work on the Soul, Briefly Summarized* wherein he inquires into the Aristotelian and Platonic definitions of the soul.

The *Epistle on the Nature of Sleep and Rest* (1950, pp. 293–311) is an independent contribution to the Aristotelian psychology tradition (*De anima*, the *Parva naturalia*, and their commentaries), where we find an allusion to Joseph's dream (see the Koran, 12.44–5). This work was translated into Latin in the twelfth century as was the *Epistle on the Intellect*. Like the chapter on sleep and rest, the chapter on the intellect is based on Greek philosophical tradition; Alkindi draws upon Plato and Aristotle at the outset of the work, but really the *De anima* of Aristotle provides the frame and content of the text. Alkindi begins by listing four different senses of the term 'intellect': the intellect always in act; the intellect in potency (this pertains to the soul); the intellect that passes in the soul from potency to act; and the intellect "that we call the second." The analogy between sense and intellect, sensation and intellection corresponds to the duality of forms as sensible and intelligible. The soul's acquired intellect comes forth from the first intellect, "the specificity of things that are always in act." Lastly, Alkindi gives a list of four intellects slightly different than those ennumerated earlier: the intellect that is the cause and principle of all intelligibles and of the secondary intellects"; the second intellect, which is in potency; the acquired intellect once it is in act "which the soul uses and makes evident to us"; and the intellect "which is evidently something apart from the soul and exists in act for a thing other than itself."

The noetic thought of Alkindi is, as we see, located properly in a line of Aristotelianism modified under Platonic influences; we find more evidence for this interpretation in an epistle recently translated, entitled *On the remembrance that the soul has of what it formerly had in the world of the intellect once it has passed into the world of perception, and its remembrance of what it had in the world of perception when it passes into the world of the intellect*

(Endress 1994). In this work, Alkindi takes up a notion, traceable to Plato, of cognition as remembrance of knowledge prior to this life. The same Platonic theme is just as evident in a text bearing a strange but significant title which shows the mixture of Platonic and Aristotelian influences, the *Discourse on the soul: a summary of Plato, Aristotle, and other philosophers* (1950, pp. 272–80). In this work, Alkindi treats, first of all, the nature of the soul, "a substance which comes from the substance of the Creator as radiance does from the sun," and shows that it is immortal. The second part of the work is both moral and eschatological; the key idea is that the soul should detach itself from the body and purify itself so as to be able to pass "into the light of its Creator" at death; if the soul is not purified, it will have to undergo various trials after death so as to obtain the vision of God, but there seems to be no notion of hell in Alkindi's scheme (Genequand 1988; Jolivet 1996). The present life is, then, a "place of passage," "a bridge" towards a life to come; this theme is taken up once again in the *Epistle on the means of keeping sadness at bay*, a work that is thematically and stylistically close to the moral exhortations of Greek literature. Alkindi exhorts us not to grow sad at the losses we must suffer in the present life, since this life is only a passageway; we ought to prepare ourselves instead for the future life and the happiness we shall merit, just as sea travellers at a port of call on an island should not remain there, forgetting that they are there only as travellers and not as inhabitants.

Finally, leaving aside the *Epistle of definitions* of questionable authenticity with its complicated distinctions, let us look at the *Epistle on the number of Aristotle's writings and what someone needs to know to begin philosophy* (1950, pp. 363–84; 1938). This is a work in which the basis of Alkindi's thought finds its expression, and its structure, which one may at first sight find surprising, is actually quite masterful. In the first part, Alkindi lists the works of Aristotle, subdivided into four categories: logic, physics, psychology, and metaphysics (the last two being covered by periphrases); except for the *Categories*, this is simply an enumeration of the works followed by a mention of the ethical writings. The second part prescribes that philosophical study should begin with the study of mathematics, that is, with the study of the classical *quadrivium*, and shows how the different branches of the latter constitute entirely the knowledge of all substances and their accidents and hence are indispensable for philosophical study. Thereafter, Alkindi passes abruptly on to a third part, distinguishing in it between "human knowledge" acquired through much effort and length of study and "divine science" which God communicates instantaneously to the prophets. To show that the two forms of knowledge are actually in accord, he devotes two entire pages to commenting upon four verses of a chapter of the Koran. Finally, in the last part of the *Epistle*, he divides the sciences of the *quadrivium* in terms of their being sciences of quantity and quality, showing how we should approach the "science of philosophy" by associating mathematical knowledge with particular works of Aristotle; he gives a summary of each of them so as to display the authorial "intention" behind them.

Along these lines, we should mention his account of the *Metaphysics*: the intention of Aristotle in that work, quite significantly, is to treat of "the unicity of God, to expound His beautiful names, and to show that He is the agent and final cause of the universe, the God and Regent of the universe." In this passage, as in the philosophical commentary on the Koranic verses that precedes it, we recognize an echo of a page of the *Book on First Philosophy* where Alkindi emphasizes that the teaching of philosophy is compatible with the message of the prophets. This problem of the relationship between religion and philosophy will find its place once again, in different forms and with different solutions, in Alfarabi, AVICENNA, and AVERROES; in this respect, as in so many others, Alkindi remains the originator of Arabo-Islamic philosophy.

Bibliography

Primary sources

(1938), "Uno scritto morale inedito di al-Kindī," in H. Ritter and R. Walzer, eds., "Studi su al-Kindi II. Uno scritto inedito di al-Kindī," *Memorie dell'Accademia Nazionale dei Lincei*, ser. 6, vol. 8, fasc. 1.

(1940), "Introduction to Aristotle," in A. Guidi and R. Walzer, eds., "Studi su al-Kindī. Uno scritto introduttivo allo studio di Aristotele," *Memorie dell'Accademia Nazionale dei Lincei*, ser. 6, vol. 6, fasc. 6.

(1950), *Al-falsafiyya*, in M. A. Abū Rīda, ed., *Rasā'il al-Kindī al-falsafiyya* [1369] (*Philosophical Treatises of al-Kindī*), Cairo.

(1998), *Oeuvres scientifiques et philosophiques d'al-Kindī*, vol. 2: *Métaphysiques et cosmologie*, ed. R. Rashed and J. Jolivet, Leiden, Cologne, and New York: Brill.

Secondary sources

Atiyeh, A. (1966), *Al-Kindī, the Philosopher of the Arabs*, Rawalpindi and New Delhi: Islamic Research Institute.

Endress, G. (1973), *Proclus Arabus. Zwanzig Abschnitte aus der Institutio theologica in arabischer Übersetzung*, Beirut: Orient-Institut der Deutschen Morgenländischen Gesellschaft; in Kommission bei F. Steiner, Wiesbaden.

——(1994), "Al-Kindī über die Wiedererinnerung der Seele. Arabischer Platonismus und die Legitimation der Wissenschaften im Islam," *Oriens* 34, pp. 175–221.

Genequand, G. (1987–8), "Platonism and hermetism in Al-Kindī's Fī al-Nafs," *Zeitschrift für Geschichte der Arabisch-Islamischen Wissenschaften* 4, pp. 1–18.

Gutas, G. (1998), *Greek Thought, Arabic Culture*, London and New York: Routledge.

Ivry, A. L. (1986), "Al-Kindī and Mu'tazila: philosophical and political reevaluation," *Oriens* 25–6, pp. 69–85.

Jolivet, J. (1971), *L'Intellect selon Kindī*, Leiden: Brill.

——(1996), "La topographie du salut d'après le Discours sur l'âme d'al-Kindī," in M. A. Amir-Moezzi, ed., *Le Voyage initiatique en terre d'islam: ascensions célestes et itinéraires spirituels* (pp. 149–58), Louvain and Paris: Peeters.

Rashed, R. (1997), *Oeuvres philosophiques et scientifiques d'Al-Kindī*, vol. 1: *L'Optique et la catoptrique*, Leiden, Cologne, and New York: Brill.

Rescher, N. (1964), *Al-Kindī: An Annotated Bibliography*, Pittsburgh: University of Pittsburgh Press.

Tornero Poveda, E. (1992), *Al-Kindī. La transformación de un pensamiento religioso en un pensamiento racional*, Madrid: Consejo Superior de Investigaciones Científicas.

Travaglia, P. (1999), *Magic, Causality, and Intentionality: The Doctrine of Rays in Al-Kindī*, (pp. 147–65), Florence: Edizioni del Galazzo.

12

Alrazi

THÉRÈSE-ANNE DRUART

Abū Bakr Muhammad ibn Zakariā' al-Rāzī (in Latin Rhazes, b. ca. 865; d. ca. 925), physician and philosopher, was Persian but wrote mostly in Arabic. Director of the hospital in Rayy (Persia), he kept a diary of clinical observations, and penned medical treatises (for instance, on smallpox) that were translated into Latin. Most of his philosophical works are no longer extant, except for *The Philosophical Life*, *The Spiritual Medicine*, *Doubts on Galen*, and a few others.

His denial of revelation and his lack of reverence for Aristotle isolated him. This independence of mind indicates that medieval Islamic philosophy is not necessarily Aristotelian.

Following a Hellenistic tradition, Alrazi conceives philosophy as the medicine of the soul which has fallen into matter but can be rescued by intellect, God's great gift to it. God's justice requires that he not privilege any one with a revelation, but that he endow everyone with the intellectual abilities to discover his existence and his main attributes of intelligence, justice, and mercy. Understanding such attributes and God's rescue of the cosmic soul grants human beings the capacity to imitate divine action by inferring the proper moral principles and their applications. For Alrazi, animal as well as human souls are rational, at least to some extent, and he accepts transmigration and shows great concern for the environment. Some of these ideas are probably grounded in his reflections on Plato's *Timaeus*, on which he may have commented.

Alrazi is philosophically unorthodox; he claims to be a follower of Socrates and Plato and to reject Aristotle's views. Nature is not really a cause since a true cause must act by choice and nature is inert. He uses a form of atomism to ground material explanations and was very interested in alchemy.

Philosophy is a way of life and demands that one serve one's fellow human beings, earn one's bread, and encourage other people to look for the truth. As passions distract us from intellectual pursuits and from being useful to others, Alrazi tries to convince us to give them up. He does not hesitate to give practical advice and to use rhetorical and emotional appeal, but also hints at serious philosophical positions and sophisticated arguments that would be found in more theoretical works. Their loss deprives us of fully appreciating the originality and depth of his unusual views.

Bibliography

Primary sources

(1939), *Opera philosophica fragmentaque quae supersunt*, ed. Paul Kraus, Cairo.
(1950), *The Spiritual Physick of Rhazes*, trans. Arthur J. Arberry, London: John Murray.

(1993), *Kitāb al-shukūk 'alā Jālīnūs*, ed. Mehdi Mohaghegh, Tehran.
(1993), "The book of the philosophic life," trans. C. E. Butterworth, *Interpretation* 20, pp. 227–36.

Secondary sources

Druart, T.-A. (1996), "Al-Razi's conception of the soul: psychological background to his ethics," *Medieval Philosophy and Theology* 5, pp. 245–63.
——(1997), "Al-Razi's ethics," *Medieval Philosophy and Theology* 6, pp. 47–71.
Stroumsa, S. (1999), *Freethinkers of Medieval Islam: Ibn al-Rāwandi, Abū Bakr al-Rāzī and their Impact on Islamic Thought*, Leiden: Brill.

13

Anselm of Canterbury

JASPER HOPKINS

Anselm (b. 1033; d. 1109) flourished during the period of the Norman Conquest of England (1066), the call by Pope Urban II to the First Crusade (1095), and the strident Investiture Controversy. This latter dispute pitted Popes Gregory VII, Urban II, and Paschal II against the monarchs of Europe in regard to just who had the right – whether kings or bishops – to invest bishops and archbishops with their ecclesiastical offices. It is not surprising that R. W. Southern, Anselm's present-day biographer, speaks of Anselm's life as covering "one of the most momentous periods of change in European history, comparable to the centuries of the Reformation or the Industrial Revolution" (1990, p. 4). Yet it is ironic that Anselm, who began as a simple monk shunning all desire for fame, should nonetheless today have become one of the most famous intellectual figures of the Middle Ages. And it is even more ironic that this judgment holds true in spite of the fact that he wrote only eleven treatises or dialogues (not to mention his three meditations, nineteen prayers, and 374 letters).

Anselm was born in Aosta, today a part of Italy but in Anselm's time a part of the Kingdom of Burgundy. Italians usually refer to him as Anselm of Aosta (when they are not referring to him as Saint Anselm), whereas almost everyone else names him Anselm of Canterbury, after the identifying seat of his archiepiscopacy. Most of what we know about Anselm's life derives from three primary sources: his own collection of his letters and from the two informative works *Vita Anselmi* (*Life of Anselm*) and *Historia novorum in Anglia* (*History of Recent Events in England*), written by Eadmer, a monk at Canterbury who was Anselm's contemporary. To a much lesser extent, further impressions of Anselm's thought may be gleaned from the *Dicta Anselmi* (*Anselm's Sayings*), compiled by Alexander, also a monk at Canterbury.

The foregoing sources tell us that Anselm's father was Gundulf; his mother, Ermenberga; and his sole sibling, his sister Richeza. After his mother's death (ca. 1050) Anselm's relation with his father became progressively more strained – to the point that he left home in 1056 and travelled within Burgundy and France, perhaps staying with relatives of his mother. In 1059, at the age of 26, he arrived at the Benedictine monastery at Le Bec, France, where he aspired to study with his compatriot, Lanfranc of Pavia, then prior of the community. Within a year of his arrival he decided, in great part through Lanfranc's influence, to take the vows of a monk and to remain at Bec. In 1063, when Lanfranc was made Abbot of the Abbey of St. Etienne in Caen, Anselm was elected to replace him as Prior of Bec. Fifteen years later (September 1078) he was chosen by his fellow-monks as abbot. And another fifteen years later (March 6, 1093) he was invested as Archbishop-elect of the see of Canterbury – invested against his personal wishes but in accordance with what he himself, along with the others, understood to be the will of God. His consecration to the office came on December 4, 1093.

Anselm became archbishop at a time when there were two rival claimants to the papacy, each having excommunicated the other. Anselm had already given his allegiance to Urban II, rather than to Clement III; England's King William Rufus (William II, son of William the Conqueror) was soon to do likewise. All too early on, Anselm quarrelled with Rufus over the service of knighthood that was owed to the king by the Canterbury archdiocese because of the lands that it held by permission (under feudalism) of the Regal Overlord. The quarrel became so grave that Anselm left England, with William's consent, for a self-imposed, three-year exile (November 1097 to September 1100), whose main purpose was to confer with the pope, Urban II. After Anselm's departure Rufus confiscated the Canterbury land-holdings. Upon Rufus's death under suspicious circumstances (August 2, 1100), Anselm was invited back to England by the new king, Henry I, Rufus's younger brother, who promised to restore the Canterbury lands. Anselm returned, yet fell into conflict with Henry over the issues of homage and of investiture. In April of 1103 Anselm again left England to take counsel of Pope Paschal II, who had become pope (August 13, 1099) during Anselm's previous absence from England, though after Anselm had left Rome. Not until September of 1106 did Anselm once again return to England, having become reconciled with Henry, whom he had threatened to excommunicate and whom Henry had threatened not to allow back into the country. Anselm died in Canterbury on April 21, 1109 and was buried in Canterbury Cathedral. After a fire his body was relocated within the cathedral, and its whereabouts forgotten.

Anselm is lastingly important not so much for his ecclesiastical resoluteness and his tenacious commitment to *libertas ecclesiae* but rather for his abiding intellectual accomplishments. The primary influences upon his thought, apart from Lanfranc's tutoring in dialectic, are AUGUSTINE, BOETHIUS, and Aristotle. Anselm knew only portions of Aristotle's philosophy, with whose thought he was familiar only through Boethius' Latin translations. In particular, he knew Aristotle's *De interpretatione* and *De categoriis*, together with Boethius' commentaries thereon. Furthermore, he knew Boethius' own works on the hypothetical syllogism (*De hypotheticis syllogismis*), the categorical syllogism (*De syllogismo categorico*), as well as Boethius' *De consolatione philosophiae* (*The Consolation of Philosophy*) and his *Tractatus theologici* (*Theological Tractates*). Likewise, he was acquainted with Cicero's *Topics* but not with Boethius' accompanying commentary. Anselm's knowledge of Plato was second-hand, mainly through Augustine's comments, though he might possibly also have read Calcidius' or Cicero's Latin translation of the *Timaeus*.

In terms of the impression that Anselm made on subsequent generations, we may be certain that his greatest impact proceeded from (1) his *Proslogion* (*An Address* [*of the Soul to God*]) (*P*) and (2) his *Cur Deus homo* (*Why God Became a* [*God-*]*man*) (*CDH*). In lesser ways, various future thinkers also took some account of (3) his doctrine of the Trinity, (4) his statements about faith and reason and (5) his early writings on truth, freedom, and evil. These are the five areas of his thought from which one may extract his essential ideas.

Proslogion and debate with Gaunilo

We must keep in mind that the *Proslogion* is a unified work, in spite of the fact that our interest in it tends to gravitate towards chapters 2 to 4, which contain the richly provocative, and extremely controversial, "ontological" argument for God's (necessary) existence. In rightly assessing the *Proslogion*, we must look beyond these initial chapters in order to take full account of what Anselm himself tells us: that the *Proslogion* (written ca. 1077–8) is an attempt to restate more simply and tersely the ideas that were previously set down in the *Monologion* (*M*) (completed in 1076). Although the *Monologion*, too, proposed considerations ostensibly enabling one to conclude that God exists (*M* 1–4), most of the *Monologion* deals with determining, *sola ratione* (i.e., by reasoning alone, apart from Scriptural revelation), the nature and the attributes of the Divine Being. Accordingly we must not forget that the *Proslogion*, likewise, focuses not just on determining *that God is* but also on determining *what God is*. In arriving at its conclusions – the same major conclusions as reached in the *Monologion* – the *Proslogion* uses a new strategy. This strategy begins with *unum argumentum* – a single consideration – and reasons from it to the existence and the nature of the one and only God. Thus Anselm makes use of a *single consideration*, not of a *single argument*; for this consideration (that God is Something than which nothing greater can be thought (of)) gives rise to several different arguments, each of which has an identity of logical structure. Oftentimes this structure is misinterpreted. One prominent historian of philosophy, for example, identifies the argument-form as syllogistic:

God is that than which no greater can be thought:
But that than which no greater can be thought must exist, not only mentally,
  in idea, but also extramentally:
Therefore God exists, not only in idea, mentally, but also extramentally.
(Copleston (1947–75), II: p. 162)

Yet Anselm's reasoning is decidedly not syllogistic but, rather, proceeds by way of *reductio ad absurdum*:

	(1)	Whatever is understood is in the understanding.
	(2)	If one understands what is being spoken of when he hears of Something than which nothing greater can be thought, then Something than which nothing greater can be thought is in the understanding.
But:	(3)	When one hears of Something than which nothing greater can be thought, he understands that which is being spoken of.
Thus:	(4)	Something than which nothing greater can be thought is in his understanding.
	(5)	Either That than which nothing greater can be thought is in the understanding only, or That than which nothing greater can be thought is in the understanding and exists also in reality.
Assume:	(6)	That than which nothing greater can be thought is in the understanding only.
	(7)	If anything is in the understanding only and does not exist also in reality, then it can be thought to exist also in reality.
So:	(8)	That than which nothing greater can be thought can be thought to exist also in reality.
	(9)	Whatever does not exist in reality but can be thought to exist in reality can be thought to be greater than it is.
So:	(10)	That than which nothing greater can be thought can be thought to be greater than it is.
Thus:	(11)	That than which nothing greater can be thought is That than which something greater can be thought – a contradiction.
Hence:	(12)	Something than which nothing greater can be thought is in the understanding and exists also in reality.

The foregoing reasoning postulates one alternate of a disjunctive proposition that exhausts the universe of discourse. From the alternate it derives a contradiction: a fact that justifies the assertion of the other alternate. Once Anselm has shown to his own satisfaction that there exists Something than which a greater cannot be thought, he turns to showing – by means of reasoning that repeats the logical structure of his existence-argument – that this Being is omnipotent, omniscient, omnipresent, merciful, just and "whatever else we believe about the Divine Substance." For example, implicit in *Proslogion* 5 is the following parallel reasoning:

(1) Either Something than which nothing greater can be thought is omnipotent, or Something than which nothing greater can be thought is not omnipotent.

Assume: (2) That than which nothing greater can be thought is not omnipotent.

(3) If anything is not omnipotent, it can be thought to be omnipotent – something which is greater.

So: (4) That than which nothing greater can be thought can be thought to be greater than it is.

Thus: (5) That than which nothing greater can be thought is That than which something greater can be thought – a contradiction.

Hence: (6) Something than which nothing greater can be thought is omnipotent.

Interestingly, Anselm continues onward to demonstrate – in *Proslogion* 15, still implicitly using the same argument-form – that Something than which a greater cannot be thought is also Something greater than can be thought. Here he means to indicate not that God cannot at all be conceived (he makes clear in *Reply to Gaunilo* 8 that God can to some extent be conceived) but that He cannot at all be comprehended, cannot at all be perfectly conceived (except by Himself), cannot be conceived as He is in and of Himself, for "we see [only] through a glass, darkly" (I Cor. 13: 12). Anselm thinks of himself as having proved (*probare* – the word he uses in his *Reply to Gaunilo*) both that, necessarily, God exists and that God exists necessarily. Implicit in his line of thought is the point that Spinoza later made explicit: that there cannot be two or more beings each of which is such that no one of them is even conceivably greater (more perfect) than the other since all of them are co-equal in power, wisdom, goodness, etc. Spinoza argues that if there were two Gods, neither would be omnipotent, since each would limit the other's power by not being at all subject to it. (And being God, requires being omnipotent.) Anselm makes a comparable point in *Proslogion* 5: Since God is Something than which nothing greater can be thought, He alone must exist only through himself, with all other things existing through him; otherwise, he could be thought to be greater, since there could be thought to be a single self-existent Creator of all else.

Anselm's interchange with Gaunilo, monk of the Abbey of Marmoutier (near Tours, France), is highly instructive both of his intent and of the actual structure of the argument-form in *Proslogion* 2–3. Nonetheless, just as Gaunilo, in attacking Anselm, misunderstands some of what Anselm writes in the *Proslogion*, so Anselm, in defending himself, misunderstands several of Gaunilo's key points. To be sure, Gaunilo misapprehends. For he construes Anselm to be claiming that "if this thing [than which nothing greater can be thought] existed solely in the understanding, then whatever existed also in reality would be greater than it." But Anselm's point is, assuredly, different: that if That than which nothing greater can be thought existed solely in the understanding, then it itself could be thought to be greater, inasmuch as it could be thought to exist also in reality, so that That than which a greater cannot be thought would be That than which a greater can be thought – an impossibility. Accordingly, this *reductio* approach allows Anselm to generate the kind of contradiction that is crucial to his strategy.

On the other hand, Anselm himself misconceives two points that are important to the relevance of Gaunilo's attack: Anselm misconstrues Gaunilo's shorthand phrase *maius omnibus* as an abbreviation for *illud maius omnibus quae sunt* ("That [Being which is] greater than all [other] existing things"); but Gaunilo means it as an abbreviated form of *illud maius omnibus quae cogitari possunt* ("That [Being which is] greater than all [else] that can be thought"), an expression that exactly captures Anselm's notion. Similarly, Anselm mistakenly accuses Gaunilo of inconsistently maintaining both that unreal things can be understood and that 'to understand *x*' means 'to apprehend with certainty that *x* really exists.' Yet, in his *On Behalf of the Fool* 2, Gaunilo is defining the meaning of *intelligere* not as *scientia comprehendere re ipsa illud existere* ('to understand with certainty that that thing exists in reality') but only as *scientia comprehendere* ('to understand with certainty') – as the editorial use of parentheses would make clear: "*quia scilicet non possim hoc aliter cogitare, nisi intelligendo (id est scientia comprehendendo) re ipsa illud existere.*"

A final clarification is necessary. For the question often arises as to whether or not Anselm regarded existence as a perfection. Kant, of course, imagines that he does. And Kant is right. For Anselm stands, to a certain extent, within the Neoplatonic tradition that considers there to be degrees of existing and degrees of participation in exemplars. During the medieval period these exemplars were regarded as existing in the Divine Mind – and regarded, more strictly, as being (in last analysis) a single Exemplar that is identical with the Word of God, the second member of the Trinity. (See *Monologion* 10, 11, and 33.) The doctrine of degrees of being – a doctrine that enters into the *Proslogion* – is best observed in the *Monologion*:

> For no one doubts that created substances exist in themselves very differently from the way they exist in our knowledge. For in themselves they exist in virtue of their own being; but in our knowledge their likenesses exist, not their own being. It follows, then, that the more truly they exist anywhere by virtue of their own being than by virtue of their likenesses, the more truly they exist in themselves than in our knowledge (*M* 36).

This same doctrine of degrees of existing underlies the *Proslogion*. Yet, whether or not one regards the argument of *Proslogion* 2–4 as sound, and whether or not one regards as dispensable to the argument the presupposition that existence is a perfection, everyone will agree that the crux of Anselm's thinking in those chapters is the following: If one understands God to be Something than which a greater cannot be thought, then in thinking of God, one cannot think of Him as not-existing. Hence, since His non-existence is inconceivable to each person who understands rightly what He is, only a Fool would *assert* to be nonexistent that very Being whose nonexistence he himself rightly finds to be inconceivable.

Of course, the question remains: Does our conceiving of a Being as inconceivably nonexistent entail that, in fact, that Being exists? This question was resolved differently by Thomas Aquinas and by Gottfried Leibniz. And the pondering of this question led Nicholas of Cusa to argue, in his *De apice theoriae* 13: 4–14 (*Concerning the Loftiest Level of Contemplative Reflection*), along lines that, clearly, are cognate with Anselm's strategy.

Atonement and original sin

Anselm's *Cur Deus homo* and *De conceptu virginali* are magnificent attempts to explain (1) why the Divine Incarnation was necessary for the redemption of human beings and (2) why, nonetheless, the Incarnation was not necessitated, though in certain respects it appears to have been so. Had Eve alone sinned, reasons Anselm, God could have created another woman, from whom Adam could have produced sinless progeny. But once Adam himself sinned, he was powerless to reproduce descendants who would be free of the guilt of original sin. Original sin, according to Anselm, is the sinfulness, or guiltiness, which each descendant of Adam incurs at his origin. For at his origin he inherits a sinful human nature. That is, when Adam sinned personally his personal sin corrupted his human nature, with the result that the nature inherited by his progeny was also a corrupted nature. In the progeny this corrupted human nature contaminated the person, so that when Adam's descendants reach the age of accountability, each of them will at some point personally choose to sin. Each Adamic descendant is held accountable only for his own personal sin – held accountable in spite of the fact that his personal sin is occasioned by his inherited sinful Adamic nature. He is not personally accountable for Adam's personal sin. However, unbaptized infants who die without having sinned personally (as none of them do sin) are still excluded from entrance into the Heavenly Kingdom, since no one with any sinfulness at all (including a sinful nature) may enter into that Kingdom. Such infants do not, however, experience punishment or damnation.

Any personal sin against God is very grave, notes Anselm; for one ought not to refuse to obey God's will even if the consequence of obedience to God were that the entire world would perish. Indeed, one ought not to disobey God even were an infinite number of such worlds as ours to perish. Anyone who does disobey God must both repent and make payment to God for that dishonoring of Him. Involved in repenting is the idea of expressing sorrow for the wrong-doing and the idea of resuming full obedience. Making payment will consist of giving to God something that will compensate for the dishonoring. But human beings have, of themselves, nothing with which to make this payment, or this satisfaction. They owe to God obedience, gratitude, good works, humble conduct, etc., by virtue of being his creatures. So these services cannot count as making satisfaction. Indeed, the satisfaction that must be made by the sinner has to be satisfaction that is greater than is that for whose sake he is obliged not to dishonor God. Since one is not supposed to dishonor God even were doing so to keep an infinite number of worlds from perishing, the sinner must render to God something whose value exceeds the value of an infinite number of worlds. Now, no human being can make this required payment of compensation. Yet, only an Adamic human being ought to make this payment, because only someone of Adam's lineage can – on behalf of himself, of Adam and of the whole human race – make payment, or repayment, to God of the debt incurred by Adam and by himself and his fellow human beings. Only a human being *ought to* make this satisfaction; but only God *can* make it; therefore, it is necessary that a God-man make it (*CDH* II, 6), reasons Anselm.

The God-man can make this payment (the making of which makes up for the human race's dishonoring of God) by letting himself be killed for righteousness's sake, i.e., by letting himself be killed rather than saving his life and abandoning the truth by telling the lie that he is not God. Here Anselm makes a further theological assumption: "that a sin which is committed in regard to his [i.e., the God-man's] person surpasses, incomparably, all conceivable sins which are not against His person" (*CDH* II, 14). But "every good is as good as its destruction is evil"; so the incomparable good of Christ's life is offered to God in payment for all conceivable sins that are not against the person of the God-man. And the sin that is against the person of the God-man – a sin that would have been, in and of itself, incomparably evil had it been perpetrated knowingly – is only a venial sin because it was done unknowingly. (Anselm does not maintain, as some interpreters have supposed, that the

Jews bear "infinite guilt" for insisting to Pontius Pilate that this execution take place. When the Jews exclaimed "His blood be upon us and upon our children" (Matt. 27: 25), Anselm regards the guilt as venial.) Thus, the merit of the God-man's death infinitely exceeds the demerit of all actual sins. Such a righteous abiding by the truth, on pain of death, deserves to be rewarded. Since nothing can constitute a reward to the God-man, who, as God, needs nothing, the reward may rightly be transferred to those to whom the God-man will have it given. It is, therefore, applied against the debt of men's sins. The God-man's death is meritorious also because the God-man, being sinless, did not deserve at any time to die.

Anselm's theory of atonement, including its underlying presuppositions, has often and extensively been studied and disputed. Some philosophers (Gombocz 1999) have questioned, for example, the soundness of the inference, to wit, that if atonement is to be made, then it must be made by a God-man; for only a man (a human being) *ought to* make satisfaction and only God *can* make satisfaction, so that only a God-man both ought to and can. One problem seems to be that the sense in which only a man (i.e., only a human being) ought to make atonement is not the sense in which the God-man ought to make atonement. For a human being of Adam's race ought to make satisfaction because he *owes* the debt that is incurred due to sin – owes it both on his own behalf and on behalf of his race. However, the sense in which the sinless God-man ought to make satisfaction is not that he himself owes – either for himself or for others – any debt that is due to sin. Rather, he ought to make satisfaction only in the sense that he wills to do so and that he ought to do what he sinlessly and meritoriously wills to do. Accordingly, Anselm stands accused of equivocation, something detrimental to his line of reasoning.

Anselm's theological claims lead him into various intriguing philosophical puzzles, puzzles that he himself recognizes as springing forth. He claims, for instance, that the God-man (whom in the end he identifies with the historical Jesus) was born of a mother (Mary) who was free of sin. And she was free of sin, he further claims, by virtue of her faith in the efficacy of his future death. But now the question arises: How is it that Jesus died freely, rather than by necessity? For since he was begotten by Mary in her purity, it seems that he was under the necessity of sacrificing himself, since otherwise Mary's faith would not have been true faith and Mary's purity would not have been true purity. (Although Anselm teaches the doctrine of the immaculate conception of Jesus, he does not teach the immaculate conception of Mary, whom he, nonetheless, speaks of [in *De conceptu virginali* 18] as "beatified with a purity than which a greater cannot be conceived except for God's.")

Trinity and Incarnation

Anselm's view of the Trinity and the Incarnation is wholly orthodox. He maintains that God is one nature (or substance or essence) in three persons (or relations or operations). These numerically three persons differ from one another irreducibly, without differing numerically from one another in nature. In other words, the numerically one Divine Nature is related to itself in numerically three different ways: as Father, as Son, as Holy Spirit. Anselm repudiates both Sabellianism and tritheism. According to the latter, there are three numerically distinct divine natures; according to the former, there is a single Divine Nature that appears at different times in the mode of Father, in the mode of Son, in the mode of Holy Spirit – these being that Nature's three, non-coexistent modes-of-being. By contrast, Anselm believes that in the Incarnation the second member of the Trinity, namely the Son of God (or Word of God), assumed a distinct human nature. Thus, he became *a* man (i.e., *a* human being); he did not become *man* as such. Anselm would not agree with the nineteenth-century theologian Ferdinand Christian Baur, who taught that "Christ as man, as God-man, is universal man. He is not a single individual but is, rather, the universal Individual" (*Die christliche Gnosis*, p. 715).

Similarly, Anselm repudiates Arianism, Apollinarianism, Docetism, Eutychianism, and Nestorianism. Arianism supposedly taught that the Father created the Son – *ex nihilo* and before all time – as the firstborn of all creatures. Thus, the Son is not of the *same* substance (*homoousios*) as the Father but is of *like* substance (*homoiousios*) with the Father. In the historical Jesus the human nature is said to *partake of* the divine nature. Apollinarianism claimed that in the historical Jesus there was no human soul, no human mind, since the human soul was replaced by the Divine Logos. Jesus did, nonetheless, have human flesh, according to the Apollinarians. By contrast, Docetism denied that the Son of God assumed a real human body; rather, he only appeared to have a body. Eutychianism viewed Christ as having but a single nature – the divine nature – into which the human nature was absorbed. And Nestorianism, in its condemned version, was viewed as affirming that Jesus had not only two natures but also two persons – persons that were united in a moral union. Moreover, Mary was said to be the bearer not of God (*theotokos*) but only of Christ (*Christotokos*), for she begot not a divine nature but only a human nature that became united to a divine nature.

It is not possible to separate the doctrine of the Incarnation from the doctrine of the Trinity, and Anselm makes no attempt to do so. Thus, his treatise *De incarnatione Verbi* treats both issues concurrently. In writing *De incarnatione Verbi* and *De processione Spiritus Sancti* (*DP*) – both of which were completed after his departure from Normandy for England – Anselm was still writing with an eye to the monks of Bec, for whom he desired to be as clear as possible. Because this was his envisioned audience, he was led to seek out illustrations that would prove elucidating to the minds of the more simple among these monks. Hence he proposes his example of the Nile river as a way of providing such elucidation. The Nile is one body of water which, nevertheless, is also three things: a spring that begets a river that proceeds into a lake. The spring is not the river or the lake; the river is not the spring or the lake; and the lake is not the spring or the river. Yet, each is one and the same Nile. Here Anselm's example is motivated by a slightly different example from Augustine's *Faith and the Creed* 9.17 (*Patrologia Latina* (*PL*) 40: 189). Finally, we must not forget that Anselm's concern with the doctrine of the Trinity is not a localized concern but is a concern that pervades his entire intellectual period: it begins to express itself in the *Monologion*; and it continues on until his late work *De processione*, completed in 1102.

In the late Middle Ages Anselm's claims about the Trinity came to be challenged on the grounds that the distinction between the members of the Trinity is not a numerical distinction – at least, not numerical in any sense in which we understand a distinction to be numerical. Meister Eckhart, for example, distinguished between God and the Godhead. And Nicholas of Cusa declared: "the Maximum is infinitely above all trinity" (*De docta ignorantia* I, 20 (61)). Or, as he says elsewhere, God is three without number, even as the oneness that is predicated of him is not mathematical oneness (*De Possest* 46 and 50).

Faith and reason

Anselm's conception of the relationship between faith and reason is best discerned from the prefacing and introductory remarks that he makes in some of his works. For example, the preface to the *Monologion* expresses his desire to conform that work to the expectation of certain monks at Bec who prescribed the following guidelines:

> that nothing at all in the meditation would be argued on Scriptural authority, but that in unembellished style and by unsophisticated arguments and with uncomplicated disputation rational necessity would tersely prove to be the case, and truth's clarity would openly manifest to be the case, whatever the conclusion resulting from the distinct inquiries would declare. They also desired that I not disdain to refute simple and almost foolish objections which would occur to me.

And at the outset of chapter 1 Anselm speaks of reaching conclusions *sola ratione*, by reason alone. Accordingly, in the *Monologion* he attempts to simplify both his style and his approach and to proceed toward giving proofs that would be rationally compelling. Other things that he tells us elsewhere cohere with this same programmatic approach, at times supplementing it, never contradicting it or veering from it. Thus, when he indicates in the *Proslogion* that his method is that of *fides quaerens intellectum* (faith seeking understanding), this method is not opposed to that of the *Monologion*, even though the style of these two works and their respective strategies are strikingly different. Yet, like the *Proslogion*, the *Monologion* is the soliloquy of a religious believer who is seeking certainty; and like the *Monologion*, the *Proslogion* is seeking the certainty that accompanies rational necessity. This latter fact is evident from Anselm's declaration in *De incarnatione Verbi* 6, where he groups the *Monologion* and the *Proslogion* together and states that he wrote each of them in order to show that "what we hold by faith regarding the divine nature and its persons – excluding the topic of incarnation – can be proven by compelling reasons apart from [appeal to] the authority of Scripture." In other words, the *Proslogion* moves via the principle of *sola ratione* just as decidedly as does the *Monologion*.

Similarly, in the *Cur Deus homo* the preface informs us that Anselm intends to pursue his argument in book one in such a way as to furnish us with a conclusion reached by rational necessity and apart from appeal to revelation – i.e., a conclusion arrived at *Christo remoto*, as if nothing were known historically of Jesus. And, likewise, the argument in book two is said to aim at clarity and at necessity of theological inference. Of course, amid all of his arguing, whether in the *Cur Deus homo* or elsewhere, Anselm never forgets that his reason needs the assistance of grace, needs to be "cleansed by faith." Thus, in *De incarnatione Verbi* 1 he alludes disapprovingly to certain men who are

> accustomed to mount up presumptuously unto the loftiest questions of faith before they possess spiritual wings through firmness of faith. Consequently, when they try to ascend to those questions which first require the ladder of faith (as it is written, "Unless you believe you will not understand"), but try to ascend in reverse order by means of first understanding, they are constrained to fall into many kinds of errors on account of their defective understanding. For it is apparent that they have no foundation of faith who, because they cannot understand what they believe, argue against the truth of this same faith – a truth confirmed by the holy Fathers. It is as if bats and owls, which see the sky only at night, were to dispute about the midday rays of the sun with eagles, which with unblinded vision gaze directly at the sun.

In this same section Anselm makes two further significant points: (1) The reason that he who does not believe will not understand is that he will not experience and, hence, will not know. (2) A mind that lacks faith and obedience will not be able to grasp higher religious and theological truths; and, moreover, "by the neglect of good conscience even the understanding which has already been given is sometimes removed and faith itself overturned."

In the commendation of the *Cur Deus homo* to Pope Urban II Anselm again quotes Isaiah 7: 9 (in the Old Latin version) to the effect that "unless you believe you will not understand." And he again seeks the rational basis of faith and, in doing so, advances *sola ratione* (*CDH* II, 22). Within the body of the *Cur Deus homo* Anselm draws his well-known distinction between *rationes necessariae* (rationally compelling reasons) and *rationes convenientes* (fitting reasons). (Yet we must remember that as early as the *Monologion*'s preface Anselm used the expression *rationis necessitas*.) Both kinds of reasons suffice to *persuade*. However, the former kind are understood to be conclusive, whereas the latter kind are taken to be conditionally compelling: they are sufficient until such time, if ever, as stronger reasons are discerned:

> I would like for us to agree to accept, in the case of God, nothing that is in even the least degree unfitting and to reject nothing that is in even the slightest degree reasonable unless something more reasonable opposes it. For in the case of God, just as an impossibility results from any unfittingness, however slight, so necessity accompanies any degree of reasonableness, however small, provided it is not overridden by some other more weighty reason. (*CDH* I, 10)

Anselm's notion of *rationes convenientes* serves to illustrate the fact that when he speaks of arguing *sola ratione*, his conception of *ratio* and *rationabilis* is very broad. It includes appeal to whatever renders a premiss or a conclusion more plausible than any alternative premiss or conclusion. In particular, it encompasses not only the reasonableness of self-evidence and of formal demonstrations but also evidence from empirical observations, conceptual judgments that are based on comparisons or analogies or parallelisms, and ideas that serve to complete a pattern of thought. As an illustration of this last point, we may note what is said in *Cur Deus homo* II, 8:

> God can create a human being in either of four ways: viz., (1) from a man and a woman (as constant experience shows); (2) neither from a man nor from a woman (as He created Adam); (3) from a man without a woman (as He created Eve); (4) from a woman without a man (something which He had not yet done). Therefore, in order for Him to prove that even this fourth way is subject to His power and was reserved for this very purpose, nothing is more fitting than that He assume from a woman without a man that man about whom we are inquiring.

Although Anselm by and large seeks to reason *sola ratione, rationibus necessariis*, and *rationibus convenientibus*, without recourse to supporting evidence from Scripture, nevertheless he does sometimes resort to filling out his line of reasoning by introducing considerations from Scripture. This point holds true especially when his topic is more theological than it is philosophical, so that he is obliged to introduce interpretations of various Scriptural texts. Thus, we see that in *De processione*, when he is arguing (against the Greeks) that the Holy Spirit proceeds from the Father and the Son, he maintains that if "proceeding" means "being given or sent," then the Holy Spirit proceeds also from the Son because he is given and sent by the Son as well as by the Father (*DP* 2). And his authority here is the Scriptural verse John 15: 26. Moreover, he once again appeals to Scripture when he vehemently asserts: "we nowhere read [in Scripture], and we wholly deny, that the Holy Spirit is the Son" (*DP* 4). (The Greeks, of course, make this same denial.) Throughout *De processione* Anselm looks to Scripture; and the reason for this viewing is that the basis for deciding whether or not to accept the *filioque* addition to the Nicene-Constantinople Creed of

381 is primarily scriptural. What is amazing, however, about the *De processione* is how *logically* it attempts to reason, how *philosophically* it approaches this theological theme.

In summary, Anselm aims – no doubt, without always succeeding – to reason very clearly about topics that are suggested to him by his reading of Scripture. Indeed, he aspires to reasoning so clearly that his opponent will be forced to use the very words of concession that in a different context Anselm himself utters: "I understand to such an extent that [even] if I did not want to believe . . . I could not fail to understand" (*P* 4).

Truth, freedom, and evil

Anselm's notions of truth, freedom, and evil are highly influenced by Augustine. In *Soliloquies* 2.2.2 (*PL* 32: 886), for example, Augustine argues that truth cannot perish, because if it perished it would still be true that it had perished; and a proposition cannot be true unless there is truth. Likewise, in his work *On Christian Doctrine* he employs at 2.35.53 (*PL* 34: 60) an Aristotelian notion of propositional falsity, when he writes: "The false is defined when we say to be false our signifying of a thing when the thing is not as it is signified to be." And in *On Free Choice* 2.12.34 (*PL* 32: 1259) he concludes that because some truths are unchangeable, there is unchangeable truth. And if truth is unchangeable, then it is eternal, so that it is identifiable as God, identifiable as Truth. Anselm follows Augustine's lead by arguing both in *Monologion* 18 and *De veritate* 1 that certain propositions (such as "Something was going to exist") have always been true, whereas other propositions (such as "Something has existed in the past") will never cease being true, so that these truths attest that truth (without which the truths could not be true) is without beginning and without end. Like Augustine, Anselm too does not hesitate to identify beginningless and endless truth as Truth itself, that is, the Eternal God.

Since God, as omniscient, eternally knows all true propositions, the truth of these propositions is eternal. Thus, the truth even of true propositions that begin to be conceived at some time by the human mind, i.e., that begin to be conceived in *time*, exists ontologically prior to the temporal conceptualization of them. Thus, such propositional truths, being eternally known by God, are themselves eternal, existing apart from all time, rather than being perpetual, existing for all time. In *De veritate* Anselm, again in a manner reminiscent of Augustine, picks up on Aristotle's notion of propositional falsehood, as well as of propositional truth, so that (for Anselm) correspondence becomes a key notion. But he goes beyond Aristotle when he affirms that things other than propositions may also be true. For truth has to do with a thing's being what it ought to be or as it ought to be, and with its doing what it ought to do as it ought to do it. Thus Anselm can ascribe truth to thoughts, to actions, to acts of will, to the senses – and even to the very being of things insofar as these things are what God wills for them to be, since otherwise they would not at all exist.

In last analysis, Anselm defines 'truth' in terms of *rectitudo*: truth is a kind of *rightness*: rightness that is perceptible only to the mind. In fact, as he notes in *De veritate* 12, truth and rightness and justice are interchangeable notions, for justice is (up)rightness-of-will kept for its own sake (only). When a will is thus upright, it "does the truth," he explains, thereby using a scriptural expression (John 3: 21). Freedom-of-will also has to do with rightness, or uprightness, so that Anselm defines such freedom as the ability to keep uprightness-of-will for its own sake (only). Thus, 'freedom' is defined in accordance with the possession of an ability and not in accordance with the possession of strong motivation. Accordingly, free will is a power (we speak even today of having "willpower"); but it is not the power of alternative choice. It is the power always to choose, or to consent to, that which is morally upright. Each one of us always has this power, supposes Anselm, even when his will is not morally upright. That is, in spite of the fact that an unjust will has *no* power to become just in and through its own acts, nevertheless once it is made just – made just by God on the basis of the confession of wrongdoing and of repentance – the will with restored uprightness does have the power to retain its uprightness.

Anselm's conception of human free will gives rise to a number of paradoxes. Three such paradoxes are especially noteworthy. First, on Anselm's theory, as we have said, an unjust will (i.e., an unrighteous will) is free even though it is powerless to will that which is morally perfect; i.e., it is powerless continually to will *that which* is morally right *because* it is morally right. Indeed, an unjust will is free only in the reduced sense that it has the residual power to keep itself just, after it has once again been made just through the divine grace of forgiveness and restoration. As Anselm claims: It is more appropriate for us to call the unjust will *free* on the basis of its residual ability than to call it *unfree* on the basis of the fact that it has no uprightness to retain and that it has no power to regain uprightness, or justice. Secondly, according to Anselm, even a will that is free in the defined sense of having the ability to keep uprightness-of-will for its own sake (only) cannot, if it is unjust, actually use this ability, since such a will has no actual uprightness to keep. Most people, however, will find it strange to speak of as *free* a will that has an *actually unusable* ability. Thirdly, it seems counterintuitive that Anselm should say, as he does, that no one can ever be compelled to will anything. This claim of his seems to indicate his own failure properly to analyze the concept of compulsion.

In spite of such paradoxical conclusions Anselm's theory of free choice is truly intriguing. It contains aspects of philosophical truth that must be patiently identified and mulled over. Above all, it represents an heroic attempt to square the demands of experience with the deliverances of reason and the teachings of Scripture. And it rightly recognizes that our choices are *motivated*: are occasioned, induced, "caused." Anselm avoids Augustine's suggestion that Satan's initial choosing to do evil resulted from a "deficient cause," for this expression conveys the impression that there was something defective with respect to Satan's nature (*De concordia* III, 10). Anselm understands Satan's initial act-of-will to constitute not an unwillingness to keep uprightness but, rather, a willingness to possess some good that Satan did not then have and was not supposed to have at that time. In willing this good he *ipso facto* willed to abandon uprightness-of-will. Just what this good was, Anselm does not claim to know (*De casu diaboli* 4). Thus, he also does not know *why* Satan willed to have it. Accordingly, he states that Satan willed what and as he did *only because he willed to* (ibid. 27). There was neither an external inducement nor an internal predisposing sinful inclination. Still, Anselm does not say that Satan's act-of-will was uncaused: he says that it was the "efficient cause of itself," an expression that he knows to be problem-filled (ibid. 27). It is his way of saying, perhaps, that Satan's *superbia* (pride) is inexplicable to us. In any event, Satan's will, like every human and angelic act-of-will, has both a *what* and a *why* (cf. *De veritate* 12). And God's "foreknowledge" of Satan's fall did not compel Satan's sinful act-of-will. (This conclusion is inferable from *De concordia*, where the interrelationship between foreknowledge, predestination, grace, and free will is insightfully discussed.)

Evil is regarded by Anselm either as *incommodum* (detriment) or as *nihil* (nothing). Evil *qua* detriment (disease, pain, hunger, etc.) is said in Scripture (Isaiah 45: 7) to be created by God, inasmuch as God wills to permit both it and the conditions that precipitate it: "I form the light and create darkness. I make peace and create evil," a verse that Anselm cites in *De concordia* I, 7. But evil *qua* nothing is privation: it is the absence of justice, or uprightness, from a will that ought to have it. Hence, moral evil, per se, is an *absence*, a form of not-being. Yet, we sometimes speak of it as if it were something. We use, for example, the expressions "Greed caused it" or "Lust caused it," where greed and lust are the absence of moderation, the absence of restraint. Hence, our statements are comparable to a statement such as "The absence of a bridle caused the horse to run wild" (*De casu diaboli* 26; cf. 24). Here we are speaking not according to fact (*secundum rem*) but after the fashion of ordinary usage (*secundum formam loquendi*) (*De casu diaboli* 11).

Anselm's least important work is the *De grammatico* (*On (an) Expert-in-Grammar*), which takes up the question of whether *grammaticus* is a quality (the quality of being expert-in-grammar) or a substance (an expert-in-grammar) and whether the word *grammaticus* signifies a quality or a substance. The question arises because Latin has neither a definite article (corresponding to our word 'the') nor an indefinite article (corresponding to our word 'a'/'an'). Anselm intended for this dialogue to provide training, of sorts, to the monks of Bec who wanted to develop skills in eristic. The topic under discussion was motivated by a passage in Aristotle's *Categories* 1 and by the section of Boethius' *Commentary on the Categories* that is entitled *De denominativis*. Anselm's keen interest in the relationship between language and reality is apparent not only in *De grammatico* but also in his *Philosophical Fragments*.

Conclusion

In the end, Anselm is deserving of the epithet "Father of Scholasticism" that has come to be conferred on him. His emphasis on furnishing argumentation, on searching out *rationes necessariae*, on distinguishing *usus loquendi* from *significatio per se* and on further distinguishing *significatio per se* from *significatio per aliud* – all of these warrant his being honored by historians, who have given him this special title. Yet, amid our admiring his clear-mindedness and succinctness, we must not lose sight (1) of his openness to having his views corrected and (2) of his humility in not wanting to be among those who "judge with foolish pride that what they are not able to understand is not at all possible" (*De incarnatione Verbi* 1).

Bibliography

Primary sources

Latin edition
(1968), *Opera omnia*, 2 tomes, ed. F. S. Schmitt, Stuttgart and Bad Cannstatt: Frommann.

Translations
Davies, Brian and Evans, Gillian R., eds. (1998), *Anselm of Canterbury: The Major Works*, New York: Oxford University Press.
Fröhlich, Walter, trans. (1990, 1993, 1994), *The Letters of Saint Anselm of Canterbury*, 3 vols., Kalamazoo: Cistercian Publications.
Hopkins, Jasper and Richardson, Herbert W., trans. (2000), *Complete Philosophical and Theological Treatises of Anselm of Canterbury*, Minneapolis: Banning.
Ward, Benedicta, trans. (1973), *The Prayers and Meditations of Saint Anselm*, Baltimore, MD: Penguin.

Secondary sources
Adams, Marilyn M. (1990), "Saint Anselm's theory of truth," *Documenti e Studi sulla Tradizione Filosofica Medievale* 1, pp. 353–72.

Augustine, Aurelius (1841ff.), Latin works as found in J.-P. Migne, ed., *Patrologia Latina* (*PL*), vols. 32–46, Paris: Vivès.

Baur, Ferdinand Christian (1967), *Die christliche Gnosis oder die christliche Religionsphilosophie in ihrer geschichtlichen Entwicklung*, Darmstadt: Wissenschaftliche Buchgesellschaft.

Copleston, F. (1947–75), *A History of Philosophy*, 9 vols., London: Burns, Oates and Washbourne.

Evans, Gillian R., ed. (1984), *A Concordance to the Works of St. Anselm*, 4 vols., Millwood, NY: Kraus International Publications.

Fröhlich, Walter (1984), "The letters omitted from Anselm's collection of letters," in R. Allen Brown, ed., *Anglo-Norman Studies 6: Proceedings of the Battle Conference 1983* (pp. 58–71), Woodbridge, NH: Boydell.

Gilbert, Paul, Kohlenberger, Helmut, and Salmann, Elman, eds. (1999), *Cur Deus homo. Atti del Congresso Anselmiano Internazionale*, May 21–3, 1998, Rome: Pontificio Ateneo S. Anselmo.

Gombocz, Wolfgang L. (1999), "Anselm von Aosta als Schrecken der 'europäischen' Anthropologie? Anmeldung der philosophischen Pflicht, 'Cur Deus homo' zu durchkreuzen," in Gerhard Leibold and Winfried Löffler, eds., *Entwicklungslinien mittelalterlicher Philosophie. Vorträge des V. Kongresses der Österreichischen Gesellschaft für Philosophie* (part 2) (pp. 73–86), Vienna: Hölder-Pichler-Tempsky.

Hopkins, Jasper (1976), "Anselm's debate with Gaunilo," in *Anselm of Canterbury*, vol. 4: *Hermeneutical and Textual Problems in the Complete Treatises of St. Anselm* (pp. 97–117), Lewiston, NY: Mellen.

Kienzler, Klaus (1999), *International Bibliography: Anselm of Canterbury*, Lewiston, NY: Mellen.

Southern, Richard W. (1988), "Sally Vaughn's Anselm: an examination of the foundations," *Albion* 20 (Summer), pp. 181–204.

——(1990) *Saint Anselm: A Portrait in a Landscape*, New York: Cambridge University Press.

Vaughn, Sally N. (1987), *Anselm of Bec and Robert of Meulan: The Innocence of the Dove and the Wisdom of the Serpent*, Los Angeles: University of California Press.

Vuillemin, Jules (1996), "Justice anselmienne et bonne volonté kantienne: essai de comparaison," in David E. Luscombe and Gillian R. Evans, eds., *Anselm: Aosta, Bec and Canterbury* (pp. 361–75), Sheffield: Sheffield Academic Press, 1996.

14

Arnaldus of Villanova

FRANCISCO BERTELLONI

Arnaldus de Villanova (b. 1238/40; d. 1311), a Catalan physician, philosopher, and theologian, was born in Valencia. He studied Latin with the Dominicans, Arabic and later theology and medicine in Naples and Montpellier. In 1276 he received the tonsure in Valencia. In his medical treatise (*Speculum medicinae*) Arnaldus re-elaborated many topics of the Salernitan medical tradition as well as others received from Galen and the Arabic tradition, but with a definite orientation towards practical application. His increasing reputation as physician earned him the position of doctor of the Kings of Aragon in 1281, and for them he wrote the *Regimen sanitatis*. Later he became the personal physician of the Kings of Sicily and Naples as well as of the pope. In 1291, Arnaldus was appointed Professor of Medicine in Montpellier.

Although he certainly devoted himself to alchemy, many works on magic and alchemy are erroneously attributed to him. Some writings on astrology, however, such as *Capitula astrologiae*, are authentic. As a theologian he distanced himself from the Dominican tradition and was strongly influenced by the spiritual Franciscans. He also rejected the use of philosophy within theology in the *De philosophia catholica*. Arnaldus was also author of numerous treatises in Catalan (e.g., *Confessió de Barcelona*, *Lliçó de Narbona*, *Raonament d'Avinyó*). From 1300, his activity as well as his writings in Latin (*Expositio super Apocalipsim*, *Tractatus de tempore adventu Antichristi*) defended the historic-eschatological ideas of Joachim of Fiore, including social reform plans and projects for the renovation of the Church and clerical life. This created difficulties for him in the university, and he was forced to flee to Rome, where he was protected by Pope Boniface VIII, whose ideas, however, he did not quite support. Later he acted as counselor at the court of Frederick III of Sicily. He died in 1311 on a shipwreck near Genoa.

Bibliography

Primary sources

(1947), *Obres catalanes*, ed. M. Battlori, Barcelona: Editorial Barcino.

(1971ff.), *Scripta spiritualia*, ed. M. Battlori et al., Barcelona: Institut d'Estudis Catalans.

(1975ff.), *Opera medica omnia*, ed. L. García Ballester, M. R. McVaught, et al., Granada: Seminarium Historiae Medicae Granatensis; Barcelona: Universitat de Barcelona.

(1994), *Arnau de Vilanova y l'arnaldisme*, in *Obra completa*, vol. III, Valencia.

Secondary sources

Battlori, M. (1954), "Orientaciones bibliográficas para el estudio de Arnaldo de Villanova," *Pensamiento* 10, pp. 311–23.

——(1951), "A. de Vilanova en Italie," *Analecta Sacra Tarraconiensia* 24, pp. 83–102.

Carreras y Artau, J. (1936), "Les obres theologiques d'Arnau de Vilanova," *Analecta Sacra Tarraconiensia* 9, pp. 217–31.

Finke, H. (1902), *Aus den Tagen Bonifaz VIII* (pp. 191–226), Münster: Aschendorff.

Manselli, R. (1953), "Arnaldo de Villanova diplomatico, medico, teologo e riformatore religioso alle soglie del secolo XIV," *Humanitas* 8–9, pp. 268–79.

Menéndez y Pelayo, M. (1880–1), *Historia de los heterodoxos españoles*, Madrid: Librería Católica de San José.

Perarnau, J. (1991), "Profetismo gioachimita catalano da Arnau de Vilanova a Vicent Ferrer," in G. L. Potestá, ed., *Il profetismo gioachimita tra Quattrocento e Cinquecento* (pp. 401–14), Rome: General Marietti Santi.

Potestá, G. L. (1994), "Dall'annuncio dell'Anticristo all'attesa del pastore angelico. Gli scritti di Arnaldo di Vilanova nel codice dell'Archivio generale dei carmelitani," *Arxiu de Textos Catalans Antics* 13, pp. 287–344.

Santi, F. (1987), *Arnau de Vilanova: l'obra espiritual*, Valencia.

15

Augustine

SCOTT MACDONALD

Aurelius Augustine (b. 354; d. 430), lived virtually his entire life within one hundred kilometers of his birthplace in Roman North Africa. He spoke and wrote the Latin of the educated Roman world but apparently could not easily manage Greek, the primary language of the philosophical traditions of antiquity. He had little formal training in philosophy. All his surviving writings were composed after his conversion to Catholic Christianity. He wrote the vast majority of them after his ordination to the priesthood in his late thirties and in service of his attempts to understand and articulate the truth he found in the Christian Scriptures and Christian doctrine. His intellectual background, profile, and circumstances are, therefore, very different from those of the great philosophers of the Greek and Roman world. He was, however, a powerful and extraordinarily prolific philosophical writer and thinker, and the legacy of ideas, arguments, and problems he left to the western world is rivaled only by those of Plato and Aristotle.

Augustine was born in the town of Thagaste (in what is now Algeria) to middle-class parents who struggled to secure a good education for their talented son. He loved Latin literature and excelled in rhetoric, the art of public speaking and performance, which seemed to him and his parents to be his ticket to advancement in the civic life of the empire. He taught for a time in Thagaste and Carthage, and then at Rome from 384 to 386. Augustine left Rome for Milan to take up the prestigious position of imperial professor of rhetoric. It was in Milan in 386 that his life took the dramatic turn that led to his conversion to Christianity, his abandoning his promising professional career, and his return to North Africa to embark on a religious life.

Augustine tells us that his first intellectual awakening was sparked by an encounter at the age of 18 with Cicero's *Hortensius*, an exhortation to philosophy that is now lost. Cicero inspired Augustine to devote himself to attaining the sort of immortality that comes with wisdom. Augustine's search for wisdom led him first to Manichaeanism, a syncretistic philosophical-religious system that impressed the young Augustine as being tough-minded and intellectually ambitious. He spent over a decade associated in some way with the Manichees. Over time, however, he became increasingly convinced that Manichaean doctrine was not only unsatisfying but also untenable. For a brief period he was tempted to believe, with the academic skeptics, that wisdom is unattainable and that the best intellectual course for him was to withhold assent where philosophical and theological matters were concerned. But Augustine's encounter with Ambrose, Milan's charismatic bishop, and with the Platonist philosophy of Plotinus and Porphyry brought an end to his dalliance with skepticism and led him straightaway to a form of intellectual Christianity. For the remaining four decades of his life, Augustine was convinced, and worked tirelessly to show, that Christianity offers the true wisdom that philosophy seeks.

Augustine's prolific career as a writer began almost immediately after his conversion in the late summer of 386. While waiting to be baptized at Milan, Augustine and a small group of friends spent the winter months of 386–7 in conversation and contemplation at the country estate of Cassiciacum. Augustine used that time to begin working out philosophical positions that would come to define his Christian philosophy. The results were the dialogues *Contra academicos*, *De beata vita*, and *De ordine*, and the self-reflective treatise *Soliloquia*.

After his baptism at Easter 387, Augustine's plan was to return to his home town to establish a monastic community of friends devoted to study and contemplation. While making his way from Milan to Thagaste by way of Rome in 387–8, he wrote a half-dozen more treatises, including two on the soul (*De immortalitate animae* and *De quantitate animae*) and the first book of what is perhaps the most important of his smaller works, *De libero arbitrio*.

Augustine began his life of monastic seclusion in 388, but it was short-lived: in 391 he became convinced that he should accept ordination as a priest and its accompanying public obligations to the Church. But in the years from 388 to 391 he wrote another half-dozen treatises, including *De magistro* and the masterful summary of his emerging understanding of the Christian view of the world, *De vera religione*. In the five years immediately following his ordination Augustine continued his philosophical reflections on Christianity, completing books two and three of *De libero arbitrio*. He also began to wrestle in earnest with the Christian Scriptures, beginning work on the *Enarrationes in Psalmos* and writing *De sermone Domini in monte*. He made several approaches to Paul's epistle to the Romans, the biblical text that above all shaped his thinking about God's grace and its interaction with the human will in salvation. Moreover, he began a treatise devoted to a theoretical account of the interpretation of Scripture, *De doctrina christiana*.

In 396 Augustine succeeded Valerius as Bishop of Hippo. He remained in that position until his death in 430. Shortly after becoming bishop Augustine wrote the *Confessiones*, his best-known work. The *Confessiones* consolidates a good deal of the philosophical progress Augustine had made in the decade since his conversion to Christianity and introduces the main themes he would go on to develop in three massive projects that occupy most of the rest of his life: *De Genesi ad litteram* (begun in 401, completed 415), *De Trinitate* (399–422/6), and *De civitate Dei* (413–426/7).

Augustine's years as Bishop of Hippo were busy with preaching, correspondence, and the day-to-day pastoral and administrative affairs of his diocese. They also led him into important ecclesiastical and doctrinal controversies. He waged a sustained battle with, and wrote several polemical tracts against, the schismatic Donatist church in North Africa. Moreover, from 412 when he first encountered the views of the British monk Pelagius, Augustine wrote voluminously against the Pelagian understanding of grace and free will. In major works such as *De spiritu et littera* (412), *De natura et gratia* (413–15), and two treatises *Contra Julianum* (421–2, 429–30), and in nearly a dozen smaller treatises Augustine worked out the views on original sin, the bondage of the human will, predestination, and divine grace that would in part define Christianity and profoundly affect its history.

Augustine died of natural causes in 430 as marauding Vandals laid siege to the city of Hippo. His native North Africa was experiencing, at the moment of his death, catastrophic upheaval of the sort Rome itself had experienced twenty years before, at the hands of the Visigoths, a catastrophe that had prompted Augustine to begin writing his great book on the workings of divine providence in human history, *De civitate Dei*. As the power, influ-

155

ence, and institutions of the late Roman empire crumbled, Augustine's vast body of writings would be preserved and passed along to thinkers of a very different world from the one Augustine himself inhabited. For more than a millennium after his death, philosophers and theologians, poets and historians would view the world through the lens of his writings.

Wisdom, happiness, and virtue

Cicero inspired a teenage Augustine to devote himself to wisdom – to be a philosopher. Augustine thereby came to believe that his leading the best life possible, his being truly happy, depended on his acquiring wisdom (*Confessiones* III. iv. 7–8). That youthful conviction became one of the foundations of his mature philosophical system. He holds consistently, from his earliest writings to his last, that happiness not only requires wisdom but is identical with the possession of it. Following the Christian Scriptures he identifies wisdom with God (the second person of the divine Trinity) and holds that true happiness consists in knowing and possessing God. Christianity, therefore, is the true philosophy: it reveals wisdom to us and gives us the means of attaining it (*De beata vita*, *De moribus ecclesiae catholicae*, *De civitate Dei* VIII. 1–8).

In his early writings Augustine draws on Platonist and Stoic traditions to develop philosophical arguments supporting and explaining these Christian conclusions. He claims that the happy life consists in living in accordance with that which is best or highest in us, and he argues that reason, that by virtue of which human beings surpass other animals, is what is highest in us. He concludes that happiness for human beings consists in living in accordance with reason, living a life in which reason rules and orders the soul. Moreover, since a person whose soul is perfectly ordered by reason is wise, the happy person will be wise, and the wise person happy (*Contra academicos* I. ii. 5; *De libero arbitrio* I. vii–ix; *De moribus ecclesiae catholicae* 4–5).

What is it to live one's life under reason's rule? The wise person both perceives the true nature of reality, including the true relative values of things, and desires things in accordance with their true value. Wisdom, then, involves knowing the truth about human and divine matters and desiring or loving things in a manner commensurate with their real value, the highest good above all and lesser goods less (*Contra academicos* I. vi. 16).

Augustine takes it as a fundamental truth that all human beings want the highest good for themselves, want to be happy (*De moribus ecclesiae catholicae* 3; *De libero arbitrio* II. 9–10; *Confessiones* X. xx. 29–xxiii. 33; *De Trinitate* XIII. iii. 6–vi. 9). But he acknowledges the obvious truth that different people have different views about what the highest good is, and so seek their happiness in different forms of life (*De libero arbitrio* II. 9; *De civitate Dei* IX. 4, XIX. 1–3; *De Trinitate* XII. 6. 8–7. 10). He recognizes both subjective and objective constraints on what can count as a genuinely happy life. First, there are irreducible subjective components to happiness: happiness requires the satisfaction of one's significant desires; one whose most important desires remain unfulfilled cannot be happy. (Augustine takes this point to rebut the claim that the skeptic can be wise or happy. Since the skeptic devotes himself wholeheartedly to seeking truth but does not – and perhaps in principle cannot – find it, his deepest desires remain unfulfilled.) Moreover, happiness is incompatible with fear and anxiety. He argues that happiness must be secure and stable precisely because the happy person cannot be subject to the fear of losing happiness against his will. The happy life therefore will essentially involve satisfaction, fulfillment, and tranquility. Second,

Augustine argues that there are objective constraints on what can count as a happy life. He observes that people whose desires are radically misdirected are unhappy and are made *more* unhappy by having their misdirected desires fulfilled. The happy person, therefore, will desire and possess genuinely fulfilling goods and, primarily and above all, that which is in fact the highest good. People whose beliefs about the highest good are mistaken and whose deepest desires and loves aim at what is not in fact the highest good must remain ultimately unhappy (*Contra academicos* I; *De beata vita*; *De civitate Dei* XI. 11).

Augustine's argument that God is the highest good relies on his understanding of the hierarchical structure of reality (see "God," below). God is the eternal and immutable being than which there is nothing better or higher. God is therefore both the supreme being and the highest good. Human beings, whose happiness consists in finding and possessing the highest good, can find true happiness only in knowing and loving God.

Broadly speaking, therefore, Augustine's ethical theory adopts the general eudaimonistic structure of the ancient Greek ethical tradition and gives it a specific theological content. Augustine fits his account of the virtues into this eudaimonistic framework: "If virtue leads us to the happy life, then I would not define virtue in any other way than as the perfect love of God" (*De moribus ecclesiae catholicae* xv. 25). The four cardinal virtues, temperance, courage, prudence, and justice are states of the soul that orient a person's love toward the highest good, sustain that orientation, and prevent its being undermined by extraneous influences or distractions (*De moribus ecclesiae catholicae* xix. 35–xxiv. 45; *De libero arbitrio* I. 13; *De civitate Dei* XIX. 4; *De Trinitate* XII. 6–8).

Sin, evil, and theodicy

On Augustine's view, the just or morally upright person is the one whose soul is perfectly ordered under the rule of reason. The person in whom reason fails to rule is in a morally bad state. Moreover, particular actions that are not properly ordered by reason are moral evils or sins. Augustine uses the word *peccatum*, typically translated by 'sin', to refer generally to bad acts for which an agent bears moral responsibility (*De libero arbitrio* I).

Augustine rejects the view that morally bad actions are bad because they are directed at intrinsically bad objects. He denies, for example, that pleasure or the food or sexual act in which a person might seek pleasure are intrinsically bad; each is, in fact, intrinsically good. The badness of an action (for example, an act of gluttony or fornication) owes rather to something on the side of the agent. Morally bad acts are disordered, and their disorder consists in the agent's inordinate desire for that at which the act aims. The basic morally bad acts, therefore, are acts of will (choices, intentions, and reflective preferences) which embody or express an agent's inordinate desire for something. Acts of gluttony are morally bad because the glutton's desire for food is out of proportion: the glutton assigns to food more value than it in fact has. But neither the desire for food nor the food desired is in itself bad (*De libero arbitrio* I. viii. 65; *De civitate Dei* XII. 8).

The disorder in our choices and intentions is what makes them bad. But it is their being acts of will that makes them subject to specifically moral appraisal. Augustine holds that human beings are morally responsible for their acts only insofar as they are voluntary, that is, insofar as they are themselves acts of will or arise from the will in the right way. We are not directly responsible for our brute desires and inclinations, what Augustine sometimes calls motions or disturbances in the non-rational part of our soul; whether or not they arise in us is typically beyond our control. We are fully morally responsible, however, for whether we make any of these brute desires our will by consenting to or endorsing them. For reason to exercise control over the soul is for it to withhold consent from illicit, inordinate, brute desires. Reason abandons its control, however, when it surrenders to illicit desires. In the former case, a person refrains from moral evil despite the presence of desire; in the latter case, he wills inordinately and thereby commits moral evil. (See "Will and personal agency," below.)

Augustine often prefers to describe morally basic acts in terms of agents' loves rather than in terms of their choices or intentions. That is because he thinks of the disorder that characterizes particular morally bad acts as expressive of an underlying and persistent state of the soul by virtue of which agents' lives have an overarching bent or directedness. Thus, despite its failure to be ordered *by reason*, a soul that is in a morally bad state is not *utterly* disordered. It is ordered instead by the agent's most deeply held desires, desires whose strength and dominance in the agent's life is out of proportion with the real value of their objects and their objects' ability to be genuinely fulfilling. The term 'love' conveys the sense in which agents' particular choices and intentions express what they care *most* about, what their lives are directed toward generally and above all. When Augustine says that the eternal law requires us to purify our love by turning it away from temporal things and towards what is eternal, he is insisting that moral conversion must transform us not only and not primarily in our particular choices and actions but in the deep, architectonic structure of our values and desires (*De libero arbitrio* I. 15).

Augustine's account of sin as inordinate desire conforms to his account of evil (or badness) in general. He holds that evil is no substance or nature but only a corruption or privation in something that is itself good. A thing's being evil does not consist in its possessing or instantiating some real property or nature additional to its own nature but, rather, in its own nature's being defective or corrupted, its lacking being to some extent. Fundamentally, *moral* evils are defective acts or states that constitute a corruption in rational nature. Augustine is careful to emphasize that moral evil is constituted by the inordinateness and not by the person, the person's will, or the object towards which the will is directed (*De libero arbitrio* II. xix. 53–xx. 54). Non-moral evil or badness is constituted by corruption or defect in non-rational natures (*De libero arbitrio* I; *De moribus Manichaeorum; Confessiones* VII. 12; *De natura boni; De civitate Dei* XI).

Augustine believes that recognizing that evil is a corruption and not a substance or nature in its own right helps resolve an apparent paradox that had kept him for a time from accepting Christianity. Augustine saw that Christianity required commitment to the following propositions:

1   God is the highest good.
2   Everything that exists (other than God) comes from God.
3   Only good comes from the highest good.
4   Evil exists.

Recognizing that these four propositions are logically inconsistent, he had concluded that Christianity could not be true (*De libero arbitrio* I. 2).

Augustine came to see that propositions (2) and (4) are too crude to express both Christian doctrine and philosophical truth. Proposition (4) expresses a truth: evil exists, but only as a corruption or privation in a nature; it is not itself a substance or nature. Moreover, proposition (2) is true insofar as it expresses the Christian doctrine that God is the independent and sovereign creator. But that doctrine, most accurately expressed, is that all the substances or natures that comprise the universe have been created by God. Thus, when (2) and (4) are carefully explicated in these ways, the four propositions are no longer inconsistent. Christian doctrine, properly understood, can acknowledge that evil infects creation without thereby asserting that evil is one of God's creatures (*De moribus Manichaeorum*; *Confessiones* VII. xii. 18–xiii. 19; *De natura boni*).

The Manichaean view that had attracted the young Augustine offered a superficially simpler and seemingly more attractive resolution of the paradox. It rejected proposition (2) altogether, postulating the existence of two fundamental realities rather than one: all the goods in the universe come from the highest good god whereas all the evils come from an evil force that is independent of and opposed to the good god. Augustine eventually realized that the superficial simplicity of the Manichaean position masked a deep incoherence. It was part of the Manichaean account that the corporeal universe is the result of a primal conflict between the good and evil powers in which the evil power had succeeded in capturing part of the good god's substance and imprisoning it in corporeal matter. An argument that Augustine attributes to his friend Nebridius displayed the incoherence as follows: The good god is the highest good; but the highest good must also be incorruptible; hence, either the Manichaean good god is incorruptible, and so not subject to attack and violation at the hands of an evil force, or the Manichaean good god is corruptible, and so not the highest good. On either option the Manichaean position is shown to be untenable. Augustine took this to be definitive reason for rejecting the Manichaean resolution of the paradox of evil and for abandoning the Manichaean views he had once held (*Confessiones* VII. ii. 3).

Augustine's account of evil as a corruption or privation allows him to hold that evil is not among the things God creates. But if God does not create evil, then it seems that it must originate somehow from within God's good creation. Augustine needs to explain how that can happen. Moreover, if God is sovereign creator and providential ruler of the universe, it is difficult to see how God can fail to be responsible, and hence culpable, for whatever evil in fact comes to exist, even if God did not directly create it. Augustine takes the biblical stories of the fall of the angels and of Adam and Eve as providing a model for an adequate explanation of evil's origins. The first evils in creation are evil acts of free will – sins. By means of the free choice inherent in their rational nature, some of the angels and the first human beings turned away from God, the highest good, loving themselves and their own good as if it were the highest good. In so doing, they acted inordinately, preferring lower goods to higher goods. Acts of that kind are irrational and hence corruptions of rational nature. They are the first corruptions in creation and the first evils (*De libero arbitrio*; *De genesi ad litteram*; *De civitate Dei* XI–XIV).

Beginning from this account of the origin of evil, Augustine develops his famous two-evils theodicy: all evil is either sin or a consequence of sin. Sin is introduced into creation by the rational creatures whose sins they are, and sinners, rather than God, bear direct responsibility for it. God is justified, however, in endowing creatures with the dangerous capacity for originating evil and permitting them to exercise it. This is in part because free will is itself a good and necessary for other great goods such as moral virtue and happiness, and in part because God providentially weaves the evil that arises from free will into a beautifully ordered whole which essentially includes the just punishment of sin and the final redemption of creation. The consequences of sin are evils to those who suffer them. They include the natural consequences of moral evil on the sinner (increased ignorance, moral blindness, disordered desire, and unhappiness) and on humanity, and the disruption of the harmony in the natural world (resulting in disease and danger from animals and natural forces). Augustine argues that these consequences are justly suffered by those who bear them, and hence that God is justified in causing or permitting them. He therefore claims to find justification for God in respect of both kinds of evil, sin and its consequences (*De libero arbitrio* I and III; *De civitate Dei* XIV. 15–28).

Will and personal agency

Augustine's account of free will plays a central role in his theodicy, but his views about the nature and significance of the will ground a general account of agency that is important for a wide range of his philosophical reflections. He recognizes that there is a distinctive sort of agency that characterizes rational beings. In virtue of it, they exercise unique control over what they do and who they are, the sort of control that makes their actions *theirs* in the most intimate sense and thereby makes them appropriate objects of moral praise and blame. He believes that if we consider our own case attentively, that is, if we consider our own actions and states from the first-person perspective, we are able to distinguish clearly between what *we do* and what merely *happens to us*. In the most obvious cases, cases of external coercion, there is as clear distinction between, for example, one's moving one's arm oneself and one's arm's moving merely because another person has bumped into one or has grabbed one's arm and forced it to move. When one moves one's arm oneself, one acts; when another person or force moves one's arm, one is acted on, something happens to one without one's doing anything oneself. In cases of the latter kind, the relevant events are not *ours* despite their occurring in our bodies; we are not their source and do not control them (*De libero arbitrio* III. 3–4).

Augustine argues that the same distinction can be drawn with regard to events that occur within our souls. One's sensory faculties can be affected by things in one's immediate vicinity in just the way one's body can be moved by a passing person or a strong gust of wind. Moreover, appetitive events and states – urges and desires – and even events in the higher cognitive faculties – mental imaginings, thoughts, and memories – can intrude into one's mental life entirely unbidden. An aroma from the kitchen, for example, can catch one by surprise – one cannot help being affected by it. But neither can one help being affected by the memory of one's childhood home that the aroma suddenly causes or the desire for a taste of the pie that is baking which immediately follows. One's soul, then, can be the locus of events that are not ours, that we are not the sources of and do not control.

In contrast with these, Augustine identifies states and activities within our souls with respect to which we are distinctively active. When one focuses one's attention in order to determine whether the aroma from the kitchen is evidence of apple or of blueberry pie, or when one chooses to go to the kitchen to have some pie, one is acting. In these cases, we are the originators of our states and activities; their occurrence and to some extent their nature is importantly in our control. For that reason, Augustine argues, the states and activities with respect to which we are active rather than merely passive are the ones that determine and express who and what we are from the moral point of view, who we are as persons or selves.

Augustine appeals to the notion of will to account for the distinctive character of these states and activities. Their being in our control is constituted by their expressing or embodying our will, and it is in virtue of possessing a will that we can be moral agents and persons. Choosing and intending are basic acts of will, and other acts – focusing one's attention, searching one's memory, moving one's arm – are ours by virtue of their being done, as Augustine says, "by will" (*ex voluntate*).

Augustine gives special attention to the connection between the sort of control over our actions that grounds moral responsibility and our ability to avoid those actions. He claims that Adam and Eve, for example, sinned – committed a morally blameworthy act – only if they could have avoided or resisted the act. He argues that an act's being an act of will or done by will is what grounds the required ability to resist. If an agent could not have resisted, then the act was not only not blameworthy but also not done by will.

But Augustine allows for non-central cases. One can be culpable for an act one cannot resist provided one's inability to resist is itself a result of prior acts one could have resisted: habits that have their roots in voluntary actions can acquire the force of necessity (*Confessiones* VIII). Moreover, Augustine holds that after the fall of Adam and Eve, and as a direct result of it, the human will is debilitated in such a way that human beings no longer have it in their direct power to resist sin. He nevertheless holds that post-fall human beings sin culpably in part because there is a means of avoiding sin available to them: God's grace. Post-fall sinners are blameworthy for not availing themselves of the special aid God provides, aid that would give them power to resist sin (*De libero arbitrio* II–III).

The control an agent has, and the responsibility an agent bears, by virtue of the power to resist an action is central to Augustine's ethics. In his view, full-fledged moral significance rests on an act of will that he calls "consent."

> There are three steps by which sin is brought to completion: suggestion, delight, and consent. A suggestion comes about through memory or a bodily sense (when we see, hear, smell, taste, or touch something). If the enjoyment of this thing delights, then if the delight is illicit, one ought to refrain from it. For example, when we are fasting and an appetite for something to eat arises in us at the sight of food, this occurs only by virtue of delight. Nevertheless we do not consent to it, and we restrain it by a command of reason which has control. But if consent had been given, the sin would be complete (*De sermone Domini in monte* I. 12. 34; cf. *De libero arbitrio* III. 10. 29; III. 25. 74–5; *De Trinitate* XII. 3. 17–18).

Augustine's conception of will is central to his ethics and moral psychology but also has an important place in his epistemology. He believes that some of the events essential to our sensory experience manifest our agency in the fundamental way our moral actions do (*De Trinitate* XI). One can to some extent directly control one's perceptions by intentionally turning one's gaze in this direction rather than that, for example, or moving one's hand in order to touch something. But Augustine argues that the will is active in and essential to perception and thought in subtler ways. He remarks that in sense perception we typically manage the potentially overwhelming barrage of sensory stimuli affecting our perceptual faculties by focusing on and giving salience to certain elements, leaving others utterly unnoticed (*De Trinitate* XI). As one observes a bird flitting from branch to branch in the woods, for example, the myriad colors and shapes of the various objects in one's broad visual field impinge on our visual faculties, but they remain unnoticed while one's attention is focused on the bird. Similarly, as one watches the bird, one might completely fail to notice the very slight pressure on one's shoulders caused by the weight of one's garment. Augustine claims, then, that it is one thing for a sensory stimulus merely to affect us, merely to impinge on our sensory faculties, but it is another for us to grasp it in the cognitively significant way that constitutes perception. He claims that the focus or directedness of one's sensory attention in cases of this sort (what he calls the *intentio animi*) is a manifestation of agency of a sort akin to the agency that makes us persons or selves. He therefore explains it as a manifestation of will: our will is what distinguishes our perceiving something in a cognitively robust way from our being merely perceptually affected by something.

161

Augustine finds a similar distinction important for understanding the phenomenon of knowing something. He argues that no external teacher can genuinely teach – that is, genuinely bring about knowledge in – a student. One's hearing or reading words or propositions is, in itself, merely to be affected by them, and teachers and books can do no more than cause us to be affected in this sort of way. By contrast, we come to know something when we ourselves see that it is true, when we grasp it for ourselves. Augustine thinks that this phenomenon of seeing something for oneself is a kind of activity that we as rational agents are capable of. He concludes that all teaching and learning occurs within the soul: as the objects of knowledge are illumined by truth itself we are in position to see them with our mind's eye (*De magistro*). The epistemic agency that characterizes knowing and understanding is therefore analogous to the sort that underlies sense perception and moral agency.

Reason, understanding, and belief

Augustine's youthful search for wisdom was guided by the epistemic principle that legitimate intellectual assent to a proposition requires certainty. He tells us that he was initially attracted to the Manichees because they promised a worldview grounded on nothing but the certainty of reason (*De utilitate credendi* 2, 21; *Confessiones* III. vi. 10). Over time he came to see that the Manichaean promise was empty. But his conviction that intellectual assent must be grounded in certainty remained unshaken, and that explains why he was next drawn to academic skepticism. The skeptics advocated withholding assent where philosophical matters are concerned precisely because they believed certainty about such matters to be impossible. Finding himself at a loss with regard to where certainty might be found, Augustine was attracted to the skeptical position (*De utilitate credendi* 20; *Confessiones* V).

His skepticism, however, was short-lived, as two important discoveries undermined his commitment to it. First, he came to believe that there are in fact truths that can be known with certainty. He offers as examples mathematical and logical truths such as '7 + 3 = 10' and 'There is one world or it is not the case that there is one world', but also propositions about value and morality such as 'What is incorruptible is better than what is corruptible' and 'We should live justly' (*Contra academicos* II. 21–6; *De libero arbitrio* II. viii, x). Convinced by Platonist arguments that he first encountered at Milan, Augustine came to believe that certain knowledge of these sorts of truths rests both on the nature of the propositions themselves and their constituents – their necessity, immutability, eternality, and mind-independence – and on our direct intellectual awareness of them.

Augustine groups together with these objective necessary truths a small group of contingent propositions such as 'I exist' and 'I seem to see white' (*Contra academicos* II; *De Trinitate* X). Certain knowledge of these propositions about our immediate experience is grounded in the nature of the mind itself and its access to its own nature, states, and activities. For example, I can be certain that I exist when I consider the matter because, even on the supposition that I am mistaken in thinking that I exist, it follows that I exist. Augustine here anticipates Descartes's famous *cogito* argument.

In *Contra academicos* Augustine undertakes, with only limited success, a detailed refutation of academic skepticism. What appears to matter most to him in that early text and throughout his later writings, is establishing that no sort of *global* skepticism can be true. Insofar as his claims to possess certain knowledge of the kinds he has drawn attention to are true, they show that some certainty is indeed possible, and hence that global skepticism is false.

The second thing that led Augustine away from skepticism was his coming to recognize that intellectual assent could be rational in the absence of certainty. He came to see that if intellectual assent requires certainty, then a vast quantity of our beliefs must be illegitimate. All our beliefs about events that occurred before we were born, geographical locations that we have never visited, and the existence and contents of other people's minds lack the requisite sort of certainty. These beliefs are grounded essentially in the testimony of others, and by its very nature testimony cannot provide certainty. Augustine, however, thinks we can be justified in holding many of these beliefs. To begin, we have a kind of practical justification for accepting other people's testimony: we could not get on in the world or in our social relationships if we were unwilling to take other people at their word (*De utilitate credendi* 23). But more significantly, we have epistemic justification for accepting some testimony: reason can help us distinguish legitimate from illegitimate, expert from bogus, authority (*De utilitate credendi* 22; *De vera religione* 45). We can, then, have good epistemic grounds for accepting what legitimate authorities tell us. But since no belief accepted on authority is known with certainty, it will follow that it can be legitimate or rational to assent to propositions that are not known with certainty (*De Trinitate* XV. 4. 21–2).

Augustine accordingly distinguishes two sorts of intellectual assent: *understanding* (*intelligere*) which is assent based directly on reason, and *belief* (*credere*) which is assent based on authority. The former sort constitutes paradigm or strict knowledge (*sapientia, scientia*). The latter constitutes mere belief or, when the justification is sufficient, knowledge only in a broad sense (*Retractationes* I. xiv. 3).

Augustine develops his account of the main epistemic concepts in terms of an elaborate analogy with vision. Reason or mind is a kind of capacity for intellectual vision, and the intellectual grasping of some object or proposition is a kind of intellectual seeing (*Soliloquia* I. vi. 12). The paradigm of epistemic justification is explained in terms of the mind's direct acquaintance with its objects. When reason sees its objects directly (and the objects themselves are of an appropriate kind), reason knows them with certainty. When Augustine defines understanding as assent based on *reason*, he is drawing on this metaphor. Assent is based on reason when reason sees the relevant objects directly or sees why the relevant objects must be as the proposition assented to asserts. By contrast, when one assents on the basis of authority, reason does not itself see the proposition's truth but instead takes another as vouching for its truth. In book two of *De libero arbitrio* Augustine asks his interlocutor, Evodius, whether he is *certain* that God exists. Evodius confesses that although he *believes* that God exists, it is not something he sees for himself. Augustine goes on to develop an elaborate proof showing both that God exists and how God is related to other things (see "God," below). The proof's purpose is to put Evodius in position to "know and understand" what he formerly merely believed.

Augustine's doctrine of illumination is an extension of the metaphor of vision. Just as our seeing material objects depends on their being illumined by the light of the sun, our intellectual vision of intelligible objects depends on their being illumined by an intelligible light, truth itself. Hence, knowledge of immutable, eternal truths requires direct acquaintance not only with certain kinds of objects but with the fact that those objects have the properties of being necessary, immutable, and eternal. Since Augustine identifies truth itself with the necessary, immutable, and eternal God, he maintains that knowledge of truth rests on divine illumination (*Soliloquia* I. viii. 15).

Augustine's doctrine of divine illumination is closely related but also intended as a clear alternative to the Platonist doctrine of recollection. Both doctrines account for our knowledge of certain kinds of objects and truths by appeal to direct intellectual awareness of them.

According to the doctrine of recollection, our souls had direct acquaintance with the relevant things in a prior existence, and our coming to know them in this life consists in our recalling what we in fact already know by virtue of past experience. For a time Augustine seriously entertained this account and its commitment to the pre-existence of the soul before its entry into the human body. But he eventually abandoned the doctrine of recollection, developing his own illuminationist account. On the latter account, our knowledge of purely intelligible objects and truths rests on our direct acquaintance with them, but that direct cognitive contact is open to us in this life and occurs whenever we grasp one of these objects or truths. The illumining of these intelligible things by truth itself makes them visible to our minds. Augustine's view that Christ is the inner teacher is an expression of this episte-mological position in Christian terms. God is truth itself which, in the form of the second person of the divine trinity, illumines our minds thereby making intellectual vision possible (*Soliloquia* I. vi. 12; *De magistro*; *De Trinitate* XII. 22–5).

Method in philosophical theology

Augustine defends and explains his own philosophical approach to Christianity by appeal to the distinction between the epistemic states of belief and understanding. He assigns priority to the revealed truths expressed in Christian doctrine and known through the Bible. Fundamentally and essentially, Christian believers, including philosophically minded believers such as Augustine himself, assent to the truths of Christianity on the basis of authority and are thereby in the state of belief with respect to those truths. Augustine argues that the biblical texts are reliable witnesses to the historical events they report, and that those events are strong evidence of divine activity and purpose (*De utilitate credendi* 32–3; *De moribus ecclesiae catholicae* 2). He therefore claims that despite its being based on authority, Christian belief is not blind or irrational but rather epistemically justified.

Augustine also holds that many of the truths of Christianity can also be understood, that is, seen to be true on the basis of reason. Philosophically minded believers therefore can profitably apply reason – philosophical analysis and argument – in investigating those truths. Moreover, believers have not merely the opportunity but also the obligation to understand the truths of Christianity to the extent that they are able. Augustine argues that failing to use reason to the fullest extent is a sinful repudiation of God's image in us (*Epistola* 120). Believers who undertake reasoned investigation of theological matters, however, must *start from* and *be guided by* their antecedent assent to the truth of Christian doctrine.

To start from one's Christian belief requires not only taking one's Christian beliefs as the *subject* of one's investigation but also taking for granted the *truth* of those beliefs. To be guided by one's Christian belief involves both exploiting the conceptual and explanatory resources of a systematic Christian worldview and working to ensure that the results of one's inquiry do not contradict Christian doctrine. When Augustine takes up the paradox of evil, for example, he takes as given the elements of Christian doctrine that constitute the paradox (including that God is the highest good and sole creator of all things) and stipulates at the outset that the results of the investigation cannot depart from Christian belief (*De libero arbitrio* I. 2). The result of that particular investigation is a resolution of the paradox, an account of the meaning of its constituent propositions that explains how they can all be true simultaneously. Typically, Augustine's investigations of this sort proceed, as this investigation does, by developing an underlying theoretical account that provides the basis for drawing crucial distinctions and the resources for constructing illuminating explanations.

In the case of the paradox of evil, he supposes that by coming to see the paradox's resolution, we acquire understanding of what we formerly merely believed. In general, when Augustine admonishes Christians to seek to understand what they believe, he intends to be advocating reasoned investigation of Christianity that starts from and is guided by Christian belief in this way. Moreover, he claims divine authority for that admonition: "Seek and you shall find," says Christ in the gospels. Augustine tells us that it is belief that seeks and understanding that finds (*De Trinitate* XV. 2).

Augustine cautions that not all the truths Christians believe are equally accessible to human understanding. Truths about the historical events reported in the Scriptures can be known only on the basis of authority and not by reason, and some truths about the divine nature are beyond our ability fully to grasp by reason. Indeed, all our thinking about the infinite supreme being must be inadequate to some extent. But even with regard to Christian doctrines where human reason must fall significantly short of full understanding, such as the doctrine of the Trinity, Augustine thinks there is point and profit in rational inquiry. His wide-ranging reflections in *De Trinitate* lead him to develop and explore extremely interesting and fertile analogies of Trinity in the nature of the human mind. He explicitly denies that any of his results there constitute anything approaching a complete explanation of the divine Trinity; but he supposes nevertheless that there is clarification and insight – understanding of a kind and to a certain extent – to be gained in the process.

God

After his conversion to Christianity Augustine never doubted that the Christian Scriptures present the truth about the divine nature. He was equally certain that the Christian Scriptures require careful investigation and explication if the truth about God that they express is to be properly understood. The tools he found most useful in this task were primarily those of Platonist philosophy. He credits Platonism with providing him important strategic and methodological principles for his thinking about the divine: they admonished him to look within his own soul rather than to the external material world, and to look with the eye of the mind rather than with the bodily senses. Indeed Platonism provided Augustine with a rich repertoire of ideas and arguments that he would use to probe and articulate the Christian conception of God.

Augustine develops his systematic account of the divine nature by pursuing two different but complementary strategies. On the one hand, he develops his conception of God by analysis of the notion of a supreme being. On the other hand, he describes an intellectual ascent that mirrors his own path to the discovery of the truth of Christianity. The ascent proceeds by drawing attention to features of the created universe that reveal God's existence and nature, culminating in a kind of intellectual glimpse of the divine nature itself.

Analysis of the divine supremacy

Augustine takes it as a kind of governing principle of his thinking about the divine nature that God must be supreme, that is, that than which nothing is higher or better: "the most genuine root of piety consists in thinking about God in the highest possible way (*optime de deo existimare*)" (*De libero arbitrio* I. ii. 5). In *De doctrina Christiana* Augustine suggests that the notion of supremacy is part of the very concept of the divine:

When the sound of the word '*deus*' strikes the ears of anyone who knows Latin, that person is prompted to think of a kind of nature that is utterly surpassing (*excellentissimam*) and immortal. For when someone thinks of that one God of gods . . . one thinks in such a way that one's thought strains to reach something than which there is nothing higher (*aliquid quo nihil melius sit*) or more sublime. (I. vi. 6–vii. 7)

Augustine allows that people can be confused or ignorant about what sort of thing really is that than which there is nothing higher, as he himself was when he followed the Manichees. Nevertheless "all agree that God is what they place above all other things" (*De doctrina Christiana* I. vii. 7). He takes the notions of being supreme, being that than which nothing is higher or better, and being the highest good to be mutually entailing.

But what sort of nature is in fact supreme? What specific attributes must characterize something than which nothing is higher? Augustine makes progress with this question by investigating what is entailed by the concept of supremacy. No supreme being can fail to possess an attribute that it is intrinsically better to have than to lack. He argues, for example, that since being incorruptible is intrinsically better than being corruptible, a supreme being cannot fail to be incorruptible. Moreover, since immutability is intrinsically better than mutability, a supreme being cannot fail to be immutable. Augustine uses this pattern of reasoning as a constructive tool, specifying, attribute by attribute, a determinate conception of the divine nature. He suggests that some of the ranking-principles on which these deductions depend are a priori truths that the attentive mind recognizes as self-evident.

Some of the ranking-principles Augustine appeals to are based on the sort of metaphysical reflections that support his view of reality as hierarchically structured. Existence that is characterized by life is better than existence that lacks it; life that is characterized by understanding is better than life that lacks it. These comparative ranking-principles can also be used in analyzing divine supremacy. Since life is intrinsically better than inanimate existence, a supreme being must be characterized by life; since a life characterized by wisdom is intrinsically better than a life lacking it, a supreme being must be characterized by wisdom; and since a life characterized by immutable wisdom is better than a life whose wisdom is mutable, a supreme being must be characterized by immutable wisdom (*De doctrina christiana* I. vii. 7).

The analysis of divine supremacy allowed Augustine to discover many of the particular attributes constitutive of the divine nature, including incorporeality, eternality, immutability, incorruptibility, inviolability, life, and wisdom. But he believed that the sort of piecemeal progress the analysis makes possible is in a certain way superficial. What he wanted was an understanding of the divine that is unifying and deeply explanatory of both the manifold divine attributes and the universe in which God ranks supreme (*Confessiones* VII. i. 1–iii. 4). That understanding came with a vision of the divine nature at the pinnacle of Augustine's intellectual ascent toward God.

Intellectual ascent

Augustine describes the intellectual ascent to God in several places (*Confessiones* VII. x. 16; xvii. 23; X). In *De libero arbitrio* Augustine presents the process of ascent as an elaborate argument. He begins there by establishing a hierarchy that sorts into general categories and then ranks relative to one another the natures that comprise the universe: existence, life, and understanding.

Therefore the nature that merely exists (and neither lives nor understands) ranks below the nature that not only exists but also lives (but does not understand) – the soul of the non-human animals is of this sort. This nature in turn ranks below the nature that at once exists, lives, and understands – for example, the rational mind of the human being. (*De libero arbitrio* II. vi. 13)

Augustine's strategy in the succeeding stages of the argument is to show that there is a nature that ranks above the rational mind, a nature whose characteristics mark it as divine. In order to discover that higher nature, Augustine ascends the hierarchy of natures, turning attention first from bodies (the first and lowest category in the hierarchy) to the soul (the nature constitutive of both the second and third categories), and then within his own soul from the sensory part (a part found in both human beings and the non-human animals) to reason: "a kind of head or eye of our soul . . . which does not belong to the nature of non-human animals" (*De libero arbitrio* II. vi. 13).

Having ascended as far as reason – that which is highest in us – he focuses on reason's distinctive perceptual capacities and the distinctive sorts of objects they put us in contact with, the objects of pure thought (see "Reason, understanding, and belief," above). He observes that those objects must be incorporeal, immutable, and independent of our minds. Moreover, since these entities and truths are immutable standards to which our minds must conform and against which our particular thoughts must be judged, they must be higher than reason (*De libero arbitrio* II. viii. 20–1; x. 28).

Augustine goes on to argue that since all these intelligible objects are immutably true, there must be a single thing – immutable truth itself – shared in common by them all. Immutable truth itself is the one over the many, or the one in which the many share or are contained. This last part of his argument is less than fully explicit, and Augustine himself acknowledges the difficulty in making it clear. In other passages he prefers the analogy of light: just as the sun is a single thing despite our seeing many things in its light, so the eye of the soul is able to see various immutable truths because of the light shed on them by the one immutable truth itself. Whatever the obscurities in this crucial last step in Augustine's argument, it is clear that he supposes that this inference completes the strategy he has been pursuing in the proof. "I had promised, if you recall, that I would prove that there is something more sublime than our mind, that is, than reason. Here it is: truth itself" (*De libero arbitrio* II. xiii. 35). That truth itself is more sublime than the human mind and that it is eternal and immutable warrants us, Augustine claims, in identifying it with God. Moreover, this identification is corroborated by and helps explain Christ's own identification of himself as truth ("I am the truth" (John 14: 6)).

The conclusion of Augustine's argument in *De libero arbitrio* is less than fully satisfying. As his interlocutor points out, proving that there is something higher than reason, even something that is eternal and immutable, is not yet to prove that God exists. That requires proving that there is something than which nothing is higher. Augustine's own intellectual ascent seems to have succeeded where his argument falls short, however, because, as he reports it, his own ascent culminated in a glimpse of the divine nature itself.

When I first came to know you, you raised me up so that I might see that what I was seeing is Being, and that I who was seeing it am not yet Being. . . . I said: "Is truth nothing just because it is not diffused through space, either finite or infinite?" And you cried from far away: "No, indeed, for I am who I am" (Exodus 3: 14). I heard in the way one hears in the heart, and there was absolutely no room left for doubt. (*Confessiones* VII. x. 16)

Augustine presents his discovery that God is Being, that which truly *is*, as a kind of intellectual vision, and he sees it as both the philosophical articulation of the scriptural divine name and as the final remedy to the long-standing ignorance that plagued his search for wisdom. He presents the identification of God as true being as more fundamental than any of the other characterizations he finds illuminating, more fundamental even than 'light', 'truth', or 'wisdom'.

What does Augustine mean when he identifies God as what truly *is*? As he conceives of it, that which truly *is* possesses its being in its own right and independently of other things. It therefore cannot fail to be. Moreover, it is the source of being for all other existing things, that on which all other beings depend for their existence. By contrast with what truly *is*, other beings exist in a dependent and contingent way. Augustine bases his understanding of the Christian doctrine of creation on this distinction. To say that other things depend on God for their being is to say that God makes them, that is, causes them both to exist and to be the kinds of things they are. In making things, God requires no aid from any other independent being and uses no pre-existing, independent matter or stuff. Moreover, God does not make things out of God's own substance; that possibility would require either that God be corrupted or that mutable, contingent creatures be equal to God. God makes things out of nothing (*ex nihilo*). The fact that things are created by God *ex nihilo* explains their contingency, mutability, and corruptibility. God gives them being, but because they are made and made from nothing, they are not true being. They are tinged with non-being, as that which truly *is* is not.

Augustine sees this conception of God as grounding his anti-Manichaean resolution of the paradox of evil (see "Will and personal agency," above). Since God is what truly *is* and the source of all being, there can be no existing nature that is distinct from and utterly independent of God. As Augustine puts it: "If you look for something strictly contrary to God, you will find absolutely nothing, for only non-being is contrary to being. Therefore there is no nature contrary to God" (*De moribus Manichaeorum* i. 1). It follows that there can be no independent divine principle opposed to God and that evil, which is contrary to the divine nature, cannot be a created nature or substance but only a corruption or privation – a kind of non-being.

The attribute that Augustine links most closely to true being is immutability. He very often discusses them together, and he takes them to be mutually entailing. His understanding of the nature of change provides the conceptual link between them. Augustine conceives of change as consisting in the loss and acquisition of being. That which changes ceases to be what it was and comes to be what it was not. But what truly *is* cannot lose or acquire being. Hence, what truly *is* must be immutable. Conversely, for something to be immutable is for it to be such that it cannot lose or acquire being. But only what truly *is* can be of that sort. Hence, what is immutable must also be what truly *is*.

Augustine's conception of change as consisting in the acquisition and loss of being also grounds his understanding of both the divine eternality and the divine simplicity. Augustine supposes that a being that experiences time necessarily changes: what one anticipates as future, one will come to experience as present, and then as past. By contrast, the divine being, that which truly *is*, cannot change in this way, and so must comprehend all things in the eternal present. "In the eternal, nothing passes, but the whole is present" (*Confessiones* XI. xi. 13). For similar reasons Augustine holds that God must be metaphysically simple.

> That nature is called simple which does not possess anything that it can lose and for which the possessor and what it possesses are not distinct in the way a vessel and the liquid it contains, a body and its color, the air and its light or heat, or a soul and its wisdom are. (*De civitate Dei* XI. x)

Augustine argues that in cases in which a thing's substance and its attributes – what it is and what it has – are not the same, it is possible for the thing to persist through the acquisition and loss of attributes. But that which truly *is* can neither lose nor acquire being. Hence, God's substance and God's attributes must be identical. "Things are said to be simple which are principally and truly divine because in things of that sort, substance and quality are the same" (*De civitate Dei* XI. x).

Finally, Augustine argues that what truly *is* is what exists or has being in the highest possible way. And since to be in the highest possible way is to be supreme, that which truly *is* must be supreme: "Once one has understood [that than which there is nothing higher] . . . one sees at once that what exists in the highest and primary way is what is said most truly *to be*" (*De moribus Manichaeorum* i. 1). Hence, the discovery that God is true being brought Augustine unprecedented certainty and understanding: it showed him the single conceptual source out of which the other divine attributes flow and by virtue of which they can be explained and fitted together into a coherent Christian conception of reality.

Soul, mind, and memory

In the *Soliloquia* Augustine expresses the desire to know nothing but God and the soul. What he learns about the soul most fundamentally is that it is created by God. That the soul is created by God he takes to be a datum of Christianity, but Augustine thinks that view is corroborated by philosophical reflection. He saw as particularly significant the mind's recognition of the existence of purely intelligible objects and truths that reveal a reality higher than our minds. Our minds are subject to truth itself and, hence, are neither the highest natures in the universe nor divine. Similarly, Augustine thought our experience of the mutability and fallibility of our own minds is conclusive evidence that we are finite, limited natures and not divine.

Augustine's first philosophical proclivities were Platonist, and so in his earlier work he takes a strongly dualist view of the relation between the soul and the body: human beings are souls that make use of a body but are not essentially embodied. He takes seriously the possibility that souls exist before their entry into the body and he holds that they are immortal, and so exist after the body's corruption. Moreover, he is inclined to view the body as a distracting and corrupting influence, as a weight preventing the soul from contemplating eternal things. Over time, however, Augustine's commitment to Christianity tempered his Platonist predilections. He insisted that matter and the body are created by God, and hence are goods; he came to think of the soul as connected with the body in an especially intimate way; and he defended the Christian doctrine of the resurrection of the body (*De civitate Dei* XIV. 3–6). Although he believes the rational soul to be a creature, Augustine nevertheless takes it to be an extraordinary creature: it is highest and best among created natures and most directly bears the divine image. The soul's highest part, that by virtue of which rational nature surpasses the natures of non-rational animals, is mind. Mind endows human beings with their specifically intellectual capabilities grounded in their capacity for direct acquaintance with intelligible objects and for perception of truth. He often calls the mind the soul's eye. Mind is also the seat of the will, and so Augustine holds that it is by virtue of possessing mind that we are moral agents and can seek for and love the highest good.

Augustine holds that among the mind's capacities is the capacity for immediate awareness of itself. That awareness explains how we can be certain that we exist, live, and think, and also that we will, remember, and judge (*De Trinitate* X. iii. 13–14). Moreover,

169

Augustine claims that the mind's knowledge of itself allows it to know that it is immaterial. He argues that, strictly speaking, knowing something entails knowing its substance; and since the mind knows itself with certainty, it must be that the mind knows its substance with certainty. Therefore, since the mind is uncertain whether it is some kind of body or some arrangement or organization of a body, the mind's substance can be none of those things (*De Trinitate* X. iii. 16).

Augustine's reflection on the nature of mind and its distinctive cognitive capacities led him to one of his most striking philosophical positions, his account of *memoria* (*Confessiones* X). Because he conceives of the mind as the eye of the soul and thinks of cognitive activity as essentially involving the mind's perceiving its objects, he feels compelled to give an account of how the mind and its objects are able to come into contact. His position is that mind encounters its objects in *memoria*. *Memoria* is typically translated as 'memory', but that translation is inappropriate since *memoria* has no essential or important connection with *past* experience. *Memoria* is both the storehouse for the materials of cognition and thought and the "place" where mind encounters its object, making cognition and thought possible. *Memoria* stores the images of things we have perceived with the senses, and it is the resource on which our mind must rely in all our thinking and conceiving that involves sensory images. *Memoria* stores the skills associated with the liberal arts, such as the principles of logic, and the principles and laws of mathematics and geometry. In these cases, *memoria* contains the objects themselves not images or mental proxies, and in *memoria* the mind has direct awareness of these intelligible objects. Moreover, *memoria* is the interior place where the mind encounters itself and is able to think about its own nature, states, and activities. And most importantly, *memoria* is the interior place where the mind encounters God.

Memoria, then, is the feature of the rational soul that makes cognition and thought possible, that accounts for our ability to imagine, think, and reason about the different kinds of objects and in the variety of ways that characterize our conscious lives as rational creatures. It is the realm of the distinctive consciousness that belongs to rational beings.

Bibliography

Primary sources

A complete chronological listing, compiled by W. Harmless, of Augustine's works together with Latin editions and English translations is available on the World Wide Web: http://www.library. villanova.edu/sermons/dates.htm. A useful bibliography of the main texts and English translations can also be found in Kirwan (1989).

Latin texts: These series, all of which are in progress, contain critical editions of many of Augustine's texts.

(1866–), *Corpus Scriptorum Ecclesiasticorum Latinorum* (several volumes devoted to Augustine), Vienna: Hoelder-Pichler-Tempsky.

(1936–), *Bibliothèque Augustinienne: Oeuvres de Saint Augustin* (in progress), Paris: Desclée de Brouwer and Etudes Augustiniennes.

(1953–), *Corpus Christianorum, Series Latina* (several volumes devoted to Augustine), Turnhout: Brepols.

A nearly complete collection of non-critical editions is printed in the *Patrologia Latina*:

Migne, J.-P., ed. (1841–2), *Sancti Augustini Hipponensis Episcopi Opera omnia*, 11 vols., *Patrologia Latina*, vols. 32–47, Paris: Vivès.

English translations: These series and anthologies contain English translations of many of Augustine's texts.

(1887–1902), *A Select Library of the Nicene and Post-Nicene Fathers of the Christian Church*, 8 vols., New York; repr. 1979, Grand Rapids, MI: W. B. Eerdmans.

(1946–), *Ancient Christian Writers*, Westminster, MD and New York: Newman Press.

(1947–), *The Fathers of the Church*, Washington, DC: Catholic University of America Press.

(1996–), *The Works of Saint Augustine: A Translation for the 21st Century*, Brooklyn, NY: New City Press.

Burleigh, J. H. S., ed. (1953), *Augustine: Earlier Writings*, Philadelphia: Westminster Press.

Burnaby, J., ed. (1955), *Augustine: Later Works*, Philadelphia: Westminster Press.

Secondary sources

Bonner, G. (1986), *St. Augustine of Hippo: Life and Controversies*, Norwich: Canterbury Press.

Brown, P. [1967] (2000), *Augustine of Hippo: A Biography*, Berkeley and Los Angeles: University of California Press.

Chadwick, H. (1986), *Augustine*, New York: Oxford University Press.

Gilson, E. (1960), *The Christian Philosophy of St. Augustine*, New York: Random House.

Kirwan, C. (1989), *Augustine*, London and New York: Routledge.

Markus, R. A., ed. (1972), *Augustine: A Collection of Critical Essays*, New York: Doubleday.

Matthews, G. B. (1992), *Thought's Ego in Augustine and Descartes*, Ithaca, NY: Cornell University Press.

——, ed. (1999), *The Augustinian Tradition*, Berkeley: University of California Press.

Menn, S. (1998), *Descartes and Augustine*, Cambridge: Cambridge University Press.

O'Daly, G. (1987), *Augustine's Philosophy of Mind*, London: Duckworth.

Rist, J. M. (1994), *Augustine: Ancient Thought Baptized*, Cambridge: Cambridge University Press.

Stump, E. and Kretzmann, N., eds. (2001), *The Cambridge Companion to Augustine*, Cambridge: Cambridge University Press.

Wetzel, J. (1992), *Augustine and the Limits of Virtue*, Cambridge: Cambridge University Press.

16

Avempace

IDRIS SAMAWI HAMID

Post-Hellenic Islamic philosophy after ALFARABI (d. 950) divides into two branches: eastern and western. The eastern branch was based primarily in Iran and spearheaded by AVICENNA (Ibn Sīnā) (d. 1037); it is marked by a greater emphasis on Neoplatonic themes. The western branch developed mostly in Muslim Spain; it is marked by a stricter though by no means slavish adherence to Aristotelianism and Farabianism. The founder of this latter branch was Avempace (Ibn Bájjah) of Saragossa (d. 1139). It reached its height with AVERROES (Ibn Rushd) (d. 1198), whose father or grandfather is said to have been a direct disciple of Avempace (and to have freed him from prison on one occasion).

Avempace's work displays a certain unevenness and incompleteness when compared to that of Alfarabi or Averroes, which is partially attributable to his involvement in the political intrigues of the day. What survives of his work demonstrates original contributions to zoology, astronomy, physics, metaphysics, epistemology, psychology, and ethics. His commentary on Aristotle's *Physics* is quite original. However, his main philosophical work is the unfinished ethico-political treatise *Governance of the Solitary* (*Tadbīr al-Mutawaḥḥid*). Moses of Narbonne wrote a commentary in Hebrew on this work. More than Averroes, Avempace openly draws from both the easterner Avicenna as well as, curiously, from the anti-philosopher ALGAZALI (d. 1111).

The aim of man in general and the philosopher in particular according to Avempace is "connection" (as opposed to "union") with the active intellect. Avempace develops this theme through his metaphysics of *form*. Form can exist without matter. There are three levels of form:

- form coupled with matter;
- particular forms abstracted from matter but not yet completely spiritualized;
- general and purely spiritualized forms, embedded in the active intellect.

The theme of progression from abstract particular forms to general spiritual forms leads to a doctrine of transcendent *monopsychism* or *unity of souls*.

In *Governance of the Solitary* Avempace considers the obstacles and opportunities facing the philosopher on his road to wisdom as well as his lonely responsibilities in the Platonic-Alfarabian utopia of the philosopher-king. These reflections were reworked by Ibn Ṭufayl (d. 1185), a junior contemporary and fellow Andalusian, in his famous philosophical novel *Hayy ibn Yaqẓān* (which, like Avempace's treatise, draws on Avicennan themes).

Much of Avempace's influence on scholasticism and beyond came from his astronomy and physics. In the former he was a critic of Ptolemy; in physics he proposed a new theory of velocity in place of Aristotle's. "Avempacean dynamics" was supported by THOMAS AQUINAS and JOHN DUNS SCOTUS (but rejected by Averroes and ALBERTUS MAGNUS). However, Avempace's formula, that the velocity of a given object is the *difference* of the motive power of that object and the resistance of the medium of motion (as opposed to their *ratio* in Aristotle's view), was adopted by Galileo in the *Pisan Dialogue*.

Bibliography

Al-Ma'sumi, Muhammad (1963–6), "Ibn Bājjah," in M. M. Sharif, ed., *History of Muslim Philosophy*, vol. 1, Wiesbaden: Harrassowitz.

Moody, E. A. (1951), "Galileo and Avempace: the dynamics of the leaning tower experiment," *Journal of the History of Ideas* 12, pp. 163–93.

Goodman, Lenn E. (1996), "Ibn Bājjah," in S. H. Nasr and O. Leaman, eds., *History of Islamic Philosophy*, vol. 1, London: Routledge.

17

Avencebrol

TAMAR RUDAVSKY

Medieval Jewish Neoplatonism provided the philosophical context for the thought of many cultivated Jews of the eleventh and twelfth centuries, many of whom were influenced by the Islamic school of Neoplatonism. Living during the height of the Arabic reign in southern Spain, Avencebrol, also known as Avicebron, and in Arabic as Solomon Ibn Gabirol (b. 1021/2; d. 1057/8), is a product of this rich Judeo-Arabic interaction, which colored Spanish intellectual life during the eleventh century. Avencebrol represents the flourishing of Jewish intellectual life in Andalusia under the enlightened reign of the Umayyad caliphate. Much of his work was written in Arabic, and many of his ideas and poetic styles reflect Arab intellectual and stylistic components.

Of Avencebrol's life we know very little. He was born in Malaga, Spain, and spent the majority of his life in Saragossa. From his poetry we can infer that he was orphaned at a young age and relied upon the patronage of others for his support. In his poems he describes himself as "small, ugly, and sickly, and of a disagreeable disposition"; in one poem he describes the terrors of his recurrent skin diseases. At the age of 16, Avencebrol came under the protection of Yekutiel ben Ishaq ibn Hasan, a Jewish dignitary at the court of the king of Saragossa. But he was known for his arrogant, sometimes virulent temper, and upon the death of his patron Yekutiel, he was soon forced out of Saragossa to Granada, and finally to Valencia. It is not clear exactly when Avencebrol died; his near contemporaries place his death anywhere from 1054 to 1070. It is most likely, however, that he died in Valencia at the age of 35 to 38.

Although Avencebrol himself boasted of having written over twenty books, only such two works are extant: *Mekor Hayyim* (*Fountain of Life*) and *Tikkun Middot ha-Nefesh* (*On the Improvement of the Moral Qualities*). At age 19, he wrote his great didactic poem *Anak*, a 400-verse compendium of Hebrew grammar. Several other works have been attributed to him over the years, but with little evidence. For example the treatise *Mibhar Peninim* (*Choice of Pearls*) is a collection of practical morality composed of 610 proverbs, maxims, and parables, but there is not sufficient evidence to determine whether Avencebrol actually composed the work. Two other philosophical treatises mentioned by him in *Mekor Hayyim* are not extant, and it is not clear whether these works ever really existed. Many of Avencebrol's hundreds of poems have been scattered throughout the Jewish liturgical and literary corpus and have not yet been fully collected. A relatively recent edition (Jarden 1971–3 and 1975–6) contains several volumes of Avencebrol's poetry.

The poetry falls into two camps, what we might term the secular and philosophical genres. The secular output is one of the first attempts in Hebrew literature to write purely non-religious poetry, unconnected to Scripture or liturgical themes. Avencebrol's knowledge of the Hebrew language is remarkable, as is reflected in the poem *Anak*. In addition, he wrote numerous elegies, love poems, and panegyrics. However, his major literary contribution consists of what we may term his "wisdom poetry." Here his work most clearly spans the interface between poetry and philosophy. In these poems Avencebrol is obsessed with the search for knowledge, the ascent and rediscovery of wisdom. The underlying motif of these poems, reflected in his philosophical works as well, is that our sojourn on this earth is but temporary, and the purpose of it is to acquire knowledge and ultimate felicity. The mystical undercurrents are much akin to Sufi poetry, as well as to themes in earlier cabalistic literature.

The best-known and most elegant example of Avencebrol's philosophical poetry is his masterpiece *Keter Malkhut*, a work that to this day forms the text for the Jewish Day of Atonement service. It comprises forty songs of unequal length, and is divided into three parts. Song nine in the first part is particularly noteworthy in that it reflects several motifs found in *Mekor Hayyim*. Part Two of the poem is cosmological in nature, and describes the sublunar elements, the throne of glory, angels, and human corporeal existence. For this cosmology Avencebrol turned to the works of the *Epistles of the Brethren of Purity* (*Rasāil ikhwān as-safā'*), and to the astronomical works of Al-Farghāni. He incorporates the basic elements of Ptolemy's *Planetary Hypotheses*: a series of concentric spheres around the earth, with the five planets, moon and sun, the zodiac, and a ninth diurnal sphere that imparts motion to all the other spheres. In *Cento* X the earth is described as an orb with the moon and four elements encircling it. The moon excites new events in our world every month, but Avencebrol cautions that "Always her own Creator's will (ratzon ha-Bore') she heeds," noting that astrological influences are subject to divine will. After describing Jupiter, Mars, and Saturn, he turns to the zodiac, whose signs have a power to affect sublunar events. In all these passages Avencebrol emphasizes that the influences that flow through the planets to the sublunar sphere do so at the will of their Creator, a motif that will reappear in *Mekor Hayyim*.

Avencebrol's major contribution to ethical literature is his work *Tikkun Middot ha-Nefesh*. This work was written in 1045 in Saragossa, and is available in the original Arabic, as well as in a Hebrew translation by Judah ibn Tibbon dated 1167. In *Tikkun Middot ha-Nefesh*, which is primarily a treatise on practical morality, the qualities and defects of the soul are described, with particular emphasis upon the doctrine of the Aristotelian mean. This mean is supported by biblical references, as well as by quotations from Greek philosophers and Arab poets. One original element in this work is Avencebrol's connection between the moral and physiological makeup of the human. That is, each of twenty personal traits is correlated to one of the five senses. Hence the body as well as the soul must participate in the person's aspirations toward felicity. In effect, Avencebrol delineates a complete parallel between the microcosm as represented by the human being and the macrocosm that is the universe.

This contrast between the microcosm and the macrocosm finds its fullest expression in Avencebrol's most comprehensive philosophical work, *Mekor Hayyim* (*Fountain of Life*). This text has had a checkered history. The original work was written in Arabic, and has come down to us in a Latin translation of the twelfth century made by John of Spain, in collaboration with DOMINICUS GUNDISSALINUS. Hebrew extracts were compiled in the thirteenth century by the philosopher Shem Tov ben Josef ibn Falaquera, and then subsequently translated into Latin under the author's name of 'Avicebrol' or 'Avicebron'. Although medieval Hebrew authors were familiar with Avencebrol's philosophy, Latin scholastics reading the *Fons vitae*, as it had become known by the thirteenth century, did not connect the work to their Spanish Jewish author. In 1857, a French scholar named S. Munk edited and translated the Hebrew extracts once again. It was while comparing the editions in

Falaquera and ALBERTUS MAGNUS that Munk noted that the appellations 'Avicebron', 'Avencebrol', and 'Avicebrol' in fact referred to the great Jewish poet Solomon Ibn Gabirol. Munk thus reintroduced him to a nineteenth-century audience.

Many scholars have mentioned the lack of Jewish content in *Mekor Hayyim*: unlike Avencebrol's poetry, this work contains virtually no references to other Jewish texts, ideas, or sources. His primary influences appear to be several Neoplatonist texts that represent a variation upon standard Plotinian cosmology. Plotinus' *Enneads* was transmitted in a variety of ways, most notably through the *Theology of Aristotle* (a paraphrase of books 4, 5, and 6 of the *Enneads*), and through doxographies, collections of sayings by Plotinus which were circulated among religious communities. The *Theology of Aristotle* exists in two versions: the shorter (vulgate) version, belonging to a later period and found in many manuscripts, and a second, longer version that exists in three fragmentary manuscripts in Hebrew script. Two other influential works are worthy of note. Proclus' *Elements of Theology* was transmitted to Jewish thinkers between the early ninth and late tenth centuries through an Arabic translation *Kalām fī māhd al-khaïr*. Known to Latin thinkers as the *Liber de causis*, it was translated in the twelfth century from Arabic into Latin, most likely by Gerard of Cremona, and was generally attributed by medieval philosophers to Aristotle. Detailed discussion of recent editions and translations of the *Theology of Aristotle* can be found in an article by R. C. Taylor (Taylor 1992). Fenton has recently discovered that Shem Tov Ibn Falaquera translated quotations directly from the original "vulgate" Arabic version of the *Theology* into his own work, making Ibn Falaquera the only medieval Jewish author to have done so (Fenton 1992). Another relevant work is the *Book of Five Substances*, attributed to Empedocles but written in the ninth century in Arabic and translated into Hebrew in the fourteenth and fifteenth centuries. This pseudo-Empedoclean work greatly influenced Avencebrol, especially in its placing of "spiritual matter" as the first of the five substances.

The form of *Mekor Hayyim* (*MH*), a dialogue between a teacher and his disciple, reflects a style popular in Arabic philosophical literature of the period. However, unlike Platonic dialogues in which the student contributes to the philosophical integrity of the argument, Avencebrol's players function primarily as literary interlocutors without much philosophical bite. The work comprises five books of unequal length, of which the third is the most comprehensive (over 300 pages in the Latin edition). A succinct summary of the work is given by Avencebrol himself in his introduction:

> Inasmuch as we propose to study universal matter and universal form, we must explain that whatsoever is composed of matter and form comprises two elements: composed corporeal substance and simple spiritual substance. The former further subdivides into two: corporeal matter that underlies the form of qualities; and spiritual matter which underlies incorporeal form. . . . And so in the first treatise we shall treat universal matter and universal form; in the second we shall treat spiritual matter. This will necessitate subsequent treatises as well. In the third we shall treat the reality of simple substances; in the fourth, the search for knowledge of matter and form of simple substances; and in the fifth universal matter and form in and of themselves. (*MH* I. 1)

Avencebrol's most creative and influential contribution in *Mekor Hayyim* is his hylomorphic conception of matter. His purpose is to show that all substances in the world, both spiritual and corporeal, are composed of matter and form. Unlike Aristotle, he postulates the existence of spiritual matter; which underlies incorporeal substances. Even intellects, souls, and angels are composed of matter and form. Types of matter are ordered in a hierarchy that corresponds to a criterion of simplicity: general spiritual matter; general corporeal matter; general celestial matter; general natural matter; and particular natural matter. Individual matter is associated with prime matter, which lies at the periphery of the hierarchy, thus epitomizing the very limits of being (*MH* 5. 4). Each level of matter is coarser ontologically than its predecessor.

How are form and matter interrelated? Avencebrol's ambivalence is reflected in two alternative responses. On the one hand he argues that form and matter are mutually interdefined and are differentiated only according to our perspective of them at a particular time; accordingly both are aspects of simple substance. On the other hand, he emphasizes the complete opposition between matter and form, suggesting that each possesses mutually exclusive properties that renders a reduction of one to the other an impossibility (*MH* 4. 2).

Avencebrol raises the issue of the infinite divisibility of matter and substance in treatise two of *Mekor Hayyim*, in the context of working out his ontologies of matter and form. Although he does not mention Zeno by name, his analysis pertains to the ultimate divisibility of the parts of substance and reflects issues raised by Zeno's paradoxes of motion. Having just maintained that each composite of substance is composed of that of which it was put together, Avencebrol asks whether the parts of substance are divisible or indivisible. In posing this question, he reflects the concern of the Islamic Mutakallimūn who had argued for the ultimate indivisibility of matter. His aim is to show that quantity exists only with substance. On the basis of this distinction, Avencebrol presents a number of arguments, in 2. 17, designed to support the divisibility of parts and concludes that "the part in question between the parts of the quantity of the world is divisible, and it is clear to me that it is divided into substance and accident" (*MH* 2. 18). His contention is that extension and indivisibility pertain to two different kinds of being: the former is associated with matter, and the latter with spirit. It is impossible to reduce the one to the other. Hence matter cannot be composed of indivisible, spaceless atoms (*minimae partes*). Inasmuch as any indivisible unit must be of a spiritual nature, once we begin to speak of spiritual matter, we leave the issues of quantity and matter behind. Avencebrol therefore envisions the possibility that all of the world might exist in a point and that extension is not essential to matter.

Having seen that matter is infinitely divisible, let us turn to Avencebrol's arguments for the divisibility of form. He clearly asserts that both finitude and divisibility pertain to form as well. Form is the principle of divisibility as well. Clearly, what distinguishes the finitude of both matter and form is the fact that they are mutually interdependent: in this context finitude signifies not so much the sense of spacial limitation as ontological dependence. Having characterized the finitude of matter and form, we are now in a position to characterize more fully the notion of infinity used by Avencebrol to describe God. By infinite in the qualitative, or substantive, sense, he means a totally independently existing entity, one that requires no ontological support. An infinite being possesses no form (4. 6), is not divisible (3. 3) and is not subject to change (3. 6).

Interestingly enough, Avencebrol says little about infinity itself, but rather devotes considerably more time to divine will, which resides in the intermediary sphere between finitude and infinity: the finite and infinite intersect in the will. In part III he offers fifty-six arguments to demonstrate the existence of a substance intermediate between God and substance. Speaking of the intelligible substance, the disciple asks, "Tell me whether the forms of these substances are finite or infinite; if they are finite, how they can have the being of an infinite force; if they are infinite, how something finite in act can issue from them?" (*MH* 4. 20). Avencebrol's response requires aligning form with the creative will: in and of itself, form is identical with will. It is only when it enters into a creative act with matter that it becomes finite. In other words, both form and will, that is to say the force that produces these sub-

177

stances, are finite by virtue of their effect and infinite by virtue of their essence. But the will is not finite by virtue of its effect except when "the action has a beginning and so follows the will; and it is infinite by virtue of its essence for it does not possess a beginning. And inversely, we say of the intelligible substance that it has a beginning because it is caused, and that it has no end for it is simple and not temporal" (*MH* 3. 57). Hence the process of creation is seen as the projection of infinite form upon finite matter, and the retention on the part of matter of a part of this infinite form. Theoretically, were form able to exist independently of matter, it would be infinite and not finite. An even more interesting question concerns the finitude of matter: if matter were able to exist independently of form, would it be infinite as well? No, for it contains within itself the grounds for finitude. So that, although form is allied with finitude, Avencebrol reserves the possibility of speaking of the infinity of form.

Finally we turn to the difficult question concerning the role of will in creation. From comments within *Mekor Hayyim*, Avencebrol apparently either wrote or intended to write a separate treatise on divine will; in any event, the notion of will plays a central role in his cosmogony. He posits the doctrine of divine will (*voluntas*) as both creative and ultimate unity; it is both the origin of multiplicity and yet itself one (McGinn 1992, p. 87). Will is the necessary medium between God and creation. Will is described as both identical with divine intelligence or essence, and as creatively productive of universal form and matter, although in some contexts it is productive of form alone. In the former case it is inactive, and is identical with divine intelligence; in the latter case, it is finite and not identical with divine essence (*alia ab essentia*). From God's will as activity are created all things. Thus will is both united to and separate from the absolute unity of God (*MH* 5. 37).

The question, then, is how to understand the relation that exists between God's essence and God's will when will is active. Is will a hypostasis separate from God, or does it acquire a being of its own? In other words, is will or intellect superior? A number of scholars have argued that for Avencebrol, God's will is superior to intellect, yielding a radical voluntarism. Schlanger goes as far as to suggest that God's will is distinct from God's essence as an independent, autonomous entity (Schlanger 1968, pp. 277–8). Activity is what accounts for the distinction between will and the divine essence. But inasmuch as the will is itself repose, how does it traverse everything and become movement? Avencebrol responds that

> This problem is beyond our research, for it is one of the most difficult in the understanding of the will. But what you must know is that the will penetrates everything without movement and acts in everything, outside of time, by its grand force and its unity. And if you wish to comprehend this more easily, think of the action of the intellect and the soul without movement and outside of time; and represent to yourself the diffusion of the light, sudden, without movement and current of time. (*MH* 5. 39)

Reflecting the discrepancies discussed earlier with respect to matter and form, Avencebrol's discussion of will is thus fraught with tension; this tension reverberates in his discussion of creation as well. Again, the question is whether his concept of will rules out a standard Neoplatonist emanationism. As we have already noted above, in the poem *Keter Malkhut* (*KM*), wisdom (*hokhmah*) and will (*hefez*) are distinct hypostases: "Thou are wise, and from Thy wisdom Thou didst send forth a predestined will (*hefez mezuman*) and made it as an artisan and craftsman to draw the stream of being from the void" (*KM* IX). In this work, then, Avencebrol appears to postulate a voluntary creation out of nothing. But in *Mekor Hayyim*, matters are less clear. In several passages he suggests that creation occurs outside of time. "It is necessary that the First Author achieve its work outside of time" (*MH* 3. 4). Speaking of simple substances and their actions, he says, "How much more grand must be the force of God which penetrates all things, exists in all things and acts on all things outside of time" (*MH* 3. 15). Talking about the difference between matter and will, he says that the will acts outside of time, without movement. That is, the action of the will has for its effect the simple substances, which are outside of time, while the simple substances have for effects corporeal substances that are in time. "The will produces outside of time the being in matter and intelligence, that is to say it produces the universal form which sustains all the forms" (*MH* 5. 37). But in other passages (*MH* 5. 41; 43) he describes creation as a necessary emanation.

In answer to the question whether matter and form are eternal or not, Avencebrol gives an ambivalent response: "matter issues from non-matter and form from non-form" (*MH* 4. 15). When describing the yearnings of matter, he argues that inasmuch as matter was created bereft of form, it now yearns for fulfillment (*MH* 5. 32). However, in other contexts, he asserts that matter subsists not even for an instant without form (*MH* 5. 42). In this latter case, matter is and always was united with form. Additionally, he offers two accounts of the actual process of creation. According to *MH* 5. 42, universal matter comes from the essence of God, and form from the divine will; whereas according to *MH* 5. 36–8, both were created by the divine will.

As in standard Neoplatonic texts, the ultimate purpose of human existence is the return of the soul to its source. Avencebrol modifies the standard picture by claiming that when the soul attaches itself to the will, it returns to the world of intellect and thus reaches the source of life. "Your intellect should distinguish most clearly matter from form, form from will, and will from movement. For if you do this, your soul will be purified, and your intellect will be enlightened and will penetrate to the world of intellect" (*MH* 5. 43). In order to achieve this level of perfection, humans must distance themselves from sensible things and turn themselves toward God. Only by turning from material existence toward will is spiritual perfection achieved. We cannot help but note that the hylomorphism so carefully delineated in Avencebrol's ontology is put aside in his quest for human perfection.

From this brief synopsis of *Mekor Hayyim*, it is clear that Avencebrol's cosmology differs from standard Muslim Neoplatonism in two important respects: in his concept of form and matter, and in his view of will. In his conception of matter, Avencebrol has both incorporated both Aristotelian and Stoic elements, the latter possibly from having read Galen. It has been suggested that the notion of spiritual matter may have been influenced by Proclus' *Elements of Theology*. Unlike Avencebrol, however, Proclus does not maintain that universal form and matter are the first simple substances after God and will. It is more likely that on this point Avencebrol was influenced by both Pseudo-Empedocles and ISAAC ISRAELI, both of whose views on matter and form are very similar to his own. Secondly, we have seen that Avencebrol places great importance upon primacy of will in the creative act. Will represents the nexus of finite and infinite, of time and eternity. Finally, it is clear that he is grappling with a notion of infinity that takes into account not only the quantitative dimension of measure, but the qualitative as well. This two-fold sense of infinity is developed in greater detail particularly by Christian scholastics, and culminates in Spinoza's famous *Letter on the Infinite*.

Avencebrol's philosophical masterpiece had a mixed reception among subsequent thinkers. Unfortunately, *Mekor Hayyim* was not translated into Hebrew during his lifetime, and the original Arabic text was soon lost. Possibly because he does not discuss issues close to the heart of the thirteenth-century Jewish world, such as faith and reason, Jewish philosophers steeped in Aristotelianism had little interest in his work. Abraham Ibn Daud attacked *Mekor Hayyim* on several levels: that it was aimed towards all religious faiths, and not for Jews alone; that it developed one single subject to excessive length; that it lacked scientific method; and finally, that it seduced Jews into error. However, *Mekor Hayyim* did influence several important Jewish Neoplatonists such as Ibn Zaddik and Moses Ibn Ezra, as well as important cabalistic figures such as Ibn Latif.

In contrast, Avencebrol's work influenced several generations of Christian philosophers. Upon the translation of *Mekor Hayyim* into Latin in the twelfth century, many scholastics read and were affected by his voluntarism, his theory of plurality of forms, and the doctrine of universal hylomorphism. Importantly, the *Fons vitae*, as it became known to the Latin schoolmen, contained elements compatible with significant themes in AUGUSTINE and BOETHIUS; it also complemented certain aspects of the twelfth-century Parisian "SCHOOL OF CHARTRES" (McGinn 1992, p. 93). Franciscans such as BONAVENTURE and JOHN DUNS SCOTUS accepted a number of Avencebrol's views. Most importantly, his hylomorphic ontology provided a way of explaining the difference between creatures and God by introducing the ontological distinction of spiritual matter. The doctrine of universal hylomorphism allowed scholastics to posit to angels a "spiritual matter" in order to distinguish them from God.

Avencebrol's doctrine of the plurality of forms in each existing subject became a controversial issue for subsequent scholastics. According to Avencebrol, all existing substances from the First Intellect down to the lowest bodies are composed of the kinds of matter and form appropriate to their substantial level in their respective domains (McGinn 1992, p. 89). Hence there can be many substantial forms in a single individual. Franciscans accepted this theory, which was compatible with their adoption of hylomorphism. Both Albertus Magnus and his student THOMAS AQUINAS rejected Avencebrol's doctrines, however, in particular the doctrine of substantial forms (See Weisheipl 1980).

Moreover, it has been argued that Avencebrol's voluntarism was adopted by thirteenth-century Augustinians as a reaction against the necessary emanationism of Muslim philosophers. According to this reading, Avencebrol wished to make divine will the supreme cause of the universe, in contradistinction to ALFARABI, AVICENNA, and the *Liber de causis* who saw the creation process as a necessary and impersonal emanation from the First Principle (See Weisheipl 1980). On this reading, Avencebrol's voluntaristic strain culminates in the extreme voluntarism of WILLIAM OF OCKHAM in the early fourteenth century. A strong case can be made, however, that Avencebrol's theory of will does not require a rejection of Plotinian and Arabic emanationism (Pessin 2000).

Avencebrol's influence continued throughout the late medieval and Renaissance period. A number of important sixteenth-century Jewish and Christian cabalists were influenced by the more esoteric conceptions of his cosmology. We can also mention the influence of Avencebrol upon the revival of Neoplatonism in the sixteenth century. There is even evidence to suggest that Giordano Bruno utilized the *Fons vitae* in developing his pantheistic cosmology. In short, the works of Avencebrol, the most original medieval Jewish Neoplatonist, came to influence scholasticism under pseudonyms, his true identity concealed as a result of his efforts to systematize the basic principles of Jewish thought without any recourse to religious dogma or belief.

Bibliography

Primary sources

Munk, Salomon (1857–9), "Liqqutim min ha-Sefer Makor Hayyim," in *Mélanges de Philosophie Juive et Arabe*, Paris: A. Frank.

Baümker, Clemens, ed. (1892–5), *Avencebrolis Fons vitae ex Arabico in latinum translatus ab Johanne Hispano et Dominico Gundissalino, Beiträge zur Geschichte der Philosophie des Mittelalters* 1/2–4, Münster: Aschendorff.

Wise, Stephen S., trans. (1901), *Tikkun Middot ha-Nefesh* (*The Improvement of Moral Qualities*). New York: Columbia University Press.

Cohen, A. (1925), *Solomon Ibn Gabirol's Choice of Pearls*, New York: Bloch Publishing Co.

Blaustein, Jacob (1926), *Sefer Mekor Hayyim* (trans. into Hebrew), Tel-Aviv: Mossad Ha-Rav Kook.

Lewis, Bernard, trans. (1961), *The Kingly Crown*, London: Valentine, Mitchell.

Jarden, Dov (1971–3), *Shirey ha-qodesh le-ribbi shelomoh 'ibn gabirol im perush*, Jerusalem: Jarden.

——(1975–6), *Shirey ha-hol le-ribbi shelomoh 'ibn gabirol im perush*, Jerusalem: Jarden.

Secondary sources

Brunner, F. (1980), "La doctrine de la matière chez Avicébron," repr. in Stephen T. Katz, ed., *Jewish Neoplatonism*, New York: Arno Press.

Dillon, John (1992), "Solomon Ibn Gabirol's doctrine of intelligible matter," in Lenn Evan Goodman, ed., *Neoplatonism in Jewish Thought* (pp. 43–59), Albany: State University of New York Press.

Fenton, Paul (1992), "Shem Tov Ibn Falaquera and the *Theology* of Aristotle," *Da'at* 29, pp. 27–39.

Kaufman, David (1962), "The Pseudo-Empedocles as a source of Salomon Ibn Gabirol," in D. Kaufman, ed., *Mehqarim be-sifrut ha'ivrit shel yemei ha-binayim* (pp. 78–165), Jerusalem: Mossad Ha-Rav Kook.

Loewe, R. (1989), *Ibn Gabirol*, New York: Grove Weidenfeld.

McGinn, Bernard (1992), "Ibn Gabirol: the sage among the schoolmen," in Lenn Evan Goodman, ed., *Neoplatonism and Jewish Thought* (pp. 77–109), Albany: State University of New York Press.

Munk, Solomon (1859), *Mélanges de philosophie juive et arabe*, Paris: A. Franck.

Pessin, Sarah (2000), "Solomon Ibn Gabirol: universal hylomorphism and the psychic imagination," Ph.D. dissertation, Ohio State University.

Rudavsky, Tamar (1978), "Conflicting motifs in Ibn Gabirol's discussion of matter and evil," *The New Scholasticism* 52, pp. 54–71.

Schlanger, Jacques (1968), *La Philosophie de Salomon ibn Gabirol: Étude d'un néoplatonisme*, Leiden: Brill.

Taylor, R. C. (1992), "A critical analysis of the structure of the *Kalām fi māhd al-Khaïr* (*Liber de causis*)," in Parviz Morewedge, ed., *Neoplatonism and Islamic Thought*, Albany: State University of New York Press.

Weisheipl, James A. (1980), "Albertus Magnus and universal hylomorphism: Avicebron," in Francis J. Kovach and Robert W. Shahan, eds., *Albert the Great Commemorative Essays* (pp. 239–60), Norman: University of Oklahoma Press.

18

Averroes

RICHARD C. TAYLOR

Abū al-Waḥīd Muḥammad Ibn Aḥmad Ibn Muḥammad Ibn Rushd al-Ḥafīd, known in Latin as Averroes (b. ca. 1126; d. 1198), was born shortly after the death of his like-named grandfather, who was *Qāḍī* (judge) and *Imām* at the Great Mosque at Cordoba and a prominent jurist of the Malikite School then dominant in Almoravid Spain and Morocco. Following in the footsteps of his grandfather and father, Averroes pursued the study of the *Shaŕiah* (religious law) and in due time was himself appointed *Qāḍī* in Seville and later Grand *Qāḍī* (chief judge) in his birthplace, Cordoba. His appointment at Seville in 1169 shortly after the death of his father seems to have followed his famous introduction to the Almohad ruler, Abū Ya'qūb Yūsuf. Yūsuf was a well-educated prince who had succeeded 'Abd al-Mu'min, follower of al-Mahdī Ibn Tūmart (d. ca. 1129–30) and victor over the Almoravids. According to the account attributed to Averroes himself via one of his students, he reported that Ibn Ṭufayl, author of the famous critical philosophical and religious novel, *Ḥayy Ibn Yaqẓān*, and physician to Abū Ya'qūb Yūsuf, introduced him to the royal court. The court was renowned for its support of intellectuals and scholars, and after formalities, Abū Ya'qūb Yūsuf asked Averroes the opinion of the philosophers on whether the heavens were eternal or created. Uncertain of the views of the prince on this controversial theological and philosophical issue, Averroes tried to excuse himself and deny he had undertaken philosophical studies. Abū Ya'qūb Yūsuf then turned to Ibn Ṭufayl and displayed such a sophisticated understanding of the issues that Averroes became at ease enough to re-enter the discussion and display his philosophical erudition. Rewarded by the court with money, robe, and mount for this appearance, Averroes later was charged by Ibn Ṭufayl to produce summaries of the works of Aristotle; this was at the instigation of the prince, who had complained of their difficulty (1967a, pp. 12–13). This is generally taken as the commission of what came to be the *Middle Commentaries* (*Talākhīṣ*), Averroes' paraphrasing of the works of Aristotle. These were preceded by the epitomizing *Short Commentaries* (*Jawāmi'*), which draw heavily on Greek and Arabic commentators for explication of Aristotle. Beginning in 1180, Averroes produced five *Long Commentaries* (*Shurūḥ* or *Tafāsīr*): *Posterior Analytics* (1180), *Physics* (1186), *De caelo* (1188), *De anima* and *Metaphysics* (1190). The start of this production of definitive *Long Commentaries* was immediately preceded by three important theological works of considerable philosophical importance: the *Decisive Treatise Determining the Nature of the Connection Between Religion and Philosophy* with *Appendix*, the *Explanation of the Sorts of Proofs in the Doctrines of Religion*, and his famous *Incoherence of the Incoherence*, a philosophical and dialectical refutation of ALGAZALI's monumental critique of the thought of AVICENNA and ALFARABI, the *Incoherence of the Philoso-*

phers. Not long after completing his *Middle Commentary on the "Republic" of Plato* in 1194 (Aristotle's *Politics* was not available in Arabic translation), Averroes fell out of favor with al-Mansur, successor to power upon the death of his father Abū Ya'qūb Yūsuf in 1184, and was exiled to Lucena with an order for his books to be burned. Shortly thereafter Averroes was restored to a position of prominence at Marakkesh, where he died in 1198. In addition to the works listed above, Averroes was also renowned for his medical work, *al-Kulliyāt* (Latin *Colliget*), works on Galen, and juridical writings.

Through the centuries, Averroes has long been prominent in the history of European philosophy and theology in the Middle Ages and Renaissance, owing primarily to the importance of the thirteenth-century and Renaissance Latin translations of some of his most analytical and mature philosophical works. The medieval Latin translations of Averroes' *Long Commentaries* on the *Physics*, *De caelo*, *De anima*, and *Metaphysics* of Aristotle provided complete texts of each of these works by Aristotle and detailed philosophical analyses drawing on works of Alexander of Aphrodisias, Themistius, and others of the Greek Commentary tradition, as well as on the work of philosophers of the Arabic *Mashsha'i* (Arabic Peripatetic) tradition such as Alfarabi, Avicenna, and AVEMPACE. In 1328 the *Incoherence* was translated into Latin, and in the Renaissance Latin translations from Hebrew of works such as the *Long Commentary on the "Posterior Analytics"* and the *Middle Commentary on the "Republic" of Plato* became available. Although Michael Scot is often associated with the translation of works by Averroes in the Middle Ages, only the translation of the *Long Commentary on the "De caelo"* is known to be his (Burnett 1999, pp. 269–70).

Preceded in Latin translation by the works of Avicenna, which gave the Latin West doctrines and arguments from a tradition strongly imbued with insights from various Neoplatonic sources, these works by Averroes taught the Latin West how to read Aristotle's own texts with depth and argumentative rigor; they showed the value of returning to the genuine thought of Aristotle himself. The Latin tradition knew Averroes' admiring statement, "I believe that this man was a model in nature and the exemplar which nature found for showing the final human perfection" (1953, p. 433) as well as his vigorous philosophical defense of Aristotelian teachings on the eternity of the world, the perishable nature of the individual human soul, the eternity of the human species, the unity of the intellect for all human beings, and the denial of knowledge of particulars by the transcendent intellectual Deity whose nature was self-thinking thought. He was also thought to have denied free will, to have denied the miraculous, and to have taught the infamous doctrine of "double truth" (Badawi 1972, p. 849).

Seen as championing these teachings, Averroes' writings in Latin were often attacked by theologians such as ALBERTUS MAGNUS, BONAVENTURE, and THOMAS AQUINAS, while those same teachings and arguments inspired the Latin Averroist movement. Its members sought some independence from religious influence for their purely philosophical project, imitating what the *Long Commentaries* seemed to present as proper philosophical methodology. In the Renaissance, interest in Averroes revived and the medieval Latin translations as well as new translations from Hebrew were made available in printings of the *Opera* of Aristotle (Averroes 1574; Cranz 1976; Davidson 1992, pp. 300–14).

The medieval Hebrew philosophical tradition was also deeply influenced by the works of Averroes, although the works translated were quite different from those in the Latin tradition and so led to quite a different understanding of his thought. The medieval Latin West had none of the theological and legal writings of Averroes (aside from a selection found in the late thirteenth-century work of RAMON LULL), with the result that major thinkers such

183

as Albert, Aquinas, Bonaventure, SIGER OF BRABANT, and others saw Averroes only as philo-sophical commentator. In sharp contrast, the Jewish tradition had translations from Arabic of the *Decisive Treatise Determining the Nature of the Connection Between Religion and Phi-losophy*, the *Incoherence of the Incoherence*, a great many of the *Short Commentaries* and, of particular importance, the *Middle Commentaries* on the *Physics*, *De caelo*, *De anima*, and *Metaphysics*, and the *Long Commentaries* on the *Posterior Analytics* and *Physics*. This gave Hebrew readers both a more complete picture of the religious thought of Averroes and yet also a less complete philosophical picture, since the Hebrew tradition was missing his most mature work as found in his important *Long Commentaries* on Aristotle's *De caelo*, *De anima*, and *Metaphysics* (Anawati 1978). This meant that Averroes' final positions on the nature of the human intellect and on the nature of the first cause as established in these last of his *Long Commentaries* remained unknown to Hebrew readers. Still, Jewish thinkers drank deeply of Averroes' reflections on the relation of philosophy and religion in the *Decisive Treatise* and *Incoherence*, often having this as a major theme of discussions, while Christians could approach the same issues only on the basis of inferences from philosophical positions found in works of Averroes available to them (Leaman 1996). There were substantial dif-ferences also in the understanding of the human intellect since, as we shall see, the sophis-ticated and controversial position of Averroes on the separate Material Intellect and separate Agent Intellect and on the perishable individual human rational power found in the *Long Commentary on the "De anima"* was unknown in the Hebrew tradition. Rather, the Hebrew tradition's most mature account was that of the *Middle Commentary*, which neither excluded personal immortality nor asserted the separate Material Intellect.

In the Arabic philosophical tradition Averroes was not the founder of a school of phi-losophy, though he did have students, among them his own sons. GILES OF ROME suggests that the sons of Averroes were at the court of Frederick II Hohenstaufen and that they may have had a hand in providing works to be translated (Burnett and Zonta 2000). For the most part, however, there is little evidence that the Arabic works of Averroes traveled to the East. Indeed, a generation after his death his works seemed to have little currency. Only much later Ibn Khaldun, who had read the *Incoherence of the Incoherence*, mentions him as an important Islamic philosopher (Burnett 1999). In the nineteenth and twentieth centuries the work of Averroes was rediscovered by nationalists and others and used to serve various political ends, to show the compatibility of religion and modern science, and also to recall days of glory when the Arabic East was more scientifically advanced than Christian Europe (von Kügelgen 1994). Today his works are sometimes used to further conservative religious or even secularist causes against Islamic fundamentalism with the claim that the *Decisive Treatise* and other writings have shown the way to the conciliation of religion and scientific and philosophical advancement. Such a so-called Enlightenment view of Averroes, however, is not a correct understanding of Averroes' thought in relation to that of the European Enlightenment nor is it an informed view of the thought of Averroes as a whole (Butter-worth 1996). Modern Arabic writers who have very much relied on works such as the *Deci-sive Treatise*, the *Incoherence*, and related Arabic writings only recently have been gaining comprehensive access to Averroes' most mature and sophisticated philosophical works, among them his *Long Commentaries* and his *Middle Commentary on the "Republic" of Plato*. As indicated, much of his work was preserved and transmitted only by way of translations into Latin and Hebrew, and is now becoming available in translations into European lan-guages and in modern editions of the older texts in Arabic, Hebrew, and Latin. For the Arabic-speaking world as well as for the rest of the world, these recent editions and trans-lations have produced both a revival of interest in the thought of Averroes and a need for a reassessment of his teachings, particularly in light of contemporary reflections on the nature of religion.

Philosophy and theology

Averroes' legal *Decisive Treatise* begins, "The purpose of this treatise is to examine, from the standpoint of the study of the Law, whether the study of philosophy and logic is allowed by the Law, or prohibited, or commanded – either by way of recommendation or as obligatory" (1967, p. 44; 1959, p. 1). Following an approach similar to that of al-Mahdī Ibn Tūmart on whose thought the ruling Almohad regime was founded (Geoffroy 1999), Averroes says that the Koran itself (59, 2) commands "reflection on beings and the pursuit of knowledge about them" (1967, p. 44; 1959, p. 1) and explains that this is precisely philosophy's method of demonstration. Other forms of reasoning, rhetorical, dialectical, or even fallacious, may hit on the truth by accident but philosophical demonstration yields certainty and necessary truth through knowledge of causes. Yet the Koran calls all people with its message even though

> the natures of men are on different levels with respect to [their paths to] assent. One of them comes to assent through demonstration; another comes to assent through dialectical arguments, just as firmly as the demonstrative man through demonstration, since his nature does not contain any greater capacity; while another comes to assent through rhetorical arguments, again just as firmly as the demonstrative man through demonstrative arguments." (1967a, p. 49; 1959, p. 49)

Central to his understanding is the principle of the unity of truth, that "Truth does not contradict truth but rather is consistent with it and bears witness to it," one that Averroes transplants into his *Decisive Treatise* without mentioning its source in Aristotle's *Prior Analytics* (Taylor 2000). With this principle and also with his Farabian view of the tripartite division of human intellectual abilities and psychological characters, Averroes argues that apparent contradictions between the necessary truth of demonstrative philosophy and the divinely inspired truth of the Koran can be resolved since Scripture bears surface and inner meanings corresponding to the differing dispositions of human beings. In the case of apparent contradictions, the nature of Scripture as a guide to proper action for all human beings must be kept in mind while an allegorical interpretation of Scripture must be brought to bear. Here the infamous issue of double truth, one of religion and the other of reason, does not arise in the thought of Averroes, thanks to this methodology which gives philosophy – where it is in possession of demonstration – priority in judging the soundness of scriptural interpretation. Ẓāhirite literalist interpretations are to be rejected for their excessive anthropomorphism as are those of Ash'arite and Mu'tazilite dialectical theologians for their false or uncertain assumptions and unfounded conclusions. Most to be condemned are those such as Algazali, who undermined beliefs of devoutly practicing Muslims by exposing members of the rhetorical or dialectical classes to allegorical interpretations suitable only for learned thinkers of the demonstrative class. What is more, Algazali publicly charged Alfarabi and Avicenna with unbelief for upholding the eternity of the world, divine ignorance of particulars, and denial of bodily resurrection; his charge was not only dangerously confusing for the unlearned, it was insufficiently grounded. In fact, the theologians' account of the world even contradicts the literal sense of the Koran and puts in its place an

185

allegorical account of creation *ex nihilo*. And Algazali's understanding of God's knowledge of particulars is an anthropomorphic denial of the unchanging, prior, and causative nature of God's knowledge. Finally regarding resurrection, interpretations of the scriptural texts vary, so "only the negation of existence [of future life] is unbelief, because it concerns one of the principles of religion" (1967a, p. 61). In all these and other matters, the mistakes of philosophers seeking truth are to be excused since they are the ones able to make the most qualified judgments possible, while the mistakes of the unqualified, the dialectical theologians, are to be condemned in themselves and for the confusion into which they lead pious Muslims. Still, while this entire approach founded on the principle of the unity of truth puts demonstrative philosophy in a position of priority and judgment in some cases, it does not claim that philosophy contains in actuality all truth and that philosophy is thereby in actual possession of the right to judge the truth of all Scriptural interpretation. Rather, Divine Revelation is a fit guide for all human beings in all their differing classes, rhetorical, dialectical, or demonstrative, into which Divine Wisdom has placed them.

Averroes went on to write his own critical theological treatise, the *Explanation of the Sorts of Proofs in the Doctrines of Religion* with chapters on the existence of God, divine unity, divine attributes, divine transcendence, divine actions in the origin of the world, prophecy, predestination, justice, and eschatology. Although he criticizes Ash'arite occasionalism for its denial of natural causality and on the grounds that it ultimately entails a denial of divine purpose, Averroes also finds inadequate the ways to God set forth by the Literalists: the Ash'arites, the Sufis and esotericists, and the Mu'tazilites (these latter to the extent that their way is of the same dialectical kind as the Ash'arites). Averroes explains that God's existence is established by the ways indicated in the Koran, the way of providence for human beings (*al-'ināyah bi-l-insān*) and the way of creation of all the world's existents by this providence (*khalqi jamī'i al-maujudāt min ajli-hā*). The argument from providence is based on two propositions: all existents in the world are conducive to the existence of human beings and this conduciveness is necessarily through an agent intending this by will (*murīdun*). Empirical observation and human reasoning powers confirm these propositions, which are already stated in the Koran, and allow for the existence of God as conclusion. The argument from creation is based on empirical consideration of animals, plants, and the heavens and is founded on the existence in potency of two fundamental principles in the natures of all human beings. First, these beings are created, something known self-evidently in the consideration of animals and plants in contrast to inanimate bodies, since we know that what is living must have something determining (*qaṭ'an*) the existence of life, namely God. In the case of the heavens, their movement, so providential for things in the sublunar realm, also indicates the presence of the Creator. Second, everything created has a creator. On the basis of this second set of two propositions reflected in the Koran and confirmed by empirical observation, Averroes again finds sufficient grounds to assert the existence of God (1998b, p. 118–19).

Averroes' *Incoherence of the Incoherence* is the third in this trilogy of theological or dialectical works aimed at bolstering the position of philosophy in the face of attacks from Algazali and other dialectical theologians. This work, which contains Algazali's complete *Incoherence of the Philosophers*, without its prefaces, prefigures the *Long Commentaries* on the works of Aristotle in their close textual study and philosophical argumentation. However, the *Incoherence* differs from the demonstrative *Long Commentaries* in its dialectical character. Averroes explains this and points those seeking demonstrative arguments to his *Commentaries*, when he writes that the *Incoherence* contains not demonstrative but persuasive statements. He continues, "It is for you to inquire about these questions in the places where they are treated in the books of demonstration . . . Nothing therefore of what we have said in this book is a technical demonstrative proof; they are all non-technical statements, some of them having greater persuasion than others, and it is in this spirit that what we have written here must be understood" (1930, pp. 427–8; 1969, pp. 257–8).

Averroes' detailed refutations of Algazali in the *Incoherence* are often powerfully critical but the positive positions he sets forth need to be read in light of this statement on the dialectical nature of the *Incoherence*. For example, his argument for possible personal immortality in the hereafter by way of transmigration of souls to celestial bodies is a dialectical argument, which he knew to be in contradiction of Aristotelian psychological principles (Taylor 1998). His arguments for the literal denomination of God as Creator on the basis of the assertion of the creative character of divine knowledge satisfies religious sensibilities but fails to be sufficiently coherent from the point of view of his *Long Commentary on the "Metaphysics"* and Aristotelian premises (Kogan 1985). And his Seventeenth Discussion on causality and miracles is dialectical and intentionally ambiguous in asserting the appropriateness of the traditional religious ascription of miracles to God in language which appears to endorse the commonplace view, while in fact he provides a naturalistic analysis for the careful and informed reader (Kogan 1981). The *Incoherence* is nevertheless a powerful, compelling, and largely successful response to the devastating critique of philosophy leveled by Algazali. But the failure of the widespread transmission of the works of Averroes to the East meant that the critique was read by few and that the attack on the philosophers by Algazali continued to have influence in Islamic religious and philosophical contexts.

God and natural philosophy

Averroes' approach in his more strictly philosophical studies of the existence and nature of God is Aristotelian. While he followed Alfarabi and Avicenna in proposing a Neoplatonic-inspired emanative scheme for the universe in his *Short Commentary on the "Metaphysics"*, Averroes rejected the Arabic version of this Neoplatonic principle decisively in the Third Discussion of his *Incoherence* and it played no role in his mature *Long Commentaries*, even though he retained its imagery and language (Kogan 1985, pp. 248ff). The order of completion of his *Long Commentaries* is significant in understanding his procedure. The first completed was the *Long Commentary on the "Posterior Analytics"*, known in Arabic as the *Book of Demonstration* (*Kitāb al-Burhān*). It was followed by the *Long Commentary on the "Physics"*, then the *De caelo*, and then by the presumably contemporaneous *Long Commentaries* on the *De anima* and *Metaphysics*. With his intensive study of the science of demonstration completed, Averroes was able to undertake detailed studies of the way in which the existence and nature of God is established.

Declining to follow Avicenna's founding of metaphysics on the mind's ability to grasp reality as divided into the necessary and the possible, Averroes traces the cause of sublunar motion to the motion of the eternal celestial bodies, as did Aristotle in the *Physics*. Averroes follows Aristotle's *De caelo* and explains that these observable and permanent heavenly bodies must themselves have matter, the same only in name with the matter in perishable early things. They can be said to have matter insofar as they have a potency, in their case a potency for unending circular movement, but their matter is not subject to substantial change given their eternal substances. The celestial body is an indestructible "matter-like substratum" which has an associated form which "is a source of infinite power whereby the substratum moves eternally" (Davidson 1992, p. 325). For Averroes this form is an incorporeal reality which causes motion in the celestial body by way of Aristotelian final causality, as is made clear in metaphysics. And it is the first or outermost celestial body that is the primary cause of the eternal motion of the universe as a whole, according to the arguments of physics. But the science of physics or natural philosophy in Aristotle's analysis deals only with that which has "within itself a principle of motion and of stationariness" (*Physics* 2.2, 192b14), that is, it concerns physical bodies, and as such is unable to explore the nature of incorporeal reality within the science of physics. This issue was important enough for Averroes to devote a separate treatise to it, his *De substantia orbis* (Averroes 1986).

For Averroes this account from physics was sufficient to satisfy the criteria of Aristotle's *Metaphysics* 6.1, where it is argued that first philosophy will be physics if it cannot be established that immaterial substance exists. It allowed for the science of *Illāhīyāt* – metaphysics or divine concerns – as the science that treats of being *qua* being, that is, all being corporeal or incorporeal, and its causes, and does so only on the condition that the existence of separate immaterial substance could be proven. For Averroes, who goes beyond the Aristotelian account, this opened the door to the investigation into the nature of incorporeal entities and ultimately the First Cause of all, Allāh. In the *Long Commentary on the "Metaphysics"* this investigation centers on Aristotle's Book Lambda of the *Metaphysics* and the *Commentary of Alexander of Aphrodisias* (1967b, pp. 1393ff; 1984, pp. 59ff) with the discovery in physics of a plurality of eternal motions and incorporeal unmoved movers. By metaphysical argument founded on Aristotle's account in *Metaphysics* 7 and 8 and probably also relying on Alfarabi (Walzer 1985, pp. 70–3), Averroes infers in his *Long Commentary on the "Metaphysics"* that these individual and separately existing immaterial forms are each an intellect insofar as they are actually existing forms without matter. He writes,

> [I]t is fully clear that these celestial bodies are alive and that among the powers of the soul they have only intellect and the power of desire, i.e. [intellect] which causes motion in place. This is perhaps evident from what I say, for it has been explained in the eighth book of the *Physics* that what causes motion belonging to the celestial bodies is not in matter and is a separate form. And it was explained in the *De anima* that the separate forms are intellect. So, consequently, this mover is an intellect and is a mover insofar as it is an agent of motion and insofar as it is the end of motion. (1967b, pp. 1593–4; cf. 1984, p. 149)

For Averroes each of these separate final causes of celestial motion, which Aristotle had called gods, is regarded as an eternal and incorruptible intellect having the nature of a pure form without matter for substantial or accidental change. Hierarchically ranked with God, the First Cause, and the First Form, as the unique substance at the highest rank, each of these separate immaterial substances has the nature of self-thinking thought. What distinguishes them from one another and from God is the note of potency which all below the First have insofar as their natures are not fully self-complete. God alone is "pure actuality", *fi'lun maḥḍun* (1967b, p. 1599; 1984, p. 151) and simple, but they are "composite things [which] surpass one another by the lack of composition and their proximity to the simple and the first in this genus" (1967b, p. 1704; 1984, p. 196), since everything except God contains a reference and relation of final causality to the complete and perfect actuality of the First Cause. The knowledge contained in these separate intellects is unique to each intellect since each is self-thinking thought and each is set in the hierarchy according to its active power of knowing, its "intellectual conceptualization," *tassawūr bi-l-'aql, imaginatio per intellectum* (1967b, pp. 1599–1600).

The perfect simplicity and ultimate transcendence of the First Cause raises the important issue of the nature of God's knowledge since his perfect self-thinking thought would

188

seem to imply the inability to know the prayers and petitions of his servants. To this question, Averroes again answers that his knowledge can be neither particular nor universal (1967b, pp. 1707–8; 1984, pp. 197–8). But what is the knowledge that God has when the only two forms of knowledge of which human beings are aware must be denied of God? The metaphysical argument about the nature of God as pure actuality of intellect does give reason for asserting knowledge in God, since knowledge is the name given for the activity of intellect. In this sense, knowledge can be predicated of God but that knowledge is purely an unchanging and eternal activity of self-knowing and radically unlike the human forms of knowing. Such being the case, it is very difficult to accept literally Averroes' contention that God knows all existing beings through his knowledge of himself as their cause.

For Averroes God is the extrinsic final and extrinsic formal cause of the universe, with his role as formal cause arising through his extrinsic final causality as the ultimate perfection of actuality toward which all reality aspires. In his philosophical account, it is through this final causality that Averroes considers that God can be called Creator in traditional religious language since creation is but

> bringing what is in potentiality into actuality. What becomes actual is destroyed in potentiality and all potentiality becomes actuality when that which is in actuality brings it out. If potentiality did not exist, there would be no agent at all. Therefore it is said that all proportions and forms exist in prime matter. (1967b, p. 1505; 1984, p. 112)

As indicated earlier, creation *ex nihilo* is regarded by Averroes as an insufficiently founded allegorical interpretation of the literal statements of the Koran, so it is not surprising that he takes refuge in this Aristotelian account of divine final causality and the drawing out of what is potential into actuality as the proper understanding of creation. This very activity of final causality, which is identical with God's perfect self-knowing in actuality, provides for the perfection in the universe and so could also be called providential, although this notion of providence is one free of intention in relation to the world. The providence benefiting the sublunar world is that of the celestial bodies which function as guides and caretakers (1967b, p. 1714; 1984, p. 200). In spite of the religious language, Averroes regards his account of providence as essentially that of Aristotle.

> It must be known to you that this is Aristotle's view concerning providence, and that the problems arising about providence are solved by (his view); for there are people who say that there is nothing for which God does not care, because they claim that the Sage must not leave anything without providence and must not do evil, and that all his actions are just. Other people refuted this theory through the fact that many things happen that are evil, and the Sage should not produce them; so these people went to the opposite extreme and said that therefore there is no providence at all. The truth in this is that providence exists, and that what happens contrary to providence is due to the necessity of matter, not to the shortcomings of the Creator. (1967b, p. 1715; 1984, pp. 200–1)

It is evident from all this that Averroes systematically revises the meaning of traditional theological language in accord with his philosophical approach and conclusions. 'Providence', 'creation', 'knowledge', 'miracle', 'immortality', and other terms familiar in the Islamic religious tradition continue to be employed by Averroes; but their conceptual content is understandable fully and properly perhaps only to philosophers, the members of the demonstrative class, because for them the meanings are not the same as those conceived by the rhetorical or dialectical classes.

189

Averroes regards his metaphysical account of God and the other separate intellectual substances in the *Long Commentary on the "Metaphysics"* to be dependent on principles discovered in the science of the soul or psychology (Taylor 1998). He explains how this is the case in the *Long Commentary on the "De anima,"* when he writes,

> as sensible being is divided into form and matter, intelligible being must be divided into things similar to these two, namely into something similar to form and into something similar to matter. This is [something] necessarily present in every separate intelligence which thinks something else. And if not, then there would be no multiplicity in separate forms. And it was already explained in First Philosophy that there is no form absolutely free of potency except the First Form which understands nothing outside Itself. Its essence is Its quiddity (*essentia eius est quiditas eius*). Other forms, however, are in some way different in quiddity and essence. If it were not for this genus of beings which we have come to know in the science of the soul, we could not understand multiplicity in separate things, to the extent that, unless we know here the nature of the intellect, we cannot know that the separate moving powers ought to be intellects. (1953, pp. 409–10)

In his metaphysical explanations Averroes required support on several principles from psychology: (1) proof is required that the immaterial separate forms asserted as immaterial movers by physics are, in fact, intellects; (2) grounds are required for the assertion of some similarity at least of an analogical kind between the human activity of knowing and the activity of separate substances (including God) which is denominated knowing; and (3) proof is required that a potency as the basis for a hierarchy could exist somehow in these separate substances. The establishment in the *Long Commentary on the "De anima"* of his controversial and complex teaching on the separate Material Intellect which is one for all humankind solved these and other epistemological problems with which Averroes had struggled for decades. In his *Short Commentary on the "De anima"* Averroes closely followed Alexander of Aphrodisias and particularly Avempace, holding that the material intellect is a function of the imagination and so perishable with the perishing of the subject in which imagination resides, namely the corporeal human individual. This position, which he labeled true and demonstrative at that time, was rejected in a second, very late, revised version of the *Short Commentary*. In his *Middle Commentary on the "De anima"*, perhaps written in 1174, Averroes seems to move beyond the position of the *Short Commentary* to assert that the material intellect is a power in each individual as a result of its relationship with the separate Agent Intellect (Davidson 1992, pp. 276–82). But these two commentaries do not provide accounts sufficient to yield the needed principles for metaphysics. Only in the *Long Commentary* does Averroes finally set forth the doctrine of the separate, unique yet shared Material Intellect with which he claimed to solve many of the difficulties thought insurmountable until then.

Unlike Avicenna, for whom the separate Agent Intellect was a "Giver of Forms," *wāhib al-ṣuwar, dator formarum*, Averroes – like Aristotle – grounded his philosophical psychology in the objects of perception, the things of the physical world, and their causal action on the senses. Those sensible objects of the world affect the senses predisposed for the reception of sensible forms or intentions (*ma'ānin, intentiones*), with the subjects receiving the sensible intentions from the things in the world, which are the grounds of truth and actuality. The internal senses then process these intentions in preparation for the acquisition of knowledge. The common sense, together with the power of imagination, forms this sensation into an image of the external sensible object and an individual intention is made available to the cogitative power. This cogitative power according to Aristotle is an individual-distinguishing power because it discerns things only in an individual way, not in a universal way. For it was explained [in Aristotle's *Sense and Sensibilia*] that the cogitative power is only a power which distinguishes the intention of a sensible thing from its imagined image. That power is one which is such that its relation to those two intentions, to the image of the thing and to the intention of its image, is just as the relation of the common sense to the intentions of the five senses. The cogitative power, therefore, is of the genus of the powers existing in bodies. Aristotle explicitly said this in that book, when he placed the individual distinguishing powers in four orders. In the first he placed the common sense, next the imaginative power, next the cogitative power, and afterwards the power of memory. He made the power of memory the more spiritual, then the cogitative, then the imaginative, and last the sensible. (1953, pp. 415–16)

Knowledge that is universal is not grasped at the level of the cogitative power since this power still concerns individuals. However, the cogitative power, unique to humans as rational animals and empowered by Intellect, works with the results of the common sense and imagination to discern the individual intention in itself to the extent possible, and then turns over the results to memory for its active processing (1953, pp. 225–6). At this stage the intention is still individuated as a "this" or intention of an individual and as such remains an intelligible in potency, not an intelligible in act. Following Aristotle's suggestions in *De anima* 3.5 and the explicit accounts of the Greek commentators Alexander and Themistius, and also Avicenna, Alfarabi, and others of the Arabic tradition, Averroes asserts that a separate and transcendent Agent Intellect is needed to bring about the actuality of knowledge experienced by human beings. The "light" of this Agent Intellect fully distills the form from the purified yet still individual intention and actualizes the form as an actual intelligible in the separate Material Intellect. In this process, *taṣawwūr bi-l-ʾaql*, *formatio* or *imaginatio per intellectum*, individual human beings provide intentions which the separate Material and Agent Intellects process into intelligibles in act. This is a conjunction or conjoining (*ittiṣāl*, *continuatio*) which brings about the acquired intellect, *al-ʾaql al-mustafād*, *intellectus adeptus*, in the individual human being. As a result of this, the individual attains the intellect in a positive disposition of knowledge, *al-ʾaql bi-l-malakah*, *intellectus in habitu*, which connects the individual human being in an abiding way with the Material Intellect where the intelligibles in act exist. This is Averroes' famous doctrine of the two subjects for the intelligibles. On the model of sensation in which sensation takes place in the power of sense residing in the sense organ with the sensible object in the world as the cause of the activity of the sensation, Averroes asserts that the intelligibles in act exist in the separate Material Intellect as in a subject. Thus they exist as eternal actualities in accord with the eternal nature of the Material Intellect itself and they also exist in human imagination as in a subject which in this case is the cause of their truth (1953, pp. 411–12). Individual human beings thus serve the Material Intellect, which is eternally being actualized by intelligibles in act thanks to the "light" of the Agent Intellect and the provision of intentions by individual human beings via sensation.

As a consequence of this, Averroes can assert that the human species, like the Material Intellect, must be eternal since humans must always exist to provide the imagined intentions, which the eternally actualizing Material Intellect along with the Agent Intellect transforms into intelligibles in act. Furthermore, it is only thanks to this unity of all humanly acquired intelligibles in the unique Material Intellect that intersubjective discourse and science are possible, since the intelligibles to which human beings refer are in this way the same for all. This is required because these intelligibles cannot exist in individuals without being individuated and particularized by the individual human in which they exist. In the

Material Intellect the intelligibles are no longer particular, but rather form one shared the-saurus in a knowledge which is unique to the Material Intellect; this itself is shared by all knowing human beings via their individual passive intellects, that is, their individual cogitative powers.

This activity of conjoining, whereby individual human beings are able conjure up knowl-edge already grasped, is something that is in the will of individuals to carry out by way of the cogitative powers of their souls. But in contrast to Avicenna, who held the rational soul to be per se intellectual and immortal and brought to perfection by a conjoining with the Agent Intellect, and in contrast to Alfarabi, who taught at one point that the human soul could be transformed from mortal to immortal by a conjoining with separate Intellect, Averroes regards conjoining as primarily an epistemological issue which does not involve mystical elements or the transformation of mortal human beings into immortal entities. Rather, for Averroes the individual human being is identified ontologically with the cogitative power that controls will, actions, and endeavors of individuals. The eternal Material and Agent Intellects in their activities are not other than human beings but they also do not transform the perishable natures of human beings by the conjoining that makes the world intelligible (Black 1999). Thus they should perhaps be said to be operationally present in individuals (Hyman 1981) even though there are metaphysical implications entailed.

A consequence is that there is no room made for the immortality of individual human beings in the mature philosophical psychology and metaphysics of Averroes. But with this new understanding Averroes does find in psychology the metaphysical principles needed for his account of a separate intellect. Insofar as human beings in fact do have knowledge of universals, Averroes accounts for this by way of his doctrine of the Material Intellect in three ways: (1) he provides an instance of a separate immaterial entity which is intellectual in nature, apparently satisfying the need for proof that the immaterial movers proved by physics are intellects; (2) he shows a relationship of identity between the activity of knowing which human beings experience and the activity taking place in the separate Material Intel-lect; and (3) he shows how the potency in the Material Intellect for receiving the intelligi-ble forms made by the "light" of the Agent Intellect acting upon the spiritualized and denuded individual intentions demonstrates that there can exist in separate immaterial intel-lects some form of potency. While his doctrine of the Material Intellect does generate new difficulties and questions, for the mature Averroes this final position solved many of the psychological and metaphysical problems that had eluded a coherent solution over his many years of study and reflection.

Religion and political philosophy

Averroes attacked *kalām* or dialectical theology in various forms as poor or unsound rea-soning, but he did not attack religion (Benmakhlouf 2000, p. 53), which he believed to be essential to the moral formation of human beings and to the enabling of human beings to attain their highest possible kind of happiness and fulfillment.

> [T]he religions are, according to the philosophers, obligatory, since they lead toward wisdom in a way universal to all human beings, for philosophy only leads a certain number of intelli-gent people to the knowledge of happiness, and they therefore have to learn wisdom, whereas religions seek the instruction of the masses generally. (1930, p. 582; 1969, p. 360)

[A]ll the learned hold about religions the opinion that the principles of the actions and regulations prescribed in every religion are received from the prophets and lawgivers, who regard those necessary principles as praiseworthy which most incite the masses to the performance of virtuous acts. (1930, p. 584; 1969, p. 361).

Like Aristotle, Averroes holds that the fullness of human excellence, both moral and intellectual, requires the involvement of parents, community, and habituation, and that moral excellence is the foundation for intellectual excellence and achievement. As he puts it in his 1194 *Middle Commentary on the "Republic" of Plato*,

[B]ut this kind of perfection – i.e. the moral, is laid down [in relation to] theoretical perfection as a preparatory rank, without which the attainment of the end is impossible. Hence, this perfection is thought to be the ultimate end because of its proximity to the ultimate end. It appears from this, then, that the human perfections are . . . all for the sake of theoretical perfection. (1974, p. 92 [72.29–34])

The role of the politician or lawgiver is to guide all society toward excellence to the extent that this is possible for individuals of varying abilities. For some that guidance will be by swaying them toward what is right and best by rhetorical presentations, while for others it may take the form of dialectical argumentation on the basis of commonly held and assumed first principles. In each case what is true and right will be what is practically valuable in realizing moral virtue in society. People of the demonstrative class require proper moral upbringing and habituation but by their methods of demonstration they may well reach philosophical conclusions that require allegorical interpretation of scriptural statements, conclusions unfit for sharing with those of the other classes lest they undermine the latter's pious and beneficial beliefs.

For it belongs to the necessary excellence of a man of learning that he should not despise the doctrines in which he has been brought up, and that he should explain them in the fairest way, and that he should understand that the aim of these doctrines lies in their universal character, not in their particularity, and that, if he expresses a doubt concerning the religious principles in which he has been brought up, or explains them in a way contradictory to the prophets and turns away from their path, he merits more than anyone else that the term unbeliever should be applied to him, and he is liable to the penalty for unbelief in the religion in which he has been brought up. (1930, p. 583; 1969, p. 360.)

Such a thing would undermine the political end of religion, which is the attainment of happiness for all members of society insofar as this is possible. To this extent, philosophers should keep to themselves demonstrative arguments that might undermine religion and its end of universal human fulfillment in accord with the abilities of each human being.

Averrroes' deep admiration for the philosophical works of Aristotle caused him to work hard to explain and solve philosophical problems from Greek thought that were still vital and current in his medieval Islamic philosophical context. Issues in Aristotelian epistemology and metaphysics continue to attract the interest of philosophers and historians of philosophy today; in light of that modern scholars would be well served to make the most of the insights of Averroes in his commentaries and other philosophical works. But it is in the area of modern philosophy of religion that the thought of Averroes can be seen to have valuable insights to offer today, both to his co-religionists and to other philosophers and theologians. Averroes argued forcefully about the nature and interpretation of texts, in particular against naive scriptural literalism as well as against insufficiently founded religious presumptions. He strived to show that the principle "Truth does not contradict truth but rather is consistent with it and bears witness to it" entails that reason and religion must ultimately be one and without contradiction, and that philosophy has a fundamentally important role to play in religion.

Bibliography

Primary sources

(1574), *In Aristotelis opera cum Averrois Commentariis*, Venice: Iunctas; repr. 1962, Frankfurt-on-Main: Minerva.

(1930), *Incoherence*, in Maurice S. J. Bouyges, ed., *Tahafot al-tahafot*, Beirut: Imprimerie Catholique.

(1953), *Commentarium magnum in Aristotelis De anima libros*, ed. F. Stuart Crawford, Cambridge, MA: Medieval Academy of America.

(1959), *Decisive Treatise, Kitāb Faṣl al-maqāl with its Appendix (Damīma) and an Extract from Kitāb al-kashf fī al-manāhij al-adilla*, ed. George F. Hourani, Leiden: Brill.

(1967a), *Decisive Treatise, On the Harmony of Religion and Philosophy: A Translation, with Introduction and Notes, of Kitāb Faṣl al-Maqāl with its Appendix (Damīma) and an Extract from Kitāb al-kashf fī al-manāhij al-adilla*, trans. George F. Hourani, London: Luzac.

(1967b), *Tafsīr mā baʾd al-ṭabīʾah*, 3 vols. in 4 parts, 2nd edn., ed. Maurice S. J. Bouyges, Beirut: Dar al-Machreq Editeurs, Imprimerie Catholique.

(1969), *Incoherence, Tahafut al-Tahafut (The Incoherence of the Incoherence)*, trans. Simon Van Den Bergh, London: Luzac.

(1974), "Middle Commentary on the *Republic*," in *Averroes on Plato's "Republic,"* trans. Ralph Lerner, Ithaca and London: Cornell University Press.

(1984), *Metaphysics: A Translation with Introduction of Ibn Rushd's Commentary on Aristotle's Metaphysics, Book Lam*, trans. Charles Genequand, Leiden: Brill.

(1986), *De substantia orbis: Critical Edition of the Hebrew Text with English Translation and Commentary*, trans. Arthur Hyman, Cambridge, MA and Jerusalem: Medieval Academy of America and the Israeli Academy of Sciences and Humanities.

(1998a), *L'Intelligence et la pensée: Grand Commentaire du De anima Livre III (429a10–435b25)*, trans. Alain de Libera, Paris: GF Flammarion.

(1998b), *Explanation, al-Kashf ʾan al-manāhij al-adillah fī ʾaqāʾid al-millah (Explanation of the Sorts of Proofs in the Doctrines of Religion)*, Beirut: Markaz Dirāsāt al-Wahdah al-ʾArabīyah. A complete translation of this is found in Alonso (1947). Now there is an English translation by Ibrahim Y. Najjar (2001): *Faith and Reason in Islam: Averroes' Exposition of Religious Arguments*, Oxford: Oneworld.

Secondary sources

al-ʾAlawi, Jamal al-Din (1986), *al-Matn al-Rushdī*, Casablanca: Dar Touqbal li-n-nashr.

Alonso, Manuel, S. I. (1947), *Teología de Averroes*, Madrid and Granada: Imprenta y Editorial Maestre.

Anawati, G. C. (1978), *Bibliographie d'Averroes (Ibn Rushd)*, Alger: Organisation Arabe pour l'Education, la Culture et les Sciences.

Arnaldez, Roger (2000), *Averroes: A Rationalist in Islam*, Notre Dame, IN: Notre Dame University Press.

Badawi, Abdurrahman (1972), *La Philosophie en Islam*, vol. 2, Paris: J. Vrin.

Benmakhlouf, Ali (2000), *Averroès*, Paris: Les Belles Letters.

Black, Deborah L. (1999), "Conjunction and the identity of knower and known in Averroes," *American Catholic Philosophical Quarterly* 73, pp. 159–84.

Burnett, Charles (1999), "The 'Sons of Averroes with the Emperor Frederick' and the transmission of the philosophical works by Ibn Rushd," in Jan A. Aertsen and Gerhard Endress, eds., *Averroes and the Aristotelian Tradition: Sources, Constitution and Reception of the Philosophy of Ibn Rushd (1126–1198)* (pp. 259–99), Leiden: Brill.

Burnett, Charles and Zonta, Mauro (2000), "Abū Muhammad 'Abdallāh Ibn Rushd (Averroes junior), *On Whether the Active Intellect Unites with the Material Intellect whilst it is Clothed with the Body*: A critical edition of the three extant medieval versions, together with an English translation," *Archives d'Histoire Doctrinale et Littéraire du Moyen Âge* 67, pp. 295–335.

Butterworth, Charles E. (1996), "Averroës, precursor of the Enlightenment?," *Alif* 16, pp. 6–18.

Cranz, F. Edward (1976), "Editions of the Latin Aristotle accompanied by the Commentaries of Averroes," in Edward P. Mahoney, ed., *Philosophy and Humanism: Renaissance Essays in Honor of Paul Oskar Kristeller* (pp. 116–28), New York: Columbia University Press.

Cruz Hernández, Miguel (1997), *Abu-l-Walid Muhammad Ibn Rushd (Averroes). Vida, obra, pensamiento, influencia*, Cordoba: Publicaciones de la Obra Social y Cultural Cajasur.

Davidson, Herbert A. (1992), *Alfarabi, Avicenna, and Averroes on Intellect*, Oxford: Oxford University Press.

Endress, Gerhard (1999), "Averrois Opera: a bibliography of editions and contributions to the text," in Jan A. Aertsen and Gerhard Endress, eds., *Averroes and the Aristotelian Tradition: Sources, Constitution and Reception of the Philosophy of Ibn Rushd (1126–1198)* (pp. 339–81), Leiden: Brill.

Geoffrey, Marc (1999), "L'Almohadisme théologique d'Averroès (Ibn Rushd)," *Archives d'Histoire Doctrinale et Littéraire du Moyen Âge* 66, pp. 9–47.

Harvey, Steven (2000), "On the nature and extent of Jewish Averroism: Renan's *Averroès et l'averroïsme* revisited," *Jewish Studies Quarterly* 7, pp. 100–19.

Hyman, Arthur (1981), "Averroes' theory of the intellect and the ancient commentators," in Dominic J. O'Meara, ed., *Studies in Aristotle* (pp. 161–91), Washington, DC: The Catholic University of America Press.

Kogan, Barry (1981), "The philosophers al-Ghazali and Averroes on necessary connection and the problem of the miraculous," in Parviz Morewedge, ed., *Islamic Philosophy and Mysticism* (pp. 113–32), Delmar, NY: Caravan Books.

——(1985), *Averroes and the Metaphysics of Causation*, Albany: State University of New York Press.

Leaman, Oliver (1996), "Jewish Averoism," in Seyyed Hossein Nasr and Oliver Leaman, eds., *History of Islamic Philosophy* (pp. 769–80), London and New York: Routledge.

——(1998), *Averroes and his Philosophy*, 2nd revd. edn., Richmond, Surrey: Curzon.

Renan, Ernest (1852) *Averroès et l'averroïsme*, in Henriette Psichari, ed., *Oeuvres complètes de Ernest Renan*, vol. 3, Paris: Calmann-Lévy, Éditeurs.

Taylor, Richard C. (1998), "Averroes on psychology and the principles of metaphysics," *Journal of the History of Philosophy* 36, pp. 507–23.

——(2000), "*Cogitatio, cogitativus* and *cogitare*: remarks on the cogitative power in Averroes," in Jacqueline Hamesse and Carlos Steel, eds., *L'Élaboration du vocabulaire philosophique au Moyen Âge* (pp. 111–46), Leuven: Peeters.

von Küglegen, Anke (1994), *Averroes und die arabische Moderne. Ansätze zu einer Neubegründung des Rationalismus im Islam*, Leiden: Brill.

Urvoy, Dominique (1998), *Averroès. Les Ambitions d'un intellectuel musulman*, Paris: Flammarion.

Walzer, Richard, trans. (1985), *Al-Fārābī on the Perfect State*, Oxford: Clarendon Press.

19

Avicenna

DAVID B. BURRELL

There are many Avicennas, as Abu 'Ali al-Husayn Ibn Sīnā (b. 980; d. 1037) was known in the West: the prolific adapter of Aristotle, accomplished in logic, who fairly defined Islamic *falāsifa* (an Arabic transliteration of 'philosophy') and was accordingly awarded the dubious distinction of *kafir* (unbeliever) by ALGAZALI (b. 1058; d. 1111), as well as the composer of allegories intended to lead the inquiring intellect to the very source of wisdom in the uncreated One. We shall see that Algazali gained even more from his predecessor's philosophy than he renounced, however, and will also come to see that the duality which we draw between "logician" and "mystic" is rather more an imposition of our settled understandings of "philosophy," whereas Avicenna's conception of his vocation will correspond more authentically to the original Socratic coinage: lover and seeker of wisdom. We shall also pursue the diverse ways in which this thinker has been received, with a view to recognizing the traces of his inquiring mind in our western traditions of philosophical inquiry, since figures like Avicenna loom larger than their life, and must be so regarded if we are to relate to them as fellow inquirers, rather than relegate them to "the past."

Avicenna was born into the domain of a Persian dynasty, the Samanids, near the city of Bukhara, located in a large oasis in what is today Uzbekistan. Although Persian, the Samanids were Sunni Muslims, so more in sympathy with the caliphate in Baghdad than with the predominantly Shi'ite ethos of Persia. In 892, they established their capital in Bukhara, and by the time of Avicenna controlled the surrounding territory of Khurasan (known as Transoxania, or what-lies-beyond-the river Oxus, to its Muslim conquerors in the early eighth century). His father served Nuh ibn Mansur, one of the last Samanid rulers, which would give the young Avicenna access to the library which nourished his voracious reading habits. In the autobiography which he dictated to his disciple al-Jurjani, Avicenna recounted his intellectual development to the time of their meeting. He had been instructed in the Koran and Arabic literature (*'adab*) as a young boy, memorizing the Koran by the age of 10, after which he was entrusted to a greengrocer to learn the arithmetic that we call Arabic, but which had originated in India. He was also introduced at this time to the study of Islamic law (*fiqh*) by a Hanafi jurist, Ismail al-Zahid (the Ascetic), so acquiring a talent for disputation that would serve him admirably in assimilating philosophical arguments. This began in an introductory way under the supervision of al-Natili, who (in Avicenna's words) "claimed to be a philosopher," yet whose tutorial ways cramped the young man's style:

> Whatever questions he posed, I would conceive it better than he did, and he warned my father against me taking up anything other than learning. I went till I had finished with him a super-

ficial reading of the logic [of Porphyry's *Isagoge*]; but he had no notion of the subtle points of the subject. (Gohlman 1974, p. 22)

In fact, he went on to study the commentaries on the remainder of Aristotle's logical works, and he outpaced his tutor, as he notes: "I read the first five or six figures with him, then took over solving the rest of the book by myself" (*Life* 22); and then went on to master Ptolemy's *Almagest*, the medieval source of cosmology and astronomy. After al-Natili left Bukhara, doubtless with some relief, Avicenna proceeded on his own to study Aristotle's *Physics* and *Metaphysics*. Momentarily stumped, especially by the latter work, he took the time to master the art and science of medicine, as set down by Galen, the Greek physician of Marcus Aurelius, whose 129 works had been translated in the previous century by a group of Nestorian Christians directed by Huynayn ibn Ishaq. It was this acquired medical skill that would grant him access to Nuh ibn Mansur's extensive library, after which he was successful in treating an undiagnosed illness of the prince a few years later.

Now in his eighteenth year, Avicenna began to take stock of what he had learned philosophically, proceeding to organize the knowledge attained syllogistically. For a year and a half, seldom sleeping through the night, he came to realize that he had in fact mastered all of philosophy as it had been presented to him, yet metaphysics seemed beyond his grasp. He had read Aristotle's work of that name forty times, he tells us, yet its import eluded his grasp. A chance encounter with a bookseller brought the slim treatise of ALFARABI (b. ca. 870; d. ca. 950) *On the Aims of Metaphysics* into his hands; this allowed him to penetrate Aristotle's puzzling work by clarifying its goal: a universal mode of knowing which seeks to identify what belongs to anything at all by virtue of its existing as a *something*. It was soon after this discovery that he gained access to the prince's library, so was able to complete his education, in gratitude for which he dedicated his first work to the prince: *Compendium on the Soul*. At this time, he tells us: "I had completed all the sciences. At that stage I could remember things better, but today the knowledge is more mature – [yet] the knowledge is the same, not reconstructed or reborn [*yatajaddidu*] in the least" (Gohlman 1974, pp. 36–8). Lenn Goodman glosses this astounding statement: "What he meant was that the framework of his understanding was firm and his central beliefs would not alter radically as he matured. There is no dialectic of conflict and contradiction for a Hegelian intellectual biographer here, but the gradual unfolding of a set of central themes which deepen as Avicenna's knowledge extends into new areas, but which did not change its course" (1992, p. 17). He was soon commissioned to compose a book bringing together all of knowledge, named *Philosophy for 'Arudi*, after the one who supported its composition. For a scholar of Islamic law and the Koran, named Abu Bakr al-Baruqi, he undertook to summarize philosophical ways of knowing in twenty volumes, as well as a compendium of ethics. Neither of these have come down to us, but the first clearly formed the basis for his later *al-Shifa* (*The Healing*).

Political unrest required Avicenna to move in search of patrons, and after some years (at 32) he found a haven in Jurjan with Abu Muhammad al-Shirazi, where he also met his companion and disciple, al-Jurjani, who coined the verse (after hearing the account of his life to that point):

> I grew great, and no city could contain me;
> When my price went up, there was no one left to buy me.

Working with al-Jurjani, however, he was able to produce a text that became a medieval classic in the West as well: the *Canon on Medicine*. His medical skills also made him attrac-

197

tive to rulers who suffered from illness; as political unrest moved him deep into Persian territory, he stayed in Rayy (near Isfahan) to treat the Buyid ruler, Majd al-Dawla, for depression, and also to compose his *Situation of the Human Soul*, his mature philosophical anthropology. This treatise argued for the immortality of the rational soul through the access which it offers to timeless reality. A few years later, he migrated to Hamadhan to serve Majd's brother, Shams al-Dawla, and to settle down to write his extensive philosophical treatise (*al-Shifa*) during the years 1015–23. After Shams's death, Avicenna sought a new patron in 'Ala al-Dawla of Isfahan; this led to accusations of treason against the successor regime in Hamadhan, from which his friends hid him, allowing him to complete the *al-Shifa*; and four months later, while in prison, he composed the allegory of the human intellect, *Hayy ibn Yaqzan*. Rescued by the forces of 'Ala al-Dawla, he remained in Isfahan from 1024 until his death in 1037, composing a paraphrase of his philosophy in Persian, the *Danesh Nameh*, known in the West through its Arabic paraphrase by Algazali as the *Intentions of the Philosophers*. He devoted some time as well to his monumental *Kitab al-Insaf* (*Impartial Judgment*), which addressed some 28,000 questions associated with philosophical thinkers from Khorasan to Baghdad, and purported to distinguish these schools. At the same time he wrote a work expressly entitled *Eastern Philosophy*, which we no longer possess, but whose title has generated a controversy which we shall address. When the text of the *Kitab al-Insaf* was seized in a pillage of Isfahan, Avicenna declined to recreate that text, but rather composed the *Book of Hints and Pointers* (*Al-Isharat wa'l-Tanbihat*), which epitomized his views on writing of philosophy, and directing his disciples to a method of appropriation of the discipline rather than imitation of others. Civil unrest was to take his life, however, as he fell ill of a colic while retreating with his patron, 'Ala al-Dawla, before the troops of Mas'ud while the treasures of Isfahan were once again looted. When his physician proved overzealous in applying Avicenna's own cure, it became clear to him that "the governor that used to rule my body is too weak to rule any longer," so his full and energetic life was complete at 56 years of age.

Avicenna's philosophical achievements: Aristotle and beyond

There can be little doubt that Avicenna wanted Hellenic philosophy to assist in the articulation of his Muslim faith. Yet he was unwilling to do what theologians are generally content to do: simply select features of that philosophy which could bolster the deliverances of the Koran. That had been the strategy employed by the Kalam thinkers, who had already put obstacles in the way of his grasp of Aristotle's intent in the *Metaphysics* by attempting to tailor that book to a treatment of God, the intellect, and the soul. In fact, however, these subjects constitute but a fraction of the work, concentrated in Book *lambda*, which is why Alfarabi's correction of that apprehension was so liberating to Avicenna: "metaphysics is that universal way of knowing which investigates what is common to all existents" (Druart 1982, p. 40). And the mode of investigation will be logical, since our exploring what is common to all existents clearly transcends the apprehension of the senses. Since the knowledge we are after is one that seeks to know what belongs to an object in virtue of the kind of thing that it is, essences will be at issue, which we apprehend by way of definition. These are the indispensable tools of inquirers in such a domain. So Avicenna would display his mastery of these tools in expounding his own "metaphysics" in his *al-Shifa: Illahiyyat*. The voice of the Koran will appear, however, in what distinguishes him from Aristotle, whose study culminates in the proof of an unmoved mover as the abiding *good* bringing about all motion in the universe precisely by being that One that all things desire, as Plato had intimated. Yet for a Koran-believer, even that will not be enough, since that One must be the source of the very being of all that is, and not simply the motion of a pre-existing universe. At the same time, however, this move can be regarded as directly in line with Aristotle's own metaphysical orientation, since the One can be articulated as the *principle* of being itself, where "principle" is exactly what metaphysics must concentrate on, with the principles of matter/form and of potency/act elucidating Aristotle's initial four causes as explanatory principles of anything which exists.

The turning point in Avicenna's analysis will be essence: that which can be articulated in a definition, and so display what links discourse to the reality of things. So a thing's reality will be known in its essence, and what distinguishes Avicenna's treatment of *essence* is the way he distinguishes three ways of taking it: as existing in individual things and so determining their kind, as understood to be shared by many such things, and as it is in itself (*Metaphysics* 1.5). This distinction exploits the ambiguity in Aristotle's own treatment of *substance*, where he constantly oscillates between the individual existing thing (Socrates or "primary substance") and its characterizing kind (human being or "secondary substance"). What distinguishes secondary substance from primary substance does not come from the essence itself, but from their differing modes of being: universality belongs to essence as it exists in the intellect, while individuality belongs to it as it exists in things. In itself, essence is simply essence: that which is predicated of an individual to locate it in the manifold realm of what exists. Moreover, if it were already universal or individual, it could not be predicated of individuals (*Metaphysics* 1.6–7), so Avicenna rightly discerns how the primitive relation of predication mirrors the structure of reality itself in Aristotle's exposition.

Where he differs so tellingly from Aristotle, however, is in addressing the very existence of anything that is, rather than simply presupposing it, as Aristotle had. Essence as such must be brought into existence, for while it remains the principle of being, in the sense that whatever is must be of a certain kind, essence itself cannot explain why things exist. What needs explaining is not the obvious fact that contingent things come into being, as a product of generation, and so can be traced to efficient causes, but the more startling assertion that the entire process exists which allows things to come to be in the way they do. So existence must come to things from another; essence can "explain" what something is by articulating its *whatness*, but not that it exists. This is either a "brute fact" or a startling assertion; Avicenna sees it as startling, while Aristotle seems to have been able to regard what makes a thing to be of lesser import than what makes it to be what it is. The price he paid, however, was simply to presume the universe itself – all-that-is – to be necessary. More coherently, Avicenna located this necessity in the one *necessary being*, itself the source of the being of everything else, which must then be *possible in itself*.

This is the celebrated distinction of *essence* from *existing*, which appears to be a genuine development from Aristotle, responding to the ambiguity noted between "first" and "second" substance. Yet it also reflects the perspective of the Koran, which seeks to elevate human consciousness to the one God by addressing the sheer contingency of all that is not God in the recurring phrase: "God said 'be' and it is." The emanation of all things from this One will itself be necessary for Avicenna, and so fail to reflect the freedom of the creator inherent to Muslim tradition; yet to have established the very need for origination proved a significant alteration of Aristotle's presumption of an everlasting (and hence "necessary") universe, and one in the direction of coherence with the Koran. He will show the cogency of distinguishing existing from essence with the odd example of a triangle: "know that you may understand the sense of 'triangle', yet doubt that it is described as actually existent; even after it is manifest to you that it is made of line and surface, yet it may not be clear to you that it exists" (1957, pp. 441–3). A triangle is an odd example precisely because one may succeed in doing geometry without ever reflecting on whether triangles exist, but his propensity for such examples reflects his abiding focus on essences, even while taking pains to call our attention to *existing* as something which must "come to" them from the One.

He will similarly try to deflect criticism from the logical consequence of his emanation scheme, which must deny God knowledge of particulars, by affording the example of an eclipse as the kind of singular that God can know (1978, bk 8, ch. 6). Yet since an eclipse is thoroughly predictable, it is hardly the kind of singular which critics would have in mind. But Avicenna's universe is presented as a necessary one, though derivatively so, since whatever emanates necessarily from the One will perforce exhibit that necessity in the connections among its parts. As we shall see, both necessities will rankle with Algazali, yet the elegance of a universe whose emanation is conceived on the model of logical deduction would never fail to attract philosophical minds, especially when the levels of distance from the One, as the intelligences come forth from it, could be identified cosmologically with the Ptolemaic system, while they could be identified psychologically with degrees of proximity to God for those "knowers" on their return journey to this One. Indeed, here we have the two dimensions of Avicenna's metaphysics, exhibited first in the cosmological outpouring from the One to originate a universe, and then in the "mystical" return of intentional beings to that One to fulfill the inbuilt powers of their intellectual natures.

There is considerable complexity to this emanation scheme, adapted from Alfarabi's *Perfect State*, yet we should offer enough of the scheme to identify its cosmological and psychological appeal:

> It is necessary that there be an intellectual substance from which proceeds an intellectual substance and a heavenly body. It is known that two only flow from one by means of two aspects. [The celebrated Neoplatonic principle that "from one only one comes."] Multiplicity of considerations and modes are impossible in the first principle, because it is one in every respect, and transcends comprising various aspects and multiple respects. But this is not impossible relative to its effects. So it is not possible that more than one proceeds from it, yet it is possible that a number of effects proceed from that. The only two different aspects here are whatever intellectual substance has: that it is, in itself, possibility of existence, and by the first, necessity of existence. It conceives itself, and it conceives the First. It is, of its state relative to the first, a principle of something; and it is, by virtue of what it has by virtue of its essence, a principle for something else. Because it is caused, there is nothing preventing it from being constituted by various parts. How could it be otherwise? It has a contingent quiddity, and an existence which is necessary by virtue of another. Moreover, it is necessary that the formal aspect of it be a principle for the formal being, and that the aspect most like matter be a principle for the being appropriate to matter. So insofar as it is conceiving the first who necessitated it, it is a principle for an intellectual substance: and by the other, a principle for corporeal substance. (*Isharat*, 645–57).

The steps are familiar from Plotinus: the One/First, in contemplating itself, produces an intelligence that contemplates both the One and itself. In that contemplation of the One, it produces a lower intelligence (or "soul") which becomes the principle for corporeal substance (or "body"). The final emanation in this series of intelligences is the "active intellect," which accounts for the forms in the world of nature, by which we come to know the natures of things, as well as the existence of the human soul. Moreover, this downward scheme will provide the steps by which that soul, exercising its intellectual part, will return to the One by dint of assimilation to the active intellect.

This symmetry between cosmology and psychology is enhanced by Avicenna's view that it is the rational soul which identifies each human being, and that it is the soul which (as a spiritual and so deathless entity) can receive influences from the intelligences that govern the motions of the universe. Although this unabashed dualism of soul and body might seem attractive to religious thinkers, this teaching is one of those for which he was excluded from the Muslim community by Algazali. For the teaching of the Koran focuses on the resurrection of the body rather than the immortality of the soul. Here is precisely where Avicenna's attempt to conciliate Neoplatonic reason with Koranic revelation failed, and dramatically so, for the disdain with which the legacy of Plotinus has viewed matter is notorious. Moreover, as we have seen, the entire cosmological scheme, itself so easily inverted to become a psychological trajectory, depends crucially on those purification methods which could align a spiritual substance – the human soul – with others on its journey home.

Doubtless what irritated Algazali was the impudence with which a philosopher could so blatantly transmute the countless references in the Koran itself to the "resurrection of the body," in his attempt to offer a reading of revelation palatable to philosophy as he had assimilated it. We shall also see how this attitude will influence and shape Avicenna's forays into a closer characterization of the "return" of the soul to its transcendent source in the One. Thus far, however, we have encountered a philosopher in the Neoplatonic tradition, skilled in logic and dialectic, and quite predictable in his philosophical anthropology. The signal contribution of his Muslim faith seems to have been the celebrated distinction of *essence* from *existing*, which attempts to factor the universe's origination in the One into the very structure of each created substance. That this origination is necessary rather than – as the Koran implies – free, need not impugn the *aseity* (or intrinsic dignity) of the One, which need gain nothing from the extensive emanations from it. What such necessity does impugn, however, as Algazali notes, is the possibility of revelation itself, for on this scheme, that would have to be an "intervention," which a necessitarian scheme must rule out in principle. It is in fact Algazali's Jewish counterpart, MOSES MAIMONIDES (b. 1138; d. 1204), who will make a special point of this implication of the necessary emanation view of origination from the One. Indeed, internal evidence would support the presumption that Maimonides was acquainted with Algazali's refutation of the "philosophers" on the vexing alternatives between the necessary and everlasting universe (which philosophy prefers), and one freely created such that there would be an initial moment of time (as the Koran implies). Avicenna opts clearly for the first.

Beyond philosophical articulation: glimpses of wisdom

So far the Avicenna we have expounded is virtually indistinguishable from Plotinus, except for the key distinction noted. Yet there seems to be another Avicenna, less content with articulation and more attuned to mystical flights of intuitive understanding, capable of assimilating knowers to the One in ways that transform the self by virtue of its proximity to the source of all being. This Avicenna was the inspiration of Suhrawardi (b. 1154; d. 1191), who is known as the father of "philosophy of illumination" from his major work, *Hikmat al-ishraqi*, which takes its name from the rising of the sun in the east. Although born more than a century after Avicenna's death, Suhrawardi's philosophical impulse can be seen as a development of later trends in Avicenna's own thinking, though hardly a simple extension of them. How can we identify these tendencies? They can be found in a work of Avicenna's of which most has been lost, entitled "The Easterners" (or "Eastern Philosophy"), and summarized in the fourth part of his *Isharat*. Here the focus is on the type of spiritual exercises needed to detach the spiritual soul from the multiple distractions of its earthly milieu (including the body), and set it on its way to conjunction with the active intellect. Knowledge of a conceptual sort (*ilm*) becomes knowing of a direct kind (*ma'arifa*), so that those who can thereby gain proximity to the One source of all are called "knowers" (*arifun*) (or "gnostics").

In this account the "knowers" are initiated into the secrets of the higher realms of intellect as they move up through the nine "stations" (a Sufi term for stages of proximity to God), which correspond to the cosmological emanations. This journey is completely other-directed, and has nothing to do with promised rewards: "the knower seeks the First Truth not for anything other than Itself and prefers nothing to the knowledge and worship of it alone" (*Isharat* 810; Inati 1996, p. 83). Moreover, once having attained to this Truth, the seekers find that "there are steps not fewer in number than those that have preceded. We have preferred brevity concerning them, for . . . discourse does not reveal anything about them. . . . He who desires to know these steps must move gradually until he becomes one of the people of witnessing and not of speaking, one of those who arrive at the Truth Itself and not those who hear the trace" (*Isharat* 841–2; Inati 1996, p. 89). The effects on their demeanor are palpable: "The knower is bright-faced, friendly, and smiling. . . . How could he not be bright-faced when he enjoys the Truth and everything other than the truth, for he sees the Truth even in everything other than the truth! Furthermore, how could he not treat all as equal when, to him, all are equal! They are objects of mercy, preoccupied with falsehood" (*Isharat* 843; Inati 1996, p. 89).

If one detects a note of *hauteur* in the final remark, it is there. The return that Avicenna envisages is reserved for those who have been able to liberate their intellect from earthly distractions, and follow its innate propensities to undertake a return journey conjoined with the active intellect – the final emanation from the One, which becomes the gate through which one returns to it. Others will remain mired in desire or honor, and unable to make this inner journey. Yet Avicenna does not hesitate to use allegory to describe this return, notably in his later writings; so he does avoid the usual propensity of Islamic "philosophers" sharply to divide proper demonstrative procedures in coming to know from the recourse to metaphor so characteristic of the Koran. The four "recitals," as Henry Corbin dubs them, all concern themselves with the *ascent* or *return* of the rational soul to its proper place, variously identified as the One, the True, or reminiscently of Plato, the Good. They are *Hayy ibn Yaqzan*, the *Book of Ascent* (*Mi'raj Nama*), *The Birds*, and *Salaman and Absal* (Corbin 1960).

The *Ascent*, designed to give a rational account of Muhammad's *mi'raj* or ascent into the highest heavens, ostensibly from the Haram ash-Sharif in Jerusalem, has not been unequivocally attributed to Avicenna, but Peter Heath argues for its authenticity. The stories are agonistic, in that the protagonists meet with obstacles in responding to the guidance of higher figures with whom they are brought into contact. Yet the direction in every case is already inbuilt, as they find themselves oriented to a quest that consumes them, and whose attraction is confirmed as they proceed. In each case, these seem to be extant allegories that Avicenna can adapt to his purposes, and which later Islamic thinkers, notably Fakhr ad-Din ar-Razi, and al-Tusi, will elaborate upon. So they are not to be treated as aberrations from a properly philosophical mode, and hence considered esoteric treatises; they assume a central place in the Islamic tradition, even while not being readily identifiable with the Avicenna known to the West for his rigorous demonstrations. So something different is going on: first, a change in idiom, and then a clear reference to the "return" already noted in the fourth part of the *Isharat*, itself a later resumé of the philosophic path to knowing. That such a compendium should issue in *ma'arifa* rather than *ilm*, as we have seen, strongly suggests that Avicenna is asserting an impulse to the philosophical spirit beyond formulation and articulation – normally taken to be the hallmarks of philosophy, and in which Avicenna excelled.

Yet the evidence suggests that we are in the presence of an evolution rather than a revolution, and that the propensity to see two Avicennas reflects our conventions about philosophical discourse more than the actual élan of his inquiry. After all, the very term 'philosophy', simply transliterated in Islamic culture as *falsafa*, means "love of wisdom," so the original élan so effectively captured in the opening assertion of Aristotle's *Metaphysics* should perdure to the end: "all human beings desire to know." The Platonic lineaments are clearly etched: *knowing* is to be contrasted with *opining*, and the activity of inquiry that leads one through opinion to knowledge is fueled, as are all activities, by *desire*; yet this desire is focused upon knowing what is the case: the truth. If this statement – offered without proof yet effectively realized in those who persist in following Aristotle's sinuous pathways – is indeed true, then it should not seem strange that the philosophical arguments he offers will end up pointing beyond themselves to a truth that defies articulation precisely because it takes the form of an immediate grasp, as Plato's *Seventh Letter* intimates.

For a modern western reader, of course, this signals a shift from "philosophy" to "mysticism," marking a transition from expression to an intellectual encounter with that which the expression seeks to express. Yet we have seen how Avicenna's rational psychology, which accentuated intuition, could aspire to conjunction with the active intellect as a yet more effective mode of knowing. As Shams Inati expresses it (in commenting on her translation of the concluding portion of the *Isharat*):

> mysticism as understood by Avicenna seems to be an inevitable result of completing or perfecting the function of being a philosopher. In this sense, once one reaches the end of the path of philosophy, the truth will be uncovered to the theoretical intellect. Even though one may distinguish between philosophy as such and mysticism – the former being scientific or indirect knowledge, the latter illuminative or direct knowledge – once one perfects the former, one finds oneself in the latter. The latter is nothing other than the inevitable fruit of the former. That is why Avicenna's type of mysticism [has been] referred to . . . as "speculative, theoretical, or philosophical." (1996, p. 63)

Yet the need for a transition of sorts would be indicated by his own shift in idiom to allegory.

The speculative or theoretical character of this final journey has been a subject of much comment. It is especially in evidence in two works composed while he was in Jurjan and in Rayy (from 1009 to 1015): the *Book of the Beginning and the Return* (*Kitab al-Madba' wa l-Ma'ad*), and the *Letter Concerning the Return* (*al-Risalat al-Adhawiyya fi l-Ma'ad*), which

Jurjani calls *The Book of the Return* (*Kitab al-Ma'ad*), and Jean Michot takes to offer Avicenna's eschatological vision for human beings. The problematic of human finality turns on the stark difference between the intellectual ascent which we have seen depicted by way of summary description in the *Isharat* and allegorically in the four "recitals," and the luxurious descriptions of paradise in the Koran. The Sufi tradition had long accepted that the Koran was speaking metaphorically, and focused less on gratification of the senses than on the delights of proximity to the True and Real One (*al-Haqq*). Yet Avicenna veers towards a dual destiny: one for those who "know" (*arifun*), and another for those quite unconscious of these dimensions of human understanding, yet faithful to the *Shar'iah*. Again, the dualism is not clearly enunciated, yet the presumption is there, as with all philosophers, that there is but one way of "returning": to trace the path of emanation back to its source. And since the emanation scheme was modeled on logical deduction, the return path would have to be similarly theoretical in character.

We might expect Algazali to resist so stark an opposition between theoretical reason and the imaginal discourse of revelation; what is yet more fascinating is Michot's adaptation of Ibn al-Arabi's dismissal of "metaphysical idolatry," using Corbin's formulation. "While [Avicenna] criticizes religious people for allowing themselves to be stopped short in paradise rather than continue to seek God alone, he himself stops short by dint of his metaphysical inquiry." This happens because of "his penchant for identifying, in the end, the intelligible dimension of being which opens itself to a wise elite, with absolute reality, which in turn, as he elaborates his philosophy, he often seems to identify, quite unconsciously, with God" (Michot 1986, p. 210). As a result, Michot's final assessment mirrors that of Algazali and of Ibn al-Arabi, as well as an earlier commentary by Louis Gardet:

> Avicenna's vision of human destiny in general as well as his imaginal eschatology, despite the willing openness which they signal, are fundamentally characterized by intellectualism. They reflect the drama of a philosophy profoundly humanist yet too convinced of the truth of reason to let itself attend to the common lot of human being, and so be truly engaged with the witness their corporeality and their beliefs can bear touching on the mystery of existence and the return to the Most High. (Michot 1986, pp. 221–2)

Yet we should hardly be surprised at Avicenna's "intellectualism," for that was his penchant and his *métier*. What seems apropos, however, is to ask – as this critique implicitly does – how indebted is this "return" to the deliverances of revelation, and how reflective is it of a *telos* inherent to philosophy itself? Moreover, while Algazali had reason to contrast these two sources of illumination and of motivation, we may be more inclined to see them as complementary. Indeed, Algazali's work intended to deconstruct philosophy reveals that what most riled him were the pretensions of philosophers to have given a seamless account; his less polemical works will display modes of reasoning and conclusions far more congenial with those of Avicenna himself, as we shall see.

Imprints upon philosophical tradition

The prevailing narrative would make Algazali's intentional "deconstruction" of *philosophy* (*falsafa*) decisive for the Islamic world, and focus on Avicenna's considerable prestige among western medieval thinkers. Yet Louis Gardet has noted how Algazali's attack was carefully circumscribed by its focus on the four conclusions that he adjudged to be contrary to

Muslim teaching; and Richard Frank reminds us in telling detail just how indebted Algazali himself was to Avicenna in his own constructive works. Moreover, the use to which this same philosophy has been put by so central a religious thinker as Fakr ad-Din ar-Razi (b. 1149; d. 1209) utterly belies the standard story, without even registering the further transformations of Avicenna worked by Suhrawari and later by Mulla Sadra (Sadr ad-Din ash-Shirazi) into their distinctive *ishraqi* mode of philosophizing. So far from disappearing from the scene, Avicenna has enjoyed a redoubtable presence in subsequent philosophical developments within Islam, while as Avicenna, his presence in the West has been at once explicit (by citation) as well as implicit in its reach. Let us first consider his complex relation with Algazali, then follow chronologically his presence in Paris and Naples, and complete the circle with the return of philosophy to the East in Suhrawardi and Mulla Sadra (b. 1572; d. 1640).

It can be thoroughly misleading to identify Algazali with the *Tahafut al-Falasifa*, whose stated aim is one of "deconstruction":

> We did not plunge into this book in the manner of those who introduce [what is constructive], but in the manner of those who are destroyers and objectors. For this reason we have named the book *The Incoherence of the Philosophers*, not *The Introduction to Truth*. (Discussion 6, Marmura 107)

Moreover, he had already composed a summary of philosophical views, by translating into Arabic (with a few examples added) Avicenna's Persian compendium of philosophy, the *Danesh Nameh*. Presented in some manuscripts as an introduction to the *Tahafut*, Algazali introduces this work (without reference to Avicenna's authorship) to his community:

> You have desired from me a doubt-removing discourse, uncovering the incoherence [lit., falling to pieces] of the philosophers and the mutual contradictions in their views and how they hide their suppressions and their deceits. But to help you thus is not at all desirable except after first teaching you their position and making you know their dogmatic structure.

The fact that this work of Algazali's was the only one translated into Latin generated the irony that western medievals placed him on a footing with "the philosophers" of Islam, while those who came to know him through the *Tahafut* identified him as the most influential destructive force operating against philosophy in the Islamic tradition. Yet in his own constructive work, Algazali can hardly be said to be anti-philosophical, as Richard Frank's fruitful use of the *Treatise Explaining the Ninety-nine Beautiful Names of God (Maqsad al-asna)* shows so clearly. While this work plunges readers into the heart of Islamic theological inquiry, Frank delineates the way in which, "while rejecting significant elements of Avicenna's cosmology, Algazali adopted several basic principles and theses that set his theology in fundamental opposition to that of the classical Ash'arite tradition" (Frank 1992, p. 11). Through a close study of this and related texts, Frank concludes that Algazali intends to

> treat the traditional formulations concerning God's creative activity in the world and Avicenna's account of the determinate operation of the orders of secondary causes as they descend from the first cause as two alternative but fundamentally equivalent descriptions of the same phenomena. To accomplish this, however, he reinterprets the former in terms of the latter and so doing rejects one of the basic tenets of classical Ash'arism, e.g., the radical occasionalism according to which no created entity, whether an atom, a body, or an accident, has any causal effect

205

[*ta'athir*] on the being of any other. . . . [H]is aim is to adapt the traditional language and formulations to his own, quasi-Avicennian vision of creation. (1992, p. 37)

All this served Algazali's fundamental aim: "to work out and to present a global theological vision that in its higher metaphysics and ethics embraces all the sciences, disciplines, and practices proper to or recognized by Islam – all levels of Muslim experience, knowledge, belief, and activity – within an integrated whole." This would demand that he "bring his own metaphysics and his essentially Avicennian conception of the nature of the rational soul and its place within the cosmic system into some kind of positive relationship with the traditional teaching of the Ash'arite school" (Frank 1994, p. 88). The strategies that Algazali uses to harmonize these often contradictory accounts are fascinating, but beyond the scope of our inquiry, which traces how present Avicenna was to the constructive phase of the development of this thinker, also known as the "Seal of Islam," as he pursued his constructive exposition of Islamic thought. What Algazali did succeed in doing, notably in his emphasis on creation as free and intentional, was to relativize the logical (and hence deterministic) model for creation by replacing the seamless picture of causality which that model offers with the insistence that created causes be ever subservient to the creator of all. So the pervasive influence of the creator-God replaces logical necessity as the binding force of nature, thus establishing the abiding presence of the *shehada*: "There is no God but God," with its operative corollary: "there is no power but God's," which his harmonizing interpretation will render: whatever does act acts by the power of the One who acts in all. This will leave the status of "secondary causes" ambiguous enough to generate a great deal of subsequent discussion, but the intent is clear: to use philosophical strategies to introduce a free creator without thereby derogating from the status of creatures.

In the West, THOMAS AQUINAS (b. 1225; d. 1274) will also employ Avicenna to highlight the creator/creature distinction by underscoring the distinction between *essence* and *existing* that Avicenna introduced into Aristotelian Neoplatonic ontology. In his early short work, *On Being and Essence*, Aquinas will repeat the argument we have seen Avicenna use to manifest how we can consider a thing without attending to the fact that it exists. He then departs from Avicenna, however, in avoiding the misleading terminology of *existing* being an "accident" because it "comes to" (Arabic: *arada*; Latin: *accidit*) the *essence*, by explicitly identifying *essence* with Aristotle's *potency*, and *existing* with *act*. Any student of Aristotle, however, will see how radical a proposal this is, for the one whom medievals revered as "the Philosopher" regularly identified *essence* with *act*. Yet Aquinas's intent is clearly to make present in each thing the action of the creator, as the one who alone can bestow *existing* (*esse*), and indeed the One whose proper effect is each thing's *existing* precisely because that One's own *essence* is simply *to exist*. So the shift to *potency* and *act* also provides a positive way of characterizing "necessary existence" by transferring the focus from *necessity* itself to the ontological constitution of the One as "cause of being." That is, Aquinas's way of characterizing divine necessity is by identifying *essence* with *esse* in God, rather than relying on any specific notion of modality. This maneuver will also permit Aquinas to present creation as an intentional act, for the actions of the One whose essence is to exist must be intentional, since that formula is but another way of designating divinity as pure act. Aquinas begins his *On Being and Essence* by citing Avicenna: "the first conceptions of the intellect are 'a being' (*ens*) and 'an essence' [*essentia*]." Yet Aquinas's way of explicating the "first conception" will differ radically (according to Étienne Gilson) from Avicenna's illuminationist account. It is not that we are visited with a concept of *being*, as though one might parse the sentence "the rose is red" as bringing together three notions: *rose*, *is*, and *red*; but rather that the various modes of predication, of which the accidental predication of color is one, all display ways of being. This way of expounding Avicenna's contention that *being* is the first conception of the intellect reflects Aristotle's insistence that "being" is said in many ways. Yet Avicenna's illuminationist view of intellect veers closer to the tripartite analysis of the example, even though the example itself cannot serve in Arabic, for lack of a copula. When combined with AUGUSTINE's recourse to divine illumination as the cause of human understanding, however, Avicenna's predilection for intellectual intuition of essences has led, in Gilson's view, to a metaphysical posture that privileges essence over "the act of existing." The ensuing development tends to replace Aristotle's insistence that "being" is said in many ways, as well as bypass Aquinas's development of the inherently analogous character of this key term, to arrive at an understanding of *being* more cognate with the univocal notion introduced by JOHN DUNS SCOTUS. Gilson's laborious tracing of this trajectory (in his 1926 extended essay) deserves critical attention, though it is corroborated by Louis de Raeymaker, as well as by Georges Anawati, OP in the Introduction to his 1978 translation of the *Illahiyyat: La Métaphysique du Shifa*.

Concluding remarks

Avicenna's status in the Islamic philosophical tradition, particularly in its return to "the East" in Suhrawardi and Mulla Sadra, can hardly be gainsaid; and his impact on medieval reflection as Avicenna is well documented. Moreover, the contrast between his way of proceeding and that of Thomas Aquinas continues to be reflected in divergent ways of executing philosophical theology. A recent work by Harm Goris, intent on bringing these strategies into conversation, summarizes the difference this way:

> Aquinas' early writings suggest that he considered the essence of the creature in itself, i.e. apart from God's creative activity, as a possible. This indicates an influence of Avicenna's essentialism. In his later works, Aquinas expressly holds a stronger view: apart from divine agency, which gives being [*esse*], the essence of the creature is not something possible by itself, it is utterly nothing. This means that Aquinas does not think the distinction between Creator and creature along the lines of the opposition between necessary being and possible or contingent being, as in Avicenna's thought, but to the more radical opposition between being and nothing. For creation is out of nothing [*ex nihilo*]; no essence as a possible subject is presupposed to God's act of giving. . . . Aquinas does not distinguish Creator from creatures in terms of natural or logical necessity and contingency; he describes the distinction in terms of causality. The whole of creation is the freely willed effect of the First Cause. (1996, pp. 290–1)

If as we have suggested, the motivation of Avicenna's distinction between *essence (mahiyya)* and *existing (wujud)* is to introduce a creator into the inherited schemata of Hellenic philosophy, then these divergent ways of characterizing the distinction of the creator from everything else will certainly affect the subsequent development of philosophy within those traditions that aver such a creator. Likewise they will affect the ways in which intentional creatures' return to their source are articulated as well. Yet however differently this unitive way may be presented, no philosophical thinker within the Abrahamic traditions can be consistent with their faith-tradition in truncating the human desire for transformation in the One. So Avicenna offers an abiding challenge to a preconception of "philosophy" in the West that finds it easy to do just that.

Bibliography

Primary sources

(1957), *Al-Isharat wa-al-tanbihat*, Misr: Dar al-Ma'arif.

(1978), *La Métaphysique du Shifa*, trans. Georges Anawati, Paris: J. Vrin; repr. 1987.

Secondary sources

Aquinas, Thomas (1968), *On Being and Essence*, trans. Armand Maurer, Toronto: Pontifical Institute of Mediaeval Studies.

Burrell, David (1986), *Knowing the Unknowable God: Avicenna, Maimonides, Aquinas*, Notre Dame, IN: University of Notre Dame Press.

Corbin, Henry (1960), *Avicenna and the Visionary Recital*, New York: Pantheon-Bollingen.

Druart, Thérèse-Anne (1982), "Le Traité d'al-Farabi sur les buts de la *Métaphysique* d'Aristote," *Bulletin de Philosophie Médiévale* 24, pp. 38–43.

Frank, Richard (1992), *Creation and the Cosmic System: Al-Ghazali and Avicenna*, Heidelberg: Carl Winter.

——(1994), *Al-Ghazali and the Ash'arite School*, Durham, NC and London: Duke University Press.

Gardet, Louis (1951), *La Pensée réligieuse d'Avicenne*, Paris: J. Vrin.

Gilson, Étienne (1926), "Pourquoi S. Thomas a critiqué S. Augustin," *Archives d'Histoire Doctrinale et Littéraire du Moyen Âge* 1, pp. 5–127.

——(1927), "Avicenne et le point de départ de Duns Scot," *Archives d'Histoire Doctrinale et Littéraire du Moyen Âge* 2, pp. 89–149.

Gohlman, William (1974), *The Life of Avicenna: A Critical Edition and Annotated Translation*, Albany, NY: State University of New York Press.

Goodman, Lenn (1992), *Avicenna*, London and New York: Routledge.

Goris, Harm (1996), *Free Creatures of an Eternal God*, Leuven: Peeters.

Gutas, Dmitri (1988), *Avicenna and the Aristotelian Tradition*, Leiden: Brill.

Heath, Peter (1992), *Allegory and Philosophy in Avicenna with a Translation of the Book of the Prophet Muhammad's Ascent to Heaven*, Philadelphia: University of Pennsylvania Press.

Inati, Shams (1996), *Avicenna and Mysticism: Remarks and Admonitions: Part Four*, London and New York: Kegan Paul International.

Janssens, Jules (1991), *An Annotated Bibliography on Avicenna (1970–1989)*, Leuven: Leuven University Press.

Marmura, Michael (1997), *Al-Ghazali: The Incoherence of the Philosophers*, Provo, UT: Brigham Young University Press.

Michot, Jean (1986), *Le Destinée de l'homme selon Avicenne: Le retour à Dieu [ma'ad] et l'imagination*, Leuven: Peeters.

Nasr, Seyyed Hossain (1996), "Mulla Sadra: his teachings," in S. H. Nasr and O. Leaman, eds., *History of Islamic Philosophy*, vol. 1 (pp. 643–62), London and New York: Routledge.

Nasr, Seyyed Hossein and Leaman, Oliver, eds. (1996), *History of Islamic Philosophy*, 2 vols., London and New York: Routledge.

de Raeymaeker, Louis (1956), "L'être selon Avicenne et selon S. Thomas d'Aquin," in V. Courtois, ed., *Avicenna Commemoration Volume*, Calcutta: Iran Society.

Ziai, Hossein (1996), "Mulla Sadra: his life and works," in S. H. Nasr and O. Leaman, eds., *History of Islamic Philosophy*, vol. 1 (pp. 635–42), London and New York: Routledge.

——(1996), "Shihab al-Din Suhrawardi: founder of the Illuminationist School," in S. H. Nasr and O. Leaman, eds., *History of Islamic Philosophy*, vol. 1 (pp. 434–64), London and New York: Routledge.

20

Bernard of Clairvaux

BRIAN PATRICK McGUIRE

Bernard of Clairvaux (b. 1090; d. 1153) was born at the castle of a prominent family of the lower nobility outside of Dijon in Burgundy and was probably educated by canons of Châtillon-sur-Seine. In 1112 he and his brothers and friends entered the reform monastery of Cîteaux under its dynamic abbot Stephen Harding. As early as 1115 Bernard was sent out as the leader of a monastic group to found a daughter house of Clairvaux in Champagne. In the 1120s he involved himself in the affairs of the Cistercian Order and began writing letters that provide a chronicle of his commitments, and by the 1130s he had emerged from his monastic environment and was beginning to play a central role in the Church, for example, in the resolving of the papal schism of Innocent II and Anacletus. Bernard refused offers of further advancement in the Church and remained Abbot of Clairvaux, a position that gave him a great degree of independence from special interests.

In the period 1130 to 1145 he traveled extensively in dealing with the affairs of the order and the Church. Wherever he went, he left behind new Cistercian foundations. According to one of his biographers, mothers hid their sons when they heard that Bernard was coming, for as soon as they heard him preach, they wanted to become monks. By the time of Bernard's death, the Cistercian Order had spread all over western Europe, to a large extent as a result of his outstanding ability to publicize the attractiveness of its monastic reform (Lekai 1977, pp. 33–51; McGuire 1991, pp. 17–38).

Bernard is remembered today for two activities in particular: first, the preaching of the Second Crusade in the 1140s, which became a total fiasco; second, the persecution of PETER ABELARD, which ended with the latter's condemnation at the Council of Sens in 1140, where Bernard's role is highly controversial (Clanchy 1999; Grane 1970). Because of this involvement, Bernard is sometimes considered to be a dark enemy of the learning and new scholastic philosophy of the twelfth century, a reactionary or fundamentalist who had no appreciation of what was happening around him, in an intellectual culture that would lead to the foundation of the first great European university at Paris.

As so often in history, myths are much less complex than realities. Bernard had his own philosophical point of view, based on his understanding of the Christian religion, but by no means hostile to all forms of learning. In his *Sermons on the Song of Songs*, delivered in chapter to the monks at Clairvaux over a period of many years, Bernard conveyed the essence of his teaching. Here he paraphrased Paul (1 Cor. 1: 23) and spoke of his own philosophy as being something "more refined and interior, to know Jesus and him crucified" (*haec mea subtilior, interior philosophia*, SC 43.4, in 1957–77, 2, p. 43).

This philosophy was "not drawn from the school of rhetoricians and philosophers" (SC 36.1, in 1957–77, 2, p. 4). Bernard thought of himself as having learned from experience. His teachers, he said, were around him in nature: "The forest and stones will teach you what you cannot hear from masters [of the schools]" (Letter 106, ibid. 7, p. 266).

Bernard, nevertheless, was expertly taught in the school of the medieval *trivium* in grammar, rhetoric, and logic. He knew how to argue and how to make his argument attractive. Étienne Gilson (1940, pp. 6–12) once claimed that Bernard imitated Ciceronian rhetoric, while Christine Mohrmann, an expert on Latin style, has claimed that AUGUSTINE was his model (1957–77, 2, p. xii). Whatever the case, Bernard's contemporaries recognized his skill with words and arguments. One of his enemies, Berengar of Poitiers, a disciple of Abelard, once attacked Bernard for forgetting that he had once done his best to win over others in intellectual competitions and in clever displays of witty invention (*acutaeque inventionis versutia*, PL 178: 1857). Such a passage indicates that Bernard had a reputation not only for literary skill but also for philosophical argument before he entered the monastery.

Bernard may have decided in his early twenties to abandon a promising career as a master in the schools for the ascetic life of the monk. In doing so, he did not feel obliged to leave behind the superb training in language and reasoning that he had received. In the words of Étienne Gilson (1940, p. 8), "in renouncing the world to enter at Cîteaux, St. Bernard renounced this Latin culture along with the rest – too late no doubt, in a sense, since he was already possessed of it." Bernard, in fact, made the best of this background when he preached and wrote about the meaning of monastic life. He spoke of the transformation of the self in the image of God through desire for Christ. In this process of interiorization, there was no need for what the desert fathers of Egypt and Syria in late antiquity demanded: *apatheia*, a removal of all attachments to others, in order to attain the Christian life. For Bernard feeling (*affectus*) comes from closeness to Christ, and provides a basis for bonds with other people, without any danger of emotionalism or anti-intellectualism. On the contrary, the affectivity of Cistercian spirituality as described by Bernard is the basis for a new understanding of the world (McGuire 1988, pp. 286–7).

Always on guard when faced with philosophical language, Bernard can seem to denigrate philosophy as such, but his enemy was rather the thought of those who used their learning for wrong purposes. He taught his monks that "all knowledge in itself is good, so long as it is founded on the truth" (SC 36.2, in 1957–77, 2, p. 5). The problem is that there is little time, so he encouraged his monks to concentrate on types of learning that would contribute to their salvation. This attitude cannot be described as anti-philosophical.

Bernard, like his fellow Cistercian abbots, wanted recruits who had received a good education and knew what they wanted. He would therefore accept only grown men into the monastery and refused to take children as oblates (Leclercq 1979, pp. 9–16). Many of the new monks would, like Bernard, have come from the schools. Such men he readily accepted, but he warned them against seeking knowledge out of curiosity, vanity, or hope of financial reward. Knowledge must be used in the service of others or for one's own inner development (SC 36.3, in 1957–77, 2, p. 5).

Bernard often linked philosophers with heretics, and he considered Abelard's philosophical distinctions to be a point of departure for heresy, especially when Abelard began to use his logical distinctions in explaining the doctrine of the Trinity. Bernard's polemics against intellectual categories for the Godhead did not mean a similar rejection of philosophical reasoning and discourse. But he required that philosophers and intellectuals in general contribute to the needs of the Church. He pointed out that he was aware of the "benefits" scholars provided the Church, "both by refuting its opponents and instructing the uneducated" (SC 36.2, in 1957–77, 2, p. 4).

Bernard thus was suspicious of any philosophy that exists for its own sake. He accepted the view, overwhelmingly present in medieval culture, that all learning is the handmaid of theology and must contribute to theological insight. As a master of invective, Bernard could make fun of philosophers and heretics who decorated themselves with words (SC 41.2, in 1957–77, 2, p. 29) and never moved beyond empty talk about indifferent matters. For Bernard such talk was "windy chatter" (*ventosa loquacitas*, SC 58.7, ibid. 2, p. 131) or "wordiness" (*verbositate philosophorum*, SC 79.4, ibid. 2, p. 274). Probably thinking again of Abelard and his followers, Bernard described philosophers as "wandering about, unable to settle down in the certitude of the truth, always learning and never coming to the knowledge of truth" (SC 33.8, ibid. 1, p. 239. cf. 2 Tim. 3: 7). As a leading scholar of Bernard has pointed out, this passage is very close to one in the *Rule of Saint Benedict*, Bernard's model for monastic life (Casey 1988, p. 37).

Without ever using the expression, Bernard believed in a "Christian philosophy" in which knowledge can provide a point of departure for spiritual insight. He shared the attitude of ANSELM OF CANTERBURY (d. 1109), originally taken from Augustine himself, that faith is a point of departure for the pursuit of understanding (*fides quaerens intellectum*; Southern 1995, p. 226). It is this faith that must be preached to the ignorant and even to heretics, although they are not to be forced to accept it: "Faith is a matter of persuasion, not of imposition" (SC 66.12, in 1957–77, 2, p. 187). Bernard added here that he was pessimistic about the usefulness of speaking with heretics, who, he claimed, "are not convinced by logical reasoning, for they do not understand it."

Bernard nevertheless had sufficient belief in the usefulness of logical reasoning to accept an invitation to preach against the dualist heretics of the Midi, as the south of France was then known, and he apparently had at least a limited success (Wakefield 1974, pp. 24–5). Here, as in other situations, Bernard was willing and able to make use of rhetoric and logic in order to convince others of his point of view.

An example of Bernard's ability to make careful distinctions and to argue in a logical manner is his little treatise *On Grace and Free Will* (1957–77, 3, pp. 165–203). This is one of the finest pieces within what can be called the literature of early scholasticism. A theological problem is discussed not only on the basis of biblical or Patristic authorities but also in terms of theses and counter-theses. For this reason, Peter Abelard cannot be considered to be the sole founder of "the scholastic method," but merely someone who sharpened a form of argumentation already present at the end of the eleventh century, used by Anselm of Canterbury and Anselm of Laon, and taken over in the next generation by thinkers such as Bernard (Southern 1995).

Bernard's masterpiece of debate and discussion is a letter to the Paris master HUGH OF ST. VICTOR concerning the necessity of baptism for salvation. Bernard argued on the basis of authorities but also used rational arguments (Letter 77, 1957–77, 7, pp. 184–200). As one monastic scholar has shown in a seminal article, Bernard as "a great champion of monastic theology – meditative and contemplative, experiential, symbolic, transcendent . . . shows himself in this one work at least a skilled practitioner of the theology of the schools – logical, speculative, impersonal and argumentative" (Feiss 1992, p. 359).

Bernard never expressed regret about the learning he brought with him to Cîteaux. He is remembered for sweeping down on the schools of Paris in the search for new recruits, but those whom he later brought with him from Paris, such as his future secretary and biographer, Geoffrey of Auxerre, were welcome to make use of their talents at Clairvaux. After the death of Bernard, the Cistercians continued to be in contact with intellectual currents in the secular schools, especially at the nascent university in Paris, and debated the advantages of a permanent connection with the city. By the 1240s they decided to establish an institution there, so that the most promising young Cistercian monks could be trained in philosophical and theological discourse. It is no accident that the name given this school was the *Collège de Saint Bernard* (Lekai 1977, pp. 80–2).

One side of Bernard's philosophical contribution, which only recently has received the recognition it deserves, is his interest in describing friendship in monastic and human life in general (McGuire 1988 and 1991). As part of his training in classical learning, Bernard would have come across texts in Cicero and other writers celebrating the importance of friendship as a basis for social life. Bernard's rhetoric of friendship in his letters shows an intimate knowledge of this literature, but one may wonder if Bernard simply made use of a rhetoric of friendship in order to get what he wanted. Thus the letters exchanged between Bernard and PETER THE VENERABLE, the Abbot of Cluny, can be looked upon either as guarded expressions of polite distance or as the manifestation of a spiritual bond.

Whatever the actual feelings involved, Bernard was able to relate to Peter the Venerable and many others the necessity of describing human feeling and the importance of emotional closeness. Right into the twelfth century, Christian intellectuals had debated the usefulness or appropriateness of friendship within the ascetic life. Bernard ignored this debate and took it for granted that his monks were his friends. His language of friendship inspired disciples like Aelred, Abbot of Rievaulx, to write the first treatise on friendship since Cicero (McGuire 1994).

Peter the Venerable seems to have known and understood Bernard well. He characterized him as a man whose worldly learning (*eruditio saecularium*) had been complemented by his knowledge of holy matters (*scientia divinarum litterarum*, in Letter 28, in Constable 1967, 1, p. 53). The second phrase hints at Bernard's reputation for knowing and using the Bible. Almost every line in his *Sermons on the Song of Songs* is redolent of biblical language, and at times the reader does not know where the voice of Bernard begins and the biblical reference ends. This effect is precisely what Bernard intended. In his mind he integrated his school knowledge of classical texts with his monastic *lectio divina* or meditation on "divine letters," the language of the Gospels, the Psalms, the Prophets, and above all of Saint Paul.

A key to understanding Bernard is the language of Paul. Both were skeptical about the philosophical learning they saw around them and yet had a fairly good knowledge of philosophy. Bernard's commitment to monasticism and Christianity can be seen in terms of Paul's warning: "See to it that no one takes you captive through philosophy and empty deceit, according to human tradition . . . and not according to Christ" (Col. 2: 8). Passages such as this show that Paul also envisioned a Christian philosophy as an alternative to the philosophy of the world.

Bernard claimed to find such a philosophy "more through wonder than through examination" (*quasi admirans, non quasi scrutans*, SC 62.4, in 1957–77, 2, p. 158). But admiration of the created world as the manifestation of God did not exclude an examination of the riches that were taken from pagan philosophers. To return to Peter the Venerable's description of Bernard, the Abbot of Cluny said that the Abbot of Clairvaux in coming to the monastery had, like the Hebrews, left Egypt. Like them, Bernard had taken the spoils with him and had been able to benefit from them (Constable 1967, 1, p. 53). This image of despoiling the Egyptians, which justified the use of secular knowledge, came originally from Augustine's *On Christian Doctrine* (bk III, ch. 40/60), and it is an excellent description of

212

the Augustinian-Bernardine attitude: to make use of the best to be found in non-Christian learning and to integrate it into a Christian way of life.

Bernard can thus be considered as a master of secular learning, which he had imbibed through a traditional education in the *trivium* of grammar, rhetoric, and logic, the last of which was probably based on BOETHIUS' commentaries on Aristotle (Gilson 1955, pp. 97–8, 106). In Bernard, however, this learning is transformed by a new rhetoric of religious devotion and desire for direct experience of God. For Bernard there could be no boundaries or distance between a Christian philosophy and a Christian theology, for all learning and understanding expresses the presence of God in the human person.

Bernard's integration of learning and spirituality fell by the wayside with the increasingly technical orientation of scholastic philosophy and theology in the thirteenth century. The growing concern with reconciling Aristotelian philosophy and Christian revelation meant that scholastic argumentation became much more refined and analytical than it had been in Bernard's time. Aside from the treatise *On Grace and Free Will*, Bernard's writings were largely ignored in the "golden age" of scholasticism (Elm 1994).

By the end of the fourteenth century, however, a growing dissatisfaction with abstract and erudite scholastic speculation on the nature of God or the limits of knowledge brought a new orientation. Scholars such as JOHN GERSON (b. 1363; d. 1429) called for a scholastic learning that concentrated on questions of concern for Christian life. The new pastoral and ethical concerns of Parisian theology inspired such teachers to return to what the monastic scholar Jean Leclercq (1982) has called "the monastic theology of the twelfth century." Bernard of Clairvaux again became a central figure, and his *Sermons on the Song of Songs* were read as guides to the life of the soul (McGuire 1998).

In our own time Bernard of Clairvaux remains important in a perennial debate between intellectual learning and affective spirituality. Advocates of the first are deeply suspicious of all forms of emotionalism and "blind faith," whereas those who seek the latter complain about the aridity of abstract philosophy. For Bernard of Clairvaux there was no doubt that his "interior philosophy" of Christ crucified had to be based on an understanding of the texts that conveyed the basis for what later might become religious experience. For Bernard it was necessary to seek both faith and understanding.

In Bernard's model the well-trained scholar enters the monastery and uses his talents to deepen the interior life and to enrich the lives of others inside and outside the community. For Bernard's successors, for whom the monastery may not be an option, the beauty and depth of his language still show the benefits to be obtained when faith and knowledge are integrated.

Bibliography

Primary sources
(1957–77), *Opera*, 8 vols., ed. J. Leclercq and H. Rochais, Rome: Editiones Cistercienses. (Translations to English are available from Cistercian Publications, Kalamazoo, MI, cistpub@wmich.edu, for example, *On the Song of Songs* (SC), 4 vols.).

(*PL*) (1844–71), *Patrologia Latina cursus completus*, ed. J-P. Migne, Paris: Vivès.

Secondary sources
Casey, M. (1988), *A Thirst for God: Spiritual Desire in Bernard of Clairvaux's Sermons on the Song of Songs*, Kalamazoo, MI: Cistercian Publications.

Clanchy, M. T. (1999), *Abelard: A Medieval Life*, Oxford and Malden, MA: Blackwell.

Constable, G., ed. (1967), *The Letters of Peter the Venerable*, 2 vols., Cambridge, MA: Harvard University Press.

Elm, K., ed. (1994), *Bernhard von Clairvaux. Rezeption und Wirkung im Mittelalter und in der Neuzeit*, Wiesbaden: Harrasowitz Verlag.

Evans, G. R. (1982), "The classical education of Bernard of Clairvaux," *Cîteaux Commentarii Cistercienses* 33, pp. 121–34.

——(1983), *The Mind of St. Bernard of Clairvaux*, Oxford: Clarendon Press.

Feiss, H. (1992), "*Bernardus scholasticus*: the correspondence of Bernard of Clairvaux and Hugh of Saint Victor on Baptism," in J. R. Sommerfeldt, ed., *Bernardus Magister* (pp. 349–78), Kalamazoo, MI: Cistercian Publications.

Gilson, E. (1940), *The Mystical Theology of Saint Bernard*, Kalamazoo, MI: Cistercian Publications; repr. 1990.

——(1955), *History of Christian Philosophy in the Middle Ages*, London: Sheed and Ward.

Grane, L. (1970), *Peter Abelard: Philosophy and Christianity in the Middle Ages*, London: George Allen and Unwin.

Lekai, L. J. (1977), *The Cistercians. Ideals and Reality*, Kent, OH: Kent State University Press.

Leclercq, J. (1979), *Monks and Love in Twelfth-century France*, Oxford: Clarendon Press.

——(1982), *The Love of Learning and the Desire for God: A Study of Monastic Culture*, New York: Fordham University Press.

McGuire, B. P. (1988), *Friendship and Community: The Monastic Experience 350–1250*, Kalamazoo, MI: Cistercian Publications.

——(1991), *The Difficult Saint: Bernard of Clairvaux and his Tradition*, Kalamazoo, MI: Cistercian Publications.

——(1994), *Brother and Lover: Aelred of Rievaulx*, New York: Crossroad.

——(1998), *Jean Gerson: Early Works*, Mahwah, NJ: Paulist Press.

Southern, R. W. (1995), *Scholastic Humanism and the Unification of Europe*, vol. 1, Oxford and Cambridge, MA: Blackwell.

Wakefield, W. L. (1974), *Heresy, Crusade and Inquisition in Southern France, 1100–1250*, London: George Allen and Unwin.

21

Berthold of Moosburg

BRUCE MILEM

Berthold of Moosburg (b. ca 1300; d. after 1361), a German Dominican, taught between 1335 and 1361 at the Dominican school in Cologne founded by ALBERTUS MAGNUS. Like his predecessors at this school, including DIETRICH OF FREIBERG and MEISTER ECKHART, Berthold articulated a philosophical position opposed in many ways to the Aristotelianism then dominant in the universities. He wanted to retrieve Platonic philosophy, especially its treatment of God and the soul. In his view Platonism harmonized perfectly with both natural reason and Christian revelation. However, since little of Plato's work was available to Berthold, he relied instead on the writings of the Greek philosopher Proclus, whom he regarded as the best of Plato's disciples. Berthold's one surviving work is a vast commentary on Proclus' *Elements of Theology*, which Berthold interprets as a systematic exposition of Plato's thought. It is, as far as we know, the only commentary on Proclus produced in the Middle Ages. All through it, Berthold draws on and modifies the ideas of his predecessors in Cologne, especially Dietrich.

Berthold says that Proclus' *Elements of Theology* "handles the universe of divine things according to its procession from the highest good and its return into it." The highest good, which Berthold, like Proclus, also calls "the One," is both the source and the ultimate goal of everything that is. It itself is not being or a being but rather surpasses being. Berthold understands this highest good and pure oneness as the trinitarian God of Christianity, though he recognizes that Proclus did not. The created universe has two kinds of being: the eternal, immaterial ideas, and material things. The ideas are "divine by essence," while material things, patterned on the eternal ideas, are "divine by participation."

In a class by itself, though, is the human intellect. It springs spontaneously and directly from God and forms an image of God. The intellect is, in a sense, infinite: it can potentially know all things, and it is the vehicle for the soul's ascent to God. As Berthold explains, one can reach God through a "laborious investigation," which starts by using reason to know material things, then rises to a contemplation of the eternal ideas, and culminates with a vision of the highest good. Ultimately, thanks to a "special grace," the soul is transported beyond the intellect into a "divine madness" and actually becomes one with God.

Berthold's work is notable for its explicit intent to revive ancient philosophical tradition, its dissent from Aristotelian scholasticism, and its synthesis of earlier German Dominican thinkers. His account of the universe and the intellect he largely borrows from Dietrich, but his emphasis on divine union is closer to Eckhart. Like so much Platonic thought, Berthold's writing ignores any distinction between philosophy and mysticism.

Bibliography

(1984–), *Expositio super Elementationem theologicam Procli*, 9 vols., Hamburg: Felix Meiner Verlag.

22

Boethius

JOHN MAGEE

Anicius Manlius Severinus Boethius (b. ca. 480; d. 524/5) had already attracted attention for his scholarship by about 507. He was named Consul in 510 and Master of the Offices in 522. Shortly thereafter he was denounced before Theoderic, which led to his incarceration, in Pavia, without trial. He was tortured and then executed (Chadwick 1981, pp. 1–68). Only the *Categories* commentary, which was under way in 510 (*PL* 64, 201 B), and *Consolatio* (ca. 524) are datable on external grounds; the *De arithmetica* (ca. 500) presumably marks the beginning of Boethius' literary career.

Where did Boethius study? Two centers of Greek learning inevitably suggest themselves as possibilities. Athens: Although it remains an open question whether Boethius made use of the commentaries of the Athenian master Proclus, it is clear that he had at least indirect access to doctrines of Proclus' teacher Syrianus. Even secure evidence to the effect that he either utilized Proclus or had direct access to Syrianus would not, however, amount to proof of a period of study in Athens, and the only directly relevant testimony suggests that Boethius in fact "entered the Athenian school" *despite* its distance (Cassiodorus 1973, *Var.* I, 45, 3). Alexandria: The evidence for Courcelle's famous theory to the effect that Boethius studied in Alexandria is inconclusive (1969, pp. 316f). The main difficulty is that, although there are indeed some points of similarity between the commentaries of Boethius and those of the Alexandrian master Ammonius, there are in fact many more differences; the similarities, moreover, may be symptomatic only of a shared tradition. Boethius must have received some instruction in Italy, but the availability of Greek material there is a subject of debate (Asztalos 1993, pp. 398–405; Ebbesen 1990, p. 376; Shiel 1990, p. 368). Did he own copies of the Greek commentaries or only manuscripts fitted out with scholia extracted from them? The scholia theory, if indeed valid, need not eliminate its competitor, for which there is strong supporting evidence.

Philosophy and the sciences

Boethius coined the term *quadruvium* for the four mathematical sciences (*De arith.* I, 1999, p. 9, 6f) and is thus one of the founders of the western tradition of departmentalized faculties. Moreover, he transmitted to the medieval schools two methods of dividing disciplines. One of them is Peripatetic (*In Isag.* I, 1906, pp. 8, 1–9, 22; *De arith.* I, 1; *Inst. mus.* I, 2; II, 3; *De Trin.* 2; *Cons.* I, 1, 4):

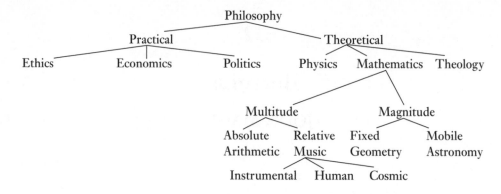

The other is generally considered Stoic (*In Cat.* 161B; *In Isag.* II, 1906, pp. 140, 23–141, 19; *In Perih.* II, 1880, p. 79, 19f; cf. *De div.*, 1998, pp. xxiii, nn. 25, 26; xxxvii, n. 8):

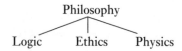

Common to both methods is the implication that philosophy is the *source* of knowledge. It is not a discipline coordinate with the rest, like a modern university department, but transcends them all. Boethius' treatises on astronomy and geometry have not survived, but in the *De arithmetica* and *De institutione musica* (incomplete) his commitment to this viewpoint is revealed. Each work looks to Plato's *Timaeus* for confirmation that the rational foundations of the universe explain the sciences (e.g., *De arith.* II, 2, 1999, p. 97, 6; *Inst. mus.* I, 1). Logic marks the point of difference between the two systems above. Is it a *part* of philosophy (Stoic view), or a *tool* (Peripatetic view)? Boethius argues for both (*In Isag.* II, 1906, p. 140, 13–143, 7): logic has its proper philosophical aims but is also what discovers and evaluates arguments for application in other areas of philosophy.

The unity of Plato and Aristotle

Boethius planned to translate, comment on, and harmonize Plato and Aristotle (*In Perih.* II, 1880, p. 79, 9–80, 6). For the last part of the project he may have been inspired by Porphyry, who wrote a treatise on the subject; unfortunately, Porphyry's work is lost and Boethius did not live to carry out his plan, so that efforts to reconstruct his thinking on the unity of Plato and Aristotle are inevitably conjectural. Cicero, another possible influence, speaks of the Academy and Peripatos as one school (*Academicae quaestiones* I, 4, 18; II, 5, 15, after Antiochus), but whereas he also adds the Stoa, Boethius maintains a strict separation of the Stoics from the Peripatetic and Academic schools. The Stoics are a muddled crowd (*Cons.* I, 3, 7; V, m. 4). Thus Plato and Aristotle are the only philosophers whom Lady Philosophy in the *Consolatio* will call her own (I, 3, 6; III, 9, 32; V, 1, 12). Two illustrations will help us to see how Boethius may have conceived of the harmonizing project.

First, to the Peripatetic division of theoretical sciences mentioned earlier Boethius applies, in *In Isagogen* I, a corresponding ontological division of intellectibles (theology), intelligibles (mathematics), and corporeals (physics), tracing the descent of souls from the top down. Despite some new terminology the passage as a whole breathes a late Platonism reminiscent of Macrobius' commentary on Cicero's *Somnium Scipionis* (I, 14, 6f), which he knew (*In Isag.* I, 1906, p. 31, 22f); gaps in the theory are filled in by, for example, the doctrine of procession and return in the *Consolatio* (III, m. 2, 34–8). Between the first and second *Isagoge* commentaries Boethius sharpened his scholarly skills, and so on the problem of universals in the second he toes the Peripatetic line (for the *Isagoge* is an introduction to Aristotle), saying that genera and species subsist in particulars but are by intellect abstracted as universal concepts; even there, however, he hints at his agreement with Plato (p. 167, 18).

Second, let us look at his theory of elements. Plato describes the bond between earth, air, fire, and water in mathematical terms (*Tim.* 31B–32B), whereas Aristotle maintains that elemental change arises from competition between contrarily opposed qualities (hot/cold, dry/moist) in a substrate (*GC* II, 4). In the *Consolatio* Boethius unites the theories. At IV, m. 6, 19–24 he targets Aristotle, referring to the struggle (*pugnantia*) between moist and dry, cold and hot, to produce fire and earth; the terms he uses (*humida siccis . . . frigora flammis*) echo those at III, m. 9, 10–12 (*frigora flammis, arida . . . liquidis*), where, however, fire and earth are described as bound by number (*numeris*), as in Plato. Again Boethius may have been influenced by Macrobius (*In somn. Sc.* I, 6, 25–7, cf. Calcidius, *In Tim.* §§317f); he was certainly not following Proclus (1903–6, 2, pp. 37, 33–38, 24, citing Ocellus).

Boethius' intention was to show that Plato and Aristotle agree on "most points, and those the most important philosophically" (*In Perih.* II, 1880, p. 80, 5f). Our examples demonstrate, however, that although he was indeed prepared to force Plato and Aristotle into agreement (division of sciences and the descent of souls, the elements), he was also prepared to concede the necessity of having to choose between them on certain fundamental matters (universals). *Consolatio* V probably tells the story best: in general, harmonizing means making Aristotle's *logic* serve Plato's *metaphysics*; which in the end makes Boethius a Platonist, "brought up," as Lady Philosophy says, "on Eleatic and Academic studies" (*Cons.* I, 1, 10). Of course, his philosophers have been touched by the school traditions, and his Platonism is particularly obscure. There is no indication that he read, for example, Plotinus, whom he mentions only once, thanks to Porphyry (*De div.* 875D). About the Peripatetic tradition more will be said presently.

Philosophical translations and commentaries

Extant are six translations, of the *Isagoge*, *Categories*, *De interpretatione*, *Prior Analytics*, *Topics*, and *Sophistical Refutations*, and five commentaries, on the *Isagoge* (two editions), *Categories* (single edition, plus a possible fragment from a lost second one), and *De interpretatione* (two editions). At the opening of the second *Isagoge* commentary, Boethius promises to translate verbatim, sacrificing rhetorical polish to untainted truth (1906, p. 135, 5–13). This policy evolved out of frustrations that arose in the course of his commenting first on Marius Victorinus' Latin version of the *Isagoge*, and it suggests that the making of new translations was not a part of his original plan (Asztalos 1993, p. 377). Although Boethius polished his translation skills over a long period of time, *De arithmetica*, which paraphrases a Greek handbook of Nicomachus, suggests that by about 500 he was already in control of a specialized technical idiom.

Boethius evidently revised all but one of his translations. Differences between the commentary lemmata of *In Isagogen* II and the continuous translation indicate a rethinking of the *Isagoge*. The *Categories* implies three stages of development, a crude preliminary translation, a revision (the commentary lemmata), and a final draft reflecting the influence of a second Greek exemplar (Asztalos 1993, pp. 371f). *De interpretatione* too is in three versions, lemmata for the first commentary, revised lemmata for the second, and a polished continuous translation. The *Prior Analytics* survives in two redactions, one of them accompanied by scholia (of Greek origin) which may point to a lost commentary. And a fragment buried in the textual tradition of *De divisione* indicates a second recension of the *Topics*. Even when Boethius was not actually translating he thought in terms of the Greek linguistic background (e.g. *De arith*. II, 4, 1999, p. 110, 99; *De div*. 878A; *C. Eut*. 3; *Cons*. III, 10, 22), and his bilingual habit brought new life to the Latin philosophical idiom. His translations have had a lasting influence, giving terms such as 'substance' and 'accident' resonances which they might not otherwise have had; modern scholars still search their rebarbative Latin in hopes of recovering the *ipsissima verba* of Aristotle and Porphyry. These translations are the backbone of Boethius' philosophical achievement.

It appears that Boethius intended to write the commentaries according to the traditional pedagogical order (*Isagoge, Categories, De interpretatione*) but changed plans along the way. The first *Isagoge* commentary is unique for its dialogue form (after Porphyry's smaller *Categories* commentary), its reliance upon Victorinus' Latin, and its hints of Platonism. Boethius' gradual rethinking of the project is evident on all counts: he allows the dialogue conceit to fade, he becomes increasingly impatient with Victorinus, and in the *second* commentary he jettisons the Platonism. After the first *Isagoge* commentary Boethius proceeded to the *Categories*, translating as he commented. That he was still finding his way is indicated by the different versions of the translation; also, it seems that his announcement of a more advanced exegesis (160A–B), and hence the idea of a second commentary, was an afterthought (Asztalos 1993, pp. 378–94; cf. Ebbesen 1990, pp. 387f). After the *Categories* Boethius returned to the *Isagoge*, composing his own translation and a new commentary. This fresh start may have consolidated his plan: henceforth Boethius would comment on his own translations (thus 1906, p. 135, 5–13 heralds a new style of translation) and would, like Porphyry, write double commentaries at two levels, for novices and veterans (see 1906, p. 154, 2–8). The *De interpretatione* commentary presupposes a double treatment (I, 1877, pp. 31, 6–32, 6; II, 1880, pp. 186, 4; 251, 8) and advertises the project of translating, commenting on, and harmonizing Plato and Aristotle (II, 1880, p. 79, 9–80, 6). Boethius' handling of the six traditional *didascaliae* (intention, utility, title, order, authenticity, part of philosophy) is more systematic in the prolegomena to the first *Isagoge* and *Categories* commentaries than it is in the prolegomena to the second *Isagoge* and both *De interpretatione* commentaries, which display a subtler selection and interweaving of themes; this may lend support to the view that the second *Isagoge* commentary postdates the one on the *Categories*.

The *Categories* and second *De interpretatione* commentaries are rich in doxographical notices, whereas for pedagogical reasons, probably, the first *De interpretatione* commentary and both *Isagoge* commentaries are by comparison jejune (cf. *In Isag*. II, 1906, p. 164, 4; 168, 14f; *In Perih*. I, 1877, pp. 132, 3–7). Although Porphyry is Boethius' main guide (*In Cat*. 160A; *In Perih*. II, 1880, pp. 7, 5–7; 219, 17f), the later commentators Iamblichus (*In Cat*. 224D–225B), Themistius (*In Cat*. 162A; *In Perih*. II, 1880, p. 4, 2f), Praetextatus (*In Perih*. II, 1880, p. 3, 7), and Syrianus (ibid., pp. 18, 26; 87, 30–88, 28; 172, 13–173, 11; 321, 21; 324, 15) figure as well. Patterns of citation in the second *De interpretatione* commentary are suggestive, for example, Porphyry is often mentioned alongside his predecessors Herminus and Alexander, who, however, rarely appear without him (ibid., pp. 93, 9–22; 98, 15; 307, 29–310, 17; 317, 9). Whenever Boethius cites Porphyry to correct the earlier commentators or Stoics we may assume that he is following Porphyry; the post-Porphyrian material must come from somewhere else.

In the *Categories* commentary Boethius adheres closely to Porphyry's exegesis (the "Question and Answer" commentary), and in the second *De interpretatione* commentary he speaks only once of being able to improve upon Porphyry (1880, p. 121, 25f.); in general, the commentaries exhibit philosophical originality only in their organization and reworking of material. We occasionally catch glimpses of Boethius at work. For example, from *De divisione* 877B–C we know that the system of diaeresis articulated at *In Isagogen* II (1906, pp. 154, 11–155, 8) is the one he eventually adopted, not the one at *In Isagogen* I (1906, p. 22, 14f). And while the *Categories* commentary is somewhat elliptical concerning Aristotle's intention, the second *De interpretatione* commentary tells a fuller story: the *Categories* is indeed about words insofar as they signify things (*In Cat.* 159C–160A), but insofar as they signify them *through the medium of thoughts* (*In Perih*. II, 1880, pp. 7, 25–8, 7). The latter interpretation, then, forms the basis for a general account of signification (Ebbesen 1990, pp. 381–3; Magee 1989).

The second *De interpretatione* commentary is a mature work reflecting some of Boethius' own philosophical preoccupations. As against Aristotle's fourteen chapters, it has six books, the third of which is devoted exclusively to *De interpretatione* 9, on future contingents. In an elaborate introduction (*In Perih*, II, 1880, pp. 185, 17–198, 21) Boethius traces the history of his subject in the Peripatos and Hellenistic schools. No other chapter of *De interpretatione* is raised to the same position of prominence; indeed, the third book of the commentary amounts almost to a separate treatise, the merits (and limitations) of which are implicitly acknowledged in the *Consolatio* (V, 4, 1). Boethius spent about two years on the commentary (*In Perih*. II, 1880, p. 421, 5), which from the fourth book on betrays his growing impatience and fatigue. Thus he promises to write a less taxing exposition in the form of a compendium (ibid., p. 251, 8f) and has difficulty remembering certain points (pp. 466, 19f; 489, 10). The sixth book is marked by two significant changes, in that the *theōria kai lexis* (*sententia et ordo sermonis*) mode of commentary associated with the *reportationes* from Ammonius' school is most in evidence and the doxographical material has vanished. The two facts may be related, since half of the sixth book treats of *De interpretatione* 14, on which Porphyry never commented (Ammonius 1897, p. 252, 8–10). But Porphyry's absence cannot fully explain the lack of doxographical material, since the sixth book mentions no authority in connection with *De interpretatione* 13 (Diodorus is the last named authority, in the fifth book (*In Perih*. II. 1880, p. 412, 16)), and in it the post-Porphyrian commentators too are silent. Is Boethius' weariness, or a failure in his source(s), the cause of the tapering off of authorities? Possibly both.

Logical monographs, topical theory

Six works complement the philosophical translations and commentaries. *De divisione* derives from the prolegomena to Porphyry's lost commentary on Plato's *Sophist*, which in turn derived from a treatise by Andronicus of Rhodes (also lost). It emphasizes the division of genera into species but treats also of the division of wholes into parts, of equivocal and ambiguous expressions into significations, and of the incidental modes of division. The *Introductio ad syllogismos categoricos* and *De syllogismo categorico* (on the titles, see De Rijk 1964, pp. 38–42, 161f) were conceived as prolegomena of some kind (761B; 793C). Although closely related, they differ in terminology and in the fact that *De syllogismo categorico* is in two books, the second of which harkens back to Eudemus, Theophrastus, and Porphyry (813C–815B; 829D). The plan for each was to rehearse doctrines from *De interpretatione* (764A; 795B) in preparation for material treated in the *Prior Analytics* (762C; 794D); our text of the *Introductio*, unfortunately, does not reach its goal. *De hypotheticis syllogismis* attempts to fill gaps left by Aristotle, Theophrastus, and Eudemus (I, 1, 3), i.e., to reclaim for the Peripatetic tradition a subject otherwise dominated by Stoics; it is one of Boethius' most complex and important works. The commentary on Cicero's *Topics* is incomplete (cf. *Diff. top.* I, 1, 5) and shares with the first *Isagoge* commentary a sharp hostility to Victorinus. In order to remedy Victorinus' philosophical shortcomings, Boethius brings Aristotle into focus, examining such issues as definition (1096B), genera and species (1105B), the modes of opposition (1119C), the Stoic "indemonstrables" (1133A), and fortune and chance (1153A). *De differentiis topicis* brings Cicero into conjunction with Themistius on dialectical topics (III, 7, 1).

Opuscula sacra

The theological tractates are what give substance to the old description of Boethius as the "first of the scholastics." In them Boethius pays tribute to AUGUSTINE (*De Trin.*, praef., 2000, p. 167, 30) and speaks of conjoining faith and reason (*Utr. pat.*, 2000, p. 185, 67) but strikes out on his own with a rigorous pursuit of Aristotelian dialectic, about which Augustine was more cautious (e.g. *De Trin.* V, 5, 6; *Confessiones* IV, 16, 28). The tractates recall the project of harmonizing Plato and Aristotle in their application of Aristotelian logic to a non-Aristotelian metaphysics. Emphasis varies widely: *De fide catholica* is unphilosophical, *Utrum pater et filius* is almost as unphilosophical; and whereas *De Trinitate* and *Contra Eutychen et Nestorium* examine tenets of Christian faith, the only tenets sustaining *De hebdomadibus* are its prefatory common conceptions, axioms redolent of Euclid rather than Moses. The prefaces to *De Trinitate*, *De hebdomadibus*, and *Contra Eutychen et Nestorium* are unapologetically esoteric: Boethius' religion is for the philosophical elite.

De hebdomadibus poses the question of how substances can be good *qua* existent given that they are not good *qua* substances. The task is to find a path between two impossibilities, i.e., that things are good by participation (in which case they are not *per se* good), and that they are substantially good (which would make them God). Boethius builds the argument up from an unfulfilled hypothesis: If there were no first good to explain existence, then goodness and existence would be only incidentally united in the created order (the "participation" impossibility), and created things, if good, would be only good, indeed, they would be *the* only good (the "substantial" impossibility). Thus the goodness of the created order is explained on the grounds that things derive existence from a primary source in which being and goodness are completely undifferentiated. In style the tract recalls Proclus, although Augustine's influence is felt as well (Chadwick 1981, pp. 206f).

The prolegomena to *De Trinitate* rehearse material treated in the commentaries: (1) generic, specific, and numerical difference, (2) the division of sciences and form/matter distinction, (3) substantial and accidental predications, (4) the categories. The argument proper takes up the category of relation (5–6). Boethius falls back on arguments developed in the *Categories* commentary (234A–237A; cf. *De div.* 884B) in order to show that relation entails no predication of substantial difference; he maintains that whereas divine unity is a question of substance, the Trinity entails a difference of relation.

Contra Eutychen et Nestorium shares with *De Trinitate* a formal division into prolegomena (1–3) and argument proper (4–8), and with *De hebdomadibus* the search for a *via media*. From Christ's two natures Nestorius infers two persons, while from his one person Eutyches infers one nature; Boethius must show that Christ is one person in and of two natures. In the main argument hypothetical reasoning is to the forefront, Boethius' technique being to introduce his opponent's assumption, state its implications, show that the implications are incongruent with commonly accepted beliefs, and so subvert the assumption (cf. *De hyp. syll.* I, 4, 3–7; *In Cic. top.* 1133C). The prolegomena are philosophically more interesting. Christ's two natures imply separate differentiae (1). But can two different natures be shown to be compatible with one person? A definition of "person" that applies to both the human and the divine is desiderated, which in turn calls for logical diaeresis (2). One division harkens back to the *Categories* (see *In Cat.* 169C–175C):

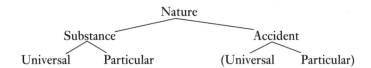

the other to the *Isagoge* (see *In Isag.* II, 1906, p. 208, 9–209, 6):

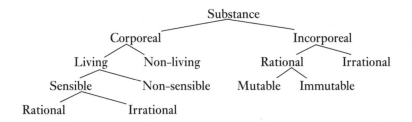

Boethius selects the genus (substance) from what is common to the two systems and the differentiae (particular, rational) from what separates them (*sic*), thus arriving at the definition that became standard in the medieval schools. The exploration of terms in chapter 3 is to show that nature = *ousia* (*essentia*) and person = *hypostasis* (*substantia*, cf. ch. 4, 2000, p. 219, 265–7). Collapsing the distinction between terms Boethius affirms that man has, and God is, "essence" (being), subsistence, substance, and person. The main difficulty stems from the term 'substance', which could be mistakenly interpreted as implying a substrate for change in the godhead; 'person', Boethius observes, is the term endorsed by ecclesiastical tradition. The union of natures in Christ does not destroy the elements of composition, as happens when water is blended with honey; rather, the human and divine remain intact, like gems and gold in a crown (7).

Philosophiae consolatio

The *Consolatio* is Boethius' most celebrated work. The *mise-en-scène* is his prison cell; while composing a poem Boethius falls into a dream (I, 1, 1), the substance of which is the ensuing colloquy. The detail of the dream is meant to evoke Plato's Socrates, who in prison dreamt of being ordered to make philosophical "music" (I, 3, 6; Plato, *Phaedo* 60E–61B, 84E–85B; *Crito* 44A). Although Lady Philosophy's description of Boethius as enchained (I, m. 2, 25) may be metaphorical (cf. I, m. 4, 18; I, m. 7, 30; III, m. 10, 2; IV, m. 2, 5), there is no reason to regard the imprisonment as a fiction (I, 3, 3; I, 4, 36).

The prosimetric form of the *Consolatio* has tended to split its audience. Some prefer the "literature," often the poetry of the first three books, others the philosophy, generally the prose of the fifth. It is wrong, says Lady Philosophy, to break apart that which is one (III, 9, 4; cf. I, 1, 5; I, 3, 7), and that the *Consolatio* is a coherent unity of literary form and philosophical content is clearly demonstrated by, among other things, its philosophical poetry (III, m. 9; III, m. 11; V, m. 4) and "literary" prose (II, 2/7). The prose/poetry tension in fact assists the development of the argument. Book I begins and ends with poetry, whereas book V begins and ends with prose; books II through IV begin with prose and end with poetry. This pattern creates formal symmetry and allows the stronger "medicine" of philosophical prose gradually to prevail. There are signs of a ring structure, for example, in the anticipation, in the passage on Fortune's wheel (II, 2, 9), of the discussion of the orb of fate/providence (IV, 6, 15–17), in the chiastic arrangement of poems in acatalectic anapestic dimeters (I, m. 5 = "Boethius"; III, m. 2/IV, m. 6 = Lady Philosophy; V, m. 3 = "Boethius"), and in the elegiac couplets to open books I and V. At the center is a unique poem in hexameters (III, m. 9), an acknowledged turning point and evocation of Plato's *Timaeus* (III, 9, 32f; Gruber 1978, pp. 22f). The formal symmetry mirrors the *philosophical* idea that the divine mind is the hub around which everything revolves (III, m. 9, 16f; III, 12, 37; IV, 6, 17). It also supports the "therapy": the gradual heightening of perspective, for example, in the shift from Fortune (I–II) to fate and providence (IV–V), exemplifies the rule that knowledge is according to the powers of the knowing subject, not the known object (V, 4, 25). By revisiting themes Lady Philosophy is able to assess her interlocutor's progress.

The labyrinthine (III, 12, 30) argument is driven by a single concern, as stated by "Boethius" in two poems of identical meter. In the first (I, m. 5) he complains of a world split between perfect order (1–24) and the chaos of Fortune (25–48), in the second (V, m. 3), of a world split between incompatible "truths" (free choice, divine foreknowledge). The second is really a reprise of the first in light of the fact that Fortune has in the meantime been removed from consideration (IV, 5–7, resuming II, 8), and Lady Philosophy's response to each brings the observation that the world follows a *single* principle of governance (I, 5, 4; V, 4, 2). Her explicitly stated task is to help "Boethius" recall that the world is indeed divinely ruled (I, 6, 7/19; III, 12, 3), i.e., to disabuse him of the dualism.

The question of the Christianity of the *Consolatio* seems lifeless today. The biblical allusions argue against apostasy or paganism (e.g., III, 12, 22 = Sap. 8: 1). One in fact arises in connection with the articulation of the main philosophical problem. When Lady Philosophy observes that "Boethius" has prayed that the peace that "rules heaven should rule the earth as well" (I, 5, 10 = I, m. 5, 46–8), she is paraphrasing Matt. 6: 10 (Klingner 1921, p. 5), a passage which Boethius quotes at *Contra Eutychen et Nestorium* 8, 2000, p. 240, 766f. We need only compare V, 3, 33–6 and V, 6, 1–14 with *De Trinitate* 4 (2000, pp. 175f, 235–48) and 6 (2000, pp. 180f, 360–5) to perceive the continuity of spiritual and rational that is so characteristic of Boethius: each work invokes the same distinction between eternity and perpetuity, the same conviction that where reason ends prayer and divine grace begin. And by implicitly placing limitations on Lady Philosophy herself (e.g., IV, 6, 38/53; V, 6, 25) Boethius reminds us that the philosophy of the *Consolatio* is not wisdom (cf. *In Isag.* I, 1906, p. 7, 12–23; *Inst. mus.* II, 2), but a preparatory *exercitatio* (III, 12, 25, after Plato, *Republic* 435A).

Bibliography

Primary sources

(1867), *De institutione musica*, ed. G. Friedlein, Leipzig: Teubner.

(1877–80), *Commentarii in librum Aristotelis ΠΕΡΙ ΕΡΜΗΝΕΙΑΣ*, 2 vols., ed. C. Meiser, Leipzig: Teubner.

(1891), *Opera omnia*, in J.-P. Migne, ed., *Patrologia Latina (PL)*, vol. 64, Paris: Vivès.

(1906), *In Isagogen Porphyrii commenta*, ed. S. Brandt, Corpus scriptorum ecclesiasticorum latinorum 48, Vienna: F. Tempsky; Leipzig: G. Freytag.

(1969), *De hypotheticis syllogismis*, ed. L. Obertello, Brescia: Paideia Editrice.

(1990), *De topicis differentiis*, in Boethius' *De topicis differentiis und byzantische Rezeption dieses Werkes. Anhang: Eine Pachymeres-Werkarbeitung der Holobos-Übersetzung*, ed. D. Z. Nikitas, Athens, Paris, and Brussels: J. Vrin.

(1998), *De divisione*, ed. J. Magee, Leiden: Brill.

(1999), *De arithmetica*, ed. H. Oosthout and J. Schilling, Corpus Christianorum series latina 94a, Turnhout: Brepols.

(2000), *De consolatione philosophiae, Opuscula theologica*, ed. C. Moreschini, Munich and Leipzig: K. G. Saur.

(2001), *De syllogismo categorico*, ed. C. Thomsen Thörnqvist, Dissertation, Göteborg University.

Secondary sources

Ammonius (1897), *Commentaria in Perihermenias Aristotelis*, ed. A. Busse, Berlin: G. Reimeri.

Asztalos, M. (1993), "Boethius as a transmitter of Greek logic to the Latin West: the *Categories*," *Harvard Studies in Classical Philology* 95, pp. 367–407.

Cassiodorus (1973), *Variarum libri XII*, ed. A. J. Fridh, in *Opera omnia*, vol. 1, Corpus Christianorum series latina 96-8, Turnhout: Brepols.

Chadwick, H. (1981), *Boethius: The Consolations of Music, Logic, Theology, and Philosophy*, Oxford: Clarendon Press.

Courcelle, P. (1967), *La Consolation de Philosophie dans la tradition littéraire: antécédents et postérité de Boèce*, Paris: Études Augustiniennes.

——(1969), *Late Latin Writers and their Greek Sources*, trans. H. E. Wedeck, Cambridge, MA: Harvard University Press.

De Rijk, L. M. (1964), "On the chronology of Boethius' works on logic I, II," *Vivarium* 2, pp. 1–49, 125–62.

Ebbesen, S. (1990), "Boethius as an Aristotelian commentator," in R. Sorabji, ed., *Aristotle Transformed: The Ancient Commentators and their Influence* (pp. 373–91), Ithaca: Cornell University Press.

Folkerts, M. (1970), *"Boethius" Geometrie II: Ein mathematisches Lehrbuch des Mittelalters*, Wiesbaden: Franz Steiner.

Fuhrmann, M. and Gruber, J., eds. (1984), *Boethius*, Darmstadt: Wissenschaftliche Buchgesellschaft.

Galonnier, A. (1997), *Anecdoton Holderi ou Ordo Generis Cassiodororum: Eléments pour une étude de l'authenticité Boécienne des Opuscula Sacra*, Louvain and Paris: Peeters.

——ed. (2002), *Boèce ou la chaîne des savoirs*, Louvain and Paris: Peeters.

Gersh, S. (1986), *Middle Platonism and Neoplatonism: The Latin Tradition*, 2 vols., Notre Dame, IN: University of Notre Dame.

Gibson, M., ed. (1981), *Boethius: His Life, Thought and Influence*, Oxford: Blackwell.

Gruber, J. (1978), *Kommentar zu Boethius De Consolatione Philosophiae*, Berlin and New York: De Gruyter.

——(1997, 1998), "Boethius 1925–1998," *Lustrum* 39, pp. 307–83; 40, pp. 199–259.

Hadot, P. (1959), "Un fragment du commentaire perdu de Boèce sur les Catégories d'Aristote dans le codex Bernensis 363," *Archives d'Histoire Doctrinale et Littéraire du Moyen Âge* 26, pp. 11–27.

Klingner, F. (1921), *De Boethii consolatione philosophiae*, Berlin: Weidmann.

Magee, J. (1989), *Boethius on Signification and Mind*, Leiden: Brill.

Marenbon, J. (2002), *Boethius*, New York: Oxford University Press.

Micaelli, C. (1988), *Studi sui trattati teologici di Boezio*, Naples: D'Auria.

Minio-Paluello, L. (1972), *Opuscula: The Latin Aristotle*, Amsterdam: Hakkert.

Obertello, L. (1974), *Severino Boezio*, 2 vols., Genoa: Accademia Ligure di Scienze e Lettere.

——ed. (1981), *Congresso internazionale di studi Boeziani: atti*, Pavia, October 5–8, 1980: Rome: Herder.

O'Daly, G. (1991), *The Poetry of Boethius*, London: Duckworth.

Proclus (1903–6), *In Platonis Timaeum commentaria*, ed. E. Diehl, Leipzig: Teubner.

Scheible, H. (1972), *Die Gedichte in der Consolatio Philosophiae des Boethius*, Heidelberg: Carl Winter.

Schmidt-Kohl, V. (1965), *Die neuplatonische Seelenlehre in der Consolatio Philosophiae des Boethius*, Meisenheim am Glan: Anton Hain.

Shiel, J. (1990), "Boethius' commentaries on Aristotle," in R. Sorabji, ed., *Aristotle Transformed: The Ancient Commentators and their Influence* (pp. 349–72), Ithaca: Cornell University Press.

Troncarelli, F. (2000), "*Mentis cogitatio*: un prologo di Boezio in un prologo a Boezio?," in J. Hamesse, ed., *Les Prologues médiévaux: actes du colloque international organisé par l'Academia Belgica et l'Ecole Française de Rome avec le concours de la FIDEM*, Rome, March 26–8, 1998 (pp. 39–86), Turnhout: Brepols.

23

Boethius of Dacia

B. CARLOS BAZÁN

Although Boethius of Dacia has been recognized since the thirteenth century as one of the main representatives – together with SIGER OF BRABANT – of "radical Aristotelianism" and as one of the principal targets of Bishop Tempier's condemnation of 1277 (Hisette 1977; Piché 1999, p. 243 n. 1), the information about his life and career is scarce. Results of the latest research on his biography (Jensen 1963; see also *Opera*, 1969, p. xxxiv) can be summarized as follows. He was born in Denmark, not in Sweden, and the dates of birth and death are unknown. He was in Paris after 1262, and taught as master of arts at the university around 1270–80. He was not cited by the Inquisition in November 1276, as were Siger of Brabant, Bernier of Nivelles, and Goswin of La Chapelle, and he may have become a Dominican priest at an unknown later date because his works are listed in the catalogue of Stams. His works were all written before 1277 (logical works around 1270; writings on natural philosophy around 1272), which suggests that his career as a master of arts had come to an end before 1277. Medieval catalogues and references made by Boethius himself to his works allow us to infer that the extant manuscripts cover only part of his writings (see Bibliography, below). Probably some manuscripts were destroyed after the condemnation of 1277, and some are still to be discovered.

Logic and epistemology

Of the numerous interesting logical developments arising from the work of Boethius of Dacia, we shall mention only some that have a strong impact on his conception of science and metaphysics. Both in his sophism *Omnis homo de necessitate est animal* and in his commentary on Aristotle's *Topics* (*Opera*, 1976a, p. 117ff) Boethius emphasizes that it is impossible to formulate true propositions about nonexistent objects. Pinborg and Ebessen (ibid., p. xxxvii) have shown the relationship of this principle with Boethius' general conception of science and its impact on both the discussion concerning the eternity of the world and the degree of necessity of physical laws. Their interpretation can be summarized as follows: the relationship between cause and effect is necessary, provided that the cause exists and is not prevented from acting by other causes; the world has been created by a free act of the divine will that science can neither explain nor state as having been posited (as existing) necessarily; consequently scientific propositions and laws concerning the world do not possess strict necessity because they refer to a state of affairs that does not exist necessarily. This leads them to conclude that "Boethius of Dacia is ahead of time on some fundamental nominalist theories" (ibid., p. xxxviii).

One of Boethius' basic epistemological principles is that a specialist in any given science can "demonstrate, concede, or deny something only in terms of the principles of that science" (Wippel 1987, p. 11). This leads to a "topography" of sciences (Piché 1999, p. 193), which assigns to each science a well-defined sphere of epistemological competence and validity restricted to what is rationally demonstrable from its principles. A particular science has nothing to say about things that fall beyond its sphere of epistemological competence; *however*, it "should deny any truth which it can neither establish nor know from its principles if it is contrary to its principles and destroys the science" (1976b, *De aet.*, p. 51; see also Putallaz and Imbach 1999, pp. 95–8). Boethius is a strong defender of the autonomy of philosophy and undertook the project of "saving" (*salvare*) the validity of what the philosophers have concluded in the light of their principles, especially when they contradict the truths of Christian revelation. Historians agree today that neither Boethius nor Siger, or for that matter any of the so-called radical Aristotelians, ever defended the absurdity of a "double truth," as Bishop Tempier accused them of doing. To clarify this point, as well as Boethius' conception of the relationship between sciences and faith, it is necessary to examine his position concerning the eternity of the world (developed in his treatise *De aeternitate mundi*) and his doctrine on human happiness (presented in his *De summo bono*). Literal quotations are taken from Wippel's translation of these works.

The eternity of the world

The doctrine concerning spheres of epistemological competence determines the methodological differences between the various sciences that examine this problem. The first sphere is that of physics or "natural" philosophy, as conceived historically by Aristotle. The principle from which it demonstrates its conclusions is nature. But nature (*physis*) produces only by way of generation, which presupposes matter already existing; in other words, physics presupposes being. The absolute positing of being (*creation*) falls beyond its sphere of knowledge. Within the perspective of generation it is impossible to postulate an absolute beginning of motion or that a first motion began to be insofar as by definition any motion is preceded by a prior one. From these principles, Aristotle concluded in book VIII of his *Physics* that the world is eternal. This proposition is valid only in reference to the principles of natural causality from which it has been inferred, i.e., its truth holds only *sub conditione*. However, since the world has been produced by the creative causality of the First Cause, which the natural philosopher is "unable to study," the same proposition should be considered "false when it is taken without qualification" (1976b, *De aet.*, p. 52), i.e., if it is taken absolutely (*absolute*) as valid beyond the scope of the natural principles from which it derives. The principles of mathematics (which includes astronomy) do not allow one to conclude that the world began to be either. But in metaphysics Boethius was a "creationist" (Van Steenberghen 1966, p. 408); the metaphysician can demonstrate by rational means the contingency of the world and consequently the existence of a First Cause of being, although he cannot demonstrate by rational means "that the world is not coeternal with the divine will" (1976b, *De aet.*, p. 54), nor can he demonstrate that the world is eternal (p. 55). Indeed, in order to do so, the metaphysician would need to penetrate the intention of the divine will and to assign such power to human reason would be not only a figment of the imagination, but also "akin to madness": "From whence does this reasoning come to man, by which he might perfectly investigate the divine will?" (ibid.). As in the case of Siger of

Brabant (1972, p. 7), the absolute transcendence of the divine will is the final limit of human knowledge.

Under these circumstances, what is the relationship between faith and reason? Given that the conclusions of a particular science are always relative to the principles from which they have been inferred (truth *secundum quid*), they might not coincide necessarily with absolute truth (truth *simpliciter*). We have seen that, in the case of physics, the philosopher, "taking into account only the powers of natural causes," concludes necessarily that the world is eternal, whereas Christian faith, "taking into account a cause which is higher than nature holds that the world could begin to be." For Boethius the two "do not contradict one another in any way," because the natural philosopher states his conclusion as valid only within a sphere determined by premises that restrict its scope. To see here a doctrine of "double truth" would require putting both conclusions at the same level and considering them true in the same respect, falling thus into a *fallacia secundum quid et simpliciter* (de Libera 1991, p. 371; cf. Aristotle, *De soph. elench.* XXV). Historians agree that Boethius did not propose a theory of double truth and that the Condemnation of 1277 misinterpreted his epistemology, which in fact is respectful of Christian faith (though questions remain with respect to the place and value that Boethius assigns to theology).

Human happiness

In his treatise *On the Supreme Good* (*De summo bono*), Boethius defines, in the spirit of Aristotle's *Nicomachean Ethics*, and in the light of natural reason, the supreme good capable of ensuring perfect human happiness. As a philosopher, his task is conceived as a purely rational inquiry (epistemological limit) concerning the good that is possible and proportionate to human nature (ontological limit). In principle his inquiry excludes, without denying it, the perspective of faith, which tends towards a perfect other-wordly happiness achieved with the help of divine grace (Piché 1999, p. 244). For Boethius, the supreme good of a human being "should be his in terms of his highest power" (1976b, *Summo bono*, p. 27), which is reason and intellect (speculative and practical). Man's supreme good and the "very essence of the good life or the happy life" (1987, p. 6) consists in "knowing the true, doing the good and taking delight in both" (1976b, *Summo bono*, p. 29). Contrary to what the Condemnation of 1277 seems to suggest, "radical" Aristotelians like Boethius were opposed to a life of sense pleasures and favored instead an intellectual eudaimonism centered on the pursuit of theoretical and practical wisdom. Quoting Aristotle, Boethius reminds us the intellect is "that which is divine in man. For if there is anything divine in man, it is right for it to be the intellect" (ibid., p. 28). According to Aristotle's *Metaphysics*, it is because the object known gives delight to the one who knows, that the first intellect (God) enjoys the most pleasurable life. By devoting his life to the knowledge of truth and the practice of good, and finding delight in doing so, human beings achieve the kind of happiness that is proportionate to their nature and get as close to God as possible in this life. This happy life is the greatest good "which man can receive from God and which God can give to man in this life"; and Boethius adds: "He who shares more perfectly in that happiness which reason tells us is possible for man in this life draws closer to that happiness which we expect in the life to come on the authority of faith" (ibid., p. 29). An epistemological parallelism can be established between *De aeternitate mundi* and *De summo bono* (de Libera 1997, p. 439). Philosophical ethics is concerned only with the good and the kind of happiness that humans can achieve as a result of their natural powers (which have been given to them by God in the act of creation); but it is not concerned with the highest kind of happiness (beatitude) that God could grant by grace and that humans could expect on the authority of faith. The equivalence between happiness and the practice of intellectual and moral virtues is an Aristotelian thesis; the idea of a progressive spiritualization of man through an ascetic intellectual life comes from ALFARABI, AVICENNA, and AVERROES (Bianchi 1990, p. 155). Against the Christian conception that a human being is unable to reach moral perfection in this life without the help of grace, owing to original sin, Boethius reaffirms the "pagan" idea that moral perfection can be achieved by the practice of intellectual and moral virtues (Piché 1999, pp. 249–50). This medieval version of Pelagianism was one of the reasons why Boethius was targeted in the Condemnation of 1277.

But that was not the only reason. Boethius stated not only the autonomy of philosophy in its own field, but also the superiority of the philosophical life over other kinds of lives. As intellectual happiness is proportional to the dignity of the object known, the philosopher enjoys the highest possible happiness, devoted as he is to contemplating the highest causes of the universe. The confluence of the highest activity (understanding – *finis quo*) and the highest object of contemplation (God – *finis cuius*) secures the superiority of the happiness enjoyed by philosophers, which in turn defines a new attitude in moral philosophy (Celano 1986, pp. 37–9). The contemplation of God leads to the love of God: "the philosopher, noting that all goods come to him from this first principle and are preserved for him insofar as they are preserved by this first principle, is moved to the greatest love for this first principle" (1976b, *Summo bono*, p. 35). That is why "the philosopher lives as man was born to live, and according to natural order" (ibid., p. 32), and, consequently, "has acquired the best and ultimate end of human life" (ibid., p. 35). By "hyper-valuing" (Piché 1999, p. 260) philosophy, Boethius gives the impression of favoring a "philosophical imperialism" (Wippel 1987, p. 8) to the detriment of other kinds of life (that of the saint, or the mystic, or the theologian), which might be considered higher by the religious believer. Indeed, as was the case in *De aeternitate mundi*, Boethius seems to leave no room for theology in *De summo bono*: the way to happiness in this life passes through philosophy; the way to happiness in the afterlife, through faith. However, Boethius' philosophical humanism is not exclusive and is required by his epistemology: it is contrary to the rational nature of philosophy to take into consideration principles that are beyond the scope of the discipline. Within this epistemological framework, his position is perfectly compatible with Christian beliefs (Van Steenberghen 1966, p. 404). As to his personal intentions, "they escape historical investigation" (Gilson 1954, p. 401).

Bibliography

Primary sources

Opera, in Corpus Philosophorum Danicorum Medii Aevi, Copenhagen: Det Danske Sprog, Og Litteraturselskab (GAD):

(1969), vol. IV-1, *Modi significandi sive Quaestiones super Priscianum Maiorem*, ed. J. Pinborg and H. Roos, adiuvante S. S. Jensen;

(1972), vol. V-1, *Quaestiones De generatione et corruptione*, ed. G. Sajo;

(1974), vol. V-2, *Quaestiones super libros Physicorum*, ed. G. Savo;

(1976a), vol. VI-1, *Quaestiones super librum Topicorum*, ed. N. G. Green-Pedersen and J. Pinborg;

(1976b), vol. VI-2, *De aeternitate mundi, De summo bono, De somnis*, ed. N. G. Green-Pedersen;

(1979), vol. VIII, *Quaestiones super IVm Meteorologicum*, ed. G. Fioravanti.

(1932), *De summo bono* and *De somniis*, ed. M. Grabmann, in "Die Opuscula de Summo Bono sive De vita Philosophie und De somniis des Boetius von Dacien," in *Archives d'Histoire Doctrinale et Littéraire du Moyen Âge* VI, pp. 287–317; 2nd edn. 1938, *Mittelalterliches Geistesleben* II, pp. 200–24.

(1962), "Das Sophisma des Boetius von Dacien 'Omnis homo de necessitate est animal' in doppelter Redaktion," ed. H. Roos, *Classica et Mediaevalia* 23, pp. 178–97.

(1963), "Ein unbekanntes Sophisma des Boetius de Dacia," ed. H. Roos, *Scholastik* 38, pp. 378–91.

(1964), *Tractatus de aeternitate mundi*, ed. G. Savo, Berlin: Quellen und Studien zur Geschichte der Philosophie IV.

(1987), *On the Supreme Good, On the Eternity of the World, On Dreams*, trans. J. Wippel, Toronto: Pontifical Institute of Mediaeval Studies.

Secondary sources

This list includes sources published after 1976. For earlier works, see the bibliography in *Opera* VI-2.

Bianchi, L. (1984), *L'errore di Aristotele. La polemica contro l'eternità del mondo nel XIII secolo*, Florence: La Nuova Italia Editrice.

——(1990), *Il vescovo e i filosofi. La condanna parigina del 1277 e l'evoluzione dell'aristotelismo scolastico*, Quodlibet 6, Ricerche e strumenti di filosofia medievale, Bergamo: Pierluigi Lubrina Editore.

Biffi, I. (1994), "Figure medievali della teologia: la teologia in Sigieri di Brabante e Boezio di Dacia," *Teologia* XIX, pp. 263–99.

Celano, A. J. (1986), "The 'finis hominis' in the thirteenth century commentaries on Aristotle's *Nicomachean Ethics*," *Archives d'Histoire Doctrinale et Littéraire du Moyen Âge* 53, pp. 23–53.

——(1987), "Boethius of Dacia: 'On the Highest Good'," *Traditio* 43, pp. 199–214.

Dales, R. C. (1982), "Maimonides and Boethius of Dacia on the eternity of the world," *The New Scholasticism* 56, pp. 306–19.

——(1984), "The origin of the doctrine of the double truth," *Viator* 15, pp. 169–79.

de Libera, A. (1991), *Penser au Moyen Âge*, Paris: Éditions du Seuil.

——(1997), "Faculté des arts ou faculté de philosophie? Sur l'idée de philosophie et l'idéal philosophique au XIIIe siècle," in O. Weijers and L. Holtz, eds., *L'Enseignement des disciplines à la faculté des Arts (Paris et Oxford, XIIIe–XIVe siècles*, Studia Artistarum IV, Turnhout: Brepols.

Gauthier, R.-A. (1984), "Notes sur Siger de Brabant (fin) II. Siger en 1272–1275," *Revue des Sciences philosophiques et théologiques* 68, pp. 3–50 (see pp. 18–20).

Ghisalberti, A. (1979), "Boezio di Dacia e l'averroismo latino," *Actas del V Congreso Internacional de Filosofía Medieval*, vol. II (pp. 765–73), Madrid: Editorial Nacional.

Gilson, É. (1954), *History of Christian Philosophy in the Middle Ages* (esp. pp. 399–402), New York: Random House.

Glorieux, P. (1971), *La Faculté des arts et ses maîtres au XIIIe siècle* (esp. pp. 112–15), Paris: Librairie Philosophique J. Vrin.

Hisette, R. (1972), "Boèce de Dacie et les questions sur la Physique du Clm 9559," *Recherches de Théologie Ancienne et Médiévale* 39, pp. 71–81.

——(1977), *Enquête sur les 219 articles condamnés à Paris le 7 mars 1277*, Philosophes médiévaux 22, Paris: Publications Universitaires; Louvain: Vander-Oyez.

Jensen, S. S. (1963), "On the national origin of the philosopher Boetius de Dacia," *Classica et Mediaevalia* 24, pp. 232–41.

Piché, D. (1999), *La Condamnation parisienne de 1277* (pp. 184–226, 243–85), (Coll. Sic et Non), Paris: Librairie Philosophique J. Vrin.

Putallaz, F.-X. and Imbach, R. (1999), *Profession philosophe: Siger de Brabant* (pp. 88–107, 123–8), Paris: Éditions du Cerf.

Siger of Brabant (1972), *Quaestiones in tertium De anima*, ed. B. Carlos Bazán, Louvain-la-Neuve: Publications Universitaires.

Van Steenberghen, F. (1936), "Boèce de Dacie," *Dictionnaire d'Histoire et de Géographie Ecclésiastiques*, vol. 9, col. 381–2.

——(1966), *La Philosophie au XIIIe siècle* (pp. 402–13), Philosophes médiévaux 9, Paris: Publications Universitaires; Louvain: Beatrice-Nauwelaerts.

——(1985), "Le débat du XIIIe siècle sur le passé de l'univers" (review of L. Bianchi, *L'Errore di Aristotele*), *Revue Philosophique de Louvain* 83, pp. 231–38.

Weijers, O. (1994), *Le Travail intellectuel à la faculté des arts de Paris: textes et maîtres (ca. 1200–1500)*, I: *Répertoire des noms commençant par A–B*, Studia Artistarum 1, Turnhout: Brepols.

Wippel, J. (1987), "Introduction," in *Boethius of Dacia: On the Supreme Good, On the Eternity of the World, On Dreams*, Toronto: Pontifical Institute of Mediaeval Studies.

232

24

Bonaventure

ANDREAS SPEER

Bonaventure (b. 1217; d. 1274) – like most of the greatest speculative thinkers during the Middle Ages such as ALBERTUS MAGNUS, THOMAS AQUINAS, or JOHN DUNS SCOTUS – thought of himself as a theologian. Can we speak therefore of Bonaventure's philosophy or is such an idea nothing more than a modern hermeneutical fancy? Étienne Gilson in characterizing Bonaventure's philosophy as one of the greatest syntheses of Christian thought, denies that this philosophy would appear to be philosophical at all, if one accepts the Aristotelian *Organon* as the sole criterion of truth with respect to philosophical questions (Gilson 1924, pp. 387, 396). But is this true?

When Bonaventure – who was born as Johannes Fidanza in Bagnoregio, a little town near Orvieto, and died at Lyon during the fourth session of the ecumenical council there – entered the university of Paris around 1235, the curriculum of the arts faculty was already modeled after the Aristotelian corpus. In this intellectual context, the question of the status of philosophy became crucial especially *vis-à-vis* the attempt to establish theology as a science following the Aristotelian model of a scientific discipline. More precisely, the Aristotelian concept of wisdom taken as the highest science, which deals with the first causes and the first principles, prompts the question of whether science can be called wisdom in the proper sense: first philosophy, i.e., metaphysics or the kind of theology based on revelation, which is therefore directive of other sciences. If one does not want to follow in this context the Augustinian model of Christian wisdom (*doctrina christiana*), then the question of the foundation of knowledge is at the very center of every attempt to establish philosophy as an autonomous discipline.

This was exactly the way in which Bonaventure, later the seventh general minister of the Franciscan order, presents the question of the contribution of philosophy to the foundation of knowledge in one of his early university treatises from Paris around 1254. In the beginning of his *Disputed Questions on the Mystery of the Trinity* he points out the conditions, in addition to the possession of divine grace, necessary for the study of the Trinity. A first condition is what Bonaventure calls the "foundation of certain knowledge." A second is the "foundation of knowledge by faith" (*Mys. Trin.*, prol., *Opera* V, 45ab). In introducing these conditions, Bonaventure raises the question concerning what these foundations are and how they can be examined. This twofold distinction concerning the foundation of knowledge evokes the distinction between philosophical knowledge that deals with a knowledge of the truth that can be characterized as "certain knowing," and theological knowledge, which provides a knowledge of truth that is worthy of belief by "pious knowing" (*Don. Spir.* IV, 5, *Opera* V, 474b). Bonaventure defines philosophy's role very clearly and it follows from his ideas about certainty. Philosophy undertakes no less than to disclose the foundation of all knowledge. Since theology requires a firm foundation for certainty, it follows that theology needs philosophical analysis (*Mys. Trin.* I, 1, *Opera* V, 45a).

This opening of a disputed question, which treats an issue at the very heart of Christian theology, could be taken as a first clarification of the question of the status of philosophy. Bonaventure is looking for the proper feature of the philosophical approach to reality that remains unquestioned from within a theological framework and does not serve merely as a part of a Christian pedagogy leading to true wisdom. This first sketch of Bonaventure might be surprising if one takes the standard view of Bonaventure as a major figure of so-called Augustinianism and even more as an anti-Aristotelian (see Speer 1997, pp. 25–9). While 'anti-Aristotelian' lacks any differentiation and must be generally judged as incorrect, 'Augustinianism' needs further clarification. What is the connection of illumination – one of the main doctrines commonly ascribed to Augustinianism – and certitude in founding knowledge, if one understands illumination not only as a theological doctrine but also as posing an epistemological problem – one that in the thirteenth century was seriously rethought and reformulated *vis-à-vis* the Aristotelian epistemology?

Pivotal for the question of certainty in knowledge is the fourth question of his *Disputed Questions on the Knowledge of Christ*, which he undertook shortly after inception as an ordinary master at Paris in the beginning of 1254: "Is what is known by us with certainty known in the eternal Ideas themselves?" Bonaventure distinguishes the two conditions for all certain knowledge: an infallibility on the part of the subject and an immutability on the part of the object (*Sc. Chr.*, q. 4c, *Opera* V, 23b). The question operative here is this: How can one know with certainty what something is? Bonaventure's answer follows Aristotle: by knowing it completely, that is, under the conditions that cover both the object known and the subject (*Chr. mag.* 6, *Opera* V, 568b–569a). But how can this requirement be met? In what follows I discuss three approaches to this problem, which concern the understanding of: (a) the eternal reason or standard (*ratio aeterna*), (b) illumination (*illuminatio*), and (c) analysis (*reductio*).

(a)   A first approach concerns how the *ratio aeterna* must be conceived. At the beginning of his response in his fourth *Disputed Question on the Knowledge of Christ*, Bonaventure discusses two positions, both of which he considers inadequate and erroneous. It is not the case that certain knowledge can exist only in the intelligible world of eternal prototypes, nor can one speak merely of the "influence" of the eternal standard (*ratio aeterna*) on human knowing. The *ratio aeterna* serves as a kind of eternal standard, without it being the case, however, that it can ever be attained in its fullest sense (*Sc. Chr.*, q. 4c, *Opera* V, 22b–23a). But created truth (*veritas creata*) is not merely unchangeable, it is unchangeable as a consequence of a foundational condition. Bonaventure thus seeks a third way between the two rejected positions: "In order to achieve with necessity a knowledge that lays claim to certainty, one seeks an eternal standard for guidance and direction, not [for use] by itself and in its perfect clarity, but together with a created standard, and in such a way that it is to some degree glimpsed by us even in our state of imperfection" (ibid., 23b). This eternal standard is the *ars aeterna*, the eternal creative art, in which things are considered according to their conceptual and specific mode of existence, that is, insofar as each constitutes a trace, an image or a similitude (ibid., 24a).

From this point of view, Bonaventure must reject the extreme positions cited in the beginning, for they ultimately lead to skeptical problems and the conclusion that "one can know absolutely nothing" (ibid., 23a). Beyond the a priori moment, an a posteriori moment or –

following the terminology of the *Posterior Analytics* – an inductive moment is indispensable for the attainment of knowledge. In order to know, the intellect must not only turn itself toward the eternal standards (*rationes aeternae*), but it must also proceed by using essences abstracted from experience (ibid., 24b). In this context the divine ideas are not the direct object of human knowledge, nor something we can perceive, but rather that through whose influence we attain certainty. The ideas, which serve as the "standard of knowledge" (*ratio cognoscendi*) insofar as they can be grasped at all by the human intellect, can only be grasped by it reflexively. As formal principles of knowing, they first guarantee certainty on the part of both the objects and the subjects of knowledge, but the specifying properties and the material principles require experience (ibid., 23b–24a; *I Sent.*, d. 35, a. 1, q. 3c, *Opera* I, 608a).

(b)   A second approach leads to the doctrine of illumination, which allows Bonaventure to develop an epistemology rooted in exemplarism and the theory of ideas. In order to illustrate this, Bonaventure takes over from AUGUSTINE the example of the godless person who can think of a concept like eternity and judge rightly regarding rules of practical living because the cause of the pagan's knowledge lies within rules "that are written down in the book of that light which is called Truth" (*Sc. Chr.*, q. 4c, *Opera* V, 23b). These rules are obviously in force quite independently of mistakes on the part of the knower. Illumination thus stresses the non-empirical origin of judgments. Not all human knowledge has its origin in experience or can all be taken as the outcome of a process of abstraction. Although Bonaventure stipulates that for the possession of perfect knowledge there is a need to trace things back "to an altogether unchangeable and fixed truth as well as to an altogether infallible light" (ibid., 23b), the influence of the light can nevertheless not be seen as having a general application. This divine light is not a cause of wealth, Bonaventure maintains, in the same way that it is a cause of knowledge. At the same time, the light of illumination should not be seen exclusively as exceptional or special, as if all knowledge were infused and no knowledge were acquired or innate (ibid., 23ab). The epistemological problem in the theory of illumination thus becomes especially pronounced when focused on the individual subject. Bonaventure elaborates on the problem of the cooperation of the infallible light of truth by distinguishing carefully between a created standard (*ratio creata*) and an eternal standard (*ratio aeterna*), between the light of the creature (*lux creaturae*) and the infallible light (*lux infallibilis*), or between created wisdom (*sapientia creata*) and uncreated wisdom (*sapientia increata*).

For the latter question, treated in the fifth disputed question on the knowledge of Christ, the point of departure is again the question of the certainty of knowledge, which is crucial for Bonaventure's thought. In a first step he distinguishes certain knowledge (*cognitio certitudinalis*) from sapiential knowledge (*cognitio sapientialis*). The distinction follows the manner of the influence and presence of the supreme light of truth on knowledge that lays claim to certainty. A merely general influence, without the immediate presence of that light, is as obviously insufficient as its mere presence without the possibility of an immediate influence (*Sc. Chr.*, q. 5c, *Opera* V, 29b). But if we know with certainty only when we comprehend all the conditions of knowledge and possess wisdom, how can the created soul come to any certain knowledge without supposing that such knowledge is attained exclusively in the state of perfection? Human knowledge, striving after certainty, must therefore have the ability to extend to that uncreated fountainlike wisdom (*sapientia fontalis*), which itself can be reached only by a godlike and, because of that, an uplifted and suitable intellect. But therefore this "forming, enabling, and uplifting principle" must in a way be proportionate and inherent. The manner in which the created intellect can participate in the uncreated wisdom in this life (*in statu viae*) is created wisdom (*sapientia creata*) (ibid., 29b).

(c) The key-word of our third approach, *reductio* (which I will translate by 'analysis') must not be understood in a purely technical or formal sense. Moreover, in Bonaventure's concept of metaphysics, analysis (*reductio*) is in a certain respect the complement of illumination (*illuminatio*). One way to be moved intellectually is to be moved by what Bonaventure calls "spiritual radiation"; its complement is to be "reduced or led back to the highest" (*Hex*. I, 17, *Opera* V, 332b). Again, one recognizes Bonaventure's epistemological approach, his analysis of the concepts and of understanding in order to disclose the metaphysical constitution of beings. In the first book of his *Commentary on the Sentences*, Bonaventure distinguishes the receiving intellect (*intellectus apprehendens*) from the analyzing intellect (*intellectus resolvens*).

The intellect does not proceed by simply accumulating data, adding one item of information to another. Instead, it regards the essence of beings, which is to say, it understands effects together with their underlying causes. Thus, the intellect no longer perceives a single thing but, rather, understands how beings are interconnected and related to their common goal (*I Sent.*, d. 28, dub. 1, *Opera* I, 504a). With reference to a full and certain understanding of a single being, *reductio* means that we must understand this not only in itself (*in se*), nor as it is in the mind (*in anima*), but also and especially insofar it is in the eternal standard (*in arte aeterna*), also known as the eternal creative art (*Sc. Chr.*, q. 4c, *Opera* V, 23b–24a). Therefore, true analysis leads not only to a "common" goal but to the "first" one. If the analysis of the intellect actually proceeds to its very end, then perceiving being as the first common concept and its general transcendental modes, the "conditions of being" (*conditiones entis*) cannot conclude the analysis. The reason is that this analysis only leads as a first step (related to the nature of a vestige) to a particular being – the extramental being of the things *extra nos* – which is mixed with potentiality and therefore limited, or as a second step (related to the nature of an image) to an analogous being – the intramental being *intra nos* – "that has the least of act because it least exists." Such analysis would only be incomplete (*semiplene*). "It remains, therefore," Bonaventure concludes, "that the being which we are considering is the divine being" (*Itin.* V, 3, *Opera* V, 308b–309a). The divine being – the being in its real firstness and purity which is absolutely certain and cannot be thought not to be – is the first known (*primum cognitum*), and serves as an a priori condition of human understanding (ibid., 308b; *Hex*. X, 6, *Opera* V, 378a).

In the third chapter of his treatise *The Journey of the Mind to God*, Bonaventure gives a further argument concerning the full analysis (*resolutio plena*). The point of departure is again the understanding of being. Since being can be understood as diminished or as complete, as imperfect or as perfect, as in potency or in act, etc., and since "privations and defects can in no way be known except through something positive," he continues, referring to AVERROES,

> therefore our intellect does not make a full and ultimate analysis of any single created being unless it is aided by a knowledge of the most pure, most actual, most complete and absolute being, which is being unqualified and eternal, and in whom are the essences of all things in their purity. For how could the intellect know that a specific being is defective and incomplete if it had no knowledge of the Being that is free from all defect? (*Itin.* III, 3, *Opera* V, 304a)

The full and complete understanding of the fully analyzing intellect (*intellectus plene resolvens*) includes not only knowledge of an eternal being as the end of the resolving intellect, i.e., a being that possesses the reasons (*rationes*) of all beings in its purity, but also the awareness that nothing can be known without referring to the divine being as the first known, i.e., without grasping the necessary causal relation expressed by truth and goodness (*II Sent.*, d. 1, p. 2, dub. 2, *Opera* II, 52a; see Speer 1999, pp. 115ff and 122).

The epistemological foundation of knowledge is closely related to Bonaventure's understanding of metaphysics and vice versa. He gives a definition of what a true metaphysics must be about in the first collation of his *Collations on the Six Days*. This was a series of public sermons delivered in Paris in April and May of 1273, which reflect the condemnation of December 10, 1270 (Van Steenberghen 1991, pp. 411–21), before he became Cardinal Bishop of Albano. With the phrase "this is our entire metaphysics" (*haec est tota nostra metaphysica*), he introduces a neat list of topics delineating the proper field of study. The topics included are: emanation (*emanatio*), exemplarity (*exemplaritas*), and consummation (*consummatio*), by which he means being "illuminated by the spiritual radiation and reduced to the highest" (*Hex.* I, 17, *Opera* V, 332b). This, taken together with the first elaboration of the systematic problems inherent in the doctrine of illumination pointed out at the beginning, is a classic expression of an exemplaristic metaphysics. Exemplarism means, as we can read in ROBERT GROSSETESTE'S *On Truth* (*De veritate*), a twofold reading of reality, a twofold knowing of things: one, knowing of things in themselves (*in se*); the other, knowing them in their exemplarity and likeness (*in exemplari vel similitudine*). Because the exemplar's essence has greater clarity, all being is understood in a more noble, clear, and lucid manner when it is understood in its exemplarity and likeness (in Baur 1912, p. 142, 9–12).

Bonaventure draws several consequences from his metaphysical principles, some of which we have already discussed. They may be summarized in four points: In particular he claims (1) that the existence of truth can never be denied because without truth, nothing can be considered or understood (*Hex.* I, 13, *Opera* V, 331b); (2) to know something, in the strict sense of the term, is to understand it with certainty (for Bonaventure, this means to understand it by means of, or in relationship to, an immutable truth) (ibid.); (3) he argues for a metaphysical parallelism, i.e., the intelligibility of things corresponds to their ontological structure, and vice versa (ibid.); and finally (4), as we have already seen, the mind's first concept is the divine being (*esse divinum*), insofar as the divine being serves as an a priori condition for the entire possibility of knowing (*Hex.* X, 6, *Opera* V, 378a). We might call these basic teachings, following Romano Guardini, "system-constituting" elements of Bonaventure's thought (Guardini 1964). Each of them is important for an accurate reconstruction of his thought.

Although exemplarism in the Augustinian tradition is deeply related to theology, one should note that for Bonaventure the starting point in the epistemological order is not theological. Moreover, the need for a second reading of reality follows on the one hand from the necessity of an immutable and incorruptible foundation of knowledge, if knowledge is to attain certainty, and on the other hand from the insight into the limitation and mutability of our knowledge when the object known is corruptible and the knowing subject is fallible. This twofold approach to the question of the certainty of knowledge gives Bonaventure's exemplarism its specific shape. The leading question is: how can one understand something with certainty, and how can there be a true demonstration that brings forth knowledge, i.e., knowledge of a singular object? The ideas in Bonaventure are principles of knowing, not the objects known; they cannot be grasped by us without an inductive element of experience and sense-perception, and then only reflexively. So, the way in which Bonaventure makes the question of certainty in knowledge the point of departure in their epistemological analyses, brings Aristotle and Augustine together. There is obviously an intrinsic philosophical interest in the foundation of knowledge that needs further clarification with respect to the understanding of the singular as well as the attainment of the principles.

I am stressing this philosophical interest because for Bonaventure the question of the foundation of knowledge is mainly related to natural reason and natural cognition (*naturalis cognitio*). This is even true for the question of illumination, which encompasses not only knowledge of principles but also of the archetypal world. Without knowing the scope of natural reason, one cannot accurately speak about grace (see *Sc. Chr.*, q. 4c, *Opera* V, 23ab). For Bonaventure, this question becomes pivotal. He, in this way, reflects the intellectual atmosphere of the thirteenth century. Around the middle of this century, this atmosphere became increasingly dominated by the debate concerning the relation of philosophy and theology *vis-à-vis* their understanding of true wisdom.

For Bonaventure, philosophy is associated with the light of natural reason (*lumen naturale*). In the fourth collation of *On the Six Days* – the one bearing on the first vision of the natural light – he gives a division of philosophy based on the three primary rays of the light of the first and highest truth, a truth that can neither be denied nor viewed as nonexistent (*Hex.* IV, 1–2, *Opera* V, 357b). This model of the three-fold truth – the truth of beings (*veritas rerum*), moral truth (*veritas morum*), and the truth of language (*veritas vocum*) – covers the traditional divisions of philosophy and serves as a model for the scope of philosophical knowledge founded on reason and acquired wisdom (*Hex.* IV, 2–3, *Opera* V, 349ab; Speer 1997, pp. 44ff). But in his *On the Six Days* the determination of the extent of philosophical knowledge points to a fundamental epistemological critique. This critique holds especially for the knowledge that is founded on reason alone, but also for the possibility of a perfect comprehension of the highest truth on the basis of an acquired and, therefore, created wisdom. "Philosophers offered these nine sciences and gave examples of them," so Bonaventure concludes, and they promised a tenth (*Hex.* V, 22, *Opera* V, 357b; *Hex.* IV, 1, *Opera* V, 349a). "They sought to reach wisdom, and truth was leading them: and they promised to give wisdom, that is, beatitude, that is, an intellect in possession of its goal" (*Hex.* V, 22, *Opera* V, 357b). But "passing from knowledge to wisdom is not assured" (*Hex.* XIX, 3, *Opera* V, 420b). Thus, it is philosophy's incompetence to direct man towards his final goal, i.e., towards happiness, that defines its limitation. This practical limit has a theoretical implication, which concerns the only undeniable place for philosophy, if one refers to the beginning of the *Disputed Questions on the Mystery of the Trinity*: the disclosing of the foundation of all knowledge (*Mys. Trin.* I, 1, *Opera* V, 45a).

The philosophical and metaphysical criticism, which becomes evident in the late Parisian sermons or collations (*Collationes*) *On the Ten Commandments* (1267), *On the Seven Gifts of the Holy Spirit* (1268), and in particular *On the Six Days* (1273), articulates nothing but philosophy's limitation in uncovering the foundation of the certainty of knowledge. Philosophy is the way to other knowledge, not the goal; "whoever comes to stay there, falls into darkness" (*Don. Spir.* IV, 12, *Opera* V, 476a). In Bonaventure, the critical attitude of the Augustinian epistemology with respect to natural human understanding fully comes to light. Knowing the whole goes hand in hand with the claim for certainty. In between, there is the place for the natural cognition in its entire finiteness. Others – for example Grosseteste, especially in his *Commentary on the Posterior Analytics* – give some place for the limited project of the weak intellect (*intellectus debilis*) which is closely related to the Aristotelian project. But Bonaventure, one generation later, points out the limits of this project. His epistemological criticism leads to a fundamental critique of metaphysics. More precisely, it gives rise to a critique of a metaphysics of the Aristotelian type from the point of view of an exemplaristic metaphysics, which goes hand in hand with the renewed concept of a Christian wisdom, a *sapientia christiana* (see *Hex*. I, 9–10, *Opera* V, 330b; Speer 2001, pp. 253–60, 273–5).

Bibliography

Primary Sources

The works of Bonaventure are quoted from the Quaracchi edition of 1882–1902: *Bonaventurae doctoris seraphici Opera omnia*, 10 vols. (and Index), Quaracchi: Collegium S. Bonaventurae.

(*Chr. mag.*) *Sermo IV: Christus unus omnium est magister* (*Opera* V, 567–574)

(*Don. Spir.*) *De septem donis Spiritus sancti* (*Opera* V, 457–503)

(*Itin.*) *Itinerarium mentis in Deum* (*Opera* V, 296–313)

(*Hex.*) *Collationes in Hexaemeron* (*Opera* V, 329–449)

(*Mys. Trin.*) *Quaestiones disputatae de mysterio Trinitatis* (*Opera* V, 45–115)

(*Sc. Chr.*) *Quaestiones disputatae de scientia Christi* (*Opera* V, 3–43)

(*I–IV Sent.*) *Commentarii in quatuor libros Sententiarum* (*Opera* I–IV)

English translations

(1960–70), *The Works of Bonaventure*, 5 vols., trans. J. de Vinck, Paterson, NJ: St. Anthony's Press.

Works of Saint Bonaventure, published by the Franciscan Institute, St. Bonaventure, NY:

(1956) II. *Itinerarium mentis in Deum*, ed. P. Boehner (repr. 1990).

(1976) III. *Disputed Questions on the Mystery of the Trinity*, ed. Z. Hayes.

(1992) IV. *Disputed Questions on the Knowledge of Christ*, ed. Z. Hayes.

(1995) VI. *Collations on the Ten Commandments*, ed. P. J. Spaeth.

(1993) *The Journey of the Mind to God*, trans. P. Boehner, ed. with introd. and notes by S. F. Brown, Indianapolis: Hackett.

Secondary sources

Baur, L. (1912), "Die philosophischen Werke des Robert Grosseteste, Bischof von Lincoln," *Beiträge zur Geschichte der Philosophie des Mittelalters* 9, Münster: Aschendorff.

Bérubé, C. (1976), *De la philosophie à la sagesse chez Bonaventure et Roger Bacon*, Bibliotheca Seraphico-Capucina 26, Rome: Istituto storico dei Cappuccini.

Bougerol, J. G., ed. (1973), *S. Bonaventura 1274–1974, Volumen commemorativum anni septies centenarii a morte S. Bonaventurae Doctoris Seraphici*, 5 vols., Grottaferrata: Collegium S. Bonaventurae.

Bougerol, J. G. (1988), *Introduction à Saint Bonaventure*, Paris: J. Vrin.

Emery Jr., K. (1983), "Reading the world rightly and squarely: Bonaventure's doctrine of the cardinal virtues," *Traditio* 39, pp. 183–218.

Gilson, É. (1924), *La philosophie de saint Bonaventure*, Études de philosophie médiévale 4, Paris: J. Vrin, English trans. 1965: *The Christian Philosophy of St. Bonaventure*, trans. by Dom I. Trethowan and F. J. Sheed, Paterson, NJ: St. Anthony's Press.

Guardini, R. (1964), *Systembildende Elemente in der Theologie Bonaventuras. Die Lehre vom Lumen mentis, von der Gradatio entium und der Influentia sensus et motus*, ed. W. Dettloff, Studia et documenta franciscana 3, Leiden: Brill.

Marrone, Steven P. (2001), *The Light of Thy Covenant: Science and Knowledge of God in the Thirteenth Century*, 2 vols., Leiden: Brill.

Speer, A. (1997), "Bonaventure and the question of a medieval philosophy," *Medieval Philosophy and Theology* 6/1, pp. 25–46.

——(1999), "*Principalissimum fundamentum*. Die Stellung des Guten und das Metaphysikverständnis Bonaventuras," in W. Goris, ed., *Die Metaphysik und das Gute. Aufsätze zu ihrem Verhältnis in Antike und Mittelalter* (pp. 105–38), Leuven: Peeters.

——(2001), "*Sapientia nostra*. Zum Verhältnis von philosophischer und theologischer Weisheit in den

Pariser Debatten am Ende des 13. Jahrhunderts," in J. A. Aertsen, K. Emery, Jr., and A. Speer, eds., *Nach der Verurteilung von 1277. Philosophie und Theologie an der Universität von Paris im letzten Viertel des 13. Jahrhunderts. Studien und Texte*, Miscellanea mediaevalia 28 (pp. 248–75), Berlin and New York: De Gruyter.

Van Steenberghen, F. (1991), *La Philosophie au 13ème siècle*, 2nd edn. (esp. pp. 177–244, 385–7), Philosophes médiévaux 28, Louvain and Paris: Peeters.

25

Dante Alighieri

TIMOTHY B. NOONE

Dante Alighieri (b. 1265; d. 1321) was born in Florence to a family associated with the "white" party of the Guelphs which became politically ascendant during the 1290s in Florence. He was, in all probablity, a notary by profession. After the death in 1290 of the woman he loved best, Beatrice, Dante found consolation in little else except philosophy, a subject he studied avidly by attending the disputations between 1291 and 1294 at the religious houses, the Dominican and Franciscan *studia generalia* in Florence. Yet by 1302 Dante's life was changed forever; he was sentenced to lifelong exile along with many other prominent members of the "white" party when the "black" party re-established themselves as the leaders of Florence.

Though he spent the remainder of his life in a variety of cities on the Italian peninsula, the exile of Dante (1302–21) was the period of his greatest literary activity. During this time, he wrote his treatise on language, defending the legitimacy of the vernacular, *De vulgari eloquentia*; his work communicating much of scholastic learning to a lay readership in a work written in Italian, *Convivio*; his literary masterpiece regarding human destiny and love, the *Divina commedia*; and his chief political work, *De monarchia*.

The *Commedia*, apart from its fascinating depiction of the fate awaiting the damned (the *Inferno*), the imperfect (the *Purgatorio*) and the blessed (the *Paradiso*) in the afterlife, is a lengthy exploration of the theme of how all virtues and vices spring from love. The importance of this theme for interpreting the poem may be seen in the use of the latter to teach moral theology in later centuries.

De monarchia presents Dante's eventual monarchism, a position that he came to after his disillusionment with the Florentine republic. In a position reminiscent of that of SIGER OF BRABANT, Dante claims that there are really two ends for human beings: happiness and blessedness; the attainment of the former is up to the temporal rulers and the latter is available through revelation entrusted to the care of the Church. Dante argues that political troubles are ultimately rooted in a failure on the part of leaders of political communities to recognize the proper end of man in the temporal sphere, namely, happiness understood as the perfection of our natural intellectual capacities (*De monarchia* I 4–I 5), and to order human affairs so as to bring about the realization of this end. Related to such a failure are the efforts of rulers other than the universal monarch to increase their own power or resources at the expense of the well-being of the ruled, and efforts on the part of religious authorities to increase their temporal sphere of influence. The ideal monarch would have universal jurisdiction, thereby removing any temptation for increasing his kingdom and thereby, too, giving a final court of appeals to disagreements in lower jurisdictions.

Monarchy would, moreover, give human beings the fullest opportunity to have the highest degree of freedom (*De monarchia* I 9–12).

Bibliography

Primary sources

(1966–7), '*La commedia*' *secondo l'antica vulgata*, 4 vols., ed. G. Petrocchi, Milan: Mondadori.
(1995), *Convivio*, 2 vols., ed. Franca Brambilla Agneo, Florence: Casa Editrice Le Lettere.
(1998), *Monarchia*, ed. and trans. Richard Kay, Toronto: Pontifical Institute of Mediaeval Studies.

Secondary sources

Bemrose, Stephen (2000), *A New Life of Dante*, Exeter: University of Exeter Press.
Hollander, Robert (2001), *Dante: A Life in Works*, New Haven and London: Yale University Press.

26

Denys the Carthusian

KENT EMERY, JR.

Denys de Leeuwis (b. 1402/3; d.1472) was born in Rijkel in Limburg. At 18 or 19 he sought to enter the Carthusians but was refused because he was too young. The prior at Roermond sent him to the University of Cologne, where he matriculated in 1421 and was promoted to Master of Arts in 1424. At Cologne he studied in "the way of Thomas Aquinas" (*via Thomae*). After leaving the university he joined the Carthusians at Roermond. Evidently not all of his confreres approved his zeal for knowledge, for in the 1440s he was prohibited from writing for several years and in 1446 he was censured at the Carthusian General Chapter for unspecified abuses, probably related to his intellectual curiosity. Denys corresponded with Nicholas of Cusa and dedicated at least three writings to him; he may have traveled with the cardinal on his papal legation through the Low Countries in 1451–2 (but see Meuthen 1993).

Denys was probably the most encyclopedic reader and prolific writer of the Middle Ages. He wrote commentaries on every book of Scripture, on the *Sentences* of PETER LOMBARD, on BOETHIUS' *Consolation of Philosophy*, and on all of the writings of PSEUDO-DIONYSIUS. He also composed works based closely on the teaching of THOMAS AQUINAS, a *Summa* of vices and virtues, over 900 model sermons, and scores of philosophical, theological, pastoral, and ecclesiastical treatises. In his writings, he cites hundreds of authors, including many ancient, Jewish, and Arabic philosophers. His massive commentaries on the *Sentences*, wherein he recites and analyzes the arguments of numerous scholastic theologians, present a dialectical history of medieval thought; reflecting the common judgment of fifteenth-century follow-ers of the *via antiqua*, however, he dismisses the opinions of "nominalists," who, entangled in terms and concepts, never attain reality, and thus are "philosophers in name only."

Denys organized his thought according to a threefold order of wisdom (perhaps adapted from HENRY OF GHENT; see Emery 2000): "natural wisdom naturally acquired" or philoso-phy; "supernatural wisdom naturally acquired" or scholastic theology; "supernatural wisdom supernaturally bestowed" or mystical theology. The three modes of wisdom are iso-morphic; formally, each mode lays the foundation for the one above. The highest form of wisdom is mystical contemplation, which, by means of an intellectual intuition of the divine being, rises above ordinary ratiocination and is suspended immediately in the blinding "darkness" of divine light. Denys's intellectual interpretation of mystical theology ran counter to the affective interpretation popular in his day.

Denys embraced many of the teachings of Thomas Aquinas, but, influenced by the writ-ings of his "most-elect teacher," Pseudo-Dionysius, ALBERTUS MAGNUS and his followers, Henry of Ghent, Boethius, and Proclus, he disputed Thomas on several key philosophical issues. Denys held that the distinction between essence and existence in creatures is "intentional" not "real"; the soul cognizes first principles immediately by self-reflection; the mind need not refer to phantasms in every act of knowledge; the soul does not "naturally desire" the beatific vision, but, lacking supernatural illumination, desires (and can achieve) a natural, philosophic felicity, the cognition of separated substances; and the mind can attain certain knowledge of the existence of God through an examination of its own being and concepts (e.g., ANSELM). These doctrines establish a natural ground in the soul that is perfected by grace and glory.

Bibliography

Primary source

(1896–1935), *Opera omnia*, ed. Monks of the Carthusian Order, 42 vols. in 44, Montreuil, Tournai, and Parkminster: Typis Cartusiae S. M. de Pratis.

Secondary sources

Emery, Kent, Jr. (1990), "Did Denys the Carthusian also read Henricus Bate?," *Bulletin de Philosophie Médiévale* 32, pp. 196–206.

——(1991), *Dionysii Cartusiensis Opera selecta 1: (Prolegomena) Bibliotheca manuscripta 1A-1B: Studia bibliographica*, 2 vols., Corpus Christianorum continuatio mediaevalis 121–121a, Turnhout: Brepols.

——(1996), *Monastic, Scholastic and Mystical Theologies from the Later Middle Ages*, Variorum Collected Studies, Aldershot: Ashgate Publishing.

——(1998), "The matter and order of philosophy according to Denys the Carthusian," in J. A. Aertsen and A. Speer, eds., Miscellanea mediaevalia 26: *Was ist Philosophie im Mittelalter?* (pp. 667–79), Berlin and New York: De Gruyter.

——(2000), "A complete reception of the Latin *Corpus Dionysiacum*: the commentaries of Denys the Carthusian," in T. Boiadjiev, G. Kapriev, and A. Speer, eds., *Die Dionysius-Rezeption im Mittelalter: Internationales Kolloquium in Sofia vom 8. bis 11. April 1999* (pp. 197–247), Turnhout: Brepols.

——(2000), "The image of God deep in the mind: the continuity of human cognition according to Henry of Ghent," in J. A. Aertsen, K. Emery, Jr., and A. Speer, eds., *Nach der Verurteilung von 1277: Philosophie und Theologie an der Universität von Paris im letzten Viertel des 13. Jahrhunderts. Studien und Texte* (pp. 59–124, esp. 92–5), Berlin and New York: De Gruyter.

Macken, Raymond (1984), "Denys the Carthusian, commentator on Boethius's *De consolatione philosophiae*," Analecta Cartusiana 118 (pp. 1–70), Salzburg: Institut für Anglistik und Amerikanistik.

Meuthen, Erich (1993), "Nikolaus von Kues und Dionysius der Kartäuser," in Ludwig Hagemann and Reinhold Glei, eds., *EN KAI ΠΛΗΘΟΣ. Einheit und Vielheit: Festschrift für Karl Bormann zum 65. Geburtstag* (pp. 100–20), Würzburg and Altenburg: Echter.

Schmitz-Perrin, Rudolf (1995), "Denys le Chartreux – théologien de la divinisation de l'homme dans la tradition de la théologie latine: présentation de textes," in James Hogg, ed., *The Mystical Tradition and the Carthusians*, vol. 3 (pp. 97–116), Analecta Cartusiana 130, Salzburg: Institut für Anglistik und Amerikanistik.

Turner, Denys (1995), *The Darkness of God: Negativity in Christian Mysticism* (pp. 211–25), Cambridge: Cambridge University Press.

Wassermann, Dirk (1996), *Dionysius der Kartäuser: Einführung in Werk und Gedenkenwelt*, Analecta Cartusiana 133, Salzburg: Institut für Anglistik und Amerikanistik.

27

Dietrich of Freiberg

ROLAND J. TESKE

Dietrich of Freiberg (b. ca. 1250; d. ca. 1310), also known as Theodoricus Teutonicus de Vriberch, was born in Saxony, entered the Dominican order, and studied in Paris probably between 1272 and 1274. He held the post of lecturer at Trier in 1280 and 1281; he later returned to Paris where he lectured on the *Sentences* until 1293. He was prior of the Dominican convent at Würzburg and later Provincial of the Dominican Province of Germany. He became a master of theology in Paris in 1296 or 1297 and continued to teach in Paris until 1300.

Dietrich's writings, which took the form of treatises rather than of longer *Summae* or *Quaestiones*, reveal his diverse interests in theological, philosophical, and scientific issues. His theological writings include *The Beatific Vision* (*De visione beatifica*), *Christ's Body after Death* (*De corpore Christi mortuo*), *The Characteristics of Glorified Bodies* (*De dotibus corporum gloriosorum*), and *Spiritual Substances and the Bodies of the Future Resurrection* (*De substantiis spiritualibus et corporibus futurae resurrectionis*). His philosophical works include *Being and Essence* (*De ente et essentia*), *Quiddities* (*De quidditatibus*), *Accidents* (*De accidentibus*), *The Origin of Predicamental Realities* (*De origine rerum praedicamentalium*), and *The Intellect and the Intelligible* (*De intellectu et intelligibili*). The best-known of his scientific works are: *Light* (*De luce*), *Colors* (*De coloribus*), and *The Rainbow* (*De iride*).

In the opening lines of his treatise on the beatific vision Dietrich appeals to Denis the Areopagite (PSEUDO-DIONYSIUS), AUGUSTINE, Proclus, and Aristotle, managing to identify the Augustinian recess of the mind with the agent intellect of Aristotle. He holds that the agent intellect surpasses the possible intellect, is the highest element in our nature, and is that by which we immediately draw near to God in the beatific vision. For, as Proclus taught, there is a continuity between the highest element of the lower and the lowest of the next highest. The treatise then explores the relations of the agent intellect to God and of the agent intellect to the possible intellect and other beings; it shows that the beatific vision cannot be attained by the possible intellect but only by the agent intellect.

For Dietrich the concept of being is most fundamental; it is that which sets something apart from nothing. His treatise, *Being and Essence*, argues against THOMAS AQUINAS'S real distinction between existence and essence in creatures. According to Dietrich the existence of a thing expresses its essence, and the essence of the thing expresses its existence, each differing only in its mode of signifying. 'Being' denotes the essence of a determinate existing individual, while 'entity' denotes the same thing abstractly. In *Quiddities* Dietrich considers such non-existential terms as *quid* (what) and *quidditas* (quiddity), the former denoting the essential mode of a being that makes it a being of a certain kind, the latter the formality by which something is a what. According to Dietrich only composite beings have a quiddity; God and the intelligences have essences, but not quiddities. Dietrich presents a hierarchical view of the universe influenced by Proclean Neoplatonism with bodies at the bottom, then souls, thirdly, the intelligences, and finally, the One.

Bibliography

Primary sources

(1977–85), *Opera omnia*, 4 vols., ed. K. Flasch, Hamburg: Felix Miner.

(1992), *Treatise on the Intellect and the Intelligible*, trans. M. L. Führer, Milwaukee: Marquette University Press.

Secondary sources

Flasch, K., ed. (1987), *Von Meister Dietrich zu Meister Eckhart*, Hamburg: Meiner.

Kandler, K.-H. (1997), "Theologie und Philosophie nach Dietrich von Freibergs Traktat, 'De subiecto theologiae,'" in J. A. Aertsen and A. Speer, eds., *Was ist Philosophie im Mittelalter?* (pp. 642–7), Erfurt: Akademie Gemeinnütziger Wissenschaft zu Erfurt.

Maurer, A. (1956), "The *De quidditatibus entium* of Dietrich of Freiberg and its criticism of Thomistic metaphysics," *Mediaeval Studies* 18, pp. 173–203.

Wallace, W. A. (1959), *The Scientific Method of Theodoric of Freiberg*, Fribourg: Fribourg University Press.

28

Dominicus Gundissalinus

R. E. HOUSER

Dominicus Gundissalinus, i.e., Domingo (son of ?) González (fl. 1150–90), translator and philosopher, was a canon of Segovia who contributed to translations done in Toledo under Archbishop John (1152–66). Avendeuth, an "Israelite and philosopher" (who was perhaps Ibn Daud, a Jew, and who was not "Master John," a fellow translator) has indicated how the translation team worked:

> Pursuant to your command, Lord [John], to translate the book of the philosopher Avicenna *On the Soul*, I have taken pains to hand over our results, so that by your munificence and my labor the Latins may come to know what heretofore remained unknown, namely, that the soul exists, what it is, what its essence and effects are like, proven by completely true arguments. Thus you have the book (ourselves taking the lead and putting each word into the vulgar tongue, while Dominic the Archdeacon turned each into Latin) translated from Arabic.

The translations were extremely literal and not without problems, but they allowed perceptive readers such as ALBERTUS MAGNUS and THOMAS AQUINAS to grasp the thought of their authors with remarkable accuracy. The manuscripts also list Dominic as co-translator with "Master John" of *Fons vitae* by AVENCEBROL and *Summa theoricae philosophiae* by ALGAZALI, and as translator of *Metaphysica* by AVICENNA. He probably translated works by ALFARABI, ALKINDI, and ISAAC ISRAELI.

As an author, Dominic confined himself to philosophy. *De divisione philosophiae* renders the breadth of philosophy in the Arabic, Aristotelian tradition. *De unitate* connects the many senses of transcendental unity with the procession of creatures from God. *De processione mundi* details that procession, which is "like the flow (*exitus*) of water emanating from its source." *De anima* presents an Avicennian account of the soul, cunningly rearranged for Christians to "understand not just through faith but also through reason." Dominic stitched together quotations from Muslim philosophers much as his contemporary PETER LOMBARD did with Christian fathers.

Reversing noun and adjective in Gilson's memorable description, "Avicennizing Augustinianism (*augustinisme avicennisant*)," Jolivet has said that Dominic developed "a practically complete metaphysical system" which set the Christian fathers "like precious building-materials, into a *secular* edifice" (1998, p. 145). But Dominic used Islamic *materials* only because he recognized their intellectual superiority to Patristic ones; the *form* and *end* of his building, however, is Christian. This made his use of Muslim philosophy paradigmatic for thirteenth-century scholastics, even though they saw better than he that the resultant structure is theology, and no longer philosophy.

Bibliography

Primary sources

(1891), *De unitate*, ed. P. Correns, *Beiträge zur Geschichte der Philosophie des Mittelalters* 11, Münster: Aschendorff.

(1903), *De divisione philosophiae*, ed. L. Baur, *Beiträge zur Geschichte der Philosophie des Mittelalters* 4/2–3, Münster: Aschendorff.

(1925), *De processione mundi*, ed. G. Bülow, *Beiträge zur Geschichte der Philosophie des Mittelalters* 2/3, Münster: Aschendorff.

(1940), *De anima*, ed. J. T. Muckle, *Mediaeval Studies* 2, pp. 23–103.

Authenticity questioned

(1897), *De immortalitate animae*, ed. G. Bülow, *Beiträge zur Geschichte der Philosophie des Mittelalters* 24/3, Münster: Aschendorff.

(1954), *De scientiis*, ed. M. Alonso, Madrid.

Secondary sources

d'Alverny, M.-T. (1982), "Translations and translators," in R. Benson and G. Constable, eds., *Renaissance and Renewal in the Twelfth Century* (pp. 444–62), Cambridge, MA: Harvard University Press.

Fidora, A. (2000), "Dominicus Gundissalinus," in *Biographisch-Bibliographisches Kirchenlexikon*, vol. 17, Herzberg: Verlag Traugott Bautz. www.bautz.de/bbkl

Jolivet, J. (1998), "The Arabic inheritance," in P. Dronke, ed., *A History of Twelfth-Century Western Philosophy* (pp. 134–48), Cambridge: Cambridge University Press.

Riet, S. van. (1972), "La traduction latine du *De anima*," in *Avicenna Latinus: liber de anima seu sextus de naturalibus I-II-III* (pp. 91*–105*), Louvain: Peeters; Leiden: Brill.

29

Durand of St. Pourçain

RUSSELL L. FRIEDMAN

Durand of St. Pourçain (b. 1270/5; d. 1334) was a Dominican friar, and is best known for having been the focus of an extensive polemic by his order, which aimed at showing how Durand had misrepresented or misunderstood THOMAS AQUINAS. Durand had welded elements from diverse sources into an innovative synthesis that departed from Aquinas on such major issues as the Aristotelian categories, philosophical psychology and theory of knowledge, and individuation.

Durand's scholastic career began sometime between 1303 and 1308, when he wrote an extensive commentary on PETER LOMBARD'S *Sentences*, the standard medieval theological textbook. This commentary contained many positions that deviated significantly from those that Thomas Aquinas had taken. Since Aquinas at this time already enjoyed a privileged status as the doctor whose theological and philosophical positions Dominicans were to defend and adhere to, Durand's work drew a great deal of criticism from fellow Dominicans, especially from the future head of the order, HERVAEUS NATALIS. As a result of this, Durand wrote a second *Sentences* commentary (1310–12), in which he adhered more strictly to a Thomist line. Despite this, and despite his receiving the doctorate in theology from the University of Paris in 1312, the Dominican order launched two investigations into Durand's orthodoxy (in 1313–14 and 1316/17) and a number of the order's members wrote against Durand in the period 1312–30. Meanwhile, Durand, after having taught at the papal curia in Avignon (1313–17), was promoted to bishop, first of Limoux, then of Le Puy, and finally of Meaux. Durand's importance is indicated by the fact that he was one of those assigned by Pope John XXII to investigate the orthodoxy of WILLIAM OF OCKHAM in 1325–6. During this later period, Durand composed a third *Sentences* commentary (1317?–27) in which he returned to many of his original positions. This is the most important text for understanding Durand's thought. In addition, he produced three Quodlibets (1313–17), and a *Treatise on Habits* (ca. 1316–17), as well as several treatises of a more purely theological or political nature. Durand is significant not merely because he is a key figure for exploring the early development of Thomism in the Dominican order, but also because his innovative and provocative philosophy and theology had an impact well into the early modern period: witness the many (about fifteen) printings of his third *Sentences* commentary between 1508 and 1595 (for more historical information, see Schabel et al., forthcoming; for a full list of Durand's works, manuscripts, and editions, see Kaeppeli 1970–93, 1: pp. 339–50).

The category of relation

The central metaphysical problem in Durand's work is the nature of the category of relation (Koch 1927, p. 193). For Durand, the ten Aristotelian categories can be divided into three basic kinds, each having a way of existing (*modus essendi*) irreducibly distinct from the other two. These kinds are: (1) things that can stand on their own (substance); (2) accidents that are absolute (quantity and quality), i.e., which have some being of their own and normally depend for their existence on their inherence in (or "being in") a subject; and (3) accidents that have no being of their own and are merely a way in which their foundation exists, i.e., a pure *modus essendi*. Included in this third kind is the category of relation, as well as the six other relational categories (action, passion, place, time, situation, and manner of being).

According to Durand, then, a relation is an internal disposition of its foundation – whether that is substance or one of the absolute accidents – towards some other thing; since it is merely a way in which its foundation exists, a relation takes all of its being from its foundation. Thus, a father and a son have an internal disposition towards each other in virtue of the causal link between them; yet the relations by which father and son are related have no being of their own, since they are merely ways in which each of their foundations exist. In his theory of relations, Durand looks back to HENRY OF GHENT and JAMES of METZ, who also considered relation (and the other relational accidents) to be a pure *modus essendi* of its foundation, and Durand has turned his back on Aquinas, for whom a relation had its own being and inhered in its foundation. Despite the fact that a relation takes all its being from its foundation, Durand maintains that it is really (*realiter*) different from its foundation, e.g., Socrates' fatherhood is really different from Socrates himself. This is because Socrates and his fatherhood have two irreducibly distinct *modi essendi* – substance versus relation – and these *modi essendi* are by their very nature really different. Nevertheless, Durand denies that a relation enters into composition with its foundation, since the relation is merely an internal disposition towards some external object; in other words, a pure *modus essendi*, such as relation, does not inhere in its foundation, and composition only results from inherence. Hence, a relation and its foundation are really distinct – they are two really distinct modes – yet do not enter into composition with each other. Throughout his career, Durand insisted further that, in creatures, real relations require the real dependence of one foundation on the other; this limits real relations to causal ones. All other relations (similarity, equality, etc.) are merely conceptual, i.e., they require a conceiving mind for their establishment.

Durand's view that a relation and its foundation are really distinct, yet do not enter into composition with each other, was one of the most problematic of his early positions, and met with a great deal of criticism (for Durand's early texts, see Müller 1968, pp. 97–8). For medieval theologians, a theory of relations was necessarily involved with the doctrine of the divine Trinity, for, according to this doctrine, the three divine persons are distinct by virtue of the relations between them (the Father is distinct from the Son because they are related to each other by the relations of paternity and filiation). But Durand's claim that a relation and its foundation are really distinct was problematic because it appears to entail that the divine relations are really distinct from their foundation, the divine essence, and this would necessarily compromise divine simplicity. Heavy criticism led Durand to tone down his statement of his position in later works, where he maintained that a relation and its foundation are really distinct in a certain sense (*secundum quid*), but not absolutely speaking (1571, *I Sent.*, d. 30, q. 2, fos. 83vb–85rb; 1965, *Quodl. Aven.*, I, 1).

Philosophical psychology

Durand's doctrine of relation was closely tied to several of his distinctive ideas in philosophical psychology. For him, a concept (or mental word, *verbum mentis*) is simply the intellect's act of understanding, and he rejects the Thomistic theory that the act of understanding produces a separate entity, which is a concept. Other medieval philosophers (e.g. JOHN DUNS SCOTUS) held that a concept is an intellectual act; but for them this act is a quality with its own being inhering in the soul. In contrast, for Durand an act is merely a *modus essendi* of its foundation: it is a relational and not an absolute accident. Thus, according to him, the act of understanding has no being of its own, since it is merely a way that its foundation, the intellect, exists. It follows that the intellect does not gain anything, nor is it altered in any concrete way, by this act; the act of understanding has no being outside the being of its foundation, but merely marks that the intellect stands in a relation to some external object; *mutatis mutandis* this is also true for the senses and each of their acts. Indeed, Durand is quite explicit that one of the considerations which led him to adopt this position was that he thought it impossible for an external material object to add an absolute accident (like a quality) to the soul. Here Durand follows an Augustinian (and ultimately Platonic) notion that the soul cannot be affected by any material object, and further that the soul is fundamentally active. For Durand, then, the object of an act of sensing or understanding is a condition for our having these acts, but it is not their efficient cause, it is only a cause *sine qua non*; the efficient cause is the active cognitive power itself. No object actuates a cognitive power in the slightest, since cognitive powers are purely active and cognize by their very nature.

Both the influence of Durand's doctrine of relation on his noetic and its Augustinian roots are most clearly seen in Durand's first *Sentences* commentary (1929, pp. 18–25). Some important consequences resulting from these are, however, also found in his later works. Since Durand maintains that cognitive powers by their very nature cognize things, the complex apparatus that had been developed in the Aristotelian tradition to explain cognition is, on his view, superfluous (in this context, among others, Durand uses the principle of parsimony often called Ockham's razor: entities should not be multiplied without necessity). For Durand, a cognitive power needs nothing but the presence of the object in order for sense or intellectual cognition to take place. Thus, he denies that there is an agent intellect, an otherwise standard part of the basic Aristotelian theory of abstractive cognition. According to this theory, in order to have intellectual cognition, it is necessary to "abstract" an intelligible "species" – a spiritual representation – from the sensible species which emanate from all extra-mental material objects. This intelligible species is then impressed upon the possible (or potential) intellect, which in turn produces a concept. It is the agent (or active) intellect that abstracts the intelligible species from the very last material representation of the object (the phantasm). The agent intellect is thus something of a bridge between the sensible and the intellectual. Durand, on the other hand, claims that the agent intellect serves no purpose and hence denies its existence: there is only a possible intellect, which, by its very nature, enters into a relation with objects of cognition (and this relation is the intellectual act itself).

One of Durand's arguments for this position is based on the way he understood universality. A basic metaphysical principle for Durand is that everything that exists is singular, and he rejects the common thirteenth-century Aristotelian idea that the form of each and every singular thing is a universal of sorts, a "universal in the thing" (*universale in re*), which the agent intellect abstracts and presents to the possible intellect. Having rejected that there is anything at all universal in things, Durand sees no reason to retain an agent intellect to abstract it; universals are formed by the possible intellect considering the object without its determining sensible characteristics. Thus, for Durand, abstraction is not a metaphysical process of stripping away layers of material conditions to get at the universal beneath them; rather, it is a purely psychological process by which the intellect considers the object with fewer and fewer determining conditions (corresponding to more and more universal concepts). A corollary of this position is that the intellect knows first and foremost the singular, and only through this psychological process does it come to grasp the universal (1571, *I Sent.*, d. 3, pt. 2, q. 5, fos. 27ra–28rb; *II Sent.*, d. 3, q. 7, fos. 140rb–141ra).

Durand further denies any type of cognitive species – sensible or intelligible – that would serve to represent external objects to a cognitive power. Since he holds that the cognitive act is simply a relation of the intellect to the object, Durand rejects all mediation between object and sensory or intellective power. He argues further that only if we first had conscious awareness of these species could they facilitate our grasping extra-mental objects; since we do not, there is no reason to posit them (1571, *II Sent.*, d. 3, q. 6, fos. 139ra–140ra). Moreover, Durand rejects yet another element of medieval psychology: habits (or dispositions). These were a device used to explain how, upon repeated exercise of an intellectual or voluntary act, that act becomes easier; a habit is a subjectively existing psychological entity that, under certain conditions, brings a faculty more promptly from potency to act. Durand, however, as we have seen, holds that cognitive powers are by their very nature active, so that, when presented with an object, they act. Therefore, he maintains that habits are entirely superfluous: intellect and will simply act, and no further psychological entities are needed to explain this fact (1930, pp. 40ff).

Finally, Durand's ideas on philosophical psychology have an impact on his theory of truth. He defines truth in a typically medieval fashion as the conformity (or adequation) of the understanding to the thing understood. Other thinkers (including Aquinas) would maintain that this conformity held between the extra-mental thing and a subjective quality of the intellect having some minimal being of its own (whether an intellectual act or the product of an intellectual act). Durand, however, rejected that the intellectual act has any being of its own: it is a way that its foundation exists and it takes all of its being from that foundation. Thus for Durand, truth is the conformity of the extra-mental thing to that same thing as it is understood, i.e., as it is an *object* of the understanding; falsity is the lack of this conformity (1571, *I Sent.*, d. 19, qq. 5–6, fos. 65va–66vb).

Conceptualism, individuation, and intellectualism

Durand has often been called a forerunner of William of Ockham's conceptualism. He is indeed a conceptualist, if by this we mean someone who holds that universality is a conceptual phenomenon. All things that have real extra-mental existence are singulars. But, although Durand is a conceptualist in this sense, on at least one related issue he differs greatly from Ockham, and from Ockham's near contemporary and fellow conceptualist PETER AURIOL. For both Ockham and Auriol, as for Durand, only individuals exist in the extra-mental world. But, whereas Ockham and Auriol maintain that there is no principle of individuation – there is no reason that one individual is distinct from another, that is simply the way things are – Durand claims that there must be a ground whereby an individual is a distinct individual, and this ground is that through which the individual exists. On this basis, Durand isolates four principles that account for individuation, two principles intrinsic to the individual in question, two extrinsic. The two intrinsic principles are the form and matter of the individual; the two extrinsic principles are the end and the agent who produced the individual. Because, according to Durand, actions are produced by singulars and terminate in singulars, Durand gives a certain pride of place to the agent as principle of individuation (1571, *II Sent.*, d. 3, q. 2, fos. 136va–137rb; Henninger 1994).

Durand again parts company with Ockham and Auriol in his intellectualism. Like these two Franciscans, but unlike Aquinas, Durand thinks intellect and will are one and the same absolute thing, diverse only because this one thing is the source of two ordered acts, understanding and willing (1571, *I Sent.*, d. 3, pt. 2, q. 4, fos. 26ra–27ra). Nevertheless, contrary to Ockham and Auriol and more in agreement with Aquinas, Durand holds that primitive freedom of choice resides principally not in the will, but in the intellect. He argues that, with regard to their own acts, intellect and will are equally free, because they are both inclined to act by their very nature. Yet in terms of true freedom of choice – i.e., the power to choose between opposites – Durand claims that it is the final judgments of the intellect that determine what we elect to do and how we elect to do it: it is how we *understand* a situation that determines what we will to do (1571, *II Sent.*, d. 24, q. 3, fos. 171vb–172vb).

Bibliography

Primary sources

(1571), *Commentary on Peter Lombard's Sentences* (3rd version, ca. 1317–27), in *D. Durandi a Sancto Porciano in Petri Lombardi Sententias theologicas commentariorum libri IIII*, Venice; facsimile reprint 1964, Ridgewood, NJ: Gregg Press.

(1929), *Quaestio de natura cognitionis (II Sent. [A] d. 3, q. 5) et Disputatio cum anonymo quodam*, ed. J. Koch, Münster: Aschendorff. 2nd rev. edn. 1935.

(1930), *Quaestiones de habitibus*, ed. J. Koch, *Durandi de Sancto Porciano, O.P. Tractatus de habitibus, quaestio quarta (De subiectis habituum)*, Münster: Aschendorff.

(1965), *Quodlibeta*, ed. P. T. Stella, Zurich: Pas Verlag.

Secondary sources

Fumagalli, M. T. B.-B. (1969), *Durando di S. Porziano. Elementi filosofici della terza redazione del 'Commento alle Sentenze'*, Florence: La Nuova Italia.

Henninger, M. G. (1994), "Durand of Saint Pourçain (B. CA. 1270; D. 1334)," in J. J. E. Gracia, ed., *Individuation in Scholasticism: The Later Middle Ages and the Counter-Reformation, 1150–1650* (pp. 319–32), Albany: State University of New York Press.

Kaeppeli, T. (1970–93), *Scriptores Ordinis Praedicatorum medii aevi*, 4 vols., Rome: S. Sabina.

Koch, J. (1927), *Durandus de S. Porciano O.P. Forschungen zum Streit um Thomas von Aquin zu Beginn des 14. Jahrhunderts*, Münster: Aschendorff.

Müller, H. J. (1968), "Die Lehre vom verbum mentis in der spanischen Scholastik," Ph.D. dissertation, Westfälischen Wilhelms-Universität, Münster.

Schabel, C., Friedman, R. L., Balcoyiannopoulou, I. (forthcoming), "Peter of Palude and the Parisian reaction to Durand of St Pourçain on future contingents," *Archivum Fratrum Praedicatorum* 71.

30

Francis of Marchia

RUSSELL L. FRIEDMAN

Francis of Marchia (b. ca. 1290; d. after 1344), known in Latin as Franciscus de Marchia or Franciscus de Esculo, was a Franciscan theologian who lectured on the *Sentences* of PETER LOMBARD at the University of Paris in 1319–20. Between 1324 and 1328, he taught at the Franciscan convent in Avignon, but immediately thereafter, as a result of his opposition to Pope John XXII on the issue of absolute poverty, Francis (along with WILLIAM OF OCKHAM and several others) took refuge with Emperor Louis of Bavaria. After capture by ecclesiastical authorities Francis recanted, no later than December 1343. He has left us a literal *Physics* commentary, a short and a long *Metaphysics* commentary, a single Quodlibet, a treatise written against John XXII, as well as several versions of a monumental and rather popular *Sentences* commentary, which remains largely unedited (for more on Francis, his life and works, see Friedman and Schabel, forthcoming).

Francis's thought is little studied, but where it has been investigated, it is strikingly original. Thus, Francis proposed an innovative way of reconciling God's foreknowledge of future contingent events with human free will, which influenced, among many others, GREGORY OF RIMINI (Schabel 2000, esp. pp. 189–220, 264–74). Francis is best known, however, for several of his positions in natural philosophy, where he shows a clear willingness to question and to discard important elements of the Aristotelian worldview. Thus Francis denied that the celestial regions were composed of matter that is fundamentally different in nature from the matter composing the terrestrial regions; heavens and earth are composed of the same sort of matter and in principle obey the same laws of cause and effect. Francis also proposed that in "violent" motion (e.g. projectile motion), what keeps the object moving is a force left behind (*virtus derelicta*) in the moving thing by the motor. Thus, when someone throws a ball, the ball gains a temporary force that keeps it in motion after it has left the hand; as this force is exhausted, the ball gradually comes to a halt. This is a forerunner to the famous "impetus" theory of Francis's successors at the University of Paris, JOHN BURIDAN and NICOLE ORESME (Schneider 1991). Francis is also noteworthy for having been among the first to accept that an actual infinite is possible. While influenced by JOHN DUNS SCOTUS, Francis is more often than not critical of Scotus's philosophical positions, even fundamental ones like the formal distinction. In his investigations, Francis often takes as his point of departure a critical evaluation of the thought of his Franciscan predecessor at Paris, PETER AURIOL.

Bibliography

Primary sources

(1993), *Improbatio contra libellum Domini Johannis qui incipit 'Quia vir reprobus'*, ed. N. Mariani, Grottaferrata: Collegium S. Bonaventurae.

(1997), *Quodlibet cum quaestionibus selectis ex commentario in librum Sententiarum*, ed. N. Mariani, Grottaferrata: Collegium S. Bonaventurae.

(1998), *Sententia et compilatio super libros Physicorum Aristotelis*, ed. N. Mariani, Grottaferrata: Collegium S. Bonaventurae.

Secondary sources

Friedman, R. L. and Schabel, C. (forthcoming), "Francis of Marchia's commentaries on the *Sentences*: Question list and state of research," *Mediaeval Studies* 63.

Schabel, C. (2000), *Theology at Paris 1316–1345: Peter Auriol and the Problem of Divine Foreknowledge and Future Contingents*, Aldershot: Ashgate.

Schneider, N. (1991), *Die Kosmologie des Franciscus de Marchia: Texte, Quellen, und Untersuchungen zur Naturphilosophie des 14. Jahrhunderts*, Leiden: Brill.

31

Francis of Meyronnes

ROBERTO LAMBERTINI

The Franciscan theologian Francis of Meyronnes (b. ca. 1288; d. 1328) was born probably in a noble family of Provence with close connections to the house of Anjou. He lectured on the *Sentences* in Paris in 1320–1. In that academic year he was engaged in a famous controversy with Pierre Roger (the future Clement VI) about the Trinity. Shortly afterwards (on May 24, 1323), the Chancellor of the University of Paris conferred the mastership in theology upon him, as commanded by Pope John XXII, who in turn had acted upon the request of the king of Sicily, Robert of Anjou. As Provincial Minister of Provence for about five years, from 1323, Francis was active in Avignon as preacher and teacher; he also served as ambassador of the pope in Gascogne. He died in Piacenza.

He left an impressive corpus of writings, which are partly unedited. In his *Commentary on the Sentences* (handed down in more than one version, among which the most famous is his revision of the first Book, known as *Conflatus*) and other works Francis proves himself to be a rather independent follower of JOHN DUNS SCOTUS. For example, he rejects PETER AURIOL'S critique of Scotus's position concerning God's foreknowledge, but sometimes blends Scotist doctrines with the positions of previous authors, such as HENRY OF GHENT. Like the *Doctor subtilis*, he advocates the univocity of being and the doctrine of the formal distinction, developing a theory of *rationes formales*, which he defends against Pierre Roger's criticism of the use of the formal distinction in the Trinity.

He took a stance (most probably before 1323) on the debate about the absolute poverty of Christ, arguing in favor of absolute poverty in a hitherto unedited *quaestio*. This did not lead, however, to a conflict with John XXII, whom Francis strongly supported in the field of political theory. For example, his *Quaestio de subiectione* (probably before 1321) defends the superiority of the pope (*hierarcha summus*) over lay authorities, including the emperor; in his *Tractatus de principatu regni Siciliae* (after 1323), Francis maintains that the feudal subordination of the Kingdom of Sicily to the pope, far from being a sign of weakness, represents an ideal situation, because in this case political power is explicitly exercised under the high sovereignty of the pope. His much-debated *quaestio* devoted to universal monarchy (*Tractatus de principatu temporali*, ca. 1320–4), which some scholars have seen as an implicit answer to Dante's *Monarchia*, maintains that a *princeps monarcha* for the whole of mankind would be the best solution in theory, but in practice it encounters many difficulties because of the wickedness of many princes. At any rate, even this universal monarch should be subject to the pope. In the field of economic theory, Francis considers private property an institution of human positive law, a sort of "apposition" added to the natural law principle of communal use; moreover, although condemning usury for religious reasons, he rejects all the traditional natural-law arguments against it. In connection with his preaching activity, Francis also left a vast number of sermons.

Bibliography

Primary sources

(1961), *François de Meyronnes – Pierre Roger, Disputatio*, ed. J. Barbet, Paris: Librairie Philosophique J. Vrin.

(1994–7), "De notitia intuitiva," ed. G. Etzkorn, in "Franciscus de Mayronis: a newly discovered treatise on intuitive and abstractive cognition," *Franciscan Studies* 54, pp. 15–50.

Secondary sources

Cheneval, F. (1995), *Die Rezeption der Monarchia Dantes bis zur Editio Princeps im Jahre 1559* (see pp. 187–194), Munich: Finke.

Langholm, O. (1992), *Economics in the Medieval Schools* (see pp. 420–9), Leiden, New York, and Cologne: Brill.

Lapparent, P. (1940–2), 'L'oeuvre politique de François de Meyronnes, ses rapports avec celle de Dante," *Archives d'Histoire Doctrinale et Littéraire du Moyen Âge* 15–17, pp. 5–151.

Rossmann, H. (1972), *Die Hierarchie der Welt. Gestalt und System des Franz von Meyronnes mit besonderer Berücksichtigung seiner Schöpfungslehre*, Werl, Westf.: D. Coelde.

Schabel, C. (2001), *Theology at Paris, 1316–1345: Peter Auriol and the Problem of Divine Foreknowledge and Future Contingents* (see pp. 149–55), Burlington, VT: Ashgate.

32

Gabriel Biel

RUSSELL L. FRIEDMAN

Gabriel Biel (b. before 1425; d. 1495) played an important role in the transmission of the medieval philosophical and theological tradition to pre- and early Reformation Europe. He was educated at several of the major universities in Germany, and was exposed to teaching according to both the *via antiqua* (emphasizing realist thinkers like THOMAS AQUINAS and JOHN DUNS SCOTUS) and the *via moderna* (emphasizing nominalist thought, particularly WILLIAM OF OCKHAM'S). From around 1460 to 1484, Biel was heavily involved in church activities, authoring an ecclesiological treatise (Biel 1968). From 1484 he taught theology at the University of Tübingen. Throughout his life he was involved in the spiritual movement known as the Modern Devotion (*devotio moderna*, also known as the Brethren of the Common Life), and a concern for pastoral duties is manifest in his works (for more on Biel, with a complete list of his writings, see Oberman 1983).

Biel's most clearly philosophical work is his *Commentary on Peter Lombard's Sentences* (Biel 1973–92), which was written from the middle 1480s on. His philosophical thought is not straightforwardly innovative, but has more of a synthetic nature; his generally recognized clarity of expression is often achieved by contrasting diverse positions with each other. Although Biel discusses a broad spectrum of thinkers, including Thomas Aquinas (see Farthing 1988), BONAVENTURE, John Duns Scotus, GREGORY OF RIMINI, and PIERRE D'AILLY, Biel's major source of philosophical and theological inspiration was William of Ockham. Thus, Ockham's nominalism is at the heart of Biel's metaphysics and epistemology (see e.g., Burkard 1974). Further, Biel follows Ockham (and, more generally, Franciscan thought) in his voluntarism: not only does Biel hold that the created will is a more noble faculty than the created intellect and that the intellect does not have a causal priority over the will, but he also maintains that all contingency in the universe ultimately derives from the freedom of the divine will (see, e.g., Grane 1961, pp. 97–148). Of the many who read Gabriel Biel's work throughout the sixteenth century, the most significant was Martin Luther, although how and how much Biel influenced Luther is not entirely clear.

Bibliography

Primary sources

(1963–7), *Canonis misse expositio*, ed. H. A. Oberman and W. J. Courtenay, 4 vols., Wiesbaden: Franz Steiner Verlag.

(1968), *Defensorium obedientiae apostolicae et alia documenta*, ed. and trans. H. A. Oberman, D. E. Zerfoss, and W. J. Courtenay, Cambridge, MA: Harvard University Press.

(1973–92), *Collectorium circa quattuor libros Sententiarum*, 4 vols. plus indices, ed. H. Rückert, M. Elze, R. Steiger, W. Werbeck, and U. Hofmann, Tübingen: J. C. B. Mohr (Paul Siebeck).

Secondary sources

Burkard, F. J. (1974), *Philosophische Lehrgehalte in Gabriel Biels Sentenzenkommentar unter besonderer Berücksichtigung seiner Erkenntnislehre*, Meisenheim am Glan: Verlag Anton Hain.

Farthing, J. L. (1988), *Thomas Aquinas and Gabriel Biel: Interpretations of St. Thomas Aquinas in German Nominalism on the Eve of the Reformation*, Durham, NC and London: Duke University Press.

Grane, L. (1962), *Contra Gabrielem. Luthers Auseinandersetzung mit Gabriel Biel in der Disputatio Contra Scholasticam Theologiam 1517*, Copenhagen: Gyldendal.

Oberman, Heiko A. (1983), *The Harvest of Medieval Theology: Gabriel Biel and Late Medieval Nominalism*, 3rd edn., Durham, NC: Labyrinth Press.

33

Gaetano of Thiene

STEPHEN E. LAHEY

Gaetano di Thiene (b. 1387; d. 1465), philosopher and physician, succeeded Paul of Venice as the foremost philosopher at the University of Padua in 1422. His interests were wide-ranging, extending from formal logic and the theoretical physics that had come to be associated with it in the Mertonian tradition, through more traditional Aristotelian metaphysics and physics, to an extended examination of cognition and the problems associated with Averroistic conceptions of the intellect. Gaetano's influence in fifteenth-century Italian philosophy was considerable; his students included Bernardo Bembo, Lauro Quirini, Johannes Argyropulos, Nicolleto Verni, and Francesco della Rovere (later Sixtus IV), and his writings elicited attention from Pomponazzi and Cajetan.

Gaetano's *Recollecte*, his commentary on WILLIAM HEYTESBURY'S *Regule* and the first 30 of Heytesbury's *sophismata*, illustrates the evolution of kinematics from fourteenth-century Oxford to fifteenth-century Italy. For the Mertonians, kinematics was an abstract field in which the logic of propositions about motion, velocity, and resistant force mattered more than the natural world, while Italian philosophers strove to trace out its implications in the natural world. For example, Heytesbury focused his discussion of *maxima* and *minima* on the logical validity of propositions indicating complications in relating power and correspondent resistance. In considering limits or boundaries of capacities, on the one hand there is a maximum weight that Socrates can carry, or a minimum that he does not. This kind of limit differs from the minimum size of an object that Plato can see from 100 yards' distance, and the maximum size of an object that he cannot see from the same distance. These four divisions describe both upper and lower limits of capacity, and the two disjuncts ((*maximum quod sic, minimum quod non*), (*minimum quod sic, maximum quod non*)) respectively describe active and passive powers. Heytesbury's analysis allows for precise consideration of the resistance a power meets within uniform and difform media such as air or water, the strengthening or weakening of a power during operation, and for inclusion of velocity and duration of movement. Gaetano's commentary on Heytesbury provides much needed explication and exemplification of the *Regule*, releasing it from the logical analysis of propositions about physical phenomena by applying Heytesbury's analytical apparatus to physical phenomena considered as such.

As a cognitive theorist, Gaetano is remembered largely for his interest in incorporating an Averroist theory of the intellect into the more conventional Christian Aristotelianism of ALBERTUS MAGNUS. While agreeing with Averroes on a number of topics, he held that AVERROES' position on the unity of the human intellect was in error because positing a common intellect led to the impossibility of individual humans having knowledge. The intellective soul, argues Gaetano, is created by God and infused into individual human beings, which position allows both for individual and immortal intellective souls, a combination not possible according to Aristotle. Gaetano's conception of the soul was to allow later thinkers, among them Johannes Argyropulos, to incorporate the nascent humanist interest in Plato's works into discussions of Aristotle's *De anima*.

Bibliography

Primary sources

(1491), *De intensione et remisione formarum*, Venice.
(1494), *Complexum expositionis Messini de tribus praedicamentis*, Venice.
(1494), *Recollectae super Sophismatibus Hentisberi*, Venice.
(1496), *Recollectae super octo libros Physicorum Aristotelis*, Venice.

Secondary sources

Clagett, Marshall (1959), *The Science of Mechanics in the Middle Ages*, Madison, WI: University of Wisconsin Press.
Valsanzibio, Silvestro da (1949), *Vita e dottrina di Gaetano di Thiene*, 2nd edn., Padua: Studio Filosofico dei FF. MM. Cappuccini.

34

Gersonides

SARAH PESSIN

Gersonides (b. 1288; d. 1344), also known as RaLBaG (the Hebrew acronym for Rabbi Levi ben Gershom) and as Leon of Bagnols, lived in Provence. His corpus includes biblical commentaries, astronomical and astrological tracts, a supercommentary on AVERROES, as well as his most comprehensive philosophical work, the *Milhamot Adonai* (or *The Wars of the Lord*, sometimes also called *Milhamot ha-Shem*). The *Milhamot's* six books address the entire range of medieval philosophical topics.

To get a good sense of how Gersonides' worldview works as a whole, it is useful to focus on his doctrine of active intellect. Treated as an existent separate from God (*pace* Alexander of Aphrodisias) and yet entirely transcending any individual's material intellect (*pace* Themistius and Averroes), the active intellect is the "rational order": God's complete plan for the sublunar realm. As such, sublunar substances are the particular – and plural – manifestations of what presents itself as a completely unified order in active intellect. Epistemologically, interaction with the various particulars of the sensory world is merely the *occasion for* knowledge, which ultimately consists in the individual's acquisition of some part of the "rational order" of active intellect (the acquisition itself being dependent upon the said individual's moral perfection). It is this doctrine of active intellect and knowledge acquisition that lies at the heart of Gersonides' doctrine of personal providence and personal immortality.

First, a person will lead a more or less providentially sanctioned life to the extent that he or she personally succeeds in acquiring knowledge from active intellect; for the more parts of the divinely ordained order one apprehends, the better able one is to live in accord with that plan. And while Gersonides denies that God can know individuals per se, his epistemology allows him a sense in which God knows the providentially attuned individual person; having acquired knowledge, that individual partakes of something *above* the vicissitudes of the particularity which is itself an object of God's knowing.

Along similar lines, it is to the extent that an individual has, in life, managed to acquire knowledge that the said individual has ensured his or her personal immortality; for, in coming to know parts of the divine order found in active intellect, the individual has acquired something that will eternally transcend the mortality of corporeal particulars. The individual lives on, then, as the sum total of his or her acquired knowledge – a sum total that will differ from individual to individual. This doctrine represents Gersonides' rejection of Averroes' rather impersonal account of human immortality, and offers a more religiously sensitive vision: the way an individual lives during life is directly responsible for the way that individual will live on after death.

Other notable features of Gersonides' thought are his simultaneous commitments to astrology and human freedom, his rejection of God's knowledge of particulars and future contingents, and his rejection of *creatio ex nihilo* in favor of God's creating the world out of a pre-existing formless matter.

Bibliography

Primary source
(1984–99), *The Wars of the Lord*, 3 vols., trans. and with notes by Seymour Feldman, Philadelphia, New York, and Jerusalem: Jewish Publication Society.

Secondary source
Wolfson, H. (1953), "Maimonides and Gersonides on divine attributes as ambiguous terms," in M. Davis, ed., *Mordecai Kaplan Jubilee Volume* (pp. 515–30), New York: Jewish Theological Seminary of America.

35

Gilbert of Poitiers

JOHN MARENBON

Gilbert of Poitiers (b. 1085/90; d. 1154) taught at Paris and, probably, Chartres, before becoming Bishop of Poitiers in 1142. Although he was the founder of a distinctive school in logic (see Anonymous 1983), Gilbert's surviving work is theological. Most important is his long commentary (1146–7, perhaps earlier) on BOETHIUS' *Theological Treatises*. One of Gilbert's aims here is to distinguish, and yet permit analogy between, the types of reasoning appropriate to natural science and to theology. He also develops a sophisticated, original metaphysics.

Gilbert's starting point is the distinction between *quo est*s and *quod est*s. An object under a description or designated by a name is a *quod est*: for example, the man, the white thing, the rational thing, Socrates. That *by* which it is that *quod est* is a *quo est*: for example, humanity, whiteness, rationality and Socrateity. *Quo est*s are what twelfth-century writers call "forms," and they are singular, not universal, ones. Socrates is, for instance a man and white by his singular *quo est*s of humanity and whiteness. Some of these *quo est*s are simple, some complex. Socrates' whiteness and rationality are simple *quo est*s; his humanity is a complex *quo est*, made up of the simple *quo est*s rationality and mortality. Most complex of all is the *quo est* by which Socrates is Socrates – the "whole property" of Socrates, Socrateity. It is composed of all the *quo est*s "which both in actuality and by nature have been, are and will be" those of Socrates (1966, pp. 144: 73–8, 274: 74–95). Although all *quo est*s are singular, most of them are exactly like other *quo est*s because they have the same effects: Socrates' rationality and humanity are exactly like Plato's rationality and humanity. But collected forms, such as Socrateity, are not exactly like any other *quo est*: they alone (and their corresponding *quod est*s) are not merely singulars, but also individuals.

Gilbert's (somewhat problematic: will not every man have the same whole property?) inclusion in whole properties of what something might be "by nature" is linked to his tendency to think of there being synchronous alternative possible states of affairs, each belonging to different providential programs, any one of which God could choose to put into effect. Gilbert was thus a precursor of JOHN DUNS SCOTUS's modal innovations (see Knuuttila 1993, pp. 211–17).

Bibliography

Primary source

(1966), *Commentaries on Boethius*, ed. N. Häring, Toronto: Pontifical Institute of Mediaeval Studies.

Secondary sources

Anonymous (1983), *Compendium logicae Porretanum*, ed. S. Ebbesen, K. Fredborg, and L. Nielsen, in *Cahiers de l'Institut du Moyen Âge Grec et Latin* 46, pp. 1–113.

Jacobi, K. (1998), "Gilbert of Poitiers," in E. Craig, ed., *Routledge Encyclopaedia of Philosophy*, vol. IV (pp. 68–72), London and New York: Routledge.

Knuuttila, S. (1993), *Modalities in Medieval Philosophy*, London and New York: Routledge.

Nielsen, L. O. (1982), *Theology and Philosophy in the Twelfth Century*, Leiden: Brill.

36

Giles of Rome

SILVIA DONATI

Giles of Rome (b. 1243/7; d. 1316) was born probably in Rome and died at the papal court in Avignon. He was the first member of the Augustinian order to become a master in theology at the University of Paris. He probably entered the Augustinian order in Rome and afterwards was sent to Paris to study philosophy and theology. He may have taken THOMAS AQUINAS's courses in theology during Aquinas's second stay at Paris in the years 1269–72. Giles's academic career was interrupted in 1277, when, in the context of the condemnation of heterodox Aristotelianism by the Bishop of Paris, Étienne Tempier, and the reaction of the Paris faculty of theology against Aquinas's doctrines, he was also subjected to a doctrinal inquiry, where he refused to recant the doctrines that had been censured. If an ancient report can be believed, Giles was the preceptor of the future king of France, Philip the Fair, during this period and it was certainly at Philip's request that Giles composed *De regimine principum* during the hiatus in his teaching. His university career resumed in 1285, when at the request of Pope Honorius IV, Giles's doctrines were re-examined by a commission of theologians appointed by the Bishop of Paris, Ranulphe de la Houblonnière. After his rehabilitation, Giles became a regent master, probably holding the chair in the years 1285–91. In 1292 he was elected General Prior of the Augustinian order. In 1295 he was made Archbishop of Bourges by Boniface VIII. He took Boniface's side in the conflict, started by the Cardinals James and Peter Colonna, over the legitimacy of Boniface's election, after the abdication of Celestine IV. Giles devoted the treatise *De renuntiatione papae* (1297) to this topic. Afterwards he supported the pope in his conflict with Philip the Fair regarding the relationship between temporal and spiritual power, defending Boniface's theocratic position in his treatise *De ecclesiastica potestate* (1301–2). Giles was among the supporters of the suppression of the Templar order, as is clear from his treatise *Contra exemptos*, which was written during the Council of Vienne (1311–12), where the abolition of the order was decided.

Metaphysics

Giles's metaphysical thought was strongly influenced by Thomas Aquinas, whose main philosophical doctrines he shares. Despite this dependence, Giles cannot properly be defined as Thomas's disciple, because he always reworks Thomas's doctrines into original formulations and often criticizes some minor points in them. A well-known example of Giles's attitude toward Thomas is the doctrine of the real distinction between essence and existence. Giles develops his own formulation of the theory of real distinction (1930 (prop. 5, 12), pp. 19–26, 66–77; 1503, q. 9, fos. 17vb–22rb), in opposition to HENRY OF GHENT, who is Giles's direct antagonist in this discussion. In contrast with Henry, who conceives existence as a mere relationship of the created essence to the Creator, Giles describes essence and existence as two *res*. E. Hocedez has pointed out the realistic connotation of Giles's conception of the real distinction (1930, pp. 51–67) in contrast to Thomas's more nuanced position. In Giles's metaphysical thought, the real distinction between essence and existence constitutes the ultimate ontological foundation for the finitude of created being, its contingency and temporality, as well as for the possibility of creation and annihilation. All composition in created beings, such as the composition of genus and difference and of substance and accident, are ultimately reduced to the composition of essence and existence. P. Nash (1957, pp. 114–15) has emphasized the essentialistic character of Giles's theory, in which existence is conceived as a posterior kind of actuality in comparison to the more basic actuality of essence. Although Giles denies that existence can be described as a predicamental accident, it is apparent that in his view existence resembles an accidental determination. In this respect, Giles' conception of essence and existence bears a closer similarity to AVICENNA'S conception of existence as an accident of essence than to the Thomistic conception of existence as the first actuality of substance.

Another Thomistic doctrine adopted by Giles is the theory of the unicity of the substantial form, according to which there is only one substantial form in substances. Concerning this theory, however, Giles's position shows some hesitations (Donati 1990, pp. 20–4; Luna 1990, pp. 158–78). A radical formulation is found in the *Errores philosophorum* (1944, pp. 8, 12), a work of uncertain authenticity probably dating from the late 1260s or early 1270s, whose author criticizes Aristotle for defending the doctrine of unicity of substantial form. In works known to be authentic dating from the same period, on the contrary, Giles supports the unicity of form in all material substances. A further witness to Giles's unreserved acceptation of the unitarian theory is the treatise *De gradibus formarum* (1278). In works dating from the intermediate period and after 1278, on the other hand, Giles shows a more reserved attitude: although he supports the unitarian theory for all other substances, he avoids taking a position in the case of human beings. Because of its connections with theological matters, such as the dogma of the Eucharist and Christological theories, the issue of the number of substantial forms in men was conceived as a philosophical problem with theological implications. Giles's oscillations on this issue are probably a consequence of the anti-Thomistic climate of the University of Paris in the 1270s and of Giles's personal involvement in the condemnation of 1277. More specifically, the *Contra gradus et pluralitatem formarum* is considered to be a reaction to the 1277 condemnation of Giles's unreserved adoption of the unitarian position in his early works (1985, pp. 89–91, 169–70, 235; Luna 1990, p. 171). On the other hand, Giles's reserved attitude in his later works is explained on the basis of the hypothesis that the theory of the unicity of substantial form in man was one of the doctrines Giles had to recant in 1285 (1985, pp. 112–13; Luna 1990, p. 171).

Like Thomas, Giles rejects the theory of universal hylomorphism, which attributes a matter and form composition to every created being, and allows this composition only in the case of corporeal substances (1581 (dist. 3, p. 1, q. 1, a. 1), vol. I, pp. 160–70). Matter is conceived by Giles as absolute potentiality. Accordingly, he rejects positions like those of Henry of Ghent and RICHARD OF MIDDLETON which attribute a certain degree of actuality to matter (Donati 1986, p. 248). Given the assumption that the only principle of distinction is actuality, from the conception of matter as absolute potentiality Giles deduces the impossibility of different kinds of prime matter. Thus, in contrast to Thomas, he attributes an essentially identical matter to sublunary bodies, which are generable and corruptible, and to celestial bodies, which are ungenerated and incorruptible (ibid., pp. 243–64). The adoption of the Thomistic theory of *materia signata quantitate* as the principle of individuation of material substances is also a consequence of the assumption of the absolute potentiality of matter. If distinction always implies actuality, matter can play the role of principle of individuation only insofar as it is informed by quantity. On the other hand, unlike Thomas, whose position shows some oscillations in this respect, Giles stays faithful to the Averroistic doctrine of indeterminate dimensions: the dimensions which, together with matter, play the role of principle of numerical plurality are not determinate, but indeterminate, that is, they are dimensions of no determinate size. According to AVERROES, these inhere in matter prior to substantial form and because they precede form in matter, they explain the numerical plurality of the supervening form by making matter divisible.

Philosophy of nature

Although in the main lines of his philosophy of nature Giles clearly belongs to the Aristotelian tradition, his views on physics show some interesting differences with Aristotle. Besides the notion of bodily extension or volume, Giles introduces a notion, previously unknown within the Aristotelian tradition, of quantity of matter, which bears some similarity to the modern concept of mass (Donati 1988b, pp. 178–91). He introduces this notion, which he conceives as a development of the Averroistic notion of indeterminate dimensions, primarily in order to explain that in the natural phenomena of rarefaction and condensation the quantity of matter remains the same, whereas the extension of bodies varies.

Besides the Aristotelian notion of place conceived as the internal surface of the containing body, called by Giles "material place," he introduces a second concept of place or "formal place," which is constituted by the distance of the located body from fixed points in the universe (Trifogli 1988, pp. 260–8). The notion of formal place is introduced by Giles in order to save the Aristotelian assumption of immobility of place in the case in which the containing body is in motion, and in the case of the last sphere, which is not contained in another body.

An original contribution to Aristotelian natural thought is also provided by Giles's discussion of natural motion in a void (Trifogli 1992, pp. 143–61). In contrast with the view prevalent among Aristotelians, Giles conceives this hypothetical motion not as atemporal, but as temporal motion. According to him, however, the time associated with natural motion in the void is not conceived, as in the Aristotelian tradition, as a continuous successive magnitude, but is characterized by a multiplicity of instants in such a way that there is no temporal extension intervening between any two of them. And since each one of these instants lacks magnitude, this kind of time is without duration and corresponds to just an instant of celestial time. The same notion of time is also used by Giles in the explanation of the movements of angelic substances.

Concerning the traditional discussion on the duration of the universe, Giles rejects the Aristotelian theory of the eternity of the world. However, a certain evolution can be detected in Giles's position, which is probably a consequence of the 1277 condemnation (Pini 2000, pp. 395–404). Before the condemnation, Giles, on the one hand, rejects Aristotle's arguments as not conclusive and based on an improper extension of the laws of nature, that is, on the erroneous assumption that every kind of production implies movement. Like Thomas Aquinas, he maintains that creation is a kind of production that does not imply motion. On the other hand, also following Thomas, he considers the hypothesis of an eternal world theoretically possible and thus the theory of temporal creation as not demonstrable. After the condemnation, in which the hypothesis of the theoretical possibility of an eternal world was censured, however, Giles shows a more reserved attitude. First, he seems to conceive eternity as incompatible with the nature of creatures, although he does not exclude the possibility of eternal creation due to God's infinite power (1985; 1939–40, pp. 128–9). Furthermore, he no longer maintains that temporal creation is not demonstrable, but only that it has not been demonstrated yet (1581 (dist. 1, pars 1, q. 4, a. 2), vol. I, pp. 54–60).

Psychology and gnoseology

Giles's psychology and gnoseology generally follow Aristotelian–Thomistic principles. In the discussion on the relationship between the soul and its faculties, in contrast with Henry of Ghent, Giles holds Thomas's position, according to which the powers of the soul are really different from the soul itself; being intermediate between the soul and its operations they cannot be identical with the very essence of the soul itself. In his gnoseology, Giles adopts Aristotelian empiricism, maintaining that knowledge derives from experience, and thus rejecting Platonic innatism. Since human knowledge originates from the senses, for Giles as for Thomas, the proper object of the human intellect are perceptible substances, which are known through abstraction. Consequently, since abstraction is a process of dematerialization and the individuating principle of perceptible substances is matter informed by dimensive quantity, Giles excludes the possibility of a direct intellectual knowledge of the individual; only the essence of perceptible substances is directly known. On the basis of similar considerations, Giles also excludes the possibility of a direct knowledge of the soul by itself; according to Giles, the soul is known only indirectly as the subject of the knowledge of other things (1500c, III, fos. 67vb–68vb). Unlike perceptible substances, God and the other separate substances, that is, imperceptible substances, cannot be grasped in their very essence by the human intellect; according to Giles, in this life there is only the possibility of an indirect knowledge, based on the knowledge of their perceptible effects. The impossibility of a direct knowledge of separate substances is the cause of a limitation in the scope of metaphysics as developed by the human intellect. Giles maintains that metaphysics *qua* science should include in its scope the consideration of the essence of separate substances. In his opinion, it is only because of the imperfect way in which the human intellect knows metaphysics that in metaphysics, as in physics, separate substances are known not in themselves, but only through their effects (Zimmermann 1998, pp. 180–1).

Like Averroes, Giles infers the necessity of an agent intellect from the analysis of abstraction. If, according to the Platonic Theory of Ideas, there were immaterial essences of perceptible substances actually existing separated from their perceptible instantiations, they would be intelligible in act, and thus there would be no need to postulate an agent intellect. But since the essences of perceptible substances exist only in their material instantiations, and thus are intelligible only in potency, an active principle must be assumed, which illuminates the phantasma and starts the process of abstraction (1500c, III, fo. 69rb). In the discussion concerning the problem of intelligible species, contrary to Henry of Ghent, who denies the existence of the species, Giles supports the traditional view, which postulates species as a necessary intermediary between *phantasmata*, that is sensible representations, and the act of intellectual apprehension (ibid., fo. 68ra). Like Thomas, Giles participates in the discussions regarding the unicity of intellect. He criticizes both the theory, which he attributes to Avicenna, of the unicity of the agent intellect (ibid., fos. 69va–69vb) and the Averroistic theory of the unicity of the possible intellect. Giles devotes the treatise *De intellectu possibili* to the rejection of the latter.

Ethics

In ethics, Giles's main doctrines are characterized by a moderate intellectualism, occupying a middle position between the voluntarism of authors such as Henry of Ghent – who support the theory of the primacy of the will over the intellect – and the intellectualism of authors such as GODFREY OF FONTAINES – who support the theory of the primacy of the intellect. According to Giles, the will is a passive power, which cannot activate itself, but requires a *bonum apprehensum*, the apprehension of an intended good, in order to be activated. In his view, however, this does not imply a denial of free will, because the will, contrary to the other powers of the soul, can determine itself after it has been activated by the apprehension of an end. Giles's moderate intellectualism is also apparent in the discussion of the relationship between intellect and will in the origin of sin. Among Giles's doctrines condemned in 1277 is the principle according to which *non est malitia in voluntate nisi sit error in ratione*. In later works Giles maintains that the evil in the will always implies an error of judgment, since whatever is wanted is wanted insofar as it is conceived as a good. On the other hand, in his view the evil in the will is not caused by the error of judgment. On the contrary, it is the error of judgment that is caused by the evil in the will, since the damage of the will due to this evil also produces an impairment in the capacity of judgment by the intellect (De Blic 1948, pp. 45–65).

Bibliography

Primary sources

(1500a), *De gradibus formarum*, Venice.

(1500b), *De intellectu possibili*, Venice.

(1500c), *Super libros De anima*, Venice.

(1503), *Quaestiones de esse et essentia*, Venice.

(1554), *De renuntiatione papae*, Rome.

(1555), *Tractatus contra exemptos*, Rome.

(1556), *De regimine principum libri III*, Rome.

(1930), *Theoremata de esse et essentia*, ed. E. Hocedez, Louvain: Museum Lessianum.

(1581), *In secundum librum Sententiarum*, Venice.

(1939–40), *Quaestiones I–XX a fratre Aegidio Romano Paduae disputatae in capitulo generali O. E. S. A. 1281*, ed. G. Bruni, *Analecta Augustiniana* 17, pp. 125–50.

(1944), *Errores philosophorum*, ed. J. Koch, trans. J. O. Riedl, Milwaukee, WI: Marquette University Press.

(1952), *Theorems on Existence and Essence*, trans. Michael V. Murray, Milwaukee, WI: Marquette University Press.

(1961), *De ecclesiastica potestate*, ed. R. Scholz, Aalen: Scientia.

(1985), *Apologia*, ed. R. Wielockx, Florence: L. S. Olschki.

Secondary sources

De Blic, J. (1948), *L'Intellectualisme moral chez deux aristotéliciens de la fin du XIIIe siècle*, in *Miscellanea moralia in hon. A. Janssens*, vol. I (pp. 45–76), Louvain: Nauwelaerts-Duculot.

Del Punta, F., Donati, S., and Luna, C. (1993), *Egidio Romano*, in *Dizionario biografico degli Italiani*, vol. 42 (pp. 319–41), Rome: Enciclopedia Treccani.

Donati, S. (1986), "La dottrina di Egidio Romano sulla materia dei corpi celesti. Discussioni sulla natura dei corpi celesti alla fine del tredicesimo secolo," *Medioevo* 12, pp. 229–80.

——(1988a), "Ägidius von Roms Kritik an Thomas von Aquins Lehre der hylemorphen Zusammensetzung der Himmelskörper," in A. Zimmermann, ed., *Thomas von Aquin* (pp. 377–96), Berlin and New York: De Gruyter.

——(1988b), "La dottrina delle dimensioni indeterminate in Egidio Romano," *Medioevo* 14, pp. 149–233.

——(1990), "Studi per una cronologia delle opere di Egidio Romano. I: Le opere prima del 1285. I commenti aristotelici," *Documenti e Studi sulla Tradizione Filosofica Medievale* 1, pp. 1–111.

Hocedez, E. (1927), "Gilles de Rome et Henri de Gand sur la distinction réelle (1276–1287)," *Gregorianum* 8, pp. 358–84.

Luna, C. (1990), "La Reportatio della lettura di Egidio Romano sul Libro III delle Sentenze (Clm. 8005) e il problema dell'autenticità dell'Ordinatio," *Documenti e Studi sulla Traditione Filosofica Medievale* 1, pp. 113–225.

Makaay, J. S. (1924), *Der Traktat des Aegidius Romanus über die Einzigkeit der substantiellen Form*, Würzburg: St. Rita Druckerei.

Nash, P. W. (1957), "The accidentality of *esse* according to Giles of Rome," *Gregorianum* 38, pp. 103–15.

Pini, G. (2000), "Being and creation in Giles of Rome," in J. A. Aertsen, K. Emery, and A. Speer, eds., *Philosophie und Theologie an der Universität von Paris im letzten Viertel des 13. Jahrhunderts*, Berlin and New York: De Gruyter.

Porro, P. (1988), "Ancora sulle polemiche tra Egidio Romano e Enrico di Gand: due questioni sul tempo angelico," *Medioevo* 14, pp. 107–48.

Strayer, J. R. (1980), *The Reign of Philip the Fair*, Princeton, NJ: Princeton University Press.

Trifogli, C. (1988), "La dottrina del luogo in Egidio Romano," *Medioevo* 14, pp. 235–90.

——(1990), "La dottrina del tempo in Egidio Romano," *Documenti e Studi sulla Tradizione Filosofica Medievale* 1, pp. 247–76.

——(1992), "Giles of Rome on natural motion in the void," *Mediaeval Studies* 54, pp. 136–61.

Wippel, J. F. (1981), *The Metaphysical Thought of Godfrey of Fontaines: A Study in Late Thirteenth Century Philosophy*, Washington, DC: The Catholic University of America Press.

37

Godfrey of Fontaines

JOHN F. WIPPEL

Godfrey of Fontaines (b. before 1250; d. 1306/9) was born in the principality of Liège, probably at the chateau of the noble family to which he belonged, at Fontaines-les-Hozémont. After pursuing philosophical studies at Paris in the faculty of arts in the early 1270s, he must have begun to study theology by August 15, 1274 (De Wulf 1904, pp. 3–16; Wippel 1981, pp. xv–xviii). His interest in the work of the masters of arts at Paris, especially the radical Aristotelians of the 1260s and 1270s, is reflected by the presence of many of their works in manuscripts in his personal library (Bibliothèque Nationale lat. 15.819, 16.096, and especially 16.297, known as his *Student Notebook*; Wippel 2001, pp. 361–5). Godfrey's teaching activities at the university as a master in the theology faculty began in 1285 and continued until about 1303–4, when he conducted his fifteenth and last quodlibetal disputation. He may have been outside the city for some time after completing *Quodlibet* XIV about 1298–9. The year of his death is uncertain, probably 1306 or 1309, but the day is known: October 29.

As a master of theology Godfrey adopted the quodlibetal disputation as his major vehicle for publication. His fifteen *Quodlibets* have all been edited in the series *Les Philosophes belges*, although the first four survive only in the form of *reportationes*, i.e., copies taken down by an auditor. Briefer versions of *Quodlibets* III and IV have also been edited. Godfrey also conducted ordinary Disputed Questions, and a number of these survive in manuscript, only some of which have been edited (Wippel 1981, pp. xxv–xxvii).

Subject of metaphysics: For Godfrey metaphysics has as its subject being as being. He was undoubtedly aware of an earlier controversy between AVICENNA and AVERROES concerning this. Avicenna had stressed the nonparticular and therefore the universal character of being as being and made this the subject of metaphysics. Averroes had emphasized it as the science that has the highest kind of being, separate or divine being, as its subject. Godfrey sides with Avicenna. He writes that being as being is the object (or subject) of metaphysics (*Quodl.* X, q. 11), and that the notion of being is first and simplest because it enters into, i.e., it is implied by, every other concept (*Quodl.* VI, q. 6) Hence it is also the most general notion. God is not to be regarded as the subject of metaphysics, even though God is the first and primary being and must be studied within metaphysics with respect to whatever natural reason can discover about him (*Quodl.* I, q. 5). Godfrey contrasts the metaphysical study of God, which he says may be described as a kind of theology, with the theology based on sacred Scripture. The latter does not have being as being as its subject, but God himself (*Quodl.* IX, q. 20; Wippel 1981, pp. 2–15).

Division of being: In *Quodlibet* VIII, q. 3 Godfrey maintains that being itself may be divided into being in the mind ("cognitive" being), which he describes as a lesser or diminished being, and real being, i.e., being outside the mind or knower. Real being is further divided into real potential being and real actual being. For a thing to enjoy real potential being is for it to have being only by reason of its cause or causes. For it to enjoy real actual being is for it to be realized in accord with its nature in completed or perfected form. Finally, a thing can enjoy real potential being either by reason of an intrinsic cause, e.g., pre-existing matter, or by reason of an extrinsic cause, e.g., a pre-existing agent (1924, pp. 38–40).

Analogy of being: In referring in *Quodlibet* II, q. 8 to being as being as the object of the intellect, Godfrey indicates that being is taken analogically and not univocally, so as to be defined in the same way in each of its applications. Hence it is primarily affirmed of substance and of all else as ordered or related to substance. Therefore, while substance and accidents differ in genus, each will fall under this analogous notion of being. In *Quodlibet* III, q. 1 he argues for the analogical character of being by showing that it is neither univocal nor purely equivocal. In *Quodlibet* XV, q. 3 he insists that if being is applied to an accident insofar as it is related to substance in some way, this does not mean that being is not intrinsically realized in its secondary instances, i.e., in accidents. He insists that there is analogy and proportion at the level of reality between these different instantiations of being, and corresponding to this, at the level of meaning (Wippel 1981, pp. 19–24).

Transcendentals: Godfrey also maintains that there are certain properties of being which are really identical and convertible with it, in other words, certain transcendental characteristics present wherever being itself is realized. He singles out the one, the true, and the good. With respect to the one, in *Quodlibet* VI, q. 16 he distinguishes between the one that serves as a principle of number and which is based on discrete quantity, and the one that is convertible with being. Only the latter is transcendental. In *Quodlibet* VI, q. 6 he notes that truth only adds a mode to being, namely, a relationship to mind or intellect. To say that something enjoys this kind of truth is simply to recognize that it can make itself known to mind or to intellect, or in other words, that it is intelligible. Consequently, truth is present in being only virtually, in that it can cause truth to be present in the intellect. Truth in the formal sense resides in the intellect (Wippel 1981, pp. 24–36).

Essence and existence: The view that in all finite beings there is a real, i.e., not merely a conceptual, distinction between, and a composition of, an essence principle and an act of existing (*esse*) or existence principle was central to the metaphysics of THOMAS AQUINAS. By the mid-1270s GILES OF ROME had developed his own version of a real distinction between essence and existence, and would be involved in a long controversy with HENRY OF GHENT concerning this. Unfortunately, at times Giles used the language of "thing" to describe essence and existence and their relationship and, though he denied that either could exist in separation from the other or that existence was an essence, by using such language he opened the theory to such misinterpretations. Henry of Ghent, on the other hand, while rejecting any kind of real distinction between essence and existence, judged it necessary to posit some-thing more than a merely conceptual or logical distinction between them. Hence he proposed a new and third kind of distinction that would fall between a real distinction and a purely conceptual distinction, namely, an "intentional distinction" (Wippel 1981, pp. 39–44).

In his *Quodlibet* II, q. 2, Godfrey comments that either essence is really identical with existence and differs from it only conceptually or intentionally, or else existence is a distinct

273

"thing," i.e., the act of the essence and really distinct from it. In *Quodlibet* IV, q. 2 he outlines in greater detail the three different positions concerning the relationship between essence and existence (*esse*). Some hold that they are really distinct and that existence enters into a real composition with essence. Yet it is not separable from essence. If a thing lacks its existential being, it also lacks essential being. According to another view they are really identical, but differ intentionally. Finally, still another position maintains that they are really identical and differ only conceptually. Hence they do not enter into composition with one another (Wippel 1981, pp. 45–6).

In *Quodlibet* III, q. 1 Godfrey had examined the evidence for each of these positions in detail. There, too, he presents the theory of real distinction between essence and existence in language that reflects the usage of Giles of Rome by referring to existence both as "something" (*aliquid*) and especially as a "thing" (*res*). Next he offers a number of arguments in support of this view which seem to be taken from Giles, especially from his *Quaestiones disputatae de esse et essentia*, and refutes them. For Godfrey essence and existence are identical, and differ only in the way they signify. Just as a concrete noun such as a 'runner' (one who runs), an abstract noun such as 'running', and the verb 'to run' differ in their mode of signifying, so too do 'essence', 'a being', and 'to exist' (*esse*). But the reality they signify is one and the same (Wippel 1981, pp. 46–66).

Godfrey next presents in detail Henry's theory of intentional distinction. As he explains in his later *Quodlibet* VIII, q. 3, according to this view real being is divided into essential being (*esse essentiae*) and existential being (*esse existentiae*). Each thing enjoys its essential being from eternity insofar as it corresponds to its appropriate exemplar idea within the divine intellect and is, therefore, a genuine or real quiddity or essence, although not an actually existing one. It may receive actual existence in the course of time owing to the intervention of the divine will (1924, pp. 34–7). Henry concludes from this that within an actually existing entity, its essence is not really distinct from its existence; but the two are not identical. Rather they are "intentionally" distinct from one another. Godfrey rejects Henry's new and third kind of distinction. There can be no intermediary distinction between the purely conceptual and the real. And in *Quodlibet* III, q. 1 he also directs a series of arguments against intentional distinction between essence and existence (Wippel 1981, pp. 85–8).

Having rejected both real distinction and intentional distinction between essence and existence, Godfrey resolutely defends their real identity. Whatever is true of essence is true of existence, and vice versa. To account for the possibility that one might be aware of something as a possible existent even when it does not actually exist, one need not postulate two really distinct or even two intentionally distinct principles. One need only appeal to the distinction between act and potency, in this case, between being that is potential and being that is actual.

Moreover, Godfrey offers a new and different application of act and potency in order to meet one kind of argument that had been offered for real distinction between essence and existence (act of being). If, as he maintains, angels are not composed of matter and form, how is one to avoid making them perfectly simple beings and therefore equal to God? Rather than appeal to any real distinction of essence and existence in such entities to account for this, Godfrey counters that one and the same being may be regarded as actual to the extent that it actually exists and yet as potential insofar as it falls short of the actuality of any higher being and, above all, of the First Being, Pure Actuality, or God. In support he cites Proposition 2 from Proclus' *Elementatio theologica*: "What participates in the One is both one and not-one." As Godfrey interprets this, anything that is different from the One can fall short of the One only by approaching (*accessus*) the not-one. Hence it is not the One itself by reason of its receding from (*recessus*) the One. Consequently, beings such as angels fall short of the One, or God, without being composed of really distinct factors. But actuality and potentiality are present in them because they possess a kind of intermediary nature and hence are "assimilated" to different points of reference, i.e., to that which is higher and more actual, and to that which is lower and more potential. Corresponding to their relationship to these different points of reference, both potentiality and actuality are to be assigned to them. Hence they may be said to be composed of potency and act, not really composed, to be sure, but by a conceptual composition. Yet this composition is not fictitious but applies to such entities by reason of the fact that they are related to these different points of reference (Wippel 1981, pp. 89–97).

One likely source for this unusual theory is SIGER OF BRABANT'S *Quaestiones in metaphysicam*, especially so since a shorter version of this was contained in Godfrey's *Student Notebook*. But an even clearer source has more recently come to light, namely, an anonymous set of questions on the *Posterior Analytics*, which was also contained in Godfrey's library (Bibl. Nat. lat. 16.096; Wippel 1984b, pp. 231–44).

Knowledge of God's existence and essence: Godfrey maintains that philosophical knowledge of God belongs more properly to metaphysics than knowledge of any other being. While he has not left detailed arguments for God's existence in his surviving writings, he holds that this conclusion can be established by philosophical reasoning. Moreover, he was obviously familiar with Aquinas's "five ways" since he copied into the margins of his personal version of Aquinas's *Summa theologiae I* an abbreviated version of the first four "ways" (Bibl. Nat. lat. 15.819, fo. 226r).

But a dispute had arisen between Averroes and Avicenna concerning whether it belongs to natural philosophy (Averroes) or to metaphysics (Avicenna) to demonstrate the existence of God. Probably influenced on this point by Siger of Brabant, Godfrey defends what appears to be a compromise position. In *Quodlibet* XI, q. 1 he observes in passing that the metaphysician's consideration of God is more eminent and more perfect than that of the natural philosopher, who merely views him as the First Mover. But God is the First Mover by reason of his total being. In *Quodlibet* V, q. 10 he maintains that one can establish God's existence by reasoning from natural things to knowledge of him as the first efficient cause of creatures or, as he puts it there, as their causal and productive principle. As he explains in *Quodlibet* IX, q. 20, natural reason can establish a number of things about God with certainty: that because he is the First Being he is simple; that he is being in actuality; that he is an intellectual being. All these things are proved in metaphysics (Wippel 1981, pp. 102–5).

In *Quodlibet* VII, q. 11 Godfrey was asked whether by the same knowledge one knows that God is and what he is. Underlying this question was Aquinas's well-known view that, when it comes to our natural knowledge of God, we can know that he is by reasoning from effect to cause. We can also know what he is not; but we cannot know what he is. Godfrey seems to have in mind Aquinas's *Summa theologiae* I, q. 3, a. 4, ad 2 because, after referring to some who say that we cannot know what God is, he notes that they hold that even when we recognize that he is, the "is" which we understand is not that act of being (*esse*) whereby God subsists in himself, but only that which signifies that the judgment "that he is" is true (1914, p. 383).

Godfrey maintains that in the case of philosophical knowledge of God, we first reach a purely nominal knowledge by drawing some kind of analogy with things we observe in the sensible world. Just as some lower beings are the principal causes of others, and some are governed by others, so we apply the name 'God' to signify something in the universe which is the first and unique cause of all else and than which nothing greater can be thought. But this purely nominal knowledge is not enough to show that what is signified by the name 'God' enjoys real being, or "that he is."

Next one may reason as Aristotle did in *Physics* VII by eliminating an infinite regress of moved movers to the conclusion that one First Mover, or God, exists, and that this being is perpetual and pure actuality (as in *Physics* VIII). This yields knowledge "that God is," but does not indicate "what he is" in any real sense (as distinguished from nominal knowledge). For this step Godfrey turns to Aristotle's procedure in *Metaphysics* XII where he takes the knowledge "that God is" as established in the *Physics* and reasons to the presence in him of certain perfections to an eminent degree. Godfrey suggests that Aristotle uses these characteristics or perfections as quasi-differences, and thereby moves from knowledge "that God is" to knowledge of "what he is" by passing from a confused and quasi-generic knowledge to a more determined and quasi-specific knowledge. Godfrey recognizes, of course, that God does not really fall into any genus or species. In light of this he rejects the view that we cannot know "what God is," although he recognizes that in this life such knowledge will always be imperfect (1914, pp. 384–6; Wippel 1981, pp. 110–15).

Eternity of the world: Before and during Godfrey's time at the University of Paris, one of the most contested points had to do with the possibility of demonstrating philosophically that the world began to be. BONAVENTURE offered argumentation to prove that the world could not have been created from eternity. Aquinas dealt with this on many occasions and always maintained that neither the eternity nor the fact that the world began to be can be demonstrated philosophically. Christians hold that the world began to be solely on the grounds of religious belief. In his *De aeternitate mundi* Aquinas concluded that an eternally created world is possible philosophically speaking (Wippel 1984a, pp. 203–14). Henry of Ghent strongly argued that one can demonstrate that the world could not have been created from eternity.

In his *Quodlibet* II, q. 3, Godfrey is asked to determine whether the world or any creature could be or exists from eternity. He develops an answer heavily influenced by Aquinas's *De aeternitate mundi* but is troubled by one of the objections raised against this possibility. If the world were eternal, an infinity of days would have preceded the present one, and God could have created something such as a stone on each of those days and kept it in existence. But this would result in an actual infinity of stones here and now. Moreover, God could unite all of these stones so as to form one infinite body. But an actually infinite body is impossible and consequently the possibility of an infinity of simultaneously existing finite bodies must be rejected and, so too, the possibility of an eternally created world (1904, pp. 72–8).

Godfrey comments that one need not restrict this objection to stones, for one can make the same point by discussing the resulting infinity of human souls had the world been created from eternity and always populated by human beings. But he does seem to regard it as impossible for an infinity of things to exist simultaneously. In response he comments that one might allow for a world inhabited by humans from eternity by postulating transmigration of a finite number of souls to many different human beings under a different dispensation wherein they are not ordered to a supernatural destiny. Or this world might have existed from eternity without always being populated by humans. However, since this world seems to be intended primarily for human beings, if humans could not have been created from eternity under the present dispensation whereby they are ordered to eternal beatitude in heaven, it may be argued with probability that this world could not have been so created by

God's ordained power. But this does not prove that no creature or no other world could have existed from eternity. And so Godfrey concludes rather cautiously that neither the claim that an eternal world is impossible nor the claim that it is possible can be demonstrated. Each may be defended as probable, and neither is to be rejected as erroneous (Wippel 1981, pp. 160–8).

Substance and accidents: Godfrey accepts the Aristotelian division of being into substance and accidents. For something to be a substance is for it to enjoy separate entity and to have a nature to which it belongs to exist not in any subject (Wippel 1981, p. 174). Godfrey also assigns to a finite substance the role of serving as a subject for accidents and, therefore, of being in potency with respect to the accidents that inhere in it.

He emphatically denies that any substance can be the efficient cause of accidents that inhere in it. It would then be in act insofar as it efficiently caused its own accidents, and in potency insofar as it served as their subject. Godfrey would always insist that nothing can be in act and potency at the same time and in the same respect. He applies this to human action, including intellection and volition, and is extremely critical of attempts by others, especially Henry of Ghent and later GONSALVO OF SPAIN, to make an exception in the case of human volition. The will cannot reduce itself from potency to act (Wippel 1981, pp. 178–83). Therefore Godfrey denies that the human will is the efficient cause of its acts of volition. The will is moved by the object that is willed insofar as that object is presented to it by the intellect. He insists that this does not result in determinism because of the indeterminacy, even the freedom, of the intellect (Putallaz 1995, pp. 184–7, 198–208, 233–47; Wippel 1981, pp. 199–201). Closely connected with this is Godfrey's defense of a real distinction between the soul and its powers. The powers of the soul are accidents and are related to its essence as accidents to substance. This means that if the immanent operations of the soul inhere immediately in such powers, whether they are the senses, the intellect, or the will, the powers themselves cannot be the efficient cause of these operations (Wippel 1981, pp. 202–7).

Abstraction: Godfrey also regards the agent intellect and the possible intellect as distinct powers of the human soul, and defends a theory of intellection based on the abstraction of potentially intelligible content from phantasms (images) produced by the internal sense known as the imagination. In *Quodlibet* V, q. 10 he makes a special effort to explain the process of abstraction. Because the possible intellect is at times only in potency with respect to an intelligible object, it must be reduced to understanding in actuality by something else. Hence the intervention of the agent intellect is needed to enable phantasms to move or to actualize the possible intellect.

Godfrey concludes, therefore, that the agent intellect operates on the phantasm simply by removing or separating one factor present therein from another, so that what has been so removed or separated or abstracted is then capable of moving the possible intellect. One may distinguish between the quiddity of a material thing as it is presented in a phantasm and its designation as this particular quiddity by reason of its individuating accidental dispositions. While the quiddity of this given thing is particular and individuated, when simply considered in itself it is not so individuated. If it could exist apart from the individuals in which it is realized, it would be intelligible (and universal) in itself. And so in the order of consideration the agent intellect separates or frees the quiddity from its individuating conditions and thereby reduces it from being potentially intelligible to being actually intelligible and therefore capable of moving the possible intellect to understand it.

277

This is the process of abstraction (Wippel 1986). On a related matter, if Godfrey at times refers to intelligible species, he denies that they are really distinct from the intellect's acts of understanding (*Quodl.* IX, q. 19; *Quodl.* X, q. 12; Wippel 1981, pp. 198–9).

Matter and form: Godfrey defends the matter-form composition of corporeal beings and rejects all efforts to assign any degree of actuality to prime matter. Prime matter is pure potentiality and can never exist without some substantial form, not even by divine power. Moreover, there can be no intermediary between prime matter and the substantial form which actualizes it. Neither matter alone nor form alone is a being, but both are principles of one and the same composite entity to which existence in the unqualified sense belongs (*Quodl.* XIV, q. 5, 1932. pp. 404–5; Wippel 1981, pp. 266–70).

Sharply controverted in the 1270s and 1280s both at Paris and Oxford was the question concerning whether there is one or more than one substantial form in an individual substance, and especially, in a human being. Aquinas was especially noted for having defended unity or unicity of substantial form in all entities, including human beings. Others maintained that to account for the different levels of perfection present in complex entities such as higher animals and humans, a number of substantial forms were required. Many combinations and varieties of this general position – plurality of forms – were developed, but all were opposed to unicity of substantial form.

This opposition was based on both philosophical and on theological grounds. On the philosophical side, those who assigned a certain degree of actuality to prime matter were usually open to plurality of substantial forms. Those who viewed any actuality in prime matter as incompatible with the substantial unity of the matter-form composite would reject plurality of substantial forms for the same reason. On the theological side, alleged difficulties, especially one concerning the continuing identity of Christ's body while in the tomb, caused opponents of unicity of substantial form to view this position as theologically unacceptable, even as erroneous and heretical. And so on March 18, 1277, the Dominican Archbishop of Canterbury, ROBERT KILWARDBY, condemned 30 articles, including several which were aimed at or touched on unicity of substantial form. In 1284 his successor as Archbishop, the Franciscan JOHN PECHAM, reissued Kilwardby's condemnation and in 1286 he issued a new and even more explicit condemnation of this doctrine (Wippel 1981, pp. 314–19).

In his *Quodlibet* II, q. 7 of Easter, 1286, Godfrey begins to address this issue by presenting in detail three general positions, each of which defends some version of plurality of forms. The third is that developed by Henry of Ghent, according to which in human beings there are two substantial forms, one educed from the potentiality of matter, and the other the spiritual and rational soul directly created by God. Godfrey directs many criticisms against Henry's position, after first noting that all the objections he had raised against other versions of plurality of forms also apply to this view. His most fundamental objection is one already formulated by Aquinas. Two substantial forms cannot combine with one another to constitute a being that is substantially one. It is of the very nature of a form to communicate actual being (*esse*). Because each substantial form must contribute actual being, Henry's theory undermines the substantial unity of the human composite. Godfrey ranks the competing theories. That which defends unicity of form in all entities is more probable. Those which defend a multiplicity of forms in all material entities are more improbable. Henry's theory is less improbable because it defends that which is less probable (plurality of forms) in fewer cases (in human beings). While Godfrey's philosophical sympathies and argumentation favored unicity of substantial form in all entities including human beings, theological difficulties kept him from defending this as certain (Wippel, 1981, pp. 321–47).

The principle of individuation: Like many of his contemporaries (see Gracia 1994), Godfrey was interested in providing a philosophically consistent explanation for the fact that many different individual material beings may be realized within the same species. His distinction between transcendental unity and numerical unity in the strict sense is central to his solution. It is by reason of its substantial form that a material substance enjoys transcendental unity or unity of being. But for that same substance to enjoy numerical unity taken strictly, it must also be quantified.

In *Quodlibet* VII, q. 5 Godfrey reasons that if the different individuals within a given species share in common in the specific nature, they cannot be differentiated by reason of that. Something else is required. This added factor would appear to be something accidental, namely quantity. But many arguments can be offered against the claim that something accidental could serve as the principle of individuation and thereby distinguish one substance from another. He proposes that even in material entities the substantial form whereby the entity is what it is should also serve as the principle of its individuation. Yet quantity has a role to play. While it is not the material or the efficient or the formal or the final cause of individuation, it does dispose matter so that it can be divided into different parts and thereby receive and individuate different substantial forms. Hence it exercises only a mediate and quasi-dispositive causality in individuation. But the formal cause of individuation is a given substance's substantial form (Wippel 1981, pp. 349–64).

Bibliography

Primary sources

(1904), *Les quatres premiers Quodlibets de Godefroid de Fontaines*, ed. M. De Wulf and A. Pelzer, in *Les Philosophes belges*, vol. 2, Louvain: Institut Supérieur de Philosophie de l'Université.

(1914), vol. 3: *Les Quodlibets cinq, six et sept*, ed. M. De Wulf and J. Hoffmans.

(1924, 1928, 1931), vol. 4: *Le huitième Quodlibet, Le neuvième Quodlibet, Le dixième Quodlibet*, ed. J. Hoffmans.

(1932, 1935), vol. 5: *Les Quodlibets onze et douze, Les Quodlibets treize et quatorze*, ed. J. Hoffmans.

(1937), vol. 14: *Le Quodlibet XV et trois questions ordinaires de Godefroid de Fontaines*, ed. O. Lottin.

Disputed Questions: Some are edited in scattered publications. See Wippel 1981, pp. xxxi–xxxii.

Secondary sources

De Wulf, M. (1904), *Un théologien-philosophe du XIIIe siècle. Étude sur la vie, les oeuvres et l'influence de Godefroid de Fontaines*, Brussels: M. Hayez.

Gracia, J. J. E., ed. (1994), *Individuation in Scholasticism: The Later Middle Ages and the Counter-Reformation, 1150–1650*, Albany: State University of New York Press.

Putallaz, F.-X. (1995), *Insolente liberté. Controverses et condamnations au XIIIe siècle*, Fribourg: Éditions Universitaires; Paris: Éditions du Cerf.

Wippel, J. F. (1981), *The Metaphysical Thought of Godfrey of Fontaines: A Study in Late Thirteenth-Century Philosophy*, Washington, DC: The Catholic University of America Press.

——(1984a), *Metaphysical Themes in Thomas Aquinas*, Washington, DC: The Catholic University of America Press.

——(1984b), "Possible sources for Godfrey of Fontaines' views on the act-potency composition of simple creatures," *Mediaeval Studies* 44, pp. 222–44.

——(1986), "The role of the phantasm in Godfrey of Fontaines' theory of intellection," in C. Wenin, ed., *L'Homme et son univers au moyen âge*, vol. 2. (pp. 573–82), Actes du septième congrès internationale de philosophie médiévale, August 30 to September 4, 1991, Louvain-la-Neuve: Éditions de l'Institut Supérieur de Philosophie.

——(2001), "Godfrey of Fontaines at the University of Paris in the last quarter of the thirteenth century," in J. Aertsen, K. Emery, and A. Speer, eds., *Nach der Verurteilung von 1277. Philosophie und Theologie an der Universität von Paris im letzten Viertel des 13. Jahrhunderts. Studien und Texte*, Miscellanea mediaevalia 28 (pp. 359–89), Berlin and New York: De Gruyter.

38

Gonsalvo of Spain

A. G. TRAVER

Gonsalvo of Spain also known as Gonsalvus of Balboa and in Latin as Gonsalvus Hispanus (d. ca. 1313) was a Franciscan philosopher and theologian, the master of JOHN DUNS SCOTUS, and the Minister General of his order. He was born in the province of Galicia in Spain, and is often confused with another Spanish Franciscan, Gonsalvus de Vallebona (or de Balboa). It is unknown when Gonsalvo entered the Franciscan order. He began his early studies in Spain, but had become bachelor of theology at Paris by 1288. In the following year, he was a legate for the Castilian royal family to Pope Nicholas IV, and in 1290 was elected provincial minister for the Franciscan province of Santiago of Compostela.

He returned to Paris in about 1297 to become a master of theology. From 1302 to 1303 he was the Franciscan regent master at Paris, and JOHN DUNS SCOTUS commented on PETER LOMBARD's *Sentences* (*Reportata parisiensia*) under his supervision. On June 25, 1303, both Gonsalvo and Scotus were forced to leave Paris, since they were cited as "dissidents" for refusing to support King Philip IV in his quarrel with Pope Boniface VIII. Gonsalvo returned to Spain where he was elected provincial minister for the Franciscan province of Castile, and in 1304 succeeded John of Murrovalle as Minister General, a position he held until his death in about 1313.

In 1304, while Minister General, Gonsalvo recommended that John Duns Scotus be promoted to the doctorate as he had known him by reputation and by "long experience." Modern historians have been puzzled by the phrase *experientia longa* and have sought to explain it either by positing a possible visit by Gonsalvo to Oxford or by conjecturing an early period of Parisian study for Scotus. But as has been recently demonstrated, we simply do not know how many years of association were required for Gonsalvo to say that he knew Scotus from long experience.

While at Paris, Gonsalvo engaged in a dispute with the Dominican MEISTER ECKHART. Eckhart had defended the thesis that "the praise of God in heaven is nobler than the love of God on earth" (*Utrum laus Dei in patria sit nobilior eius dilectione in via*). Gonsalvo rejected this idea and asserted the opposite. In this debate, Eckhart defended his personal view and that of his order. On the question of the primacy of the intellect or the will, the Dominicans emphasized the intellect, while the Franciscans laid stress on the will, and hence love, as an activity of the will.

Gonsalvo's literary record is not extensive. His commentary on the *Sentences* no longer survives and his scholastic works include *Quaestiones disputatae et de quodlibet* and the *Conclusiones metaphysicae* (once attributed to Scotus). In addition, he wrote a treatise on the precepts of the Franciscan Rule, some polemical works against the followers of PETER OLIVI, and sponsored the compilation of the *Catalogue of General Ministers*, also known as the *Gonsalvinus*.

Gonsalvo's *Quaestiones* date from his Paris regency. In them, he attacks several positions held by GODFREY OF FONTAINES and the Dominicans JOHN (Quidort) OF PARIS and Peter of La Palu. Philosophically, Gonsalvo belonged to the Franciscan School and upheld the traditional Augustinian themes such as the supremacy of the will over the intellect, hylomorphism in both angels and men, and the plurality of forms in man. Like Olivi, Gonsalvo denied the necessity of divine illumination in intellectual knowledge.

Bibliography

Primary source
(1925), *Quaestiones disputatae et de quodlibet*, ed. L. Amorós, Quaracchi: Collegium S. Bonaventurae.

Secondary sources
Gracia, Jorge J. E. (1969), "The agent and possible intellects in Gonsalvus Hispanus' Question XIII," *Franciscan Studies* 20, pp. 5–36.

Longpré, E., OFM (1924–5), "Gonsalve de Balboa et le B. Duns Scot," *Études Franciscaines* 36, pp. 640–5; 37, pp. 170–82.

——(1930), *Le B. Jean Duns Scot O.F.M. pour le Saint Siège contre le Gallicanisme*, Quaracchi: Collegium S. Bonaventurae.

Martel, Benoît, OFM Cap. (1968), *La Psychologie de Gonsalve d'Espagne*, Paris: Librairie Philosophique J. Vrin.

Wolter, Allan B. (1995), "Duns Scotus at Oxford," in *Via Scoti: Methodologica ad mentem Joannis Duns Scoti* (I, pp. 183–92), Rome: Edizioni Antonianum.

39

Gregory of Rimini

JACK ZUPKO

Gregory of Rimini (b. ca. 1300; d. 1358) was an Augustinian theologian of the later Middle Ages who played a crucial role in the transmission of philosophical ideas from Oxford to Paris, as well as developing influential positions of his own on the genesis of human knowledge and the necessity of grace for salvation. His teachings and his readings of authoritative texts were self-consciously Augustinian, but not in a reactionary way. Gregory was fully conversant with, and indeed, made his own contributions to, the many doctrinal and methodological advancements of his own day. He was in this sense a "modern," bringing a distinctively Augustinian voice to the rich intellectual life of fourteenth-century Paris.

Gregory was born around 1300 in the town of Rimini on the Adriatic coast of Italy. There he joined the monastic order of the Hermits of St. Augustine and began his scholarly training, eventually moving on to study theology at the University of Paris (1323–9). After more than a decade of teaching, first at Paris and then at Augustinian houses of study in Bologna, Padua, and Perugia, he returned to Paris in 1342 to prepare his lectures on the *Sentences* of PETER LOMBARD, which he delivered in the following academic year. Gregory used his preparation year to make himself thoroughly familiar with the work of English theologians such as WILLIAM OF OCKHAM, WALTER CHATTON, and ADAM OF WODEHAM, whose writings were just becoming available at Paris. His *Sentences* commentary shows an extensive knowledge of Wodeham in particular. In 1351 he returned to his home in Rimini as regent master of the Augustinian *studium* there and prior of the monastery. He was unanimously elected Prior General of the Augustinian Order in 1357, but died only a year later on a visit to Vienna.

Gregory composed a number of philosophical and theological works, but the most important by far is his *Lectura in primum et secundum libros Sententiarum* (Lectures on Books I and II of the *Sentences* (of Peter Lombard)). Virtually everything we know about Gregory's teachings comes from this text. Lombard's *Sentences* contains four books, but if Gregory did lecture on Books III and IV during his second sojourn at Paris, the text has been lost. He also wrote philosophical treatises on the intension and remission of forms and on the four cardinal virtues, as well as theological works and scripture commentaries. But again, his philosophical reputation rests upon his *Sentences* commentary, of which we now have a reliable critical edition (Trapp 1979–84).

As Gregory's modern editor, Damasus Trapp, remarked, "Modern Augustinianism begins only with Gregory of Rimini" (Trapp 1956, p. 158). Trapp insisted that it was a mistake to think of Gregory's Augustinianism as a throwback to an earlier time, an attempt to recover the methods of twelfth-century theologians. Instead, he suggested that Gregory advocated a historico-critical approach to theology, which used common sense and a careful attention to authoritative texts to respond to the excessive devotion to logical subtlety (*subtilitates*) he perceived in the work of radical nominalists such as JOHN OF MIRECOURT, whose teachings were condemned at Paris in 1347. For this reason, Trapp gave no credence to a much-quoted early sixteenth-century description of Gregory as the "*antesignanus nominalistarum* (standard-bearer of the nominalists)."

As a characterization of Gregory, Trapp's point is well taken. Gregory's writings are filled with quotations from AUGUSTINE, and his erudite discussions of these and other works, including those of his opponents, set a new standard for the critical use of texts among later medieval authors. Indeed, his quotations are so accurate that they have enabled modern scholars to identify Wodeham's *Lectura secunda*, as well as giving us some idea of the content of Wodeham's lost London lectures on the *Sentences*, which Gregory had available to him while preparing his commentary (Courtenay 1978, pp. 123–31). But doctrinal relationships with his Parisian contemporaries have been harder to determine. William J. Courtenay (1972–3; 1974) has shown that Gregory himself held one of the views for which Mirecourt was condemned, making it unlikely that he thought of himself as some kind of anti-nominalist. Indeed, it seems clear that 'nominalist' is no more than a family-resemblance term as applied to fourteenth-century philosophers, since, depending upon the figure in question, it can signify many other things besides an opposition to real universals. Thus it is important to try to understand Gregory's thought on its own terms, without typecasting his role in medieval intellectual history.

The signification of propositions

Like most fourteenth-century theologians, Gregory begins his *Sentences* commentary with a comprehensive discussion of whether theology is a science in the Aristotelian sense of that term. Can doctrinal truths be deductively ordered into a complete body of knowledge, like the natural sciences? In the latter sphere, lower or subalternate sciences (e.g., psychology) are said to borrow their principles from higher or subalternating sciences (e.g., physics), and to reach their proper conclusions by means of the theory of demonstration set out in the *Posterior Analytics*. Those who, as THOMAS AQUINAS, assume that theology is a deductive science, tend to see it as an extension of the Aristotelian method "upwards" into the discourse of revealed truth. But opponents of this view, such as GODFREY OF FONTAINES and HENRY OF GHENT, pointed to the fact that, unlike natural science, theological propositions are held on the basis of faith, not evidence, and hence they are not properly scientific (Brown 1999, pp. 195–201).

Gregory took a middle path in this dispute, arguing that theology is a science, though not strictly speaking. Articles of faith, such as "God is one," are not truly known because our belief in them is not based on their luminous self-evidence, or produced from other such principles via demonstrative proof (*I Sent.* prol. q. 1: 20–1; 51). Rather, following Augustine, Gregory contends that properly theological discourse must be based on the propositions of sacred Scripture, or what can be deduced from them. But if the movement from theological principles to conclusions is deductive, then theology at least formally constitutes a rational discourse, and so it can be considered a science in this sense (ibid.: 18–20). The difference between theological and natural science is chiefly one of content: theology is based on the Bible, whereas the natural sciences find their principles in the "text" of nature. Likewise, our readings are in each case guided by different authorities: by the writings of the Church Fathers (especially Augustine) in theology, by the philosophy of Aristotle in the natural sciences.

In the course of discussing the status of theology as a science, Gregory pauses to consider the proper object of scientific knowledge in general, and in doing so, unwittingly introduces the University of Paris to one of the most controversial ideas of fourteenth-century English theology. This is the idea that when we know something scientifically, what we know is neither an extra-mental thing nor a proposition (which were the views defended by the English Franciscan theologians Walter Chatton and William of Ockham, respectively), but a *complexe significabile* (= lit. "propositionally signifiable"), or state of affairs capable of being signified by a proposition. Until fairly recently, it was thought that Gregory himself was the source of this doctrine, but Gedeon Gál (1977) demonstrated that, although it was Gregory's version of the doctrine that was most widely known at Paris, he actually got the idea from the *Sentences* commentary of Adam of Wodeham. Wodeham, another English Franciscan, had intended the doctrine as a compromise between the views of his confreres Chatton and Ockham, which he believed were saddled with irremediable difficulties. The question at issue here is the old Aristotelian one of how scientific knowledge could be both necessary and about an ever-changing and evidently contingent world. Briefly, Wodeham did not think that scientific knowledge could be about things (*contra* Chatton) because our beliefs about the world are too complex to be mapped onto a simple ontology of things. We can assent not just to the fact that things are, but also that they are in a certain way (e.g., snow and ice not only exist, but they are cold). Alternatively, propositions are epistemically too derivative to serve as objects of scientific knowledge (*contra* Ockham). Our assent to propositions is carried further to what those propositions signify, since, according to Aristotle, to know is to know the causes of a thing, and propositions, *qua* propositions, are not the causes of any thing. Wodeham concludes that the total object of our assent in scientific knowledge must be "the total significate of the proposition necessitating the assent" (Wood and Gál 1990, p. 193).

Wodeham states this conclusion with some trepidation because, besides running against the opinions of two of the most famous theologians of his day, it could easily be interpreted as violating the law of parsimony by introducing a new kind of thing. Wodeham is adamant, however, that these *complexe significabilia* are not "things" in any sense of the term, but modes of being. Now in making this doctrine his own, Gregory manages to miss some of the subtlety in Wodeham's argument. For reasons that are unclear and which may come down to the fact that he simply did not share the same concern about parsimony that was so important in the original Franciscan debate, Gregory allows that *complexe significabilia* can be things in two of the three senses he assigns to that term (*I Sent.* prol., q. 1: 8–9). The fallout at Paris was swift and predictable. When other masters, especially those outside the faculty of theology, learned about the doctrine by reading Gregory's work, they tended to dismiss it using the razor. Thus, we find John Buridan remarking that "everything can be easily explained without positing such *complexe significabilia*, which are not substances, nor accidents, nor subsistent per se, nor inherent in anything else. Therefore, they should not be posited" (Buridan 1518, 31ra). Perhaps Gregory found affinities between the doctrine and his view of theology as a science concerned with propositions of sacred Scripture, but if so, these considerations were lost on Arts Masters such as Buridan, who found nothing to redeem *complexe significabilia* as an explanation of knowledge in the natural sciences (Zupko 1994–7).

Intuitive cognition and the need to posit a species of cognition

Gregory's other teachings likewise reveal an independent thinker responding to the views of English theologians – sometimes agreeing with them but just as often disagreeing – and bringing their ideas to the attention of his Parisian audience. He was particularly concerned to refute Ockham's theory of cognition, versions of which were already being defended at Paris by his colleagues, John Rathe Scotus and Francesco of Treviso (Tachau 1988, p. 358). Ockham had dismissed the widely accepted teaching that the causal mechanism of intellectual and sensory cognition is a species propagated in the medium between the cognizer and the object of cognition, arguing instead that there is a simple act of cognition by which the cognizer is intuitively or non-discursively aware of the object. This led Ockham to claim, incredibly, that just as we can have intuitive knowledge of the existence of a particular object when it does in fact exist, so we can also know intuitively that an object does not exist when it does not. Regardless of his reasons for it, most mid-fourteenth-century theologians found the doctrine highly controversial and associated it specifically with Ockham.

Gregory led the charge against the doctrine at Paris, arguing that Ockham's elimination of species made it impossible to explain not only sense perception but also higher modes of cognition such as memory and thought, which can function in the absence of their objects (*II Sent.* d. 7, q. 3: 138–40). He defends his position using a characteristic mix of authoritative and experiential arguments. Three passages are quoted showing that Augustine clearly assumes the existence of species. The third of these, from *De genesi ad litteram* (12.16.33), would have reinforced for his readers the novelty of Ockham's position: "when we see some body we have not seen before," Augustine says, "its image [*imago*] begins to exist in our soul, which we remember when that body is absent." Next, Gregory quotes Aristotle's *De anima* III (432a9–10) remark that "phantasms are like sensible species [*sensibilia*]" to the intellective soul, a sentiment he notes is echoed in AVERROES. These authorities are then bolstered by a number of commonsense arguments in which Gregory outlines his view that the generation of species in acts of cognition is part of the natural order, as anyone who heeds the testimony of experience can plainly see. For "if the species representing a thing were completely erased," he observes, "experience teaches that no recollection of it could be produced in us naturally, unless some other species representing it were already formed in us."

Gregory regards species as natural for a simple reason. Since objects wax and wane in the natural order, it makes sense that "nature, or rather, the author of nature," should "assist us so that we can know a thing which is absent or not yet existing by means of something similar to it, which is present to us." As for Ockham's claim to the contrary, "it has no evidence to support it [*nullam habet apparentiam*]." Gregory has little tolerance for *subtilitates* that fly in the face of common sense. As he indicates later in his commentary, the elimination of species threatens to undermine our knowledge of the external world:

> For it is absurd to think that I would not be naturally certain whether the fire that burns my hand (assuming it does) is really there or only apparent, or further, that I would not be certain that it heats me and burns me; or whether you are now sitting here, and whether I am now speaking and hearing my voice, and other things of this kind, which, when we assume them, destroy all knowledge [*scientia*] whose principles are taken from sense, since knowledge consists of certain and evident concepts [*notitia*]. What is more, it follows that the whole of life and social intercourse would no more proceed on the basis of certain and evident judgment than the work of those who, when they are asleep, speak of some things from their dreams as if they were real and busy themselves with other things they think are really outside them. The con-

sequence is immediately obvious, because from the fact that [on Ockham's view] we can have a sensation of this kind [i.e., intuitive] without the object present and, by the same reasoning, without the object existing, it is impossible for me to be certain through some concept [*notitia*] that it is existing and present when it is, rather than when it is not . . . (*I Sent*. d. 3, q. 1, additio 11: 325)

To Ockham's objection that there would be no point in positing species if they were of the same nature as the object of cognition, Gregory replies that they are of a different nature, though related to their objects by essential agreement or qualitative similarity. His elaboration of this claim suggests that we must pay careful attention to particular examples of cognition before attempting to classify them. We can see, for example, that sometimes creatures are able to recognize differences between objects that are essentially the same, while failing to recognize differences between similar objects whose essential agreement is small:

> An example should make this obvious. Everyone agrees that a wolf and a sheep are less dissimilar in terms of essential agreement than a wolf and a statue of a wolf, and yet a lamb certainly distinguishes between a wolf and a sheep, and indeed, even between its mother and another sheep – which agree still more essentially – although not between a wolf and a statue of a wolf. For if the lamb were to see a well-made statue of a wolf, it would flee from it just as if it were a real wolf. Many other examples like this could be given. (*II Sent*. d. 7, q. 3: 140)

For Gregory, the evident judgment of our intellect reflects another kind of authority, the authority of nature, whose deliverances can be harmonized with the arguments of Aristotle and Augustine.

What is striking in Gregory's development of his position is not the fact that he cites authorities (virtually everyone did), but the skill and accuracy with which he marshals authoritative arguments, which he sees as seconded by natural reason. Two centuries before Gregory, ALAN OF LILLE had cautioned students of theology that authority has a nose of wax that can be bent any way one wishes. Gregory responds with an exemplary reading of authoritative texts, stabilizing their voices through careful citation and commonsense articulation.

God's power to change the past

Gregory is among the small minority of medieval theologians who held that divine omnipotence includes God's ability to make the past not to have happened, a view which he shared with his English contemporary THOMAS BRADWARDINE (Courtenay 1972–3, pp. 154–65). His position is developed cautiously, by means of arguments opposed to the "many moderns" according to whom "every affirmative proposition about the past, if true, is necessary" (*I Sent*. d. 42–44, q. 1, additio 155: 364). In contrast, Gregory held that the proposition, 'Adam was created [*Adam fuit creatus*]' is true, "even though it is contingent and able never to have been true [*potest numquam fuisse vera*]." His position seems based on the idea that we can never produce a contradiction by denying any such true proposition about the past, together with the assumption that God views the whole of creation at once, from eternity:

> Everything that God could have willed from eternity, He now can have willed from eternity, and what He could have not willed, he is able not have willed. Therefore, although He has willed from eternity to produce Adam, He is able not to have willed it, and He is able to have willed not to produce [Adam], just as he has been able from eternity. (*I Sent*. d. 42–4, q. 1, additio 155: 362)

The way Gregory expresses it, God's being 'able not to have willed [*potest non voluisse*] to produce Adam' is ambiguous between 'make it [now] such that Adam never existed' and '[timelessly] will Adam's non-existence' (notice that the indexical 'now [*nunc*]' drops out of the particular example above). Gregory does not think that God would make it the case now that Adam both existed and did not exist, for that would be a contradiction, and not even God can make a contradiction true. In the same way, God cannot erase from the Book of Life the name of someone He has already willed to save (which Gregory interprets as God's making the same name both written and not written), although He can, by virtue of His absolute power, actually save someone who has never been destined to be saved (ibid., 369). Gregory evidently wants to ensure that God's freedom to create or annihilate from eternity is not trumped by such creaturely, perspectival considerations as the necessity of the past, although he does not speculate on what this would mean for us metaphysically. Indeed, he closes the main part of his discussion in a way that is surprisingly ambivalent about his main thesis: "Take note: I have set out the arguments and responses on both side of the question, but which of these is to be preferred is something I leave to the judgment of the doctors [of theology]" (ibid., 384).

The composition of continuous magnitudes

Gregory also made an original contribution to the great fourteenth-century debate over the composition of continua, i.e., lines (continuous in one dimension), surfaces (continuous in two), and bodies (continuous in three). Most of the debate focused on lines and points, and especially on the questions of how points can be said to compose a line, whether such points are indivisible, infinitely many, and so on. Now one might wonder why we would find a dis-cussion of continuous magnitudes in a *Sentences* commentary, which is, after all, a work of theology, rather than in a work of natural philosophy such as commentary on Aristotle's *Physics*. But the debate was in fact conducted in both settings. In theology, it arose in thought experiments designed to test the limits of properties traditionally ascribed to God, such as omniscience and immutability, as well as in questions about whether angels could be said to be in a place.

Gregory did not write a *Physics* commentary, but he did devote considerable attention to the continuum problem. In response to Distinctions 35–6 of Book I of the *Sentences*, which ask about God's knowledge of creatures, most theologians examined the question of whether we can conclude by natural reason that God understands things other than himself. This immediately raised the worry about whether God is in a state of potentiality with respect to his knowledge of everything other than himself, since creatures are mutable, constantly moving from states of potentiality to actuality. This is how the question first comes up in Gregory, where an objector argues that God could never know all of the parts of a continuous magnitude – i.e., know them as "divided and distinct" – if continua are infinitely divisible, since the actual division of such a magnitude could never be completed (*I Sent.* d. 35–6, q. 1: 213–14). Indivisibilists such as the late thirteenth-century English theologian HENRY OF HARCLAY had argued on these grounds that continua must be composed of infinitely many indivisible points. But the majority of thinkers found Henry's position incoherent – e.g., the adjacent points which make up a line must have a "left side" and a "right side," but anything with distinct sides is divisible – and so held with Aristotle that the parts of a continuous magnitude are always further divisible. Accordingly, they used sophisticated logico-semantic techniques to distinguish between the different senses in which a continuum can be divided, which helped them to reconcile their divisibilism with God's knowing every part of a continuum (Murdoch 1982; Zupko 1993).

But Gregory would have none of this. In his view, the problem with existing accounts is that they all conceive of divisibility as a physical process, whereas God's knowledge is simple, eternal, and perfect – not based on any kind of process at all. As Richard Cross (1998) has shown, Gregory uses this idea to argue that a continuum is composed of infinitely many extended parts, which we should think of as "overlapping" rather than adjacent: each part contains other parts, and no division will produce infinitely many equal parts or point-like indivisibles. All of the parts of a continuous magnitude are themselves magnitudes (*II Sent.* d. 2, q. 2: 288). Gregory proposes that we should think of God conceiving the divisions of a continuous magnitude as already completed, in all of its myriad ways:

> And just as every continuum in fact has infinitely many potential parts, and each [part of it], however small, includes infinitely many [parts] (and no part can be understood to be an indivisible; nor is there a potential infinity of such [indivisible] parts), so I say that in God's conception, the continuum is totally actually divided into parts, of which each is also totally actually divided, and includes infinitely many actually divided [parts]. (*I Sent.* d. 35–6, q. 1: 224; Cross 1998, p. 102)

If God knows each of the parts of an infinitely divisible continuum as already perfectly (conceptually) divided, then God's knowledge does not depend on any process of division. In addition, God is acquainted with the continuum as a kind of indivisible, for a continuum that has been "totally actually divided" is indivisible in the sense that it cannot be further divided, i.e., it lacks any potentiality for further division. It is almost as if Gregory wants us to think of continuous magnitudes as wholes in the same way that he thinks of propositions as wholes: just as the signification of a proposition is not reducible by semantic analysis to the significations of its grammatical or logical parts, so the totality of a line is not reducible by physical division to its component parts. God does not know the line by knowing each of its infinitely many parts, but by immediately knowing the entire line as composed of "infinitely many actually divided parts." There is thus an interesting resonance between Gregory's holistic understanding of continuous magnitudes, and his view that the proper object of scientific knowledge is the *complexe significabile*, or total state of affairs capable of being signified by a proposition.

Bibliography

Primary source

(1979–84), *Lectura super Primum et Secundum Sententiarum*, vols. I–VI, ed. A. Damasus Trapp, OSA, et al., Berlin and New York: De Gruyter.

Secondary sources

Buridan, John (1518), *In Metaphysicen Aristotelis quaestiones argutissimae*, Paris. Repr. (1964) as *Kommentar zur Aristotelischen Metaphysik*, Frankfurt-on-Main: Minerva. (Note: the publication date of the incunabula edition is incorrectly given as 1588 on the frontispiece of the reprint.)

Brown, Stephen (1999), "The intellectual context of later medieval philosophy: Universities, Aristotle, arts, and theology," in John Marenbon, ed., *Medieval Philosophy* (pp. 188–201), vol. III of *Routledge History of Philosophy*, London and New York: Routledge.

Courtenay, William J. (1972–3), "John of Mirecourt and Gregory of Rimini on whether God can undo the past," *Recherches de Théologie Ancienne et Médiévale* 39, pp. 224–56; 40, pp. 147–74.

——(1974), "Nominalism and late medieval religion," in Charles Trinkhaus and Heiko A. Oberman, eds., *The Pursuit of Holiness in Late Medieval and Renaissance Religion* (pp. 26–59), Leiden: Brill.

——(1978), *Adam Wodeham: An Introduction to his Life and Writings*, Leiden: Brill.

Cross, Richard, (1998), "Infinity, continuity, and composition: the contribution of Gregory of Rimini," *Medieval Philosophy and Theology* 7, pp. 89–110.

Gál, Gedeon (1977), "Adam of Wodeham's question on the '*complexe significabile*' as the immediate object of scientific knowledge," *Franciscan Studies* 37, pp. 66–102.

Murdoch, John (1982), "Infinity and continuity," in N. Kretzmann, A. Kenny, and J. Pinborg, eds., *The Cambridge History of Later Medieval Philosophy* (pp. 564–91), Cambridge and New York: Cambridge University Press.

Tachau, Katherine (1988), *Vision and Certitude in the Age of Ockham: Optics, Epistemology, and the Foundations of Semantics, 1250–1345*, Leiden, New York, and Cologne: Brill.

Trapp, A. Damasus OSA (1956), "Augustinian theology of the 14th century: notes on editions, marginalia, opinions and book-lore," *Augustiniana* 6, pp. 146–274.

Wood, Rega and Gál, Gedeon eds. (1990), *Adam de Wodeham, Lectura secunda in librum primum Sententiarum*, St. Bonaventure, NY: Franciscan Institute.

Zupko, Jack (1993), "Nominalism meets indivisibilism," *Medieval Philosophy and Theology* 3, pp. 158–85.

——(1994–7), "How it played in the *Rue de Fouarre*: the reception of Adam Wodeham's theory of the *complexe significabile* in the arts faculty at Paris in the mid-fourteenth century," *Franciscan Studies* 54, pp. 211–25.

40

Guido Terrena

FRANCISCO BERTELLONI

Guido Terrena (d. 1342) was born in Perpignan. The first signs of his intense activity are evident in Paris. He becomes student of GODFREY OF FONTAINES, *magister theologiae* in 1312, regent master of the Carmelites until 1317, teacher of JOHN BACONTHORPE and Provincial of the Order. From 1318 to 1321 he is General Prior of the Order, from 1321 to 1332 Bishop of Majorca, and from 1332 to 1342 Bishop of Elna. His main works are the *Commentaries on Peter Lombard's Sentences* (only fragments survive), *Quodlibeta*, *Quaestiones ordinariae*, *Quaestiones disputatae*, several commentaries on Aristotle (*De anima*, *Metaphysics*, *Physics*, and *Ethics*) and on the *Decretum Gratiani*, a *Summa de haeresibus*, and *De perfectione vitae angelicae*.

At the beginning of fourteenth century, influenced by his teacher Godfrey of Fontaines, Guido develops a strongly intellectualist Thomism and defends intellectual abstraction and knowledge's objectivity. He is opposed to the Augustinian illumination theory and upholds the object's active character and the intellect's primacy over the will in a free act. His solution to the problem of universals is close to nominalism, although it was criticized by WILLIAM OF OCKHAM. Guido develops a middle position between realism and terminism by reducing the unity of the species to a similarity between individuals. He also denies the real distinction between essence and existence, defends the principles of act and potency, and considers form as the principle of individuation. Guido claims that the foundations of natural law and *ius gentium* are to be found in the nature of beings. Despite the relevance of his philosophical and theological works, the most outstanding aspect of his intellectual personality is his theoretical compromise with the ecclesiastical conflicts of his time. In fact, he acquired renown as the first theorist of the pope's doctrinal infallibility (Tierney 1972). In the controversy on poverty, he defends Pope John XXII's position against the Franciscans. He died in Avignon.

Bibliography

Primary sources

(1926), *Quaestio de magisterio infallibili R. Pontificis*, ed. B. M. Xiberta, Münster: Aschendorff.

(1972), "Quarti quolibet prima quaestio; Quinti quolibet prima quaestio; Secundi quolibet prima quaestio," ed. Jorge J. E. Gracia, in "Tres *quaestiones* de Guido Terrena sobre los trascendentales," *Analecta Sacra Tarraconensia* 45, pp. 87–130.

(1973), "Quodlibeto IV, q. 2: Si la unidad de la especie es real," trans. Jorge J. E. Gracia, in "Guido Terrena y la unidad real del universal: Quodlibet IV, q. 2," *Diálogos* 9, pp. 117–31.

Secondary sources

Fournier, P. (1938), *Histoire littéraire de la France*, vol. 37 (see pp. 1–38), Paris: Imprimerie Nationale.

Gracia, Jorge J. E. (1973), "The convertibility of unum and ens according to Guido Terrena," *Franciscan Studies* 33, pp. 143–70.

Lohr, C. H. (1968), "Medieval Aristotle Latin commentaries," *Traditio* 24, pp. 190–1.

Marcuzzi, P. G. (1979), "Una soluzione teologicogiuridica al problema dell'usura in una questione 'de quolibet' inedita di Guido Terrena," *Salesianum* 41, pp. 647–84.

Melsen, J. (1939), *Guido Terrena (1260?–1342) jurista*, Rome.

Tierney, B. (1972), *Origins of Papal Infallibility, 1150–1350* (see pp. 238–72), Leiden: Brill.

Turley, T. (1975), "Infallibilists in the Curia of Pope John XXII," *Journal of Medieval History* 1, pp. 71–101.

——(1978a), "Guido Terreni and the *Decretum*," *Bulletin of Medieval Canon Law*, NS 8, pp. 29–34.

——(1978b), "The ecclesiology of Guido Terreni," Ph.D. dissertation, Cornell University.

Xiberta, B. M. (1924), "De magistro Guidone Terreni, priore generale ordini nostri, episcopo Maiorensi et Elnensi," *Analecta Ordinis Carmelitarum* 5, pp. 113–206.

——(1925), "De doctrinis theologicis M. Guidonis Terreni," *Analecta ordinis carmelitarum* 6, pp. 233–76.

——(1932), *Guido Terrena Carmelita de Perpinyá*, Barcelona: Institutió Patxot.

41

Hasdai Crescas

TAMAR RUDAVSKY

Although Hasdai Crescas (b. ca. 1340; d. 1410/11) had no interest in science per se, he was embroiled in precisely the same set of scientific issues that occupied scholastic philosophers after the condemnation of 1277. Crescas was born in Barcelona and studied with the famed philosopher Nissim ben Reuben Girondi. In 1389 he assumed the post of rabbi of Saragossa. In 1391, responding to riots against the Jews, Crescas wrote a polemic *Sefer bittul Iqqarei ha-Nozrim* (*The Book of the Refutation of the Principles of the Christians*, 1397–8) in which he argues that major Christian principles such as original sin, the Trinity, and transubstantiation are all self-contradictory and philosophically absurd. His major work *Sefer Or Adonai* (*The Book of the Light of the Lord*, 1405–10), finished several months before his death, is a polemic against his two Aristotelian predecessors, MAIMONIDES and GERSONIDES. In this work, Crescas sought to undermine the Aristotelian cosmology and physics that pervaded the works of his predecessors.

In an attempt to weaken Aristotle's hold upon Jewish philosophy, and to uphold the basic dogmas of Judaism, Crescas subjects Aristotle's physics and metaphysics to a trenchant critique. Crescas rejects Aristotle's theory of place and argues that place is prior to bodies: in contradistinction to Aristotle's conception of place, space for Crescas is not a mere relationship of bodies but rather the "interval between the limits of that which it surrounds" (Wolfson 1929, p. 195). Space is seen by Crescas as an infinite continuum ready to receive matter. Because this place or extension of bodies is identified with space, there is no contradiction in postulating the existence of space not-filled with body, i.e., the vacuum (see pp. 38–69). Crescas, in fact, assumes that place is identical with the void, on the grounds that "place must be equal to the whole of its occupant as well as to [the sum of] its parts" (p. 199).

Further, Crescas rejects Aristotle's theory of time, arguing that "the correct definition of time is that it is the measure of the continuity of motion or of rest between two instants." By *hitdabequt* Crescas means to emphasize that time is not to be identified with physical motion or bodies, but with the duration of the life of the thinking soul. Time is "indeed measured by both motion and rest, because it is our conception (*tziyurenu*) of the measure of their continuity that is time" (Wolfson 1929, p. 289). On this basis Crescas concludes that "the existence of time is only in the soul" (ibid.). It is because humans have a mental conception of this measure that time even exists. The continuity of time depends only upon a thinking mind, and is indefinite, becoming definite only by being measured by motion. Were we not to conceive of it, there would be no time. It is in this context that Crescas comes closest to reflecting his near scholastic contemporaries PETER AURIOL and WILLIAM OF OCKHAM, both of whom develop a subjective theory of time.

The *Light* contains as well a theory of physical determinism. Crescas lists six fundamental doctrines: God's knowledge of particulars, Providence, God's power, prophecy, human choice, and the purposefulness of the Torah. Against Gersonides, he affirms God's knowledge of future contingents, even those determined by human choice. He then argues that human freedom is only apparent and not genuine: humans think they are free because they are ignorant of the causes of their choices. Human responsibility for action lies not in the actual performance of the action, but rather in the agent's acceptance of an action as its own. The feeling of joy an agent feels at acquiescing to certain actions, e.g., fulfilling the commandments, is the reward for that action. So too, God experiences joy in giving of himself to the world.

Many scholars have tried to trace the formative influences upon Crescas' doctrine of will. In his recent study of Crescas' *Sermon on the Passover*, Ravitsky has argued that Crescas' discussion of will appears to reflect a connection to Latin scholasticism in its acceptance of Scotist ideas regarding the moral and religious primacy of the will (Ravitzsky 1998, p. viii). After noting important similarities and differences between AQUINAS'S and Crescas' conceptions of belief, Ravitsky turns to a comparison of JOHN DUNS SCOTUS and Crescas, arguing that both philosophers reject their predecessors' insistence upon an intellectualist conception of belief which leads to ultimate felicity, and replace it with a conception of belief based on the primacy of will (pp. 54–60).

Harvey suggests that Crescas' work was "perhaps connected in some way with the pioneering work in natural science being conducted at the University of Paris" (Harvey 1980, p. 23). More specifically, Harvey has compared the works of the two contemporaries NICHOLAS ORESME and Crescas, arguing that they are the two most important philosophers representing the new physics. Working in Pamplona in the 1330s, both argue for the existence of many worlds; both claim that many worlds do not imply existence of more than one God; both argue that generation and corruption in the sublunary world is evidence for successive worlds. Crescas himself describes his analysis and critique of Aristotelian science as having "no small benefit for this science" (Wolfson 1929, p. 180). In fact, it can be argued that Crescas' critique of Aristotle helped lay the groundwork for the abandonment of Aristotelian science in subsequent centuries.

Bibliography

Primary sources
(1990), *The Light of the Lord (Sefer Or Adonai or Or Ha-Shem)*, ed. Shlomo Fisher, Jerusalem; first printed 1555, Ferrara.
(1992), *The Refutation of the Christian Principles*, trans. and with introduction and notes by Daniel J. Lasker, Albany, NY: State University of New York Press.

Secondary sources
Feldman, Seymour (1980), "The theory of eternal creation in Hasdai Crescas and some of his predecessors," *Viator* 11, pp. 289–320.
Harvey, Warren Zev (1980), "The term *hitdabbekut* in Crescas' definition of time," *Jewish Quarterly Review* 71, pp. 44–7.
——(1998), *Physics and Metaphysics in Hasdai Crescas*, Amsterdam: J. C. Gieben.

Pines, Shlomo (1967), *Scholasticism after Thomas Aquinas and the Teachings of Hasdai Crescas and His Predecessors*, Jerusalem: Israel Academy of Sciences and Humanities.

Ravitzky, Aviezer (1998), *Sermon on the Passover (Derashat ha-Pesach le-Rab Hasdai Crescas u-Mehqarim be-Mishnato ha-Pilosofit)*, Jerusalem: Israel Academy of Sciences and Humanities.

Wolfson, H. A. (1929), *Crescas' Critique of Aristotle*, Cambridge, MA: Harvard University Press.

42

Henry of Ghent

R. WIELOCKX

Henry of Ghent (d. 1293) was Archdeacon of Bruges (1277) and of Tournai (from 1279/80), and stands out as regent master in theology at the University of Paris (1276–1292/3). In the years after the death of THOMAS AQUINAS and before the arrival of JOHN DUNS SCOTUS, he was the leading Augustinian, while GODFREY OF FONTAINES was the dominant Aristotelian.

Henry explicitly states (*Quodlibet* II, 9; 1983, pp. 66–7, ll. 6–26) that he was a member of the theological commission consulted by Tempier, the Bishop of Paris, while drafting the famous Syllabus of March 7, 1277. Tempier also consulted others, in addition to the masters in theology. In fact, with the support of the legate and the diocesan staff, Tempier sometimes ignored the *unanimous* advice of Henry and the other masters (Wielockx 1985, pp. 97–120). Nevertheless, the formulation of one article in particular of the Syllabus bears the stamp of Henry of Ghent's phraseology (Gauthier 1947/8, p. 220). Moreover, the notorious conflict between the mendicant orders and the secular clergy made Henry a protagonist once again (Laarmann 1999, pp. 27–8, 29–31; Porro 1996a, pp. 380–8).

The *Quodlibeta* I–XV and *Summa (Quaestiones ordinariae)* I–LXXV are certainly authentic and important, in contrast to doubtfully authentic attributed works (Laarmann 1999, pp. 42–9).

Godfrey of Fontaines's library reveals the coexistence of early and revised versions of some of Henry's *Quodlibeta* and *Quaestiones ordinariae*, the earlier version usually in full page, the revised version in the margins. C. Luna (1998, pp. 172–86, 220–36) discovered an otherwise-unknown, early version of *Quodlibet* X, 7, not even present in Godfrey of Fontaines's library. As to the suggestion that Henry may have first published *Summa* I–LXI in 1289 (Marrone 1996, pp. 208–9), two observations are in order. First, Godfrey of Fontaines already had a copy of *Summa* I–XXVI in his possession by 1276–7 (Wielockx 1985, pp. 17–41). Second, the supposed editorial unit *Summa* I–LXI displays the presence of incompatible teachings regarding, for instance, noetics: the admission of *species impressa* (impressed mental picture of the thing) in *Summa* I and III and its denial in *Summa* XXXIII, XXXVI, LVIII (Nys 1949, pp. 52–60, 67–70, 94–8).

Metaphysics: from creatures to creator

J. Paulus (1938, pp. 52–66) presented a devastating and influential interpretation, in which he argued that Henry's notion of analogy suffered from internal contradiction. Whereas

Henry's explicit and somewhat marginal theory of analogy proceeded in good Aristotelian tradition from things to ideas, from creatures to Creator and tended ultimately towards equivocality, the main stream of his metaphysical effort led him to deduce the notion of God from that of being, and the understanding of creatures from the notion of God. This attempt would imply that what comes first objectively also comes first in our knowledge and would assume, in line with AVICENNA and paving the way for Duns Scotus, that the notion of being is univocal.

The excellent monograph by J. Gómez Caffarena (1958) and the work of W. Hoeres (1965) put things in a different light, and, more recently, J. Decorte (1996) has uncovered the weakness of J. Paulus's views.

Henry consistently admits that creatures come before God in the order of "reason," unlike what happens in the order of "nature," where God comes first (*Summa* XXIV, 7–9). Since human knowledge is both nature and reason, it mirrors the order of nature and the order of reason as well. In human knowledge as nature, even when there is not yet any act of knowledge and, hence, any concrete object of knowledge, knowledge is characterized by its proper capacity and by the specificity of its potential or "formal" object (*ratio intelligendi*). On this level of intellectual knowledge, its first (formal) object is the most undetermined. Thus the Undeterminable Undetermined (*esse subsistens*: Subsistent "Beingness") comes before the determinable undetermined (being as participated) and both the subsistent and the participated come before the participating being (see also *Quodlibet* XV, 9). In human knowledge as reason, however, which is characterized by its "material" object, the first we know is "this being" or "that good," which escapes from being merely determined, since it is not simply "this" or "that," but "this *being*" or "that *good.*" Inasmuch as this first "material" object is somehow undetermined, it is not entirely dissimilar from the determinable undetermined (participated being) or the Undeterminable Undetermined (Subsistent "Beingness"). Accordingly, the knowledge of "this being" is also an analogous, indirect, and at first undiscerned knowledge of God. After this first distinct knowledge of a determined being, we come to know distinctly, by a first abstraction, the determinable undetermined being and, still later, by a second abstraction, we come to discern the Undeterminable Undetermined "Beingness." In our knowledge as reason, therefore, God is not the first, but the last we discern.

As for the charge that he admits univocity, Henry clearly does not deduce the notion of God by external differentiation from a supposedly univocal notion of being (*Summa* XXI, 2, 1520, fos. 124G–I, 124O–125S, 125V; Decorte 1996; Laarmann 1999, pp. 104–16). According to Henry, Avicenna's contention that being is the first notion to impress itself on the human mind is either wrong or it simply means that the Subsistent "Beingness" (*esse*) and not any supposedly separate being in general is the first object of human knowledge as nature and the first indirect object of human knowledge as reason. Henry, moreover, does not in any way deduce the understanding of creatures from the notion of God. He employs a distinction found also in the so-called *Summa fratris Alexandri* and thereby rejects any univocal community or likeness between Creator and creatures (*convenientia univocitatis* or *similitudinis*) that may exist between genus and species or between species and individuals. He only admits a community of analogy or imitation (*convenientia analogiae* or *imitationis*) between them.

Creatures

Two of Henry's most famous contributions to metaphysics concern essence. He not only attributes a distinct being to the essence of creatures, *esse essentiae* (essential being), but also admits that their essence is composed of *esse essentiae* and *essentia* or – according to the dominant terminology of his later works – *aliquitas* (somethingness). Both points deserve a closer look.

Should existence in actuality account for this specific *esse essentiae* of creatures? How then does one explain the fact that, although they all supposedly exist in actuality, no essence is exactly any other? Should, moreover, the existence in God's creative mind explain this specific *esse essentiae*? How then does one account for the fact that the divine idea of this essence (the human being, for instance) is *not* the divine idea of that essence (the dog, for instance) (*Quodlibet* II, 1; *Quodlibet* IX, 2)? Should, finally, the existence in the creature's mind explain anything here? But, in this mind, fictive realities (*res a reor reris*), like "goatstag" or "golden mountain," coexist with real realities (*res a ratitudine*), like "a human being" or "a dog" (*Quodlibet* VII, 1–2; 1991, p. 27, ll. 59–67). It seems, then, that Henry is positing an intermediary being between "being in actual existence" and "being in the mind" (*Quodlibet* III, 1; 1518, fo. 61r–vO; Wippel 1982, p. 403). As to its actual existence, the being characteristic of the essence of creatures will undoubtedly have to rely on things in actual existence and, as to its existence in the mind, it will have to be grounded in the Creator's thinking or it will have to be present to the created mind. In itself, however, the *esse essentiae* of creatures is irreducible except to God's own *esse essentiae* of which they are an imitation.

Henry is close to AVICENNA here, not only because any quiddity is in some way self-sufficient (*Equinitas est equinitas tantum*: to be a horse is just to be a horse: Avicenna, *Metaph.* V, 1, 1980, p. 228, l. 33), but also because he invokes the authority of Avicenna from his very first presentation of the *esse essentiae* (*Quodlibet* I, 9, 1979, p. 53, ll. 64–8; Avicenna, *Metaph.* VI, 1, 1980, p. 295, ll. 89–90). Neither is he far from the Neoplatonic tradition. According to Proclus, being is basically the unparticipated "Beingness" that, at the top of the intelligible universe, transcends all participated and participating beings, even though it is itself both finite and infinite because it is less simple than the One. According to the anonymous author of the *Liber de causis*, being is not merely actual existence, but the universal specificity previous to the more particular specificity of life and to the still more particular specificity of intellect.

It seems likely, then, that it is the *esse essentiae* itself that inspired Henry to introduce the "intentional distinction" for which he is famous, since his first presentation of *esse essentiae* coincides with his first presentation of a new kind of intermediary distinction between sheer real distinction and mere mental distinction (Macken 1981, pp. 769–76). He is careful in making clear the property of each. For instance, between substance and accident, there is a real distinction. Between the thing defined and its definition, as between a human being and a rational animal, there is only a distinction of reason. The distinction between a genus and its difference, as between animal and rational, is more than a purely mental one and less than a real one. This type of difference Henry calls "intentional" (*Quodlibet* X, 7; 1981, pp. 164–6).

Henry clearly agrees that, in creatures, there is an intentional distinction between their essence and their *esse existentiae* (existential being). In his early writings (*Quodlibet* I, 9), however, he seems to have admitted a mental distinction between *esse essentiae* and *essentia* in creatures. Henry soon became aware (*Summa* XXVIII, 4 and second redaction of XXI, 4) that whereas, in God, Essence and Beingness (*esse*) do not impose any limitation on each other, in creatures, on the other hand, their essential being implies that they are some essence, but not that they are specifically this special essence and not that other one. Their being-this-special-essence, conversely, is always a restriction of their being-any-essence, which in itself is open to more than just this one essence (Gómez Caffarena 1958, pp. 101–4). Although "to be a human" and "to be a dog" are both infinite within the borders of their specificity (since, in being human or respectively in being dog, nothing is lacking to either of them), neither of them, however, realizes all that "being an animal" can be or, even less, all that "to be an essence" can be (*Summa* XXVI, 1). Their *esse essentiae* can never be synonymous with their *essentia/aliquitas*. The distinction between them must be stronger than just a mental one (*pace* Porro 1996c, pp. 235–6).

The creator

Henry refuses to admit that God's existence is immediately evident to humans and affirms that humans can doubt God's existence (*Summa* XXII, 3). Hence he undertakes to prove that God exists.

Although he agrees to some extent with AVERROES that the existence of God is demonstrated in physics, Henry is convinced that it belongs to metaphysics to show "*secundum Avicennam et secundum rei veritatem*" (in accordance with Avicenna and with truth) that this God whose existence is demonstratively established in physics is the Beingness (*esse*) that subsists in itself and is thus, by definition, one – in fact the true God (*Summa* XXII, 5; 1520, fo. 134D).

The demonstration in physics (*Summa* XXII, 4) unfolds *via causalitatis* (arguing from causality) and *via eminentiae* (arguing from eminence) (Laarmann 1999, pp. 155–74; Porro 1990, pp. 94–9).

The *via causalitatis* makes use of efficient, formal, and final causality. As to efficient causality, Henry develops three arguments: motion leads to the certainty of an unmoved mover; possible being requires a necessary one; things coming about (by others) make clear that there is a first cause. In a remark reminiscent of an argument advanced by SIGER OF BRABANT, Henry does not fail to note with care that all the proofs advanced on the basis of causality may very well compel one to deny the possibility of infinite regress and to arrive at the substantiation of a first cause. None of those proofs, however, is able to show that the respective first cause must be the same as the first cause demonstrated in other arguments. Only a proof of a necessary unique first cause would be able to show that the ultimate end is the first truth and the one efficient universal cause.

The *via eminentiae* relies, first, on the reduction from the diminished to the perfect good and, second, on the comparison of degrees of truth.

The metaphysical proof in Henry's understanding (Laarmann 1999, pp. 256–71; Porro 1990, pp. 117–21) works with a kind of fusion of Avicenna and AUGUSTINE: "*secundum Avicennam et Augustinum*" (*Summa* XXII, 5, fo. 134C–D). Whereas in Avicenna, transcendentals (being etc.) are the first notions to impress themselves on the mind (*Metaph.* I, c. 5; Van Riet 1977, p. 31, ll. 2–3), in Augustine (*De Trinitate* VIII, iii, 4) the understanding of transcendentals as realized in creatures (this good etc.) is a privileged way for arriving at the knowledge of God. Unlike the proof by formal causality or the *via eminentiae*, the metaphysical proof no longer deals merely with a being superior to and prior to creatures. Rather, it shows that in creatures being is always participated (restricted), and the essence, accordingly, finite. In contrast, God is the utmost in simplicity, the identity of Beingness (*esse*) and Essence (*Summa* XXII, 5; 1520, fo. 135E). And knowing scientifically this characteristic simplicity, one by the fact itself knows that God must be one (*Summa* XXV, 2–3), which allows the metaphysical proof to achieve what the physical proofs leave unachieved.

299

True, Aristotle, in Book Lambda of the *Metaphysics*, succeeds in showing that the governor of the universe is in fact one because the order of the universe is one. But this argument only concludes that God is one in fact and not that he must be one by definition. It only works on the premiss that the universe is one and not that it must be one in all hypotheses. In the hypothesis of the existence of more than one universe, therefore, Aristotle, Henry says, would reckon with the possibility of several first principles, each presiding over its respective universe (*Summa* XXV, 3, 1520, fo. 153E).

More concretely, the metaphysical proof (*Summa* XXIV, 6) develops in three main steps: the most general knowledge; the more general one; the general one. Since the final result of this proof is no more than *general* knowledge, we are left with the sense that the conclusion reached is far from being the distinct and immediate face to face vision of God in his essence, which is the object of Christian hope. It is immediately evident also that the metaphysical proof moves from the knowledge of creatures to that of the Creator. The first step (most general knowledge) indeed moves *via causalitatis* from the effect (the complex) to the cause (the simple). The second (*via eminentiae*), as a step from creatures toward the Creator that transcends them, necessarily supposes the logically previous notion of creatures. The third (*via remotionis*), in its capacity as a negation, supposes in turn that the quality to be denied in God is acknowledged as present in creatures.

The most general step of knowledge comprehends three moments. In a first moment humans know this good here or that good there (clearly in creatures). Thanks to the imitation by this good of the unrestricted Good and thanks to the analogy of our notions of this good and the unrestricted Good, the transcendentals as realized in creatures and known by us from the outset are already a way, indistinct and still most general, of knowing God in knowing creatures. The second moment of the most general knowledge, by a first abstraction, leaves out the "this" and the "that" from "this good" and "that good." The relatively unrestricted "good" which this abstraction grasps is both universal and participated (restricted). This grasping of the *bonum universale et participatum* is, in fact, much like the crucial metaphysical analysis of the essence of creatures inasmuch as they are finite, namely participated (determinable) in their *esse essentiae* and determined in their respective restrictive essences. The third moment of the most general knowledge, by a second abstraction, reaches the conclusion that the Creator must be beyond the composition that is characteristic of finiteness and, hence, is *bonum per essentiam et subsistens* (the Good by essence, subsistent in itself). This Good cannot be diminished, unable as it is to be received in anything else, which would of necessity be less good. Not being determined or even determinable by anything else, it is and can be only subsistent in itself.

The second step of thought (*via eminentiae*) consists of realizing a little less in general and a little more in particular which kind of attributes belong to the one subsistent in itself. Even though humans may feel in general that God is somehow the one subsistent in itself, some of them may nevertheless be mistaken. This apparently occurs when some humans consider God to be a creature or, even more crudely, a piece of wood or stone.

The third step of thought (*via remotionis*) consists of understanding that all deficiency and all perfection mixed with imperfection is a composite and that *every* composite is an imperfection, which is denied to Simplicity, to absolute Perfection. At this point it is impossible to think that God is perfect simplicity only in his essence. Denying at this level the real or even intentional composition of a participated *esse essentiae* and a finite essence, we deny on the same ground the real or even intentional composition of *esse existentiae* and essence. When attributed to God, Being, Essence, and Existence can be distinguished only by mental distinction, however one grounded in reality.

300

A spiritualistic anthropology

Avicenna links in one spiritualistic anthropology his views on the human soul as substance (as opposed to form informing matter) and on some human self-knowledge independent of the senses. Henry, who is comparable with him regarding these two points, insists, in addition, on free will in humans.

From the very beginning of his career (*Quodlibet* I, 4) Henry prefers to accept a double substance in a human being. This preference is the more remarkable because he holds, from the beginning to the end of his teaching, that there is only one substantial form in all other composites. In his first years, he does not absolutely exclude, however, either Thomas Aquinas's thesis or the special variant proposed by GILES OF ROME (*Theoremata de corpore Christi*): matter, defined as three-dimensionality, accounts for the continuity of individuation of the body of Christ even if, at the moment of death, his intellectual soul was separated from the body. The events of March 1277 influenced Henry's further development on this point. Since Henry probably refrained from either approving or reproving the censure imposed by the other Masters in Theology on the thesis of Giles of Rome ("In any composite, there is only one form"), Bishop Tempier and his staff were left with uncertainty about Henry's personal position. The master was soon summoned to the papal Legate, Simon de Brie, in the presence of Tempier and his diocesan staff. He was requested to declare his position. When he revealed that he was inclined to admit anthropological dimorphism, the legate, after consultation with Tempier and his staff, required him to recant, publicly and academically, his indulgent attitude toward Aquinas's thesis. A few days later, the bishop, supported by the legate, had the Masters in Theology gather to examine a number of Thomas's positions. When the masters (except for the two Dominicans) unanimously rejected the Thomistic thesis "There is only one substantial form in man, namely the intellectual soul," Henry joined the majority position, thus giving up his initial tolerance. Throughout the rest of his career Henry remained faithful to this rejection of the unicity of the substantial form (the intellectual soul) in a human being. Thus, in his riper years, Henry held that, in a human being, along with the form of corporeality, there is a second substantial form (the intellectual soul containing the capacities of sensitive and vegetative life) which actualizes matter through the mediation of the *forma corporeitatis* (Wielockx 1985, pp. 169–70, and 1988).

There is a first actual (and later habitual) intellectual self-knowledge of the human soul, anterior to the active intellectual reflection on the reception of sensible species from the outward object. On this point Augustine's *De Trinitate* is closely scrutinized and, as generally acknowledged, correctly understood by Henry (Laarmann 1999, pp. 462–3; Macken 1972, p. 101).

The results of T. Nys's monograph (1949) are generally accepted. They show that Henry, regarding human knowledge in general, progressively abandons the doctrine of an intellectual *species impressa* (an impressed mental picture of the outward thing), first (*Quodlibet* III) in the case of the vision of God *per essentiam* (beatific vision), and then (*Quodlibet* IV) in all other cases. The general suppression of the *species impressa* is concurrent with a second evolution in Henry's thinking. In his earlier writings, Henry, in company with Aristotle, considers that the formation of the concept occurs by one simple abstraction. From *Quodlibet* IV onward, he develops the Augustinian doctrine, as found also in the so-called *Summa fratris Alexandri* and BONAVENTURE: the completely formed mental word is a fully worked out definition and thus mirrors the hierarchy of the internal composition of the essence of the thing (*res*). It is the final result of a formation process that, in the vein of the *ars definitiva*, evolves from the intellectual presence of the object known through a series of conscious acts of both the intellect (possible and, under some circumstances, agent) and the will.

As to divine illumination, the thesis of M. Gogacz (that illumination is irrelevant for Henry) and of J. Paulus (that it becomes progressively irrelevant for Henry) cannot be retained. V. Sorge (1988, p. 183) is right in stressing the importance of divine illumination throughout Henry's career. Anticipating an observation of S. P. Marrone (1985, pp. 145–7, and 1996, p. 207), R. Macken (1972, pp. 98–104) noted that, along with a proof (of illumination) relying on the insufficiency of the human subject to grasp "sincere truth," there is a second proof based on objective relationships. The characteristic object of the act of intellectual understanding being the *aliquitas* (the "somethingness" or definite essence), every intellection must also somehow understand everything to which the *aliquitas* refers by its very nature: its *esse essentiae* (participated being) and the in-itself subsistent divine Paradigm. This entails three important consequences. First, there is (also) a common object of created knowledge and creative knowledge: *Sunt enim eadem cognita: et praedicta intellecta in phantasmatibus et incorporeae rationes in ipsa veritate aeterna: non sunt enim aliud quam ipsae naturae et essentiae rerum*: "The things known are indeed the same, namely, on the one hand, those things understood (by humans) in the phantasmata and, on the other hand, the incorporeal specificities in the eternal truth: they are nothing else, indeed, than the natures and essences of things" (*Quodlibet* IX, 15; 1983, p. 262, ll. 29–31). Second, as Gómez Caffarena (1958, p. 261) pointed out, since a finite essence cannot be itself unless it points and tends to its less restricted but still participated *esse essentiae* and since this dynamism proves in the end to be the attraction of the in-itself subsistent Beingness (*esse*), the "metaphysics of human inquietude" is ultimately also "metaphysics of the desire of God" (see also Sorge 1988, p. 182–3: "exemplaristic finalism"). Third, as Marrone (1985, pp. 145–7, and 1996, pp. 207–8) proposed, it may be hard and even impossible to disentangle the Aristotelian side (the place given to quiddity in the theory of scientific knowledge as presented in the *Posterior Analytics*) and the Augustinian side (divine illumination) of Henry's personal thinking, which may very well be a genuine synthesis. Marrone (1996, p. 201) also suggested that Henry "allowed himself to do away completely" in his mid-career (*Summa* XXXI–XXXIV) with some earlier statements on divine illumination. It seems useful, however, to distinguish between silence on illumination and its denial. While Henry, in later versions, sometimes cancels out explicit references to illumination, he never denies it; indeed in *Quodlibet* IX, 15, he insistently reinstates it. And, as Marrone (1996, p. 208) himself notes, what Henry "fully realized" in *Quodlibet* IX, 15, was "present in seed as early as article 34 of the *Summa*."

In line with his spiritualistic conception of a human being, Henry is always careful to underline the free character of the human intellectual soul's activity. From his first academic acts onward, he is adamant in his criticism of Thomas Aquinas's understanding of freedom as "inclination," however spontaneous and internal. Accordingly, Henry never tires of telling us that freedom is instead an "initiative" (Wielockx 1985, pp. 127–30, 185–7, 191–3). As can be seen in *Quodlibet* IX, 5, which belongs among the most representative pages ever written in the scholastic debate on the understanding of human freedom, this conviction led Henry to criticize the principle: *omne quod movetur, ab alio movetur* ("all that is moved, is moved by something else").

Bibliography

Primary sources

(1518), *Quodlibeta Magistri Henrici Goethals a Gandauo, doctoris Solemnis, Socii Sorbonici, et archidiaconi Tornacensis, cum duplici tabella. Venundantur ab Iodoco Badio Ascensio, sub gratia et priuilegio ad finem explicandis*, 2 vols., Paris; repr. 1961, Heverlee (Louvain): Bibliothèque SJ.

(1520), *Summae Quaestionum Ordinariarum Theologi recepto praeconio Solennis Henrici a Gandavo, cum duplici repertorio, Tomos Prior/Posterior. Venundantur in aedibus Iodoci Badii Ascensii, cum Priuilegio Regio ad calcem explicando*, 2 vols., Paris; repr. 1953. New York: Franciscan Institute.

Of the Louvain (University Press) edition *Henrici de Gandavo Opera omnia* (Ancient and Medieval Philosophy, De Wulf–Mansion Centre, Series 2) the following are in print:

(1979–91): *Quodlibet* I, II, VI, VII, IX, X, XII (q. 1–30), XII (q. 31), XIII.

(1991–8): *Summa (Quaestiones ordinariae)* XXXI–XXXIV, XXXV–XL, XLI–XLVI.

Secondary sources

Decorte, J. (1996), "Henry of Ghent on analogy. Critical reflections on Jean Paulus' interpretation," in W. Vanhamel, ed., *Henry of Ghent* (pp. 71–105), De Wulf–Mansion Centre, Series 1, 15, Louvain: Peeters.

Ehrle, F. (1885), "Heinrich von Gent. Beiträge zu den Biographien berühmter Scholastiker, I," *Archiv für Litteratur [sic] und Kirchengeschichte des Mittelalters* 1, pp. 365–401.

Gauthier, R.-A. (1947/8), "Trois commentaires averroïstes sur l'*Ethique à Nicomaque*," *Archives d'Histoire Doctrinale et Littéraire du Moyen Âge* 16, pp. 187–336.

Gogacz, M. (1961), *Problem istnienia Boga u Anzelma z Canterbury: Problem prawdy u Henryka z Gandawy*, Lublin and Tow: Naukowe Katolickiego Uniwersytetu Lubelskiego.

Gómez Caffarena, J. (1958), *Ser participado y ser subsistente en la metafísica de Enrique de Gante*, Analecta Gregoriana 93, Rome: Gregoriana.

Hoeres, W. (1965), "Wesen und Dasein bei Heinrich von Gent und Duns Scotus," *Franziskanische Studien* 47, pp. 121–86.

Laarmann, M. (1999), *Deus, primum cognitum. Die Lehre von Gott als dem Ersterkannten des menschlichen Intellekts bei Heinrich von Gent († 1293)*, Beiträge zur Geschichte der Philosophie und Theologie des Mittelalters NF 52, Münster: Aschendorff.

Luna, C. (1998), "Nouveaux textes d'Henri de Gand, de Gilles de Rome et de Godefroid de Fontaines," *Archives d'Histoire Doctrinale et Littéraire du Moyen Âge* 73, pp. 151–272.

Macken, R. (1972), "La théorie de l'illumination divine dans la philosophie d'Henri de Gand," *Recherches de Théologie Ancienne et Médiévale* 39, pp. 82–112.

——(1981), "Les diverses applications de la distinction intentionnelle chez Henri de Gand," in W. Kluxen, ed., *Sprache und Erkenntnis im Mittelalter* (pp. 769–76), Berlin: De Gruyter.

Marrone, S. P. (1985), *Truth and Scientific Knowledge in the Thought of Henry of Ghent*, Cambridge, MA: Medieval Academy of America.

——(1996), "Henry of Ghent in mid-career as interpreter of Aristotle and Thomas Aquinas," in W. Vanhamel, ed., *Henry of Ghent* (pp. 184–209), De Wulf-Mansion Centre, Series 1, 15, Louvain: Peeters.

Nys, T. (1949), *De werking van het menselijk verstand volgens Hendrik van Gent*, Leuven: Nauwelaerts.

Paulus, J. (1938), *Henri de Gand: Essai sur les tendances de sa métaphysique*, Études de philosophie médiévale, 25, Paris: J. Vrin.

Porro, P. (1990), *Enrico di Gand. La via delle proposizioni universali*, Vestigia, Studi e strumenti di storiografia filosofica 2, Bari: Levante Editori.

——(1996a), "An historiographical image of Henry of Ghent," in W. Vanhamel, ed., *Henry of Ghent* (pp. 373–403), De Wulf-Mansion Centre, Series 1, 15, Louvain: Peeters.

——(1996b), Bibliography, in W. Vanhamel, ed., *Henry of Ghent* (pp. 405–34), De Wulf-Mansion Centre, Series 1, 15, Louvain: Peeters.

——(1996c), "Possibilità e *esse essentiae* in Enrico di Gand," in W. Vanhamel, ed., *Henry of Ghent* (pp. 211–253), De Wulf-Mansion Centre, Series 1, 15, Louvain: Peeters.

Van Riet, S., ed. (1977, 1980, 1983), *Avicenna latinus. Liber de philosophia prima sive scientia divina*, 3 vols., Leuven: Peeters; Leiden: Brill.

Sorge, V. (1988), *Gnoseologia e teologia nel pensiero di Enrico di Gand* (Definizioni, 4), Naples: Loffredo.

Vanhamel, W., ed. (1996), *Henry of Ghent: Proceedings of the International Colloquium on the Occasion of the 700th Anniversary of his Death (1293)*, De Wulf-Mansion Centre, Series 1, 15, Louvain: Peeters.

Wielockx, R. (1985), *Aegidii Romani Opera omnia: III,1: Apologia. Edition et commentaire*, Florence: L. S. Olschki.

——(1988), "Autour du procès de Thomas d'Aquin," in A. Zimmermann, ed., *Thomas von Aquin. Werk und Wirkung im Licht neuerer Forschungen* (pp. 413–38), Berlin: De Gruyter.

Wippel, J. F. (1982), "Essence and existence," in N. Kretzmann, A. Kenny, and J. Pinborg, eds., *The Cambridge History of Later Medieval Philosophy* (pp. 385–410), Cambridge: Cambridge University Press.

43

Henry of Harclay

MARK G. HENNINGER

Henry of Harclay (b. ca. 1270; d. 1317), Chancellor of the University of Oxford (1312–17) and theologian, was master of arts by December 1296. Although he was then a member of the secular clergy, not being ordained a priest until the following year, he was particularly influenced by the Franciscan tradition, particularly as mediated by JOHN DUNS SCOTUS. Harclay did his theological studies at the University of Paris shortly after 1300 when Duns Scotus was teaching there, and the strong influence of the Subtle Doctor is seen in Harclay's still unedited commentary on the *Sentences* of PETER LOMBARD: he takes solutions verbatim from Scotus, frequently uses Scotus's arguments and adopts many of his positions. Still, he was not a slavish disciple, but, as an acute commentator, offered independent criticisms which may have influenced Scotus's final edition of his own commentary, the *Ordinatio*.

Harclay returned to the University of Oxford, becoming master of theology sometime before 1312, and in December of that year he was confirmed by the Bishop of Lincoln as Chancellor of the University of Oxford. During these years Harclay disputed a number of questions, in his *Quaestiones ordinariae*, a series of twenty-nine questions in which he exhibits more independence and maturity than in his early Parisian *Sentences* commentary.

Harclay was a particularly active chancellor, faithfully solicitous in maintaining the good order of the university. On May 20, 1315, he received from the king the confirmation of a number of important privileges that Henry III had left to the university. On May 28 of that year, for example, Edward II instructed the mayor of Oxford to admit the chancellor and procurators of the university to the periodic testing of beer; this invitation had sadly fallen into disuse, to the detriment of the beer and of the students and faculty at the university. Also in his role as chancellor, Harclay became embroiled in bitter controversies between the university and the Dominicans over a number of privileges the latter claimed. He threw himself into the battle on the side of the university, being among those who drew up new regulations that restricted the privileges, and on behalf of the university he traveled to the papal court at Avignon to find a settlement. These controversies with the Dominicans are mirrored in his constant anti-Thomist stance throughout his later *Quaestiones*. Toward the end of his life, these controversies rekindled, and Harclay traveled once again to Avignon where he died on June 25, 1317.

In his *Quaestiones ordinariae*, Harclay shows himself familiar with and sharply critical of many of the positions and arguments of his contemporaries on a wide variety of theological and philosophical issues, including predestination and divine foreknowledge, the ontological status of divine ideas, universals, and relations, the univocal concept of being, the eternity of the world, the plurality of substantial forms in humans, the formal distinction, whether anyone can predict the end of the world, the immortality of the soul, and various moral questions. Harclay was not interested in constructing a system, but was a widely-read and independent, critical thinker, whose great strength lay in questioning opinions and propositions that to others were self-evident, and in supporting his own position with numerous clear arguments.

Ontology: universals and relations

These traits are seen in his *quaestio* on universals in which he criticizes Scotus's theory of "common natures" existing extra-mentally in many singular things. Harclay's alternative position is clear: "I say . . . that in extra-mental reality nothing is a thing unless it be singular, and commonness is not in extra-mental reality" (Gál 1971, p. 211, n. 67; all translation are mine). For Harclay, numerical singularity is a necessary condition for anything existing extra-mentally. And he defines singularity in terms of incommunicability, that is, it is logically impossible that a singular thing exist simultaneously in numerically many things. In this sense, then, Harclay denies that any extra-mental thing is common to many. To understand this denial, it is necessary to examine his account of the property of commonness or a unity less than individual attributed by some to a common nature. Instead of positing such a common nature, Harclay offers an alternative account of universals based on really distinct singular things and their relations of similarity.

Henry takes "real unity" for numerical identity and holds that a and b are really distinct if and only if a and b are not really one. Hence if a and b are really distinct, they cannot be really one strictly speaking. This is fundamental to Harclay's position.

But 'unity' is an equivocal term that is said at times of the similarity between really distinct things. For example, an equilateral triangle and an isosceles triangle are said to be one figure. The term 'one' does not denote a real unity properly speaking, since for Harclay real unity implies numerical identity, and an equilateral triangle is not numerically identical with an isosceles triangle. 'One' said of the triangles indicates rather some similarity obtaining between the numerically two triangles by virtue of which they are both called one figure.

Harclay's doctrine of universals can be called a resemblance theory, and he is intent on establishing two points: (1) 'unity' is in fact often used to refer only to similarity, and (2) similarity necessarily implies distinction, the opposite of identity or unity strictly speaking.

He establishes (1) by referring to texts of Aristotle, BOETHIUS, Scripture, AUGUSTINE, and others. Regarding (2), he relies on a commonly accepted medieval view of relation. Sentences of the form 'aRb' ('a is really related by R to b') are true only if (1) a and b are really distinct extra-mental things and (2) there is a real foundation in a for R. For Harclay, as for many other scholastics (though not for WILLIAM OF OCKHAM), a real distinction of relata is a necessary condition for a real relation such as similarity.

Hence if a is really related by a relation R of similarity to b, then a and b are really distinct. But then there can be no "real unity" between a and b. In another question, that of the univocal concept of being, he says that the similarity between two things can increase to infinity, but there will be no greater unity between them, for similarity always presupposes distinction.

Extra-mentally, then, there are really distinct singular things that resemble each other in various ways. These cause a variety of concepts in our mind. Central to this last is his contention that, with respect to concepts, a singular extra-mental thing is an equivocal cause. "A thing in itself in some way brings about diverse concepts and diverse considerations of it in the mind; and therefore it is not necessary that to the diverse considerations in the mind there correspond diverse things in reality" (Gál 1971, p. 227, n. 103).

In the question on the univocal concept of being, Harclay gives another reason for the diversity of concepts. When some effect depends essentially on two causes, if one cause varies while the other does not, there follows a variation in the effect. But our concepts depend on the intellect as well as on the object. Hence with various "dispositions" in the intellect of the knower there will follow various concepts, more or less distinct. Harclay would agree with Ockham that the belief that distinctions in concepts must be mirrored by distinctions in reality is one of the most basic errors in philosophy.

In the question on universals, he summarizes: "In this way I say that each thing posited outside the soul by that fact is singular. And this singular thing is apt to move the intellect to conceiving it confusedly and to conceiving it distinctly. And I call a 'confused concept' that concept by which the intellect does not distinguish this thing from that" (Gál 1971, p. 216, n. 79). Socrates can move the intellect to conceive him as a man, and the intellect in using that "confused" concept "man" does not distinguish Socrates from Plato.

Regarding Harclay's conceptualism, the following points should be noted. First, he holds not only that every extra-mental thing is singular, but the confused concept is also singular, for the concept as a quality in the soul is just as singular and incommunicable to many as any extra-mental thing. In addition, Harclay teaches that both the confused concept and, surprisingly, the singular extra-mental thing are universal. The concept is universal because it represents many confusedly so that through it the intellect cannot distinguish one singular from another of the same kind. And because the singular can be conceived in a confused manner, Harclay claims that it is universal. William of Ockham and WALTER BURLEY later criticize Harclay's view that one and the same thing can be both singular and universal.

Second, Harclay insists that these confused concepts are not mere poetic figments with no foundation in reality. The foundation for these "philosophical figments" is the real relation of similarity among individuals. His *quaestio* on real relations helps us understand better this extra-mental foundation for universal concepts.

To follow Harclay here, it is essential to keep in mind that the principal assumption of the late medieval view of relations is that a real relation is an Aristotelian accident. This fact is at the root of the strangeness many find in medieval theories of relation. Today we might talk of one relation R of color similarity between two pieces of white chalk, a and b. But for the medievals, if there are two really distinct substances, there must be two really distinct accidents. Being an accident, a relation is not an entity that somehow hovers between the two things related. In the chalk example, then, one relation of color similarity R of a to b is based on an accident, the quality of whiteness in a. A numerically distinct relation of similarity R' of b to a is based on a numerically distinct accident of whiteness inhering in b. There are two relations, one in each of the things related, and each has a "foundation," the quality of whiteness inhering in the piece of chalk. The medieval controversy was over the ontological status of such "relational accidents," like similarity, and how they differed from the "absolute accidents," for example, whiteness.

In his early *Sentences* commentary, Harclay had followed Duns Scotus in adopting a strongly realist position on real relations, but in a lengthy later *quaestio* he argues against this view and devotes much energy to defending his own position, one closer to that of William of Ockham. Harclay's later theory of relation can be contrasted with Scotus's in the following way. According to Scotus, if R is a real relation, then sentences of the form 'aRb'

307

('*a* is really related to *b*') are true if and only if (1) *a* and *b* are really distinct extra-mental things, (2) there is a real foundation in *a* for *R* to *b*, and (3) there exists an extra-mental "relative thing" *R* inhering in *a* that is really distinct from its foundation. Further, sentences of the form '*R*-ness exists', as 'Similarity exists', are true if and only if there exists an extra-mental "relative thing" really distinct from, but inhering in, its foundation.

As mentioned, Harclay had held this ontology in his *Sentences* commentary, though even there he voices reservations. But in his later *quaestio* he develops his own theory holding that if *R* is a real relation, then sentences of the form '*aRb*' are true if and only if (1) *a* and *b* are really distinct extra-mental things, (2) there is a real foundation in *a* for *R* to *b*, and (3) there exists a real relation *R*, a non-inhering condition of *a* towards *b*. And sentences of the form '*R*-ness exists' are true if and only if there exists a mind-independent condition "in" (non-inherence) one thing towards another. Two points should be noted: There is no need to posit a third "relative thing" really distinct from, but inhering in *a*, and the condition of *a*'s being related to *b* is mind-independent.

Betraying his realist Scotist background, Harclay claims that in a certain sense it can be admitted that when something becomes really related to another, some "thing" comes to the former, but it does not inform its foundation, as an "absolute" accident as whiteness informs a substance. He believes that whatever in some way exists independently of the mind can be called a "thing," and this is true of a real relation, a non-inhering accident. He calls a real relation a "condition [*habitudo*] or the fact of being associated [*societas*] or a concurrence together [*simultas*] or coexistence [*coexistentia*] or in whatever way we wished to call [it]" (Henninger 1987, p. 98, n. 51). In sum, it is this mind-independent non-inhering condition Harclay calls a "real relation."

We can also ask, What are the truth conditions for sentences of the form '*R*-ness exists'? On the one hand, he has rejected an ontology of relations by which substitutions for '*R*-ness' name some extra-mental relative thing that inheres in a foundation. On the other hand, he does not have an ontology like PETER AURIOL for whom relations are concepts in an intellect. Harclay insists repeatedly that real relations exist independently of the mind. Neither of the ontologies just described is his: Harclay states: "So a relation posits nothing in its foundation, and yet it is a thing not made by the intellect" (Henninger 1987, p. 98, n. 52). For Harclay, statements of the form '*R*-ness exist' are true if and only if there exists a mind-independent condition "in" (non-inherence) one thing towards another.

But although a real relation is not an extra-mental relative thing that inheres in its foundation, neither is it identical with its foundation. Harclay says:

> Whiteness and similarity, however, are not the same, but rather radically different. For that condition of association and concurrence is of a nature different from whiteness. And I say that a relation has no stronger being than has that concurrence or association. And that association posits nothing in it [i.e., the subject], but only affirms a condition of it with respect to another. (Henninger 1987, p. 98, n. 52)

The foundation is of a nature different from the relation. For example, the former may be an inherent absolute accident, as whiteness, but the latter, the relation of color similarity, is only a condition of the white thing. Despite the difficulty in expression, Harclay's intuition is that a real relation has an extra-mental ontological status that is not reducible to that of absolute things. On the reality of relations, then, Harclay is representative of a middle way, adopting neither a strongly realist ontology like Duns Scotus nor a conceptualist ontology of relations as Peter Auriol's.

It is real relations that provide the extra-mental foundation for confused and so universal concepts. For two things, such as Socrates and Plato, are really distinct and individual, but "still something common to them can be abstracted, for such things can be similar or agreeing; therefore one common concept on the part of the intellect is able to correspond to both" (Gál 1971, p. 221, n. 92).

Harclay's conceptualism and his relational account of the commonness characteristic of universal concepts allow him to posit an extra-mental world of only singular things, that is, things that are incommunicable: logically incapable of existing simultaneously in numerically many things. With such an ontology, Harclay feels no constraint to give a positive account of individuation. Having banished Scotus's common nature from his ontology along with any real unity less than numerical, he maintains that each thing posited extra-mentally by that fact is singular.

Harclay uses his theory of relations in other areas to depart from tradition. Most if not all scholastics before Harclay had argued that though creatures are really related to God, he is not really related to them, for this would entail change in him. When Harclay wrote his early *Sentences* commentary, he adopted Scotus's ontology of real relations in which something taking on a real relation, a "relative thing," was really changed by it. In his long and involved later *quaestio* on relations, however, Harclay argues that something changes only if there is a change in it, if by "in" is meant inherence. But according to his new ontology of relations, a real relation does not inhere, but is a mind-independent condition, as explained above. Hence Harclay sees no reason to follow theological tradition on this point and argues that when creatures come to exist, God becomes as really related to them as they are to him, since no change is effected in God. In this *quaestio*, he took the authoritative texts and arguments that had grown up around the problem of the ontological status of relations, including his own early Scotistic view, worked through them very carefully, and developed his own novel position.

Before leaving these ontological questions, it should be noted that Harclay was Chancellor at Oxford when William of Ockham was studying there, and Ockham quotes verbatim from Harclay's *quaestio* on universals which, as we have seen, is critical of Scotus. On relations, there is evidence that Ockham may have held a Scotist position as he began his philosophical career, but changed very soon afterwards during his course of studies. I believe that as Harclay's work on universals influenced Ockham, so also did his work on relations, since not only are there similarities in position, but also in the arguments and in their order of presentation.

Still, regarding Harclay's ontology, it would be rash to see him positing a world of "radical individuals," ontological blocks devoid of further ontological distinction or composition. Harclay's treatment of the singular as really one or numerically identical in his *quaestio* on universals is one side of a more complex ontology that is emerging as more *quaestiones* of Harclay are edited.

This is clear from Harclay's fine-grained discussion of various types of formal identity and distinction (Henninger 1981), and his discussion of the plurality of forms (Maurer 1974). In the first, he distinguishes (at least in the Trinity) various grades of formal non-identity within what is really numerically one, and so the profound influence of Scotus is seen even in Harclay's later teaching. In the second, Harclay posits within one singular thing, like a human, a plurality of substantial forms. Hence, in one way a human is made up of several beings; he even calls these substantial forms "individuals." In another way the final form received completes the composite substance, giving it a certain unity, making it one and not many entities.

Morality: the virtues and the will

Another area in which Harclay uses his theory of relations is in determining the ontological status of moral virtue. Traditionally following Aristotle, the scholastics viewed moral virtue as a species of habit, an acquired quality that is relatively permanent and inclines the agent to perform definite types of acts with ease, accuracy, and consistency. A moral virtue, then, is one of the nine Aristotelian accidents, a quality, and is distinguished from the power possessing it.

Harclay departs from this traditional view of moral virtue in the course of answering the *quaestio*, "Are moral virtues in the intellective appetite, i.e., the will, or in the sensitive appetite?" (*Quaest. ordin.*, MS Borgh. 171, fos. 27v–28v). For Harclay, virtue is a kind of moral health, however imperfect it may be in this wayfarer's life, and it consists primarily in the proper subordination and obedience of the sensitive appetite to the will. But if moral virtue is interior health, then for Harclay it is not some additional quality added to what is healthy. Just as exterior health is the result of the correct proportion or relation of the four humors in the body, so interior health is nothing but the correct relation of obedience of the sensitive appetite to the will. If the sensitive appetite is not too hot and rebellious nor too flaccid and insensitive, but instead has a proper relation of obedience, only then is a person morally healthy. "And so health, which is nothing but the above-mentioned relation, is moral virtue" (ibid., fo. 28r).

He gives three separately necessary and jointly sufficient conditions for a moral virtue's existing in the soul. The first is right judgment in the intellect about what is to be done, whereas the second is a choice in the will conforming to the intellect's judgment. But a third condition is also necessary, since virtue must issue in acts performed easily and consistently. And so there also must be

> a relation of obedience in the lower sensitive appetite, so that the sensitive appetite may be in itself disposed to be drawn easily to the judgment of reason. I say that of those three, the due relation is moral virtue, such that that virtue is like a certain musical harmony. I assert, then, that moral virtue is no one absolute quality, but a relation of many things. (MS Borgh. 171, fo. 28r)

As is his custom, especially when departing from tradition, Harclay gives a battery of arguments against the received position. In one argument, he assumes that by absolute divine power any one quality can exist without another. But then, he reasons, if health were a quality, it could exist by divine power in a non-existing body, or in a body with no heat at all, which he takes to be absurd. Or else it would be possible by divine power for health not to be in a body perfectly suited with the requisite proportion of humors and heat.

As in his discussion of universals, Harclay here uses his theory of relations to argue for an ontology more parsimonious than that of his mentor Duns Scotus. Harclay does not have a clear and comprehensive semantic theory like that of William of Ockham, who relentlessly uses his theory of connotative terms to reduce the number and kind of ontological entities. But Harclay does use his theory of relations, God's absolute power, and his own original interpretation of authorities, especially Aristotle and Augustine, to the same end.

With regard to the human will, Harclay inherited strong views from Scotus. THOMAS AQUINAS and others had argued that the human will is a natural power that has its own proper object, the good. Any good less than the final and perfect good, i.e., God, can be the object of a free choice precisely because that good is limited. But if a human soul were to see God, as do the blessed in heaven, its will would "necessarily" be moved by its natural desire for the good and would love God. But are the blessed in heaven still free? Or as Harclay asks in a lengthy *quaestio*, "Could those who believed Christ to be the true God have deliberately killed him?" (*Quaest. ordin.* MS Worcester F.3, fos. 201r–207r).

Harclay divides his *quaestio* into three articles, each dealing with the powers of the will with respect to different objects. The first concerns the final end, God, apprehended by the soul as a particular object, not in the way some generally wish happiness for themselves. Harclay asks and discusses whether the will can knowingly hate God. Aware that he is going against the common opinion, he answers affirmatively. The second article is about the same final end: having shown that the will can hate God who is clearly apprehended, he then asks if the will is able to refrain completely from all acts of either loving or hating God, and he reasons boldly that it can. The third article concerns the means to the final end, the choices made in this life, whether when the intellect is apprehending some such good to be done, can the will (*pace* Socrates) choose the opposite. Following the majority of scholastics, he answers affirmatively.

In the course of the long discussion, he stresses the difference between "natural powers," which in the presence of their proper objects must act, as fire burns in the presence of the combustible, and a rational power which need not act in the presence of its proper object, as the will need not act in the presence of the good, whether finite or infinite. This native liberty of the will, to choose among alternatives and also to refrain from any act of willing, remains with the blessed in heaven. Can the blessed, then, choose to sin and turn from God? "I concede that for its part the will can sin, but God supports it lest it sin, and this is its reward. So by its power, as actually supported by God, the will cannot sin, but by the absolute power of the will it can sin" (MS Worcester F.3, fo. 204r). And further, he holds that in heaven the will can freely desire that God so graciously maintain it in its love of God, and so even among the blessed "the will from its nature always remains free for this or that alternative" (ibid.).

However cogent, this response shows Harclay to be part of the broad movement away from various forms of necessitarianism that occurred after the condemnations of the 1270s. This is also seen in his *quaestiones* on the contingency of creation and the immortality of the human soul (Maurer 1957). In the first, he argues against Thomas Aquinas that only God is a necessary being, all other beings, including angels, are equally contingent; there are no degrees of necessity and contingency. This position underlies the teaching in his *quaestio* on the immortality of the soul: no creature is by nature necessary and hence immortal, for all created beings tend to revert to nothing. This is as true of human souls as of any creatures, including angels. But we know with certainty from Scripture and tradition, not from the philosophers, that the human soul is in fact immortal. And for Harclay the true explanation for this remarkable fact is that God by his act of will and grace preserves our souls in existence forever.

Conclusion

It would be wrong to see Harclay simply as one of the earliest representatives of the school of Scotus. Though strongly influenced by Scotus in his early years, Harclay's relation to the Subtle Doctor is complex: while in his later *quaestiones* he criticizes key doctrines of Scotus, including that of "common nature," he also uses with great facility Scotus's formal distinction. Though Harclay was not himself a Franciscan, he was certainly part of the

Franciscan intellectual tradition, and a study of Harclay helps to understand its development, particularly in the first two decades of the fourteenth century in England and at Oxford.

Finally, a study of Harclay reminds us that before pronouncing on a thinker's membership in a school or movement, we must read carefully the texts and be constantly prepared for surprises. For example, in Harclay's *quaestiones* on the eternity of the world, we find that he held rather non-traditional views on infinity and the "continuous" (Dales 1983, 1984; Murdoch 1981). He argued in his own way that not all infinities are equal, that they can be added to and subtracted from without affecting their infinity, and that certain forms of an actual infinite are possible. Further, a number of fourteenth-century thinkers, including WILLIAM OF ALNWICK, ADAM OF WODEHAM, and THOMAS WILTON, attacked him, along with WALTER CHATTON, for being "atomists," i.e., for their non-traditional view that continua, whether of lines, distances, time, or motions of any kind, are composed of "atoms," i.e., indivisibles. Harclay follows his own counsel here as in other topics.

As more of Harclay's questions are edited and compared, we find his teaching is more complex than expected. Our understanding of Harclay will be greatly enhanced by the critical edition and English translation of the *Quaestiones ordinariae* being prepared for the series *Auctores Britannici Medii Aevi*.

Bibliography

Primary sources

Manuscripts

Quaestiones ordinariae: Vatican Library Borghese 171, fos. 1r–32v; Worcester, Cathedral Library F. 3, fos. 186v–220v; Assisi, Biblioteca Comunale 172, fos. 125r–131v, 133r–136r, 149r–153v; Tortosa Cathedral 88, fos. 74v–94v; Florence, Biblioteca Nazionale Fondo principale II.II.281, 94r–101v.

Commentary on the First Book of the Sentences: Vatican Library Lat. 13687, fos. 13v–97v; Casale Monferrato, Biblioteca del Seminario Vescovile MS b 2, fos. 1r–84r.

Editions

Dales, R. C. (1983), "Henricus de Harclay: quaestio *Utrum mundus potuit fuisse ab eterno*," *Archives d'Histoire Doctrinale et Littéraire du Moyen Âge* 50, pp. 223–55.

Gál, G. (1971), "Henricus de Harclay: *Quaestio de significato conceptus universalis*," *Franciscan Studies* 31, pp. 178–234.

Henninger, M. (1980), "Henry of Harclay's questions on divine prescience and predestination," *Franciscan Studies* 40, pp. 167–243.

——(1981), "Henry of Harclay on the formal distinction in the Trinity," *Franciscan Studies* 41, pp. 250–335.

——(1987), "Henry of Harclay's question on relations," *Mediaeval Studies* 49, pp. 76–123.

Maurer, A. (1954), "Henry of Harclay's question on the univocity of being," *Mediaeval Studies* 16, pp. 1–18.

——(1957), "Henry of Harclay's questions on immortality," *Mediaeval Studies* 19, pp. 79–107.

——(1974), "Henry of Harclay's disputed question on the plurality of forms," in J. R. O'Donnell, ed., *Essays in Honor of Anton Pegis* (pp. 125–59), Toronto: Pontifical Institute of Mediaeval Studies.

Secondary sources

Dales, R. C. (1984), "Henry of Harclay on the infinite," *Journal of the History of Ideas* 45, pp. 295–301.

Henninger, M. (1989), *Relations: Medieval Theories 1250–1325*, Oxford: Clarendon Press.

Murdoch, J. (1981), "Henry of Harclay and the infinite," in A. Maierù and A. Paravicini Bagliani, eds., *Studi sul XIV secolo in memoria di Anneliese Maier* (pp. 219–61), Rome: Edizioni di Storia e Letteratura.

Pelster, F. (1924), "Heinrich von Harclay, Kanzler von Oxford und seine Quästionen," *Miscellanea Francesco Ehrle I* (Studi e Testi 37), pp. 307–56.

44

Hervaeus Natalis

ROLAND J. TESKE

Hervaeus Natalis (b. 1250/60; d. 1323), also known as Harvey Nedellec, was born in Brittany, joined the Dominicans in 1276, was present in Paris at St. Jacques in 1303, lectured on the *Sentences* in 1301–2 or 1302–3, and became Master of Theology in 1307. He supported Philip the Fair against Pope Boniface VIII on the question of papal jurisdiction; he was elected provincial of France in 1309 and master general of the Dominicans in 1318. As head of a commission to investigate the works of DURAND OF SAINT POURÇAIN, he found 91 objectionable propositions. He opposed various teachings of JAMES OF METZ, PETER AURIOL, and HENRY OF GHENT. Though he wrote a defense of the teachings of THOMAS AQUINAS, his own views did not reflect those of Aquinas on the real distinction in creatures between existence and essence, on the five ways of proving the existence of God, and on the principle of individuation. Hervaeus worked hard for the canonization of Thomas Aquinas, but died at Narbonne on his way to the ceremony that marked his success.

Earlier in the twentieth century, Hervaeus was heralded as the first real Thomist, but more recent studies have shown that, despite his enthusiastic support for Aquinas, Hervaeus was more of an eclectic than a Thomist. He, in fact, seldom mentions Aquinas, is unaware of his distinction between existence and essence in created beings, and has only two proofs for the existence of God, one terminating at the first efficient cause and the other at the most perfect being. Hervaeus draws a distinction between the subjective being of the act of knowing and the objective being of the object of cognition, attributes a certain numerical unity to the species, and assigns as external cause of a being's individuation its efficient cause and as the internal cause of its individuation its whole essence along with its accidents. Thus far, Hervaeus' thought has been studied more in relation to others, such as Aquinas and JOHN DUNS SCOTUS, rather than in itself.

Bibliography

Primary sources

(1959), *De iurisdictione*, ed. L. Hödl, Munich: M. Hueber.

(1966), *In quattor libros sententiarum commentaria* with *De potestate papae*, Farnborough: Gregg.

(1966), *Quodlibeta*, Ridgewood, NJ: Gregg.

(1999), *The Poverty of Christ and the Apostles*, trans. J. D. Jones, Toronto: Pontifical Institute of Mediaeval Studies.

Secondary sources

Allan, E. (1960), "Hervaeus Natalis: an early 'Thomist' on the notion of being," *Mediaeval Studies* 22, pp. 1–14.

Conforti, P. (1997), "Hervé de Nédellec et les questions ordinaires *De cognitione primi principii*," *Revue Thomiste* 97, pp. 63–82.

——(1999), "'Naturali cognitione probare': natural and theological knowledge in Hervaeus Natalis," in J. A. Aertsen and A. Speer, eds., *Was ist Philosophie im Mittelalter?*, Berlin: De Gruyter.

Henninger, M. (1994), "Hervaeus Natalis (b. 1250/60; d. 1323) and Richard of Mediavilla (b. 1245/49; d. 1302/07)," in J. J. Gracia, ed., *Individuation in Scholasticism* (pp. 299–318), Albany: State University of New York Press.

Mannath, J. T. (1969), "Harvey of Nedellec's proofs for the existence of God: *De cognitione primi principii*," *Salesianum* 31, pp. 46–112.

Trottmann, C. (1997), "Verbe mentale et noétique thomiste dans le De verbo d'Hervé de Nédellec," *Revue Thomiste* 97, pp. 47–62.

Wengert, R. G. (1983), "Three senses of intuitive cognition: a quodlibetal question of Harvey of Nedellec," *Franciscan Studies* 43, pp. 408–31.

45

Heymeric of Camp

PETER J. CASARELLA

Heymeric, also known as Heymericus de Campo and Heymeric van de Velde (b. 1395; d. 1460), studied at the University of Paris where he helped revive ALBERTUS MAGNUS'S approach. Later he taught at Cologne and Louvain, and was considered by some as the founder of the Albertist "way" in Cologne. He was the first to introduce a theological perspective into the philosophy of the "neo-Albertists" (Kaluza 1995, p. 226). He also helped to preserve and pass on the doctrines of RAMON LULL, a less conventional interest that led to a close association with NICHOLAS OF CUSA.

Heymeric resolutely defends Albert in his early work of 1424–5, a treatise entitled *Unresolved Questions [Problemata] Dividing Albert the Great and Saint Thomas.* In Cologne, Albertists and Thomists rejected the denial of the real existence of universals by "Epicurean" nominalists, but the differences between the realist schools were just as divisive. In the thirteenth question, for example, Heymeric treated the Aristotelian "active intellect" (*De anima*, 430a10–19). And he stated that, through their relation to it, men can know directly pure essences, separated substances, and God (in short, the totality of all things). Heymeric contrasts this position with the Thomist view that a conversion to material phantasms is necessary in all acts of knowledge.

His mature works are less polemical. The *Treatise on the Seal of Eternity of all the Arts and Sciences* (written between 1432 and 1435 at the Council of Basel) uses an elaborate geometrical symbolism as an image of every human science. "Through a glass darkly" the human intellect can proceed from the sensible image to eternal truths. The *Book of a Hundred Theologies* (completed after 1453) catalogues the philosophical theologies of the fifteenth century. Heymeric ascribes the diversity of approaches to the incommensurability of the human knower with divine self-knowledge. The human intellect, he maintains, is no less moved by wonder to know.

Recent scholarship shows that Heymeric forged an influential current of philosophical realism, advocated a return to more ancient doctrines, and guided others to a new synthesis of philosophy and theology. With the publication of the critical edition of his works (now in preparation), an even more differentiated picture will undoubtedly emerge.

Bibliography

Primary source
(1496), *Problemata inter Albertum Magnum et Sanctum Thomam ad intelligentiam utriusque opinionis multum conferentia*, Cologne.

Secondary sources

Colomer, E. (1963), "Heimeric van de Velde entre Ramón Llull y Nicolas de Cusa," in J. Vincke, ed., *Spanische Forschungen der Görres-Gesellschaft*, vol. 21 (pp. 216–32), Münster: Aschendorff.

Hoenen, M. J. F. M. (1990), *Heymeric van de Velde: Eenheid in de tegendelen*, Baarn: Ambo.

——(1995), "Heymeric van de Velde († 1460) und die Geschichte des Albertismus: Auf der Suche nach den Quellen der albertistischen Intellektlehre des *Tractatus problematicus*," in M. J. F. M. Hoenen and A. de Libera, eds., *Albertus Magnus und der Albertismus. Deutsche philosophische Kultur des Mittelalters* (pp. 303–31), Leiden: Brill.

Imbach, R. (1983), "Das *Centheologicon* des Heymericus de Campo und die darin enthaltenen Cusanus-Reminisizenzen," *Traditio* 39, pp. 466–77.

Kaluza, Z. (1995), "Les débuts de l'albertisme tardif (Paris et Cologne)," in M. J. F. M. Hoenen and A. de Libera, eds., *Albertus Magnus und der Albertismus: deutsche Philosophische Kultur des Mittelalters* (pp. 207–95), Leiden: Brill.

46

Hildegard of Bingen

BRUCE MILEM

Hildegard of Bingen (b. 1098; d. 1179), a Benedictine nun, was exceptional for her vigorous personality and wide-ranging achievement. Her work encompassed medicine, drama, music, and politics. Throughout her life she had elaborate, allegorical visions about God, humanity, and creation. In three books she carefully described and interpreted her visions in detail, drawing on her knowledge of traditional doctrine and contemporary theology.

These three visionary works present a synthesis of Christian doctrine that is both orthodox and creative. Constant Mews suggests that Hildegard shares with ANSELM the desire to justify Christian doctrine on the basis of self-evident truths instead of relying solely on the authority of Scripture. But rather than appealing to abstract concepts like being or substance, as Anselm does, Hildegard uses organic concepts drawn from nature. This reflects her basic theological perspective, which conceives of God not only as creator but also as life itself. Her favorite term for life is the Latin word *viriditas*, or greenness, which has connotations of vitality, abundance, fecundity, and dynamic health, precisely the qualities she finds in God. The divine life also includes the rationality expressed in the Word, the second person of the Trinity. Hildegard sees the life and rationality of God mirrored in the created universe, which she envisions as an egg or a wheel, an organic ensemble of different parts arranged in harmonious order.

Humans occupy an important place in creation. Each is made in the image of God as a single individual with three aspects: body, soul, and intellect. Hildegard's inclusion of the body as part of the image indicates her favorable judgment of it. Each human being is also a microcosm. Every smallest detail of the body symbolically represents some aspect of nature, morality, and the supernatural. But, Hildegard says, because of their sinfulness, people have become blind to the evidence of God's creative presence in the world around them. The only way to regain that vision and enjoy true life is to obey the moral teaching of the Church and strive for virtue.

Hildegard also has a distinctive treatment of gender and sexuality. On the one hand, she entirely accepts a hierarchical view common in the Middle Ages which grants men authority over women. But, on the other hand, she argues that both sexes are complementary, metaphysically equal, and incomplete without each other. Focusing as ever on life, she bases her view on the necessity of both sexes to reproduction.

More than any other medieval thinker, Hildegard puts life at the center of her theology. For many people today, her ideas, though reflecting her time, address modern concerns about the environment, sexual equality, and embodiment.

318

Bibliography

Primary sources

(1987), *Book of Divine Works, with Letters and Songs*, Santa Fe: Bear and Company.
(1990), *Scivias*, trans. Columba Hart and Jane Bishop, intro. by Barbara Newman, New York: Paulist
Press.

Secondary source

Mews, C. (1998), "Religious thinker: a frail human being," in B. Newman, ed., *Voice of the Living
Light: Hildegard of Bingen and her World* (pp. 52–69), Berkeley: University of California Press.

47

Hugh of St. Victor

MICHAEL GORMAN

Hugh of St. Victor (b. 1097/1101; d. 1141) was a canon regular who entered the Abbey of St. Victor in Paris. Probably a student of WILLIAM OF CHAMPEAUX, he became a leading master in the abbey's school.

His writings encompass a wide range of commentaries, treatises, and mystical works. The two most important are *De sacramentis christianae fidei*, the first theological *summa*, and *Didascalicon*, which proposed an influential framework for scientific inquiry and biblical interpretation. Hugh's works (along with some inauthentic works) can be found in Migne (*Patrologia Latina*, vols. 175–7) and are being critically edited at the Hugo von Sankt Viktor Institut in the Philosophisch-Theologische Hochschule Sankt Georgen in Frankfurt.

Hugh was a master in a school and counts as a scholastic author, even though he comes before the rise of university scholasticism and before the Latin West's rediscovery of the integral Aristotle. A careful thinker, he often pauses to indicate which things are known, which things are matters for speculation, and which things cannot be settled. The greatest testimony to the breadth of his mind is that of BONAVENTURE in the *De reductione artium ad theologiam* (n. 5, ed. Quar. V 321b). According to Bonaventure (who introduces Hugh in *Paradisio* XII.133), the three branches of theology are doctrine, morals, and mysticism; their best practitioners were AUGUSTINE, Gregory the Great, and PSEUDO-DIONYSIUS, and they were succeeded by ANSELM, BERNARD OF CLAIRVAUX, and RICHARD OF ST. VICTOR on account of their reason, preaching, and contemplation; "but Hugh had all of these."

Like most medieval authors, Hugh is more a theologian than a philosopher. His main categories and concerns are determined by the Christian faith, he appeals to revelation freely, and he seldom engages in independent philosophical inquiries. At the same time, however, he does distinguish philosophy from theology, and he sees a real (if secondary) role for reason acting without special guidance from faith in an attempt to grasp the works of institution (see below); we can, therefore, speak truly of his philosophical views. This article will focus on them, but not without giving due attention to his overall theological vision and some of his theological positions.

Hugh's overall vision

At some risk of oversimplification, we can identify three principles at work in Hugh's thought. The first is the chronological distinction between institution and restoration. Institution is God's work of creating everything in its original state; restoration refers to

320

God's subsequent work of bringing everything back from evil to even greater good (*De sacr.* I, prol.; see also I.6.10). Attention to this chronological scheme is important for understanding Hugh's views on various topics, most importantly human nature, which is in a different state before and after the fall. The second principle is semiotic. For Hugh, all creatures are signs of God, and man is an especially good sign of God; further, certain creatures are used by God as signs, above all in Scripture. This semiotic network ties reality together in a way that allows man's knowledge to mount from creature to creator. The third principle is causal. For Hugh, all things are bound up in causal networks. All things are caused by God and exist according to his will, and part of what he wills is that there be hierarchical causal relations among creatures as well (*De sacr.* I.2.2).

Of these three principles, the causal is the most basic. All creation is as it is, and develops as it develops, as a result of God's creative will; within God's arrangement of things, creatures exert causal powers on each other. The chronological principle explains the pattern according to which God's works unfold. The semiotic principle explains how man comes to know all this. (For a somewhat different view of Hugh's system, see Hofmeier 1964, pp. 297–302.)

Sources

Hugh knew many Patristic authors, both eastern and western, but he had little or no direct knowledge of Plato or Aristotle. Writing over a century before the rediscovery of the full Aristotelian corpus naturally put him at a handicap in comparison with thirteenth-century authors, but it is well to remember how much material of philosophical interest is to be found in the Fathers, much of it introduced in the course of debates over the Trinity, the Incarnation, and Pelagianism. Hugh was thus familiar with reflection on topics such as substance, person, nature, relation, causation, and moral psychology. As for more immediate sources, he is familiar with the works of other early scholastic authors and sometimes is at odds with them; PETER ABELARD in particular comes in for criticism.

Division of the sciences

Hugh's division of the sciences reflects his respect for the whole range of human intellectual endeavor. "The arts" or "philosophy" has four divisions: theoretical, practical, mechanical (to include this is a Hugonian innovation), and logical (*Didasc.* II). At the first level of subdivision, theoretical philosophy is divided into theology, physics, and mathematics; practical is divided into solitary, private, and public; mechanical is divided into fabric-making, armament, commerce, agriculture, hunting, medicine, and theatrics; logic is divided into grammar and argument.

Biblical interpretation

Most important is the study of Scripture. Everything in the Bible is to be interpreted either literally (historically), allegorically, or tropologically (morally); many but not all passages in Scripture have two or even three of these meanings (*Didasc.* 5.2). Hugh is careful to add that not only biblical words but also the things referred to by biblical words have meaning;

for example, in 1 Pet. 5: 8, 'lion' means a lion, and the lion means the devil. The *Didascal-icon* explains the place of scriptural study in the whole of human inquiry and tells how to study the Bible; the *De sacramentis* provides the theological understanding without which the reader of the Bible is bound to go astray (*De sacr*. I, prol.).

God

For Hugh, God is neither wholly known by us nor wholly unknown (*De sacr*. I.3.2). We know about God in two basic ways, reason and revelation; each of these is subdivided into external and internal indications of God's existence (*De sacr*. I.3.3). Hence we can know of God through reason by reflecting on external creatures (*De sacr*. I.3.10; I.2.12; I.3.28) or by reflecting on our own minds (*De sacr*. I.3.6–9; I.2.13); likewise, we can know about God through external teaching or internal inspiration (*De sacr*. I.3.3). All these ways find their unity in the fact that it is the one God who makes himself known through them all, an example of how philosophy finds its place in the broader context of faith (see Schutz 1967, pp. 286–304).

Hugh reduces the basic divine attributes to power, will (goodness), and wisdom (*De sacr*. I.2.6; I.3.29), and he does not seem to feel the need to reduce them to one trait, such as infinity or perfection. Throughout, Hugh shows an awareness of what will later be called analogy, i.e., he is aware that God's attributes are both similar and dissimilar to the corresponding attributes found in creation (*De sacr*. I.3.28; I.2.13).

Steering a safe path through the trinitarian controversies of his time, Hugh discusses appropriation of common names, argues that the Trinity is reflected in creation but not in such a way that we could have discovered it without revelation, and presents the view that the trinitarian persons are united in nature and distinguished by opposed relations (*De sacr*. I.3; II.1.4).

Creation

Hugh follows Augustine in holding that time began with creation (*De sacr*. I.1.6). He also holds that the world began in a relatively unformed state and was later given (more) form by God (*De sacr*. I.1.6). He holds that evil is privation (*De sacr*. I.1.10) and that God could have created the world differently (*De sacr*. I.1.3). He discusses the angels in *De sacr*. I.5 and also in his commentary on Pseudo-Dionysius' *Celestial Hierarchy*, emphasizing their inequality. He seems to be steering clear of the view that angels have spiritual matter, which anticipates a debate in the later Middle Ages (*De sacr*. I.1.4–6; I.5.7).

Providence and evil

Not surprisingly, Hugh holds that God governs all of creation. This raises difficulties that call on much of his skill. In *De sacr*. I.2.14–22, Hugh notes that God has foreknowledge of all things. It seems, however, that if God knows infallibly all that will happen, then (a) things must turn out the way he foresees their turning out, which makes all events necessary, and (b) the truth of his knowledge depends on their turning out that way, which makes God posterior to creatures. The heart of Hugh's solution is a distinction between foreknowledge and providence; one can have foreknowledge of things over which one has no control, whereas one can have providence only of things over which one has control. God's knowledge is not merely foreknowledge but providential foreknowledge. The source of the difficulty was that how things turn out and God's knowledge of how they turn out co-vary; if God knows that it will rain, it will rain, and if it will rain, God knows that it will rain. If that is all we say, then there is no way to tell which is causally prior, the rain or God's knowledge thereof. But once we see that God's knowledge is providential, i.e., that it concerns what he has control over, we can see the direction of causation: things happen the way they do because God has providential knowledge that they will so happen, not vice versa. This solves both problems. God is not posterior to created happenings, and that his knowledge is providential ensures that in fact the opposite is the case. As for created happenings, they are contingent, because God could have willed them to happen otherwise; in that contrary-to-fact case, his providential foreknowledge would have been other than it was.

Another problem concerning providence is posed by evil. For Hugh the issue is not whether the existence of evil counts against the existence of God but how both God and evil can exist (*De sacr.* I.4.1–8). He distinguishes what God permits (his permissive will) from what God brings about (his operative will). Second, he distinguishes something's being good (or evil) in itself from something's being such that it is good (or evil) for it to exist. This yields four logical possibilities and allows Hugh to account for the existence of evil. Some things are evil in themselves, but nonetheless it is good for them to exist; the death of an animal, which is evil in itself but provides food, might be a good example. Such evils God does not create, but he does permit them, as it is better for there to be not only the kinds of good that arise from good things whose existence is good, but also the kinds of good that arise from evil things whose existence is good.

So what God does and what he permits both reveal his will. But a further problem arises when we consider his commands and prohibitions, many of which are disobeyed (*De sacr.* I.4.9–25; cf. I.5.30–2). If they are disobeyed, does this not mean that God's will is thwarted? If not, if God's commands are disobeyed only in accordance with his will, how are they not deceptive signs of that will, at least in those cases in which God's will is for them not to be obeyed? Hugh argues that God's commands tell us what we should do, what would benefit us; some choose evil, however, and God permits this when the evils chosen are things such that it is good (for others' benefit) for them to be. Thus, as Hugh explains, God does not cause evil, but he orders it for the sake of good (*De sacr.* I.5.32).

Human nature and ethics

Hugh has a strong doctrine of man as the image of God (*De sacr.* I.6.2; I.5.3). He sees man as including both soul and body, but he has a strong tendency to identify man with the soul alone (*De sacr.* I.6.1–3); a tendency to think of form as accidental (*De sacr.* I.3.15) may be preventing him from seeing the soul as the body's form. He thus emphasizes the division between body and spirit, with the latter commanding the former and the former (ideally) obeying. He seems to associate man's natural good with bodily good and his supernatural good with spiritual good, without leaving much room for any natural perfections of the mind.

Salvation

The work of restoration is spread out over a long expanse of time, starting right after the fall, even before the first revelation to the Jews. All of it is the work of Christ, whom Hugh compares to the captain of an army, some of whose soldiers go on before him and some of whom come behind (*De sacr.* I prol. 2). Nothing but the best is good enough for man (*De sacr.* I.6.6), and his end state after redemption is higher than it was before the fall (*De sacr.* I.6.10).

Hugh's Christology is basically orthodox; he shows good mastery of the basic Patristic teachings on person and nature, although his zeal to overcome certain heterodox tendencies of his day led him to exaggerate Christ's human knowledge (*De sacr.* II.1.6; cf. Poppenberg 1937, p. 112.)

Very noteworthy is Hugh's teaching on the sacraments. It was he who made the decisive contribution to Christian theology of characterizing a sacrament in the full sense as not just a sign but a sign instituted by Christ for the purpose of conveying what it signifies (*De sacr.* I.9.2). Sacraments in this sense are found not only within Christianity but throughout all salvation history, and in them we find united the main principles of Hugh's thought: sacraments both signify the restorative work of God and bring it about.

Hugh understands the Church (*De sacr.* II.2) on the basis of St. Paul's metaphor of the body of Christ, whose animating spirit is the Holy Spirit and each of whose members has its own function to fulfill for the sake of the whole. The two "sides" of this body are the clergy and the laity; the clergy are devoted to spiritual matters and the laity are devoted to the things of this life. This spiritual/temporal distinction is not a distinction between the Church and the world, at least not in the Christendom Hugh knew; it is in a sense a distinction within the Church, as both secular and spiritual power are under Christ's authority. The secular is subordinated to the spiritual (*De sacr.* II.2.4), but the secular power's sphere has to be respected by the spiritual, which qualifies the sense in which the spiritual power can possess material things (*De sacr.* II.2.7).

Spiritual teachings

The central spiritual problem is the restlessness of the human heart, which pursues the many changing things of this changing world. This restlessness is an effect of the fall, which robbed man of the loving contemplation by which he was aware of God's presence in a way that unified his thoughts and actions and made them good. In the next life we hope to attain the beatific vision, which goes even beyond that pre-lapsarian contemplation; in this life we can only strive, with the help of supernatural grace, to recover loving contemplation (*De arca Noe morali* I, prol.). Using the image of Noah's Ark, Hugh describes how one should float above the changing waters of the world in the ark of the recollected soul, in a life of contemplation where thought and action are directed to God (*De arca Noe morali*, II, 2–5, in *PL* 176).

Influence and importance

Hugh had a great influence over the members of his own school, RICHARD OF ST. VICTOR above all. In an even more long-lasting way, he influenced PETER LOMBARD, whose impact

324

on later scholastic thought is hard to overstate; this gives Hugh a tremendous if indirect influence over the entire course of scholastic thought. As for direct influence, this tended to wane after the twelfth century, although he was certainly read and appreciated by later authors, such as Bonaventure, THOMAS AQUINAS, and others, especially on specific points, such as his definition of sacraments.

If Hugh sometimes lacks the great sophistication of later scholastic thinkers, at the same time the relative lack of complexity of his thought makes it easier for him to achieve and expound an overall vision without getting distracted by technical issues. His caution and prudence are attractive, and when he does go into details, his discussions are often quite interesting and instructive. He balances concern for the natural with a concern to place it in the greater supernatural context. Finally, his appropriation of the tradition of the Church Fathers and what he has of Greek philosophy is an example of how much can be accomplished by someone who is more interested in learning and passing on the truth than in being original (see *De sacr.* I.2.22).

Bibliography

Primary sources

(1854), *Opera omnia*, in J.-P. Migne, ed., *Patrologia Latina* (*PL*), vols. 175–7, Paris: Vivès.

(1951), *On the Sacraments of the Christian Faith* [*De sacramentis christianae fidei*], trans. R. Deferrari, Cambridge, MA: The Medieval Academy of America.

(1961), *The Didascalicon*, trans. J. Taylor, New York: Columbia University Press.

(1962), *Selected Spiritual Writings*, trans. by a religious of Congregatio Sanctae Mariae Virginis, New York: Harper and Row.

Secondary sources

Bonaventure (1882–1902), *De reductione artium ad theologiam*, in *Doctoris seraphici S. Bonaventurae Opera omnia*, vol. V, Quaracchi: Collegium S. Bonaventurae.

Hofmeier, J. (1964), *Die Trinitätslehre des Hugo von St. Viktor*, Munich: Max Hueber Verlag.

Illich, I. (1993), *In the Vineyard of the Text: A Commentary to Hugh's Didascalicon*, Chicago: University of Chicago Press.

Poppenberg, P. E. (1937), *Die Christologie des Hugo von St. Victor*, Münster: Herz Jesu-missionshaus Hiltrup.

Schütz, C. (1967), *Deus absconditus, Deus manifestus: Die Lehre Hugos von St. Viktor über die Offenbarung Gottes*, Rome: Herder.

F. Vernet (1927), "Hugues de Saint-Victor," in A. Vacant, E. Mangenot, and E. Amann, eds., *Dictionnaire de théologie catholique*, vol. 7, no. 1 (pp. 240–307), Paris: Librairie Letouzey et Ané.

48

Isaac Israeli

SARAH PESSIN

Isaac Israeli (b. ca. 855; d. ca. 955) lived in North Africa. In addition to medical tracts, his corpus includes a number of philosophical texts, among them *The Book of Definitions*, *The Book of Elements*, and *The Book of Substances*. A mix of Arabic Aristotelianism and Neoplatonism, these works clearly reveal the influence of ALKINDI, and (as Altmann and Stern (1958) maintain) of "Ibn Hasday's Neoplatonist." The latter is a moniker devised by Stern to refer to the unknown author whose (non-extant) work(s) he posits to explain similarities between parts of Israeli, the longer version of the *Theology of Aristotle*, and passages in Ibn Hasday.

Israeli's positions on given topics are often unclear; not only is much of his corpus available to us only in fragmentary form, but, even among those fragments, inconsistencies seem to abound. One example is his equivocation on the nature of Wisdom and Intellect: at times, they seem to be identical (representing the highest level beneath the Godhead), at times they appear to lose that distinction to first matter, and at times they emerge as entities distinct from one another.

Furthermore, lack of agreement about the relationship between some of Israeli's claims and Plotinian Neoplatonism contributes to further uncertainty regarding how best to interpret Israeli's views. Where in Plotinus we find a One emanating forth into Intellect, Soul, and Nature, in Israeli, we find a Willing God followed by a "created" Intellect, three Souls and "Sphere" (a reality which sometimes, but not always, appears to overlap with Plotinus' Nature); additionally, Israeli at times speaks of a first form and first matter preceding even Intellect. While these might seem clear departures from pagan emanationism, a sustained examination leaves unclear whether or not these differences in Israeli's language can be taken to represent genuine philosophical departures from a Plotinian worldview. And so, for example, while all agree that Israeli is committed to emanation as regards the relationship between Intellect and the levels of reality that follow from it, there is no agreement on how Israeli regards the relationship between God and Intellect. While Altmann argues that Israeli is here committed to a decidedly non-Plotinian creation *ex nihilo*, Wolfson maintains that even this relationship may be seen as one of emanation.

These difficulties aside, what characterizes Israeli as a Neoplatonist is not only his interest in a mystical union as the end-goal of human existence, but (a) the particular metaphors he uses to describe that phenomenon, and (b) the extent to which the mechanics of that union are understood precisely in terms of a characteristically Neoplatonic cosmology.

Bibliography

Primary source

(1937–38), *Liber de definitionibus*, ed. L. T. Muckle, in *Archives d'Histoire Doctrinale et Littéraire du Moyen Âge* 11, pp. 299–340.

Secondary sources

Altmann, A. (1979), "Creation and emanation in Isaac Israeli: a reappraisal," in I. Twersky, ed., *Studies in Medieval Jewish History and Literature* (pp. 1–15), Cambridge, MA: Harvard University Press.

Altmann, A. and Stern, S. M. (1958), *Isaac Israeli: A Neoplatonic Philosopher of the Early Tenth Century*, London: Oxford University Press.

Wolfson, H. A. (1973), "The meaning of *ex nihilo* in Isaac Israeli," in Harry Austryn Wolfson, *Studies in the History of Philosophy and Religion*, ed. I. Twersky and G. H. Williams, vol. 1 (pp. 222–33), Cambridge, MA: Harvard University Press.

49

Isidore of Seville

SANDRO D'ONOFRIO

Isidore (b. ca. 560; d. 636), Bishop of Seville at the beginning of the seventh century, is primarily known for his *Etymologies*, which is an extensive and wide-ranging encyclopedia divided into twenty books, in which he tried to summarize all the knowledge available to him at the time. This work seeks to reveal the nature of things through a study of the etymology of the terms we use to refer to them. It begins by discussing the seven liberal arts, and continues with medicine, universal history, the sacred books and offices of the Church, and many other subjects such as geography and the practical arts.

It is a commonplace to say that Isidore was the last candle of classic learning at the beginning of the Dark Ages, for he was a scholar and supporter of ancient learning in an intellectually poor world. The amount of information found in the *Etymologies*, or in his other encyclopedia, the *De natura rerum*, is impressive, but he often restates views that are not quite clear to him and his etymologies range from the true to the ridiculous.

Isidore's aim, following the example of late Roman encyclopedists, such as Varro and Pliny the Elder, seems to be primarily the compilation of ancient learning for the sake of its preservation and use in instruction of the clergy. Isidore does not add information from his own age, but restricts himself to the compilation of materials available to him from prior times. However, it is clear from such works as the *Differentiae* and the *Synonyms* that he also aims to reconcile Christian theology with secular learning. These two works precede the *Etymologies* and are not devoted merely to the clarification of the meaning of words, but also to the elucidation of theological and spiritual issues. In the first book of the *Differentiae*, Isidore presents more than six hundred synonyms in order to explore their meanings; in the second, he is concerned with the meaning of theological terms in particular. Among Isidore's other works are *De fide catholica*, *Liber numerorum*, *De ecclesiasticis officiis*, *De ordine creaturarum*, *Allegoriae*, and *Sententiarum libri tres*. In the theological works he uses the grammatical tools he borrows from the *trivium* and applies them to biblical exegesis. Despite the subordinate role that secular learning plays in his work, the importance he gives to science makes him a precursor of scholasticism.

Bibliography

Primary source

(1797–1803), *Opera omnia*, 7 vols., ed. Faustino Arévalo, Rome: A. Fulgonius.

Secondary sources

Brehaut, Ernest (1964), *An Encyclopedist of the Dark Ages: Isidore of Seville*, New York: B. Franklin (contains a translation of the *Etymologies*).

Fontaine, Jacques (1959), *Isidore de Seville et la culture classique dans l'Espagne visigothique*, 2 vols., Paris: Études Augustiniennes.

Madoz, José (1960), *San Isidoro de Sevilla; semblanza de su personalidad literaria*, ed. Carlos García Goldaraz, León: Consejo Superior de Investigaciones Científicas, Centro de Estudios e Investigaciones S. Isidoro.

329

50

James of Metz

RUSSELL L. FRIEDMAN

James of Metz was a Dominican theologian active around 1300. We know nearly nothing about his life, but from comparison with contemporary works we can deduce that James lectured on the *Sentences* of PETER LOMBARD at least twice, the first time about 1300–1, the second about 1302–3. On the basis of these two lecture series, several versions of a written *Sentences* commentary were composed. Most of this work still remains unedited, surviving in some twelve manuscript copies (see, on James and his works, Köhler 1971, pp. 1–66). While modern scholarship has shown that James was not a doctrinaire anti-Thomist, nevertheless, on many philosophical and theological issues he parted ways with THOMAS AQUINAS. In fact, a short treatise exists that replies to many aspects of James's thought from a Thomist point of view; this treatise was probably written in the first decade of the fourteenth century by the future Master General of the Dominican order, HERVAEUS NATALIS.

James was an eclectic thinker, influenced by, among others, HENRY OF GHENT and PETER OF AUVERGNE. Thus James, clearly under the influence of Henry of Ghent, held that relation is not an accident with its own being that inheres in its foundation, but rather is merely a way that its foundation exists (a *modus essendi*); a relation, then, takes all of its being from its foundation and does not enter into composition with it (Decker 1967, pp. 438–60). James also rejected Aquinas's position that matter or quantity is the principle of individuation, maintaining instead that this principle is the individual's form (Köhler 1971, pp. 226–51, with text editions 515–22; Ullrich 1966, pp. 266–71). A final example: James held that a concept is the intellectual act, and not the product of that act (Decker 1967, pp. 531–6; Ullrich 1966, pp. 306–54). Although on many philosophical issues James had a clear influence on his more famous confrere, DURAND OF ST. POURÇAIN, nevertheless there is no evidence that James was Durand's official teacher (*pace* Koch 1929).

Bibliography

Decker, B. (1967), *Die Gotteslehre des Jakob von Metz. Untersuchungen zur Dominikanertheologie zu Beginn des 14. Jahrhunderts*, Münster: Aschendorff.

Koch, J. (1929), "Jakob von Metz O.P., der Lehrer des Durandus de S. Porciano O.P.," *Archives d'Histoire Doctrinale et Littéraire du Moyen Âge* 4, pp. 169–229; repr. 1973 in J. Koch, *Kleine Schriften*, vol. 1 (pp. 133–200), Rome: Edizione di Storia e Letteratura.

Köhler, T. W. (1971), *Der Begriff der Einheit und ihr ontologisches Prinzip nach dem Sentenzenkommentar des Jakob von Metz O.P.*, Rome: Herder.

——(1974), "Wissenschaft und Evidenz. Beobachtungen zum wissenschaftstheoretischen Ansatz des Jakob von Metz," in T. Köhler, ed., *Sapientiae procerum amore* (pp. 369–414), Rome: Herder.

Ullrich, L. (1966), *Fragen der Schöpfungslehre nach Jakob von Metz, O.P.*, Leipzig: St. Benno-Verlag.

51

James of Viterbo

MARK D. GOSSIAUX

James of Viterbo (b. ca. 1255; d. 1307/8) was a member of the Augustinian order and a
master in the theology faculty at the University of Paris from 1293 to 1300. His most important philosophical works are his four *Quodlibetal Questions* and his *Quaestiones de divinis
praedicamentis* (Questions on the divine categories). In general, James's thought falls within
the Neo-Augustinian movement of his day. Although he admits that there is a real distinction between a creature's essence and its existence, James understands this in a manner quite
different from that of GILES OF ROME or THOMAS AQUINAS. Existence is related to essence as
the concrete to the abstract. In its primary signification it means the same thing as essence;
in its secondary signification it denotes the essence as it is joined to all of the accidents necessary for its actual existence. Thus a creature is distinguished from God by having within
itself a composition of substance and accidents. In his understanding of the categories James
draws upon BOETHIUS to establish a distinction between those categories that signify a thing
(*res*), and those that signify circumstances or modes of a thing. Ultimately for James the
created world is composed of three kinds of things, namely substances, quantities, and qualities. The remaining categories denote various conditions and relations of these things.

Although James agrees with Aquinas that the soul and its powers are really distinct, he
often parts company with him over the nature of intellect and will. For James the will is
superior to the intellect, human happiness consists more in an act of the will than in an act
of the intellect, and the agent intellect is not really distinct from the possible intellect. James
also maintains that intellect and will are self-movers. He explains this by positing various
"aptitudes" or incomplete actualities within the soul, which serve to incline it to a complete
act. In a similar vein, James develops a theory of seminal reasons to account for the origin
of substantial form. James accepts two basic tenets of Aristotelian hylomorphism, namely,
that there is a composition of matter and form in all sensible substances, and that all substantial forms (with the exception of the human soul) are educed from the potentiality of
matter. Matter, however, is not purely passive; it contains seminal reasons, which James
construes as inchoate forms and active principles in matter. This "form in potency" is really
distinct from matter and inclines matter to actuality.

Bibliography

Primary sources
(1968–75), *Disputationes de quodlibet*, 4 vols., ed. E. Ypma, Würzburg: Augustinus-Verlag.
(1983–6), *Quaestiones de divinis praedicamentis*, 2 vols., ed. E. Ypma, Rome: Augustinianum.

Secondary sources

Casado, F. (1951–3), "El pensamiento filosófico del Beato Santiago de Viterbo, *La Ciudad de Dios* 163, pp. 437–54; 164, pp. 301–31; 165, pp. 103–44, 283–302, 489–500.

Gossiaux, M. D. (1999), "James of Viterbo on the relationship between essence and existence," *Augustiniana* 49, pp. 73–107.

52

Jean de la Rochelle

GÉRARD SONDAG

Jean de la Rochelle (b. 1190/1200; d. 1245), master of arts, Franciscan, and then master of theology, is especially known for the part that he played in the redaction of the *Summa fratris Alexandri*, a work that exercised quite a strong influence upon the theology of the thirteenth century. He seems to have been the principal redactor of books I (On God) and III (On the incarnate word; law and precepts; on grace and the virtues) of the *Summa*. He also produced treatises on moral theology (*The Capital Sins* and *Questions on Grace*), commentaries on Scripture (two inaugural lectures of courses on the Bible), a number of sermons, and two more properly philosophical treatises (*The Treatise on the Different Divisions of the Powers of the Soul* and the *Summa de anima*).

For Jean de la Rochelle, theology is essentially wisdom (*sapientia*). Taking as his paradigmatic example St. Anthony of Padua, Jean deems that three things are required for a theologian: knowledge, a holy life, and teaching. Someone who teaches Scripture should have a solid doctrinal formation, but should also "embody in himself sacred knowledge by his good will and moral actions, before practicing his profession upon others through teaching and preaching."

At a time when Parisian theologians tended to eschew philosophical studies, Jean emphasized their usefulness, so long as such studies were pursued for a good end: even as the Philistines forebade the Hebrews from forging swords and spears (1 Sam. 13: 19), so the demons would like to turn Christians away from the study of philosophy and the art of reasoning, "fearing that they might acquire thereby acute and perceptive minds."

Summa de anima is based primarily upon the pseudo-Augustinian work *On the Spirit and the Soul*, as is evident in its distinction between intellect (*intellectus*) and intelligence (*intelligentia*); above the level of intellect, that knows creatures, there is the intelligence that knows unchanging truth and goodness, that is to say, God.

Jean de la Rochelle introduces into his account of intellectual cognition, however, a theory of abstraction of Aristotelian inspiration, while nonetheless retaining certain Avicennian doctrines. Sensible features are reorganized in the imagination (the *phantasia* of Aristotle). Thereafter, considering the constitutive features of sensible items, the "estimative" faculty (*aestimativa*) retains the similarities discovered and eliminates the differences so as to isolate the corporeal form; but the latter is not, at this stage of cognition, entirely removed from the sensible realm. Finally the intellect strips away the corporeal form from motion and the conditions associated with the matter and singularity of objects, and thus "grasps it purely, as a simple and universal notion." Once we arrive at this final stage of abstraction, the form is predicable of all individuals of the same species and is the fully formed universal. The

334

influence of AVICENNA upon Jean de la Rochelle's doctrine of the degrees of abstraction is noticeable. Furthermore, the differences among the various operations of the intellectual soul, which arise from differences in their respective objects, imply a distinction among the faculties of the soul and the soul itself, although the faculties are substantially identical to the soul.

Ideas such as these, which will be found later in the philosophy of mind of JOHN DUNS SCOTUS, are sufficient to indicate the originality of the thought of Jean de la Rochelle in philosophical psychology; too often has Jean been relegated to the status of a mere popularizer.

Bibliography

Primary sources

(1995), *Summa de anima*, ed. Jacques Guy Bougerol, Paris: J. Vrin.
(1964), *Tractatus de divisione multiplici potentiarium animae*, ed. Pierre Michaud-Quantin, Paris: J. Vrin.

Secondary source

Gilson, Étienne (1955), *History of Christian Philosophy in the Middle Ages*, New York: Random House.

53

Jerome of Prague

JONATHAN J. SANFORD

Jerome of Prague (b. 1370/1; d. 1416), was a close friend and disciple of John Hus. In 1399 Jerome journeyed to Oxford, where he studied Wyclif's works. He copied Wyclif's *Dialogue* and *Trialogue*, and carried them back with him to Prague, making him the first to spread Wyclif's most important theological works to Bohemia. After returning to the university in Prague he promoted Wyclif's realism and anti-clericalism. Owing to an edict in Prague against Wyclif's doctrines, Jerome moved to the University of Paris where he became master of arts. There he became an even more entrenched realist, which put him at odds with the predominantly nominalist faculty. Jerome was forced to flee Paris and in 1406 went first to Heidelberg, and then to Cologne, both of which places he was again forced to flee.

Prague was more receptive to Hus and his followers in 1407 when Jerome returned there. He played an important role in the quodlibet of 1409 in which the question of universals was examined. After 1409 Jerome appears to have taken the lead in the reform movement, and began traveling to promote the movement. In 1410 he appeared in Vienna to answer charges of heresy. He was condemned, but fled. Jerome was a vehement opponent of the papal indulgence of 1412, and after he had organized a number of public protests his ideas took a more radical turn. For example, he supported lay priesthood and iconoclasm (Betts 1969, pp. 216, 220–1). Jerome secretly traveled to the Council of Constance in 1415 in order to support Hus. He was persuaded to leave, but was captured and detained for a year. At trial he at first withdrew his support for the doctrines of Wyclif and Hus, but later recanted and was burned at the stake.

Jerome wrote little, but was known as a great orator and dedicated proselytizer of the reform movement. Only a few of his speeches survive (Höfler 1856–66, vol. 2), and his biographical data are drawn mainly from the documents of the Council of Constance (Hardt 1696–1742).

Bibliography

Primary sources

(1696–1742), *Magnum oecumenim Constanciense concilium*, 7 vols., ed. H. von der Hardt, Frankfurt, Leipzig, and Berlin.

(1856–66), *Geschichtschreiber der hussitischen Bewegung in Böhmen*, 3 vols., ed. C. Höfler, Vienna.

Secondary sources

Bernard, P. (1958), "Jerome of Prague, Austria and the Hussites," *Church History* 35, pp. 3–22.

Betts, R. R. (1969), "Jerome of Prague," in G. H. Bolsover, P. Brock, and O. Odložilík, eds., *Essays in Czech History* (pp. 195–235), London: Athlone Press, University of London.

Kaluza, Z. (1994), "Jérôme de Prague et le *Timée* de Platon," *Archives d'Histoire Doctrinale et Littéraire du Moyen Âge* 61, pp. 57–104.

Vilém, H. (1995), "Der Streit zwischen Hieronymus von Prag und Johann Gerson: Eine spätmittelalterliche Diskussion mit tragischen Folgen," in S. Włodek, ed., *Société et Église* (pp. 77–89), Rencontres de philosophie médiévale 4, Turnhout: Brepols.

337

54

John Baconthorpe

RICHARD CROSS

John Baconthorpe (b. 1290; d. 1345/8), English Carmelite friar, read the *Sentences* at Paris before 1318, and was regent master in the theology faculty by 1323. He edited his *Sentences Commentary* in about 1325; his *Quodlibetal Questions* date from 1323–4 (*Quodlibet* I), 1324–5 (*Quodlibet* II), and 1330 (*Quodlibet* III). He was the Carmelite Provincial of England in 1327–33, and later taught in Cambridge and probably in Oxford, dying before 1348.

Baconthorpe adopts a sophisticated if eclectic Thomist stance. Some of the notable points of disagreement with THOMAS AQUINAS, however, spring from Baconthorpe's self-conscious faithfulness to the Paris and Oxford condemnations of 1277. Most notable is Baconthorpe's acceptance of HENRY OF GHENT's view that the will is an active power with the liberty of indifference, a power that can move itself in the absence of any prior cause, and, in accordance with the Parisian condemnation, can will against any object presented to it by the intellect. Baconthorpe rejects too Aquinas's claim that there is only one substantial form in human beings, holding that a human being has a bodily form in addition to an intellective soul. The explicit motivation here is ROBERT KILWARDBY's Oxford condemnation of the view that an embryo does not retain identity before and after the creation of its intellective soul. The Parisian condemnation leads Baconthorpe to accept that angelic presence in the material world cannot be reduced merely to an angel's operation; this operation requires a prior non-bodily contact between the angel and the place where the angel brings about its effect. Although he does not cite it, Baconthorpe rejects in accordance with the Parisian condemnation Aquinas's view that there cannot be many angels of the same species, and he rejects too Aquinas's reason for this view – namely, that matter along with quantity individuates material substances. Baconthorpe argues that form individuates, though he rejects JOHN DUNS SCOTUS's haecceity theory, on the grounds that, as Aquinas held, common essences do not have any being in themselves. Existing essences are *eo ipso* individuals, instances of otherwise nonexistent common essences.

Baconthorpe diverges too from Aquinas in ways that reflect the later transformation of debates after Aquinas by Henry of Ghent, Duns Scotus, and PETER AURIOL, Baconthorpe's three favorite opponents. Combating Scotus's extreme rejection of any sort of extra-mental relation between God and creatures, Baconthorpe holds that God is really related to his creatures. Any relation that requires the real existence of its end term is real, and God's being creator requires the existence of creatures. God's knowledge of future contingents is also entirely dependent on the free choices of creatures that timelessly cause this knowledge in God. Furthermore, creatures are known by God through their eternally having ideal or representative being, distinct from the divine essence, in the divine mind. Baconthorpe modifies Aquinas's account of the composition between essence and existence, holding that they are distinct not really but only in terms of their degree of reality. Finally, Baconthorpe, like Henry of Ghent, rejects the existence of intelligible species prior to any intellectual act; actual cognition results directly from the action of the agent intellect on the phantasm.

Baconthorpe's *Sentence* commentary is notable for many discussions of the opinions of Aristotle and especially of AVERROES, and unusually an occasional tendency to determine a question *secundum philosophos* as well as, or instead of, a purely theological discussion of the issues. Baconthorpe's thorough account of his named theological opponents makes the work a very useful resource for ascertaining the state of theological debate in Paris during the 1310s.

Bibliography

Primary source
(1618), *Quaestiones in quatuor libros sententiarum et quodlibetales*, 2 vols., Cremona.

Secondary sources
Wippel, John F. (1994), "Godfrey of Fontaines (b. ca. 1250; d. 1306/09), Peter of Auvergne (d. 1303), and John Baconthorpe (d. 1345/48)," in Jorge J. E. Gracia, ed., *Individuation in Scholasticism: The Later Middle Ages and the Counter-Reformation 1150–1650* (pp. 221–56), Albany: State University of New York Press.

Xiberta, Bartholomaeus Maria (1931), *De scriptoribus scholasticis saeculi XIV ex ordine Carmelitarum*, Bibliothèque de la Revue d'Histoire Ecclésiastique 6, Louvain: Bureaux de la Revue.

55

John Buridan

GYULA KLIMA

Although John Buridan (b. ca. 1295; d. 1361) was one of the most famous philosophers of his time, relatively little is known about his life with certainty. He was born somewhere in the diocese of Arras in Picardy. The scarcity of information on his early life and the fact that he probably completed his early studies in the College of Cardinal Lemoine as the holder of a stipend provided for poor students may indicate that he was of humble origins. If this is true, then his life exemplifies the possibility of a brilliant, and even financially rewarding, academic career in late medieval society based solely on talent and personal achievement.

When Buridan received his license to teach (after 1320), he joined the arts faculty of the University of Paris, where he taught for the rest of his life. Diverging from the usual career path of his time, he never moved on to what were regarded as the more advanced faculties (roughly the equivalents of modern graduate, or professional schools), namely, theology, law, or medicine. This, however, in no way diminished his academic stature or professional influence: he served twice as rector of the university (in 1327/8 and 1340), and became one of the most influential philosophers of the period.

Buridan's professional influence was to be felt not only as a result of his scholarly output, but also through his teaching and administrative actions. His nominalist doctrine was widely disseminated through the works of his students (or younger colleagues) who themselves also became very influential. As for his administrative actions, the strange fact that as rector he signed an apparently anti-nominalist statute (in 1340) meant to curb certain theoretical excesses of Ockhamists at the university will at once make sense, if we see it as an effort to protect his own *calm* nominalism, deliberately kept by him within the doctrinal confines of philosophical research, without venturing into controversial issues in theology (Moody 1971).

Nevertheless, although he prudently distanced himself from the Ockhamist theologians of his university (especially NICHOLAS OF AUTRECOURT, whom he consistently confronted on a number of logical, metaphysical, and epistemological points), Buridan's logical and philosophical doctrine is markedly Ockhamist in the sense that Ockham's nominalist innovations (Klima 1999b) in Buridan's doctrine became integrated into an original, philosophically as well as pedagogically, highly effective system. Indeed, one may safely assert that whatever in WILLIAM OF OCKHAM had been merely programmatic, controversial, and tentative, in Buridan's hands became systematic, uncontroversial, and operative, both in teaching and in philosophical and scientific research.

As to its form, Buridan's scholarly output mostly consists of question-commentaries on Aristotle's works, and some independent treatises. The treatises include two major works in

340

logic, the *Summulae de dialectica* (in the subsequent references: *SD*), and the *Treatise on Consequences*, along with some minor treatments of some difficult questions in natural philosophy. The question-commentaries cover the whole extent of Aristotelian philosophy, ranging from logic to metaphysics, to natural philosophy, to ethics. The question format, focusing on the thorough discussion of certain difficult or controversial points in connection with Aristotle's text, rather than on its detailed exposition, allows Buridan to develop his own comprehensive philosophical system, applying the characteristic conceptual tools he developed in his logical works. Indeed, it is precisely this conceptual apparatus, most systematically presented in his *Summulae*, that provides the unifying perspective of Buridan's thought in any field of philosophical inquiry.

Accordingly, the subsequent discussion of Buridan's philosophy will naturally fall under the headings of logic, metaphysics/physics, and ethics, the first and most detailed discussion being reserved for Buridan's logic, in particular, his *Summulae*.

Logic

Buridan's *Summulae*, following the teaching practice of the time, is written in the form of a running commentary on an authoritative text, in this case, PETER OF SPAIN'S *Tractatus*, also known as *Summulae dialecticales*. However, because of certain irreconcilable conflicts between the realist master's text and Buridan's nominalist doctrine, for his *Summulae* Buridan completely reorganized Peter's text, and at some points simply replaced and supplemented it by his own. So in these passages Buridan is actually commenting and expanding on his own, more succinct formulations in the main text (Klima forthcoming).

What primarily allows us to characterize Buridan's logic as *nominalist* is Buridan's *semantic* doctrine, which describes the relationships between language, mind, and reality. Indeed, we may say that the gist of Buridan's nominalism consists in achieving ontological parsimony by using his semantic theory to show how we can map a great number of radically different linguistic categories onto a reduced number of ontological categories. In order to achieve this ontological reduction Buridan's main tactic, following Ockham, is to map linguistic categories onto ontological ones by means of conceptual structures, thus constituting a *mental language* (Klima 1991). Since the concepts of the mind, according to Buridan, are but individualized qualities of singular substances, admitting them into his ontology does not in any way compromise the simplicity of his system of ontological categories, which contains only three really distinct kinds of permanent entities, namely, substances, their quantities, and their qualities. (Some further types of entities, namely, successive *motions* and not really distinct *modes*, will be considered below in connection with Buridan's metaphysics.)

To understand the significance of Buridan's reduction of the categories of permanent entities to these three, and the semantic theory whereby he achieved this reduction, we should contrast it with a brief, schematic account of what may be called the prevailing realist doctrine of the time. (For detailed comparative discussion, see Klima 1999a.)

According to this realist doctrine in its most extreme form, Aristotle's ten categories provide a division of real beings into ten mutually exclusive classes of singular entities. Universals, as such, even in this tradition were not regarded as real, mind-independent entities, but rather as objects of the mind, founded on the abstractible characteristics of singular entities (i.e., their forms, or natures). Thus, reality primarily consists of primary substances (namely, material substances, that is, bodies, and immaterial substances, such as angels and God), their quantities (such as the dimensions of bodies), their qualities (such as colors, shapes, or natural abilities), their relations (anything by which one thing is related to another, such as their equality, or similarity), their actions and passions (such as causing or undergoing change), their time (i.e., *when* they are), their places (i.e., *where* they are), their positions (such as standing or sitting), and their habits (in the sense of having some garment or equipment on them, such as being dressed, armed, or saddled).

According to the nominalists, what yields the apparently unlimited proliferation of these entities is what they regard as the realists' mistaken semantic conception. For according to this conception, the concrete common terms of human languages signify precisely the inherent, non-substantial entities listed above, informing individual substances. What verifies these terms of individual substances is the *actual inherence* of these entities in their subjects. This is why this theory is often referred to in the secondary literature as *the inherence theory of predication*. For example, the predication 'Socrates is wise' is true according to this conception, if and only if wisdom actually inheres in Socrates, that is, if Socrates' wisdom is actual. But since the same goes for all sorts of predications, in all categories, the theory does seem to be committed to various weird entities, such as Socrates' now being admired by philosophy students, because philosophy students now admire him, or his non-asininity, because Socrates is not an ass.

Quite characteristically, whereas Ockham waged an all-out war against this doctrine, Buridan often satisfies himself (and his students) by simply declaring that the doctrine is wrong and he does not follow it. (2001, 3.6.1; 1983, pp. 129, 149, 145.) He shows the strength of his own theory by explaining how it is able to provide a satisfactory account of the semantic properties of our common terms *without* committing us to the sorts of weird entities noted above.

In the first place, Buridan, following Ockham, distinguishes absolute and appellative (or connotative) common terms. A common absolute term is one that is subordinated to a common absolute concept, namely, an act of our minds by which we conceive of a number of things indifferently, disregarding their individual or specific differences, but without conceiving them in relation to other things. According to Buridan, absolute terms are all the terms that belong in the category of substance, and some of the terms that belong in the categories of quantity and quality. Appellative terms are those that are subordinated to connotative concepts, i.e., concepts by which we conceive things indifferently, but in relation to other things. Buridan also makes a distinction between simple and complex concepts, the latter being those that are made up from the former. The important point to note about this distinction is that the simplicity of a spoken or written term of our languages does not guarantee the simplicity of the corresponding concept. Finally, he also uses the old distinction between categorematic and syncategorematic terms, applied also to mental terms, i.e., concepts, in the sense that a categorematic term is one by which we signify/conceive things, whereas the function of syncategorematic terms is to modify the representative function of the categorematic terms to which they are applied, and to join them in complex phrases (complex concepts), as do the terms (concepts) of logical connectives, such as 'all', 'not', 'and', 'is' (in its function of a copula, joining two terms in a proposition) (2001, 4.2.3).

With these distinctions in hand, Buridan can easily eliminate all real distinctions between things apparently demanded by the realist theory, in favor of distinctions between concepts by which we conceive of the same things in different ways.

For example, take the proposition 'Socrates is a father'. According to the realist theory, this predication is true if and only if Socrates' fatherhood is actual. Accordingly, the term 'father' in this proposition is construed as signifying an inherent relation somehow connecting Socrates to his children. One of the thorny questions inevitably emerging here is whether Socrates has as many fatherhoods as children, or he is related to them all by the same fatherhood. This type of question had serious theological significance, when it was raised concerning the filiations of Christ relating him (temporally) to the Holy Mother and (eternally) to the Heavenly Father.

Buridan's account, on the other hand, does not necessarily give rise to such thorny questions. (This does not mean, however, that such questions cannot be raised in the framework of his theory.) For on his account the predicate term of this proposition need not be construed as signifying an inherent relation. For him, the term 'father' is simply a connotative term, which means that it is subordinated to a concept in our minds by which we conceive of men in relation to their children. Accordingly, the term 'father' does not signify the inherent fatherhood(s?) of these men, but it signifies these men, connoting their children. Therefore, the proposition in question is true if and only if Socrates is one of these men, i.e., if Socrates is identical with a man having at least one child. In general, in this framework, such a simple affirmative predication is true if the terms of the proposition stand for the same thing or things. This is why this theory of predication is often referred to as the *identity theory*. As can be seen, in this framework the simple relative term 'father' is analyzed as being subordinated to the complex concept of a man having at least one child. This analysis allows Buridan simply to sidestep the problems generated by positing inherent fatherhoods, for the term subordinated to this concept obviously need not signify such a strange entity, but those men who have at least one child.

To be sure, despite the nominalists' claims to the contrary, the realist semantics they opposed was not necessarily committed to the proliferation of strange entities, since it was still open for the realists to identify the significata of various terms from several categories, as they did in a number of metaphysically justified cases. Nevertheless, whereas the metaphysical questions of the possibility of such identifications necessarily emerge in the realist framework, Buridan's nominalist framework does not necessarily give rise to such questions, although they may be raised whenever there is a metaphysically justified need to do so, as we shall see in the discussion of Buridan's metaphysics.

The situation is similar in the case of another semantically motivated ontological issue between nominalists and realists, namely, the question of the ontological status of the significata of whole propositions. According to the realist theory heavily criticized by Buridan, what a proposition as a whole signifies is something distinct from both the proposition itself and the things signified by its terms. What the proposition signifies is in fact something that cannot even be signified in any other way but by means of the complex combination of terms that make up the proposition, which is why it is called a *complexe significabile* (literally, something that is "complexly signifiable," i.e., signifiable in a complex manner) (Ashworth 1974, pp. 55–62).

Buridan finds this doctrine metaphysically mistaken, and even theologically unacceptable (for such entities would have to be neither created nor uncreated, and would still have to be co-eternal with God). However, again, besides showing why he finds this theory unacceptable, his main effort is spent on showing why it is completely unnecessary to posit such *complexe significabilia* in the first place (2001, *Sophismata*, c. 1, *fifth sophism*; c. 2, *conclusions* 3–8).

To be sure, Buridan does not verbally deny that there are *complexe significabilia*. In fact, he declares: "all beings in the world are complexly signifiable; further, every being, however simple it may be, is signifiable complexly. For example, God, who is the most simple being, is signified complexly by the expression 'God is God'" (*Sophismata*, c. 1, *to the fifth sophism*). But the example in this brief quote is telling: for Buridan what is signified in a complex manner by the proposition 'God is God' is the most simple being, God himself, who of course is also signifiable by the simple noun 'God'. So what is signified by this proposition is not some strange entity (signifiable *only* in this complex manner, distinct from God, and residing in a separate ontological realm not subject even to God's power), but God himself. In fact, Buridan claims that the contradictory proposition 'God is not God' also signifies God (2001, 1.1.6; 4.2.3; *Sophismata*, c. 1, *to the third sophism*).

But how can this be? How can these contradictory propositions signify the same? Buridan's answer lies in his two–tiered semantics: these propositions signify the same thing outside the mind, but they signify different propositions in the mind. To put the point in modern terms, we have sufficiently "fine–grained" structures in the mind to account for the semantic differences of these propositions, whence we need not posit any further differences in reality to account for these semantic differences. In particular, these two propositions are mapped in the mind onto different mental propositions, i.e., different acts of thought with different representative functions, which are determined by their different constituents. The difference in conceptual structure, namely, the fact that the one contains a negation operating on the copula, whereas the other does not, guarantees that their semantic values will be opposite, namely, true versus false, respectively; still, they will represent only one and the same simple thing outside the mind, only in different ways, namely, affirmatively versus negatively. (For more details, see Klima 1991 and Klima, forthcoming.)

So, Buridan's semantic framework allows him, in the first place, to reduce the signification of propositions to the ultimate *significata* of their terms, while preserving their semantic distinctness on the mental level. In the second place, he is able to reduce the significations of all categorematic terms to the ultimate significata of absolute terms, by identifying them with the ultimate *significata* and/or *connotata* of appellative terms, whether the latter are simple or complex. Finally, he can also account for the signification of syncategorematic terms within his restricted ontological framework, by identifying their *significata* as individual acts of individual human minds, namely, the syncategorematic concepts of these minds, which merely operate by modifying the representative function of the categorematic concepts of the same minds, and by joining them in more complex concepts.

Metaphysics and physics

With this semantic apparatus in place, Buridan could in principle endorse a much simpler ontology than he actually does. In fact, he could interpret all linguistic categories as ultimately signifying just one category of entities, namely, individual substances. (An Ockhamist theologian, JOHN OF MIRECOURT, was censured for holding precisely this thesis. See Adams 1985.)

He could achieve this reduction by claiming that the only absolute terms are in the category of substance, and analyze all other terms as being subordinated to either simple or complex connotative concepts, whereby the mind conceives of individual substances in relation to each other. However, further, non–logical considerations prevent Buridan from such a radical ontological reduction. In fact, much of his metaphysics and physics can be characterized as providing reasons for positing some non–substantial entities, in particular, in order to provide a comprehensive account of physical change (Normore 1985).

To be sure, change can in some cases easily be accounted for without positing some distinct, inherent, non–substantial entity in the changing subject. For instance, when someone becomes a father, then he does not have to acquire a relational entity, a fatherhood. It is enough that he begets a child, and thus, once the child is born, he can come to be conceived, and so signified, in relation to his child, in terms of the relative concept, and the corresponding spoken and written term 'father'. So, the person can come to be called something that he was not before, without having to posit a new inherent entity in him. But similar considerations apply, for example, in changing shape. When a straight piece of wire is bent, and so what was straight becomes curved, we need not assume that a shape-thing, a straightness, was destroyed, and a new shape-thing, a curvedness, came to be. All we have to say is that the extremes of the wire came to be closer to each other than they were before, when they were maximally distant. Here, again, analyzing away the apparently simple terms 'straight' and 'curved' in favor of the connotative complex terms and the corresponding concepts of the extremes being maximally distant and being closer (i.e., less than maximally distant), Buridan can easily explain away the apparent need for inherent entities to explain change. To be sure, Buridan also acknowledges the need to talk about the different *ways* or *modes* in which things are, when they are one way or another, but he does not take these modes as entities really distinct from the entities they characterize (Adams 1985; Klima 1999a).

However, there are cases in which, according to Buridan, this eliminative tactic just cannot work. In the first place, there is the supernatural case of transubstantiation, where the substance of the bread is turned into the body of Christ, whereas its accidents remain without a substance to inhere in, and thus are sustained by divine power alone. These accidents, the sensible qualities of the bread, clearly cannot be identified with their subject, if they remain in existence, while their subject does not.

Again, one cannot explain away a purely qualitative change in terms of the locomotion of the parts of their subject, as we could do in the case of change of shape, unless one is committed to the view that material substances are just complexes of tiny material parts, arranged in different ways (i.e., in different *modes*) to produce this or that sensory impression, which is the atomist doctrine of Democritus and Melissus. But atomism (notably revived by Nicholas of Autrecourt in Buridan's time) is rejected by Buridan as an "obscure and dangerous" doctrine, sufficiently refuted by Aristotle (1989, III, q. 11, p. 122).

Furthermore, Buridan advances a number of arguments in his questions on the *Physics* which show that quantity, despite Ockham's claim to the contrary, also has to be distinct from substance (1964, lb. IV, q. 11). Buridan takes the phenomena of compression and rarefaction to be inexplicable without such distinction, again, excluding the possibility of atomism (which is precisely the theoretical background of the explanation of these phenomena in the modern kinetic theory of gases).

Finally, the most notable illustration of Buridan's admitting into his ontology some entity demanded by his physical considerations is provided by his famous *impetus* theory, which remained influential until it became replaced by the modern conception of inertial motion (1964, lb. VIII, q. 12). Buridan's *impetus* is an impressed force left behind in the moving body by its mover, which accounts for the continuing motion of the moving body even when it is no longer moved by its mover, as in the case of projectile motion. Buridan's *impetus* theory provided an appealingly simple and coherent explanation of countless phenomena of motion that the "standard" Aristotelian theory (attributing the continuation of projectile movement to the medium of motion) could not adequately explain. (For further details, see Clagett 1959, pp. 505–40 and Grant 1977, pp. 50–5.)

But similar considerations apply to Buridan's analysis of the operations and powers of the soul. Buridan sticks to his parsimonious ontology in maintaining the thesis of the unity of substantial forms. For him, it is one and the same substantial form in man, the human soul, that performs vegetative, sensitive, and intellective functions, and not three distinct forms. This same form is merely signified in different ways by the terms 'vegetative', 'sensitive', and 'intellective', connoting different powers of the same soul. Nevertheless, he thinks we cannot properly account for the operations of these powers, unless we distinguish them from the substance of the soul. Furthermore, he also argues that in the operations of these powers we have to distinguish between the dispositions of their acts, their retained habits, and the acts themselves. So, contrary to what one might expect on the basis of his general Ockhamist ontological stance, he endorses intelligible species (*species intelligibiles*), as the first dispositions of primary acts of thought, and intellectual habits (*habitus intellectuales*), as the carriers of intellectual memory, distinct from the acts of thought (*actus intelligendi*) (1989, III, q. 15).

Ethics

Buridan's ethics, perhaps curiously for the modern reader, but very much in line with Aristotle's philosophy, is an organic continuation of his physics and metaphysics. In J. J. Walsh's succinct formulation, Buridan "professes a full-fledged moral naturalism – naturalism in the sense that moral knowledge is held to stem from the nature of things" (Walsh 1966, p. 5). However, this should not be so surprising, if we keep in mind that ethics primarily considers human actions with respect to good and evil, and human action is just one specific, although in many ways peculiar, kind of action in general.

The most important and both ontologically and ethically relevant peculiarity of human action as such is that it is free. But how do we know this, if at all? Buridan does not think we can demonstratively know that the will is free. He finds all arguments for this conclusion probable, but not demonstrative, just like the philosophical arguments for the immateriality of the human soul. Yet this does not mean that we do not know these conclusions, besides having to hold them firmly on the basis of faith, with an appropriate degree of certainty. In fact, the certainty is just the appropriate kind, namely, the immediate experience and evidence of our ability to choose to act otherwise, under any given circumstances, other things being equal. So, in this case, just as in his polemic with Nicholas of Autrecourt's skepticism in general, Buridan's strategy is to point out that the high demands of demonstrative certainty are simply inappropriate concerning certain questions and in certain fields (2001, 8.4.4; Zupko 2002, c. 15).

That the will is free, however, does not mean that its acts are random or fortuitous. It only means that, given its nature, its acts are not determined by circumstances in the way the actions of natural agents are determined. Still, the choice of the will itself is not completely undetermined.

Free will is a power that can only belong to intellectual agents, i.e., agents that by their intellects are able to conceive of different alternative courses of action. (Indeed, for Buridan, just as for THOMAS AQUINAS, the will is simply "intellectual appetite.") The freedom of the will is manifested in its ability to choose from the alternatives presented to it by the intellect as possessing certain values, namely, one being better than the other. In this setting, one of the controversial issues between (Thomist) *intellectualists* and (Scotist) *voluntarists* was whether the intellect, by setting these values on different alternatives, determines the choice of the will, namely, whether the will would always (rationally) choose the alternative that is presented as the best by the intellect, or it is free to choose (irrationally) some lesser good, contrary to the judgment of the intellect.

Buridan seeks a middle ground between these two alternatives by introducing a third one, namely, the will's ability to defer choice. For example, when two alternatives, A and B, are presented by the intellect in such a manner that A seems to be a better choice than B, the will's first act of agreement with A does not necessitate its choice of A, for before actually choosing A, the will also has the choice of sending back the whole issue for reconsideration to the intellect, which in the second round may come up with a different evaluation. After all, we are not omniscient, and the first judgment of the intellect may have been based on insufficient information. However, although this analysis of free choice seems to move away from intellectualism pure and simple, Buridan's doctrine is still closer to intellectualism than voluntarism. For what motivates the will's deferment of choosing either alternative presented to it by the intellect, is the *intellectual* consideration of the possible insufficiency of information.

In any case, it is definitely not the intellect's presentation of the alternatives alone that determines the choice of the will. In addition to the judgment of the intellect, and the will's inclination to choose what appears to be the best (unless uncertainty prevails), the virtues and vices of the agent contribute to the determination the will's choice. To be sure, the virtues and vices are not strictly determinants, but rather acquired habits that influence choice, inclining the will in one way or another. Virtues, for Buridan, are acquired qualities of the soul with a certain degree of latitude, pretty much on a par with other natural dispositions and habits that influence or determine the operations of natural agents. So, in light of Buridan's general naturalistic attitude toward psychology, including moral psychology, it should come as no surprise that he often explains virtue as a kind of *impetus*: just as a heavy body in motion has a tendency to keep a certain direction despite forces that try to push it off course, so too, the virtues (and vices) of human persons give a certain general direction to their choices.

Bibliography

Primary sources

(1964), *Subtilissimae quaestiones super octo Physicorum libros Aristotelis*; repr. of the Paris, 1509 edn., Frankfurt: Minerva.

(1966), *Sophisms on Meaning and Truth*, trans. T. K. Scott, New York: Appleton-Century-Crofts.

(1982), *John Buridan on Self-Reference: Chapter Eight of Buridan's Sophismata*, ed. and trans. G. E. Hughes, Cambridge: Cambridge University Press.

(1983), *Quaestiones in praedicamenta*, ed. J. Schneider, München: Verlag der Bayerische Akademie der Wissenschaft.

(1985), *John Buridan's Logic: The Treatise on Supposition; The Treatise on Consequences*, trans. P. King, Dordrecht, Boston, and Lancaster: D. Reidel.

(1989), "John Buridan's philosophy of mind: an edition and translation of book III of his *Questions on Aristotle's 'De anima'* (Third Redaction)," ed. and trans. J. A. Zupko, Ph.D. dissertation, Cornell University.

(2001), *Summulae de dialectica*. (Includes a new translation of Buridan's *Sophismata*, and his *Treatise on Supposition*, trans. G. Klima.) Yale Library of Medieval Philosophy, New Haven: Yale University Press.

Secondary sources

Adams, M. M. (1985), "Things versus 'hows', or Ockham on predication and ontology," in J. Bogen and J. E. McGuire, eds., *How Things Are* (pp. 175–88), Dordrecht: D. Reidel.

Ashworth, E. J. (1974), *Language and Logic in the Post-Medieval Period*, Dordrecht: D. Reidel.

Clagett, M. (1959), *The Science of Mechanics in the Middle Ages*, Madison: University of Wisconsin Press.

Grant, E. (1977), *Physical Science in the Middle Ages*, New York: Cambridge University Press.

Klima, G. (1991), "Latin as a formal language: outlines of a Buridanian semantics," *Cahiers de l'Institut du Moyen Âge Grec et Latin* 61, pp. 78–106.

Klima, G. (1999a), "Buridan's logic and the ontology of modes," in S. Ebbesen, ed., *Medieval Analyses in Language and Cognition* (pp. 473–95), Copenhagen: Royal Danish Academy of Sciences and Letters.

Klima, G. (1999b), "Ockham's semantics and ontology of the categories," in P. V. Spade, ed., *The Cambridge Companion to Ockham* (pp. 118–42), Cambridge: Cambridge University Press.

Klima, G. (forthcoming), "The *Summulae* of John Buridan: Introductory essay," in J. Buridan (forthcoming title).

Moody, E. A. (1971), "Ockham, Buridan and Nicholas of Autrecourt," in J. Ross, ed., *Inquiries into Medieval Philosophy* (pp. 275–315), Westport, CT: Greenwood Publishing.

Normore, C. (1985), "Buridan's ontology," in J. Bogen and J. E. McGuire, eds., *How Things Are* (pp. 189–203), Dordrecht: D. Reidel.

Walsh, J. J. (1964), "Is Buridan a sceptic about free will?," *Vivarium* 2, pp. 50–61.

——(1966), "Nominalism and the *Ethics*: some remarks about Buridan's commentary," *Journal of the History of Philosophy* 4, pp. 1–13.

Zupko, J. (2002), *John Buridan: Portrait of a 14th-century Arts Master*, South Bend, IN: Notre Dame University Press.

56

John Capreolus

KEVIN WHITE

John Capreolus, or Jean Cabrol (b. ca. 1380; d. 1444), was born in the Rouergue in southern France, where he joined the Dominican order. In 1407 he entered the University of Paris as bachelor of *Sentences*, graduating as master of theology in 1411. He taught at Dominican houses in Toulouse and Rodez, finishing his *Defensiones theologiae divi Thomae Aquinatis* in 1432, and dying in Rodez in 1444.

His "arguments in defense of Aquinas's theology," a series of 190 "questions" correlated to the distinctions of PETER LOMBARD's *Sentences*, show wide knowledge of THOMAS AQUINAS's works. An introductory remark indicates a division of questions into three formal parts: conclusions (of which the *Defensiones* presents 755), objections, and solutions:

> before I come to the conclusions, I preface one thing I wish to be held as supposed through the whole reading: that I intend to introduce nothing of my own, but only to recite opinions that seem to me to have been from the mind of St. Thomas; and not to adduce – except rarely – any proofs beyond his own words for the *conclusions*. But I do propose to adduce in their proper places *objections* of Auriol, Scotus, Durandus, John of Ripa, Guido of Carmelo, Varro, Adam, and others who attack St. Thomas; and to *solve* them by what St. Thomas said. (I, Prol.)

Thus Capreolus proposes to defend Aquinas against early fourteenth-century attackers, many of whose arguments he seems to have taken from PETER AURIOL.

The art of judicious quotation is central to Capreolus's elaborate method of "question." For example, "Are habitual virtues necessary to man?" (III, D.23). A brief negative and a brief affirmative argument are stated. Two conclusions – habits are necessary to man; human virtues are habits – are established, each with a quotation from Aquinas's *Summa theologiae* and one from his *Sentences* commentary. "Objections" of DURAND OF ST. POURÇAIN against the first conclusion, and of Auriol and "others" against the second, are quoted, then "solved" with quotations from Aquinas's *Sentences* commentary, *Summa theologiae*, disputed and quodlibetal questions, and commentary on *Physics*. The negative argument is answered with a quotation from *Summa theologiae*.

During the period 1483–1589 three editions, a compendium, and five epitomes of the *Defensiones* appeared. Renaissance Thomists called Capreolus their "prince" (*princeps Thomistarum*). Twentieth-century Capreolus scholarship focused largely on metaphysical themes and the question of Capreolus's fidelity to Aquinas. In 1992 an international conference held in Rodez discussed Capreolus's context, doctrine, and influence.

Bibliography

Primary sources

(1900–8), *Thomistarum principis Defensiones Theologiae Divi Thomae Aquinatis*, 7 vols., ed. C. Paban and T. Pègues, Tours: Cattier; repr. 1967, Frankfurt-on-Main: Minerva.

(2001), *On the Virtues*, R. Cessario and K. White, eds., Washington, DC: The Catholic University of America Press.

Secondary sources

Bedouelle, G., Cessario, R., and White, K., eds. (1997), *Jean Capreolus en son temps (1380–1444)*, *Mémoire dominicaine*, numéro spécial n. 1, Paris: Éditions du Cerf.

Grabmann, M. (1956), "Johannes Capreolus O.P., der princeps Thomistarum (†1444), und seine Stellung in der Geschichte der Thomistenschule," in *Mittelalterliches Geistesleben: Abhandlungen zur Geschichte der Scholastik und Mystik*, vol. 3 (pp. 370–410), Munich: Hueber.

57

John Dumbleton

EDITH DUDLEY SYLLA

John Dumbleton (b. ca. 1310; d. ca. 1349) was a fellow of Merton College, Oxford, in 1338 and 1347–8, and was in Paris in 1345–7 where he became a master of arts and a master of theology. He was the author of *Summa logicae et philosophiae naturalis* (*Summa* of logic and natural philosophy), a work planned in ten parts, but perhaps never completed; it provides the best available synthesis of the views of mid-fourteenth-century Oxford natural philosophers concerning the fields covered by the Aristotelian corpus, including physics, generation and corruption, cosmology, and psychology. The work is extant in over twenty typically large and well-produced manuscripts, the most complete of which end in the midst of Part IX, lacking the planned Part X, which would have covered universals or Platonic Ideas. Perhaps because the work was never printed, it was less influential on the continent than were other works of the Oxford Calculators, such as THOMAS BRADWARDINE'S *On the Ratios of Velocities in Motions*, WILLIAM HEYTESBURY'S *Rules for Solving Sophisms*, and RICHARD SWINESHEAD'S *Book of Calculations*, for which it provides illuminating background material.

Whereas the works of the other Oxford Calculators are frequently shaped by their connection with the disputations that formed a large part of the arts curriculum at Oxford in the mid-fourteenth century, Dumbleton's *Summa* is more directed to expounding the truths of natural philosophy, together with the relevant conceptual tools. Like the other Calculators, Dumbleton followed the ontological parsimony often associated with WILLIAM OF OCKHAM, denying the real existence of mathematical indivisibles such as points, lines, and planes, and asserting that substances and qualities are the only categories of things that can exist independently, even by the absolute power of God. Dumbleton followed JOHN DUNS SCOTUS in advocating the addition-of-part-to-part theory of the intension and remission of forms and backed this advocacy with a cogent defense of the Aristotelian conception of continuity. In helping to further the development of measures of motion with respect to cause and effect, Dumbleton took an Aristotelian approach to mathematical physics, assuming that mathematical quantities are abstracted by mathematicians from the substances or qualities in which they inhere.

Bibliography

Primary sources

Compendium sex conclusionum, MS Paris, B. N. Nouv. Acq. Lat. 625, fos. 70v–71v.
Summa logicae et philosophiae naturalis, MSS Cambridge, Peterhouse 272, fos. 1–111; Cambridge, Gonville and Caius 499/268, fos. 1–162; Vatican lat. 6750, fos. 1–202.

Secondary sources

Molland, A. G. (1974), "John Dumbleton and the status of geometrical optics," in *Actes du XIIIe Congrès International d'Histoire des Sciences 3/4*, Moscow: Editions "Naouka"; repr. in A. G. Molland (1995), *Mathematics and the Medieval Ancestry of Physics*, Aldershot, Hampshire and Brookfield, VT: Variorum.

Sylla, E. (1970–91), *The Oxford Calculators and the Mathematics of Motion, 1320–1350: Physics and Measurement by Latitudes* (pp. 130–44; 565–625, outline of Parts II–VI), New York and London: Garland/Harvard Dissertations in the History of Science.

——(1973), "Medieval concepts of the latitude of forms: the Oxford Calculators," *Archives d'Histoire Doctrinale et Littéraire du Moyen Âge* 40, pp. 251–71.

——(1991), "The Oxford Calculators and mathematical physics: John Dumbleton's *Summa logicae et philosophiae naturalis*, parts II and III," in S. Unguru, ed., *Physics, Cosmology and Astronomy, 1300–1700: Tension and Accommodation* (pp. 129–61), Boston Studies in the Philosophy of Science 126, Dordrecht, Boston, and London: Kluwer.

Weisheipl, J. A. (1959), "The place of John Dumbleton in the Merton school," *Isis* 50, pp. 439–54.

——(1968), "Ockham and some Mertonians," *Mediaeval Studies* 30, pp. 199–207.

58

John Duns Scotus

STEPHEN D. DUMONT

The Franciscan theologian and philosopher John Duns Scotus (b. ca. 1266; d. 1308) ranks with THOMAS AQUINAS and WILLIAM OF OCKHAM as one of the most important and influential thinkers of the scholastic period. A notoriously difficult and highly original thinker, Scotus's nuanced and technical reasoning earned him the epithet "Subtle Doctor" from his own contemporaries. Among his more distinctive views were the univocity of the concept of being, the elimination of divine illumination, and a very strong voluntarism, according to which the will is the only truly rational power and the origin of so-called synchronic contingency. Scotus developed many of his positions in explicit, critical reaction to the neo-Augustinian synthesis of HENRY OF GHENT, the most important theologian of the preceding generation and noted critic of Aquinas. As such, Scotus is a pivotal figure in scholasticism, representing the shift between the thirteenth-century project of assimilating Greek and Arabic sources, as exemplified by ALBERTUS MAGNUS, BONAVENTURE, and Aquinas, and the fourteenth-century focus on contemporary opinion evident in Ockham.

Relatively little is known of Scotus's life and career. Of Scottish origin, he began his lengthy theological training at Oxford about 1288, but was transferred by the order in 1302 to the more prestigious University of Paris to complete his degree. His studies at Paris were shortly interrupted when he, together with much of the Franciscan convent, was ordered out of France by Philip the Fair for siding with Pope Boniface VIII in their dispute over taxation of church property. It is generally assumed that Scotus returned to Oxford during the year of exile from France. Back in Paris by April, 1304, Scotus continued his studies and was promoted to Master of Theology in 1305. He was regent theologian in the Franciscan chair at Paris until 1307, when he was again transferred, this time to the Franciscan house of studies in Cologne, where he died at the age of 42. This means that the bulk of Scotus's substantial writings were produced over a period of only about ten years.

Scotus's corpus can be divided into two parts: his mostly earlier commentaries on Aristotle and his certainly later works in theology. Scotus wrote question-style commentaries on the Aristotelian logic (*Categories, Porphyry, On Interpretation*, and *Sophistical Refutations*), the *De anima*, and the first nine books of the *Metaphysics*. Whereas these philosophical works are generally taken to be early, perhaps written when he was a Master of Arts, the dating of the *Metaphysics* has long been a matter of controversy. The current view is that it was revised over a period of time and some sections are late. Scotus's reputation, however, rests mainly on his theological writings, and of these the most important are his commentaries on the *Sentences* of PETER LOMBARD, a required text for the scholastic degree in theology. From Oxford Scotus has two commentaries on the *Sentences*, an earlier one termed the *Lectura* (i.e., his preliminary lectures on Lombard), which he then greatly expanded into his *magnum opus*, the *Ordinatio* (i.e., revised lectures). His corresponding commentary from Paris survives in the reports of students or secretaries, and is hence called the *Reportatio parisiensis*, although one copy alleges to having been examined by Scotus himself. The chronological relationship between these latter two commentaries remains an important point of dispute, since at places the *Ordinatio* and *Reportatio parisiensis* differ significantly. The standard view has been that the *Ordinatio*, as Scotus's crowning achievement, incorporated both the *Lectura* and *Reportatio parisiensis*, and thus was the latest and most mature of the three. Increasingly, however, scholars are of the view that Scotus wrote a substantial portion of the *Ordinatio* before leaving Oxford for Paris in 1302, which would make the *Reportatio* his latest commentary, at least in part. In addition to his *Sentences*, Scotus has two sets of university disputations termed *Collationes*, one each from Oxford and Paris, and a magisterial *Quodlibet* (i.e., a public disputation open to any topic) held during his regency at Paris. Finally, there are two treatises: the *Treatise on the First Principle*, which may not have been completed by Scotus, given that half of it is taken from the *Ordinatio*, and the *Theoremata*, whose authenticity has been disputed.

It should be noted that the works of Scotus have suffered more than those of any other scholastic thinker from confused transmission and damaging misattributions. In part this seems to have resulted from his early death, which left some of his works, particularly his *Ordinatio*, incomplete and in the course of revision. Already in the fourteenth century his texts were conflated to supply missing material. It has taken nearly a century of research to establish Scotus's authentic canon and tease apart the various redactions of his theological works. Even at that, definitive interpretation on points remains difficult, since a large portion of his corpus still exists only in the unreliable sixteenth-century edition of Luke Wadding.

Metaphysics

Although other areas of his thought, such as physics and especially ethics, have received increasing attention, Scotus is generally regarded as having made most of his contributions in metaphysics. Among these must be counted the doctrine of the univocity of being, his proofs for the existence of God, the formal distinction, and his theory of individuation. While strictly speaking his concept of will could be considered under metaphysics, it will here be treated under ethics.

Univocity of the transcendentals

The thirteenth century accepted as metaphysical bedrock Aristotle's claim that 'being' was not a univocal predicate but equivocal by reference (*pros hen*; *ad unum*) or, in their terminology, analogous. The scholastics generally understood analogy as a middle ground between strict univocity, where 'being' would have the same meaning (*ratio*) in all its instances, and pure equivocity, in which its meanings would be totally disparate and unconnected. As analogous, 'being' would have different but related meanings, applying primarily and properly to God and secondarily or by extension to creatures. Analogy was thus seen to strike the balance needed to ensure, on the one hand, that God transcends creatures, which univocity would disallow, and, on the other, that he is naturally knowable, which pure equivocity would make impossible.

In a move recognized even by his contemporaries as radical, Scotus broke with this canonical view and held, to the contrary, that there has to be some notion of being and the other transcendentals univocal to God and creatures, as well as to the ten categories. Scotus formulated his position in reaction to the version of analogy developed by Henry of Ghent, who brought out more explicitly the difficulties facing the doctrine in accounting for natural knowledge of God. Following Aquinas's claim in his discussion of analogy that being did not have a single *ratio* or formal notion, Henry repeatedly stressed that being ultimately resolved into two separate and irreducible notions (*rationes*): that of infinite being proper to God and the universal concept of being common to the ten categories, which is finite and proper to creatures. That is, according to Henry, there could be no third notion or *ratio* of being apart from these two proper concepts, for such would be univocally common to God and creature and eliminate divine transcendence.

Scotus argued to the contrary that a univocal concept of being is required to sustain the traditional claim of natural knowledge of God. In particular, he maintained that Henry could not consistently assert that being resolves only into two proper notions, having no conceptual element in common, and at the same time uphold the possibility of deducing any knowledge of God from creatures. Scotus's most famous argument is that from "certain and doubtful concepts," as his contemporaries labeled it. It took direct aim at Henry's repeated assertion that there could be no concept of being separate from the two analogous and proper notions applicable exclusively to God and creature. An intellect certain about one concept, but doubtful about others, has a concept about which it is certain, different from the concepts about which it is doubtful. But we can be certain that God is a being, while doubting whether God is infinite or finite being. Therefore, the concept of being is different from, and hence univocal to, the concepts of infinite and finite being. Scotus takes the first premiss to be evident, for a given intellect cannot be both certain and doubtful of the same thing. The second premiss is true *de facto*, because past thinkers, such as the pre-Socratics, disagreed as to whether the first principle was finite or infinite, or even material or immaterial. Yet, in attempting to establish one of these alternatives, no philosopher ever doubted that the first principle is a being. Being must therefore have a separate, distinct concept from those that apply properly to God and creature.

The point of Scotus's argument is that since it is a matter of doubt whether God is an infinite or finite being, this must be determined by demonstration. Yet such a demonstration must begin from something certain about God, for otherwise it would proceed from premisses doubtful in all respects. Thus, unless the concept of being is admitted as certain, apart from the doubtful concepts of infinite and finite which are themselves the object of demonstration, no reasoning about God will be possible.

Scotus applied a similar analysis to the traditionally accepted methods of reasoning from creatures to God, including Anselm's doctrine of "pure perfections" and the Pseudo-Dionysian ascent through removal and eminence, arguing that all required a common, univocal notion of being or some other attributable perfection. Indeed, Scotus claimed that in practice all the theologians took a univocal concept of being for granted, although they explicitly denied it.

It is important to appreciate that Scotus was not rejecting altogether the doctrine of analogy. He of course admitted that the concepts of infinite and finite, or created and uncreated, being proper to God and creature are analogous, and that the later are related respectively as primary and secondary. Rather, his fundamental point was that the concept of being could not be merely analogous. Unless some underlying concept of being were common to the analogous, proper ones, then they would in fact turn out not to be analogous at all but purely equivocal. Natural knowledge of God would thus be impossible. What Scotus did reject was reliance on the analogous relationship itself as sufficient to account for any proper concept of God on the grounds that knowledge of a relation is posterior to any knowledge of the terms related. Analogy of itself therefore cannot explain, but rather already presupposes, a knowledge of being as proper to God and creatures.

Proofs for the existence of God

Scotus's proof for the existence of God is the longest and most complex of the later medieval period. Revised over the course of his career, it exists in four versions and in its fullest form runs to hundreds of pages and dozens of conclusions. The proof is so long and complex because Scotus requires that a demonstration for the existence of God reach not just a first cause but an actually infinite being, as this represents the highest concept of God attainable by natural reason. Accordingly, Scotus's proof has two main steps. The first argues that there is a first efficient cause, a first final cause, and a most perfect or eminent being – the so-called triple primacy – and that they coincide in a single nature. The second step is to show that this primary being is actually infinite.

The most important and extensive argument in the first step is that for a first efficient cause. In a significant move, Scotus stipulates that he is concerned only with efficient causality in the metaphysical sense of a cause of being, and explicitly leaves aside Aristotle's proof of a prime mover in *Physics* VIII on the grounds that such need not reach anything other than subordinate entities, such as celestial intelligences or souls. While Scotus's formal argument itself is brief and standard – from an empirically given effect it is necessary to conclude to a first efficient cause upon pain of infinite regress in causes – it is considerably expanded in response to two fundamental objections.

The first is that the argument begs the question in assuming that an infinite regress of causes is impossible. In response, Scotus does not immediately give arguments against an infinite regress, but first defines the precise causal relations concerned in such arguments. At issue, says Scotus, is not simply a series of essential as opposed to accidental causes, for these can be infinite. The father is an essential cause of the son, and the grandfather of the father, but these could extend to infinity, as both Aristotle and AVICENNA held. Rather, the relevant series is the hierarchy of essentially ordered causes that must be simultaneously present to result in a given effect, for no one admits that these can be infinite. Such essentially ordered causes have three features. The first is that the posterior cause depends upon the prior for the very exercise of its causal power. From this it follows, secondly, that the prior cause must be of a nature and order different than the posterior, for no cause depends upon another of the same nature for its efficacy. Finally, all essentially ordered causes must be simultaneously present to produce an effect, for otherwise some causal nature necessary for the effect would be missing. (Thus the series of individual agents, such as past generations of parents, are not essentially ordered causes with respect to a given offspring, for they are not simultaneously required for its production.)

Having so stipulated the causal relations at issue, Scotus gives several brief arguments against infinite regress based on Aristotle's *Metaphysics* II and Avicenna's *Metaphysics* VIII. An interesting exception is the final argument, which aims to establish only that a first efficient cause is possible. Scotus argues that since efficient causality does not in itself imply imperfection, it is possible for it to exist without imperfection. But if there is an infinite regress in efficient causes, then all would be dependent on some prior cause, and efficiency could never be found without imperfection, contrary to assumption. Therefore, a first efficient cause in the sense defined must be possible. Scotus will exploit this seemingly weaker result to construct a strict, necessary proof in response to the second objection.

The second objection is that the argument lacks the requisite necessity of strict demonstration because it begins from the contingent premiss that some effect exists. Scotus responds that the argument can be recast with modal premisses to meet the requirement of necessity. In this way, the argument would begin from the possibility of an effect and conclude to the possibility of a cause. The actual existence of a first efficient cause can then be deduced from its possibility. As established in the last argument against an infinite regress, a first efficient cause is at least possible. But if such a first cause is possible, it must actually exist. The reason is that if it does not exist, it could only be possible if some other cause could bring it into existence. But a first efficient cause can depend on no prior cause, either for its existence or its ability to cause. Accordingly, if such a first cause does not actually exist, it would be impossible for it to exist, contrary to what has been demonstrated. Therefore, a first efficient cause exists. Alternatively, Scotus says, the same conclusion can be reached by the other traditional arguments recorded against an infinite regress, but they would begin from contingent albeit evident premisses.

The critical second step of the proof is to show that the primary nature demonstrated in the first part is actually infinite by means of each of its properties as a first efficient cause, an ultimate end, and a most perfect being. Once again, the arguments from efficiency are the most developed. Scotus critically considers two such standard proofs, one based on the first efficient cause as the origin of motion (i.e., as prime mover), and the other as the origin of being (i.e., as creator). The former argument, derived from Aristotle's *Physics* VIII, is that the first mover is infinite in power because it eternally moves the world. Even apart from its false assumption that the world is eternal, Scotus says that the argument does not hold as its stands. It does not follow that a cause is infinite in power simply because it produces a finite effect or succession of such effects – in this case the rotations of the heavens – over an infinite duration. Scotus, however, thinks that the Aristotelian argument can be salvaged if it is revised to show that the prime mover must simultaneously possess the totality of power required to produce all of its effects realizable over an infinite time. This follows from its nature as a first cause, for if it does not already possess the power to produce some effect, it cannot derive it from anything else. Thus, since the first mover must possess at once the power to produce all of its effects, which are infinite in number, it is infinite in power. In the second standard argument, the first efficient cause is seen to be infinite in power because the "distance" between non-being and being traversed in the act of creation *ex nihilo* is infinite. Scotus rejects this reasoning outright, arguing that contradictories have no intermediate and consequently no intervening "distance."

Given the weaknesses of the standard arguments for the infinity of the first cause considered as mover and creator, Scotus constructs his own from exemplar causality, that is, from the first efficient cause considered as an intelligent agent. This requires the lengthy proof of three preliminary results: that the first cause has an intellect and will, that its intellectual and voluntary acts are identical to its essence, and that it knows all that can be known both distinctly and in act. From this Scotus argues that since the divine intellect knows distinctly and in act all that can be known, it knows these things all at once, for an intellect knows successively only if it moves from confused to distinct or from potential to actual knowledge. But the things that can be known are infinite. Therefore, since the intellect of the first efficient cause knows an infinity of things actually and at once, it is actually infinite.

Formal distinction

The generally realist orientation of thirteenth-century philosophy typically saw the need for some class of intermediate distinction that was not merely "rational," or the work of reason alone, but less than fully real, to provide an objective basis for our discrete concepts of one and the same thing. For instance, Aquinas held that our different concepts arose not merely from the mind but had "a foundation in the thing" (*fundamentum in re*), whereas Henry of Ghent admitted an "intentional" distinction (*distinctio intentionalis*), according to which our concepts or "intentions" actually distinct in the mind exist as potentially distinct in the thing. In line with such realism, Scotus recognized a "formal distinction" between what he variously called realities (*realitates*), entities (*entitates*), or formalities (*formalitates*) within one and the same thing (*res*) corresponding to our different concepts of it. Scotus's formal distinction, or more accurately formal non-identity, is not real in the full sense, since formally distinct entities cannot exist apart but only as really identical within the same individual. It is, however, more real than the corresponding distinctions of Aquinas and Henry, because it is found in a thing (*ex parte rei*) prior to the action of any intellect whatever, human or divine. Broadly speaking, then, Scotus defines a formal distinction as that holding between really identical (i.e., inseparable) entities in the same thing whose definitions (i.e., concepts) are such that one is not included in the other, or, if their simplicity precludes strict definition, then what stands for the definition of one is different from that of the other.

Scotus gives the formal distinction wide application in both theology and philosophy. In theology, Scotus argues that the personal properties of the Trinity are each formally distinct from the divine essence and that the divine attributes (e.g., goodness, wisdom, etc.) are formally distinct from each other. In philosophy, Scotus holds that genera and their specific differences, species and their individual differences, the soul and its powers, being and its transcendental attributes, and certain kinds of relations and their foundations, are in each case formally distinct. Scotus defends the controversial application of the formal distinction to God by arguing that it does not of itself entail real composition. The formally distinct divine attributes, for instance, are really identical not because they exist as parts united in a composite but because they are all infinite. In creatures, on the other hand, formally distinct entities, such as genera and differences, are really identical because they only exist in some third thing (i.e., a species or individual) united as act (difference) and potency (genus).

The above depiction of Scotus's formal distinction is that found in his Oxford works. In his Parisian commentary on the *Sentences*, however, he recasts the distinction in connection with its application to the persons of the Trinity. There Scotus defines the formal distinction as a type of "qualified" or diminished distinction (*distinctio secundum quid*) that is compatible with an "unqualified" or absolute identity, a terminology absent from his parallel Oxford discussion. This revision has been interpreted to mean that Scotus no longer saw the formal distinction as requiring extra-mental entities or formalities. Even if this interpretation is accurate, it is unclear whether Scotus abandoned his commitment to real formalities in all applications of the formal distinction, or just in the special case of the divine persons.

Universals and individuals

Scotus's most famous philosophical application of the formal distinction was to the problem of universals, where he argued that a specific nature had its own entity and unity apart from the factor that rendered it individual. Scotus's realism on this score was extensively criticized by William of Ockham, whose nominalist program strongly denied any formal distinction within an individual that would impute some extra-mental reality to a universal. Although Scotus and Ockham are typically seen as the chief opponents in the realism-nominalism debate of the fourteenth century, Scotus's stance on universals was far from the most extreme of the period. Even Ockham himself ranked Scotus's position as last in its degree of realism, and for this reason appears to have paid it serious attention.

Scotus takes up the problem of universals as part of an extensive discussion of the principle of individuation. This had become a highly developed and controversial topic after the condemnations of 1277, which tended to undermine the standard Aristotelian view that matter individuated by asserting that God could multiply instances of a form without matter and create individuals within a species of immaterial form (i.e., angels). Scotus's own treatment of individuation betrays this background as he raises it not in the older context of the status of universals but under the topic of angels or separate substances. His procedure is to reject at length five standard opinions on the cause of individuation, which he strategically orchestrates to culminate in his own view.

The first and for Scotus most problematic opinion holds that a specific nature, such as horseness or humanity, is of itself singular, so that no distinct principle of individuation is required. This view is based on the Aristotelian commonplace that a nature (or form) exists in an absolute sense as singular outside the mind but only in a qualified way as universal in the mind. Since what belongs to a thing absolutely does so of itself, a nature is of itself singular. On this view, then, no additional cause of singularity is to be sought over and above those factors that produce the nature into actual existence, as if the nature were first realized as universal and then some intervening cause rendered it individual. Rather, some further cause – the intellect – is needed to account for its universality.

The principal burden of Scotus's entire discussion of individuation is to establish against this view that a specific nature taken in itself is not singular but common. For this he has two main arguments, both of which reveal his realism. The first maintains that making a nature individual of itself is inconsistent with its role as the proper object of the intellect, according to which it is known as universal. The reason is that the proper object of a power must really precede the act of that power as its cause. But on the above view, the nature of itself is singular prior to any act of the intellect. Therefore, for the intellect to understand the nature as universal would be to grasp it under an aspect opposed to that which it has as object. In brief, if the nature taken absolutely and in itself is singular, knowledge of it as universal or common is impossible.

Secondly, Scotus maintains that a nature of itself must have a unity that is real but less than the numerical unity of the particular. Scotus argues that this so-called "minor unity" of a specific nature is required to support numerous relations that are generally taken to be real in the sense that they are not mind-dependent but nonetheless cannot be based on numerical unity, since, according to Aristotle, there is no essential ordering of individuals in a species. Thus, for instance, contrariety is real because it is a principle of physical change. Yet things are not contrary insofar as they are numerically one, for then there would be as many basic sets of contraries as individuals. Similarly, if the only real unity were numerical, then all diversity would strictly speaking be between individuals. This is clearly false, because then all things would be equally diverse, so that Socrates would differ no less from Plato than from this rock. Since these considerations show that the specific nature must have a real unity less than numerical, it cannot be of itself individual.

Given the above arguments that a nature of itself cannot be singular, Scotus concludes that it must be of itself common. By this, however, Scotus does not mean that the nature of itself is the universal as found in the mind. Rather, Scotus says, the community of the nature taken in itself is to be understood as expressed by Avicenna in his famous dictum that "horseness is nothing else but horseness alone; of itself, it is neither one nor many, neither universal nor singular." That is, universality and particularity lie outside the definition in which are expressed only the essential constituents of a nature. Scotus sees this neutrality of the nature in itself to be required for essential predication where an identity is asserted between subject and predicate. If horseness included universality as an essential constituent, then it could never be predicated of an individual horse, for nothing individual is a universal in the sense of being predicable of many. If it included singularity, then horseness could only be asserted of one instance. Thus, Scotus maintains that, although the specific nature is never realized except intentionally in the mind as a universal or really outside the mind as a singular, taken absolutely and in itself it includes neither mode of being. It is this common nature so considered as absolute of, and prior to, either universality or singularity that is the object of the intellect, the metaphysical notion of essence, and the significate of terms in essential predication.

Since the nature in itself is neither singular nor universal, a cause of its singularity outside the mind must be located, just as the intellect is the cause of its universality in the mind. There are four main candidates: negation (Henry of Ghent), existence (a common view), quantity (GILES OF ROME), and matter (standard interpretation of Aristotle). Henry had maintained that since to be individual meant "not divisible into further instances" and "not identical with others," individuation results from a twofold negation. Scotus rejects this on the grounds that negation can never be an ultimate cause or explanation, since it always presupposes something positive. Henry thus begs the question, for what is sought is precisely that principle whereby something is made individual in the sense of being indivisible and non-identical with others.

The second view, that existence individuates, is based on the axiom that act distinguishes. Since individuation is the ultimate distinction and existence the ultimate act, actual existence must be the principle of individuation. In an interesting move, Scotus concedes that existence is the ultimate actuality, but denies that it is relevant to individuation. Extending the Avicennian distinction between essence and existence, Scotus argues that since actual existence is an accident in the broad sense of lying outside the entire framework of the categories – the Porphyrian tree in traditional terms – it is posterior to the descent of the category of substance into individual instances. In other words, it is not the specific nature that is directly in potency to actual existence but rather an individual of that species. What is sought then is the principle that causes a substance to be individual, not the principle that causes an individual substance to exist.

In a similar line of reasoning, Scotus rejects the categorical accident of quantity as the principle of individuation. Here Scotus argues from the Aristotelian doctrines that accidents are really posterior to substance and that the primary sense of substance is the individual. It follows a fortiori that quantity is posterior to the individual substance and hence cannot be the principle of individuation. In his *Metaphysics* Scotus extends this argument more generally to the traditional Boethian view that individuation results from the conglomeration of all accidents. Finally, Scotus denies that matter can individuate, since what is itself indeterminate and indistinct cannot be a principle of distinction.

The general force of these arguments is that individuation must result from a principle intrinsic to the individual substance itself. It thus cannot be an accident of any kind, whether one of the other categories or actual existence, for these are posterior to the individual substance. Nor can it be the intrinsic principles of matter, form, or even the resulting composite, insofar as they are taken as natures, for so taken they are common and hence prior to individuation. Scotus concludes that the principle of individuation must be a further difference in the substantial order added to the specific nature. This further difference, which Scotus calls an "individual difference," is related to the specific nature in a manner analogous to the way in which the ultimate specific difference is related to its genus. Thus, just as the ultimate specific difference renders the species of which it is a part incapable of division into further species, so the individual difference renders the singular absolutely indivisible. Further, the specific difference is formally distinct from, and actual with respect to, the genus, because this is the least real distinction that can provide an objective basis for such concepts. So too, the individual difference is actual with respect to the specific nature and formally distinct from it. The individual difference, of course, is not another specific difference, for it adds no further quidditative reality (i.e., "whatness" or essence) but rather is the ultimate reality of a quiddity. Tradition has designated this individual difference the haecceity or 'thisness', a term used sparingly by Scotus himself.

To summarize, Scotus holds that a specific nature taken absolutely and in itself is neither universal nor particular but has its own minor unity and reality prior to either condition. Thus both the universality and singularity of a nature require explanation, not just its universality alone. On the one side, this means that Scotus sharply distinguishes the community that a nature has in itself from the universality that results from the action of the intellect. The universality conferred by the mind is a greater unity than a nature has in itself, for it renders the self-same nature predicable of several instances. Only in this qualified sense is Scotus willing to admit the Aristotelian maxim that "the intellect makes the universal." On the other side, it means that the Porphyrian descent of substance by way of real division does not stop with a specific nature but extends down into the constitution of the singular substance itself with the addition of a further, individuating difference. In this, Scotus broke with the Greek tradition that made the specific nature the focus of being and intelligibility and the individual itself only an incidental object of intellectual knowledge. Perhaps the most significant result of Scotus's doctrine of individuation is that it makes the individual *qua* individual essentially intelligible, at least in principle, although Scotus denied such knowledge is possible for our intellect in the present state.

Epistemology

Like most of his contemporaries, Scotus conformed to the general scholastic interpretation of Aristotle according to which all knowledge originates from the senses, and the agent intellect, abstracting from the sense image, produces an intelligible species in the possible intellect that represents the object known. (The need for a separate intelligible species, however, was denied by many, including Henry of Ghent, at least later in his career, and GODFREY OF FONTAINES.) Despite these general agreements with his contemporaries, Scotus's epistemology was marked by several influential innovations, including a decisive rejection of the theory of divine illumination and the introduction of an intellectual intuition.

Rejection of illumination

Although recent research has shown that the scholastic commitment to the theory of divine illumination, which accorded some essential role to the divine ideas in human cognition, had progressively weakened by the time of Scotus, his critique all but eliminated the doctrine. As in many other areas, Scotus's precise target was Henry of Ghent, who had mounted an elaborate defense of illumination in the wake of Aquinas's reduction of it to a general influence present in the Aristotelian agent intellect. As Scotus reports in detail, Henry argued against Aquinas that the Aristotelian apparatus of abstraction is insufficient to achieve infallible knowledge of truth and needs to be supplemented by a special illumination. Appealing to the accepted Aristotelian distinction between simple apprehension (i.e., conceptualization) and composition and division (i.e., judgment), Henry says that by the former we know "that which is true" (*verum*). That is, in simple apprehension we conceive a real thing outside the mind. For this no special illumination is needed, as there is no error in simple apprehension, and abstraction suffices. But to know a thing that is "true" or real is not to know its "truth" (*veritas*), for truth is conformity to an exemplar or model, and this can only be seen in a judgment involving a comparison of one thing to another. As even Plato realized, Henry claims, a thing has two exemplars against which it can be compared or measured: a created exemplar, which is its form existing in the soul as the result of abstraction, and an uncreated exemplar, which is its form existing eternally and immutably in the divine mind. But no comparison of a thing to a created exemplar acquired through abstraction by the human mind will yield infallible knowledge of truth. First, the created exemplar cannot be immutable, since the object from which it is abstracted is itself constantly changing. Second, the intellect itself in which the created exemplar exists is mutable. Given the mutability of both the knowing subject and object, Henry concludes that no matter how much we universalize a sensible form by abstraction, it can never be a basis for infallible knowledge of truth. Since the dignity of a human being demands such knowledge, some access to the uncreated exemplar in the divine mind is therefore required. (Henry, like all illuminationists, goes to lengths to explain how this does not involve a direct intuition of God in the present life.) In rough terms, Henry was attempting to integrate Augustinian illumination with Aristotelian abstraction by having the former operate at the level of judgment and the latter at the level of conceptualization.

As with Henry's other efforts at accommodation, Scotus saw this attempt as fraught with inconsistency. According to Scotus, far from ensuring certitude, Henry's theory of illumination actually led to a deep and irremediable skepticism. Thus, even granting Henry that the thing itself from which the created exemplar is abstracted is constantly changing – a position Scotus regards as false and tantamount to the error of Heraclitus – no amount of illumination can give us certitude about it. On Henry's reasoning the apparent function of illumination is to allow us to see the wholly mutable thing itself as immutable. In that case, illumination results in no knowledge at all, for then the thing would be apprehended contrary to the way it really is. Similarly, if the human mind itself is so mutable that it makes the created exemplar subject to change, then for the same reason no illumination can prevent the mind from erring. Since illumination itself must somehow exist in the mind, it would be no less subject to change. Furthermore, according to Henry, illumination is supposed to occur by means of cooperation between the changeable, created exemplar and the unchanging, uncreated exemplar. But if there are two causes cooperating in the production of knowledge, certitude can never be greater than the weaker of the two causes. For example, when one premiss is necessary and the other contingent, only a contingent conclusion can follow.

For Scotus, then, unless the human cognitive apparatus and the object are of their nature so constituted as to be capable of producing certitude, no intervention of illumination could render them such. Scotus was in fact following a caution issued as early as BONAVENTURE – that if illumination is given too large a role and made the total cause of certitude, then skepticism results – but pushed it to exclude any role whatever for illumination in natural certitude.

Having eliminated illumination as a factor in certitude, Scotus gives a positive account of how fully certain knowledge is possible without it. According to Scotus, we can have infallible knowledge of (1) first principles and all things deduced from them, (2) induction from experience, and (3) our own acts. Given these, Scotus goes on to argue for (4) the reliability of sense knowledge. As for (1), Scotus argues that self-evident propositions are those in which the subject and predicate terms are so identical that it is evident that the one necessarily includes the other. Therefore, when the intellect grasps these terms and unites them in a proposition, it has infallible certitude that the proposition is true, i.e., that the identity (or non-identity) of the subject and predicate asserted in the proposition "conforms," as Scotus puts it, to the meaning of the subject and predicate terms. Against Henry, then, Scotus maintains that the "conformity" at issue in truth given through judgment is that of a proposition to the meaning of its terms, not that of a created to the uncreated exemplar. From this is guaranteed the certitude of conclusions deduced from such propositions, for the certitude of a conclusion depends only upon the certitude of the principles and evidence of the valid argument form. Scotus himself raises the standard objection that the certitude of self-evident propositions cannot be assured because the meanings of the terms themselves ultimately originate from the senses, which can be deceived. He replies that the senses are not the cause but merely the occasion of the truth of these kinds of propositions, for such are not known to be true from sensing that the terms are united in reality, but solely from the meaning of the terms themselves. Thus, even if the senses were deceived as to whether this particular thing was black or white, once the concepts of black and white are known, the intellect knows with certitude that black is not white.

(2) But of course not all universal propositions are known to be true as either self-evident from their terms or as necessarily deduced from them. Some are known from experience, which reveals regular connections between things, such as that a type of herb cures a certain disease or that a certain positioning of the planets results in an eclipse. Thus Scotus maintains secondly that we can have infallible knowledge of what is regularly observed by the senses. Even though we do not observe all cases of some occurrence, and even though we do not observe that it obtains in every single case, but only in most, we can have infallible knowledge that it obtains universally from the following principle: "Whatever occurs frequently from a non-free cause (i.e., not from a will) is the natural effect of that cause." This principle itself is not known by extrapolation from sense experience, but is self-evident from its terms, for by definition a cause that is non-free cannot frequently produce an effect contrary to what it is apt to produce. In this way, Scotus sought to underwrite the standard understanding of Aristotle's conception of scientific demonstration, according to which experience (*empeiria*; *experientia*) reveals the fact of a connection and analysis reveals its cause.

(3) Scotus argues that there is infallible certitude of our own acts, such as understanding, sensing, etc., maintaining that we are as certain as these as we are of self-evident, necessary propositions. That such acts are contingent is not an impediment to certitude about them, for Scotus argues that even among contingent propositions there must be some that are immediately evident, otherwise there would either be an infinite regress in the ordering

363

of such propositions or a contingent proposition would follow from a necessary one, both of which are impossible.

(4) Finally, Scotus argues that the senses are reliable, so that external objects are as we perceive them to be. He does so by applying the above principle that whatever occurs frequently from a non-free cause is the natural effect of that cause. Thus, where the senses agree in their perceptions of an object and where such repeated perceptions yield the same results, we can conclude from this principle that the perception has the object as its natural cause and hence the object is as it appears. If the senses disagree, as when sight indicates that the stick in the water is broken, Scotus says that this error can be detected by other senses in cooperation with some proposition which is true from its terms (or one deduced from them). In this case, the sense of touch together with the self-evident proposition, "A hard object is not broken by contact with a softer object," yields certain knowledge that the stick is not broken. In sum, Scotus replaces the corrective function of illumination with self-evident propositions whose certitude is immune from the variability of sense knowledge.

Intuitive cognition

Despite the importance of his rejection of illumination, Scotus's most significant epistemological innovation was the distinction between intuitive and abstractive cognition. As defined by Scotus, intuitive cognition is knowledge of an object insofar as it is actually existing and present to the intellect. Abstractive cognition is knowledge of the object insofar as it abstracts from actual existence or nonexistence. It is important to stress, first of all, that both intuitive and abstractive cognition are acts of the intellect proper. They do not differ in that the senses grasp the particular by intuition and the intellect the universal by abstraction; "abstractive" does not here refer to Aristotelian abstraction of the universal. Rather, both types of cognition have as their object the essence or quiddity as opposed to the sensed particular. The difference is that in intuition, it is evident to the intellect that the object itself as existing and present is the cause of knowledge, whereas in abstractive cognition the intelligible species goes surrogate for the existing object. Second, Scotus is specific that "intuitive" is not here equated with "non-discursive." Some abstractive knowledge can be "intuitive" in this sense, since it can be non-discursive.

Scotus argues that the intellect must be capable of intuitive cognition on the grounds that a perfection found in a lower power must be found in a higher power of the same type. But the particular senses have intuitive, sensible cognition of the particular as present and existing, while the imagination knows the same object abstractively by means of the sensible species, which can remain in the absence of the sensible thing itself. The same twofold cognitive capacity must, by parity, be found in the intellect. (Despite this argument, it has long been a matter of dispute to what extent Scotus admitted intuitive cognition in the present life.)

For Scotus, then, the intellect has a direct apprehension of an intelligible object insofar as it is the actually existing and present cause of its cognitive act. The chief philosophical use to which Scotus puts intuitive cognition is to supply certitude for contingent propositions. For example, as just indicated, Scotus claims that by means of intuitive cognition we are as certain about our own acts as we are about necessary, self-evident propositions. After Scotus, the entire fourteenth-century preoccupation with certitude was regularly cast in terms of intuitive cognition, most famously in the question of whether God could cause an intuitive cognition of a nonexistent object.

Ethical theory

The defining feature of Scotus's ethical theory is the central role given to the will. Indeed, it is fair to say that the medieval conception of the will culminated with Scotus and that he drew out more explicitly than anyone had before its fundamental inconsistencies with the Aristotelian account of morality and action. This is perhaps nowhere more evident than in Scotus's separation of morality from eudaimonism, but clear as well in his denials of the connection of prudence and moral virtue and of the necessity of the natural law, at least as it comprised precepts governing relationships between created beings.

Intellect and will

Beginning with Aquinas, the medieval discussion of the will focused on its causal relation to the intellect and in particular on whether it was a self-moving power, a concept wholly inimical to Aristotle. Aquinas allowed the will to be a self-mover in the qualified sense that once it had been put in act by the intellect as regards an end, it could move itself to will the means to that end. Aquinas's balanced but mixed solution gave rise to a polarized debate that persisted to Scotus. On the one side, Henry of Ghent rejected Aquinas's account as deterministic, arguing that if the intellect were permitted to "move" the will in any sense of causing its act, then all freedom would be destroyed. Rather, Henry said that the appetible object in the intellect is merely a necessary condition for the will to move itself to act. At the other extreme was Godfrey of Fontaines, who upheld a strict and universal application of Aristotle's prohibition against self-motion, denying any to the will.

In his question on the problem Scotus surveyed these opposed positions of the previous quarter-century. As analyzed by Scotus, the debate was over the efficient cause of volition. He interpreted Henry as holding that the will is the total efficient cause of its act and Godfrey that the object is the total cause. Scotus argued that neither extreme position could be correct, for if the object is the total efficient cause of the act of willing, then volition would not be within the power of the will. Our actions would accordingly not be voluntary. On the other side, if the will is the total cause, then the will would be in a continuous state of volition, for on this view the will alone would be sufficient to cause its act. In response to the debate, Scotus claims to take a middle way between the two extreme views, which either accord no causality to the will or none to the object, by appealing to his doctrine of partial causes. According to Scotus, both the will and the object concur as partial co-causes of volition, so that together they cooperate as a total efficient cause of willing. Scotus says that there are three ways in which several causes can cooperate to form the total cause of a single effect. First, several causes of the same nature (*ratio*) can concur to produce an effect that they would not if taken in isolation, such as several men pulling a ship. This is not relevant to the intellect and will, since there is not an essential but only an accidental order among causes of the same type. Secondly, several agents concur when one depends upon a prior cause for its power and efficacy. Again, this is not relevant, because the intellect and the will do not derive their causal efficacy from each other. Finally, several causes can concur to produce an effect even though they are different in kind, as opposed to the first case, and even though neither draws its own ability to cause from the other, as opposed to the second case. In this third relationship, both are required but one is related to the other as the more principal agent, as male and female in reproduction. This applies to the will and intellect, since the will requires the intellect for its act, but the will is the more principal agent, endowing volition with its free and contingent character.

STEPHEN D. DUMONT

This carefully balanced view of the intellect and will cooperating in volition is that of Scotus's early Oxford lectures on the *Sentences*, the *Lectura*. When lecturing on the *Sentences* at Paris, however, Scotus appears to have developed some sympathy for the more voluntaristic position of Henry that the will is the total cause of its act, a position in fact shared by many prominent Franciscans. Because Scotus did not complete that section of his *magnum opus*, the *Ordinatio*, that would have contained this question on the will, the exact relation between the *Lectura* and Parisian treatments on this point has perhaps been the most contested and confused single issue in all of Scotistic scholarship.

Will as the power for opposites

Regardless of the degree to which Scotus may have endorsed the concept of the will as a total cause of its act, it is clear that he did not regard the will's relation to the intellect as the fundamental issue in its freedom. Scotus would have admitted the will to be free to act against a practical judgment of the intellect no matter how correct – a point unequivocally asserted in the condemnations of 1277 – whether a causal role was assigned to the intellect or not. Rather, the critical issue was not the ability of the will to choose the opposite of what the intellect dictated but the manner in which the will itself was capable of eliciting opposite acts. The standard view, contained in the question on free choice in Peter Lombard's *Sentences*, maintained that choice was free only with respect to something in the future, not in the past or the present. On Lombard's account, what is in the present is already determined, nor is it in our power, when something actually is, to make it be or not be. This may be possible at some future moment, but it is impossible for anything not to be while it is, or to be something else while it is what it is. Even before Scotus another noted voluntarist, PETER OLIVI, had recognized that this was simply an application of Aristotle's dictum in the *Perihermenias* that "Everything that is, when it is, necessarily is," to free choice, and that it spelled determination for the will. As Olivi argued, deferring the capacity of free choice to do otherwise to some future moment did nothing to preserve freedom, since when that future moment arrived and became the present, the will would be as incapable of doing otherwise at that future moment as it was before. Thus, unless the will were capable of doing otherwise at the very moment at which it willed, it never would be so capable.

Scotus, doubtless aware of Olivi's insight, gave it a more rigorous defense and systematic development within the available framework of modal propositions. Thus, according to Scotus, there is a twofold freedom (*libertas*) of the will arising from its ability for opposites. The first, which is evident, is the capacity to have opposite acts over time. Scotus says that freedom in this sense is not a perfection, for it is a feature of any mutable subject that it can have opposed states successively. There is, however, a second, less evident power for opposites in the will without succession (i.e., apart from change of actual states over time). Scotus argues for this less evident power for opposites without succession as follows. Consider a created will that exists only for an instant and in that instant has an act of willing. Now that will cannot produce that volition necessarily, for then the will would be a absolutely necessary cause, which is impossible. The reason is that the nature of a cause is exhibited at no other time than at the moment when it acts. Thus, if a will existing at an instant causes necessarily, it would so cause at every instant, which is contradictory to the notion of a will. Therefore, since the will causes contingently in that instant, there must be a potency for the opposite at that same instant, and thus a potency for opposites without succession.

With Scotus, then, the will became an active power for opposites in the strong and innovative sense that, at the moment when it is actually willing, it retains the real capacity to will the opposite. Scotus's general point is that if there is to be the notion of an essentially and intrinsically contingent cause, then the accepted doctrine that an essential cause must be simultaneous with its effect entails that, at the very moment the will effects a volition, there must be a possibility for its opposite. In this Scotus, and Olivi before him, pushed voluntarism well past the plane of previous discussion where freedom of the will was understood in terms of the will's ability to act contrary to the intellect, and examined the underlying basis for a free act within the will itself. More broadly, Scotus's new notion of will and attached conception of contingency has been recognized as constituting an important break with ancient conceptions of modality, which understood contingency in terms of the possibility for actual states at different times, rather than in terms of an actual state and the possibility for its opposite at the same time. In advancing this new, so-called synchronic theory of contingency, Scotus has been seen as anticipating Leibniz's notion of possible worlds.

Will as a rational power

One of the central texts in medieval discussions of the will was *Metaphysics* IX. 2 where Aristotle distinguished between rational agents that could produce contrary effects and non-rational (i.e., natural) agents limited to a single effect. Thus, fire can produce only heat, but a knowledge of medicine can produce both health and disease. The more intellectualist approach, such as found in Aquinas, took this to mean that the root cause of freedom is to be found in the ability of the intellect to conceive opposites. In a lengthy commentary on Aristotle's text, however, Scotus argued to the contrary that, since the will is a power capable of opposites, it is not only a rational power, but the only rational power. For Scotus, the primary and most fundamental division of all active powers is into the equivocates of nature and will. A natural agent is one that is of itself determined to act. That is, a natural power will issue in a single act necessarily and to its greatest capacity unless impeded. A voluntary or free power is not determined of itself to act, so that it may issue in a contrary act or in no act at all. By 'not determined of itself' Scotus really means that the will is self-determining. Its indeterminacy to act is not a defect owing to an insufficiency of power, so that it requires activation by something else, but a perfection that results from a super-sufficiency of power that makes it capable of contrary effects. Given this primary division of nature and will, Scotus places the intellect on the side of natural powers because it must necessarily assent to what is true. Thus, on Aristotle's definition, the intellect is not strictly speaking rational. The will consequently became the only truly rational power, where "rational" is contrasted with "naturally determined." In a complete reversal of the intellectualist and Aristotelian model in which appetite was seen to be rational by its relation to the intellect, Scotus concluded that the intellect was rational only in the qualified sense that it is required as a precondition for the action of the will.

The two affections of the will

The will, however, is not only an active power capable of acting in opposite ways, but an affective power that is an inclination to the good. Here too, Scotus sought to protect the will from any natural determinism by denying that it could be defined solely as an intellectual appetite. According to Scotus, if the will were simply, as Aquinas and others had described it, an inclination consequent upon the intellectual apprehension of the good, then it would be no more free than the sense appetite, for the intellect is no less a natural power than the

367

sense. Adopting ANSELM's distinction between an affection for the advantageous (*affectio commodi*) and affection for justice (*affectio iustitiae*), Scotus says that there must be a twofold inclination in the will if it is to be a free appetite. As interpreted by Scotus, the former is the inclination to self-fulfillment characteristic of natural desire. In other words, it is the intellectual appetite of the rational agent to its own good or happiness. Again, Scotus says, if the will were nothing else than this, it could not be free. What is required for freedom is the addition of an affection for the just, which is not an inclination for the good of the agent but for the good in itself. It serves to moderate the otherwise unrestrained and natural drive of the rational agent toward its own self-fulfillment present in the *affectio commodi* by inclining the will to love the supreme good, God, for his own sake or other lesser goods for their own worth. Scotus calls the affection for the just the "innate freedom of the will" because it enables the will to transcend the determinism of natural appetite to self-perfection, which, in the rational agent, is no less a natural appetite for being intellectual. In denying that the will construed as a rational desire for happiness is a free appetite, Scotus is generally interpreted as having taken the significant step of separating morality from eudaimonism.

Virtue and natural law

Such a strong voluntarism was not without its ramifications for Greek ethical theory, and Scotus did not hesitate to draw them out. Two in particular are notable. First, Scotus rejected in principle the connection of prudence to moral virtue, a key element of Aristotelian ethics. Scotus's basic argument was that since prudence can be generated without moral virtue, they are not necessarily connected. According to Scotus, when the intellect issues a correct moral command, the will is free not to elicit any act at all. Since no moral virtue is generated unless the will acts, prudence can be generated in the intellect through dictates of right reason without necessarily producing the corresponding moral virtue in the will. Scotus's position follows from two voluntarist positions, both contrary to Aristotle: that the moral virtues reside in the will, not the sensitive appetite, and that the will need not follow even a completely correct moral judgment of the intellect. It should be stressed that Scotus was here concerned only to establish that prudence did not *necessarily* require moral virtue, even if they were ordinarily connected, as a direct consequence of the will's freedom with respect to the intellect. But this point of principle was significant and beyond even what Henry of Ghent, who required a connection of the virtues at some level, would admit in his voluntarism.

A more far-reaching result was Scotus's position that the natural law, at least as it governed moral obligations to created beings, is not necessary. Specifically, Scotus held that the body of natural or moral law as revealed in the Decalogue is contingent as regards the second table. In this Scotus was in explicit disagreement with Aquinas, who held that both tables were immutable, so that when, for instance, God commanded Abraham to kill Isaac, there was no genuine setting aside of the fifth commandment. Scotus, to the contrary, held that God could dispense with the second table so that the same act under the same circumstances that was forbidden under the Decalogue could be made permissible by God. Their disagreement was not over the meaning of natural law, for both defined it as first principles of practical reason or dictates deduced necessarily from them. They differed on what fell under this definition. For Scotus, only those precepts concerning God are such because only God is necessarily good. All creatures are good contingently, so that no moral precept concerning them is necessary. Thus, Scotus limits natural law in the strict sense defined above to only those precepts concerning God in the first table. The second table is part of the natural law only in an extended sense of being highly agreeable with, but not a necessary consequent of, the first table. Ultimately, Scotus's motivation was to protect divine will against limitation or constraint by creatures.

Bibliography

Primary sources

Editions

(1891), *Opera omnia. Editio nova, juxta editionem Waddingi XII tomos continentem*, 26 vols., Paris: Vivès.

(1950–), *Opera omnia studia et cura Commissionis Scotisticae ad fidem codicum edita praeside P. Carolo Balic*, 11– vols., Vatican City: Typis Polyglottis Vaticanis.

(1997–), *Opera philosophica*, 3– vols., St. Bonaventure, NY: Franciscan Institute. (Originally planned for the Vatican *Opera omnia*, but now published separately.)

(1998–), *Opera omnia. Editio minor*, 2– vols., Alberobello: Aga.

Translations

(1975), *God and Creatures: The Quodlibetal Questions*, trans. F. Alluntis and A. B. Wolter, Princeton, NJ: Princeton University Press.

(1986), *Duns Scotus on the Will and Morality*, trans. A. B. Wolter, Washington, DC: The Catholic University of America Press.

(1987), *Philosophical Writings: A Selection*, trans. A. B. Wolter, Indianapolis: Hackett; repr. of 1962 edn.

(1997), *Questions on the Metaphysics of Aristotle*, trans. A. B. Wolter and G. Etzkorn, St. Bonaventure, NY: Franciscan Institute Press.

Secondary sources

Cross, R. (1999), *Duns Scotus*, New York: Oxford University Press.

Frank, W. A. and Wolter, A. B. (1995), *Duns Scotus, Metaphysician*, West Lafayette, IN: Purdue University Press.

Williams, T., ed. (forthcoming), *The Cambridge Companion to Duns Scotus*, Cambridge: Cambridge University Press.

Wolter, A. B. (1946), *The Transcendentals and their Function in the Metaphysics of Duns Scotus*, Washington, DC: The Catholic University of America Press.

Wolter, A. B. and Adams, M. M., eds. (1990), *The Philosophical Theology of John Duns Scotus*, Ithaca, NY: Cornell University Press.

59

John Gerson

JAMES B. SOUTH

John Gerson (b. 1363; d. 1429) was born at Gerson-les-Barbery and studied philosophy and theology at the College of Navarre. A student of PIERRE D'AILLY, he received his theology doctorate in 1394. Almost immediately after, he became Chancellor of the University of Paris. While chancellor, he reached a point in 1400 where he threatened to resign and sent a remarkable letter to the faculty at Navarre complaining that the overwheening pride of theologians and the academic politics he was forced to endure had become intolerable to him and that he could no longer make the moral compromises that they required. As a result, he was able to institute a series of reforms that involved students reading less of Book I of the *Sentences* of PETER LOMBARD and instead stress the later books that focus on moral and church issues. He also proposed eliminating disputes of sophistical questions. At the Council of Constance (1414–17), Gerson played a major role and his views on the nature of papal authority were central to the deliberations. His work *On Ecclesiastical Power* was written shortly afterwards.

Gerson is best known for his adherence to conciliarism, the view that in ecclesiastical matters the pope is not the locus of power. Instead, he believed that a representative assembly of the Church, a general council, possesses supreme authority. He also extended this conclusion to secular society. He argued that despite their different origins, the Church and secular society share a common structural feature. Thus, while the Church is of divine origin and secular society has a purely human origin, nonetheless they are both "perfect" societies and in both the ultimate source of authority over members resides in some representative assembly. As a result, a ruler cannot be greater than the community over which he exercises authority. Both the pope and a prince are merely ministers entrusted with the care of their respective societies. Accordingly, neither holds a right over their subjects. Indeed, the notion of a "subjective right," that is, one that attributes to the possessor of something the freedom to do with it as she wills, is one to which Gerson appeals when he claims that neither pope nor prince has a right over any subject.

In *On Mystical Theology*, Gerson set forth a criticism of the scholastic approach to theology, contrasting it with traditional mystical theology. Scholasticism relies, he thought, on the outward vestiges of God's actions and this fact leads to an emphasis on the use of reason at the expense of affectivity. The ultimate issue at stake is the way we think about God: scholastics think of God as "truth" while mystical theologians cling to God as "good." Indeed, Gerson goes so far as to suggest that it is only through the affective side that we can come to experience God in some manner above nature. The famous analogy he uses is that just as fire causes water to boil over, so too love allows the mind to ascend to knowledge it could not reach alone. Finally, the superiority of the affective path is most obvious because it is available to anyone, not just the sophisticated theologian.

Bibliography

Primary sources

(1960–73) *Oeuvres complètes* [1401–26], 10 vols., ed. P. Glorieux, Paris: Desclée.
(1998) *Early Works* [1401–08], ed. and trans. B. P. McGuire, New York: Paulist Press.

Secondary sources

Combes, A. (1963), *La Théologie mystique de Gerson. Profil de son évolution*, Rome: Desclée et Socii.
Pascoe, L. B. (1973), *Jean Gerson: Principles of Church Reform*, Leiden: Brill.

60

John of Jandun

JAMES B. SOUTH

John of Jandun (b. 1285/9; d. 1328) was born in Reims, in the Champagne region. We know several definite dates in his life and can extrapolate others from those. We know, for example, that he was teaching in Paris in 1310 as a master in the arts faculty. That puts his birth at sometime in the 1280s, though it is impossible to be precise about the year. In 1315 he was part of the original faculty at the newly formed College of Navarre. At Paris, Jandun developed a close acquaintance with MARSILIUS OF PADUA who was rector at the university from late 1312 through March 1313. While it is unlikely that Jandun had a large influence on the argument of Marsilius's work, apparently he was considered by Pope John XXII to be as dangerous as Marsilius. In 1326, Marsilius was exposed as the author of *The Defender of Peace*, and both Jandun and Marsilius fled to the court of Ludwig of Bavaria. On September 6, 1326, Pope John XXII issued the first of a series of condemnations concerning Marsilius and Jandun, culminating on October 23, 1327, when both were excommunicated as heretics. Meanwhile, Jandun accompanied Ludwig to Italy and was present when Ludwig was crowned Holy Roman Emperor at Rome on May 1, 1328. Shortly after being named Bishop of Ferrara in May 1328 by Ludwig, Jandun died late in the summer, at Todi.

Jandun is one of the most important thinkers in the Latin Averroist tradition and played a key role in the transmission to later thinkers in the fifteenth and sixteenth centuries of that important thread of medieval philosophical speculation. In fact, already by the second quarter of the fourteenth century his writings were being read and discussed in Bologna. The great number of manuscripts and, later, printed editions, are evidence of his influence on the development of Italian Aristotelians up to Galileo's time.

Jandun's writings cover a wide spectrum of Aristotelian thought and include sets of questions on the *Physics*, *De anima*, *Metaphysics*, *Parva naturalia*, and the *De caelo*. In addition, he composed special works on particular topics such as the notion of the agent sense, the principle of individuation, and the priority of universal knowledge to particular knowledge. His first writing can be dated to around 1310 and treated the issue of the "agent sense," an issue that continued to be debated into the late sixteenth century and in which his treatment of the issue was a standard view to be discussed.

Despite his indebtedness to AVERROES, whom he calls the "most perfect and subtlest" of philosophers after Aristotle, he is not afraid to take original positions. Recent scholarship and careful readings of his texts show that he frequently made subtle changes in his thought from work to work and was not afraid to follow a position to its logical conclusion. At the same time, he was perfectly willing to admit that he was unable to come to a settled opinion on a topic. He was well informed of debates in theological circles, and engaged in discussions and polemics with theologians at Paris. Although Jandun wrote on many topics within natural philosophy and metaphysics, many of his most original and notable views revolve around questions of human cognition. These psychological views were to have the strongest influence on later thinkers.

Faith and philosophy

Jandun is one of the most notable proponents of the view that philosophy and theology proceed in different ways and that the conclusions appropriate to philosophy might, and frequently do, contradict the teachings of theology. It is crucial to note that nowhere does Jandun state that the conclusions of philosophy and the truths of theology constitute two separate and contradictory sets of truths. Instead, his position arises from a methodological standpoint that gives primacy of place in philosophical argumentation to sensory experience, in contrast to a supernatural method that appeals to principles beyond what is sensible as is appropriate in theology. He repeatedly contrasts the evidence of the senses to the authority of the saints, to what is handed down in Sacred Scripture, and to faith. Indeed, Jandun suggests that much harm is done by theologians who misuse the methods of philosophy without a proper understanding of natural philosophy and, in his work *Treatise on the Praises of Paris*, he points out that incessant theological disputation weakens the sincere confession of the articles of faith. In short, Jandun proposes that the best way to defend the faith is not by producing arguments that are weak, sophistical, or based on what is not sensible, but rather to lay out the truths of faith and assent to them with reverence. He remarks in passing that this reverent assent is made easier when one has listened to the truths of faith from childhood.

The sincerity of Jandun's professions of faith is a matter of some dispute. Certainly, he has been seen by many as a kind of prototype of the freethinker, but that is almost certainly an anachronistic perspective. Instead, it is much more likely that he means what he says: the methods of the theologian and the methods of the philosopher are very different and following a philosophical method and interpreting the texts of Aristotle is a unique type of exercise that is not intrinsically destructive of faith. Included among the many claims that he thinks can be known only by faith and not by the evidence of the senses, are the immortality of the individual human soul, the resurrection of the body, the infinity of the power of God, the creation of the world by God, the fact that accidents remain in the sacrament of the altar, and that God knows objects other than himself.

The issue of the "agent sense"

Jandun is perhaps most famous for his defense of the need to postulate an agent sense power to explain how sensation takes place. On one standard Aristotelian-inspired account of sensation, the sensible object produces a likeness of itself (called a sensible species) that subsequently is received in the sense power. The reception of the sensible species in the sense power is thus viewed as sufficient to account for the act of sensing. Jandun, though, argues that the reception of the species is insufficient for the production of sensation because the species would lack the nobility to cause an act in the soul or its powers and so he concludes that the species is merely the immediate *receptive* principle of sensation. However, no principle can be both immediately receptive and active. Consequently, there must be some immediate active principle of sensation and that is what he calls the agent sense. This agent sense is a separate power of the sensitive soul and acts only after the receptive power has received a species. It is notable that Jandun does not view the agent sense as compromising the essential passivity of the process of sensation and sees himself making more plausible the Aristotelian assertion that sensation is a passive operation. The key fact that he points to in order to save the passivity of sense is that the action of the agent sense is itself received in the passive sense power and thus ultimately the passive sense power is responsible for sensing.

The controversy over intelligible species

Jandun provides an interesting account of the production of intelligible species consistent with his Averroistic tendencies. He is committed to making a sharp distinction between the intellect on the one hand and the properly human internal sense powers on the other hand. Intelligible species are those mental representations through which the intellect knows objects in the world, and he argues that the internal senses are the primary cause of their production. These internal senses play the crucial role of mediating between our discrete external sensory experience and our intellectual cognition, and Jandun follows Averroes in delineating four such powers: common sense, imagination, sense memory, and the cogitative power. The basic idea is that imagination preserves the content of prior external sensations, which have been unified by the common sense, while the cogitative power is aware of the non-sensed species. The standard example of a non-sensed species is the awareness of danger that the sheep has when seeing a wolf. He reserves to memory the role of preserving these sorts of non-sensed species. In addition to the cogitative power's role of knowing non-sensed species, it is also the internal sense power that knows the sensed species. Because it knows both the sensed and the non-sensed species, its activity is most important for our intellectual knowledge and Jandun holds that its acts of knowing are dispositive for the production of the act of the potential intellect when it knows.

One of the most striking claims he makes in his *Questions on the De anima* concerns the relation between phantasm, agent intellect, and potential intellect. He argues that the agent intellect is not productive of the intelligible species, but only of the act of thinking and he argues that the abstractive power of the agent intellect is nothing more than its causing the potential intellect's act of knowledge. The consequence of this view is that the phantasm produced by the cogitative power's act of awareness is solely responsible for the generation of an immaterial and universal intelligible species. In other words, he completely rejects views that see the function of the agent intellect as consisting in abstracting an intelligible species from a phantasm existing in the internal sense power. The agent intellect merely renders the intelligible species actually knowable so that the potential intellect can know the quiddities of things. Unfortunately, he provides no account of how it is that the cogitative power produces an intelligible species. After all, the sensitive soul and the intellective soul are two distinct forms, the former a form of the body, the latter wholly immaterial. It is unclear how an immaterial universal species can simply arise from the material phantasm representing a singular object. While Jandun's view leaves an explanatory gap of some significance in his account of cognition, his willingness to criticize various authoritative positions on the question is evidence of his independent mind and his willingness to follow where his argument takes him.

The agent intellect and human happiness

Jandun holds that the agent intellect and the potential intellect are essential parts of the intellective soul, although he does not think that they are two substances. He argues that the intellective soul is itself a single separate substance united to the human body and not multiplied numerically according to the number of humans beings who exist. This intellective soul, a separate form distinct from the sensitive soul, operates within the human body and its operation is analogous to the way that a sailor operates within his ship. Jandun recognizes that this account of the relation of the intellective soul calls into question the unity of the human person, but believes that it is inspired by Averroes's thought, has too many positive points in its favor to discard, and is congruent with the teaching of Aristotle.

When the potential intellect is informed by an intelligible species, it is properly described as the "intellect in habit." However, it is also the work of the potential intellect to know conclusions that are based on self-evident propositions. If we include these conclusions along with its intelligible species, we can then properly call the potential intellect the "speculative intellect." Once the speculative intellect has arisen in this way, the agent intellect unites to the potential intellect as its true form. This union in turn provides the potential intellect with the resources it needs to ascend to a knowledge of all the other separate substances including, ultimately, God, the most perfect of all substances. This knowledge is not just a series of propositions that we can predicate of God, but is an intuitive knowledge of God's essence, a "state of attainment" that provides us with the greatest delight and happiness available to humans. However, he also sees a political dimension to this wisdom since he suggests that either a ruler or an adviser to the ruler ought to have this kind of intuitive knowledge in order to promote the well-being of the community. Of course, since this work of the potential intellect is an action of a form separate from the sensitive soul and is not unique to any human being, this intuitive knowledge of separate substances and God only equivocally belongs to the individual human.

Bibliography

Primary sources

(1505), *Super parvis naturalibus Aristotelis quaestiones perutiles ac eleganter discussae*, ed. M. Zimara, Venice: Heirs of Octavianus Scotus.

(1552), *In libros Aristotelis De caelo et mundo quae extant quaestiones subtilissimae*, Venice: Iuntas.

(1553), *Quaestiones in duodecim libros Metaphysicae iuxta Aristotelis et magni Commentatoris intentionem disputatae*, Venice: Hieronymus Scotus; repr. 1966, Frankfurt: Minerva.

(1587), *Super libros Aristotelis De anima subtilissimae quaestiones*, Venice: Heirs of Hieronymus Scotus; repr. 1966, Frankfurt: Minerva.

(1587), *Super octo libros Aristotelis de physico auditu subtilissimae quaestiones*, Venice: Iuntas; repr. 1969, Frankfurt: Minerva.

(1867), *Tractatus de laudibus Parisius*, in Le Roux de Lincy and L. M. Tisserand, eds., *Paris et ses historiens aux XIVe et XVe siècles* (pp. 32–79), Paris: Imprimerie Impériale.

(1961), *Quaestio de habitu intellectus*, in Z. Kuksewicz, "Les trois 'Quaestiones de habitu' dans le ms. Vat. Ottob. 318. Editions des textes de Jean de Jandun, Guillaume Alnwick et Anselme de Côme (?)," *Mediaevalia Philosophica Polonorum* 9, pp. 3–30.

(1963), *Quaestio de principio individuationis*, in Z. Kuksewicz, "*De principio individuationis* de Jean de Jandun," *Mediaevalia Philosophica Polonorum* 11, pp. 93–106.

(1965), *Quaestio de infinitate vigoris Dei*, in Z. Kuksewicz, "*De infinitate vigoris Dei* des Pariser Averroisten Johannes de Janduno," *Manuscripta* 9, pp. 167–70.

(1965), *Quaestio utrum forma substantialis perficiens materiam sit corruptibilis*, in Z. Kuksewicz, ed., *Averroïsme polonais au XIVe siècle: edition des texts*, Ossolineum: Editions de l'Académie Polonaise des Sciences.

(1970), *Quaestio de notioritate universalium*, in Z. Kuksewicz, "La *quaestio de notioritate universalium* de Jean de Jandun," *Mediaevalia Philosophica Polonorum* 14, pp. 87–97.

(1980), *Quaestio utrum aeternis repugnet habere causam efficientem*, in A. Maurer, "John of Jandun and the divine causality," *Mediaeval Studies* 17, pp. 198–207; repr. 1990 in A. Maurer, *Being and Knowing: Studies in Thomas Aquinas and Later Medieval Philosophers* (pp. 275–308), Toronto: Pontifical Institute of Mediaeval Studies.

(1988), *Sophisma de sensu agente*, in A. Pattin, ed., *Pour l'histoire du sens agent: la controverse entre Barthélemy de Bruges et Jean de Jandun, ses antécédents et son évolution* (pp. 118–65), Louvain: Presses Universitaires de Louvain.

(1988), *Tractatus de sensu agente*, in A. Pattin, ed., *Pour l'histoire du sens agent: la controverse entre Barthélemy de Bruges et Jean de Jandun, ses antécédents et son évolution* (pp. 166–222), Louvain: Presses Universitaires de Louvain.

Secondary sources

Ermatinger, C. J. (1969), "John of Jandun in his relations with arts masters and theologians," in *Arts libéraux et philosophie au moyen âge* (pp. 1173–84), Montreal: Institut d'Études Médiévales; Paris: J. Vrin.

Grignaschi, M. (1958), "Il pensiero politico e religioso di Giovanni di Jandun," *Bollettino del'Istituto Storico Italiano per il Medioevo e Archivio Muratoriano* 70, pp. 425–96.

Jung-Palczewska, E. (1987), "Jean de Jandun, a-t-il affirmé la nature active de l'intellect possible? Problème d'une contradiction dans la question 6 du livre III *De anima* de Jean de Jandun," *Mediaevalia Philosophica Polonorum* 27, pp. 15–20.

Kuksewicz, Z. (1968), *De Siger de Brabant à Jacques de Plaisance: La théorie de l'intellect chez les averroïstes latins des XIIIe et XIVe siècles*, Wrocław: Éditions de l'Académie Polonaise des Sciences.

MacClintock, S. (1956), *Perversity and Error: Studies on the "Averroist" John of Jandun*, Indiana University Publications, Humanities Series 37, Bloomington: Indiana University Press.

Mahoney, E. P. (1986), "John of Jandun and Agostino Nifo on human felicity (*status*)," in C. Wenin, ed., *L'Homme et son univers au moyen âge*, 2 vols., Philosophes médiévaux 26, vol. 1 (pp. 465–77), Louvain-la-Neuve: Editions de l'Institut Supérieur de Philosophie.

——(1987), "Themes and problems in the psychology of John of Jandun," in J. F. Wippel, ed., *Studies in Medieval Philosophy* (pp. 273–88), Studies in Philosophy and the History of Philosophy 17, Washington, DC: The Catholic University of America.

Maurer, A. (1955), "John of Jandun and the divine causality," *Mediaeval Studies* 17, pp. 185–207; repr. 1990 in A. Maurer, *Being and Knowing: Studies in Thomas Aquinas and Later Medieval Philosophers* (pp. 275–308), Toronto: Pontifical Institute of Mediaeval Studies.

Pacchi, A. (1958–60), "Note sul commento al 'De anima' di Giovanni di Jandun," *Rivista Critica di Storia della Filosofia* 13: pp. 372–83, 14: pp. 437–57, 15: pp. 354–75.

Schmugge, L. (1966), *Johannes von Jandun (1285/89–1328): Untersuchungen zur Biographie und Sozialtheorie eines lateinischen Averroisten*, Pariser Historische Studien 5, Stuttgart: Anton Hiersemann.

Vitali, M. C. and Kuksewicz, Z. (1984), "Notes sur les deux rédactions des *Quaestiones de anima* de Jean de Jandun," *Mediaevalia Philosophica Polonorum* 27, pp. 3–24.

61

John of Mirecourt

MAURICIO BEUCHOT

John of Mirecourt (fl. ca. 1345, also known as *monachus albus*, the white monk) taught at the Cistercian College of St. Bernard in Paris (a renowned center for nominalism at the time) achieving most fame around 1345. He wrote the *Principium* and a two-version commentary on the four books of the *Sentences* of PETER LOMBARD, on which he lectured between 1334 and 1336. Mirecourt was attacked by Johannes Normanus, a Benedictine also known as *monachus niger* (the black monk). In 1346, sixty-three of the propositions from Mirecourt's *Lecture* on the *Sentences* were singled out as suspicious. Mirecourt composed a *Declaratio* explaining the meaning of his propositions on the *Sentences* and defending himself of the charges. However, Robert of Bardis – a Florentine friend of Petrarch and university chancellor at the time – condemned between forty and fifty of the propositions in 1347 in an action supported by the faculty of theology. Mirecourt wrote a second apology without success. After his condemnation, nothing further is known about him.

PETER OF CANDIA places Mirecourt among the followers of WILLIAM OF OCKHAM (*filii*, *imitatores Ockami*) and "nominalists" in this sense of the term. Like his contemporary NICHOLAS OF AUTRECOURT, Mirecourt underwent an "intellectual crisis" of sorts and embraced an extreme version of nominalism leading to phenomenalism. Mirecourt accepted the view that metaphysics can achieve only probability; he thought that the propositions of metaphysics are indemonstrable without the aid of revelation.

Principles of knowledge

There are two kinds of certain or indubitable knowledge, namely, knowledge of the first principle, which is the principle of non-contradiction, and secondly, the immediate intuition of one's existence. In regards to the later, Mirecourt's position is close to that of AUGUSTINE, for whom the act of doubting one's existence, in and of itself, demonstrates to the doubter his or her own existence.

In regard to knowledge of the first principle, Mirecourt asserts (as did Autrecourt) that the principle of non-contradiction and the analytic judgments reducible to it are the most indubitable of all things known. It is impossible, Mirecourt asserts, not to see the evidence of the first principle. Mirecourt calls this evidence "special" evidence. Any principles deducible from the first principle share the special evidence proper to this principle. The principle of causality, however, is not analytic and therefore it is not known with special evidence.

Analytic knowledge of the first principle has the highest degree of evidence in its support, followed by knowledge by experience, or synthetic knowledge. Mirecourt distinguishes between internal and external (or empirical) synthetic knowledge. Internal knowledge is first-person knowledge of one's existence. This knowledge is evident in the sense indicated, namely, that doubting one's own existence entails a contradiction. The evidence through which we know the existence of everything else is derived from the evidence which supports this first-person knowledge. On the other hand, knowledge based on experience of external things (external or empirical knowledge) is neither evident nor indubitable. External things are known intuitively and immediately, that is, without the mediation of the species or representative beings (e.g. subjective and objective idols such as those posited by PETER AURIOL, among others). However, the evidence through which we know external things is not logical but merely physical. Mirecourt calls this evidence "natural." Natural evidence eliminates fear of error, provided one assumes God's general or ordinary power (that is, excluding miracles, which belong to God's absolute power). The external, or empirical knowledge that connects us with the world lacks the guarantee that analytic knowledge and knowledge of one's existence possess. Some spirit, even God himself, could always come disguised as an evil genius and give us the illusion that there are external things when in fact there are none. On this point, Mirecourt anticipates Descartes's concerns.

As we have seen, Mirecourt distinguishes between two sorts of evidence, namely, special and natural. The first makes us assent without vacillation, free of any presupposition, conjecture, or opinion. This assent excludes faith, which implies an act of the will. Assent based on special evidence cannot lead us into falsehood. Assent based on natural evidence, in contrast, can always lead us into falsehood owing to the possibility of some miracle. Although natural evidence makes us assent without vacillation, it is weaker than special evidence because it can result in falsehood not only if one assumes God's general influence or ordinary power but also the possibility of miracles, which belong to God's absolute power.

Degrees of knowledge

A created intellectual being can understand with special evidence analytic propositions or tautologies (the truth of which is evident from the meaning of the terms), because such propositions share the special or logical evidence that belongs to the first principle. Examples of these propositions are: 'If God is, God is', 'If man is, animal is'. All propositions logically deducible from the first principle (or from other evident propositions) are also supported by special evidence. It is evident that, if P and "P implies Q" are evident, Q is equally evident. The principle of causality is not reducible to the principle of contradiction and for this reason knowledge of this principle is weaker than knowledge of the first principle.

A created intellectual being can also understand with special evidence that something exists and that he exists. If he did not exist, he could not even doubt and, since he doubts, he exists. Furthermore, he has special evidence that he understands, knows, deduces, and so on. However, in these cases the special evidence is limited because a man can only know with special evidence his own existence. Knowledge of things such as that whiteness exists, that a man exists, and that two or more things exist, lacks special evidence, since it is not self-evident that there is a contradiction when something that seems to be so is not so. Likewise, propositions asserting future contingents lack special evidence.

Empirical propositions only have *natural* or physical evidence. These propositions describe with certainty what appears to be the case and cannot happen otherwise except through a miracle. Most of the condemnations against Mirecourt were prompted by this excessive use – in Ockhamist fashion – of the *potentia Dei absoluta*, that is, of the notion of God's willing and somewhat capricious intervention. Mirecourt exalts the absolute omnipotence of God, a point on which he is close to Ockham and THOMAS BRADWARDINE. However, he extends this view farther: asserting, for instance, that God could make it so that the world that exists has never existed. Although Mirecourt grants that we know by faith this not to be so, reason could never prove it. Everything in the physical and moral realms depends on the entirely free will of God. No being or law surpasses God's will and omnipotence. Everything occurs because God wills it, it occurs in the manner in which God wills it, and God could annihilate everything. Nonetheless, faith teaches us that he will not annihilate everything and we must accept what faith tells us.

A created intellectual being can know with *natural* evidence that whiteness exists, that a man exists, that an ox exists, and many other things. And he can know with *natural* evidence that there are truths for which there is no evidence. For instance, an angel can know through evidence that God is three and that men know this only through faith. An angel knows that a proposition that is not evident for somebody, who knows it by faith, is true. On the basis of our experience, we have knowledge of those beings external to us: man exists; white and black exist; some causes produce some effects; and so on. But through a miracle, God could make us see objects not present, accidents without substance, and so on.

Intermediaries of knowledge and modes of knowing

Mirecourt also discusses *esse subjectivum* (the subjective being or psychological fact of knowing) and *esse objectivum* (its objective being or discernible content) and uses Ockham's razor to simplify the account of epistemic entities, such as the intelligible species and subjective and objective beings. Mirecourt contends that if an *esse objectivum* must be known by means of an intermediary, this intermediary, in turn, must be known through another intermediary and so on ad infinitum. But, because an intermediary can be neither substance nor accident, it has to be a fictitious being (*esse fictum*), which is to say, pure fiction.

Aside from knowing through the understanding, Mirecourt says that humans can know with their will. Here he picks up an unusual idea from ADAM OF WODEHAM, though without defending it too decisively. Mirecourt does not deny that knowledge precedes will; rather, he affirms that sometimes what is willed encompasses what is known and can even produce it.

Physics: atomism

Regarding physics or natural philosophy, Mirecourt explains the structure of the corporeal world by an appeal to atomism, as did Autrecourt. He denies causality and holds that accidental movements produce the combinations of atoms and these combinations, in turn, produce the changes in things. Mechanistic physics replaces Aristotelian, qualitative physics.

Mirecourt also thought that it is possible for there to be substances without accidents, and that these could be the only substances composing the universe. Nevertheless, he pointed out that we know by faith that accidents are different from substances.

In humans, the acts and faculties of the soul are not separable from the soul. The eternity of the world, though unacceptable to faith, is probable to reason. There is no connection between probability and truth.

Existence and the properties of God

The proofs for God's existence, even though stronger than those to the contrary, are not fully demonstrations. Mirecourt uses St. AUGUSTINE'S argument against skepticism (if I doubt, I exist) and a second argument based on it to demonstrate the existence of God: If something exists, it is either independent or dependent. If independent, then God exists, since independence is a characteristic of God. If dependent, then it depends on something else and, because there cannot be an infinite succession of dependent beings, there must be a being that is prior and independent, and this being is God. However, this argument is not conclusive or demonstrative because the impossibility of an infinite succession of beings is not self-evident. All proofs for the existence of God are based in experience and for this reason they can only provide synthetic or natural evidence, not analytic or special evidence. Mirecourt wrote in his defense that, although this does not limit the validity of the proofs for God's existence, such proofs could not yield absolute certainty given the principles involved in them.

Propositions opposed to the articles of faith can be more probable than these articles. Mirecourt distinguishes between what is true and what is probable. An article of faith can be true for the believer while its negation can be more probable for the dialectician.

With respect to God's knowledge of future contingents and his predetermination of human acts, Mirecourt sticks to the principle that God wills that everything that is be the way it is. Even what is contingent is so, because God makes it this way and wills it this way. Everything depends absolutely on God's free and divine will, and this exalts his omnipotence.

Ethics

Everything that exists is so because God wills it, in the classical sense of having God's consent or approval. Furthermore, everything that exists stems from God's efficacious will, which acts as it wants exactly because God wills it that way. Everything that occurs is produced and sustained by God's will. In this manner, Mirecourt arrives at ROBERT HOLCOT'S view, that God efficaciously wills sin and even produces it in the sinner. It is not that God sins, but that he wills everything that is. Thus, when man sins, God wills even this. Ultimately, with efficacious will God makes the sinner sin. Sin is the lack of rectitude in the sinful act. God could supply this rectitude if he willed it. But God does not provide it, and to this extent God allows sin. God can be said to be the cause of sin, for his permissiveness amounts to his volition. By consenting, that is, by not preventing the sin in the sinner, God wills and in some sense causes the sinner.

Mirecourt says that, even under a state of grace, there are temptations that can be overcome only through a miracle. For instance, he says that a man cannot resist having sexual relations with another man's wife unless a miracle intervenes. For this reason, such an act can be neither adultery nor a sexual sin. Man is not responsible for sins such as this, because the miracle required to avoid them does not happen.

Since a free causal action of a being on another being cannot be demonstrated, Mirecourt adopted the determinism of Bradwardine and, with it, embraced an extreme positivism in morals and law. Good and evil are rooted in God's law, not in the nature of things. Furthermore, God is the author of all our acts, including the sinful acts, and this makes God the author of our sins.

In Ockhamist fashion, Mirecourt also held that the prohibition of hatred towards others is commanded by God only temporarily, and that God could have it that hatred, even towards himself, did not take away merit. In addition, he says that a good intention can diminish sin even to the point of suppressing the ill circumstance that would otherwise attach to the sinful act, although a good intention can also worsen sin.

Conclusion

Mirecourt appears indebted to Bradwardine's determinism, but at times he seems to be moved by a desire to analyze theological concepts in the most abstract of terms. There is excessive Ockhamist dialectics in his work, and it is not always easy to determine to what extent Mirecourt's issues were serious problems or just mental games. But one thing is certain: Mirecourt's assertions scandalized the faculty of theology of Paris and provoked his condemnation.

Bibliography

Primary sources

(1922), "Declaratio," ed. A. Birkemmajer, in "Ein Rechtfertigungschreiben Johanns von Mirecourt," *Vermischte Untersuchungen zur Geschichte der mittelalterlichen Philosophie, Beiträge zur Geschichte des Philosophie des Mittelalters*, XX 5 (pp. 91–128), Münster: Aschendorff.

(1958), "In I Sent., qq. 2–6," ed. A. Franzinelli, "Questioni inedite di Giovanni de Mirecourt sulla conoscenza (Sent. I, q. 2–6)," in *Rivista Critica di Storia della Filosofia* 13/3, pp. 319–40.

(1978), "In I Sent., qq. 13–16," ed. M. Parodi, in "Questioni inedite tratte del I libro del Commento alle Sentenze di Giovanni di Mirecourt (q. 13–16)," *Medioevo* 3, pp. 237–84.

Secondary sources

Deniflé, J. and Châtelain, E., eds. (1889), *Chartularium Universitatis Parisiensis*, vol. 1 (see esp. 610–11), Paris.

Michalski, K. (1923), "Die vielfachen Redaktionen einiger Kommentare zu P. Lombardus," in *Miscellanea Franz Ehrle*, I (pp. 226–36), Rome: Biblioteca Apostolica Vaticana.

——(1969), *La Philosophie au XIVe siècle. Six études*, ed. and with introduction by K. Flasch, Frankfurt: Minerva.

Parodi, M. (1978), "Recenti studi su Giovanni di Mirecourt," *Rivista Critica di Storia della Filosofia* 33, pp. 297–307.

Stegmüller, F. (1933), "Die zwei Apologien des J. de Mirecourt," in *Recherches de Théologie Ancienne et Médiévale* 5, pp. 40–78, 192–204.

Vignaux, P. (1938), *La Pensée au Moyen Âge*, Paris: A. Colin.

62

John of Paris

RUSSELL L. FRIEDMAN

John of Paris (d. 1306), also known as John Quidort, was a Parisian Dominican theologian and philosopher. He has been described as "the most versatile and most distinctive figure of the old Parisian Thomist school at the end of the thirteenth century" (Grabmann 1922, p. 3). John's independent Thomism seems to have surfaced around 1282–4, when he almost certainly wrote the *Correctorium "Circa"* (1941), one of the Dominican works of the period which defend the teachings of THOMAS AQUINAS from the criticism of William de la Mare's *Correctorium*. Sometime between 1292 and 1296, John lectured on the *Sentences* of PETER LOMBARD at Paris; student notes (reports) of these lectures survive, and the lectures on books I and II have been critically edited (1961–4). Several points of John's thought in his *Sentences* commentary were provocative enough to elicit condemnation (for further literature and more on dating, see Friedman, forthcoming). John became master of theology at Paris in 1304; his magisterial teaching on the Eucharist was condemned, and he died while an appeal was in process.

John wrote a large variety of works throughout his career (for a full list of his works, manuscripts, editions, and translations see Kaeppeli, 1970–93, 2, pp. 517–24). Without question, John's most famous philosophical work is his treatise on political theory of 1302, *On Royal and Papal Power* (see ibid., p. 522, n. 2578). In this work, John follows a middle course between those who claimed that the Church was barred all temporal power and possessions and those who claimed that the Church had an inherent superiority to the state even in temporal affairs. John instead supports a dualism of Church and state: they do not relate as superior and inferior, but each is supreme in its own field of endeavor, the Church in spiritual matters, the state in temporal. John follows Aristotle in holding that it is human nature to form societies and states; thus, the state has an intrinsic value as a guardian of the people's well-being, its value is by no means derived from or subordinate to the Church. Despite this dualism, John holds that the Church can possess temporal goods and power, but as a concession or gift from the state; the state, on the other hand, has a spiritual role to play, since its end is the common good of the people (including salvation).

Bibliography

Primary sources
(1941), *Le Correctorium Corruptorii "Circa" de Jean Quidort de Paris* ed. J. P. Muller, Rome: Herder.
(1961–4), *Commentaire sur les Sentences. Reportation Livre I–II*, ed. J. P. Muller, OSB, Rome: Herder.

Secondary sources

Friedman, R. L. (forthcoming), "The *Sentences* Commentary, 1250–1320: General trends, the impact of the religious orders, and the test case of predestination," in G. Evans, ed., *Medieval Commentaries on the Sentences of Peter Lombard* (pp. 41–128), Leiden: Brill.

Grabmann, M. (1922), "Studien zu Johannes Quidort von Paris O.Pr.," in *Sitzungberichte der Bayerischen Akademie der Wissenschaften*, Munich; repr. 1979, in M. Grabmann, *Gesammelte Akademieabhandlungen*, vol. 1 (pp. 69–128), Paderborn: F. Schöningh.

Kaeppeli, T. (1970–93), *Scriptores Ordinis Praedicatorum medii aevi*, 4 vols., Rome: S. Sabina.

63

John Pecham

GIRARD J. ETZKORN

John Pecham (b. ca. 1230; d. 1292), an English Franciscan philosopher and theologian, defender of Augustinian doctrines, was born in Patcham, near Brighton, Sussex. Educated as a youth at the Benedictine monastery at Lewes, he joined the Franciscans at Oxford sometime during the 1250s. He continued his education at Oxford and was sent to Paris in the 1260s to complete his theological studies. He became regent master in the Franciscan chair of theology at Paris in the spring term of 1270. Pecham returned to England sometime after 1271 and was appointed the eleventh Franciscan to be regent master of theology at Oxford. He held this position until 1274, when he was elected the ninth minister provincial of the Franciscans in England. In 1277, he was appointed as lecturer to the papal curia until he was named Archbishop of Canterbury on January 27, 1279, the office he held until his death on December 8, 1292.

Pecham's philosophical career represented a concentrated effort to defend the traditional views of AUGUSTINE and ANSELM (among other theologians) against what was perceived as a growing tendency towards heterodox Aristotelianism exemplified in such doctrines as the eternity of the world, a single intellect for all humankind, and a divinity which had no knowledge of individual beings. As a student in the late 1260s Pecham was undoubtedly present at the sermons of BONAVENTURE, who had alerted his listeners to the growing threat of unorthodox Aristotelianism. If Pecham was not directly involved in compiling the list of 13 errors condemned in 1270 by Stephen Tempier, Bishop of Paris, he certainly would have agreed that the condemned propositions were erroneous. Together with William de la Mare, Pecham was one of the first Franciscans to oppose THOMAS AQUINAS, whose opinions were viewed as compromising Christian doctrine and being all too deferential to Aristotle and AVERROES. This same tendency continued in the followers of Pecham, namely MATTHEW OF AQUASPARTA, ROGER MARSTON, Bartholomew of Bologna, William of Falagar, and, later VITAL DU FOUR.

As a true follower of Bonaventure, Pecham in his writings shows a fundamental allegiance to Augustine while accommodating the philosophy of Aristotle where possible. In the critically edited texts of the works that have survived, Pecham shows little interest in logic or metaphysics. His writings reveal a preoccupation with the theory of knowledge, with philosophical psychology, and with natural philosophy and science (see 1918; 1948; 1989). In his theory of knowledge, Pecham supported divine illumination with regard to first principles, claiming that the human intellect needed the "eternal reasons" with regard to the certitude of intellectual and moral first principles although not with respect to their contents. In contrast to Aquinas, Pecham held that the human (as well as the angelic and divine) intellect had a direct knowledge of singulars. According to the Thomistic interpretation of the Aristotelian adage that the senses know the singular and the intellect the universal, the intellect must reflect on the imagination which receives its image from the senses and then abstract the universal from the phantasm. In response, Pecham argues that the intellect abstracts either knowingly or unknowingly. If knowingly, then it had direct knowledge of the singular in the first place; if unknowingly, then how can it be called intellectual knowledge at all? In addition to a set of disputed questions on the soul (1918), Pecham also wrote a treatise on the soul (1948). In the former, he dismisses traducianism which would have the human soul come from either the divine substance, or the bodies of the parents, or develop from a sensitive soul. Nor were all human souls created at the beginning of time, as Origen held. Rather each and every soul is created directly by God and infused into the body. Pecham vigorously defends the immortality of the soul, claiming that this can be demonstrated by seven irrefutable arguments. At the same time, he is opposed to multiple souls in the human being. There is only one (intellective) human soul, which, however, encapsulates the vegetative and sensitive functions as grades of a single intellectual "form." He strenuously attacks as heretical the view of Averroes, which denied that each human had his or her own rational soul. Such an opinion jeopardized immortality and rendered the statement "I understand" impossible, as Aquinas had pointed out.

The powers of the soul, though multiple, are not really distinct from one another or from the soul. The vegetative grade of the form is distinguished into nutritive, augmentative, and generative. The sensitive grade has motive and apprehensive powers, the latter being distinguished into external (the five senses) and internal powers comprising the "common sense," the imagination, the aestimative (determining what is friendly or hostile), and the memory. The intellectual soul likewise has apprehensive and motive powers, the apprehensive being the agent intellect, the "possible" intellect, and the intellectual memory. The rational appetite or will comprises concupiscible and irascible powers whereby it seeks the good and flees the harmful, powers which it shares with the sensitive grade. Freedom is not a separate power of the will; nevertheless, the will is so free that it can withhold consent in the face of the dictates of the (practical) intellect. This virtual containment of the various powers in the one intellectual soul anticipates, it would seem, the formal distinction of JOHN DUNS SCOTUS.

In the realm of natural philosophy, Pecham emerges as an opponent of Aquinas on several issues. In Aristotle's view every composite substance was made up of matter and form. Aquinas had held that prime matter, as the basis for substantial change, was pure potentiality. Pecham held that (1989, *Quodlibet* IV, q. 1) it was essentially and really distinct, so that by his divine power God could create prime matter distinct from any form whatever. Aquinas likewise held that there was but one substantial form in the human being (ibid., q. 25) uniting the soul to the body. Pecham responded with his theory of multiple grades, i.e., vegetative and sensitive, which persisted as (substantial) components of the human composite. Thus the bodily, vegetative and sensitive "forms" are not successively "corrupted out" by the advent of the higher forms, as Aquinas would have it, but they remain as grades of the higher form. Pecham may have been the first to introduce the grades theory as a refinement of "tri-animism" or the plurality of substantial forms. While his treatise on this subject is apparently lost (Douie 1952, p. 280 n. 2), the salient points of his theory undoubtedly survive in his faithful disciple ROGER MARSTON's *Quodlibet* II, q. 22. Pecham likewise disagreed with Aquinas's view on the eternity of the world. The latter held that de facto the world was created in time, but that there is nothing theologically or philosophically repugnant to the world's being created from all eternity (1975; 1993; Bukowski 1979).

Following in the footsteps of Bonaventure, Pecham believed that creation from all eternity was fundamentally contradictory.

Pecham was likewise interested in science. He wrote both a treatise on optics and a *Perspectiva communis* (1970) which later became a textbook on the subject. He is also the author of a treatise on the spheres, eleven sets of disputed questions (2002), and a tract on mystical numbers (1985). In addition, he wrote numerous treatises on Franciscan spirituality (Brady; Teetaert 1933), including a tract on evangelical poverty. Much of Pecham's work (Doucet 1933; Spettmann 1919) survives only in manuscripts, particularly his commentary on the *Sentences* of PETER LOMBARD, the last three books of which appear to have been lost. A comprehensive assessment must await the critical edition of these works.

Bibliography

Primary sources

(1885), *Registrum epistolarum Fr. Ioannis Peckham*, 3 vols., ed. C. T. Martin, in *Rerum Britannicarum Scriptores*, London.

(1918), *Quaestiones de anima*, ed. H. Spettmann, *Beiträge zur Geschichte der Philosophie des Mittelalters* XIX-5, Münster (also includes *Quaestiones de beatitudine corporis et animae* and *Quaestiones de anima* excerpted from Pecham's commentary on book I of Lombard's *Sentences*).

(1928), *Summa de esse et essentia*, ed. F. Delorme, Rome: Studi Franciscani.

(1948), *Tractatus de anima*, ed. G. Melani, Florence: Studi Franciscani.

(1970), *Perspectiva communis*, ed. D. Lindberg, Madison, WI: University of Wisconsin Press.

(1972), *Tractatus de perspectiva*, ed. D. Lindberg, St. Bonaventure, NY: Franciscan Institute.

(1975), *Quaestio disputata "De aeternitate mundi,"* ed. O. Argerami, *Patristica et Mediaevalia* 1, pp. 82–100.

(1985), *De numeris misticis*, ed. B. Hughes, *Archivum Franciscanum Historicum* 78, pp. 3–28, 333–83.

(1989), *Quodlibeta quattuor*, ed. G. Etzkorn and F. Delorme, *Bibliotheca Franciscana Scholastica* 25, Grottaferrata.

(1993), *Quaestiones de aeternitate mundi*, ed. I. Brady and V. Potter, New York: Fordham University Press.

(2002), *Quaestiones disputatae*, ed. G. Etzkorn, H. Spettmann, and L. Oliger, *Bibliotheca Franciscana Scholastica* 28, Grottaferrata.

Secondary sources

Bibliographia Franciscana (1931–1970), Index (pp. 312–13), ed. C. Van de Laar, Perugia.

Brady, I. (1974), "Jean de Pecham," *Dictionnaire de Spiritualité* 8, pp. 645–9.

——"John Pecham and the background of Aquinas's *De aeternitate mundi*," in *St. Thomas Aquinas (1274–1974)* (pp. 11–71), Commemorative Studies, 2: Toronto: Pontifical Institute of Mediaeval Studies.

Bukowski, T. (1979), "J. Pecham, T. Aquinas et al. on the eternity of the world," *Recherches de Théologie Ancienne et Médiévale* 46, pp. 216–21.

Callebaut, A. (1925), "Jean Peckham OFM et l'augustinisme," *Archivum Franciscanum Historicum* 18, pp. 441–72.

Crowley, T. (1951), "John Peckham OFM Archbishop of Canterbury: versus the new Aristotelianism," *Bulletin of the John Rylands Library* 33, pp. 242–55.

Doucet, V. (1933) "Notulae bibliographicae de quibusdam operibus Fr. Ioannis Pecham, OFM," *Antonianum* 8, pp. 307–28, 425–59.

Douie, D. (1952), *Archbishop Pecham*, Oxford: Clarendon Press.

Ehrle, F. (1889), "J. Peckham über den Kampf des Augustinismus und Aristotelismus in der zweiten Hälfte des 13 Jahrhunderts," *Zeitschrift für katholische Theologie* 13, pp. 172–93.

Etzkorn, G. (1989), "John Pecham, OFM: a career of controversy," in *Monks, Nuns, and Friars in Mediaeval Society* (pp. 71–82), Sewanee: Press of the University of the South.

Lindberg, D. (1965), "The *Perspectiva communis* of John Pecham: its influence, sources, and content," *Archives Internationales d'Histoire des Sciences* 18, pp. 37–53.

——(1968), "Bacon, Witelo, and Pecham, the problem of influence," *XII Congrès Internationale d'Histoire des Sciences* III, pp. A: 103–7.

Spettmann, H. (1919), "Die Psychologie des Johannes Pecham," *Beiträge zur Geschichte der Philosophie des Mittelalters* 20, pp. 1–102, Münster: Aschendorff.

Teetaert, A. (1933), "Pecham, Jean," *Dictionnaire de Théologie Catholique* 12 (pp. 100–40), Paris: Letouzey et Ane.

Wielockx, R. (1985), "Jean de Pecham," *Catholicisme* X (pp. 1005–7), Paris: Letouzey et Ane.

64

John Philoponus

JAMES B. SOUTH

John Philoponus (b. ca. 490; d. ca. 570) was born in Alexandria and was a pupil of Ammonius at his school there. He was also known as John the Grammarian, either because he studied philology before undertaking his philosophical studies or because he was professor of philology. Philoponus was evidently born a Christian and over the course of his career his writings show adherence to many controversial views that are outside the mainstream of Aristotelian or Neoplatonic thought. His writings consist of commentaries on the writings of Aristotle, philosophical treatises, and theological works. In several of his commentaries, he expounds the thought of Aristotle in a rather straightforward way using a basic Neoplatonic framework. However, in others he takes issue with Aristotle as well as with important themes in Neoplatonic thought. Most notably, John rejects the eternity of the world and argues that matter itself is created. In his three treatises on the issue of the eternity of the world, he accepts views that are not present in some of his other works. For example, in some of his works, he holds to the view that the human soul is pre-existent. However, he explicitly rejects that view in the works on the eternity of the world, though it is unclear exactly why this change of thought occurs.

John's views in physics are striking, since he rejects Aristotle's account of projectile motion. Instead of the Aristotelian view that the air behind a projectile is responsible for its motion, John holds that a motive force can be impressed on a projectile. He also rejects the Aristotelian notion of a fifth element since such an element would be eternal. His influence in the Middle Ages was quite extensive. AVICENNA and AVERROES knew his writings and refer to him frequently. THOMAS AQUINAS possessed a translation of part of Philoponus's commentary on the *De anima*. It was not until the Renaissance that many of his writings were reintroduced to the West and many of his ideas about physics were noted with favor by Galileo.

Bibliography

Primary sources

(1887–8), *On Aristotle's Physics*, in H. Vitelli, ed., *Commentaria in Aristotelem Graeca* XVI–XVII, Berlin: Reimer. English editions: (1993), *On Aristotle's Physics 2*, trans. A. R. Lacey; (1994), *On Aristotle's Physics 3*, trans. M. Edwards; (1994), *On Aristotle's Physics 5 to 8*, trans. P. Lettinck; all published London: Duckworth.

(1897), *On Aristotle's On the Soul*, in M. Hayduck, ed., *Commentaria in Aristotelem Graeca* XV, Berlin: Reimer.

(1905), *On Aristotle's Prior Analytics*, in M. Wallies, ed., *Commentaria in Aristotelem Graeca* XIII 2, Berlin: Reimer.

(1909), *On Aristotle's Posterior Analytics*, in M. Wallies, ed., *Commentaria in Aristotelem Graeca* XIII 3, Berlin: Reimer.

(1987), *Philoponus, Against Aristotle on the Eternity of the World*, trans. C. Wildberg, London: Duckworth.

Secondary sources

Sorabji, R. R. K., ed. (1987), *Philoponus and the Rejection of Aristotelian Science*, London: Duckworth.

Verbeke, G., ed. (1966), *Jean Philopon, Commentaire sur le de anima d'Aristote, traduction de Guillaume de Moerbek*, Corpus Latinum commentariorum in Aristotelem Graecorum III, Paris: Éditions Béatrice-Nauwelaerts.

Verrycken, K. (1990), "The development of Philoponus' thought and its chronology," in R. R. K. Sorabji, ed., *Aristotle Transformed* (pp. 233–74), London: Duckworth.

65

John of Reading

KIMBERLY GEORGEDES

John of Reading (b. ca. 1285; d. 1346), an English Franciscan theologian at Oxford, lectured on the *Sentences* as a bachelor prior to 1320, and became the university's forty-fifth regent master about 1320/1. In 1322 he became master of theology at the Franciscan *studium* in Avignon, where he also advised John XXII on theological issues. He apparently never returned to England prior to his death at Avignon. His *Sentences* commentary was only partially revised before his death, and survives complete in only one manuscript: Florence B. N. conv. soppr. D. IV. 95.

Reading was an early disciple of JOHN DUNS SCOTUS at Oxford. He was also the first theologian to challenge WILLIAM OF OCKHAM'S and PETER AURIOL'S new epistemology. Reading lectured on the *Sentences* at Oxford prior to Ockham, who cited him in his own lectures on the *Sentences*. That Ockham was in turn cited by Reading in the revision of his commentary indicates that he took into account the views of Ockham and other younger contemporaries as he became aware of them (Tachau 1988, pp. 166–7).

Reading is essentially Scotistic in epistemology and maintains that intuitive and abstractive cognition are two distinct modes of cognition. He argues that intuitive cognition is not necessarily causally or temporally prior to abstractive cognition. He opposes Scotus in arguing that one need not posit an intellectual counterpart to sensitive intuitive cognition in this life. He follows Scotus, however, in defending the necessity of *species in medio*, and the species derived from them in the senses and intellect. He steadfastly defended this against Ockham, arguing that Ockham fails to demonstrate his claim about species and that the intellectual intuitive cognition posited by Ockham is superfluous (Tachau 1988, pp. 166–79).

Reading appears to agree with Ockham on the possibility of the intuition of a nonexistent, and argues that this leads to skepticism because existential certitude is in no way the basis for scientific knowledge. Both also agree on the fact that this is a supernatural possibility, although Reading also allows for it to be a natural occurrence based on optical experience (Tachau 1988, pp. 169–72).

Despite the superficial agreements, there are some significant differences between Reading and Ockham. Exploring Reading's work further will enhance our knowledge of the relationship between Scotism and Ockhamism in the fourteenth century.

Bibliography

Primary sources
(1966), *Super Sententias*, Prologue, q. 2, in Stephen Brown, "Sources for Ockham's Prologue to the *Sentences*," *Franciscan Studies* 25, pp. 36–65.

(1969), *Super Sententias* I, 4, 3, q. 3, in Gedeon Gál, "Quaestio Ioannis de Reading de necessitate specierum intelligibilium defensio doctrinae Scoti," *Franciscan Studies* 29, pp. 191–212.

(1981), *Super Sententias* I, 2, qq. 2 and 3, in Girard Etzkorn, "John Reading on the existence and unicity of God, efficient and final causality," *Franciscan Studies* 41, pp. 110–221.

Secondary sources

Brown, Stephen and Gál, G. (1970), "Introduction," in S. Brown and G. Gál, eds., *Ockham, Scriptum in Librum Primum Sententiarum Ordinatio*, in *Opera theologica*, vol. II (pp. 18*–34*), St. Bonaventure, NY: St. Bonaventure University Press.

Etzkorn, Girard (1977), "Introduction," in Girard Etzkorn, ed., *Ockham, Scriptum in Librum Primum Sententiarum Ordinatio* (*OTh* III) (pp. 16*–18*), St. Bonaventure, NY: St. Bonaventure University Press.

Gál, Gedeon, OFM (1969), "Quaestio Ioannis de Reading de necessitate specierum intelligibilium defensio doctrinae Scoti," *Franciscan Studies* 29, pp. 66–156.

Longpré, E. (1924), "Jean de Reading et le B. Jean Duns Scot," *La France Franciscaine* 7, pp. 99–109.

Tachau, Katherine H. (1988), *Vision and Certitude in the Age of Ockham: Optics, Epistemology, and the Foundations of Semantics, 1250–1345*, Leiden: Brill.

66

John of Salisbury

C. H. KNEEPKENS

John of Salisbury (b. 1115/20; d. 1180) was born in Old Sarum (near the present Salisbury, Wiltshire), and died at Chartres. In 1136 John traveled to Paris to pursue his studies at the Mont-Saint-Geneviève. He stayed for about twelve years at Paris and probably at Chartres, where he studied under the most prominent scholars of his time, among whom were thinkers such as PETER ABELARD, Alberic of Paris, Robert of Melun, William of Conches, Thierry of Chartres, GILBERT OF POITIERS, Robert Pullen, and PETER HELIAS. From 1141 to 1148 he gave private instruction. John spent several years of the period between 1148 and 1162 in the service of the Archbishop of Canterbury. During 1163–70 he was in exile in France because of the conflict in England between Archbishop Thomas Becket, whose secretary he was, and King Henry II. He stayed at Reims in the abbey of St. Rémi, where his friend, Peter of Celle, was the abbot. Although he hoped to return to England, he remained loyal to the archbishop and was one of his important advisers. In 1170 he was back at Canterbury, where he stayed until 1176. After the murder of Becket, he stayed in England at several locations. On August 15 of 1176 he was consecrated Bishop of Chartres. His works comprise the *Entheticus*, the *Policraticus*, the *Metalogicon*, the *Historia Pontificalis*, a collection of letters, and two short hagiographical works.

John's works are marked by his acquaintance with the Holy Scripture and ancient and early Christian authors, although several of the ancient writings to which he refers were only known to him through the medieval collections of sayings known as *florilegia*. They display a thorough sense of scholarship, a gentle humanity and deeply rooted feeling for moderation, and a moral engagement. Above all he proved himself to be an independent thinker in politics. His oldest work is the *Entheticus de dogmate philosophorum*, a didactic poem consisting of 926 elegiac disticha. This was written between 1154 and 1162, and contrary to what used to be believed, it is now generally accepted that it was conceived as an independent work. Although the meaning of its title is not clear, this work is primarily concerned with the nature of true wisdom and ideal philosophy, which for John should be rooted in classical authors and the Bible. It discusses three main themes. The first is the contempt for a superficial instruction and the importance of a thorough education based on a solid program of study in pursuit of true, i.e., Christian, philosophy and wisdom. This is in fact the central motif underlying the whole poem.

The second section deals with ancient philosophical schools (Stoicism, Epicureanism, the Peripatetics, and Academics) and what John considered to be the leading philosophers of antiquity (i.e., Pythagoras, Socrates, Plato, Aristotle, and Cicero) and their main doctrines, paying especial attention to their epistemological, cosmological, and ethical views.

John's deep affinity with the Chartrian Neoplatonic tradition is particularly felt in his discussion of Plato, to whom he had access only through a few sources such as the incomplete translation of, and commentary on, Plato's *Timaeus* by Calcidius, Macrobius' commentary on the Dream of Scipio, AUGUSTINE, and BOETHIUS. Aristotle is regarded as the pre-eminent logician, for John was one of the first twelfth-century thinkers who had the complete *Organon* at his disposal. Nonetheless, among pagan philosophers Plato is given first place. John ends with the thesis that without faith reason will fail: he is only truly wise and a true philosopher who, guided by the Holy Scriptures, leads an active Christian life.

The third section of the work discusses true favor (*gratia*), faith (*fides*), and good morals (*boni mores*), and the negative consequences for society when the king, his court, the judges, and the ecclesiastical dignitaries (of Canterbury) do not care about these three. The poem ends with a praise of the true wisdom and love that should be the goal of the Christian philosopher.

The *Policraticus sive De nugis curialium et vestigiis philosophorum* was completed in September 1159, and there has been a lengthy debate about the meaning of the title, which may mean "of many forms of government" or "the book that masters many (philosophical) authors." This is a prose work in eight books concerned with applied political and social philosophy, and dedicated to Thomas Becket. It offers a synthesis of the classical tradition and contemporary ideas on social philosophy, and social criticism in a Christian setting. The question of its relation to the so-called *Institutio Traiani*, mentioned by John as his source for books five and six and attributed by him to Plutarch, has not yet completely been settled. In all probability, the *Policraticus* was the most influential of all his writings during the Middle Ages. John's aim in it is to show that the court of any Christian ruler, be it ecclesiastical or secular, must be dominated by true philosophy and wisdom in order to create for every member of the state a good and happy life on earth as a preamble to eternal beatitude. His view of the state and society was highly influenced by Chartrian Neoplatonism's generally accepted principle that art imitates nature: the macrocosm is the model for the state, which, in turn, with constitutional law, belongs to the domain of positive, and not natural law, and is, therefore, a human artifact. John saw the state as an organism, a public cosmos, with the king or prince at its head, and he added a fourth category to the traditional Platonic view of the state and its three classes, namely, the peasants and craftsmen. Another important addition to the traditional view is that, according to John, each social class had its own duties and receives the conditions to fulfill its task from the other classes. Although as a twelfth-century thinker, John looked at society from one all-embracing Christian perspective, he accepted a clear distinction between the secular and ecclesiastical domains and between the responsibilities of their respective dignitaries. The king is ultimately responsible for the *bonum commune*, and so he has the central and main position in the state. It is his duty to preserve the physical and spiritual security of his subjects, and while ruling them he has to exercise moderation. The good king voluntarily submits to the King of kings, and by doing this he becomes his representative on earth. The tyrant, however, displays the behavior of Satan: his only motive is to obtain the first and best place for himself. John warns princes that the inhabitants of the state have the right, even the duty, to protect themselves against such a bad ruler.

In composing the *Policraticus*, John made extensive use of the method of *exempla*. Consequently, notwithstanding the fact that the work has a coherent, well-thought-out structure at a deeper level, it makes, at first sight, a muddled impression, especially since these examples have been derived from various sources, such as Holy Scripture and several ancient and early Christian authors. However, these examples are an integral part, together with

393

rational argumentation, of John's demonstrative strategy. They are not used merely as illustrative stories. The persons and events presented are stripped of the temporal particularities surrounding them, and are presented as timeless models, which serve to create and develop knowledge for the reader.

In most manuscripts, the *Policraticus* is preceded by a poem called the *Entheticus minor*. It consists of 153 elegiac disticha (306 lines), and is written in a style that is considered more refined and polished than that of the *Entheticus maior*. This is generally accepted to be the preface to the *Policraticus*, and it is divided into two main parts. The first, covering lines 1–156, describes the journey to the chancellor, who is the addressee of the *Policraticus*, and an exchange with him; the second, which consists of lines 157–304, starts with a *laudatio* of Canterbury as a religious center and prays for the return from France of Becket, advising him how to behave prudently and what kind of people he should avoid meeting.

In October of the same year John published the *Metalogicon*, a defense of logic as a fundamental part of any philosophy instruction. This work, divided into four books, shows John's thorough knowledge and love of logic when this is understood broadly. For him, the liberal arts are restricted to the *trivium*, which obtain a central position in his educational program. Book 1 has an introductory character and also deals with the role of grammar in the curriculum. John starts with what, in all probability, was usual during that period, namely, an attack on superficial and hasty instruction. His adversary is the still elusive Cornificius. John points to the importance of the liberal arts in general for a thorough education, and insists on the basic role of logic, taken broadly as the art of speaking and arguing well, in education. Although grammar and poetics are artificial and therefore not the same for all people, they are considered to play a preparatory, but essential role in all serious instruction. Their respective tasks are discussed and he emphasizes that they are necessary for correct speech, which, in turn, is indispensable for the good practice of philosophy and a virtuous life. This book contains the famous paragraph about the teaching method of BERNARD OF CHARTRES (bk. 1, ch. 24).

Book 2 consists of a general introduction to logic understood in a strict sense (*dialectica*). The importance of dialectic as a method is shown: it is the discipline that teaches how to avoid unskilled argumentation. Furthermore, its place among the sciences is elucidated. Some central notions, such as the dialectical proposition, are discussed, and various positions concerning universals are presented, and their authors identified, in a section that is of paramount importance for our knowledge of the development of logic in the first part of the twelfth century. This discussion enables us to discern the main lines of the views on this topic at the time and to connect the names of particular thinkers to particular views: the "vocalists," for whom universals are *voces* (Roscellinus), the "sermocinales," for whom they are *sermones* (Abelard), and so on, including several realist positions. (In an abbreviated form, the same material is found in the *Policraticus*.)

Books 3 and chs. 1–23 of book 4 constitute a kind of aid to the study of the Organon, and testify to the fact that John had the complete logical works of Aristotle at his disposal. Book 4, chs. 24–9 demonstrate how to teach, use, and interpret generally the works of the Organon, while the remaining chapters (30–42) are taken up by a discussion of the nature of truth and reason.

The *Historia Pontificalis* describes a part of the ecclesiastical history of western Europe from 1148 to 1152, when John was in close contact with the papal court. It has been preserved in only one manuscript and is incomplete. It deals mainly with the Second Crusade, and the confused political situation of Europe as a result of its disastrous outcome. Although this work has a restricted scope and is not comprehensive, it presents often a fresh and valuable insight into contemporary events. For the trial of Gilbert of Poitiers in 1148, for example, John appears to be our only objective source.

John's *Letters* comprise 325 items, which fall into two parts. The first (1–135) covers the letters written during the time John was a secretary at the archiepiscopal court of Theobald at Canterbury, and most of these letters were written in the archbishop's name. The other part is of utmost importance to the Becket dossier, but contains also interesting and even unique information about other contemporary events. John's correspondence is a fine testimony to John's use of biblical and classical texts, his mastery of the Latin language, and his clear and elegant style, and it displays his ability as a adviser in political affairs.

John's hagiographical writings are only of minor interest. He composed a *Life of St. Anselm* in 1163 in support of his canonization, but this is in fact nothing more than an abbreviation of the work by Eadmer. Shortly after Becket's canonization in 1173, John also wrote the short *Vita et passio Sancti Thomae Martyris*.

Bibliography

Primary sources

(1855), *Vita beati Anselmi*, in J.-P. Migne, ed., *Patrologia Latina*, vol. 199 (col. 1009–40), Paris: Vivès.

(1875–85), *Vita beati Thomae*, in James Craigie Robertson, ed., *Materials for the History of Thomas Becket, Archbishop of Canterbury (canonized by Pope Alexander III, AD 1173)*, 7 vols. (see 1876, vol. II, pp. 301–22), London: Longman.

(1909, 1978), *Policraticus sive De nugis curialium et vestigiis philosophorum libri III*, ed. Clement Charles Julian Webb, Oxford: Clarendon Press.

(1938, 1972), *Frivolities of Courtiers and Footprints of Philosophers. Being a translation of the first, second, and third books and selections from the seventh and eighth books of the Policraticus of John of Salisbury*, trans. Joseph B. Pike, Minneapolis: University of Minnesota Press; New York: Octagon Books.

(1955, 1979), *Letters*, ed. and trans. W. J. Millor and Christopher N. L. Brooke (vol. 1: *The Early Letters*; vol. 2: *The Later Letters*), Oxford: Oxford University Press.

(1956), *Historia Pontificalis: Memoirs of the Papal Court*, trans. with intro. and notes by Marjorie Chibnall, London: Nelson (repr. 1986, Oxford: Oxford University Press).

(1987), *Entheticus maior and minor*, 3 vols., ed., with trans. and notes by Jan van Laarhoven, Leiden: Brill.

(1990), *Policraticus*, trans. Cary J. Nederman, New York: Cambridge University Press; repr. 1995.

(1991), *Metalogicon*, ed. John Barrie Hall and K. S. B. Keats-Rohan, Turnhout: Brepols.

(1993), *Policraticus*, ed. K. S. B. Keats-Rohan, Turnhout: Brepols.

Secondary sources

Brooke, Christopher (1984), "John of Salisbury and his world," in Michael Wilks, ed., *The World of John Salisbury* (pp. 1–20), Oxford: Published for the Ecclesiastical History Society by Blackwell.

Chibnall, Marjorie (1984), "John of Salisbury as historian," in Michael Wilks, ed., *The World of John Salisbury* (pp. 169–77), Oxford: Published for the Ecclesiastical History Society by Blackwell.

Guth, Klaus (1978), *Johannes von Salisbury (1115/20–1180): Studien zur Kirchen-, Kultur- und Sozialgeschichte Westeuropas im 12. Jahrhundert*, St. Ottilien: Eos-Verlag.

Jeauneau, Edouard (1984), "Jean de Salisbury et la lecture des philosophes," in Michael Wilks, ed., *The World of John Salisbury* (pp. 77–108), Oxford: Published for the Ecclesiastical History Society by Blackwell.

Kerner, Max (1977), *Johannes von Salisbury und die logische Struktur seines Policraticus*, Wiesbaden: Steiner.

Laarhoven, Jan van (1994), "Titles and subtitles of the *Policraticus*: a proposal," *Vivarium* 32, pp. 131–60.

Liebeschütz, Hans (1950), *Mediaeval Humanism in the Life and Writings of John of Salisbury*, London: University of London.

Luscombe, David (1984), "John of Salisbury in recent scholarship," in Michael Wilks, ed., *The World of John Salisbury* (pp. 21–37), Oxford: Published for the Ecclesiastical History Society by Blackwell.

Martin, Janet (1984), "John of Salisbury as classical scholar," in Michael Wilks, ed., *The World of John Salisbury* (pp. 179–201), Oxford: Published for the Ecclesiastical History Society by Blackwell.

Moos, Peter von (1984), "The use of exempla in the *Policraticus* of John of Salisbury," in Michael Wilks, ed., *The World of John Salisbury*, Oxford: Published for the Ecclesiastical History Society by Blackwell.

——(1988), *Geschichte als Topik: das rhetorische Exemplum von der Antike zur Neuzeit und die historiae im "Policraticus" Johanns von Salisbury*, Hildesheim and New York: G. Olms.

Nederman, Cary J. (1989), "Knowledge, virtue and the path to wisdom: the unexamined Aristotelism of John of Salisbury's *Metalogicon*," *Mediaeval Studies* 51, pp. 268–86.

Struve, Tilman (1984), "The importance of the organism in the political theory of John of Salisbury," in Michael Wilks, ed., *The World of John Salisbury* (pp. 303–17), Oxford: Published for the Ecclesiastical History Society by Blackwell.

Webb, Clemens Charles Julian (1971), *John of Salisbury*, New York: Russell & Russell (repr. of 1932 edn.).

Wilks, Michael, ed. (1984), *The World of John Salisbury*, Oxford: Published for the Ecclesiastical History Society by Blackwell.

67

John Scotus Eriugena

CARLOS STEEL AND D. W. HADLEY

John the Scot (b. ca. 800; d. ca. 877), the "Irishman" (or Eriugena – "of Irish birth" – as he liked to call himself), is one of those many scholars who migrated from Ireland to the European continent during the Carolingian period. He is first mentioned in a document around 850 concerning the predestination controversy, initiated by the monk Godescalc with his claim that all human beings are eternally predestined to either eternal life or damnation. Hincmar, the powerful Archbishop of Reims at the time, asked the scholar who "resided at the palace" of Charles the Bald to write a refutation of this heretical doctrine. The treatise that followed, *De divina praedestinatione*, is not the usual theological controversial work with quotations from traditional authorities; rather it attempts to show that the doctrine of double predestination is "not acceptable to reason." Even the notion of "predestination" is only understandable when taken in a metaphorical sense, for we should not attribute to God any pre-knowledge or pre-destination because these involve temporality. Requested as a refutation of a heresy, this work immediately provoked indignation in the ecclesiastical milieu; it was even condemned, as people were scandalized by the endeavor to answer a theological question using "principles of dialectical reasoning," whereby "true philosophy and true religion are identical."

In Eriugena's opinion, all theological errors come "from ignorance of the liberal arts, which have been established by the divine Wisdom as its companions and investigators." The study of the liberal arts was indeed in Carolingian culture the foundation of all education, and Eriugena himself probably started his career as a teacher of the arts at the palace. However, it was his intensive contact with the Greek theological tradition that opened his mind to an entirely different world than the one he knew through his Latin authorities (mainly AUGUSTINE). At the request of the king – John remained in royal favor throughout his career – he made a complete translation of the works of Dionysius the Areopagite (followed later by a commentary on PSEUDO-DIONYSIUS' *The Celestial Hierarchy*). This translation, an extraordinary philological accomplishment, would serve for centuries as the standard version of Dionysian writings in the West and the main channel for the spread of its Neoplatonic theology. It also had a profound impact on John himself: he was to become deeply influenced by Dionysius' Neoplatonic understanding of God and creation.

Eriugena also translated two works of MAXIMUS CONFESSOR (d. 662), the first great commentator on Dionysius, and an important treatise on human nature by Gregory of Nyssa, *De imagine*. Such close contact with these great Greek speculative minds liberated Eriugena from a too literal interpretation of Christian doctrine and further compelled him to explore it more deeply. Having been nourished from the best sources of both the Latin and the Greek traditions, Eriugena then began composing his own theo-philosophical synthesis, the *Periphyseon*. He also wrote a thoughtful commentary on the Gospel by the most speculative of all Apostolic writers, St. John.

After 870, nothing of historical certainty is known of Eriugena, although William of Malmesbury states that he relocated to England because of suspicions raised by his original work.

Periphyseon

The *Periphyseon* is undoubtedly Eriugena's masterpiece. He labored on it for many years, making substantial additions and corrections to an earlier version, as we see from the manuscript tradition. In the oldest manuscripts (Bamberg phil. 2/1 and Reims 875) of the ninth century, we find many corrections and additions in the text which are due to two different Irish hands. It is now generally accepted that the first hand is Eriugena's own writing, the second his secretary's. Those corrections were integrated into the later copies of the text, while new additions were made by a later reader. The Greek title, *Periphyseon* (On natures), invented by the author himself, reminds us of the long tradition of treatises "On nature" beginning as far back as the pre-Socratics. Nature here stands for the whole universe, encompassing both being and non-being, and in this work Eriugena examines its "divisions," that is, its articulation into a manifold of species from the most general to the most particular, and its "unification" from the utmost manifold to absolute simplicity. The work is written in the literary form of a dialogue between Master and Disciple, wherein the latter plays an active intellectual role. Notably, it is not solely a speculative but also a beautiful literary work. Nor is it simply a speculative work of philosophical dialectic; it is also a work of Christian hermeneutics, being an attempt to understand the meaning of the truth as revealed in Sacred Scripture. The pertinent text of Scripture is Genesis 1–3, which gives the account of the creation of the world, culminating in the creation of humanity in the image of God, the description of paradise, and the narrative of the fall. The *Periphyseon* stands in the tradition of the many Patristic works commenting on the six days of creation (the "hexaemeron"). Through his commentary upon the biblical text, Eriugena develops a cosmology, anthropology, and doctrine on the origin of evil.

Already Plato (see *Phaedrus* 265d) had identified division and collection as the two main procedures of dialectics: "to bring a dispersed plurality under a single form . . . to divide into forms following the natural articulation." In the Neoplatonic tradition these procedures are no longer understood as merely logical, but as the very movements of reality in its procession from the One to multiplicity and in its return into unity. Hence, dialectics is not just a human invention but rather the movement of nature itself in its division and unification; or, in Christian terms, its creation and redemption. Eriugena excellently formulates this Neoplatonic view, which underlies his whole system of thought, in the prologue of his translation of Maximus's *Ambigua*:

> What is meant by procession is the multiplication of the Divine Goodness into all things that are, descending from the highest to the lowest, first through the general essence of all things, then through the most universal genera, then through the less universal . . . to the most particularized; and then this same Divine Goodness returns by gathering itself together from the infinitely varied multiplicity of the things that are, through the same stages to that most unified unity of all things which is God.

This is precisely the task of a dialectical understanding of nature: to grasp both the division of nature and its recollection into unity, that is, to consider nature both in its procession from, and in its return to, the uncreated divine nature, which is its origin and end.

At the beginning of the *Periphyseon*, John introduces his famous fourfold division of nature, which will provide the main structure for the entire discussion. Applying the dialectical method of dividing a genus into species by differences, the Master comes up with a division that can be applied to the whole universe, or Nature. The most fundamental difference we can introduce in Nature is that between "creating" and "being created," both of which can be taken positively and negatively. Applying these four differences we discover the four fundamental species of Nature: that which creates and is not created; that which is created and creates; that which is created and does not create; that which is not created and does not create. The first species is God, the uncaused cause of everything. Its *opposite* species (that which is created and does not create) stands for the sensible world, comprehending the numerous sub-species of animals and plants that come to be through creation in times and places. Now, in the Christian tradition most authors have considered only these two species, which are absolutely distinguished, thus understanding the universe through their opposition, that is, through the opposition of the creator and the creation. Not so Eriugena. The most original feature of his thought is his demonstration that the distinction between the creative and created nature can never be absolute. To begin with, the creation could never exist in itself; it is but a participation in (or, a manifestation of) the divine nature. Further, there is a species of Nature (the second from above) that has the attributes of both: it is both created and creative. This is the level of the primordial ideas wherein God has from all eternity produced the world in its most general ideal structure (before it is manifested in time and place and individualized in matter). Those ideas are not only the objects of God's thought but also produced by him in his Word, although, as such, they cannot be identical with him (who is in his absolute nature beyond all forms of being). Finally, there is the fourth nature, which seems to be "impossible," for what neither creates nor is created logically cannot be. Yet, as the Master explains, this species must be understood again as God, for only the divine nature can be properly called uncreated. We must consider God, then, not only as the cause or origin from which all things proceed through creation, but also as the end of all things which seek him for their eternal and immutable rest:

> For the reason why the Cause of all things is said to create is that it is from it that the universe of those things which have been created after it and by it proceeds through a wonderful and divine multiplication into genera and species and individuals, and into the differentiations and all the other features which are observed in created nature: but because it is to the same cause that all things that proceed from it shall return, when they reach their end, it is therefore called the end of all things and is said neither to create nor to be created. (*Periphyseon* II, 526C–D)

Eriugena's understanding of procession and return as the fundamental motions of all reality is indebted to the Neoplatonic tradition with which he became acquainted through Dionysius and Maximus. In his *Elements of Theology*, Proclus thus formulates the fundamental principle of "the cyclical activity" of all beings: "all that proceeds from something, returns by nature to that from which it derived its existence" (*El. Theol.* prop. 33–4). It should be noted that, for Proclus, this cyclical process has no temporal meaning. In all eternity, everything comes from the One and returns to it. Time is a process limited to the sensible world, though even that world as a whole has no origin in time and will not cease to be. When, however, Christian thinkers adopted Neoplatonic metaphysics, they tended to interpret this cyclical process in an historico-temporal sense. Thus Eriugena understands the procession of all things as the creation of the world, which sets the beginning of time; further, he views the return as not just a metaphysical reversion of all things to the origin of their being, but also as an eschatological process, which will happen at the "end of times" and lead to the suppression of space and time and, indeed, the whole sensible universe. Eventually, then, the entire created nature will no longer exist as distinguished from uncreated nature, for what will God create when everything returns to Him?

In the original planning of the *Periphyseon*, four books were projected, each corresponding to one of Nature's four divisions. However, because of its many digressions and recapitulations, a fifth book was added to discuss the return of all things into God, a subject left unfinished in the fourth book.

God and the primordial causes

The *Periphyseon*'s initial description of God is as "the uncreated creating nature." Of the four major divisions of reality, the divine nature stands first within the whole of Nature. In absence of this divine maker, nothing else exists, for God is "inseparable from every universe that He has created" (III, 621B). Yet God is not simply one species among many, because as the "principal cause," which brings forth out of nothing the diverse orders of being, he transcends all beings. Properly speaking, then, Eriugena's God is *anarchos*, without beginning, and "transcends everything that is or can be" (III, 620D). Because of this transcendence, the divine cause is "more obscure than the others"; indeed, "that Nature . . . can neither be spoken of nor understood" (I, 463A–B). Hence, John urges, one should either treat divinity with respectful silence or speak only in the manner appropriate to divinity. He explains this manner by first drawing upon the Dionysian distinction between cataphatic (or affirmative) and apophatic (or negative) theology. The former makes affirmations concerning God, transferring to the creator the meaning of all created things, whether "Truth, Goodness, Essence, Light, Justice, Sun, Star, Spirit, Water, Lion" or things contrary to nature, such as "being drunken . . . foolish . . . mad" (I, 458B). The latter denies that any of these affirmations can properly define God, thereby preserving his incomprehensible "nature." Eriugena further emphasizes this ineffability by systematically reviewing the ten Aristotelian categories, showing that their capacity to describe natures is "wholly extinguished" in respect to the Divine Essence, for this is neither "genus nor species nor accident" (I, 463C).

In his recognition of the transcendent unknowability of God, Eriugena is consciously following earlier Christian philosophers. He follows the tradition still further by emphasizing that, even those affirmations that seem most properly predicated of God (e.g., Essence, Goodness, Truth), are in fact only metaphorical. The symbolic language used by biblical authors – e.g., 'I saw the Lord sitting' (I, 446D) – is one example of what must be taken metaphorically. But John borrows even more from Dionysius in his explanation of the nature of the "super-affirmative" names of God. He advises that one might consider "more than goodness" or "super-essential" to be proper names for God, given that they follow from apophatic revisions of cataphatic statements. But it is not so: such "more than" or "super-" statements combine a negation and an affirmation, and thereby incorporate both of these distinct branches of theology; for instance, 'God is essence', followed (appropriately) by 'God is not essence', becomes 'God is super-essential'. While such propositions are rightly seen as overcomings of any supposed opposition of cataphatic and apophatic theology, what is signified by the 'more than' is simply the meaning of a prior negation and affirmation. In this way, such terms preserve inviolable the incomprehensible character of divinity even while acknowledging the metaphorically transferable meanings of all creatures to their creator. From this unification of the two ways of speaking about the ineffable follows Eriugena's ultimate name of God as 'He is He Who is More-than-being' (I, 487B).

The metaphorical connection between created being and the uncreated Creator indicates that John's four divisions of Nature are more closely bound than the introduction of the *Periphyseon* first suggests. In fact, John goes on explicitly to identify "Nature" and "God," and he just as explicitly describes all four divisions of Nature as modes of the circular process of the divinity proceeding from and returning to itself. More particularly, the second division of Nature – *creata et creans* – emerges as another appearance of the Creator. This second species of Nature is created in the uncreated Word, wherein God, who is to himself unknown, eternally expresses himself in thinking. This eternal Word, which resembles the Plotinian *nous*, is properly the creating "Artificer" of the world. Eriugena locates in it an array of active exemplars – the *primordiales causae* – standing above all particulars in the sensible realm. Serving as the ontological grounds for these particulars, they enable creatures to be precisely what they are as existents. Even further, these causes are the sole true beings: they exist most fully because the understanding of all things, Eriugena argues, is all things in their fullness. From this metaphysical vantage point, one will not be surprised by his description of real humanity as intellectual: "the substance of the whole man [is] nothing else but the concept of him in the Mind of his Artificer" (IV, 768B). Consequently the world of effects, as we ordinarily say, must be seen solely as existing in the "world of ideas," for the former is ontologically derivative of the latter. This view raises the question whether the former actually exists as a separate creation – and how.

God and the world: theophany

Eriugena answers the question of the created nature's being through his arresting view that in creating the world God in fact creates himself. His position is best understood by beginning with the fact that this sensible world exists only through participation in the Divine Nature and the primordial causes wherein the Divine Nature expresses itself. That is, for Eriugena, corporeal things have no proper subsistence on their own, and exist only as compounds derived from intelligible principles, their true substance being an eternal idea in the mind of the Creator. He directly states that "there is no visible or corporeal thing which is not the symbol of something incorporeal and intelligible" (V, 866A).

For God to create means, then, that he provides being not solely at some primordial beginning point, but in an ongoing eternal giving that becomes here and now dynamically active: God, as creator, now serves as the ontological constituent of all, and nothing, whether sensible or intellectual, can be said to exist apart from divinity. Thus, to be, for a creature, is to be a participant in the divine being, and God is in the world, then, "so far as it is understood to have being" (III, 679A). From this position follow Eriugena's many stunning statements that God is the essence of each being; that all things exist only within him; that God and creatures are "one and the same" (III, 678C); that "He alone is everything that in existing things is said to be" (I, 518B). For, at every stage of his discussion of God and the world, Eriugena affirms in no uncertain terms that *to be is to be theophany*, that is, a "God-showing." The ontological activity of divinity in its creative relation to the world demands that to exist

401

as a creature means to exist as a manifestation: "everything that is understood and sensed is nothing else but the apparition of what is not apparent, the manifestation of the hidden . . . the comprehension of the incomprehensible . . . the materialization of the spiritual, the visibility of the invisible" (III, 633A).

Beginning from the Creator rather than the creature, Eriugena puts this same point in the arresting way noted above: God's creation of the world is God's creation of himself. That is to say, God himself is created in the coming to be of the world. Hence, to see the world as it is, is to see it as the self-revelation and self-making of that which before creation lay hidden, unknown, nonexistent. In light of the panoramic display of beauty, order, and life which is created reality, this hidden and Divine Essence beyond essence has itself become created and particular, visible and knowable. The infinite has made itself finite: "that Nature . . . is in an admirable manner created in all things which take their being from it" (I, 454C), even while through this self-making all else comes: "God is everything that truly exists because He Himself makes all things and is made in all things" (III, 633A). This doctrine of the self-creation of God, though intimated in some Greek Christian thinkers (e.g., Maximus), is Eriugena's most provocative speculative thought.

"Man: how great a thing and great a name, the image of divine nature" (V, 821C)

In the circle of emanation (through multiplication) and return (through unification) the human being occupies a central place. Indeed, John finds that, in creating human nature as a rational animal, God created the whole universe. Man is the "container," the "workplace," the connecting intermediary (*medietas*) of the whole universe preventing its falling into separate sensible and intelligible realms. For human nature comprehends body, vital powers, sensitivity, imagination, reason, intellect: "In it all creatures visible and invisible, the whole spread of creation, is understood to inhere" (IV, 763D). For this reason the human creation is introduced at the end of the *hexaemeron*, on the sixth day. It serves as the culmination of the creation of the whole universe, for while man is created in the genus "animal," he is not as a species encompassed by this genus but still transcends it, insofar as he is an intellectual being. "Man is an animal . . . man is not an animal": that we can make such contradictory statements is no surprise, since in this respect humankind resembles the Divine Nature in whose image it was made. Of God, too, we can (and must) make both affirmations and negations.

Human beings stand above even the angels because only they have been made as the "image of God." With Gregory of Nyssa, Eriugena locates this image particularly in the ability to transcend all that is animal, that is, man's intellectual nature. Man resembles the divine nature in all respects but one: in being created. Thus he has, just like God (though in a created manner), omnipotence and omniscience, which fact Eriugena demonstrates through a most original analysis of the creative role played by human knowledge in the constitution of the world, imitating and continuing on an inferior level, that of the effects (the third species of nature), the divine creation: "Just as the Creative Wisdom . . . beholds all the things which are made in it before they are made, and that very contemplation of the things to be made is their true and eternal immutable essence, so the created wisdom, which is the human nature, knows all things which are made in it before they are made and that very knowledge is their true and indestructible essence" (IV, 778D). Like the Divine Mind, the human mind is prior to all the things known; therefore, the human soul resembles its

Divine Creator in its eternal a priori knowledge, found in itself, of all things created. There remains this difference: all things exist as primordial causes or substantial forms in the divine understanding but as effects in human knowledge. Yet, when the human soul circles around God, it produces in itself the reasons by which "it knows and creates (*praecognoscit et prae-creat*) in advance" all things (II, 577B). As God is more than the ideas wherein he manifests himself, ever remaining in his absolute incomprehensibility, so is man. He never understands what he really is, but only knows with certainty "that he exists." In fact, true human nature is an eternal essence known only to God.

Through the Fall, however, this connatural knowledge has been lost and the soul has fallen into ignorance of itself and of the riches it contains. Humanity turned away from the Creator, dishonoring its natural dignity and making itself similar to the beasts: now we not only suffer hunger, disease, pain, decay, but also copulate and propagate sexually in a bestial manner. This animality, argues Eriugena, does not belong to the image of God, for in his original plan God had wanted to create humans similar to angels without needing for their multiplication a sexual behavior akin to that of irrational beasts. Furthermore, God originally created humanity as sexless, not divided into male and female. It is in this sexless state that man will rise again at the resurrection, "for man is more than sex" (II, 534A). But because God had foreseen from all eternity that humans would abuse their freedom and sin, and thus fall from the status of equality with the angels to the level of the beasts, he modified his original plan and introduced in the creation of human beings the consequences of sin before it occurred. In this, God is like a masterful engineer who, foreseeing possible problems and failures with his design, builds remedies into his system in advance. Thus, the sexualized animal body of man (involving all its pain and passion, sickness, and corruption) was created together with his original rational nature, though remaining external to his true essence, a *superadiectum* added as a remedy and a penance for sin. Eriugena stresses that this additional nature is also God's own creation, however, and must not be condemned (as the Manichees erred in doing).

This last consideration guides John's interpretation of the larger story of paradise, his discussion of the tree of knowledge, the sleep of Adam, and of course the division of the sexes by the creation of Eve. The division of the sexes is seen as the corporeal manifestation of the divorce in the sinner, man, between the intellect and the senses. It will be overcome when, at the resurrection, all shall rise in a perfect, sexless, spiritual body. Because by creating man God created the whole universe, it is fitting that return of all things also begins with the return of humanity in the resurrection.

Last things

A philosopher must not only explain, advises John, how creatures proceed from God through multiplication from the universal species into individuals, but also trace their return "by the same stages through which the division had previously ramified into multiplicity, until it arrives at that One which remains inseparably in itself and from which that division started" (II, 526A). The reason for this is that "the end of every movement is in its beginning: it is concluded in no other term but that origin out of which its movement began, and to which it ever seeks to return in order that therein it may cease and have rest" (V, 866C). Thus the fifth and final book of the *Periphyseon*, entirely devoted to the return of all things, begins with cosmological, biological, and logical examples demonstrating that movement from a beginning to an ending point is a universal law of Nature. For John, these mirror the metaphysical movements of created things from out of their ontological source back into it.

This cycle of procession and return can be interpreted strictly metaphysically: created things only exist insofar as they *simultaneously* proceed from their Divine Cause, remain in it, and revert upon it as their ultimate end. Return and procession will then both be seen as constitutive movements of being. The most common interpretation, however, locates the climax of the procession-return cycle in the historically future eschatological events described in, for example, the Book of Revelation. The procession that is the coming into being of the world is now seen as moving gradually back into divinity, away from the confusions of sensible experience, out of the dissipations of sin and of non-being, towards fuller unity, clarity, and joy in the Word of God.

Eriugena conceives of this return as taking place in stages. Following the writings of Maximus, he first distinguishes the movements, rendered possible by the Incarnation of Christ, of creatures into their spiritual causes: male and female shall be unified into sexless humanity; then, through the inclusion of all corporeality in the spiritualized human nature, the sensible earth will again be made one with paradise; then the earth and the heaven shall be unified, and the sensible shall no longer be distinguished from the intelligible, as all effects will have returned into their primordial causes and, finally, through their causes, into the Divine Nature. One should notice, however, that in this return the inferior levels do not cease to exist, but are "preserved in the better essence." Even in the ultimate transformation of all creation into God, ontological distinction will remain, as Eriugena illustrates with his favourite examples; as iron, when melted in the fire, seems to be converted into fire, so that it appears to be nothing but fire even as the substance of the metal is preserved; as air, when illuminated, seems to become entirely light and yet remains distinguishable as air (V, 879A–B).

Eriugena makes a clear distinction between the *general* return, which is the common, natural destination of the whole creation in its return to God, and the *special* return, which is the beatification (and deification) only granted to the angels and to blessed human beings. The general return is as it were implied in the natural process of *exitus* and *reditus*. But it is thanks to God's grace and human free will that some of those who return may be blessed with the richest self-disclosures of divinity. At the "end," all human beings, blessed and damned alike, will return to the perfection of the same human nature (including acquisition of a spiritual body). Yet they will be individually distinguished not by differences in nature, body, or place (even hell and heaven are no longer different "places"), but by a different access each shall be granted to God's deifying self-revelation. Those who led a righteous life will be allowed to eat from the Tree of Life and to see God in differing gradations of his theophanies. The damned, on the contrary, will be refused access to that Tree, and will be eternally tormented with the "empty dreams" (V, 945A) of those things which incited their desires while still living: their punishment is their incapacity to satisfy those desires after death. Thus, the righteous and wicked alike will be confronted by "appearances," "but those of the righteous will be the representations of divine contemplation" while the unrepentant "will be given over to phantasies of mortal things and manifold false appearances" (V, 945C, D). In this way, notes John, God shall punish in man what he has not created (i.e., the human vices) and, therefore, the created nature will be eternally perfect despite the fact that both the unrepentant and redeemed will have been enfolded back into divinity. It is this doctrine of the "special return" that makes it possible for Eriugena to preserve, within his speculations on the ultimate return of all things, the individual diversity of human persons. Though it is sometimes suggested that the return to God is nothing but a recapturing of an original lost state, Eriugena's emphasis on grace and the diversity of its gifts shows that the personal history, responsibility, and choices of each human being will be preserved. For all eternity, each of us will be what he made of his life. For, as Eriugena says, "one singular human being is more precious than the whole sensible universe" (IV, 784C).

Eriugena in his time and beyond

Eriugena is most certainly an original thinker, although this may be due more to his bold, new articulations of standing doctrines rather than to making new discoveries. His foremost achievement is found in the doctrine of the self-creation of God, which later attracted the admiration of idealist philosophers such as Schelling and Hegel. He defends what may be called a Platonic idealism wherein all reality is contained in the divine ideas rather than in sensible existence. Provocative also are his anthropological doctrines, which place man in the center of creation, his interpretation of the origin of the sexes, his views on the origin of evil, and his daring spiritualistic interpretation of the body's resurrection. Eriugena stands apart from all of his contemporaries in his confident declarations of the unity of true philosophy and true religion and the harmony of reason and authority.

Although his works have been continually read since their composition, Eriugena's general influence has been limited. He gained a number of admirers, especially in the twelfth century, but these Eriugenians of varying stripes found themselves at odds with church authorities, and in fact at this time the *Periphyseon* was condemned by papal bull (1225) and copies of it were burned. Subsequently, up until the nineteenth century and his rediscovery by German idealists, the influence of Eriugena's systematic thinking was minimal. His foremost influence on the later Middle Ages, then, derives from his translation work, as his translations of the Dionysian corpus provided the textual basis for the work of thirteenth-century philosophers, such as THOMAS AQUINAS, upon apophatic theology. Still, this influence was enhanced by Eriugena's own very Dionysian doctrines, especially in his understanding the "sensible world" as a self-revelation of God.

Though standing at the beginnings of medieval culture, Eriugena may be for many modern readers more stimulating than many acclaimed scholastic writers from the thirteenth to the fifteenth centuries. Though more well-known at present than Eriugena, and despite their many philosophical and theological accomplishments, these thinkers no longer enjoyed the freedom to engage in such daring speculations, nor demonstrated such persuasive and eloquent rhetoric, as we find abundantly in the writings of John Scotus Eriugena.

Bibliography

Primary sources

(1853), *Periphyseon*, in J.-P. Migne and H. J. Floss, eds., *Patrologia Latina*, vol. 122, Paris: Vivès.

(1969–72), *Homely and Commentary on St. John*, ed., with French trans., by E. Jeauneau, in *Sources Chrétiennes*, vols. 151 and 189, Paris: Éditions du Cerf.

(1978), *De divina praedestinatione*, ed. G. Madec, Corpus Christianorum continuatio mediaevalis 50, Turnhout: Brepols.

(1987), *Periphyseon*, trans. I. P. Sheldon-Williams and revised by J. J. O'Meara, Montreal: Bellarmin.

(1996–2000), *Periphyseon*, ed. Edouard Jeauneau, Corpus Christianorum continuatio mediaevalis 161–4, Turnhout: Brepols.

Secondary sources

Proceedings of the Society for Eriugenian Studies (starting with *The Mind of Eriugena* (Dublin, 1973) and continuing with a tenth forthcoming volume from Leuven University Press, *History and Eschatology in Eriugena and his Age*) contain contributions by leading scholars.

Brennan, M. (1989), *A Guide to Eriugenian Studies*, Fribourg, Switzerland: Editions Universitaires; Paris: Editions du Cerf. A supplement to this bibliography for the years 1987–96 and 1997–2000 has been compiled by G. van Riel, in the proceedings of two conferences in Leuven and in Maynooth of the Society for the Promotion of Eriugenian Studies.

Carabine, D. (2000), *John Scot Eriugena*, Oxford: Oxford University Press.

Moran, D. (1989), *The Philosophy of John Scottus Eriugena*, Cambridge: Cambridge University Press.

68

John Wyclif

JOHN D. KRONEN

John Wyclif (b. ca. 1320; d. 1384) was a late medieval philosopher, theologian, and proto-reformer of the Church. He took his doctorate in theology in 1372, eighteen years after he entered Oxford. After publishing his famous treatise on the Eucharist in 1380, Wyclif was condemned by a commission of the university, and ended his days at the rectory at Lutterworth. He was formally condemned as a heretic after his death by the Council of Constance (1415).

For his attacks on the papacy and the doctrine of transubstantiation, as well as for his championing of Scripture as the sole ultimate norm of theological truth, Wyclif has long been praised by Protestants as "the Morning Star of the Reformation." Anthony Kenny has questioned this tradition (Kenny 1985, pp. 106–9), arguing that Wyclif was distinguished from the Reformers of the sixteenth century by his doctrine of justification and by his scholasticism. These points are well taken, but Kenny overlooks the fact that the attacks which both Wyclif and Luther leveled against nominalism and the theology of the medieval Church flowed from a common Augustinianism.

Indeed, it could be argued that Wyclif was the last great medieval exponent of Augustinianism, differing from earlier Augustinians only in that he drew theological conclusions from the Augustinian tradition that were inimical to the Church of his day (Robson 1961, p. 25). For example, from the Augustinian doctrine of grace, he drew the conclusion that the Church consists of the elect and has no visible nature that can be tied to the pope or the hierarchy (Stacey 1964, pp. 99–101). This probably explains why he was condemned as a determinist, even though he was neither more, nor less, a determinist than many before him (Kenny 1985, p. 31).

In other matters as well, Wyclif was an Augustinian. In opposition to the nominalism which reigned at Oxford during his day, Wyclif maintained an older view, according to which God creates by making an external manifestation of the eternal archetypes in his mind, and does so in such a way that every created substance is essentially constituted by a universal nature, which it shares with every other created substance that is specifically or generically like it (Kenny 1985, pp. 14–15). Wyclif held that the common natures of things are formally distinct from the individuals they constitute, though he also held that, *as they exist in individuals*, they are numerically the same as such individuals (1984). Wyclif held that God could not destroy any individual, as doing so would involve the destruction of all universal natures.

Finally, Wyclif was an Augustinian in maintaining that real love is not centered on the self. For him, morality demands that we love the humanity in every human, the common nature which we all share and which is of greater value than our individual selves.

Wyclif was a voluminous writer in both Latin and English, but many of his works have not yet been edited. The only translation in English of any of his Latin works is the treatise *On Universals*, by Anthony Kenny. This is part of his greatest work, the *Summa de ente*, a large and rather disorganized compendium of theological and philosophical questions. In spite of its awkward organization, this work reveals that Wyclif was possessed of a keen and subtle mind. A careful study of his thought is long overdue.

Bibliography

Primary sources

(1883), *John Wyclif: Polemical Works*, ed. R. Buddensieg, London: Trübner.

(1883–1922), *Wyclif's Latin Works*, 36 vols., London: The Wyclif Society.

(1930), *De ente: libri primi tracta primus et secundus*, ed. S. H. Thomson, Oxford: Oxford University Press.

(1962), *De Trinitate (On the Trinity)*, ed. Du Pont Breck, Boulder: University of Colorado Press.

(1978), *Selections from English Wycliffite Writings*, ed. A. Hudson, Cambridge: Cambridge University Press.

(1985), *De universalibus*, vol. 1, Latin text ed. I. Mueller; vol. 2, a translation: *On Universals*, trans. A. Kenny and P. Spade, Oxford: Clarendon Press; New York: Oxford University Press.

Secondary sources

Dahmus, J. H. (1952), *The Prosecution of John Wyclyf*, New Haven: Yale University Press.

Kenny, A. (1985), *Wyclif*, Oxford and New York: Oxford University Press.

McFarlane, K. B. (1952), *John Wycliffe and the Beginnings of English Non-conformity*, London: The Wyclif Society.

Manning, B. L. (1966), "John Wyclif," in *Cambridge Medieval History*, 2nd edn., vol. VII (pp. 486–507, 900–7), Cambridge: Cambridge University Press.

Robson, J. H. (1961), *Wyclif and the Oxford Schools*, Cambridge: Cambridge University Press.

Stacey, J. (1964), *John Wyclif and Reform*, Philadelphia: Westminster Press.

69

Landulph Caracciolo

CHRISTOPHER SCHABEL

The Franciscan Landulph Caracciolo, born in Naples, probably lectured on the *Sentences* at Paris in the academic year 1318–19, just after PETER AURIOL (1316–18) and before FRANCIS OF MARCHIA (1319–20) and FRANCIS OF MEYRONNES (1320–1), all of whom are better known. By February 1325, when Landulph was Franciscan provincial minister of Terra Laboris in southern Italy, he was master of theology. Landulph became Bishop of Castellammare in 1327 and was Archbishop of Amalfi from 1331 until his death in 1351.

Landulph's major philosophical work is his popular commentary on the *Sentences*: over two dozen extant manuscripts contain at least one of the four books, and book II was printed in Venice before 1500. Landulph was the first Parisian Franciscan to come to JOHN DUNS SCOTUS's defense against Peter Auriol. In contexts like epistemology, future contingents, and predestination, Landulph provided intelligent and sometimes compelling "Scotistic" rebuttals of Auriol. Landulph's successors at Paris in the 1320s, 1330s, and 1340s, such as the Augustinian MICHAEL OF MASSA, the Cistercian PETER CEFFONS, and the Carmelite Paul of Perugia, recognized this and frequently cited Landulph by name. He was still cited in the early sixteenth century, so his impact was long-lived.

Landulph did not always offer a solution to philosophical problems that would dissolve Auriol's critique of Scotus, but it appears that Landulph himself understood this, and was content at times to show Auriol's position to be no improvement on Scotus's. Thus Landulph would respond to Auriol, "This difficulty follows from *every* position, because *every* position posits that . . ." One controversial Scotistic device that Landulph used in an interesting way is the "division" of an instant of time into "instants of nature." Using this device, Landulph tried to avoid the difficulties of the Aristotelian explanation of how and at which instant change occurs between contradictory states, as from non-being to being or rest to motion. For Simo Knuuttila, Landulph's answer was that "contradictory terms of change, which *can* be present in the same instant of *time*, belong to different instants of *nature*," and "*real* contradictions should be considered as instantaneous overlappings of states of affairs, which in the *conceptual* order are mutually exclusive and jointly exhaustive" (1993, p. 161).

Bibliography

Heynck, V. (1961), "Der Skotist Hugo de Novo Castro, OFM," *Franziskanische Studien* 43, pp. 244–70.
Knuuttila, S. (1993), *Modalities in Medieval Philosophy*, London: Routledge.
Scaramuzzi, D. (1931), "L'immaculato concepimento di Maria. Questione inedita di Landolfo Caracciolo, OFM (†1351)," *Studi Francescani* 28, pp. 33–69.

Schabel, C. (1999),"Landulphus Caracciolo and a Sequax on divine foreknowledge," *Archives d'Histoire Doctrinale et Littéraire du Moyen Âge* 66, pp. 299–343.

——(2001), *Theology at Paris 1316–1345: Peter Auriol and the Problem of Divine Foreknowledge and Future Contingents*, Burlington, VT: Ashgate.

——(2002), "Landulph Caracciolo and Gerard Odonis on predestination: opposite attitudes toward Scotus and Auriol," *Wissenschaft und Weisheit: Franziskanische Studien zu Theologie, Philosophie und Geschichte* 65, pp. 62–81.

70

Marsilius of Inghen

MAARTEN J. F. M. HOENEN

Marsilius of Inghen (b. ca. 1340; d. 1396) was born in Nijmegen (Low Countries) and died in Heidelberg. In 1362 he became master of arts at the University of Paris. In 1379 he left Paris and reappeared in 1386 at Heidelberg as master of arts and first rector of the university. Shortly before he died, he finished his theological studies, which he had begun in 1366 at Paris.

Marsilius wrote logical treatises and commentaries on Aristotle (*Organon*, *Physica*, *De generatione et corruptione*, *Metaphysica*), the Bible, and the *Sentences* of PETER LOMBARD. His writings survive in a large number of manuscripts, and some were printed in the fifteenth and sixteenth century. Marsilius had a large personal library, with 237 volumes containing scholastic writings and treatises of classical authors.

In his logic and commentaries on Aristotle, Marsilius followed in the footsteps of WILLIAM OF OCKHAM and JOHN BURIDAN, but in a critical manner. He considered sense data as the foundation of human knowledge and defended the nominalist opinion that there are no universals outside the human mind. Metaphysics is the highest form of natural knowledge, since it deals with the first and most universal principles. Using his natural capacities (*lumen naturale*, natural light), man is able to have true knowledge of God. This applies especially to Aristotle, whose thinking is the paradigm of human natural thinking according to Marsilius. Man can prove that God exists and has knowledge and a will, but he cannot demonstrate that God has free choice, is infinitely powerful, and can create from nothing. To prove this, man needs the supernatural light of the Christian faith (*lumen supernaturale*). If man is not guided by faith but follows the principles of natural knowledge, he will find the opposite of truth, namely that God acts necessarily, has only limited powers, and cannot create from nothing.

Marsilius' influence was enormous. In the fifteenth and sixteenth centuries he was considered as one of the most important proponents of nominalism, together with Ockham, Buridan, and GREGORY OF RIMINI. His works on logic and commentaries on Aristotle were used as textbooks at many universities. The style of his thinking was characterized as clear, modest, and easy to understand (*stilus humilior*) and was recommended as an antidote against Wyclifism and Hussitism. In 1499 the doctors of the *via moderna* at the University of Heidelberg published a book with epigrammata by such famous humanists as Jacob Wympfeling celebrating the ingenuity of Marsilius. Humanistic epigrammata can also be found in the printed edition of his *Commentary on the Sentences* (Strasbourg 1501). Marsilius's theology became widely known and he was quoted by such Spanish theologians as Francisco de Vitoria, Domingo de Soto, Luis de Molina, and Francisco Suárez on matters concerning divine foreknowledge and grace.

411

Bibliography

Primary sources

(1983), *Treatises on the Properties of Terms*, ed. E. P. Bos, Dordrecht: D. Reidel.

(2000), *Quaestiones super quattuor libros Sententiarum*, 2 vols., ed. M. Santos Noya, Leiden: Brill.

Secondary sources

Hoenen, M. J. F. M. (1989–90), "Marsilius von Inghen: bibliographie," *Bulletin de Philosophie Médiévale* 31–2, pp. 150–67, 191–5.

——(1993), *Marsilius of Inghen: Divine Knowledge in Late Medieval Thought*, Leiden: Brill.

Hoenen, M. J. F. M. and Bakker, P. J. J. M., eds. (2000), *Philosophie und Theologie des ausgehenden Mittelalters. Marsilius von Inghen und das Denken seiner Zeit*, Leiden: Brill.

Markowski, M. (1988), "Katalog dziel Marsyliusza z Inghen z ewidencja rekopisow," *Studia Mediewistyczne* 25, pp. 39–132.

Ritter G. (1921), *Marsilius von Inghen und die okkamistische Schule in Deutschland*, Heidelberg: Carl Winter.

71

Marsilius of Padua

FRANCISCO BERTELLONI

Marsilius of Padua (b. 1280; d. 1343) was born in Padua, son of a notary from a bourgeois family of the flourishing city. He probably studied law, then medicine and arts (philosophy), and was rector of the University of Paris between 1312 and 1313. During his stay in Paris, Marsilius became acquainted with the conflict over the papal *plenitudo potestatis* in the struggle between the French King Philip IV (d. 1314) and Pope Boniface VIII (d. 1303), and with the dispute between the spiritual Franciscans and Pope John XXII (d. 1334). Both conflicts were treated again in the first and second *dictio* of the *Defensor pacis* (*DP*), which was finished before June 1324.

In the first half of the thirteenth century, particularly during the reign of Emperor Frederick II (d. 1250), the conflicts between the spiritual and temporal powers began to display some new aspects that resulted in qualitative changes in the development of medieval political theory. On the one hand, the *Mirror of Princes* literary genre, which was more descriptive than argumentative, lost its popularity. On the other hand, this genre began to be replaced by treatises with more theoretical power. Frederick II tried to defend the empire's autonomy from the papacy with the theory of the *duo regimina*, papal and imperial. The empire is independent, it does not receive its authority from the pope but straight from God (*a deo culmen imperii obtinemus*). Both authorities rule in different and independent dominions and neither of them can be reduced to the other. Moreover, they complete each other in the fulfillment of different functions (*se ad invicem complectuntur*). Political argumentation suffered a radical metamorphosis and increased both in quantity and quality. The causes of this development are at least three: (1) the arrival of Aristotle's writings on ethics and politics in the West, (2) the institutional consolidation of the universities and, above all, (3) the introduction of systematic theory and argumentation, which is to a great extent a consequence of the two previous causes.

As a result of this process, a series of treatises on political theory appeared, the first of which may be *De regimine principum* by THOMAS AQUINAS. These texts inaugurated a tradition in political literature that can be described as the "theory of the duality of powers." This approach assumed different shapes: indirect subordination of the temporal power to the spiritual (Thomas Aquinas); direct subordination and reduction of the temporal power to the spiritual (GILES OF ROME); relative independence (JOHN OF PARIS); and absolute independence (DANTE ALIGHIERI). In different degrees and forms, all these authors can be included in a theoretical model that stated the existence of *two coactive powers*. In current language, this means simply two sovereignties. In the *DP*, Marsilius of Padua definitely splits from this tradition and tries to show that sovereignty is only one (I, xvii), that it cannot be divided, and that it does not reside in the pope but in the *legislator humanus*.

The political thought of Marsilius has both theoretical and practical grounding. All his writings are examples of the simultaneous influence of both theoretical and historical factors. In fact, the intellectual seed of the *DP*, Marsilius's most important work, can be traced back to the 1314 German election for emperor. The pretenders were Ludwig of Bavaria and Frederick of Habsburg. Although the majority of the electing princes selected Ludwig, both candidates were crowned in different places. After some undecided battles, both emperors decided to submit themselves to the decision of Pope John XXII, who delayed the final verdict. The victory of Ludwig of Bavaria in the battle of Mühldorf in 1322 set a new political stage. While Ludwig began to exert influence upon Italian politics, the pope encouraged him to abandon the imperial throne under threat of excommunication. The pope claimed his holy consent was a necessary requisite for the authentic coronation of the emperor. According to Ludwig, on the contrary, the only source of imperial power was the will of the electors. Excommunicated by the pope in 1324, Ludwig reacted in Sachsenhausen by issuing a document in which: (1) he attributed arbitrariness to the pope for having rejected the decision of the electors; (2) accused him of heresy for denying the absolute poverty of Christ and the apostles; and (3) recognized the General Council as the legitimate representative of the Church, while endowing it with the power of examining the pope's heresy and implementing his deposition.

Marsilius concluded the *DP* in June 1324 and dedicated it to Ludwig of Bavaria. In fact, the treatise is ideologically biased, since a great part of its argumentation constitutes, in fact, a theoretical legitimation of the political ambitions of Ludwig. Marsilius explains the reason for the title *The Defender of Peace* at the end of the treatise: "It discusses and explains the principal causes whereby civil peace or tranquillity exists and is preserved and whereby the opposed strife arises and is checked and destroyed" (III, iii).

This work develops two well-articulated theories: (1) a theory of peace and (2) a theory of the state. The latter illustrates the order among the different parts of the state. Both theories aim to solve the nuclear problem of the treatise, namely, the recovery of lost peace by a state that avoids the disputes between its parts and aims to restore its specific function to each part.

From the beginning, it is clear that the *DP* is the result of two traditions. The first understood political theory in organic terms, which explains Marsilius's use of an image of the natural world in the comparison of the body politic with an organism (hence the health of the body deserves social and political organization in order to have peace). The second tradition understands knowledge as a systematic and gradual access to the causes of phenomena. It is indeed notable throughout the treatise that Marsilius understands political phenomena in terms of causality: he both analyzes *political events* in terms of causality and also conceptualizes the *relations* between phenomena in terms of causal relationships. Thus, the steps of the *DP*'s argument are solidly grounded in a theoretical and causal way.

To these two traditions, the organic and the causal, two methodological characteristics of the *DP* must be added. The first concerns the way Marsilius develops his *scientia politica*. On this point, Marsilius distances himself from Aristotle: whereas for the Stagirite the argumentation on moral philosophy, i.e., ethics and politics, deals only with probabilities, for Marsilius politics constitutes a rational and apodictic science, based on the principles of Aristotelian natural philosophy, which can only have *necessary* consequences. The second characteristic is concerned with the nature of the argumentative resources specific for each of the parts or *dictiones* of the *DP*: in the first one, he expounds his political theory in a rational way, in the second one, on the contrary, he bases his arguments on the revealed truth.

Dictio I starts with a strong defense of civil peace and a reference to the conflicts that put it in danger. Marsilius describes a conflict that Aristotle did not know, and the cause of which is in his mind a doctrine (i.e., a theoretical formulation), which he characterizes as a *perverted* and *sophistic opinion*. This doctrine, he notes, "came to be adopted as an aftermath of the miraculous effect produced by the supreme cause long after Aristotle's time; an effect beyond the power of the lower nature and the usual action of causes in things" (I, i, 3). The supreme cause is God, the admirable effect beyond the usual action of causes in things is the divine Incarnation of the Son, and the perverted opinion is a doctrine wrongly derived from this admirable fact. This opinion states that, from the priesthood instituted by Christ derives a power, that is to say a jurisdictional authority, beyond the purely sacramental, spiritual, or religious dominion. In fact, Christ only ordained the apostles "as the teachers of his law and as ministers of the sacraments according to it, bestowing on them through the Holy Ghost the authority of this ministry, which authority is called 'priestly' by faithful Christians" (I, xix, 5). However, beyond this authority, another merely human authority, derived not from a divine but from a human institution, must exist: "This latter authority is the pre-eminence of the one among them over the others . . . for this authority is not given immediately by God, but rather through the will . . . of men" (I, xix, 6). This is an authority of human origin, "which was given to priests by man in order to avoid scandal after the number of priests had multiplied" (I, xix, 6).

Notwithstanding the human origin of this pre-eminence, however, the bishops of the Roman see have used the so-called authority of the keys (Matthew 16: 19) to alter the exclusively sacramental nature of this authority, attributing to it a coercive character. In this way, they pretend that it has power not only over priests, but also over secular princes:

> Because of the prerogative which this disciple or apostle seemed to have over the others, inasmuch as he was given the keys before the others . . . some of the bishops who succeeded him in the apostolic or episcopal seat at Rome . . . declare and assert that they are over all the other bishops and priests in the world, with respect to every kind of jurisdictional authority. And some of the most recent Roman bishops make this claim not only with regard to bishops and priests, but even with regard to all the rulers, communities and individuals. (I, xix, 8)

Marsilius concludes this part of the treatise with the identification of the cause of the dispute, namely, the perverted opinion that assumes the name of *plenitudo potestatis*, i.e., plenitude of power:

> This wrong opinion of certain Roman bishops and also perhaps their perverted desire for rulership, which they assert is owed to them because of the plenitude of power given to them, as they say, by Christ. This is that singular cause which we have said produces the intranquillity or discord of the city or state. (I, xix, 12)

Marsilius shows that this papal claim constitutes an usurpation by the ecclesiastical part over the governmental part of the city (*civitas*). The claim is the cause of disorder and uneasiness in the city. Consequently, the claim lacks legitimacy. To show this, Marsilius proposes a radical revision of the relationships between the temporal and the ecclesiastical powers, which he accomplishes mainly by exploring three topics: (1) the analysis of the origin, causes, and end of the *civitas*; (2) the presentation of a theory of law that constitutes the foundation of the state; and (3) the exposition of his theory of the parts of the *civitas*, including the consideration of the ecclesiastical part as a *pars inter partes* (i.e., a single part among other parts).

415

When he explains the origin of the *civitas* as a social and political entity, Marsilius presents himself as a naturalist in an Aristotelian fashion, although he complements this naturalism with a kind of natural realism of Ciceronian coinage. In fact, Marsilius admits the natural origin of the gregarious instinct that makes humans desire the union with other humans in society, but he interprets this natural instinct as a proclivity to overcome the risks of self-destruction: "Man . . . is born bare and unprotected from excess of the surrounding air and other elements, capable of suffering and of destruction" (I, iv, 3). In other words, society is the result of the human necessity of self-preservation: "he [i.e., man] needed arts of diverse genera and species to avoid the afore-mentioned harms. But since these arts can be exercised only by a large number of men, and can be had only through their association with one another, men had to assemble together" (I, iv, 3). Immediately after he moves from society and sociability to the city as a political organization in which the authority of one rules over the others. Here he suggests a distinction between sociability and politicity (the natural disposition of man to govern and being governed): "But since among men thus assembled there arise disputes and quarrels which, if not regulated by a norm of justice, would cause men to fight and separate and thus finally would bring about the destruction of the state, there had to be established in this association a standard of justice and a guardian or maker thereof" (I, iv, 4).

The main goal of the neutralization of discord and the restoration of peace is the recovery of the city as an adequate and necessary place for the attainment of civil happiness. This is equivalent to a *bene vivere* or sufficient life. This rational justification of the inclusion of human happiness as reachable and attainable in the *civitas* is apodictic. The only possible object with which the theory of politics can deal in a scientific way is this happiness insofar as it is attainable in this world. In fact, we can talk about eternal happiness, but its existence has never been proved in a demonstrative way: "But as to the first kind of living and living well or a good life, that is, the earthly, and its necessary means, this the glorious philosophers comprehended almost completely through demonstration" (I, iv, 3). In order to attain happiness in this life, the city is necessary: "Hence for its attainment they concluded the necessity of the civil community, without which this sufficient life cannot be obtained" (I, iv, 3). This is the reason why Marsilius organizes the whole of *Dictio* I around the true necessities of the *universitas civium*, which, following Aristotle, he calls *bene vivere*. The object of the Marsilian *scientia politica* is, precisely, to develop a theory of the city that makes possible, in this world, the satisfaction of the human necessities and the attainment of this *bene vivere* understood as a perfect end, complete and independent of any other end. According to Marsilius, this end is only possible in the *civitas*, and consists in human happiness.

The totality of the citizens or the *universitas civium* gathered in the Marsilian city gives itself its own law, and, therefore, its own order: "the legislator, or the primary and proper cause efficient of the law, is the people or the whole body of citizens, or the weightier part thereof, through its election or will expressed by words in the general assembly of the citizens" (I, xii, 3). Marsilius reveals himself as a real innovator when he defines law by stressing its coercive dimension. This is a necessary condition in the formal process of its sanction. Law is not law because of its eudaimonological character, that is, because its content is good or bad, just or unjust. Rather, the essence of law rests on a norm that identifies it both with the will of those who establish it and with its character as a coactive precept. In this way, coercion is for Marsilius a formal requisite and a *conditio sine qua non* of the law. Law "may be considered according as with regard to its observance there is given a command coercive through punishment or reward to be distributed in the present world, or according as it is handed down by way of such a command; and considered in this way it most properly is called, and is, a law" (I, x, 4). The people or the totality is also called *legislator humanus*. In contrast with Aristotle, the *universitas civium* or *legislator humanus* is now a whole of self-governed Christians ruled by their own will, which suggests the presence of an element of consent in the theory of the Marsilian *civitas*.

The *Dictio* I of the *DP* introduced at least three important innovations in political thought: the transference of the *potestas iurisdictionalis* to the *universitas civium*, the transformation of the people into an efficient cause of the law, and the definition of the law as a coercive precept. If the goal of Marsilius was to recover the order of the city and to create the conditions for the attainment of human happiness in this life, he widely accomplished it by uprooting the *potestas coercitiva* and the governmental function from the institution that so far had exercised it, namely, the priesthood. In the Marsilian view, the priesthood not only loses its jurisdictional faculties, but is also deprived of its pre-eminent character as a result of being considered a mere part among the many parts of the *civitas*. In this way, the priesthood is subordinated to the will of the *universitas civium*. Making use of the Aristotelian idea of the natural organism (with the harmonic organization among its parts), the priesthood is thought as a part among parts, whereas sovereignty and power are redefined as one and indivisible, making the risks of conflict between powers disappear.

Dictio II is almost three times longer than *Dictio* I. In this second discourse, Marsilius seeks to confirm the theses already proved in *Dictio* I, but this time on the basis of eternal revealed truth (*testimonia veritatis in aeternum fundata*), rather than by means of arguments based on principles of reason. This is why this *Dictio* abandons the philosophical style of *Dictio* I in order to introduce what may be called the ecclesiology of the *DP*. At this point Marsilius criticizes theocratic thought, by making use of its very arguments, but with an opposite goal. On the one hand, Marsilius dismantles the papal ecclesiology; on the other, he offers a substitutive ecclesiology inspired in his own interpretation of biblical texts.

Marsilius' argumentation starts with Christ's institution of the holy order, the priesthood, which is transmitted by priests to their successors by sacrament. In virtue of this sacrament, the priesthood (one of the parts of the city) fulfills only spiritual functions, and its main goal is to prepare the flock in this world to reach happiness in the other. For this reason the sacerdotal power of "binding or untying" is not coercive. From this characterization of the holy order as a sacrament that does not establish a primacy of one priest among the others, Marsilius moves forward to the definition of the Church as a non-hierarchical institution, that is, as a community consisting of "the whole body of the faithful who believe in and invoke the name of Christ" (*DP*, II, ii, 3). This community includes both the clergy and laymen. Any exercise of ecclesiastical functions that implies superiority of one priest over others is foreign to those exclusively spiritual functions, and if any kind of pre-eminence is to be established among priests, it can only have its source in the will of the human legislator. Moreover, priests lack any power to punish sinners; only civil law, when it is enforced by he who has coercive power, can punish certain sins, such as heresies or schisms.

Marsilius defends also the absolute poverty of Christ and the apostles. Absolute poverty consists, after the life-example of Christ and the apostles, in the individual and common renunciation to the right of property and the ownership of goods. Hence, the possession of any property within the Church is considered as radically contrary to the spirit and ideal of evangelic life.

Marsilius takes then another step toward the government of the Church. The Church must be understood as a human institution whose government is exercised through a General Council representative of all Christians. Although all parishioners have the right to

417

take part in the General Council gathered together by the *supremus legislator fidelis*, it is better that every community, region, or province of Christianity bestow its authority on its respective legislator, in such a way that he, as its representative, may deliberate and legislate concerning Christian doctrine and liturgy. Legislators give legal character to the decisions of the General Council in matters of faith, and their decisions must be accepted even by priests.

The brief *Dictio* III presents, as a conclusion, a list of propositions that summarize the political content of the whole treatise.

At the beginning, the *DP* had a rather limited circulation in the University of Paris, but its posterior diffusion, its repercussions in the pontifical Curia in Avignon, and the imminent reprisals on the ground of its antipapal contents made Marsilius, together with JOHN OF JANDUN, flee to the court of Ludwig of Bavaria in Munich in 1336. The treatise was condemned in 1327 by the bull, *Licet iuxta doctrinam*, of John XXII. In it the pope condemns five theses of the *DP*, developed for the most part in *Dictio* II, rather than in *Dictio* I: (1) all belongings of the Church are subject to the emperor; (2) Christ did not establish any kind of leadership in the Church; (3) it is the emperor's duty to correct or depose the pope; (4) all priests (including the pope) have equal authority; (5) neither the pope nor the Church have any coercive power, except when it is received from the emperor. The papal condemnation of these ecclesiological theses (notice that the theoretical-political ones were not condemned) restrained the influence of the *DP* and anticipated the directions that the repercussion of the treatise were to take. Its fortune in the immediately following centuries was more related to its ecclesiological position than to its political doctrines (Piaia 1977).

Ludwig was crowned Emperor of the Romans in Rome in 1328. Immediately afterwards he substituted Pope Nicholas V for John XXII. John of Jandun was appointed Bishop of Ferrara and Marsilius, papal assessor on spiritual matters. However, Ludwig's imperial dream was very short. His military inferiority to the papal armies made him flee from Rome to Munich, where he gathered an interesting group of intellectual figures, such as Marsilius, Michael of Cesena (former General of the Franciscans), and WILLIAM OF OCKHAM. The last one, also Franciscan, was accused of heresy and had to flee from the Curia at Avignon to find asylum in the imperial court. As a result of his conversations with Ockham, Marsilius wrote a new and shorter treatise, entitled *Defensor minor*. In fact, in his *Dialogus* (1340) Ockham had expressed his disagreement with the Marsilian theses that denied all jurisdictional power to the pope. In 1341 Marsilius published his *Defensor minor* to answer Ockham's criticisms (Dolcini 1988). Some years later, Ludwig asked Pope Benedict XII for the annulment of an early marriage of the Austrian countess Margareth Maultasch in order to make possible her new marriage with his son Ludwig. The papal refusal made Ludwig ask Ockham and Marsilius to write something on the issue. This produced the 1341–2 *Tractatus de iurisdictione imperatoris in causis matrimonialibus*. Finally, before his death, in 1343, Marsilius wrote the *Tractatus de translatione imperii*, an essay that tries to refute, on historical grounds, the curial interpretation that the legitimacy of the *translatio imperii* resides in the papal *auctoritas*.

The originality of the political thought of Marsilius is multiple. Two aspects must be especially stressed. First, he was the first Christian medieval theorist who tried to find a solution to the conflicts between the spiritual and civil powers (avoiding the problems of any dualistic solution), by means of changing the place of the coactive power from the spiritual to the temporal realm. In other words, Marsilius's political theory is an attempt to recover the unity of sovereignty. Second, after a long tradition of medieval writings that, under the mask of political theory, had only and scarcely formulated a theory on the relationships between the spiritual and the temporal powers, Marsilius's *DP* is the first political treatise that offers a theory of the *civitas*, i.e., of the state understood as the only possible location for the full realization of man. Finally, and most important, Marsilius defines the conflict between powers in a entirely new way by introducing a theory of the *civitas*, that mediates between the two antagonists of a conflict apparently insoluble.

Bibliography

Primary sources

(1922), *Defensor minor*, ed. C. K. Brampton, Birmingham: Corrish Brothers.

(1928), *The Defensor pacis of Marsilius of Padua*, ed. C. W. Previté-Orton Cambridge: Cambridge University Press.

(1932–3), *Defensor pacis*, ed. R. Scholz, Hanover: Hahn.

(1951), *The Defender of Peace*, vol. I: *Marsilius of Padua and Medieval Political Philosophy*, ed. A. Gewirth, New York: Columbia University Press.

(1956), *The Defender of Peace*, vol. II: *The Defensor pacis*, trans. and with an introduction by A. Gewirth, New York: Columbia University Press.

(1979), *Oeuvres mineures: Defensor minor, De translatione imperii*, ed. C. Jeudy and J. Quillet, Paris: Editions du Centre National de la Recherche Scientifique.

(1993), *Marsiglio of Padua: Writings on the Empire, Defensor minor and De translatione*, trans. C. J. Nederman, Cambridge: Cambridge University Press.

Secondary sources

Battaglia, F. (1928), *Marsilio da Padova e la filosofia politica del medioevo*, Florence: Monnies.

Bigongiari, D. (1964), *Essays on Dante and Medieval Culture: Critical Studies on the Thought and Texts of Dante, St. Augustine, St. Thomas Aquinas, Marsilius of Padua and Other Medieval Subjects*, Florence: L. S. Olschki.

Coleman, J. (1983), "Medieval discussions of property, *ratio* and *dominium* according to John of Paris and Marsilius of Padua," *History of Political Thought* 4, pp. 209–28.

de Lagarde, G. (1970), *La Naissance de l'esprit laïque au déclin du moyen âge*, vol. III: *Le Defensor Pacis*, Louvain and Paris: St. Paul Trois Châteaux.

Dolcini, C. (1988), "Marsilio contra Ockham. Intorno a una recente edizione del *Defensor minor*," in C. Dolcini, *Crisi di poteri e politologia in crisi* (pp. 269–89), Bologna: Partron.

Gewirth, A. (1948), "John of Jandun and the *Defensor pacis*," *Speculum* 23, pp. 267–72.

——(1979), "Republicanism and absolutism in the thought of Marsilius of Padua," *Medioevo* 5, pp. 23–48.

Haller, J. (1984), "Zur Lebensgeschichte des Marsilius von Padua," in J. Haller, *Abhandlungen zur Geschichte des Mittelalters* (pp. 335–68), Essen: Magnus.

Lewis, E. (1963), "The 'Positivism' of Marsilius of Padua," *Speculum* 38, pp. 541–82.

Miethke, J. (1989), "Marsilius von Padua. Die politische Theorie eines lateinischen Aristotelikers des 14. Jahrhunderts," in H. Boockmann, B. Moeller, and K. Stackmann, eds., *Lebenslehren und Weltentwürfe im Übergang vom Mittelalter zur Neuzeit* (pp. 52–76), Göttingen: Vandenhoeck and Ruprecht.

——(1993), "Literaturbericht über Marsilius von Padua (1958–1992)," *Bulletin de Philosophie Médiévale* 35, pp. 150–65.

Munz, P. (1960), "The 13th-century and the ideas of Marsilius of Padua," *Historical Studies* 9, pp. 156–72.

Nederman, C. J. (1981), "Marsiglio of Padua as political theorist: ideology and middle-class politics in the early fourteenth century," *University of Ottawa Quarterly* 51, pp. 197–209.

——(1990), "Medieval law and power, nature, justice and duty in the *Defensor pacis*: Marsiglio of Padua's Ciceronian impulse," *Political Theory* 18, pp. 615–37.

——(1991), "Knowledge, consent and the critique of the political representation in Marsiglio of Padua's *Defensor pacis*," *Political Studies* 39, pp. 19–35.

——(1992), "Character and community in the *Defensor pacis*: Marsiglio of Padua's adaptation of Aristotelian Moral Psychology," *History of Political Thought* 13, pp. 377–90.

Passerin d'Entrèves, A. (1959), *The Medieval Contribution to Political Thought: Thomas Aquinas, Marsilius of Padua, Richard Hooker*, New York: Oxford University Press.

Piaia, G. (1977), *Marsilio da Padova nella Riforma e nella Contrariforma*, Padua: Antenore.

——(1999), *Marsilio e dintorni*, Padua: Antenore.

Pincin, M. (1967), *Marsilio*, Turin: Giappicelli.

Quillet, J. (1970), *La Philosophie politique de Marsile de Padoue*, Paris: J. Vrin.

Reeves, M. (1965), "Marsilius of Padua and Dante Alighieri," in B. Smalley, ed., *Trends of Medieval Political Thought* (pp. 86–104), Oxford: Oxford University Press.

Rubinstein, N. (1965), "Marsilius of Padua and Italian political thought of his time," in J. Hale, R. Highfield, and B. Smalley, eds., *Europe in the Late Middle Ages* (pp. 44–75), Evanston, IL: Northwestern University Press.

Siegmund, P. E. (1962), "The influence of Marsilius of Padua on XVth century conciliarism," *Journal of the History of Ideas* 22, pp. 392–402.

Tierney, B. (1991), "Marsilius on rights," *Journal of the History of Ideas* 52, pp. 5–17.

Torraco, S. (1992), *Priests as Physicians of Souls in Marsilius of Padua's Defensor pacis*, San Francisco: Mellen Research University Press.

72

Martin of Dacia

JOSÉ LUIS RIVERA

Martin de Dacia (d. 1304), sometimes Martinus Dacus, was a Danish scholar, master of arts and theology at the University of Paris around 1250–88, and the author of *Modi significandi*, a very influential treatise on grammar. He studied and taught arts and theology at the University of Paris until his appointment as Chancellor of King Erik VI Menved of Denmark in 1287–8. After sixteen years of service to the king, he died on August 10, 1304 at Paris (Roos 1952, pp. 47–71).

Martin of Dacia represents a relatively early stage in the systematization of a "scientific" approach to the study of grammar around the "modes of meaning" (*modi significandi*) subsequently refined in the works of BOETHIUS OF DACIA, RADULPHUS BRITO, Siger of Courtrai, and THOMAS OF ERFURT. The first step to turn grammar into a demonstrative science was to identify the object or set of objects composing its genus. Martin of Dacia identifies the *modi significandi* or "modes of meaning" of traditional grammarians as the genus of scientific grammar; and as a result, he tries to explain the rules of grammar, and to distinguish grammar from other sciences (especially from logic), in terms of the *modi significandi*.

The definition of the *modus significandi* follows the path established by Aristotle's correlation among *things, affections of the soul,* and *words* outlined in *Peri Hermeneias* (1, 16a4–8). According to Martin, there are modes of real being (*modi essendi*), which are "properties of things outside the mind" (*proprietates rei . . . extra intellectum*), modes of understanding in the mind (*modi intelligendi*), which are the properties of things insofar as they are understood by the mind (*intellectus*), and modes of meaning (*modi significandi*), which are the properties of things insofar as they are signified by words (*Modi significandi*, I.3, 4: 7–12). The properties corresponding to modes of being, understanding, and meaning are "essentially the same," but "accidentally different." They all are the properties of real beings, but their "modality" depends on their "location": they are modes of being in the thing, modes of understanding in the mind, and modes of meaning in words. Their "identity" is analogous to the identity of Socrates in different places: Socrates is essentially the same, whether in the choir or in the forum; he only changes position (*Modi significandi*, II.7, 6: 6–19).

Martin proposes that there are modes of meaning corresponding to the traditional eight parts of the sentence (noun, pronoun, verb, adjective, adverb, participle, conjunction, and preposition). In the rest of the book, Martin tries to show how these modes of meaning explain the rules governing the construction of sentences. Martin's view is that the work of the grammarian consists in defining the modes of meaning on the basis of the different functions fulfilled by a word, and in explaining the rules governing the construction of sentences. Later "modists" will challenge Martin's explanations, but not this basic assumption.

The modes of meaning also help to determine the difference between logic and grammar. Grammarians study nouns and verbs as having modes of meaning that allow the construction of the sentence, and logicians study them as indicating logical relations (*In Perihermeneias* q. 17, 254: 30–255: 3). Thus the modes of meaning only explain the syntactical properties of noun and verb as parts of the sentence, but not their role in the construction of syllogisms. Consequently, grammarians can only provide rules to determine whether a given sentence is constructed correctly, and logicians can only provide rules to determine the validity of an inference: they do not interfere with each other.

Finally, Aristotle's standards of scientific demonstration and a long tradition of Neoplatonic interpretation of the *logica vetus* led Martin to endorse a strong form of metaphysical realism. This is clear when Martin says that the mode of understanding of the abstract noun precedes the mode of meaning of the concrete noun (*In Praedicamentorum*, q. 10, 168: 23–5). In short, Martin's theory seemed a plausible solution for two problems: how to claim that grammar is a science, and how to distinguish it from logic. Other "modists" developed further his approach until the advent of nominalist accounts.

Bibliography

Primary source

(1961), *Opera*, ed. Heinrich Roos, Corpus philosophorum danicorum medii aevii, II, Copenhagen: Gad.

Secondary sources

Maierù, Alfonso (1994), "The philosophy of language," in Giulio Lepschy, ed., *History of Linguistics*, vol. 2: *Classical and Medieval Linguistics* (pp. 272–315), London and New York: Longman.

Roos, Heinrich (1952), *Die Modi Significandi des Martinus de Dacia*, Copenhagen: A. Frost-Hansen; Münster: Aschendorff.

Bursill-Hall, G. L. (1971), *Speculative Grammars of the Middle Ages*, The Hague and Paris: Mouton.

Pinborg, Jan (1982), "Speculative grammar," in N. Kretzmann, A. Kenny, and J. Pinborg, eds., *The Cambridge History of Later Medieval Philosophy*, Cambridge: Cambridge University Press.

73

Matthew of Aquasparta

R. E. HOUSER

Matthew of Aquasparta (b. ca. 1240; d. 1302), of the noble Bentivenghi family of Aqua-sparta, Italy (patrons of the convent of S. Fortunato in nearby Todi), joined the Franciscan order about 1260. There he doubtless met Benedict Caetani (later Pope Boniface VIII) who in 1260 became canon of the cathedral under his uncle Peter, Bishop of Todi, and Jacomo de' Benedetti, a prominent poet who, after his wife died, became Fra Jacopone da Todi.

Matthew was sent to the University of Paris about 1268, just as Franciscans were attacked by secular masters of theology, such as Gerard of Abbeville, who rejected their way of life, and by radical Aristotelians in the faculty of arts, such as SIGER OF BRABANT. Matthew took inspiration from BONAVENTURE, Minister General of the Order (1257–73), who defended mendicancy in *Apologia pauperum* (1269) and set Aristotle in his proper place in *Collationes in Hexaemeron* (spring, 1273). A second inspiration was JOHN PECHAM, holder of the Franciscan chair of theology (ca. 1269–71) and leader of Bonaventure's feisty lieutenants. Pecham criticized the Aristotelianism of THOMAS AQUINAS, as did William de la Mare, who held the Franciscan chair in 1273–76 and wrote a *Correctorium fratris Thomae* in 1279. Matthew learned the rhetoric of moderation from Bonaventure and more conservative practice from Pecham.

Matthew studied in Paris in about 1268–73, and his *Commentum in Sententiis* is still unedited. A tract written before the Council of Lyons (1274) is noteworthy for saying "the plenitude of power resides in the Roman Pontiff" (1957a, p. 424.20). He probably incepted as master of theology in 1273, with a *principium* on the science of theology. Its conception of authority underlies his whole career. The "utility" of theology comes from its end: beatitude; its "faculty" comes from its matter: God's law. The "authority of the Master" comes from "the God of glory and majesty," theology's "special (*praecipuus*) teacher." Inner illumination "is rendered authentic and confirmed" through God's "prodigious deeds of nature [studied in philosophy] and grace [as seen in Scripture]"; through special inspiration; and tradition. Hence the authority of masters, bishops, popes. Finally, there are three "conditions" for the theologian becoming a "disciple": "First the disciple must enter the school and humbly subject himself to the Master, not contradict what he hears but piously and faithfully assent to it, for this is the loftiest doctrine"; second, "fervently desiring and through desire diligently investigating" this doctrine; and finally achieving "purity of vision and tranquillity of mind" (1957a, pp. 22–8). This humility led Matthew to embrace a well-developed Franciscan tradition and to be suspicious of change, "for from intellectual pride come all errors, all eccentric opinions, all impious and profane innovations" (1962b: 41).

Matthew taught at Bologna and Paris before his appointment to the *studium* of the papal curia (1279–87), where he succeeded Pecham, who was made Archbishop of Canterbury on January 28, 1279. Since a notary's record places "Br. Matthew doctor in theology" at Bologna in August, 1273, just before the beginning of the academic year (1956: 6*), it is likely that he first taught in Bologna (ca. 1273–7), then at Paris (ca. 1277–9), in the aftermath of the condemnation of March 7, 1277. His scholarly life ended in May, 1287, when he was elected Minister General at the Franciscan General Chapter in Montpellier.

The literary record from Bologna is sparse, as befits a first appointment. Bits of "a question disputed at Bologna" about God are preserved (1935, p. lxxxvi). *De anima* 1–13 may well come from Bologna, since it contains no references to the condemnation of 1277 (1961, pp. 11–12).

In *De anima* Matthew embraces the twin doctrines of universal hylomorphism and the plurality of substantial forms (1961, pp. 168, 65; cf. 1957b, p. 180). Following these general principles, humans are composites of body and soul, "an intellectual spirit so conjoined to the body that it is the form and perfection of the body" (25). Matthew placed himself between Aquinas's single substantial form, "the intellective or rational soul, which is the specific human form giving sensible being and vegetative being and even corporeal being" (59) and the exaggerated realism of Plato's "three souls in one man" – the "rational" soul situated in the head, "desire" in the heart, and the "nutritive" soul in the liver. His view follows "the common position of the theologians, that the soul is one in substance, having three consubstantial and connatural powers, through which it produces life, sensation, and intellectual being, so that the soul in itself totally and in all its powers is created by God, and in this creation is poured into a body formed and perfectly organized" (108). Matthew's view requires delayed animation and a plurality of forms to prepare the body for the infusion of the rational soul; God as efficient cause of the infused rational soul; and agent and possible intellects which are parts of the individual soul, not cosmic forces. He can agree verbally with the Thomist teaching that the soul is both "an individual substance (*hoc aliquid*)" and the "form and perfection of the body."

Typical of Matthew's approach is his argument for the immortality of the soul, based on the Dionysian hierarchy of "four grades of beings": things that only are, that also live, and perceive, and understand. Bonaventure used this hierarchy to argue from "footprints" in the world to the existence and incorruptibility of "supercelestial things": God and angels (*Itin.* 1.13). Matthew moves in the opposite direction. Assuming a "supreme grade of being" which "cannot be corruptible" because it is so "noble and high," he concludes on Dionysian grounds about the human soul: "since it is intellectual, it cannot be mortal." Demonstration of this conclusion is based on "consideration of its essence" in terms of the hierarchical structure of reality. This is not the last instance in which Matthew appeals to the Dionysian hierarchy.

The chronology of his Parisian and curial disputations is based on an autograph manuscript (Assisi 134; cf. Todi 44) where Matthew set out the texts of 21 groups of questions in what seems to be chronological order, since it intersperses ordinary and quodlibetal questions. Those he disputed as master in Paris are: *De fide* qq. 1–8; *De cognitione* 1–10; *De anima separata* 1–3; *Quod. I*; *De anima separata* 4–9; *De anima beata* 1–8. *De fide* and *De cognitione*, which contain two offhand references to the condemnation of 7 March 1277 (1957a: 160, 203), are likely to have begun that fall (1277–8). The questions about separated souls are painstakingly structured around positions "excommunicated *recently* by the present lord Bishop of Paris [Étienne Tempier], following the common consensus of all the Masters" (1959, pp. 26–7) and thus probably disputed during the following academic year (1278–9).

Matthew returned to Paris as a man with a mission to defend Franciscan tradition in a highly polemical setting. His way of doing so can be traced in the new form taken by the "responses" of his Parisian disputations. After setting out the full range of positions on a question, stating his own view clearly, and arguing for it, as he had previously done, Matthew invariably completes his response by appending an extended quotation from AUGUSTINE, one designed to legitimize what he has proven through other, often Bonaventurean, arguments. Matthew's so-called "Augustinianism" consists in appealing to the authority of St. Augustine, something quite different from taking his philosophical inspiration there.

The disputed questions *De fide* and *De cognitione* are conceived as a unit to show how faith and reason operate together. *De fide* q. 1 situates the truth that humans can attain certain knowledge between the hyper-realism of the Old Academy and the skepticism of the New. The rest of *De fide* concerns certitude coming from faith. Religious belief is necessary for salvation (q. 2), which is why "the sane truth dictates and right reason confirms" that salvation is found "only in the one true faith and law of Christianity" (q. 3, 1957a: 70, 78). The nature of faith is then clarified through causal analysis (qq. 3–8) and seen to be so important that one can both know and believe a given truth about God at one and the same time (q. 5, 1957a, p. 135).

In *De cognitione* Matthew widens the argument of Bonaventure's *De scientia Christi*, q. 4, which assumed illumination theory and asked which of its proponents had given its best account: Plato, AVICENNA, or Augustine. For Matthew, the goal is to attain a mean between Plato, who held the forms are the " total and only cause of knowing" and Aristotle, who "said the whole cause of knowing comes from below, by way of sense, memory, and experience." Under the authority of Augustine and the inspiration of Bonaventure, Matthew takes a middle position: "whatever is known with certain intellectual knowledge is known in its eternal reasons and in light of the first truth." Exactly what is and what is not due to God he then determines with precision: "The *material* cause of knowing comes from exterior things, from where the species of the things known derive"; divine ideas do not provide the content for knowledge, which is empirical. "But the *formal* cause partly comes from within, that is, from the light of [human] reason" working through the abstractive process to produce universal concepts and judgments, "and partly it comes from above, from eternal rules and reason, but by way of completion or consummation," where God acts as efficient cause, adding the formality of *certitude* to human cognition. Only the certitude of knowledge comes from God (q. 2, 1957a, p. 240), a Bonaventurean position perhaps clearer here than in Bonaventure himself.

Matthew's disputations in 1278–9 seem conceived to support the authority of "the common opinion of the Masters," which the Bishop of Paris had used in the condemnation. Matthew begins oddly; qq. 1–3 of *De anima separata* are devoted to motion and separated souls, where one would expect consideration of the state of separation itself. The reason is that Matthew has his eye on the view, advocated by Aristotelians like Siger and Aquinas, that angels and separated souls are completely immaterial, which was condemned because it makes creatures too much like God.

It is the prerogative of God to move bodies at will, so in q. 1 Matthew attacks the condemned view (Hissette 1977, p. 132) that angels and separated souls can do this, too. Once it has left the body, the human soul cannot act as a mover or re-enter the body on its own volition (1959, p. 10), because the soul can move the body only when united as its form. In qq. 2 and 3 Matthew attacks another condemned view advocated by Aquinas and Siger, that substances separated from bodies – whether angels or human souls – do not in their substance and nature exist in a place, but are only in place reductively "through operation" (Hissette 1977, pp. 53, 54, 55). The fundamental error here is trying to make creatures too

425

much like God by separating them from all matter. All creatures are "contained within the single circumference of the one highest heaven," a fact that the doctrine of universal hylomorphism embraces. Since spiritual substances contain matter, by nature they are "in place," they "move from place to place," and do so "successively" not instantaneously. Matthew then draws equally anti-Aristotelian conclusions about their knowledge. "A separate soul acquires knowledge from inferior things," a view "more sane and catholic and more in concord with Sacred Scripture" than that of Aquinas (q. 4; 70). As a corollary, distance impedes the knowledge separated souls can have of corporeal things (q. 5; 85). The line of argument running through these questions is designed to support the condemnation through attacking the contrary views of prominent Aristotelians.

When he turns to souls enduring the torments of hell, Matthew follows the Fathers, contrary to Avicenna's "completely erroneous" rejection of sensible pains in hell. The damned suffer from the sensible "fire of Gehenna" and from the even more painful "worm of conscience" within. The distinction is important, for unbaptized children suffer the absence of God only interiorly, they endure no physical suffering (qq. 6–9).

In *De anima beata*, Matthew takes up the roles of intellect and will in the beatific vision. The intellect plays a subordinate, "dispositive" role, while the will is "completive" in a complex act involving both. The intellect sees the divine essence immediately, but the divine essence does not become the "form of the intellect" as Dominicans held, for so unifying the creature's mind to God would undercut the ontological simplicity of God (qq. 6–8). To get to these traditional topics, however, Matthew moves through two other issues which *do* arise out of the condemnation. Bishop Étienne Tempier had rightly condemned the claim "that felicity is had in this life and not in another" (Hissette 1977, p. 172), because "however much [the philosophers] disputed about the end of 'the good', they could not attain that to which only *divine authority* leads" (1959, p. 186). A rational creature attains beatitude only in the "uncreated good" and needs a glorified body to do so (qq. 1–2). There follow qq. 3–5 about equality among beatified souls, where Matthew uses angels as a metaphysical test case. PSEUDO-DIONYSIUS had clearly held that "among angels there is inequality" within a species, which is contrary to the Avicennian and Thomistic doctrine that each angel constitutes a unique species, a view condemned "by the whole college of the Masters of the faculty of theology" (1959, pp. 260–1). Likewise, within the human species there is such inequality of nature that some souls enjoy more, others less beatitude and glory, a difference derived not from the body but from "their very natures." Such inequality, far from being an embarrassment, "is right due to the multitude of forms and the form of beauty found in the city of the highest heaven" (236). Once again Dionysian hierarchy opens the way to the vision of the common good which came to preoccupy Matthew after he left Paris.

All Matthew's other disputations were done at the curia (1279–87). In chronological order: *De ieiunio* 1–3; *Quod. II*; *De productione rerum* 1–4; *Quod. III*; *De prod.* 5–6; *Quod. IV*; *De prod.* 7–9; *De providentia* 1–4; *Quod. V*; *De prov.* 5–6; *De gratia* 1–8; *Quod. VI*; *De gratia* 9–10. Outside the chronological list are: *De incarnatione* 1–9; *De legibus* 1–6; *De anima* 1–6; *De morte Christi*.

Especially important philosophically are *De productione rerum* and *De providentia*, again conceived as a unit where philosophical reason joins revelation to study God as principle and overseer of creation. "Since production presupposes a cause" Matthew begins with the existence of God, one of those common axioms known to all humans (*communis animorum conceptio*). For as soon as we hear the term 'God' our "mind immediately conceives and so assents to his existence." It does not follow, however, that arguments for God's existence are useless, and Matthew distinguishes two routes such proofs can take (1956, p. 11).

Along the inner route he construes the ontological argument as dialectical reasoning of the sort used to defend indemonstrable first principles. What makes the proposition 'God exists' axiomatic is that "the cause of the predicate is completely included in the subject," that is, in "the definition (*ratio*) of 'first and supreme being'." He then uses a Bonaventurean formulation to clarify the ontological inference: "Just as 'if the best is the best', then it follows that 'the best is' . . . so also 'if the first and supreme being is first and supreme being', then it necessarily follows that 'the first and supreme being is', because the first and supreme being is fully actual and complete" (1956, pp. 11–12).

The second is an exterior route divided along the broad contours of Aristotelian causality. Three avenues open up for demonstrating God's existence from effects, since "God is efficient, formal, and final cause of creatures" (1956, *De productione rerum*, p. 241). Two arguments use efficient causality, one taken from the origin of creatures, a second from their beginning in time. Three more arguments are taken from formal causality: one from the gradations in creatures, another from their imperfections, and a third from their mutability. Finally, two arguments use final causality, one taken from the governance of the world, and another from its order (1956, pp. 12–18). Matthew associates each argument with a particular Christian thinker and his arguments based on formal and final causality show he learned something from Aquinas. Like Bonaventure, Matthew outlines every possible route to God, and he finds no need to choose between dialectical arguments for God's existence as a principle and demonstrative arguments for the same conclusion, so long as the two types of arguments are not confused.

The remaining questions concern the nature of God as creator, who must possess every formal perfection bestowed on creatures (1956, q. 2) and must be the one universal cause "of all other things" (q. 3). God must then produce things "by means of creation, or, from nothing" (q. 4). Muslim emanation is rejected because God produces creatures "immediately," not through a co-creator, since even for God it is impossible "to communicate the power of creating to a creature" (qq. 5–6). Muslim and Jewish philosophers also failed to recognize that the extrinsic procession of creatures presupposes an internal procession of persons within God (q. 7; cf. Bonaventure, *Itin.* 6.2). Matthew ends his questions *De productione rerum* by noting how utterly different are creator and creature. Creation changes God not at all (q. 8), while in creatures it is so great a transformation that the very notion of an eternal creature or an eternal world is a contradiction in terms (q. 9).

Though he rejects mediate creation, in *De providentia* Matthew embraces a kind of mediate governance based on Dionysian hierarchy. "Thus I say indubitably that God rules and disposes, or administers, the whole of creation so that through mediating superiors he administers and rules inferiors, through more perfect mediators the less perfect, through the nobler the more ignoble, and what requires this is the nature of the good, the beauty and order of the universe, and his own perfection" (1956, p. 323). Hierarchy is set into the very nature of creation, from the arrangement of the heavens to the order within our souls, and humans have a duty to arrange their own institutions accordingly. There is an eternal law, upon which is founded the natural law, which in turn requires a written law. Each subsequent law depends upon the higher, prior law, and makes it more useful to ignorant, sinful men (1959, pp. 443, 466, 486). Hierarchy is not a theoretical construct but forms the fundamental principle Matthew uses to guide his stewardship of the Church.

As Minister General of the Franciscans (May 1287 to 29 May 1289) Matthew took a conciliatory approach to the Spirituals. He rehabilitated PETER OLIVI and John of Parma. After the death of Pope Honorius IV (April 3, 1287), a divided conclave and the deaths of six cardinals in the summer heat brought the first Franciscan pope, Nicholas IV (February 22,

1288–April 4, 1292), who appointed Matthew cardinal on May 16, 1288 and in 1291 named him Cardinal-Bishop of Porto. The "missionary Pope" sent Franciscans as far away as China, but in Rome Nicholas was subservient to the aristocratic Colonna family and lampooned as enclosed in a column (the Colonna symbol) with only his tiara and head showing. Under Nicholas, Matthew became penitentiary, a sensitive post which involved absolution of papal censures and granting of dispensations.

Upon the death of Nicholas IV the papal throne lay vacant for 27 months owing to a dispute between Orsini and Colonna cardinals. Finally, on July 5, 1294 Cardinal Latino Malabranca OP revealed that a saintly hermit, Pietro del Morrone, had prophesied divine retribution if the cardinals left the Church headless any longer. He proposed the hermit as pope and Matthew, along with the other cardinals, agreed, perhaps in hope that Celestine V would be the longed for "angel Pope," ushering in a new age of the Holy Spirit. It was not to be. Celestine recognized his own incapacity and on December 13, 1294, in full consistory before Matthew and the other cardinals, he abdicated. This long crisis cemented the trust between Matthew and Matteo Caetani, elected Pope Boniface VIII on Christmas Eve, 1294.

Boniface's pontificate split the two Franciscans he had met in Todi as a young canon. Jacopone wrote: "Behold, a new Lucifer on the papal throne, | Poisoning the world with his blasphemies," while Cardinal Matthew became Boniface's chief lieutenant, playing the role he had seen Pecham perform so well for Bonaventure in Paris.

Boniface's pontificate was marked by an ongoing dispute with King Philip IV (r. 1285–1314). The French called him "the Fair," but in Matthew's eyes he looked like Emperor Frederick II (d. 1250), who had espoused "the most dangerous of all [moral] errors," namely, that "in every sect, whatever it believes and however it lives, salvation can be obtained as long as one does not violate its customary law," the source of his insubordination to papal authority (1957a: 70, 77–8). Once Boniface chose Matthew as chief adviser and theoretician for papal policies, it was almost inevitable that the dispute with Philip would rise to the level of first principles, where compromise quickly became impossible. This quarrel produced the finest scholastic writing on political theory – by GILES OF ROME, JOHN OF PARIS, DANTE – and created a political stand-off between Church and state. Humble but resolute, Matthew stood at the center of the whole dispute.

The conflict opened when Boniface asserted papal authority in *Clericis laicos* (February 24, 1296), to prevent taxation of the clergy. Philip replied by cutting off the pope's income from France, and Boniface backed down. After a lengthy process supervised by Matthew and two other cardinals, which generated "more codices than a mule could carry," Boniface canonized Louis IX, Philip's grandfather, on July 11, 1297, with Cardinal Matthew preaching.

Boniface was weakened in his fight with Philip by a dispute with the Colonna family, who joined with Spiritual Franciscans in spring 1297, issuing a series of manifestos which began by questioning Boniface's election and ended by accusing him of murdering Celestine V. Matthew lined up Franciscan support for Boniface, including Spirituals such as Olivi; on December 14, 1297 Matthew was made papal legate; and on February 20, 1298 he began preaching a crusade against the Colonnas, who surrendered by September 1298. Jacopone da Todi was clapped in jail, where he continued to inveigh against Boniface.

The first jubilee year in papal history (1300), was declared in part to reassert papal authority. On Epiphany (January 6), "Lord Matthew of Aquasparta preached, before the Pope and the cardinals, and before all, in the Church of St. John Lateran, that the Pope is the sovereign master (*sire*) over all things temporal and spiritual, whatever they are, in the place of God, by reason of the gift that God made to St. Peter, and to the Apostles after him" (*PL* 185: 1901a). Matthew was made papal legate over Florence on May 23, 1300, finally entering the city on December 15, 1301, from which he exiled Dante, among others (January 23, 1302).

By this time, the dispute had entered a new and deadly phase. On October 24, 1301 Bernard Saisset, Bishop of Pamiers, was arrested, tried, and convicted in Philip's presence, a direct violation of canon law. Boniface replied on December 5, 1301 with *Ausculta fili*: "Listen, son, to the commands of a father, heed the teaching of a master who holds on earth the place of Him who alone is Lord and Master," and also commanded the French bishops to attend a council in Rome called for November, 1302. In response, Philip convened the first meeting of the Estates General at Paris, April 10, 1302, where his adviser Pierre Flotte used forgeries to say that Boniface claimed feudal lordship over France. The nobility wrote to the cardinals, the clergy to the pope; and Philip's envoys were received in full consistory on June 24, 1302, where Matthew replied for the cardinals and Boniface in his own right.

In his address, Matthew took his theme from Jeremiah 1:10, which had become a proof text for papal power: "See I have set you this day over nations and over kingdoms, to pluck up and to break down, to destroy and to overthrow, to build and to plant." This theme applied to Jeremiah and John the Baptist, but it "can be said more truly of Christ and his Vicar St. Peter and his successors the supreme Pontiffs." Matthew then developed a legal argument that includes a memorable comparison based on the story of Absalom, who tried to usurp David's kingship with the connivance of Achitophel, the archetypal evil counselor. Boniface was like David, who held both spiritual and temporal power in Israel, Philip was like Absalom, led astray by Pierre Flotte, his Achitophel.

Matthew then began his theological argument on an impassioned, personal note: "So I stand for this truth, which I would dare to defend against the whole world and would dare to give my life: that the supreme Pontiff who is the vicar of St. Peter does have the plenitude of power." Three arguments in support of this conclusion followed.

"Christ, who was lord of the universe, bestowed his own power on Peter and his successors. Thus he said 'Feed *my* sheep' – not these or those but *my* sheep, and 'I give to you the keys to the kingdom of heaven'." These two biblical texts argue from the universal extent of the Church's authority, broader than any human power and symbolized by the keys, to the conclusion that all lesser powers must be subordinated to the one power of the Church. The reasoning is scholastic: a particular cause is subordinated to a universal cause. To try to avoid the argument by denying the universality of ecclesiastical and therefore papal power is also to deny "the Catholic Church, the communion of saints, the forgiveness of sins," an article of the Apostles' Creed. *Unam sanctam* would begin with this same article, as found in the Nicene Creed.

As he customarily did in theology, Matthew followed with a purely rational argument: "Even if you omit everything said thus far, I assume one [principle], that for everything in the whole universe there is some one supreme thing": one creator for the world, one father for each family, one captain for each ship. Deny this Neoplatonic principle and you produce disorder, making the community of God a two-headed monster. Matthew then reminded Philip's legates of Noah's ark; inside there was one ruler – Noah himself – while the flood produced chaos outside. The ark is a symbol of the Church, "the bark of Christ and Peter," outside of which there is no salvation. Since reason demands there be "one ruler and one head" for every hierarchy, it follows that the one head – the pope – "must be lord of all, temporal and spiritual, one who has the plenitude of power."

Matthew's last argument addressed the temporal sword, for Matthew knew a letter had been concocted by the king's advisers putting in Philip's mouth this insult to the pope: "Let your great fatuity know that in temporalities we are subject to none." The cardinal replied that "jurisdiction" covers law and right (*de iure*), but also actions taken to enforce the law (*actus et usus*). In spiritual matters, Christ gave to Peter and the supreme pontiffs full jurisdiction in both respects. The supreme pontiff "can *judge* every temporal matter *in respect of sin*" or "*de iure*," but Jesus said to Peter, "put your sword back in its sheath" (John 18: 11), which withdrew from Peter and his successors the right of enforcement – but only enforcement. It does not follow that Church and pope have no jurisdiction at all. To say less would deny the Church's right to judge the moral character of human actions and consequently deny two fundamental articles of faith: that Christ "will judge the living and the dead" and that the Church is "the communion of [morally virtuous] saints."

Subsequent events proved just how perceptive was Matthew's distinction. On October 30, 1302, with only 36 of 78 French bishops attending, Boniface's council opened, without Matthew, who had died the previous day. There is no documentary record on the cause of death, but it is humanly impossible not to think that the failure of his episcopal brothers to support the pope must have helped bring down Matthew, then by all evidence at the height of his powers. Within the month came *Unam sanctam*, clearly Boniface's tribute to his lieutenant and so close in style and substance to Matthew's address of the previous June that Matthew himself must have had a hand in drafting it (1962b: 14*–23*). Bereft of Matthew's advice and courage, Boniface succumbed to Philip's next attack, dying on October 11, 1303. Matthew's tomb, by the school of John Cosmati, is found in the Franciscan Church of Aracoeli in Rome.

The Franciscan *Chronica xxiv generalium* described Matthew as "a man of great achievement (*vir magnae sufficientiae*)" (1935: xi), achievement that rests squarely on his conception of authority. In matters of theory, Matthew followed Bonaventure and Dionysius with the zeal of a disciple. But he also made use of the more ancient authority of Augustine to cap an argument or solidify a doctrine, though here one senses more institutional solidarity than love and conviction. The same distinction characterized Matthew's practical life as a cardinal. He was in awe of the institution of the papacy and completely supported Pope Boniface's claims to "plenitude of power," supplying him with his best arguments, acting on his behalf, even preaching a crusade against the Colonnas. But one suspects Matthew was the instrument, not the disciple of Boniface. In practical life he was the disciple of only one human authority – the little plain man from Assisi. For Francis's practical genius had kept his new and eccentric way of life doctrinally orthodox and on the right side of papal power, while his most fervent disciples, the Spirituals – not least among the crosses Cardinal Matthew had to bear – failed utterly in this regard.

Bibliography

Primary sources

Unedited works

See Introduction, by V. Doucet (1935), in *Introitus to the Book of Numbers* (pp. xi–clx); *Brevis expositio of Ecclesiastes, Commentum in I, II, IV Sententiarum* (later *Additiones ad I Sent.* and a concordance of the *Sent.*); *Breviloquium de Trinitate*; *Postillae* on *Psalms, Job,* and *Apocalypse*; *Sermons*; *Quodlibetal Questions*.

Edited works

(1909), *Commentum in I Sententiarum* D. 2.2.1, ed. A. Daniels, in *Quellenbeiträge und Untersuchungen zur Geschichte der Gottesbeweise im xiii Jahrhundert, Beiträge zur Geschichte der Philosophie und Theologie des Mittelalters* 8.1–2 (pp. 52–63), Münster: Aschendorff.

(1934), *Commentum in I Sententiarum*, Prol. q. 7, ed. L. Amorós, *Archives d'Histoire Doctrinale et Littéraire du Moyen Âge* 9, pp. 284–5.

(1935), *Quaestiones disputatae de gratia*, ed. V. Doucet, Bibliotheca Franciscana Scholastica Medii Aevi 11, Quaracchi: Collegium S. Bonaventurae.

(1936), *Commentum in II Sententiarum*, D. 19.1, ed. S. Vanni Rovighi, in *L'immortalità dell'anima nei maestri francescani del secolo XIII*, vol. 23 (pp. 255–72), Milan: Publicazioni dell'Università Cattolica del Sacro Cuore.

(1956), *Quaestiones disputatae de productione rerum et de providentia*, ed. G. Gál, Bibliotheca Franciscana scholastica medii aevi 17, Quaracchi, Florence: Collegium S. Bonaventurae. (Contains *Quaestio 9 de productione rerum*, pp. 3–227; *Quaestio 6 de providentia*, pp. 231–395.)

(1957a), *Quaestiones disputatae selectae: quaestio de fide et de cognitione* (repr. of 1903 edn.), Bibliotheca Franciscana Scholastica Medii Aevi 1, Quaracchi, Florence: Collegium S. Bonaventurae. (Contains *Introitus ad s. scripturam*, pp. 3–22; *Introitus ad s. theologiam*, pp. 23–33, probably Matthew's principium as a master of theology; *Quaestio 8 de fide*, pp. 35–198; *Quaestio 10 de cognitione*, pp. 199–406; *Tractatus de processione spiritus sancti*, pp. 407–32.)

(1957b), *Quaestiones disputatae de incarnatione et de lapsu aliaeque selectae de Christo et de eucharistia* (repr. of 1914 edn.), Bibliotheca Franciscana Scholastica Medii Aevi 2, Quaracchi, Florence: Collegium S. Bonaventurae. (Contains *Quaestio 9 de incarnatione*, pp. 3–192; *Quodlibeta V*, q. 4, II, qq. 4–6, VI, q. 3, pp. 195–213; Disputations *in aula* and *in vesperiis*, pp. 213–30; *De morte Christi*, pp. 230–41; *Commentum in II Sententiis*, d. 21.2.1–2, d. 30.1.1–2, d. 31.2.1, pp. 244–304.)

(1957c), *Quaestiones de anima 6*, ed. A.-J. Gondras, *Archives d'Histoire Doctrinale et Littéraire du Moyen Âge* 24, pp. 203–352.

(1959), *Quaestiones disputatae de anima separata, de anima beata, de ieiunio, de legibus*, ed. G. Gál, A. Emmen, I. Brady, and C. Piana, Bibliotheca Franciscana Scholastica Medii Aevi 18, Quaracchi, Florence: Collegium S. Bonaventurae. (Contains *Quaestio 9 de anima separata*, pp. 3–176, and *Quaestio 8 de anima beata*, pp. 177–362; *Quaestio 3 de ieiunio*, pp. 363–428, and *Quaestio de legibus*, pp. 429–571.)

(1961), *Quaestiones disputatae de anima 13*, ed. A.-J. Gondras, Paris: J. Vrin.

(1962a), *Sermones de beata Maria virgine*, ed. C. Piana, Bibliotheca Franciscana Ascetica Medii Aevi 9, Quaracchi, Florence: Collegium S. Bonaventurae.

(1962b), *Sermones de S. Francisco, de S. Antonio, et de S. Clara*, ed. G. Gál and C. Piana, Bibliotheca Franciscana ascetica medii aevi 10, Quaracchi, Florence: Collegium S. Bonaventurae.

(1994), *Sermo de promotione ad aliquam dignitatem*, ed. L.-J. Bataillon, in "Le cardinalat vu par un futur cardinal: un sermon de Matthieu d'Aquasparta," *Archivum Franciscanum Historicum* 87, pp. 129–34.

Secondary sources

Hissette, Roland (1977), *Enquête sur les 219 articles condamnés à Paris le 7 Mars 1277*, Louvain: Publications Universitaires.

Matteo d'Aquasparta. Francescano, filosofo, politico, Atti del xxix convegno storico internationale, Todi, 11–14 ottobre 1992 (1993), Spoleto: Centro Italiano di Studi sull'alto Medioevo.

74

Maximus Confessor

ERIC D. PERL

Maximus Confessor (b. 580; d. 662), a Byzantine monk, is known principally for his defense of orthodox Christology against the imperially-sponsored monothelite and monoenergist heresies, for which he was exiled and mutilated. His thought, which transcends any distinction between philosophy and theology and unites the spiritual and intellectual traditions of Origen, the Cappadocian Fathers, PSEUDO-DIONYSIUS, and post-Chalcedonian Byzantine Christology, offers a comprehensive vision of reality founded in the mystery of Christ.

Maximus adopts the Neoplatonic doctrine of remaining, procession, and reversion: all things are pre-contained in God, are unfolded from him into creation, and return to him as their end. Creation is the pouring out or distribution of God to all things as the distinct "logos," or determinative principle, of each, at once its cause of being and its purpose or end. The logos of each thing is the presence in it of *the* Logos, God the Word: "The one Logos is the many logoi, and the many the one" (*Ambigua* 7, in *PG* 91, 1081B). Creation is thus analogous to Incarnation, a "thickening" of the Word (*Amb.* 33, 1285C–1289A), his self-presentation in created mode. Since all creation is contained in human nature, man is "microcosm and mediator" (Thunberg 1965), the locus wherein all creation comes together and is deified. Consequently, the intrinsic nature of creation is fulfilled in the Incarnation and its correlate, the incorporation of man, and in man all things, into God. This

> both deifies man to God . . . and hominifies God to man, by a fair inversion, and makes man God by the deification of man, and God man by the hominification of God. For always and in all the Word of God . . . wills to effect the mystery of his embodiment. (*Amb.* 7, 1084CD)

Therefore, the unconfused hypostatic identity of divine and human natures in Christ

> is the blessed end on account of which all things were constituted . . . God the Word become man . . . reveals in himself the end on account of which the things that are made . . . received beginning in being. For on account of Christ, that is the mystery of Christ, all the ages, and the things in the ages, take in Christ their beginning and end of being. (1980, *QT* 60, 621AB)

Maximus became a dominant influence in subsequent Byzantine thought, and was a major source for JOHN SCOTUS ERIUGENA, who translated some of his works into Latin and incorporated large extracts from them into his *Periphyseon*. In recent years, Maximus has been celebrated not only for his profound Christology, but also for his articulation of a philosophically and theologically coherent vision of "the cosmic Christ," of God the Word incarnate as not merely the redeemer of fallen man but the first principle and final end of all reality.

Bibliography

Primary sources

(1865), *Ambigua*, in *Opera omnia*, ed. R. P. Franc Combelis, in *Patrologia Graeca*, vols. 90–1, Paris: Migne.

(1980), *Quaestiones ad Thalassium*, ed. Carl Laga and Carlos Steel, Turnhout: Brepols.

Secondary sources

Balthasar, Hans Urs von (1961), *Kosmische Liturgie; das Weltild Maximus' des Bekenners*, 2nd edn., Einsiedeln: Johannes-Verlag.

Thunberg, Lars (1965), *Microcosm and Mediator*, Lund: C. W. K. Gleerup.

——(1985), *Man and the Cosmos*, Crestwood, NY: St. Vladimir's Seminary Press.

75

Meister Eckhart

JAN A. AERTSEN

Meister Eckhart (b. ca. 1260; d. 1328) was and is the most controversial thinker of the Middle Ages. He was the first distinguished master of theology against whom inquisitorial proceedings were constituted, and to the present day his thought has received widely divergent interpretations. The controversial character of his work partly stems from the fact that Eckhart occupies a special position within medieval intellectual history: he was not only a scholastic academic, but also active outside the university as a preacher and spiritual director for religious communities. This fact is reflected in the bilingualism of his work. Eckhart published not only in Latin, but also wrote treatises in the vernacular language that were destined for a non-academic audience.

Eckhart had a brilliant academic career. After entering the Dominican order, he studied theology at the *studium generale* of the order in Cologne and at the University of Paris. In 1294 Eckhart was named prior of the Dominican house in Erfurt and vicar general of Thuringia. In 1302–3 he was master of theology in Paris and in the next years he held executive positions within his order in Germany. A token of the high prestige the Meister enjoyed is that in 1311–13 he occupied for a second time the chair of theology at Paris that was reserved for foreign Dominicans – an honor also bestowed upon THOMAS AQUINAS.

In the next decade (1313–23), Eckhart worked in Strasbourg, where he was charged with the *cura monialium*, the spiritual care of the communities of Dominican nuns in the southern part of Germany. In this function, he was confronted with various religious lay movements, such as that of the Beguines. Eckhart's own utterances, such as his defense of preaching for "the unlearned," suggest that the difficulties at the end of his life go back to this period.

When in 1324 Eckhart returned to Cologne, probably as head of the *studium generale*, the Archbishop of Cologne started an inquiry into his doctrines on suspicion of heresy. Eckhart rejected all accusations in his "Rechtfertigungsschrift" and appealed to the pope in Avignon, but died before the conclusion of the trial. In the bull *In agro dominico* of March 17, 1329, Pope John XXII condemned 28 propositions taken from his works and sermons; 17 he declared to be erroneous or tainted with heresy, the other 11 he described as "offensive, very temerarious and suspect of heresy" (for the text of the bull, see Meister Eckhart 1980, pp. 77–81).

Eckhart's influence was exercised primarily through the German sermons and treatises that established his long-standing fame as a mystic and spiritual master. Another, more academic Eckhart, however, emerged when Heinrich Denifle rediscovered his Latin works in 1886. That rediscovery raised the controversial issue of the relation between the German ("mystical") Eckhart and the Latin ("scholastic") Eckhart. In recent literature, there is a strong reaction to the view that sees Eckhart primarily as a mystic. "Mysticism," it is argued (Mojsisch 2001), is a harmful model for our understanding of Eckhart, because it suggests an opposition to "scholasticism" and thereby isolates him from his contemporaries. Furthermore, mysticism today mostly denotes a kind of "irrational" experience, which is utterly foreign to Eckhart's works. He is not a theologian of "extasies"; his procedure is strictly rational. He intends to develop a "philosophy of Christianity," which relates him to modernity, in particular to German idealism.

The almost completed critical edition of Eckhart's Latin and German works (since 1936) has laid a new basis for the study of his thought. Although the edition has not yet resolved all problems of authenticity, especially with respect to the German sermons, it corroborates the thesis that there is no fundamental opposition between the German and Latin Eckhart. The following account will focus on the unity of his thought and its distinctive features.

Eckhart's project: the *Opus tripartitum*

Eckhart presents a comprehensive design of his thought in the *Opus tripartitum*; this text must therefore be the basis of any interpretation. As the title indicates, the work is divided into three parts: The *Opus propositionum* (*Work of Propositions*), which would contain, as Eckhart states, "more than one thousand propositions"; the *Opus quaestionum* (*Work of Questions*), organized after the model of the *Summa* of "the illustrious friar" Thomas Aquinas; and the *Opus expositionum* (*Work of Expositions*), consisting of commentaries on both Testaments of Sacred Scripture and of sermons (*LW* I, pp. 149–51).

Eckhart's project, which has no equivalent in the Middle Ages, distinguishes three forms of thought: propositions, questions, and expositions. The last two belong to what Eckhart calls "school exercises" (*actibus scholasticis*, *LW* I, p. 148); the "propositions" represent another tradition, the ideal of an axiomatic system, derived from the Neoplatonist Proclus (*Elementatio theologica*) and the anonymous *Book of Causes*. What is new in Eckhart's project is the connection of both traditions. One may wonder whether the incorporation of the *Work of Propositions* into the project does not imply a criticism of scholasticism. The "scholastic" method is marked by the *quaestio*. In response to a concrete question, certain principles and distinctions are put forward. Consider, for example, Thomas's proofs for the existence of God in the second question of the first part of the *Summa theologiae*. His "five ways" are all causal arguments, but what causality is and the manner in which it is differently conceived remain implicit to a large extent.

In this respect, a preliminary remark made by Eckhart in the General Prologue about the order of the *Opus tripartitum* is revealing. "The second work, and so too the third, are so dependent on the first, namely the *Work of Propositions*, that without it they are of little use, because the explanations of questions and the expositions of scriptural texts are usually based on one of the propositions" (*LW* I, p. 156). Eckhart next explains his manner of proceeding in the whole *Opus* through an example. He deals with the first proposition (which is the main thesis of the work), "Being is God" (*Esse est Deus*), the first question "Does God exist?", and the first text of Scripture, "In the beginning God created heaven and earth." He successively shows how the proposition is explained, how the question is solved by it, and how the scriptural text is elucidated by the same proposition (*LW* I, pp. 156–65). In the conclusion of the General Prologue Eckhart stresses the "rational" character of his procedure:

435

Finally, notice that all, or almost all, the questions concerning God are easily solved through the first proposition stated above, if the inference is well made; and most of what is written about him, even obscure and difficult matters, is clearly explained by natural reason. (*LW* I, p. 165)

From the Prologue, it appears that Eckhart's grand project acquires its systematic foundation in the *Work of Propositions*. The pressing problem for the study of Eckhart is that the *Work of Propositions* has not come down to us; probably the Meister never completed it. We only possess fragments of the *Opus tripartitum*: the General Prologue, the prologues to the first and second work (but not the works themselves) and considerable parts of the third Work: scriptural commentaries (on Genesis, Exodus, the Book of Wisdom, and the Gospel of John) and a collection of sermons. But despite the serious lacunae, the General Prologue and the Prologue to the *Work of Propositions* provide insight into the objectives of Eckhart's project.

Work of Propositions

In the General Prologue, Eckhart announces that the *Work of Propositions* would consist of fourteen treatises corresponding to the basic terms of which the propositions are composed. He also mentions the titles of the treatises:

The first treatise is about Being (*esse*) and being (*ens*) and its opposite, which is nothing.
The second, about unity and the one and its opposite, which is the many.
The third, about truth and the true and its opposite, which is the false.
The fourth, about goodness and the good and its opposite, evil.
The fifth, about love and charity and its opposite, sin.
The sixth, about the noble, virtue and right, and their opposites, the base, vice and wrong.
The seventh, about the whole and its opposite, the part.
The eighth, about the common and indistinct and their opposite, the proper and distinct.
The ninth, about the nature of the superior and its opposite, the inferior.
The tenth, about the first and the last.
The eleventh, about idea and reason and their opposite, the unformed and privation.
The twelfth, about "that by which it is" (*quo est*) and the contrasting "that which is" (*quod est*).
The thirteenth is about God himself, the highest Being, who "has no contrary except non-being," as Augustine says.
The fourteenth, about substance and accident. (*LW* I, pp. 150–1)

These titles indicate the basic terms of Eckhart's thought. They put forward perennial metaphysical themes, but also typically theological topics. The subject of the fifth treatise is not only *amor*, but also *caritas*, that is, Christian love. The title of the tenth treatise is of biblical provenance, it is about "the first and the last," the alpha and omega (Apoc. 1: 8 and 22: 8). From a reference in a scriptural commentary (*LW* I, p. 649), we know that the thirteenth treatise, which is about God, would deal with the divine Trinity.

A first feature of the *Work of Propositions* is that, in contradistinction to Aquinas's methodological separation of philosophy and Christian theology, it pursues a model of integration which is marked by an agreement between nature and Scripture. In the prologue of his most important commentary, that on the Gospel according to John, Eckhart states: "It is the intention of the author – as it has been indeed in all his works – to expound by means

436

of the natural arguments of the philosophers the doctrines taught by holy Christian faith and the Scriptures of the two Testaments." Conversely, he wants "to show how the truths of natural principles, inferences and properties are clearly intimated in the very words of Scripture expounded with the help of those natural truths" (*LW* III, p. 4). Eckhart's model of integration assumes the idea of the concordance of revelation and reason. The Christian truth is explained by a metaphysical proposition, but, on the other hand, Scripture contains "the keys to metaphysics, natural science and ethics" (*LW* I, p. 453).

The *Work of Propositions* is divided into fourteen treatises. There is no evidence at all for the claim that Eckhart's treatises correspond to the fourteen books of Aristotle's *Metaphysics* (cf. Aertsen 1999), so we need another principle of ordering.

Metaphysics of the transcendentals

The treatises I–IV of the *Work of Propositions* are about "being," "unity," "truth," and "goodness." They belong together, because they deal with the *transcendentia* (transcendentals), a doctrine that was developed in the thirteenth century. These terms signify that which is common to all things; because of their commonness they "transcend" the Aristotelian highest genera or categories. Most of Eckhart's remarks in the Prologues are related to these *termini generales*. Since the *Work of Propositions* is fundamental for the two other parts of the *Opus*, we may conclude that Eckhart's grand project finds its philosophical foundation in a "metaphysics of the transcendentals" (to use an expression of Josef Koch, 1973, p. 413). There is no other medieval work in which the doctrine of the transcendentals has such a prominent place.

The phrase 'metaphysics of the transcendentals', however, has the disadvantage that it does not sufficiently express the particular nature of Eckhart's doctrine. Several thinkers in the thirteenth and fourteenth centuries consider being and its transcendental properties as the proper subject of metaphysics. But in comparison to his contemporaries, Eckhart's doctrine of the transcendentals has distinctive features.

A first feature becomes evident when we take a closer look at the titles of the treatises I–IV. It is striking that in each case they refer to the transcendentals in a twofold way: by an "abstract" term ('being' (*esse*), 'unity', 'truth', and 'goodness') and by a "concrete" term ('being' (*ens*), 'the one,' 'the true,' and 'the good'). An *abstractum* signifies a perfection as separated from its concrete subjects; in Eckhart, however, the "abstractness" is not the result of an abstracting act of the human intellect, but rather expresses the ontological state of the perfection, its subsistence and identity.

In the General Prologue, Eckhart's first observation underlines the ontological priority of the *abstracta*. General terms like 'being', 'unity', 'truth', and 'wisdom' should not be conceived after the manner and nature of accidents. They are not posterior to their subjects but prior to them (*LW* I, pp. 152–3). In the thirteenth century, for example, in Aquinas, the focus of the doctrine of the transcendentals was on the *concreta*, on that which is (*ens*), is one (*unum*), is true (*verum*), and is good (*bonum*). In Eckhart, the center of interest moves to the abstract transcendentals.

This shift is connected with another distinctive feature of his doctrine, the identification of the transcendentals with God. The first proposition of the *Opus* reads: 'Being is God'. In the Prologue to the *Work of Propositions*, his first *notandum* is that 'God alone is properly being, one, true, and good' (*LW* I, p. 167). Eckhart gives the impression that this statement is a traditional teaching by adducing a great deal of references from Scripture, philosophers, and Church Fathers such as AUGUSTINE and Dionysius the Areopagite. It is true that, for instance, in Aquinas the transcendental names are at the same time divine names, but this traditional aspect of the doctrine acquires in Eckhart a new accent.

In the thirteenth century, one of the main problems of the doctrine of the transcendentals was the relation between these terms and that which is proper to God. In what sense can transcendentals be said of God? For Eckhart, the transcendentals are God's *propria*; for all other things, they are "strangers and foreigners" (*LW* III, pp. 83–4). For him, the question is rather: To what extent can transcendentals be said of finite things?

At this point in our analysis, we have to discuss a controversial issue in the study of Eckhart. How can the main thesis of the *Work of Propositions*, *Esse est Deus*, be reconciled with his view in the first Parisian question (1301/2), in which he contradicts the identification of Being and God? The subject in the Parisian question is: "Whether being and understanding (*intelligere*) are the same in God?" (*LW* V, pp. 39–48). Eckhart develops a series of arguments supporting the priority of understanding of being, arguments which can be read as a critique of medieval theo-ontology. 'Being' means to be caused, and is therefore, according to the famous fourth proposition of the *Book of Causes* ('The first of created things is being'), the mark of the finite world. God is not *esse* but *intelligere*.

In order to solve this contradiction, many scholars assumed a development in Eckhart's thought after the Parisian question. According to the commonly accepted chronology of Eckhart's works, the project of the *Opus tripartitum* was designed during his second regency in Paris (1311–13). But that chronology has been challenged by Loris Sturlese's recent discovery of another manuscript of Eckhart's Latin works in Oxford. His inquiry into the new materials suggests that the origins of the *Opus tripartitum* also go back to the period of Eckhart's first Parisian professorship (Sturlese 1995).

The new chronology undermines the idea of a development in Eckhart's thought. It seems plausible that he did not consider the divergent propositions in the Parisian question and the *Work of Propositions* as mutually exclusive alternatives. It is notable that in the Parisian question he leaves room for another semantics and another meaning of 'being': "Being" does not befit God, unless you mean by 'being' the purity and fullness of being (*LW* V, p. 45).

In the order of the *Work of Propositions*, treatises V and VI certainly belong together. The object of "love" is the good; the sixth treatise deals with "the moral good (*honestum*) and virtue." Both treatises are connected with treatises I–IV, not only through the mediation of the good, but also in an immediate way. It is noteworthy that when, in the General Prologue, Eckhart lists the "general terms," not only 'being' (*esse*), 'unity', 'truth', and 'goodness' are mentioned, but also 'wisdom'. In other texts, he also mentions 'justice', which is his paradigm of virtue, among "the most general perfections." The term 'perfection' seems to connote a more encompassing notion, which includes the traditional transcendentals and spiritual perfections.

The inclusion of spiritual perfections in the doctrine of the transcendentals is in itself not new. We find something similar in JOHN DUNS SCOTUS, who came to Paris in the same year as Eckhart (1302). Another distinctive feature of Eckhart's doctrine of the transcendentals is the central place of *moral* perfections.

The special place of ethics in Eckhart becomes clear in a university sermon which he gave during his first stay in Paris. In this sermon, he presents a threefold division of theoretical philosophy, for which he appeals to BOETHIUS. But Eckhart's presentation contains a significant modification; philosophy is divided into mathematics, physics, and "ethics or theology" (*LW* V, p. 90). The identification of philosophical theology (or metaphysics) and ethics is another aspect of Eckhart's integration model. In his project, the contemplative life is not separated from the active life. Eckhart is not only a *Lesemeister* ("lector"), but above all a *Lebemeister*. The ethical "appeal" is one of the reasons for the enduring fascination of his thought.

Guiding principles

As we have seen, treatises I–VI of the *Work of Propositions* form a unity that is based on a metaphysics of the transcendentals. The next six treatises also belong together – while treatises XIII (on God) and XIV (on substance and accident) conclude and summarize the work. The inner connection between treatises VII–XII is not immediately evident, because the notions they deal with are quite different from each other. But all of them are concerned with structural principles that determine and clarify the relationship between God and creature, explained in the first six treatises. This concern becomes obvious in the three distinctive features of Eckhart's metaphysics of the transcendentals: the identification of these notions with God, the shift from the concrete to the abstract transcendentals, and the inclusion of moral perfections in the doctrine.

Treatise VIII is "about the common (*communis*) and indistinct and their opposites, the proper and distinct." Commonness is the mark of the transcendentals. Is not a consequence of Eckhart's identification of the transcendentals with God that God is common? Indeed, Eckhart draws the conclusion, *Deus communis est* (*LW* IV, p. 51), but this statement has by no means a pantheistic connotation in his thought. He points out that it is precisely this commonness that constitutes God's transcendence and his difference from creatures.

Eckhart's argument is based on one of his central ideas, the distinction between "being" (*ens*) and "this or that being" (*ens hoc aut hoc*). Notice, he argues, that all that is common, insofar as it is common, is God, and that all that is not common, insofar as it is not common, is created. Every creature is something distinct, a "this" or "that," restricted to a genus or species (e.g., "man" or "stone"). God, however, is not something distinct, but rather common to all things; he is outside and beyond every genus (*LW* IV, pp. 51–2).

If the transcendentals are "foreign" to all creatures, is it then not a consequence that they are a pure nothing? In the General Prologue, Eckhart makes a preliminary remark that clearly refers to treatise IX on the "superior" and "inferior." "The prior and superior takes absolutely nothing from the posterior, nor is it affected by anything in it. On the contrary, the prior and superior influences the inferior and posterior and descends into it with its properties and assimilates it to itself" (*LW* I, p. 154). Because the transcendentals are proper to God, God alone is the cause of being, unity, truth, and goodness in all things. Creatures have being and the other transcendental properties completely from God.

The transcendentals are said "analogously" of God and creatures. In Eckhart's understanding of analogy, the perfections are as such only in one of the *analoga*, God; they are not rooted in creatures themselves. Eckhart denies any relative autonomy to creatures. In themselves, that is, separated from God, they are "nothing." This view determines the structure of treatises I–IV; they deal with the transcendentals and their opposites: "nothing," "many," "false," and "evil." This dialectical structure reflects the opposition between God and creatures when the latter are separated from God. Outside of being, which is God, there is nothing.

But this "nothingness" is not Eckhart's final word on the matter. There exists another relation between God and creatures, for which the relation between the abstract transcendental and the concrete subject is the model. It is a causal relation and a relation of participation. As *beings*, finite things participate in the transcendentals that are proper to God. To be, for a creature, is to receive being. Eckhart emphasizes that the reception of being is a permanent process, a continuous influx. Creatures have being and yet always receive it. This relationship is well expressed in a text from Ecclesiasticus (24: 21), commented upon by Eckhart, "Those who eat me, still hunger." Insofar as a creature is (and is one, etc.), it always "eats"; insofar as it is not of itself but through some else, it always "hungers."

In medieval thought, ethics occupies a major place, because it is concerned with the return of rational creatures to the principle from which they have come forth. The "first" is the "last" (the title of Eckhart's tenth treatise). Man's final end consists in the union with God. In order to become a *homo divinus*, a human being should "detach" itself from all that is creaturely. "Detachment" is the ethical consequence of Eckhart's metaphysical view that the distinction between God and creature has to be understood as the distinction between "being" and "this or that being." Every creature is a particular being, something distinct. God, however, is not something distinct; all that is common, insofar as it is common, is God. Therefore, it is man's highest virtue to detach and empty himself from all particularity. Detachment is the condition of his transformation into God and becoming a son of God (*filius Dei*).

The birth or generation of God in the human soul is a characteristic teaching of Eckhart. The philosophical ideal of man's divinization experiences a Christian transposition through the doctrine of the Incarnation. Man can become divine, because God has become man. The process of purification, detachment, and of the union with the One can be described as "mysticism," because the term is then used in the sense it has in the Dionysian tradition of "mystical theology." What Eckhart presents is not a report of an individual experience but a "rational" inquiry into the conditions of man's union with God.

The philosophical foundation of his account rests on the analysis of one of the general perfections that Eckhart connects with the transcendental notions, "justice." As he himself points out, his analysis of the relation between abstract justice and a concrete just (man) touches the core of his thought. "Whoever understands the doctrine of justice and the just understands everything that I am saying" (*DW* I, p. 105). In the return to God, man has to detach himself from that which is creaturely, from every particularity. He should become just *as just*. The process of detachment is the condition for another relation between the abstract and the concrete, not the relation between God and creature but that between Father and Son. "The Father begets his Son as the just one." Justice and the just, insofar as he is just, are entirely one; they differ only in that the justice bears and the just is born (*LW* II, p. 392). This relationship of the abstract to the concrete is Eckhart's model for the birth of God in the soul, which is the most adequate expression of man's union with him.

The German Eckhart

The German Eckhart is not different from the Latin one. Their fundamental agreement is demonstrated by his most influential German treatise *Das Buch der göttlichen Tröstung* (*The Book of Divine Consolation*), probably written about 1315 (*DW* I, pp. 471–97). The first (and most important) part of it is a profound metaphysical investigation.

In this part, Eckhart analyzes the relation between the concrete, general (or transcendental) perfections and the abstract ones. "One should know how the wise and wisdom, the true (man) and truth, the just and justice, the good and goodness refer to each other and are related to each other." He explains their relationship by means of the example of goodness. "Goodness is neither created nor made nor born, but it bears and brings forth the good (man); and the good, insofar as he is good, is not made and uncreated, and yet born child and son of goodness." The last sentence was attacked by the Archbishop of Cologne in the trial against Eckhart. In his defense (in the *Rechtfertigungsschrift*), Eckhart underlines that the meaning of his statement is determined by the key term *inquantum*. The good, *insofar as* it is good, is uncreated.

He next emphasizes the dynamic unity of the good and goodness. "The good and goodness are but one goodness, entirely one in all things, apart from bearing and being born . . . All that belongs to the good (man) he receives from goodness and in goodness. There he is and lives and dwells, as the Son says in Scripture (John 14: 10): 'The Father dwells in me and does the works'."

What has been said of the relation between the good and goodness also applies to the other general perfections. It is equally true of the truthful (man) and truth, of the just and justice, of the wise and wisdom. Eckhart goes on to say that it is equally true "of the Son of God and God the Father, of everything that is born of God and that has no father on earth, in which nothing that is created is born, nor anything that is not God." We see here how his reflection on the transcendental perfections prepares the doctrine of the birth of God in man. This doctrine is suggested by the text in the Gospel of John (1: 12–13): "To all those is given the power to become sons of God who were born, not of the blood or the will of the flesh or the will of man, but of and from God alone."

By "the will of man," Eckhart understands the highest powers of the soul, the immaterial faculties of intellect and will. Yet, since they themselves are not God, but were created in the soul and with the soul, they must be stripped (*entbildet*) of themselves and transformed (*überbildet*) into God alone, and born in God and from God, so that God alone may be their father, for in this way they are sons of God and the only-begotten son of God. A man so fashioned, God's son and the son of justice insofar as he is just, has everything that pertains to justice.

The conclusion of Eckhart's investigation reverts to one of his other basic thoughts, the idea of the concordance of revelation and reason. "From this teaching, which is written in the holy Gospels and recognized in the natural light of the rational soul, man finds true consolation in all his sufferings."

The Book of Divine Consolation contains all the main themes of the Latin Eckhart. It gives, as it were, a summary of the elements that are constitutive of his project. First, the German treatise presupposes the *Opus tripartitum*. This fact substantiates the thesis that the *Opus* provides the key to Eckhart's thought. Second, *The Book of Divine Consolation* confirms the role Eckhart attributes to natural reason, his "rationalism." In his project, which aims at the integration, not the separation, of philosophy and Christian theology, a principal aspect is the idea of the concordance of revelation and reason. Third, the treatise endorses the view that the metaphysics of the transcendentals is the philosophical foundation of the entire project. Finally, *The Book of Divine Consolation* shows the integration of metaphysics and ethics in Eckhart. Man's return to God requires detachment and transformation into God. Eckhart's analysis of the relation between justice and the just, that is, the relation between an abstract perfection and its concrete subject, explains the birth of God in man.

441

Bibliography

Primary sources

(1936ff), *Meister Eckhart*, vol. I: *Die deutschen Werke* (*DW*), vol. II: *Die lateinischen Werke* (*LW*), Stuttgart: Kohlhammer (the critical edition).

(1980), *Meister Eckhart: The Essential Sermons, Commentaries, Treatises, and Defence*, ed. and trans. E. Colledge and B. McGinn, New York: Paulist Press.

(1986), *Meister Eckhart: Teacher and Preacher*, ed. and trans. B. McGinn, F. Tobin, and E. Borgstadt, New York: Paulist Press.

Secondary sources

Aertsen, J. A. (1999), "Meister Eckhart, eine ausserordentliche Metaphysik," *Recherches de Théologie et Philosophie Médiévales* 66, pp. 1–20.

Goris, W. (1997), *Einheit als Prinzip und Ziel. Versuch über die Einheitsmetaphysik des "Opus triparti- tum" Meister Eckharts*, Leiden, New York, and Cologne: Brill.

Koch, J. (1973), *Kleine Schriften* I, Rome: Storia e Letteratura.

Largier, N. (1989), *Bibliographie zu Meister Eckhart*, Freiburg: Universitätsverlag.

——(1998), "Recent work on Meister Eckhart: positions, problems, new perspectives, 1990–1997," *Recherches de Théologie et Philosophie Médiévales* 65, pp. 147–67.

McGinn, B. (2001), *The Man from whom God hid Nothing: Meister Eckhart's Mystical Thought*, New York: Crossroad.

Mojsisch, B. (2001), *Meister Eckhart: Analogy, Univocity and Unity*, trans. O. F. Summerell, Amsterdam: Grüner.

Sturlese, L. (1995), "Meister Eckhart in der Bibliotheca Amploniana. Neues zur Datierung des *Opus tripartitum*," in A. Speer, ed., *Die Bibliotheca Amploniana: ihre Bedeutung im Spannungsfeld von Aristotelismus, Nominalismus und Humanismus* (pp. 434–46), Miscellanea mediaevalia 23, Berlin and New York: De Gruyter.

76

Michael of Massa

CHRISTOPHER SCHABEL

Little is known about the life of the Italian Augustinian hermit Michael of Massa (d. 1337). Born in the Siena area, he was his province's *definitor* in 1332, and he probably died in Paris, where he had lectured on the *Sentences*. Although his *Sentences* commentary on books I–II, his major philosophical work, survives in only a handful of manuscripts, Courtenay notes that "Michael of Massa's *Quaestiones in Sententias* remains one of the richest unedited and, for the most part, unstudied texts of the fourteenth century" (1995, p. 191). Massa's commentary was once dated to about 1325, but recently it has been shown that he is much more likely to have lectured in the 1330s, and indeed the written version was not yet completed at Massa's death. Since his commentary on book I was abbreviated twice in the fifteenth century, it had a long-term impact.

Massa's commentary on book II – the normal theological forum for natural philosophy – is an important witness to the reception of WILLIAM OF OCKHAM's physical theories at Paris. This work, extant only in one manuscript, is the first or one of the first to mention the existence of "Ockhamists" at the University of Paris, an issue of some significance and controversy. The fact that book II has now been dated to the mid-to-late 1330s rather than the mid-1320s suggests that Ockham's physics did not become a subject of controversy until a couple of years before the Paris arts faculty restricted the use of Ockham's works in 1339.

Although his commentary on book II appears never to have been cited, his book I had an impact within his order, most importantly on GREGORY OF RIMINI, one of the most influential thinkers of the late Middle Ages. Massa leaned away from the Dominican-oriented philosophy of GILES OF ROME and Gerard of Siena and towards the Franciscan school, and perhaps helped found an independent school of philosophy among the Augustinian Hermits. In the context of the problem of divine foreknowlege and future contingents, for example, Massa shows himself to be a close adherent to the doctrine of FRANCIS OF MARCHIA, OFM. It was probably Massa's treatment of the issue, building on and criticizing where necessary that of Marchia, that was the inspiration for Rimini's exhaustive and influential rejection of PETER AURIOL's stance. In particular, Rimini's defense (against Auriol) of the applicability of the principle of bivalence to propositions about future contingents resembles Massa's own. Future research will tell whether Massa had an impact on other aspects of Rimini's thought.

Bibliography

Primary source

(1998), "*In I Sentences*, dd. 35–38," ed. C. Schabel, in "Questions on future contingents by Michael of Massa, OESA," *Augustiniana* 48, pp. 165–229.

Secondary sources

Courtenay, W. (1995), "The *Quaestiones in Sententias* of Michael de Massa, OESA: a redating," *Augustiniana* 45, pp. 191–207.

Hödl, L. (1975), "Studien zum nominalistischen Schöpfungsbegriff in der spätscholastischen Theologie des Michael de Massa OESA (†1337)," *Cassiciacum* 30, pp. 234–56.

Trapp, D. (1956), "Augustinian theology in the 14th century: notes on editions, marginalia, and booklore," *Augustiniana* 6, pp. 146–274.

——(1965), "Notes on some manuscripts of the Augustinian Michael de Massa (†1337)," *Augustinianum* 5, pp. 58–133.

77

Moses Maimonides

ALFRED L. IVRY

Moses ben Maimon, known in the Latin West as Maimonides (b. 1138; d. 1204), is acknowl-edged as the most important Jewish philosopher of the Middle Ages, if not of all time. This is not to say that he is medieval Jewry's most rigorous philosopher (a title that should go to GERSONIDES, 1288–1344), but that his work had the greatest influence on those who followed him, an influence that is felt to this day.

Maimonides was born in Cordoba, Spain (the Arabic Andalusia, or Al-Andalūs), which belonged then to the Moorish Almoravid empire. He was born into a prominent rabbinic family that counted seven generations of communal leaders. In 1148 the Almohads, another Moorish dynasty, overran Andalusia and forced all non-Muslims to convert or leave the country without their possessions.

The Maimon family disappears from the historical record for about twelve years, sur-facing eventually in Fez, North Africa, the Almohad capital. Maimonides becomes a public figure at this time, owing to a spirited written defense of his dissembling coerced co-religionists in Andalusia. In this "Letter on Apostasy" (1977, p. 65), he urges these proto-Marranos to emigrate to countries where they can reaffirm their belief in Judaism, and argues that they should be welcomed back.

After this incident, the Maimon family sailed east to Palestine, before settling in Egypt, about 1165. There they found a tolerant Fatimid Muslim society, and a sizable Jewish com-munity. Settling in Fustat, adjacent to the new capital of Cairo, Maimonides began writing commentaries and interpretations of Jewish law of a strikingly original kind. He completed a commentary on the Mishnah (the earlier stratum of the Talmud) in 1168, and in 1170 wrote the *Book of the Commandments*, identifying and organizing the 613 commandments of Jewish law.

As the leading rabbinical authority of his time, both in Egypt and beyond, Maimonides' guidance was sought on many religious and political issues. The ensuing life-long corre-spondence is voluminous. It includes essays on messianism and resurrection that attempt in part to avoid conflict with popular notions of these concepts that he found philosophi-cally unacceptable.

Maimonides may have received official recognition of his status in the Jewish commu-nity at various times in the new Ayyubid regime of Saladin, which came to power shortly after the Maimon family arrived in Egypt. He soon also served the new regime as physician to the royal court, a position that gave him access to intellectual circles in Cairo. He wrote medical treatises which show his familiarity with Muslim and classical, mostly Galenic, sources. About 1180 he produced a monumental code of Jewish law, the *Mishneh Torah* (which can be translated as "The Reiteration of the Torah"). Then, between 1185 and 1190, Maimonides wrote the *Guide of the Perplexed*, his philosophical *magnum opus*. Written in Arabic with Hebrew characters, that is, Judeo-Arabic (1929), the *Guide* was translated into Hebrew even in Maimonides' lifetime, and became the most studied, controversial, and influential work of medieval Jewish philosophy.

The *Guide* is Maimonides' second work of a largely philosophical kind, the first being a *Treatise on Logic* (1938) which he is thought to have penned as a young man. Maimonides' knowledge of philosophy and science is evident, however, throughout his rabbinic as well as medical writings.

Maimonides read the Greek authors he so admired in Arabic translations and paraphrases made in the ninth century. He read his Aristotle and (abridgements of) Plotinus with the assistance of a rich body of commentaries and original compositions produced by Muslim *falāsifa* in the intervening 300 years (1963, pp. lvii–cxxxiiv). Jewish philosophy, in contrast, was barely out of its swaddling clothes at the time, and much of it too formally theological and Neoplatonic for him.

Maimonides was particularly taken with the logical and political writings of ALFARABI (d. ca. 950), though he also learned much from the ontology and prophetology of AVICENNA (d. 1037) and the epistemology of AVEMPACE (d. 1139). He approved of the Aristotelian commentaries written by his contemporary AVERROES (b. ca. 1126; d. 1198), but the extent of his familiarity with the Cordovan's work remains an open question (1977, p. 135; 1963, p. cviii).

Maimonides' *Treatise on Logic* is culled mostly from the logical treatises of Alfarabi (1938, p. 19; Kraemer 1991, p. 81). Its originality lies mostly in the organization of the material Maimonides had at his disposal and the structure that he gave to the subject, which is indicative of the perspective in which he viewed it.

The "art of logic," as Maimonides calls the treatise, is construed in broad terms, with minimal explanations. It is not meant to teach the subject, for as Maimonides says in his preface (1938, p. 34), many introductions already do that. He writes allegedly at the request of a person who apparently is a Muslim legal scholar, well educated in the Arabic language (and presumably its diverse literatures), but not familiar with the technical language of logic. This person wants to be given a brief explanation of its terminology, nothing more.

This strange request, and the way Maimonides responds to it, opens a window on the challenge philosophy presented to many intellectuals (Jews as well as Muslims) in the Islamic world. These were men who were familiar and comfortable with the "religious sciences" of their faith – scriptural exegesis, Arabic (or Hebrew) grammar, law, and theology – but who were unfamiliar and uncomfortable with the "secular sciences" of the classical heritage. They feared and desired such foreign knowledge, and particularly wanted to be able to follow the reasoning insisted upon by the philosophers. Philosophy, they knew, had its own methodologies through which the world was construed and described, metastructures which had to be learned, beginning with their names – if only to be rejected afterwards.

The struggle had already been joined in the tenth century, with rival claims of logicians and grammarians for the priority of their fields. Maimonides begins his first chapter of the *Treatise on Logic* with an (undeclared) attempt to put this ongoing conflict to rest, by showing how both fields run on parallel tracks, logic having its own grammar. He returns to this theme in chapter 13, again stressing the complementary nature of the two disciplines. Whereas Maimonides first explained such terms as subject, predicate, and proposition, he now speaks of the various classes of nouns, of univocal, equivocal, amphibolous, and metaphorical terms; these are distinctions that will preoccupy him later, when writing the *Guide*.

446

It is in the next, final chapter of the treatise that Maimonides serves notice to the grammarians and all non-philosophers of the priority of logic to all individual grammars, it being a sort of universal grammar. Following Alfarabi, he says (1975, p. 158; Kraemer 1991, p. 80), that 'logic' (Arabic *mantiq*, similar in semantic range to the Greek *logos*) is an equivocal term. It refers to the activities of the rational faculty in general, as well as to both the "inner" speech (or "inner reason", *al-nutq al-dākhil*) of apprehended intelligible thoughts, and to the "external" speech, or reason, which these intelligible ideas assume in language.

Language (every language) thus corresponds to thought and is ruled by it, even as the intelligible ideas, the contents of thought, are governed and guided by the rational faculty. Aristotle has described all aspects of this "art" of logic to perfection in the *Organon*, Maimonides states, having himself described the key terms of these books in the preceding chapters of this treatise.

There we indeed find the definitions of words, sentences, and propositions, their modes and relations; the nature and various figures of the syllogism; and the names of the Aristotelian categories. Maimonides presents these last as the *summa genera* for all "existing things" (*al-mawjūdāt*), in contrast to the (Porphyrian) predicables that are called universal "notions," (literally, "intentions," *al-ma'ānī*), i.e., mental constructs. For Maimonides it is clear that the art of logic uses data provided by our senses and our thoughts to construct a theory of meaning that underlies our understanding of semantics and linguistics; logic provides a necessary tool with which to reason in all areas of science.

In chapter 8 of the treatise (1975, p. 156), Maimonides tackles another long-standing and delicate issue with which philosophers had to contend: the status of assertions made in the name of faith, having the authority of tradition. Following Alfarabi again, Maimonides says that these statements are like others "which are known and require no proof of their validity." These propositions are those that are based on (healthy) sense perceptions or "first (and subsequent) intelligibles," as well as on "generally accepted opinions," propositions of a moral sort.

In order to be considered valid, traditions need only verify the general trustworthiness of the bearer, Maimonides says, apparently accepting thereby the standards of proof established by religious authority. He soon qualifies this statement, however, acknowledging that both "generally accepted opinions" and traditions are not always universally accepted; which is to say, they are not valid necessarily. The truly sound, or "certain" propositions, are those based on the data of our sense perceptions and the intelligible concepts that our rational faculty possesses. "Experience" can be relied upon also, he concedes, though presumably only to the degree it conforms to the preceding criteria.

Maimonides' following discussion of syllogisms, distinguishing with Aristotle between demonstrative, dialectical, and rhetorical proofs, associates dialectic with one or both premisses being of the "generally accepted" or conventional sort, and rhetoric with one or both premisses being based on tradition. In this way, it becomes clear he considers neither syllogism truly certain and necessarily true, a realization which will play a central role later in Maimonides' writing of the *Guide*, but which may be seen as already informing his rabbinic writings.

For Maimonides, as we have seen, the art of logic encompasses more than Aristotle's *Organon* and Porphyry's *Isagoge*. Logical constructs depend in part upon our perceptions of the physical world, and therefore it is necessary to identify its major categories. In chapter 9 of the treatise (1938, p. 55), Maimonides discusses Aristotle's four causes. Sensitive to the apprehensions of his reader(s), Maimonides states that (though) the final cause of man is the "attainment of ideas" (literally, the "apprehension of intelligibles"), the efficient cause of his formal nature, that of having a rational faculty, is God. This, Maimonides adds, is also the view of the philosophers, though they consider him the remote cause only, and search always for the proximate (physical) cause.

Maimonides in the *Guide* adopts the philosopher's view, and, taking the biblical prophets as philosophers, believes they too understood God as a remote cause. Maimonides explains their use of language that depicts God as an immediate, proximate cause of events to be a necessary stratagem, in effect a rhetorical appeal attuned to popular belief. Maimonides himself often refers to God in such terms also in the *Guide*, and almost exclusively so in his rabbinic writings. We should therefore view him in this modality as he viewed the biblical prophets.

It is also significant that, whereas Maimonides in this chapter of the treatise identifies God as the agent for bringing forms into existence, he does not refer to him at all in his discussion of matter. The material cause is traced down to the four elements, and beyond that to prime matter. The relation of prime matter to God is not discussed, foreshadowing Maimonides' difficulty with this issue in the *Guide*, apropos the question of the origin of the universe. The *Treatise on Logic* may thus offer some support to those who see him inclined towards the philosophers' view of the eternity of matter.

The importance for logic of understanding the concepts through which the philosophers classify the physical world is brought out forcefully in chapter 11 of the treatise, when Maimonides says (1938, p. 55) that "anyone who cannot distinguish between the potential and the actual, between *per se* and *per accidens*, between the conventional and the natural, and between the universal and the particular, is unfit to reason," that is, unable to discourse upon matters (*ghayr mukhātab*).

This charge would have been particularly wounding to the jurist for whom Maimonides wrote the treatise, a person known for his eloquent command of Arabic. Maimonides is here challenging him and the entire class of theologians in Islam, the *mutakallimūn* (the practitioners of *kalām*, dialectical theology) who denied these distinctions. These theologians are Maimonides' adversaries in the *Guide*, posing as serious a challenge to his belief in philosophy as the philosophers do to his belief in revelation. Maimonides here already asserts his staunch opposition to their claims.

Chapter 14, the final chapter of the treatise, follows its opening discussion of the full extent of the term 'logic', above discussed, with a full if brief discussion of the term 'philosophy' itself. Maimonides thus closes the treatise with a classification of the sciences along Aristotelian lines. Here the most striking feature is his description of political philosophy, or "science," as he calls it, which includes ethics, economics, and politics. "True happiness," he claims, is found in the governance of a city, in the moral education of its citizens, and in the creation of just laws for the society. In saying this, Maimonides again follows Alfarabi (Kraemer 1991, p. 97), lending support to those like Leo Strauss who advocate a political reading of the *Guide*. Whether it represents the mature Maimonides' view of the final perfection of the ideal man, his ultimate happiness, is another question.

Maimonides closes his remarks on political science with the observation that in ancient times men posited laws (*nawāmīs*, the Greek *nomoi*) to govern their societies, but "in these times . . . people are governed by the divine commands." Maimonides thus gives religious law, and the regime which is built upon it, pride of place over secular law and society, offering a statement which would do much to appease his addressee. It would also resonate with Maimonides' Jewish readers, and in a summary fashion reflects Maimonides' own belief.

In one sense, Maimonides is merely stating the obvious, given the nominally theocratic underpinning to Islamic and Jewish society in his time. In another sense, however,

Maimonides is closing the door on political theory, not willing to entertain the sort of assessments of political regimes that Plato initiated and that Alfarabi paraphrased and adapted. Nevertheless, as stated, Maimonides was drawn to Alfarabi's political as well as logical writings, and made ample use of them, even going so far as to copy passages verbatim from him.

This Farabian influence is evident in two self-contained compositions found within larger works, the first being a treatise on ethics in eight chapters (called as such; see 1975, pp. 60–104) which serves to introduce Maimonides' commentary on the treatise "Aboth" ("Fathers"), in his *Commentary on the Mishna*; the second being Maimonides' *Book of Knowledge*, which is the first of the fourteen books which comprise his code of Jewish law, the *Mishneh Torah*. The *Eight Chapters* is heavily indebted to Alfarabi's *Aphorisms of the Statesman* (also known as *Selected Aphorisms*; see Davidson 1977, p. 120), which itself draws ultimately upon Aristotle's *Nicomachean Ethics*; while the *Book of Knowledge* is closely modeled upon Alfarabi's *Opinions of the People of the Virtuous City* and related works (Kraemer 1979, p. 109), in which the influence of Plato's *Republic* is marked.

There are overlapping ethical teachings in both of Maimonides' compositions, though marked differences as well, structural as well as substantive. *Eight Chapters* emphasizes the psychic basis for moral behavior, locating it, as was customary, primarily in the appetitive faculty of the soul, the source of our desires and fears. Much of the treatise uses a medical analogy to discuss the proper treatment of the soul, which is to establish equilibrium in the soul by means of a dialectical employment of mutually undesirable opposite extremes (Chapter 4, in 1975, p. 67). There are, as Aristotle has said, rational or intellectual virtues as well as moral ones, and Maimonides recognizes (though he does not dwell on it) the role of the practical intellect in distinguishing between base and noble actions. A prophet, we are told in chapter 7, must have acquired all the rational virtues, and most of the moral virtues, before he can prophesy, his will governed by his intellect.

The will is free, Maimonides says in the last chapter of this composition, declaring that it is God's will that man perform his actions voluntarily. Inveighing against the *mutakallimūn* of Islam, Maimonides insists that God's will was manifested directly during the six days of creation only, and since then "all things act continuously in accordance with their natures" (1975, p. 87). Nature thus functions autonomously, however ultimately dependent upon God, its physical principles having been established by him. These principles can be learned, Aristotle primarily has taught them, and they presumably offer our understanding of the natural world a sense of demonstrable certainty and necessary truth.

Maimonides has no sympathy, however, with the theologians who speak of "rational laws" that govern moral behavior (1975, p. 80). The virtues and vices that are so identified, however widely agreed upon, are just that: "well-known," conventional agreements that have no universal premises with which to establish their necessary truth value.

Maimonides recognizes that many of the things that both Jews and Gentiles condemn are regarded, within the Jewish tradition, as declared bad by God. This does not change their epistemic status, however, for Maimonides; propositions invoking them remain reasonable, though not demonstrable assertions. Maimonides here identifies such actions as murder, theft, fraud, harming an innocent man, repaying a benefactor with evil, and degrading parents.

As opposed to these widely agreed upon moral judgments, Maimonides acknowledges a category of commandments in Scripture that has no obvious moral entailments, the injunctions accepted on the basis of the authority of tradition, which "if it were not for the Law, they would not be bad at all" (1975, p. 80). As such, they pose an ethical problem for

449

Maimonides, only partially resolved by his identification of the person who obeys them with Aristotle's "continent man" (*Nicomachean Ethics* VII).

Maimonides believes that a Jew who follows the law, whether in the form of rational or a-rational commandments, chooses voluntarily to do so, but he does not dwell in Aristotelian fashion on the issue of choice, or for that matter, deliberation. The good has been revealed, in every area of life, and one should feel obligated to accept that.

The section devoted to ethics in the *Book of Knowledge*, called by its translator "Laws concerning character traits" (1975, pp. 27–58), posits that Jewish law assists in finding the desirable mean between undesirable extreme expressions of each trait, or virtue. As such, the treatise is necessarily political, part of a grand scheme which Maimonides, adapting Alfarabi, designs to create a shadow polity, to strengthen a people in exile. Maimonides is in the position here of the Platonic and Farabian philosopher-statesman, identifying the values necessary for his people's survival and welfare, and locating the corresponding laws (Kraemer 1979, p. 109).

There is a certain irony here, since the role model Maimonides affirms in this treatise, as well as in the earlier *Eight Chapters*, is far from being a political figure, as that term is usually used. Rather, he is the sage who is preoccupied with the study of the law, the scholar whose consuming goal is knowledge of the Lord. Such a person is involved with others in society, and fulfills his obligations towards them, but he remains psychologically detached. He is not averse to the pleasures of this world (in which he is commanded to participate), but he is essentially indifferent to them.

This stance is the opposite of Aristotle's ideal man, the gentleman who is psychologically as well as physically engaged in the world, a benefactor of his society and a proud seeker and recipient of its honors. This man has a positive attitude to the physical world and enjoys the political challenges that he faces. He may recognize that true happiness ultimately is found in intellectual contemplation (*Nicomachean Ethics*, X. 7 1178a7), but that does not dissuade him from enthusiastic participation in the governing of his society. This man is a political animal, and accepts himself, in part, as such.

Maimonides tacitly dissents from Aristotle in these matters. This may be due in part to the particular circumstances in which Jews lived in Maimonides' time, that of a tolerated but threatened minority, a people whose faith was often challenged, and before whom the temptation of assimilation and apostasy was all too real. Maimonides could not, under these circumstances, adopt Alfarabi's posture of a disinterested political theorist, or endorse a humanistic, triumphalist ethical image. His writings on ethics and politics reflect in part the reality of Jewish history, of a life in political and existential exile.

There are nevertheless many moral virtues that Maimonides shares with Aristotle, via Alfarabi (Davidson 1977, p. 122). These include the virtues of moderation, justice, gentleness, contentment, courage, and even wittiness (*Nicomachean Ethics* II. 7; 1975; 1912, p. 67). Maimonides includes as well the Aristotelian virtues of liberality and magnificence, but whereas the Stagirite distinguished between the two on the basis of the size of their donations (*Nicomachean Ethics* IV. 2), the magnificent man being a great public benefactor, Maimonides considers liberality in terms of private expenditures, and magnificence (which he renders closer to "generosity" (*karam*)) in terms of charitable acts towards others (1975, p. 98).

Maimonides thereby shows his discomfort with honoring the person of great means who lavishes his wealth upon public institutions, expecting in return – and for Aristotle deserving of – recognition of his greatness and prestige. Similarly, Aristotle's "proud" man, though possessing all the virtues, is very concerned with being honored (*Nicomachean Ethics* IV. 3

1123b30), and therefore has no place in Maimonides' scheme. He replaces him with the man whose humility is beyond anything Aristotle would admire, for it is a humility that is self-abasing in the extreme.

Maimonides is explicit about this in chapter 2 of the "Laws concerning character traits" in the *Book of Knowledge* (1975, p. 31), building upon the biblical characterization of Moses in Numbers 12: 3 as "very humble," and upon Talmudic condemnations of arrogance. The Talmud also contains condemnations of anger, and Maimonides fully concurs in this. One should be trained not even to feel anger, let alone to show it, he believes. A parent or community leader may feign anger, as a pedagogic technique, but should not succumb to the emotion.

In taking these positions, Maimonides not only deviates from the Aristotelian mean that is his behavioral and ethical guideline in general, but also from the Aristotelian image of a healthy, virtuous person (Frank 1990, p. 272). This is a person whose emotional responses to life are apposite to the situations confronted, a person who is not inhibited in expressing a full range of feelings. This person has a sense of self-worth and self-esteem that Maimonides' man would lack, that he would see as vanity, even as idolatry in that it regards man as the center of his world. Friendship, for example, the deep, disinterested love for another person that is so valued by Aristotle (*Nicomachean Ethics* VII. 3 1156b6), is left out of Maimonides' list of virtues. He believes that one should love one's neighbor as oneself, be generous, kind, and courteous; but the sort of friendship of which Aristotle speaks should be reserved for one's relation with God.

Beyond his admiration for much of Aristotle's ethics, then, and particularly the idea of virtue as a mean between extremes, ultimately Maimonides has a perspective on man's place in the world different from that of Aristotle and Alfarabi. Maimonides' ideal man is not just a sage who is wise in the ways of both philosophy and the law, he is also, and even more so, a *hasid*, a pious man who goes beyond the letter of the law, an extremist in devotion and a border-line ascetic. Maimonides' *hasid* approaches rejection of the pleasures and benefits that life has to offer, and has a profound sense of his and mankind's unworthiness.

For Maimonides, Jewish law itself tends to the extreme, with the intention to bring people thereby towards the mean in their conduct. The law therefore addresses the average person, and Maimonides believes it does so in an exemplary and all-encompassing way. At the same time, he is clearly attracted to the more extreme manifestations of piety, those that distance a person from his family and society, and bring him into closer proximity with God.

Maimonides' ethics, accordingly, are twofold. While the commandments are seen as instrumental in character formation, some more obviously so than others, they are also understood to be invested with a sanctity revealed at Sinai that makes them, and the life lived in observance and study of them, into ends, or rather quasi-ends, in themselves. The true end of life, the purpose of man's existence, for Maimonides as for the classical rabbinic tradition, is to know God and walk in his ways.

For Maimonides, as for his philosophical predecessors, metaphysics precedes ethics and grounds it. This is made explicit in the structure of the *Book of Knowledge*, where the very first section of the book, the "Laws concerning the basic principles of the Torah," precedes the "Laws concerning character traits." In the "Laws concerning the basic principles of the Torah," the first commandment and most fundamental principle of the faith, according to Maimonides, is to know that there is a God, and that he alone is responsible for bringing all else into existence (2000, p. 141).

Maimonides supports this principle with one (abbreviated) proof, which assumes an eternal universe in which the outermost sphere of the heavens is always in motion (together with all the spheres within the cosmos), thereby requiring an eternal mover. This is the one, unique and incorporeal deity, whose essence we cannot comprehend, but whom we are commanded to love and fear.

These responses are elicited, according to Maimonides, by an awe-inspiring appreciation of nature, perceiving it as bearing witness to God's wisdom; accompanied by a sense of personal insignificance and profound intellectual limitations. However limited, Maimonides has here sketched out an argument from design, which he believes all people can grasp. It is through "reflection" or "contemplation" (*hitbonnenut* in Hebrew, the root letters of which entail the cognitive act of discernment) that one is led to appreciate the natural world and to realize its dependence upon God.

The love and fear of God (which fear is awe when properly understood, the Hebrew term *yir'ah* admitting both meanings) are, then, dependent upon our knowledge of him, which is only attainable through our understanding of the natural world. Accordingly, Maimonides proceeds, in this first section of his *Book of Knowledge*, to present an outline of mostly Aristotelian views of physics and metaphysics, all considered as part of the foundations of the Torah.

Maimonides appropriates the philosophical heritage by asserting that it is part of the ancient Jewish tradition as well, but kept secret to all but a select few because of the profundity (and no doubt volatility) of the subject (Lerner 2000, p. 146). He adopts Talmudic references to the "account of the chariot" and the "account of creation" (probably originally referring to mystical or Gnostic ideas), to (mostly) Aristotelian metaphysics and physics respectively. This invoking of the authority of tradition provides him a defense (or so he vainly hoped) against the charge of innovation and importation of foreign ideas into Judaism.

Maimonides believes the proper understanding of God requires awareness that the biblical descriptions of him in corporeal terms are not to be taken literally (Lerner 2000, p. 142). As the rabbis had said, "the Torah speaks in the language of the sons of man," which Maimonides regards as both a linguistic and political necessity. It offended him, however, that people of his time continued to hold a fundamentalist view of Scripture, and that they refused to believe that the prophets' descriptions of God in anthropomorphic terms were intended as metaphors. He himself is more cautious in this work than he is in the *Guide*, apparently willing to present angels as immaterial beings separate from the intelligences of the spheres (Lerner 2000, p. 144); and to claim later in the book that each word of the Torah came directly from God himself.

Maimonides here presents dogmatically issues that he qualifies greatly in the *Guide*. Among them is the claim that the human soul, being innately separate from the body, survives death, knows its creator, and endures forever (Lerner 2000, p. 152). Later, however, Maimonides excludes a variety of types from immortality, considering them doomed by virtue of holding false beliefs. Among these unfortunate persons is one who commits no transgression, but simply separates himself from the community, being indifferent to the plight of his people (Hymanson 1962, p. 85a).

It is clear from such statements that Maimonides is writing a code of law that is meant to have political muscle, however unrealistic under present circumstances some of its ordinances are. He believes that observance of the commandments, and the ethical life that they entail, is a prerequisite for doing philosophy, and that they have a beneficial effect upon the world as a whole (Lerner 2000, p. 153).

It is in the *Guide of the Perplexed*, his final work, that Maimonides tackles in philosophical depth many of the issues that he has summarily mentioned in his earlier writings. It is here too that his more prolonged analyses reveal the uncertainty he feels in positions held before with apparent confidence. This raises the question whether Maimonides' thinking has evolved over the years, and particularly in the relatively short span of time that passed between his writing the *Mishneh Torah* and the *Guide*; or whether Maimonides deliberately misrepresented certain views in his rabbinic writings, for political purposes. As taught by Alfarabi in a tradition going back to Plato, and as indirectly endorsed by Maimonides in *Guide* III: 32 (1963, p. 526), it is at times incumbent upon the leader of a state (or people) to deceive the masses for their own good, and in order to retain their confidence in him.

A third possibility is that Maimonides began the *Guide* with one set of philosophical beliefs, and in the course of subjecting them to close inquiry was obliged to modify his views. He seldom actually admits to his own perplexities, having written the book to relieve a former favorite student of the perplexities the young man had. Still, it may be taken as a general maxim that one writes a work of this sort for oneself as much as for another, and that Maimonides is working out his own dilemmas too in this confrontation of theology and philosophy.

It is the theology of the *Mutakallimūn*, the Muslim adherents of *kalām*, and their Jewish followers, that Maimonides confronts in the *Guide*. It is their teachings that have perplexed his student and brought him to Maimonides in the first place (Dedication; 1963, p. 4). As the now distant pupil is reminded in the book's dedication, Maimonides would not help him before instructing him in the "proper methods" by which truth could be established and "certainty" arrived at in an orderly, not accidental manner. Presumably he managed to do this, as well as to begin to explain his hermeneutical approach to the Bible and midrashic literature, before circumstances compelled the young man to depart.

The *Guide* is thus written for one who has reached a certain level of philosophical and scientific sophistication, one who has studied, we are told, logic, mathematics, and astronomy. The reader also is expected to have been introduced to physics and metaphysics of an essentially Aristotelian kind, and to be familiar as well with the basic tenets of Neoplatonism. Maimonides usually employs concepts from both these philosophical traditions without explaining them.

Maimonides does explain, in the introduction to the first part of the *Guide*, that the purpose of the book is to explain the biblical prophets' use of language. The reader should recognize that individual terms have more than univocal meanings, and that entire passages should be seen as philosophical parables.

This is a lesson that the alleged addressee of the *Guide* would have learned already, indicating that Maimonides is aware that not all his readers will be as sophisticated as his former pupil. He is writing for a wider audience than he claims, and this may account for much in the *Guide* which is not persuasive philosophically, and which he would have known to be such. This does not mean that the work essentially is one of theology, not philosophy, but that there are elements of both in the *Guide*. Maimonides does not believe there is a fundamental schism between Jerusalem and Athens, as Leo Strauss (1984) has argued, and certainly he sets out in the *Guide* to resolve the apparent conflict between faith and reason.

Philosophy is part of the Jewish tradition, he reiterates (I: Introduction; 1963, p. 6), having already said so in the *Mishneh Torah*. Knowledge of physics and metaphysics is necessary for apprehending God as much as we may, thereby reaching individual perfection, and – through observance of his laws – bettering our political state. Due, however, to the profundity of the subject and the limitations of our understanding, Maimonides says, philosophy has been communicated in the Bible and Jewish tradition in parables and riddles. Terms are often employed equivocally to accommodate the masses, while enabling the "perfect man, who is already informed," to understand their deeper meanings.

453

Maimonides comes, then, to assist the reader to understand the philosophical teachings of Judaism, many of which he believes concur with those of Aristotle, particularly in the natural sciences and in sub-celestial physics. Loyal to his alleged predecessors, and facing circumstances similar to theirs, Maimonides will not, however, be particularly forthcoming in his explanations. Moreover, he informs the reader that the book, while composed with utmost care so that every word is in its place, contains deliberate contradictions and contrary statements (I: Introduction; 1963, p. 17). These are necessitated, he claims, for pedagogical reasons, or are due to the profound, or obscure (the same word in Arabic) nature of the subject.

This last reason has alerted readers since medieval times to the presence in the *Guide* of an esoteric doctrine, and much scholarship in the twentieth century followed Leo Strauss (1987) in attempting to identify contradictory and contrary positions within the work. Where discovered, the standard procedure has been to assume Maimonides' genuine view is the unorthodox position, which is usually the one he mentions less frequently.

Thus Maimonides has been seen by diverse scholars as believing in an eternal and not created universe, in an impersonal and not historic deity, and in a collective and not personal immortality. Some scholars have concluded he is an agnostic or a skeptic, despite his apparent dedication to the philosophical enterprise.

Certainly, the work itself begins, after the introduction, on a decidedly nonphilosophical, even dogmatic note. Maimonides follows his avowed purpose of explicating biblical language to didactically deny all anthropomorphic expressions in Scripture, going through most of the first forty-nine chapters of the first part of the *Guide* to do so. The first terms he clarifies are 'image' and 'likeness' as used in Genesis 1: 26, "let us make man in our image, after our likeness." This has led people to imagine God has a man's form, Maimonides states, whereas the terms really refer to the essential nature of God and man, namely, intellect.

In the second chapter of the *Guide*, Maimonides informs the reader that the intellect that God and man have in common (to whatever degree) is the theoretical intellect; that indeed it was God's intention originally to create a perfect universe, a paradise in which man would have no need for a practical intellect. Adam at first, in this reading, was to be concerned only with propositions that yielded certain (since necessary) knowledge, in which he could discriminate between truth and falsehood; and he had no need and no faculty for distinguishing between generally accepted (but not universal and hence not necessary) propositions, the basis for judgments of good and evil.

This parabolic reading of the fall, whatever its philosophical merit, well conveys Maimonides' estimation of the inferior status of *praxis* to *theoria*. He recognizes that postlapsarian man has to attend to socio-economic, ethical, and political issues, and much of the third part of the *Guide* is his attempt to show, in a necessarily nondemonstrative way, that the commandments of Judaism do that, and in an exemplary manner. Maimonides' preference for theoretical contemplation is clear, however. As brought out in the closing chapter of the *Guide*, "true human perfection . . . consists in the acquisition of the rational virtues . . . the conception of intelligibles which teach true opinions concerning the divine things" (III: 54; 1963, p. 635). It is thus metaphysical knowledge that ultimately returns man to Eden and to the divine realm, granting him "permanent perdurance" there. However, as he has indicated earlier, in *Guide* I: 74 (1963, p. 221) the soul which survives death has no individual aspects of personality, being comprised of the universal ideas or "intelligibles" a person has acquired, which are eternal.

Maimonides' most sustained philosophical arguments are found in the middle of the *Guide*. First he brings out the full implications of his crusade against anthropomorphisms by a thorough analysis of the difficulties involved in predicating anything of God; then he embarks on arguments for the existence, unity, and incorporeality of God, posing his views as responses to those of his intellectual adversaries, first the *mutakallimūn*, then the *falāsifa*.

Maimonides makes it clear that the logic of God's absolute unity precludes any meaningful attribution, which would have the effect of dividing the divine essence into a composite being having subject and predicate. He regards all propositions with positive attributes as either tautologies or shorthand ways of negating the privations of these attributes. Thus, to assert that "God is living" is to mean that he is not dead; saying that he is "powerful" means he is not powerless, 'knowing' means not ignorant, and 'willing' means not inattentive or negligent (I: 58; 1963, p. 135).

It is doubtful, however, if Maimonides' doctrine of negative attributes avoids the syntactic and hence logical entailments of positive attribution (Stern 2000, p. 210). He understands that the very structure of language does not allow us to articulate in any way, or to discursively comprehend, God's unique essence. We cannot attribute a relationship of any sort between God and the world without infringing on the utter simplicity of his being. Even the actions we attribute to God, which Maimonides is most prepared to tolerate, realizing their necessity for popular religion, he considers projections of our own responses to events; God being impervious to change or affect of any sort (I: 53; 1963, p. 121).

This image of God is necessitated for Maimonides by philosophical proofs for the existence of such a being, incorporating Aristotelian arguments for a first unmoved mover of self-contained intelligence with Avicennian arguments for a necessary being whose essence is existence and who endows the world with its existence. Yet, adopting Avicennian and ultimately Neoplatonic doctrines, Maimonides goes beyond Aristotle and his own stated views on divine attributes, to affirm an active role for God in the world. He is the emanating principle of all existence, the governing source of the order found in the world, and as such may be called a providential and all-knowing deity.

Maimonides has thus affirmed and denied God's involvement with the world. Even the affirmation, however, does not allow Maimonides to present God in the personal, volitional terms the Bible offers. This is what the theologians of *kalām* do offer, and Maimonides' explicit rejection of them is striking. He opposes the *mutakallimūn* mainly because of their anti-scientific science and what we could call their purely formal logic; their doctrine of atomism and Occasionalism in which objects have no inherent properties whatsoever, and everything is dependent upon the constant and unilateral exercise of the divine will. Anything imaginable is possible, according to them, as long as it is not self-contradictory (I: 73, p. 206).

Maimonides thus understands the *mutakallimūn* to believe logic has no necessary relation to the physical world, all propositions being equally possible and equally fanciful. He rejects this understanding of logic, with its indifference to the distinctions between demonstrative and nondemonstrative syllogisms. For Maimonides, as for all the philosophers of his day, it is only the apodictic syllogism, with its necessary premises drawn from experience in the world, which offers absolutely certain truth. That said, it has not escaped the attention of scholars, and probably of Maimonides himself, that most of his arguments in the *Guide* are dialectical in nature, a fair number are rhetorical, and few in fact are demonstrative.

As a good Aristotelian, Maimonides believes the possible has natural limitations and natural causes which the intellect, and not the imagination, can determine. It is the order and continuity in nature that allows us to pursue knowledge, and to rely on our senses and intellect. He concludes his discussion of the views of the *mutakallimūn* by saying "they have abolished the nature of being" in their arguments for creation in time, yet "the demonstrations (of the existence, unity and incorporeality of God) . . . can only be taken from the permanent nature of what exists, a nature that can be seen and apprehended by the senses and the intellect" (I: 76; 1963, p. 231).

Maimonides' faith in science and demonstration thus seems unshaken at first, and enables him to go to Aristotle and his successors for most of his proofs concerning God. He lists and approves of the basic tenets of Aristotelian physics in the introduction to the second part of the *Guide*. It is only the data that Ptolemy and later Muslim astronomers have compiled challenging Aristotle's model of celestial motion (II: 9, 11), that give him grounds to believe Aristotle's arguments for an eternal universe are not demonstrably true, and which allow him to offer an alternative scenario positing creation from nothing. He feels he needs creation to buttress the notion of divine will, and for that reason would be prepared to accept Plato's cosmogony, were it demonstrated to his satisfaction (II: 25; 1963, p. 328).

Maimonides bases his argument for creation *ex nihilo* on the thesis that it is logically possible to claim that the laws of physics and logic, though eternal *a parte post*, did not exist prior to the creation of the world, such that creation would not have been logically impossible. In so arguing, however, Maimonides adopts *kalām* methodology, reasoning from a self-contained logic that is totally removed from any physical, and correspondingly rational, correlation. It is likely Maimonides was aware of this, and this may well be one of the secrets of the *Guide*.

Perhaps it is his inability to argue convincingly for creation, together with his awareness of the inadequacy of Aristotelian-based celestial physics, that strengthens Maimonides' claims concerning the limitations of the human intellect to know anything with certainty beyond the sublunar realm. Yet, for all his disclaimers, Maimonides appears to believe much can be said, if only with a probable degree of truth, about both the heavens and their master. He does not publicize the logical status of his assertions, however.

Creation is mostly important to Maimonides in that it allows him to affirm the miracle of revelation, particularly that at Sinai, the source and guarantor of the Law. Yet Maimonides knows that the biblical account of God's interventions in history, and the entire assumption of miracles, wreaks havoc with his conception of God and of nature. Sinai, and the Torah as a whole, is therefore presented in good part as the record of Moses' unique, though still limited, understanding of God; even as the theophanies experienced by the other prophets in the Bible testify to their individual powers of comprehension. While all other prophets express their understanding of God in imaginative terms, Moses is said to have had direct and purely intellectual communion with God, rendering Mosaic prophecy and the Law which ensues from it unsurpassable and eternally valid.

This claim is politically necessary for Maimonides, but conflicts with the historic rationale he offers elsewhere in the *Guide* for certain biblical practices and laws, such as sacrifices. More significantly, claiming unique status to Mosaic prophecy overlooks the Torah's conventional use of language and its unavoidable association with the imaginative faculty. Moses' authentic communication with the divine has to be beyond linguistic expression, beyond discursive thought. The Torah as we have it, divinely inspired as it is, is still a human document (Ivry 1995, p. 295). This is one of the deepest secrets of the *Guide*.

Maimonides makes an attempt to safeguard the inimitability of the Torah by claiming a nearly superhuman status for Moses. Others, like philosophers, who are continually absorbed in knowing as much as can be known of eternal truths, may reach a similar level, one in which no harm can befall them (III: 51; 1963, p. 625). Maimonides means by this that the physical misfortunes that may occur to such persons are not significant to them, they are in another place, in a divine and eternal realm of being.

In ways such as these, Maimonides expresses an essentially naturalistic philosophy, accommodating it to the demands of traditional religion as best he can, aided by Neoplatonic modifications of Aristotelian doctrine. Maimonides' concern for upholding the law of his people is paramount throughout his writings, even if ultimate happiness and immortality depend upon metaphysical knowledge.

Maimonides' use of the tools of philosophy brought the discipline into prominence within the Jewish community, which has been divided ever since in its interpretation of his beliefs. In Latin translation, the *Guide* made an impact on scholastic thought as well, particularly for what was judged to be its attempts to modify a strictly Aristotelian approach to philosophy. On the other hand, Spinoza, for all his criticism of Maimonides' adherence to the Law, was much taken with his naturalism.

Bibliography

Primary sources

(1912), *The Eight Chapters of Maimonides on Ethics (Shemonah perakim): A Psychological and Ethical Treatise*, ed. Joseph I. Gorfinkle, New York: Columbia University Press.

(1929), *Moses Maimonides: Delālah al-Hā'irīn*, ed. S. Munk, Jerusalem: Azriel Press.

(1938), *Maimonides' Treatise on Logic*, trans. I. Efros, New York: American Academy for Jewish Research.

(1962), *Mishneh Torah: The Book of Knowledge*, trans. M. Hyamson, Jerusalem: Boys Town Publishers.

(1963), *The Guide of the Perplexed*, 2 vols., trans. S. Pines, Chicago: University of Chicago Press.

(1975), *Ethical Writings of Maimonides*, ed. R. L. Weiss and C. E. Butterworth, New York: New York University Press.

(1977), *Letters of Maimonides*, trans. L. D. Stitskin, New York: Yeshiva University Press.

(2000), *Maimonides' Empire of Light*, ed. R. Lerner, Chicago and London: University of Chicago Press.

Secondary sources

Davidson, H. (1977), "Maimonides' *Shemonah Peraqim* and Alfarabi's *Fusūl al-Madanî*," in A. Hyman, ed., *Essays in Medieval Jewish and Islamic Philosophy* (pp. 116–33), New York: Ktav Publishing House.

Frank, D. (1990), "Anger as a vice: a Maimonidean critique of Aristotle's ethics," *History of Philosophy Quarterly* 7/3, pp. 269–81.

Ivry, A. (1995), "Ismā'ili theology and Maimonides' philosophy," in D. Frank, ed., *The Jews of Medieval Islam* (pp. 271–99), Leiden: Brill.

Kraemer, J. (1979), "Alfarabi's *Opinions of the Virtuous City* and Maimonides' *Foundations of the Law*," in *Studia Orientalia* (pp. 107–53), Jerusalem: The Magnes Press.

——(1991), "Maimonides on the philosophic sciences in his treatise on the art of logic," in J. Kraemer, ed., *Perspectives on Maimonides* (pp. 77–104), Oxford: Oxford University Press.

Pines, S. (1963), Translator's introduction, in *Moses Maimonides: The Guide of the Perplexed*, vol. I (pp. lvii–cxxxiv), Chicago: University of Chicago Press.

Stern, J. (2000), "Maimonides on language and the science of language," in R. S. Cohen and H. Levine, eds., *Maimonides and the Sciences* (pp. 173–226), Dordrecht: Kluwer.

Strauss, L. (1984), "Jerusalem and Athens," in L. Strauss, *Studies in Platonic Political Philosophy* (pp. 147–73), Chicago: University of Chicago Press.

——(1987), *Philosophy and Law*, trans. F. Baumann, Philadelphia: Jewish Publication Society.

78

Nicholas of Autrecourt

MAURICIO BEUCHOT

Nicholas of Autrecourt, or Ultracuria (b. ca. 1300; d. after 1350), was born in Maas, diocese of Verdun. Between 1320 and 1327 he studied philosophy, law, and theology at the Sorbonne. After 1327 he taught theology at the University of Paris, where he also lectured on the *Sentences* of PETER LOMBARD and on Aristotle's *Politics*. In addition to his commentaries to these works, he wrote nine polemical letters against Bernard of Arezzo, two of which have been preserved, and one to a certain Aegidius (Giles), also extant.

In 1338 Autrecourt obtained a prebend's stall in the Cathedral of Metz. In 1339 the University of Paris issued a decree against Ockhamists, alleging that they were dogmatizing the doctrines of the *Venerabilis Inceptor*. Autrecourt was involved in this attack, which was instigated by JOHN BURIDAN. With Buridan's appointment as rector of the university in 1340, the decree became inconvenient to Autrecourt, even though he departed on important points from the nominalism of WILLIAM OF OCKHAM (Moody 1975; Scott 1971). In the same year, Autrecourt was called to an inquiry at the papal court in Avignon. The process was delayed but in 1346 he was sentenced to burn his writings in Paris. The sentence was carried out in 1347, and his academic degrees were voided. Yet when Autrecourt was appointed Dean of Metz in 1350 he was still referred to as licensed in theology. It is not known when he died.

In addition to the aforementioned letters and commentaries, Autrecourt wrote a treatise which begins *Exigit ordo executionis*, and another one entitled *Utrum visio creaturae rationalis beatificabilis per Verbum possit intendi naturaliter*, which fits the style of the discussions about the intension and remission of forms and qualities.

Critical and skeptical environment

Despite the prevailing image of medieval philosophy as realist and naive in regards to knowledge, there were skeptical trends during the period, which have often been assimilated to "nominalism" in general. However, there were different varieties of criticism and skepticism besides strict Ockhamism. It is therefore necessary to distinguish different kinds of medieval nominalism and to speak, instead, of nominalisms.

Autrecourt should be understood in this context. He has been called "the Hume of the Middle Ages" (Dal Pra 1951; O'Donnell 1942; Rashdall 1907; Weinberg 1948) because of the vigor and radicalism of his skepticism and criticism. Although he was not a nominalist in the Ockhamist sense, he lived in the strongly critical intellectual climate of the time. As we shall see, Autrecourt decried metaphysical knowledge, even knowledge of the external world, and rejected the concepts of "substance" and "cause," which had been the pillars of metaphysics and the general theory of knowledge in the Middle Ages.

Nominalism and skepticism

The seeds of modern criticism and skepticism are found in medieval nominalism. Nominalism of various sorts was pervasive in the Middle Ages and the opposite of realism, which also had different varieties. This opposition reached its highest point during the fourteenth and fifteenth centuries. Nominalism was opposed to realism mostly in regards to metaphysics, as it denied the firm and stable essences on which realism grounded the being of things. However, the opposition extended to epistemology, since it was on the strength of essences that realism had lent support to the safe, immutable knowledge of things in themselves. Against realism, nominalism emphasized the individual (as opposed to the universal, which it did not admit), dispersion in plurality, and change in processes. These were the characteristics of individuals, empirical and material individuals that nominalism emphasized. Accordingly, nominalists favored empiricism more than did thinkers of other orientations, such as Platonic-Augustinian realism (represented in thinkers such as ROGER BACON and ROBERT GROSSETESTE) and Aristotelian realism (represented in thinkers such as ALBERTUS MAGNUS and THOMAS AQUINAS).

In some respects, the empiricism of the nominalists was logical. It involved accepting the primacy of logical and empirical truths while denying any strong connection between logic and the natural sciences, because the principles of logic do not stem from anything empirical. Most nominalists cultivated and made significant contributions to the empirical sciences (natural and historical sciences) and to formal logic. By contrast, only some realists, such as Roger Bacon and Albert Magnus cultivated the natural disciplines. Because of their empiricist orientation, the nominalists questioned metaphysical knowledge. Some of them, such as Buridan, reduced metaphysics to the study of a single word, namely, the word 'being' and its logico-semantic properties. More radical nominalists progressively undermined other metaphysical concepts, such as "essence," "substance," and "cause," arguing their lack of epistemic content. Nominalists began a critique of knowledge that would become extreme in modern times, and initiated the sort of skepticism that later thinkers, such as Hume, would further develop (Dal Pra 1952, pp. 389–402).

Autrecourt's skepticism was too extreme for the prevailing way of thinking of his time, but in relation to the skepticism of antiquity and modern philosophy, Autrecourt's version is weak. It lacks the radical character of Pirron's skepticism; it does not measure up to the Academy's moderate version; and it does not have the vigor of Hume and Bayle's skepticism. Nevertheless, Autrecourt succeeds in leaving metaphysics and the principles of empirical knowledge in crisis.

Varieties of nominalism

Testimonies of Autrecourt's doctrines are found in the decree of condemnation, in his recantations, and in his extant letters and treatises. Some of Autrecourt's rivals left allusions to his doctrines. Buridan, for instance, defended some of Ockham's theses against Autrecourt.

459

The nominalism of Autrecourt is not simply a variety of Ockham's; on several important points, he departed both from Ockham and from other Franciscans, such as Bernard of Arezzo and Buridan. At the same time, he was influenced by various forms of nominalism. Among these we can mention the nominalism of PETER ABELARD, which reduces universals to linguistic entities yet admits divine exemplar ideas, and that aspect of Ockham's nominalism that denies the reality of universals but accepts that they are concepts. Still another variety that also influenced Autrecourt is the extreme version embraced by Roscelin and Johannes Maior, for whom universals are but words, *flatus vocis*, and written signs.

The differences between Autrecourt and Ockham are the former's stricter critique of knowledge, and his stronger skepticism, which springs from principles already held by him. Ockham postulated that we have intellectual knowledge of individual things, that is, an intuitive, certain, and evident knowledge of singular entities. Autrecourt denies that we can have evident knowledge of individual things external to the mind. According to him, evident knowledge encompasses only what is immanent to the spirit or known internally.

Principles

The only thing Autrecourt accepts as known with evident certitude is the principle of non-contradiction (which he regards as the first principle) and what is reducible to it. This principle is internal to the mind and governs the life of the spirit. Anything not reducible to the principle is not known with any evidence. "All the certitude we possess is resolved into this principle, and the principle itself is not resolved into anything else as a conclusion is resolved into its premise" (1908, p. 6; Weinberg 1948, p. 14).

In his second polemical letter to Bernard of Arezzo, Autrecourt says that he is surprised that this Franciscan Ockhamist should have said – in public and against the Dominicans (their intellectual rivals) – that he could know abstract immaterial substances. Autrecourt argued that he could know neither abstract nor concrete (that is, material and individual) substances.

Autrecourt's argument against Arezzo is built around the principle of non-contradiction. He gives this principle the following formulation: "Contradictory statements cannot be true at the same time" (1908, p. 6). Obviously, by casting it in terms of truth-value, Autrecourt intends to show that the principle of non-contradiction implies the principle of excluded middle. The principle of non-contradiction is the most basic of all principles (of reasoning) and the only evident principle. Everything known with certitude is based – mediately or immediately – on this principle. Everything not reducible to it lacks all certitude or evidence.

One of the conclusions of Autrecourt's argumentation against Arezzo is as follows: "It is possible, without any contradiction, that something seems to you to be so without being so; therefore, you cannot have evident certitude of its being so" (1908, p. 7; Weinberg 1948, pp. 14–15). What Autrecourt means here is that knowledge of appearances cannot be based on the principle of non-contradiction. This principle can ground only knowledge stemming from reason. Furthermore, the Ockhamists are mistaken in supposing that beings are known through intellectual intuition, or through an act oriented directly to what lies outside the mind. On the contrary, beings are known through inference, and logical inferences are never a sufficient foundation for empirical knowledge. Thus empirical knowledge cannot be guaranteed.

460

Autrecourt argues at length to show that, because the principle of non-contradiction is evident and irrefutable, it is the only thing of which we are certain. All other knowledge, including empirical knowledge, is always threatened by uncertainty.

From these points Autrecourt derives six corollaries which, he contends, undermine all knowledge not stemming from reason. These principles are the scaffolding of his skepticism:

1 "The certitude of evidence which we have in the natural light of reason is certitude without qualification. For since this certitude is ours in virtue of the first principle, truth neither contradicts it nor can contradict it. Therefore, if anything is demonstrated by the natural light it is demonstrated without qualification" (Weinberg 1948, p. 17).

2 "The certitude of evidence has no degrees: if we are certain of two conclusions we are no more certain of one than of the other" (Weinberg 1948, p. 17). For certitude derives its force from the same first principle. Although some truths are reducible to this principle mediately and others immediately, in the end the certitude belonging to each of them is the same. Thus, a geometer can say that he is equally certain of his first conclusion, and of the second, and of the third, and so on, according to the law of *de primo ad ultimum* (scholastic logicians called the transitivity of the conditional an inference *de primo ad ultimum*; in a series of propositions joined by the relation of inference, the epistemic properties of the propositions (e.g., certitude) carry on from one proposition to another).

3 "With the exception of the certitude of faith, there is no other certitude except that of the first principle, or the certitude that can be resolved in the first principle" (1908, p. 8). The certitude that is but of one kind and without gradations belongs only to what has no trace of falsity or doubt, that is, only to the first principle (Weinberg 1948, p. 18).

4 "Any syllogistic form is immediately reducible to the first principle" (1908, p. 8). This is so because the conclusion is reducible to the first principle either immediately or mediately. If reducible immediately, the thesis is thereby proved. If reducible mediately, either we have an infinite regress or we arrive at a conclusion that is in turn immediately reducible to the first principle (cf. Weinberg 1948, p. 18).

5 "In every consequence immediately reducible to the first principle, both the antecedent and the consequent are really identical, whether in whole or in part" (1908, p. 8). Otherwise, Autrecourt says, it would not then be immediately evident that the antecedent and the opposite of the consequent cannot both be true (cf. Weinberg 1948, p. 18).

6 "In every evident consequence reducible to the first principle by however many intermediaries, the consequent is really identical with the antecedent or with a part [of what is] signified by it" (1908, p. 9). If a consequent is proven by, say, three antecedents, that consequent can be shown to be identical to the third antecedent or a part of it (by the fifth corollary) and eventually, to all other antecedents (for, by the rule of *de primo ad ultimum*, the antecedents can be shown to be identical with one another). Eventually, the consequent can be shown to be identical to the first antecedent of the series, that is, to the first principle (cf. Weinberg 1948, p. 19).

For Autrecourt, everything that is evident is also tautological and thus cannot ground empirical knowledge. We find here a dichotomy between analytic and synthetic (as in Hume), or tautological and factic (as in Wittgenstein). Tautological knowledge is the only evident knowledge but it is formal, lacks any connection with the real world, and hence is empty. What is known through the first principle is analytic and devoid of factual information (see Moody 1975, p. 154).

The basis of Autrecourt's skepticism can be seen in the following statement: "From the knowledge that a thing exists it cannot be inferred with evidence reducible to the first principle or to the certitude of the first principle, that some other thing exists" (1908, p. 9). Autrecourt advances the following argument to prove this point: A consequence in which the consequent is not identical with the antecedent or a part of it cannot be known with the evidence of the first principle. For, were the antecedent and the opposite of the consequent true at the same time, something would be both affirmed and denied of the same thing. A stronger argument is that no inference can yield an identity broader than the identity holding between the extreme and middle terms of a syllogism, since the extreme term can be correctly inferred only through the middle term. This would not be so if from the fact that a thing is a being it followed that something else is also a being. "In fact, the predicate of the conclusion and the subject [of the major premiss] signify what is really identical, whereas in reality they are not really identical to the middle term which has been put as something else" (1908, pp. 10–11).

According to Autrecourt, it follows that Aristotle did not possess evident knowledge of any substance other than his own soul. Aristotle (or, perhaps, Bernard of Arezzo) did not have evident knowledge of any substance, whether material and concrete or abstract. In this context, "substance" should be understood as something different from the sensible objects given in experience, otherwise Aristotle would have known something prior to any inference, which is impossible. If substances were perceived intuitively, the uneducated (*rustici*) would know that substances exist. Similarly, essences are not inferred from the things perceived to exist prior to discursive thought, because from one thing it cannot be inferred that another thing exists (1908, p. 12).

In Autrecourt we see a reaction against Aristotelianism from within Aristotelianism itself. The objections against Aristotle would not operate *a fortiori* had Autrecourt been a Platonist instead of an Aristotelian. The fact is that he embraced some Platonist views. One such view is that only knowledge of the principle of non-contradiction is evident.

Autrecourt says that Aristotle hardly had any certitude of his conclusions regarding physics and metaphysics. Furthermore, he said that Aristotle did not even have probable knowledge. The "fool-proof" argument Autrecourt offered for this is that one does not have certitude of a consequent unless that consequent is known evidently, that is, unless both the consequent and its antecedent are true. From the things that appear to us prior to any inference, it does not follow that other things (e.g., substances) exist.

There is certitude only with respect to the self. If we carve a stone or a piece of wood, this act presupposes a belief on our part. This belief, however, can lack a referent. It would be possible that, as a result of an exercise of divine power, there is the appearance of things, but no substance corresponding to the appearance. For a consequence is evident if and only if it is logically impossible for the antecedent and the opposite of the consequent to be both true. We may remark that, in referring to God's omnipotence as a possible source of falsehood, Autrecourt makes reference to a "liar God" very similar to Descartes's notion.

With Autrecourt's critique of substance and causality, the medieval metaphysical edifice collapses. Without a metaphysical foundation, knowledge becomes progressively encapsulated in idealist immanentism and leads to skepticism.

The subject of Autrecourt's first critique is "substance." The subject of the second critique is "causality." The critiques are related. We shall discuss the critique of substance first, following the order in which it is presented in the condemnatory documents.

In Autrecourt's recantations (1346) we find the famous proposition, that from the fact that something is known it is not possible to derive certitude or evidence with respect to some other thing. From this proposition Autrecourt concluded that we should not attempt to explain sensible appearances (*apparentia naturalia*), or phenomena by an appeal to substances, which are non-sensible, non-empirical entities. Appearances are the only things we can guarantee, everything else is an arbitrary construction. This point bears on Autrecourt's attack on Aristotle. "From these things I made the effort of proving that Aristotle did not have evident knowledge of any substance . . . because this he would have had before any discourse, which cannot be so" (1908, p. 12). We know the reason for this already. First, substances do not appear intuitively, otherwise even the uneducated would know them. Secondly, substances are not known through discourse. Substances are not inferred from perceptual data existing prior to discourse, for one thing cannot be inferred evidently from another thing. For these reasons Autrecourt rejects all metaphysical theories concerning change in beings.

In regards to physical knowledge, it cannot be said that Autrecourt is skeptical because he advances an atomist theory which is already a theory of reality, no matter how arbitrary a construct "reality" may be for him. Autrecourt explains everything in terms of local movements of atoms, somewhat in the fashion of modern physics (e.g., of Gassendi's physics): "There is only local movement in natural things, that is, congregation and dispersion" (Denifle and Chatelain 1891, pp. 582). When this movement follows the congregation of natural atomic bodies (*corpora athomalia*), the bodies bond with one another and participate in the nature of a base or individual. In this case the movement is called generation. When the bodies disperse, the movement is called corruption. When moving atoms do not seem to influence the movement of the base, even in what could be called its natural operation, the movement is called alteration. Autrecourt's doctrine assumes substantial realities which are not known evidently (these are somewhat similar to Kant's noumena) and reduces knowable reality to phenomena or appearances.

Critique of the principle of causality

The bases of Autrecourt's critique of causality are found in the second letter to Bernard of Arezzo. The fully developed version of the critique is found in the condemned propositions. Realizing that he had not dealt with the principle of causality, Autrecourt proceeded to justify this by first denying the principle of final causality (teleology) and then the principle of causality in general. In regards to the former, Autrecourt denies "that somebody knows evidently that some thing is the end of another thing" (Denifle and Chatelain 1891, p. 577). The proof offered is that any proposition affirming some finality or teleology in things is not reducible to the first principle, therefore we do not have infallible knowledge of teleology. In regards to causality in general, Autrecourt denies that, "if one thing (effect) exists, it follows that another thing (cause) must exist." In the recantations, Autrecourt grants having asserted just this: "I also said in the aforementioned letter that no demonstration can be such whereby from the existence (of the cause), the existence of the effect is demonstrated" (1908, p. 12). For Autrecourt, any argument seeking to demonstrate causality is fallacious. If the thing whose existence is being inferred is different from the thing given in experience, "then we transpose the legitimate scope of the principle of contradiction in affirming of the subject a predicate for which nothing proves that it belongs to the subject necessarily" (ibid.).

As with substance, our knowledge of causality is merely belief. Empirical knowledge lacks evidence and is more akin to religious belief, or faith. We only have certitude or evidence in

463

the case of rational knowledge, and inasmuch as this knowledge is derivable from the first principle, which is the foundation of all certitude.

If there is no certitude regarding the principle of causality, the existence of the external world is dubious, at best. The human being in this terrestrial life – before going to heavenly life, where as a result of his vision of God he will have evidence of everything –"cannot have evident knowledge of the existence of things, that is, an evidence reducible to the certitude of the first principle" (Denifle and Chatelain 1891, p. 385). The access to external reality and to any realism (understanding by 'realism' the acceptance of the existence of a realm independent of our mind) is foreclosed. In all, we are left only with the evidence of our own existence as something mental, ideal, or spiritual. "We have neither certitude nor evidence of any material substance, only the certitude of our own soul" (Denifle and Chatelain 1891, p. 577). Knowledge of any reality external to the mind is foreclosed. This precludes metaphysics and reduces empirical knowledge to knowledge of phenomena. The proofs for the existence of God lose all value, since they are based on the idea of causality. God can only be accepted through faith.

Anthropology and ethics

We have seen that Autrecourt departs from Aristotelian metaphysics and arrives at a version of atomistic physics. Everything, even the human body, is reducible to atoms with local movement. From the movement of grouping, bodies are generated. From the movement of separation, corruption results. The human soul is both *sense* and *intellect*. These remain united to the body but are immortal. Because different conglomerates of atoms (bodies) can become united to the soul, Autrecourt is committed to a sort of metempsychosis or trans-migration of souls. There are acts of understanding and acts of will. However, from the acts of the soul we cannot infer the corresponding powers or faculties, or affirm that there is intelligence or will.

Autrecourt rejected the notion of a final cause. There is no evident knowledge that one thing is the end of another. Yet skepticism about natural reality may lead man to what is of most interest to him, namely, the cultivation of virtue, or man's ethical side. It is not clear, though, which sort of ethics could be defensible in Autrecourt's theoretical framework, save for one entirely based on religious faith.

Conclusion

Nicholas of Autrecourt is one source of modern skepticism. Whether or not he ought to be regarded as a direct source of modernity may be controversial, but the main ideas of modern skepticism are, no doubt, found in his views. Not in vain has Autrecourt been called "the Hume of the Middle Ages." In a similar way to the British philosopher, Autrecourt rejected metaphysics and knowledge of substances and causality. His physics lead him into a phe-nomenalism akin to the phenomenalism of Hume and even Kant. Autrecourt held that the essences (noumena) of things are unknowable. Beyond appearances (phenomena) the phys-ical world cannot be known with any evidence. Autrecourt's atomism resembles the versions of Gassendi and Hume. They all subscribed to that variety of skepticism known as academic skepticism, which fully matured in modern times.

Bibliography

Primary sources

(1908), "Briefe zu B. von Arezzo", in J. Lappe, ed., "Nicholas von Autrecourt. Sein Leben, seine Philosophie, seine Schriften," in *Beiträge zur Geschichte der Philosophie des Mittelalters*, 6/2, Münster: Aschendorff.

(1939), "Exigit ordo executionis (Tractatus universalis magistri Nicolai de Ultracuria ad videndum an sermones Peripateticorum fuerint demonstrati," in J. R. O'Donnell, "Nicholas of Autrecourt," *Mediaeval Studies* 1, pp. 179–280.

(1994), *Nicholas of Autrecourt: His Correspondence with Master Giles and Bernard of Arezzo*, trans. L. M. De Rijk, Studien und Texte zur Geistergeschichte des Mittelalters 42, Leiden: Brill.

Secondary sources

Dal Pra, M. (1951), *Nicola di Autrecourt*, Milan: Fratelli Bocca.

——(1952), "La fondazione del empirismo e le sue aporie nel pensiero de Nicola di Autrecourt," *Rivista Critica di Storia della Filosofia* 5, pp. 389–402.

Denifle, J. and Chatelain, J., eds. (1891), *Chartularium Universitatis Parisiensis*, vol. 2, Paris; repr. 1964, Brussels: Culture et Civilisation.

Kaluza, Z. (1995), "Nicolas d'Autrecourt: ami de la verité," *Histoire littéraire de la France*, vol. XLII, fasc. 1, Paris: Institut (Académie des Inscriptions et Belles-lettres).

Maccagnolo, E. (1952), "Metafisica e gnoseologia in Nicolas d'Autrecourt," *Rivista di Filosofia Neoscolastica* 45, pp. 36–53.

Moody, E. A. (1975), "Ockham, Buridan and Nicholas of Autrecourt" [1947], *Studies on Medieval Philosophy, Science and Logic* (pp. 127–60), Berkeley, Los Angeles, and London: University of California Press.

O'Donnell, J. R. (1942), "The philosophy of Nicholas of Autrecourt and his appraisal of Aristotle," *Medieval Studies* 4, pp. 97–125.

Rashdall, H. (1907), "Nicholas of Ultracuria, a mediaeval Hume," *Proceedings of the Aristotelian Society* 8, pp. 1–27.

Scott, T. K. (1971), "Nicholas of Autrecourt, Buridan and Ockhamism," *Journal of the History of Philosophy* 9, pp. 15–41.

Vignaux, P. (1931), "Nicolas d'Autrecourt," *Dictionnaire de théologie catholique*, vol. XI, cols. 562–87, Paris: Letouzey et Ane.

Weinberg, J. (1948), *Nicholaus of Autrecourt: A Study in Fourteenth-century Thought*, Princeton, NJ: Princeton University Press for the University of Cincinnati.

79

Nicholas of Cusa

LOUIS DUPRÉ AND NANCY HUDSON

At the threshold of the modern age stands a towering, ambiguous figure, Nicholas of Cusa (b. 1401; d. 1464). This meteoric thinker, clearly the most original mind of the fifteenth century, has been called the gatekeeper to the modern world. Yet having had no real predecessors or genuine followers, he properly belongs neither to the past nor to the future. In some respects, he anticipates much of modern thought: a heliocentric cosmology, a new way of posing the relation between finite and infinite in the universe, the importance of the mathematical a priori in the study of the world, even, to some degree, the position of the human subject as the source of knowledge. Yet some, including Hans Blumenberg, regard him as the last medieval thinker, citing his dependence on scholastic philosophy and his unique combination of Neoplatonism and nominalism. Also, his firm resolve to retain theology at the heart of philosophy and the decidedly mystical inspiration of his thought reveal an intellectual attitude more common in the High Middle Ages. Yet his theory of an infinite, centerless universe in which the human subject functions as the spiritual center prepared the late medieval mind for accepting the imminent new cosmology. Was he the last of the "ancients" or the first of the moderns? Should he be viewed as a Platonist or nominalist? To answer these questions and others, including ones about the orthodoxy of his intellectualism it is necessary to study his later mystical works as well as his early, more theoretical texts. For Cusanus, epistemological theory leads naturally to mystical metaphysics.

To a surprising degree for such a prominent public figure, he leaves us in the dark about his early years, apart from his birth in Kues. We possess little reliable information about his family life and studies before he went to study at the University of Padua, at the time a center of advanced empirical science as well as of serious Aristotelian philosophy. Nicholas registered in the faculty of law but spent much of his six-year residence studying mathematics, physics, and astronomy. Not long after completing his theological studies at the University of Cologne he became secretary of Ulrich von Manderscheid, who had been elected Archbishop of Trier. Soon his sponsor sent him to the Council of Basel to plead his case against a rival candidate, appointed by the pope, for that same bishopric. At that momentous gathering Cusanus unambiguously embraced the position of the majority party, claiming that the Council holds the ultimate spiritual authority in the Church, against the one advanced by the minority party representing the supremacy of the pope. As the Council lingered on, Cusanus attempted to assist it in reaching a decision by preparing a lengthy, historically erudite brief for the conciliar party, *De concordantia catholica*. In this stunning display of canonical and Patristic learning he defended the conciliar position as strongly as it has ever been defended. The memory of Constance (1414–18) still remained fresh with him, as it remained with all the Fathers, when the Council had to break the deadlock created by three rival claimants to the papal see.

When the conciliar party, however, unable to impose its view, began to use force on members of the minority, the same concern for unity and peace that had inspired him in the first place moved Nicholas to change his position. His concern for ecclesiastical unity fully alienated him from the conciliarists when they refused to honor the demand of the Greek Church, desirous to be reunited with the Latin one, to meet in a neutral Italian city rather than in France or Germany. The Council, Nicholas felt, had ceased to represent the universal Church and had turned into a political faction. In such a case, he concluded, the party in alliance with the Roman pontiff must be held to be the *sanior pars* (sounder part), since the pope alone is able to resolve otherwise irresoluble differences – a clear reversal of the situation faced in Constance. In his later *De pace fidei* Cusanus justified his position by locating the formal principle of unity – the *complicatio* (enfolding) which the Church *explicates* (unfolds), as he put it in the language of *De docta ignorantia* – in the pope rather than the Council.

Soon after leaving the Council Cusanus accepted a papal diplomatic mission to Constantinople to prepare for the imminent council with the Greek Church that was to take place in Ferrara and Florence (1439). It was on his return from Constantinople to Venice that Nicholas received the sudden insight that directly inspired his major work, *De docta ignorantia*, and indirectly all others.

Cusanus seeks an understanding of the infinite, which he calls "the Maximum" or that than which there can be nothing greater. The mind attains ordinary knowledge by moving from what it knows to what is yet unknown but analogous with previously established knowledge. The infinite, however, "escapes comparative relation." The Maximum is complete "fullness" insofar as it comprehends everything. Nothing exists outside of the Maximum. Knowledge reached through analogy, however, requires the opposition of one thing to another in order for a comparison to be made. Because the Maximum *includes* everything, nothing can be set apart from it for comparative purposes. Thus, the infinity of the Maximum rules out the ordinary process from the unknown to the known. It also means that the Maximum can never be fully comprehended or encompassed by the mind. It always remains beyond the mind's grasp. Nevertheless, we may learn about it, as long as our learnedness consists of knowing that we do not know. The very recognition of the limitations of the human mind in the light of the infinite is learned ignorance.

Learned ignorance, however, is not equivalent to ignorance. Although the Absolute One cannot be known in itself, it is an object of knowledge insofar as it exists in the plurality of all things. As the self-manifestation of the absolute, the universe and all it contains can tell us about it. Cusanus cites Hermes Trismegistus: if God is to be named, either he would have to be called by every name or else all things would have to be called by God's name (*De docta ignorantia* I, 24: 75).

On Learned Ignorance is divided into three books: Book I deals with the *maximum absolutum* (the Absolute Maximum or God); Book II discusses the universe as the manifestation of the Maximum; Book III, a more theological text, is about Christ. The first book describes the Maximum, which Cusanus alternatively terms "God." Since the Maximum is all that can be, nothing surpasses it. But if it *does* envelop all possibility of being within itself, nothing can be less than it either. That is, all potential existence is encompassed by the Maximum; nothing exists or can exist independently of it. Even the smallest thing in the universe is wholly encompassed by the Maximum. Therefore, the Maximum also earns the appellation "Minimum." The two terms are alternate designations for the Infinite; they coincide.

467

Cusanus justifies this coincidence by pointing out that, given the inclusivity of the Maximum, it is inconceivable that anything should oppose it, not even the inverse concept of the Minimum. Any polarity between the Infinite and an opposite would threaten the Infinite with a dualistic limitation. Hence opposites in their extreme degree coincide.

The coincidence of opposites in the absolute entails the mind's learned ignorance of it, not just because the Maximum exceeds human thought, but because its very nature confounds the mind. The way in which the infinite dis-closes itself closes us to precise knowledge of it. At the same time, the notion of a coincidence of opposites distinguishes learned ignorance from a simple philosophical skepticism that denies the possibility of knowledge of the absolute.

In contrast to traditional negative theology, which holds that the only true statements about God are negations, learned ignorance avoids total silence. The *via negativa* compares the absolute with the self and the world, and then removes all finite predicates like corporeality, sensation, and the imagination. Once all are removed we can only say what God is *not*. Not only does this render all relationship with the absolute impossible, but it remains trapped in the same self-referentiality as analogy. This pathway of "removing boundaries" (*De quaerendo Deum*, V, 49) tells you nothing about God, but is only a pathway "*within yourself.*"

Rather than halting at the rejection of all predicates, Cusanus moves to the coincidence of all predicates and their denials. Hence his ignorance about God is not bare but *learned*. If God *manifests* himself in creation, we must certainly know something positive about its Creator. The paradoxical language of coincidence opens up new possibilities for religious language, for it overcomes the most basic obstacle to our thinking about God: the law of non-contradiction. By disclosing the limits of reason, the paradox speaks of the absolute and of our relationship to it.

Cusanus' paradoxes follow those MEISTER ECKHART employs in his commentaries on Exodus and on the Book of Wisdom. But Cusanus integrates them within his theory of the coincidence of opposites. This theory, the main subject of *De docta ignorantia* and one assumed in all the later works, allows him to claim that, despite God's total ineffability, God remains the *exemplar* of all finite reality which he enfolds within himself. The inherence of all things in the divine nature authorizes the mind to refer to that nature by ordinary symbols, since all *participate* in the divine reality. The justification for religious symbolization lies, beyond similarity, in God's presence at the core of all things. True, occasionally Cusanus speaks of "a likeness of God and the world" (*De docta ignorantia*, II, 5 and the very title of II, 4) Yet *likeness* here does not refer to a similarity of appearance – which Cusanus has repeatedly ruled out – but to a larger parallel between the fact that the *uni*verse is composed of a multiplicity of things and the One God's existence in plurality.

Sometimes Cusanus presents even his paradoxes in symbols. Thus in *De visione Dei* he compares the seeing of an image with the "vision" of God. In the former case, the power of viewing resides with the observer, not with the image. The image is entirely dependent on the observer. In the latter case all these relationships become inverted: the icon is the source of the "vision" and the observers are reduced to the role of images. Paradoxically, the beholder sees himself only *in* God. God as object coincides with God as the supreme subject, and God's immanence with his transcendence. Symbols such as these are more than mere analogies: they become so altered as to undermine their very definition.

Cusanus concedes the inadequacy of all God-talk, while at the same time asserting the validity of the mind's symbolizing activity. The symbol, unlike the image representation, serves to lift the mind to a different mode of "seeing" once ordinary seeing and thinking have collapsed. This leads to a new and different affirmation. Since negating the content of all symbols is as much a finite act as the affirmation itself, the negation itself must be negated. The same divine presence that induced the mind to create symbols and to deny their ultimate appropriateness with respect to God, forces it to move beyond its own negation. Ultimately the mind asserts the presence of the absolute *within* the relative. Precisely because of the coincidence of all qualities in God, God can be the exemplar of all things without being similar to any of them. The mind alone is created "into the image and likeness" of God.

At the heart of Cusanus' use of symbol is his view of the mind and its constructive activity as the primary image of God. In *De docta ignorantia*, Cusanus considers only mathematical constructions. Different geometrical figures, if extended into infinity, coincide. Sphere, circle, triangle, even straight line all lose their oppositions when infinitely protracted. Now a mathematical infinite obviously differs from an ontologically infinite. Yet, disregarding the difference in nature, Cusanus concentrates exclusively on the symbolic significance of the mathematical relation between finitude and infinity. Nor does he equate the numerical *one* with divine simplicity. But one presupposes the other.

Mathematical symbolism appears particularly appropriate to Cusanus because, while bearing no resemblance to the reality it investigates, it nevertheless, in a non-intuitive way, assists the mind in conceiving it. The purely constructional nature of mathematics prevents the mind from seeking illusory resemblances where none are possible. But the use of mathematics commends itself to Cusanus also for a positive reason. Number is "the first exemplar of spirit," since God is threefold in unity, and science indicates that the world follows arithmetical, geometrical, musical, and astronomical models. (*De coniecturis* I, 4; and *De docta ignorantia* II, 13.) In choosing the path of numbers, then, the mind follows the plan of God's own creative activity as much as we are capable of knowing it.

Cusanus develops this notion in *De coniecturis* (*On Conjectures*, 1442–3). By directly imitating divine creativity, particularly in mathematical knowledge, the mind itself turns into an image of God. To be sure, Cusanus insists, numbers and geometrical figures are inherently finite and, as such, alien to God's essence. But at least they evoke the proportion that exists among different facets of the ideal model of the cosmos operative in God's creative act. Our own quantitative articulation of this proportion merely functions as a finite reconstruction of an infinite, inimitable knowledge. Rather than imitating an inimitable divine "model" the mind in its own way progressively construes an intelligible cosmos. The divine mind creates by conceiving; our mind assimilates by conceiving in notions and conjectures, moving from the *explicatio* (unfolding) of the creature's diversity towards the *complicatio* (enfolding) of the divine unity. "Mind is the primary image of the Divine Enfolding [Being]" (*Idiota de mente*, ch. IV). On the level of reason the mind, beyond "comprehending" ideas (the function of the understanding, *ratio*), constitutes their intelligible unity.

The shift that occurs from *De docta ignorantia* to *De coniecturis* runs in the direction indicated by Eckhart: from similarity to identity. Identity through participation appears to be the fundamental principle underlying the metaphysics of unity adopted in *De coniecturis*. But Cusanus does not follow Eckhart in attributing to the entire creation a similarity with God. The mind alone may be called an image of God. It acts "like" God as it converts "traces" (BONAVENTURE'S *vestigia*) or signs into *symbols* of its own participation in God. The act of knowing brings a mere multiplicity to an ideal unity. In *De docta ignorantia* Cusanus had shown how the absolute Maximum conditions all cognitive acts. In *De coniecturis* and such later works as *De non-aliud* and *De visione Dei*, he stresses how only the *presence* of the

469

One enables the mind to subsume all otherness under unity – the very essence of knowing. Each cognitive act implicitly symbolizes God's presence, without ever knowing God directly. The mind then is an "image" of an unknown original. Cusanus follows the long-standing Neoplatonic reading of the verse of Genesis "He created them into His own image" as referring to the presence of the divine Logos in the soul. In and through this presence the mind is capable of thinking, that is, measuring and combining things with one another.

Thus, Cusanus' epistemology leads to a mystical metaphysics. Though Neoplatonic in inspiration it substantially differs from Plotinus' thought in that the divine act of creation, is one of free choice. (Still, Nicholas often formulates the Creator/creation distinction in terms of *Unitas/alteritas, complicatio/explicatio*, and *Non-aliud/aliud*, rather than in the language of creation.) Most importantly, he denies the Neoplatonic hierarchy of which the stages become progressively more distant from the One. This is a crucial alteration of Neoplatonic emanationism. The celestial realm is no purer expression of God than the terrestrial. In fact, the created order *in its entirety* consists of God's unfolding what he is "enfolded."

The idea that the One unfolds itself immediately at each individual stage of the multiple gives creation as a whole a divine status. In contrast to Platonic thought, created things are not shadows of what is truly real, nor is their being mediated through emanations that proceed from the One. They are not attenuated versions of divine realities, but they exist in their own right. Since Cusanus frequently uses Platonic terminology, it is important to keep the distinction in mind which a cursory reading of his work could lead one to overlook.

The *complicatio-explicatio* (enfolding-unfolding) formula itself makes clear that Nicholas has not merely dressed a Platonic ontology in Christian clothes. It indicates that the same reality which is God enfolded is that of the actual world. The fact that God has unfolded himself in creation and that creation is and remains enfolded in God is sufficient to dispel all doubts as to its ontological status. In various ways, Nicholas repeats the idea that in God, created things are God, and, in creation, God is creation.

In his profound theological treatise, *De li non aliud*, Cusanus describes God as the very principle through which things are identical with themselves. The absolute cannot stand in a relation of otherness to any relative being. Though God entirely surpasses his creation to the point of being unknown in himself, he cannot be defined through the derived category of "otherness." The absolute must define both itself and all the rest. Eckhart had declared God to coincide with Being. This implies that in its *essential* Being the creature is not other than God. Eckhart had escaped the pantheistic consequences of his thesis by distinguishing that essential *esse* from the creature's *existence*, which limits it and differentiates it from its divine *esse*. Nor does that essence consist in the limiting characteristics which separate the nature of one creature from that of another. For Eckhart, self-identity cannot be defined in a purely negative way, as it is by Spinoza when he defines *determination* as *negation*. It consists essentially in a positive mode of being which transcends distinctiveness and which by the same token constitutes the link of identity with the divine Being.

In *De li non aliud* Cusanus follows Eckhart's line of argument in declaring self-identity to be characteristic of God's Being not only in its uniqueness but also in its unfolded presence in creation. How does creation still differ from its Creator? In *De li non aliud* Cusanus interprets the traditional position that God is in all things even though he is none of them, by referring to God's absolute priority in the order of being. All things coincide with their divine Being before being themselves. As their created being remains totally dependent on God, God remains innermost in their own being. In God's "complicated" Being, antecedent to creation, all things may be said to be in an undifferentiated way. In the "explicated" divine Being, however, God is *in* all things all that they are.

As *causa sui* (original cause) and first principle God cannot be defined by anything else. God coincides with himself in a manner that excludes any reference to otherness. But, as origin of all that is, God must define all created things as well. Now, as that which defines itself and everything that is, God cannot be "other" than what he defines. Though Cusanus refers to the relation between God and the creature as one of causality, he specifies the causal relation through the more intimate form of participation. If the creature participates in God in its very being, God can be no other with respect to it. Otherness implies a lack, but God lacks nothing that the creature is or has. Indeed, as God's "explicated" Being, creation is nothing but "the manifestation of the Creator defining Himself" (*De li non aliud*, "Propositiones," §12).

The term 'Not-other' illustrates both the absoluteness of divine causation and its imma-nent presence in the effect. God is not the cause merely of the actual being of things, but also of their possibility. God creates possibility as well as actuality. "In Not-other we see clearly how it is that in Not-other all things are Not-other antecedently [to being them-selves] and how it is that in all things Not-other is all things" (*De li non aliud* 6, 22). The divine presence to and in the created order constitutes its very identity: "in all things Not-other *is* all things."

In *De dato patris luminum* Cusanus includes in the idea of participation in *being* that of form. "In every existing thing the form *is* the being, so that the very form which gives being *is* the being which is given to the thing" (II, 98). This clearly distinguishes his position from scholastic philosophers such as THOMAS AQUINAS, who used the terminology of participa-tion. For Aquinas also, God is *ipsum esse* (being itself). But when Cusanus refers to God as *forma formarum* or *absolute form* he shifts ontological perfection from existence to essence. For St. Thomas, the highest perfection resides in individual existence which the essence does not include. That being remains entirely on the side of *form* is what distinguishes the entire Neoplatonic tradition most decisively from the more existential Thomist one. For St. Thomas, a real distinction between essence and existence may have appeared indispensable for safeguarding the contingent nature of created being, a contingency missing in any conception of reality based upon *intrinsically necessary* forms. For Cusanus, as for all who had undergone the impact of nominalist theology, formal perfection itself had lost that intrinsic necessity, dependent as it had become upon the unlimited and inscrutable power of an omnipotent creator. This allowed the cardinal without scruples to embrace the form-essentialism of Platonic and Neoplatonic philosophies.

In favoring a Platonic ontology Cusanus may have followed the trend of the Renaissance – when the complete works of Plato and Plotinus came to be known again in the West and began to be translated. But the choice may also have been inspired by the greater mys-tical potential of a philosophy that allowed him to convert an efficient causal relation into a more immanent formal one. Though Cusanus' position includes nominalist as well as Neoplatonic elements, it remains distinct from both in its fundamental principles.

This appears clearly in the third book of *De docta ignorantia*, where he presents a unique exemplarism. Every particular is finite; it embodies various forms but never actually *is* the full concrete embodiment of those forms because of its finitude and variability. The coinci-dence of finite being with the absolute in the incarnational union of Christ's human nature and divine Maximality constitutes an exemplar of all things. Rather than attempting to analyze Cusanus' exemplarism into either a nominalist or realist position on universals, it may be preferable to recognize that through his Christology Cusanus avoids being restricted

471

to either alternative. Christ is the Form of forms, the Maximum Exemplar in whom all universals are united.

Similarly, Cusanus' theory of participation is uniquely his own. Absolute Unity is at once participable and imparticipable. In itself, it is imparticipable and incommunicable. In *otherness*, it is participable. Insofar as it is imparticipable, Absolute Unity is distinct from multiplicity. It is only because there are two discrete terms that participability, something that happens between two things, is a possibility. The separateness that is a prerequisite for participation originates in a fundamental imparticipability. In this sense, then, imparticipability and participability, far from contradicting one another, are mutually reinforcing. This does not mean, however, that Cusanus has adopted a Proclean Unity with two levels, the highest imparticipable, the lowest participable. It is not as though there was imparticipable unity alongside an other that then performs the action of participating in the unity. *Alteritas* (otherness) is not a principle that accounts for multiplicity, but simply *is* the participation. Participation *is* the existence of Unity in otherness. In Cusanus' fluid dialectic the top term (God) informs the bottom term (the world and all of its elements).

The divine presence and the participatory-nonparticipatory relationship between God and creation make Cusanus' thought essentially mystical. He fully develops this aspect of his theology in *De visione Dei* (1453). In this work of his mature age, he presents the human vision of God as it coincides with God's own vision of the soul. The title itself with the ambiguous genitive *Dei* hints at the closeness between God's vision, where God is subject, and the vision of God, where God is object.

· In the mystical vision, God's vision and one's own vision coalesce. Since God's "sight *is* an eye, i.e., a living mirror, it sees within itself all things. Indeed, because it is the Cause of all visible things, it embraces and sees all things in the Cause and Rational Principle of all things, viz., in itself" (*De visione Dei* 8: 32). Cusanus illustrates the finite vision of God by comparing it to an icon whose glance follows the observer as he moves. As he gazes on the icon, the observer sees, first of all, his own nature projected. But seeing it he realizes that it is the icon who constitutes his being and that of all other things. Thus the observer's vision of the icon becomes the icon's vision of the observer, and, finally, the icon's vision of himself. The active human performance of seeing becomes the passive role of being mirrored. The cognitive metaphor of vision is transformed by Cusanus into an ontological one. His mystical metaphysics concludes the epistemological development of *De docta ignorantia*.

The very image of *vision* is, of course, thoroughly Neoplatonic. It is the root metaphor in Plotinus as well as in Proclus and PSEUDO-DIONYSIUS. In Plotinus' *Nous* the coincidence of Intelligence and Intelligibility makes the Soul aspire to a vision in which *seeing* consists in *being seen*. Cusanus, following Eckhart, reinterprets the metaphoric pair in a creationist sense.

The cognitive quality of Cusanus' understanding of the mystical vision situates his position on an issue hotly debated among his contemporaries, whether the union of the soul with God consists exclusively in an affective state of mind (as the thirteenth-century Carthusian, Hugh Balma, had argued) or whether the intellect plays an essential part in it and indeed creates its preliminary condition (as JOHN GERSON had claimed). This had been the very question the Benedictines of Tegernsee, to whom the work was addressed, had raised: *Utrum anima devota sine intellectus cognicione, vel etiam sine cogitacione previa vel concomitante, solo affectu seu per mentis apicem quam vocant synderesim Deum attingere possit?* (Whether the devout soul, without the cognition of the intellect, or even without either previous or concomitant thought, is able to attain to God by love alone or through the apex of the mind, which they call synderesis.)

Vincent of Aggsbach, who had attacked Gerson and was to attack *De visione Dei*, had correctly perceived that the entire issue turned on the interpretation of Pseudo-Dionysius' "dark contemplation." How could what surpassed all understanding be cognitive? On the other hand, how could one love without knowing what to love? For Cusanus, intellectual apprehension precedes unitive love. What renders this apprehension "dark" is that knowledge at its highest point destroys its own distinctions and becomes a conscious *not-knowing*. The intellect discerns that it enters a region where contradictories coincide and, hence, where the usual clarity of knowledge no longer pertains. Negative theology does not suspend all cognitive activity, however. For the mind *perceives* that it enters a realm of darkness. But once it does so, its negative insight, far more than the conclusion of an intellectual argument, rallies all mental powers, the affective as well as the cognitive, into a new, comprehensive experience. While *De docta ignorantia* uses symbols and proofs in addressing reason, *De visione Dei* appeals to the affective powers of the soul as well.

The mystical quality of Cusanus' works receives a solid intellectual foundation in his purely theoretical works. Grace and nature remain continuous for Cusanus. The mind's cognitive *conatus* (undertaking) leading to a collapse of its distinctions, methods, and powers, is, from the beginning motivated by an implicit desire of an obscure vision of the One who is beyond all distinctions, methods, and human potential. Yet that intellectual drive by itself does not attain a genuine vision of God. To do so grace must transform the mind's active striving into passive contemplation. Not until that point has the mind reached the end of its thinking process. In *De filiatione Dei* Cusanus declares the human spirit to contain a divine seed that allows it to grow into full conformity with God's Son (§53). The soul's natural aspirations remain unfulfilled until she reaches this *theosis* (deification) whereby she partakes in God's own nature.

What were the sources of Cusanus' mystical theology? The thought of Pseudo-Dionysius, the sixth-century Neoplatonist, may well form the most archaic layer. Perhaps nowhere does that appear more clearly than in *De deo abscondito*. But Nicholas read Dionysius' *Mystical Theology* as it had been received and interpreted by a long Christian tradition. In his case that included the reading of his Albertist masters at the University of Cologne and, later, that of Eckhart. The Albertist interpretation reached him primarily through the brilliantly original HEYMERIC OF CAMP. Rudolf Haubst, who did pioneering work on Cusanus' early history, claims that the seeds of the *coincidentia oppositorum* may be found in ALBERTUS MAGNUS' commentaries on Pseudo-Dionysius and on the Neoplatonic *Liber de causis*, commentaries on which Heymeric had based his own *Compendium divinorum* (1422–4).

Even more decisive than the Cologne Albertism was the impact of Eckhart's theology. The Rhineland mystic was, of course, committed to a more radically Neoplatonic thought than St. Albert and his followers had been. In Eckhart's religious vision all creatures possess their primordial Being in God the Son, divine Image of the Father. Thus their immanent Being coincides with God's own nature. Yet beside this ontological identity with God, which it shares with all other creatures, the soul as a spiritual entity displays a unique *similarity* to God. Spiritual life for Eckhart, then, consists in bringing the mind's created likeness to the greatest possible conformity to that uncreated Image with which it coincides in the "spark" of the soul.

Cusanus, even as the Rhenish mystic, proposes a sort of inverted analogy of being in which, contrary to the Thomist one, the finite must be interpreted through the infinite, rather than the other way around. Indeed, the finite has its entire reality within God. Cusanus refuses to qualify the identity between God and creation: "There is not one world which with the Father is an eternal world and another world which through descent from

473

the Father is a created world" (*De dato patris luminum* III, p. 106). Not surprisingly, statements such as these raised questions about Cusanus' orthodoxy among his contemporaries. He defended himself competently (see his *Apologia doctae ignorantiae*, 1449). Indeed, the questions are easily answered if one reads his work as a whole, rather than concentrating on any single statement. Cusanus was a thoroughly dialectical thinker, unparalleled in his ability to hold together what for others remained unbridgeable oppositions, such as those between immanence and transcendence, monism and dualism, logic and mystical theology.

Bibliography

Primary sources

(1932–), *Opera omnia. Iussu et auctoritate literarum Heidelbergensis ad codicum fidem edita*, Leipzig and Hamburg: Felix Meiner.

(1979), *Idiota de mente, de sapientia*, in Clyde Lee Miller, trans., *The Layman: About Mind*, The Janus Library Series 7, New York: Abaris Books.

(1981), *De docta ignorantia* (*On Learned Ignorance*), in Jasper Hopkins, trans., *Nicholas of Cusa on Learned Ignorance: A Translation and Appraisal of De docta ignorantia*, Minneapolis: Arthur J. Banning Press.

(1981), *Directio speculantis seu de non aliud* (*On God as Not-other*), in Jasper Hopkins, trans., *Nicholas of Cusa on God as Not-other: A Translation and an Appraisal of De li non aliud*, Minneapolis: University of Minnesota Press.

(1985), *De visione Dei* (*The Vision of God*), in Jasper Hopkins, trans., *Nicholas of Cusa's Dialectical Mysticism: Text, Translation, and Interpretative Study of De visione Dei*, Minneapolis: Arthur J. Banning Press.

(1989), *The Layman on Wisdom and the Mind*, M. L. Fuehrer, trans. and ed., Ottawa: Dovehouse Editions.

(1993), *De coniecturis* (*On Conjectures*), in William F. Wertz, trans., *Toward a New Council of Florence: "On the Peace of Faith" and Other Works by Nicholas of Cusa*, Washington, DC: Schiller Institute.

(1994), *De filiatione Dei* (*On Divine Sonship*), in Jasper Hopkins, trans., *A Miscellany on Nicholas of Cusa*, Minneapolis: Arthur J. Banning Press.

(1994), *De quaerendo Deum* (*On Seeking God*), in Jasper Hopkins, trans., *A Miscellany on Nicholas of Cusa*, Minneapolis: Arthur J. Banning Press.

(1996), *The Layman on Mind*, in Jasper Hopkins, trans., *Nicholas of Cusa on Wisdom and Knowledge*, Minneapolis: Arthur J. Banning Press.

Secondary sources

Hopkins, Jasper (1978), *A Concise Introduction to the Philosophy of Nicholas of Cusa*, Minneapolis: University of Minnesota Press.

Sigmund, P. E. (1963), *Nicholas of Cusa and Medieval Political Thought*, Cambridge, MA: Harvard University Press.

80

Nicole Oresme

EDWARD GRANT

Nicole Oresme (b. ca. 1320; d. 1382) was born near Caen in Normandy. He is first mentioned on June 19, 1342, in a letter from the papal court at Avignon to the four nations of the arts faculty of the University of Paris. In this recently discovered letter, Oresme is offered a benefice and is referred to as a master of arts. He was thus a master of arts by the academic year 1341–2, which indicates that he matriculated in the arts faculty during the 1330s, much earlier than previously thought. In 1348, his name appears on two lists at the University of Paris, once on a list of members of the Norman nation, and again in a list of holders of theology scholarships in the College of Navarre. In 1356, he became a doctor in theology and also grand master of the College of Navarre. Oresme held numerous church offices during his lifetime. He was appointed Archdeacon of Bayeux in 1361, but abandoned it when his request to retain the grand mastership of the College of Navarre was rejected. On November 23, 1362, he was made a canon at Rouen, at which time he presumably resigned as grand master of Navarre. Shortly after, on February 10, 1363, he was appointed canon at Sainte-Chapelle in Paris, which was followed more than a year later (March 18, 1364) with an appointment as Dean of the Cathedral of Rouen. With the potent influence of King Charles V of France, Oresme was made Bishop of Lisieux in 1377.

Oresme's relationship with King Charles is noteworthy. Somehow, by 1356, he had come into contact with the royal family, when King John II, Charles's father, utilized Oresme's services in coping with problems of national finance. Partly on the basis of these experiences, Oresme composed a famous treatise on money (*Tractatus de mutationibus monetarum*; and a later French version *Traictié de la monnoie*). While engaged in his duties for the crown, Oresme probably came to know the dauphin, the future Charles V, who was probably between 15 and 17 years of age. When Charles became king (r. 1364–80), one of his first acts was to appoint Oresme Dean of the Cathedral Church of Rouen.

Sometime around 1370, Charles commissioned Oresme to translate four of Aristotle's treatises from Latin into French. Between 1372 and 1377, Oresme translated the *Nicomachean ethics*, *Politics*, *Economics*, and *On the Heavens*. In his preface to the *Ethics*, Oresme says that the king wished to use the first three treatises to make his councillors and courtiers better at governing. Oresme offers no reason for translating *On the Heavens*, but he interspersed a section by section French commentary, which became his last known work. Oresme had a very high regard for *On the Heavens*, which he makes evident in the final two lines of a four-line Latin poem which serves as the conclusion of his French translation:

> For never in this world was there a book
> On natural philosophy more beautiful or more powerful.
>
> (Menut 1968, p. 731)

Oresme belongs to a small group of theologian–natural philosophers whose contributions to natural philosophy exceed their contributions to theology. Oresme's profound understanding of natural philosophy and mathematics and his contributions to these fields is second to none in the Middle Ages. He wrote treatises on all of Aristotle's natural philosophy books (including *Physics*, *On the Heavens*, *On the Soul*, *Meteorology*, and *On Generation and Corruption*), using the questions format that was typical of medieval scholastic commentaries on Aristotle, but also making a straightforward commentary, as in his French translation of *On the Heavens*.

Contributions to science, natural philosophy, and mathematics

In *Le Livre du ciel*, Oresme presents his most mature judgment on the possible existence of other worlds and whether an infinite void space might exist beyond our world. He shows that Aristotle's arguments against the possibility of a plurality of worlds are inconclusive, since God, by his absolute power, could create them any time he pleases, although Oresme did not believe that God had actually done so. Against Aristotle's argument that all existent matter comprises our world and none can possibly exist beyond it, Oresme offers a customary rebuttal that "God could create *ex nihilo* new matter and make another world" (Menut 1968, p. 175). He also rejects Aristotle's claim that the earth of another world would tend to move towards the center of our world. He does this by abandoning Aristotle's absolute sense of the terms 'up', 'down', 'light', and 'heavy', and redefining the meaning of 'up' and 'down'. For Oresme, a body is said to be "heavy" and "down" when light bodies surround it. The surrounding light bodies are said to be "up." In this way, heavy and light bodies and the directions up and down could be interpreted independently of the natural places of bodies. Oresme concludes that if God created a piece of earth in the heavens, that piece of earth would have no tendency to move towards the center of our world. Thus all worlds would be closed systems, quite independent of one another.

Against Aristotle's argument that no place or void can exist beyond our world, Oresme proclaims that "the human mind consents naturally . . . to the idea that beyond the heavens and outside the world, which is not infinite, there exists some space whatever it may be, and we cannot easily conceive the contrary" (Menut 1968, p. 177). Oresme regarded this space as an actually existent infinite void, because he identified it with God's real, infinite immensity.

In his *Le Livre du ciel* Oresme also considers whether the earth rotates daily on its axis. Although he ultimately agreed with Aristotle that the heavens rather than the earth rotate daily, he believed that neither experience nor reason could demonstrate either alternative. Going beyond the earlier account of his teacher JOHN BURIDAN, Oresme presents an impressive array of arguments in favor of the earth's rotation that Nicholas Copernicus himself did not surpass in his *On the Revolutions of the Heavenly Orbs* (1543). Invoking relativity of motion, Oresme argued that we perceive the local motion of a body only when it assumes a different position relative to another body. If a man were carried around by the heavens and could see the earth in some detail, it would seem to him that the earth moved with a daily motion, just as we, on earth, viewing the rotating heavens, attribute the daily motion to the heavens. To the argument that if the earth rotated from west to east, a noticeable wind should blow constantly from the east, Oresme counters that the air rotates with the earth and therefore would not blow from the east. Similarly, some argued that because an arrow shot into the air falls back approximately to the place from whence it was shot, and does not fall to the west, it follows that the earth does not rotate. Oresme countered that this argument was inconclusive because if the earth rotated, the arrow would share the earth's rotation and fall back to the place from which it was launched. Thus the same effects would occur whether or not the earth had a daily axial rotation. Oresme offered additional plausible, though non-demonstrative, arguments in favor of the earth's axial rotation. For example, it would be simpler if God caused the daily rotation of the heavens by causing the small earth to rotate, rather than making the monumentally large heavens revolve at enormously higher speeds. To the biblical argument that God aided the army of Joshua by making the sun stand still over Gibeon (Joshua 10: 12–14), thus demonstrating that the heavens rotate and the earth is at rest, Oresme suggests that God could also have performed his miracle by temporarily halting the earth's rotation. Both Galileo and Kepler presented explanations of the Joshua miracle, with Kepler's arguments resembling Oresme's. At the end of his lengthy discussion, Oresme concludes, apparently on biblical grounds, that the heavens move and not the earth, and does so even though he was convinced that the arguments in favor of the earth's rotation were more plausible than the alternative. In this instance, he accepted the idea that some false propositions might be more probable than some true propositions.

Oresme made his most significant and spectacular contributions in his numerous treatises, where he had greater opportunity to elaborate on themes that interested him. A few of his major contributions involved both natural philosophy and mathematics. One of the most significant themes Oresme pursued concerned mathematical commensurability and incommensurability and their application to terrestrial and celestial motions. In his *Treatise on Ratios of Ratios* (*Tractatus de proportionibus proportionum*), probably written in the 1350s, Oresme developed the mathematical ideas in THOMAS BRADWARDINE'S *Treatise on Ratios* of 1328. Using Euclid's theory of proportionality in the fifth book of the *Elements*, Oresme develops the concept of a "ratio of ratios," which is actually what we, though not Oresme, call the exponent. For example in the relationship $A/B = (C/D)^{p/q}$, the exponent, p/q, is a "ratio of ratios" that relates the two ratios A/B and C/D. If p/q is rational, then ratios A/B and C/D, which may be rational or irrational, or one rational, the other irrational, must be commensurable and represent a "rational ratio of ratios." For example, $(2/1)^{1/2}$ and $2/1$ are commensurable and form a rational ratio of ratios because $2/1 = [(2/1)^{1/2}]^{2/1}$; similarly, $27/1 = (3/1)^{3/1}$ is also a rational ratio of ratios because the exponent $3/1$ relates the two ratios $27/1$ and $3/1$. But $6/1$ and $3/1$ form an "irrational ratio of ratios," because $6/1 \neq (3/1)^{p/q}$, where p/q is rational. In fact, p/q must be irrational.

Oresme also introduces probability considerations in demonstrating that any two given unknown ratios are more likely to be incommensurable than commensurable. He takes 100 rational ratios from $2/1$ to $101/1$ and relates them two at a time. For example, $2/1$ and $3/1$ form an irrational ratio of ratios, namely $3/1 \neq (2/1)^{p/q}$, whereas $2/1$ and $4/1$ form a rational ratio of ratios, namely $4/1 = (2/1)^{p/q}$, where $p/q = 2/1$. These 100 ratios taken two at a time form 9,900 possible ratios of ratios. Since Oresme is only interested in ratios of greater inequality, where the numerator is greater than the denominator, only half of the ratios of ratios are relevant, namely 4,950. Of these ratios, Oresme shows that only 25 are rational, while the other 4,925 are irrational. Thus when a set of 100 rational ratios are posited, the ratio of irrational to rational ratios is 4925/25, or 197/1. As one takes more and more rational ratios, the odds that any given "ratio of ratios" is irrational increases.

It was by means of "ratios of ratios" that Oresme, and before him Thomas Bradwardine, represented velocities of motion produced by ratios of force and resistance, the latter usually conceived as a mobile body of some kind. Although Oresme did not use symbolic representation, we may represent his verbalizations as $F_2/R_2 = (F_1/R_1)^{v_2/v_1}$, where F is a force applied to a resistance, R, and v_2/v_1 is the ratio of velocities that is generated by the two force-resistance ratios. Oresme applied this formulation to terrestrial speeds and then to motions of celestial orbs. Although Oresme accepted prevailing opinion and assumed that "an intelligence moves by will alone and with no other force, effort, or difficulty, and the heavens do not resist it" (Grant 1966, p. 293), he nevertheless applied ratios of force and resistance to the heavens by analogy with terrestrial forces and resistances and arrived at his monumental conclusion that "When two motions of celestial bodies have been proposed, it is probable that they would be incommensurable, and most probable that any celestial motion of the heaven [that you might choose] would be incommensurable to the motion of any other [celestial] sphere that you might choose" (Grant 1966, p. 305).

In his later *Treatise on the Commensurability or Incommensurability of the Celestial Motions*, Oresme ignores force–resistance relationships and confines himself to purely kinematic theorems, involving distances traversed, times, and velocities. So impressive were Oresme's numerous theorems that a modern mathematician declared that some of them "have their counterpart in the modern theory of ergodic dynamical systems" (Von Plato 1981, p. 190). Oresme recognized that he had not demonstrated the incommensurability of the celestial motions, but had simply shown that it was mathematically probable. But it was sufficient to convince him that prognosticative astrology was inherently implausible, as we find in his *Ad pauca respicientes*, where he observes that "assuming any incommensurability in motions, which is probable, every future disposition, as long as it came from the present, would be unknown." However, because one cannot be certain whether any pair of motions is commensurable or incommensurable, it follows that "who is ignorant of the antecedent is necessarily ignorant of the consequent." On the basis of his numerous arguments about celestial incommensurability, Oresme was convinced that "it follows from all these things that astrology is vain" (Grant 1966, p. 427). To show how vain astrology really is, Oresme composed numerous treatises on the subject and sought to weaken its foundations as much as possible, in no small measure because astrologers exerted too great an influence on his sovereign, Charles V.

In his *Le Livre du ciel*, Oresme also used the probability of celestial incommensurability to counter Aristotle's claim that whatever had a beginning must also come to an end; and whatever comes to an end must have had a beginning (see Menut 1968, p. 199).

"The intension and remission of forms" was a well-developed medieval subject in which natural philosophers attempted to quantify all kinds of variable qualities, both visible and invisible. Parts of forms were added and subtracted as if they were extensive, mathematical magnitudes. The mathematical treatment of qualities was highly developed at Oxford University. In the 1330s and 1340s at Oxford University, motion was treated as if it were a variable quality like color or taste. In the course of their deliberations, scholars at Merton College, Oxford, devised definitions of uniform motion, uniformly accelerated motion, and instantaneous motion, definitions on which Galileo did not improve. By an ingenious use of these definitions, they also derived the mean speed theorem, which equated a uniformly accelerated motion with a uniform motion, enabling the former to be expressed by the latter. The Mertonians gave an arithmetic proof, which can be represented by its modern equivalent as $s = 1/2\ at^2$, where *s* is distance traversed, *t* is time, and *a* is uniform acceleration.

Sometime around 1350 Oresme wrote the most important medieval treatise on the intension and remission of forms or qualities. In this highly mathematical work, titled *Treatise on the Configuration of Qualities and Motions*, Oresme represented variable qualities by geometric figures. His most spectacular contribution, however, was a geometric proof of the mean speed theorem in which he represented uniformly accelerated motion from rest by a right triangle, and employed a rectangle to represent uniform motion, which was assigned the speed acquired at the middle instant of the uniform acceleration. Oresme showed that the triangle and rectangle are equal in area and therefore a body moving with a velocity that is uniformly accelerated from rest would traverse the same distance as a body moving during the same time with a uniform speed equal to the middle instant of the uniform acceleration. Oresme's proof and diagram were printed in numerous editions of the sixteenth century and probably influenced Galileo in his *Two New Sciences* (1638).

In his *On Seeing the Stars* (*De visione stellarum*), recently edited and translated in a Ph. D. dissertation by Danny E. Burton, Oresme considers atmospheric refraction and makes a spectacular contribution to the history of science. Oresme first rejects two traditional views in optics – held by Ptolemy, ALHACEN, ROGER BACON, and Witelo – that a light ray is refracted only at the interface of two media of differing densities *and* that no refraction could occur in a single medium whose density varies uniformly. By contrast, Oresme argues that refraction of light does not require a single refracting interface between two media of differing densities. It will be refracted along a curved path when it is in a single medium of uniformly varying density. For example, if air increases in rarity as it is more distant from the earth, light would pass through it along a curved path. To deduce a curved path, Oresme used his knowledge of convergent infinite series, assuming that successive refractions produced successive line segments and that as the line segments increased to infinity they form a curved line (Burton 2000, pp. 40–55).

In his analysis of Oresme's text, Danny Burton, who first discovered Oresme's contribution to our understanding of atmospheric refraction, observes that Robert Hooke and Isaac Newton were previously thought to have first argued that light is continuously refracted as it moves along a curved path through a uniformly decreasing medium. However, "while the definitive demonstration of the curvature of light in the atmosphere was Hooke's and Newton's, the original argument for such curvature was Oresme's" (Burton 2000, p. 53).

Attitude towards nature

Oresme's attitude towards nature was shaped by the fact that he was both a natural philosopher and a theologian. He firmly believed in the regularity of nature and assumed that a particular natural cause would always produce its particular natural effect. Consequently, he strongly opposed those who were quick to invoke magical and supernatural explanations for what he regarded as natural phenomena. But he also doubted the certainty of natural knowledge, emphasizing human limitations in its acquisition. He believed that many propositions in natural knowledge required as much of an act of faith as did the truths of revelation.

Bibliography

Primary sources

(1966), *Nicole Oresme: "De proportionibus proportionum" and "Ad pauca respicientes,"* ed. and trans. E. Grant, Madison: University of Wisconsin Press.

(1968), *Nicole Oresme and the Medieval Geometry of Qualities and Motions: A Treatise on the Uniformity and Difformity of Intensities known as "Tractatus de configurationibus qualitatum et motuum,"* ed. and trans. M. Clagett, Madison: University of Wisconsin Press.

(1968), *Nicole Oresme: Le Livre du ciel et du monde*, ed. and trans. A. D. Menut, ed. A. J. Denomy, Madison: University of Wisconsin Press.

(1971), *Nicole Oresme and the Kinematics of Circular Motion: Tractatus de commensurabilitate vel incommensurabilitate motuum celi,"* ed. and trans. E. Grant, Madison: University of Wisconsin Press.

(2000), "Nicole Oresme's "On Seeing the Stars" (*De visione stellarum*): A critical edition of Oresme's treatise on optics and atmospheric refraction, with an introduction, commentary, and English translation," ed. and trans. D. E. Burton, Ph.D dissertation, Indiana University, Bloomington.

Secondary sources

Grant, E. (1993), "Jean Buridan and Nicole Oresme on natural knowledge," *Vivarium* 31, pp. 84–105.

Von Plato, J. (1981), "Nicole Oresme and the ergodicity of rotations," in Ingmar Pörn, ed., *Essays in Philosophical Analysis Dedicated to Erik Stenius on the Occasion of his 70th Birthday*, Acta Philosophica Fennica 32, pp. 190–7.

81

Paul of Pergula

STEPHEN E. LAHEY

Paul of Pergula (d. 1455), student of PAUL OF VENICE, is known for advocating an ontology-free logic. Medieval thinkers believed that written and spoken propositions conventionally signified a correspondent mental proposition, which itself naturally signifies in a universal mental language its object, whether mental or extra-mental. For Ockham, simple supposition, in which a term refers to a universal like 'man' in 'Man is a species', referred to concepts only, while Paul of Venice further precluded a realist ontology by eliminating simple supposition altogether. Paul of Pergula pursued this in his *Logica*, his introduction to the elements of reasoning and language. This text introduces the reader to: (1) supposition theory, how terms function in linguistic propositions as representative of their referents and as the formative material elements of propositions; (2) how propositions refer to states of affairs both outside of and within language; (3) how propositions follow as consequences from antecedent propositions; (4) *obligationes* rules; and (5) *insolubilia* rules. The last two topics were genres of medieval logic concerned with puzzles resultant from logical disputation and problems of reference connected to problematic statements like the liar's paradox.

In his description of the kinds of supposition, Paul of Pergula's refusal to admit ontology into logic is clear; the subject term in 'Man is a species' has personal supposition, but its reference is determined by the predicate 'is a species'. In this case, the predicate describes how instances of signification of the subject term are related, a relational property of terms, not things. Thus, 'man' in 'Man is a species' has no referent outside of the proposition. It is neither an extra-mental universal nor a universal concept. This is not to say that Paul is silent about propositions referring to acts of the mind, or *officiables*; these, he says, point to confused mobile supposition. For example, in the proposition 'I want peace', 'peace' refers to what I want in any given case, and the cases that there are are this case, or that, and so on.

Paul differs from his predecessors in his explication of consequences as well. Consequences, the term commonly used to describe implication, entailment, and inference relations between propositions, are grounded in Boethian logic. WALTER BURLEY, Pseudo-Scotus, and ALBERT OF SAXONY expanded consequences literature to encompass all deductive logic by including syllogistic proposition relations, but Paul, perhaps attempting to simplify what had become a complex field, omits syllogistic inference. As with other later medieval logicians, though, Paul appears to have been sensitive to views on these topics. For example, if you know you are dead, then you are dead (one cannot know the false), and if you know you are dead, then you are not dead (the dead cannot know anything), so you do not know you are dead (If p, then q; if p then ~q; therefore ~p). Also of note is that Paul assumes De Morgan's theorem, as did JOHN BURIDAN, in his explications of the relation of propositions.

Bibliography

Primary source

(1961), *Logica et Tractatus de sensu composito et divisio*, ed. M. A. Brown, St. Bonaventure, NY: Franciscan Institute.

Secondary source

Boh, Ivan (1965), "Paul of Pergula on suppositions and consequences," *Franciscan Studies* 25, pp. 30–89.

82

Paul of Venice

ALAN PERREIAH

Paul of Venice, also known as Paolo Nicoletto Veneto (b. 1369; d. 1429), was an Augustinian who taught in Padua in the early Renaissance (Perreiah 1986, chs. 1, 2). He composed twenty works extant in over 260 manuscripts (MSS census in ibid., ch. 3). These cover theological topics as well as most areas of Aristotelian thought, namely logic, physical theory, philosophy of mind, metaphysics, ethics, and politics. Paul's influence may be measured by the number of copies made of his most important works: *Lectura super librum Posteriorum analyticorum* (53 MSS), *Summa naturalium* (53 MSS), *Lectura super librum De anima* (12 MSS), *Quaestio de universalibus* (9 MSS), *Logica parva* (81 MSS). In physical theory Paul's works set a standard at the famous School of Padua, yet they are more remarkable for clear exposition than innovation. By contrast, in metaphysics he knows current Oxford thought and advances some important theses, e.g., on universality (Conti 1996). Paul's greatest contribution was in logic. His lectures on *Posterior Analytics* influenced scientific theory throughout Italy. His *Sophismata* and *Quadratura* (collections of sophisms for dialectical practice) are large works, but were not widely circulated. *Logica parva* (over 80 manuscripts and 25 editions) was by far Paul's most important work. It transmitted Oxford logic to Italy where it was the leading textbook for nearly two hundred years (1984). The encyclopedic *Logica magna* has been attributed to Paul of Venice; but serious discrepancies in doctrine between that work and Paul's known works render that attribution debatable (Perreiah 1986, chs. 4, 5).

The *Logica parva* advances a theory of logical form. The first chapter introduces the distinction between categorematic and syncategorematic terms. This distinction supports an analysis of a sentence into logical and non-logical components, and the former define its logical form. The rules of *suppositio* (ch. 2) provide a system of notation for the oral medium enabling the dialectician to articulate precisely the logical forms of sentences. The rules of *consequentia* (ch. 3) show the inference patterns between sentences on the basis of their logical forms. Finally, the rules of *probatio* (ch. 4) supply protocols for exhibiting the truth-conditions for sentences of determinate logical form. The rules of *obligatio* (ch. 5) give a regimen for training students in dialectic. The rules of *sophismata* (ch. 6) show how to respond to sophisms in dialectical debate. The major theses and rules of chapters 1 and 3 are subjected to rigorous criticism and response (chs. 7, 8). The coherence and practical utility of this theory help to explain the resilience of scholastic logic as an alternative to humanist rhetoric throughout the Renaissance.

Bibliography

Primary sources

(1971), *Logica magna, Tractatus de suppositionibus*, trans. A. R. Perreiah, St. Bonaventure, NY: Franciscan Institute.

(1978), *Logica magna, Tractatus de veritate et falsitate propositionis et Tractatus de significato propositionis*, ed. F. Del Punta, trans. M. M. Adams, Oxford: Oxford University Press.

(1979), *Logica magna, Tractatus de terminis*, trans. N. Kretzmann, Oxford: Oxford University Press.

(1980), *Super primum Sententiarum Johannis de Ripa lecturae abbreviatio*, ed. F. Ruello, Florence: L. S. Olschki.

(1984), *Logica parva*, trans. A. R. Perreiah, Washington, DC: The Catholic University of America Press; Munich: Philosophia Verlag.

(1988), *Logica magna, Tractatus de obligationibus*, ed. and trans. E. J. Ashworth, Oxford: Oxford University Press.

(1990), *Logica magna, Capitula de conditionali et de rationali*, ed. and trans. G. E. Hughes, Oxford: Oxford University Press.

(1990), *Logica magna, Tractatus de hypotheticis*, ed. and trans. A. Broadie, Oxford: Oxford University Press.

Secondary sources

Conti, A. D. (1996), *Esistenza e verità*, Rome: Istituto Storico Italiano per il Medio Evo.

Perreiah, A. R. (1986), *Paul of Venice: A Bibliographical Guide*, Bowling Green, OH: Philosophy Documentation Center.

83

Peter Abelard

JOHN MARENBON

Peter Abelard (b. 1079; d. 1142) is the most famous, and probably the subtlest and most adventurous, of twelfth-century philosophers. He made important contributions to logic, metaphysics, ethics, and the philosophy of religion.

Abelard, the eldest son of a minor aristocrat at Le Pallet, was born near Nantes in Brittany. He decided when young to pursue a career as a logician rather than as a knight. After studying with Roscelin, with whom he would later quarrel violently, he was drawn to Paris (ca. 1100), which was not yet otherwise an outstanding scholastic center, by the fame as a logician of WILLIAM OF CHAMPEAUX, master at the Cathedral School of Notre Dame. Abelard learned from William, but he also found that he could out-argue him, and Abelard began his own school of logic, in rivalry with William and his followers. By 1113, after an abortive attempt to learn theology from the famous Anselm, teacher at Laon, Abelard succeeded in becoming master of the School of Notre Dame. It was probably during this period (ca. 1115–16; cf. Marenbon 1997, pp. 41–3) that he wrote his first major logical work, the *Dialectica*, a treatise covering all the areas of logic studied at the time.

It was during this period too that Abelard met, seduced and (secretly) married Héloïse, the niece of Fulbert, a canon of Notre Dame. Héloïse, perhaps in her twenties when the affair began, and well-known for her literary learning, may have helped to expand Abelard's interests beyond the area of logic, to which they had up until then been mostly confined (Clanchy 1999, pp. 169–70). But it was the castration of Abelard organized by Fulbert which, in its repercussions, did most to change Abelard's intellectual horizons. Abelard's reaction to the castration was to force Héloïse to enter a nunnery and himself to become a monk of St. Denis. But he gave up neither teaching nor writing. Not long after he entered St. Denis (ca. 1119), he issued a set of long, intricate logical commentaries on Porphyry, Aristotle, and BOETHIUS, the *Logica (ingredientibus)*, and about five or six years later he produced another, importantly different commentary on Porphyry's *Isagoge* (Introduction) to logic, the *Glossulae* (sometimes called *Logica nostrorum petitioni sociorum*). But, as a monk, Abelard thought he should also write about Christian doctrine, and at St. Denis he found himself for the first time with access to a large library to help him do so. His first theological work, a discussion of the Trinity known as the *Theologia summi boni* (1120) was promptly condemned and burned at the Council of Soissons in 1121. But Abelard was undaunted and expanded the work into his *Theologia Christiana* (ca. 1125–6) and finally revised it into the *Theologia scholarium* (ca. 1134).

Abelard had left St. Denis shortly after the Council of Soissons, after quarreling with his confreres. He obtained permission to set up his own monastery, which he finally called the Paraclete: students flocked there to be taught by Abelard. In about 1126, Abelard accepted an invitation to become abbot of St. Gildas, an unruly monastery in a remote part of his native Brittany. Probably during his time there – a miserable period, during which he tried and failed to reform the monastery – he wrote his *Collationes* ("Comparisons," also known as *Dialogue between a Christian, a Jew and a Philosopher*).

In the 1130s, probably by early in 1133, Abelard returned to the Paris schools. His second Parisian period, which lasted until 1138, was one of his most productive: as well as the *Theologia scholarium*, he wrote a commentary on Paul's letter to the Romans, gave lectures over the whole range of theology which were written up as his *Sententie*, and wrote his *Scito teipsum* ("Know thyself," also called his *Ethics*). He gave some lectures on logic, but his main concentration was on theology (and so on questions in ethics and the philosophy of religion). In the late 1130s, Abelard's teaching was attacked by BERNARD OF CLAIRVAUX and his followers. At the Council of Sens (June 1140), where Abelard had hoped to expose the accusations against him as unjust, Bernard managed to present him as a heretic. Abelard appealed, unsuccessfully, to Rome, and was offered refuge by PETER THE VENERABLE, Abbot of Cluny. He died at Chalon-sur-Saône, a dependency of Cluny, in 1142. (See Clanchy 1999 for a full biography; Marenbon 1997, pp. 7–95, and Mews 1995 for briefer accounts of his life and works.)

Logic

Abelard's work as a logician was bound up with lecturing on the seven books of the early twelfth-century logical curriculum: Aristotle's *Categories* and *On Interpretation*, Porphyry's *Isagoge* (Introduction) to the *Categories*, and four logical textbooks by Boethius. Even his *Dialectica*, ostensibly an independent treatise, derives from such lectures. Much of Abelard's more formal work in logic is highly technical and difficult to summarize, but it is possible to give an idea of his innovative thinking about propositionality.

Aristotle's syllogistic, known in the twelfth century mainly through Boethius, provided medieval logicians with a formal system of *term* logic. Although in antiquity *propositional* logic had been developed by the Stoics, it was hardly transmitted to the Middle Ages. According to the scholar who has worked most closely on this area, Abelard should take the credit for rediscovering it (Martin 1991; cf. Martin 1987). Unlike his main source, Boethius, Abelard considers a "hypothetical syllogism," such as 'If it is day, it is light; it is day; so, it is light' as depending on the link between whole propositions, rather than terms. Abelard considers that a conditional (an 'if . . . then . . .' statement) is true if and only if the antecedent "of itself requires" the consequent: not only is it impossible for the antecedent to be true and the consequent false, but the antecedent also contains the meaning of the consequent (*Dialectica* III, 1; 1970, pp. 284: 1–4; cf. Martin 1987, pp. 385–93). A conditional such as 'If it is a rose, it is a flower', meets this requirement. The connection it asserts cannot, however, be explained in terms of particular roses and flowers, because it would be true even if none existed (and Abelard does not accept that there are universal roses or flowers; see below). Nor, obviously, is it just a connection between strings of words (*propositiones*), nor between thoughts, since I might think of a rose, without thinking of a flower. Abelard concludes, then, that the connection is between *dicta* (1919–27, pp. 365: 31–370: 3) A *dictum* is that which is said by a sentence. Abelard is a little unclear, however, whether *dicta* are roughly what philosophers nowadays call "propositions," or rather states of affairs:

truth-bearers or truth-makers (cf. Marenbon 1997, pp. 202–9). Despite this uncertainty, and problems over the ontological status of *dicta* (see below), Abelard's concept of the *dictum* shows how carefully he thought about the semantics necessary for propositional (as opposed to term) logic.

Metaphysics

In his logical works, Abelard was not just concerned with formal logic. The ancient texts – especially the *Categories* and *Isagoge* – gave him the opportunity to develop a distinctive metaphysics, linked to his semantics and logic.

Abelard takes it for granted that things in nature belong to natural kinds, each of which has fixed, distinguishing characteristics. Unlike many of his contemporaries, however, he does not accept that real species and genera (or any other sort of universal) exist. He rejects all the theories designed to explain how a thing can be one and many, as a universal must be (1919–27, pp. 10: 17–16: 18; 1933, pp. 513: 15–522: 9; cf. de Libera 1999, pp. 305–67; Tweedale 1976, pp. 89–132). According to him, therefore, everything is a particular. Abelard's distinctive metaphysics is the result of applying this nominalism to the scheme set out in the *Categories* and *Isagoge*. Aristotle distinguishes between substances (roughly speaking, independent things) and accidents, which he divides into nine categories (quantity, quality, relation, where, when, posture, having, doing, and being-done-to); and between whether the substances and accidents are particular or universal. Accidents are non-essential properties. Porphyry also discusses essential properties, which he called *differentiae*, because they distinguish one species or genus of things from another: rationality and mortality, for instance, are the *differentiae* of human beings. Abelard and his contemporaries use the word 'form' (*forma*) to cover both accidents and *differentiae*.

According, then, to the twelfth-century realist reading of the *Categories*, the basic constituents of the world are substances and forms, and things of each of these sorts exist as particulars and universals. Particular substances are things such as John Marenbon and Shergar the horse; universal substances are species, such as man and horse, and genera, such as animal; particular forms are things such as the particular whiteness by which John Marenbon is white and the particular rationality by which he is rational (even though he is exactly the same shade of white and rational in exactly the same way as many others); universal forms are whiteness and rationality. Abelard holds that only two of these four sorts of items exist: particular substances and particular forms. When Aristotle and Porphyry talk about universal substances and forms, he considers that they are talking about a way in which words can be used, but not about a type of thing: in the true sentence 'Man is an animal', 'man' is being used as a universal word, but it does not thereby follow that there is any thing in reality which is the species man (cf. Marenbon 1997, pp. 101–16).

This metaphysical scheme raises two obvious problems, which Abelard tries to tackle. First, how are particular forms and substances related? Second, how can Abelard explain the truth of sentences involving universal words, when he claims that there are no universal things?

According to Abelard, forms differ from substances by a relative lack of independence. Every form that exists is a form belonging to some substance or other (John Marenbon's rationality, Shergar's brownness). But Abelard makes clear that, although a particular form that informs one substance cannot subsequently inform another, any of the particular forms that inform a given substance might not have informed that substance, but another one: I may have been rational by the particular rationality by which, as a matter of fact, you are rational (1919–27, pp. 84: 14–21, 92: 22–9, 129: 33–6; cf. Marenbon 1997, pp. 119–22). The dependence of forms on their substances does not, therefore, stop them from being, at least in theory, distinct things. It might seem, therefore, that in the final analysis substances are aggregates of forms, since it is by having certain differential forms (*differentiae*) that a substance is the substance it is: a man is man through having particular forms such as rationality, mortality, being-able-to-perceive-through-the-senses. Yet, although he some-times writes as if bodily substances were simply aggregates of body and various differential forms, elsewhere Abelard explicitly states that particular substances do each have an essence, which has its own identity independent of any of the forms, including differential ones, which belong to it (*Dialectica* III, 2; 1970, pp. 420: 30–421: 8; cf. Marenbon 1997, pp. 128–30).

This is the scheme Abelard put forward in his *Dialectica* and *Logica*. By the mid-1120s, Abelard appears to have pared down his ontology still further so far as accidental (though not differential) forms are concerned. He came to doubt that relations (*Theologia Christiana*, IV, 154–8, 1969b, pp. 342: 2434–344: 2532) and, perhaps, most other accidents, except for some in the categories of quality and of action, can be considered things at all (Marenbon 1997, pp. 138–61).

Abelard provides a complex explanation of how, given that everything is particular, sen-tences about universals can be true. His main concern (in common with his contemporaries, and the passage from Porphyry's *Isagoge* which posed the problem of universals) is with words for universal substances. How, for instance, do we explain the truth of *Socrates est homo* ('Socrates is (a) man')? The problem was not seen to be one about reference – because twelfth-century logicians were happy to say that *homo* refers to the particular substance, Socrates – but about signification. Signification is a causal, psychological notion: a word '*w*' signifies *x* by causing a thought of *x* in the listener's mind. The signification of *homo* in *Socrates est homo* is clearly universal: the *x* of which it causes a thought is a universal man, not a particular one. But how can it do so, if every thing is particular? Abelard's strategy in the *Logica* (1919–27, pp. 20: 15–22: 24) is to say that what is signified by a universal word is not a *thing* at all, and so it can be universal! Universal words cause two different effects in the minds of their listeners. They produce a thought – which is a thing, a particular accident – but they also cause a mental image. The mental image, which is a confused, common conception (for example, 'man' produces a confused conception of what humans have in common, not the image of any particular man) is not a thing. These common con-ceptions are what universal words signify – universals, indeed, but non-things.

The idea behind this discussion is that in an act of cognition there can be distinguished (1) the act of cognition itself; (2) the object in the world which the cognition is about; (3) the object (= 2) *as envisaged in the cognition under a certain mode of presentation*. Abelard reasonably enough considers that (3) is not an extra item in the world to be counted in addi-tion to (1) and (2), and that the mode of presentation is in some cases universal rather than particular. On Abelard's view, therefore, "a universal does not exist in the outside world. Its existence, rather its being given, is just due to some productive way of thinking" (De Rijk 1980, p. 149). Nonetheless, the classification of things into species and genera is a real feature of how they are. Men, for example, "come together in being a man" or, as Abelard often (e.g. 1919–27, p. 20: 3–4) puts it, "in the *status* of man" (the condition of being a man). But, as Abelard is quick to emphasize (1919–27, pp. 19: 25–9, 20: 1, 6), a *status* is not a thing.

Some historians (following Jolivet 1981b, p. 194) contend that, despite Abelard's nomi-nalism, the basis for the meaning of universal words is provided by Platonic Ideas in God's mind. There is good reason to reject this interpretation. Abelard would, indeed, have accepted that God grasps universals perfectly and infallibly and so has Platonic Ideas in his mind, but not that they play a part in human understanding of universals. He considers that, unlike God, men do not grasp universals completely or always correctly – a position which fits well with the view that the significates of universal words are confused, common conceptions (1919–27, pp. 22: 28–23: 30). Nonetheless, the mechanics of how words are imposed on objects ensure that the extension of a substance-word is exactly matched to the substances of that sort. Although, for example, the person who, looking at Shergar, decides that 'horse' should be the word for animals of that sort may not know the *differentiae* that distinguish horses from other substances, by the act of imposition 'horse' is assigned as the word for all substances that have the structure of *differentiae* that Shergar in fact has (*Dialectica*, V, 2; 1970, p. 595: 26–8). Since Abelard accepts unproblematically that all substances belong to fixed natural kinds, 'horse' will henceforth be the word for all and only horses.

Altogether, Abelard wishes to preserve the main features of how he believes Aristotle conceives the world in his *Categories*, but to do so with more ontological parsimony than most of his contemporaries. The problem with his account lies in the lack of an explanation of how non-things, such as *status*, which Abelard needs in order to frame his theory, can be reduced to the basic constituents of the world, particular substance and non-substance things. And, in one passage from the *Glossulae* (1933, 570: 29–573: 5), rather than tackle this problem, Abelard seems to give up his nominalism and allow for universals which are in some sense real, though only in the case of *differentiae*, not that of substances (cf. Marenbon 1997, pp. 198–201). There is a similar, perhaps even graver problem, with the metaphysics of another of Abelard's metaphysical innovations, the *dicta* of sentences (*dicta propositionum*) discussed above. Like *status*, *dicta* are not things, according to Abelard (1919–27, 369: 37–9; cf. 366: 37–8), although they are "quasi-things." But a reductive account of *dicta* in terms of things would be very difficult to give, because *dicta* do not depend on the existence of any thing. (For the fullest study of Abelard on universals, and an analysis in some ways different from the above, see de Libera 1999, pp. 281–498.)

Ethics

Abelard elaborated his ethical theory in the last ten years of his life, in his commentary on Romans, the *Collationes*, and *Scito teipsum* (of which only the first book, on sin, is complete). His moral theory is also outlined in the *Sententie* based on his lectures. (See De Gandillac 1975; Marenbon 1997, pp. 250–97.)

For Abelard, people act well or badly according to whether they show love or contempt for God. They show him love by obeying his commands and contempt by disobeying them. This account depends on divine commands being known to everybody, since no one can show love or contempt by merely happening to obey or disobey an injunction of which he is unaware. Abelard's mechanism for this universal knowledge of divine commands is natural law: he believes that every mentally competent adult, everywhere and in all periods of history naturally knows God's main moral commands (for example, the prohibition of murder, theft, and adultery, and the injunction to love God and one's neighbor). Moreover, he considers that everyone is endowed with conscience (*conscientia*), which he takes as the ability to see how these general commands apply to particular actions.

This underlying view results in a tension. On the one hand, the moral quality of an action depends, not directly on the sort of action it is, but on whether the agent is doing it in contempt for God, in which case it is a sin (Abelard tends to concentrate on sin; his discussion of meritorious actions is more sketchy). It follows that it can never be concluded simply from the fact that I have done A – where 'A' is an external description of an action, such as 'killed a man', 'taken goods which are not mine' – that I have sinned. On the other hand, the basis of Abelard's ethics are divine commands which prohibit or enjoin certain sorts of actions. The universality of natural law and conscience rules out the possibility of people being able to, for instance, steal or murder without thereby showing contempt for God, because they do not know that God forbids such actions. They cannot but know.

Moreover, Abelard is quite clear that contempt for God is involved whenever his commandments are knowingly broken. A person does not have to perform an act *for the sake of* showing contempt for God for his act to be an act of contempt for God. Indeed, Abelard accepts that very often, when people sin, they do so reluctantly. I want to sleep with Fifi; I would far prefer that she were not married and that I could sleep with her without committing adultery; still, I choose to sleep with her rather than not. According to Abelard I have sinned, although unwillingly (*Commentary on Romans* III; 1969a, pp. 206: 35–207: 682). In *Scito teipsum* (1971, pp. 4: 26–10: 27) he introduces a terminology to make this analysis clearer. I do not *wish* to sin, Abelard says, but I *consent* to it. Someone consents to an action when he will perform it unless thwarted.

Abelard is often described as emphasizing intentions in ethics, by contrast with his contemporaries. Yet, in one sense, most early-twelfth-century moral thinkers placed far more weight on intentions than Abelard. They analyzed the different stages of a sinful action, from thinking about it, being tempted, actively contemplating performing it and, finally, actually doing it. Even the first stages involves some sin, but at each stage the degree of sin increases. For Abelard, none of the early stages carries any guilt; on the contrary, he holds that someone who is strongly tempted, but does not consent to sinful action, is more praiseworthy than someone who feels no temptation. Such a person is showing love for God, by resisting temptation to disobey him, not contempt (1971, p. 12: 3–13). By the same token, a person is no less guilty because a sinful action which he is ready to perform is thwarted, since his contempt for God is the same as if it had not been. Consent (to a forbidden action) is, then, the measure of sin.

Abelard's ethical theory has little room for a substantive conception of the good life for man, based on distinctively human virtues. Rather, Abelard uses the scheme of virtues (prudence, justice, courage, temperance, and their sub-divisions), taken mainly from Cicero, to provide a moral psychology (*Collationes*, II, 111–39; 2001, pp. 128–48). Prudence is seen as an aid to virtue, not a virtue itself. Roughly speaking, a just action is that which follows the course of divine commandment. But Abelard considers that people are very often led away from performing just actions, either by fear or pleasure. Courage is the settled state by which we are not stopped from acting well by fear; temperance is the settled state by which pleasure does not succeed in tempting us to do what is forbidden or not to do what is enjoined.

Philosophy of religion

Abelard contributed to what is now described as "philosophy of religion" in two different ways. First, he put forward solutions to the classic problems about the concept of an omnipotent, omniscient, eternal, and wholly benevolent being. Particularly interesting are two unusual positions he takes about God, goodness, and evil. Most of Abelard's contemporaries held that evil is merely a privation of goodness; so-called evils, such as sickness, blindness, and sin, are not things, they thought, but rather absences. In the *Collationes* (II, 224; 2001, p. 220; cf. Introduction, p. lxxxi), however, Abelard recognizes the existence of these and other evil things. But he maintains a distinction between 'good' as applied to things, and 'good' as applied to *dicta* about those things. As he emphasizes: it is good that there is evil, but evil is not good. The benevolence of an omnipotent and all-wise God is evident at the level of *dicta* – how things are – and it can accommodate evil at the level of things (an awkward position perhaps if Abelard is also committed to reductionist explanation in terms of things). In the *Theologia Christiana* (V, 30–2; 42–3; 1969b, pp. 358: 424–359: 456; 366: 586–611) and *Theologia scholarium* (III, 27–56; 1987, pp. 511: 373–524: 771), Abelard also develops the doctrine, which he knows is unusual and will not be popular, that God cannot do more or differently from what he does. God always does what it is fitting for him to do, so that to do something other than what he does do would mean *not* doing something which is fitting for him to do.

Second, Abelard examined penetratingly the nature of faith and its relationship to reasoning. In Book II of the *Theologia Christiana* (not paralleled in the other versions of the work), Abelard devotes himself to praising the wisdom and virtue of the ancient Greeks and Romans, especially their philosophers. They were pagans, he says, in name only; through their reasoning they knew of the triune God and they lived exemplary lives. The *Collationes* is designed to look at the claims of reason and different faiths more closely. In a dream vision, Abelard is asked to judge between the cases made by a Jew, a Christian, and a Philosopher. The Philosopher is the representative of reason, but the other two interlocutors, although they follow revealed laws, present thoroughly reasoned arguments for their views, and they all treat each other with respect, as colleagues engaged in investigating the truth. The Jew puts forward a rationalized version of Judaism. Only the commands to love God and one's neighbor, and what they imply, are important for salvation; the external ceremonies and observances of the Old Law are valuable merely as instruments that help Jews to obey these central commands, by setting them apart from others, and as ways of showing especial devotion and obedience to God. The Christian accepts a good deal of the Philosopher's reasoning about the nature of the highest good, including his account of the virtues. But he gradually succeeds in arguing the Philosopher towards the position that the highest good for people is the love for God which they will have most fully after their death. The Christian goes on to put forward a very untraditional account of heaven and hell: they are not places, and the wicked do not receive the physical punishments that a literal reading of the Bible would indicate. Taken together with the bold attempt in the *Theologia summi boni* (I, cap. ii, 1–5; 1987b, pp. 86: 10–88: 62) – nuanced, but never abandoned in later versions of the work – to equate God's triunity with the three aspects of his perfection (his power, wisdom, and love), the *Collationes* suggests that underlying Abelard's work is a very bold attempt to set Christianity on a rational basis.

Abelard's place in medieval philosophy

In the second half of the twelfth century, Abelard had a school of followers (called the "*nominales*") who followed and developed what they took to be his characteristic logical doctrines. His approach to theology certainly influenced PETER LOMBARD and other twelfth-century theologians, whose work would determine the way theology was studied in the later medieval universities. Yet the direct influence of Abelard's writings was slight. In the century after his death, the aims and context of metaphysics, ethics, and logic were changed by the rediscovery of almost all Aristotle's works. In more recent times, where Abelard has been remembered as more than the lover of Héloïse, his reputation has been that of a brilliant logician who went on, in later life to apply his logical tools to questions of Christian doctrine. He has been seen as a critical, even destructive thinker, with an important role in the development of the scholastic method, but not, except in logic, as an original, creative philosopher (e.g. Jolivet 1982, p. 363; cf. Marenbon 1997, 340–9). There is, indeed, an *element* of truth in such a characterization. Abelard did not, like THOMAS AQUINAS or JOHN DUNS SCOTUS, set out a single, coherent system of thought, covering the main areas of philosophy and theology. But he did advance interesting and original positions in a number of philosophical fields. In the first half of his career, he elaborated a nominalist metaphysics. In the second half, he developed both a theory of ethics and a boldly rational approach to Christian doctrine.

Bibliography

Primary sources

(1919–27), *Logica*, ed. B. Geyer, in *Peter Abaelards Philosophische Schriften* I, *Beiträge zur Geschichte der Philosophie und Theologie des Mittelalters* 31/1–3, Münster: Aschendorff (trans. Paul V. Spade as "From the 'Glosses on Porphryry' in his *Logica ingredientibus*" (1994), *Five Texts on the Mediaeval Problem of Universals*, Indianapolis and Cambridge, MA: Hackett).

(1933), *Glossulae*, ed. B. Geyer, *Peter Abaelards Philosophische Schriften* II, *Beiträge zur Geschichte der Philosophie und Theologie des Mittelalters* 31/4, Münster: Aschendorff.

(1958), *Logica* (authentic ending of *De interpretatione* commentary), ed. L. Minio-Paluello, in *Twelfth-century Logic* II: *Abaelardiana inedita*, Rome: Edizioni di storia e letteratura.

(1969a), *Commentary on Romans*, ed. E. M. Buytaert, in *Petri Abaelardi opera theologica* I, Corpus Christianorum continuatio mediaevalis 11, Turnhout: Brepols.

(1969b), *Theologia Christiana*, ed. E. M. Buytaert, in *Petri Abaelardi opera theologica* II, Corpus Christianorum continuatio mediaevalis 12, Turnhout: Brepols.

(1970), *Dialectica*, 2nd edn., ed. L. M. De Rijk, Assen: Van Gorcum.

(1971), *Scito teipsum*, ed. D. E. Luscombe, in *Peter Abelard's Ethics*, Oxford: Oxford University Press.

(1987a), *Theologia scholarium*, ed. C. J. Mews and E. M. Buytaert, in *Petri Abaelardi opera theologica* III, Corpus Christianorum continuatio mediaevalis 13, Turnhout: Brepols.

(1987b), *Theologia summi boni*, ed. C. J. Mews and E. M. Buytaert, in *Petri Abaelardi opera theologica* III, Corpus Christianorum continuatio mediaevalis 13, Turnhout: Brepols.

(2001), *Collationes*, ed. J. Marenbon and G. Orlandi, *Abelard's* Collationes, Oxford: Oxford University Press.

Secondary sources

Clanchy, M. (1999), *Abelard: A Medieval Life*, Oxford: Blackwell.

De Gandillac, M. (1975), "Intention et loi dans l'éthique d'Abélard," in *Pierre Abélard, Pierre le Vénérable: les courants philosophiques, littéraires et artistiques en Occident au milieux du xlle siècle* (pp. 585–608), Paris: Éditions du Centre National de la Recherche Scientifique.

de Libera, A. (1999), *L'Art des généralités: Théories de l'abstraction*, Paris: Aubier.

De Rijk, L. M. (1980), "The semantic impact of Abailard's solution of the problem of universals," in R. Thomas, ed., *Petrus Abaelardus (1079–1142): Person, Werk und Wirkung* (pp. 139–50), Trierer theologische Studien 38, Trier: Paulinus Verlag.

Jolivet, J., ed. (1981a), *Abélard en son temps*, Paris: Les Belles Lettres.

——(1981b), "Non-réalisme et platonisme chez Abélard," in J. Jolivet, ed., *Abélard en son temps* (pp. 175–95), Paris: Les Belles Lettres.

——(1982), *Arts du langage et théologie chez Abélard*, 2nd edn., Études de philosophie médiévale 57, Paris: J. Vrin.

Marenbon, J. (1997), *The Philosophy of Peter Abelard*, Cambridge: Cambridge University Press.

Martin, C. (1987), "Embarrassing arguments and surprising conclusions in the development of theories of the conditional in the twelfth century," in J. Jolivet and A. de Libera, eds., *Gilbert de Poitiers et ses contemporains*, History of Logic 5, Naples: Bibliopolis.

——(1991), "The logic of negation in Boethius," *Phronesis* 36, pp. 277–304.

Mews, C. J. (1995), *Peter Abelard*, Authors of the Middle Ages II 5, Aldershot: Variorum.

Thomas, R., ed. (1980), *Petrus Abaelardus (1079–1142): Person, Werk und Wirkung*, Trierer theologische Studien 38, Trier: Paulinus Verlag.

Tweedale, M. M. (1976), *Abailard on Universals*, Amsterdam: North-Holland.

84

Peter Auriol

LAUGE OLAF NIELSEN

Peter Auriol (b. ca. 1280; d. 1322) was born near Cahors in southern France. Scarcely anything is known of his early life but he may have studied in Paris around 1304 and heard JOHN DUNS SCOTUS there. Some time before 1311, he entered the Franciscan order, and he lectured in the order's houses of study in Bologna (1312) and Toulouse (1314). In May 1316 Auriol was sent to pursue his academic career at the University of Paris, where, in the fall of 1316, he commenced lecturing on PETER LOMBARD's *Sentences*.

Auriol's ideas provoked strong opposition from several masters of theology, especially from the Dominican HERVAEUS NATALIS. In the early summer of 1318, Auriol finished his lectures on the *Sentences*, and, with the support of Pope John XXII, became a master. In 1320 the Franciscans elected Auriol provincial minister of Aquitaine; nevertheless he remained in Paris where he continued his academic activities. In February 1321 he was nominated Archbishop of Aix-en-Provence, and in June he was consecrated in Avignon by Pope John XXII. It is not clear whether Auriol ever took up his new office, since he died in Avignon at the beginning of the following year.

Auriol's first work was a treatise on evangelical poverty in which he sought to steer a middle course between spirituals and conventuals. Auriol's only writing of a solely philosophical nature is the incomplete and still unpublished treatise on the principles of philosophy, which dates from his early years as a teacher. Auriol's reasons for abandoning the project are still unclear; it has been argued that the decision of the Council of Vienne on the relationship between man's body and soul frustrated Auriol's enterprise (Teetaert 1935, cols. 1819ff). During his time in Toulouse Auriol composed two treatises on Mariology, which document his debates with Dominican contemporaries (Duba 2000).

While in Toulouse Auriol also started his first, monumental commentary on Lombard's first book of the *Sentences*, which was finished in Paris in late 1316 or early 1317 and was dedicated to Pope John XXII. Auriol's lectures in Paris are reflected in a second set of commentaries on the *Sentences*, of which the commentary on the third book is incomplete. The transmission of these commentaries in medieval manuscripts presents numerous difficulties of literary criticism, owing to the fact that each commentary has survived in more than one stage of development (Heynck 1969; Nielsen 2001). Auriol's intense discussions with contemporaries are amply documented in his Parisian commentaries on the *Sentences*, and they are also prominent in a *Quodlibet* published in 1320.

As master, Auriol composed a handbook of scriptural interpretation, in which he attempted to identify the main doctrinal point made by each of the books in the Bible. Presumably the work was finished in 1319; it enjoyed great popularity and was printed in

1475. Several independent commentaries on biblical books have been ascribed to Auriol but their authenticity is not yet determined.

Epistemology: intentional being

Auriol is best known for his claim that acts of intellection posit a special mode of being in their objects. He calls this mode "objective," "intentional," or "apparent being." The key idea behind this conception is not hard to grasp but precisely identifying its role in and, significance for, human cognition is not without problems.

Auriol adopts Aristotle's position that intellectual cognition rests on, and is inextricably tied to, sense perception. As a consequence, Auriol denies the existence of innate ideas, just as he rejects all appeals to a realm of eternal reasons or immutable ideas. Sense and intellect are fully sufficient to account for human cognition, and this is due to the fact that they complement each other and agree in basic structure. Though the senses and the intellect belong to different parts of man, i.e., body and soul, both sense perception and intellectual cognition require an object towards which the act of sensing or cognizing is directed. Sensing and thinking are always focused on something, and without an object such acts would be nothing. This distinctly intentional nature of human cognition is the explicit foundation of Auriol's epistemology.

With regard to sense perception, Auriol subscribes to the view that material objects emit likenesses of themselves, and that these so-called sensible species travel through the medium, e.g., air, and are received in the external organs of sense. This does not imply, however, that sense perception is a purely passive process. In order to bring about sense perception, it is required that the senses be directed towards some particular object, and that the sensible species received from this particular object be given priority over the multitude of species emitted from nearby objects. Thus, without the information provided by the objects through sensible species there would be nothing to sense, but without the attentive focusing of the perceiver the information provided by sensible species would be of no use and present no particular object. At the end of the process of sensation, the object is presented to the internal sense organs, and its likeness is stored in sensory memory.

In order to substantiate the formative role played by the sensible or material soul in sensory perception, Auriol draws attention to the fact that the senses are not always veridical, and that objects do not always appear as they are. Auriol adduces several examples of, in particular, visual deception; e.g., to somebody sailing on a river the trees on the riverbank appear to move, or an oar partially submerged in water seems to be broken. Since the trees on the bank remain firmly rooted irrespective of the moving ship, and the oar remains intact even when it is stuck into water, Auriol considers it to be an established fact that the senses may, and occasionally do, err. On this basis, Auriol points out that an incongruence between external reality and its appearance to the sensible soul cannot be due to the external object or its emitted likenesses. What causes the incongruence is either a deformity or illness in the physical sense apparatus or a mistaken formation of the object by the soul. That the soul's formative role in sense perception is revealed precisely by instances of the failing of the senses does not induce Auriol to adopt a general distrust of sense perception.

According to Auriol, the intellect exerts a similarly formative role in intellectual cognition. To Auriol, it is evident that an act of intellection is by nature focused on some particular object, and by being directed towards the object, the intellect posits it in intentional or apparent being. In its proper mode of operation, the intellect deals with natures or what is true in general, whereas sensory perception is concerned solely with particulars. Illustrating the progression from the realm of sense to that of intellect, Auriol adduces the example of the perception of a rose. On the lower level, the senses apprehend the particular rose, and by focusing on the rose – in contradistinction to what surrounds the rose – the sensible soul unites the various sense impressions and posits the rose in intentional being in the inner sense. In order to grasp the nature of the rose, the intellect is called upon. With Auriol, the intellect is fully capable of working directly with the contents of the sensible soul, and by inspecting the particular rose placed in intentional being in the material part of the soul, the intellect proceeds to its act. This act first identifies its proper object in the rose, i.e., the nature or essence of the rose, and brings this forth in apparent or intentional being and, subsequently, presents the rose in its intentional mode of being to the intellect. What results from this is the actual cognition of the nature of roses, i.e., the concept of a rose (1956, pp. 696ff).

The basic outline of Auriol's conception of man's attainment of knowledge is readily identified, just as it is obvious that the intentional character of cognition implies that man's free will is an indispensable and directive force in man's quest for knowledge. However, his motives for stipulating "intentional being" as a necessary element in the cognitive process are quite complex.

Auriol views intentional or objective being as a golden key to a host of problems in epistemology. Since he insists on the intentional character of intellectual cognition, it is impossible for him simply to identify the intellectual act and its object, as, for example, WILLIAM OF OCKHAM was later to do. In the final analysis, such a solution would, according to Auriol, entail turning all intellectual acts into reflexive ones; thinking about objects would, on these terms, amount to nothing more than thinking about thoughts. On the other hand, the intellect's object cannot be equated with something that is freely produced or dreamt up by the intellect or another power of the soul; in that case, intellectual acts would have no connection with external reality and be of scant value.

Furthermore, intellection is of essences or natures as its proper objects, and general truth is what the intellect aims at. Nevertheless, general truths should serve to promote man's understanding of the world of particulars. These twin stipulations preclude identifying the objects of intellectual knowledge with either Platonic Ideas or external particulars by themselves. Platonic Ideas are not acceptable candidates to Auriol, because they would have to be separate from particulars and thus have no immediate significance for understanding the corporeal world. On the other hand, extra-mental objects are not simply identical to natures or essences and, for this reason, they do not conform to what is required of objects of intellection.

What kind of being accrues to an object of intellection is not a simple question either. Such an object is neither a fiction nor a real attribute or quality of the soul. To Auriol, the latter possibility is ruled out by the consideration that such a real mental entity would interpose itself between the intellect and the external world and prevent the intellect from having direct contact with particulars. Thus, it would make all intellectual cognition internal to man. This would obtain even if it were granted that the quality had been brought forth by an extrinsic cause and was said to mediate between acts of intellection and the external world.

On these negative premises, Auriol argues that the object of intellectual cognition belongs to the intellectual act in such a way that the object is contained in, and posited by, the act. This should not be taken to mean that the object of intellection is a placeholder for the particular real object that is perceived. Instead, Auriol claims that the intentional object is simply *identical* to the extra-mental object that was presented by the senses. Since external objects are not present in the human intellect in their real being, Auriol has to explain in greater detail what is implied by this identity. He does this by adding the modification that an act of intellection places its object in a special mode of being, namely apparent, intentional, or objective being. Objective being is something that accrues to particulars insofar as they are conceived by an intellect and become intentional objects. Receiving this kind of being does not in any way change or add to the objects in their real being. Taking on objective being is a consequence of the way in which the human intellect works in perceiving entities in external reality.

Auriol insists that particulars and the concepts to which they give rise are numerically identical. Taking the example of the rose, one cannot count the rose in its real being and the rose as an intentional object of the intellect as two different things; the rose is only one, but by being conceptualized by an intellect it acquires this special mode of being. In itself, being an intentional object is not a "something," and Auriol even goes so far as to say that it is nothing (*nihil*). The implication of this is that intentional or apparent being does not exist and cannot even be conceived of in isolation from the act that brings it forth. For this reason, Auriol does not shrink from claiming that the intentional object is composed of the intellectual act and the particular object cognized. Accordingly, an act of intellection conceptualizes a particular object by giving it another mode of being, and in this mode of being the object appears to the intellect as a nature or an essence (1956, pp. 704ff).

While objective being would seem to solve some of the problems Auriol perceived in competing theories of cognition, it does make it incumbent on Auriol to explain the obvious incongruence between external objects that are particulars, and objective being that is general or of natures and accrues to objects as cognized. To this Auriol's answer is that the perception of, for example, any single rose is fully sufficient for generating the concept of the nature or essence of roses. This unitary concept may, accordingly, be applied to any object that gives rise to the very same concept, i.e., all other roses. Consequently, the generality that is a characteristic of concepts does not belong to particulars as such, and it is based on the fact that all particulars of a certain kind give rise to the same act of intellection (1605, *Comm. in II*, cols. 63a and 109a–b).

Clearly, maintaining this stance is only possible for Auriol because of his conviction that intuition – as opposed to abstraction – is the basic way in which the intellect forms concepts. In this connection "intuition" should not, however, be taken to imply that man's intellect understands in the same way as do incorporeal and separate intelligences, namely angels. Auriol is convinced that man's intellect in its present state does not enjoy intuitive cognition in the strict sense of the term insofar as its acts are inextricably bound to the testimony of the senses and to the presence of the perceived object in the material part of the soul (1952, pp. 209ff). On the other hand, being linked to the material soul does not prevent the intellect from having the ability to form concepts on the basis of only one particular.

Auriol's view of the generality of concepts presupposes that concepts function in the same manner as words, and that they signify particulars. This implies that the structure of thinking or intellectual cognition should be understood along the lines of language, and in thinking concepts function as names which the intellect combines into meaningful sequences that have the same predicative structure as spoken or written language. Auriol

497

made this point on several occasions and appealed to the authority of AUGUSTINE, but he failed to develop a theory of mental language. He did, however, explain that the referential aspect of concepts makes it possible to decide which names or concepts correspond to which particulars since this is a matter of deciding what acts the various particulars give rise to (see Friedman 1999).

Ontology I: individuals and concepts

Auriol was unwavering in his basic conviction that generality is a property of concepts and words, and that the world of external reality is populated solely by individual objects. Over against the realistic ontologies of such figures as THOMAS AQUINAS and John Duns Scotus he provided a strong defence of the primacy of individual substances, and this he conducted on several fronts.

In the first place, Auriol maintained that objects are singular by themselves, and that singularity is a basic fact that needs no further explanation. According to his appraisal, seeking an explanation for singularity is simply irrational. In order to identify a principle of singularity or individuation, Auriol claims, it would be necessary to stipulate that singularity arises because of an ontological principle that is unique to each object. An explanation of singularity in terms of a general principle of individuation would invariably imply that one and the same principle confers singularity on a multitude of singulars, and that objects are distinguished by something that is common to them; but this is plainly self-contradictory. Consequently, a principle of individuation should be unique to each single object, and, inversely, every single object should be assumed to possess and result from its own individuating property. Irrespective of how one were to characterize such a property, Auriol argues, it would be imperative to ask how the singularity of each individuating property comes about. If an infinite regress is to be avoided, no answer can be provided except that an individuating property is individual or single by virtue of itself. But, as Auriol underscores, this conclusion reveals the utter futility of seeking a principle of individuation. Maintaining that an object is singular or individual because it results from or is endowed with a proper principle of individuation which is itself singular, amounts to nothing more than duplicating what should be explained; and this is tantamount to explaining nothing at all (1605, *Comm. in II*, cols. 112bff).

Secondly, Auriol defends the priority of individuals by arguing for the fundamental unity of single substances. He concedes that substances are made up of form and matter, and that form and matter are real components that come together so as to constitute substances. Nevertheless, this should not be taken to imply that it is possible to treat form and matter independently of each other. Form and matter are not realities of which man has direct cognition; they are ontological principles that are known only discursively on the basis of change in the world of nature. Substances are corrupted and undergo change, and for this reason it is legitimate to assume that there is a material principle that serves as the substrate for change, whereas form is the principle that determines the nature of change. This does not, however, warrant viewing substances as juxtapositions or collections of form and matter. In themselves, form and matter are not complete beings or things, whereas the substances that result from the composition of form and matter are unitary and complete beings. In this manner, Auriol insists, the union of form and matter results in some third thing, namely, a substance, and a substance is a homogeneous being in which it is not possible to single out the formal or material component (1605, *Comm. in II*, cols. 174aff). As a consequence of this, Auriol

generally avoids talking of forms as inhering in substances. Saying that the form of rationality inheres in, for example, Socrates, is, according to Auriol, just another way of saying
that Socrates is rational (see 1605, *Comm. in IV*, col. 110b).

In the third place, Auriol defends the unity of substances against attempts to posit a plurality in substances on the level of their formal principles. Seen from Auriol's perspective,
the question of the unity or multiplicity of substantial forms, which had vexed numerous
thirteenth-century thinkers, is completely futile and rests on a misunderstanding of funda-
mentals. Auriol recognizes that we have several concepts of one and the same substance, and
that many of these concepts express essential or invariable characteristics of the substance.
Furthermore, there is a certain order to these concepts, and this order is reflected in the
definition of an object. In the case of human substances, we have concepts such as "living
being," "animal," "rational," "able to laugh," and "man." When we define man as a rational animal that, on occasion, exhibits a sense of humor, we order these concepts according
to genus, difference, species, and proper characteristic. One of the fundamental mistakes of
realist ontologies is, according to Auriol, that this multiplicity of concepts is assumed to
provide information about the ontological principles that make an object such as a human
being into an object of this particular kind. Instead of seeking the explanation for the multiplicity of concepts in the essential principles of things, one should, according to Auriol,
focus on the way in which these concepts arise, and how they are ordered. The fact is that
every single thing is apt to give rise to several sense impressions and, on the level of intellect, to several concepts. Spotting an animal from afar one may form the concept of a living
being that moves on its own accord, and this gives rise to the concept "animal." Observed
at closer range the animal proves to be able to communicate and to engage in rational conversation; and on this basis, the concept of "rational animal" or "man" is formed. In other
words, concepts of the essential characteristics of things are dependent, according to Auriol,
on the way in which we perceive things. This does not imply that these concepts are
fictitious, since it is the objects themselves that give rise to them. Moreover, the relative
ordering of concepts does not reveal the inner ontological constitution of things, but
merely reflects the lesser and greater scope and adequacy of concepts; adding the difference
"rational" to the generic concept of "animal" yields a more precise concept of human
being (see Friedman 1997).

Ontology II: accidents

Besides essential characteristics, individuals possess variable or accidental properties such
as gaining weight or acquiring a tan. Such properties are accidental inasmuch as they do not
necessarily belong to a substance and do not affect the substance's unity or essential being;
they merely affect its appearance. Auriol analyzes characteristics of this sort along the same
lines as essential ones. According to him, accidents are real in the sense that they truly belong
to the substances they modify. This should not, however, be construed to imply that accidents are formal principles that inhere in substances, or that they are entities with only
diminished being. As Auriol explains, accidents modify substances in the sense that they
"permeate" the substances and determine the way in which they appear or are "terminated."
For this reason, such accidents have no being except that of the substances to which they
belong. Separating the changeable properties from a substance is not possible insofar as this
would introduce plurality into the substance and confer an, albeit relative, independence on
their variable characteristics (1605, *Comm. in IV*, cols. 109aff). With this interpretation,

Auriol does not aim to obliterate or weaken the distinction between what is essential and what is accidental, but to emphasize the priority and unity of primary substances.

How many kinds of accidental characteristics are there? To this, Auriol's answer is simple: all real or mind-independent properties can be classified in the categories of quality and quantity. Accordingly, the remaining – the so-called circumstantial or relational – Aristotelian categories do not contain real objects or their concepts. Predicates or concepts that belong to these Aristotelian categories Auriol views as purely mental; characteristics of these kinds are ascribed to objects solely on the basis of man's perception and have no immediate counterparts in the external world. With great acumen, Auriol analyzes, in particular, the category of relation, and he emphatically refutes the view that a relation is a real attribute that belongs to one object and extends towards another. The relation of similarity that obtains between, e.g., two white things, should not be taken to imply that the two substances acquire the property of similarity by being compared. In themselves, the two substances are white; it is the human mind that realizes they are similar, and in so doing establishes a relationship of similarity between the two things (1596, cols. 667bff; cf. Henninger 1989).

The categories of action and passion are, with Auriol, exceptional cases. Concepts classified in these categories are not purely mental, but reflect realities in the external world (notwithstanding Teetaert 1935, col. 1856). Auriol identifies the fundamental reality expressed by concepts of action and passion as efficient causality. That something brings about change in another object is a basic fact of experience and cannot, according to Auriol, be ascribed to man's perception. Against the Thomist view that efficient causality should be identified with motion, Auriol objects that motion is a phenomenon in corporeal reality, whereas efficient causality is certainly also verified in the spiritual realm; e.g., man's will is undeniably an agent and an efficient cause of man's intellections and bodily actions, whereas motion plays no role. Equally, Auriol rejects the competing view of the Scotists, namely, that efficient causality is a relation between an agent and a patient. If this were the case, Auriol argues, there would be no difference between the process by which a cause brings about an effect and the resulting relationship between cause and effect. But common experience brings out this difference, Auriol argues. Being the father of a son is a static relation between two substances and does not imply change. On the other hand, generation or conception is a dynamic process that brings about change in the world, i.e., the formation of the offspring. Consequently, identifying the static relationship between father and son with the activity or transitory process by which the son is brought into existence, is an obvious mistake.

Auriol's basically Aristotelian ontology of substance did not make it easy for him to determine the ontological status of efficient causality. The problem claimed his attention throughout his academic career, and he experienced great difficulties in finding a terminology that could accurately convey his view. To him, it was a basic fact that the ontological reality implied by efficient causality does not properly belong to either cause or effect. The cause is not enriched in its being or properties by acting as a cause, just as the patient or effect is not the foundation of this reality. This implies that efficient causality should be seen as a sort of middle entity between cause and effect. Though it originates and proceeds from the cause, it does not reside in the cause; and though it is directed towards the patient, it is not a property of the patient or effect. For these reasons, Auriol at one point stated that the reality in efficient causality is a non-absolute form and an intermediary between cause and effect. Neither term, however, fits in seamlessly with the fabric of Auriol's ontology, which does not attach great explanatory force to forms in general and explicitly rejects the reality of relational entities. The search for a suitable terminology led Auriol to adopt and modify BOETHIUS' distinction between what is (*id quod*) and that by which something is (*id quo*).

Thus Auriol claimed that substances are that which is, whereas efficient causality is that by way of which substances and their properties are brought about. Moreover, Auriol insisted that efficient causality is best expressed by verbs inasmuch as their mode of signifying is particularly well suited to express transitory processes, whereas nouns should properly be used to signify the permanent results of processes (1596, cols. 604bff; 1605, *Comm. in IV*, cols. 124bff; *Quodl.*, cols. 11bff).

Auriol's interpretation of efficient causality was not favorably received by his contemporaries, who accused him of compromising the very framework of Aristotelian ontology. The fierce criticism did not, however, induce Auriol to abandon his position. To him, the dynamic character of efficient causality is attested by experience, and it is a revealing indication of the fact that substances are active entities that interact in the world of external reality. Put in modern terms, Auriol's insistence on the unique status as well as the dynamic and transitory character of efficient causality should be seen as an attempt to come to terms with the concept of force.

Auriol's historical significance

In medieval philosophy Auriol's importance derives not least from the circumstance that his work challenged several of the basic assumptions of thirteenth-century thought and ushered in new avenues of inquiry in epistemology as well as ontology. Modern scholarship has mainly focused on Auriol's insistence on the intentional character of human cognition and his meticulous charting of the processes by which man's concepts are formed. Often his thought has been characterized as "conceptualistic" (cf. Dreiling 1913), and this is certainly justified, provided that it be kept in mind that Auriol's stance in epistemology is squarely based on, and presupposes, his ontology of individuals.

In many respects, Auriol takes on the guise of a less than faithful disciple of John Duns Scotus. Auriol adopted numerous of Scotus's distinctions, and to a large extent he spoke the language of the Subtle Doctor (see Kobusch 2000). However, with Auriol the words had fundamentally changed their meaning. Often what Scotus found to be true of the essential order of extra-mental objects, Auriol verified of concepts. Scotus's ontology of formalities and the formal distinction were firmly rejected by Auriol. This did not, however, prevent Auriol from adopting Scotus's method of essential analysis, and he delighted in identifying the varying contents of, and fine differences between, related concepts. An illustrative example of Auriol's complex relationship to Scotus is their widely diverging assessments of the so-called transcendentals. Auriol was as convinced as Scotus of the difference between transcendentals such as being, unity, and goodness. While Scotus viewed the transcendentals as formally distinct, Auriol held them to be only rationally so. Names such as 'being', 'good', and 'one' signify one and the same thing, but they differ in the way they signify this object: 'being' is the least precise of names and may be applied to everything that exists; 'good' indicates that the object passes muster with respect to some standard of goodness or usefulness; whereas 'one' applies to what has not been divided. In Auriol's parlance, words such as 'being', 'good', and 'one' have the same signification, i.e., the truly existing thing, but differ with respect to connotation, i.e., some other entity or standard that the particular thing is being compared to or viewed together with (see 1995, and Brown 1965).

Affinities between Auriol and his slightly later confrere, William of Ockham, are immediately apparent. While Ockham appears to have been acquainted with at least some of Auriol's works, it is unlikely that Auriol knew of Ockham or his teaching. Though Ockham was severe in his criticism of Auriol, especially in epistemology, this circumstance should not obscure the fact that they followed parallel paths in their assaults on the positions of the realists. Both strove to do full justice to the Aristotelian concept of substance and to purge philosophical explanation of superfluous entities. Equally, in epistemology they both struggled with such problems as the elimination of intellectual species and the veracity of intuitive cognition. Fundamental to both was the conviction that concepts signify, and that consignification or connotation provides a key to properly distinguishing between related concepts. In this connection, one of the more prominent differences between Auriol and Ockham comes to the fore. Whereas supposition theory was one of Ockham's preferred tools in philosophical analysis, Auriol only rarely employed this logical device. Possibly, this difference is related to Auriol's reservations *vis-à-vis* logical reasoning and his insistence on the fundamental role of experience. Though 'experience' with Auriol often refers to man's inner experience, he repeatedly stressed sense experience as the only trustworthy source of knowledge of the external world (cf. Teetaert 1935, cols. 1848–9).

Later scholastic theologians and philosophers rarely agreed with Auriol (see Schabel 2000). Yet GREGORY OF RIMINI found Auriol's thought so much of a challenge that he felt compelled to devote large parts of his own work to carefully refuting Auriol. Even in the fifteenth and sixteenth centuries, Auriol continued to inspire and provoke opposition, and the great defender of Thomist thought, JOHN CAPREOLUS, singled him out as one of his prime targets. A telling testimony to the high esteem in which Auriol was held in this period is the printing of his scholastic works at the turn of the sixteenth and seventeenth centuries.

Bibliography

Primary sources

(1596), *Commentariorum in primum librum Sententiarum pars prima et secunda*, Rome.

(1605), *Commentariorum in secundum, tertium et quartum Sententiarum et Quodlibeti tomus secundus*, Rome.

(1952), *Scriptum super primum Sententiarum, Prologue: Distinction I*, ed. E. M. Buytaert, Franciscan Institute Publications, Text Series no. 3, St. Bonaventure, NY: Franciscan Institute.

(1956), *Scriptum super primum Sententiarum: Distinctions II–VIII*, ed. E. M. Buytaert, Franciscan Institute Publications, Text Series no. 3, St. Bonaventure, NY: Franciscan Institute.

(1995), *De unitate conceptus entis*, ed. Stephen F. Brown, in *Petrus Aureoli: De unitate conceptus entis* (*Reportatio Parisiensis in I Sententiarum*, dist. 2, p. 1, qq. 1–3 et p. 2, qq. 1–2), *Traditio* 50, pp. 199–248.

Secondary sources

Boehner, P. (1948), "*Notitia intuitiva* of non-existents according to Peter Aureoli OFM (1322)," *Franciscan Studies* 8, pp. 388–416.

Brown, S. F. (1965), "Avicenna and the unity of the concept of being: the interpretations of Henry of Ghent, Duns Scotus, Gerard of Bologna and Peter Aureoli," *Franciscan Studies* 25, pp. 117–50.

Dreiling, R. (1913), "Der Konzeptualismus in der Universalienlehre des Franziskanerbischofs Petrus Aureoli (Pierre d'Auriole) nebst biographisch-bibliographischer Einleitung," *Beiträge zur Geschichte der Philosophie des Mittelalters* 11/6, Münster: Aschendorff.

Duba, W. (2000), "The immaculate conception in the works of Peter Auriol," in R. L. Friedman and L. O. Nielsen, eds., *Peter Auriol*, *Vivarium* 38/1 (special issue), pp. 5–34.

Friedman, R. L. (1997), "Conceiving and modifying reality: some modist roots of Peter Auriol's theory of concept formation," in C. Marmo, ed., *Vestigia, imagines, verba: Semiotics and Logic in Medieval Theological Texts (12th–14th Centuries)* (pp. 305–22), Turnhout: Brepols.

——(1999), "Peter Auriol on intentions and essential predication," in S. Ebbesen and R. L. Friedman, eds., *Medieval Analyses in Language and Cognition* (pp. 415–30), Copenhagen: The Royal Danish Academy of Sciences and Letters.

Friedman, R. L. and Nielsen, L. O., eds. (2000), *Peter Auriol, Vivarium* 38/1 (special issue).

Henninger, M. G. (1989), *Relations: Medieval Theories 1250–1325*, Oxford: Oxford University Press.

Heynck, V. (1969), "Die Kommentare des Petrus Aureoli zum dritten Sentenzbuch," *Franziskanische Studien* 51, pp. 1–77.

Kobusch, T. (2000), "Petrus Aureoli. Philosophie des Subjekts," in T. Kobusch, ed., *Philosophen des Mittelalters* (pp. 236–49), Darmstadt: Primus.

Nielsen, L. O. (2001), "Peter Auriol's way with words: the genesis of Peter Auriol's Commentaries on Peter Lombard's First and Fourth Books of the *Sentences*," in G. R. Evans, ed., *Medieval Commentaries on Peter Lombard's Sentences* (pp. 149–219), Leiden: Brill.

Schabel, C. (2000), *Theology at Paris, 1316–1345: Peter Auriol and the Problem of Divine Foreknowledge and Future Contingents*, Ashgate Studies in Medieval Philosophy, Aldershot: Ashgate.

Teetaert, A. (1935), "Pierre Auriol ou Oriol," *Dictionnaire de théologie catholique*, vol. XII, part 2 (cols. 1810–81), Paris: Letouzey et Ané.

85

Peter of Auvergne

ROBERT ANDREWS

Peter of Auvergne (d. 1304) was a secular master at the University of Paris in the thirteenth century. If he is the same Peter of Auvergne as was named Bishop of Clermont by Boniface VIII on January 21, 1302, he was born at Crocq (Crocy) in south-central France.

He is credited with writing commentaries on all of the extant works of Aristotle, as well as a commentary on PETER LOMBARD's *Sentences*, and several *Quodlibetal Questions*, although the usual reservations must be made about the authenticity of the works ascribed to him. His renown among his contemporaries was such that a number of works were falsely attributed to him; in at least one manuscript the attribution to SIGER OF BRABANT was erased and replaced with the name of Peter. Many of his genuine works remain unedited.

In logic, Peter is associated with the modists, or speculative grammarians, whose central tenet was a parallelism among language, thought, and world. Logic and linguistic studies thereby gained an enhanced role, since knowledge of language could lead to unmediated knowledge about the external world. Peter's logical commentaries influenced RADULPHUS BRITO, SIMON OF FAVERSHAM, and thereby indirectly JOHN DUNS SCOTUS.

In metaphysics and natural philosophy, Peter shows the influence of THOMAS AQUINAS, and his work was used to fill out several unfinished works of Thomas's, although there is no evidence for the claim occasionally made that Peter was once Thomas's pupil. Peter is concerned to accommodate the revealed truths of theology within his metaphysics. He holds that designated (*signata*) matter is the principle of individuation, and subscribes to the unity of substantial form.

In theology, Peter follows HENRY OF GHENT and GODFREY OF FONTAINES, and often adopts their criticisms of Aquinas. For instance, under the influence of Godfrey, he revises his opinion on the principle of individuation, and in *Quodlibet II* question 5 holds it to be form.

Bibliography

Primary sources

Andrews, R. (1987), "Petrus de Alvernia: *Quaestiones super Praedicamentis*. an edition," *Cahiers de l'Institut du Moyen-âge Grec et Latin* 55, pp. 3–84.

Celano, A. (1986), "Peter of Auvergne's Questions on Books I and II of Aristotle's *Nicomachean Ethics*: a study and critical edition," *Mediaeval Studies* 48, pp. 1–110.

Ebbesen, S. (1986), "*Termini accidentales concreti*: texts from the late thirteenth century," *Cahiers de l'Institut du Moyen-âge Grec et Latin* 53, pp. 37–150.

——(1993), "*Animal est omnis homo*: questions and sophismata by Peter of Auvergne, Radulphus Brito, William Bonkes, and others," *Cahiers de l'Institut du Moyen-âge Grec et Latin* 63, pp. 145–208.

Pinborg, J. (1973), "A new MS of the questions on the *Posteriora analytica* attributed to Petrus de Alvernia (Clm. 8005) with the transcription of some questions related to problems of meaning," *Cahiers de l'Institut du Moyen-âge Grec et Latin* 3, pp. 1–54; 10, pp. 48–62.

Secondary sources

Ebbesen, S. (1988), "Concrete accidental terms: Late 13th century debates about problems relating to such terms as '*album*'," in N. Kretzmann, ed., *Meaning and Inference in Medieval Philosophy: Studies in Memory of Jan Pinborg*, Dordrecht: D. Reidel.

Galle, Griet (2000), "A comprehensive bibliography on Peter of Auvergne," *Bulletin de Philosophie Médiévale* 42, pp. 53–79.

Grech, G. M. (1964), "Recent bibliography on Peter of Auvergne," *Angelicum* 41, pp. 446–9.

Monahan, A. P. (1954), "The subject of metaphysics for Peter of Auvergne," *Mediaeval Studies* 16, pp. 118–30.

86

Peter of Candia

CHRISTOPHER SCHABEL

A fine example of the possibilities presented by the mendicant orders' international *studia* system, the Greek Peter of Candia, also known as Petros Philargis (b. ca. 1340; d. 1410), was born in Venetian Crete. Orphaned as a small child and educated by the local Franciscans, he formally entered the order in 1357. His intelligence opened doors: he studied arts at the Franciscan *studium* in Padua, then theology at the *studia* in Norwich, Oxford, and Paris, where he lectured on the *Sentences* in 1378–80 and became master in 1381. He returned to Italy to found the University of Pavia, then became successively Bishop of Piacenza (1386), Vicenza (1388), and Novara (1389), Archbishop of Milan (1392), cardinal (1405), and finally Pope Alexander V at the Council of Pisa (1409). His leading role in the conciliar movement and at the council says much about his political philosophy, but his papacy failed to end the Great Schism.

Candia has an interesting place in the history of philosophy. The only Greek pope since the early Middle Ages, he foreshadows the influx of Greek scholars into Italy that began about 1400. He was conscious of his Greek identity, and considered Plato and Aristotle his compatriots. In Italy he had close links to the humanists Coluccio Salutati, Umberto Decembrio, and Pier Candido Decembrio. He had a humanist impact on scholastics, and a scholastic impact on humanists.

More importantly, Candia's popular *Sentences* commentary, never printed but surviving in over three dozen MSS, was a conduit through which later scholars learned of the ideas of the great, primarily Franciscan, masters of the first half of the fourteenth century. To take the example of future contingents, PETER DE RIVO knew PETER AURIOL's position via Candia, who according to Rivo presented Auriol's theory more clearly than had Auriol himself. In the twentieth century, the philosophical study of the problem of future contingents really begins with Ehrle's book (1925) on Candia's *Sentences* commentary.

Candia's role as a conduit must be emphasized, because his role as a philosopher was negligible. Thus he concludes his very lengthy discussion of future contingents, "I, like, a little dog, have started the hare for you. Capture it through whatever path of the aforesaid ways you wish." Realizing he was adopting a contradictory position on the fundamental subject of the univocity of the concept of being, Candia remarks, "If I here maintain the contrary, it is not because I consider one position to be truer than the other, but in order to illustrate several ways of conceiving the problem, for the convenience of those who desire to eat sometimes bread and sometimes cheese." As Étienne Gilson remarks, this successful political and intellectual diplomat did not take philosophy so seriously, and exemplifies the "speculative lassitude" of the later fourteenth century.

Bibliography

Brown, S. F. (1976), "Peter of Candia's sermons in praise of Peter Lombard," in R. S. Almagno and C. L. Harkins, eds., *Studies Honoring Ignatius Charles Brady, Friar Minor* (pp. 141–76), St. Bonaventure, NY: Franciscan Institute.

——(1991), "Peter of Candia's hundred-year 'History' of the theologian's role," *Medieval Philosophy and Theology* 1, pp. 156–90.

——(1994–7), "Peter of Candia on believing and knowing," *Franciscan Studies* 54, pp. 251–76.

Ehrle, F. (1925), *Der Sentenzenkommentar Peters von Candia des Pisaner Papstes Alexander V*, Münster: Aschendorff.

Emmen, A. (1954), "Petrus de Candia, O. F. M. *De immaculata Deiparae conceptione*," in *Tractatus quatuor de immaculata conceptione B. Mariae Virginis* (pp. 235–359), Quaracchi: Collegium S. Bonaventurae.

Schabel, C. (1998), "Peter of Candia and the prelude to the quarrel at Louvain," *Epeterida tou Kentrou Epistemonikon Erevnon* 24, pp. 87–124.

87

Peter Ceffons

CHRISTOPHER SCHABEL

The Cistercian theologian Peter Ceffons lectured on the *Sentences* at Paris in 1348–9, four years after his confrere JOHN OF MIRECOURT. Ceffons later became Abbot of Clairvaux. A single, beautiful manuscript, Troyes, Bibliothèque municipale 62 (formerly Clairvaux I 11), preserves his main surviving work, the unedited commentary on the *Sentences* (along with an introductory letter, printed in Trapp 1957). Ceffons had interesting ideas in such areas as cosmology, but he has been little studied and apparently had little direct impact himself. Thus Ceffons's importance for the history of philosophy lies mostly in the information he gives us about the intellectual climate at Paris in his day.

Ceffons is important as a witness to the absorption of new English ideas and methods (e.g., propositional and mathematical analysis) into Parisian thought in the 1340s starting with the *Sentences* lectures of GREGORY OF RIMINI (1343–4). Ceffons displays more direct knowledge of English theologians than had Rimini, Mirecourt, and others. Indeed, Ceffons's "modern" practice of citing explicitly and accurately the works of English thinkers was not to be surpassed until the Augustinian John Hiltalingen of Basel two decades later. An example of Ceffons's knowledge is that he correctly recognizes the origins of the important epistemological notion of a state of affairs that is only signifiable by a proposition, "the *complexe significabile*," in the English theologians WALTER CHATTON (early 1320s) and ADAM OF WODEHAM (early 1330s). That Ceffons also had a good grasp of earlier Parisian scholars such as LANDULPH CARACCIOLO (ca. 1320) demonstrates that Parisian thought in the 1340s was not completely subservient to British trends.

The influx of "English subtleties" into Parisian thought provoked a negative reaction from Pope Clement VI and separate condemnations of the ideas of NICHOLAS OF AUTRECOURT and John of Mirecourt in the mid-1340s. In his introductory letter to his *Sentences* commentary, Ceffons charges that the instigators of the condemnations were "three old foreign heresy-hunting witches," who were "slandering what they have not understood." Subtlety could enter the head of one of them about as easily as "a fully loaded elephant could get through a finger ring." Ceffons's stinging ridicule of the ignorance of the conservative opponents of English methods helps explain why eventually the victory would go to the liberals.

Bibliography

Primary source

Commentary on the Sentences, MS Troyes 62.

Secondary sources

Eldredge, L. (1978), "Changing concepts of Church authority in the later fourteenth century: Pierre Ceffons of Clairvaux and William of Woodford, OFM," *Revue de l'Université d'Ottawa* 48, pp. 170–8.

Genest, J.-P. (1984), "Pierre de Ceffons et l'hypothèse du Dieu trompeur," in Z. Kaluza and P. Vignaux, eds., *Preuve et raisons à l'Université de Paris: Logique, ontologie et théologie au XIVe siècle* (pp. 197–214), Paris: J. Vrin.

Murdoch, J. (1978), "*Subtilitates Anglicanae* in fourteenth-century Paris: John of Mirecourt and Peter Ceffons," in M. P. Cosman and B. Chandler, eds., *Machaut's World: Science and Art in the Fourteenth Century, Annals of the New York Academy of Sciences* 314, pp. 51–86.

Trapp, D. (1957), "Pierre Ceffons of Clairvaux," *Recherches de Théologie Ancienne et Médiévale* 24, pp. 101–54.

88

Peter Damian

JONATHAN J. SANFORD

Peter Damian (b. 1007; d. 1072), saint, doctor of the Church, and ascetic, was one of the foremost clerical reformers of the eleventh century. In 1035 Peter entered religious life in Fonte Avellan, a congregation of hermits, and in 1043 was elected prior. He dedicated himself first to reforming his own congregation, and then turned his attention to abuses within the Church at large. *Liber gomorrhianus* (ca. 1051), and *Liber gratissimus* (ca. 1053), are two of his more significant reform writings. One of the main themes both in Peter's life and his spiritual writings is that of striking the right balance between the active and contemplative life. For biographical information see Dressler (1954) and McNulty (1959, pp. 11–53).

Peter is notorious for his condemnatory epigrams concerning philosophy. He claimed that the first grammarian was the devil, who taught Adam to decline *deus* in the plural. He also claimed that philosophy should serve theology as a servant serves her mistress (1867, *PL* 145, p. 603). The phrase *philosophia ancilla theologiae* ("philosophy is the handmaiden of theology") does not, however, appear in his writings. Peter argued that monks need not learn philosophy, and that philosophical knowledge certainly is not required for salvation (otherwise Jesus would have chosen philosophers as apostles). These epigrams do not, however, do justice to the scope and depth of Peter's writings. His animosity to philosophy is due in part to his view that logic is concerned only with the implications of statements, and is not indicative of the structure of reality.

Peter's *De divina omnipotentia* (ca. 1067) has received the most attention from philosophers. In it Peter argues that God's omnipotence is such that he can bring it about that a past event did not occur. Peter's argument has often been derided for its failure to recognize the ontological version of the principle of non-contradiction. Holopainen (1996, pp. 6–43) has recently given Peter's text a more sympathetic reading, arguing that modal subtleties in Peter's argument have been overlooked. Gaskin (1997) rejects this reading in favor of the traditional interpretation.

Bibliography

Primary sources
(1867), *Opera omnia*, in J.-P. Migne, ed., *Patrologia Latina* (*PL*), vols. 144 and 145, Paris: Vivès.
(1943), *De divina omnipotentia et altri opuscoli*, ed. P. Brezzi, trans. B. Nardi, Florence: Vallecchi.
(1959), *Selected Writings on the Spiritual Life*, trans. P. McNulty, London: Faber and Faber.
(1982), *Book of Gomorrah*, trans. J. P. Payer, Waterloo: Wilfrid Laurier University Press.

Secondary sources

Dressler, F. (1954), *Petrus Damiani, Leben und Werk*, Studia Anselmiana 34, Rome: Herder.

Gaskin, R. (1997), "Peter Damian on divine power and the contingency of the past," *British Journal for the History of Philosophy* 5, pp. 229–47.

Holopainen, T. (1996), *Dialectic and Theology in the Eleventh Century*, Leiden, New York, and Cologne: Brill.

89

Peter Helias

C. H. KNEEPKENS

Peter Helias (b. ca. 1100; d. after 1166) was born in the neighborhood of Poitiers. He became a student of Thierry of Chartres at Paris in the 1130s and a renowned teacher of grammar and rhetoric. He returned to Poitiers about 1155, where he died.

Peter composed a commentary on Cicero's *De inventione* and a *Summa super Priscianum*, a widely used textbook on Priscian's *Institutiones*. Other works traditionally attributed to him are spurious. Most of his works relay heavily on the gloss commentary tradition, especially on William of Conches, but his *Summa* is the starting point of a new didactic approach in the teaching of grammar. This is a well-structured textbook, not a gloss or commentary, that offers the opportunity to discuss coherently, albeit within the framework of Priscian, the major linguistic topics, and provides readers with clear definitions of pertinent concepts.

In the early twelfth century, the search for the explanatory principles, or causes of invention, of linguistic phenomena came into vogue, and found its culmination in Helias's discussion of morphology. It was believed that the answer to the question of why a certain linguistic phenomenon was invented had to supply insights into its presence and function in language.

In semantics, Peter came under the influence of Thierry of Chartres in particular. For his doctrine of substance, he adopted, via Thierry, the three meanings or levels of substance that stemmed from BOETHIUS' theological treatises; moreover he transposed the notion of *complexivus* from Thierry's reflections on the categories in theology into grammar. The latter move was part of his efforts to reduce the haphazard appeal to equivocation to explain linguistic facts. The same intention underlies his discussion of surnames. Although a surname signifies the proper qualities of many people and is common to many, it is not equivocal. Peter came to this conclusion after an examination of the cause of its invention followed by a detailed analysis of nominal signification.

He introduced a distinction between the secondary grammatical categories that contribute to the (general) meaning of words, such as number and case (*secundariae significationes*), and other accidents, such as gender and conjugation (*proprietates communes*). The importance of this distinction became clear in the early thirteenth century, when the notion of secondary meanings developed into the *significatio generalis* of parts of speech.

In syntax, an innovation of paramount importance was the clear-cut distinction between construction at word level and a construed sentence. The former stimulated an interest in binary combinations, and created new perspectives in syntax; it made dependency grammar possible. In his definition of the construed sentence, Peter Helias introduced semantic well-

formedness as a criterion for acceptability and rejected sentences of the type "he has hypothetical shoes with categorical laces" as nonsensical.

Bibliography

Primary source
(1993), *Summa super Priscianum*, ed. L. Reilly, Toronto: Pontifical Institute of Mediaeval Studies.

Secondary sources
Fredborg, K. M. (1988), "Speculative grammar," in P. Dronke, ed., *A History of Twelfth-century Western Philosophy* (pp. 177–95), Cambridge: Cambridge University Press.

Hunt, R. W. (1943), "Studies on Priscian in the eleventh and twelfth centuries," *Mediaeval and Renaissance Studies* 1, pp. 194–231.

Kneepkens, C. H. (2000), "Grammar and semantics in the twelfth century: Petrus Helias and Gilbert de la Porrée on the substantive verb," in M. Kardaun and J. Spruyt, eds., *The Winged Chariot* (pp. 237–75), Leiden: Brill.

Pinborg, J. (1967), *Die Entwicklung der Sprachtheorie im Mittelalter, Beiträge zur Geschichte der Philosophie und Theologie des Mittelalters*, Texte und Untersuchungen 42/2, Münster: Aschendorff; Copenhagen: Ame Frost-Hansen.

Rosier, I. (1987), "Les acceptions du terme 'substantia' chez Pierre Helie," in J. Jolivet and A. de Libera, eds., *Gilbert de Poitiers et ses contemporains* (pp. 299–324), Naples: Bibliopolis.

513

90

Peter Lombard

PHILIPP W. ROSEMANN

Peter Lombard (b. 1095/1100; d. 1160), Bishop of Paris, is the author of what has been called "one of the least read of the world's great books" (D. Luscombe, cited in Colish 1994, p. 8). The *Sententiae in quattuor libris distinctae* ("Sentences divided into four books") served as the standard theological textbook of the Latin West from the thirteenth until the sixteenth century. During that time, it was part of the duties of every aspiring master of theology to lecture on the *Sentences*. The history of much of scholastic thought could therefore be written as the history of commentaries on this book.

The *Sentences* mark a decisive step in the development of scholastic method. Since Patristic times, Christian thinkers had been trying to reconcile texts: first, the Old and the New Testament, but over the centuries an increasing number of authoritative texts attached themselves to this core. Building a tradition meant to merge these texts into a convincing whole – not an easy task, given their diverse provenance from western and eastern Christianity, as well as Greek and Roman sources. By the time of Peter Lombard, powerful tools for textual interpretation had come into existence. Scripture was accompanied by the *Glossa ordinaria*, or "standard gloss," a selection of excerpts from the most influential exegetes. In his work *Sic et non* (*Yes and No*), Peter Abelard compiled authoritative quotations concerning 158 controversial theological points; the prologue provided a catalogue of interpretive methods for their reconciliation.

Drawing on this, and other, material, the *Sentences* go a step further. They not only compile biblical texts with authoritative interpretations from different sources, attempting to harmonize them, but arrange these texts systematically, according to a logical order. Other authors tried to create similar theological systems, but Peter Lombard's arrangement proved most convincing. The four books of the *Sentences* follow a conceptual logic set out at the beginning of book one, where Peter introduces an Augustinian distinction between things and signs; and again between things to be enjoyed and to be used. God is the only thing to be enjoyed (book one is devoted to the triune God). Creation proceeds from him, and thus is to be used, precisely as a sign pointing back to God; the human being, however, should both be enjoyed for its own sake and used as a sign (book two). Christ, the God-man, brings thing and sign into perfect harmony (book three). Finally, the sacraments are signs that help the believer reach salvation (book four).

If theological (and philosophical) discourse became more recognizably "scientific" in the twelfth century, Peter Lombard's *Sentences* made a crucial contribution to this development.

514

Bibliography

Primary source

(1971–1981), *Sententiae in IV libris distinctae*, 2 vols., ed. I. C. Brady, Grottaferrata: Editiones Collegium S. Bonaventurae ad Claras Aquas.

Secondary sources

Colish, M. L. (1994), *Peter Lombard*, 2 vols., Leiden: Brill.

Grabmann, M. (1911), *Die Geschichte der scholastischen Methode*, vol. 2: *Die scholastische Methode im 12. und beginnenden 13. Jahrhundert*, Freiburg: Herder.

Stegmüller, F. (1947), *Repertorium commentariorum in Sententias Petri Lombardi*, 2 vols., Würzburg: Schöningh.

91

Peter Olivi

FRANÇOIS-XAVIER PUTALLAZ

The work of the Franciscan Peter John Olivi (b. ca. 1248; d. 1298) is closely linked with the dramatic events that marked his life and his posthumous destiny. Flattered by those who venerated him as a saint, loathed by others who saw him as an agitator, he has never ceased to fascinate historians exactly as he did his contemporaries. One event may serve as a symbol of this. When he died on March 14, 1298, Olivi was buried in the choir of the Franciscan church at Narbonne. It is said that, on the anniversaries of his death, pilgrims flocked to the place, even more numerous than to the tomb of St. Francis. Such a popular cult might have led to his canonization, had his work not been suspected of heterodoxy. The Franciscan order itself decided to put a stop to it. In 1318, Olivi's remains were removed, and the tomb destroyed.

His ideas had no better fortune. His anthropology (on the soul, form of the body) was indirectly questioned at the Council of Vienne in 1311–12; four Franciscans of spiritual tendency, said to be inspired by Olivi, were burnt at the stake in Marseilles on May 7, 1318; and Pope John XXII condemned his *Apocalypse* commentary on February 8, 1326. During this time, his reputation continued to grow in the south of France, since Beguines in Languedoc and Provence considered him a prophet whose travails had conferred on him the seal of authenticity.

But what were the causes of such a combination of popularity and notoriety?

How should philosophers be read?

Born at Sérignan around 1248, Peter Olivi joined the Franciscans of Béziers at the age of 12, then studied in Paris from 1267 to 1272. This was the time when the rediscovery of Aristotelian thought was helping to bring to a head the greatest intellectual crisis the Middle Ages had known. Before returning to Languedoc to take up the post of lector in the Franciscan convents of Narbonne and Montpellier, Peter formed an opinion about the role that should be given to philosophy in the acquisition of knowledge.

His remarks on Aristotelianism seemed to follow directly the line that had been established by BONAVENTURE between 1267 and 1271. Philosophers spread three mortal errors: they state that there is a single intellect for all men, that the world is eternal, and that every event takes place by necessity. Like Bonaventure, Olivi knew that these three errors derive from having the human mind rely only on itself. Bonaventure had said it, and Olivi made

516

it a theme of the *De perlegendis philosophorum libris*, and showed how pagan philosophers should be approached.

His entire plan is defined by the words of the Apostle Paul: "Hath not God made foolish the wisdom of this world?" (1 Cor. 1: 20). Indeed, insofar as pagan philosophers enjoyed the remains of intellectual light with which humans were originally graced, they were able to discover scraps of truth. But, ignorant of the fact that original sin had darkened this light in them, they laid down as absolute their obscured insights; in this way they became slaves to vanity, rashly confusing error and truth. This is why the Christians, who enjoy the privilege of revelation, can avoid the mistakes of these philosophers and can read them with authority:

> Thus, since this philosophy is folly, it must be read cautiously, and since it contains a spark of truth, it must be read with discernment. Because of its vanity, it must be read rapidly and be used as a means rather than as an end or a conclusion. Given its limitations, and because it is naive and childish, the reader must function as its master, not as its slave; we must in fact be its judges, not its followers (1941, n. 3, pp. 37–8).

Folly, spark of truth, vanity, and limitations: these are four expressions that define Olivi's philosophic plan from 1275 to 1280, when he composed the treatise.

Pagan philosophy is *folly*, for it is full of errors; its principles are corrupt and its conclusions, instead of leading to the veneration of divine majesty, replace it with idols. The philosophers resemble those false prophets who believe only in the senses, to the extent that all of their search is tainted by their blind trust in sensory data.

All of their search? Not exactly, for natural intelligence has retained some glimpses capable of some small *truth*. Thus philosophers were able to develop the speculative sciences (sciences of nature, mathematics, and metaphysics), study ethics, and attempt to construct rational arguments. In these sciences they have made fewer errors. Indeed, Olivi is even inclined to admit that there is some worth in the philosophy of language; insofar as it does not directly concern faith, it is not a threat to it and may be of use in the study of the Scriptures.

In other areas however, the philosophers were almost invariably wrong and taught *in vain* in that, unable to look to God as their master, they displayed presumption and pride. The aim they identify for human life was sterile, for they did not imagine the vision of God: if the final aim of humans is no more than earthly happiness, then events affect the wise man and the foolish in the same way.

Hence it is easy to establish the *limitations* and the insignificance of the philosophers' investigations. It would be superfluous to repeat Olivi's list of their innumerable errors, arising from their misunderstanding of true human nature. Next to the unity of intellect and the eternity of the world, the greatest errors concerned those spiritual realities that remain outside the reach of the senses. Philosophers not only called these separate intelligences gods, they knew nothing of the divine persons or of free creation. They, therefore, taught a false doctrine of bliss and, consequently, a false morality: "It is not surprising," Olivi concludes, "because all of them were shamefully mistaken as to the cult of the true God, to the extent that all became equally slaves to idolatry" (1941, n. 23, p. 44).

Olivi's virulent criticism of pagan philosophy, a philosophy so prized by some contemporary theologians, comes from his visceral hatred of idolatry. Idolatry! This is the keyword. Its seed is present whenever reason overestimates itself; whenever too much credit is given to the philosophy of the world; whenever we read texts not as masters but as slaves.

517

Aristotle is but an illustration of this. He is not the target, however, but rather the "Christians, professional theologians, and members of religious orders, who so appreciate the words of Aristotle that they almost adore them" (*II Sent.*, q. 6; 1922–6, I: p. 131). They have made Aristotle a god of this world, taking him as the infallible measure of truth (ibid., q. 27; I, 1922–6, p. 479). Olivi resents this idolatrous cult of Aristotle.

The dangers of philosophy

Here is the first indication of one of Olivi's major intuitions: to avoid error, one must practice philosophy as a master, not as a slave, and freedom alone protects Christian thinkers from the many slaveries of this world. The intellectual life is not their true destiny; as charity is greater than knowledge, so philosophical and theological knowledge has no validity but in the exact measure in which it serves love (1964, q. 3, p. 149). This explains the contemptuous tone adopted by Peter towards the pretentious philosophy of the world.

Yet the historian is surprised to discover that Olivi's immense opus (Ubertino de Casale says that it is seventeen times longer than Peter Lombard's *Sentences*) is full of philosophical debates. Why did a theologian who wrote *De perlegendis philosophorum libris* expend so much effort discussing philosophy? How is one to reconcile these two sides of Olivi: his virulent criticism of vain philosophy on the one hand, and the innumerable pages of philosophy that he left behind him, on the other? This cannot be explained in psychological terms, by assumed modesty or hypocrisy. Olivian thinking is, on the contrary, committed to this very coherent attitude: it is precisely in order to emphasize the negligible character of philosophy that he engages it on its own ground. The demonstration that opposing arguments destroy each other in their pretention to truth proves that neither has much weight. To discuss philosophy is both to denounce its derisory nature and to show that Christian freedom is practiced elsewhere: in love, and not in intellectual exercise.

This throws some light on the troubles encountered by Peter Olivi throughout his life. During the 1280s, he had already had to defend himself against another Franciscan who denounced him to the minister general of the order. The criticism was on theological grounds (on grace), but several of the nineteen accusations concerned philosophical doctrines. He was criticized, for example, for affirming the identity between quantity and substantial form. Olivi defended himself in a first vindicatory letter, showing that he had merely tried to undermine Aristotle's arguments because they were given too much credit. "In presenting these texts and arguments," he wrote, "I wished above all that Aristotle's sayings should not be adopted as if they were infallible principles" (1998, p. 56).

But the danger did not come only from Aristotle. It came also from those who attempted to impose a contrary opinion. In the end, the anti-Aristotelians also gave too much credit to philosophy, thinking that it contained the truth. The only correct approach is, therefore, to discuss arguments and raise doubts: dialectics is a means of preserving revealed truth insofar as it destroys the force of rational arguments. Olivi states this clearly:

> But as to human opinions arrived at through human reason alone, if they are proffered by great and trustworthy persons, I receive them with a humble and obedient heart: but, were I given the whole world, I would not adopt them as articles of the Catholic faith . . . ; that would be to venerate the words of men as idols; thus does one risk the birth of sects and schisms, and that men might say: "I am of Paul, I of Aristotle, and I of Thomas." (1998, p. 61)

Olivi himself experienced the weight of human opinions. In fact, his vindicatory letter did not have the desired effect. His writings were examined, and a commission of seven members appointed by Bonagratia, the general of the order, drew up a list of errors, then sent Olivi a letter with their seven seals, setting out the principles he was ordered to accept. Olivi attempted to respond, but in vain; without even a hearing, his works were forbidden, the *Letter of the Seven Seals* was read in all the convents of his province and his university career came to a sudden stop in 1283. He was confined to the region of Montpellier where, deprived of his writings, he was unable even to answer his accusers.

Two years later, he wrote a long vindicatory letter, of identical tone, but with presumably more effect. In 1287, the new minister general of the order, MATTHEW OF AQUASPARTA, rehabilitated Olivi. He was appointed lector at the convent of Santa Croce in Florence, where he had a decisive influence on his disciple, Peter of Trabibus and also, indirectly, on DANTE ALIGHIERI.

The long Apology of 1285 throws light on the Olivian conception of philosophy and on the limits of obedience due to human authority. He repeats that he sets little value on philosophy, and that is why he is mostly content to present (*recitare*) the arguments without passing any judgment and without adopting any of them. It is in just this way that philosophy should be practiced: "I have presented these various opinions, " he said, "without holding any one . . . ; they have not seemed to me less apt than others to explain and defend our faith" (1935, p. 405). The discussion of philosophical doctrines is not, therefore, directed against Aristotle alone: it attacks all philosophical idolatry, including anti-Aristotelianism. Danger arises also, then, from theologians and members of the Franciscan Order. Those who believe they are defending the faith by unilaterally attacking Aristotle, fall into another kind of idolatry. This danger is the more subtle in that it takes the form of a crusade for truth:

> I will not develop my attack further, but I leave that to the zealots of the Catholic faith; in fact, although the philosophers–Sadducees have said dreadful things about our rational nature, the Pharisees who oppose them do so with zeal, but it is an ill-advised zeal, as the Apostle Paul says. For they oppose the Sadducees in such a way that they do grave harm to the spirit of Christ. (II *Sent.*, q. 51; 1922–6, II: p. 125)

Poverty in the apocalyptic march of history

Olivi had an acute sense of this danger, which was the more serious for being masked by an argument in favor of faith. This danger, among others, seemed to him a sign of the coming of the Antichrist. Olivian thinking cannot be understood, therefore, outside the heritage of Joachim of Fiore and the theology of history developed by Bonaventure, who saw in St. Francis an irreplaceable "herald of God," a latter-day Elijah announcing the end of history.

In the eighth of his *Quaestiones de perfectione evangelica*, Olivi explicitly links his philosophical attitude to the defense of Franciscan poverty and to a sense of history. Did not Aristotle make an apology for prosperity in his *Ethics*, believing wrongly that wealth is the means and the instrument of happiness? This is an exclusively human doctrine, says Olivi; "in my view it is the foundation and the cause of the error of the Antichrist, as are all these errors" (1989, q. 8, p. 170). Olivi interprets in this way the intentions of providence, which brought about the wisdom of St. Francis and his order at a time when the Church was facing the most threatening conflicts of her history. The gravity of the situation demanded that the

519

message of Christ should be thenceforth spread throughout the world in its radical austerity (ibid., p. 152). Whence, the two major principles that gave rise to both the fame and the ruin of Olivi: the apocalyptic march of history and the role of evangelical poverty.

It is of course the *Apocalypse* commentary, condemned in 1326, that contains the essentials of this teaching. Dividing history into several periods, Olivi situates his own time as the completion of the age of the Father and of the Son: then comes the age of the Spirit, giving shape to the gentle contemplation of monks and members of religious orders. This contemplation is presented as true charity, revitalizing the knowledge of church doctors and ensuring the revival of evangelical life. Strictly intellectual theology had had its day and was now unfit for the new age that was beginning. St. Francis occupied a privileged place in this process, because he renewed a way of life founded by Christ. Thus all those who practiced evangelical perfection were laid open to many attacks: they were assailed by the opponents of poverty outside the order (known as "the mendicants' dispute") but, more especially, inside it.

The economic upheavals of Europe and the impressive rise of the Franciscan Order in fact made difficult the absolute poverty envisaged by St. Francis. The order itself was established, acquired wealth, and many of its members held high office, as masters, bishops, or cardinals. In the time of St. Bonaventure, the Franciscan brothers had already caused scandal: their richly decorated buildings became a source of criticism. There arose at once a bitter argument within the Franciscan Order which led, in the fourteenth century, to a break between conventuals and the spiritual partisans of absolute poverty, a terrible dispute that tragically culminated in the burnings of 1318 at Marseilles.

Olivi directly took part in this upheaval as his entire work bears witness, in particular the *Tractatus de usu paupere* written in the 1280s, just before he was condemned. In Olivi's opinion, the adversaries of poverty had entered the very heart of the Franciscan Order; for, although they had banned all private or collective property, they did not accept the need of an additional practice of poverty (*usus pauper*) in the use of the goods at their disposal. Indeed, Olivi believed that the *usus pauper* was an integral part of the Franciscan vow. To refuse it, as his adversaries did, was to attack the evangelical spirit itself, for voluntary poverty bears fruit in the development of the evangelical virtues. If wealth and property form an obstacle to the grace and love that unite human beings to God (1989, q. 8, p. 127), poverty fosters humility, for the persons who embrace it freely accept contempt: they are willing to seem vile in the eyes of other human beings.

The extolling of liberty

An immoderate love of riches ties humans to this world and impairs their true freedom; poverty, on the other hand, sets them free. We may thus understand Olivi's resentment of those philosopher-theologians who give too much importance to Aristotle and the sensory world, who are deeply attached to the cultural, intellectual, social, and economic riches of this world. Faith alone allows us to read philosophers in freedom; poverty alone confers on us the sovereign liberty to which we aspire.

Olivi thus appears to be the thirteenth-century writer who most extolled freedom. According to him, it is not intelligence that is the essence of humanity, otherwise humans would be reduced to nothing but "intelligent beasts" (*II Sent.*, q. 57; 1922–6, II: p. 338): it is not intellect, but freedom that makes for personality. In fact, human life, in its entirety, is an experience of freedom, for the latter is what gives it dignity: "All existence that is neither free nor personal is incomparably inferior to a free and personal existence" (ibid., q. 1; 1922–6, I, p. 11). If one were given a choice between being reduced to an inferior reality or plunged into nothingness, one would prefer to become nothing; our deepest senses cry out that everything else is nothing, compared with freedom (ibid., q. 57; 1922–6, II, p. 334).

Human beings are so free that they are defined by their autonomy: they are free precisely because they are not of the world. This is what dictates Olivi's attitude towards wealth, social ambition, and authority. It is also the reason why every injury to Christian freedom announces the battle of the Antichrist. The fleshly church enters the heart of the Church of Christ, it invades the great monastic centers, the most sensitive areas, all the way to the papacy. Those who live fully according to the Gospel will therefore be attacked by enemies who appear to wield legitimate power. Pope Boniface VIII, who in 1295 had just demoted Raymundus Gaufredus, the minister general who favored the spirituals, may even have been, in Olivi's eyes, the historic figure of the pseudo-pope mentioned in the *Apocalypse Commentary*. However that may be, it is clear that Olivi's thinking contained a critical egalitarian indictment of all overly pretentious human hierarchies, and that it was not to the taste of John XXII when, in the 1320s, he took issue with the entire Franciscan Order.

An economic thought

Several aspects of Olivian thinking concerned with epistemology have been closely studied by historians in the twentieth century. On this point, Olivi joins the mainstream of the Augustinian tradition, denying that any object can have an immediate influence on the human soul. He develops a very dynamic doctrine of knowledge, assuming that the mind regulates itself with respect to the object it wishes to know. In this process, the mind alone is active and the object plays the part of "terminative cause": the mind models itself on the object, as a beam of light penetrating a spherical object adapts itself to the contours of the sphere (*II Sent.*, q. 72; 1922–6, III: p. 36). This theory of knowledge was in perfect harmony with Olivi's anthropology. Olivi defended a classical doctrine of plurality of forms, emphasizing what he called the *colligantia potentiarum*, i.e., the unity of the various human faculties which, rooted in one spiritual matter, intermingle with and complete each other. This doctrine was so hard to understand that Olivi was accused of holding that the intellective soul informs the body only through the sensory faculty.

Without looking into these well-known doctrines, I prefer to bring up a fundamental aspect of Olivian thought which gives him a prominent place in the history of economic ideas. This may appear surprising in a Franciscan, but it is consistent with the Olivian plan considered as a whole. In fact, because freedom consists in a natural capacity for the things of this world, it is the foundation, for members of religious orders, of the voluntary renunciation of all possessions and, for tradespeople, the opportunity to make use of goods or exchange them. So, around 1293–4, Olivi wrote a treatise *De contractibus* (formerly known by its subtitles: *De emptionibus et venditionibus, de usuris et de restitutionibus*), of which a new edition is being prepared.

During his last stay in Narbonne (1292–8), Olivi devoted much time to pastoral work. *De contractibus* contains in several elements the influence of these practical activities; he adapted the treatise to the economic conditions familiar to the merchants of Languedoc. Olivi seems to have intended this work for his co-religionists, to guide them in their confessional practices. Not only does the term 'capital' seem to appear for the first time in history in this text, but also Olivi emphasizes the voluntary and contractual dimensions of commercial exchange. If the price of an object were in fact fixed a priori before any exchange, then either all merchants would be sinners or no one would ever wish to exchange anything. In reality, a fair price must result from the free consent of both buyer and seller. This domain of human activity is not therefore ruled exclusively by natural laws insofar as it must contain a margin of uncertainty and contingency: "This type of estimation of the value of ordinary objects can rarely or never be made, except by conjectural and probable opinions . . . It contains little certitude and much ambiguity, in accordance with the type of knowledge that relies on opinions" (1980, q. 1, dist.). This is the source of the fluctuation of more or less fair price margins.

Conclusion

Olivi wrote his *De contractibus* at a time when the local authorities of Narbonne were attempting to take charge of the local economy, for which the treatise "offers the strongest possible legitimation, by showing that divine law transfers to human communities the care of establishing the norms of justice in this domain" (Piron 1999, p. 700). It has been pointed out that this work develops one of the first complete concepts of the notion of "value," and that it gave birth to a new economic consciousness whose elements modern thought has only recently been able to synthesize.

But it is in its entirety that the work of Olivi has been, for some years, the object of discovery and re-evaluation. His thinking is particularly characterized by an acute sense of human freedom and individuality. Olivi stands out as one of the major figures of the thirteenth century, preparing the way for the new ideas introduced by JOHN DUNS SCOTUS and WILLIAM OF OCKHAM (Bettoni 1955, p. 508–15). Olivi especially displays a sense of the singular, which makes him a decisive link in the discovery of the individual in the Middle Ages (Bérubé 1964, p. 100–6), in his phrase in the *Epistola ad fratrem R.*: "*Sic sentio, sic et loquor*" (1998, p. 63). This knowledge of self, privileged above all else, made Olivi an astonishingly free thinker in the hierarchical society of his time, causing him to become, in self-defence, the inspirer of grave spiritual and social dissidence, both within the Franciscan Order and among the lay Beguines of Languedoc and Provence.

By placing Olivi among the great thinkers of the late thirteenth century, historians have committed themselves to re-evaluating this period. They began by noting that Olivi's thinking did not enjoy support from civil or religious institutions, and that his works did not receive the attention they deserved. This neglect is now being repaired since the celebration of the 700th anniversary of his death, in 1998, when two publishing projects were undertaken: first the *Collectio Oliviana*, of which Grottaferrata has recently published the first two volumes, second, the publication by Brepols of many completely unknown commentaries. There is no doubt that these efforts will bear fruit, arousing among historians that mixture of repulsion and attraction that has always made Olivi one of the most fascinating thinkers of the Middle Ages.

Bibliography

Primary sources

(1922–6), *Quaestiones in secundum librum Sententiarum*, 3 vols., ed. B. Jansen, Quaracchi: Bibliotheca Franciscana Scholastica Medii Aevi.

(1935), *Responsio fratris Petri Ioannis* [Olivi] *ad aliqua dicta per quosdam magistros Parisienses de suis Quaestionibus excerpta*, ed. D. Laberge, *Archivum Franciscanum Historicum* 28, pp. 130–55, 374–407.

(1941), *De perlegendis philosophorum libris*, ed. F. Delorme, *Antonianum* 16, pp. 37–44.

(1964), *Quaestiones de perfectione evangelica*, q. 3: *An studere sit opus de genere suo perfectum*, in A. Emmen and F. Simoncioli, eds., "La dottrina dell'Olivi sulla contemplazione, la vita attiva e mista," *Studi Francescani* 61, pp. 113–67.

(1980), *De contractibus. De emptionibus et venditionibus, de usuris et restitutionibus*, ed. G. Todeschini, Rome: Istituto Storico Italiano per il Medio Evo (in preparation: a new edition by S. Piron).

(1989), *Quaestiones de perfectione evangelica*, q. 8: *An status altissime paupertatis sit simpliciter melior omni statu*, in J. Schlageter, ed., *Das Heil der Armen und das Verderben der Reichen. Petrus Johannis Olivi OFM. Die Frage nach der höchsten Armut*, Werl: Dietrich-Coelde-Verlag.

(1998), *Epistola ad fratrem R.*, ed. R. S. Piron, *Archivum Franciscanum Historicum* 91, pp. 33–64.

Secondary sources

Bérubé, C. (1964), *La Connaissance de l'individuel au Moyen Âge*, Montreal: Presses de l'Université de Montréal; Paris: Presses Universitaires de France.

Bettoni, E. (1955), *Le dottrine filosofiche di Pier di Giovanni Olivi. Saggio*, Milan: Vita e Pensiero.

Boureau, A. and Piron, S., eds. (1999), *Pierre de Jean Olivi (1248–1298), Pensée scolastique, dissidence spirituelle et société* (pp. 390–9), Paris: J. Vrin.

Burr, D. (1976), "The persecution of Peter Olivi," *Transactions of the American Philosophical Society* 66, pp. 5–98.

——(1989), *Olivi and Franciscan Poverty*, Philadelphia: University of Pennsylvania Press.

——(1993), *Olivi's Peaceable Kingdom: A Reading of the Apocalypse Commentary*, Philadelphia: University of Pennsylvania Press.

Flood, D. (1971), *Poverty in the Middle Ages*, Werl: Dietrich-Coelde-Verlag.

Gieben, S. (1968), "Bibliographia oliviana (1885–1967)," *Collectanea Franciscana* 38, p. 167–195.

Manselli, R. (1955), *La "Lectura super Apocalipsim" di Pietro di Giovanni Olivi, Ricerche sull'escatologismo medioevale*, Rome: Istituto Storico Italiano per il Medio Evo.

Piron, S. (1999), "Parcours d'un intellectuel franciscain. D'une théologie vers une pensée sociale: l'œuvre de Pierre de Jean Olivi (ca. 1248–1298) et son traité *De contractibus*," unpublished thesis, Paris: École des Hautes Etudes en Sciences Sociales.

Putallaz, F.-X. (1995), *Insolente liberté. Controverses et condamnations au XIIIe siècle*, Paris and Fribourg: Éditions du Cerf, Éditions Universitaires.

——(1996), *Figures franciscaines: de Bonaventure à Duns Scot* (pp. 167–73), Paris: Editions du Cerf.

Vian, P. (1989), *Pietro di Giovanni Olivi, Scritti scelti*, Rome: Citta Nuova.

92

Peter de Rivo

CHRISTOPHER SCHABEL

Born Peter van den Becken, the controversial Flemish philosopher Peter de Rivo (b. ca. 1420; d. 1500) spent most of his life at the University of Louvain, where he began his studies in 1437. Promoted to master of arts in 1442, he then studied theology and lectured on the *Sentences* in 1448–9, but he was not made master of theology until 1477. Rivo composed commentaries on many of the works of Aristotle and treatises on the calendar, over which topic he was involved in a dispute in his later years, but he is most famous for his involvement as an arts master in the "quarrel over future contingents at Louvain."

Although the quarrel's prehistory goes back to 1446, the real argument began in 1465 when Rivo defended PETER AURIOL's (ca. 1320) unpopular position on future contingents in a quodlibetal debate. To save free will, Rivo denied any determination in future contingents prior to their coming about. For Rivo, as for Auriol, this entailed a denial of the applicability of the principle of bivalence to propositions about future contingents: right now, "the Antichrist will come" is neither true nor false, but simply neutral, Rivo claimed. Along with this, Rivo adopted the other elements of Auriol's theory, for example that God's knowledge is not properly speaking "foreknowledge" and imposes no predetermination on the future, because it does not precede the future but is rather "indistant" from the "actualities" of future contingents. Nevertheless, it was Rivo's rejection of bivalence that always played the most important role in his extensive and interesting writings on the subject. Rivo did bend a little when treating prophecy, admitting different types of "truth" in future contingent propositions, but he completely rejected any truth (or falsity) "of logical vigor" in such propositions.

Rivo quickly drew fire from a long-time opponent, the Louvain theologian Henry of Zomeren. When the university at first supported Rivo, in 1470, Zomeren turned to his patron Cardinal Bessarion for help. Eventually the faculties of theology at Paris and Cologne became involved, but it was the opposition of Bessarion's circle of intellectuals in Rome that proved Rivo's downfall. This group included such figures as Fernando de Cordoba and Francesco della Rovere, and the latter's elevation to the papacy as Sixtus IV in 1471 led to the eventual condemnation of Rivo's (and Auriol's) stance in 1474.

Bibliography

Primary sources

(1950), *La Querelle des futurs contingents (Louvain 1465–1475)*, ed. L. Baudry, Paris: J. Vrin; trans. in 1989 as *The Quarrel over Future Contingents, Louvain, 1465–1475*, by R. Guerlac, Dordrecht: Kluwer.
(1997), *Cardinal Bessarion, De arcanis Dei*, ed. G. J. Etzkorn, Maestri Francescani 8, Rome.

Secondary sources

Laminne, J. (1906), "La controverse sur les futurs contingents à l'Université de Louvain au XVe siècle," *Bulletin de la Classe des Lettres et des Sciences Morales et Politiques et de la Classe des Beaux-arts* (pp. 372–438), Académie Royale des Sciences, des Lettres et des Beaux-arts de Belgique, Brussels: Hayez.

Schabel, C. (1995, 1996), "Peter de Rivo and the quarrel over future contingents at Louvain: new evidence and new perspectives," *Documenti e Studi sulla Tradizione Filosofica Medievale* 6 (Part I), pp. 363–473; 7 (Part II), pp. 369–435.

93

Peter of Spain

GYULA KLIMA

The author of the *Summulae*

Until recently, there was a general agreement among scholars concerning the identity of the author of one of the most successful academic books ever, the *Summulae dialecticales*. According to the commonly accepted opinion, the author was Petrus Iuliani, who became Pope John XXI, a man of science almost to the point of neglecting his papal duties in favor of his research, whose papacy came to an abrupt end after only eight months, when the ceiling of his newly-built private study in the Viterbo palace collapsed upon him in 1277. The so-called Byzantine thesis concerning the authorship of the *Summulae*, according to which it is a Latin translation of an original Greek work by the eleventh-century Byzantine scholar, Michael Psellos, by now is a mere curiosity of intellectual history. Study of the sources has definitively shown that the Greek work mistakenly attributed to Psellos is in fact a Greek translation of the Latin work, prepared by Gennadios Scholarios in the fifteenth century (De Rijk 1972, pp. lxi–lxviii). However, careful study of the historical evidence by Angel d'Ors (d'Ors 1997) successfully revived another tradition concerning the authorship of the *Summulae*, often referred to as the "Dominican thesis." Indeed, d'Ors's study has established that the identification of the author of the *Summulae* with John XXI is probably a relatively late tradition, and the evidence supporting the Dominican thesis, according to which the author was a Dominican friar, is much stronger. However, d'Ors found the evidence insufficient for a definitive positive identification of the actual person. Some sources refer to the author by the name of Petrus Alfonsi, others as Petrus Ferrandus, but there may be other candidates as well. Therefore, until the issue of authentic authorship is settled, the name 'Peter of Spain' (and its equivalents, Petrus Hispanus, etc.) should be used simply as an abbreviation of the definite description 'the author of the *Summulae*'. In any case, this is the policy this article will follow.

Peter of Spain was justifiably famous for authoring the *Summulae*. The work was on the core curricula of many universities for centuries, until it became one of the prime targets of humanist mockery of "scholastic barbarisms," and was gradually eliminated from university curricula with the rest of the scholastic output. But Peter was also famous for authoring another important logical work, under the title *Syncategoreumata*, dealing with the properties of syncategorematic terms, i.e., various types of logical connectives.

The rest of this article will be devoted to a doctrinal analysis of the *Summulae*, focusing on its original contribution to the characteristically medieval doctrine of the properties of terms, and – also drawing on the doctrine of the *Syncategoreumata* – pointing out its significance concerning the problem of universals and philosophical realism in general.

The *Summulae* and the realism of Peter of Spain

The *Summulae* is a systematic logical work consisting of twelve tracts, which fall into two main groups: (A) those providing the standard Aristotelian-Boethian teachings of the so-called *logica antiqua* (comprising the materials of *logica vetus* and *logica nova*), and (B) those providing the doctrine of the so-called *logica modernorum*, the original medieval contribution to logical theory (cf. De Rijk 1962, pp. 14–17).

The tracts according to this grouping are the following:

(A)
1   On introductory matters (*De introductionibus*), Tract I.
2   On predicables (*De predicabilibus*), Tract II.
3   On categories (*De predicamentis*), Tract III.
4   On syllogisms (*De syllogismis*), Tract IV.
5   On topics (*De locis*), Tract V.
6   On fallacies (*De fallaciis*), Tract VI.
(B)
7   On suppositions (*De suppositionibus*), Tract VII.
8   On relatives (*De relativis*), Tract VIII.
9   On ampliations (*De ampliationibus*), Tract IX.
10   On appellations (*De appellationibus*), Tract X.
11   On restrictions (*De restrictionibus*), Tract XI.
12   On distributions (*De distributionibus*), Tract XII.

The tracts belonging to the *logica antiqua* provide a simple, elementary exposition of Aristotelian-Boethian logic, as it was adopted in the twelfth-century logical literature (cf. De Rijk 1972, pp. lxxxviii–xcv).

It is the tracts of the *logica modernorum* that contain Peter's contribution to the characteristically medieval theory of the properties of terms, analyzing and classifying their semantic functions. The tract on suppositions first defines the primary semantic property of terms, which has to precede their supposition, namely, signification.

According to Peter, signification is the conventional representation of some thing by an utterance. Therefore, only those terms have signification that signify some thing, i.e., categorematic terms (namely, such terms that can meaningfully be the subject or predicate of propositions, while not taken to stand for themselves). Indeed, Peter goes on to argue that since every thing is either particular or universal, and since syncategorematic terms, such as 'every' and 'some', do not signify either a universal or a particular thing, they do not signify some thing, and so they do not have signification in this strict sense. Nevertheless, as we shall see, this does not mean that these terms are absolutely meaningless. In fact, Peter will argue that although such terms do not signify things, they do signify certain modes of the things signified by categorematic terms. For now, however, we should just note Peter's unabashed talk about universal things in this argument.

Peter divides signification into the signification of substantive things, performed by substantive nouns, and the signification of adjective things, performed by adjective nouns or verbs. He insists that this distinction does not characterize modes of signification, but modes of things. Whatever these things and their modes are, Peter states that it is on account of the difference between these two types of signification that we have to distinguish between *supposition* and *copulation*.

Supposition is the taking of a substantive term for something, whereas copulation is the taking of an adjective term for something, i.e., its referring to something. This is why signification is prior to supposition. Since only a term can refer, supposition (i.e., reference) can only belong to a term, that is, an utterance that already has signification.

Peter first divides supposition into discrete and common supposition. Discrete supposition belongs to discrete terms, i.e., terms that on account of their signification can apply only to one thing, such as proper nouns, or common terms determined by a demonstrative pronoun and an act of pointing. Common supposition belongs to common terms, i.e., terms that on account of their signification can apply to several things.

Common supposition is further divided into natural and accidental supposition. Natural supposition is the taking of a common term for all those things that fall under it, be they past, present, or future. Although Peter does not say much about this type of supposition, its significance is clear in natural science, where we want to make universal claims about natural phenomena regardless of whether they are actual at the time of making the claim or not. For example, 'Every lunar eclipse is the interposition of the earth between the sun and the moon' should be true, even when there is no lunar eclipse. Accidental supposition is the taking of a term in a proposition for something, as determined by the propositional context.

Accidental supposition is further divided into simple and personal supposition. (In medieval logic it was also common to distinguish material supposition, when a term stands for itself, as in ' "Man" is a noun', but Peter omits this type of supposition from consideration.

According to Peter, in simple supposition a common term refers to the universal thing it signifies. For example, in the proposition 'Man is a species' the term 'man' stands for what it signifies, namely, man in general, and not any particular man, since obviously no particular man is a species. Furthermore, the predicate terms of universal affirmative propositions also have simple supposition. For example, in 'Every man is an animal', the term 'animal' cannot be taken to stand for any particular animal, for obviously no particular animal is every man.

Personal supposition is defined by Peter as the taking of a common term for its inferiors. It is divided into *determinate* and *confused*, the latter of which is further subdivided into *mobile* and *immobile supposition*. Determinate supposition is had, for example, by the subject of a particular proposition such as 'Some man is running'. Such a supposition is called determinate, for although the term 'man' stands in it for all men, it is verified for just any one of them (i.e., it is true, if this man is running, or that man is running, etc.). Confused supposition, according to Peter's definition, is the taking of a common term for many things, with the mediation of a universal sign. For example, the subject term of 'Every man is an animal' has confused, mobile, and distributive supposition, for the term obviously stands for all men, and, contrary to determinate supposition, the proposition is true only if the predicate is verified for all of them (i.e., it is true, if this man is an animal *and* that man is an animal, etc.). Peter goes on to distinguish this type of confused supposition, which he calls *confused by the necessity of the sign*, from another type, which he calls *confused by the necessity of the thing*.

It is clear that the subject term of 'Every man is an animal' is distributed for all men because of the use of the universal sign 'every'. But, Peter argues further that, since each man has his own essence and his own animality, the copula 'is' and the predicate term 'animal' should also be taken to stand for all those essences and all those animals, not by the necessity of the sign, but by the necessity of the thing.

The term confused by the necessity of the sign is taken *distributively*, for it is taken to stand for all men, but it has confused and *mobile* supposition, because one can "descend" to any of its inferiors by a valid inference, such as this: 'Every man is an animal; therefore, Plato is an animal'. By contrast, the term confused by the necessity of the thing has confused but immobile supposition, for under this term no such descent is possible: the inference 'Every man is an animal; therefore, every man is this animal' is not valid.

However, in Peter's discussion of simple supposition it was precisely this property of the predicate term of this sentence that allowed him to conclude that this term had simple supposition. In general, Peter's criterion there to detect whether a term had simple supposition seemed to be whether the term could be taken to stand for any one of its particulars, preserving the truth of the proposition. So which kind of supposition applies here?

Peter first addresses this problem by pointing out that attributing both simple and immobile personal supposition to the same term is not inconsistent. For the term has simple supposition insofar as it stands for the nature of the genus predicated of its species, but it has confused supposition insofar as the nature of the genus is multiplied in the supposita of the species.

But Peter is not satisfied with this solution in that he finds it impossible that a term should have confused personal supposition in the predicate position. He argues as follows. In 'Every man is an animal' a genus is predicated of one of its species. But the nature of the genus multiplied in the supposita of the species is not a genus. Therefore, it is not the nature of the genus multiplied in the supposita of the species that is predicated here. But the predicate of this sentence stands for what is predicated, which is not the nature of the genus multiplied in the supposita of the species. Hence it cannot have confused supposition insofar as it would require this multiplication.

Peter's consequent rejection of the aforementioned distinction between the two types of confusion (which he found in one of his sources, cf. De Rijk 1972, p. lxxi) gives us a clearer insight into Peter's semantic conception. Here he states that although from the point of view of logic, the nature signified by 'man' in its supposita is one, in reality each man has his own humanity, and these humanities are distinct on account of the matter they inform. Likewise, the nature signified by the term 'animal' in individual humans is one from the point of view of logic (*secundum viam logice*), but is multiplied in these individuals in reality (*secundum viam nature*). So, the multiplication of animalities has nothing to do with the semantic function of the predicate of 'Every man is an animal'; indeed, we find the same multiplication of animalities even when we consider 'Every man is white' or 'Every man is black'.

So Peter's apparently naively realist talk about universal things need not be taken at face value. It is only the proper way of talking for the logician, who is discussing things insofar as they are conceived by us, and consequently signified by our terms. But since we are able to conceive of singular things in a universal manner, by abstracting from their differences, and consequently are able to signify them in the same way, the logician is entitled to talk about what our common terms signify as a universal thing, while keeping in mind that the thing in question is not a real thing, but something universally conceived and signified. (Cf. also 1992, pp. 46–9 and 104–5.)

To summarize Peter's conception by means of an example, the term 'man' signifies human nature in general, and this is what it stands for when it has simple supposition, as in 'Man is a species' or 'Every philosopher is a man'. But the same term stands for the individuals

GYULA KLIMA

having this nature (each one its own), when the term has personal supposition, whether determinate, as in 'A man is an animal' or confused, mobile and distributive, as in 'Every man is an animal'. However, Peter rejects the suggestion that the predicate term of this sentence, besides having simple supposition would also have personal (confused and immobile) supposition, not because he thinks these two kinds of supposition are incompatible, but because he argues that this predicate simply does not have the latter semantic function.

All this squarely places Peter of Spain in the moderate realist camp concerning the problem of universals. However, there is more to Peter's realism. If in a very general sense we take a realist to be someone who is willing to allow a one-to-one mapping of linguistic categories to ontological categories (at least, in most, and significant cases), as opposed to a nominalist who would reduce his ontological commitment by arguing for many-to-one mappings, then Peter will appear to be a realist even in this general sense. To be sure, his realism is certainly mitigated by his distinction between what one can talk about *secundum viam logice* and what there really is *secundum viam nature*. Nevertheless, the way he talks about substantive and adjective things, and especially about the signification of syncategorematic terms, is revealing. The things he is talking about may not be things of nature pure and simple, but things-as-conceived-and-signified. But then, as far as Peter's semantics is concerned, there might be just as many, or almost as many, such "quasi-things" as there are different ways of signifying real things (disregarding, e.g., synonymies).

This is quite clear not only in Peter's remarks on adjective and substantive things referred to above (which after all reflects a genuine distinction between substances and accidents), but especially in his treatment of the signification of syncategorematic terms and propositions. As far as the latter are concerned, he does not hesitate to talk about what is signified by a proposition, and referred to by the corresponding sentential nominalization, as a thing, which may have its own accidents. (1972, p. 195.) As for syncategorematic terms, Peter both in the last tract of the *Summulae* and in the *Syncategoreumata* insists that, although syncategorematic terms do not signify subjectible and predicable things, which are signified by categorematic terms, nevertheless, they do signify certain modes of these things. To be sure, he adds, these modes do not belong to these things as they are in themselves, but insofar as they are subjectible or predicable, which is why they need not stick with their things in syllogisms in different propositions. For example, consider

Every white man is running
Socrates is a white man

Socrates is running

In this syllogism, the disposition 'white' of the subject 'man' belongs to the thing in itself, so it has to be repeated in the other premiss in order to get a valid inference. However, the further disposition 'every' need not be repeated (i.e., we do not have to assume 'Socrates is every white man' as the second premiss) in order to obtain a valid inference. In Peter's view, this is so because 'every' signifies a disposition that determines the subject in relation to the predicate, for it signifies that the predicate applies to all supposita of the subject.

The remaining tracts of the *Summulae* deal with the supposition of relative pronouns (tr. VIII), the modifications of supposition in various propositional contexts (tr. IX, XI, XII), and supposition for the actually existing supposita of a term, distinguished by the name of appellation (tr. X), in marked contrast with JOHN BURIDAN'S later interpretation of appellation.

530

Bibliography

Primary sources

(1972), *Tractatus, called afterwards Summule logicales*, ed. L. M. De Rijk, Assen: Van Gorcum.

(1992), *Syncategoreumata*, ed. L. M. De Rijk, trans. J. Spruyt, Leiden: Brill.

Secondary sources

De Rijk, L. M. (1962), *Logica modernorum: A Contribution to the History of Early Terminist Logic*, vol. I: *On the Twelfth Century Theories of Fallacy*, Assen: Van Gorcum.

——(1972), Introduction, in *Peter of Spain*, Assen: Van Gorcum.

d'Ors, A. (1997), "Petrus Hispanus O.P. Auctor *Summularum*," *Vivarium* 35, pp. 21–71.

94

Peter the Venerable

JONATHAN J. SANFORD

Peter the Venerable, also known as Pierre Maurice de Montboissier (b. ca. 1092; d. 1156), was elected Abbot of Cluny in 1122. He brought about reforms within the congregation of Cluny, but resisted the more anti-intellectual trends of many of his contemporaries, the most notable of whom was BERNARD OF CLAIRVAUX. Peter was noted as one of the most reasonable and peaceful men of his day. He will always be remembered for securing reconciliation for Abelard and welcoming him into Cluny for the last two years of his life. For biographical information see Torrel and Bouthillier (1986, pp. 3–104), and Constable (in 1967, vol. 2, pp. 233–348).

In 1142 Peter journeyed to Spain, where he became interested in the work of the Toledan translators, and commissioned the first translation of the Koran into Latin. Subsequently, Peter composed his polemic against the Islamic faith, *Liber contra sectam sive haeresim Sarracenorum*. He earlier had composed two other polemical works, one against the views of the heresiarch Peter de Bruis, *Tractatus contra Petrobrusianos haereticos* (ca. 1134); and another addressed to Jews, *Liber adversus Judaeorum inveteratam duritiem* (ca. 1143). As Kritzeck (1964, pp. 26–7, 196) notes, Peter's books addressed to the Jews and to Muslims are marked by their good will as well as by the pains he took to familiarize himself with the Talmudic and Islamic literary traditions. Peter sought more to persuade than to castigate.

Peter's writings include other theological works, rules for the congregation of Cluny, letters, and verse. His works were first collected and published by Pierre de Montmartre in 1522. Besides bequeathing his own literary efforts, Peter saw to the substantial growth of his monastery's collection of manuscripts, a collection which included many classical texts.

Bibliography

Primary sources

(1890), *Opera omnia*, in J.-P. Migne, ed., *Patrologia Latina*, vol. 189, Paris: Vivès.

(1964), *Liber contra sectam sive haeresim Sarracenorum*, in J. Kritzeck, ed., *Peter the Venerable and Islam*, Princeton, NJ: Princeton University Press.

(1967), *The Letters of Peter the Venerable*, 2 vols., ed. G. Constable, Cambridge, MA: Harvard University Press.

(1968), *Contra Petrobrusianos hereticos*, ed. J. Fearns, Corpus Christianorum continuatio mediaevalis 10, Turnhout: Brepols.

(1985), *Adversus Iudeorum inveteratam duritiem*, ed. Y. Friedman, Corpus Christianorum continuatio mediaevalis 58, Turnhout: Brepols.

Secondary sources

Constable, G. and Kritzeck, J., eds. (1956), *Petrus Venerabilis (1156–1956): Studies and Texts Commemorating the Eighth Century of his Death*, Studia Anselmiana 40, Rome: Herder.

Kritzeck, J. (1964), *Peter the Venerable and Islam*, Princeton, NJ: Princeton University Press.

Orbán, A. P. (1993), "Wie zitiert Petrus Venerabilis in seiner Korrespondenz die klassisch lateinischen Autoren?," *Philogus* 137, pp. 295–307.

Torrell OP, J.-P. and Bouthillier, D. (1986), *Pierre le Vénérable et sa vision du monde*, Leuven: Spicilegium Sacrum Lovaniense.

95

Philip the Chancellor

R. E. HOUSER

Philip the Chancellor (b. 1165/85; d. 1236) was truly a "Renaissance" figure: poet, preacher, master of theology, ecclesiastical politician. He was made archdeacon by one noble cousin in 1202 and Chancellor of Notre-Dame by another in 1217. The chancellor's right to confer the *licentia docendi* placed Philip in the midst of controversies at the University of Paris, and under his governance Dominicans attained two chairs in theology, Franciscans one. One of his sermons is a plea to scholars to return to Paris during the great strike (1229–31), finally ended by Pope Gregory IX (*Parens scientiarum*). His main theological work is *Summa de bono* (1225–8).

Since everything God made was "very good" (Gen. 1: 31), Philip took goodness as his organizing principle and divided his work into two major sections: one on creation, the "good of nature," the other on ethics, the "good of grace." The omnipresence of goodness, however, seems to contradict Luke 18: 19: "No one is good but God alone." So Philip turned to the "philosophers" and began his *Summa* with the first scholastic treatment of the transcendentals. "Being," "one," "true," and "good" have two sides. They are "utterly universal (*communissima*)" and predicable "of all things." But they also are "appropriated" to God, because their own *proper natures* are found only in God: "Thus, in the First is absolute good, in others there is relative good (*secundum quid*)." The transcendentals, then, reconciled these scriptural texts and also provided a model for Philip's metaphysics and ethics.

The "good of nature" makes every creature exist on two levels. Each has transcendental traits, universal conditions for its very existence, but also has a specific nature "appropriated" to it. These natures fall into three groups: angels or purely "intellectual creatures"; "corporeal creatures"; and humans, made "out of corporeal and intellectual" parts.

The "good of grace" Philip studied first in angels, then in humans. Since actual grace produces virtue, the study of morality becomes the study of virtue. Philip envisioned an exhaustive hierarchy of virtues and vices, topped by seven fundamental virtues: three "theological" and four "cardinal." The latter are both *general* virtues, a set of "universal conditions" for good action, and *specific* virtues "appropriated" to limited areas of moral life. All other virtues are *specific* virtues and "parts" of the seven. Thus, just as every creature exhibits two distinct senses of being – *transcendentals* and its *specific* essence – so also two distinct senses of virtue govern every good action – *general* cardinal virtues and *special* virtues.

Philip's distinction between the two senses of cardinal virtue became axiomatic for the ethics of ALBERTUS MAGNUS and THOMAS AQUINAS, as much as his two modes of being did for their metaphysics.

534

Bibliography

Primary sources

(1985), *Summa de bono*, ed. N. Wicki, Bern: Francke.

(1972), *Sermons of Philip the Chancellor*, in *Repertorium der lateinischen Sermones des Mittelalters für die Zeit von 1150–1350 (Autoren L-P)*, ed. J. Schneyer, *Beiträge zur Geschichte der Philosophie und Theologie des Mittelalters* 43/4, Münster: Aschendorff.

Secondary sources

Aertsen, J. (1996), *Medieval Philosophy and the Transcendentals: The Case of Thomas Aquinas*, Leiden: Brill.

Lumpe, A. (1994), "Philipp der Kanzler," *Biographisch-Bibliographisches Kirchenlexikon*, vol. 7 (pp. 481–5), Heraberg: Verlag Traugott Bautz. www.bautz.de/bbkl.

MacDonald, S. (1992), "Goodness as transcendental: the early thirteenth-century recovery of an Aristotelian idea," in Jorge J. E. Gracia, ed., *The Transcendentals in the Middle Ages*, *Topoi* 11/2, pp. 173–86.

Principe, W. (1975), *Philip the Chancellor's Theology of the Hypostatic Union*, Toronto: Pontifical Institute of Mediaeval Studies.

96

Pierre d'Ailly

RICHARD A. LEE, JR.

Pierre d'Ailly, also known in Latin as Petrus de Alliaco (b. ca. 1350; d. 1420), Cardinal of Cambrai, was born at Compiègne, studied at the College of Navarre at Paris, receiving the title Doctor of Theology in 1381. He was active in the administration of the university and participated in the Council of Constance, which finally put an end to the Great Schism.

D'Ailly follows WILLIAM OF OCKHAM in maintaining that outside the soul only singulars exist and that universals are merely signs that signify individuals. These universals are concepts that have being as accidents of the soul. Universals are caused by the things they signify, i.e., by the individuals conceived or known through them. It is not required that the thing be in the soul for us to know it, "but only its similitude or representation" (*Tractatus de anima*, c. 12, p. 2). This similitude is a confused representation of the singular thing, abstracting from its accidents and extraneous conditions.

D'Ailly accounts for our knowledge of singulars, on one hand, by recourse to Ockham's idea of "intuitive knowledge," and, on the other, by asserting, against Ockham, knowledge by way of sensible species that affect the medium through which the thing is sensed. The thing sensed causes the medium to take on its visible aspect. This chain of causation continues all the way to the soul, which gets immediate knowledge of the thing by way of these species. This knowledge is called "intuitive."

Developing another Ockhamistic notion, d'Ailly argues that certitude is available for us when the knowledge we have of things is "evident" (1500, *Q. in I Sent.*, q. 1). For d'Ailly there are two kinds of evidence available to us: absolute, which we have of the principle of non-contradiction and truths derived from it, and conditioned, which we have of all other truths. Evidence means assent to a truth such that the intellect cannot err or be deceived. Conditioned evidence relies on the customary course of nature and the general influence of God, while absolute evidence provides certain, infallible grounds for our assent to matter, i.e., it has no conditions. Yet d'Ailly clearly maintains that once God has created an ordered universe, God is bound to that order. Therefore, even our conditioned evidence (e.g., evident knowledge of a singular, sensible thing) is evident and thus certain, given the right state of the sensory medium and the sensory organs.

These two types of evidence rely on the distinction between God's ordered power (*potentia ordinata*) and absolute power (*potentia absoluta*). D'Ailly, in his introductory *Principium* to the *Questions on the Sentences*, clearly indicates that God as creator is also the first lawgiver, establishing through a free act of the divine will binding laws for human action as well as an order for the universe. As creator and lawgiver, God maintains the order that has been created. Just as we are bound to the laws God has established, even though we cannot further ground these laws in reason, so too we are bound to a natural order that has been established, even though that order is contingent and not further explicable by reason.

Bibliography

Primary sources
(1500), *Quaestiones in I, II, et IV Sententiarum*, Venice.
(1505), *Tractatus de anima*, Paris.

Secondary sources
Ackerman Smoller, Laura (1994), *History, Prophecy, and the Stars: The Christian Astrology of Pierre d'Ailly 1350–1420*, Princeton, NJ: Princeton University Press.
Pluta, Olaf (1987), *Die philosophische Psychologie des Peter von Ailly: Ein Beitrag zur Geschichte der Philosophie des späten Mittelalters*, Amsterdam: B. R. Grüner.

97

Pierre de Maricourt

JOSÉ LUIS RIVERA

Pierre de Maricourt, also known in Latin as Petrus Peregrinus de Maharncuria (fl. ca. 1267) was a French scientist, the author of the *Letter on the Magnet* (*Epistula de magnete ad Sigerium de Foucaucourt*), a short treatise on the properties and uses of magnetite, and a *New Construction of a Particular Astrolabe* (*Nova compositio astrolabii particularis*). Maricourt also mentions a treatise *On the Properties of Mirrors* (*De operibus speculorum*, see *De magnete* II.2, p. 353), of which nothing else is known.

Most of our meager information concerning Maricourt is derived from Roger Bacon (*Opus majus* IV.2, 1897, I.116; *Opus tertium* 11, 1859, pp. 35, 13, 43ff). Although the identity between the "Magister Petrus" mentioned by Bacon and Pierre de Maricourt may be problematic (Schlund 1911a: 445–9, 455), it is strongly supported by the estimated date of *Nova compositio* (after 1263; cf. 1995, p. 113), *De magnete* (dated on August 8, 1269), and Bacon's writings (before 1267). In any event, *De magnete* and *Nova compositio* seem to confirm Bacon's report on Maricourt's preference for the practical aspects of scientific research and his mathematical competence.

De magnete is perhaps the most interesting work of Maricourt. It is not clear whether all his information is the product of his own observations or was at least partly derived from earlier sources, but his letter was the main source of information about magnetism in Europe until William Gilbert's own *De magnete* (1600). The letter is divided in two parts: the first discusses the properties of magnets, and the second proposes the construction of some devices based on these properties. Maricourt is the first known scientist to use the word 'pole' in his description as a reference to the geographical poles (*De magnete* I.4, pp. 73–7), to describe magnetic fields (I.4, pp. 78–89), and to provide a method to determine the poles of the magnet (I.4–5, pp. 90–118). He describes carefully the basic laws of attraction (I.6, pp. 120–43), the magnetization of iron (I.7, pp. 150–61), and the change of polarity by a stronger magnetic field (I.8, pp. 163–77). On the basis of his observations, Maricourt challenges some applications of the ancient principle of the attraction of the opposites (I.6, pp. 144–6), and proposes that the orientation of the magnet depends on the disposition of the celestial bodies (I.10, pp. 260–5) instead of the existence of deposits of magnetite (I.10, pp. 239–45).

However, perhaps the most interesting feature of *De magnete* is Maricourt's description of the background of the researcher. Maricourt states that the construction of scientific instruments is irreplaceable for the transmission of the science of the magnet (cf. I.1, pp. 32–4). To achieve this knowledge it is not enough to "know the nature of things," not enough "not being ignorant of the motions of heavens," but it is also necessary "to be proficient in

538

manual works" (I.1, pp. 43–4), for "by means of his manual skill [the researcher] can correct in no small amount the errors that could never be corrected by natural or mathematical [knowledge] alone if he lacks 'manual ability', and in difficult works we rely heavily on manual ability, and in general we can achieve nothing without it" (I.2, pp. 48–9). Moreover, Maricourt appeals to the "evidence of experiment" (I.6, p. 147), the "truth proved by experience" (I.7, pp. 160–1), and the "experienced truth" (I.9, p. 220) to support his conclusions. Finally, he explains to his reader that if some of the experiments described in the letter are unsuccessful, "impute your failure to your own lack of skill rather than to a defect of nature" (I.10, pp. 277–8). These traits seem to anticipate the attitude of scientists in the seventeenth century.

Bibliography

Primary source

(1995), *Opera: Epistula de magnete, Nova compositio astrolabii particularis*, ed. Loris Sturlese and Ron B. Thomson, Pisa: Scuola Normale Superiore.

Secondary sources

Bacon, Roger (1859), *Opus tertium*, ed. John S. Brewer, London: Longman, Green, and Roberts.

——(1897), *Opus majus*, ed. Henry Bridges, Oxford: Clarendon Press.

Schlund, Erhard, OFM (1911a), "Petrus Peregrinus von Maricourt. Sein Leben und seine Schriften. Ein Beitrag zur Roger Baco-Forschung," *Archivum Franciscanum Historicum* 4, pp. 436–55.

——(1911b), "Petrus Peregrinus von Maricourt. Sein Leben und seine Schriften. Ein Beitrag zur Roger Baco-Forschung (Fortsetzung)," *Archivum Franciscanum Historicum* 4, pp. 633–43.

——(1912), "Petrus Peregrinus von Maricourt. Sein Leben und seine Schriften. Ein Beitrag zur Roger Baco-Forschung (Schluss)," *Archivum Franciscanum Historicum* 5, pp. 22–40.

98

Pseudo-Dionysius

ERIC D. PERL

Pseudo-Dionysius the Areopagite (fl. ca. 500), was a Byzantine philosopher-theologian who wrote under the name of Dionysius the Areopagite, an Athenian converted to Christianity by St. Paul's sermon on "the unknown God" (Acts 17: 34). His true identity is unknown, but he was probably a Syrian and almost certainly a monk. The *corpus Dionysiacum*, as his works are often called, consists of four treatises (*On Divine Names*, *On Mystical Theology*, *On the Celestial Hierarchy*, *On the Ecclesiastical Hierarchy*) and ten letters. The writer (henceforth called Dionysius) refers in these works to various others, but whether these were actually written but have not survived, or are merely part of his fictive identity, is uncertain. The corpus was translated into Latin in the ninth century, and throughout the Middle Ages was received with little question as the work of the disciple of St. Paul. Its sub-apostolic authorship was first seriously questioned in the fifteenth century and definitively disproved in the nineteenth, principally because it shows extensive and unmistakable influence of the late pagan Neoplatonist Proclus (412–85). Other evidence dates the corpus between 476 and 532. More recently, it has become clear that Dionysius' thought is no mere superficial "Christianization" of Proclus, but draws on and synthesizes several distinct but interrelated traditions, including not only Neoplatonic philosophy but also the Alexandrian school of Philo, Clement, and Origen; the Cappadocian Fathers, especially Gregory of Nyssa; and the spiritual and liturgical traditions of Egyptian and Syrian monasticism. Despite their author's pseudonymity, Dionysius' works have continued to be widely studied and valued, not only because of their powerful influence on later thought, but also for their intrinsic philosophical and theological significance.

God beyond being

The starting point of Dionysius' philosophy is the doctrine that God is "beyond being" (*hyperousios*), the ground of all beings but not himself any being, and so also absolutely unknowable and ineffable. "For if all acts of knowledge are of beings and have their limit in beings, that which is beyond all being also transcends all knowledge" (1990–1, *De divinis nominibus* (*DN*) I.4, 593A). Dionysius himself offers no philosophical justification for this position, but it is grounded in Neoplatonic arguments which must be understood if we are to grasp Dionysius' philosophy. The Neoplatonic doctrine that the One or the Good, the first principle of reality, is beyond being and knowledge, is a direct consequence of the fundamental law that to be is to be intelligible. This law goes back at least as far as Parmenides,

540

and is central to the thought of Plato and to all Neoplatonism. It affirms that whatever is, is able to be thought, to be apprehended by the mind. It would be incoherent to postulate a being which cannot be thought, for to do so would already be to think such a being. Intelligibility, therefore, is co-extensive with being, or indeed is its very meaning: that which is, is that which can be apprehended by the mind. From this it follows that to be is to be determinate, or finite, for only a definite, finite "this" can be grasped by the intellect. Further, any being *is* in virtue of the determination, the totality of features or attributes, whereby it is what it is, and thus is intellectually graspable. Every being, therefore, is both finite and derivative, dependent for its existence on its determination.

Consequently, the first principle of reality cannot be any being. If it were, it would be finite and hence not first but dependent on its determination. It would, moreover, share an attribute, namely being itself, with all other beings. It would be one member within the totality of all things rather than the source of that totality, and the shared attribute would be anterior to both the supposed first principle and all other things. Consequently Neoplatonism maintains that the source of all things is not any being, any object of thought, but is rather "beyond being" and beyond the grasp of intellect. This Plotinian argument, although not presented in Dionysius' works, underlies the whole of his thought and furnishes the starting point whose implications he unfolds.

The doctrine of God as beyond being and knowledge does not mean that true discourse about God consists merely in negative propositions, such as 'God is not' or 'God is unknowable'. Negation is an intellectual activity and as such still identifies God in conceptual terms. It is no more correct to say "God is not" than to say "God is." To deny existence, or any attribute, of God, is still to treat him as a conceptual object, defined by the possession or privation of various attributes. To say "God is unknowable" is in effect to identify him as an unknowable being and to lay claim to some knowledge of him. Hence Dionysius says that God is "beyond every negation and affirmation" (1990–1, *De mystica theologia* (*MT*) I.2, 1000B; cf. *MT* V, 1048B). God is not simply ineffable and unknowable, but beyond ineffability and unknowing (*hyperarrētos, hyperagnōston*, 1990–1, *DN* I.4, 592D). "Negative theology," for Dionysius as for Plotinus, consists therefore not in negations but in silence. We must "honor the hidden of the divinity, beyond mind and being, with unsearchable and sacred reverence of mind, and ineffable things with a wise silence" (*DN* I.3, 589AB). The mind's union with God "comes about in the cessation of every intellectual activity" (*DN* I.4, 593C; cf. *DN* I.4, 592CD), in complete "non-activity of all knowledge" (*MT* I.3, 1001A; cf. III.1, 1033C). This is no mere "mystical" effusion, but a rigorous philosophical deduction from the intelligibility of being. A "God" who either is or is not anything at all, who could be grasped by the mind whether positively or negatively, would not be God but a finite and therefore created being. "And if anyone, having seen God, understood what he saw, he did not see [God] himself, but something of those things of his which are and are known" (1990–1, *Epistolae* (*Ep.*) 1, 1065A). Every intellectual activity is an apprehension of some being, and therefore of something finite and created, not of God.

Creation as theophany

This philosophical insight raises the problem of how we can speak or think meaningfully of God at all. (See *DN* I.5, 593AB.) Dionysius' answer is that we can "name," or know, God, from all created things (i.e., all beings whatsoever) as their "cause" (*DN* I.5, 593D; I.6, 596A). To call God "cause" would appear to identify him as a being, as finite, as intelligible. But Dionysius understands the term 'cause' in a distinctively Neoplatonic sense. Since to be is to be determinate, any being depends for its existence on its determination, so that its determination is its cause of being. Hence, for Dionysius, God is the creator of all things as their constitutive determination, making each thing to be by making it *what* it is. Thus he is the being (i.e., "beingness") of all beings (e.g., *DN* V.4, 817C, 817D; *De coelesti hierarchia* (*CH*) IV.1, 177D), by which they are beings; the life of living things (*DN* I.3, 589C), by which they are living; and, in short, "all things in all things" (*DN* I.7, 596C). All the determinations or perfections of all things – and hence the entire content of creation – are God creatively present in them. Thus God can be "named," or known, only as he is causally present in all creatures. These causal perfections, which Dionysius variously calls "powers," "participations," "processions," "manifestations," or "names" of God, are God as he is participated in, i.e., is present in all creatures, as their constitutive determinations.

This Neoplatonic idea of creation as determination avoids making God, as cause, into another being beside his creatures. Since all the perfections of all things are differentiated presentations of God, it follows that God pre-contains all things in himself, without distinction (*DN* I.7, 597A). God is the "enfolding" of all things, and all things are the "unfolding" of God. He is not another thing, but "all beings and none of beings" (*DN* I.6, 596C), or, better, "all things in all things and nothing in any" (*DN* VII.3, 872A). He is "all things in all things" in that the whole of reality is the differentiated presence of God, and "nothing in any" in that he is not himself any one thing, distinguished from others within that whole and constituted by this distinction. Thus he is at once utterly transcendent and utterly immanent: transcendent in that he is not any being, not included within reality as any member of it; immanent in that he is immediately present to all things as their being and all their perfections.

The creation of the world, then, the production or emergence of all things from God, is the differentation, distribution, or impartation whereby God is differently present to all things and thus makes them be. (See *DN* II.11, 649BC.) God is not a differentiated being, but the very Differentiation in virtue of which each creature is itself and so is. He is named

> the Different, since God becomes providentially present to all things and "all things in all things" for the preservation of all . . . Let us consider the divine difference . . . as the single multiplication of himself and the uniform processions of his multiple generation to all things. (*DN* IX.5, 912D)

In understanding creation as differentiation, Dionysius follows the Neoplatonic doctrine of remaining and procession. 'Remaining' refers to the containment of effects in their causal determination, without distinction, while 'procession' means the differentiation whereby the effects are constituted as realities distinct from each other and thus from the cause. Hence the production of the world, for Dionysius as for the Neoplatonists, is the manifestation in intelligible multiplicity of its principle, not the making of other beings additional to that principle. Thus creation is nothing but theophany, the manifestation of God: the divine Nothing is known in all things as their intelligible perfections.

Goodness, beauty, and love

In Neoplatonic metaphysics, the effect not only remains in and proceeds from its cause, but also reverts or returns to it. For the constitutive determination of a being is also its goodness or end. To be is to be good, because any being is what it is, and so is, by fulfilling its proper nature, by being good in its proper way. Therefore, every being tends towards its determination, its cause of being, as its goodness, and any being is only insofar as it achieves this perfection. Thus the procession of all things from their cause and their return to it, the *exitus-reditus* cycle characteristic of Neoplatonism and adopted by Dionysius, is a dynamic expression of participation, the relation of that which is determined, the "effect," to its constitutive determination, the "cause."

God, as the determination of all things, is therefore at once their source and their end. 'The Good' thus names God as the determinative principle in which all things are contained, from which all proceed, and to which all return.

> The Good is . . . that from which all things subsist and are brought forth as from an all-perfect cause, and in which all things are held together as in an all-powerful foundation . . . and towards which all things are reverted, as each to its proper end. (*DN* IV.4, 700AB)

The characteristic activity of each being, its enactment of its own nature, and hence its very existence, is its reversion to God in its proper mode.

> It is the Good . . . which all things desire, the intellectual and rational beings cognitively, the sensitive sensitively, those without a share in sense-perception by the implanted motion of vital desire, and those which are lifeless and merely exist by the mere fitness for existential participation. (*DN* IV.4, 700B)

Since the proper activity of each being is its reversion, this reversion to God, no less than its procession from him, is its being created: to be, for each creature, is to revert to God, the Good, in its proper way. "All things by desiring the Beautiful and Good do and wish all that they do and wish" (*DN* IV.10, 708A); and the most fundamental act of any being, of which all other acts are specifications, is to be. Thus all things exist only insofar as they desire or tend towards God as their goodness.

This goodness is also their beauty. For Dionysius, as for Plotinus and Augustine, the beauty of each thing is the form, the determination in it, which is what makes it to be. Thus, just as to be is to be good, so to be is to be beautiful. Each being is by being beautiful in its proper way. "From this Beautiful is being to all beings, each being beautiful according to its proper determination [*logon*]" (*DN* IV.7, 704A). And this constitutive beauty is God himself in the creature as its perfection, at once its source and its end. As Beauty, God creatively distributes himself to all things and creatively draws all things to himself.

> The Beautiful beyond being is called Beauty on account of the beauty imparted from itself to all beings in the manner appropriate to each . . . and as calling [*kaloun*] all things to itself, wherefore it is called Beauty [*kallos*]. (*DN* IV.7, 701C)

All the aspects of divine causation are encapsulated in this name:

> The Beautiful is the principle of all things as making cause . . . and limit of all things, and cherished, as final cause, since for the sake of the Beautiful all things come to be; and paradigmatic [cause], in that all things are determined according to it. (*DN* IV.7, 704A)

In short, each thing is what it is, and so is, insofar as it proceeds from and reverts to – i.e., participates in – God as Goodness and Beauty.

The cycle of procession and return underlies Dionysius' account of God as Love (*eros*). The name 'Love' signifies, first, God's creative procession or self-distribution to all things.

> Love, the very benefactor of beings, pre-existing in excess in the Good, did not permit itself to remain unfertile in itself, but moved itself to productive action, in the excess which is generative of all things. (*DN* IV.10, 708AB)

And again,

> Divine love is ecstatic ... The very cause of all things, by the beautiful and good love of all things, through excess of erotic goodness, becomes out of himself in his providences towards all beings ... and is led down from being above all things and beyond all things to being in all things, according to an ecstatic power beyond being, without going out from himself. (*DN* IV.13, 712AB)

Since God is not any determinate, self-contained being, but the creative differentiation of all things, his being "in himself" consists in his being "out of himself" and "in all things" as their constitutive determinations. Like the name 'Different', the name 'Love' describes God as the distribution which establishes all things.

But 'Love' refers to reversion as well as procession. All things are only insofar as they revert towards God as Beauty and Goodness, so that the creature's very being is its reversion to, its desire or love for, God. And this love of the creature for God, in virtue of which the creature is, is God's attracting it to himself as its perfection. The entire cycle of procession and reversion, involving God's self-distribution to the creature, the creature's emergence from God, the creature's movement towards God, and God's drawing the creature to himself, is participation, the relation of the creature to God as its constitutive determination. This cyclical metaphysical motion, which is the very being of all things, is what Dionysius describes as the "whirling circle" of divine love (*DN* IV.14, 712C–713A).

Evil

Drawing heavily on Proclus, Dionysius offers a characteristically Neoplatonic solution to the problem of evil, much like those of Gregory of Nyssa and AUGUSTINE. Evil is not a positive attribute, but only a deficiency of goodness and, therefore, of being, in a creature which to some extent is good and is. "All beings, insofar as they are, are good and from the Good; and insofar as they are deprived of the Good, they are neither good nor beings" (*DN* IV.20, 720B). On this ground Dionysius, like Proclus, firmly rejects the notion that matter is evil or the source of evil. (See *DN* IV.28, 729AB.) Evil, rather, lies in the failure of any being to fulfill its constitutive nature, to perform its proper activities, and thus fully to be. The demons, for example, "are not evil by nature, but by the lack of the angelic goods" (*DN* IV.23, 725B), i.e., the constitutive perfections proper to them as angels. "The evil in them is from the falling away from their proper goods, and a change, the weakness ... of the perfection befitting them as angels" (*DN* IV.34, 733C).

Since the goodness and being of every creature is its reverting to or loving God in its proper way, any creature is evil, i.e., fails to be, insofar as it fails to love God. Dionysius adheres to the Platonic principle that all activity is motivated by desire for some good, and hence ultimately for God, as the Goodness of all good things. (See *DN* IV.19, 716C; IV.31,

544

732C.) Even seemingly evil actions, such as those performed in lust or anger, aim at some good, or they would not take place at all.

> And he who desires the worst life, in wholly desiring life, and that which seems best to him, by the very fact of desiring, and desiring life, and looking to a best life, participates in the Good. (*DN* IV.20, 720BC)

All beings, therefore, insofar as they have any desire and thus any activity, any being at all, desire goodness, love God, and are good. Even the demons

> are not altogether without a share in the Good, insofar as they are and live and think, and in short, there is some motion of desire in them . . . In that they are, they are both from the Good, and are good, and desire the Beautiful and Good, desiring the realities, to be and to live and to think. (*DN* IV.23, 725BC)

Conversely, insofar as any being desires evil, it is desiring nothing, and to that extent failing to desire and hence to be. "And if they do not desire the Good, they desire non-being. And this is not desire, but a failure of what is truly desire" (*DN* IV.34, 733D). Evil, then, consists not in any positive activity, but in a failure to love God and so to act, i.e., to be.

Hierarchy

The hierarchical ordering of creation follows from Dionysius' understanding of the relation of creatures to God. He explains that the different divine "names" or processions are not a multiplicity of quasi-divine entities intermediate between creatures and God, but are rather God himself as he is present in different creatures. (See *DN* V.2, 816C–817A; XI.6, 953C–956A.) Thus, while each one is God, the processions are hierarchically ranked in order of universality. Goodness is highest because as Goodness God is present in all beings and non-beings (the latter category apparently means matter); Being is next, since it is present in all beings; next comes Life, which is present in all living beings; next Wisdom, which is present in all cognitive beings. (See *DN* V.1, 816B.) The order of the divine processions is therefore a mirror image of the ranks of creatures:

Goodness
Being
Life
Wisdom

cognitive living beings
living beings
mere beings (inanimate objects)
matter

The lower processions are included within the higher as their specifications, so that nothing can possess a higher perfection without also possessing the lower ones: living things, in possessing life, also have being, and cognitive things, in possessing cognition, also have being and life. In fact, all these processions are higher and lower modes of the same divine presence that constitutes all things. Thinking, for example, is the higher mode of living and

545

being proper to cognitive things, while mere being is the lower mode of living and thinking proper to inanimate objects. (See *DN* V.3, 817B.) The increasing specification extends to the determinative principles or *logoi* of particulars, whereby each individual creature is itself and so is.

> In the cause of all things the paradigms of all beings pre-exist . . . Paradigms . . . are the being-making [*ousiopoious*] *logoi* of all beings, which pre-exist uniformly in God, which theology calls pre-determinations . . . determinative and creative of beings, according to which the beyond-being both predetermined and produced all beings. (*DN* V.8, 824C)

Here Dionysius has, in effect, a doctrine of "forms of individuals" which are contained in more universal forms as their specifications.

Thus God is present in each thing, or each thing participates in God, "analogously" (*analogos*) or "according to its rank" (*kat' axian*): God is in each thing in the distinct mode proper to and constitutive of that thing. Divine justice consists not in an egalitarian leveling but rather in the hierarchical order whereby each creature is established in its proper place. (See *DN* VIII.7, 896AB). Hence there is no conflict between the hierarchical ordering of creation and the immediate presence of God to all things. Each creature participates directly in God precisely by filling its proper place in the hierarchy of beings. Since God is not any being but "all things in all things and nothing in any," he does not stand at the summit of that hierarchy, but transcends and permeates the whole:

> The goodness of the Godhead which is beyond all things extends from the highest and most venerable substances to the last, and is still above all, the higher not outstripping its excellence nor the lower going beyond its containment. (*DN* IV.4, 697C)

Knowledge

"Wisdom," the distinctive perfection of all cognitive beings (angels, humans, and animals), is subdivided into intellection, discursive reason, and sense perception. These are not three different faculties with three different objects, but higher and lower ways of apprehending reality. Again, the higher power includes the lower in itself, so that, for example, "the angels know things on earth, knowing them not by sense perception (although they are sensible things), but by the proper power and nature of the deiform intellect" (*DN* VII.2, 869C). Here Dionysius follows Proclus' doctrine that whatever is known is known according to the mode of the knower, not of the object. The modes of cognition are distinguished, in standard Neoplatonic manner, by the degree of unity in which each apprehends reality. Intellection is the most and sense the least unified mode of cognition, but even sense perceptions are "an echo of wisdom" (*DN* VII.2, 868C) in that they are an apprehension, however dim or dispersed, of reality, the manifestation of God. As the soul ascends from sense to discursive reason to intellection, it gathers its content into ever greater unity. At the peak, when absolute unification is achieved, intellectual knowledge passes over into the silence of unknowing.

> Souls, uniting and gathering their manifold reasonings into one intellectual purity, go forward in the way and order proper to them through immaterial and partless intellection to the union above intellection. (*DN* XI.2, 949D; cf. *MT* III, 1033BC)

546

Thus the soul's "mystical" encounter with God in the "cessation of intellectual activities" is in continuity with the cognitive ascent. The union with God in unknowing is not opposed to the intellect's function of knowing beings, but is rather its goal and consummation.

There is no fundamental opposition, then, between sense and intellect, for they are higher and lower modes of the same activity, the apprehension of reality. Nor is it the case that God is known by intellect but inaccessible to sense. Rather, God is the object of every cognition, including sense perception, and of none, even intellection: of none, because he is not any being, any object for the mind; of all, because all being, all that is available to cognition in any mode, is nothing but a finite presentation of God.

> God . . . is known by knowledge, and by unknowing, and of him there is intellection, and reason, and science, and touching, and sense-perception, and opinion, and imagination, and name . . . and he is neither thought, nor spoken, nor named . . . and he is all things in all things and nothing in any, and he is known to all from all and to none from any. (*DN* VII.3, 872A)

Symbolism

Since, apart from creation, God is not an object for any mode of cognition, and is known only as finitely manifested in beings, he can be known only through created symbols. Any non-symbolic knowledge would necessarily be knowledge of some being, not of God. "It is not possible for the thearchic ray to illuminate us otherwise than anagogically cloaked in the variety of the sacred veils" (*CH* I.2, 121B). Paradoxically, God can "illuminate" us, i.e. be presented or revealed to us, only insofar as he is "veiled" or concealed from us. A symbol, in that it expresses God but is not God himself, at once presents and leaves him behind, and thus makes God known without objectifying him as a being. Only in a symbol can he be encountered without his inaccessibility being violated, and hence only in a symbol can true divinity be encountered at all. Dionysius expresses this twofold nature of symbolism, at once revealing and concealing, in his use of the word *probeblesthai*, which means both "present" and "shield." Created symbols are *probeblēmena*, presentations/shields of God (*Ep.* 9.1, 1105BC), and the entire order of being, the whole of creation, is set forth (*probebletai*) as a symbol of God, a presentation which shields and a shield which presents (*DN* V.5, 820A; V.6, 820C).

Consequently, far from denigrating symbolic knowledge of God in favor of an (impossible) non-symbolic encounter, Dionysius exalts symbols as our only access to the inaccessible divinity.

> We must, then . . . cross over into the sacred symbols in a way befitting the sacred, and not despise them, because they are the offspring and impressions of the divine marks, and manifest images of the ineffable and supernatural visions. (*Ep.* 9.2, 1108C)

Dionysius' doctrine of creatures as symbols of God is thus another version of creation as theophany, of God's absolute transcendence and immanence.

Christological consummation

It is artificial to abstract the "philosophical" content of Dionysius' thought from its "theological" aspects, for Dionysius recognizes no such distinction, but has a single, undifferentiated vision of reality in its relation to God. Thus his metaphysics cannot be fully understood apart from its consummation in Christ, nor can his doctrines of Christ, salvation, the Church, and the sacraments be understood apart from his metaphysics. Dionysius presents the incarnation in terms of symbolism and theophany, and thus in continuity with the metaphysics of creation:

> The beyond-being, out of his hiddenness, for revelation to us, has come forth, becoming a being in a human way. But he is hidden after the revelation, or, to speak more divinely, even in the revelation; for this is the hidden mystery of Jesus, inexpressible by any word or mind; but what is said remains ineffable, and what is thought, unknowable. (*Ep.* 3, 1069B)

The expression Dionysius repeatedly uses in reference to the Incarnation, "the beyond-being becomes a being" (*ho hyperousios ousiōmenos, ousiōthe*; *Ep.* 4, 1072B) could equally, in light of his metaphysics, refer to all creation. Incarnation, God becoming manifest as a being, is therefore the model for all creation, which thus shares in this "incarnational" nature. And since the world's fall into evil is a loss of being, its salvation in Christ is its restoration to the fullness of being, to its status as theophany. The "ecclesiastical hierarchy," the liturgical, sacramental life of the Church, is the realization and fulfillment of reality as symbol, as the presence and manifestation of the inaccessible, unmanifest God.

The importance of Dionysius as a source for later medieval philosophy can hardly be overstated. His thought was largely adopted by JOHN SCOTUS ERIUGENA and had a powerful influence on MEISTER ECKHART and NICHOLAS OF CUSA. He was also the principal channel by which Neoplatonism – a more authentic and philosophically sophisticated Neoplatonism than Augustine's – entered more "mainstream" medieval philosophy. The present brief survey has brought to light many themes that are familiar in thirteenth-century scholasticism: the radical transcendence of God, and the inadequacy of all thought and language with regard to him; the transcendentals, especially goodness, beauty, and being; creation as a system of signs or symbols of God; participation; hierarchy; the procession of all things from God and their return to him; the metaphysics of divine love; and evil as deficiency of being. In some cases through adoption, in others by transformation of his ideas, scholastic philosophy draws extensively on Dionysius, and none of these classic themes can be adequately understood without reference to him.

Even more important than Dionysius' influence, however, is the intrinsic value of his thought. His uncompromisingly ontological approach to all topics, including love, evil, symbolism, and mystical union, is a needed alternative to the subjective, epistemological, moral, and psychological approaches that characterize so much of modern thought. Most importantly, he understands divine transcendence in such a radical way, surpassing any form of "ontotheology," that it coincides with immanence. This enables us to avoid both the monism that identifies God with the world and the dualism that posits him as another being alongside it. Thus we can affirm God's transcendence without separating him from the world, and regain the classical vision of the sacred, symbolic cosmos, filled with and manifesting transcendent divinity. The metaphysics of creation as theophany thus lets us return from the modern, scientific-technological stance to a contemplative-liturgical stance towards the world. Finally, the doctrine of procession and return, the dynamic expression of this metaphysics, offers a rationally grounded, philosophical vision of reality as the Great Dance, in which beauty is the beginning and end of all things and love is the foundation and moving principle of being.

Bibliography

Primary source

(1990–1), *Corpus Dionysiacum*, 2 vols., ed. B. R. Suchla, G. Heil, and A. M. Ritter, Berlin and New York: De Gruyter.

Secondary sources

Balthasar, Hans Urs von (1984), "Denys," in *The Glory of the Lord: A Theological Aesthetics*, vol. 2: *Studies in Theological Style: Clerical Styles*, trans. Erasmo Leiva-Merikakis, ed. Joseph Fessio and John Riches, San Francisco and New York: Ignatius Press.

Golitzin, Alexander (1994), *Et Introibo ad Altare Dei: The Mystagogy of Dionysius Areopagita with Special Reference to his Predecessors in the Eastern Christian Tradition*, Thessalonica: Patriarchikon Chidryma Paterikon.

99

Radulphus Brito

GORDON A. WILSON

Radulphus Brito, also known as Ralph the Breton (b. ca. 1270; d. ca. 1320), sometimes also identified as Raoul de Hotot (Radulphus de Hoitot), was probably born in Brittany. By 1296 he was already a master of arts in Paris and he joined the masters in the theology faculty by 1311. In 1315 he became "provisor" of the Sorbonne, a position he maintained until his death.

It is unfortunate that few works of Brito are edited and available to current scholars, because he was both prolific and influential. His philosophical works reflect his career in the arts faculty. He authored questions on Priscian, the *Isagoge* of Porphyry, the *Categories*, *Peri hermeneias*, *Sex principiorum*, *De divisione* of Boethius, *De differentiis topicis* of Boethius, *Prior Analytics*, *Posterior Analytics*, *Topics*, *Sophistical Refutations*, *De anima*, *Physics*, *Meteorologica*, and *Parva mathematicalia*, as well as *Sophismata* and possibly *Questions on the Metaphysics*. His more theological works include *Questions on Lombard's Sentences I–III*, *Quaestiones in vesperis* (Evening Questions), and a *Quodlibet*. Of these, only his *Questions on Book III of De anima*, the questions on Boethius' *Topics*, *Questions on Priscian minor*, the prologues to his *Questions on the Old Logic* and to his *Questions on the Sophistical Refutations*, some *sophismata*, and a long section from the *Questions on Porphyry's Isagoge* have been edited.

Brito had an influence in Paris and elsewhere. He was considered the most important of a group of logicians known as *modistae*, thinkers who were committed to the notion that scientific knowledge was knowledge of the universal. He was particularly studied in Italy, and in the 1400s some of his work was translated into Greek by Gennadios. He is perhaps best known today for his epistemology and semantic theory, especially his ideas concerning second intentions and universals. However, because so much of his work remains in manuscript form and unedited, much of his philosophy is unavailable and unstudied.

Bibliography

Primary sources

(1974), *Quaestiones in Aristotelis librum tertium De anima*, ed. W. Fauser, in *Der Kommentar des Radulphus Brito zu Buch III De anima*, Beiträge zur Geschichte der Philosophie und Theologie des Mittelalters NF 12, Münster: Aschendorff.

(1975), *Sophisma "Aliquis homo est species,"* ed. J. Pinborg, in "Radulphus Brito's sophism on second intentions," *Vivarium* 13, pp. 119–52.

(1978), *Sophisma 'Rationale est animal'*, ed. S. Ebbesen, in "The Sophism *Rationale est animal* by Radulphus Brito," *Cahiers de l'Institut du Moyen-âge Grec et Latin* 24, pp. 85–120.

(1978), *Quaestiones super libros Topicorum Boethii*, ed. N. J. Green-Pedersen and J. Pinborg, in "Radulphus Brito: Commentary on Boethius' *De differentiis topicis* and the sophism *Omnis homo est omnis homo*," *Cahiers de l'Institut du Moyen-âge Grec et Latin* 26, pp. 1–92.

(1978), *Sophisma 'Omnis homo est omnis homo'*, ed. N. J. Green-Pedersen and J. Pinborg, in "Radulphus Brito: Commentary on Boethius' *De differentiis topicis* and the sophism *Omnis homo est omnis homo*," *Cahiers de l'Institut du Moyen-âge Grec et Latin* 26, pp. 93–114.

(1980), *Quaestiones super librum Porphyrii*, ed. J. Pinborg, *Cahiers de l'Institut du Moyen-âge Grec et Latin* 35, pp. 56–142.

(1980), *Quaestiones super Priscianum minorem*, ed. H. W. Enders and J. Pinborg, in *Grammatica speculativa* 3/1–2, Stuttgart and Bad Cannstatt: Fromman-Holzboog.

(1981–2), *Quaestiones super Artem veterem* and *Quaestiones super librum Elenchorum*, ed. S. Ebbesen and J. Pinborg, in "Gennadios and western scholasticism: Radulphus Brito's *Ars vetus* in Greek translation," *Classica et Mediaevalia* 33, pp. 263–319.

Secondary sources

Ebbesen, S. and Pinborg, J. (1981–2), "Gennadios and western scholasticism: Radulphus Brito's *Ars vetus* in Greek translation," *Classica et Mediaevalia* 33, pp. 263–319.

McMahon, William E. (1981), "Radulphus Brito on the sufficiency of the categories," *Cahiers de l'Institut du Moyen-âge Grec et Latin* 39, pp. 81–96.

Pinborg, J. (1967), *Die Entwicklung der Sprachtheorie im Mittelalter*, *Beiträge zur Geschichte der Philosophie und Theologie des Mittelalters*, Texte und Untersuchungen 42/2, Münster: Aschendorff; Copenhagen: Frost-Hansen.

——(1972), *Logik und Semantik im Mittelalter. Ein Überblick*, Stuttgart and Bad Cannstatt: Frommann-Holzboog.

——(1980), "Radulphus Brito on universals," *Cahiers de l'Institut du Moyen-âge Grec et Latin* 35, pp. 56–142.

100

Ralph Strode

KIMBERLY GEORGEDES

Ralph Strode (fl. 1360–87) was an English logician at Oxford, and a fellow of Merton College in about 1360. While at Oxford he knew Wyclif, whom he engaged in discussions on theological issues. In the 1370s he gave up his academic career to become a lawyer and took a position in London, where he made the acquaintance of Chaucer. Strode died in 1387 (1973, pp. iii–iv).

While at Merton College, Strode wrote a series of treatises on logic, which were intended as a basic textbook for students: *De arte logica, De principiis logicalibus, Tractatus suppositionum, Consequentiae, Obligationes,* and the *Tractatus insolubilium.* They are collectively known as the *Logica* and survive as a whole in only one manuscript (Oxford Bodleian *Canonici Miscellaneous* 219), although some of the individual treatises are found separately elsewhere.

Strode's influence as a logician did not emerge until nearly fifty years after his death, and then primarily in Italy, where his *Consequentiae* and *Obligationes* had the greatest impact. There are over forty manuscripts of the former, all apparently of Italian origin, and most of which are still in Italian libraries. The *Consequentiae* were also edited by three different scholars and underwent ten printings in Italy in the fifteenth and sixteenth centuries. The *Obligationes* exists in at least eleven Italian manuscripts and underwent at least six printed editions in Italy. Fifteenth-century Italian commentators on Strode contributed to an understanding of his logic (1973, pp. iv–viii).

Bibliography

Primary source
(1973), *Tractatus de consequentiis*, ed. and trans. Wallace K. Seaton, in "An edition and translation of the *Tractatus de consequentiis* by Ralph Strode, fourteenth-century logician and friend of Geoffrey Chaucer," Ph.D. dissertation, University of California, Berkeley.

Secondary sources
Blackley, F. D. (1967), "Ralph Strode," in *New Catholic Encyclopedia*, vol. XII, p. 71.
Maierù, Alfonso (1982), "Le Ms. Oxford Canonici Misc. 219 et la *Logica* de Strode," in Alfonso Maierù, ed., *English Logic in Italy in the 14th and 15th Centuries* (pp. 87–110), Rome: Bibliopolis.
Spade, Paul Vincent (1975), *The Mediaeval Liar: A Catalogue of the Insolubilia-Literature*, Toronto: Pontifical Institute of Mediaeval Studies.

101

Ramon Lull

CHARLES H. LOHR

Ramon Lull (b. 1232/3; d. 1316) was born on the island of Majorca, which was taken in the Reconquista by James I of Aragon. In his youth, Lull was attached to the royal court, especially to that of James's son, the future James II of Majorca.

First period (about 1263–74)

At the age of 30 years (in about 1263) Lull had a vision of Christ crucified, which led him to abandon the worldly life he had been leading and to attempt to bring infidels to Christianity by writing a book about the true faith. He left Majorca, made pilgrimages to Rocamadour and Santiago de Compostela, finally returning to Barcelona, where he met the Dominican Raymond of Penyafort, who, as general of the order and then as adviser to James I, had encouraged the foundation of houses of the order for the study of the Arabic language and Muslim theology. In accordance with this program, Penyafort advised Lull not to study at Paris, as he had planned, but rather in his native Majorca.

There Lull began nine years of study (1265–74): Latin, Arabic (with a slave whom he had bought), philosophy, theology, and medicine, seeking a new way to present the Christian faith to nonbelievers. Lull had observed that two of the principal missionary efforts organized by the Dominican order in the kingdom of Aragon – the disputation of 1263 with the Jews in Barcelona (in which Ramon de Penyafort participated) and the attempt of the celebrated Dominican missionary, Raymond Martí, to convert the Muslim sultan of Tunis in 1268/9 – were futile because of the Dominican refusal to seek positive proofs of articles of the Christian faith. The vast *Libre de contemplació en Déu* of 1273/4 (*OE* II, *OO* IX–X), one of Lull's first works, represents his earliest attempt to find a new approach to the problem of God. The work offers almost 11,000 prayers in 365 chapters, 30 prayers per day for each of the days of the year. The *scala creaturarum* which is found in the *Libre* (prime matter, the firmament, elements, metals, plants, angels, men (dist. X–XI cap. 30–59)) betrays Lull's indebtedness to Neoplatonist speculation.

Second period (about 1274–89)

Lull's formative period culminated in the "illumination" at Mount Randa in Majorca, in about 1274, where he discovered the method of writing his book against the errors of the infidels: not as an Aristotelian theoretical science concerned with immutable truths, as the Dominicans had done, but rather as a productive art concerned with possibles to be realized. The first form of the Art is found in the *Ars compendiosa inveniendi veritatem* (Majorca, about 1274; *OO* I). In this early form sixteen fundamental principles (the divine names: good, great . . .) regarded as common to the three religions, Judaism, Islam, and Christianity, are employed for the purpose of discovering the true religion. The principles are grouped in multiples of four (elemental theory playing a basic role) and various combinatory figures are used to show the way in which the Art may be applied generally to the four university faculties of philosophy, theology, medicine, and law.

Although these ideas are at variance with Dominican apologetics, Lull did adopt the Dominican idea of the establishment of language schools for his missionary purpose. In 1276 he founded the monastery of Miramar on the north coast of Majorca, for the instruction of missionaries. From this time on Lull undertook, although residing principally at Majorca and Montpellier, frequent voyages in the effort to have monasteries founded on the model of Miramar. But this foundation was, owing to political difficulties, of short duration and his voyages were mostly in vain. An idea of Lull's missionary approach may be gained from the *Libre del gentili i dels tres savis* of this period, 1274–6 (*OE* I, *NE* II, *OO* II), a dialogue between the religions, in which a Muslim, a Jew, and a Christian present the teachings of their respective faiths – with remarkable tolerance – in the presence of a pagan scholar, who is brought to a belief in God, but makes no further commitment.

During this period, Lull composed some of his best-known works, writing in Catalan: *Doctrina pueril* (of 1274–6; *Ob* I); *Orde de cavalleria* (about 1279–83; *Ob* I, *OE* I); *Blanquerna* (Montpellier, 1283; *Ob* IX, *OE* I), a novel which includes the *Libre d'amic e amat*, a mystical dialogue; *Libre d'intenció* (1283; *Ob* XVIII, *OO* VI), which distinguishes, in accord with the notion of the Art as productive, two intentions of an action: God should be loved for himself (first intention), while all other things are only means – instruments – to this end (second intention), with sin reversing this order; and *Felix* or *Libre de meravelles* (Paris, 1288–9; *OE* I).

The *Ars demonstrativa* and the *Liber chaos* (both about 1283, in Montpellier) together presented Lull's view of the cosmos, including the possibles in the mind of God the Creator. They sought to give his Art the certitude of an Aristotelian science by adding to the Aristotelian proofs *quia* and *propter quid* a third form of proof valid for the infinite divine attributes, a method further developed later in the *Liber de demonstratione per aequiparantiam*, of 1305. The *Ars demonstrativa* also added, in accord with Lull's method of invention, a great number of topical questions and continued the attempt to apply the Art to the four university faculties. But in this effort the Art became so complicated that it was rejected by the students of Paris on Lull's first visit there, in 1288–9.

Third period (1290–1308)

Lull's experience in Paris led him to revise the Art, simplifying its elements in the *Ars inventiva veritatis* (Montpellier, 1290; *OO* V; the work was translated into Arabic in 1291). This work groups the principles of the Art in multiples of three, rather than the previous four. The absolute principles are definitively reduced to nine (*bonitas, magnitudo, duratio; potentia, sapientia, voluntas; virtus, veritas, gloria*), and nine relative principles (*differentia, concordantia, contrarietas; principium, medium, finis; maioritas, aequalitas, minoritas*) are introduced. This system is one of Lull's greatest contributions to the history of philosophy.

The *scala creaturarum* is included in the *Ars inventiva* in the form of nine "subjects" (*elementativa, vegetativa, sensitiva, imaginativa, rationalis, moralis [instrumentalis], caelestialis, angelica, divina*), whereby the insertion of imagination as a step in the *scala* makes it possible for us to situate Lull's ideas, not within contemporary Latin, but rather Muslim and Jewish, thought.

The fact that the principles are defined in terms of Lull's theory of the correlatives of action (principle, term, and bond: "*Bonitas est id, ratione cuius bonum agit bonum*") enables us to place Lull, more precisely, in the context of Sufi speculation. The *Ars inventiva* is composed in accordance with topical invention, but it is clear from the section *De punctis transcendentibus* (dist. III, reg. 8) that Lull conceived his Art first of all as a method of ascent. It proceeds by a double *transcensus*, a transcending of sense-knowledge by the ascent from the positive to the comparative degree of the principles (*bonum → melius*) and by a transcending of rational knowledge by the ascent from the comparative to the superlative degree (*melius → optimum*). At this highest degree of knowledge the differences constituting the first two degrees of the various divine names, as they are manifest in creation, are transcended. At this degree the mystic encounters – as in ANSELM OF CANTERBURY – the God in whom he can no longer distinguish between goodness and greatness; God is both the best and the greatest *in superlativitate*. These ideas were applied by Lull to mystical theology in the *Ars amativa* of this period (1290; *OO* VI, *Ob* XVII).

From 1290 to 1297, Lull used Montpellier as a home-base, but lived mostly in Italy, having received a licence from the Franciscan general to preach in the convents of the order. In 1292 Lull made a visit to the papal court, where he wrote one of his many tracts on the crusade, the *Libre de passatge*. In the same year, he planned a first missionary voyage to North Africa, going from Genoa to Tunis. But shortly before his departure, he was seized with fear at the idea of his possible martyrdom. After a long psychological crisis, which ended with his deciding on a Franciscan, rather than the Dominican, approach to the missions, he embarked for Tunis, where he regained his composure and began discussions with Muslim theologians about the true religion. Arrested by the authorities and banished from the country, he returned to Naples, where, in 1293–4, he received permission to preach at Muslim places in the area.

In Naples, Lull completed his *Tabula generalis* (begun in Tunis and Naples 1294; *OO* V, *Ob* XVI), a work that developed the combinatory aspect of his Art. He substituted nine fundamental questions (*utrum, quid, de quo, quare, quantum, quale, quando, ubi, quo modo/cum quo*) for the original *regulae* of the *Ars inventiva* and associated the letters B to K with the principles, the subjects, and the questions of the Art respectively, so as to facilitate the combinations of the generalized *tabula*. Using the four figures of the *Ars inventiva*, Lull drew the fourth figure out to 1,680 combinations.

In Naples, in 1294, Lull also wrote the *Liber de quinque sapientibus* (*OO* II), an interreligious dialogue, in which a Latin theologian, using Lullian methods, disputes with a Greek about the procession of the Holy Spirit, with a Nestorian about the unity of the person in Christ, with a Jacobite (monophysite) about the two natures in Christ, and with a Saracen about the Trinity and Incarnation. A mystical tract, *Flores amoris et intelligentiae* (1294; *OO* VI, *Ob* XVIII), was dedicated to Pope Celestine V, with a petition for his missionary plans. When Celestine abdicated in December of the same year, Lull followed the new pope, Boniface VIII, to Rome, composing during his stay there (in 1295–6) a monumental encyclopedia, the *Arbor scientiae*, in which he presents his conception of all the contemporary disciplines as arts concerned with production, rather than as Aristotelian sciences concerned exclusively with theoretical knowledge (*Ob* XI–XIII).

After a brief sojourn in Montpellier, in 1296–7, Lull visited Paris for a second time in 1297–9, writing a great many works (edited in part in *OL* op. 76–81). At this time, he began a prolonged effort to rewrite the traditional liberal disciplines as productive arts, in accordance with a movement begun already in Islamic philosophy: *Tractatus novus de astronomia* (Paris, 1297; *OL* op. 79), *Geometria nova* (1299), rhetoric (1301), logic (1303), and even metaphysics and physics (both Paris, 1310; *OL* 156–7). In *De astronomia*, he worked out a system of astrology, calculating stellar influences through their effects on the elements. Extending the tree symbolism in his *Arbor philosophiae amoris* (Paris, 1298; *OO* VI, *Ob* XVIII, *OE* II), he pleaded for a philosophy valid not only for theoretical science, but also for the active love of God.

Having failed to persuade Philip the Fair of the importance of his projects, Lull left for Barcelona in 1299, receiving there permission to preach in the synagogues and mosques (*OL* op. 87–89). In 1300 he returned again to his native Majorca where he was also able to preach to the Muslims (*OL* op. 90–6). Having then learned that the Il-Khan of Persia was planning to attack Syria, Lull undertook a voyage to Cyprus in the vain hope that he might win the Mongol emperor for Christianity. In Cyprus, in 1301–2, Lull found it impossible to interest the King of Cyprus, Henri II de Lusignan, in his missionary projects, but he was able to write several works (*OL* op. 97–100), especially *Rhetorica nova* and *De natura*, and to meet with the ill-fated Master of the Templars, Jacques de Molay.

Returning by way of Majorca and Montpellier, Lull visited Genoa in 1303, writing there, among other things, the *Logica nova* (*OL* op. 101, *NE* IV), a general logic meant both for the sciences and for the arts. From 1303 to 1305 Lull resided at Montpellier, where he wrote *OL* op. 105–22, finishing especially *Ars magna praedicationis* (1304; *OL* op. 118); *Liber de ascensu et descensu intellectus*, where the subjects of the Art serve as steps in the *scala creaturarum* on the way of the intellect's ascent to God; *Liber de demonstratione per aequiparantiam*, which treats specifically the third form of proof described above; and *Liber de fine*, a further proposal for the crusade (all in 1305; *OL* op. 120–2).

In the years 1305 and 1306 he visited Paris, Barcelona (*OL* op. 123–4), Montpellier (*OL* op. 125), and Lyons (where he met Pope Clement V). In 1307, Lull sailed from Majorca for Bougie (in North Africa). Taking there a more confrontational approach in his discussions with the Muslim clerics, he was imprisoned for six months and then expelled from the country. On the return voyage, he lost all his property in a storm off Pisa.

In Pisa in 1308 he completed his *Ars generalis ultima* (begun 1305 in Lyons; *OL* op. 128), the definitive form of his Art, in which all the elements (the absolute and relative principles along with the subjects of the *Ars inventiva*, the questions of the *Tabula generalis*, and the figures of the earlier Arts) are brought together and combined systematically. The alphabet of the Art is now as follows:

Litterae	Principia absoluta	Principia relativa	Subiecta	Regulae
B	bonitas	differentia	Deus	utrum
C	magnitudo	concordantia	angelus	quid
D	duratio	contrarietas	caelum	de quo
E	potestas	principium	rationalis anima	quare
F	sapientia	medium	imaginativa	quantum
G	voluntas	finis	sensitiva	quale
H	virtus	maioritas	vegetativa	quando
J	veritas	aequalitas	elementativa	ubi
K	gloria	minoritas	instrumentativa	quomodo/cum quo

He also produced a short form of the Art in his *Ars brevis* (1308; *OL* op. 126), and provided a Latin account of his debate with a Muslim scholar at Bougie in his *Disputatio Raymundi christiani et Hamar saraceni* (1308; *OL* op. 131), along with various other works (*OL* op. 130–3).

In 1308–9 Lull was in Montpellier, where he composed *OL* op. 127, 134–53 in preparation for a visit to Paris, and finished a tract *De acquisitione Terrae Sanctae* (1309, *OL* op. 146 in prep.), in which the missionary method of the Dominicans (based on the Aristotelian theory of science) is explicitly rejected. He also visited Genoa, Marseilles (where he seems to have consulted with ARNALDUS DE VILLANOVA), and Avignon (where he again met Clement V).

Final period (1309–16)

During the years 1309–11 Lull resided in Paris, where he enjoyed considerable success, his Art being approved for lectures by the faculties of arts and of medicine. He wrote there some thirty works (*OL* op. 154–89), especially against Latin Averroism. The *Liber facilis scientiae* (*OL* op. 176) proposed Lull's final method of proof by way of contradictory syllogisms, a method further developed in *De novo modo demonstrandi* of 1312 (*OL* op. 199). This method is meant to advance from belief to understanding without having to appeal to the essences of things (as in the syllogism on which the method of the Dominicans was based). The question that is implicit in every belief is first expressed as two contradictory hypotheses, concluding that one of the hypotheses is true by drawing out the consequences of the other and showing that they are impossible. The *Vita coaetanea* (Paris 1311; *OL* op. 189), a sort of autobiography, dating also from the end of this period, proposed three causes to the king and the university: the establishment of schools for oriental languages, measures against the opinions of AVERROES, and the unification of the military orders for the recovery of the Holy Land.

At the Council of Vienne (1311), Lull presented these causes, gaining an important success in that chairs for the teaching of Hebrew, Arabic, and "Chaldean" were to be established at Paris, Oxford, Bologna, Salamanca, and the papal court. At Vienne, Lull composed *OL* op. 190–3. After the council Lull moved to Montpellier (1311; *OL* op. 194) and then to Majorca (1312–13) where he composed a body of sermons and various other works (*OL* op. 195–211). His last will and testament (Majorca, 1313; *OL* op. 212) repeats a wish expressed at the end of the *Vita* that three collections of his works be made at Paris, Genoa, and Majorca to assure their preservation and diffusion.

In 1313–14 Lull was in Messina, hoping vainly to gain the support of the Catalan king of Sicily, Frederick III, for his projects. Here he wrote *OL* op. 213–50. Finally, in 1314–15, Lull visited Tunis, then an important commercial center under the powerful influence of Catalonia. Here he composed a great number of short works (*OL* op. 251–80, some lost), some of them written in Arabic and addressed to the sultan, who pretended to be ready to convert to Christianity; they concern especially the doctrines of the Trinity and Incarnation. The last two of these works date from December 1315. Lull died early the next year, probably in Tunis. He is buried in Palma in the Church of St. Francis.

Bibliography

Primary sources
(*OO*) (1721–42), *Opera omnia*, vols. I–VI, IX–X, ed. I. Salzinger (vols. VII–VIII never appeared), Mainz; repr. 1965, Frankfurt-on-Main: Minerva.

(*OL*) (1959–67), *Opera latina*, ed. F. Stegmüller et al.; vols. I–V, Palma de Mallorca: Maioricensis Schola Lullistica; (1975–), vols. VIff., Turnhout: Brepols.

(*Ob*) (1906–50), *Obres*, ed. S. Galmés et al., 21 vols., Palma de Mallorca: M. Font.

(*OE*) (1957–60), *Obres essencials*, 2 vols., Barcelona: Maioricensis Schola Lullistica.

(*NE*) (1990), *Nova edició de les obres de Ramon Llull*, Palma de Mallorca: Patronat Ramon Llull.

(1985), *Selected Works of Ramon Llull, 1232–1316*, 2 vols., ed. A. Bonner, Princeton, NJ: Princeton University Press.

Secondary sources

Brummer, R. (1976), *Bibliographia lulliana: Ramon-Llull-Schrifttum 1870–1973*, Hildesheim.

Carreras y Artau, T. and J. (1939–42), *Historia de la filosofía española: Filosofía cristiana de los siglos XIII al XV*, 2 vols.; I, pp. 231–640 (Lull), II, pp. 7–437 (Lullism); Madrid: Real Academia de Ciencias Exactas, Físicas y naturales.

Colomer, E. (1961), *Nikolaus von Kues und Raimund Llull aus Handschriften der Kueser Bibliothek*, Berlin: De Gruyter.

Gayà, J. (1979), *La teoría luliana de los correlativos: Historia de su formación conceptual*, Palma de Mallorca: Maioricensis Schola Lullistica.

Hames, H. (2000), *The Art of Conversion*, Leiden: Brill.

Hillgarth, J. N. (1971), *Ramon Lull and Lullism in Fourteenth-century France*, Oxford: Clarendon Press.

Madre, A. (1973), *Die theologische Polemik gegen Raimundus Lullus*, Münster: Aschendorff.

Platzeck, E.-W. (1962–4), *Raimund Lull: Sein Leben, seine Werke, die Grundlagen seines Denkens*, 2 vols., Düsseldorf: L. Schwann.

Pring-Mill, R. D. F. (1961), *El microcosmos lul.lià*, Palma de Mallorca: Editorial Moll.

Rogent, E. and Duran, E. (1927), *Bibliografia de les impressions lul.lianes*, Barcelona: Institut d'Estudis Catalans; repr. Hildesheim: Gerstenberg.

Sala-Molins, L. (1974), *La Philosophie de l'amour chez Raymond Lulle*, Paris: Mouton.

Salleras, M. (1986), "Bibliografia lul.liana, 1974–1984," *Randa* 19, pp. 155–98.

Urvoy, D. (1980), *Penser l'Islam: les présupposés islamiques de l'art de Lull*, Paris: J. Vrin.

Yates, F. A. (1982), *Lull and Bruno: Collected Essays*, vol. I, London: Routledge and Kegan Paul.

102

Richard Brinkley

KIMBERLY GEORGEDES

Little is known of Richard Brinkley (fl. 1350–73), an English Franciscan theologian and logi-cian active in Oxford. He wrote a commentary on the *Sentences*, parts of which, along with selections from his *Quaestiones magnae* and *Quaestiones breves* have been edited by Z. Kaluza. The date of Brinkley's *Sentences* commentary is uncertain, but probably between 1352 and 1360. Kaluza has determined that the work was known in Paris by 1362 or 1363, and was cited by Étienne Gaudet, and John Hiltalingen of Basel, among others (Kaluza 1989, pp. 188–212). Brinkley also authored the now lost *Determinationes* (Gál and Wood 1980, pp. 76–7).

Brinkley is best known for his *Summa logicae.* Gál and Wood have placed the date of this work between 1360 and 1373 (p. 78), although Fitzgerald argues for 1356–63 (1987, pp. 3–12). Brinkley composed the *Logic* at the request of his superiors as a basic text for begin-ning logic students, it possibly being intended to replace WILLIAM OF OCKHAM's *Summa logicae.*

The *Logic* consists of seven treatises: (1) *On terms*; (2) *On universals*; (3) *On the categories*; (4) *On supposition*; (5) *On propositions*; (6) *On insolubles*; and (7) *On obligations*. The text belongs to the tradition of modern or terminist logic. Brinkley represents the general trend of logicians at Oxford from the 1350s insofar as he was a realist on the question of univer-sals, and he understood simple supposition to stand for common natures in things. More-over, he affirmed the real (extra-mental) existence of the categories. Brinkley also criticized another trend among some of his contemporaries, which was to emphasize the priority of written and spoken terms and propositions over mental concepts and propositions. More-over, his work in general defends the perspectivist view of epistemology against the Ockhamist view of intuitive cognition.

Bibliography

Primary sources

(1969), *De insolubilibus*, ed. Paul V. Spade, in *An Anonymous Fourteenth Century Treatise on Insolubles: Text and Study*, Toronto: Pontifical Institute of Mediaeval Studies.

(1987), *De significato propositionis*, ed. and trans. Michael J. Fitzgerald, in *Richard Brinkley's Theory of Sentential Reference: De significato propositionis from Part V of his Summa nova de logica*, Leiden: Brill.

(1995), *Obligationes*, ed. Paul V. Spade and G. Wilson, in *Richard Brinkley's Obligationes: A Late Fourteenth-century Treatise on the Logic of Disputation*, Münster: Aschendorff.

Secondary sources

Andrews, Robert (1998), "Richard Brinkley," in Edward Craig, ed., *Routledge Encyclopedia of Philosophy*, vol. 2 (pp. 19–21). New York: Routledge.

Gál, G. and Wood, R. (1980), "Richard Brinkley and his *Summa logicae*," *Franciscan Studies* 40, pp. 59–101.

Kaluza, Zénon (1989), "L'oeuvre théologique de Richard Brinkley, OFM," *Archives d'Histoire Doctrinale et Littéraire du Moyen Âge* 56, pp. 169–273.

Spade, Paul Vincent (1991), "Richard Brinkley's *De insolubilibus*: a preliminary assessment," *Revista di Storia della Filosofia* 46, pp. 245–56.

——(1993), "Opposing and responding: a new look at *positio*," *Medioevo* 19, pp. 233–70.

——(1994–7), "The logic of *sit verum* in Richard Brinkley and William of Ockham," *Franciscan Studies* 54, pp. 227–50.

103

Richard of Campsall

KIMBERLY GEORGEDES

Richard of Campsall (b. ca. 1280; d. ca. 1350), a secular theologian at the University of Oxford in the early fourteenth century, was arguably one of the most important philosophers there just prior to WILLIAM OF OCKHAM. Recent research reveals that several views described as Ockhamist by the end of the fourteenth century possibly originated with Campsall. A fellow of Balliol College prior to 1306, in 1306 Campsall became a fellow of Merton College. By 1308 he was a regent master of arts. He probably read the *Sentences* at Oxford in 1316–17 (prior to Ockham). From 1322 to 1324 he was regent master of theology and in 1325–6 he served as *locum tenens* for the chancellor. How long he lived is open to question, but Synan argues that he lived until about 1350/60 (1952, pp. 1–2).

Campsall's extant works include his *Quaestiones super librum Priorum analeticorum* (ca. 1308), the *Contra ponentes naturam* (on universals), a short treatise on form and matter (*Utrum materia possit esse sine forma*), and *Notabilia de contingencia et presciencia Dei*, all of which were probably written about 1317 or 1318 (Tachau 1987, p. 110). Campsall's *Sentences* commentary is not extant, but WALTER CHATTON, ADAM OF WODEHAM, Rodington, ROBERT HOLCOT, and Pierre de Plaout cite him in their *Sentences* commentaries.

In the *Questions* on the *Prior Analytics* Campsall maintains that training in logic is the basis for all other sciences. He discusses three major topics: syllogism, consequences, and conversion. The subject of logic is the syllogism, and knowledge of consequences and conversion is necessary for the study of syllogism, especially for converting "imperfect" syllogisms into "perfect" syllogisms (1968, pp. 21–2). In the area of supposition theory, Campsall proposes views usually first attributed to Ockham, for example, his distinction between simple and other types of supposition. For Campsall, a word has "simple" supposition when it stands for a concept in the mind. His conception of supposition was important for another innovation regarding paralogisms involving the Trinity and the insufficiency of Aristotelian logic for dealing with such problems. Gelber has elucidated this issue, and was the first to draw attention to Campsall's use of "Anselm's rule." Utilizing this rule, Campsall maintains that the result in trinitarian paralogism is the fallacy of accident, a view also maintained by Ockham. Campsall's use of "Anselm's rule" greatly influenced Holcot in his decision to complement Aristotelian logic with the "logic of faith," which makes up for the insufficiencies of Aristotle's logic (Gelber 1974, pp. 260–70).

Campsall proposes an "Ockhamist" view regarding universals. He argues that universals are not part of existing things, but are singular intentions in the intellect. Campsall, as a conceptualist, maintains that "the relationship of a universal intention to many singulars is not grounded in the structure of those singulars but in the capacity of one universal sign to represent many singulars" (1982, p. 12).

Campsall's views on intuitive and abstractive cognition are a response to JOHN DUNS SCOTUS, and were adopted by Rodington and Holcot. Campsall argues that "intuitive" and "abstractive" cognition are two terms for the same cognition, depending on whether the object is present (intuitive) or absent (abstractive) (Tachau 1982, pp. 194–5).

Bibliography

Primary sources

(1968), *The Works of Richard Campsall*, vol. 1: *Questiones super librum Priorum Analeticorum: MS Gonville and Caius 668*, ed. Edward A. Synan, Toronto: Pontifical Institute of Mediaeval Studies.

(1982), *The Works of Richard Campsall*, vol. 2, ed. Edward A. Synan, Toronto: Pontifical Institute of Mediaeval Studies.

Secondary sources

Gelber, Hester (1974), "Logic and the Trinity: a clash of values in scholastic thought, 1300–1335," Ph.D. dissertation, University of Wisconsin.

Synan, Edward A. (1952), "Richard of Campsall, an English theologian of the fourteenth century," *Mediaeval Studies* 14, pp. 1–8.

Tachau, Katherine H. (1982), "The response to Ockham's and Aureol's epistemology (1320–1340)," in A. Maierù, ed., *English Logic in Italy in the Fourteenth and Fifteenth Centuries* (pp. 185–217), Rome: Bibliopolis.

——(1987), "The influence of Richard Campsall on fourteenth-century Oxford thought," in Anne Hudson and Michael Wilks, eds., *From Ockham to Wyclif* (pp. 109–23), Oxford: Blackwell.

104

Richard Fishacre

R. JAMES LONG

Richard Fishacre (b. ca 1205; d. 1248) was the first Dominican master at Oxford to be educated exclusively in England. Originally from the diocese of Exeter, the young Fishacre was drawn to the *studium* at Oxford, and it was probably there that he first encountered the Dominicans and became one of the "catches" of which Jordan of Saxony, the Minister General, boasted. As a student at the first Oxford Blackfriars, he came under the tutelage of Robert Bacon, the first Dominican master in theology at the young *studium*, and incepted probably by 1240. His commentary on PETER LOMBARD'S *Sentences* was the first of that genre composed at Oxford (ca. 1241–5) and, although commenting on Lombard's work became in time the exclusive province of bachelors, the evidence suggests that Fishacre's commentary – like that of several Parisian masters before him – was the work of a master (Long and O'Carroll 1999, pp. 15–26, 39–40).

Whether Fishacre succeeded Robert Bacon as the sole regent master or whether they both held chairs simultaneously is not altogether certain. We know from the testimony of Nicholas Trivet that Fishacre lectured with (*legens una cum*) his former master, but the lecturing may have been in different venues, one in the "university" and the other in the Dominicans' convent (Long and O'Carroll 1999, 26–7).

Death came for both friar Richard and his mentor in the same year; Fishacre would have been in his early forties. In one of the very few autobiographical references in his writings, Fishacre protests in the prologue to his commentary that he was laboring under a twofold handicap: a lack of knowledge and a weakness of body. A colophon in the form of a prayer in one of the manuscripts makes the same point. These personal glimpses, if they are taken as more than commonplaces, can be seen as intimations of Fishacre's weak constitution and hence premonitions of his demise at a relatively young age (Long and O'Carroll 1999, pp. 27–8).

In metaphysics, Fishacre's view of reality can be located comfortably within the Christian Neoplatonic tradition: being is essence. The divine being is completely what it is, simple and immutable; the metaphysical scandal is change, and to the extent that creatures change, they are shot through with non-being (*In I Sent.* 8.1).

Yet there are unexploited suggestions of something more. In an isolated yet telling passage and in the tradition of AVICENNA, Fishacre identifies existence as an accident. Our *esse*, he says, is neither form nor matter nor the composition thereof, but *esse* is consequent upon the composition and is therefore the act of the essence, in short, an accident. God's *esse* is *truer* than ours and is identical with his substance. Our *esse*, in fact, is midway between being and non-being, because our being is to die (*In I Sent.* 8.1).

Given this Neoplatonic metaphysics, it is not surprising to find Fishacre an enthusiastic champion of ANSELM's *Proslogion* argument. His list of ten arguments for God's existence includes three that are patently variations on the Anselmian argument. He recasts the first of these in terms of divine simplicity:

> If there be something most simple, it would be identical with its being; otherwise it would have its being and something else besides and consequently would not be the most simple. Therefore, if anything be most simple, it would exist; but the most simple is the most simple; therefore it exists. (Long 1987, pp. 176–7)

Of divine attributes, God's infinity is the focus of Fishacre's attention. According to Leo Sweeney, Fishacre is the first western thinker to attach such importance to this attribute. Taking up the doctrine condemned at Paris in 1241, namely, that neither men nor angels will ever behold the divine essence, Fishacre frames the problem in terms of the infinite distance between creature and Creator. In the beatific vision, creatures are lifted across the infinite distance (*elongatio*) separating their limited intellect and the infinitude of divine essence. It is, moreover, precisely this matter of distance that becomes Fishacre's most telling argument for God's infinite power: there is an infinite distance between nothingness and prime matter (in other words, between nothing and something); but the greater the distance to be spanned the greater the power required; therefore, creation *ex nihilo* requires infinite power (Sweeney and Ermatinger 1958, pp. 194–208).

Talk of the human creature's knowledge of God gives rise to a discussion of knowledge in general, and here we find ourselves in a world that Aristotle would not have recognized. The species of a thing, which Fishacre calls the "word by which the exterior thing speaks to me," reaches as far as my innermost sentient power (the common sense) – but no farther. It is axiomatic that the inferior cannot act on the superior, and thus "the word" (*verbum*) cannot beget itself in the mind. Rather, and here Fishacre invokes the authority of AUGUSTINE,

> the soul in marvelous fashion and with equally marvelous speed produces in itself a similitude of that species which is in the common sense – that is, it makes itself like and conforms itself to that received species, just as light conforms itself to the water with which it comes into contact. (*In II Sent.* 7.5)

Since there is nothing common between the physical and the spiritual, the similitude of the sensible species within the soul is the product of the soul itself. As a given piece of wood is able to be configured in an infinite variety of ways, the intuiting of one of which in act belongs to the artisan, so likewise infinite likenesses of things are part of the natural endowment of the soul; yet, like the artisan, the soul comes to awareness of one while leaving all the others out of its consideration (Sweeney and Ermatinger 1958, p. 229).

Incredibly, Fishacre manages to enlist Aristotle's authority. The soul, he says, is able to read the sensible likenesses impressed on the instrument of the common sense, the heart. In this way all of our knowledge begins from the senses, and to the extent that our senses fail us our knowledge will be deficient (*In II Sent.* 7.5).

Notwithstanding his attempts to recruit Aristotle, Fishacre remains deeply committed to an Augustinian doctrine of innate ideas. Although no more explicit in his explanation than was Augustine, he reverts to this teaching in several texts. Memory is twofold, he says: one belonging to the possible intellect – and this is memory in the ordinary sense – and the other belonging to the agent intellect. The latter is a *habitus*, a permanent disposition, of all the intelligible forms in the mind from the time of its creation. Thus angels and humans before the Fall were created knowing everything. If we did not have habitual knowledge of everything, how could Aristotle assert that we had the desire to know everything (*In II Sent.* 16.2).

The soul, finally, is like a *tabula* "a slate," but not a *tabula rasa*. On the canvas of the soul are to be found the likenesses of things, like pictures, which are illuminated by the divine Light. In this life, however, the soul focuses on the pictures, not on the canvas, much less the Light: the soul knows neither itself nor God directly. It is owing to the presence in the soul of all forms that Aristotle can say: "The soul is in a way all existing things" (*In II Sent.* 16.2).

This view is rooted in a philosophy of human nature for which Fishacre is remotely indebted to Augustine, but more proximately to ROBERT GROSSETESTE. Typically, soul and body are considered separate substances; however, it is not the case that a human being is essentially a soul and the flesh merely a garment, notwithstanding the opinion of Avicenna and "certain theologians" (*In II Sent.* 31.1).

In defining the soul, however, Fishacre resorts to a stratagem first attempted by Avicenna, and in his own time by ALBERTUS MAGNUS: namely, the soul is a *forma coniuncta* (a conjoined form) according to its being, but a *forma separata* (a separated form) according to its essence; the human form thus occupies a middle position between the elemental form and the angelic (*In II Sent.* 2.2).

This duality of forms entails on the one hand a spiritual life which we share with angels, free from animal necessities, and on the other an animal life devoted to the body. This *affectio* or devotion for bodiness – not any body, he makes clear, but one "suitable to itself" – is what distinguishes the human from the angelic form; no angel, good or bad, is thus favorably disposed towards the body. So strong is this love for the body, in fact, that if the soul were deprived of its body in eternity, it would be eternally miserable (*In II Sent.* 17.3). Whether this *affectio ad corpus* is essential enough a difference to constitute the human soul as a species distinct from the angel, Fishacre admits he does not know, but thinks that it does not. Weighing in Fishacre's hesitation is the authority of Augustine, who asserted that the angel and human soul are equal in nature, though unequal in function (*In II Sent.* 3.2).

Although the doctrine is not developed systematically or in much detail, Fishacre's discussion of a rational and a sensible form in the human composite amounts to at least tacit acceptance of the plurality of forms. He is careful to describe the three contemporary opinions on the subject, but then hesitates to embrace any of the three (*In II Sent.* 24.2). Elsewhere, however, he speaks of the form by which the soul is an intellectual being as more noble than that being by which it is devoted to the body. Since nature always subordinates the less noble form to the more noble, the form by which the soul is devoted to the body is subordinated to the form by which the soul understands. But this is surely to posit the coexistence of at least two forms in the human soul (*In II Sent.* 24.3).

Between the soul's essence and its operations, Fishacre posits the faculties or *virtutes*, which, following the trinitarian division inherited from Augustine, are three in number: memory, understanding, and will (*In I Sent.* 3.7). Since the first two are collapsible, however, Fishacre finds Grosseteste's dyad of *aspectus* and *affectus*, apprehending and willing, a sufficient taxonomy (1972, pp. 96–8).

His discussion of reason and will eventually yields to the issue of *liberum arbitrium*, the free choice of the will. Devoting more pages in his Commentary to this question than any other, Fishacre's discussion constitutes a self-standing treatise on the subject, dependent on

Grosseteste's treatment, yet displaying a remarkable subtlety and originality. How is this power, called *liberum arbitrium*, related to reason and will? As its very name implies, it is related to both faculties. But is it anterior or posterior to them? Peter Lombard thought it was posterior to reason and will and rooted in them.

To the objections to this view, Fishacre answers in a unique and cleverly nuanced way. Since free choice is in the intellectual creature but not in the brute, it will be rooted properly in that element by which the former is superior to the latter. But that which is proper to an intellectual creature is its ability to reflect – that is, to "bend back" upon its own activity. Free choice, therefore, is the turning back on oneself poised on the brink of willing and passing judgment. Because *liberum arbitrium* is the medium between the apprehension and incomplete will on the one hand and the completed will or consent on the other, it is defined by both extremes (Long 1995, pp. 879–91).

As to the other half of the *binarium famosissimum*, namely universal hylomorphism or the doctrine of spiritual matter, Fishacre, like the majority of his contemporaries, was unquestionably a proponent. The human soul and the angel are composed of matter and form. But it is in his teaching concerning the latter that Fishacre works out the full implications of spiritual matter – almost as if angels constituted a kind of metaphysical testing ground (Long 1998, pp. 241–51).

If an angel were a form without matter, it would be con-penetrable with other spiritual substances, that is, an angel itself would be in the mind of one understanding it, not merely a similitude of it. The result is that, without matter as a check on its permeability, if one angel were to understand all the other angels, all angels would be present in the mind of that one angel (*In I Sent.* 8.4). This is a most curious argument and makes sense only if Fishacre understands matter as a kind of secondary matter or dross, and not in the Aristotelian sense of first matter or *hyle*.

Matter also accounts for individuality in an angel. The argument is as follows: the property that makes an angel *this* particular angel is either an accident, a (specific) difference, or matter. If an accident, then individuals differ by accidents alone, and if substances can be imagined without accidents, they will be the same substance. If, however, angels differ by specific difference, then each angel will belong to a distinct species – an option Fishacre thinks so little of that he does not even bother to refute it. By a process of elimination, he decides that angels are individuated through matter. In an angel, however, there is little matter and much form (ibid.). Furthermore – and here the influence is clearly Grosseteste's – insofar as all form is light, and an angel is almost wholly form, it is almost wholly light (*In II Sent.* 2.1).

Although an angel has matter, it is incorruptible because of its form. The form of a composite is not so noble that it terminates and completes every inclination of matter to another form and therefore, is subject to corruption. The form that is intellect, however, is so noble that it altogether completes matter, so that there is no inclination to another form left in the matter. Angels are thus naturally mortal owing to their matter, but naturally immortal owing to their form. God alone, lacking matter of any sort, is immortal *simpliciter* (*In II Sent.* 3.3).

Whatever the details of his metaphysics and psychology – and it is fair to say that Fishacre did not work out all of the details – his most original contributions are in the area of natural philosophy, which he sees as propaedeutic to theology. As he explains in the prologues to the first two books of the Commentary, the book of nature provides visual examples to supplement the hearing of Scripture.

It is here, moreover, that he is most indebted to Aristotle. Although he feels no hesitation in disagreeing with Aristotle, he is convinced nevertheless that the Philosopher is in possession of the truth about the created realm. Realizing that the sacred text can bear more than one interpretation, and noting indeed that the Fathers not infrequently disagree on the meaning of a text, Fishacre insists that

> they, that is the holy expositors, [with respect to disputed passages] be mindful only that they show that whatever truth be found in the writings of Aristotle is not contrary to Scripture, in order that it may thus be plain to all that this our Scripture be not contrary to the truth in any detail. (*In II Sent.* 13.2)

Thus the theologian who is properly grounded in philosophy should yield to the authority of the *physicus* in the latter's own proper realm, not only better to understand the sacred text, but also to deny to nonbelievers the occasion to ridicule the faith itself.

Far from being confined to the hexaemeral questions in the *Sentences* Commentary, there is growing evidence that Fishacre's interest in natural philosophy intensified in his post-Commentary period. There is a question on the ascension of Christ, a treatise on heresies, and even a number of university sermons, all of which make use of the new learning to discover more about the sacred text. There are in addition four lengthy discussions of questions suggested by the hexaemeron (on light, on the nature of the heavens, on the eternal duration of the world, and on the waters above the firmaments) that were not a part of the first redaction, but that were apparently composed afterwards and inserted into the Commentary. The growing sophistication of these questions bears eloquent witness to Fishacre's continued absorption with philosophy up to the time of his death (Long and O'Carroll 1999, pp. 33–6).

Daniel Callus once wrote that it would be an exaggeration to claim Fishacre was an ardent Aristotelian, and that is certainly true (Callus 1943, p. 229). But his failure fully to embrace the new learning was more a matter of ignorance than ideology. Fishacre gladly invokes Aristotle's biological works, which were more easily absorbed and had no rivals. With the rest of the natural philosophy he had only a passing and indirect acquaintance, most probably through a *florilegium* (Long 1996, pp. 54–5).

Could he then fairly be labeled an Augustinian? In the sense in which all of western Christian philosophy is a series of footnotes to Augustine, yes; in the sense in which he is consciously an adherent to a school of thought, clearly not. Augustine is obviously Fishacre's pre-eminent authority, and he never explicitly parts company with his teaching. At times, moreover, he hesitates to embrace positions owing to the perceived opposition of Augustine or, in not a few cases, pseudo-Augustine. Yet Fishacre has views that are decidedly non-Augustinian: his teaching on spiritual matter, the plurality of forms, and the impossibility of direct knowledge of the soul, for example.

The safest course is to avoid labels and see Richard Fishacre as an adventurous thinker, deferential to the established authorities, at least in his youthful work (the *Sentences* commentary), but showing signs of an emerging independence of mind in the works that can be dated towards the end of his career.

Bibliography

Primary sources
(1972), "The science of theology according to Richard Fishacre: edition of the prologue to his *Commentary on the Sentences*," ed. R. J. Long, *Mediaeval Studies* 34, pp. 71–98.

(1998), "Fishacre and Rufus on the metaphysics of light: two unedited texts," ed. R. James Long and Timothy B. Noone, in *Roma, Magister mundi, itineraria culturae medievalis: mélanges offerts au Père L. E. Boyle*, vol. 1 (pp. 517–48), Louvain-la-Neuve: Fédération Internationale des Instituts Médiévales.

Secondary sources

Callus, D. A. (1943), "Introduction of Aristotelian learning to Oxford," *Proceedings of the British Academy* 29, pp. 229–81.

Dales, R. (1995), *The Problem of the Rational Soul in the Thirteenth Century*, Leiden: Brill.

Long, R. J. (1987), "Richard Fishacre's way to God," in R. Link-Salinger et al., eds., *A Straight Path: Studies in Medieval Philosophy and Culture: Essays in Honor of Arthur Hyman* (pp. 23–36), Washington, DC: The Catholic University of America Press.

——(1995), "Richard Fishacre's treatise *De libero arbitrio*," in B. C. Bazán, E. Andújar, and L. G. Sbrocchi, eds., *Moral and Political Philosophies in the Middle Ages*, vol. 2, Ottawa: Legas.

——(1996), "The reception and use of Aristotle by the early English Dominicans," in J. Marenbon, ed., *Aristotle in Britain during the Middle Ages* (pp. 51–6), Turnhout: Brepols.

——(1998), "Of angels and pinheads: the contributions of the early Oxford masters to the doctrine of spiritual matter," *Franciscan Studies* 56, pp. 239–54.

Long, R. J. and O'Carroll, M. (1999), *The Life and Works of Richard Fishacre OP: Prolegomena to the Edition of his Commentary on the "Sentences,"* Munich: Bavarian Academy of Sciences.

Sweeney, L. and Ermatinger, C. J. (1958), "Divine infinity according to Richard Fishacre," *The Modern Schoolman* 35, pp. 191–235.

105

Richard Fitzralph

KIMBERLY GEORGEDES

One of the most important figures in the late 1320s, Richard Fitzralph (b. ca. 1300; d. 1360) was at Oxford by 1315, became a master of arts ca. 1322, read the *Sentences* probably in 1327–8, and was a bachelor of theology by 1329. After a year in Paris, Fitzralph returned to Oxford where he became a doctor of theology in 1331 and served his regency in 1331–2. He served as chancellor of the university from 1332 to 1334, during which time he was involved in the Stamford schism. In 1334 he went to Avignon, where he became involved in the controversy over the beatific vision. In 1335 he was appointed Dean of Lichfield, and in 1346 he was elected Archbishop of Armagh, a post he held until his death. Between 1335 and 1360, he traveled to England and Avignon several times to argue causes in defense of his archdiocese. From approximately 1350 to 1360 he was involved in a controversy against the mendicant orders.

Fitzralph's *Sentences* commentary followed the typical pattern of the early fourteenth century, and concentrated primarily on topics of Books I and II, including creation, the mind and its faculties, future contingents, and God's omnipotence. His views combined a moderate Augustinianism with moderate realism, and certain Averroist tendencies (Walsh 1981, pp. 49–54). On the issue of free will, Fitzralph strove to find a middle road between extreme Augustinianism and the apparent semi-Pelagianism of the nominalist school, and argued for the primacy of man's free will with a moderated acceptance of predestination. He also sought a middle course between the views of JOHN DUNS SCOTUS (to whom he was often in opposition) and THOMAS AQUINAS regarding the primacy of the will over the intellect (ibid., pp. 57–9).

At Avignon, Fitzralph argued against John XXII that the blessed have a total vision of God prior to the Last Judgment. Regarding intuitive and abstractive cognition, Fitzralph accepted the process of the multiplication of species, as well as the creation of species impressed on the senses and intellect, and stored in memory. He disputed, however, the identity of the impressed species with acts of sensation, cognition, or intellection. Fitzralph seems to have been opposing Rodington on this issue rather than WILLIAM OF OCKHAM. With regard to the mendicant controversy, Fitzralph's basic ideas were that God's grace provides the foundation for all valid lordship and authority, and those who abuse the rights and privileges of their position should be deprived of them. JOHN WYCLIF adopted his views on grace and dominion.

Fitzralph's three major works are his *Commentary on the Sentences* (1330s), the *Summa contra Armenos* (1340s) and the treatise *De pauperie salvatoris*, supplemented with the *De mendicitate* (1350s). Fitzralph's works influenced scholars both at Oxford and Paris, including ROBERT HOLCOT, ADAM DE WODEHAM, JOHN OF MIRECOURT, PETER CEFFONS, GREGORY OF RIMINI, and John Wyclif.

Bibliography

Primary source

(1890), *De pauperie salvatoris*, in R. Lane Poole, ed., *Wyclif's Latin Works*, vol. 8 (pp. 257–476), London: Trübner.

Secondary sources

Gwynn, Aubrey (1940), *The English Austin Friars in the Time of Wycliff*, London: Oxford University Press.

Hammerich, L. L. (1938), *The Beginning of the Strife between Richard Fitzralph and the Mendicants*, Copenhagen: Levin and Munksgaard.

Leff, Gordon (1963), *Richard Fitzralph, Commentator of the Sentences*, Manchester: Manchester University Press.

Robson, J. A. (1966), *Wyclif and the Oxford Schools*, 2nd edn., Cambridge: Cambridge University Press.

Walsh, Katherine (1981), *Richard Fitzralph in Oxford, Avignon and Armagh*, Oxford: Clarendon Press.

106

Richard Kilvington

EDITH DUDLEY SYLLA

Richard Kilvington (b. 1302/5; d. 1361), was a master of arts by 1331, a fellow of Oriel College, Oxford, in 1333. He was granted papal dispensation as son of a priest to be ordained and hold a benefice with cure of souls; was a bachelor of theology by 1335; and in the employ of Richard of Bury, Bishop of Durham in 1342 and 1344. A doctor of theology by 1350 and perhaps as early as 1338, Dean of St. Paul's London in 1354, he was a junior contemporary of THOMAS BRADWARDINE and WALTER BURLEY, whose work exemplifies the Oxford Calculatory tradition. WILLIAM HEYTESBURY, who, like Kilvington, wrote an influential set of *Sophismata*, may have been one of Kilvington's students. Kilvington composed works tied to Aristotle's *Physics, On Generation and Corruption*, and *Ethics*, and to PETER LOMBARD'S *Book of Sentences*, each consisting of a few long questions. His *Sophismata* is his only work up to the present to receive a printed edition, but his other works were also well known in his day, and his positions were noted by later fourteenth-century authors.

Kilvington's sophismata typically consist of a sophisma sentence, a case or hypothesis upon which interpretation of the sentence is to be based, arguments for and against the truth of the sentence, and resolution ending with replies to the arguments for the opposing side. Most of the sophismata involve physics and their solutions may involve mathematics as well as logic. Thus the first eleven sophisms involve comparisons of whiteness and of processes of whitening, along with theories of first and last instants. It is argued, for instance, that if the first sophisma, 'Socrates is whiter than Plato begins to be white' is true, so will the second sophisma, 'Socrates is infinitely whiter than Plato begins to be white' be true. Recent research on Kilvington's Aristotelian commentaries, as well as on his *Sophismata*, has begun to shed new light on activity in the arts faculty at Oxford in the 1320s.

Bibliography

Primary sources

(1990), *The Sophismata of Richard Kilvington. Introduction, Translation, and Commentary*, ed. N. Kretzmann and B. E. Kretzmann, Cambridge: Cambridge University Press.

(1990), *The Sophismata of Richard Kilvington*, ed. N. Kretzmann and B. E. Kretzmann, Oxford and New York: Oxford University Press for the British Academy.

Secondary sources

Bottin, F. (1973), "Analisi linguistica e fisica Aristotelica nei *Sophysmata* di Richard Kilmyngton," in C. Giacon, ed., *Filosofia e politica, et altri saggi* (pp. 125–45), Padua: Antenore.

Caroti, S. (1995), "Da Walter Burley al *Tractatus sex inconvenientium*: la tradizione inglese della discussione medievale *De reactione*," *Medioevo* 21, pp. 279–304.

Jung-Palczewska, E. (2000), "Works by Richard Kilvington," *Archives d'Histoire Doctrinale et Littéraire du Moyen Âge* 67, pp. 181–223.

Kretzmann, N. (1977), "Socrates is whiter than Plato begins to be white," *Nous* 11, pp. 3–15.

——(1982), "Richard Kilvington and the logic of instantaneous speed," in A. Maierù and A. Paravicini-Bagliani, eds., *Studi sul XIV secolo in memoria di Anneliese Maier* (pp. 142–75), Rome: Edizioni di Storia e Letteratura.

——(1988), *Tu scis hoc esse omne quod est hoc*; Richard Kilvington and the logic of knowledge," in N. Kretzmann, ed., *Meaning and Inference in Medieval Philosophy* (pp. 225–45), Dordrecht: Kluwer.

Wilson, C. (1956), *William Heytesbury: Medieval Logic and the Rise of Mathematical Physics*, Madison: University of Wisconsin Press.

107

Richard of Middleton

RICHARD CROSS

Richard of Middleton (b. ca. 1249; d. 1302) was a Franciscan friar. It is unknown whether he was English or French. He studied at Paris, and was appointed in 1283, while still a bachelor, to a Franciscan commission set up to examine the writings of PETER OLIVI. He was regent master of the Franciscan *studium* in Paris from 1284 to 1287. On September 20, 1295 he was made Franciscan provincial master of France. In addition to his *Sentences* commentary, Richard produced some forty-five disputed questions (still largely unpublished) and three sets of *Quodlibets*. Richard's thought owes a great deal to his three great predecessors BONAVENTURE, THOMAS AQUINAS, and HENRY OF GHENT, and he eclectically synthesizes from all three, rejecting where he sees fit. The result is nevertheless a coherent and impressive whole, that continued to be regarded as authoritative into the fifteenth century. His own original contributions are to be found principally in the area of natural philosophy.

Metaphysics and epistemology

Richard accepts a form of moderate realism on the question of universals that is very close to that found in Aquinas. He argues that every extra-mental item is singular. The universal is merely a concept: the essence of a species *as understood*. This same essence *as existent in extra-mental reality* is simply all the individual instances of the essence; there is no sense in which the essence *in itself*, prior to its universality (as understood) and particularity (as existent in extra-mental reality), has any sort of being (*In I Sent.* 36.2.2). In line with this, Richard explicitly rejects Henry of Ghent's theory that there is a realm of essences caused by God, external to him, that has some sort of minimal existence (*esse essentiae*) prior to the existence of particular instances of such essences (*In I Sent.* 35.1.1). The universal itself is a relation: a concept that is related indifferently to any extra-mental item that falls under it (*Quod.* 1.7).

   Richard rejects, however, Aquinas's theory that individuation is to be explained by extended matter. Accordingly, he accepts that there can be many angels of the same species (*In II Sent.* 3.5.1 and 2). Understanding individuality as indivisibility, Richard adapts Henry of Ghent's theory that indivisibility is nothing more than the negation of divisibility (*In II Sent.* 3.4.1). Like Henry, he claims that indivisibility entails distinction from all other items. But Richard adds a further component to Henry's theory, consistent with Richard's Thomist version of moderate realism. Created things are individuated in some sense by their act of existence: an essence as individual is just an essence existent in extra-mental reality (*In I Sent*. 24.1.2; *In II Sent*. 3.4.1 ad 4).

Following Henry, Richard holds that existence adds a relation to essence: a relation to God's efficient causality, causing instances of the essence in extramental reality (*In II Sent*. 3.1.1). He follows Aquinas in holding that relations are not things; they have existence "towards" something without in any sense being inherent accidents (*Quod*. 1.9). Since existence is a relation, and relations are not in any sense things, Richard rejects any sort of real distinction between essence and existence: an existent essence is just an individual, extramental, essence; individuation and existence coincide, and nothing needs to be added to an individual essence to explain its existence. Richard borrows some arguments from Henry to show that existence cannot be really distinct from essence. The strongest one is related to the famous "third man" argument of Parmenides. Suppose existence has to be added to essence in order to explain the existence of the essence. Is this existence *essentially* existence? If so, it is God; if not, then it itself requires an explanation of its existence, and this will lead to a vicious regress. According to Henry, there is an *intentional* distinction between essence and existence, a *definitional* distinction that requires some distinction in its object that is less than real but more than merely mind-imposed. Richard rejects any such distinction midway between real and rational, and hence rejects Henry's claim that there is an intentional distinction between essence and existence. According to Richard, the distinction between essence and existence is merely rational or mind-imposed: it does not correspond to any distinction in the existent individual (*Quod*. 1.8).

An existent essence is an *ens* – a being. *Ens* as such – the analogical concept under whose extension everything falls – is the first object of human cognition (*In Sent*. 1.3.3.3). *Ens* is a transcendental property, one that transcends, or applies to all, the categories. Following Bonaventure, Richard holds that the transcendental property of *goodness* is prior to *ens* (*In II Sent*. 1.5.2). Following this line of thought, Richard argues against Aquinas that will is a higher faculty than intellect (*In I Sent*. 1.2.1). One reason for this is the Bonaventurean one that it is better to love God than to know him (*In II Sent*. 24.1.5). But Richard's cognitive psychology also allows him to conclude that will is a higher faculty than intellect. He argues that will, unlike intellect, can command: will commands intellect, and is actively required for certain mental acts (*In II Sent*. 24.1.5). We have to want to think of something in order to think of it. Intellect merely shows and persuades will. Intellect is also a necessary condition for volition (*In I Sent*. 12.1.4). But its causal role is no more than dispositive: the will is a self-mover (*In II Sent*. 24.1.5), and Richard holds, against Aquinas, that it has the liberty of indifference in relation to any object presented to it by a judgment of the intellect, whether the good in general or some particular good (*Qu. disp*. 15.3). But he holds too that the will only has a role to play in choosing between goals in cases where there are *reasons* for acting in one or more ways (*In II Sent*. 38.2.4): the will necessarily desires the ultimate goal of happiness, irrespective of any particular judgment as to the *content* of this happiness. The will necessarily wills happiness, but it can will against any general or specific moral good presented to it by the intellect. But presented with God, the ultimate goal of human existence and the necessary beatific cause of human happiness, the will naturally wills him, without either coercion or freedom (*In II Sent*. 38.2.1).

Richard rejects Aquinas's view that there is a real distinction between intellect and will, or between these two powers and the soul itself. Following Henry, Richard claims that the only distinction is in terms of different relations: intellect and will are simply different functions of the soul, the soul's being related to different sorts of act that it can produce, and to the different objects of these acts. These different relations are only rationally distinct from the soul itself (*In I Sent*. 4.1.2.1).

Like Aquinas, Richard holds that divine illumination has no place in human cognition (*Qu. disp*. 13 (pp. 234–8)). He thus rejects Bonaventure's view, and accepts instead Aquinas's abstractive account of cognition, ultimately derived from Aristotle. The intellect is a *tabula rasa*, and all human knowledge derives from the senses (*In II Sent*. 25.5.1). More precisely, we know substances by the mediation of their accidents – for Richard their *perceptible* features (*In II Sent*. 24.3.3). In accordance with Richard's moderate realism, the universal is the essence as understood – the *concept*. This universal exists potentially in the phantasm (*In I Sent*. 22.1.2), and is abstracted – actualized – by the agent intellect (*In I Sent*. 3.2.1). The passive intellect then receives the impressed intelligible species (*In II Sent*. 24.3.2). Actual knowledge occurs when the agent intellect causes an act of understanding to inhere in the passive intellect. This act of understanding is the mental word, and Richard identifies it as the expressed species, actively caused by the agent intellect and inherent in the passive intellect (*In I Sent*. 27.1.1). The abstracted universal has *esse repraesentativum*: it represents the common essence of the things that fall under it (*In II Sent*. 3.3.1); the phantasm, likewise, represents the extra-mental individuals themselves (*In II Sent*. 25.5.1). Since the universal is present potentially in the phantasm, Richard holds, against Aquinas, that the intellect can reflect on the phantasm in such a way as to gain direct intellectual knowledge of singulars (*In II Sent*. 25.5.1). But this knowledge of singulars is the result of the potential existence of the (universal) intelligible species in the phantasm; against MATTHEW OF AQUASPARTA, it is not the result of the existence of a singular species representing a singular object. So it would be a mistake to think of Richard as a precursor of JOHN DUNS SCOTUS's theory of the intuitive knowledge of the individual. Likewise, Richard rejects Bonaventure's theory that the soul has direct self-knowledge, without the mediation of universal species. The soul has self-knowledge through its knowledge of universal species: it reflects on its own acts of cognition, and thereby has self-knowledge (*In I Sent*. 3.2.2; *In I Sent*. 3.6.1).

Richard follows Aquinas's exegesis of Augustinian claims to the effect that we know created truth only "in the eternal truth." This means not that God directly illuminates the soul to allow it to know created truths. Rather, God brings it about that the agent intellect has the power to abstract species by means of a natural intellectual light directed onto the phantasm. This intellectual light is a created accident of the soul, wholly distinct from God. Since the intellectual light somehow contains the form of things, the light is able to function effectively in abstracting intelligible species – universals – from the phantasm. This possession of the forms of things does not amount to any sort of innate knowledge; it is just what allows the agent intellect to perform its function successfully (*Qu. disp*. 13 (pp. 242–4)).

Our natural knowledge of God is derived empirically too (*In II Sent*. 25.5.1). Since all creatures represent God in some sense, we can argue from the existence and nature of these effects to the existence and nature of their cause (*In I Sent*. 3.1.1). Against Bonaventure, Richard rejects Anselm's ontological proof, and accepts instead the sort of a posteriori arguments championed by Aquinas, taking as his starting point the notions of cause, motion, goal-directedness, order, and adding to Aquinas's list the notions of conscience, and of the rational desire for the good (*In I Sent*. 3.1.3). Like Aquinas, Richard rejects any real distinction between the divine attributes: the divine attributes are simply different ways in which the simple divine essence is represented to created minds (*In II Sent*. 1.2). While the concept of *ens* is common to God and creatures, it is not a simple or univocal concept, but rather analogical: as ascribed respectively to God and creatures, there is no common concept included in its intension (*In I Sent.* 8.4.2). God is an *ens* – a being – because he is *esse* – existence itself; a creature is an *ens* only insofar as it imitates the *esse* of God. *Esse* too is analogical, divided into created and uncreated, and with no common concept included in its intension (*Quod.* 1.9).

God has ideas of all things, universal and singular, and these ideas are merely rationally distinct from each other (*In I Sent.* 35.2.3 and 4). Such ideas are identical with the divine essence: they are this essence as it is imitable by creatures. God knows the future by causing it: the contingency of future events results merely from the fact that God's decision to cause any event is contingent (*In I Sent.* 38.1.3). (Richard makes no attempt to integrate this doctrine with his claim that the human will has the liberty of indifference.) Following Bonaventure closely, Richard holds that creation from eternity is impossible – and thus the created universe must have had a beginning if it exists at all – because creation entails the acquisition of existence after nonexistence (*In II Sent.* 1.3.4). Equally, the unintelligibility of an actual infinity entails that such an infinity cannot be made (*In I Sent.* 43.6); and this in turn entails that the created universe cannot have existed for ever (*In II Sent.* 2.3.4).

Natural philosophy

Richard's own distinctive contributions can be found in the area of natural philosophy. Most notably – though understandably not a suggestion taken up by any of his major successors – is Richard's distinction between two senses of 'matter': first, matter properly so-called, the (passive) thing that enters into composition with form; and secondly, the pure potentiality from which forms are "educed." The first of these is recognizable from standard Franciscan accounts of matter: it has some sort of actuality, and can by divine power exist without form. If it did not have any sort of actuality, it would make no sense to think of it as entering into composition with anything else. The second, however, is distinctive to Richard's theory, and is supposed to help explain why it is that the generation of a material composite does not involve the *creation* of substantial form *ex nihilo*. Richard argues that there is a purely passive principle that somehow "contains" forms in such a way that one and the same form can exist first potentially and then actually. This principle is pure potentiality: the forms are not included in it actually; neither does it make any active contribution to the generation of the substance whose form is educed from it (*In II Sent.* 2.1.1 and 2; *In II Sent.* 12.1.4). Thus, while it plays a similar role in Richard's theory to the role that the *rationes seminales* play in Bonaventure's theory – namely, as a way of avoiding the position that substantial forms have to be created – it differs from Bonaventure's theory. According to Bonaventure, *rationes seminales* are *active* principles included in matter. Richard's second kind of matter is a purely *passive* principle (*In II Sent.* 14.3.3; *In II Sent.* 18.1.2). But Richard's matter differs from Aquinas's prime matter since, unlike that, it somehow contains forms in such a way that one and the same form can exist first potentially and then actually. Richard accepts too a form of universal hylomorphism, holding that angels also include some sort of matter – not the corporeal matter or the pure potentiality thus far described, but incorporeal, unextended matter. Richard holds that this angelic matter is necessary in order to explain how an angel can move. In order to move, an angel must include active and passive components: an active component to be the mover, and a passive component to be moved (*In II Sent.* 3.1.2).

Unlike Aquinas, but in accord with the standard Franciscan line from the 1280s, Richard holds to the plurality of forms in material objects. He maintains that the plurality of forms is required empirically in order to explain the generation of complex animate objects (*In II Sent*. 17.1.5). In addition to accepting the plurality of forms, Richard holds too that substantial forms admit of degrees: forms can be educed to greater or lesser degrees from the pure potentiality of the second sort of matter (*In II Sent*. 14.2.2). Richard makes use of these two theories to explain the way in which the elements exist in compounds of them. He holds that compounds of the elements (earth, fire, air, and water) are caused by the *interpenetration* of unaltered elements. These elements exist in lower degrees in the compound; there is no contradiction in supposing that contrary *incomplete* elements can exist together in one compound. Since the elements and their qualities are remitted, they form together an intrinsic principle of corruptibility (*De gradu* (1951, pp. 119–32)). The whole view represents a sophisticated development of AVERROES' theory of chemical composition, according to which the elements and their qualities exist in a compound, but in a "remitted" or fragmented state.

Richard's most significant innovation is his theory of the augmentation of qualities. According to it, the increase and decrease of qualities such as color and heat is explained on the analogy of a quantity. Richard distinguishes between two sorts of quantity: the *extension* of a substance (*quantitas molis*) and the degree of *intensity* of a quality (*quantitas virtutis*). Increases and decreases of the degree of a quality are understood as increases or decreases of the virtual quantity of the quality, analogous to increases and decreases in extension (*In I Sent*. 17.2.1). This quantitative theory of qualities was later taken up and developed by Scotus, and proved important in facilitating the formulation of the "mean speed theorem" of acceleration by the Mertonian mathematicians of the early fourteenth century, a theorem that in turn led to the development of the theory of inertia by Galileo. Although the basic insight developed by Richard was taken up by Scotus, Scotus did not agree with all the elements of Richard's theory. In particular, Scotus denied Richard's claim, itself owing something to Henry of Ghent's theory, that lower degrees of a quality are in potency to higher degrees. Richard holds that this potency theory is necessary to explain the unity of any higher degree of a quality (*In I Sent*. 17.2.2). Scotus claims instead that not all cases of real composition require a composition of the potential with the actual. Richard denies the theory developed by GILES OF ROME that there is a quantity of matter that is independent of extension. For Richard, any quantity that is not the virtual quantity of a quality is identified as extension. He has no inchoate notion of mass.

Ethics

Richard shows no trace of the sort of divine command theory of ethics that was to be developed by some Franciscans at the beginning of the fourteenth century. Actions are commanded by God because they are good, and prohibited because they are bad. Thus, he holds that the eternal law is the result of divine practical reason discerning, as it were, which courses of action are good, and which are bad (*In III Sent*. 29.1.10; *In III Sent*. 40.2.1). Natural law is the eternal law as understood by human beings. All of this is like both Aquinas and Bonaventure. But Richard agrees with Bonaventure against Aquinas that conscience should be understood as a habit, not an act: our habitual understanding of the precepts of natural law (*In II Sent*. 39.2.2).

Bibliography

Primary sources

(1591), *Super quatuor libros Sententiarum . . . quaestiones*, 4 vols., Brescia.

(1591), *Quodlibeta*, Brescia.

(1874), *Quaestio disputata* 13, ed. Fidelis a Fanna, in *De ratione cognoscendi, seu Utrum quidquid certitudinaliter cognoscitur a nobis cognoscatur in rationibus aeternis*, Turin: Marietti.

(1951), *De gradu formarum*, ed. Roberto Zavalloni, in *Richard de Mediavilla et la controverse sur la pluralité des formes* (pp. 35–108), Philosophes médiévaux 2, Louvain: L'Institut Supérieur de Philosophie.

Secondary sources

Cunningham, F. A. (1970), "Richard of Middleton, O.F.M. on *esse* and *essence*," *Franciscan Studies* 30, pp. 49–76.

Henninger, Mark G. (1989), *Relations: Medieval Theories 1250–1325* (ch. 4), Oxford: Clarendon Press.

——(1994), "Hervaeus Natalis (b. 1250/60; d. 1323) and Richard of Mediavilla (b. 1245/49; d. 1302/07)," in Jorge J. E. Gracia, ed., *Individuation in Scholasticism: The Later Middle Ages and the Counter-Reformation 1150–1650* (pp. 299–318), Albany, NY: State University of New York Press.

Hocedez, Edgar (1925), *Richard de Middleton: sa vie, ses oeuvres, sa doctrine*, Spicilegium Sacrum Lovaniense, Etudes et documents 7, Louvain: 'Spicilegium Sacrum Lovaniense' Bureaux; Paris: Honoré Champion.

Lechner, Josef (1925), *Die Sakramentenlehre des Richard von Mediavilla*, Münchener Studien zur historischen Theologie 5, Munich: Josef Kösel, Friedrich Pustet; repr. 1975, Hildesheim: H. A. Gerstenberg.

Rucker, P. P. (1934), *Der Ursprung unserer Begriffe nach Richard von Mediavilla: Ein Beitrag zur Erkenntnislehre des Doctor Solidus*, Beiträge zur Geschichte der Philosophie und Theologie des Mittelalters 31/1, Münster: Aschendorff.

Zavalloni, Roberto (1951), *Richard de Mediavilla et la controverse sur la pluralité des formes*, Philosophes médiévaux 2, Louvain: L'Institut Supérieur de Philosophie.

108

Richard Rufus of Cornwall

REGA WOOD

Richardus Rufus Cornubiensis (fl. 1231–56) was the first teacher of metaphysics, physics, and psychology we can identify at the University of Paris. Paris was the intellectual center of the western world. But when Rufus started lecturing on the Aristotelian *libri naturales*, a ban that prevented the Parisian faculty from teaching them had just gone out of effect. Still, Rufus was able to teach most of them before he gave up his position as a secular master of arts in 1238 to become a Franciscan. As a Franciscan novice, he moved to Oxford to begin studying theology. In about 1250, he lectured on PETER LOMBARD's *Sentences* at Oxford. After lecturing on Lombard again at Paris, Rufus returned to England to become the fifth Oxford Franciscan master of theology in about 1256.

Rufus played a crucial role in the development of scholastic philosophy: its methods, doctrines and priorities. He is not only the author of the earliest surviving lectures on Aristotle's *Metaphysica, Physica, De generatione et corruptione*, and *De anima*, but the first Oxford bachelor of theology to lecture on Peter Lombard's *Sentences* and the author of the first treatise directed against AVERROES. In addition to a number of minor works, Richard Rufus is the author of nine major works: two *Metaphysics* commentaries, commentaries on Aristotle's *Physics, De generatione et corruptione*, and *De anima*, a *Contra Averroem*, a *Speculum animae*, and *Oxford* and *Paris Sentences Commentaries*. His *Meteorology* commentary has been lost.

Previous accounts of the introduction of Aristotle in the West suggested that early lectures on Aristotelian natural philosophy took the form of elementary paraphrases of the Aristotelian text, lacking philosophical originality. Now it appears that from the start some lectures on Aristotle were critical and exciting. But this is only what we should have expected. How else could the study of Aristotle's metaphysics and natural philosophy have gone from being proscribed works to required reading in a period of little more than twenty years?

(1) Rufus' lectures on *Physics* and *De generatione et corruptione* were probably delivered before 1235. References in his theological works to the Aristotelian commentaries indicate that they were certainly written when he was a secular master, and hence before 1238, when he joined the Franciscan order. Discovered in Erfurt in 1983, the *Physics* commentary was frequently attacked by ROGER BACON. Bacon, whose long series of Aristotle lectures were delivered soon after Rufus left Paris in 1238, was a much more orthodox Aristotelian. He rejected many of Rufus' opinions – for example, views on Platonic Ideas, on place, and on impetus – but Bacon also asks and answers most of the questions put by Rufus.

Rufus' and Bacon's commentaries devote little space to summary and division of the text. In their place is a series of short questions and distinctions. Brief as they are, these questions raise major issues in western natural philosophy. Rufus' *Physics* commentary challenges the Aristotelian account of projectile motion, for example. Anneliese Maier located the medieval origins of impetus theory in the works of Roger Bacon. As she noted, Bacon did not advocate impetus theory, but set out to refute it. What she did not know was that the view he set out to refute was Rufus'. Employing what is more accurately described as "imprint theory," Rufus addresses a problem for Aristotelian physics: In projectile motion, contrary to Aristotle, violent motion appears to continue in the absence of contact between mover and moved object. Bacon accepts Aristotle's claim that substantial contact is necessary, so he explains projectile motion in terms of the projector's effect on the medium, not its impact (*virtus*) on the projectile (*Phys.* 8, Bacon 1935, 13: 338).

Rufus sees problems with this account. Though there is continued contact between the projector and the medium, the projectile will continue in motion even if the projector stops moving at once. For example, a ball will continue to fly through the air after the batter stops his action. So if projectile motion is continued by the medium, then when the projector is at rest, the medium must move itself; but bodies as bodies do not move themselves according to Aristotle, not even bodies of air or water. How, then, can the medium move itself after the mover has ceased to move? Worse: how can the same medium move projectiles at different speeds and in opposite directions? Rufus answers by positing an imprint in the projectile and resilience in the medium. The violent motion involved in throwing imprints something on the projectile when it moves it: a quality, form, or something else; it is not clear to Rufus just how to describe the imprint in Aristotelian terms. More Aristotelian is his account of the action of the medium. Air's form dictates how distant its parts are from each other. The projector pushes them apart, farther apart than air's form permits. Because air is resilient, the parts rebound. A response to violent motion, the rebound pulls the parts too close together. Successive, gradually decelerating rebounds result in a tremor that assists and accommodates motion in more than one direction.

Rufus' advocacy of imprint theory did not go unrecognized. In the fourteenth century, a more immediately influential advocate of the theory, FRANCIS OF MARCHIA, attributed the view to an ancient scholastic author, named Richard, whom he associated with BONAVENTURE. Maier unconvincingly identified this author as RICHARD OF MIDDLETON, who, however, was not a contemporary of Bonaventure and did not discuss projectile motion. Rediscovering Richard Rufus' *Physics* commentary not only supplies the right 'Richard', but it also explains some of the peculiarities of Marchia's theory. Like Rufus, and unlike his contemporaries, Marchia claims that violent motion impacts the medium as well as the projectile.

The definition of place is another subject about which Roger Bacon disagreed with Rufus. The point at issue was how to account for the immobility of place. Since Aristotle defines local motion as a change of place, place must remain fixed when motion occurs. And yet Aristotle also defines place as the boundary of a containing body, a body that can move. Ancient and medieval authors confronted the resulting problem most unavoidably in the case of the location of the heavens. As Averroes says (*Phys.* 4.43), JOHN PHILOPONUS poses the great problem for Aristotle's theory of place: if all motion is in a place, the outermost sphere must be in a place, since it is manifest that the heavens move. According to Averroes, Philoponus seeks to force us to admit either that something can move without being in a place, or that place is a *vacuum*.

Confronting this dilemma, some medieval authors argued that the heavens did not move, while others postulated the existence of a *vacuum*; but most sought alternative accounts of the immobility of place. Rufus' solution was to concede that in some sense the outermost heaven is not in a place and to present a relational account of the immobility of place. We need not suppose that when a containing medium (such as air) moves, the houses it bounds are thereby moved. Rather, different parts of the same medium – or, for that matter, another medium – retain a constant relation to the center of the earth. Since this relation is fixed and immobile, what is contained in a medium that moves need not itself be said to move. In the case of the heavens, the outermost surface of the outermost sphere moves constantly. Its parts are in different places, but as they move, each part is replaced by another part that occupies the same relation to the center of the universe; these relations are fixed and unchanging. Rufus' relational account of place was eventually adopted even by Roger Bacon, who was subsequently followed by THOMAS AQUINAS.

(2) Rufus' *De generatione et corruptione* commentary further develops views stated in the *Physics* commentary. His account of medial resilience that accounts for the movement of air and water in projectile motion is one example. Another is the theory of substantial trans-formation. As in the *Physics* commentary, Rufus distinguishes between receptive and active potential. Not prime matter, but matter in active potential is the substrate of change. Depart-ing from Averroes, Rufus and subsequently Bacon and other scholastic authors describe not just qualitative intensification and remission, but modal, substantive intensification and remission – degrees of actuality. As in the case of projectile motion, Rufus most influenced Francis of Marchia. Like Rufus, Marchia describes not just pure privation and simple actu-ality, but incomplete actuality conjoined with unrealized potential. Both authors character-ize the potential presence of elements in the case of elemental composition as confused. Rufus thus anticipates what Anneliese Maier in her ground-breaking study of medieval views on the structure of material substance, *An der Grenze von Scholastik und Naturwissenschaft*, calls the "one true" solution to the problem of elemental composition for those who accepted Averroes' claim that the elements themselves are subject to intensifi-cation and remission.

(3) In 1952 Manuel Alonso SJ edited most of books 2 and 3 of Rufus' next major work, a *De anima* commentary, from Madrid 3314. Alonso attributed the work to PETER OF SPAIN, an attribution R. Gauthier rightly rejected. R. Wood corrected the attribution on the basis of Erfurt Quarto 312, a manuscript that includes the missing first book.

In his *De anima* commentary, Rufus drew attention to the problem of identifying the agent and the possible intellects. How can the same thing be active and passive in regard to the same object? Rufus thought that in some sense they were the same, but he was also con-fident that they were different parts of that intellect. How to characterize the relationship was a major philosophical problem for him. Departing more confidently from the early thir-teenth-century views, Rufus identified human knowledge exclusively with the understand-ing of the possible intellect. We do not have access to the understanding of the agent intellect except insofar as it illuminates the species supplied by sensation. Contrary to Bacon, Rufus also held that the agent intellect was a part of the human soul, not God or a separated substance.

(4) Two sets of lectures by Rufus on the *Metaphysics* survive: *Memoriale in Metaph.* (*MMet.*) and *Dissertatio in Metaph. Aristot.* (*DMet.*). *DMet* was first attributed to Rufus by Auguste Pelzer, as V. Doucet notes. Fr. Gedeon Gál OFM was the first person to study the *Metaphysics* commentary in detail. His careful investigation revealed that it was an impor-tant source of Rufus' *Oxford Sentences Commentary*. But the manner in which Rufus cites his own earlier work suggested to Gál that it could not be by the same author. Gál found

the *Metaphysics* commentary cited as the work of a secular master. He concluded that the two works were by different authors.

Further investigation persuaded Gál instead that Rufus probably was an author who referred to his own works in the third person when rejecting views he formulated as a secular master before becoming a Franciscan. That probability became a certainty in the 1980s when at Timothy Noone's request, the Prefect of the Vatican Library, Fr. Leonard Boyle OP, using ultraviolet light, read a thirteenth-century ascription in the Vatican manuscript to Richard Rufus of Cornwall. Rufus' reuse of substantial sections of his earlier *MMet.* made it easy to establish the attribution of what now appears to be the earliest surviving commentary on any of the *libri naturales*.

Rufus' *DMet.* opens with a discussion of the Aristotelian dictum 'all men by nature desire to know' and includes an exploration of the question: What is truth? It also deals with the beginning of the world. Focusing on creation accounts, Noone's dissertation provides an edition of part of book *lambda*. Unlike Christian theologians, Aristotle argues that time and motion must be eternal because before every motion there is another motion. Rufus replies by characterizing *ex nihilo* creation as the first change, prior to which there was neither motion nor change. Creation took place at once or instantaneously, since in instantaneous change or transmutation, what is changing is also changed. This claim about transmutation comes from Averroes (*Phys.* 8.23) and appears in Rufus' *Physics* lectures, *De mutatione*, and his *Oxford Sentences Commentary*, as well as in *DMet.* However Robert Plevano, who studied treatments of the problem of instantaneous change in thirteenth-century Europe, found it in no other author.

(5) Averroes was the most important influence on Rufus' teaching of Aristotle. Nevertheless, before writing his second *Metaphysics* commentary, Rufus distanced himself from Averroes; his *Contra Averroem* is the earliest surviving western criticism of Averroes. In early thirteenth-century Europe, Averroes was regarded very sympathetically in the West as the orthodox Arab opponent of AVICENNA. Concerned to refute Avicenna's view that the active intellect is separate from the human soul, the Bishop of Paris, WILLIAM OF AUVERGNE, called Averroes the noblest of philosophers.

The first question of Rufus' treatise against Averroes concerns separated intelligences and the problem of universals. Surprisingly, Rufus prefers Plato's account to that of Aristotle. Rufus distinguishes between common natures and ideas. He identifies common natures as Aristotelian universals inhering in external objects. Ideas, by contrast, are the mind-dependent exemplars according to which external objects were formed by God. Rufus sees them as capable of separate existence, in the sense that they can exist independently of the external objects that exemplify them. This interpretation of the separate existence of Platonic forms has been advocated by such modern students of Plato as Gail Fine. Unlike Fine and the moderns, however, Rufus, like other medievals, follows the Augustinian view that locates ideas primarily in the mind of God.

Rufus' ground for preferring Plato to Aristotle is the account Plato provides of knowledge. According to Rufus, Plato's was the right solution to the problem posed by Heraclitus (*Met.* 1.6.987a32). According to Heraclitus, there cannot be demonstrative knowledge of the world, since its objects are constantly in a state of flux. Assuming that there is demonstrative knowledge (or "science," as the medievals call it), Rufus holds that Plato was right to posit ideas. Since science is about what is necessary, unchanging and fixed, its objects must be ideas, not contingently existing, external objects. Our knowledge of external objects is based on the ideas they exemplify, ideas that exist independently of the changeable world of sensible experience.

The second question of *Contra Averroem*, "De causa individuationis," presents a theory of individuation based on individual forms, similar to the views presented by JOHN DUNS SCOTUS in his *Metaphysics* commentary, views that later influenced Leibniz. For Rufus, as for Scotus, a theory of identity that permits real but not formal predication is an important conceptual tool. In the case of individuation, it explains the relation between specific and individual forms. Individual forms are really, but not formally, the same as specific forms. Specific forms are principles of shared identity; they pertain to common natures capable of instantiation (*multiplicabilis*). By contrast individual forms pertain to the same natures as they are actually instantiated (*actu multiplicata*).

Rufus also argues against alternative theories of individuation. He claims that the cause of individuation cannot be an accident or an aggregation of accidents, since individual, primary substances are ontologically prior to accidents. Though he allows a role for matter as an occasional cause of individuation, Rufus argues that even determinate matter cannot by itself be the principle of individuation. Being an individual means being distinct and united, both functions of the active principle of substance – form – not matter, the passive principle.

(6) The *Speculum animae* is the fullest statement of Rufus' epistemological views. In this ambitious treatise Rufus attempts to explain what Aristotle means when he says that "in some manner the soul is every thing" (*De an*. 3.8.431b20–21). Rufus asks in what sense the soul becomes an object when it understands or senses that object. He rejects the view his predecessors based on Patristic authorities: The soul is everything because it shares being with rocks, life with animals, and understanding with angels. He also denies that the dictum is literally true. That leaves Rufus in a difficult position, since he holds that species in the soul are really identical with the common natures exemplified in external objects. If the material in the sensory soul combines with the sensible species, why doesn't the soul become green when it perceives something green?

There are two elements in Rufus' reply: one is to postulate a different kind of being for sensible species. They are not natural beings, in the sense that they are not included in the Aristotelian categories; for they are neither substances nor accidents. Because they are different kinds of entities, when they combine with the soul, what is produced is not the object itself but cognition. The second element of Rufus' reply is to argue that what is formally distinct may be really identical. Species-beings have the same real nature, but are not formally predicable of the objects they image for the soul. This safeguards the claim that what we perceive is really the same as external objects. In some sense the soul really is all things, but it does become a tree when we perceive or understand trees.

(7) Preserved in only one manuscript, Balliol 62, the *Oxford Sentences Commentary* was first attributed to Richard Rufus by Franz Pelster, who recognized it as the first commentary on Peter Lombard's *Sentences* by an Oxford bachelor of theology. In 1987, Peter Raedts published an excellent study of this work, *Richard Rufus of Cornwall and the Tradition of Oxford Theology*. References to events at Paris in the 1240s and to Frederick II's excommunication in the commentary establish its date, roughly 1250.

One important philosophical contribution made by Rufus in his *Oxford Sentences Commentary* is a modal argument for the existence of God. Rufus rejected Anselm's famous ontological argument as "subtle" but "sophistical." In its place he advanced a modal argument based on the concept of God as an independent being (*a se et non ab alio*). The existence of independent beings is either necessary or impossible. Therefore, if an independent being can exist, it does exist. Like Rufus' views on individuation, his argument for the existence of God was accepted and modified by Duns Scotus, who also found in Rufus' formal predication a model for his own formal distinction (Gál 1956, pp. 182, 189).

Sententia Oxon. also presents important arguments against the eternity of the world. Still considered compelling by some today is the argument against the eternity of the world, which ROBERT GROSSETESTE (*In Phys.* 8, p. 154) attributed to "Master Richard." This argument was advanced in antiquity by Philoponus (whose views on this topic Rufus did not know) and associated in the medieval period with St. Bonaventure (who wrote about fifteen years after Rufus). As presented in Rufus' *Physics* commentary, the argument simply points to an inconsistency between the definitions of 'infinity' and 'past time'. By definition, past time has been traversed, but it is impossible to traverse an infinite number of days or years, therefore past time cannot be infinite. In the Oxford commentary Rufus buttresses the controversial premiss, all past time has been traversed – that is, has been present – by demonstrating what he takes to be an unacceptable consequence of the view that past time is infinite. If past time is infinite, then some past time was never present. However far we go back in time, we can never go far enough that all of the past will have been present, since there is no "all of the past." So Rufus could ask: In what sense is time past, if it never was present?

Despite its simplicity, many authors have found this argument persuasive. Immanuel Kant (in the "First antinomy of pure reason") held that it could be evaded only by denying that there is any fact of the matter about how old the world is. Even today, some contemporary cosmologists – such as G. J. Whitrow – consider it the strongest argument against the beginninglessness of the world.

(8) The *Paris Sentences Commentary*, like the *Oxford Sentences Commentary*, was first discovered by Franz Pelster. It is another massive work, though it consists chiefly of long excerpts from and critiques of St. Bonaventure's *Sentences Commentary*. It is cited as *Abbreviatio*, but that is misleading, since the Paris commentary presents Rufus' independent views as well quoting and replying to those of Bonaventure.

Though these lectures were famous, they are little studied. For many problems – for example, individuation and universals – an earlier work provides a fuller treatment. The topic of relations may be a case in which Rufus' fullest account is found in the *Paris Sentences Commentary*. Rufus denied that relations were ontologically distinct from related objects (Gál 1975, p. 154). Unlike other topics where Rufus' enduring influence is through Duns Scotus, Rufus' views on relations were rejected by Scotus. Here Rufus' influence is to be traced through PETER OLIVI and WILLIAM OF OCKHAM, the most celebrated proponent of this view.

The Paris lectures are described as "solemn" by Roger Bacon. They were delivered shortly after Bonaventure's *Sentences Commentary* (1250–2), which they quote, not long after Rufus' arrival in Paris in 1253, and before his departure for England to become the Franciscan regent master of theology at Oxford. At the same time Rufus was lecturing there, Thomas Aquinas was a bachelor of theology at Paris. A comparison of Aquinas's treatment of angelic individuation with Rufus' suggests that the changes Aquinas (*II Sent.* 3.1.1) made in the definition of form, allowing a sense in which form or quiddity rather than matter accounted for angelic potentiality, are best appreciated as a response to Rufus' views on individuation.

For both authors, the problem with form is the result of Aristotle's departures from Plato. In the Platonic system, actuality and generality correspond; the most universal forms are also most real. So there is no problem with a definition of form that combines quiddity and actuality. But with Aristotle what is most actual is the particular, not the universal, so there will inevitably be problems with the definition of form. Both Rufus and Thomas maintained the basic Aristotelian insight: the particular is most actual. And that allegiance leads both of them to alter the definition of form. Rufus chose to maintain at all costs the identification of form with act and consequently was forced to posit as the ultimate abstract form, a form lacking quiddity. Individual forms are pure act according to Rufus. Thomas takes the opposite approach. Maintaining the definition of form in terms of quiddity, he is forced to posit forms that are identified with potentiality. The ultimate individuating act, he calls being or *esse* and distinguishes from essential form. Though they disagree about the solution, Thomas and Rufus agree that radical steps are necessary to meet the problem.

Conclusion

Rufus has seldom been seriously studied since the Middle Ages, yet this is not the first attempt to assess his significance in the history of philosophy. In the 1290s, Roger Bacon, who is one of our principal sources of biographical information on Rufus, had already weighed the evidence. Bacon tells us that Rufus' influence was still increasing forty years after his death. But though he was famous among the "vulgar multitude," Bacon claims that the "wise repudiated his insanity" (1988, p. 86).

What was wrong with Rufus from Bacon's point of view? He tells us that Rufus held mistaken views on existential import, and we know that the two disagreed about the problem of universals and a variety of other topics. Commenting on Aristotle, Bacon generally followed Averroes more closely and less frequently departed from orthodox interpretations of Aristotle. But that does not explain the hostility with which Bacon viewed Rufus. The harshness in Bacon's tone is due in part to his own difficulties. Disappointed in his own projects after he joined the Franciscan Order, Bacon turned to the papacy, advocating a complete reform of the educational system, promoting the study of languages, mathematics, optics, and experimental science. He severely criticized not only Rufus, but ALBERTUS MAGNUS, ALEXANDER OF HALES, and Thomas Aquinas.

Bacon was the author of Greek and Hebrew grammars; he was widely read in Arabic philosophy; he was convinced of the value of mathematics and committed to an allegorical approach to theology. By contrast Rufus probably could read only Latin; among the Arabs he admires only Averroes; he shows no interest in mathematics. Even in logic the two men disagreed: Rufus asserted and Bacon denied that true assertions could be made about empty classes.

Bacon would have been less disturbed about Rufus, however, if Rufus had been a poor logician. But Rufus was an excellent logician, and Rufus was to carry the day. Even the many logicians who agreed with Bacon rather than Rufus on the question of empty classes, saw the enterprise of philosophy and theology in the same terms Rufus did. Like Rufus, they omitted allegorical moralizing from their lectures on theology. They shared his relatively narrow knowledge of the history of philosophy and his weaknesses in language and mathematics.

The subsequent history of scholasticism is Roger Bacon's nightmare come true. Not only did Rufus' influence on thirteenth- and early fourteenth-century scholasticism increase, but it also extended beyond the Middle Ages in the works of his fellow Franciscans, Duns Scotus, Ockham, and Francis of Marchia. Bacon was doubtless correct to see in Rufus a great danger to his views about philosophy and theology. What Bacon did not see was the brilliant possibilities that were to be developed in the Franciscan tradition of unorthodox

Aristotelianism in the High Middle Ages. Bacon failed in his efforts to turn back the clock. The future belonged to Richard Rufus.

Bibliography

Averroes (1550), *Aristotelis opera cum Averrois Cordubiensis commentariis*, 12 vols., Venice: apud Junctas.

Bacon, Roger (1935), *Opera hactenus inedita*, vol. 13: *Questiones s. lib. octo Physic.*, ed. F. Delorme and R. Steele, Oxford: Clarendon Press.

——(1988), *Compendium of the Study of Theology*, ed. T. S. Maloney, Leiden: Brill.

Doucet, V. (1948), "Prolegomena," in *Summa theologica "Alexandri,"* vol. 4.1, Quaracchi: Collegium S. Bonaventurae.

Eccleston, Thomas (1951), *Tractatus de adventu Fratrum Minorum in Angliam*, ed. A. G. Little, Manchester: Manchester University Press.

Fine, G. (1993), *On Ideas*, Oxford: Oxford University Press.

Franciscus de Marchia (1968), *Sent.* 4.1.1, in A. Maier, ed., *Zwei Grundprobleme der scholastischen Naturphilosophie* (pp. 171–80), Rome: Edizioni di Storia e Letteratura.

Gál, G. (1950), "*Commentarius in Metaphysicam Aristotelis* cod. Vat. lat. 4538, fons doctrinae Richardi Rufi," *Archivum Franciscanum Historicum* 43, pp. 209–42.

——(1956), "Viae ad exsistentiam Dei probandum in doctrina Richardi Rufi," *Franziskanische Studien* 38, pp. 177–202.

——(1975), "Opiniones Richardi Rufi Cornubiensis a censore reprobatae," *Franciscan Studies* 35, pp. 136–93.

Gauthier, R. (1982), "Le traité De anima et de potenciis eius," *Revue des Science Philosophiques et Théologiques* 66, pp. 3–55.

——(1982), "Notes sur les débuts [1225–1240] du premier 'Averroïsme'," *Revue des Sciences Philosophiques et Théologiques* 66, pp. 321–74.

——(1984), "Préface: Les Commentaires de la Vetus," in Aquinas, *Opera omnia iussu Leonis* 45.1 (pp. 236*–237*), *Sententia Libri De anima*, Rome: Commissio Leonina; Paris: J. Vrin.

Karger, E. (1998), "Richard Rufus on naming substances," *Medieval Philosophy and Theology* 7, pp. 51–67.

Maier, A. (1952), *An der Grenze von Scholastik und Naturwissenschaft*, Rome: Edizioni di Storia e Letteratura.

——(1968), *Zwei Grundprobleme der scholastischen Naturphilosophie*, Rome: Edizioni di Storia e Letteratura.

Noone, T. B. (1987), "An edition and study of the *Scriptum super Metaphysicam*, bk. 12, dist. 2: a work attributed to Richard Rufus of Cornwall," Ph.D. dissertation, University of Toronto.

——(1993), "Richard Rufus on creation, divine immutability, and future contingency in the *Scriptum super Metaphysicam*," *Documenti e Studi sulla Tradizione Filosofica Medievale* 4, pp. 1–23.

——(1993), "Roger Bacon and Richard Rufus on Aristotle's *Metaphysics*," *Vivarium* 35, pp. 251–65.

Pelster, F. (1926), "Der älteste Sentenzenkommentar aus der Oxforder Franziskanerschule," *Scholastik* 1, pp. 50–80.

——(1933), "Neue Schriften des englischen Franziskaners Richardus Rufus von Cornwall," *Scholastik* 8, pp. 561–8.

——(1936), "Die älteste Abkürzung und Kritik von Sentenzkommentar des hl. Bonaventura," *Gregorianum* 17, pp. 195–223.

Plevano, R. (1993), "Richard Rufus of Cornwall and Geoffrey of Aspall: two questions on the instant of change," *Medioevo* 19, pp. 167–232.

Raedts, P. (1987), *Richard Rufus of Cornwall and the Tradition of Oxford Theology*, Oxford: Oxford University Press.

Teske, R. (1994), "William of Auvergne on the individuation of human souls," *Traditio* 49, pp. 77–93.

Wood, R. (1992), "Richard Rufus of Cornwall on creation: the reception of Aristotelian physics in the West," *Medieval Philosophy and Theology* 2, pp. 1–30.

——(1992), "Richard Rufus of Cornwall and Aristotle's Physics," *Franciscan Studies* 52, pp. 247–81.

——(1994), "Richard Rufus: Physics at Paris before 1240," *Documenti e Studi sulla Tradizione Filosofica Medievale* 5, pp. 87–127.

——(1995), "Richard Rufus' *Speculum animae*: epistemology and the introduction of Aristotle in the West," in A. Speer, ed., *Die Bibliotheca Amploniana im Spannungsfeld von Aristotelismus, Nominalismus und Humanismus*, Miscellanea mediaevalia 23 (pp. 86–109), Berlin: De Gruyter.

——(1996), "Angelic individuation: according to Richard Rufus, St. Bonaventure and St. Thomas Aquinas," in A. Speer, ed., *Individuum und Individualität im Mittelalter*, Miscellanea mediaevalia 24 (pp. 209–29), Berlin: De Gruyter.

——(1996), "Individual forms: Richard Rufus and John Duns Scotus," in L. Honnefelder, R. Wood, and M. Dreyer, eds., *John Duns Scotus: Metaphysics and Ethics* (pp. 251–72), Leiden: Brill.

——(1997), "Richard Rufus and the classical tradition," in L. Benakis, ed., *Neoplatonisme et philosophie médiévale* (p. 231–53), Rencontres de philosophie médiévale 6, Turnhout: Brepols.

——(1997), "Roger Bacon: Richard Rufus' successor as a Parisian physics professor," *Vivarium* 35, pp. 222–50.

——(1998), "The earliest surviving western medieval *Metaphysics* commentary," *Medieval Philosophy and Theology* 7, pp. 39–49.

109

Richard of St. Victor

KENT EMERY, JR.

Richard of St. Victor (d. 1173) probably was born in Scotland. It is not certain whether he entered the Abbey of Augustinian Canons Regular at St. Victor near Paris before the death of HUGH OF ST. VICTOR in 1141 or early in the 1150s. If Richard was not Hugh's personal student he was his intellectual disciple. Richard spent the rest of his life at St. Victor, living under the rule of St. Augustine, teaching and preaching within the abbey and writing his many exegetical, doctrinal, and contemplative works. He was elected sub-prior of the abbey in 1159 and prior in 1162.

Richard conceived his intellectual activities in terms of the program of human and divine studies that Hugh of St. Victor established at the abbey. That program was ordered according to the three senses of Scripture: literal (or historical), allegorical, and tropological (or moral). The spiritual meanings of the Scriptures (allegorical and tropological) are founded on a correct understanding of the literal sense, which communicates the natural truths pertaining to the "works of creation" and records the actual events, persons, episodes, etc., in the history of salvation. Allegorical interpretation uncovers the way in which the "works of creation" signify and correspond with the salvific "works of restoration" wrought by the incarnate Christ, how the historical events, law, and the prophets of the Old Testament are fulfilled in Christ and his teaching in the New Testament and signify spiritually the Christian mysteries of faith. In the events and signs of Scripture tropological interpretation discovers the moral doctrine of Christian faith and the order of the spiritual life, crowned by the contemplation that anticipates the life of glory in eternity. In sum, the Victorine intellectual program, established by Hugh of St. Victor and pursued by his followers, closely aligns the historical narratives, things, and signs of the Scriptures with rationally ordered bodies of theological, moral, and contemplative doctrine.

The influence of Hugh's systematic pedagogy is evident in Richard's major exegetical work, the *Liber exceptionum* (probably composed before 1159), a collection of writings that serves as an introduction to the reading of Sacred Scripture. In terms of the overall intellectual program of St. Victor, Richard specialized in the moral doctrine of the spiritual life and the theory of contemplation, that is, in the "tropological" meaning of Scripture. His main tropological writings are *The Twelve Patriarchs* (*De duodecim patriarchis*) and *The Mystical Ark* (*De arca mystica*), probably composed, in the order indicated, sometime between 1153 and 1162. To modern readers, Richard's manner of scriptural interpretation in these works might appear "subjective" and "accommodated," as an imposition, convenient or fanciful, of extra-scriptural rational schemes on selected scriptural narratives and images. One must remember, however, the presuppositions of Richard's interpretative theory: (1) inspired by a divine, eternal, omniscient author, the Scriptures are the source of inexhaustible and polysemous truthful meanings, discoverable by pure and illumined readers; (2) the divine author's fullest meaning and intent are conveyed through the spiritual senses of Scripture, which are grounded in the literal or historical truths that the sacred writings record and which must be determined accurately (by means of the liberal arts); (3) according to the principles of abundance and polysemy, the tropological sense is as "real" as the allegorical or doctrinal sense; (4) indeed, the tropological sense is inseparable from the allegorical sense and is its intended outcome, inasmuch as it pertains to the way in which the mysteries of salvation wrought by Christ are internally assimilated and enacted by individual Christians; (5) the truthfulness of tropological interpretations is measured by their harmony with divinely revealed and naturally discovered truths, and with their internal coherence and appropriateness, that is, the way in which images and concepts are shown to relate and correspond with each other in a proportionate order (such order is itself a mark of truthfulness).

For Richard, the tropological sense embraces anthropological, psychological, moral, and noetic doctrines. His anthropology is first of all scriptural and historical. In several writings (following Hugh) he teaches that the soul's rational force (*vis*) was created in the image of God and its affective force in the likeness of God; originally the human body also reflected the divine nature and was destined to immortality. By the Fall, however, human reason was corrupted by ignorance, the affections by concupiscence, and the body by infirmity and death (*Liber exceptionum*). Likewise, free choice (*liberum arbitrium*), the spiritual power whereby one chooses between good and evil, was created in the image of God insofar as it is free and in the likeness of God insofar as it is directed by right reason. In the Fall, by free choice Adam rebelled against the highest Good and accordingly the lower powers of his soul rebelled against free choice, thereby diminishing its power (*De statu interioris hominis*). The fallen human soul may be restored by receiving and adhering to the teachings of divine revelation and by cooperating with the inner workings of divine grace. The light of divine wisdom remedies the soul's ignorance, divine charity heals its concupiscence, and practice of the virtues alleviates the body's infirmity although it cannot prevent death. Likewise, the divine precepts guide free choice, and consideration of the punishments due sin, the promises of pardon and grace and the rewards of glory motivate its right operation and strengthen its resolve (see Châtillon 1987, pp. 632–4).

In *The Twelve Patriarchs* (called *Benjamin minor* by later readers; see below), Richard propounds a systematic doctrine concerning the nature and operations of the soul's affective and rational powers (*affectio et ratio*), the details and order of which are revealed in the scriptural narration (Gen. 29: 15–35: 29) of the twelve sons born to Jacob in his successive marriages with Leah, Bala (the handmaiden of Rachel), Zelpha (the handmaiden of Leah), and Rachel. Exegetically, Richard establishes precise correspondences between the figures of the scriptural narrative, the etymological meanings of their names, their characters and actions, on the one hand, and the nature of the soul's powers, their operations, and the virtues that perfect them, on the other. Broadly speaking, the dim-sighted Leah signifies the soul's affective power, which comprehends the senses, passions, will, and the love of justice. Her children and those of her handmaiden Zelpha represent the individual affections of the soul (*affectus, affectiones*) and the virtues that perfect them. Broadly speaking, the formerly sterile but beautiful Rachel signifies the rational and cognitive powers of the soul and the love of wisdom. Her handmaiden Bala signifies the imagination, which links the spiritual power of reason with the senses and through them with the exterior world. Bala gives birth to two sons, who represent the use of images in meditations on the punishments inflicted on sinners

589

and the rewards bestowed on the just. Strictly speaking, Rachel represents the abstractive and discursive rational power. She first gives birth to Joseph, who signifies the virtue of discretion, which governs and orders all of the powers and virtues of the soul to their proper end and which imparts self-knowledge.

When each of its powers and their offspring are perfected by their proper virtues and are coordinated by the virtue of discretion, the soul is prepared for contemplation. Then Rachel gives birth to Benjamin, and dies in doing so. Contemplation is twofold: "above reason but not beyond reason," and "above and beyond reason"; in the first, Benjamin kills his mother when he contemplates mysteries about God above the natural capacity of reason; in the second, he is transported beyond himself and all human understanding to contemplation of mysteries (e.g., the Trinity) which one may know only through a divine showing.

In *The Mystical Ark* (called *Benjamin maior* by later readers), Richard elaborates the theory of contemplation sketched briefly in *The Twelve Patriarchs*. "Contemplation," according to Richard, "is a free, penetrating gaze of the mind, suspended in wonder, into manifest-displays of divine wisdom" (*Contemplatio est libera mentis perspicacia in sapientiae spectacula cum admiratione suspensa*; 1979, *MA* 1.4, *PL* 196: 67d). In contemplation, according to corresponding hierarchical orders of knowing and being, the rational spirit's (*animus*) imaginative, reasonable (*ratio*), and intellective (*intelligentia*) powers apprehend and behold, respectively, sensible (created and visible), intelligible (created and invisible), and "intellectible" (uncreated divine) realities.

Richard's doctrine of contemplation comprises six genera or degrees of speculation, which are signified "mystically" in the features of the Ark of the Covenant and Sanctification mounted by seraphim and placed within the Tabernacle of Moses (Exod. 37: 1–10, Ps. 132: 18). (For Richard the term 'mysticism' is not strictly synonymous with contemplative theory, the highest subject of tropological interpretation, but refers as well to the hidden allegorical sense; see 1979, *MA* 1.1, *PL* 196: 63.) The first genus of contemplation is "in the imagination according to imagination," wherein one wonders at the order and form of sensible realities and the power, wisdom, and generosity of their creator. The second genus is "in the imagination but according to reason," wherein one considers the rational principles that underlie and unify physical things, their order, disposition, causes, modes, and benefits. The gentile philosophers partook these kinds of contemplation in an "external way." Their speculations, however, were full of errors and generated endless questions and disputes. They could not discover any work that God performed from beginning to end, and although they could know the physical principles of things they were ignorant of their rational principle, the divine judgments and justice, so that they attributed to the goddess Fortuna what is the effect of divine providence. The third genus of contemplation is "in reason according to imagination," wherein by means of the similitudes of visible things one rises to a speculation of invisible realities. The fourth genus is "in reason according to reason," wherein the rational spirit (*animus*), wholly detached from the imagination, intends and reasons about (*ratiocinatione*) what cannot be known through sensible experience, namely, the human soul and the angels, according to their existence, operations, acquired goodness, and future blessedness. Moreover, in this degree the "pure intelligence" (e.g., without recourse to imagination) operates for the first time and is able "to understand itself through itself." The first four degrees of contemplation are attainable by human "industry" assisted by God; the last two depend solely on the light of divine grace shining in the "fine point of the intellect" (*acies intellectus*). The fifth genus of contemplation is "above reason but not beyond it," wherein by means of a divine revelation in the mind one cognizes "what human reason cannot fully comprehend and what cannot be investigated sufficiently by reasoning" but with which reason can "sufficiently concur," namely, the nature and simple essence of the divinity and its attributes. The sixth genus is "above and beyond reason" and seemingly "against reason," wherein by an "irradiation of divine light" in the "simple intelligence" (i.e., without recourse to reasoning) one "intuits" divine realities that seem wholly contrary to reason (the Trinity, Incarnation, Eucharist), unless it be supported by a mixture of faith (1979, *MA* 1.3–9, 2.2, 9, *PL* 196: 66c–75d, 80b–81c, 87a–88a).

Richard's philosophical psychology and cognitive theory evidently derive from Neoplatonic sources. Identifying his sources is difficult, for he seldom cites authorities explicitly but weaves their teachings synthetically into his text. The thought of AUGUSTINE and Hugh is present throughout. One may also detect terms and ideas deriving from BOETHIUS, PSEUDO-DIONYSIUS, and perhaps JOHN SCOTUS ERIUGENA, most of which however he could have found in the writings of Hugh (Châtillon 1987, p. 630). Historically, the question of his knowledge of Pseudo-Dionysius is especially important. Throughout the later Middle Ages Richard was judged to be a leading (perhaps the foremost) authority among the Latins in the "mystical theology" invented by the Areopagite. BONAVENTURE, for example, identifies him as the follower of Dionysius and the modern exemplar of the "anagogic" or "mystical" mode of theology. (The structure of Bonaventure's *Journey of the Mind into God* owes much to Richard's six degrees of contemplation.) Likewise, JOHN GERSON says that Richard was "as if the first after Dionysius" to treat mystical contemplation and "reduce it to an art and doctrine." Richard certainly knew Pseudo-Dionysius' *Celestial Hierarchy*, perhaps through the commentary on the same work by Hugh of St. Victor. His six genera of contemplation, moreover, evince some correspondence with the three modes of theology – symbolic, intelligible, and mystical – taught by Pseudo-Dionysius in *The Divine Names* and elsewhere. The first three kinds (especially the third), involving the imagination, correspond with the Areopagite's "symbolic theology." The fifth kind, in terms of its purely spiritual, illumined cognition and its object (the divine unity and attributes) corresponds closely with Dionysius' "intelligible theology." These correspondences might lead one to expect that Richard's sixth kind would correspond with Dionysius' "mystical theology," wherein according to the "negative way" the mind rises in "darkness" above all understanding into union with God. Rather, Richard's sixth kind corresponds with the highest mode of "affirmative" theology mentioned by Dionysius, which he claims to have treated in a lost or fictitious work, *The Divine Characters*: the "discrete theology" that concerns the distinctions of the trinitarian persons. Indeed, the terms and images of the "negative way" are scarcely present in *The Mystical Ark*; as in Augustine's contemplative writings, the emphasis is on increasing degrees of light and intelligibility. In general, it appears that Richard interpreted the Dionysian teachings within the framework of Augustine's authoritative theological paradigm; for example, he seems consciously to reconcile the former's terms and metaphors of spiritual ascent with the latter's terms and metaphors of introspection and penetration to the depths of the mind. Thus one should understand that the "summit of the mind" (*summum mentis*) and the "innermost bosom of the mind" (*intimum mentis sinum*) are one and the same, and that it is one and the same (like Moses) to ascend to the "peak of the mountain" (*verticem montis*) and to enter "the innermost, most secret chamber of the ark of the tabernacle" (*in tabernaculo foederis . . . intimum et secretissimum locum*, 1979, *MA* 4.23, *PL* 196: 167a–b; cf. *MA* 1.3, *PL* 196: 67b, where *sinum mentis, animi acies*, and *oculus mentis* are synonymous).

The association between Richard and Pseudo-Dionysius was confirmed by another monk at St. Victor (until ca. 1218), Thomas Gallus (later Abbot of Vercelli, d. 1246). In his interpretations of Dionysius' *Mystical Theology*, Thomas frequently takes recourse to Richard's *The Mystical Ark* and adapts the teaching of one to the other (Javelet 1962–3; Théry 1939, pp. 162–3). It was Thomas who established the interpretation of Dionysius' mystical ascent above all understanding as an affective, loving union with God that leaves intellect behind. Such an affective interpretation of mystical theology had been anticipated by Hugh of St. Victor and thereafter was adopted by Bonaventure and many others. It is not clear that Richard can be implicated in this interpretation. His contemplative theory in *The Mystical Ark* focuses mainly on intellectual cognition. Throughout his writings, however, he treats the rational and affective powers of the soul as inseparably linked: love and desire motivate the search for wisdom, and understanding elicits love and desire, so that affection accompanies each degree of contemplation. In his *Four Degrees of Violent Charity* (*De quatuor gradibus violentae caritatis*, composed after *MA*), Richard defines the ascent to union with God in terms of love and charity; his degrees of love have some rapport with his degrees of contemplation in *The Mystical Ark*. Overall, it seems that Richard conceives the rational and affective powers of the soul as reciprocal and isomorphic in the ascent to contemplative union with God.

Although later scholastic theologians seldom did so, Richard's treatise *On the Trinity* (*De Trinitate*) should be related to the highest degrees of contemplation in *The Mystical Ark*. In the latter, Richard makes clear that cognition of the Trinity comes only through an illumination of divine grace that presupposes and is supported by faith. Accordingly, in *On the Trinity* he adopts Anselm's method of a "faith seeking understanding." Such an understanding, which "lies between faith and vision" (Anselm), discovers "necessary reasons" for the existence of God, the unity of the divine attributes, the essential identity of the divine persons and the distinctions and interrelations among them. Richard's "necessary reasons" do not refer to any certitude of evidence in the knowing subject nor may his arguments be construed as "demonstrations" in any Aristotelian sense; rather, the "necessity" of the reasoning derives from the object of speculation, the eternal, immutable being of God. Richard conducts his investigation by means of a conceptual logic of perfection based on divine attributes revealed in Scripture and confirmed by reason. God is Love or Goodness in itself, which by nature is wholly self-giving. God is also Glory itself and Felicity itself, which likewise communicate themselves wholly. This threefold communicative fullness requires that there be one who gives himself exhaustively and equally, one who receives and gives back himself exhaustively and equally, and one who receives from both exhaustively and equally. In the first person, Love is "gracious," in the second "gracious and obliged (to the first)," and in the third "obliged" to both. A fourth existential category of "one who gives nothing and receives nothing" is inconceivable. Thus the circle of self-giving and receiving is consummated in three persons, each of whom possesses the shared divine existence incommunicably and independently.

Significantly, in his inquiry Richard does not resort often to Augustine's analogies between the trinitarian persons and the powers of the soul (such speculation would pertain to the fourth degree of contemplation in *MA*). Further, he judges Boethius' definition of a 'person' ("an individual substance with a rational nature") as inadequate to the divine reality, insofar as it can imply that each person is a separate substance. He thus reformulates a definition that safeguards their essential identity: a "person is one existing by itself alone, according to a certain mode of singular existence" (*De Trinitate* 4.24; 1959, p. 284; cf. Châtillon 1987, p. 610). Scholastic theologians regarded Richard as an authority among the Latins (with Augustine and Boethius) in trinitarian speculation; aspects of his thought were received sympathetically and developed by ALEXANDER OF HALES, ALBERTUS MAGNUS,

592

Bonaventure, HENRY OF GHENT, and JOHN DUNS SCOTUS, but were evaluated more critically by THOMAS AQUINAS.

In sum, following the intellectual tradition established by Hugh of St. Victor, Richard of St. Victor conceived an ordered Christian wisdom, "above philosophy but not without it," firmly affixed to the tropological sense of Sacred Scripture. Throughout the later Middle Ages and into early modern times he remained a leading authority on the theory of contemplation and mystical theology (admired by DANTE, among others). The model of his enterprise, which unites speculation with scriptural exegesis in a seamless garment, not long after his death began to unravel into separate strands of theological discourse, exegetical, scholastic, and mystical.

Bibliography

Primary sources

(1855), *Opera omnia*, in *Patrologia Latina cursus completus (PL)* 196, ed. J.-P. Migne, Paris: Vivès.

(1951), *Sermons et opuscules spirituels inédits 1: texte latin, introduction et notes*, ed. Jean Châtillon and William-Joseph Tulloch, trans. Joseph Barthelemy, Paris: Desclée De Brouwer.

(1955), *Épître à Séverin sur la charité; le quatre degrés de la violente charité (De quatuor gradibus violentae caritatis)*, ed. and trans. Gervais Dumeige, Paris: J. Vrin.

(1958), *De Trinitate*, ed. Jean Ribaillier, Paris: J. Vrin.

(1958), *Liber exceptionum: texte critique avec introduction, notes et tables*, ed. Jean Châtillon, Paris: J. Vrin.

(1959), *La Trinité: texte latin, introduction et notes*, ed. and trans. Gaston Salet, Paris: Editions du Cerf.

(1967), *De statu interioris hominis*, ed. Jean Ribailler, in *Archives d'Histoire Doctrinale et Littéraire du Moyen Age* 34, pp. 7–128.

(1967), *Opuscules théologiques: texte critique avec notes et tables*, ed. Jean Ribaillier, Paris: J. Vrin.

(1979), *The Twelve Patriarchs, The Mystical Ark (MA), Book Three of The Trinity*, trans. Grover A. Zinn, New York: Paulist Press.

(1986), *Trois opuscules spirituels de Richard de Saint-Victor: textes inédits accompagnes d'études critiques et de notes*, ed. Jean Châtillon, Paris: Études Augustiniennes.

(1997), *Les Douze Patriarches ou Benjamin minor: texte critique et traduction*, ed. and trans. Jean Châtillon et Monique Duchet-Suchaux, intro. by Jean Longère, Paris: Editions du Cerf.

Secondary sources

Andres, F. (1921), "Die Stufen der Contemplatio in Bonaventuras *Itinerarium mentis ad Deum* und in *Benjamin major* des Richards von St. Viktor," *Franziskanische Studien* 8, pp. 189–200.

Aris, Marc-Aeilko (1996), *Contemplatio: philosophische Studien zum Traktat Benjamin maior des Richard von St. Viktor, mit einer verbesserten Edition des Textes*, Frankfurt-on-Main: J. Knecht.

Châtillon, Jean (1987), "Richard de Saint-Victor," *Dictionnaire de spiritualité ascétique et mystique, histoire et doctrine*, vol. 13 (pp. 593–654), Paris: G. Beauchesne.

Colker, Marvin L. (1962), "Richard of St.-Victor and the anonymous of Bridlington," *Traditio* 18, pp. 181–227.

DiLorenzo, Raymond D. (1982), "Imagination as the first way to contemplation in Richard of St. Victor's *Benjamin minor*," *Medievalia et Humanistica* 11, pp. 77–96.

Dumeige, Gervais (1952), *Richard de Saint-Victor et l'idée chrétienne de l'amour*, Paris: Presses Universitaires de France.

Javelet, Robert (1962–3), "Thomas Gallus et Richard de Saint-Victor," *Recherches de Théologie Ancienne et Médiévale* 29, pp. 206–33; 30, pp. 88–121.

Lubac, Henri de (1959–64), *Exégèse médiévale: les quatre sens de l'Écriture*, 4 vols., Paris: Aubier.

Robilliard, J. A. (1939), "Les six genres de contemplation chez Richard de Saint-Victor et leur origine platonicienne," *Revue des Sciences Philosophiques et Théologiques* 28, pp. 229–33.

Théry, Gabriel (1939), "Thomas Gallus: aperçu biographique," *Archives d'Histoire Doctrinale et Littéraire du Moyen Âge* 12, pp. 141–208.

Zinn, Grover A. (1977), "Personification allegory and visions of light in Richard of St. Victor's teaching on contemplation," *University of Toronto Quarterly* 46, pp. 190–214.

110

Richard Swineshead

EDITH DUDLEY SYLLA

Richard Swineshead, fellow of Merton College, Oxford, in 1344, master of arts in 1355, was the author of the *Book of Calculations*, because of which he is best known as "the Calculator." In addition, some fragments by him on motion and on the heavens are preserved in Cambridge, Gonville and Caius College MS 499/268.

Differences between the extant manuscripts of the *Book of Calculations* indicate that it may have been composed in parts over several years, most probably in the 1340s. Its sixteen treatises are: I. On the intension and remission of forms; II. On difformly qualified [bodies]; III. On the intensity of an element having two qualities not equally intense; IV. On the intension and remission of mixed [bodies]; V. On rarity and density; VI. On the velocity of motion of augmentation; VII. On reaction; VIII. On the power of a thing; IX. On the difficulty of action; X. On the maximum and the minimum; XI. On the place of an element; XII. On lights; XIII. On the action of lights; XIV. On local motion; XV. On a non-resisting medium and on the increase of power and resistance; XVI. On the induction of the maximum degree. The entire work demonstrates the application of logical and mathematical approaches to physical problems typical of the Oxford arts faculty in the mid-fourteenth century and associated with disputations on sophismata.

Mathematically, the most important influence on the *Book of Calculations* was THOMAS BRADWARDINE'S *On the Ratios of Velocities in Motions*, with its approach to operations on ratios according to which continuous ratios are "added" by taking the ratio of the first antecedent to the last consequent (so, for instance, the ratio A:B added to the ratio B:C equals the ratio A:C). This approach and Bradwardine's associated rule for relating forces, resistance, and velocities, is elaborated in Treatise XIV and subsequent treatises. Other treatises on the measurement of the effects of alteration, local motion, and augmentation follow paths blazed by WILLIAM HEYTESBURY'S *Rules for Solving Sophismata*. The *Book of Calculations* was influential on the continent in the later fourteenth century and again in the fifteenth and sixteenth centuries, when it was printed several times in Padua, Pavia, Venice, and elsewhere. As late as 1509 Alvarus Thomas of Lisbon published his *Book of the Triple Motion*, devoted in large part to explaining Bradwardine's approach to ratios and Swineshead's calculations. In the seventeenth century, Leibniz credited Swineshead as being among the first to introduce mathematics into scholastic natural philosophy.

Bibliography

Primary source
(1477), *Liber calculationum*, Padua, and (1520) Venice.

Secondary sources

Clagett, M. (1950), "Richard Swineshead and late medieval physics," *Osiris* 9, pp. 131–61.

Hoskin, M. A. and Molland, A. G. (1966), "Swineshead on falling bodies: an example of fourteenth century physics," *British Journal for the History of Science* 3, pp. 150–82.

Murdoch, J. E. and Sylla, E. D. (1976), "Swineshead, Richard," in *Dictionary of Scientific Biography*, vol. 13 (pp. 184–213), New York: Charles Scribner's Sons.

Sylla, E. D. (1982), "The Oxford Calculators," in N. Kretzmann, A. Kenny, and J. Pinborg, eds., *The Cambridge History of Later Medieval Philosophy* (pp. 540–63), Cambridge: Cambridge University Press.

——(1991), *The Oxford Calculations and the Mathematics of Motion*, Harvard Dissertations in the History of Science, New York and London: Garland Publishing.

111

Robert Grosseteste

NEIL LEWIS

Robert Grosseteste ("Lincolniensis") (b. ca. 1168; d. 1253) rose from humble origins in England to fame as bishop, theologian, translator, student of nature, and philosopher. He became a master of arts in the late twelfth century, but the details of his life before about 1225 remain largely unknown. In the late 1220s he was teaching at Oxford, but around 1230/1 he renounced his secular career to become the first teacher of the Oxford Franciscans, although he did not join the order. In 1235 he was elected to the powerful position of Bishop of Lincoln. After his death several unsuccessful attempts were made to secure his canonization.

Grosseteste was one of the few Latin thinkers in the Middle Ages to know Greek. In the late 1230s he began producing Latin translations of Greek theological texts, most notably the writings of PSEUDO-DIONYSIUS. He also translated Aristotle's *Nicomachean Ethics* and parts of *De caelo*. His theological writings include commentaries on Scripture, sermons, letters, and a large collection of theological dicta. His theological masterwork is the *Hexaëmeron*, a commentary on Genesis 1–2.

Grosseteste wrote several works on natural science, addressing issues in optics, the rainbow, comets, the sun's heat, the sphere of the universe, and similar topics. He also played a key role in the assimilation of Aristotle's works, producing the first medieval Latin commentary on the *Posterior Analytics* and an incomplete commentary on the *Physics*. Commentaries on the *Sophistici elenchi* and *Prior Analytics* have also been attributed to him.

With the exception of *De libero arbitrio*, his philosophical writings are short. They focus on issues of joint philosophical and theological concern including truth, God as form, soul and body, causation, potency and act, the eternity of the world, future contingency, and free will. These writings and the commentaries on Aristotle probably date from about 1220–35.

Influences

The greatest influence on Grosseteste was St. AUGUSTINE, from whom he drew a broadly Neoplatonic outlook. But Grosseteste was also deeply influenced by the new ideas on natural philosophy and cosmology present in Aristotle and Arabic thinkers. His thought, like that of many in his day, frequently contains conflicting elements, yet he is unusually aware of tensions between his Augustinian outlook and Aristotle's teachings, and usually takes the latter to have a limited validity within a more encompassing Augustinian framework.

597

Grosseteste's philosophical influence was strongest at Oxford. The Franciscans RICHARD RUFUS OF CORNWALL, ROGER BACON, Thomas of York, and WILLIAM OF ALNWICK used his writings and held him in the highest regard. He also strongly influenced the Dominican RICHARD FISHACRE, as well as THOMAS BRADWARDINE, WALTER BURLEY, Thomas Buckingham, and JOHN WYCLIF.

Exemplarism, truth, and knowledge

Grosseteste took from Augustine the idea that God contains eternal exemplars or models of all things in his mind. Creatures are changeable and begin to exist, but their models are eternal and without beginning. Because he has such models in his mind, God may be described as the form of all things in the sense of form as "that through which a thing is what it is" (1912, p. 108). Grosseteste identifies these divine models with Plato's Ideas.

In creation God by his will forms matter in accordance with these eternal models. In itself matter lacks form and cannot remain fitted to such models. Creatures continue to exist only because God continually fits matter to their models. A creature's existence is simply its dependence on God, not some kind of metaphysical component added to its essence. God alone truly exists or has being. WILLIAM OF OCKHAM and JOHN BURIDAN understood Grosseteste to reject a distinction between essence and existence.

Grosseteste's exemplarism is closely related to his account of truth and knowledge. In *De veritate* he unites theological and logical conceptions of truth. He concludes that truth in general is a kind of conformity. The eternal Word is the supreme truth, being in conformity to the creatures that it says, but these creatures also are true, being in conformity to their models in the Word. This conformity, as ANSELM had said, is a rightness perceptible by the mind alone, and also, as Augustine had remarked, the creature's being, since a thing's being is its adherence to the Word and this adherence is its conformity to its eternal model.

All that exists conforms to its model and so in a sense nothing can be false. But things have two kinds of being, and while they fully have the first kind – the conformity just mentioned – they may not fully have the second kind in that they may fail to be perfect. A human being is a true human being, being composed of body and rational soul, but may be false in being vicious or mendacious. Similarly, all propositions are true in being the kind of thing they are, but some are false in that they fail to signify what in fact is the case.

Turning to knowledge of truth, Grosseteste appeals to Augustine's doctrine of illumination. "Since," he writes, "the truth of anything whatsoever is its conformity to its reason in the eternal Word, clearly all created truth is viewed only in the light of the Supreme Truth" (1912, p. 137). To know created truth we must view the reason or model to which a thing conforms, which requires that God, the Supreme Truth, illuminate the thing known, its model, and our minds. Indeed the Supreme Truth is most fundamentally visible to the mind, as the sun is to the eye, but most human beings fail to see the Supreme Truth himself, as though seeing things in the sunlight but not the sun itself. Vision of this Truth, the face-to-face vision of God, will be granted only to the pure of heart.

Commentary on the Posterior Analytics

Grosseteste's *Commentary on the Posterior Analytics* had the greatest influence of his philosophical writings, being standardly appealed to throughout the Middle Ages. The *Posterior Analytics* presented medieval thinkers with an account of knowledge quite different from anything found in Augustine. Aristotle provides an account of scientific knowledge (*scientia*) modeled on the paradigm of Euclidean geometry. To have such knowledge is to have formulated a deductive system consisting of demonstrations, a special kind of proof. At the basis of the system are fundamental premisses or "principles," which are true, necessary, universal, and prior. They are not demonstrated but are grasped by intellect (*intellectus*), "the mental habit by which we can accept principles."

Grosseteste takes the *Posterior Analytics* to provide criteria to judge whether a given proof provides scientific knowledge, not to provide a method for discovering principles or demonstrations. But he is quite aware that in this work Aristotle holds that it is ultimately from sense experience that the mind acquires the universal concepts and principles required by scientific knowledge. Grosseteste grants that fallen human beings must acquire knowledge by the uses of the senses; under these conditions Aristotle provides a valid account. Yet under Augustine's influence Grosseteste observes that "it is possible for any kind of knowledge to exist without reliance on the senses." God and the angels have complete knowledge and yet lack senses, and even in human beings there is a part of the soul, distinct from reason and intellect, that "needs no physical instrument to perform its proper operation." This, the intellective part or *intelligentia*, "would have complete knowledge without reliance on the senses through an illumination produced by a higher light" if it were not "darkened and burdened by the bulk of the corrupt body" (1981, p. 213). This corruption in turn is due to the misuse of the will in the Fall. Indeed all human intellectual shortcomings have their root in the will. Grosseteste remarks that the mind (*aspectus*) can reach no further than the will (*affectus*), and so "when the soul's love and desire are directed at the body and physical enticements, they must draw the mind with them and turn it from its light" (1981, p. 216).

Grosseteste does not take the *Posterior Analytics* to provide an account of knowledge that competes with illumination theory. Aristotle presents criteria for proofs to count as providing scientific knowledge, but in having such knowledge, Grosseteste thinks, one's mind is illuminated. Indeed, Grosseteste holds that all cognition involves mental illumination. In knowledge, for example, there is a mental vision of intelligible items in their purity, but even in opinion the mind is illuminated, although it grasps intelligible items only as they are mixed up with the appearances of changeable things.

It is true, Grosseteste thinks, that "only in mathematics is there scientific knowledge and demonstration in the strongest and primary sense." But Aristotle also uses a broader notion of demonstration having application in "natural science, logic . . . and moral philosophy." Grosseteste was intrigued with the question of how principles of demonstrations in natural science are acquired. Crombie (1953) has argued that Grosseteste went beyond Aristotle and was the first in the Latin West to propose an experimental method in science, and that in doing so he instigated a methodological revolution that laid the foundations for the development of modern science.

Whether Crombie is right has been subject to vigorous debate, but it cannot be denied that Grosseteste was aware of something like the use of controlled experiment in which a hypothesis is confirmed after surviving attempts at falsification. He gives the example, drawn from Arabic sources, of how, after repeated observation, we estimate that scammony draws out red bile. Reason is then "woken up" and begins to wonder if this is so. Reason turns to experience and gives someone "scammony to ingest while setting aside and removing other causes that purge red bile" (1981, p. 215). After doing this a number of times, we form the experimental universal principle that scammony as such draws out red bile. Grosseteste undoubtedly saw the value of such a method. Yet his own scientific

599

writings are no more the product of such an experimental method than are most others in the Middle Ages.

Body and soul

Grosseteste identifies three kinds of soul – vegetative, sensitive, and rational – which correspond respectively to plants, brute animals, and human beings. Vegetative souls account for the capacity to process nutriment; sensitive souls for the capacity for local motion and sense perception; and rational souls for the capacity for higher cognitive functions. In earlier works Grosseteste may have held that human beings have a plurality of distinct souls, but in his later works he instead seems to hold that the rational soul encompasses the functions of all three.

The rational soul, as Augustine had said, is a substance, yet like Aristotle Grosseteste also calls souls substantial forms and describes them as perfections of an organic body. The rational soul is immortal, non-physical, and mover of the body, but does not relate to the body simply as a mover, as Plato had thought, but also forms with the body the unity that is a human person.

In *De statu causarum* Grosseteste claims that the souls of brute animals come into existence on the basis of physical forms in bodies and are destroyed when such forms are destroyed. Rational souls, however, are created out of nothing by God and infused directly into organic bodies, and can continue to exist even when physical forms and indeed the body itself are destroyed.

In *De intelligentiis* Grosseteste notes that because it is non-physical the rational soul cannot have a place or position in the body. Loosely speaking it may be said to have a position in the heart, where the physical movements it uses in ruling the body begin, or in the brain, where the physical movements it uses in moving the body and sense experience begin. But strictly speaking the position attributed to the soul in such statements belongs to the root of the physical movement produced by the soul, not to the soul itself. Indeed the soul simultaneously exists everywhere in the body in a way akin to that in which God simultaneously exists everywhere in the world. Yet the soul acts on the body. Following Augustine, Grosseteste holds that the soul can move the bodily members only if it directly moves something in the body that is almost non-physical in nature, what he calls a "physical spirit." He describes this spirit as a kind of light, adopting Augustine's view that light is an instrument the soul uses in acting through the body. The soul moves this spirit by its desires or affections, and this spirit, in turn, moves the nerves and muscles, which move the coarser parts of the body. But the body, being less noble than the soul, cannot act on the soul. With Augustine Grosseteste holds that the body's movements do not cause changes in the soul but are just *occasions* for such changes. The soul moves itself on the occasion of such movements.

Free will

Like most medieval thinkers Grosseteste typically uses the term 'free decision' (*liberum arbitrium*) rather than 'free will' (*libera voluntas*). This notion involves a duality, the term 'free' pointing to the will and 'decision' to some kind of rational judgment.

Of particular importance in Grosseteste's treatise *De libero arbitrio* is the question whether free decision requires an ability to sin. PETER LOMBARD had defined it as "a readily exercisable capacity of reason and will by which good is chosen with the help of grace and evil without its help" and thereby suggested that free decision implies an ability to choose both good and evil. But St. Anselm had defined it as "the ability to keep rightness of will for its own sake" and expressly asserted that it does not imply an ability to sin.

Why, Grosseteste wonders, did they end up with such different accounts? The answer, he thinks, turns on the fact that "the Creator of all things cannot possibly share anything with a creature." Thus no terms may be used in the same sense (*univoce*) of God and creatures. Yet terms applied to them need not be purely equivocal. The rational creature "is a close trace, similarity, and image of its Creator" and this is a sufficient basis for some terms applying to God and the rational creature to have a common definition.

When defining free decision Anselm had considered the close, imitative similarity between God and rational creatures and, because God cannot sin, crafted a definition that implied no ability to sin. Lombard had instead focused on the rational creature and crafted a definition of free decision not as it is in itself, but in relation to the capacities it provides rational creatures, with the help of grace, in their fallen state.

Lombard's definition does not imply, Grosseteste claims, that a capacity to sin and not to sin is essential to free decision. This capacity for moral choice is grounded upon, but incidental to, the essential nature of free decision. God has free decision but cannot sin, and those who are to be confirmed in good will have it and be unable to sin.

Yet nor should we conclude from Anselm's definition that free decision does not imply a capacity to will opposites. Any agent with free decision must be able to will opposites, provided this ability is understood as the ability to will "either one of opposites considered nakedly . . . without relation to God's pleasure or displeasure," that is, not as morally good or evil. The moral goodness and evil of things is not intrinsic to the things themselves, Grosseteste thinks, but is instead defined in relation to God's will: "things are right because he wills them."

So conceived free decision is a kind of capacity, but the term also suggests a psychological process. Grosseteste takes a decision to be a kind of rational judgment that naturally precedes an act of will and proposes to it that something should be chosen or rejected. Such a judgment is a necessary condition of willing, but is not sufficient, for "reason itself imposes no necessity on the will to choose or reject what it judges in this way." As he puts it, "the will ought naturally of its own account subject itself to reason's judgment and comply with it; however, it does not submit to a necessity to comply but it is left in its power to comply or not" (1912, p. 227). In proposing this doctrine and also adopting Anselm's view that the will moves itself, Grosseteste denies that the will can be determined by the intellect. JOHN DUNS SCOTUS would later propose a similar view.

Future contingency and modality

Freedom of decision requires that our future deeds and true propositions predicting them be contingent, not necessary. But there are formidable arguments against future contingency. In his important discussion of this issue in *De libero arbitrio* Grosseteste provides a generalized form of argument against future contingency, which can be filled out in various ways. It appeals to the logical principle that in an argument in which the premises entail the conclusion, if the premises are necessary so too is the conclusion. Grosseteste notes then that if we can find necessary premises that entail ostensibly future-contingent

601

propositions, then those propositions in fact are not contingent after all. Such premisses may be of different kinds. Using the standard example of a true future-contingent proposition 'The Antichrist will exist,' Grosseteste notes that they may refer to God's knowledge ('God knows that the Antichrist will exist') or to prophecy ('It has been prophesied that the Antichrist will exist') or may simply be past-tensed propositions about the future ('It was the case that the Antichrist will exist'). For any true future-contingent proposition, Grosseteste thinks, there are indeed true premisses of these kinds that entail it. If these premisses are necessary, so too is the alleged future-contingent proposition they entail.

Grosseteste sets out arguments against future contingency in this way so that they will be immune to the by then standard response that they confuse necessity of an entailment with the necessity of the proposition about the future that is entailed. No such confusion is present in the arguments Grosseteste presents. A response to them must be along different lines.

One response Grosseteste considers is to reject the principle that necessity is transmitted by entailment. He does not adopt this radical course, however. Instead he grants that premisses of the kind mentioned are indeed necessary and that *all* truths about the future are, as the arguments seek to show, necessary in the same sense. His strategy is to argue that the sense of necessity in question is harmless, being compatible with the kind of contingency required by freedom of decision.

The account of differing conceptions of necessity and contingency that Grosseteste proceeds to offer marks an important point in the history of these modal notions. Grosseteste holds that the necessity attaching to truths about God's knowledge, prophecy, the past, and truths about the future is *unchangeability of truth*. "In the same proposition," he notes, "in one respect there is necessity because its truth cannot cease to be." Yet "in another respect there is contingency, because the proposition that is true could, without beginning, have not been true" (1991, p. 51). That is, such propositions are contingent in the sense that although they cannot *change* in their truth-value, they could have had a different truth-value all along. This idea marked an important shift away from thinking of necessity and contingency in terms of time and change towards a so-called "synchronic" conception. Views along these lines were to be developed later by Duns Scotus, perhaps under Grosseteste's influence.

To explain the idea that a proposition could have had a different truth-value Grosseteste turns to the notion of eternity. When we say that a proposition that is true at time t could have been false then or that it has a capacity to be false without beginning, we are considering things from the standpoint of eternity prior to time, and envisaging the possibility of a different world in which the proposition would have been false at time t. Grosseteste describes such propositions as having eternal capacities for truth and falsity and explains such eternal capacities of propositions in terms of God's eternal capacities to know or will them or appropriately related propositions. Thus he grounds the kind of future contingency he thinks is required for human freedom in God's eternal capacities to know and will opposites. His sophisticated discussion of the sense in which a timeless and hence immutable being such as God could have genuine capacities to know and will opposites, marked an important step in philosophical theology and prefigured ideas to be developed by later thinkers, and especially by Duns Scotus.

Cosmology

De luce, Grosseteste's cosmological masterpiece, presents something like a "big-bang" conception of the genesis of the physical universe. This universe, as Aristotle had described it in *De caelo*, consists of a finite system of nested spheres carrying the stars and planets, under which are the spheres of the four elements fire, air, water and earth in descending order.

Aristotle, according to Grosseteste, took the universe to have existed without a beginning. As a Christian, however, Grosseteste was committed to its having begun, and the Bible provides a hint of the nature of its genesis in the words "let there be light." Grosseteste developed this thought, explaining the physical universe as the product of the action of a primordial point of light at the moment of creation.

According to the account he gives, which has come to be known as the "light metaphysics," all bodies are metaphysical composites of a first matter and a corresponding first form, "corporeity." Neither first matter nor first form is a body. Each lacks all dimension and magnitude. Bodies *result* from the composition of first matter and first form. When metaphysically simple first form and first matter are combined they instantaneously give rise to a three-dimensional body. And since the cosmos is spherical, this body must be spherical. But Grosseteste observes that a simple point of light instantaneously multiplies itself in all directions in a spherical shape in a process of infinite self-replication. He therefore identifies light with first form, and holds that at the beginning of the universe a simple point of light drew simple matter out along with itself into a spherical three-dimensional body.

This initial self-multiplication of light and matter produced the outermost sphere of the cosmos. Once produced the outermost sphere emitted *lumen*, a light-like body, back into the center, from which it was instantaneously multiplied outward, rarefying itself as much as possible under the outermost sphere to produce the second sphere. Repetition of this process resulted in a cosmos consisting of a dense spherical mass in the center and twelve nested spheres enclosing it. In the nine outer spheres – the celestial spheres – *lumen* was completely dispersed and rarefied, leaving these spheres capable only of circular motion. But the incomplete dispersal and rarefaction of *lumen* under the celestial spheres left the four elemental spheres, in which change of all kinds remained possible. Indeed Grosseteste goes on to argue that all kinds of change and all form is the product of the action of light.

Underlying this account are radical ideas about infinity and the ultimate structure of magnitudes. Grosseteste holds that the *infinite* multiplication of a simple point of light will yield an item of finite size. He takes Aristotle to have held that the finite multiplication of a simple could not do this, but not to have denied that an infinite multiplication could. In fact Grosseteste claims that infinities come in different sizes and distinguishes different-sized infinite multiplications of light. Bodies of different sizes are the product of different-sized infinite multiplications of light. Grosseteste claims that infinities can stand to one another in all proportions, both those expressible as numerical ratios and those not so expressible (the latter explaining incommensurable magnitudes).

Aristotle, as well as most medieval thinkers, rejected the idea of different-sized infinities. They also rejected the idea that magnitudes are literally composed of sizeless indivisible items. Yet Grosseteste also claims that the different-sized infinities corresponding to different physical magnitudes are the different infinite numbers of indivisible sizeless points generated by the infinite multiplication of light, and that these points make up the magnitudes as their ultimate parts. In proposing this view he is quite aware of Aristotle's claim that magnitudes are made up only of magnitudes, but he thinks that the notion of a part has several meanings depending on the kinds of mathematical relationships parts have to their wholes. Aristotle, he claims, means by 'part' any item a *finite* number of which compose a whole. In this sense it is true that only magnitudes are parts of magnitudes, but this is not true, Grosseteste claims, if by part is meant an item an *infinite* number of which compose a whole.

Grosseteste's conception of light as the fundamental formal feature of physical reality, which accounts not only for the large-scale structure of the universe but also for all change and form, led him to hold that physical reality has an underlying mathematical structure, for geometrical optics shows that light acts in accord with mathematical laws. Grosseteste is the first in the West to emphasize the fundamental importance of mathematics in the natural sciences. He notes in *De natura locorum* that "once the rules, roots, and foundations are given through the power of geometry, the diligent observer of natural phenomena can provide the causes of all natural effects in this way" (1912, p. 65). His emphasis on the importance of mathematics greatly influenced Roger Bacon and probably also the Merton school at Oxford in the fourteenth century, whose members made important applications of mathematics to natural philosophy.

The mathematical structure of physical reality also accords with the biblical statement that God "has arranged all things in number, weight, and measure" (Wisdom, 11: 21). God is a measurer who has created a universe of determinate magnitude and dimensions. But, Grosseteste notes in his commentary on the *Physics*, God must measure in a manner quite different from the way in which human beings do. We stipulate a given magnitude as a unit measure and then assign numerical values to other magnitudes in relation to it. This form of measurement is conventional and relative. But according to Grosseteste God measures in an absolute, non-conventional way by counting the infinite numbers of indivisibles contained in physical magnitudes. A line of two cubits, for example, contains twice the infinite number of points as a line of one cubit. Only God, to whom the infinite is finite, can measure in this way.

Time and eternity

The notion of eternity, we have seen, plays an important role in Grosseteste's account of future contingency. It also is crucial, he thinks, to an understanding of the essential nature of time. Aristotle's definition of time as "a number of motion in respect of before and after" serves the purposes of the student of nature but fails to capture the essence of time, which must be understood in reference to eternity.

Grosseteste notes that Aristotle and the philosophers knew that eternity existed but did not understand it clearly, "but viewed it under the appearance of temporal extension, as though looking at it from afar" (1963a, p. 264). Because their desires were directed at the transitory physical world they conceived of eternity as infinite temporal extension, whereas it is in fact a timeless mode of being. In line with BOETHIUS Grosseteste holds that an eternal being has its whole life at once (*simul*). It does not exist in time and thus has no temporal before or after in its existence. Both God and angels are eternal in this sense, for they have their whole lives at once. But temporal things do not exist wholly at once. Their existence is spread over time, only an instantaneous slice, as it were, being present. This suggests to Grosseteste the definition of time as "the privation of the at-once of eternity from the totality of existence" (1963b, p. 96). That is, for there to be time is for there to be things whose existence does not adhere, as Grosseteste puts it, as a whole with the at-once of eternity. Only an instantaneous slice of a temporal thing's existence ever adheres with the at-once of eternity. The present instant may be defined as "the adherence of some existence with the at-once of eternity." Grosseteste goes on to imply that temporal reality consists entirely of the present instant and its contents and that time has an objective flow constituted by the continuous replacement of one adherence of existence with the at-once of eternity by another.

The eternity of the world

Aristotle's failure to understand eternity also led, Grosseteste thinks, to the grave error that time, motion, and the world are eternal, in the sense of having existed infinitely in the past without a beginning. Grosseteste had no sympathy with the interpretation of Aristotle being proposed by some that Aristotle had simply meant that the world did not begin in a natural way and had not meant to rule out a supernatural beginning. "In setting Aristotle up as a catholic" they run the danger "of making heretics of themselves" (1986, p. 61). Both Richard Fishacre and Richard Rufus were heavily influenced by Grosseteste's discussion of the eternity of the world.

In his discussion of this issue in *De finitate motus et temporis* Grosseteste expounds Aristotle's arguments in *Physics* 8.1 and explains why they fail. Aristotle, he claims, had argued that if there had been a first movement, it would have existed after not existing. Therefore, before it existed, it would have existed in potentiality. But such a potentiality can be actualized only by a movement. So before the first movement, there would have to have been another, which is absurd. Therefore there cannot be a first movement.

The problem with Aristotle's argument stems from the word 'after'. It would work if 'after' meant "at a later time" and it was granted that for some period of time before the first movement there was no movement. Then a movement could only occur if there were an earlier movement actualizing its potentiality to exist. But 'after' may also refer to the non-temporal sense in which time is after eternity, a sense Aristotle, being preoccupied with the sensible world, had failed to recognize. Grosseteste denies that the first movement existed after not existing in the temporal sense of 'after'. Instead it existed after not existing in the sense that it existed in time but did not exist in eternity, which is prior to time. The first movement came into existence with the world and time, but this coming into existence was not a natural change of any kind and required no change in its cause, God.

Bibliography

Primary sources

Editions

(1912), *Die philosophischen Werke des Robert Grosseteste, Bischofs von Lincoln*, ed. L. Baur, *Beiträge zur Geschichte der Philosophie des Mittelalters* 9, Münster: Aschendorff.

(1963a), *De finitate motus et temporis*, ed. R. C. Dales, *Traditio* 19, pp. 245–66.

(1963b), *Commentarius in VIII libros Physicorum Aristotelis*, ed. R. C. Dales, Studies and Texts in Medieval Thought, Boulder, CO: University of Colorado Press.

(1981), *Commentarius in Posteriorum Analyticorum libros*, ed. P. Rossi, Corpus philosophorum medii aevi 2, Florence: L. S. Olschki.

(1986), *Hexaëmeron*, ed. R. C. Dales and S. Gieben, Auctores Britannici medii aevi 6, London: Oxford University Press.

(1991), *De libero arbitrio*, ed. N. T. Lewis, in "The first recension of Robert Grosseteste's *De libero arbitrio*," *Mediaeval Studies* 53, pp. 1–88.

Translations

MacDonald, Scott (forthcoming), *Robert Grosseteste's Commentary on Aristotle's Posterior Analytics*, New Haven: Yale University Press.

McKeon, R. (1930), *Selections from Medieval Philosophers*, 2 vols., New York: Charles Scribner's Sons. Vol. 1 contains translations of *On Truth* (*De veritate*), *On the Truth of Proposition* (*De veritate propositionis*), and *On the Knowledge of God* (*De scientia Dei*), pp. 263–87.

Martin, C. F. J. (1996), *Robert Grosseteste: On the Six Days of Creation: A Translation of the Hexaëmeron*, Auctores Britannici Medii Aevi 6, Oxford: Oxford University Press.

Riedl, C. C. (1942), *Robert Grosseteste on Light (De luce)*, Medieval philosophical Texts in Translation 1, Milwaukee: Marquette University Press.

Secondary sources

Crombie, A. C. (1953), *Robert Grosseteste and the Origins of Experimental Science 1100–1700*, Oxford: Clarendon Press.

Dales, R. C. (1986), "Robert Grosseteste's place in medieval discussions on the eternity of the world," *Speculum* 61, pp. 544–63.

Eastwood, B. S. (1966), "Medieval empiricism: the case of Robert Grosseteste's optics," *Speculum* 43, pp. 306–21.

Lewis, N. (1996), "Power and contingency in Robert Grosseteste and Duns Scotus," in L. Honnefelder, R. Wood, and M. Dreyer, eds., *John Duns Scotus: Metaphysics and Ethics* (pp. 205–25), Leiden, New York, and Cologne: Brill.

McEvoy, J. (1982), *The Philosophy of Robert Grosseteste*, Oxford: Oxford University Press.

——ed. (1995), *Robert Grosseteste: New Perspectives on his Thought and Scholarship*, Instrumenta Patristica 27, Steenbrugis in abbatia S. Petri: Brepols.

——(2000), *Robert Grosseteste*, New York: Oxford University Press.

Marrone, S. P. (1983), *William of Auvergne and Robert Grosseteste: New Ideas of Truth in the Early Thirteenth Century*, Princeton, NJ: Princeton University Press.

Serene, E. F. (1979), "Robert Grosseteste on induction and demonstrative science," *Synthèse* 40, pp. 97–115.

Southern, Sir R. W. (1992), *Robert Grosseteste: The Growth of an English Mind in Medieval Europe*, 2nd edn., Oxford: Clarendon Press.

112

Robert of Halifax

KIMBERLY GEORGEDES

Robert of Halifax, OFM (b. ca. 1300; d. after 1350) belonged to the generation of English theologians after WILLIAM OF OCKHAM. Halifax entered the Franciscan order about 1318, and was sent to Oxford about 1324 where he read the *Sentences* sometime between 1333 and 1340. Relatively unknown today, he was known to many of his contemporaries in England and the continent. His popularity on the latter is attested to by the survival of his *Sentences* commentary in sixteen partial or complete manuscripts, all located on the continent. He was the 56th Franciscan lector at Cambridge in about 1336. Towards the end of the 1340s Halifax returned to Yorkshire where he was licensed to hear confessions in 1349 and 1350.

Halifax's only known work, his *Commentary on the Sentences*, illustrates two trends of the period, (1) the use of new analytical tools reflecting mathematical and physical interests, and (2) a concentration on a few questions, which were dealt with in depth, rather than on the entire *Sentences*. These trends were particularly associated with the English theologians of the second quarter of the fourteenth century.

Much of Halifax's *Commentary on the Sentences* is devoted to the discussion of light, vision, and cognition. Halifax adhered more closely to JOHN DUNS SCOTUS's views than had anyone at Oxford since the 1320s. He was a perspectivist, and his references to ROBERT GROSSETESTE and PSEUDO-DIONYSIUS suggest the importance of Neoplatonic light metaphysics. He argues for *species in medio* against Ockham. Halifax utilizes the distinction between intuitive and abstractive cognition and adheres to Scotus's definition of these terms (Tachau 1982, pp. 432–6).

The topic of enjoyment and use was of great interest to fourteenth-century thinkers, and Halifax's question on whether there is a middle act of the will between enjoyment and use drew a considerable attention from his contemporaries (Courtenay 1973, p. 142).

Bibliography

Courtenay, William J. (1973), "Some notes on Robert of Halifax, O.F.M.," *Franciscan Studies* 33, pp. 133–42.

Lang, Albert (1930), *Die Wege der Glaubensbegründung bei den Scholastikern des 14. Jahrhunderts*, Munich: Hueber.

Maier, Annaliese (1949), *Die Vorläufer Galileis im 14. Jahrhundert*, Rome: Edizioni di Storia e Letteratura.

Murdoch, John (1975), "From social into intellectual factors: an aspect of the unitary character of late medieval learning," in J. Murdoch and E. D. Sylla, eds., *The Cultural Context of Medieval Learning* (pp. 271–348), Dordrecht and Boston: D. Reidel.

——(1978), *"Subtilitates Anglicanae* in fourteenth-century Paris: John of Mirecourt and Peter Ceffons," in M. Cosman and B. Chandler, eds., *Machauts World: Science and Art in the Fourteenth Century* (pp. 51–86), New York: New York Academy of Sciences.

Tachau, Katherine (1982), "The problem of the *species in medio* at Oxford in the generation after Ockham," *Mediaeval Studies* 44, pp. 394–443.

113

Robert Holcot

KIMBERLY GEORGEDES

An English theologian, Robert Holcot (b. ca. 1290; d. 1349) entered the Dominican order at Northampton, and in about 1326 went to Oxford. Holcot's *Sentences* commentary probably dates from 1331–3, while his *Quodlibets* and *Sex articuli* were probably written during the next two years. In 1332 he was licensed to hear confessions in the diocese of Lincoln. He completed the revision of his *Sentences* commentary by about 1336. He also produced several biblical commentaries, which were widely circulated and popular, particularly his commentary on the Book of Wisdom. Holcot was under the patronage of Richard of Bury (Bishop of Durham, 1333–45). In 1343 he returned to Northampton, where he died (Smalley 1956, pp. 5–9).

Although a Dominican, Holcot's views owe a good deal more to the debates between WILLIAM OF OCKHAM and WALTER CHATTON than to THOMAS AQUINAS, while Holcot's debates with Crathorn served to refine his ideas. Holcot was also influenced by RICHARD OF CAMPSALL, John of Rodington, Hugh Lawton, and RICHARD FITZRALPH.

One of Holcot's significant innovations concerns whether Aristotelian logic was sufficient for dealing with theological problems, particularly the Trinity. Holcot, building upon the work of predecessors, particularly Campsall, proposed a two-fold logic, *logica naturalis* and *logica fidei*. Holcot maintained that Aristotelian logic was applicable only to the natural order, and that the rules of logic pertaining to theological issues constitute a separate branch of logic. He has been accused of skepticism (for this and other positions), but Hoffman has argued that Holcot specifically designated this new logic as rational, subject to rational understanding and rules, a supplement to, not a replacement for, Aristotelian logic. Thus there is no fundamental rift between faith and reason for Holcot, and his application of logic to theology allowed for more subtle refinements, not for its reduction to fideism (Gelber 1983, pp. 265–73; Hoffman 1972, pp. 23–63).

Although once thought to be one of Ockham's closest disciples, Holcot disagreed with Ockham about epistemology and psychology. Regarding intuitive cognition, Holcot allowed for the intuitive cognition of an existent object present to the knower, but against Ockham maintained that both sensible and intelligible *species* are necessary for cognition. Holcot claimed that the connotation of the term 'intuitive' precludes intuitive cognition of a non-existent even by supernatural means. Holcot appeared to follow Campsall and Rodington in holding that intuitive and abstractive are different connotations of the same cognition – that is, depending on whether the object is present or not.

609

Bibliography

Primary sources

(1518), *In quatuor libros Sententiarum*, Lyons; repr. 1967, Frankfurt: Minerva.

(1958), *Utrum theologia sit scientia*, ed. J. T. Muckle, in "*Utrum theologia sit scientia*: a quodlibet question of Robert Holcot, O.P.," *Mediaeval Studies* 20, pp. 127–53.

(1964), "Quodlibet 1, q. 6: *Utrum deus posset scire plura quam scit?*," ed. E. A. Moody, in "A quodlibetal question of Robert Holkot, O.P., on the problem of the objects of knowledge and of belief," *Speculum* 39, pp. 53–74.

(1971), "Quodlibet 1, q. 6: *Utrum deus posset scire plura quam scit?*," ed. William J. Courtenay, in "A revised text of Robert Holcot's Quodlibetal dispute on whether God is able to know more than he knows," *Archiv für Geschichte der Philosophie* 53, pp. 1–21.

(1983), *Quaestiones de quodlibet*, ed. Hester Gelber, in *Exploring the Boundaries of Reason: Three Questions on the Nature of God by Robert Holcot, OP*, Toronto: Pontifical Institute of Mediaeval Studies.

(1993), *Conferentiae*, ed. Fritz Hoffman, in *Die Conferentiae des Robert Holcot O.P. und die akademischen Auseinandersetzungen an der Universität Oxford 1330–1332*, Münster: Aschendorff.

(1995), "Quodlibet 3: *Quaestiones de futuris contingentibus*," ed. P. Streveler and K. Tachau, in *Seeing the Future Clearly: Questions on Future Contingents* (pp. 59–195), Toronto: Pontifical Institute of Mediaeval Studies.

Secondary sources

Hoffman, Fritz (1972), *Die theologische Methode des Oxforder Dominikanerlehrers Robert Holcot*, Münster: Aschendorff.

Incandela, Joseph M. (1994), "Robert Holcot, O.P., on prophecy, the contingency of revelation and the freedom of God," *Medieval Philosophy and Theology* 4, pp. 165–88.

Kennedy, L. A. (1993), *The Philosophy of Robert Holcot, Fourteenth-century Skeptic*, Lewiston, NY: Mellen.

Schepers, H. (1970–2), "Holkot contra dicta Crathorn," *Philosophisches Jahrbuch* 77, pp. 320–54; 79, pp. 106–36.

Wey, J. C., ed. (1949), "The *Sermo finalis* of Robert Holcot," *Mediaeval Studies* 11, pp. 219–23.

114

Robert Kilwardby

A. BROADIE

Robert Kilwardby (b. ca. 1215; d. 1279), English philosopher and theologian, enrolled as an arts student at Paris in about 1231, graduating about 1237. For about seven years from about 1238, while regent master in arts at Paris, he composed *Priscianus minor*, *De accentu*, and *Barbarismus Donati*, commentaries on Aristotle's *Organon*, on Porphyry's *Isagoge*, on the anonymous *Liber sex principiorum*, and on BOETHIUS' *Liber divisionum*. Possibly during this period he also wrote his commentary on the first three books of Aristotle's *Nicomachean Ethics*. He joined the Dominican order in about 1245 and thereafter, perhaps on his arrival at Oxford, began his theology studies. He composed *De ortu scientiarum* (*On the Rise [or Origin] of the Sciences*) about 1250. Also in Oxford he composed *De tempore* (*On Time*) and *De spiritu fantastico* (*On Imagination*). Also during his Oxford days he commented on the *Sentences* of PETER LOMBARD. For about five years from about 1256 he was regent in theology at Oxford, following which, in 1261, he was elected Prior Provincial of the English Dominicans. Pope Gregory X nominated him Archbishop of Canterbury in October 1272, and in 1278 he was named Cardinal Bishop of Porto. He died in 1279 in Viterbo while working in the papal service.

His historical fame rests principally on his act of proscription in March 18, 1277, eleven days after Étienne Tempier's more famous condemnation in Paris. Kilwardby prohibited the teaching at Oxford of just thirty propositions, fourteen of them concerning grammar and logic, and sixteen concerning natural philosophy. Among the propositions proscribed by Kilwardby were those affirming that a necessary truth requires the constancy of its object (which he held to be false, because God's knowledge of contingent truths is itself necessarily true), and that only what exists can be the subject of a demonstration (which he held to be false, because it is possible to formulate a demonstration about a nonexistent essence).

He also condemned the proposition that there is no active potency in matter. This proposition is of particular interest since, as against it, he argued on behalf of the Augustinian doctrine of "seminal reasons" for, according to Kilwardby, matter contains, as a kind of seed, an internal principle of motion. This doctrine relates to Kilwardby's thoughts on the contentious question of the principle of motion of the heavenly bodies. There had been a common view that the heavenly bodies were moved by angels, intelligences, or souls. Earlier in the thirteenth century John Blund had rejected it on the grounds that heavenly bodies move by their nature and not by an act of a soul. Kilwardby accepted Blund's position and expanded it in the course of a response to questions sent to him (as well as to ALBERTUS MAGNUS and THOMAS AQUINAS) by John of Vercelli. The first five questions concern the motion of celestial bodies, and particularly concern the role of angels in such motion.

Kilwardby replied that celestial bodies have a natural tendency to rotational motion. The nature of the bodies is of course God-given, but once given, the explanation for the motion lies in the body and not with God. God is therefore only indirectly the mover, and angels play no part whatever in the story. His description of the nature of the inner principle of motion is in terms of the Augustinian concept of rational seeds.

There are other important indications of Augustinianism in Kilwardby, for example, in his accounts of time and sense knowledge. Kilwardby discusses the question where time is, and focuses on two possible answers. One, associated with Aristotle, is that time is outside the mind, and the other, associated with Augustine, is that time is inside. As regards Aristotle, Kilwardby attends to the doctrine that time is "the number (or 'reckoning' or 'countability') of motion in respect of the earlier and the later" and focuses particularly on the diurnal circular motion of the sun because that is the most basic motion, the one that gives us our basic unit of time, the day.

Since diurnal motion occurs whether or not any perceptual being notices the celestial bodies in their courses, it seems that time, defined in terms of such motion, is entirely external to the mind. But Kilwardby asks whether there could be time if there were no mind counting and distinguishing it. The formulation hints at trouble for the externalist's position, for the counting or measuring of diurnal motions hints at the existence of a counter or a measurer. It might be replied that the countability of celestial motion does not actually require someone to be counting, but Kilwardby goes deeper than that, with the help of Augustine, who held that "earlier and later do not exist anywhere except where they exist together . . . But they exist nowhere at the same time except in the mind" (*De termino*, para. 3). For Kilwardby the possibility that some events are later than others depends upon the fact that in relation to a given now something lies in the past and some other event lies in the future, and that what lies in the past is earlier than what lies in the future, and that there can be no now except in relation to a conscious being for whom there is a now. Kilwardby writes:

> Augustine stated that time exists only in the mind, and according to him time is a certain extension, not of something existing outside the mind but of an affection of the mind present to it and left behind in it by things passing by.' (*De termino*, para. 4)

But Kilwardby stops short of wholehearted endorsement of this position, since Aristotle's externalist view of time has to be respected. So he adopts a compromise position on the basis of a distinction between time existing as unlimited and undetermined and as limited and determined. Defining a measure of motion, a day, or an hour, requires a mental act. Before a day is defined, there is no day, that is, no day considered as a determinate unit of measure of motion. Yet of course there were days before there was a defined measure. But these were, in Kilwardby's language, unlimited and indeterminate and hence do not presuppose the existence of a mind. The externalist view and the internalist view are therefore both correct.

A second area of Kilwardby's thought where Augustine plays a major role is in the discussion of the nature and functioning of the faculty of imagination as expounded in the *De spiritu fantastico*. Kilwardby seeks to identify the causal agent by which images of sensible things are impressed on sense. An obvious candidate is the body which is sensed, but this proposal runs up against Augustine, who affirms: "It is not sensible to think that a body can make something in a soul, for a soul does not stand in a matter-relation to a making body" (*De spiritu fantastico*, para. 47). For that which makes is in every way more excellent than the thing out of which it makes something. Augustine teaches that a soul cannot stand to a body in the relation of matter to form, and the implication of this teaching is that a body cannot impose an image upon a soul. Indeed Kilwardby believes the universe to be a hierarchy in which the direction of government is downward from the more perfect and more excellent to the less. In this hierarchy the lower cannot act upon the higher. If, then, a body cannot be the efficient cause of an image in sense, what can? Kilwardby's answer is that sense itself forms in itself the image of the sensible thing, and he supports this with authoritative texts from Augustine.

The broad picture is this: the sensible object produces an impression on the organ of sense, and the sensory soul, an active principle, goes forward to meet the organ of sense. The image in the sensory soul is a consequence of the soul's attention to the impression made on the sense organ by the sensible object.

Against this it might be objected that since the image in the sense organ is the means by which the image in the sensory soul is effected, the image in the sense organ is, after all, the efficient cause of the image in the soul. But Kilwardby replies by deploying the distinction between an essential and an accidental cause:

> For the act of the artificer is essentially the cause of the statue, but the adze is the accidental cause as the necessary instrument by means of which the art is exercised. Likewise, the mind going out to meet the passivities of the body is essentially the cause of cognition; the sensible things and the sense organ are an accidental cause like an instrument or instruments used by the mind in order to become informed. (*De spiritu fantastico*, para. 123)

Throughout his discussion of sensing and imagining Kilwardby's discussion is more on the side of Augustine than Aristotle. The latter is of course frequently invoked, but Kilwardby's predilections are in the open: "St Augustine was much more sublimely enlightened than Aristotle, especially in spiritual matters" (ibid., para. 98).

However, another of Kilwardby's works of the Oxford period, the *De ortu scientiarum*, is largely but not entirely an exposition of Aristotle, bearing few marks of Augustinianism. In it Kilwardby considers speculative philosophy under three heads, natural, mathematical, and divine. Natural philosophy deals with mobile things and material things insofar as they are mobile. Mathematical philosophy deals with mobile and material things, not as such but after abstracting them from motion and matter, thus leaving in the frame the geometrical and the arithmetical properties of things. Divine philosophy considers things that are entirely immobile and separated from matter. As regards this last heading Kilwardby distinguishes between divine science and human, the former being "that which is handed down to men by God, its author" (*De ortu scientiarum*, para. 1). The example of divine science that Kilwardby has in mind is, of course, the Bible. There is evident tension between this concept and Aristotle's concept of divine philosophy in that for Aristotle the divine philosophy is about divine things, and human beings are the authors of it as a result of having worked things out by their unaided reason.

As regards natural science there are points of obscurity in Kilwardby's exposition. He holds that mobile body is the subject of natural science but has to attend to the fact that the science apparently deals with many other things also, such as matter, form, privation, place, time, mind (or soul), and the first mover. His response is to say that natural science considers a mobile body in respect of its form, matter, and privation. Furthermore all mobile bodies are in time, and the science must therefore deal with time. In addition a naturally mobile body has within itself a principle of motion, which is considered by natural science.

613

Also the motive principle of animate things is their soul, which is likewise studied by that science. And the motive principle of the celestial bodies is the prime mover, so natural science considers the prime mover *qua* principle of motion of celestial bodies.

This last point is problematic for two sorts of reason. First, Kilwardby distinguishes between divine science and natural, and evidently regards them as mutually exclusive. Yet God is the prime mover, and in that case the prime mover is surely the object of divine science rather than of natural. This may however constitute a reason to doubt that the two sciences are after all mutually exclusive.

Secondly, Kilwardby's statement 'The motive principle of a heavenly body is the prime mover' appears to sit uneasily with his condemnation at Oxford of the proposition that there is no active potency in matter, and with his associated teaching that celestial bodies have a natural tendency to rotational motion. On this account, derived from the 1277 Oxford Condemnation, the motive principle of a celestial body is internal to it. It is, however, possible to argue that Kilwardby did not change his mind between writing the *De ortu* and issuing the Condemnation, for of course God as creator is also the prime mover of the universe and of everything in it. There is within each celestial body, and as part of the nature of the body, a principle of circular motion. But the body has the nature it has in accordance with the intention of the creator of that body, and hence there is no tension between the claims that the motive principle of a celestial body is internal to the body and that the motive principle of the body is the prime mover. There is, however, reason to be uneasy about this interpretation, for God is the prime mover in respect of all bodies, celestial or otherwise, but it is only with reference to celestial bodies that Kilwardby invokes the prime mover as the principle of motion. And why should he do that if not because it is only celestial bodies that do not have an inner principle of motion?

Kilwardby lists three sorts of substance – the uncreated, the created spiritual, and the created corporeal – and holds that they are all subjects of the first philosophy or first science. Accidents also have a kind of substance or substantiality, though not of themselves. Nevertheless their substantiality, such as it is, is sufficient to bring accidents within the ambit of the first philosophy, whose overall subject matter is defined by Kilwardby, following Aristotle, as being *qua* being.

Kilwardby's account of the subject matter of the first philosophy implies that God and human beings are subjects of the first philosophy, for they are substances and the first philosophy deals with substance. Yet Kilwardby states both that every science has just one subject, and also that creature and creator have nothing in common. There is an apparent tension here, which is dealt with by Kilwardby on the basis of the fact that whereas the unity of a science requires the unity of the subject, the subject does not have to be entirely univocal in every way. The unity of analogy is sufficient. *Being*, the subject philosophy, extends to God and creatures, for being and substance are predicated analogically of God and creatures. Being and substance belong to God essentially and primarily and more, and belong to creatures by participation and secondarily and less. There is therefore something in common between God and creatures. The model Kilwardby invokes is that of the form that informs the artificer's art and also informs the matter on which the artificer works. The world, therefore, and God, artificer of the world, have sufficient in common in respect of their being to permit the one science, first philosophy, to deal with both God and creatures.

In the latter stages of the *De ortu* Kilwardby turns to the first three of the liberal arts, grammar, logic, and rhetoric, the arts of language or of discourse, and begins with a general observation about the arts, namely that use precedes art. People counted before the rise of arithmetic, measured before the rise of geometry, and before the rise of astronomy people based their units of time on observation of the motion of the celestial bodies. Likewise, people spoke, wrote, and reasoned before the arts of grammar, logic, and rhetoric arose. These arts, argues Kilwardby, were the last to have arisen, because speech and reasoning were used in the development of the other arts, and people gradually came to realize that the perfection of the other arts depended upon the development of the arts of speech and reasoning. With the development of the latter arts it becomes easier to determine which expressions are most appropriate if one is to be understood, and which arguments are most effective if one is to get at the truth.

As regards logic there is a problem, for, as Kilwardby puts the point, it seems that what is common to all sciences is proper to none. But reasoning is common to all sciences, for without reasoning there is no science. There cannot, therefore, be a science whose subject is reasoning itself. The short answer to this problem is that the same thing can be in one way common to many things and in another way proper to one. Thus a knife has one essence and many uses. Likewise reasoning is proper to logic in so far as reasoning is the essence or subject of logic, but it is common to all sciences in respect of use. Reasoning therefore can be considered either in itself, and such a consideration is the business of logic, or else it can be considered as supportive of all other sciences. And for this reason logic is properly called the art of arts and the science of sciences.

The *De ortu scientiarum* is not a pioneering work in any sense, even though it is perhaps one of the best introductions to philosophy to have been produced during the Middle Ages. Its chief merit lies in its presentation of a particularly clear account of the state of the art of philosophy at a time of great intellectual turmoil in the universities. It is too early for a definitive judgment of Kilwardby's philosophy as a whole. Aside from biographical works, particularly centering on the Oxford Condemnation of 1277, Kilwardby scholarship is in general of two distinct sorts, namely theological studies and critical editions. A detailed study of Kilwardby's philosophy is yet to be written.

Bibliography

Primary sources

(1976), *De ortu scientiarum*, ed. Albert G. Judy, Oxford: British Academy.

(1982–95), *Quaestiones in libros Sententiarum*, ed. Johannes Schneider, Elizabeth Gössmann, Gerhard Leibold, and Richard Schenk, Munich: Verlag der Bayerischen Akademie der Wissenschaften.

(1987), *On Time and Imagination, De tempore, De spiritu fantastico*, ed. Osmund Lewry, Oxford: Oxford University Press for the British Academy.

(1993), *On Time and Imagination*, Pt. 2, *Introduction and Translation*, ed. A. Broadie, Oxford: Oxford University Press for the British Academy.

Secondary sources

Lewry, Osmund (1981), "The Oxford condemnations of 1277 in grammar and logic," in H. A. G. Braakhuis, C. H. Kneepkens, and L. M. de Rijk, eds., *English Logic and Semantics from the End of the Twelfth Century to the Time of Ockham and Burleigh*, Nijmegen: Ingenium.

——(1981), "Robert Kilwardby on meaning: a Parisian course on the *Logica vetus*," in J. P. Beckmann, ed., *Sprache und Erkenntnis im Mittelalter*, Berlin: De Gruyter.

——(1983), "Robert Kilwardby on imagination: the reconciliation of Aristotle and Augustine," *Medioevo* 9, pp. 1–42.

115

Roger Bacon

JEREMIAH HACKETT

The basic facts of Bacon's chronology are still in dispute. On one reading of a single crucial text and some additional evidence, the following would be a likely outcome: born 1214, educated Oxford 1228 to 1236, professor, University of Paris 1237–47, private scholar 1248–56, possible return to Oxford, Franciscan at Paris, 1256 to about 1280, Franciscan at Oxford from about 1280 to about 1292 (according to Little, Maloney, Hackett). On the second reading, the following: born 1220, educated Oxford 1234 to 1242, professor, University of Paris 1243–8, private scholar, 1248 to about 1255, possible return to Oxford, Franciscan at Paris 1256 to about 1280, Franciscan at Oxford 1280 to about 1292 (according to Crowley, Easton, Lindberg).

The scholarly context and philosophical issues

Bacon's philosophical commentaries are normally situated in the 1240s and they reflect concerns with the new logic at Paris and commentary on the "new" Aristotle (see below). At some stage after 1247, Bacon devoted his own financial resources to new experimental studies and to the training of others. He became acquainted with new translations of significant scientific and experimental texts such as Ibn al-Haytham's *Optics* and the pseudo-Aristotle, *Secretum secretorum*. Between 1254 and 1280, he would master these works and they would become for him, together with related texts such as Aristotle's *Meteora* and Seneca's *Quaestiones naturales*, the centerpiece of a new and more radically "experiential-experimental" philosophy. In *De multiplicatione specierum*, he outlined a philosophy of nature. He provided an account of vision and perception in the *Perspectiva* based on a geometric optics using most of the significant Greek, Roman, and Islamic texts. He took the mathematical-physical account of vision and built it into an Aristotelian-Avicennian-Augustinian philosophy of mind. All of this is situated in a deterministic astrological cosmos taken from both ALKINDI and ALBUMASAR.

The general context for this new philosophy (ca. 1250–92) is Bacon's situation at the University of Paris in the 1260s and his return to Oxford about 1280. It is clear from his many remarks "on his own misfortunes" that he had been an exile from teaching soon after he joined the Franciscans (ca. 1256). He resented this fate. Through the offices of Cardinal Guy le Gros de Foulques (his patron, later Pope Clement IV, 1265–8), he wrote the *Opus maius*, the *Opus minus*, and the *Opus tertium*. In addition to these, he wrote the *Communia naturalium* and the *Communia mathematica*. His diatribe on the scholarly disputes of his time, the *Compendium studii philosophie*, written in 1271, provides an insight into Bacon's own vociferous and strongly held prejudices concerning the scholars and translators of his times. Since the important research of Stuart C. Easton, it has long been held that Bacon's basic notion of science was dependent for the most part on the pseudo-Aristotelian work, the *Secretum secretorum*. Steven J. Williams has now shown that this is a later work, begun in Paris in perhaps the 1260s and completed at Oxford after 1280.

Bacon's last work, the *Compendium studii theologiae* (ca. 1292) (*CST*) is not complete. The modern editions consist only of parts one and two, and these deal with both scholarly sources and the issues in philosophy of language as it relates to theology. The content has much in common with the work on language in the 1260s, specifically *De signis*. This work sheds much light on the actual context of Bacon's philosophy in the 1260s: the rise of Latin Averroism. From this and other works from the 1240s one can now demonstrate that Bacon has taken up the "Averroist" themes while he was a master of arts. These arguments would be repeated by Bacon in his later post-1260 works. He attacks "Averroes and those who follow him," and he uses a selection of authors from Greek, Latin, and Islamic sources for this purpose.

There is some evidence from the *CST* and related works that, within the Franciscan Order, Bacon entered into profound disagreement with BONAVENTURE and his disciple, RICHARD RUFUS OF CORNWALL on some central philosophical ideas, especially on the notion of habitual being, essence, and empty names. But the disagreements seem to be more than merely intellectual; they seem to be intensely personal and perhaps also political. Indeed, it would seem that Bonaventure may have set limits on Bacon's work in Paris between 1267 and 1273. Yet, with the exception of astrology and *scientia experimentalis*, Bacon is in general agreement with the tone and direction of Bonaventure's *reduction of the arts to theology*. The critical edition of the works of Richard Rufus (ed. Rega Wood et al.) should provide the basis for a critical study of the relationship between Bacon, Bonaventure, and Rufus.

During the 1260s, Bacon, in admiration of the experimental studies of PIERRE DE MARICOURT, wrote both propaganda and many scientific treatises in defense of a "new" understanding of philosophy. In Bacon's view, philosophy ought to be more practically orientated. Above all, it has the task of formulating the rules for a science of nature, and it involves the application of mathematics to the discovery of the secrets of nature. The outcome would be practical: the development of new technologies for the benefit and welfare of human life specifically in health-care, military technology, and war. His moral-political thinking is aimed at the education of the prince.

Bacon's influence and importance as a thinker

It is now apparent from modern studies that Roger Bacon prepared the issues which would soon after be taken up by JOHN DUNS SCOTUS, WILLIAM OF OCKHAM, and the Parisian and Oxford debates of the early fourteenth century. And yet his personal studies from the 1260s would in time be overshadowed by the major public teaching texts of contemporaries such as Bonaventure, THOMAS AQUINAS, HENRY OF GHENT, and GILES OF ROME. Bacon's own contribution found its continuity in the works of JOHN PECHAM, RICHARD OF MIDDLETON, and the other English Franciscans up to, and including, Scotus and Ockham. More importantly, his major work on *Perspectiva* was taken up by both Pecham and Witelo. The doctrinal synthesis of these three major optical writers would be foundational up to, and including, Kepler. Indeed, the latter would name his foundational work for modern optics,

Paralipomena ad Witelonem (*Supplement to Witelo*). Bacon's sketch for a better theory of the rainbow was taken up in 1307 by Theodoric of Freiberg who integrated Bacon's work into a full formal theory of the rainbow. This account would provide Descartes with a theoretical background for his new mathematical account of the rainbow in the mid-seventeenth century.

The publication of Bacon's optics, medicine, and astrology made him known in the early seventeenth century. The *Perspectiva* was published at Frankfurt in 1614. The *Opus maius* as a whole was first published in London in 1733 by Samuel Jebb, a contemporary of Bishop Berkeley and was known to Berkeley in the 1730s. The revival of interest in Bacon in the early nineteenth century began in France with the discovery by Victor Cousin of MS Amiens 406 containing his Aristotelian commentaries, and the subsequent study of Emile Charles. This discovery provided the only evidence until recently for Bacon's commentaries on Aristotle. The discovery by Silvia Donati of a second version of Bacon's *Physica* commentary is important for a critical understanding of Bacon as an Aristotelian commentator (see Donati in Hackett, 1997a).

Roger Bacon as a logician and an Aristotelian commentator

The extant writings of Roger Bacon on logic, semantics, and grammar are both unique and important. We do not possess a series of commentaries on the *Organon* of Aristotle, but we have the *Summa grammatica, Summa de sophismatibus et distinctionibus,* and *Summulae dialectices.* It was the view of the late Jan Pinborg that these three works are important witnesses to the development of grammar, semantics, and logic at both Oxford and Paris in the first half of the thirteenth century.

Bacon takes up the traditional concerns with Donatus and Priscian in the study known as "speculative grammar." In particular, Bacon takes up the manner in which RICHARD KILWARDBY linked the study of grammar to the *Physica* of Aristotle. While noting the importance of rules for linguistic construction, Bacon insists that grammatical and logical rules cannot be mechanically applied. Above all, one must take into account the signifying intention of the speaker. This, of course, involves an element of free will and new impositions of meaning. Yet, governing rules apply not only to the normal use of language, but also to the variations introduced by authorial intention: "It is not the sign which signifies but rather the speaker by means of the language."

Alain de Libera provides a very precise summary of Bacon's place in the history of logic (de Libera, in Hackett 1997b). The literary forms, collections of distinctions and *summae,* point to the older tradition at Oxford and Paris. There are no disputed questions. One can distinguish two different stages in his logic. First, there are the works of the 1240s, which are contemporary with writings of other scholars on the *Logica modernorum*: the *Summa de sophismatibus et distinctionibus* (*SSD*) and *Summulae dialectices* (*SD*). Second, there are those works in semantics, signs, and logic that arise out of a concern with the role of language in theology within a project for reform of Christian society: *De signis* (*DS*) (1266–7), and *Compendium studii theologiae* (*CSP*) (1292). These later works involve the introduction of new elements, in particular a synthesis of AUGUSTINE and Aristotle (the theologians and the teachers of the arts) and of themes from "modism." Because of his long life, one can witness the development of thirteenth-century logic in Bacon's works all the way from the logic of WILLIAM OF SHERWOOD and the Oxford *Text-Books* to the difficult philosophical speculations of Henry of Ghent, PETER OLIVI, and Duns Scotus. There is scholarly dispute about the attribution to Roger Bacon of two other treatises on syncategorematic words.

The *SSD* belongs to a literary genre found in Paris during the first half of the thirteenth century, the *Distinctiones sophismatum*. It compares with the *Tractatus de distinctionibus communibus in sophismatibus accidentibus* attributed to Matthew of Orleans, the *Distinctiones "notandum,"* the *Abstractiones* of Hervaeus Sophista, the tracts on *Distinctiones sophismatum* as well as "anonymous" treatises described by De Rijk and Braakhuis. Briefly, the *Distinctiones* have the task of listing the rules to be used in the practice of sophisms and setting out the context, while the *Syncategoremata* set out the logical conditions for the proper use of syncategorematic words.

For the most part, the text deals with the problems of universal quantification, that is, with the syncategorematic word *omnis*. In particular, Bacon gives close attention to signs that present specific difficulty such as 'infinite', 'whole', and negative signs. For the most part, the *SSD* does not show much originality; rather it covers the common subject matter of logic. Yet it does treat some topics with great intensity and daring, in particular the problem of "inclusion" or as we would say "scope" in quantification. In dealing with such propositions as 'Every animal is either rational or irrational', the thirteenth-century logicians used a theory of natural sense by which the order of presentation of the terms in a proposition provided semantic information. It is in his treatment of this issue that Bacon exhibits great originality. He insists in taking into account: (1) the signifying intention of the speaker, (2) the linguistic expression, and (3) the sense which the hearer provides. These three essential elements are expressed in the idea of the "production of speech" (*generatio sermonis*). The thesis of *SSD* is twofold: an expression ought to contain elements that allow a listener to make an interpretation corresponding to the intention of the speaker, and since there will always be difficulties in identifying meaning; the actual expression may not fully account for the intention of the speaker. Thus, one needs a "production of speech" analysis.

This analysis includes: (1) the expression of a statement is accidental; formally and materially, it contains only a relative sense; (2) the linear order of a statement does not give the listener all the necessary information about the logical form; (3) only the order brought about in the mental operations preceding the spoken expression permits a distinction between the material and formal elements. This allows for the assignation of the logical form, which constitutes the sense, to a mental proposition. This kind of analysis implies that every mental proposition, both for the speaker and listener, is *an interpretation*. The signification of a statement is always a function of understanding. This analysis, which emphasizes the threefold aspect of inter-locution – the freedom of the speaker/hearer, the nature of language, and the constraints of communication – prepared the ground for the more mature theory in *DS, CSP, CST*.

De Libera thinks that the *SD* was written at Oxford in about 1250, although he notes that there are some correspondences to Parisian teaching in the text. The title given by Steele is somewhat misleading. The title in the Seville MS reads: *Summulae super totam logicam*. And this is the real scope of the work. It is a mature work, written by a teacher who has broad philosophical interests; it is not the work of a beginner. Indeed, it towers over some contemporary works in the manner in which it handles the "new" Aristotle and a variety of new works in philosophy and science. The work is most important for two novel semantic positions: (1) the doctrine of univocal appellation and (2) the doctrine of the predication in regard to "empty classes." Bacon insists that a word cannot univocally apply to a being and non-being. This is his fundamental semantic teaching, which is found in the later works, and which is worked out in detail in *SD*. In this, he argues against the common teaching of the schools, specifically at Paris. For the common teaching, a word has a natural meaning and once the meaning is given, it remains. Thus, the word 'Caesar' once established can be used of both the living Caesar and the dead Caesar. For Bacon, on the contrary, a term only names present things. There is nothing in common between an entity and non-entity or between present, past, and future. Terms have only present appellation and appellation to past and future are only made accidentally. Thus, Bacon rejects the doctrine of "natural supposition." In its place, he argues for an intra-propositional supposition related strictly to present objects in regard to signification and original imposition, and open to past and future by means of the verbal tense. This is "supposition through itself for present things." Thus, he is forced to reject such statements as *Omnis homo de necessitate est animal, homine non existente; Cesar est homo, Cesare mortuo*. There are echoes of this topic in SIGER OF BRABANT's *Quaestiones* from the 1260s, where he rejects the position of Bacon. Following ALBERTUS MAGNUS and others, Siger holds that the natural sense of things is not affected by the passage of time or natural change. It would appear that Bacon's rejection of predication in regard to empty classes was criticized by Robert Kilwardby on March 18, 1277. Neither did Bacon's position receive acceptance at Paris.

A second major aspect of *SD* is the complex theory of determination involved in the composition and division of propositional sense. Bacon sets out a series of rules. In this, Bacon draws on the tradition of Latin grammar from Priscian, and traditional grammatical commentary. It is important to note that Bacon makes use of all of the *trivium* in his examination of language. It is by means of his doctrine of "construction" that Bacon justifies the basis of his view of appellation and his rejection of natural supposition and of "verbal restriction," as well as the pride of place that he gives to "supposition for present things" and to ampliation. Thus, the central doctrine of the imposition of meaning for present things is fundamental. Meanings can of course change and do so even tacitly. It follows that one has need for a linguistic analysis and study of context to figure out univocal meaning. Words can also of course be extended metaphorically to cover non-present things. In this work, one finds a combination of influences from both Oxford "terminist logic" and Parisian "premodist grammar," of around 1250.

Roger Bacon's "new" experimental philosophy, 1260–92

From *Opus maius I*, it is clear that Bacon is writing his new program for theological study for Pope Clement IV in the context of a polemic at the University of Paris. Briefly stated, Bacon, like Aquinas, wishes to cut a middle way between the condemnations of Aristotle and Arabic sciences on the part of some canonists and theologians and the "rationalized" Aristotle presented by some masters of arts at the university. In brief, Bacon proposes to take up Aristotle into a doctrinal synthesis that includes elements of Stoicism and Platonism.

In *Opus maius II*, Bacon presents an account of the origins of wisdom. This has correspondences to the first book of the pseudo-Grosseteste's *Summa philosophiae*, and argues that both *philosophia* (Islamic *falsafa*) and canon law are the two main instruments for the interpretation of theology. Philosophy as a specific school-subject is therefore subordinate to the general search for wisdom. That is, philosophy as an academic subject is a specialized use of reason which acts as an instrument on the way towards wisdom. Wisdom, which includes both poetry and philosophy, was originally given to the prophets and patriarchs, and was then transmitted through the Greeks and through Islam, and it has now reached a point of development in Christian times. There is thus a history of wisdom and truth, the lineaments of which are taken from Josephus, Augustine, and ISIDORE OF SEVILLE. One can see here that Bacon engages on a destruction of the new scholastic method of the *Sentences* from within. That is, he argues, in what by 1260 is a "conservative" position, that the text of Scripture and the faithful exegesis of the text must always take precedence over the "rationalizations" of the *summae* and books of *Sentences*. The kernel of this position is evident in his application of language analysis to theology. There is also a history of anti-wisdom symbolized by the figure of Nimrod. This is the history of the disintegration of language due to the sin of pride. The great philosophers, Socrates, Plato, Aristotle, Plotinus are seen as the ones who have criticized this false mythological anti-theology. Finally, the development of arts and sciences finds its *telos* in moral philosophy. That is, the whole end of the arts and sciences is to bring about the moral and religious development of the human race.

The *Opus maius III* (and its related texts, *Compendium studii philosophiae*, *Compendium studii theologiae*) presents Bacon's new understanding of the role of language in theology. It is in the context of this general theory of language that Bacon presents his new general "theory of signs" in a section titled *De signis*, a work discovered and edited by Fredborg, Neilsen, and Pinborg (1978). The subsequent studies have mapped out the significance and novelty of Bacon's position.

Bacon's account of language and signs

In keeping with his idea of a history of wisdom, Bacon presents the science of the wisdom languages as the primary science. It is on the basis of this science that further linguistic thinking proceeds. This theory has practical uses in the Church: divine office, sacraments, preaching, the time of the Antichrist. Further, it has direct import on trade, missions, and on the conversion process. Bacon owes this "necessary knowledge of languages" to the influence of Augustine. Broadly speaking, one notices two levels of emphasis: Bacon is interested in the power of letters and words, including their "magical powers." He is also interested in this natural power of words as a multiplication of species. Yet, he situates this latter factor in the primary context of the will of the speaker, and following AVICENNA holds that nature will obey the thoughts of the soul. One can summarize, and state that Bacon, in his theory of language and signs, synthesizes the concerns of Augustine (*De dialectica*, *De doctrina Christiana*, *De magistro*), the theologians, Aristotle, and Islamic writers on language, signs, rhetoric and poetics. In fact, Bacon radically alters the traditional account of the *trivium*. There are echoes of the new humanistic concerns with grammar and poetry. Bacon presents a theory of the development of languages that has much in common with the views of DANTE. There is a sketch of a comparative linguistics, and Latin is seen as a universal technical language.

When one learns that Bacon wrote both Greek and Hebrew grammars and had some acquaintance with Arabic, one realizes that he is a person who would have been strange to the normal practices of the philosophers in the medieval university. Here, study was confined to grammar, logic, and rhetoric in Latin alone. In Bacon's view, there were three levels of language knowledge: first, the elements of Latin grammar; second, the reasoned grammar of the philosophical student of language; and third, the knowledge of languages, especially of the languages of wisdom. Only the first two were studied in the medieval university.

621

Bacon's definition of sign draws on two definitions of Augustine from *De dialectica* and *De doctrina Christiana*. A sign is "that which when offered to the senses or the intellect designates something else to that intellect." There is a two-fold relationship, that of sign to the intellect for whom it signified (the interpreter) and that of sign to what is signified. Bacon subordinates the latter to the former. As I. Catach-Rosier puts it, "the speaker is at all times free to re-impose the signs, that is to give them a new meaning: signification is thus subordinate to the decision of the speaker." The traditional medieval position as presented in RICHARD FISHACRE, Kilwardby, and Bonaventure is here inverted. For these theologians, the relation of sign to signified is an essential one. That is, once a sign has been instituted, it is essential and it is not subject to change. The relation of sign to signified once established is the foundational relation. It remains even if there is no interpreter, and it grounds the nature of the sign as sign. For Bacon, a sign such as a restaurant sign even if it has a meaning when instituted, has no meaning if there is no one around for whom it signifies. It exists only in potency. Bacon's division of signs is as follows:

1   Natural signs: example: smoke, fire
2   Signs directed by the soul in order to signify:
    (a)   Signifying conventionally, in the mode of the concept
       •   linguistic signs
         by way of imperfect deliberation: interjections
         by way of perfect [completed] deliberation: other parts of speech
       •   non-linguistic signs (the language of gestures, signs made by monks, signboards, etc.)
    (b)   Signifying naturally, in the mode of affect
       •   products of the sensitive soul: sounds emitted by animals
       •   products of the rational soul: groans, exclamations, cries of pain

As a result of this theory, analogy and metaphor become important for Bacon as the human imposition of meaning is both deliberate and tacit.

Opus maius IV deals with the applications of mathematics to both nature and human concerns, specifically theological concerns. Bacon begins with a claim that logic reduces to mathematics, that is, to concerns with quantity. He presents a digest of his teaching in his fundamental philosophy of nature, the *De multiplicatione specierum* (*DMS*). "By 'species' we do not mean Porphyry's fifth universal; rather this name is meant to designate the first effect of any naturally-acting thing." As Bacon shows, the word 'species' is equivalent to other different words which have application in human psychology and agency such as: idol, phantasm, simulacrum, appearance, form, intention, and shadow of the philosophers. "It is called 'virtue' with respect to generation and corruption; and thus we say that every agent produces its virtue in a recipient. It is called 'impression' because it resembles impressions" (*DMS*, 4).

To summarize: Bacon provides a theory of natural univocal agency in which notions of floating "spiritual" intentions are rejected. That is, every natural agent produces its likeness or species as a natural fact. And further, this agency operates according to strict material processes which are only truly knowable in a mathematical manner. One notices here a criticism of AVERROES and of some major Latin scholastic thinkers including Aquinas. In part two of this work, Bacon sets out the manner in which one can have a thorough geometrical understanding of nature according to lines, figures, and numbers. This work is fundamental for his optics and for his philosophy of human life.

In his attempt to prove the utility of mathematics to his contemporaries, Bacon provides a critical theory of the uses of mathematics in applied astronomy (astrology), an account of the uses of mathematics in theology (chronology, measurement of sacred art works), an account of world geography in reference to mission, and a brief precis of Albumasar's astrology.

Opus maius V contains the physiological and mathematical basis for Bacon's theory of mind. Part one consists of a remarkable synthesis of ALHACEN, Avicenna, Aristotle and some medical authors, such as Galen and Constantine the African. He provides a detailed sketch of the role of the senses, the *sensus communis*, imagination, memory, and *fantasia*, and he adds a detailed account of the role of discriminative reason in both animal and human knowledge. Most significant is what is missing: there is no theory of abstraction. But Bacon does not have need for one, for his theory of knowledge is evidentialist. And it is supported by a strong doctrine of illumination in which the *dator formarum* illumines the mind of the individual when the appropriate physio-psychological state has been engendered. The influence of Avicenna, Augustine, and Aristotle is obvious. To grasp the context of these remarks, they should be read together with his comments in *Communia naturalium*, I, iv, where he provides a criticism of his contemporaries and defends the positions of philosophers and English theologians. In particular, he uses his philosophy of mind with its emphasis on the primacy of the individual knower to criticize the "Latin Averroist" notion of one potential intellect for the human race. Also, he attacks Aquinas's notion of one simple intellectual form and defends a doctrine of spiritual matter in humans and angels. One has the impression of reading someone who is writing for the moment and is commenting on the formal work of others.

Part two of the *Perspectiva* consists of Bacon's interpretation of Alhacen's *Optics*. Bacon presents a thorough account of direct, reflected, and refracted vision. He clearly understands the implications of this new "intromission" doctrine of vision for a theory of perception, but he has reservations. On the basis of his view that the eye and mind are not purely passive receivers of images, he takes over from ROBERT GROSSETESTE a theory of extramission and purges it of its anthropomorphic garb. From the viewpoint of a cohesive and comprehensive physical theory of impact, this could be seen as an incoherence. But when one places, as Bacon does, a physical-mathematical theory in the context of competing philosophies of mind, one can understand what Bacon is attempting. He is seeking to graft the physical-mathematical theory into a dualism of soul and body such as is found in Augustine and Avicenna. And he reads Aristotle in the light of these thinkers. From the viewpoint of a philosophy of mind, the *Perspectiva* is of fundamental importance. Part three has to do with the "allegorical": moral uses of perspective teaching in morals and religion. Thus, geometrical analogies can be used for the purposes of moral teaching, a practice taken up by Pierre de Limoges.

Opus maius VI, de scientia experimentali is closely connected with *Opus maius V*. It provides a sketch for a theory of experiment. Both together provide Bacon's model for an experimental science. Bacon changes Aristotle's notion of experience in the light of Ibn al-Haytham. From his brief exegesis of Aristotle's *Posterior Analytics* II.19, *Metaphysics* I.1, and *Nicomachean Ethics* VI, Bacon comes up with an inversion of Aristotle's doctrine of the subordination of experience to reason. Bacon manages to read Aristotle in such a way that the person of direct visual experience has, in some cases, greater precision than the person of "knowledge." It follows from this that "inference" (*argumentum*) alone will not suffice; it must be based on, and confirmed by, experiences. There are two kinds of experience: the first is human and philosophical, that is, experiences of nature and human behavior. The second is moral and religious. In this case, Bacon provides a phenomenology of moral and religious experience. While for him the latter is superior, both are the result of a revelation of truth, a notion drawn from Augustine and pseudo-Ptolemy. Bacon's goal in *Opus maius VI* is to present the rules for a practical science of nature analogous to the rules of logic for formal reasoning. His motivation is to provide a method which will distinguish "a true science and art of nature" from the deceptions of magicians.

The central example used to exhibit this new scientific method is a sketch for an account of the theory of the rainbow. Bacon claims that natural philosophy alone or even *perspectiva* alone cannot lead to a deductive theory of the rainbow. One has need of detailed and particular experiences. What he means is that a combination of very detailed observations and precise mathematical calculations will be necessary for the theory. He draws on Aristotle, Seneca, Avicenna, and AVERROES for his "description" of the rainbow, and he draws on the inspiration of Ibn al-Haytham's mathematical optics for the idea that one must carefully measure the phenomenon. Thus, he succeeds in giving a correct account of the highest altitude of a rainbow (42 degrees). His account of reflection and refraction is important. Although he favors a theory of reflection, he does correct Grosseteste's account of refraction, and also provides a theory of the halo.

Following this example, Bacon proceeds to talk about the importance of scientific instruments, the need for "experiment" in medicine and the importance of chemistry. He concludes with a model for a philosophical chancellor, one who will use the findings of the sciences for the just regime of government and for the development of the Christian *respublica*.

Opus maius VII, entitled *Moralis philosophiae* is a single volume in itself. It presents a view of the arts and sciences as being in the service of human action, that is, human moral agency. Part one consists of a presentation of ancient pagan, Jewish, and Islamic accounts of natural theology as a pre-vision of revealed doctrine. Part two is a brief sketch of Islamic social thought. Part three, the most extensive part, is a general theory of the virtues based on a subordination of Aristotle's virtue theory to an overall Stoic doctrine of virtue. This section is important for its digest of Seneca's *De ira*, and related works. Bacon presents a theory of virtue opposed to that of Aquinas. It is clear from the surviving autograph that Bacon was writing under a deadline. His various editorial notes indicate that he was primarily concerned with providing the ruler with what he held to be a solid moral-political theory as an education for the prince. Part four deals with an astrological sociology of religions. Part five deals with the uses of language, particularly rhetoric and poetics in political life, morals, and religions. This is a very important synthesis of Islamic rhetoric and poetics (Averroes, ALGAZALI, ALFARABI) with the Latin tradition of Cicero and Horace. Here again, Augustine is a major influence. Part six consists of a brief few pages on forensic rhetoric.

Bibliography

Primary sources

(1909–40), *Opera hactenus inedita*, ed. Robert Steel and Ferdinand Delorme, Oxford: Clarendon Press.

(1978), *Opus maius: De signis*, in K. M. Fredborg, Lauge Nielsen, and Jan Pinborg, eds., "An unedited part of Roger Bacon's *Opus maius: De signis*," *Traditio* 34, pp. 75–136.

(1983), *De multiplicatione specierum* and *De speculis comburentibus*, in David C. Lindberg, ed., *Roger Bacon's Philosophy of Nature: A Critical Edition, with English Translation, Introduction and Notes of De multiplicatione specierum and De speculis comburentibus*, Oxford: Clarendon Press.

(1986 and 1987), *Summulae dialectices*, in Alain de Libera, ed., Les *Summulae dialectices* de Roger Bacon, *Archives d'Histoire Doctrinale et Littéraire du Moyen Âge* 53 (pp. 139–289); 54 (pp. 171–278).

(1988), *Compendium of the Study of Theology*, in Thomas S. Maloney, *Roger Bacon: Compendium of the Study of Theology: Edition and Translation with Introduction and Notes*, Leiden: Brill.

(1993), *Geometria speculativa*, in George Molland, ed. and trans., "Roger Bacon's *Geometria speculativa*," in M. Folkerts and J. P. Hogendijk, eds., *Vestigia mathematica*, Amsterdam and Atlanta: Editions Rodolpi.

(1996), *Perspectiva*, in David C. Lindberg, ed., *Roger Bacon and the Origins of Perspectiva in the Middle Ages: A Critical Edition and English Translation of Bacon's Perspectiva with Introduction and Notes*, Oxford: Clarendon Press.

(forthcoming), *Opus maius VI, Tractatus de experientia*, ed. Jeremiah Hackett.

Translations

Linden, Stanton J., ed. (1992), *The Mirror of Alchemy*, New York: Garland Press.

Maloney, Thomas S., trans. (1994), *Three Treatments of Universals by Roger Bacon*, Center for Medieval and Early Renaissance Studies, SUNY, Binghampton, NY: State University of New York Press.

——(forthcoming), *Roger Bacon's Summulae dialectices*.

Secondary sources

Alessio, Franco (1959), "Un secolo di studi su Ruggero Bacone (1848–1957)," *Revista Critica di Storia della Filosofia* 14, pp. 81–102.

Berubé, Camille (1976), *De la philosophie à la sagesse chez Saint Bonaventure et Roger Bacon*, Rome: Istituto Storico dei Cappuccini.

Catach-Rosier, I. (1997), "Roger Bacon and grammar," in J. Hackett, ed., *Roger Bacon and the Sciences: Commemorative Essays* (pp. 67–102), Leiden, New York, and Cologne: Brill.

de Libera, A. (1997), "Roger Bacon et la logique," in J. Hackett, ed., *Roger Bacon and the Sciences: Commemorative Essays* (pp. 103–32), Leiden, New York, and Cologne: Brill.

Ebbesen, Sten (1970), "Roger Bacon and the fools of his time," in *Cahiers de l'Institut du Moyen Âge Grec et Latin* 3, pp. 40–4.

——(1979), "The dead man is alive," *Synthese* 40, pp. 43–70.

Hackett, Jeremiah (1995), "*Scientia experimentalis*: from Robert Grosseteste to Roger Bacon," in James McEvoy, ed., *Robert Grosseteste: New Perspectives on his Thought and Scholarship* (pp. 89–119), Turnhout: Brepols; Steenbrugis: Abbatia S. Petri.

——ed. (1997a), *Roger Bacon and Aristotelianism*, *Vivarium* 35/2 (September), pp. 129–35.

——ed. (1997b), *Roger Bacon and the Sciences: Commemorative Essays*, Leiden: Brill.

——(1997c), "The published works of Roger Bacon," *Vivarium* 35/2 (September), pp. 315–20.

——(1998), "*Experientia, Experimentum* and the perception of objects in space," in Jan A. Aertsen and Andreas Speer, eds., *Raum und Raumvorstellungen im Mittelalter*, Miscellanea medievalia 25 (pp. 101–20), Berlin: De Gruyter.

Hackett, Jeremiah and Maloney, Thomas S. (1987), "A Roger Bacon bibliography (1957–85)," *The New Scholasticism* 61, pp. 184–207.

Hedwig, Klaus (2000), "Roger Bacon: *scientia experimentalis*," in Theo Kobusch, ed., *Philosophen des Mittelalters* (pp. 140–51), Darmstadt: Primus.

Kukssewicz, Z. (1982), "The potential and agent intellect," in Norman Kretzmann, Anthony Kenny, Jan Pinborg, eds., *The Cambridge History of Later Medieval Philosophy* (pp. 595–601), Cambridge: Cambridge University Press.

Maloney, Thomas S. (1982),"Roger Bacon on *The significatum of words*," in L. Brind'Amour and E. Vance, eds., *Archéologie du signe* (pp. 187–211), Toronto: Pontifical Institute of Mediaeval Studies.

——(1983), "The semiotics of Roger Bacon," *Mediaeval Studies* 45, pp. 120–54.

——(1984), "Roger Bacon on equivocation," *Vivarium* 22, pp. 85–112.

——(1997), "A Roger Bacon bibliography (1985–95)," in Jeremiah Hackett, ed., *Roger Bacon and the Sciences: Commemorative Essays* (pp. 395–403), Leiden: Brill.

116

Roger Marston

GORDON A. WILSON

Roger Marston (b. ca. 1235; d. ca. 1303), a Franciscan, studied in Paris from 1269 to 1272 under his fellow Franciscan masters, JOHN PECHAM, Eustachius Atrebatensis, and William de la Mare. Marston was present during the 1270 meeting of Parisian masters where his teacher, Pecham, and other masters challenged THOMAS AQUINAS on his position concerning the unicity of substantial human forms. He witnessed this critique by Pecham, and the subsequent refinement of some beliefs by Thomas. Marston began his teaching career in Oxford around 1276, moved to Cambridge before 1285, and in his capacity of minister provincial for the English Franciscans from 1292 to 1298 he helped to promote the young Franciscan, JOHN DUNS SCOTUS. His commentary on PETER LOMBARD'S *Sentences* is lost, and his only surviving philosophical writings are his *Quaestiones disputatae* and four *Quodlibeta*. In the latter, disputations *de quolibet*, about "whatever," Marston treats diverse topics in theology, philosophy, and canon law.

Marston flourished during the last third of the thirteenth century, a period of some turmoil at the universities. At Paris, he was aware of the tensions between mendicants and secular masters. Just before Marston began his studies at Paris, the French king sent the royal archers to protect the priory of St. Jacques, when the Dominican Florent of Hesdin began his teaching career. He would have known opposition to the mendicants by the seculars and he would have been aware of the intervention by the pope himself to get the Dominican, Thomas Aquinas, and the Franciscan, BONAVENTURE, accepted back into the theology faculty in 1257. In the early 1280s Pope Martin IV, in his bull, *Ad fructus Uberes*, gave to the Dominicans and Franciscans the privilege of hearing confessions without receiving the prior permission of local secular clergy. When the bishops of France asked the masters in theology at Paris, who were mainly secular clergy, to help them respond, bitter disputes resulted between the secular masters and the mendicant masters. Even though he was in England at the time, Marston defended the granting of this privilege to the mendicants in his *Quodlibeta*. Because a written *Quodlibet* was based upon *public* disputations, that Marston addressed this topic in his *Quodlibeta* indicates that at this time Franciscans, in spite of opposition from the secular clergy, were not prohibited from treating this issue publicly.

Marston was also a witness to clashes between the Dominicans and the Franciscans. He was already at Oxford when certain philosophical and theological propositions were condemned in 1277 both at Paris and Oxford. John Pecham opposed what he considered to be new-fangled innovations in theology which had resulted from incorporating some Aristotelian principles into theological reflection. Marston had not only witnessed Pecham's exchange with Thomas in 1270 at Paris, but also knew of Pecham's *Quodlibet quatuor* and Pecham's continued opposition to Thomas even when Pecham had moved to lecturing at the papal curia. Marston was already teaching at Cambridge when, as Archbishop of Canterbury, Pecham issued his condemnation of 1286.

Marston was such a careful disciple of his master Pecham that at times he took whole passages from him and presented them as his own. While this may reflect negatively on Marston's originality, it also could be understood as leading to the development of what may be called a "Franciscan" intellectual trend in the late 1200s. This "Franciscanism," of which Marston is representative, developed in the wake of Pecham's exchange with Thomas, the condemnation of 1277, William de la Mare's work, *The Correction of Brother Thomas* and the Dominican responses it provoked. A sign of this "Franciscan" attitude may also be seen in the requirement established by the Franciscan General Chapter of 1282 that all Franciscan readers of Thomas's *Summa* consult William de la Mare's *Correction*. In a letter of December 20, 1284, Pecham even remarked that disagreement between Franciscans and Dominicans was so pronounced that the two mendicant orders disagreed on every debatable point of doctrine. This "Franciscanism" may be characterized as conservative (in the sense of being reluctant to depart from what had seemed to serve medieval Christian thinkers so well prior to the introduction of Aristotle's *libri naturales* into the university), or as a neo–Augustinianism (as opposed to Averroistic Aristotelianism) which included, for example, beliefs in a type of illumination theory, the primacy of the will, and the "being" of matter.

Marston's epistemology did not rely solely on the empiricism of Aristotle, but it incorporated Augustinian language of illumination. For Marston, the material elements of knowledge arise from sensation or the imagination, but the formal elements, i.e., invincible evidence for the truth, cannot arise from sensation or the imagination, but can only be supplied by the "eternal reasons" or illumination. Marston believed that this illumination was the same as the agent intellect of Aristotle, but he denied that there was one agent intellect for all rational beings and insisted, contrary to AVERROES, that each individual had his or her own.

In psychology Marston, like many Franciscans before and after him, argued (contrary to Thomas Aquinas) that the will, not the intellect, was the primary faculty of rational beings. The will is free, Marston emphasized as Pecham had earlier, and if it is free it is not determined by anything, not even by the intellect judging certain objects as good and desirable. Marston rejected Thomas's unicity theory of forms as his teachers John Pecham and William de la Mare had previously, and he attacked HENRY OF GHENT's dymorphism. For Marston, there is a plurality of grades of forms, according to which the vegetative and sensitive forms do not recede with the infusion of the rational soul, as Aquinas and others maintained, but these forms remain as grades of the rational soul that is the ultimate form of the human being.

In physics, Marston rejected the Aristotelian notion of an eternally created world and he argued against those, like Thomas Aquinas, who even entertained the possibility of an eternally created world. Matter, for Marston, had some being – the *"prope nihil"* of Augustine – and as a created nature it has an essence. He, like Pecham, opposed the more Aristotelian position of Thomas Aquinas and others who maintained that matter was just a principle of physical being and thus did not, without form, "exist." Furthermore, Marston defended the Augustinian notion of *rationes seminales* against those like Thomas Aquinas who rejected it.

In metaphysics, Marston has been regarded by M. DeWulf as a proponent of universal hylomorphism, a belief that all created beings, including spiritual beings like angels, are

627

composed of matter and form. This theory has its origins with the Franciscan, Bonaventure, and it became one of the characteristics of the "Franciscan" philosophical trend after Bonaventure's death in 1274. Marston certainly maintained the hylomorphic nature of material beings and, while G. Etzkorn has rightly cautioned that this alone does not commit Marston to a universal hylomorphism, R. Hissette has subsequently maintained the view upheld by De Wulf. Finally, aside from this issue, Marston opposed the Thomistic notion that there is a "real" distinction between essence and existence.

Marston's philosophical thought, heavily influenced by his teacher Pecham, represents a deliberate opposition to what many Franciscans believed to be the unjustified introduction of Averroistic and, in the case of Thomas Aquinas, of Aristotelian tenets into the intellectual reflections of the day. Because many Franciscans before him first formulated these positions, Marston may lack originality, but in re-articulating these ideas he continued a Franciscan trend during the latter part of the 1200s, which prepared the way for Duns Scotus.

Bibliography

Primary sources

(1932), *Quaestiones disputatae*, Bibliotheca Franciscana scholastica medii aevi VII, Quaracchi: Collegium S. Bonaventurae.

(1994), *Quodlibeta quatuor*, ed. G. Etzkorn and I. Brady, Bibliotheca Franciscana scholastica medii aevi 26, 2nd edn., Grottaferrata: Collegium S. Bonaventurae.

Secondary sources

Belmond, S. (1934), "La théorie de la connaissance d'après Roger Marston," *La France Franciscaine* 17, pp. 153–87.

Bonafede, G. (1939), "Il problema del *'lumen'* in fratre Ruggero di Marston," *Rivista Rosminiana de Filosofia e di Cultura* 33, pp. 16–30.

Cairola, J. (1951), "L'opposizione a S. Tommaso nelle *'Questiones disputatae'* di Ruggero Marston," *Scholastica ratione historico-critica instauranda in Bibliotheca Pontificii Athenaei Antoniani* VII, pp. 447–60.

Daniels, A. (1911), "Anselmzität bei dem Oxforder Franziskaner R. von Marston," *Theologische Quartelschrift* 93, pp. 35–59.

Delorme, F. (1934), "Questions de Jean d'Erfurt et de Roger Marston. Autour du canon *Omnis utriusque sexus*," *Studi Francescani* 31, pp. 319–55.

Etzkorn, G. (1962), "The grades of the form according to Roger Marston, O.F.M.," *Franziskanische Studien* 44, pp. 418–54.

Etzkorn, G. and Brady, I. (1994), "Prolegomena," in *Roger Marston, Quodlibeta quatuor*, ed. G. Etzkorn and I. Brady, Bibliotheca Franciscana scholastica medii aevi 26, 2nd edn. (pp. 5*–87*), Grottaferrata: Collegium S. Bonaventurae.

Gilson, É. (1933), "Roger Marston, un cas d'augustinisme avicennisant," *Archives d'Histoire Doctrinale et Littéraire du Moyen Âge* 8, pp. 39–42.

——(1934), "Sur quelques difficultés de l'illumination augustinienne," *Revue Néoscholastique de Philosophie* 36, pp. 321–31.

Glorieux, P. (1979), "Marston (Roger) (d. 1303)," in *Catholicisme Hier Aujourd'hui Demain* 8 (pp. 724–5), Paris: Letouzey et Ané.

Hissette, R. (1971), "Les doctrines métaphysiques de Roger Marston," unpublished dissertation, University of Louvain.

——(1972), "Roger Marston, a-t-il professé l'hylemorphisme universel?", *Recherches de Théologie Ancienne et Médiévale* 29, pp. 205–23.

Hissette, R. (1980), "*Esse-essentia* chez Roger Marston," in *Sapientiae doctrina, Mélange de théologie et de littérature médiévales offerts à Dom Hildebrand Bascour, O.S.B.* (pp. 110–18), Louvain: Imprimerie Orientaliste.

Pelster, F. (1928), "Roger Marston, OFM (d. 1303), ein englischer Vertreter des Augustinismus," *Scholastik* 3, pp. 526–56.

Prezioso, F. (1950), "L'attività del soggetto pensante nella gnoseologia di Matteo d'Acquasparta e di Ruggiero Marston," *Antonianum* 25, pp. 259–326.

Zavalloni, P. (1951), *Richard de Mediavilla et la controverse sur la pluralité des formes*, Louvain: Editions de l'Institut Supérieur de Philosophie.

117

Saadiah

SARAH PESSIN

Saadiah (b. 882; d. 942), or Saadiah Gaon, or Saadiah ben Joseph Gaon, known in Arabic as Sa'id ibn Yusuf, or al-Fayyūmi) was born in Fayyoum (upper Egypt), and lived in Egypt, Palestine, Baghdad, and Aleppo.

A ground-breaking figure in many aspects of Jewish thought, Saadiah was a pioneer in Hebrew lexicography and grammar, wrote an extensive Arabic translation of (as well as commentaries on) the Bible, was an accomplished Talmudist well-versed in astronomy who – as the head of the Jewish academy of Sura in Babylon – played a key role in (a very controversial) Jewish calendrical reform, and wrote a large corpus of renowned Hebrew liturgical poetry. In addition to these many achievements, Saadiah provides a foundation for much subsequent Jewish medieval philosophical discussion. His philosophical ideas can be seen in his various biblical commentaries, as well as in two of his Arabic works in particular: the *Tafsīr Kitāb al-Mabādī* (*Commentary on the Book of Creation*, the first known commentary on the Hebrew esoteric work, the *Sefer Yeẓirah* (*The Book of Creation*)), and the *Amānāt wal-i'tiqādāt* (often translated as *The Book of Beliefs and Opinions*, or *The Book of Doctrines and Beliefs*, and known in its Hebrew translation as the *Sefer [ha-]Emunot ve[ha]-Deot*), his premier philosophical work and arguably the first comprehensive presentation of a Jewish philosophy.

Saadiah puts forth his detailed philosophical corpus in the service, he tells us, of reinforcing and correcting the beliefs of his co-religionists. In line with his efforts to clarify a Jewish belief system, we find him involved in explicit denunciation of trinitarian theology in his treatment of God's attributes in the *Amānāt*, as we also find him engaged in polemics against the Karaites (a Jewish sect renouncing the authority of Rabbinic Judaism, or Oral Law).

Saadiah's work reveals Islamic and Greek influences. He is greatly influenced by the Islamic *kalām* theologians – especially by the Mu'tazilites on the absolute unity of God and justice (the first topics addressed in *Amānāt*). Saadiah does not, however, accept *kalām* atomism (an occasionalist view on which every moment is recreated anew by God), opting instead for a more traditional creation *ex nihilo*. His writing additionally evidences knowledge on his part of a host of Greek traditions, though his philosophical presentation is often dogmatic and uncritical (e.g., he employs Aristotelian principles to argue for non-Aristotelian conclusions, as can be seen in his four arguments in support of creation *ex nihilo*).

A staunch rationalist, Saadiah makes an influential division of biblical precepts: into those that could *not* be arrived at by reason alone, and those whose general character could (eventually) be reached by reasoned reflection. In his rationalism, Saadiah treats the revealed

630

biblical text as subordinate to philosophy: where a biblical passage seems contrary to reason, it must be interpreted (allegorically or otherwise) in accord with reason.

Bibliography

(1894), *Tafsīr Kitāb al-Mabādī*, Arabic text, ed. and trans. into French by Mayer Lambert, Paris: E. Leroux.

(1948), *The Book of Beliefs and Opinions*, translated from the Arabic and Hebrew by S. Rosenblatt, New Haven: Yale University Press.

118

Siger of Brabant

B. CARLOS BAZÁN

Immortalized by DANTE in the *Divina commedia* (Paradiso, canto X, 133–8), condemned by conservative theologians like JOHN PECHAM, Siger of Brabant (b. ca. 1240; d. after 1282) has been surrounded by legend. Contemporary historiography has drawn a more sober and more relevant picture of this prominent figure of thirteenth-century philosophy. A synthesis of all previous scholarship on the subject is found in F. Van Steenberghen's monumental monograph *Maître Siger de Brabant* (1977); it was adjusted, especially with respect to the early years of Siger's career and his role in the faculty of arts in Paris, by R.-A. Gauthier (1983 and 1984); a more recent balanced account, based on well-established data has been presented by F.-X. Putallaz and R. Imbach (1997).

The exact date and place of Siger's birth are unknown. It is assumed that he was born around 1240 at a village in the Duchy of Brabant. He acquired his initial education in Liège, where he became a canon of Saint-Paul Church, a position that secured for him the means to attend the University of Paris, where he joined the Picard "nation" of the faculty of arts around 1255–7. By that time, the new statutes of the faculty of arts had incorporated into the curriculum of studies the full range of Aristotle's writings, which had been banned from "lectures" since 1215. Siger acquired an extensive knowledge of Aristotelian philosophy, of which he became one of the most distinguished representatives. Siger's name appears for the first time in a sentence of arbitration dated August 27, 1266, by which the pontifical legate Simon de Brion put an end to the conflict opposing the French and Picard nations. Gauthier's recent research questions previous interpretations of this document according to which Siger was a "leader" and a "trouble-maker" in the conflict. But the document allows us to infer that by 1266 Siger was already master of arts, a position that he retains until the end of his career. This vocational choice reveals the beginning of a new professional attitude among some of the *artistae*, who decided to remain in a faculty of "philosophy" rather than to pursue studies in the "higher" faculties of theology, law, or medicine. In his courses Siger – and other masters of arts such as BOETHIUS OF DACIA – interpreted Aristotle's texts in a way that was considered contrary to Christian faith. BONAVENTURE denounced the danger of this "radical" interpretation as early as 1267 and, in 1270, THOMAS AQUINAS wrote the treatise *On the Unicity of the Intellect*, where he confronted the Averroistic interpretation of Aristotle's *De anima* adopted by Siger. On December 10, 1270, Bishop É. Tempier condemned thirteen philosophical propositions concerning four fundamental errors: unicity of the intellect, moral determinism, eternity of the world, and the denial of divine providence. The faculty of arts reacted to the condemnation with new statutes (April 1, 1272) forbidding that ideas contrary to the faith be taught by masters of arts. But the faculty was divided at the time, owing to a conflict related to the election of the rector. Called again to solve it, Simon de Brion gave his sentence of arbitration on May 7, 1275; in it, one of the factions in conflict is defined as being led by Siger. Because the statutes of 1272 were approved by the other faction, led by Albericus of Reims, many scholars believed that Siger was leading an ideological opposition to the more moderate group. Gauthier's research suggests rather that Siger played a minor role and that the conflict was strictly corporative. On November 23, 1276 the French Inquisitor, Simon du Val OP, asked the prior of the Dominicans in Liège to summon Siger, together with Goswin of la Chapelle and Bernier of Nivelles, to appear before his tribunal at the diocese of Noyon on January 18, 1277. The causes of the suspicion of heresy are not clear in the document. As the three masters are said to have left the kingdom of France, we may infer that by the end of 1276 the university career of Siger was over and that he was in Liège pursuing his career as a canon (not in Rome, where he would have fled seeking the protection of the pope, as the legend has it). There are reasons to think that the three masters were acquitted of the crime of heresy. The last information concerning Siger's life is found in the letter that John Pecham addressed to the University of Oxford on November 10, 1284, where he recounted that Siger had been killed by his demented secretary, after February 22, 1282, while at the pontifical curia in Orvieto. With this letter begins Siger's legend because, by suggesting that Siger's miserable death was the punishment inflicted by God on the one responsible for the doctrine of the unity of the substantial form (a doctrine which in fact is a fundamental thesis of Thomas Aquinas and which had been condemned by Pecham a month before), the conservative theologian promoted Siger to the rank of a major figure. Years later, Dante would see in Siger a victim of injustice, who deserved to be rewarded by being in paradise in the company of Thomas, ALBERTUS MAGNUS, Gracian, ISIDORE OF SEVILLE, Bede, and other major figures of medieval intellectual life.

Siger's writings include logical works (*Impossibilia, Quaestiones logicales, Sophismata*); question commentaries on Aristotle's treatises (*In III De anima, De generatione, Meteora, Physics, Metaphysics*); a commentary on the *Liber De causis*; and personal writings (questions on natural philosophy and on ethics, and the treatises *De necessitate et contingentia causarum, De aeternitate mundi*, and *De anima intellectiva*). Many of these are the result of Siger's teaching at the faculty of arts and were often transmitted by students' notes (*reportationes*), a fact that should be taken into account when reading these works. The logical writings are related to scholarly exercises required by the curriculum in arts, but contain also parts that were written by Siger. Commentaries on Aristotle's writings and on *De causis* are the result of "lectures" on texts also imposed by the curriculum. The personal treatise *De anima intellectiva* is Siger's reply to Thomas Aquinas's *De unitate intellectus contra averroistas* (1270) and does not seem to be directly related to teaching (the same applies to Siger's *Compendium de generatione*). Agostino Nifo reported the existence of a previous reply, a lost treatise called *De intellectu*. As previously stated, Siger's works were published between 1265 (*Q. in III De anima*) and 1274–6 (*Q. super librum De causis*). When I edited the *Q. in III De anima*, I considered them to be posterior to Thomas Aquinas's *Quaestiones de anima*, which were supposed to have been disputed in Paris early in 1269. It seemed to me unlikely that Thomas would have discussed AVERROES' "monopsychism" in the serene way he did, had Siger already published in Paris his own commentary containing the same doctrine. Gauthier's research (1983) and my own conclusion concerning Thomas's *Quaestiones* (they were in fact disputed in Italy, in 1266–7) allows us to conclude now that nothing prevents Siger's *Q. in III De anima* from being dated in 1265.

Philosophy as a "professional" project

Siger chose to remain a master of arts. His initial philosophical attitude should be understood in the light of what was happening in the faculties of arts in the 1260s, particularly in Paris. Though initially excluded from the university curriculum in Paris by ecclesiastical authorities, Aristotle's writings became an official component of the curriculum in arts (1255 in Paris, earlier in Oxford and Toulouse). Masters of arts were required to lecture on these works and give a faithful explanation of their content. Owing to the poor quality of the available translations and the difficulties encountered in understanding the doctrines, the masters of arts (and of theology) did not hesitate in using Averroes' commentaries to clarify the meaning of a complex world-vision that was foreign to them (the Latin West had been cut off from Greek philosophy for centuries). Averroes' literal commentaries, with all kinds of references to the Peripatetic tradition, were the best interpretive tools. Faculties of arts became the forum for an extraordinary dialogue of cultures that makes the thirteenth century one of the most interesting periods of western philosophy. The masters of arts produced some remarkable pieces of Aristotelian scholarship and some of them, such as Siger of Brabant, Boethius of Dacia, and Albericus of Reims, found that a life devoted to philosophy could be taken as a valid intellectual project, worthy of being assumed as definitive (*ibi statur*), not as a simple step to "higher" studies. In his initial writings, Siger sought exclusively to explain Aristotle's texts as faithfully as possible, using Averroes' method of internal consistency of the doctrine to solve the various aporiae left by Aristotle. Siger's exegetical work shows his conception of philosophy as an autonomous and purely rational activity, capable of satisfying the human need for truth and certitude which are components of human perfection, and as a form of inquiry respectful of the philosophical tradition represented by Aristotle (Van Steenberghen 1977, pp. 223–4). Not that Siger limited his work to historical interpretation of texts; he knew that the goal of philosophical inquiry is not the truth of texts, but the truth of being: *philosophus intendit finaliter cognitionem veritatis* (1974b, *Q. morales*, 4, p. 102). He distinguished "between the way of natural reason on the one hand, and determining the mind of Aristotle, on the other," which indicates that Siger allowed "for two distinct but complementary functions for a philosopher" (Wippel 1998, pp. 490–6). The problem was that in his search for the truth of texts he discovered oppositions between what he considered to be the authentic Aristotelian doctrine and some of his Christian beliefs. Aware of the conflict, challenged by alternative interpretations of the same texts proposed by Thomas Aquinas, and alerted of the danger of heterodoxy by the Condemnation of 1270, Siger was forced to explain in detail the purpose and scope of his work.

Philosophy and faith

For Thomas Aquinas, who considered Aristotelian philosophy a great achievement of human reason and a formidable instrument worth incorporating into Christian culture, the reconciliation between faith and Aristotelian philosophy was an essential task. That is why in his treatise *On the Unity of the Intellect against the Averroists* (1270), Thomas challenged Siger on the strictly exegetical level, stating that the Averroistic reading of Aristotelian texts was absolutely contrary to their true meaning (*repugnare omnino*). This "conflict of interpretations" must be kept in mind when trying to understand Siger's reaction.

Siger replied with his treatise *On the Intellective Soul*, where he claimed that he wanted to determine "what should be said according to the texts of the philosophers, not what he thinks on his own behalf" (1972b, *De anima intellectiva*, p. 70), and to establish "only the intention of the philosophers, mainly Aristotle, even if he had stated things that are contrary to the truth and wisdom which have been transmitted by revelation but cannot be concluded by reason" (ibid., p. 83). This is not a methodological excuse. In fact, Siger had no other choice, given the nature of Thomas's challenge. When he accepted this challenge, Siger thought that historical truth should not be hidden, even if it contradicts the absolute truths of faith. There is no reason to doubt his honesty when he claimed that in case of conflict between faith and reason, truth is on the side of faith; there is no reason either to think that he ever subscribed to the absurd notion of "double truth." He simply insisted on the autonomy of philosophy in its own field and elaborated a quite consistent explanation of the conflict between philosophy and revealed truth. Philosophical propositions that oppose faith (truth) are only probable inferences; in many occasions the opposition takes place between absolute truth provided by faith and philosophical propositions whose truth-value and scope are relative to the limited principles used as premises. In those cases it is superfluous to deny the conflict and it can be deflated as not opposing truths of the same level; when kept in its epistemological field of validity, natural reason is capable of truth and does not contradict faith. Aristotle is not the only authority in philosophy and all philosophers, including Aristotle, were human and subject to error; human reason is particularly weak in dealing with the realm of separate substances and the transcendence of the first cause, and falls more easily in error in those domains. When common men do not have the instruments to refute those probable philosophical propositions that oppose revealed truth, it is legitimate for them to adhere to faith, because the authority of philosophers is not absolute (Bazán 1980a, pp. 234–54).

For Siger, absolute truth is on the side of Christian faith; philosophy is an autonomous discipline capable of truth, whose exclusive rational resources limit the scope and necessity of its conclusions. That is why he concluded that "the intention of the Philosopher (Aristotle) should not be hidden, even if it is contrary to truth" (1981, *Q. in Metaph.*, p. 139). Nothing allows us to doubt the sincerity of these declarations.

Theory of knowledge

Siger embraced the moderate realism prevailing in the thirteenth century. Realities are individual and concrete, but they are potentially universal, owing to the common determinations that can be abstracted by the intellect. The universal exists in actuality only at the level of thought. The posteriority of concepts *vis-à-vis* reality raises the metaphysical problem of the foundation of the universal. To the question whether the proposition 'Man is an animal' is true if no individual men exist (that both Platonism and exemplarism would answer affirmatively), Siger answered by saying that the hypothesis is absurd because in the Aristotelian perspective of nature the human species is eternal (Van Steenberghen 1977, pp. 265–9). Within this framework he examined the elements of language. Aristotle in the *Perihermeneias* seemed to suggest that a word signifies a concept. For Siger, things are the primary object of words, not concepts. Common terms signify only the essence of things, not all the other determinations that accompany a thing in real existence. The essence is the foundation of the signifying unity of the common term. Siger added that terms signify things not only as they are, but also as they are understood: terms signify not only the essence (the universal), but also the essence as abstracted (its universality). A concept is thus the secondary object of the term, and is co-signified by the term (Bazán 1980b, pp. 13–21; Putallaz and Imbach 1997, p. 86).

Metaphysics

The Aristotelian inspiration of Siger's metaphysics was, as in many other thirteenth-century thinkers, carefully complemented by Neoplatonic theses (*Liber de causis*, AVICENNA). The subject of metaphysics as "first philosophy" is being *qua* being, its transcendental properties, and the first principles. The first being or first cause, as well as separate substances, seem to be also part of the subject of metaphysics for Siger (1981, *Q. in Metaph.*, p. 37; Aertsen 1996, p. 394). As such it can be called "divine science" or "philosophical theology" (1981, p. 39). Siger offered a complete theory of transcendentals (*ens, unum, verum, bonum*); "being" is the first, evident, clear, and certain notion of the intellect (1981, p. 187), and is predicated analogically (1981, pp. 103–4, 171). 'Being' and 'one' signify the same thing, but are not synonyms because 'being' signifies the thing as having the act of being (*actus essendi*), while 'one' signifies it as undivided in itself (*indivisum in se*) (1981, p. 174). Siger had difficulties understanding the relationship between the transcendentals "being" and "thing." According to Thomas Aquinas, the term *ens* ('being') and the term *res* ('thing') designate the same concrete existing being but are grounded in different ontological components of this being: *ens* relates to its act of being (*esse*), *res* to its essence (*essentia*); accordingly both terms differ *ratione*, because their grounds are really distinct ontological principles, but not in *re*, because they designate the existing subject as a whole. Siger did not accept Thomas's real distinction between *esse* and *essentia*, probably owing to the influence of Averroes, who had criticized Avicenna's quite different distinction. For Siger the act of being belongs to the essence of creatures and is in no way added to their essence. Consequently, 'being' and *res* could not signify two concepts of the mind (1981, *Q. in Metaph.*, Intro. q. 7, p. 45 and Van Steenberghen 1977, pp. 287–9). Things, however, are not pure act. Their plurality implies that there is in them a composition of being (*esse*) and potency to be (*potentia ad esse*), which measures their participation in being and consequently their multiplicity. Between the two principles there is only a conceptual distinction: the composition means that "being" does not belong to the definition of the creature (or that the creature does not exist by virtue of its essence). As Van Steenberghen has shown (1977, p. 291), this *potentia ad esse* that characterizes the creature is not an ontological principle distinct from *esse*, but designates the metaphysical dependence of the creature *vis-à-vis* its creator.

The existence of God is evident for whoever could grasp his essence (1974b, *Impossibilia*, p. 70), but for us this essence is beyond our understanding. Consequently God's existence must be demonstrated. The physical proofs (Aristotle), and those based on the analysis of the necessary and the possible (Avicenna), seemed unsatisfactory to Siger. Having reached by a *resolutio secundum rationem* the transcendental concept of being, he proceeded to a *resolutio secundum rem* leading to the cause of being *qua* being, to the first cause of all caused being (1981, *Q. in Metaph.*, p. 359). The metaphysical nature of this undertaking is determined by the question itself: Is there a unique efficient cause of being for all beings? Indeed, Siger considered that because no creature *is* its being, but only *participates* in being, a creative first cause of being is required. Although all the proofs elaborated by Siger are a posteriori and, consequently, reach only the existence of God, not his essence, the metaphysical nature of the proofs allows for the inference of some essential properties of the first cause of being: it must be a pure act of being (infinite), and consequently it must also be simple, eternal, and one. Siger also stated that the first cause knows itself and this knowledge is its substance, as Aristotle had proven, and that its perfection requires that its action be voluntary (Van Steenberghen 1977, p. 302). Siger's metaphysics is then *creationist*. God is the efficient cause of being, the final cause of the universe, and the exemplary cause of everything that exists. The distinction between philosophical theology and sacred theology was carefully established by Siger (1981, *Q. in Metaph.*, pp. 359–61).

The eternity of the world

Siger's particular way of understanding the composition of *esse* and *potentia ad esse* conditions in what sense we should understand the metaphysical dependence that affects all creatures. Siger accepted that individual corruptible substances have *potentia ad non esse* (physical contingency), but the world as a whole, species, and separate substances have only *potentia ad esse*. Though dependent in their being on the first cause, their ontological status is defined only by the possibility of being, not by the possibility of not being, and what does not have the possibility of not being must necessarily be (contingency never reaches the metaphysical level according to Van Steenberghen). The case of the human intellect is a different subject: Siger states clearly that, even if it is a separate substance, the intellect is in itself corruptible by nature (1972b, *Q. in IIIm De anima*, p. 17). Confronted with the problem of the eternity or temporality of the world and of species, Siger reaffirmed his fundamental thesis that the world is created (it has an *esse ab alio*) and that the first cause is free. As a natural philosopher, whose object is the nature of things, he must conclude that the world has been created eternally because it does not have potency to non-being. But as a metaphysician he has to consider this conclusion to be only *probable*, not necessary, because the world proceeds from the will of God, which is free and beyond the reach of human reason: "Who would dare to investigate the disposition of his will?" (1972b, *Q. in IIIm De anima*, p. 7). For the same reason (the inscrutability of the divine will), philosophy cannot provide proofs of the temporality of the world and of species. The causality of nature (the only one that is accessible to rational inquiry) presupposes matter already existing and proceeds by a series of indefinite generations and corruptions (1972b, *De aeternitate mundi*, pp. 116–17). In brief, philosophy cannot prove absolutely that the world is eternal or that it began to be, and is limited to a conclusion that should not be considered necessary because it is reached through the analysis of a type of causality (that of nature) that is subordinated to the free will of God, which is a higher causality. Siger's position is thus consistent with his conception regarding the relationship between faith and reason. There is no opposition between the absolute truth of faith (the world began to be), and the relative and merely probable conclusion of philosophy. Though undeniable, the truth of faith cannot be demonstrated by philosophical arguments (Putallaz and Imbach 1997, p. 88).

The unicity of the intellect

The unicity of the intellect was recognized by the masters of arts as a typically Averroistic doctrine, but they rejected it in spite of the fact that they kept using Averroes' commentaries as their most useful interpretive tool. This was the situation until around 1260. Siger of Brabant seems to have been the first master of arts who embraced the thesis of the unicity of the intellect in his *Quaestiones in IIIm De anima*, written around 1265 (see above). This text represents Siger's initial and most radical position, but by no means his last. From the Aristotelian premises that the intellect is immaterial and that matter is the only principle of numerical multiplication within a species, Siger concluded that the intellect is a unique separate substance common to all humankind (1972b, *Q. in IIIm De anima*, p. 28). It has two faculties, the agent and receptive intellects (for Averroes each one of them was a separate substance). Given its nature, the intellect can only be the direct effect of the first cause and, as such, it must be eternal (ibid., pp. 5–6). Because it has been created, its eternity – as its being – depends from the first cause, but in itself it could be reduced to nothingness (ibid., p. 17). In order to understand material reality, the receptive intellect, being the lowest of the separate substances, depends on sensible images (ibid., p. 51), from which the agent intellect abstracts the intelligible forms and makes them intelligible in act. This dependence establishes an operational union (ibid., p. 3), not a substantial one, between the separate intellect and human beings, who participate in the act of intellectual understanding only as providers of images (ibid., pp. 52–3). The substantial form of human beings is truly the sensitive soul. Siger used the expression 'composite soul' (*anima composita*) to refer to the union between the separate intellect and the individual sensitive soul.

It must be added that even in this initial stage Siger's noetics was in crisis owing to the difficulties he encountered in explaining the role of images as intermediaries (Bazán 1981, pp. 443–5). The crisis deepened after Thomas Aquinas criticized the Averroistic doctrine as being a corruption of Aristotle's theory on the intellect. Siger replied with his *De anima intellectiva*, where he adjusted significantly his original Averroistic interpretation. The human soul is defined only by the receptive intellect (the agent intellect regains the status of a separate substance that it had enjoyed in the Peripatetic tradition). The intellect is not united to the body substantially (*in essendo*), but as an intrinsic operational principle (*intrinsecus operans*). The act of intellection can be attributed to man neither because it takes place in the body, nor because the images are in the body, but because the intellective soul by its very nature operates intrinsically in the body. The act of intellection should be attributed to this whole composite, not to any of its parts. The notion of form, used by Aristotle to define the nature of the soul, should be taken in a broader sense (*extensive*) when applied to the *intrinsecus operans* (*De anima intellectiva*, ch. iii).

With respect to the unicity or multiplicity of the intellect, Siger reaffirmed that according to faith, which cannot lie, the intellects are multiple, but that from a philosophical perspective there are arguments both in favor and against multiplicity, which explains why the philosophical tradition is divided on this subject. Siger admitted that he had serious doubts for a long time about what should be stated according to natural reason and about Aristotle's position on the matter, and concluded that in such state of doubt one should adhere to faith, which is more powerful than any human argument (ch. viii). The last stage of Siger's evolution is reached in his *Quaestiones super librum de causis*. Historians have underlined the orthodoxy of Siger's position in this writing, the complete rejection of Averroistic monopsychism, and the dependency on Thomas's anthropology. Indeed, Siger completely inverted his original position and asserted that the intellective soul is truly the substantial form of the human composite. However, this statement should not be taken as equivalent to Thomas's position, because for Siger the soul that is the form of the composite is, at the same time, a substance in itself, a *hoc aliquid*, in medieval terms (1972a, *Q. in De causis*, p. 182). Siger, indeed, reverted to the traditional anthropological dualism that was pervasive during the first half of the thireenth century, an eclectic compromise between Aristotelianism and Neoplatonism that served Christian thinkers well, but whose internal consistency is questionable and was criticized by Thomas (Bazán 1997).

Well into the fifteenth century, the Brabantine master became, together with Averroes and Thomas Aquinas, an unavoidable point of reference for those who continued searching for the deepest meaning of Aristotelian noetics.

Bibliography

Primary sources

(1948), *Questions sur la Métaphysique. Texte inédit*, ed. C. A. Graiff, Louvain: Editions de l'Institut Supérieur de Philosophie.

(1954), *De necessitate et contingentia causarum*, ed. J. J. Duin, in J. J. Duin, *La Doctrine de la Providence dans les écrits de Siger de Brabant* (pp. 14–50), Louvain: Editions de l'Institut Supérieur de Philosophie.

(1966), *Quaestiones metaphysice tres*, ed. J. Vennebusch, in *Archiv für Geschichte der Philosophie* 48, pp. 163–89.

(1972a), *Quaestiones super librum De causis*, ed. A. Marlasca, Paris: Publications Universitaires; Louvain: Béatrice-Nauwelaerts.

(1972b), *Quaestiones in IIIm De anima, De anima intellectiva, De aeternitate mundi*, ed. B. C. Bazán, Paris: Publications Universitaires; Louvain: Béatrice-Nauwelaerts.

(1974a), *Quaestiones in Physicam*, ed. A. Zimmermann, Paris: Publications Universitaires; Louvain: Béatrice-Nauwelaerts, pp. 143–183.

(1974b), *Sophisma Omnis homo de necessitate est animal, Quaeritur utrum haec sit vera: homo est animal nullo homine existente, Quaestiones logicales, Impossibilia, Quaestiones morales, Quaestiones naturales (Lisbonne), Quaestiones naturales (Paris), Compendium De generatione*, in B. C. Bazán, ed., *Siger de Brabant, ecrits de logique, de morale et de physique*, Paris: Publications Universitaires; Louvain: Béatrice-Nauwelaerts.

(1981), *Quaestiones in Metaphysicam (Munich-Vienne)*, ed. W. Dunphy, Louvain-la-Neuve: Editions de l'Institut Supérieur de Philosophie.

(1983), *Quaestiones in Metaphysicam (Cambridge-Paris)*, ed. A. Maurer, Louvain-la-Neuve: Editions de l'Institut Supérieur de Philosophie.

Secondary sources

This list includes sources published after 1977. For earlier sources, see Van Steenberghen (1977), *Maître Siger de Brabant*.

Aertsen, J. (1996), *Medieval Philosophy and the Transcendentals*, Leiden, New York, and Cologne: Brill.

Bazán, B. C. (1975), "La unión del intelecto separado y los individuos según Sigerio de Brabante," *Patristica et Mediaevalia* 1, pp. 5–35.

——(1979), "La signification des termes communs et la théorie de la supposition chez Maître Siger de Brabant", *Revue Philosophique de Louvain* 77/35, pp. 345–72.

——(1980a), "La réconciliation entre la raison et la foi était-elle possible pour les aristotéliciens radicaux?," *Dialogue* 19, pp. 235–54.

——(1980b) "La théorie de la signification chez Siger de Brabant," in *Progress in Linguistic Historiography: Papers from the International Conference on the History of the Language Sciences*, Ottawa, August 1978, ed. Konrad Koerner, Amsterdam: Benjamins.

——(1981), "*Intellectum speculativum*: Averroes, Thomas Aquinas and Siger of Brabant on the intelligible object", *Journal of the History of Philosophy* 19/4, pp. 425–46.

——(1997), "The human soul: form and substance? Thomas's critique of eclectic Aristotelianism," *Archives d'Histoire Doctrinale et Littéraire du Moyen Âge* 64, pp. 96–126.

——(2000), "Was there ever a first Averroism?," *Geistesleben im 13. Jahrhundert*, Miscellanea mediaevalia 27, pp. 31–53.

Bianchi, L. (1984), *L'errore di Aristotele. La polemica contro l'eternità del mondo nel XIII secolo*, Florence: La Nuova Italia Editrice.

——(1990), *Il vescovo e i filosofi. La condanna parigina del 1277 e l'evoluzione dell'aristotelismo scolastico*, Quodlibet 6, Ricerche e strumenti di filosofia medievale, Bergamo: Pierluigi Lubrina Editore.

Biffi, I. (1994), "Figure medievali della teologia: la teologia in Sigieri di Brabante e Boezio di Dacia," *Teologia* 19, pp. 263–99.

Bukovski, T. P. (1990), "Siger of Brabant, anti-theologian," *Franciscan Studies* XXVIII, pp. 57–82.

Dales, R. C. (1991), *Medieval Discussions of the Eternity of the World*, Brill's Studies in Intellectual History XVIII, Leiden, New York, Copenhagen, and Cologne: Brill.

——(1995), *The Problem of the Rational Soul in the Thirteenth Century*, Leiden, New York, and Cologne: Brill.

de Libera, A. (1991), *Penser au Moyen Âge*, Paris: Éditions de Seuil.

——(1994), "Introduction," in *Thomas d'Aquin: l'unité de l'intellect contre les averroïstes*, Paris: Garnier-Flammarion.

Gauthier, R.-A. (1983), "Notes sur Siger de Brabant. 1. Siger en 1265," *Revue des Sciences Philosophiques et Théologiques* LXVII/2, pp. 201–32.

——(1984), "Notes sur Siger de Brabant (fin) II. Siger en 1272–1275," *Revue des Sciences Philosophiques et Théologiques* LXVIII, pp. 3–50.

Hissette, R. (1977), *Enquête sur les 219 articles condamnés à Paris le 7 mars 1277*, Philosophes Médiévaux XXII, Paris: Publications Universitaires; Louvain: Vander-Oyez SA.

Imbach, R. (1981), "Averroistische Stellungnahmen zur Diskussion ueber das Verhältnis von *esse* und *essentia*. Von Siger von Brabant zu Thaddaeus von Parma", in A. Maierú and A. Paravicini Bagliani, eds., *Studi sul XIV secolo in memoria di Anneliese Maier* (pp. 299–339), Rome: Edizioni di Storia e Letteratura.

——(1996), "Notule sur le commentaire du *Liber de causis* de Siger de Brabant et ses rapports avec Thomas d'Aquin," *Freiburger Zeitschrift für Philosophie und Theologie* XLIII, pp. 304–23.

Mahoney, E. (1974), "Saint Thomas and Siger of Brabant revisited," *Review of Metaphysics* XXVII, pp. 531–53.

Maurer, A. (1988), "Siger of Brabant and theology", *Medieval Studies* L, pp. 257–78.

Pattin, A. (1987), "Notes concernant quelques écrits attribués à Siger de Brabant," *Bulletin de philosophie médiévale* XXIX, pp. 173–7.

Piché, D. (1999), *La Condamnation parisienne de 1277* (Coll. Sic et Non), Paris: Librairie Philosophique J. Vrin.

Putallaz, F.-X. (1992), "La connaissance de soi au moyen âge: Siger de Brabant," *Archives d'Histoire Doctrinale et Littéraire du Moyen Âge* LIX, pp. 89–157.

——(1995), *Insolente liberté. Controverses et condamnations au XIIIe siècle*, Pensée Antique et Médiévale, Vestigia XV, Fribourg and Paris: Editions Universitaires/Éditions du Cerf.

Putallaz, F.-X. and Imbach, R. (1997), *Profession Philosophe: Siger de Brabant*, Paris: Editions du Cerf.

Van Steenberghen, F. (1977), *Maître Siger de Brabant*. Paris: Publications Universitaires; Louvain: Vander-Oyez S.A.

Wielockx, R. (1994), "Autour du commentaire (P) de Siger de Brabant à la *Métaphysique*," in A. Zimmermann, ed., *Scientia und ars im Hoch- und Spätmittelalter* (pp. 240–56), Miscellanea Mediaevalia XXII–1, Berlin and New York: De Gruyter.

Wippel, J. (1995), *Medieval Reactions to the Encounter between Faith and Reason* (The Aquinas Lecture LIX), Milwaukee: Marquette University Press.

——(1998), "Siger of Brabant: What it means to proceed philosophically," in J. A. Aertsen and A. Speer, eds., *Was ist Philosophie im Mittelalter?* (pp. 490–6), Berlin and New York: De Gruyter.

119

Simon of Faversham

JOHN LONGEWAY

Simon of Faversham (b. ca. 1260; d. 1306) was a commentator on Aristotle's works, particularly those on logic and the soul. He was educated at Oxford, and although his commentaries seem to reveal a residence at Paris in the 1270s and 1280s, reflecting in particular the influence of PETER OF AUVERGNE, he spent the rest of his life at Oxford, where he became chancellor in 1304. He has often been identified as a follower of THOMAS AQUINAS, and certainly knows Aquinas and often follows his views, but his mature work shows considerable independence of thought. He often follows GILES OF ROME in his commentary on the *Sophistici elenchi*, and in his account of the nature of logic in his *Posterior Analytics* commentaries. In his second question-commentary on the *Posterior Analytics*, Question 49, he explicitly attacks Thomas and follows HENRY OF GHENT on the real distinction between essence and existence (he does not attribute his view to Henry), though he had followed Aquinas in Question 20 of his commentary on the *Categories*, written much earlier in his career. The new orientation is marked by his adoption of the phrase *esse in effectu* for existence, borrowed from AVICENNA (*On First Philosophy* V, 1), and though Simon, like Henry, avoids the consequences of Avicenna's treatment of essence and existence objected to in AVERROES, neither Simon nor Henry is the radical Aristotelian that Thomas is.

Simon may have started life as a Thomist, but as he matured, he moved much closer to the Augustinian view. In his comments on Aristotle a fundamentally Augustinian, even Avicennan, approach often obtrudes itself, and when he follows Aquinas, he often seems to apply typically Augustinian phraseology too literally to non-Augustinian doctrines, so appearing rather clumsy and immature – if, that is, he is taken as an expositor of the Master's thought. (One observes this, for instance, in Simon's short work, "Sophism: A universal is an intention.") But all these conclusions must be regarded as preliminary. The definitive work on Simon's thought is yet to be written.

Bibliography

Primary sources

(1934), *Quaestiones super tertium De anima*, ed. D. Sharp, in "Simonis de Faversham," *Archives d'Histoire Doctrinale et Littéraire du Moyen Âge* 9, pp. 307–68.

(1957), *Opera omnia*, vol. 1: *Opera logica*, tomus prior, (1) *Quaestiones super libro Porphyrii*, (2) *Quaestiones super libro Praedicamentorum*, (3) *Quaestiones super libro Perihermeneias*, ed. Pasquale Mazzarella, Padua: Cedam.

(1969), *Universale est intentio*, ed. Tetsuo Yokoyama, in "Simon of Faversham's *Sophisma: universale est intentio*," *Mediaeval Studies* 31, pp. 1–14.

(1984), *Quaestiones super librum Elenchorum*, ed. Sten Ebbeson, Thomas Izbicki, John Longeway, Francesco del Punta, Eileen Serene, and Eleonore Stump, Toronto: Pontifical Institute of Mediaeval Studies.

Secondary sources

Longeway, John (1977), "Simon of Faversham's Questions on the *Posterior Analytics*: A thirteenth-century view of science," Ph.D. dissertation, Cornell University.

Wolf, F. J. (1966), "Die Intellektslehre des Simon von Faversham nach De anima Kommentaren," Inaugural dissertation, University of Bonn.

120

Thomas Aquinas

BRIAN DAVIES

Thomas Aquinas (b. 1224/6; d. 1274) was the greatest European philosopher of the thirteenth century. Many would say that he was the greatest philosopher of the Middle Ages. Original, brilliant, and sophisticated, he wrote on a huge range of topics. He was especially interested in metaphysics, philosophy of religion, philosophy of the human person, and ethics.

His intellectual stature was recognized even during his own lifetime, and many of his medieval successors deemed him weighty enough to be studied and discussed at considerable length. His teachings had a particularly significant influence during and immediately after the time of the sixteenth-century Catholic Counter-Reformation (mostly because St. Ignatius Loyola directed that Jesuit students in formation should be grounded in Aquinas's principles). In recent years, his thinking has been especially respected in Roman Catholic centers of philosophical training (and other Roman Catholic educational institutions). Pope Leo XIII recommended it in his encyclical *Aeterni Patris* (1879). The Second Vatican Council did the same, as did Pope John Paul II in his encyclical *Fides et Ratio* (1998). Largely owing to writers such as M.-D. Chenu OP (1895–1990) and Étienne Gilson (1884–1978), who inspired generations of students to look at medieval texts in a serious and rigorous way, Aquinas has for many years been consistently respected and written about by those connected with several important contemporary centers of medieval scholarship (e.g., the Pontifical Institute for Mediaeval Studies in Toronto). Though little read or appreciated by most English-speaking philosophers from (roughly) the time of John Locke to the mid-1960s, he has also recently enjoyed a considerable measure of renewed philosophical attention in British and American philosophical circles.

Aquinas was born in the Kingdom of Naples during the reign of the Emperor Frederick II. In 1230 or 1231 he was sent to the Abbey of Monte Cassino, where he lived and studied for about eight years. His family probably hoped that he would succeed to high office in the abbey, but military conflict between Frederick II and Pope Gregory IX made Monte Cassino a center of imperial–papal rivalry. So in July 1239 Aquinas went to study at the recently founded university (or *studium generale*) in Naples. Here he began to learn about the writings of thinkers such as Aristotle, AVERROES, and MAIMONIDES. He also encountered the Dominican order of friars, which he joined sometime between 1242 and 1244. By the middle of 1246 he was a Dominican student in Paris, where he transcribed lectures of ALBERTUS MAGNUS on Denys (or PSEUDO-DIONYSIUS) the Areopagite. He subsequently moved to Cologne, where he continued to work under Albert. By 1256 he was back again in Paris, where his role now changed from that of student to teacher.

To begin with he lectured on the *Sentences* of PETER LOMBARD (b. 1095/1100; d. 1160). In 1256 he became a master in theology, which obliged him to lecture on the Bible and to preside over a series of theological discussions referred to as *Quaestiones disputatae* (Disputed Questions). He also began to produce the earliest of the works for which he is best known today: a commentary on Lombard's *Sentences*, the disputed question *De veritate* (*DV*) (*On Truth*), the work known as *De ente et essentia* (*On Being and Essence*), and a commentary on Boethius's *De Trinitate* (*On the Trinity*). Also during this time he embarked on his lengthy *Summa contra Gentiles* (*SG*).

Discussing the purpose of the *Summa contra Gentiles*, Aquinas says that he aims "by the way of reason to pursue those things about God which human reason is able to investigate" (*SG* I, 9, 4). And that is what he also does in his *Summa theologiae* (*ST*), which he began around 1265–8 and which remained unfinished at the time of his death. Commonly deemed to be his greatest achievement, it contains three long treatises (or "parts") divided into subsections called "Questions" and "Articles." It ranges over topics such as God, creation, angels, human nature and happiness, grace, virtues, Christ, and the Christian sacraments.

Aquinas's early biographers do not seem to have been very interested in sorting out the details of his career from around 1256. But we can be sure that he vacated his teaching position at Paris before 1260, that he lived and taught for a time at Orvieto in Italy, and that in 1265 he was assigned to establish a Dominican house of studies in Rome. By 1269 he was again teaching in Paris. And throughout these years he was (typically) a prolific writer. In Orvieto, for instance, he composed his *Catena aurea* (*Golden Chain*), a continuous commentary on the four Gospels composed of quotations from the Church Fathers. He also produced an edition of a liturgy for the newly created feast of Corpus Christi and a commentary on the Old Testament book of Job. In Rome, as well as beginning the *Summa theologiae*, he worked on his disputed question *De potentia* (*DP, On the Power of God*), his theological synthesis known as the *Compendium theologiae* (*Compendium of Theology*), his political treatise *De regno* (*On Kingship*), and a commentary on Aristotle's *De anima* (*DA, On the Soul*). Having returned to Paris in or around 1268, Aquinas continued with the *Summa theologiae*. He also produced the disputed question *De virtutibus* (*On Virtues*), the *De aeternitate mundi* (*On the Eternity of the World*, a discussion of the question 'Did the world have a beginning?'), and the *De unitate intellectus* (*On the Unity of the Intellect*, a critique of Averroes on the mind). He also began to write commentaries on the gospels of Matthew and John, and on Aristotle's *Physics*, *Nicomachean Ethics*, and *Metaphysics*.

In 1272 Aquinas was deputed to establish yet another Dominican study house. He chose to do so in Naples, where he continued to teach and write. Here he forged on with the *Summa theologiae* (now into its third part). He also probably lectured on St. Paul's letter to the Romans and on the Old Testament book of Psalms. But in December 1273 he abandoned his usual routine and neither wrote nor dictated anything else. Late in 1273 he was instructed to attend the second Council of Lyons. On the way to Lyons he became seriously ill. He is reported to have said: "If the Lord is coming for me, I had better be found in a religious house," so he was taken to the Abbey of Fossanova, where he died on March 7, 1274.

Does God exist?

The philosophy of Aquinas is first and foremost a theistic one. According to him, God is "the beginning and end of all things" (Introduction to *ST* I, 2). But why suppose that there is a God? Some (notably ANSELM OF CANTERBURY and René Descartes) have said that the existence of God can somehow be proved on the basis of the concept of God. In their view, 'God does not exist' is demonstrably self-contradictory. Others have said that God is a direct object of human experience. But Aquinas takes a different line. He finds no demonstrable contradiction in the proposition 'God does not exist'. And, so he says, "the awareness that God exists is not implanted in us by nature in any specific way" (*ST* I, 2, 1). His consistently held conclusion is that we can only know that God exists by inference from the world as we know it by means of our senses. In his view,

> The knowledge that is natural to us has its source in the senses and extends just so far as it can be led by sensible things; from these, however, our understanding cannot reach to the divine essence . . . We arrive at a knowledge of God by way of creatures. (*ST* I, 12, 12; 88, 3)

Aquinas does not think that those who believe in God's existence are somehow unreasonable if they cannot produce sound inferential arguments for their position. There is nothing, he says, "to stop someone accepting on faith some truth which that person cannot demonstrate, even if that truth in itself is such that demonstration could make it evident" (*ST* I, 2, 2 ad.1). But, so he holds, knowledge that God exists (or, at least, an explicit knowledge that God exists) can only be arrived at indirectly. To be more precise, his view is that we can only know that God exists by a process of causal reasoning. "Any effect of a cause", he says,

> demonstrates that that cause exists, in cases where the effect is better known to us, since effects are dependent upon causes, and can only occur if the causes already exist. From effects evident to us, therefore, we can demonstrate what is not evident to us, namely that God exists. (*ST* I, 2, 2)

How does Aquinas think that we can do this? In his famous "five ways" (*ST* I, 2, 3) he offers a series of much discussed arguments each of which concludes that there is indeed a God. All of these begin by drawing attention to some general feature of things known to us on the basis of experience (e.g., change, causal dependency, generation and perishing, degrees of goodness, and the workings of things in nature). They then suggest that none of these features can be accounted for in ordinary mundane terms, that we must move to a level of explanation that transcends any with which we are familiar. According to the five ways, questions we can raise with respect to what we encounter in day-to-day life raise further questions the answer to which can only be thought of as lying beyond what we encounter.

But it would be wrong to take the five ways as Aquinas's last word on the question 'Can we know that God exists?' They are best read as forming only the prelude to a long discussion in the *Summa theologiae*, one which only ends around *ST* I, 49. They also need to be viewed in the light of what Aquinas says in works other than the *Summa theologiae*, especially his *De ente et essentia* and his *Summa contra gentiles*. And with these points in mind, perhaps the best thing to say is that Aquinas chiefly holds that we can know that God exists since we are right to be struck by the question 'How come anything at all?'.

When we ask "How come?" the objects of our concern are usually fairly specific. We may, for example, wonder what accounts for some particular local phenomenon (as in 'How did the Empire State building come to be?' or 'Why did John's nose turn red?'). Sometimes, however, the range of our inquiry may be wider. Someone might explain how the Empire State building came about, but we might then ask why there should be any buildings or anything out of which they might be made. Someone might explain why John's nose turned

645

red, but we might then ask why there should be any people with noses or anything with the power to affect them.

And we might deepen the level of our inquiry yet further. For we might ask, not "What in the world accounts for this, that, or the other?," but "Why any world at all?" How come the whole familiar business of asking and answering "How come?"?

For Aquinas, this is a crucial question, perhaps the most important question of all. For him, "How come any universe?" is a pressing and legitimate query, one to which there must be an answer. And he gives the name 'God' to whatever the answer is. God, for Aquinas, is the reason why there is any universe at all. In *De aeternitate mundi* and elsewhere he denies that philosophy can show that the world ever *began* to be. So he does not hold that God must exist since something must have got the universe going *at some time in the past*. But he continually insists that everything we can conceive of or understand is continually dependent on God for its sheer existence (*esse*). The ancient philosophers, he says, asked causal questions about things in the world, but some "climbed higher to the prospect of being as being" and "observed the cause of things inasmuch as they are beings, not merely as things of such a kind or quality" (*ST* I, 44, 2). At the end of his *Tractatus Logico-Philosophicus*, Ludwig Wittgenstein declares: "Not *how* the world is, is the mystical, but *that* it is" (Wittgenstein 1922, 6.44). For Wittgenstein, *how the world is* is a scientific matter with scientific answers. But, he insists, even when the scientific answers are in, we are still left with the *thatness* of the world, the fact *that* it is. As Wittgenstein himself puts it: "We feel that even if *all possible* scientific questions be answered, the problems of life have still not been touched at all" (ibid., 6.52). And Aquinas is of the same mind. We can, he thinks, explore the world and develop an account of what things in it are. But when we have finished doing that, so he also wants to say, we are still left with a decidedly non-scientific question: How come something rather than *nothing*?

What is God?

Yet how is one to answer such a question? Wittgenstein thought it hopeless even to try. He found it striking *that* the world is. But this thought lead him to silence. When we have finished asking scientific questions, he says, "there is then no question left, and just this is the answer" (Wittgenstein 1922, 6.52). Aquinas, by contrast, does not give up so easily. In various texts he seeks to explore what can be said about whatever it is that accounts for there being any world at all. And he argues that there are grounds for asserting that God is (among other things) perfect, good, eternal, one, living, knowing, and omnipotent. But he also frequently denies that we can understand what it is for God to be all of this. God, he maintains,

> is greater than all we can say, greater than all we can know; and not merely does he transcend our language and our knowledge, but he is beyond the comprehension of every mind whatsoever, even of angelic minds, and beyond the being of every substance. (*Super Librum Dionysii De divinis nominibus* (*DN*) I, iii, 77)

How does Aquinas reconcile these apparently conflicting lines of thinking? A helpful way of reading him is to see him as regularly working in terms of a distinction between understanding that a statement of the form 'God is X' is true, and understanding what it is that makes such statements true. I can understand that it is possible to travel to the moon. But

'It is possible to travel to the moon' is true because of various astronomical facts, and facts known to physicists, none of which I (as it happens) understand. The statement is also true because there are now various kinds of equipment and technology, of which I (as it happens) have no serious knowledge (I can refer to them, but I could not give you a lecture on them). So it seems that I can understand that certain statements are true without understanding what makes them true. And that, Aquinas holds, is the position of us all when it comes to assertions concerning God. On his account, true statements of the form 'God is X' are true because of what God is in himself. But we cannot, so he thinks, understand what this amounts to. Or, as he sometimes puts it, we cannot understand God's *essentia*, or essence (meaning that we cannot, with respect to God, have anything like what we have when we single things out in the world and develop a scientific account of them). According to Aquinas, "The divine substance surpasses every form that our intellect reaches. Thus we are unable to apprehend it by knowing what it is" (*SG* I, 14).

And yet, Aquinas also suggests, it does not therefore follow that we cannot speak meaningfully and truly about God. For a start, so he reasons, we can be quite clear as to what God *cannot* be. Having argued for God's existence in the *Summa theologiae*, Aquinas immediately observes: "We cannot know what God is, but only what he is not; we must therefore consider the ways in which God does not exist" (*ST* I, Introduction to Question 3). And a lot that he writes, both in the *Summa theologiae* and elsewhere, follows this advice to the letter. Hence, for example, he argues that God cannot be material, changeable, limited, or temporal (since things like this are part of the world and since the reason for there being a world at all cannot resemble them in these respects). He also argues that God cannot be thought of as a member of a species or genus (as an instance of a kind as, for example, two kangaroos are instances of a kind). Or, as Aquinas himself puts it, God and his nature cannot be thought of as different. You and I are human beings. Neither of us could intelligibly be described as *being* human nature. We are things that exemplify it, just as we exemplify and are not identical with the various attributes that make us to be human. For Aquinas, however, God *is* his nature and is "identical with his own godhead, with his own life and with whatever else is similarly said of him" (*ST* I, 3, 3). Why? Because God cannot be something material and because, so Aquinas thinks, there can only be different members of a kind (like two kangaroos) where the members are materially distinct (*ST* I, 3, 3). In arguing in this way, Aquinas does not mean to suggest that, for example, sentences like 'God is wise' and 'God is powerful' are identical in meaning (he denies this explicitly in texts such as *ST* I, 13, 4). But he is concerned to stress that expressions like 'the wisdom of God' and 'the power of God' are really ways of referring to one single thing, something which can be rightly referred to as God.

Aquinas also famously holds that there can be no difference either between God and his existence. God, he says, is "His own existence" (*ST* I, 3, 4) or "subsistent being" (*ipsum esse subsistens*). Having asked whether *Qui Est* (*The One Who Is*) is the most appropriate name for God, Aquinas replies that it is because it signifies "existence itself" (*ipsum esse*). "Since the existence of God is his essence," he suggests, "and since this is true of nothing else . . . it is clear that this name is especially appropriate to God" (*ST* I, 13, 11). Some things, he says, "have existence simply by being the natures they are: yet existence is still something they *have*, it is not what they are – the incorporeal beings we call angels are of this kind." Yet, he continues: "Finally, there is the way of being that belongs to God alone, for his existence is what he is" (*ST* I, 12, 4).

For many of those who have written on Aquinas, this doctrine of his is especially profound and of deep philosophical import. According, for instance, to Fr. Norris Clarke SJ,

"The crown of the entire Thomistic vision of the universe is the notion of God as infinitely perfect pure Plenitude of Existence, ultimate Source and Goal of all other being' (Clarke 1995, p. 24). But Aquinas's teaching that God and his existence are identical (that the nature of God is to be) has also been much contested, chiefly in the light of the claim (notably defended by philosophers such as Immanuel Kant, Gottlob Frege, and Bertrand Russell) that existence should not be thought of as an attribute or property of individuals, let alone one with which something might actually be identified. Interestingly, however, there are reasons for supposing that Aquinas would have been comfortable with this claim, for he does something to defend it in his own right (Davies 1997). And though he frequently says that everything other than God "has being" while God "is Being," he is not thereby seeking to identify God with some general or particular property. Rather, he is out to insist that God cannot be something dependent, something made to be, something with respect to which we might ask "How come this, rather than nothing?" Aquinas's teaching that God is *ipsum esse subsistens* is part of an account of what God is not. It is not offered as a description of God. Its purpose is to stress that, if we really think it right to ask "How come anything at all?," we cannot reasonably settle for an answer that refers us to something that might never have been.

In other words, and in keeping with Aquinas's claim that we must "consider the ways in which God does not exist," his conclusion that God is *ipsum esse subsistens* is a piece of negative (or apophatic) philosophical theology: part of an account of what should *not* be said of God. And the same is true of much else that he writes even when he seems to be making and defending apparently affirmative statements about God. Hence, for example, he argues that God is perfect. But he does so because he thinks that God *cannot* be subject to improvement (*ST* I, 4, 2). He holds that God is eternal. But he does so because he thinks that God *cannot* be something changeable (*ST* I, 10, 2). He concludes that God is One. But he does so on the ground that there *cannot* be two Gods (*ST* I, 11, 3 and 4). He claims that there is knowledge in God. But he does so by contending that God is *not* something material (*ST* I, 14, 1). When commenting on Denys the Areopagite he says:

> The most perfect [state] to which we can attain in this life in our knowledge of God is that he transcends all that can be conceived by us, and that the naming of God through remotion (*per remotionem*) is most proper . . . The primary mode of naming God is through the negation of all things, since he is beyond all, and whatever is signified by any name whatsoever is less than that which God is. (*DN*, iii, 83–4)

Readers of Aquinas need firmly to bear in mind that this is a teaching which he never abandoned and which he frequently appeals to or takes for granted (Davies 1998).

Yet Aquinas also holds that we can make lots of literally true and positive assertions about God. For, he says, at least some words can be used of God and creatures "in an analogical way" (*ST* I, 13, 5). By this he means that there are words we can use when talking both of God and creatures without their signifying exactly the same thing, but without their signifying something entirely different either. If I say that Utah is rocky and that Colorado is rocky, I am using the word 'rocky' to signify exactly the same property. Or, as Aquinas would say, I am using it "univocally." If I say that baseball players use bats and that bats are mammals with wings, I am using the word 'bat' to refer to things which are totally different. Or, as Aquinas would say, I am using it "equivocally." But is there a kind of half-way house between the univocal and equivocal use of words? Aquinas suggests that there is, and he calls it "analogical." Suppose that someone says: 'I love my wife', 'I love a juicy steak', 'I love the music of Vivaldi', and 'I love the work I do'. Is 'love' to be understood here as signifying exactly the same thing (as having the same sense) in each case? Surely not. Is it to be understood as signifying something entirely different? Again, surely not. And, reasoning along these lines, Aquinas suggests that some things we say about God can be taken literally without signifying exactly what they do when we say the same about what is not divine.

Why? Basically because he thinks that we often have particular philosophical grounds for using the same words when talking of God and creatures without speaking either univocally or equivocally (as he argues in texts such as *ST* I, 2–12). He also argues that we may rightly apply certain words both to God and to creatures because of "the order that creatures have to God as to their source and cause in which all the perfections of things pre-exist transcendently" (*ST* I, 13, 3). According to Aquinas, one cannot give what one has not got. In his view, a productive cause expresses itself, or shows itself forth, in its effects, which can therefore be said to be like it. And since he takes everything other than God to be an effect produced by God, he argues that what we find in the created realm can give us reason for speaking positively of God in some ways rather than others. In particular, he reasons, we can apply to God terms that signify perfections in creatures: terms such as 'good'. "Any creature, in so far as it possesses any perfection," he says, "represents God and is like to him, for he, being simply and universally perfect, has pre-existing in himself the perfections of all his creatures" (*ST* I, 13, 2).

At the same time, however, Aquinas also insists that God transcends the world of natural things and that attributes truly ascribed to him are not present in him as they are in creatures. On Aquinas's account, God, strictly speaking, does not *have* attributes. Indistinguishable from his nature and existence, he is whatever it takes to bring it about that there are any things with attributes. Since Aquinas holds that all such things have their existence from God, and since he thinks that effects always somehow resemble their productive causes, he concludes that there is a likeness of creatures to God, and that this fact can serve to justify much that we say of him. Yet the likeness between creatures and God is not, for him, that between members of a natural kind, or members of different natural kinds. So, as one of Aquinas's best contemporary commentators puts it:

> For St. Thomas, when we speak of God we do not know what we are talking about. We are simply taking language from the familiar context in which we understand it and using it to point beyond what we understand into the mystery that surrounds us and sustains the world we do partially understand. (McCabe 1992, p. 58)

God and creatures

How does Aquinas think of God as relating to his creation? In several places he says that, though creatures are really related to God, God is not really related to creatures (*ST* I, 13, 7; *SG* II, 11; *DP* VII, 8). In doing so, however, he is not denying that, if A is related to B, then B can be described as related to A. He does not mean that one cannot make true statements about God and creatures that seem to imply a relation between them. Rather, he is concerned to affirm that God is in no way *changed* or *modified* by his act of creating or by the changes that creatures undergo. On Aquinas's account, God is essentially immutable, and creatures make no difference to him. But God, he argues, makes all the difference to creatures. Reflecting on the notion of creation (*ST* I, 45, 1), he observes that it cannot be thought of as the bringing about of a change in anything since it involves the coming into existence of things from *nothing* (*ex nihilo*). So he does not think that God makes a difference to creatures simply by bringing them into being. He thinks that before they exist they are not there to have any difference made to them. He does, however, hold that God makes a difference to creatures by accounting for all the different things that happen in the created order. Or, as he puts it: "God exists in everything . . . as an agent is present to that in which its action is taking place" (*ST* I, 8, 1).

In other words, Aquinas has a strong doctrine of divine providence. On his account, nothing happens that does not fall within God's plan. He allows for the occurrence of chance events since he thinks that something may happen which "is not strictly speaking a single reality or event, for instance, as when a boulder falls and a landslide starts, or as when a man digs a grave and finds a cache" (*ST* II, II, 95, 5). But he does not think of events like these as completely inexplicable or as wholly uncaused. And, so he argues, they ultimately derive from God's governing of his created order. For God, he says,

> is not simply a particular cause with respect to one class of things, but the universal cause of all being. Therefore even as nothing can exist that is not created by God, so also nothing can exist that is not ruled by him. (*ST* I, 103, 5)

On Aquinas's account, there are many created things that are able to bring about effects. If created things exercised no genuine causal power, he argues, and if God were the only real cause, we would all be subject to a massive illusion and what we take to be causal agents "would seem to have a pointless existence" (*ST* I, 105, 5). And yet, so he also thinks, no created cause can be what it is and do what it does without God, as Creator, working in it. "The divine power," he maintains

> must needs be present to every acting thing . . . God is the cause of everything's action inasmuch as he gives everything the power to act, and preserves it in being and applies it to action, and inasmuch as by his power every other power acts. (*DP*, III, 7)

According to Aquinas, created causes are real causes. But they are all instruments of God. Or, as Aquinas often says, they are all "secondary causes." When I write a letter using a pen, the pen is a genuine cause of the words that appear on the paper. But it is exercising its causality by virtue of me (which is why one can say that, though the pen produces the words, I am writing the letter). In a similar way, so Aquinas affirms, the effects of created causes are truly *their* effects. But they are also, as we might put it, the *doing* of God (McDermott 1989, pp. xxxvii and xlvii).

An important consequence that Aquinas derives from this conclusion is that even the freely chosen actions of human beings are caused by God. Some philosophers have argued that people can be free only if their actions have absolutely no cause outside themselves. But this is not Aquinas's view. For, so he argues, though people can act freely, it is unthinkable that any created event, including whatever we take to be there when human choosing occurs, should come to pass without God making it to be. Why? Because of what we have already seen him teaching about God as Creator. For him, God is the cause of the existence of everything, the reason why there is something rather than nothing, the source of *esse*. And since Aquinas takes human free actions to be perfectly real, he concludes that they must, like anything else, be caused to exist by God. One may, of course, say that, if my actions are ultimately caused by God, then I do not act freely at all. Aquinas, however, would reply that my actions are free if nothing *in the world* (nothing *created*) is acting on me so as to make me perform them, not if God is not acting in me. In terms of this account (which constitutes one of Aquinas's most original and provocative contributions to philosophy of religion and philosophy of human action) I am free not *in spite* of God but *because of* God since he is the cause of all that is real in both free created agents and non-free created agents. Or, as Aquinas argues:

> Free decision spells self-determination because man by his free decision moves himself into action. Freedom does not require that a thing is its own first cause, just as in order to be the cause of something else a thing does not have to be its first cause. God is the first cause on which both natural and free agents depend. And just as his initiative does not prevent natural causes from being natural, so it does not prevent voluntary action from being voluntary but rather makes it be precisely this. For God works in each according to its nature. (*ST* I, 83, 1)

The human creature

Aquinas is sometimes called "the Angelic Doctor" since he wrote much about the nature and activity of angels (*ST* I, 50–64). Although he thinks of angels as lofty and exalted in God's scheme of things, however, and even though he regards them as in some ways superior to people, it is the human creature to which he gives most of his attention as he reflects on what God, as Creator, has brought about. Yet what does Aquinas take people to be? Perhaps as good an answer as any is to say that he thinks of them as embodied spirits or as mind enmeshed in matter. In the philosophy of writers such as Plato and Descartes, people are essentially non-material thinking things which are linked, yoked, or attached to what is physical. In the philosophy of many contemporaries, they are nothing but material objects in motion. For Aquinas, on the other hand, people are something in between: neither wholly immaterial considered as the individuals they are; nor purely material entities. For him, they are essentially physical things which also function at a non-physical level. Or, as he often observes, they are creatures with a certain kind of *soul*.

According to Aquinas, to say that something has a soul (*anima*) is just to say that it lives. For him (as for Aristotle), anything living can be said to have a soul (to be *animate* as opposed to *inanimate*). "Inquiry into the nature of the soul," he explains, "presupposes an understanding of the soul as the root principle of life in living things within our experience" (*ST* I, 75, 1). So he takes plants and non-human animals to have souls. Yet he also thinks that there is a radical difference between these and human beings. To be sure, so he agrees, they resemble each other in certain ways. All of them grow and move, for instance. And though plants lack sensation, people and non-human animals do not. Unlike my roses and my cats, however, people can understand and reflect or think accordingly – a fact that leads Aquinas to hold that they are more than the sum of their bodily functions. Why? Because, he argues, thought and understanding cannot be identified with any particular physical object.

Why not? Aquinas's answer is that particular physical objects are not intrinsically intelligible and can only be raised to the level of intelligibility by something that is not itself a particular physical object. In his view, you do not understand what a thing is just by coming across instances of it which impinge on your senses. For him, no material thing is actually understandable considered on its own. Rather, the world is potentially intelligible, and it becomes intelligible as we "abstract" from sense data and thus come to understand things apart from their individuality. "A thing is knowable," says Aquinas, "in so far as it is separated from matter." And, so he concludes, the subject in which the thing exists as known must be immaterial. "A thing must be received by a knowing intellect in an immaterial way.

651

For this reason . . . a nature capable of knowing is found in proportion to their degree of immateriality" (*DV* II, 2). For Aquinas (in contrast to philosophers such as David Hume and John Locke), the model for knowing is not so much *seeing* as *talking*. Rather as Wittgenstein came to do, he denies that an object could ever be the meaning of a word. On his account, meaning (and, therefore, understanding) emerges as subjects able to know escape from or transcend the particularity of the way of existing had by what is physical. Or, as he commonly puts it, understanding is of *forms*, and it occurs as these come to be in a non-material subject. According to him, when I understand what, for example, a lemur is, I have in me the nature of a lemur (its "form," as Aquinas would say). But I do not have it as the lemur does. For Aquinas, lemurs (and other material things) have their forms (their natures) just by being material things of the kind they are (they have them *materialiter*). According to Aquinas, however, I can have forms in a different way (*intentionaliter*): as one who understands what lemurs (and other things) are (*ST*, I, 75, 2).

Yet Aquinas does not therefore conclude that I am something non-material. He says that the human soul, considered as "the principle of the act of understanding" is not a material object. He even says that it is something that "subsists in its own right" (*ST* I, 75, 2). But he also says that the soul is but a *part* of the whole human being. For human beings, on Aquinas's reckoning, are not just knowers. They are also things with bodies, things which can move (like plants) and feel (like non-human animals). And they are so *essentially*. Speaking in an Aristotelian vein, Aquinas observes that "the nature of a specific type includes whatever its strict definition includes." And, so he continues: "In things of the physical world, this means not only form, but form and matter" – from which he concludes that "it belongs to the very conception of 'man' that he have soul, flesh and bone" (*ST* I, 75, 4). Aquinas frequently refers to the view that human beings are essentially substances different from bodies (a notion that he ascribes to Plato). But he firmly rejects it. For him, people are naturally a composite of the immaterial and the material. Or, as he usually puts it, the human soul is "the form of the human body" (*ST* I, 76, 1), by which he means that our existence as knowers is what makes our bodies to be the special things that they are, namely bodies of intellectual animals (bodies of people as opposed to bodies of plants or non-human animals). In terms of this picture, I am not soul *plus* body. I am an *ensouled body*. There is, Aquinas argues, "no more reason to ask whether [the human] soul and body make one thing than to ask the same about the wax and the impression sealed on it . . . Just as the body gets its being from the soul, as from its form, so too it makes a unity with this soul" (*DA* II, 1). For this reason Aquinas argues that, if people are to live after their death, the soul must be reunited to the body. Since he holds that the human soul is something subsistent, and since he thinks that (being immaterial and being the principle of life in people) it cannot be destroyed in the ways that bodies can, he agrees that it might survive the corruption of the body. But, so he adds: "Soul is not the whole human being, only part of one: my soul is not me." For Aquinas, the union of soul and body "is a natural one, and any separation of soul from body goes against its nature . . . so if soul is deprived of body it will exist imperfectly as long as that situation lasts" (*Super Epistolam ad Corinthios* (*EP*) 15).

Human action

Largely because of their dissatisfaction with views of the human person such as those presented by Plato and Descartes among others, many contemporary philosophers have found much to admire in Aquinas's account of what human beings are. But he has much more to say about them than is summarized above. For people, as he describes them, are more than an amalgam of body and soul. They are actors or agents, which, so he thinks, raises questions. What is involved in human action? Can people ever do anything other than they do? Is their behavior subject to evaluation of some kind? Aquinas has things to say on these matters also.

Action in general

Aquinas holds that all living things are, in a sense, self-moving. "To live," he says, "is attributed to some beings because they are seen to move themselves, but not to be moved by another" (*SG* I, 97; *ST* I, 18, 1–3). But, he thinks, different living things move in different ways. So what is happening when human beings move? According to Aquinas, their movements are often exactly like those of plants and non-human animals since, for example, they grow and instinctively react to their environment. In his view, however, they can also move on the basis of understanding. For Aquinas, understanding (unlike, for instance, an individual's particular sensation) is expressible in judgments or statements that everyone (in principle) can share. Though I cannot have your toothache, I can, says Aquinas, have your thoughts (I can think the same thoughts as you). And, so he adds, since statements can be true or false, knowledge can lead us to recognize alternatives, on the principle that to understand a statement is also to understand its negation. So Aquinas also holds that people have the ability to *act* as well as *react*. Unlike plants and non-human animals, they can behave with alternatives in mind. According to Aquinas, human behavior differs from that of non-human things since it can sometimes proceed with reason and in a way that invites the question 'With a view to what are you doing that?' He also thinks that when human behavior is of this kind, it is always a case of people seeking what they take to be good.

According to Aquinas: "The goodness of a thing consists in its being desirable" (*ST* I, 5, 1). In his view, goodness is that to which things are drawn or attracted. It is something to which they tend. In saying so, he does not, of course, mean that if X "turns me on" then X is clearly good. Rather, his point is that we can make nothing of the suggestion that something is good without introducing the notion of attractiveness or desirability. He thinks, for example, that a *good* radio is one you would be *attracted* to if you wanted what people normally look for in radios (as opposed, say, to objects of art, or things with which to prop the door open). He also thinks that goodness is something to which *everything* naturally tends. In the case of people, however, he holds that this tending can sometimes be governed, not just by instinct or nature, but also by understanding, by what is *thought* to be good. It can express a person's will. For Aquinas, indeed, genuine human actions (as opposed to reflex motions and bodily behavior in which we engage casually and unthinkingly) always express the will of the people who perform them. And will, so he holds, is always bound up with understanding. According to Aquinas, there is no operation of the will which is not also an operation of the reason. He also thinks that there is no operation of the reason which is not also an operation of the will. In his view, what we find attractive (what we will or are drawn to as we act) depends on how we think of things, so that human action involves an interweaving of being attracted and understanding that cannot be unraveled in practice. We think of what we are attracted to thinking of, and we are attracted to what we think of.

Actions in particular

What is going on as people act in particular circumstances? Aquinas maintains that (whether consciously or otherwise) they engage in examples of "practical reasoning" (*ratio practica*), i.e., reasoning with a view to behavior, as opposed to reasoning concerning what is the case (which he calls "speculative reasoning" (*ratio speculativa*)). According to Aquinas, genuine human actions involve choice or decision (*electio*), which expresses both how we think and what we want or are drawn to. Or, as Aquinas often says, choice is the fruit of deliberation (*consilium*), and both choice and deliberation arise from habits or dispositions (*habitus*) of various kinds. For him, action starts with desire for something one finds attractive (this is where will comes in). But how is that something to be achieved? Here, says Aquinas, we may need to reflect on a strategy of means and ends (this is where deliberation comes in). And, so he argues, our desires, and how we go about seeking to fulfill them, will depend on the kind of people we are, on our characters or settled personalities (which is where habits or dispositions come in). According to Aquinas, each of us have patterns of action, or settled ways of acting, to which we tend as individuals. On his account, our choices reflect the people we have become. Or, as Aquinas frequently argues, they reflect or display our *virtues* and *vices*.

Does Aquinas's account of wanting and choosing commit him to the view that human beings must always do exactly what they do? Does it entail that there is no such thing as genuine human freedom? Some philosophers have argued that, if our actions flow from our desires or characters then they cannot really be free. It is therefore important to stress that, as noted above, this is not Aquinas's position. Indeed, so he holds, human freedom is a pre-condition of practical reasoning. If people are not free to make decisions, he argues, "counsels, precepts, prohibitions, rewards and punishment would all be pointless" (*ST* I, 83, 1). Also, so he maintains, freedom is entailed by the fact that human actions are done for reasons. Why? Because, he says, it belongs to the very nature of practical reason to deliberate with an eye on alternatives, and because reasons for action can never compel assent. Or, to put things another way, Aquinas thinks that there is an important difference between theoretical reasoning and practical reasoning.

Consider the argument:

> If all human beings are mortal
> and if all Belgians are human beings
> then all Belgians are mortal.

Here we cannot but accept the conclusion given the premisses supplied. And no additional information can leave us with any alternative but to accept it. We accept it necessarily.

But now consider the argument:

> I want to get to London.
> If I travel on this plane it will get me to London.
> So I should catch this plane.

Might additional information leave me unable to conclude other than that I should catch the plane? Obviously not. What if I learn that, if I catch this plane, I shall be traveling on a vehicle likely to be boarded by terrorists? If I consider the plane under that description, then I will (unless I am a complete idiot) not conclude that I should catch it. And yet, so Aquinas suggests, when reflecting on the world, we can always view it under different descriptions. So he also holds that we can engage with it not because we are forced to think about it in only one way. For him, people have freedom of choice since they can interpret the world in different ways and act in the light of the ways in which they interpret it.

In this sense, he maintains, their actions can be governed by reasons that are fully their own.

Virtues and vices

According to some thinkers, moral philosophy should be chiefly concerned with notions such as duty and obligation. But Aquinas is of a different mind. His moral philosophy focuses on the notion of happiness. For him, the best moral thinking will help us to become fulfilled and content considered as the creatures that we are. He also thinks that becoming thus content and fulfilled depends on our acquiring a variety of virtues and is inhibited by the presence in us of corresponding vices. For Aquinas, therefore, the key ethical concepts are those of virtue and vice rather than those of duty or obligation. In this respect, his moral thinking is much more in tune with that of Aristotle and contemporary "virtue ethicists" than it is with that of writers such as Kant.

Aquinas maintains that there is a sense in which we cannot help but seek happiness. Why? Because, as we have seen, he thinks of everything as tending to its good; but also because he thinks that the good for a thing is something that perfects or completes it and, in this sense, renders it happy. Yet he also holds that we might fail to seek happiness. We cannot but aim at what we take to be good, he holds. But we can make mistakes when it comes to what is really good for us. Why? Because, Aquinas thinks, we might fail to grasp that people, as a matter of fact, are so constituted that only certain ways of acting can lead them to be genuinely satisfied and at peace. His idea is that not just any behavior is humanly perfective or fulfilling and that serious reflection is needed so that we can make good decisions about what to aim for in practice. "When we speak of 'good' and 'evil' in human acts," he observes, "we take the 'reasonable' as our standard of reference . . . Acts are termed 'human' or 'moral' in so far as they issue from reason" (*ST* I, II, 18, 5).

In elaborating on this conclusion, Aquinas holds that practical reasoning (like speculative reasoning) must start with some basic premises which can be seen to be true without argument. "There is," he says, "a natural disposition of the human mind by which it apprehends the principles of theoretical disciplines." And, so he adds, "there is a natural disposition concerned with the basic principles of behavior" (*DV* XVI, 1). For example, says Aquinas, we can see, straight off, that good is to be done and evil avoided. We can then, he thinks, employ this judgment when reflecting on particular circumstances. But how are we to know what, in the concrete, is good or bad? At one level, Aquinas holds that there are no easy answers to this question. "Discourse on moral matters," he suggests, "is subject to uncertainty and variation," and "it is all the more uncertain if one wishes to descend to bringing doctrine to bear on individual cases in specific detail." "Judgement concerning individual cases," he says, "must be left to the prudence of each person" (*Sententia Libri Ethicorum (E)* II, 2). In general, however, Aquinas thinks that there are certain ways of behaving that help us to be humanly fulfilled. And this is where his notion of virtue comes in. A virtue (*virtus*), he says, is "a good quality of mind by which one lives righteously, of which no one can make bad use" (*ST* I, II, 55, 4). Or, as he also observes, a virtue "is a *habitus* which is always for good."

In other words, according to Aquinas, people may have abilities, tendencies, or capacities that contribute to their flourishing as people. Correspondingly, so he adds, they may have abilities, tendencies, or capacities that contribute to their human diminishment (i.e., vices). In his detailed working out of this thesis, Aquinas draws heavily on Aristotle. But his overall treatment of goodness in people adds elements of his own. Hence, for example, while

Aristotle sees ethical thinking as a quest for a happiness to be found only in this life (he calls it *eudaimonia*), Aquinas views our happiness in this life as a stage on the way to a happiness that is only complete as creatures are united to God (a state that he calls "beatitude" (*beat-itudo*)). Then again, while Aquinas and Aristotle are in much agreement when it comes to what may be listed under the headings "Virtues" and "Vices", Aquinas extends the list to include what he calls "supernatural virtues." Both, for example, hold that, in order to be humanly fulfilled, people need prudence, temperance, justice, and courage. For Aquinas, however, they also need faith, hope, and charity, virtues that he takes to be strictly unattainable by merely human effort (he calls them "infused virtues"). Also unlike Aristotle, Aquinas will often contrast virtuous behavior not with what is *vicious* but with what is *sinful*. "A certain imitation of bliss is possible in this life," he argues, "if human beings perfect themselves in the goods firstly of contemplative and secondly of practical reason. This is the happiness Aristotle discusses in his *Ethics*." For Aquinas, however, God is the ultimate (even if unrecognized) object of human desire. And his approach to human conduct is always governed by this conviction. So, again in contrast to Aristotle, he views all human actions as either in or out of tune with what he calls "Eternal Law." According to Aquinas, "Law is nothing but a dictate of practical reason issued by a sovereign who governs a complete community" (*ST* I, II, 91, 1). And since he holds that "the whole community of the universe is governed by God's mind," he takes right practical reason to be ultimately of theological significance. At the end of the day, Aquinas sees all that we do as conforming, or as failing to conform, with the goodness that God is essentially.

Aquinas the philosopher

Should a book on medieval philosophy really include a chapter on Aquinas? He never called himself a philosopher. In his writings, "philosophers" always fall short of the true and proper "wisdom" to be found in the Christian revelation. So some have suggested that he is best thought of as a theologian, not a philosopher. According to Mark Jordan, for instance, Aquinas "almost always [wrote] in what is self-evidently the voice of a theologian . . . [who] . . . chose not to write philosophy" (Jordan 1993, pp. 232ff). And there is much to be said in defense of this conclusion. Many of Aquinas's writings are devoted to obviously theological topics and are written by one whose interest in them is primarily that of a practicing Christian. And, even when Aquinas seems to be writing with an eye not directly targeted on matters of Christian doctrine, he evidently has Christian interests at the back of his mind. If a philosopher is someone whose literary output is the work of one who is not, first and foremost, a Christian believer, and if philosophers only write with little or no religious commitment, then Aquinas is certainly not a philosopher. Rather, he is someone with a serious Christian agenda.

But those with such an agenda can write in very different ways. They can proceed with no sense of what a rigorous argument looks like. Or they can write on the assumption that there are really no serious philosophical questions to be asked either about the meaning of Christian teachings or about the grounds on which they are held. They can also suppose that non-Christian thinkers have little to offer to Christians, and they can avoid discussing some of the questions that have most preoccupied philosophers. Yet Aquinas does not write in any of these ways. Even his most explicitly theological works display high standards of logical rigor. They are also full of probing and intelligent questions concerning the significance and truth of Christian claims. And Aquinas's writings as a whole draw heavily on (and, arguably, improve on) the thought of many non-Christian authors, such as Plato, Aristotle, Proclus, Averroes, AVICENNA, and Maimonides. They also frequently contain extensive and sophisticated discussions of what would normally be thought to be key philosophical issues.

For reasons such as these, one need have no hesitation in conceding that there is indeed such a thing as the philosophy of Aquinas. And it is profound, shrewd, ingenious, and astute. According to Bertrand Russell: "There is little of the true philosophic spirit in Aquinas . . . Before he begins to philosophize, he already knows the truth; it is declared in the Catholic faith" (Russell 1946, p. 484). Much more typical of the way in which Aquinas is viewed by philosophers today, however, is the verdict of Anthony Kenny, one of the best known of twentieth-century non-Christian analytical philosophers. According to him, Aquinas is "one of the dozen greatest philosophers of the western world" (Kenny 1969, p. 1). As Kenny goes on to say, Aquinas's philosophy of nature "has been antiquated, in great part, by the swift progress of natural science since the Renaissance." And "his philosophy of logic has been in many respects improved upon by the work of logicians and mathematicians in the last hundred years." But "his metaphysics, his philosophical theology, his philosophy of mind and his moral philosophy entitle him to rank with Plato and Aristotle, with Descartes and Leibniz, with Locke and Hume and Kant." No student of medieval philosophy can afford to ignore him. But the same goes even for students of philosophy as it is practiced today.

Bibliography

Primary sources
The definitive text of Aquinas's writings is being published by the Leonine Commission, established by Pope Leo XIII in 1880, which has now produced editions of Aquinas's most important works. Publications of Aquinas's writings prior to the Leonine edition include *Opera omnia* (Parma, 1852–73) and *Opera omnia* (Paris, 1871–82). Most of Aquinas's writings have also been published in manual size by the Casa Marietti (Turin and Rome). The best English edition of the *Summa theologiae* (with notes and commentaries) is the Blackfriars edition (61 vols., Latin and English with notes and introductions, 1964–80). This translation is, unfortunately, sometimes unreliable. For a more literal rendering of the text, see *St. Thomas Aquinas Summa theologica* (translated by the Fathers of the English Dominican Province, London, 1911 and Westminster, MD, 1981).

The preceding text refers to works of Aquinas thus:
De veritate (*DV*)
Quaestiones disputatae De potentia (*DP*)
Sententia Libri De anima (*DA*)
Sententia Libri Ethicorum (*E*)
Summa theologiae (*ST*)
Summa contra Gentiles (*SG*)
Super Epistolam Primam Pauli Apostoli ad Corinthios (*EP*)
Super Librum Dionysii De divinis nominibus (*DN*).

Primary sources for the life of Aquinas can conveniently be found in:
Ferrua, A., ed. (1968), *Thomae Aquinatis vitae fontes praecipuae*, Alba: Edizioni Domenicane.
Foster, Kenelm, ed. (1959), *The Life of Thomas Aquinas: Biographical Documents*, London: Longmans, Green; Baltimore: Helicon Press.

Secondary sources
Aertsen, Jan (1988), *Nature and Creature: Thomas Aquinas's Way of Thought*, Leiden: Brill.
Anscombe, G. E. M. and Geach, P. T. (1961), *Three Philosophers*, Oxford: Oxford University Press.

657

Bourke, Vernon J. (1921), *Thomistic Bibliography: 1920–1940* (The Modern Schoolman), St. Louis, MO.

Burrell, David (1979), *Aquinas, God and Action*, Notre Dame, IN: University of Notre Dame Press.

Chenu, M. D. (1964), *Towards Understanding Saint Thomas*, trans. A. M. Landry and D. Hughes, Chicago: H. Regnery Co.

Chesterton, G. K. (1933), *St Thomas Aquinas*, London: Sheed and Ward.

Clarke, W. Norris (1995), *Explorations in Metaphysics*, Notre Dame, IN: University of Notre Dame Press.

Copleston, F. C. (1955), *Aquinas*, Harmondsworth: Penguin Books.

Davies, Brian (1992), *The Thought of Thomas Aquinas*, Oxford: Clarendon Press.

——(1997), "Aquinas, God and Being," *The Monist* 80/4, pp. 500–20.

——(1998), "Aquinas on What God is Not," *Revue Internationale de Philosophie* 52/204, pp. 207–25.

Elders, Leo J. (1990), *The Philosophical Theology of St. Thomas Aquinas*, Leiden and New York: Brill.

——(1993), *The Metaphysics of Being of St. Thomas Aquinas in a Historical Perspective*, Leiden and New York: Brill.

Finnis, John (1998), *Aquinas: Moral, Political, and Legal Theory*, Oxford: Oxford University Press.

Gallagher, David, ed. (1994), *Thomas Aquinas and His Legacy*, Washington, DC: The Catholic University of America Press.

Gilson, Étienne (1957), *The Christian Philosophy of St Thomas Aquinas*, New York: Random House.

Goris, J. M. J. (1996), *Free Creatures of an Eternal God*, Utrecht and Leuven: Peeters.

Hankey, W. J. (1987), *God in Himself: Aquinas's Doctrine of God as Expounded in the Summa Theologiae*, Oxford: Oxford University Press.

Ingardia, Richard, ed. (1993), *Thomas Aquinas: International Bibliography 1977–1990*, Bowling Green, OH: Philosophy Documentation Center, Bowling Green State University.

Jordan, Mark (1993), "Theology and Philosophy," in Norman Kretzmann and Eleonore Stump, eds., *The Cambridge Companion to Aquinas* (pp. 232–51), Cambridge: Cambridge University Press.

Kenny, Anthony, ed. (1969), *Aquinas: A Collection of Critical Essays*, Garden City, NY: Anchor Books.

——(1969), *The Five Ways: Saint Thomas Aquinas' Proofs of God's Existence*, London: Routledge and Kegan Paul.

——(1980), *Aquinas*, New York: Hill and Wang.

——(1993), *Aquinas on Mind*, London and New York: Routledge.

Kretzmann, Norman (1996), *The Metaphysics of Theism: Aquinas's Natural Theology in 'Summa Contra Gentiles' I*, Oxford: Oxford University Press.

Kretzmann, Norman (1999), *The Metaphysics of Creation: Aquinas's Natural Theology in 'Summa Contra Gentiles' II*, Oxford: Oxford University Press.

Kretzmann, Norman and Stump, Eleonore, eds. (1993), *The Cambridge Companion to Aquinas*, Cambridge: Cambridge University Press.

Mandonnet, P. and Destrez, J. (1960), *Bibliographie Thomiste*, 2nd edn., rev. M.-D. Chenu, Paris: J. Vrin.

Martin, C. F. J. (1997), *Thomas Aquinas: God and Explanations*, Edinburgh: Edinburgh University Press.

McCabe, Herbert (1992), "The Logic of Mysticism – I," in Martin Warner, ed., *Religion and Philosophy*, Cambridge: Cambridge University Press.

McDermott, Timothy, ed. (1989), *St Thomas Aquinas, "Summa theologiae," A Concise Translation*, Westminster, MD: Christian Classics.

McInerny, Ralph (1982), *St Thomas Aquinas*, Notre Dame, IN and London: University of Notre Dame Press.

——(1990), *A First Glance at St. Thomas Aquinas: A Handbook for Peeping Thomists*, Notre Dame and London: University of Notre Dame Press.

——(1992), *Aquinas on Human Action*, Washington, DC: The Catholic University of America Press.

Miethe, Terry L. and Bourke, Vernon J. (1980), *Thomistic Bibliography, 1940–1978*, Westport, CT and London: Greenwood Press.

O'Rourke, Fran (1992), *Pseudo-Dionysius and the Metaphysics of Aquinas*, Leiden: Brill.

Person, Per Erik (1970), *Sacra Doctrina: Reason and Revelation in Aquinas*, Philadelphia: Fortress Press.

Russell, Bertrand (1946), *A History of Western Philosophy*, London: Allen and Unwin.

Torrell, Jean-Pierre (1996), *Saint Thomas Aquinas*, vol. 1: *The Person and his Work*, Washington, DC: The Catholic University of America Press.

Van Steenberghen, Fernand, *Le Problème de l'existence de Dieu dans les écrits de S. Thomas D'Aquino*, Louvain-La-Neuve: Editions de l'Institut Supérieur de Philosophie.

Weisheipl, James A. (1974), *Friar Thomas D'Aquino: His Life, Thought, and Work*, Garden City, NY: Doubleday; republished 1983 with corrigenda and addenda, Washington, DC: The Catholic University of America Press.

Westberg, Daniel (1994), *Right Practical Reason: Aristotle, Action, and Prudence in Aquinas*, Oxford: Clarenden Press.

Wippel, John F. (1984), *Metaphysical Themes in Thomas Aquinas*, Washington, DC: The Catholic University of America Press.

——(2000), *The Metaphysical Thought of Thomas Aquinas*, Washington, DC: The Catholic University of America Press.

Wittgenstein, Ludwig (1922), *Tractatus Logico-Philosophicus*, trans. C. K. Ogden, London: Kegan Paul, Trench, Trubner.

121

Thomas Bradwardine

STEPHEN E. LAHEY

Thomas Bradwardine (b. ca. 1290; d. 1349), briefly Archbishop of Canterbury, known as *Doctor Profundus*, was in the forefront of both scientific analysis at Merton College and the revival of Augustinian theology in the early fourteenth century. While a *magister artium*, he wrote treatises on proportion, speculative arithmetic and geometry, continuity, and memory, as well as several other aspects of natural philosophy. As he developed, Paul's statement, "So it depends not on human will or exertion, but on God who shows mercy" (Rom. 9: 16) compelled him, in his *De futuris contingentibus*, to reject WILLIAM OF OCKHAM's belief that God knows future events as future contingents; this work was to become the nucleus for *De causa Dei contra Pelagium*. He left Oxford in 1335 and joined the circle of Bishop de Bury of Durham, which included ROBERT HOLCOT, RICHARD FITZRALPH, and RICHARD KILVINGTON. During his later years, Bradwardine served as confessor to Edward III, and became Archbishop of Canterbury in July, 1349; he died of the plague on 26 August that year.

De causa Dei refutes the Ockhamist position that God's knowledge of future events is not as certain as it is of past and present ones by explaining how God's perfect knowledge and unmediated causal primacy directs created acts, with special attention to human free will (1964, I, 35, 308C). Bradwardine refutes every imaginable species of Pelagianism by examining God's will and knowledge, causality, modality, and the relation of predestination and grace to freedom. Bradwardine's treatment of each is grounded securely in the primacy of God's unmediated causal influence over creation, giving *De causa Dei* the structure of a bicycle wheel, with each of the separate yet related topics serving as the spokes that radiate from the topic of God's absolute power over creation. Bradwardine argues that predestination and human free willing are not mutually exclusive by defining freedom to be consonant with the divine will, as had AUGUSTINE, but innovates in his exploration of the divine coefficiency in all created action. Insofar as any act, even that of a human will, is law-governed, the divine will acts as coagent in that act. Instances of evil human willing are not excluded here; "all evil acts of the [human] will are from God according to the substantial act but not according to their deformity" (1964, II, 26, 564B). This enables Bradwardine to explain that divine providence is commensurate with predestination, the eternal prevolition of God or the foreordination of the divine will as regards the future (1964, II, 45, 421A). The doctrine of the divine coefficiency of action completely rules out humans doing any good on their own, which in turn prevents the Pelagian from holding that we can merit salvation or grace of any sort. "No one is predestinate or damned because of works that he does or anything else in his life, nor is any one saved or damned because of his works

. . . salvation and damnation comes from the will of God, invariable in all things" (ibid., 45, 427B).

Bibliography

Primary sources

(1964), *De causa Dei contra Pelagium et de virtute causarum ad suos Mertonenses libri tres*, ed. H. Savile, Frankfurt-on-Main: Minerva; repr. of 1618, London.

(1955), *Tractatus de proportionibus*, ed. and trans. H. Lamar Crosby, in *Thomas Bradwardine, his Tractatus de proportionibus*, Madison: Wisconsin University Press.

Secondary sources

Leff, Gordon (1957), *Bradwardine and the Pelagians*, Cambridge: Cambridge University Press.

Oberman, Heiko (1957), *Archbishop Thomas Bradwardine*, Utrecht: Kemink and Zoon.

Dolnikowski, Edith W. (1995), *Thomas Bradwardine: A View of Time and a Vision of Eternity*, Leiden: Brill.

122

Thomas of Erfurt

MAURICIO BEUCHOT

Thomas of Erfurt (fl. ca. 1300) wrote the celebrated *De modis significandi sive grammatica speculativa*. This work was traditionally attributed to JOHN DUNS SCOTUS until Grabmann demonstrated the correct authorship in 1922. Little is known about Thomas's life. The *Speculative grammar* deals with the modes of signifying (*modi significandi*), that is, with the signification and consignification of words or meaningful expressions. The signification of a word is its elementary semantic sense. The consignification of a word is the specific syntactic sense it has within the sentence structure, that is, the word's role or function in the sentence.

Thomas divides grammar into etymology or analogy (which is the present-day lexicography) and *diasynthetica* (which is the present-day syntax). The first studies word-classes (*pars orationis*), which in Latin are eight. The second one studies the rules of composition pertaining to them.

The modes of signifying of each word-class are divided into essential and accidental. A word-class as such comes into existence through the essential modes, whereas it acquires accidental modes through its relationship with other word-classes. The essential modes of signifying of each word-class are divided into general, subaltern, and special (as in Porphyry's tree). This division depends on whether the mode of signifying belongs to a given word-class with all its subdivisions or with only some of them. Accidental modes are divided into absolute and respective modes. An absolute mode relates a word-class with the property of the thing it signifies; a relative mode relates a word-class with another class, in such a way that either one of these word-classes depends on the other.

In regard to *diasynthetica* (syntax of composition) the eight Latin word-classes admit of construction, congruity, and completion. Construction is the union of constructibles on the basis of the mode of signifying pertaining to them. Every construction requires two constructibles.

In semantics, Thomas explores the signification of word-classes and not just their consignification. Thus, for instance, the noun, whether proper or common, signifies something like an entity: the proper noun implies individuation, and the common noun implies self-subsistence. On the other hand, the adjective implies something that is in another thing (that is, something to be found in another thing), etc. Construction signifies the composition, or make-up, of the mind. Congruity gives the sentence enough sense, and completion gives it full sense.

Thomas also discusses issues that we now regard as belonging to pragmatics (a part of semiotics). One of them is the attribution of meaning to a noun by language users, where

Thomas distinguishes among cases in which the attribution is due to signification and cases in which it is due to consignification. Thomas also discusses the effects of different linguistic uses on the mood of the listener.

Bibliography

Primary source

(1972), *Grammatica speculativa*, ed. G. L. Bursill-Hall, London: Longman.

Secondary sources

Bursill-Hall, G. L. (1971), *Speculative Grammars of the Middle Ages*, Paris and The Hague: Mouton.

Grabmann, M. (1922), "De Thoma Erfordiensi, auctore *Grammaticae* quae Joanni Duns Scoti adscribitur, speculativa," *Archivum Franciscanum Historicum* 15, pp. 273–7.

Pinborg, J. (1967), *Die Entwicklung der Sprachtheorie im Mittelalter*, Copenhagen: Arne Frost-Hansen.

——(1972), *Logik und Semiotik im Mittelalter*, Stuttgart: Frommann-Holzboog.

Rosier, I. (1983), *La Grammaire spéculative des modistes*, Lille: Presses Universitaires de Lille.

123

Thomas of Sutton

GYULA KLIMA

Thomas of Sutton (b. ca. 1250; d. ca. 1315), whose main literary activity falls within the period between THOMAS AQUINAS's death (1274) and his canonization (1323), was one of the profoundest early defenders of Aquinas's doctrine, while it was still regarded as radically innovative and highly controversial.

We have very scant reliable information on Sutton's life. He was ordained deacon at Blithe by Walter Giffard, the Archbishop of York, on September 20, 1274. Sutton entered the Dominican order, and became a friar in Oxford by 1282. He had probably been a fellow of Merton College before he entered the order. There he was closely associated with two other Dominicans, Richard Knapwell and William Hothum, who were also heavily involved in the defense of Thomistic positions. Sutton incepted as a master in Oxford some time between 1291 and 1300, and lectured there till his death (Roensch 1964, pp. 44–51, 237–47).

Sutton is an authentic early Thomist, a judgment warranted not only from the number of issues he addressed in this spirit in his quodlibetal and ordinary disputes, but also from the fact that several of his opuscula survived by having been mistakenly attributed to St. Thomas himself. Most notable among these is Sutton's *De pluralitate formarum* (*On the Plurality of Forms*), in which he presents an astute defense of the Thomistic thesis of the unity of substantial forms. Sutton's greatest merit in his defense of this and other central Thomistic positions (such as the real distinction between essence and existence in creatures, the analogy of being, the pure potentiality of prime matter, designated matter as the principle of individuation, the pure spirituality of immaterial substances, etc.) is his ability to reduce the differences with his opponents, such as HENRY OF GHENT, JOHN DUNS SCOTUS, and RICHARD OF MIDDLETON, and to disagreements over certain fundamental metaphysical principles. For example, Sutton reduced the originally psychological thesis of the unity of substantial forms – which had been further deepened and broadened by Thomas Aquinas – to a metaphysically and anthropologically central doctrine. For him the individual unity of a human being is only possible through the determination of a single act of substantial being caused by a single substantial form (Klima 2000).

Bibliography

Primary sources
(1969), *Quodlibeta*, ed. M. Schmaus and María González-Haba, Munich: Verlag der Bayerische Akademie der Wissenschaften.

(1977), *Quaestiones ordinariae*, ed. J. Schneider, Munich: Verlag der Bayerische Akademie der Wissenschaften.

(1980), *De pluralitate formarum*, in *S. Thomae Aquinatis Opera omnia*, ed. P. Mandonnet, Stuttgart and Bad Cannstatt: Fromman-Holzboog.

Secondary sources

Klima, G. (2000), "Thomas of Sutton on the nature of the intellective soul and the Thomistic theory of being," in J. Aertsen, K. Emery, and A. Speer, eds., *Nach der Verurteilung von 1277. Philosophie und Theologie an der Universität von Paris im letzten Viertel des 13. Jahrhunderts* (pp. 436–55), Berlin and New York: Kluwer.

Roensch, F. J. (1964), *Early Thomistic School*, Dubuque, IA: Priory Press.

124

Thomas Wilton

CECILIA TRIFOGLI

Thomas Wilton (fl. ca. 1312) was a fellow of Merton College from about 1288 until 1301, and master of arts at Oxford from 1301 until 1304, when he left in order to pursue theological studies at Paris, becoming master of theology in 1312. He was a prominent figure in Paris at the beginning of the fourteenth century. He had debates with DURAND OF ST. POURÇAIN over the nature of intellection, PETER AURIOL over the nature of relation, WALTER BURLEY over intension and remission of forms, and WILLIAM OF ALNWICK over the relation between the possible intellect and the human individual. He has been characterized frequently as an Averroist on the basis of his theory of the separation and unicity of the possible intellect (Kuksewicz 1968).

Wilton's ontology is strongly realist and has remarkable similarities with those of JOHN DUNS SCOTUS and Walter Burley, the last of whom names Wilton as his master. He holds that a relation is a real thing distinct from the individuals related. He even maintains that the extra-mental existence and the distinction of the individuals related are not necessary conditions for an extra-mental relation. For example, in his view, the relation of lordship is real, but the individuals related by it are one and the same, i.e., the creature. Furthermore, matter has real relations to non-existing forms (Henninger 1990). He argues that motion is a thing distinct from the mobile substance and the forms or places successively acquired by this substance during motion, and rejects AVERROES' view that motion can be reduced to the state finally acquired through motion (Trifogli 1995). Similarly, he claims that time is a quantity that inheres in motion and is really distinct from it, thereby denying AVERROES' theory of the dependence of time on the human soul (Trifogli 1990).

Bibliography

Wilton's principal works are commentaries on Aristotle's *Physics* and *De anima* and a *Quodlibet*. These works have not been edited, except for a few questions scattered among various journals.

Dumont, S. D. (1998), "New questions by Thomas Wylton," *Documenti e Studi sulla Tradizione Filosofica Medievale* 9, pp. 341–81.
Henninger, M. G. (1990), "Thomas Wylton's theory of relations," *Documenti e Studi sulla Tradizione Filosofica Medievale* 1, pp. 457–90.

Jung-Palczewska, E. (1996), "Wylton's solution of the Aristotelian problem of God's infinite power," in J. Marenbon, ed., *Aristotle in Britain during the Middle Ages* (pp. 311–23), Turnhout: Brepols.

Kuksewicz, Z. (1968), "De Siger de Brabant à Jacques de Plaisance: la théorie de l'intellect chez les Averroïstes latins des XIIIe et XIVe siècles," Wroclaw, Warsaw, and Cracow: Ossolineum, pp. 176–201.

Trifogli, C. (1990), "Il problema dello statuto ontologico del tempo nelle *Quaestiones super Physicam* di Thomas Wylton e di Giovanni di Jandun," *Documenti e Studi sulla Tradizione Filosofica Medievale* 1, pp. 491–548.

——(1995), "Thomas Wylton on motion," *Archiv für Geschichte der Philosophie* 77, pp. 135–54.

125

Ulrich of Strassburg

KENT EMERY, JR.

Ulrich Engelbert (b. ca. 1220; d. 1277) was born in Strassburg (Strasbourg). He joined the Dominicans around 1245 and was a student of ALBERTUS MAGNUS, first at Paris and then in the *studium generale* of the order in Cologne (1248–54), where he was a fellow student of THOMAS AQUINAS. When he finished his studies, he was appointed lector in theology at the Dominican convent in Strassburg. In 1272 he was elected provincial of the Teutonic Province of the order. In 1277 the General Chapter relieved him of his duty so that he could finish his studies in theology at Paris, where he became a bachelor in the *Sentences*. He died shortly after he arrived in Paris and never became a master.

Ulrich's major work is the *Liber de summo bono* (*Book on the Highest Good*, composed 1265–72, sometimes called *Summa de bono*), which he intended to be used for teaching theology in Dominican *studia* in the province. The work comprises eight books (subdivided into tractates and chapters), the last two of which have not survived (or were not written) and the sixth of which is unfinished: (1) on the principles of the science of the highest Good, or theology; (2) on the essence of the highest Good and the properties that flow from it; (3) on the divine persons taken "in common"; (4) on the Father and creation; (5) on the Incarnation and the mysteries that pertain especially to the Son; (6) on the Holy Spirit, grace, the gifts and the virtues; (7) on the sacraments; and (8) on beatitude.

The order and form of *De summo bono* reflect the influence of Neoplatonic sources. The work descends from the properties and operations of the highest Good to creatures, and then treats their return to God through human intellects (the "exit and return" of Proclus). Accordingly, the subject of theology is "God, insofar as he himself is the Alpha and Omega, the beginning and end" (cf. Albertus Magnus). The form of the discourse is axiomatic, as in Proclus and others, presenting a linked chain of principles upon which subordinate articles depend. Further, the work is ordered according to modes of theology specified by PSEUDO-DIONYSIUS: book 2 is a thematic commentary on the "united" theology of *The Divine Names*; book 3 treats what the persons share and operate "in common," and books 4–6 treat the "discrete" theology of the divine persons, considered according to their singular appropriations.

By means of these structural devices, Ulrich sought to systematize the philosophical and theological pedagogy of his teacher, Albertus Magnus, and to consolidate its problematic: the reconciliation of Aristotle, Plato, and Christian wisdom according to a hierarchy of cognition. Thus, as regards the nature of God, Ulrich identifies the "Being Itself" of AUGUSTINE, the "self-diffusive Good" and "the One above (created) being" of Pseudo-Dionysius, and the Intellect whence all forms flow of the Islamic Peripatetic philosophers. Likewise, as regards the soul, he synthesizes Augustine's teachings concerning the "hidden recess of the mind," the elevating intellectual light of Pseudo-Dionysius, and the agent intellect of Peripatetic philosophers, wherein the mind may be joined to separated substances and even to God himself. The agent intellect, the "likeness" of the "first and pure Intellect," is "inserted" naturally into the human soul; so the mind was created to know divine realities and to be united with them by its light, which is composed with the light of Intelligences and the divine Light. The mind's divine likeness remains in human nature after the disrupting accident of the Fall. By means of this intact natural light, the science of theology is founded on "most universal first principles, which are evident (*per se*) to us even without faith and are antecedent to its articles, and through which the articles and everything else in this science can be proved" (*Summa de bono* 1.2.3). The light of faith, emanating from Christ and infused supernaturally by God, extends the quantity of what the mind knows (e.g., the Trinity, the Incarnation), and intensifies and more limpidly illumines its cognition of divine realities (see esp. de Libera 1986, 1994). Ulrich's treatment of the "supernatural" mysteries (books 4–6) relies more on standard Latin theological authorities.

Bibliography

Primary sources

(1926–7), "La *Somme* de Ulrich de Strasbourg," ed. Jeanne Daguillon, *La Vie Spirituelle, Supplément* 14: 19–37, 89–102; *Supplément* 15: 56–67 (an edition of Lib. 6, tract. 4, caps. 7–11, from Paris, Bibliothèque Nationale, MS. lat. 15091).

(1930), *La "Summa de bono", Livre 1. Introduction et édition critique*, ed. Jeanne Daguillon, Paris: J. Vrin.

(1955), "Summa *De Bono* of Ulrich of Strasbourg, Liber II: Tractatus 2, Cap. I, II, III; Tractatus 3, Cap. I, II," ed. F. Collingwood, in J. R. O'Donnell, CSB, ed., *Nine Mediaeval Thinkers: A Collection of Hitherto Unknown Texts* (pp. 293–307), Toronto: Pontifical Institute of Mediaeval Studies.

(1987), *De summo bono: Liber 2, Tractatus 1–4*, ed. Alain de Libera, in Corpus philosophorum Teutonicorum medii aevi I.2.1, Hamburg: Felix Meiner Verlag.

(1987), *De summo bono: Liber 4, 1–2, 7*, ed. Sabina Pieperhoff, in Corpus philosophorum Teutonicorum medii aevii I.4.1, Hamburg: Felix Meiner Verlag.

(1989), *De summo bono: Liber 1*, ed. Burkhard Mojsisch, in Corpus philosophorum Teutonicorum medii aevi 1. 1, Hamburg: Felix Meiner Verlag.

Secondary sources

Backes, Ignaz (1935), *S. Thomae de Aquino Quaestio de gratia capitis (Summae p. III q. 8) accedunt textus inediti S. Albert Coloniensis et Ulrici de Argentina*, Bonn: P. Hanstein.

——(1975), *Die Christologie, Soteriologie und Mariologie des Ulrich von Strassburg: Ein Beitrag zur Geistesgeschichte des 13. Jahrhundert*, 2 vols, Trier: Paulinus-Verlag.

Breuning, Wilhelm (1959), *Erhebung und Fall des Menschen nach Ulrich von Strassburg*, Trier: Paulinus-Verlag.

de Libera, Alain (1985), "Ulrich de Strasbourg, lecteur d'Albert le Grand," *Freiburger Zeitschrift für Philosophie und Theologie* 32, pp. 105–36.

——(1994), *La Mystique Rhénane d'Albert le Grand à Maître Eckhart*, (see pp. 99–162), Paris: Éditions du Seuil.

Grabmann, Martin (1926), *Des Ulrich Engelberti von Strassburg O. Pr. (d. 1277) Abhandlung De pulchro: Untersuchungen und Texte*, Munich: Verlag der Bayerischen Akademie der Wissenschaften.

Lescoe, Francis J. (1979), *God as First Principle in Ulrich of Strasbourg: Critical Text of 'Summa De Bono', IV, 1, based on hitherto unpublished mediaeval manuscripts and philosophical study*, New York: Alba House.

Sturlese, Loris (1996), *Storia della filosofia tedesca nel mediaevo: il seculo XIII* (pp. 159–80), Florence: L. S. Oschki.

126

Vital du Four

A. G. TRAVER

Vital du Four, also known as Vitalis de Furno (b. ca. 1260; d. 1327) was a Franciscan philosopher and theologian, and later cardinal, who played a prominent role in the controversy over the Franciscan conception of *usus pauper*.

Of Gascon ancestry, Vital was born at Bazas in Aquitaine, about 60 kilometers southeast of Bordeaux. He entered the Franciscan order at an early age and went to study theology at Paris from 1285 to 1291. He studied there under the masters James of Quesnoy and probably Raymond Rigault.

He taught at the Franciscan *studium generale* at Montpellier from 1292 to 1296. While there, he edited the *Lectura* of his master James of Quesnoy. In 1296 Vital was transferred to the University of Toulouse where he taught for the next eleven years. During his regency at Toulouse, he produced his *Speculum morale totius Sacrae Scripturae*, a popular moralizing explanation of the Old and New Testaments (1305).

In 1307 he was elected the Provincial of Aquitaine. At the request of his order's superiors, he played a large role in the debates surrounding the teachings of his confrere, PETER OLIVI, who had died in 1298.

Vital argued against the position of the Spiritual Franciscans and was rewarded for his skill as a diplomat by being made cardinal-priest by Pope Clement V in 1312. Though steadily in favor for a number of years with Clement's successor, the controversial Pope John XXII, Vital opposed him on the delicate issue of evangelical poverty during the 1320s, before eventually submitting to the papal declarations.

Vital belonged to the pre-Scotistic Franciscan school, and was eclipsed by his contemporary JOHN DUNS SCOTUS. In fact, until recently one of his works, *De rerum principio*, had been attributed to Scotus. Vital's extant works include three quodlibetal questions, six disputed questions *De rerum principio*, six disputed questions *De anima et eius potentiis*, a *Commentary on the Sentences*, and eight disputed questions *De cognitione*. His non-philosophical works include the *Speculum morale totius Sacrae Scripturae*, *Postilla super Apocalipsim* (a compilation of nine commentaries on Revelations), several polemical works dealing with the issue of poverty, sermons, and some letters.

Philosophically, Vital shares many doctrines with his contemporaries and immediate predecessors, including MATTHEW OF AQUASPARTA, JOHN PECHAM, ROGER MARSTON, HENRY OF GHENT, GILES OF ROME, and the little-studied Raymond Rigault. Vital follows the main Bonaventurian doctrines including the intellectual cognition of the singular, the plurality of forms in the soul, and the direct and intuitive self-knowledge of the soul about its existence and essence. He rejects THOMAS AQUINAS's distinction between essence and existence and holds that the essence of real beings is identical with their existence; actual existence is the very essence of the thing as related to its efficient cause. It has recently been demonstrated that Vital relied heavily on Giles of Rome's *De esse et essentia* both in content and in structure for his *De rerum principio*.

Bibliography

Primary sources

(1639), *De rerum principio*, in *Johannis Duns Scoti Opera omnia*, ed. L. Wadding, Paris: Vivès.

(1927), *Quaestiones disputatae*, in F. M. Delorme, ed., "Le cardinal Vital du Four, huit questions disputées sur le problème de la connaisance," *Archives d'Histoire Doctrinale et Littéraire au Moyen Âge* 2, pp. 151–337.

(1947), *Quodlibeta tria Vitalis de Furno*, ed. F. M. Delorme, Rome: Pontificium Athenaeum Antonianum.

Secondary sources

Dumont, Stephen D. (1984), "Giles of Rome and the *De rerum principio* attributed to Vital du Four," *Archivum Franciscanum Historicum* 77, pp. 81–109.

Lynch, J. E. (1972), *The Theory of Knowledge of Vital du Four*, St. Bonaventure, NY: Franciscan Institute Press.

Mann, William E. (1991), "The best of all possible worlds," in Scott MacDonald, ed., *Being and Goodness: The Concept of the Good in Metaphysics and Philosophical Theology* (pp. 250–77), Ithaca, NY: Cornell University Press.

Putallaz, François-Xavier (1990), "La connaissance de soi au moyen âge: Vital du Four," *Collectanea Franciscana* 60, pp. 507–37.

127

Walter Burley

M. C. SOMMERS

Walter Burley (b. 1274/5; d. in or after 1344) philosopher, secular priest, known as the *Doctor planus et perspicuus*, was born possibly at Burley in Wharfedale or Burley near Leeds, Yorkshire. He studied and taught at Oxford for a period somewhere between 1294 and 1309, becoming master of arts by 1301 and fellow of Merton College by 1305. While at Oxford, he heard JOHN DUNS SCOTUS lecture on the *Sentences* (?1298–9) and perhaps was a fellow student of WILLIAM OF OCKHAM in theology (ca. 1307–8).

Burley studied theology at Paris (ca. 1309–23) and became a "Doctor of Sacred Theology" by 1324, but left Paris by the beginning of 1327.

From his first exposure to William of Ockham's *Sentences* commentary (Oxford 1317–18), Burley opposed him on a number of important issues in logic and natural philosophy, an engagement that was not one-sided. In the *Summa logicae*, Ockham both uses and attacks Burley's *De suppositionibus*. Burley counterattacks in his second version of *De puritate artis logicae* (after 1323). While Ockham's *Logic* is organized in the traditional way around terms, propositions, and arguments, Burley's is organized around general rules for consequences, thus giving priority to propositional logic.

Ockham held that (1) universals do not exist *in re* and (2) are not constitutive parts of the essence of individuals. Burley countered that (1) universals exist *in re*, although not apart from singulars, though he eventually ceded ground to Ockham on (2), holding that the universal form merely discloses the individual's essence, e.g., "human." As well as resisting Ockham's reduction of *res* to singular things, Burley objects to Ockham's reduction of Aristotle's categories to substance and quality.

Sometime after 1334, Walter Burley joined the household of Richard de Bury, Bishop of Durham, who became the patron of Burley's renewed career as a scholar. Between 1334 and 1340, he completed commentaries on the *Ethics* (Venice 1481), the *Physics*, the *Ars vetus* (Venice 1497), and the *Politics*. In the *Physics* and *Ars vetus* are found Burley's references to the *moderni*, those thinkers, encountered first during his Paris years, who threaten the purity of the font of all philosophy: Aristotle.

The *De vita et moribus philosophorum*, attributed to Burley, was thought to have been the work of his "retirement" in southern France and Italy (after 1340), but his authorship of this work is now in doubt. In 1341 he engaged in a *disputatio* at Bologna, an event which has been connected with his supposed Averroism. Burley, however, did not hold any position as true which contradicted "the truth of the Christian faith." Whether Burley returned to England to the rectory at Great Chart, Kent, obtained on June 19, 1344, or died abroad, is not known.

Bibliography

Primary sources

(1955), *"De puritate artis logicae tractatus longior" with a revised edition of the "Tractatus brevior,"* ed. P. Boehner, St. Bonaventure, NY: Franciscan Institute.

(1997), *Questions on the De anima of Aristotle by Magister Adam Burley and Dominus Walter Burley*, ed. Edward A. Synan, Leiden: Brill.

(2000), *Walter Burley's Quaestiones super librum Posteriorum*, ed. Mary C. Sommers, Toronto: Pontifical Institute of Mediaeval Studies.

Secondary sources

Martin, C. (1964), "Walter Burley," in William A. Hinnebusch et al., *Oxford Studies Presented to Daniel Callus* (pp. 194–230), Oxford: Clarendon Press.

Wood, Rega (1988), "Studies on Walter Burley 1968–88," *Bulletin de Philosophie Médiévale* 30, pp. 233–50.

Wood, Rega and Ottman, Jennifer (1999), "Walter of Burley: his life and works," *Vivarium* 37, pp. 1–23.

128

Walter Chatton

GIRARD J. ETZKORN

Walter Chatton (b. ca. 1285; d. 1343) was born in the town of Chatton in Northumbria. He entered the Order of Friars Minor at an early age. The next biographical item has him being ordained a subdeacon by John of Halton, Bishop of Carlisle in 1307. Walter Chatton became the 53rd Franciscan regent master at Oxford in 1330. The rest of his career (1333–43) was spent in Avignon where he served as an examiner of the writings of Thomas Waleys and DURAND OF ST. POURÇAIN under Popes Benedict XII and Clement VI. The latter appointed him to the Welsh See of St. Asaph, thinking that the incumbent David of Bleythn had died. Walter Chatton, however, died late in 1343 before the See of St. Asaph had become vacant.

In his writings Chatton may be said to espouse positive theology, that is to say he regularly bade his listeners to return to what the terms of the Scriptures, the Fathers of the Church, and what theological tradition signified, rather than what God might have done by his absolute power. The opponents referred to by Chatton in his lectures are predictable. In almost every question of any distinction, he cites WILLIAM OF OCKHAM and PETER AURIOL, less frequently ADAM OF WODEHAM who was most likely the *reportator* of Chatton's first set of lectures on the *Sentences*. Occasionally, Walter also argues against the views of RICHARD OF CAMPSALL. Regularly, though not always, Chatton defends and supports the opinions of JOHN DUNS SCOTUS, to whom he refers as "our doctor" or *doctor subtilis* or simply "Scotus." In his approach to philosophical theology, he frequently invokes a hermeneutical principle which is a foil to Ockham's razor and which Walter actually called "my proposition," namely that when a proposition is made true by things, if two are not sufficient, then a third must be posited, and so forth. Another oft-invoked principle involves God's omnipotence. Chatton's wording reads (and this indeed is an excursion into "hypothetical theology"): "Nothing should be denied to God's power, unless it involves an obvious contradiction."

In the realm of philosophy, Chatton may safely be categorized as a realist. The ten Aristotelean categories, for example, have correspondingly real bases, unlike Ockham for whom only substance and quality enjoy extra-mental reality. Walter fills a lot of folios in defending the extra-mental reality of quantity and relations. In the area of natural philosophy, Chatton regards the continua, both permanent and successive, as composed of indivisibles, with the proviso that while the ultimate parts are in the continua, they are there only as indivisible potentially. In this he is acutely aware that this position is counter to Aristotle and the majority of his philosophical ancestors and contemporaries.

As far as philosophical psychology is concerned, Chatton assiduously defends the need for sensible and intelligible species in human cognition, unlike Ockham who denies species and opts for habits which, as far as Chatton is concerned, amounts to the same thing. He likewise repeatedly rejects Ockham's *fictum* theory of knowledge, stating that concepts are simply acts of knowledge. Regarding one's knowledge of singulars, Walter states that initially we have sensible knowledge of singulars, which can be intellectualized by composition and division. Universals are concepts with bases in reality. We can have reflexive intellectual acts ad infinitum. Against Richard of Campsall, who claimed that intuitive and abstractive cognition are not really distinct, Walter counters with twelve difficulties requiring the real distinctness of intuitive cognition. For Chatton, there is only one rational soul in man, unlike Ockham who posited both sensitive and intellectual souls. Walter favors Scotus's view of the need to posit a principle of individuation, which is alternately called an individual property or an individual difference. The term *haecceitas* is not used.

Walter defends the univocal concept of being as essential for proving the existence of God and this, in response to Peter Auriol's critique of Scotus, is a metaphysical and not merely a logical concept. Chatton claims to prove the existence of God and likewise his unicity, holding that the notion of two infinite beings involves a contradiction.

In spite of Ockham's opposition and Wodeham's criticisms, Chatton's philosophical and theological views constitute a significant contribution to the intellectual ferment of the first third of the fourteenth century.

Bibliography

Primary sources

(1966), *Quaestio utrum quantum et continuum componantur ex indivisibilibus sicut ex partibus integrantibus*, ed. J. E. Murdoch and E. A. Synan, *Franciscan Studies* 26, pp. 234–66.

(1989), *Reportatio et Lectura super Sententias*, Prologue, ed. Joseph C. Wey, Toronto: Pontifical Institute of Mediaeval Studies.

(2002), *Reportatio in I Sent.*, dist. 1–9, ed. Joseph C. Wey and Girard J. Etzkorn, Toronto: Pontifical Institute of Mediaeval Studies.

(2002), *Reportatio in I Sent.*, dist. 10–48, ed. Joseph C. Wey and Girard J. Etzkorn, Toronto: Pontifical Institute of Mediaeval Studies.

Secondary sources

Auer, J. (1953), "Die 'skotische' Lehre von der Heiligewissheit: Walter von Chatton der erste 'Skotist'," *Wissenschaft und Weisheit* 16, pp. 1–19.

Brown, S. F. (1985), "Walter Chatton's Lectura and William of Ockham's *Quaestiones in libros Physicorum Aristotelis*," in W. A. Frank and G. J. Etzkorn, eds., *Essays Honoring Allan B. Wolter* (pp. 81–93), St. Bonaventure, NY: Franciscan Institute.

Brampton, C. K. (1963), "Gauthier de Chatton et la provenance des Mss. Lat. Paris Bibl. Nat. 15886 et 15887," in *Études Franciscaines* 13, pp. 200–5.

Etzkorn, G. J. (1977), "Walter Chatton and the absolute necessity of grace, (*Lectura* I d. 17 q. 1 et *Reportatio* I d. 17 q. 1)," *Franciscan Studies* 37, pp. 32–65.

——(1987), "A heretofore unknown Quodlibet of Walter Chatton," in *Bulletin de Philosophie Médiévale* 29, p. 230.

Fitzpatrick, N. A. (1971), "Walter Chatton on the univocity of being: a reaction to Peter Aureoli and William of Ockham," in *Franciscan Studies* 31, pp. 88–177.

Maurer, A. (1984), "Ockham's razor and Chatton's anti-razor," in *Mediaeval Studies* 46, pp. 463–75.

129

William of Alnwick

STEPHEN D. DUMONT

The English Franciscan and theologian William of Alnwick (b. ca. 1275; d. 1333) was a disciple and close associate of JOHN DUNS SCOTUS. He studied and obtained the licence in theology at Paris and taught at the Franciscan house at Oxford and subsequently at Montpellier, Bologna, and Naples. His works include a *Commentary on the Sentences* (unedited) given at Paris by 1314, a set of questions on intentional being (*De esse intelligibile*), a *Quodlibet*, and a lengthy set of some twenty-eight disputations called *Determinationes* (unedited) held at Bologna in 1322–3. Alnwick's works are replete with references to contemporary discussions and are the basis upon which some early fourteenth-century debates have been reconstructed. They show an especially intimate knowledge of Scotus's works, at times supplying important clarifications of specific texts or arguments. Alnwick probably functioned as Scotus's secretary and attested that he recorded one of Scotus's *Collationes*. He also compiled the so-called *Additiones magnae*, an edition of Scotus's own Parisian lectures on the *Sentences*.

Doctrinally, Alnwick was an independent student of Scotus, generally defending his positions as they were subjected to criticism and development in the first quarter of the fourteenth century, particularly among Franciscans. Thus, in his early *Sentences*, Alnwick can be found answering Scotus's first critics, such as Richard of Conington, and then in his later *Determinationes* replying to the next generation of criticisms by PETER AURIOL. Alnwick's defenses of Scotus, however, were not uncritical, nor was he without his own, independent contributions. In some cases, Alnwick would partially agree with Scotus. For instance, he defended Scotus's position on the univocal concept of being against the criticism of Conington, who tried to reinstate HENRY OF GHENT's version of analogy originally targeted by Scotus. Alnwick nevertheless then proceeded to reject what Scotus saw as a necessary consequence of univocity, namely, that ultimate differences and the other transcendentals could not include the concept of being. In other cases, Alnwick parted company with Scotus altogether, as when he reverted to Henry of Ghent's view on the compatibility of faith and demonstration or rejected Scotus's reasoning that the immortality of the soul was not strictly demonstrable. In a more independent vein, Alnwick was the first to respond to an early fourteenth-century version of atomism called "indivisibilism," advanced initially by HENRY OF HARCLAY and then later upheld by the Franciscans WALTER CHATTON and Gerald Odonis. This theory rejected Aristotle's fundamental prohibition against composing the continua of time, space, and motion out of indivisible units. Alnwick is recognized to have developed a significant and influential response to Harclay by applying propositional analysis to the problem of the division of the continuum.

Bibliography

Primary source

(1937), *Quaestiones disputatae de esse intelligibili et de quolibet*, ed. A. Ledoux, Quaracchi: Collegium S. Bonaventurae.

Secondary sources

Dumont, S. D. (1987), "The univocity of the concept of being in the fourteenth century: John Duns Scotus and William of Alnwick," *Mediaeval Studies* 49, pp. 1–75.

Noone, T. B. (1993), "Alnwick on the origin, nature, and function of the formal distinction," *Franciscan Studies* 53, pp. 231–61.

130

William Arnaud

STEPHEN E. LAHEY

William Arnaud, known in Latin as Guillelmus Arnaldus (fl. mid-thirteenth century) was Archdeacon of Lanta and master of arts at Toulouse (1235–44). It is possible that Arnaud became Bishop of Carcassonne in 1248 and died in September, 1255, but not certain, owing to the prevalence of the name 'Arnaldus' in southern France in the thirteenth century. It is certain that Arnaud was not the Inquisitor Guillelmus Arnaldi OP, who was murdered by townspeople in 1242. Arnaud was one of the earliest commentators on PETER OF SPAIN'S *Tractatus* or *Summule logicales*, producing the *Lectura tractatuum*, as well as commentaries on Aristotle's *Prior* and *Posterior Analytics*. Arnaud's logic exemplifies, and likely is the first instance of, the "modist" logic associated with late thirteenth-century Paris. Parisian logic had been dominated by Peter of Spain's attention to natural supposition, according to which a given term considered in itself stands in a proposition for all things to which it can possibly refer. Peter devalued appellation, in which reference applies only to presently existing things, and emphasized restriction in its place, which provides rules by which natural supposition can be narrowed down to more specific kinds of cases in which spatially and temporally modifying predicate elements can be included.

ROGER BACON took issue in the 1250s with Parisian logicians by describing a problem that arose from their emphasis on natural supposition; does the term 'man' refer to some human nature present in the same way in all men, past, present, and future? If so, as advocates of natural supposition seem to hold, then a term can naturally supposit for beings and non-beings alike, which Bacon believed to be impossible. Whereas Peter of Spain holds that a substantive term like 'man' is not common to all, without regard to whether or not they exist, Arnaud's explanation is that, in a sentence like 'Caesar is a man', the term 'man' refers to a form that is preserved in extant men, whether or not Caesar himself is alive, meaning that the statement's truth does not entail the actual existence of Caesar. This leads to larger issues: given Arnaud's innovation on Peter of Spain's position, is it possible that he would argue that the form "man," predicable of Caesar despite his nonexistence, has a reality beyond the being of existing individual men? Arnaud responds with a moderate realist position that the human intellect abstracts the intelligible species from the perceived form, which intelligible species is not directly predicable of the thing understood, but corresponds to the nature of the thing. That is, when I perceive Socrates as a man, the object of my understanding is the abstracted intelligible "man," which corresponds naturally to the formal nature of Socrates, although the "man" I understand is not a constitutive element of Socrates' being. Arnaud's explication of Peter's supposition theory contributed significantly to the "modist" approach of analyzing logic using Aristotle's conception of how understanding occurs within the soul, an approach that typified later thirteenth-century Parisian logic.

Primary source

(1969), *Glosses on Peter of Spain's De suppositione*, in L. M. De Rijk, "On the genuine text of Peter of Spain's *Summule logicales*," *Vivarium* 7, pp. 120–62.

131

William of Auvergne

ROLAND J. TESKE

William of Auvergne (b. 1180/90; d. 1249) was born at Aurillac in the province of Auvergne. Little is known of his early life, though by 1223 he was at the University of Paris with a master's degree in theology and was a canon of the cathedral of Notre Dame. When Bartholomaeus, the Bishop of Paris, died on October 20, 1227, William was so displeased by the canons' choice for the new bishop that he went to Rome and appealed to Pope Gregory IX. The pope was apparently impressed by William, ordained him priest, and appointed him Bishop of Paris on April 10, 1228. William continued as Bishop of Paris until his death on March 30, 1249.

After a student riot in 1229 over a tavern bill, during which several students were killed by police sent by the queen regent, Blanche of Castille, the masters and students at the university went on strike because William failed to obtain redress for the violation of the students' rights. The masters appealed to Rome and obtained from the pope greater independence of the university from the Bishop of Paris. During the strike William appointed the first Dominican, William of Cremona, to a chair in theology. He also allowed ALEXANDER OF HALES to retain his chair when he joined the Franciscans in 1236. In January of 1241 William condemned ten propositions in philosophy and theology as heretical – a move indicative of his concerns over some teachings at the university and foreshadowing the more extensive condemnations by Bishop Étienne Tempier some thirty years later.

William's *Teaching on God in the Mode of Wisdom* (*Magisterium divinale et sapientiale*) is his principal work; it was only early in the twentieth century that J. Kramp, following the lead of Valois, showed that seven of his works, which were published separately in the printed editions of his writings, actually formed this huge *summa*-like opus. The parts of the *Magisterium* are: *The Trinity* (*De Trinitate*), *The Universe of Creatures* (*De universo creaturarum*), *The Soul* (*De anima*), *Why God became Man* (*Cur Deus homo*), *The Faith and the Laws* (*De fide et legibus*), *The Sacraments* (*De sacramentis*), and *The Virtues and Morals* (*De virtutibus et moribus*). Other works by William of philosophical interest include *The Immortality of the Soul* (*De immortalitate animae*), two works entitled *Good and Evil* (*De bono et malo*) and *Grace and Free Will* (*De gratia et libero arbitrio*).

William is the first thinker in the thirteenth century to make an extensive and systematic use in his writings of the newly translated Greek and Islamic philosophy. He explains in the Prologue to *The Trinity* that this sacred and divine teaching is communicated in three ways: by the acceptance of a prophecy or revelation, by the obedience of faith, and by knowledge through proofs and inquiry. "The third mode is that of those who philosophize" (*Trin.* Prologue). William assures his readers that he everywhere aims at demonstrative proofs and does not appeal even to the words of Aristotle as an authority (*Soul* ch. 1, pt. 1). There are two reasons for *The Teaching on God in the Mode of Wisdom*: "the honor and glory of the creator," which is its chief end, and "the destruction of errors . . . by which one is turned from the ways of truth and the paths of rectitude" (*Univ.* Ia–Iae, ch. 1). The goals of philosophy in the mode of wisdom are "the exaltation of the creator and the perfection of our souls, which is nothing but the brilliance of the sciences and beauty of the virtues" (ibid., Preface). In these two, William adds, consists the whole of religion, and when that religion has been brought to completion, it will be the glory of our souls. In fact, the image and likeness of God to which our souls were created "is brought to its ultimate act by philosophizing" (*Trin.* ch. 26), and that ultimate act is the glorified intellect's vision of God (Teske 1998, pp. 281–3).

In the first twelve chapters of *The Trinity*, a work bearing the subtitle: *The First Principle*, William makes extensive use of AVICENNA's metaphysics to prove the existence of God and to come to some understanding of his principal attributes. He develops an argument for the existence of a being necessary through itself in clear dependence upon Avicenna's argument that moves from beings possible through themselves, but necessary through another to a being necessary through itself. Such a being, William argues, while appealing to BOETHIUS, is absolutely simple. Its being (*esse*) and what it is are identical, though in every other being, being is other than what is. Thus he follows Avicenna in holding that being is accidental to everything other than God and also anticipates the real distinction between being and essence in all creatures, a distinction that is found more clearly articulated in THOMAS AQUINAS (Caster 1995, pp. 186–9). William even claims that being necessary through itself is the most proper name of God (*Univ.* IIa–IIae, ch. 10), and when he presents his account of the divine attributes he follows the order in which Avicenna presents them in *Metaphysics* VIII, 4 (Judy 1975, pp. 364–5). Being necessary through itself is alone uncaused; it is stripped of all accidents; it is not a common attribute, and it has no quiddity or definition.

Even in the second and larger part of *The Trinity*, which attempts to prove the existence of three persons in God and to come to some understanding of their origin and distinction and of the proper way to speak of them, William uses Avicennian principles. For example, he uses the principle "From something one insofar as it is one only something one can come," in order to show that the Father can generate only one Son (*Trin.* ch. 14).

Despite his extensive debt to Avicenna, William rejected the teaching of the great Islamic thinker on many points. As William said, probably here equating Avicenna with Aristotle, as he often did, "But though on many points we must oppose Aristotle, as is truly right and just, and this is the case in all the statements in which he speaks contrary to the truth, so he should be accepted, that is, upheld in all those points on which he is found to have held the correct view" (*Soul* II, 12). While William accepted Avicenna's argument for the existence of God and his view of the ontological structure of the created world, he firmly rejected many features of Avicenna's account of the origin of creatures from God. Avicenna held that creatures emanate from the First, a name for God that William also uses, in a necessary and eternal outpouring in which the First produces the first intelligence, which in turn produces the second, and so on until the tenth and last intelligence, which created everything in the sublunar world, including human souls. William, on the other hand, insisted that only God creates, that he creates freely, that he immediately creates everything apart from himself, and that he did not create a world without a temporal beginning.

According to William, God, who is being by his essence, is the source of all beings other than himself, which are beings by participation. Just as if there were only one source of light, all illumination would come from it, so God is the one source of being from whom all other beings come (*Univ.* Ia–Iae, ch. 30). William rejects every teaching that ascribes the act of creation to any cause but God, but he is especially opposed to the Avicennian doctrine that the tenth intelligence is the creator of human souls, the source of their being, their knowledge, and their ultimate happiness. For such a view equivalently makes that intelligence the God of human souls (ibid., ch. 21).

William develops the concept of divine omnipotence as power that is not limited to one of two opposites and that cannot cease or be prevented; he says that the omnipotence of God "means that he can neither be forced to do what he does not will nor be prevented from doing what he wills" (*Trin.* ch. 9). Thus omnipotence implies will, and will in turn implies knowledge and wisdom. William claims all things are subject to the power of God "because nothing comes from him except through his will, and he only holds in being what he wills and when he wills and how he wills; nor can he be prevented or forced" (*Trin.* ch. 9).

William derived his doctrine on the divine will from the Jewish philosopher, AVENCEBROL (Ibn Gabirol), whom William calls the most noble of philosophers (*Trin.* ch. 12) and whom he suspects to be really a Christian (*Univ.* Ia–Iae, ch. 26). For in the *Fountain of Life* Avencebrol linked the divine will with the divine word, which he tended to hypostatize. Hence, William came to think of the Word of God as the will, by which God created all things. Through his doctrine of God's will William was able to introduce into his Avicennian world the radical contingency of everything other than God (Caster 1996b, p. 37).

William's doctrine of the divine will also allows him to argue that the world is not, as Avicenna had taught, eternal, "because we must admit that it was created or made or drawn from its possibility into actuality" (*Trin.* ch. 10). In *The Trinity* William briefly argues against the Aristotelian and Avicennian arguments for the eternity of the world, but in *The Universe of Creatures* he does much more. He first develops a short treatise on eternity and time in which he distinguishes eternity, which is not only without beginning and end, but also without before and after, from time, which has both beginning and end as well as before and after (*Univ.* Ia–IIae, chs. 1–5). Then he both answers at length objections against the eternity of the world and proposes arguments to prove the finiteness of the world's past (*Univ.* IIa–Iae, chs. 7–11). William, like BONAVENTURE after him, held that the finiteness of the world's past time could be demonstrated and was not merely an article of faith, as Thomas Aquinas held.

William claims that philosophers "erred, attributing more to nature than it can do and not realizing that nature's total power is completely subject to divine choice" (*Trin.* ch. 11). William says not only that there is no necessity in nature, but also that natures are unable to produce other things by themselves. At times William seems to speak like an occasionalist. He says, for example, that creatures are causes only in an improper sense, that is, in the way a window is a cause of the illumination of a house or in the way a riverbed is the cause of the water that flows through it (*Trin.* ch 11). At other times, however, William clearly seems to ascribe a genuine causality to secondary causes. Miller (1998, pp. 272–7) argues that those who have branded William as an occasionalist have overstated their case and have failed to see the instances in which he speaks of the causality of creatures.

In his *De universo* William examines philosophical questions about the created universe in two principal parts. In the first of these he examines questions about the material universe or the universe in general, while in the second he deals with the spiritual universe. The first principal part has three sections. In the first of these, after an introductory chapter, William argues against the Cathars, that is, the Manichees of William's age, destroying their

682

claim that there are two first principles, one good and the other evil. William's argument against them is developed first in terms of Avicenna's metaphysics of the First as "being necessary through itself" and absolutely simple. Without any appeal to Scripture or ecclesiastical teaching, William shows the impossibility of two simple first principles, one of which is good and the other evil. William also argues that there is no sense of "evil" in which evil could be a principle.

In chapters 11 through 15 William argues that the universe is one in opposition to some unidentified thinkers who held a plurality of universes. Here William perhaps had in mind those who thought of an afterlife in another material world separate from this world. In chapter 16 William begins a long discussion of how the universe proceeded from the First. After exploring various images of the production of the universe, William settles on the view that the world proceeded from the First by his eternal Word by which the First freely created the world, though he did not create all things at once. In chapter 24 William describes the error of Aristotle and his followers regarding the creation of the first intelligence and the heavenly bodies. He, of course, has in mind most of all Avicenna who taught that, since from what is one only something one can come, there can come from the First only one being, namely, the first intelligence. This intelligence in turn produces the second intelligence and so on until the tenth intelligence, which is the creator of human souls, is reached. The second section deals with the question of the eternity of the world, and the third section is mainly concerned with divine providence.

The second principal part of *The Universe* deals with the spiritual universe, that is, with the Aristotelian separate substances, the good angels, and the bad angels. William argues for the strict spirituality of the separate substances and good angels, though he has some doubts about the devils. He seems to have been one of the first, if not the first, in the Latin West to break away from the Augustinian view, later bolstered by Avencebrol, that everything apart from God is composed of matter, though Weisheipl (1979, p. 260) argues to the contrary that universal hylomorphism was the novelty.

William found the account of the separate substances or intelligences in Avicenna to be deficient in a number of ways. They were, he claimed, merely intelligences without wills and, hence, incapable of moral goodness or moral evil; they were thought of as having the power to create, which belongs only to God. And, worst of all, they were far too few in number to serve as attendants in the heavenly court, for no earthly king would settle for a mere ten courtiers. Apart from such differences in their functions and number, the separate substances of Avicenna are ontologically the same as the Christian angels, namely, pure forms.

In the third part of his *Magisterium*, namely, *The Soul*, William devotes 163 folio pages to the human soul. Though he is familiar with Aristotle's *De anima*, he is most influenced by Avicenna's *The Sixth Book on the Natural Sciences, or the Soul (Liber sextus de naturalibus, seu de anima)*, in both positive and negative ways. In the Prologue he expresses astonishment that anyone would regard the study of the human soul as part of the natural sciences and insists that the science of the soul as the image of God must fall under the divine and sapiential sciences along with God himself, of whom the soul is the image. *The Soul* is divided into seven chapters. In the Prologue he tells his readers that he will in the first chapter establish the existence of the soul, while in chapter 2 he will examine its essence and essential characteristics. In chapter 3 he will deal with the question of parts of the soul, and in chapter 4 he is to raise the question of a plurality of souls in a single human being. In chapter 5 he plans to deal with the manner in which the soul comes into being, and in chapter 6 to examine the state of the soul in relation to the body. Finally, in chapter 7 he will discuss the soul's noble powers in relation to God.

In chapter 1 William quotes Aristotle's definition of soul as "the first act of a physical, organic body potentially having life," but his understanding of that definition immediately places him in a clearly Platonic or Avicennian framework, since he interprets 'physical, organic body' as meaning a body made by nature as an instrument for the soul. Moreover, he can find no meaning for 'body potentially having life' except the body that remains after death. Though William quotes with approval Aristotle's claim that the soul is form and the body matter, he insists that the soul is the whole human being, not a part. He, nonetheless, notes that the soul would not constitute a human being if it were not united to a suitable organic body.

He argues for the existence of the soul in two ways. First, he claims that anyone who denies the existence of his soul knows that he denies this. Hence, such knowing must be present in him either according to the whole of him or according to a part. He regards it as absurd to hold that the whole of oneself knows; hence, knowing is present in a part, and that part knows and understands properly and essentially. But that part cannot be a body; hence, it must be an incorporeal, living substance, and that is what he means by a soul. Secondly, he argues from the instrumental character of the body that, since no instrument exists for its own sake, but for the sake of the worker who uses it, there must be present in the body a worker who uses the members of the body and has command over the body. This worker, then, must be a non-bodily substance that has command of the body and uses its members; that is, this worker must be a soul.

Twice William appeals to Avicenna's thought-experiment in which one is asked to suppose "a man in the air with his face covered and who is without the use of any sense and who had not used any sense" (*Soul* ch. 2, pt. 13). William argues that such a flying man will know that he exists though he will not know that he is a body or has any bodily parts. Hence, he will know that he is not a body or any part of a body. Later William uses the same argument to show that the soul is the whole human being, not just a part of it (*Soul* ch. 3, pt. 11). As William sees it, the body is organic, that is, instrumental; he appeals to images of an inhabitant and a house, of a helmsman and a ship, of an artisan and his workshop, and of a prisoner and his cell in order to illustrate the relation of soul to body.

Like the separate intelligences, the human soul is an immaterial or spiritual substance. It is indivisible into parts, or simple. The powers or potencies of the soul are not accidents of the soul, but identical with the soul and differentiated only in terms of their operations. There are many powers of the soul – at least fifteen. Besides the powers of the five external senses, there are the internal senses: the estimative, memorative, and imaginative powers, and common sense; there is also the higher apprehensive or intellective power and the higher moving or appetitive power, namely, the will, and the lower moving powers, namely, the concupiscible and irascible powers. Each of these powers, however, is identical with the soul, not a part or accident of the soul.

William's main interest lies in the higher apprehensive and moving powers, namely, the intellect and the will. He uses the image of the will as king or emperor in the whole kingdom of the soul. If the soul is rightly ordered, the will has command (*imperium*) over all the other powers, including the intellective power, which serves as a counselor to the will (Teske 1994a, pp. 64–7). William expresses astonishment that Aristotle has all but completely neglected the will in his writing on the soul, though he devoted so much time to the intellective power, which is far less noble (*Soul*, ch. 3, pt. 7). The will is absolutely free to will or not to will, and William compares its absolute power of willing to the omnipotence of the creator, though in our fallen state the lower apprehensive and appetitive powers often rebel against the will's reign (*Soul*, ch. 5, pt. 15). William clearly sides with the voluntarist tradition in making the will or noble moving power the highest power in the soul that commands even the intellect (Teske 1996, p. 937).

William was concerned with Avicenna's account of the individuation of the human soul since, as he saw it, human souls would on Avicenna's account lose their individuality upon separation from their bodies. On the other hand, William seems not to have grasped the problem of the individuation of souls as it arises in the Aristotelian context and simply insists that souls were created by God as individual and remain that way after death (Teske 1994b, p. 93).

William devotes much of chapters 5 and 6 of *The Soul* as well as *The Immortality of the Soul* to proofs of the human soul's immortality, something that he regards as basic to morality and religion (*Immort.* 1). Though he regards the animal soul as an incorporeal substance, he insists that the soul of an animal ceases to exist at the death of the body since it has no operations that can be carried out without the body. The human soul, on the other hand, has operations for which the body is not required as an instrument or tool, such as the operations of the intellective power in the apprehension of intelligible things. William appeals to states of ecstasy or rapture as clear examples of the soul's independence of the body, for he regards such states as ones in which the soul quite literally stands outside the body and is rapt up in special illuminations (*Soul* ch. 5, pt. 22). He draws further arguments for the immortality of the human soul from various attributes of God, such as his goodness, providence, justice, magnificence, and generosity.

Much of William's treatment of the intellective power argues against the views of others, especially Aristotle and Avicenna, though William is also positively influenced by them. William is deeply opposed to the Aristotelian – or perhaps Averroist – doctrine of an agent intellect and to the Avicennian doctrine of an agent intelligence. The Aristotelian position implies a division between the material or receptive intellect and the agent or productive intellect within the soul, and the indivisibility of the soul rules out any such parts (Teske 1995, p. 222). The doctrine of an agent intelligence, which William attributes to Aristotle, is unacceptable for other reasons, some of which we have already seen. But William also rejects the role of such an intelligence in the acquisition of human knowledge because it makes the human intellect merely the passive recipient of knowledge rather than the active seeker and acquirer of knowledge. If our intellect acquired knowledge passively through receiving it from the agent intelligence, we would have no need to study, to read books, to attend lectures, or to do anything else but to receive the illumination from that intelligence (*Soul* ch. 5, pt. 8).

Sensation requires the reception of sensible forms, but consists in the judgment upon these forms, which is an activity of the soul. So too, intellectual knowing is not merely the reception of intelligible forms, whether from an agent intelligence or from God, but is an activity of the intellective power. The human soul stands at the horizon of two worlds with God above and the sensible world beneath and receives illumination from both. From God it receives the first principles of the sciences and of morals. For William the role of divine illumination is greatly reduced, as Marrone (1983, pp. 46 and 51) shows. But the intellective power is also illumined from the side of the sensible world in three ways: by sensation, by abstraction, and by connection or conjunction. Through sensation the intellective power attains the sensible accidents of things, but must infer from them the existence of an underlying substance. Through abstraction the intellective power omits various details so that an image of a particular individual becomes representative of any individual of its kind. And through connection one infers effects from causes and causes from effects (*Soul* ch. 7, pt. 7).

685

The intellective power is active in knowing. William frequently appeals to Aristotle's "quickness of wit" for finding connections or middle terms and is fond of the example from Chrysippus of the spider that infers the presence of prey and food from one striking of one thread in its web. So too, he appeals to AUGUSTINE's claim about the soul's being able to form images in itself from itself. The intellective power builds up in itself habits of the sciences; once the habit of a science has been generated, the soul can bring it from itself into act (*Soul* ch. 7, pt 8).

In *The Virtues and Morals*, William sets out first to attain certain knowledge in this area, but aims to add to the clarity of knowledge the pleasing attraction by which our souls are drawn to perfection and armed against vices. He examines Cicero's definitions of virtue as "a habit of a well-ordered mind," which he discusses in the light of Aristotle's views, views that he knew mainly, it seems, from the second and third books of the *Nicomachean Ethics* (Jüssen 1995, p. 20). He argues that a well-ordered human life must pay honor to God, be beautiful in itself, and be useful or beneficial for others (*Virtues*, ch. 2). William discusses intellectual habits, or sciences, as well as both moral and theological virtues and the contrary vices.

Though William's thought and work has been to a large extent overshadowed by Bonaventure and Aquinas, the great philosopher-theologians who followed him, he did influence such thinkers as HENRY OF GHENT, and his work remains worth studying if only because it allows us to appreciate the early reception of Avicenna in the West and the greatness of William's immediate successors.

Bibliography

Primary sources

Editions

(1897), *De immortalitate animae*, ed. G. Bülow, in *Beiträge zur Geschichte der Philosophie des Mittelalters* 2/3, Münster: Aschendorff.

(1946), *Tractatus Magistri Guillielmi Alvernensis de bono et malo*, ed. J. R. O'Donnell, *Mediaeval Studies* 8, pp. 245–99.

(1954), *Tractatus secundus Guillielmi Alvernensis de bono et malo*, ed. J. R. O'Donnell, *Mediaeval Studies* 16, pp. 219–71.

(1963), *Opera omnia*, 2 vols., ed. F. Hotot, with *Supplementum*, ed. B. Le Feron, Frankfurt-on-Main: Minerva (originally published 1674, Orleans and Paris).

(1966), *Il "Tractatus de gratia" di Gugliemo d'Auvergne*, ed. G. Corti, Rome: Lateran University.

(1976), *De Trinitate: An Edition of the Latin Text with an Introduction*, ed. B. Switalski, Toronto: Pontifical Institute of Mediaeval Studies.

(1998), *De l'Ame (VII, 1–9)*, trans. J.-B. Brenet, Paris: J. Vrin.

Translations

(1989), *The Trinity, or the First Principle*, trans. R. J. Teske and F. C. Wade, Milwaukee: Marquette University Press.

(1991), *The Immortality of the Soul*, trans. R. J. Teske, Milwaukee: Marquette University Press.

(1998), *The Universe of Creatures*, trans. R. J. Teske, Milwaukee: Marquette University Press.

(2000), *The Soul*, trans. R. J. Teske, Milwaukee: Marquette University Press.

Secondary sources

Caster, K. J. (1995), "The real distinction in creatures between being and essence according to William of Auvergne," Ph.D. dissertation, Marquette University.

——(1996a), "The distinction between being and essence according to Boethius, Avicenna, and William of Auvergne," *The Modern Schoolman* 73, pp. 309–32.

——(1996b), "William of Auvergne's adaptation of Ibn Gabirol's doctrine of the divine will," *The Modern Schoolman* 74, pp. 31–42.

Davis, L. D. (1973), "Creation according to William of Auvergne," in G. Steckler and L. Davis, eds., *Studies in Mediaevalia and Americana* (pp. 51–75), Spokane: Gonzaga University Press.

Judy, A. (1975), "Avicenna's 'Metaphysics' in the *Summa contra Gentiles*," *Angelicum* 52, pp. 340–84, 541–86.

Jüssen, G. (1995), "Die Tugend und der gute Wille: Wilhelm von Auvergnes Auseinandersetzung mit der aristotelischen Ethik," *Philosophisches Jahrbuch* 102, pp. 20–32.

Marrone, S. P. (1983), *William of Auvergne and Robert Grosseteste: New Ideas of Truth in the Early Thirteenth Century*, Princeton, NJ: Princeton University Press.

Miller, M. (1998), "William of Auvergne on primary and secondary causality," *The Modern Schoolman* 75, pp. 265–77.

Moody, E. A. (1975), "William of Auvergne and his treatise *De anima*," in *Studies in Medieval Philosophy, Science, and Logic* (pp. 1–109), Berkeley and Los Angeles: University of California Press.

Teske, R. J. (1990), "William of Auvergne on the eternity of the world," *The Modern Schoolman* 67, pp. 187–205.

——(1993), "William of Auvergne and the Manichees," *Traditio* 48, pp. 63–75.

——(1994a), "The will as king over the powers of the soul: uses and sources of an image in thirteenth century philosophy," *Vivarium* 32, pp. 62–71.

——(1994b), "William of Auvergne on the individuation of human souls," *Traditio* 49, pp. 77–93.

——(1995), "William of Auvergne's rejection of the agent intelligence," in W. J. Carroll and J. J. Furlong, eds., *Greek and Medieval Studies in Honor of Leo Sweeney, S.J.* (pp. 211–35), New York: Peter Lang.

——(1996), "William of Auvergne on freedom of the will," in B. C. Bazán, E. Andújar, and L. G. Sbrocchi, eds., *Moral and Political Philosophies in the Middle Ages*, 2 vols. (II: pp. 932–8), New York: Legas.

——(1998), "William of Auvergne on the relation between reason and faith," *The Modern Schoolman* 75, pp. 279–91.

——(1998), "William of Auvergne's rejection of the Platonic archetypal world," *Traditio* 55, pp. 117–30.

Weisheipl, J. A. (1979), "Albertus Magnus and universal hylomorphism: Avicebron," *Southwestern Journal of Philosophy* 10, pp. 239–60.

132

William of Auxerre

JACK ZUPKO

William of Auxerre (b. ca. 1140, d. 1231) was a master of theology at Paris who developed the first great synthesis of Christian theology and the philosophy of Aristotle. Through careful study and teaching of texts that had only recently become available in the Latin West, William acquired a detailed understanding of the metaphysics, natural philosophy, and ethics of Aristotle, as well as of the Islamic philosophers AVICENNA and AVERROES. His work showed how Aristotle's principles could be used to explain theological doctrine. In the short run, this helped to curb reactionary responses to Aristotle on the part of church authorities, who were naturally suspicious about this massive intrusion of pagan philosophy into the faculty of theology. William's reputation was such that, in 1231, he was appointed by Pope Gregory IX to a commission charged with reforming the study of Aristotle among the theologians (the teaching of Aristotle had been banned once – to little effect, it seems – at Paris in 1210), though he died before he was able to complete this project. More significantly, William's engagement with Aristotle raised the practice of philosophical theology to a new level of sophistication, culminating in the great theological *Summae* of THOMAS AQUINAS several decades later.

Of William's surviving works, the most important philosophically is the *Summa aurea* (*Golden Compendium*), a systematic treatment of theological topics loosely patterned after the *Sentences* of PETER LOMBARD. William begins by specifying what he takes to be the relation between faith and natural reason. First, he says, natural reason "confirms and augments" faith in the faithful, just as temporal goods, while not providing the ultimate reason why we should love God, augment and confirm charity in those who possess it; second, natural reason permits us to defend the faith against heretics; and third, it brings simple folk to the faith (*Summa aurea* I, Prologue: 15–16). For William, the theologian is kept from heresy by the discriminate use of reason: "wishing to express what pertains to divinity using reason, we proceed on the basis of reasons suitable [to the faith], not those which belong strictly to natural things. For heretics have been deceived in this way, because they have wanted to apply to divinity reasons proper to natural things, as if they were equating nature with its Creator" (ibid., 18). William offers four proofs for the existence of God, the last of which quotes Anselm's argument from *Proslogion* 3, except that William's conclusion identifies the necessarily existing being not as simply "God" but as "the *summum bonum* or God" (ibid., 23). William's use of transcendental concepts such as being, goodness, truth, and unity to express the divine attributes was very influential among thirteenth-century theologians, and was further developed by PHILIP THE CHANCELLOR, ALEXANDER OF HALES, BONAVENTURE, and Thomas Aquinas. He also originated the theological distinction between perfect happiness, which is uncreated and proper to God, and imperfect happiness, which pertains to human beings. In addition, William was one of the first to use what later became the distinction between God's absolute and ordained powers, holding, with GILBERT OF POITIERS, that God could, absolutely speaking, change the past.

Bibliography

Primary source

(1980–7), *Summa aurea*, vols. I–VII, ed. Jean Ribaillier, Paris: Centre National de la Recherche Scientifique; Grottaferrata: Editiones Collegium S. Bonaventurae ad Claras Aquas.

Secondary sources

Arnold, Johannes (1995), *"Perfecta communicatio": Die Trinitätstheologie Wilhelms von Auxerre*, Beiträge zur Geschichte der Philosophie und Theologie des Mittelalters NF 42, Münster: Aschendorff.

MacDonald, Scott (1992), "Goodness as a transcendental: recovery of an Aristotelian idea," in *The Transcendentals in the Middle Ages*, ed. Jorge J. E. Gracia, *Topoi* 11, pp. 173–86.

Principe, Walter H., CSB (1963), *William of Auxerre's Theology of the Hypostatic Union*, Toronto: Pontifical Institute of Mediaeval Studies.

133

William of Champeaux

JOHN MARENBON

By 1100, William of Champeaux, master of the school of Notre Dame at Paris, was considered the leading logician of his day. Until very recently, his work as a logician has been known only indirectly, mainly from the comments and attacks of his famous pupil, PETER ABELARD. On the questions about universals raised in Porphyry's *Isagoge*, William argued (Abelard 1967, p. 65: 82–9) that particulars of the same species share a single essence which makes them the sort of things they are ("material essence realism"). Abelard's criticisms early in the 1100s forced William to abandon this position and adopt an "indifference" theory: every human, for instance, is the same in that what makes them each a human does not differ (see ibid.; Lottin 1959, p. 192: 116–20). Among the other views attributed to William are the idea that sentences have two distinct senses, a grammatical and a dialectical one (Abelard 1969, pp. 271ff), and the figurative interpretation of present-tense sentences about things which no longer exist ('Homer is a poet' means "The work which Homer composed in his function as a poet exists": Abelard 1970, p. 168: 11–16).

Recently, a whole group of logical works has been attributed, on good grounds, to William (Iwakuma 1999, pp. 101–23). Before 1100, William was already strongly interested in the technical side of logic. He produced a set of straightforward, technical *Introductions* and, in the earliest version of his commentary on the *Isagoge* he did not enter into the question of universals. Later versions by him of this commentary show his progress from essential essence realism to an indifference theory, whilst in his commentary on the *Categories* he tries to work out more generally his realist position in universals and its semantics. He also commented on *On Interpretation* and BOETHIUS' *On Topical Differences*.

In addition, William is author of over fifty theological "sentences": short discussions of issues ranging from the nature of evil, to simony, and heresy (Lottin 1959, pp. 189–227). The most philosophically intricate are those about divine prescience and human free will (nos. 238–9). He argues that future contingent events are determinate and necessary, as foreseen by providence, but only in the way that all events now happening are necessary and determinate (Boethius' "conditional necessity," though the term is not used); with regard to the human agents who act in them, however, the events are not necessary.

Bibliography

Primary source
Iwakuma, Y. (1993), "The *Introductiones dialecticae secundum Wilgelmum* and *secundum G. Paganellum*," *Cahiers de l'Institut du Moyen-âge Grec et Latin* 63, pp. 45–114.

William of Champeaux as reported in Peter Abelard

Peter Abelard (1967), *Historia calamitatum*, ed. J. Monfrin, Paris: J. Vrin.

——(1969), *Scritti di logica*, ed. M. dal Pra, Florence: Nuova Italia.

——(1970), *Dialectica*, 2nd edn, ed. L. M. de Rijk, Assen: Van Gorcum.

Lottin, O. (1959), *Psychologie et morale au XIIe et XIIIe siècles*, Gembloux: Duculot.

Secondary sources

Biard, J., ed. (1999), *Langage, sciences, philosophie au XIIe siècle*, Paris: J. Vrin.

Iwakuma, Y. (1999), "Pierre Abélard et Guillaume de Champeaux dans les premières années du XIIe siècle: une étude préliminaire," in J. Biard, ed., *Langage, sciences, philosophie au XIIe siècle* (pp. 93–123), Paris: J. Vrin.

134

William Crathorn

ROBERT PASNAU

William Crathorn (fl. 1330s) provides an interesting illustration of the changing nature of philosophical theology in the early fourteenth century. An Englishman, Crathorn lectured at Oxford on PETER LOMBARD's *Sentences* during the academic year 1330–1 (see Tachau 1995). The resultant series of questions (ostensibly on book one of the *Sentences*) is a disparate bunch, focusing largely on epistemology, the Trinity, and the categories.

Though a Dominican friar, Crathorn had views that bear no resemblance to those of his confrere THOMAS AQUINAS. Out of respect for authority, Crathorn regularly quotes "our doctor St. Thomas," but these homages are often accompanied by a tortured exegesis designed to bring Aquinas's ideas into line with his own. In spirit, Crathorn's work is much closer to that of WILLIAM OF OCKHAM. Though constantly attacking the details of Ockham's views, and often taking up antithetical positions, Crathorn is nevertheless strongly influenced by Ockham's skeptical tendencies and unorthodox metaphysics.

The first of Crathorn's questions on the *Sentences* is the most striking of the set, and illustrates his philosophical tendencies. Over fourteen lengthy conclusions, he advances a series of highly idiosyncratic, even bizarre claims, including:

1 Cognition occurs through sensible and intelligible species, but not through acts of cognition, because our cognitive powers are entirely passive and hence perform no actions (concl. 1). (Since there are no cognitive acts, Crathorn goes on to deny that there can be any distinction between intuitive and abstractive cognition: "they are the same thing entirely, since intuitive knowledge is the cognitive power itself, and so is abstractive knowledge" (1988, p. 132).

2 Sensible species are the things we immediately perceive, and are straightforward likenesses of external objects, and hence literally have color, sound, shape, etc. (concl. 7). (He draws on perspective theory to account for the case of size.)

3 The senses alone cannot give us "evident and entirely infallible knowledge" of the existence of any external object or quality (concl. 8–9).

4 Such knowledge is achievable indirectly, by reasoning that "God does nothing groundlessly and supernaturally so as to lead human beings into error" (concl. 12).

Of course, many of these conclusions would seem commonplace by the seventeenth century. But Crathorn was mostly ignored by his contemporaries, or even ridiculed, especially at the hands of his fellow Dominican and rival, ROBERT HOLCOT, who wrote in one typical remark that he replied to Crathorn's arguments "with weariness and shame . . .

692

There is nothing in them that ought to move a student to anything except, perhaps, to laughter."

Bibliography

Primary sources

(1988), *Quästionen zum ersten Sentenzenbuch*, ed. F. Hoffman, *Beiträge zur Geschichte der Philosophie und Theologie des Mittelalters* NF 29, Münster: Aschendorff.

(2002), "*In Sent.* Q. 1," trans. R. Pasnau, as "On the possibility of infallible knowledge," in R. Pasnau, ed., *Cambridge Translations of Medieval Philosophical Texts*, vol. 3: *Mind and Knowledge* (pp. 245–301), Cambridge: Cambridge University Press.

Secondary sources

Pasnau, R. (1997), *Theories of Cognition in the Later Middle Ages*, New York: Cambridge University Press.

Tachau, K. H. (1995), "Introduction," in P. A. Streveler and K. H. Tachau, eds., *Seeing the Future Clearly: Questions on Future Contingents by Robert Holcot*, Toronto: Pontifical Institute of Mediaeval Studies.

135

William Heytesbury

JOHN LONGEWAY

William Heytesbury (b. before 1313; d. 1372/3) was a fellow of Merton College, Oxford, from 1330, where, with RICHARD KILVINGTON, RICHARD SWINESHEAD, THOMAS BRADWARDINE, and JOHN DUMBLETON, the Mertonian "Calculators," he worked with logical puzzles about motion and the continuum.

Heytesbury's work deals chiefly with sophismata, statements occurring within formal disputations, the truth of which were at issue under specified assumptions. The respondent must agree to or deny the sophisma, and then answer his opponent's questions, granting whatever follows deductively from his admissions, without falling into contradiction. (See WILLIAM OF SHERWOOD.) Heytesbury published a general collection, *Sophismata*, a collection of *Sophismata asinina* rotating around the sophism 'You are a donkey', *Rules for Solving Sophismata, On Compounded and Divided Senses* (in Kretzmann and Stump 1988), and other logical works.

The *Rules for Solving Sophismata*, his most significant work, contains six chapters. The first deals with insoluble sentences, self-referential paradoxes such as 'What I am now uttering is false' (in Spade 1979). The second, "On knowing and doubting" (in Kretzmann and Stump 1988), deals with intensional contexts. For instance, it presents the sophisma 'You know the king is seated'. Given that the king is seated, and you know that a sentence asserting this is true, you still may not know what the sentence says. The third chapter deals with problems connected with relative pronouns, and the fourth with paradoxes involving the terms 'begins' and 'ceases'. The fifth, "On maxima and minima," (in Longeway 1984) discusses sentences about the limits of capacities measured on linear continua, and the sixth deals with change and motion.

Heytesbury's central interest is the logic of continua and infinite divisibility, a pursuit nowadays identified as part of mathematics. His puzzles are logical, and Heytesbury works, like other logicians who treated sophismata, *secundum imaginationem* (according to imagination), allowing any consistent set of propositions whatever to be assumed for the presentation of a sophisma, regardless of metaphysical or physical possibility. He treated qualities such as heat and whiteness as measurable on a continuous range, and accustomed thinkers to the notion that any quality varying in "intension" could be conceived quantitatively. Ancient physics envisioned quantitative treatments only of spatial dimensions, time, and motion, and so Heytesbury's work helped lay the logical groundwork for sixteenth- and seventeenth-century breakthroughs in such areas as the physics of heat and temperature. In the sixth chapter of his *Rules*, Heytesbury developed the mathematics of uniform acceleration, proving that uniformly accelerated bodies will, in a given period of time, cover the

694

same distance they would have covered traveling at a uniform velocity one-half the sum of initial and final velocities. Domingo de Soto noted the theorem's application to free fall in 1555, and Galileo benefited from the medieval discussion of uniform acceleration to which William contributed, though he probably was not directly acquainted with his work.

Bibliography

Primary sources

Kretzmann, Norman and Stump, Eleonore, eds. (1988), *The Cambridge Translations of Medieval Philosophical Texts*, vol. 1: *Logic and the Philosophy of Language*, Cambridge: Cambridge University Press.

Longeway, John (1984), *William Heytesbury: On Maxima and Minima*, Dordrecht: Kluwer.

Spade, Paul Vincent (1979), *William of Heytesbury on Insoluble Sentences*, Toronto: Pontifical Institute of Mediaeval Studies.

Secondary source

Wilson, C. (1960), *William Heytesbury: Medieval Logic and the Rise of Mathematical Physics*, Madison, WI: University of Wisconsin Press.

136

William of Ockham

TIMOTHY B. NOONE

We know relatively little about the life of William of Ockham (b. ca. 1285; d. 1347). He is believed to have been born in Ockham, a small village in the county of Surrey not far from London. He is known to have been made subdeacon in 1306 at Southwark, near London, and to have received a license to hear confessions by 1318; from these dates his probable date of birth (1285) is inferred. Apparently an early entrant into the Franciscan order, Ockham probably began his studies at Oxford in 1309. Between 1314 and 1316, he lectured on the Bible, and between 1317 and 1319 he lectured on the *Sentences* of PETER LOMBARD at Oxford. Although he participated in the disputations and even gave the inaugural lecture required for a master of theology (*magister regens*), he never received the degree. Instead, he was sent to London to teach philosophy to the younger members (*iuniores*) of the Franciscan order. It was during his stay in London (1321–3) that he held the disputations that were more usually conducted by a master of theology, namely, quodlibetal questions, wrote parts of his *Summa logicae*, and revised the earlier lectures on the *Sentences*, thereby producing a finished version or *Ordinatio* for the first book. By 1324, however, complaints by the former chancellor of Oxford, John Lutterell, regarding Ockham's orthodoxy caused him to be summoned to the papal court in Avignon. The papally-instituted commission declared in 1326 that some 51 propositions contained in Ockham's theological writings deserved censure, although they were never formally condemned by the pope. While waiting in Avignon for the conclusion of the proceedings against him, Ockham became heavily involved in the poverty controversy – a fierce debate regarding whether Christ and his apostles had owned anything – that was a vital issue to the mission of the Franciscan order. Because he sided with the position taken by the order at its 1321 Perugia chapter and was encouraged to defend it by the Minister General Michael of Cesena, Ockham shared the latter's fate when the situation in Avignon became perilous and the Michaelist party fled (1328). Arriving eventually at Munich along with Michael of Cesena, Ockham spent the rest of his life writing on ecclesiology, Church–state relations, the limits of legitimate authority, and the limits of papal power. Ockham apparently died in 1347 without ever being reconciled with the Church from which he had been excommunicated because of his defense of the Michaelist position.

The body of Ockham's writings is divided into two parts, corresponding to the two parts of his life: his philosophical and theological works are devoted to issues in speculative theology and philosophy, with a heavy emphasis, in the case of the philosophical works, on logic, metaphysics, and the philosophy of mind; his political works are not all that concerned with theoretical issues but focus instead on the immediate sources of political power and the role of government, both ecclesiastical and secular, in a Christian society. For the past century, most scholarship has focused on the philosophical and theological writings, which are now available in critical edition; the political writings are still being prepared for publication and have only been the focus of intensive scholarly attention since the last decades of the twentieth century.

The present essay will treat mainly of Ockham's philosophy as found in his philosophical and theological writings, for these have been the most carefully studied and contain the bulk of what we know about Ockham's thought. Ockham's *Summa logicae* has been and should be considered a landmark in the history of logic; in terms of the subject matter it presents, Ockham's logic is, on the one hand, the culmination of centuries of refinements by earlier medieval logicians and, on the other, quite original in its manner of identifying and articulating the highest order inference and equivalency rules within the framework of a novel semantics. Yet since the present volume is not a guide to the history of logic, but to the history of medieval philosophy in general, the treatment of Ockham's logic will be subordinated to the study of his other philosophical ideas.

The areas that we shall single out for special attention in Ockham's philosophy are the theory of universals, ontological reduction, philosophical theology, and his ethics. In examining Ockham's views on these topics, we shall see Ockham's commitment to a set of principles. Which of these principles is supreme, or whether any of them is privileged from a philosophical standpoint, is debatable, but that Ockham appeals regularly to them to settle philosophical problems is beyond contention. The first of these principles, perhaps, is that the world is composed of singulars and singulars only and each of these singulars, whether substance or accident, God or angel, is singular through and through. Second, if any two created things are really distinct, and not merely distinct by reason, it is logically possible for one of them to exist apart from the other at least through an exercise of the absolute power of God; the latter is constrained only by the principle of non-contradiction. Third, the world of creatures is utterly contingent. Fourth, there is the so-called Ockham's razor (really a principle tracing its origin back to Aristotle's *Physics*): never posit any more entities than necessary. Fifth, there is a principle of methodology allied to that of the razor: we should not affirm a proposition unless it is self-evident, properly deduced from self-evident propositions, a teaching of faith, a proposition deduced from a teaching of faith, or a matter or sense-experience or deduced from the same. The strictness with which Ockham applies the last three principles is sometimes remarkable, as we shall see.

Universals, logic, and philosophy of mind

Background

Ockham is often associated with the extensive medieval treatment of the problem of the universals and the position known as nominalism. As Philotheus Boehner, the pioneering editor of Ockham's philosophical works, often remarked, however, Ockham's position is really a form of conceptualism, that is, Ockham holds that universals are concepts primarily and are to be identified with spoken or written words only secondarily (Boehner 1958, pp. 156–74). Yet to see the extent that Ockham's position is novel, even radical, in the setting of the medieval discussion of the problem of universals, we need to examine briefly the sources and scope of that discussion. Then we shall turn to Ockham's critique of all forms of realism, the dominant approach to universals of which he recognizes at least four different forms. Understanding the theory that Ockham advances in lieu of the common view requires some

697

acquaintance with his own logic of terms on the one hand, especially his theory of supposition, and his philosophy of mind on the other. Once we are sufficiently apprised of his views on the relation of logic and reality and his account of the formation of our concepts, we shall turn finally to his own theory.

The medieval problem of universals arose out of the remarks of the Neoplatonist Porphyry in the opening section of the *Isagoge*, his introduction to the *Categories* of Aristotle. There Porphyry points out that the truly important question, philosophically speaking, in regard to universals, such as species and genera, is to know whether they are mind-independent realities or simply conceptions of the mind; whether, if they are mind-independent, they are corporeal or incorporeal; and whether, if they are incorporeal, they exist separately from sensible things or only subsist within them (Porphyry, *Isagoge* c. 1). Beginning with BOETHIUS' treatment of the questions in his two commentaries on the *Isagoge*, the medievals had some taste for one of the issues that separated the two great classical philosophers, Plato and Aristotle. Though he favored a Platonic solution to the problem in his own independent works, Boethius presented in his commentaries a version of an "Aristotelian" solution according to which the universal is a composite thought based on the essential similarities of things. Yet early medieval authors had little idea of precisely how appealing such an "Aristotelian" view of universals might be, because they had no direct acquaintance with the works of Aristotle wherein the corresponding philosophical psychology and metaphysics were given expression. During the twelfth and thirteenth centuries, as the works of Aristotle and his Islamic commentators made their appearance in the Latin West, medieval philosophers began to develop different accounts of universals, but all rooted to an increasing degree in the psychology of Aristotle's *De anima* and the metaphysics of substance and form sketched out in his *Categories* and *Metaphysics*. Perhaps the most influential source for the problem of universals as it was developed by thirteenth-century thinkers was AVICENNA'S *Metaphysics*. In key passages of this work, the Islamic philosopher identified universals as natures that enjoyed some ontological status of their own and were indifferent to existing both in particular things outside the soul and as thoughts in an intellect. Avicenna's outlook encouraged thirteenth-century philosophers, despite their other disagreements, to subscribe nigh on universally to a two-level metaphysics consisting of concrete, individual substances in which natures, somehow distinct from those substances, had their foothold in reality.

Philosophical sources of reflection only account, however, for some of the material that figured in thirteenth century discussions of universals. Problems in theology, especially as they were formulated in Lombard's *Sentences*, were also a strong stimulus for discussion. Solutions advanced to cope with the problem of the multiplicity of divine ideas were the occasions for advancing distinctions that were applied to similar difficulties in dealing with the problem of universals. One type of distinction recognized by thirteenth century theologians was a pure distinction of reason, the kind that obtains between a physical motion considered either as the action of the agent or what the patient is undergoing. At the other extreme was a real distinction which obtained when the two terms of the distinction either did, or at least could, exist independently of each other. Hence in its crisp formulation in HENRY OF GHENT'S writings and in most theological works thereafter, a real distinction entails separability, at least in principle, of the things said to be really distinct.

In between these extremes, there were various intermediate distinctions proposed. THOMAS AQUINAS, among others, argued that certain items were distinct in reason but with some ground for the distinction present in the things themselves. Henry of Ghent and others contended that since two terms such as 'rational' and 'animal' were distinct in meaning or intention, there must be, corresponding to such a distinction, intentionally distinct features

within a thing, though Henry tended to vacillate on the crucial issue of whether intentionally distinct items were as such prior to, or only consequent upon, human intellectual
activity.

Most importantly for Ockham's thought, the Franciscan JOHN DUNS SCOTUS had crafted
his formal distinction to cover the weaknesses perceivable in Henry's approach. Though
Scotus varied in his terminology and tended in his later writings to consider the formal distinction a subspecies of real distinction, Scotus's formal distinction may still be said, from
a comparative perspective, to be between the extremes of a distinction of reason and a real
distinction based on the separability criterion. Those features of a given thing are formally
distinct that, although really identical in a given substance, answer to non-overlapping
descriptions or definitions and hence are distinct prior to the acts of mind that so formulate the respective descriptions or definitions. The commonest example in Scotus's writings
is derived from Henry: "rational" and "animal" are formally distinct, though really identical features of a human being because they are distinct in their definitions, though equally
necessary and essential for being human. The Subtle Doctor proposes a similar distinction
between the divine attributes, which, though undefinable strictly speaking, answer to
differing descriptions.

Ockham

Ockham's recounting of opinions advanced by realists begins with the view of WALTER
BURLEY, a fourteenth-century author whose views on universals parallel in many respects
the opinions advanced in the thirteenth century by ROGER BACON. Burley's opinion holds
that universals (e.g., man) are really existing things outside the conceiving mind, distinct
both from the individual substance in which they are found, such as Socrates, and from any
other universal appertaining to that same individual substance (e.g., animal). Furthermore,
the opinion holds that these universal things are as numerous within an individual substance
as are the essential predicates belonging to that substance and they are not rendered numerically many or multiplied through the multiplication of individual substances (*Ordinatio*
I d. 2 q. 4; 1970, pp. 100–1). Many arguments are advanced on behalf of this opinion,
but the most telling are rooted in the Aristotelian conceptions of definition, science, and
signification.

Definitions are primarily of substances and universals, according to Aristotle, not
individuals. Hence, there must be universal substances in individual things in addition to
their singular substances to serve as the proper objects of such definitions. Furthermore, a
real science bears upon real things, i.e., things that exist apart from acts of thinking, and it
is by treating such real things that real sciences are distinguished from rational sciences,
such as dialectic. But since no science deals with singulars, it seems that there must be universal things grounding such real sciences. Finally, a spoken word such as 'man' must signify
something as its primary significate. But it cannot signify some given individual, such as
Socrates, inasmuch as it signifies no more one individual than another. Therefore, it must
signify a universal thing (ibid., pp. 101–2).

Ockham vehemently rejects this opinion, saying it is "entirely false and absurd" and
advances a philosophical argument employing the notion of real distinction seen above
(*Ordinatio* I d, 2 q. 4; 1970, p. 108). If the universal "man" were some really distinct thing,
it would be capable of existing apart from individual human beings since it is claimed to be
distinct from and prior to individual human beings, according to Burley; or at least it could
be kept in existence separately through the divine power (ibid., pp. 108–15). Ockham thinks

the arguments on behalf of the opinion, too, are of little merit. Definitions are not primarily of things but rather of terms. True, definitions are of terms insofar as they are capable of standing for things, but Ockham sees no reason, as we shall see more fully below, why such terms cannot stand for individual substances. Sciences, even so-called real sciences, are collections of psychological habits that deal primarily with propositions and not things. What makes real sciences distinct from rational sciences is not that the former deal with things and the latter with intentions or mental acts, but rather that the former are collections of psychological habits dealing with propositions having terms that stand for things existing apart from the mind, whereas the latter are collections of habits dealing with propositions having terms that refer to mental acts, contents, or both. Finally, a species-term such as 'man' does not signify one thing in the sense of one individual thing more than any other individual thing. But it does signify any given human, whether Plato, Socrates, or any other, insofar as the individual thing instantiates the concept of man, which itself is a natural sign for human beings (ibid., 130–40).

The second opinion is of unknown authorship, but can be plausibly claimed to be similar to that of WILLIAM OF ALNWICK, one of Duns Scotus's early disciples. This opinion is different from the first in that it claims the universal is not only a really distinct thing from individuals, but is also really multiplied in the individual substances in which it is found. The nature signified by the term 'man' is really distinct both from the individuating difference contracting the nature to become Socrates' humanity and from the individuating difference contracting the nature to become Plato's humanity; but the nature and the individuating difference do constitute respectively Socrates and Plato whose humanities or human natures are now, thanks to the individual differences making them distinct from all other entities of their kind, numerically distinct from each other (*Ordinatio* I d, 2 q. 5; 1970, pp. 154).

Ockham disposes of this opinion rather quickly. If Socrates' humanity is really distinct from Plato's humanity, it will have to be distinct from Plato's humanity by something intrinsic to itself, i.e. in its own right. Accordingly, even if we remove the individuating differences from consideration, the two humanities will be really distinct from each other in their own right. But they cannot be specifically distinct from each other because that would entail that Socrates and Plato belong to different species. Hence they must be numerically distinct from each other and thus they are, contrary to the opinion's whole tenor, each numerically singular and one thing apart from individual differences. Another difficulty raised against the view is similar to an objection against the first opinion: if the humanity of Socrates is really distinct from the individuating difference that partially constitutes the individual substance Socrates, there would be no contradiction in one of these items existing apart from the other, something Ockham thinks absurd (*Ordinatio* I d, 2 q. 4; 1970, pp. 154–9).

The third opinion is the one rightly ascribed to Duns Scotus in Ockham's judgment, as opposed to the first two that are sometimes wrongly taken to be Scotus's, and the Venerable Inceptor expends a considerable amount of effort expounding it. The opinion holds that a universal is not a thing (*res*), but a nature (*natura*) that is really the same as the individuating difference that contracts it to being one individual, though it is formally distinct from that difference, since the nature is of itself neither individual nor universal, being incompletely universal in the thing and entirely universal only in the mind. The key claim in the Scotistic theory is that a nature is an ontological feature of an individual thing. According to Scotus, a nature, unlike an individual substance, is not of itself this but becomes this through something added to it, namely, the singular entity or thisness that renders it this; a nature is not numerically one of itself but is deemed denominatively one thanks to its presence in an individual substance; a nature becomes fully universal only in the mind because, despite the fact that community belongs to the nature in its own right, the full indifference whereby the nature is predicable of many and hence fully universal is only in the mind; and, finally, the nature has minor unity in the manner of an essential property (*Ordinatio* I d, 2 q. 6; 1970, pp. 161–7).

Though Ockham praises Scotus's sophistication and brilliance, he cannot abide such a view of universals. Instead, he advances two basic lines of criticism that are, in turn, supported by numerous arguments. One line of attack is to say that it is impossible within the realm of creatures for a nature to be formally distinct from the contracting difference unless it also is really distinct. This approach is based on the principle that all contradictories are equally contradictory. Hence if there is some property or feature that must or should be affirmed of X but denied of Y, X and Y are distinct things. Ockham takes this law of egalitarian contradictories to apply to creaturely entities in such a way that it is both necessary and sufficient to show their real distinction But, in the Scotistic account of universals, universals that are said to be formally distinct are said to be distinct precisely because they have properties or features that are non-overlapping or non-interchangeable. Therefore, the Scotistic position on universals entails that universals claimed to be formally distinct are actually really distinct; or, if the formal distinction between nature and individual difference does work, it works a little too well since it entails that any two things purportedly really distinct need only be formally distinct.

The second line of criticism advanced by Ockham is that Scotus's position is internally inconsistent even supposing that one would grant the formal distinction. For example, Scotus argues that the nature is supposed to have its own minor unity that is compatible with numerical unity but distinct from it and lesser than it. Yet a nature only exists as Socrates' humanity in the case of Socrates or Plato's humanity in the case of Plato and in such instantiations the nature participates in or has, at least denominatively, numerical unity. But if a nature only exists in an individual in which it has numerical unity, then it only has numerical unity and not some less-than-numerical unity (*Ordinatio* I d, 2 q. 6; 1970, pp. 173–4; 177–80; 189).

The final kind of realism considered by Ockham breaks down into three different opinions, the second and third of which were held, respectively, by Thomas Aquinas and HENRY OF HARCLAY. To take Aquinas's version, the thing whose nature is singular in act outside the soul is, when present in the intellect, universal and it is according to one consideration universal and according to another consideration singular. Yet all three versions of the opinion hold that universals are really present in singulars (Ockham takes 'individual' and 'singular' to be interchangeable in such discussions; see *Summa logicae* I c. 19; 1974, 65–7), and in that sense they are varieties of realism. They differ from the first three opinions by holding that universals and singulars differ only according to reason (*ratio*), whereas the first three opinions claim that universals and singulars differ either really or formally (*Ordinatio* I d, 2 q. 7; 1970, pp. 226–9).

Ockham's fundamental criticism of these opinions is that, however the point is stated regarding singulars and universals differing solely according to reason, singularity and universality cannot belong to the self-same thing in the same respect and, consequently, the universal and the singular cannot be identified wholesalely. There must, accordingly, be a distinction between the singular and the universal. Such a distinction is either: (1) between two formally distinct realities, but this is Scotus's view and has already been discarded; or (2) between two really distinct things, the claim of the first two rejected opinions; or (3) between two beings of reason, but this is not plausible because the singular is no being of reason; or

701

(4) between a real being and a being of reason, but in this case the universal is a being of reason and this position is no longer realism (*Ordinatio* I d, 2 q. 7; 1970, pp. 235–7).

Having discarded every known form of realism, Ockham offers a conceptualist theory instead. His own view draws many of its key elements from salient points in his theory of how terms signify and stand for things and from his account of modes of cognition. Let us then review these two aspects of Ockham's thought prior to returning to his theory of universals.

Terms are the immediate parts of a proposition, that is, the parts which, functioning as either subjects or predicates, taken together with the copula constitute propositions. Terms are either written, spoken, or mental and are, at their appropriate levels, essential and con- stitutive parts of their respective kinds of expression (*oratio*). Written and spoken language, however, differs in kind from mental insofar as the former is composed of con- ventional signs and the latter of natural signs; written and spoken signs can, and often do, change their signification, but mental signs do not. Thus a mental term in a mental sen- tence is naturally capable of standing for (*supponere*) what it signifies. Though Ockham acknowledges that spoken and written signs are subordinated to mental signs, he follows Scotus and departs from Aquinas in maintaining that spoken and written signs, on the one hand, and mental signs, on the other, equally signify things and not mental impressions or concepts (*passiones animae*) (*Summa logicae* I c. 1; 1974, pp. 7–9).

Ockham draws upon the work of earlier logicians for his division of terms, and especially for his discussion of their signification and supposition (Brown 1997, pp. 1039a–1044b). Among the important divisions of terms are the division into categorematic and syncate- gorematic, that is, into terms that have a clear and definite signification, such as 'dog' or 'man', and terms that rather qualify such terms, functioning in the order of language like zero in mathematics, e.g., 'all', 'some', and 'only' (*Summa logicae* I c. 4; 1974, pp. 15–16). Categorematic terms in their turn are divided into absolute and connotative. Absolute terms signify whatever they signify equally and directly, in the way 'animal' signifies each and every human, cow, etc.; these terms have, or at least can have, a real definition. Connotative terms such as 'just' or 'white', on the other hand, signify one thing primarily and other things secondarily and have only a nominal definition (ibid. I c. 10; 1974, pp. 35–8).

Another notable division of terms is between concrete terms such as 'just' and 'white' and abstract terms such as 'justice' and 'white'. Sometimes such terms are distinct in that the concrete term signifies a subject of a quality or feature connoting that quality and the abstract term signifies the quality itself; this is clearly the case with 'white' which signifies the subject of whiteness while connoting whiteness and 'whiteness' which signifies the quality without reference to the subject. Sometimes such terms are distinct in that one stands for the part and the other for the whole of what is being talked about. A third kind of relation among concrete and abstract terms may be seen in cases where the two terms do not refer to either the same whole or parts of that whole but are related as cause and effect, sign and signified, or place and what belongs to a place (*Summa logicae* I c. 5; 1974, pp. 16–18).

Philosophically the most telling of the observations that Ockham makes in connection with abstract and concrete terms is that, especially in regard to terms in the categories of substance and certain kinds of quality, concrete and abstract terms are synonyms, though many believe that they are not. To take an example of a pair of concrete and abstract terms, the term 'man' and the term 'humanity' do not differ in terms of the thing to which they refer or the definition they carry. Both signify individual human beings. True, philoso- phers and theologians sometimes use the abstract member of the pair (e.g., 'humanity') as a substitute for a reduplicative expression such as 'man insofar as he is man'; yet if they think that there is some distinctive being corresponding to such abstract terms, they are mistaken. To think that there is some entity underlying such expressions is, to Ockham's mind, the error characteristic of philosophers such as Scotus who think there is a form whereby man is man that has distinctive ontological features (*Summa logicae* I c. 6–8; 1974, pp. 19–34).

Signification is a function of terms that holds good even when they are used independently of propositional context, whereas supposition is a function that terms, whether subject or predicate, perform only in and through a proposition.

Following a long-standing tradition, Ockham distinguishes between personal, simple, and material supposition. Personal supposition occurs when a term stands for what it signifies. Examples are the terms 'human being' and 'animal' in the proposition 'Every human being is an animal'; the term 'spoken noun' in the sentence 'Every spoken noun is a part of speech'; and the term 'species' in the sentence 'Every species is a universal'. Note that personal supposition has nothing to do with reference to a person, or, for that matter, to things that exist outside the mind. Terms such as 'species' and 'noun' are meant to refer to concepts and words respectively and so are not being used in any exceptional way when they occur in the propositions exemplified.

Simple supposition obtains when a term stands for the concept to which it is subordinated. An example, and a revealing one for the problem of universals, is the case of 'man' in the 'Man is a species'. According to Ockham, in this proposition 'man' does not refer to a common human nature, but rather it stands for the concept "man" that exists in the human mind.

Material supposition happens when a term stands for itself or another token-term of the same type. In English, examples are 'man' in 'Man is a three-lettered word' and 'dog' in 'Dog is monosyllabic'. Both 'man' and 'dog' are meaningful in the mentioned propositions but neither stands for what it was instituted to signify nor for the concept to which it is subordinated (*Summa logicae* I c. 64; 1974, pp. 195–6).

Ockham develops an elaborate division and subdivision of personal supposition into discrete and common supposition. To articulate these divisions and subdivisions with pertinent examples is not to our present purpose, but we need to note why Ockham bothers to develop this scheme: by doing so, he can show the precise truth conditions for different propositions and can argue that, in the case of both the subject and the predicate, all true affirmative propositions involve an identity of reference for the subject and the predicate and require for their truth nothing more than individual things (*Summa logicae* I c. 70; 1974, pp. 209–12).

The other prominent factor in Ockham's theory of universals is his account of our intellectual acts. Like nearly all other scholastics, Ockham was committed to the view that, in the present life, our intellectual knowledge begins with sense experiences. Unlike the majority of scholastics before him, however, Ockham thought that the first act of our intellectual awareness is not an abstract concept or an awareness that prescinds from the here and now, but rather a direct and immediate intellectual awareness of the things around us (*Ordinatio* I prol. q. 1; 1967, p. 27).

Our knowledge begins with what Ockham calls "intellectual intuitive cognition," an expression used previously by Scotus and others but to which he gives a new meaning. Intuitive cognition, for Ockham, is the kind of intellectual awareness whereby we can know whether or not a thing exists, whether it is present or absent, and whether or not it inheres in a subject. In contradistinction, abstractive cognition is the kind of cognition whereby we cannot tell whether or not a thing exists, is present or absent, or is inherent in a subject. Ockham is clear that intuitive and abstractive cognition do not differ in terms of their content; intuitive cognition does not involve some propositional content unavailable in abstractive cognition. Rather, they differ only in that intuitive cognition yields evident knowledge of contingent truths, such as existence/nonexistence, presence/absence, and inherence/non-inherence. Furthermore, intuitive cognition is foundational: it is through the simple and direct intellectual awareness that we have of things in intuitive cognition that we are able to have abstract awareness (*Quodlibet*, I q. 13; 1980, pp. 72–8).

Bearing in mind some of these points, let us return to the solution Ockham gives for the problem of universals. What are universals for Ockham? Certainly not extra-mental entities distinct from extra-mental individuals, for every thing outside the mind is singular. In the first version of the *Ordinatio*, whose discussion we have been following, Ockham presents four non-realistic theories. One of these is genuine nominalism in that it holds that universals exist in the mental order on the model of conventionally established spoken sounds and written inscriptions. Ockham soundly rejects this opinion as implausible precisely because concepts are natural signs of things, not founded in convention.

The three remaining opinions share all three of the following: (1) the universal is, as a feature of the mind, singular and numerically one; (2) with respect to things outside the mind, this intra-mental thing is universal, common, and indifferent to many singulars; and (3) in the latter respect, the universal is a sort of natural likeness (*quasi naturalis similitudo*). One of these three opinions can be discarded immediately because it proposes that a species, a means of abstractive cognition, is the universal existing in the mind. A species would become an intermediary between knower and known and thus could never gain the Venerable Inceptor's allegiance, whose views in philosophical psychology demand, as we have seen, direct realism with intuitive cognition assuring our immediate contact with things (*Ordinatio* I d. 2 q. 8; 1970, pp. 267–71). This process of elimination leaves two theories: the *fictum* theory and the *intellectio* theory.

In the first version of the *Ordinatio* and his other earlier writings, Ockham held that universals are *ficta*, mental objects that represent real or imagined beings. Perhaps the best way to render the term *fictum* in English is to use the English word 'model'. The universal is proposed in the *fictum*-theory as something that has no subjective being, i.e., the kind of being that a form inhering in its subject has, whether in the mind or anything else. Instead it has merely objective being, that is, being as an object of awareness. To be in this sense is nothing more than to be known (*eorum esse est cognosci*). But the universal does have objective being within the mind that somehow conforms to the subjective being a thing in the world has.

To explain how this works, Ockham invites us to consider the intellect perceiving something outside the mind and fashioning or constructing (*fingit*) a maximally like thing in the mind in such a way that, if it had not simply the power to construct psychologically but also to make, the mind would produce another thing in the world maximally like the original thing it perceived. As we might expect, Ockham introduces an artistic analogy to explain his theory: after seeing a house, a builder might see a house and fashion a house in his mind maximally like the house he saw, which, when built, would only be numerically distinct from the first house, so that the house in the builder's mind is a model for other houses. Likewise, Ockham suggests, the universal is a model formed by abstraction, a process which he describes as a kind of making up something (. . . *per abstractionem, quae non est nisi fictio quaedam*), and a model that indifferently refers to many singulars outside the mind; thanks to its maximal similarity in the realm of objective being to any of these things outside the mind, the universal can stand for any of these things that are maximally like it in subjective being (*Ordinatio*, I d. 2 q. 8; 1970, pp. 271–2).

Ockham argues on behalf of this theory on many grounds. One of the chief considerations is that such a *fictum*-model could serve as the term of the act of understanding and hence endow this act with an object when no singular is understood to fall under the universal in question. The model could also be the property bearer for certain predicates, such as 'species' in the proposition 'Man is a species', which clearly cannot, because of the rejection of realism, be attributed to anything outside the soul. Furthermore, the exemplar could be the one thing predicable of many, so that it could be the referent that fully verifies the definition of the universal. Finally, the model would function as placeholder for the innumerable instances of a sortal concept, when, clearly, the individual instances are not something that any knower could be expected to know (ibid., pp. 273–81).

Although Ockham is not very forthcoming about the process of formation of universals, another consideration on behalf of the *fictum*-theory would be that it could fit into a plausible account of concept formation. Through intuitive cognition we become aware of a given thing and naturally fashion a model of it and because other things are maximally similar to the model fashioned on the basis of the first thing, we can apply that model to them as well. Thus, using the model as a means, we predicate the same concept of the second thing and so forth. Entities that are not so maximally alike could be the objects of less exacting models and this might explain the hierarchy of generic and specific concepts.

But there are many puzzles and questions about the *fictum*-theory, some of which Ockham raises himself. One puzzle he does not mention is the difficulty of reconciling the active-formative function he attributes to the mind in the context of this theory with his general emphasis on the passivity of cognition. A problem he does mention, and which is recurrent enough to explain in part why he changes his mind on the issue, concerns the status of something that has merely objective being. Another persistent question concerns whether the *fictum* might not be rather like a species in the final analysis, something that becomes a hindrance to cognition insofar as it functions as an intermediary between the act of cognition and its extra-mental object. Finally, the theory seems to fall foul of the razor and the divine causality principles; we do not need *ficta* provided we have a human mind and the appropriate acts of understanding, whereas conversely we can have the relevant acts without *ficta* on the assumption that God supplies the necessary causality since it is not contradictory for him to do so (*Ordinatio*, I d. 2 q. 8; 1970, pp. 281–3; *Quodl.* IV q. 35; 1980, p. 473; Pasnau 1997, pp. 277–89).

In lieu of the *fictum*-theory, Ockham comes to propose the *intellectio*-theory. This is the view that a universal is simply an act of understanding whereby we are aware of things in terms of their more or less generalizable features. Ontologically speaking, this view allows Ockham to say that all universals are in the category of quality. Moreover, thanks to his theory of mental signs and supposition, he can escape from such apparent difficulties as the consequence that all the categories would be accidents and the consequence that the same thing would be found in two different categories. To address the first of these consequences, Ockham distinguishes, as usual, between the semiotic and the ontological dimensions. True, all universals are accidents without exception in that they are qualities of the mind, but this does not mean that they are natural signs only of, or principally of, things in the accidental categories. In answer to the second of these consequences, Ockham simply appeals to the distinction between personal supposition, on the one hand, and simple and material supposition, on the other. For example, in the proposition 'Substance is a quality', if the subject term exercises simple or material supposition, i.e., stands for a concept or for itself as a

705

concept, then the proposition is true, since *ex hypothesi* all concepts are qualities; if, however, the subject term of the proposition stands for something through personal supposition, the proposition is false.

Ontological reduction

For Ockham, metaphysics has both being *qua* being and God as its subject; contrary to the tenor of the controversy between Avicenna and AVERROES and its continuation by their Latin partisans, the Venerable Inceptor sees no problem with any science, including metaphysics, having two (or more) subjects (Ockham, *Expositio in lib. Phys.* I c. 18; 1985, p. 208). After all, there are no formal structures organizing things outside the mind or, for that matter, thematic unities that bind together strings of syllogisms. A science in the most precise sense is just a single syllogism with the subject of its conclusion serving as the subject of the science. Since there are many syllogisms in what we generally call a science, science in this sense has many subjects (*Expositio in lib. Phys.* Prol.; 1985, pp. 8–9; Ockham, *Quodl.* V q. 1; 1980, 475–80).

As one of the subjects of metaphysics, 'being' can be understood to mean either that which actually exists or that for which it is not repugnant to exist outside the mind. In the second, less restricted sense, being embraces everything that is not nothing. 'Being' is, for Ockham as for Scotus, univocal, though its univocity does not extend to all subjects of which it can be predicated. 'Truth', 'unity', and 'goodness' are transcendental terms in addition to 'being'; that is, they are terms of universal extension, though with different intensions (*Summa logicae* I c. 10; 1974, p. 38; I c. 38–9; 1974, pp. 106–11).

Apart from these transcendental terms, the vocabulary of being in Ockham is rather limited. He does not recognize any distinction between essence and existence; any thing is its essence and it only is such an essence when it exists. To claim that existence is an onto-logically distinct feature of a thing apart from its essence is tantamount to claiming that essence and existence are two things. Moreover, were essence and existence really distinct, God could preserve one without the other and thus they would be separable from each other (*Summa logicae* III–2 c. 27; 1974, pp. 553–5; *Quodl.* II q. 7; 1980, pp. 141–5).

The metaphysics of Ockham is focused not so much on the study of transcendental terms and their features as upon two major themes. One theme is delimiting the categories of being. Here Ockham is quite original, arguing that there are really only two categories, sub-stance and quality; the remainder of the categories are merely categories of thought rooted in the way we think about being rather than the way things are. The second theme is that of philosophical theology. Let us begin with the first theme.

Ockham was by no means the first to suggest that the ten Aristotelian categories did not correspond isomorphically to distinct features of reality. PETER OLIVI, for example, had argued as much in his *Quaestiones logicales* and elsewhere. Henry of Ghent, too, expressed what became a common view of the categories when he argued that there are three real things (*res absolutae*) designated by the different categories, namely, substance, quantity, and quality, while the remaining seven categories are relative beings, entities rooted in the three absolute categories. On the other hand, Scotus had reaffirmed the traditional view, arguing that all ten categories are both conceptual and real. Ockham's approach stands out because he reduces the number of real categories to substance and quality, arguing that the other categories can be effectively mapped onto the two real ones. Ockham's persistent attempt to reduce the number of entities needed to explain how our thought and language map onto the world is referred to by scholars as his ontological reductionism.

To see exactly how this works, let us examine briefly one of the categories that Ockham wishes to eliminate from the realm of being: quantity. In general, categories, whether both real and conceptual or merely conceptual, arise when we ask certain questions about things, such as, 'How big is it?', 'Where is it?' and so forth. This means that the division of the categories arises in answer to questions and therefore is primarily a division of names and concepts, not things (*Quodl.* IV q. 23; 1980, pp. 570–3).

But how do we eliminate quantity from the status of a real category? To take the latter question first, simplicity would seem to demand it, for in an existing physical substance with intrinsic parts we have all we need to satisfy the truth conditions for propositions that appeal to quantity. For example, the proposition 'A material substance is in place in such a way that its parts are in parts of that place and the whole of it in the whole place', holds true on the basis of the different parts of a given sensible substance without invoking some ontologically distinct accident of quantity. A more complicated argument for the same conclusion is that, if the distance of one part of the substance from another were caused by quantity as an accident, then the posterior (the putatively real accident of quantity) would explain and cause the prior (the parts of the physical substance), which is absurd since it is neither among the latter's efficient or final causes. Furthermore, the substance could still be extended without any quantity insofar as God could supply his causality in lieu of the supposed quantity-accident and the substance's parts would still be distant from each other (*Quodl.* IV q. 24; 1980, pp. 413–14).

After Ockham completes the ontological reduction of the categories the only properly real ones that remain are substance and certain qualities such as color (from the third species of quality), virtue (from the first species of quality), and abilities and inabilities (the second species of quality). In these cases, the mental term through which we think about them picks out directly or denotes something in the world, which could be pointed to and spoken of with a demonstrative pronoun. But, in the cases of the other categories, there is no such direct reference. Instead, the pertinent mental terms connote either substances or certain of their qualities in a certain respect. So, for example, two white things may properly be said to be alike, but that simply connotes two substances that are white in relation to the intensity of whiteness – say 3 lumens – and involves the mental comparison of the degree of their respective whitenesses.

Philosophical theology

Ockham argues against the standard approaches to proving God's existence and attributes favored by such medieval authors as Thomas Aquinas and Duns Scotus. Scotus, in particular, constructed an elaborate proof of God's existence that attempted to establish the threefold primacy of a first efficient cause, a first final cause, and most eminent nature, included a proof of divine infinity, and concluded with a demonstration that there could be only one God. Ockham takes issue with each of these points.

To start with the last, Ockham doubts we can show divine unicity. Perhaps we could if we could first establish that God existed in the sense of something better than anything else. But we cannot do so because every purported proof involves something not knowable by human reason, such as that there is only one world or universe. Ockham grants, however, that if we could establish God's existence in this sense divine unicity would follow. In a more positive vein, Ockham thinks that we might show that God exists as that than which nothing is more perfect, which he considers a distinct description of God. Yet this cannot yield divine

707

unicity because there still could be an indefinite number of things that fit this description (*Quodl.* I q. 1; 1980, pp. 2–4).

Divine infinity cannot be established either for Ockham. Targeting some of the reasoning used by Scotus to show divine infinity, Ockham claims that a finite incorruptible power could, just as well as an infinite one, cause the successive motion of the heavens, and since there is no infinite effect in intensity there is no direct basis for the inference to intensive infinity on the part of the cause. Also, given the right combination of active and passive factors in an infinite series of successive finite effects, a finite power is entirely suitable to explain our experience. Finally, God cannot be shown to know things other than himself and thus we cannot reason from his knowing an infinite number of things to his having infinite knowledge (*Quodl.* II q. 2; 1980, pp. 112–16).

Interestingly enough, Ockham exploits the very immanence of the doctrine of nature in Aristotle to buttress his case regarding the last point. Natural causes and effects have a determinate pattern of activity. But if natural causes are determined to a given effect, no further explanation beyond nature is required to explain their activity. Ockham remarks along these lines that it is only things like arrows (cf. Thomas Aquinas's fifth way) that stand in need of determination and direction. As a counterexample to Aquinas's arrow, Ockham suggests that fire burns given the correct conditions without anyone's intending it to do so. The explanation and causal efficacy of the universe might be similarly internal to it, as the activity of burning is to fire (ibid., pp. 115–16).

Returning to the issue of proving God's existence, we know that Ockham will disallow any inference to the unique God of the Bible because he has denied that we have adequate evidence upon which to infer the unicity of the universe. Yet it is not altogether clear what kind of inference he unequivocally allows. For example, in the opening *Quodlibet*, he accepts that we can show (*demonstrari*) God's existence since there cannot be an infinite series of entities each of which would be more perfect than the other (*Quodl.* I q. 1; 1980, p. 3). In *Quodlibet* II q. 1 and *Quodlibet* III q. 4, he denies that we can show that God is an immediate efficient cause of other things (*Quodl.* II q. 1 and *Quodl.* III q. 14; 1980, pp. 107–8 and 213). In both texts, some kind of persuasive, i.e., dialectical, argument is recognized as legitimately concluding to God's existence (*Quodl.* II q. 1 and *Quodl.* III q. 4; 1980, pp. 109 and 215). Regarding final causality, matters are somewhat clearer: no inference to a first final divine cause can be established because the mover of the outermost heaven, such as an intelligence, could just as well have itself as its own end, while, on the other hand, the very regularity of natural things blocks us from inferring that their actions are on account of an end distinct from themselves. The best we can do along the lines of final causality is to reflect that we experience ourselves doing things for God's sake so as to honor him. Though Ockham interprets Aristotle as positing God only as a final cause, such an inference on Aristotle's part appears unwarranted (*Quodl.* IV q. 2; 1980, pp. 302–3, 309).

In his *Questions on the Physics*, Ockham advances the argument for God's existence for which he is most famous. Though he doubts one can show God is the producer of things, he does think that the conservation of things implies God's existence. The reasoning is that, though once a thing is produced its maker need not continue to be, if a thing is in need of being conserved in existence, its conserver must exist at each and every moment that the conserved thing does. Either the first conserving thing is itself conserved or not. If not, it is the unconserved conserver. If so, we may ask about its conserver and so forth. There cannot be an infinite series of such conserving conservers because they would all have to exist simultaneously and thus would constitute an actual infinity of entities, something that Ockham deems impossible. Hence there must be a first unconserved conserver (*Quaest. In libros Phys.* q. 136; *Op. phil*, 1984, pp. 767–9). It is unclear how exactly this apparent proof in the order of efficient causality can be reconciled with Ockham's claim mentioned earlier that we cannot show God's existence as an efficient cause of other things, whether mediately or immediately; despite its tone, perhaps Ockham's reasoning here is meant to be simply dialectical.

In regard to divine attributes, Ockham allows, as noted above, no formal distinction or even a distinction of reason with a foundation in reality. This leaves him to explain how divine attributes are distinct. First, he distinguishes two senses of the term 'divine attribute'. In one sense, a divine attribute is the divine perfection itself completely indivisible, and, in this sense, we should not say that this divine perfection is in God but rather is God. In another sense, divine attributes are predicates or signs that can be predicated of God, and as such they might be better regarded as concepts or names of attribution since they are perfections themselves. Second, Ockham subdivides divine attributes in the second sense into three groups: (1) some, such as 'intellect' and 'will', signify the divine essence absolutely and affirmatively; (2) some connote something else as well as the divine essence, such as 'creator' or 'creative'; (3) some are negative, such as 'immortal' or 'incorruptible'. All of these concepts denote the divine essence, but they are distinct from each other as concepts or descriptions. We need such attributes to talk about God and they expand our proper, though complex, notion of God. But we must understand they do not pick out, even in the case of the first group of names, any distinct respect or aspect or feature in God since he remains utterly simple (*Ordinatio* I d. 2 q. 2; 1970, pp. 61–9; *Quodl.* III q. 2; 1980, pp. 208–11).

Ethics

Ockham's ethical thought has aroused severe criticism at times, especially among those who blame him for the decline and eventual disappearance of scholastic philosophy and theology from western culture. Yet, despite the impression such assessments might convey, Ockham is, in many respects, traditional regarding his ethical theories.

To the question whether there can be a demonstrative moral science, Ockham replies, after distinguishing two senses of 'moral science', in the affirmative. Moral science involves both a positive and non-positive dimension. Under the positive dimension, fall human positive and divine positive laws and interpretations of their application to human conduct. In one respect, these two positive parts of moral knowledge deal with the same thing, namely, what is good or bad precisely as determined by a superior. The non-positive part of moral knowledge, on the other hand, does not involve the command of the superior, but rather has the same force as self-evident propositions or arguments derived from self-evident propositions and matters known by experience. In fact, when Ockham gives instances of such moral knowledge, he often refers to self-evident moral principles such as 'Morally fine acts are to be done'. The human positive part of moral knowledge is not demonstrative insofar as it relies on the merely contingent and indeterminate character of human law as its starting point, while the divine positive part relies on the contingent decisions of the divine will and their revelation to us in Scripture. But the non-positive part of moral knowledge meets the requirements of demonstrative science since it originates from self-evident propositions (*Quodl.* II q. 14; 1980, pp. 177–8).

In a long question on the connection among the virtues, Ockham presents his account of virtue and moral goodness. There is a proportionality between acts and virtues: if acts are specifically distinct, so are the habits they tend to produce and vice versa. Acts, moreover, correspond to objects distinct in kind. The only act that is necessarily, rather than incidentally, virtuous is an act of the will; indeed, no other act besides an act of the will is, properly speaking, virtuous and consequently no other habit is either (Ockham, *Quaes. variae*, q. 7, art. 1; *Op. theol.* 1984, pp. 323–30).

Distinguishing four senses of 'prudence', Ockham first describes prudence as a kind of generic moral knowledge that is equivalent to moral science. The second sense of 'prudence' is more practical, consisting in evident knowledge that is immediately directive of action and involves awareness of a particular as falling under a universal precept. The third sense of 'prudence' is clearly distinct from general moral knowledge or science insofar as it involves knowing by experience some particular proposition. And the final sense of 'prudence' is the aggregate of all directive knowledge as immediately applicable to living well, whether that is gained by reasoning and reflection or experience. Clearly the fourth and final sense of 'prudence' is not a single type of knowledge and this allows Ockham to claim that there will be as many types of prudence in the fourth sense as there are moral virtues. This leaves room for a certain disconnection between the virtues, permitting Ockham to claim that a person can have a practical knowledge of how to control himself so as not to imbibe too much, but nonetheless be entirely lacking in the practical knowledge to exercise another virtue such as bravery (*Quaes. variae*, q. 7 art. 1; *Op. theol.* 1984, pp. 323–30).

Regarding moral virtues properly speaking, that is, bravery, temperance, and justice, Ockham distinguishes five degrees in which they may be possessed by a moral agent. The first degree is had if one is willing to perform righteous acts in accord with right reason with the appropriate circumstances and for the sake of the nobility of the deed or for the sake of peace. Yet it is important to understand something here: the intellect commands such a deed and is the rule of right reason, but moral virtue is in the will. The will's tendency to conform itself in the manner specified is the virtue. The second degree occurs when someone wills to perform a righteous act in accord with right reason with the appropriate circumstances and for the sake of the nobility of the deed, but will not cease to perform the deed even at the pain of death. The third degree occurs when someone wills according to all the conditions specified above, and does it not for the nobility or the worthiness of the act but solely because the act is commanded by right reason. The fourth degree involves the same conditions and circumstances, but now the person does it solely because of the love of God; this is the complete Christian moral virtue spoken of by the saints. The fifth and highest degree occurs when someone wills an act according to the conditions outlined above, but when the end is not the crucial factor; rather the person wills formally to perform a deed, or to suffer one, that exceeds the human state and is against human natural inclination, or, failing that, at least it exceeds the human sphere and natural inclination in respect of the circumstances of the act. The highest degree can be achieved either by a Christian or a non-Christian insofar as no formal love of God need be involved in the intentionality of the act (*Quaes. variae*, q. 7 art. 2; *Op. theol.* 1984, pp. 330–7).

How are the virtues related, then, for Ockham? They are not intimately connected in the way described by Aquinas or even in quite the way that Henry of Ghent thought. At the most general level, all moral virtues spring from and are connected in the agent's awareness of certain very general principles such as "Every good should be done" or "Everything commanded by right reason should be done." But beyond that they are loosely tied. For example, if someone has the virtue of justice in the third degree or the fourth degree, she will be inclined to perform an act of bravery should the occasion arise since she is already committed strongly to performing acts just because they are commanded by right reason or for the love of God respectively. But if she only has justice in the second degree, she might not be so inclined to perform an act of, say, temperance, since controlling one's sense appetites might not be required to bring about justice in a given setting. Hence, one of the conclusions that Ockham draws is that no moral virtue in any degree necessarily requires another virtue in another degree, though it may incline the agent towards it. In fact, at their lower levels, the virtues are so disconnected that the first two degrees of moral virtue are able to exist together in a given person with a vice opposing one of the other virtues. Furthermore, the virtue of prudence is related to the moral virtues in such a way that, although one cannot have virtue in any degree without prudence, prudence in the first sense, i.e., the kind of prudence that is equivalent to moral philosophy, is able to exist without any virtuous act or habit. This is also true of prudence in the second sense (*Quaes. variae*, q. 7 art. 3; 1984, pp. 347–55, 367–76). In general, we may say that Ockham emphasizes the extent to which moral judgment and development is based on experience and is suspicious of any efforts to discount the role of acquaintance with the particulars of moral living in the acquisition of moral virtue (Wood 1997, p. 56).

Scholars and philosophers both, however, have encountered troubles reconciling some of Ockham's stronger statements about what God could command in the moral sphere with the tone of his treatment of virtue as well as his commitment to a demonstrative non-positivistic moral science (Maurer 1999, pp. 525–39). Recall that Ockham distinguishes between positive moral science and non-positive moral science in such a way that divine positive commands are contained under the former division and universal moral principles are found under the latter. Yet, in several texts in his *Sentences* commentaries, Ockham allows that God could command the opposite of practically any act currently contained under his ordered power. Ockham's reasoning on such occasions is that God cannot be disallowed from doing what seems to involve no contradiction. In light of such texts, we might find it difficult to maintain any firm commitment on Ockham's part to a non-postivistic demonstrative moral science standing apart from positive divine precepts. Perhaps the best thing to say is that, in such instances, we find a tension between the ethical theory of Ockham and the metaphysical and theological framework he provides for that ethical theory.

Note

I would like to thank Claude Panaccio (Université de Trois Rivières), André Goddu (Stonehill College), and Gyula Klima (Fordham University) for their generosity in commenting upon a preliminary draft of the present article.

Bibliography

Primary sources
(1940–97), *Opera politica*, 4 vols., ed. H. S. Offler, et al., Manchester: Manchester University Press.
(1967–88), *Opera theologica*, 10 vols., ed. Gedeon Gál, et al.; (1967) vol. I, ed. S. Brown and G. Gál; (1970) vol. II, ed. S. Brown and G. Gál; (1980) vol. IX, ed. J. Wey; (1984) vol. VIII, ed. G. Etzkorn, F. Kelley, and J. Wey, St. Bonaventure, NY: Franciscan Institute.
(1974–88), *Opera philosophica*, 7 vols., ed. Philotheus Boehner, Gedeon Gál, et al.; (1974) vol. I, ed. P. Boehner, S. Brown, and G. Gál; (1984), vol. VI, ed. S. Brown; (1985) vol. IV, ed. V. Richter and G. Leibold, St. Bonaventure, NY: Franciscan Institute.

Secondary sources

Adams, Marilyn McCord (1987), *William Ockham*, Notre Dame, IN: University of Notre Dame Press.

Alféri, Pierre (1989), *Guillaume d'Ockham: Le singulier*, Paris: Minuit.

Boehner, Philotheus (1958), *Collected Articles on Ockham*, ed. Eligius M. Buytaert, St. Bonaventure, NY: Franciscan Institute.

Brown, Stephen (1997), "Sign conceptions of logic in the Latin Middle Ages," in Roland Posner, Klaus Robering, and Thomas Sebeok, eds., *Semiotik: Ein Handbuch zu den zeichentheoretischen Grundlagen von Natur und Kultur*, vol. I (pp. 1035–46), Berlin and New York: De Gruyter.

Gál, Gedeon (1982), "William of Ockham died 'impenitent' in April 1347," *Franciscan Studies* 42, pp. 90–5.

Goddu, André (1984), *The Physics of William of Ockham*, Leiden and Cologne: Brill.

Maurer, Armand (1999), *The Philosophy of William of Ockham: In the Light of its Principles*, Toronto: Pontifical Institute of Mediaeval Studies.

Panaccio, Claude (1991), *Les Mots, les concepts et les choses: La sémantique de Guillaume d'Occam et le nominalisme d'aujourd'hui*, Montreal: Bellarmin; Paris: J. Vrin.

Pasnau, Robert (1997), *Theories of Cognition in the Later Middle Ages*, Cambridge: Cambridge University Press.

Spade, Paul Vincent (1999), *The Cambridge Companion to Ockham*, Cambridge: Cambridge University Press.

Wood, Rega (1997), *Ockham on the Virtues*, West Lafayette, IN: Purdue University Press.

137

William of Sherwood

JOHN LONGEWAY

William of Sherwood (b. 1200/5; d. 1266/71) was born in Nottinghamshire, England and was a master at Oxford by 1252. He is known to us as a logician, though lost theological works, a commentary on the *Sentences* of PETER LOMBARD, and *Theological Distinctions* are reported. He seems to have spent his life in England. Later generations took little note of William, but he enjoyed some fame in his own time, and was praised by ROGER BACON as a finer logician than ALBERTUS MAGNUS, no doubt in part because of his substantial agreement with Bacon's own theory of supposition (Braakhuis 1977).

William's *Introduction to Logic* (ca. 1250?) consists of six chapters corresponding to the works on the logical syllabus of his day. The first, corresponding to Aristotle's *On Interpretation*, concerns the syntax of statements, logical oppositions, immediate inferences, and modal terms. The second, on the five predicables, genus, species, *differentia*, property, and accident, summarizes the *Isagoge* of Porphyry. The third, on syllogisms, corresponds to Aristotle's *Prior Analytics*. The fourth, on "dialectical" reasoning, draws on BOETHIUS' *On Different Topics* (*De differentiis topicis*), and deals with deductive arguments dependent on principles involving such terms, specific to no particular science, as 'part' and 'cause'. The sixth, on fallacy, is developed from Aristotle's *Sophistical Refutations*.

The most significant material in the *Introduction* is found in the fifth chapter, on the semantics of statements, which discusses the four "properties of terms," signification (*significatio*), supposition (*suppositio*), copulation (*copulatio*), and appellation (*appellatio*). This represents an entirely medieval development in logic. In William's version, signification, the presentation of the signified form to the understanding, belongs to a term independently of its occurrence in any particular sentence, and corresponds loosely to our notion of the meaning of a word. William supposes the signification of the term must usually be known, but will not be sufficient by itself, to see what the term means within a specific sentential context. He assumes that all statements reduce to categorical statements, and the meaning of the subject or predicate of a categorical statement within a sentence is its supposition there. A term "supposits" a form if it signifies the form "as something subsisting and capable of being ordered under something else." But knowing what a term supposits in a sentence is still not enough to capture its meaning there. We also need to know what it supposits *for*, roughly, what it refers to. A term "supposits for" something when it is in virtue of that something's falling under the predicate (or belonging to the subject) that the term may be considered to fall under it (or belong to it). For instance, if we were to say 'An animal is walking', the form of animal would be signified by the term 'animal', and supposited by it, but the term would supposit *for* individual animals, since it would only be in virtue of an individual animal's walking that 'An animal is walking' would be true, or 'animal' would fall under 'is walking'. It is what is true of what its terms supposit for that makes a sentence true.

A term can have different kinds of supposition. The term 'animal' may always signify the form of animal, but it need not supposit that form. In 'Animal is trisyllabic', it supposits itself, that is the term rather than the form it signifies. This is *material supposition*. If it supposits what it signifies, it may supposit for what it signifies, as in 'Animal is a genus', 'Humanity is the noblest of creatures', or 'Pepper is sold here and at Rome', examples of the three modes of *formal, simple supposition*. If it supposits what it signifies for something falling under what it signifies, this is *formal, personal supposition*, as in 'An animal is walking'. Personal supposition divides into *confused supposition*, which occurs when a term supposits for more than one thing, as in 'Every animal perceives', and *determinate supposition*, when it supposits for one (undetermined) thing alone, as in 'An animal is running'. Confused personal supposition may either be *mobile*, if one can apply the predicate truly to each item supposited for, as in 'Every animal perceives', from which we infer "This animal perceives," or *immobile (merely confused)*, if one cannot make such an inference, as in 'Every donkey is an animal', from which we cannot conclude "Every donkey is *this* animal."

Copulation is the property corresponding to supposition that belongs to purely adjectival terms, such as 'white'. Such terms signify accidents. In connection with them, William talks of being "of this sort," "of every sort," "of some sort," and argues that such an accidental term signifies only in conjunction with a substantive term. One cannot say 'Of every sort perceives', for the statement is ill-formed, but only, perhaps, 'Animals of every sort perceive'. So simple copulation is not possible. In effect, William wants a device to allow a kind of quantification over predicates occurring within a sentence in an adjectival clause, so that we can say, for instance, '(Some) people of every sort are Christians', meaning "(Some) people of this sort (= who are of this sort) are Christian, and (some) people of that sort are Christian, and . . . ," but he does not allow that the predicates are somehow to be treated as subjects here. If one wants to say something about white, say 'White is an accident', then 'white' has supposition, not copulation. If the term is to have copulation, we must restrict ourselves to saying something about what we say is white, not something about white.

Indeed, William seems convinced that a particular must enter into every actual state of affairs, and so there are only truths about particulars, and a sentence can only be made true by the state of particulars. One might object that he seems to allow that a form is to be viewed as a kind of particular in one mode of simple supposition, as in 'Animal is a genus', but drawing on William's discussion of genus in chapter 2, one might read 'Animal is a genus' as 'Animal is predicable of several things differing in species in respect of their essence', so that 'Animal is a genus' would be made true by the truth of a pair of statements about particulars, such as 'This cat is an animal essentially', and 'This donkey is an animal essentially'. His theory of supposition differs from PETER OF SPAIN'S, for instance, in that it does not presuppose even moderate realism, but will survive as a logical theory within a nominalist context. It is this neutrality on metaphysical issues that particularly commended it to Roger Bacon.

Appellation occurs when a term is taken to supposit only for things that actually exist at the present time.

The theory of supposition was used to do much of the work done in modern logic by quantification theory, and it implied an account of the validity of syllogism, but there are important differences from modern logic. In particular, no artificial logical language was envisioned within which the syntax precisely mirrored the semantics. Logic was done in ordinary Latin, and in the quest to make Latin itself an ideal logical language logicians resorted to a plethora of barbarous locutions to cover the necessary logical distinctions, particularly distinctions of scope, and to associated rules of semantic interpretation not at all reflecting ordinary speech and writing. William is only at the beginning of this development and often allows a locution to remain ambiguous, only noting the ambiguity, where later logicians specify artificial grammatical distinctions, often based on word order, so as to provide exceptionless rules of validity in terms of Latin syntax.

In practice, the rules often revolve about mobile and immobile supposition. For instance, the introduction of an affirmative distributive sign such as 'every' before the subject term renders the predicate term merely confused, but the introduction of a negative distributive sign, such as 'no', before the subject, confuses the predicate distributively. Hence from 'No donkey is a plant', we can conclude 'No donkey is this plant', but we cannot conclude 'Every donkey is this animal' from 'Every donkey is an animal'. In his *Treatise on Syncategorematic Words*, William extends his logic beyond simple categorical sentences by considering the introduction of words other than the subject and predicate terms into a sentence, words capable of altering the supposition of the predicate and subject terms. Such "syncategorematic" terms may have no signification of their own, but contribute to the meaning of the sentence by altering the meaning of the terms with signification occurring within it. Such terms include 'whole', 'all', 'but', 'only', and others of this sort, but also such terms as 'begins' and 'ceases'.

For example, William claims that the phrase 'infinitely many' is sometimes syncategorematic, when used in respect of a predicate, and sometimes categoric. So if one says 'Infinitely many men are hauling a boat' one may mean "infinitely many men" categorically, in which case one means that a single boat is being hauled by an infinite number of men. If 'infinitely many' is used here syncategorematically, the intention is that some boat is being hauled by a group of more men than whatever number you care to name. So if twenty men are hauling one boat, twenty-one men another, twenty-two men a third, and so on ad infinitum, in the syncategorematic sense, "infinitely many men are hauling a boat." This may seem implausible in the example at hand, but one can see how it would play out advantageously in mathematical contexts. So 'It is true an infinitely small time after five o'clock', reading 'infinitely small' syncategorematically, means it is true immediately after five o'clock, but avoids any reference to an infinitesimal time. Again, one can refer to the infinitely long time it takes to run Zeno's racetrack in the same way without attempting a reference to an actual infinity. All this would have come out of reflection on Aristotle's treatment of infinity in his *Physics*.

Sentences involving 'begins' and similar words must be "exposited," that is, their true logical form must be revealed, making it clear under what conditions they are true or false. This means they must be broken down into a logical combination of categorical propositions, and in the problematic cases that interest William, there is usually a concealed negation which immobilizes the supposition of one of the terms. Thus, he says, 'Socrates begins to be white', might be exposited as 'Socrates was not white before now, but is now white', or as 'Socrates is not now white, but immediately after this he will be white'. If Socrates, who has been looking at a man all morning, happens to catch sight of a second man just at ten o'clock, does he then begin to see a man or not? Later authors (for instance, WILLIAM OF HEYTESBURY) distinguished the two possibilities here with word order, so that 'a man Socrates begins to see' will be true under the described conditions, but 'Socrates begins to see a man' will not. William simply notes the ambiguity, and describes the difference in scope as a matter of categorical versus syncategorematic use of the word 'begins'. In any case, one can see that the implicit negation in 'begins' bars the inference from 'Socrates begins to see all these men now' to 'Socrates begins to see this one among these men now', just as the negation in 'Not all these men are awake' bars us from concluding "This one among these men is not awake."

In laying out how these words affect the meaning of a sentence, and other logical points, William often introduces sophismata, which are problem statements a student might be asked to establish or refute in the course of a disputation. A set of background conditions is proposed, which the student must grant as long as that set is consistent, and then the sophism is proposed, and the student must respond to it; moreover, he must reply to all further statements proposed by his opponent, either by affirming a given statement if it follows from what he has granted, or by denying it if it is inconsistent with what he has granted (thereby assigning it its true value) or declaring it uncertain if that is unknown, if it is logically independent of what he has so far granted. If the student can avoid falling into contradiction, he will illustrate a mastery of the logical points at issue.

In addition to the *Introduction* and the *Syncategorematic Words*, several smaller treatises have been attributed to William of Sherwood: *Obligations*, *On the Assumption of Contraries*, and *Insolubles*.

"Insolubles" are self-referential paradoxes, evident in statements such as 'I am now uttering a falsehood'. The sentence cannot be true, of course, for if it is, it is false, but it cannot be false either, since then it must be true. William mentions several approaches to these paradoxes. It may be held that the one who utters such a sentence "says nothing." But the statement is grammatical, and its meaning is clear enough so that we can argue from it. One might hold that the statement has to refer to some statement other than itself, because a term cannot supposit for a whole of which it is a part, so that the term 'falsehood' in the statement must refer to some other sentence than the sentence it is in. But this rule seems to reject perfectly harmless sentences, such as 'Every name signifies some substance with a quality', in which the term 'name' surely must be taken to supposit for itself as well as other names. William himself agrees that the term 'falsehood' in the problem sentence cannot refer to the sentence it is in, but for another reason. He invokes the principle of charity, holding that the sentence should be read in such a way that at least it *could* be true. The sentence turns out to be false, then, since, while uttering it, one is not uttering some other falsehood, and it does not follow from this that the sentence is true.

The treatise concerning the assumption of contraries deals with sophismata that assume two conditions hold, and then introduce a third assumption which, while consistent with each of the two conditions assumed, is inconsistent with the two together. William says the resolution of such sophismata consists in showing that the contrary of the illegitimate assumption follows from the assumed conditions, in order to deny it and avoid contradiction (cf. Aristotle, *Topics* VIII 13). The first sophisma assumes that 'Every Marcus faces someone, and only someone, not equal to himself', and 'Tullius is equal to Marcus alone'. These two assumptions are consistent with one another, but then the sophisma is introduced, i.e., 'Socrates faces Tullius alone'. This is consistent with each of the two assumptions, but not with both together (Socrates cannot be Marcus, or other than Marcus), and so if one grants this, one is easily forced into contradiction.

The treatise on obligations (i.e., the obligations of the respondent in a logical disputation) deals with a variety of sophismata. Many arise simply because the respondent in the debate gives the wrong response in a logically complex situation, and are similar to those in the treatise on the assumption of contraries. But peculiar to this topic are paradoxes that depend on the influence of the pragmatic context on the meanings of, or logical relations between, the statements granted. In such an exercise a sophisma might refer to the respondent in such a way as to produce a difficulty, often of the self-referential sort found in insolubles. For instance, it is assumed that you, the respondent, have never granted that God exists, but instead hold it to be uncertain that it is true. The questioner now asks you if God exists. The proposition is logically unrelated to what has been granted already, so one must assign it its known truth value. Ordinarily this produces no problems, because the respondent loses the debate only if he is trapped in a contradiction, and no contradiction will arise from following this rule. But here, if you grant that God exists, you are asked if it is the case that you have never granted that God exists. The problem disappears if the case is put into the third person ('Socrates has never granted that God exists'), but as it is, *you* have just granted that God exists, which seems to produce a contradiction. Other puzzles concern the point of view from which one speaks. You are to respond "for Browny," a donkey, to the proposition, 'You are a donkey'; does this mean you respond as Browny would, affirming it, even though it is false, or as Browny would have you do to win the disputation, 'I am not'?

Bibliography

Primary sources

(1963), *De obligationibus*, ed. Romuald Green, in "The logical treatises *De obligationibus*: an introduction with critical texts of William of Sherwood (?) and Walter Burley," Ph.D. dissertation, Louvain University.

(1966), *Introduction to Logic*, trans. Norman Kretzmann, in *William of Sherwood's Introduction to Logic*, Minneapolis: University of Minnesota.

(1968), *Treatise on Syncategorematic Words*, trans. Norman Kretzmann, in *William of Sherwood's Treatise on Syncategorematic Words*, Minneapolis: University of Minnesota.

(1970), *Insolubilia*, ed. M. L. Roure, in "La problématique des propositions insolubles au XIIIe siècle et au début du XIVe, suivie de l'édition des traités de W. Shyreswood, W. Burleigh et Th. Bradwardine," *Archives d'Histoire Doctrinale et Littéraire du Moyen Âge* 37, pp. 248–61.

(1976), *De petitionibus contrariorum*, ed, L. M. De Rijk, in "Some thirteenth century tracts on the game of obligation. III, The tract *De petitionibus contrariorum*, usually attributed to William of Sherwood," *Vivarium* 14, pp. 26–49.

Secondary sources

Braakhuis, H. A. G. (1977), "The views of William of Sherwood on some semantical topics and their relation to those of Roger Bacon," *Vivarium* 15, pp. 111–42.

Stump, E. (1980), "William of Sherwood's treatise on obligations," *Historiographia Linguistica* 7, pp. 249–61. Reprinted 1989, in *Dialectic and its Place in the Development of Medieval Logic* (pp. 177–93), Ithaca, NY and London: Cornell University Press.

138

William of Ware

RICHARD CROSS

The English Franciscan William of Ware (fl. 1290s) commented on the *Sentences* in the Franciscan *studium* at Oxford probably at the same time as JOHN DUNS SCOTUS was a student there. William's work, as well of being of great intrinsic interest, provides a crucial staging-post between HENRY OF GHENT and Duns Scotus. William frequently agrees with Henry of Ghent; when he does not, the positions he espouses often resemble those taken a few years later by Scotus, who was himself intimately acquainted with William's work. When not covertly using William as a guide for his own thought, Scotus frequently engages with him. In addition to his close reading of Henry, William discusses opinions from all of his great predecessors from the second half of the thirteenth century, as well as providing useful accounts of many of his lesser Oxonian Franciscan contemporaries. The extent and nature of the diffusion of manuscripts of his commentary have led scholars to believe that it came to be used as a standard textbook in Franciscan houses in the fourteenth century – a function for which its thoroughness, clarity, and high quality make it eminently suitable.

According to William, the subject of metaphysics is *ens inquantum ens*, understood as including God as knowable without revelation. Metaphysics is a theoretical science: revealed theology, contrariwise, is practical, having as its object God considered as the goal of human life. God's existence can be shown by natural reason on the basis of cosmological and teleological arguments, though unlike THOMAS AQUINAS William holds that the argument from motion is the weakest of the arguments, since it entails – counterfactually – that neither angels nor the human will could be self-movers.

William holds, against Henry of Ghent, that natural human knowledge does not require divine illumination. He accepts instead an abstractive account of cognition. Like Henry of Ghent, he holds that the phantasm is made to be known by the action of the active intellect, though unlike Henry he holds that intelligible species, representing extra-mental objects, are required in the passive intellect in order for the intelligence to elicit an act of understanding or mental word. William accepts the primacy of the will; intellect is merely a necessary condition for willing, and the will's act cannot be necessitated. God cooperates in the acts of his creatures merely by giving them certain causal powers.

God's nature can be known in this life, at least to the extent that he has certain intensively infinite perfections, and that these attributes, while really the same, are somehow extra-mentally distinct from each other (they differ *ratione omni intellectu circumscripto*). William makes use of this sort of distinction when discussing the way in which the powers of the soul are distinct from it: while not accidents of the soul, they are not merely the soul's being thought of as related to different objects, as Henry believed. But William does not appeal to this sort of distinction when talking about individuation, as Scotus later does. William holds natures are individuated through themselves (*per se*): any extra-mental nature is *eo ipso* both existent and individual (hence too no distinction between essence and existence). Universals are *post rem* – though William does not hold that the quiddity of a thing is reducible merely to a concept.

William accepts that prime matter, as the substrate of change and the effect of God's creative activity, has some actuality of its own, such that God could cause it to exist without form. Animate bodily creatures have two substantial forms: a bodily form and an animating soul. This explains how an animal's corpse apparently survives the death of the animal. But like WILLIAM OF OCKHAM after him, William argues that the composite substance is not anything over and above the sum of its matter and form(s). William holds that on the death of a human being, whose body and immortal soul both standardly survive, all that is corrupted is the relation that binds them together in the living composite. In accordance with the insight, William accepts that relations are things.

Bibliography

Primary sources

(1927), *Quaestio de unitate Dei*, in P. Muscat, "Guillelmi de Ware quaestio inedita de unitate dei," *Antonianum* 2, pp. 335–50.

(1930), *Quaestio de gratia creata et increata*, in A. Ledoux, "De gratia creata et increata juxta Quaestionem ineditam Guillelmi de Ware," *Antonianum* 5, pp. 148–56.

Secondary sources

Gál, Gedeon (1954), "Gulielmi de Ware, O.F.M. Doctrina philosophica per summa capita proposita," *Franciscan Studies* 14, pp. 155–80, 265–92.

Hödl, L. (1990), "Literar- und problemgeschichtliche Untersuchungen zum Sentenzenkommentar des Wilhelm von Ware O.F.M. (nach 1305)," *Recherches de Théologie Ancienne et Médiévale* 57, pp. 97–141.

Select Topical Bibliography

General histories

Armstrong, Arthur H., ed. (1970), *The Cambridge History of Later Greek and Early Medieval Philosophy*, Cambridge: Cambridge University Press.

Beckmann, Jan P. (1987), *Philosophie im Mittelalter: Entwicklungslinien und Paradigmen*, Hamburg: Felix Meiner.

Boehner, Philotheus and Gilson, Étienne (1952, 1954), *Die Geschichte der chrislichen Philosophie: von ihren Anfängen bis Nikolaus von Cues*, 2 vols., Paderborn: F. Schöningh.

Brehier, Émile (1965), *The Middle Ages and the Renaissance*, trans. Wade Baskin, Chicago: Phoenix.

——(1967), *Histoire de la philosophie*, 7th edn., vol. 1: *L'Antiquité et le moyen âge*; vol. 3: *Moyen âge et renaissance*, brought up to date by Maurice de Gandillac, Paris: PUF.

Copleston, Frederick Charles (1961), *Medieval Philosophy*, New York: Harper Torchbooks.

De Rijk, L. M. (1985), *La Philosophie au Moyen-âge*, Leiden: Brill.

De Wulf, Maurice (1934–47), *Histoire de la philosophie médiévale*, 3 vols., 6th edn. Paris: J. Vrin.

——(1935, 1937), *History of Medieval Philosophy*, trans. Ernest C. Messenger, 2 vols., 3d edn., London: Longmans, Green & Co.

Gilson, Étienne (1955), *A History of Christian Philosophy in the Middle Ages*, New York: Random House.

Haren, Michael (1985), *Medieval Thought: The Western Intellectual Tradition from Antiquity to the Thirteenth Century*, London: Macmillan.

Knowles, D. (1999), *The Evolution of Medieval Thought*, 2nd edn., London: Longman.

Kretzmann, Norman, Anthony Kenny, and Jan Pinborg, eds. (1982), *The Cambridge History of Later Medieval Philosophy: From the Rediscovery of Aristotle to the Disintegration of Scholasticism, 1100–1600*, Cambridge: Cambridge University Press.

Leff, Gordon (1958), *Medieval Thought: St Augustine to Ockham*, Baltimore: Penguin Books.

Luscombe, David (1997), *Medieval Thought*, Oxford: Oxford University Press.

Maurer, Armand A. (1962), *Medieval Philosophy*, New York: Random House.

Marenbon, John (1983), *Early Medieval Philosophy (480–1150)*, London: Routledge & Kegan Paul.

——(1987), *Later Medieval Philosophy (1150–1350)*, London: Routledge & Kegan Paul.

Vignaux, Paul (1959), *Philosophy in the Middle Ages*, trans. E. C. Hall, London: Burns and Oates.

Weinberg, Julius R. (1964), *A Short History of Medieval Philosophy*, Princeton, NJ: Princeton University Press.

Specific histories

Boehner, Philotheus (1943, 1944), *The History of the Franciscan School*, St. Bonaventure, NY: Franciscan Institute.

Cohn-Sherbok, Dan (1996), *Medieval Jewish Philosophy: An Introduction*, Richmond, Surrey: Curzon.

Corbin, Henry (1993), *History of Islamic Philosophy*, trans. Liadain and Phillip Sherard, London and New York: Kegan Paul International.

Dronke, Peter, ed. (1988), *A History of Twelfth-century Western Philosophy*, Cambridge: Cambridge University Press.

Fakhry, Majid (1983), *A History of Islamic Philosophy*, New York: Columbia University Press.

——(2000), *A Short Introduction to Islamic Philosophy, Theology and Mysticism*, Oxford: Oneworld.

Frank, Daniel H. and Leaman, Oliver (1997), *History of Jewish Philosophy*, London and New York: Routledge.

Goodmann, Lenn E. (1999), *Jewish and Islamic Philosophy: Crosspollinations in the Classic Age*, New Brunswick, NJ: Rutgers University Press.

Husi, Isaac (1958), *A History of Mediaeval Jewish Philosophy*, 2nd edn., New York: Meridian.

Holopainen, T. (1996), *Dialectic and Theology in the Eleventh Century*, Leiden: Brill.

Leaman, Oliver (1985), *An Introduction to Medieval Islamic Philosophy*, Cambridge: Cambridge University Press.

Morewedge, Parviz (1981), *Islamic Philosophy and Mysticism*, Delmar, NY: Caravan Books.

Nasr, Seyyed Hossein and Leaman, Oliver, eds. (1996), *History of Islamic Philosophy*, London and New York: Routledge.

Nielsen, Lauge Olaf (1982), *Theology and Philosophy in the Twelfth Century*, Leiden: Brill.

Sheikh, M. Saeed (1982), *Islamic Philosophy*, London: Octagon Press.

Sirat, Colette (1985), *A History of Jewish Philosophy*, Cambridge and New York: Cambridge University Press.

Van Steenberghen, Fernand (1970), *Aristotle in the West: The Origins of Latin Aristotelianism*, trans. Leonard Johnston, Louvain: Nauwelaerts.

——(1991), *La Philosophie au XIIIe siècle*, 2nd rev. edn., Louvain and Paris: Editions Peeters.

Watt, W. Montgomery (1985), *Islamic Philosophy and Theology: An Extended Survey*, Edinburgh: Edinburgh University Press.

Wippel, John. F. (1987), *Studies in Medieval Philosophy*, Washington, DC: The Catholic University of America Press.

Medieval logic

Ashworth, Jennifer (1978), *The Tradition of Medieval Logic and Speculative Grammar from Anselm to the End of the Seventeenth Century: A Bibliography from 1836 Onwards*, Toronto: Pontifical Institute of Mediaeval Studies.

Boehner, Philotheus (1952), *Medieval Logic: An Outline of its Development from 1250 to c. 1400*, Chicago: University of Chicago Press.

Broadie, A. (1993), *Introduction to Medieval Logic*, 2nd edn., Oxford: Oxford University Press.

Bursill-Hall, G. L. (1971), *Speculative Grammars of the Middle Ages*, The Hague and Paris: Mouton.

De Rijk, L. M. (1967), *Logica modernorum*, Assen: Van Gorcum.

Henry, D. P. (1972), *Medieval Logic and Metaphysics*, London: Hutchinson University Library.

Kretzmann, Norman (1988), *Meaning and Inference in Medieval Philosophy: Studies in Memory of Jan Pinborg*, Dordrecht and Boston: Kluwer.

Pinborg, Jan (1972), *Logik und Semantik im Mittelalter: ein Überblick*, Stuttgart and Bad Cannstatt: Frommann-Holzboog.

——(1984), *Medieval Semantics: Selected Studies on Medieval Logic and Grammar*, ed. Sten Ebbesen, London: Variorum Reprints.

Spade, Paul Vincent (1975), *The Medieval Liar: A Catalogue of the Insolubilia Literature*, Toronto: Pontifical Institute of Mediaeval Studies.

Stump, Eleonore (1989), *Dialectic and its Place in the Development of Medieval Logic*, Ithaca, NY: Cornell University Press.

Metaphysics, being and its properties

Aertsen, J. (1996), *Medieval Philosophy and the Transcendentals: The Case of Thomas Aquinas*, Leiden: Brill.

Gracia, Jorge J. E., ed. (1992), *The Transcendentals in the Middle Ages, Topoi* 11, 2.

Honnefelder, Ludger (1990), *Scientia transcendens: Die formale Bestimmung der Seiendheit und Realität in der Metaphysik des Mittelalters und der Neuzeit*, Hamburg: Felix Meiner.

Knuuttila, S. (1993), *Modalities in Medieval Philosophy*, London: Routledge.

MacDonald, Scott (1991), *Being and Goodness: The Concept of the Good in Metaphysics and Philosophical Theology*, Ithaca, NY: Cornell University Press.

Wolter, Allan B. (1946), *The Transcendentals and their Function in the Metaphysics of Duns Scotus*, St. Bonaventure, NY: Franciscan Institute.

Universals and individuation

Berubé, Camille (1964), *La Connaissance de l'individuel au Moyen Âge*, Paris: Presses Universitaires de France.

Klima, G. (2000), "The medieval problem of universals," in E. N. Zalta, ed., *The Stanford Encyclopedia of Philosophy* (Fall 2000 edition), URL: http//plato.stanford.edu/entries/universals-medieval.

de Libera, Alain (1996), *La Querelle des universaux*, Paris: Editions du Seuil.

Gracia, Jorge J. E. (1988), *Introduction to the Problem of Individuation in the Early Middle Ages*, 2nd rev. edn., Munich: Philosophia Verlag.

——, ed. (1994), *Individuation in Scholasticism: The Later Middle Ages and the Counter-Reformation, 1150–1650*, Albany, NY: State University of New York Press.

Padellaro De Angelis, Rosa (1971), *Il problema degli universali nel XIII e XIV secolo*, Rome: Elia.

——(1972), *Conoscenza dell'individuale e conoscenza dell'universale nel XIII e XIV secolo*, Rome: Elia.

Stegmüller, Wolfgang (1978), *Das Universalien-Problem*, Darmstadt: Wissenschaftliche Buchgesellschaft.

Tweedale, Martin (1976), *Abailard on Universals*, Amsterdam: North Holland Publishing.

——(1999), *Scotus vs. Ockham: A Medieval Dispute over Universals*, Lewiston, NY: Edwin Mellen Press.

Relations

Henninger, M. (1989), *Relations: Medieval Theories 1250–1325*, Oxford: Clarendon Press.

Philosophical psychology and epistemology

Dales, R. (1995), *The Problem of the Rational Soul in the Thirteenth Century*, Leiden: Brill.

Day, Sebastian (1947), *Intuitive Cognition: A Key to the Significance of the Later Scholastics*, St. Bonaventure, NY: Franciscan Institute.

Hairi Yazdi, Mahdi (1992), *The Principles of Epistemology in Islamic Philosophy*, New York: State University of New York Press.

Marrone, Stephen (2001), *The Light of Thy Countenance: Science and Knowledge of God in the Thirteenth Century*, Leiden, Boston, and Cologne: Brill.

Pasnau, R. (1997), *Theories of Cognition in the Later Middle Ages*, New York: Cambridge University Press.

Tachau, K. (1988), *Vision and Certitude in the Age of Ockham: Epistemological Foundations of Semantics*, Leiden: Brill.

Natural philosophy and medieval science

Bakar, Osman (1999), *The History and Philosophy of Islamic Science*, Cambridge: Islamic Texts Society.

Grant, E. (1977), *Physical Science in the Middle Ages*, New York: Cambridge University Press.

Lindberg, David (1976), *Theories of Vision from al-Kindi to Kepler*, Chicago: University of Chicago Press.

McMullin, Ernan, ed. (1965), *The Concept of Matter in Greek and Medieval Philosophy*, Notre Dame, IN: University of Notre Dame Press.

Sylla, E. D. (1982), *The Oxford Calculators and the Mathematics of Motion*, New York: Garland Publishing.

Philosophical theology

Courtenay, William J. (1984), *Convenant and Causality in Medieval Thought: Studies in Philosophy, Theology, and Economic Practice*, London: Variorum Reprints.

——(1990), *Capacity and Volition: A History of the Distinction between Absolute and Ordained Power*, Bergamo: Pierluigi Lubrina.

Davidson, Herbert A. (1987), *Proofs for Eternity, Creation, and the Existence of God in Medieval Islamic and Jewish Philosophy*, Oxford and New York: Oxford University Press.

Grant, Edward (2001), *God and Reason in the Middle Ages*, Cambridge: Cambridge University Press.

Morewedge, Parviz (1979), *Islamic Philosophical Theology*, Albany: State University of New York Press.

Rudavsky, Tamar, ed. (1985), *Divine Omniscience and Omnipotence in Medieval Philosophy: Islamic, Jewish, and Christian Perspectives*, Dordrecht and Boston: D. Reidel.

Schabel, C. (2000), *Theology at Paris 1316–1345: Peter Auriol and the Problem of Divine Foreknowledge and Future Contingents*, Aldershot: Ashgate.

Wolter, Allan B. (1990), *The Philosophical Theology of John Duns Scotus*, ed. Marilyn McCord Adams, Ithaca and London: Cornell University Press.

Time, creation, and the eternity of the world

Bianchi, L. (1984), *L'errore di Aristotele. La polemica contro l'eternità del mondo nel XIII secolo*, Florence: La Nuova Italia Editrice.

Dales, R. C. (1991), *Medieval Discussions of the Eternity of the World*, Leiden: Brill.

Rudavsky, Tamar (2000), *Time Matters: Time, Creation, and Cosmology in Medieval Jewish Philosophy*, Albany: State University of New York Press.

Ethics

Fakhry, Majid (1994), *Ethical Theories in Islam*, Leiden: Brill.

Lottin, O. (1942–60), *Psychologie et morale au XIIe et XIIIe siècles*, 6 vols., Gembloux: Duclot.

Potts, Timothy C. (1980), *Conscience in Medieval Philosophy*, Cambridge and New York: Cambridge University Press.

Political philosophy

Kreisel, Howard T. (1999), *Maimonides' Political Thought: Studies in Ethics, Law and the Human Ideal*, Albany: State University of New York Press.

Mahdi, Muhsin (2001), *Alfarabi and the Foundation of Islamic Political Philosophy*, Chicago: University of Chicago Press.

Malloy, Michael P. (1985), *Civil Authority in Medieval Philosophy: Lombard, Aquinas, and Bonaventure*, Lanham, MD: University Press of America.

Wilks, M. J. (1963), *The Problem of Sovereignty in the Later Middle Ages: The Papal Monarchy with Augustinus Triumphus and the Publicists*, Cambridge: Cambridge University Press.

General collections of texts

Collins, James Daniel, ed. (1960), *Readings in Ancient and Medieval Philosophy*, Westminster, MD: Newman Press.

Fairweather, Eugene R., ed. (1970), *A Scholastic Miscellany: Anselm to Ockham*, New York: Macmillan.

Frank, Daniel H., Leaman, Oliver, and Manekin, Charles H., eds. (2000), *The Jewish Philosophy Reader*, London and New York: Routledge.

Hyman, Arthur and Walsh, James J., eds. (1973), *Philosophy in the Middle Ages: The Christian, Islamic, and Jewish Traditions*, Indianapolis and Cambridge: Hackett.

Katz, Joseph and Weingartner, Rudolph, eds. (1965), *Philosophy in the West: Readings in Ancient and Medieval Philosophy*, New York: Harcourt, Brace, and World.

Kaufmann, Walter and Baird, Forrest E., eds. (1994), *Medieval Philosophy*, Englewood Cliffs, NJ: Prentice Hall.

Lerner, Ralph, Mahdi, Muhsin, and Fortin, Ernest L., eds. (1963), *Medieval Political Philosophy: A Sourcebook*, New York: Free Press of Glencoe.

McKeon, Richard, ed. (1929), *Selections from Medieval Philosophers*, 2 vols., New York: Charles Scribner's Sons.

Shapiro, Herman, ed. (1964), *Medieval Philosophy: Selected Readings from Augustine to Buridan*, New York: Modern Library.

Schoedinger, Andrew B., ed. (1996), *Readings in Medieval Philosophy*, Oxford and New York: Oxford University Press.

Wippel, John F. and Wolter, Allan B., eds. (1969), *Medieval Philosophy: From St. Augustine to Nicholas of Cusa*, New York: Free Press.

Index of Names

Only name references of philosophical or closely related significance are indexed. Name references included here as nouns occasionally appear adjectivally in the text, e.g. "Aristotelian" rather than "Aristotle." Some alternative names, including several not mentioned in the text, are provided in parentheses.

Index of Subjects

names of God, 6–7, 400

natural philosophy (physics), 96, 566–7, 573; and knowledge of God, 275

natural science, 597

nature, 119–22, 398–401, 449, 455–6; autonomous, 40; common, 306, 359–60, 407, 583; distinct from God, 40–1; divine, 165; and grace, 473; human, 402–3; order of, 297; regularity of, 479; as singular, 359; three kinds, 534; unity and being of, 9; universal, 407

necessary reasons, 592

necessitarianism, 311

necessity, conditional, 690; divine, 206; of every event, 516

negation (negative theology), 541

negation, as individuating, 360

negative way, 591

Neoplatonism, 457; and mysticism, 41

Nestorianism, 145

nominalism (nominalists), 9–10, 228, 258, 284, 291, 340–4, 359, 377, 411, 458–60, 471, 487–9, 697

novum organum, 16

objects, nonexistent, 227; sensible, 190

occasionalism, 120, 186, 205, 455, 682

Ockham's razor, *see* parsimony, principle of

omne quod movetur, ab alio movetur, 302

omnipotence, divine, 287, 510, 674, 682

One, 131, 199–202, 215, 326, 398, 429, 540

ontological argument, 5, 139–42, 575

operation, 425; of angels, 338

pantheism, 107, 470

Paradigm, divine, 302

paradox of evil, 158, 164

parallelism, of language, thought and world, 504

parsimony, principle of ("Ockham's razor"), 9, 251, 285, 502, 697, 705

participation, 222, 299–300, 542–4; of creature in God, 471–2

particular, the, 585

past, infinite, 584

Patristic sources in philosophy, 29

Pelagianism, 660

perfection, 438–41; moral, 230

person, 223, 324

perspectivism, 559

phantasm, 316, 374

phenomenalism, 464

philosophical theology, 164–5

philosophy (or reason) and theology (religion, faith), 1, 3–5, 11, 18–20, 55, 65–7, 88, 93–4, 98, 106, 111, 130, 134, 145–8, 152, 184–7, 193–4, 198, 211–13, 229–30, 233, 234, 339, 373, 377, 392–3, 397, 405, 426, 432, 436–7, 441, 453, 466, 567, 631, 634–5

philosophy, analytic, 11; continental, 11; autonomy of, 34, 228; Christianity as, 156; division of, 438–9; and the end of man, 96, 238, 393; excellence of, 68–9, 130; flourishing in Middle Ages, 1; "handmaiden to Scripture," 35; in relation to other disciplines, 218; "interior," 209–10, 213; medieval: subdivisions, 1–3; practical orientation of, 617; of religion, 490–1; speculative, divisions of, 613; techniques of, 34

physical spirit, 600

physics, fundamental concepts of, 133

physiology, and morality, 175

place, 268, 293, 580–1; natural, 476; of separate substances, 425

Platonism, 20, 38, 93, 165, 215

pluralism, religious, 115

plurality of substantial forms, 278, 306, 309, 521, 577, 670

plurality of worlds, 476

poetics, 111

poetry, philosophical, 174–6

political philosophy, 192–4, 448–9

positivism, 380

possibles, in the mind of God, 554

potency and act, *see* act and potency

potency to be, 636

poverty, 256, 417, 519–20

power, absolute (*potentia absoluta*), 379, 536, 689, 711; agent sense, 373–4; coercive, 417; cogitative, 190–2, of God, 69; ordered (*potentia ordinata*), 536; plenitude of, 415, 423, 429–30; political, 382

powers, duality of, 413, 418–19; intellectual, 112; natural, 229–30

predestination, 33, 305, 397, 409, 660

predicables, 447

predication, and reality, 199; inherence theory of, 342; modes of, 207; relative, 32; theories of, 82

premisses, contingent, 357

primacy of will, 569

Inter - we agree (Kraus)

But applic - less clear, Kraus, Parker
Muller. But still work to do

Gen. answ given is "—" Muller. But is it
true of Cal?

Sometimes to be sure (Parker) But this
article will arg. C employs another
approach - speci'ly he ... He didn't restrict
locus of sp sense to intentio anct. but he
was first to see it as locus.

METHOD

CONCL.
Return to beginning — While we agree
Kraus, perhaps this article has added
some prec. to his arg - # 4. that is, not
only C paid attn to anct. intentie but
specifically he looked to sp. meaning
of anctor.

1 This is helpful b/c it joins interpr.
   and applic, which is what we think
   reformers did.

2 Also this shows — applic abs, basic
   to C's approach